# Nineteenth-Century
# Literature Criticism

# Guide to Gale Literary Criticism Series

| For criticism on | Consult these Gale series |
|---|---|
| Authors now living or who died after December 31, 1959 | *CONTEMPORARY LITERARY CRITICISM (CLC)* |
| Authors who died between 1900 and 1959 | *TWENTIETH-CENTURY LITERARY CRITICISM (TCLC)* |
| Authors who died between 1800 and 1899 | *NINETEENTH-CENTURY LITERATURE CRITICISM (NCLC)* |
| Authors who died between 1400 and 1799 | *LITERATURE CRITICISM FROM 1400 TO 1800 (LC)* <br><br> *SHAKESPEAREAN CRITICISM (SC)* |
| Authors who died before 1400 | *CLASSICAL AND MEDIEVAL LITERATURE CRITICISM (CMLC)* |
| Black writers of the past two hundred years | *BLACK LITERATURE CRITICISM (BLC)* |
| Authors of books for children and young adults | *CHILDREN'S LITERATURE REVIEW (CLR)* |
| Dramatists | *DRAMA CRITICISM (DC)* |
| Hispanic writers of the late nineteenth and twentieth centuries | *HISPANIC LITERATURE CRITICISM (HLC)* |
| Poets | *POETRY CRITICISM (PC)* |
| Short story writers | *SHORT STORY CRITICISM (SSC)* |
| Major authors from the Renaissance to the present | *WORLD LITERATURE CRITICISM, 1500 TO THE PRESENT (WLC)* |

ISSN 0732-1864

*Volume 45*

# Nineteenth-Century Literature Criticism

Excerpts from Criticism of the
Works of Novelists, Poets, Playwrights,
Short Story Writers, Philosophers, and Other
Creative Writers Who Died between 1800
and 1899, from the First Published Critical
Appraisals to Current Evaluations

**Joann Cerrito**
Editor

**Jim Edwards**
**Judith Galens**
**Alan Hedblad**
**Jelena O. Krstović**
**Marie Lazzari**
**Lawrence J. Trudeau**
Associate Editors

## Gale Research Inc.

*An International Thomson Publishing Company*

I(T)P

NEW YORK • LONDON • BONN • BOSTON • DETROIT • MADRID
MELBOURNE • MEXICO CITY • PARIS • SINGAPORE • TOKYO
TORONTO • WASHINGTON • ALBANY NY • BELMONT CA • CINCINNATI OH

## STAFF

Joann Cerrito, *Editor*

Jim Edwards, Judith Galens, Alan Hedblad, Jelena O. Krstović, Marie Lazzari,
Brian St. Germain, Lawrence J. Trudeau, *Associate Editors*

Deron Albright, Thomas Carson, Catherine C. DiMercurio, Kathryn Horste,
Daniel Marowski, Sean McCready, Paul Sassalos, Debra A. Wells, *Assistant Editors*

Marlene H. Lasky, *Permissions Manager*
Margaret A. Chamberlain, Linda M. Pugliese, *Permissions Specialists*
Diane Cooper, Maria Franklin, Pamela A. Hayes, Arlene Johnson, Josephine M. Keene, Michele Lonoconus,
Maureen Puhl, Keith Reed, Shalice Shah, Kimberly F. Smilay, Barbara A. Wallace, *Permissions Associates*
Jennifer A. Arnold, Susan Brohman, Brandy C. Merritt, *Permissions Assistants*

Donna Craft, Paul Lewon, Maureen A. Puhl, Camille P. Robinson, Sheila Walencewicz, *Editorial Associates*

Victoria B. Cariappa, *Research Manager*
Mary Beth McElmeel, Tamara C. Nott, *Research Associates*
Shirley Gates, Michele McRobert, Amy T. Roy, Laurel D. Sprague,
Amy Beth Wiezorek, *Research Assistants*

Mary Beth Trimper, *Production Director*
Catherine Kemp, *Production Assistant*

Cynthia Baldwin, *Production Design Manager*
Barbara J. Yarrow, *Graphic Services Supervisor*
Sherrell Hobbs, *Macintosh Artist*
Willie F. Mathis, *Camera Operator*

Library of Congress Catalog Card Number 84-643008
ISBN 0-8103-8936-3
ISSN 0732-1864

Printed in the United States of America
Published simultaneously in the United Kingdom
by Gale Research International Limited
(An affiliated company of Gale Research Inc.)
10　9　8　7　6　5　4　3　2　1

I(T)P™

The trademark **ITP** is used under license.

# Contents

Preface  vii

Acknowledgments  xi

# Preface

Since its inception in 1981, *Nineteenth-Century Literature Criticism* has been a valuable resource for students and librarians seeking critical commentary on writers of this transitional period in world history. Designated an "Outstanding Reference Source" by the American Library Association with the publication of its first volume, *NCLC* has since been purchased by over 6,000 school, public, and university libraries. The series has covered more than 300 authors representing 26 nationalities and over 15,000 titles. No other reference source has surveyed the critical reaction to nineteenth-century authors and literature as thoroughly as *NCLC*.

## Scope of the Series

*NCLC* is designed to introduce students and advanced readers to the authors of the nineteenth century, and to the most significant interpretations of these authors' works. The great poets, novelists, short story writers, playwrights, and philosophers of this period are frequently studied in high school and college literature courses. By organizing and reprinting commentary written on these authors, *NCLC* helps students develop valuable insight into literary history, promotes a better understanding of the texts, and sparks ideas for papers and assignments. Each entry in *NCLC* presents a comprehensive survey of an author's career or an individual work of literature and provides the user with a multiplicity of interpretations and assessments. Such variety allows students to pursue their own interests; furthermore, it fosters an awareness that literature is dynamic and responsive to many different opinions.

Every fourth volume of *NCLC* is devoted to literary topics that cannot be covered under the author approach used in the rest of the series. Such topics include literary movements, prominent themes in nineteenth-century literature, literary reaction to political and historical events, significant eras in literary history, prominent literary anniversaries, and the literatures of cultures that are often overlooked by English-speaking readers.

*NCLC* continues the survey of criticism of world literature begun by Gale's *Contemporary Literary Criticism (CLC)* and *Twentieth-Century Literary Criticism (TCLC),* both of which excerpt and reprint commentary on authors of the twentieth century. For additional information about *TCLC, CLC,* and Gale's other criticism series, users should consult the Guide to Gale Literary Criticism Series preceding the title page in this volume.

## Coverage

Each volume of *NCLC* is carefully compiled to present:

- criticism of authors, or literary topics, representing a variety of genres and nationalities
- both major and lesser-known writers and literary works of the period
- 7-10 authors or 4-6 topics per volume
- individual entries that survey critical response to an author's work or a topic in literary history, including early criticism to reflect initial reactions, later criticism to represent any rise or decline in reputation, and current retrospective analyses.

# Organization

An author entry consists of the following elements: author heading, biographical and critical introduction, list of principal works, excerpts of criticism (each preceded by an annotation and followed by a bibliographic citation), and a bibliography of further reading.

■ The **Author Heading** consists of the name under which the author most commonly wrote, followed by birth and death dates. If an author wrote consistently under a pseudonym, the pseudonym wil! be listed in the author heading and the real name given in parentheses on the first line of the biographical and critical introduction. Also located at the beginning of the introduction to the author entry are any name variations under which an author wrote, including transliterated forms for an author whose language uses a nonroman alphabet.

■ The **Biographical and Critical Introduction** outlines the author's life and career, as well as the critical issues surrounding his or her work. References are provided to past volumes of *NCLC* in which further information about the author may be found.

■ Most *NCLC* entries include a **Portrait** of the author. Many entries also contain reproductions of materials pertinent to an author's career, including manuscript pages, title pages, dust jackets, letters, and drawings, as well as photographs of important people, places, and events in an author's life.

■ The list of **Principal Works** is chronological by date of first publication and identifies the genre of each work. In the case of foreign authors with both foreign-language publications and English translations, the English-language version is given in brackets. Unless otherwise indicated, dramas are dated by first performance, not first publication.

■ **Criticism** in each author entry is arranged chronologically to provide a perspective on changes in critical evaluation over the years. All titles of works by the author featured in the entry are printed in boldface type to enable the user to easily locate discussion of particular works. Also for purposes of easier identification, the critic's name and the publication date of the essay are given at the beginning of each piece of criticism. Unsigned criticism is preceded by the title of the journal in which it appeared. Publication information (such as publisher names and book prices) and parenthetical numerical references (such as footnotes or page and line references to specific editions of works) have been deleted at the editors' discretion to provide smoother reading of the text.

■ Critical excerpts are prefaced by **Annotations** providing the reader with information about both the critic and the criticism that follows. Included are the critic's reputation, individual approach to literary criticism, and particular expertise in an author's works. Also noted are the relative importance of a work of criticism, the scope of the excerpt, and the growth of critical controversy or changes in critical trends regarding an author. In some cases, these annotations cross-reference excerpts by critics who discuss each other's commentary.

■ A complete **Bibliographic Citation** designed to facilitate location of the original essay or book follows each piece of criticism.

■ An annotated list of **Further Reading** appearing at the end of each entry suggests secondary sources on the author. In some cases it includes essays for which the editors could not obtain reprint rights.

# Cumulative Indexes

- Each volume of *NCLC* contains a cumulative **Author Index** listing all authors who have appeared in Gale's Literary Criticism Series, along with cross-references to such biographical series as *Contemporary Authors* and *Dictionary of Literary Biography*. Useful for locating authors within the various series, this index is particularly valuable for those authors who are identified with a certain period but who, because of their death dates, are placed in another, or for those authors whose careers span two periods. For example, Fyodor Dostoevsky is found in *NCLC*, yet Leo Tolstoy, another major nineteenth-century Russian novelist, is found in *TCLC* because he died after 1899.

- Each *NCLC* volume includes a cumulative **Nationality Index** which lists all authors who have appeared in *NCLC*, arranged alphabetically under their respective nationalities, as well as Topics volume entries devoted to particular national literatures.

- Each new volume in Gale's Literary Criticism Series includes a cumulative **Topic Index**, which lists all literary topics treated in *NCLC, TCLC, LC 1400-1800*, and the *CLC* Yearbook.

- Each new volume of *NCLC*, with the exception of the Topics volumes, contains a **Title Index** listing the titles of all literary works discussed in the volume. In response to numerous suggestions from librarians, Gale has also produced a **Special Paperbound Edition** of the *NCLC* title index. This annual cumulation lists all titles discussed in the series since its inception and is issued with the first volume of *NCLC* published each year. Additional copies of the index are available on request. Librarians and patrons have welcomed this separate index: it saves shelf space, is easy to use, and is recyclable upon receipt of the following year's cumulation. Titles discussed in the Topics volume entries are not included in the *NCLC* cumulative index.

# Citing *Nineteenth-Century Literature Criticism*

When writing papers, students who quote directly from any volume in Gale's Literary Criticism Series may use the following general forms to footnote reprinted criticism. The first example pertains to material drawn from periodicals, the second to material reprinted from books:

[1]T.S. Eliot, "John Donne," *The Nation and Athenaeum*, 33 (9 June 1923), 321-32; excerpted and reprinted in *Literature Criticism from 1400-1800*, Vol. 10, ed. James E. Person, Jr. (Detroit: Gale Research, 1989), pp. 28-9.

[2]Clara G. Stillman, *Samuel Butler: A Mid-Victorian Modern* (Viking Press, 1932); excerpted and reprinted in *Twentieth-Century Literary Criticism*, Vol. 33, ed. Paula Kepos (Detroit: Gale Research, 1989), pp. 43-5.

# Suggestions Are Welcome

In response to suggestions, several features have been added to *NCLC* since the series began, including annotations to excerpted criticism, a cumulative index to authors in all Gale literary criticism series, entries devoted to criticism on a single work by a major author, more illustrations, and a title index listing all literary works discussed in the series.

Readers who wish to suggest authors or topics to appear in future volumes, or who have other suggestions, are cordially invited to write the editors.

# Acknowledgments

The editors wish to thank the copyright holders of the excerpted criticism included in this volume, the permissions managers of many book and magazine publishing companies for assisting us in securing reprint rights, and Anthony Bogucki for assistance with copyright research. We are also grateful to the staffs of the Detroit Public Library, the Library of Congress, the University of Detroit Mercy Library, Wayne State University Purdy/Kresge Library Complex, and the University of Michigan Libraries for making their resources available to us. Following is a list of the copyright holders who have granted us permission to reprint material in this volume of *NCLC*. Every effort has been made to trace copyright, but if omissions have been made, please let us know.

## COPYRIGHTED EXCERPTS IN *NCLC*, VOLUME 45, WERE REPRINTED FROM THE FOLLOWING PERIODICALS:

## COPYRIGHTED EXCERPTS IN *NCLC*, VOLUME 45, WERE REPRINTED FROM THE FOLLOWING BOOKS:

**PHOTOGRAPHS AND ILLUSTRATIONS APPEARING IN *NCLC*, VOLUME 45, WERE RECEIVED FROM THE FOLLOWING SOURCES:**

William Sturgis Bigelow Collection; courtesy, Museum of Fine Arts, Boston: **p. 272.**

# Edward Bulwer-Lytton

## 1803-1873

(Full name Edward George Earle Lytton Bulwer-Lytton; also wrote under the pseudonym Pisistratus Caxton) English novelist, dramatist, poet, essayist, short story writer, historian, and translator. For additional information on Bulwer-Lytton's career, see *NCLC,* Volume 1.

## INTRODUCTION

Bulwer-Lytton was one of the most popular of Victorian authors, renowned for his proficiency in several literary genres and his adaptability to diverse themes and styles. He found his greatest success as a novelist, producing works that appealed to popular taste through shrewd observation of English society. For example, the depiction of the social-climbing dandy in *Pelham* was read with enthusiasm throughout Europe, while the Victorian public's curiosity regarding criminal prosecutions was the primary motivation for the Newgate novel *Eugene Aram.* Although Bulwer-Lytton's literary subjects brought him great popularity, critics were largely unsympathetic, and his reputation declined rapidly after his death. Nevertheless, Bulwer-Lytton is now recognized as an important nineteenth-century novelist for his observations concerning Victorian society.

Bulwer-Lytton was born in London to a family of the landed gentry. His father died four years after his birth, leaving the upbringing of Bulwer-Lytton to his mother. Though he learned to read and write at an early age, his interest in school was minimal and his performance mediocre. While he was at Ealing studying the classics, he fell in love for the first time with a young woman, who was soon forced into marriage with someone else; for the remainder of his life, Bulwer-Lytton upheld the memory of their relationship as a paradigm of ideal love. At Trinity College, Cambridge, in 1825, he published a collection of poems, winning the Chancellor's Medal for "Sculpture." Bulwer-Lytton earned a B.A. in 1825, and an M.A. eight years later. In the 1820s, Bulwer-Lytton cut a dashing figure in the high societies of both Paris and London, establishing his reputation as a fashionable, young dandy. At this time, he had a brief and frustrating affair with Lady Caroline Lamb, a former mistress of Byron. Shortly afterwards, he met and married Rosina Doyle Wheeler despite the strong protestations of his mother, who revoked his allowance.

The financial necessities of his marriage provided the impetus Bulwer-Lytton needed to begin writing seriously. In 1827, he published the novel *Falkland*, a popular success that provided the funds he needed to complete his first major work, *Pelham*. For the latter novel, Bulwer-Lytton drew on his experiences in English society; the novel was greatly admired by the public and credited with initiating the wearing of black evening dress for gentlemen. Bulwer-Lytton also made regular contributions to a variety of periodicals. He became the editor of the "New Monthly" in 1831, which led to the development of a lifelong friendship with another contributor, Benjamin Disraeli. Concurrently, Bulwer-Lytton initiated a decade-long career in Parliament, where he aligned with other liberals in support of such issues as the reform of criminal punishment; he expanded his ideas on this matter in the Newgate novel *Eugene Aram.* Meanwhile, his marriage had grown increasingly acrimonious, and was finally dissolved in 1836. Bulwer-Lytton then turned to the theater, producing plays that were, like his novels, extremely popular with the public, though generally disparaged by the critics. *Richelieu*, written in 1839, reveals his interest in European history. Upon his mother's death in 1843, Bulwer-Lytton inherited the Knebworth estate and adopted the surname of Lytton. He then completed *The Caxtons*, a realistic depiction of middle-class life. Charles Dickens reassured him that it was the best novel he had ever written, an opinion that was confirmed by critical praise for the work. Bulwer-Lytton additionally wrote two sequels to the novel, and in the final phase of his career, he explored issues as various as the existence of supernatural forces in *A Strange Story*, and utopian concepts in *The Coming Race.*

Bulwer-Lytton is studied almost exclusively for his novels,

1

which provide a broad panorama of nineteenth-century literary tastes and a forum for the expression of Victorian ideas. Beginning with *Pelham*, the most significant of his social novels, he created an innocuous young dandy who embarks upon entertaining misadventures as he explores the fashionable circles of high society. Henry Pelham is not as superficial as he appears, however, for Bulwer-Lytton bestowed an acute social conscience upon him, one that provides a running commentary on Victorian sensibilities.

In his Newgate, or crime novels, Bulwer-Lytton continued to conform to popular tastes without sacrificing his reformist principles. In *Eugene Aram*, he resurrected the historical case of an actual murderer, applying a humanistic interpretation to his protagonist by investing him with extensive learning and a strong moral character. Bulwer-Lytton further suggests that Aram should not be blamed for his actions by creating a lowly and debased victim, whose death is seen as beneficial to society. Through the prosecution of Aram, the author demonstrated his position against capital punishment.

Turning to the genre of the historical novel, Bulwer-Lytton created *The Last Days of Pompeii*, his most successful work of this type. Despite the absence of the strong factual foundation and attention to detail characteristic of his other historical works, he was concerned with bestowing authenticity on *The Last Days of Pompeii*—but his greater aim was to entertain with vivid descriptions of the doomed city. In later works, particularly *Rienzi*, a novel based upon the life of a fourteenth-century Italian political reformist, Bulwer-Lytton produced his most historically accurate novels.

While he had previously directed his writing toward the cultured elite, Bulwer-Lytton's primary objective in publishing *The Caxtons* was to capture the imagination of a new and wider audience: the Victorian middle class. To accomplish this, he purposefully turned away from heroic figures and extraordinary situations, depicting average people in domestic settings. The novel revolves around young Pisistratus Caxton's adventures in Australia, where he emigrates in hope of making a fortune to restore his family's former financial condition.

Bulwer-Lytton next forayed into the realm of the supernatural, a subject of considerable interest and study for him and many Victorians. In *A Strange Story*, he develops a dramatic conflict between the representatives of two diametrically opposed forces: Dr. Allen Fenwick is a man of science, and thus a man of reason, unable to believe in anything which is not tangible; his alter ego, Margrave, is a charming practitioner of the occult, determined to control powerful, unseen forces to obtain a potion which will ensure him eternal youth. He manages to persuade Dr. Fenwick to help him achieve his goal, and in the process is destroyed by the demonic forces he sought to manipulate without any regard to his soul. Fenwick's fate is different, for he emerges unscathed due to his acknowledgement of the inexplicable. These characters are symbolic of Bulwer-Lytton's objections to the theory of evolution; and, through Fenwick's acceptance of the existence of the unknown, the author asserts his own faith in Christianity.

Darwin's theory of evolution was an important issue among the Victorians; Bulwer-Lytton would return to this theme in his depiction of utopia in *The Coming Race*. The hero of this work is a young American, who discovers a strange underground world named Vril-ya, inhabited by people who consider themselves to be the descendants of frogs. The unnamed American falls under the protection of Alph-Lin, who guides him through the seemingly perfect civilization. All is well until the traveller begins to gain the interest of several women, all of whom would like to marry him. Others from the community find the idea of a union between separate races unthinkable, and the decision is made to kill the American. He is saved by one of his would-be suitors and returned to his own land. The dangers of the Darwinian theory of survival of the fittest are apparent in this novel, wherein the fittest are not the most humane, and would not guarantee a functional utopia.

Victorian critics did not share the popular enthusiasm for Bulwer-Lytton's works, generally condemning them for a lack of sincerity and apparent stylistic flaws. Twentieth-century critics, while recognizing the weakness of his novels, argue they are not merely the product of a desire for popular success, but demonstrate the author's unique artistic vision. Bulwer-Lytton, though no longer considered one of the major nineteenth-century novelists, is still renowned for his revealing portrait of Victorian society.

## PRINCIPAL WORKS

*Ismael: An Oriental Tale, with Other Poems* (poetry) 1820
*Falkland* (novel) 1827
*Pelham; or, the Adventures of a Gentleman* (novel) 1828
*Paul Clifford* (novel) 1830
*Eugene Aram: A Tale* (novel) 1832
*England and the English*. 2 vols. (history) 1833
*Godolphin* (novel) 1833
*The Last Days of Pompeii* (novel) 1834
*Rienzi, the Last of the Roman Tribunes* (novel) 1835
*Ernest Maltravers* (novel) 1837
*Alice; or, the Mysteries: A Sequel to "Ernest Maltravers"* (novel) 1838
*Richelieu: Or, the Conspiracy* (drama) 1839
*Money: A Comedy* (drama) 1840
*Zanoni* (novel) 1842
*The Last of the Barons* (novel) 1843
*Harold, the Last of the Saxon Kings* (novel) 1848
*The Caxtons: A Family Picture* (novel) 1849
*King Arthur: An Epic Poem*. 2 vols. (poetry) 1849
*"My Novel," or, Varieties in English Life* [as Pisistratus Caxton] (novel) 1852
*What Will He Do with It?* [as Pisistratus Caxton] (novel) 1858
*Novels of Sir Edward Bulwer-Lytton*. 47 vols. (novels) 1859-1874
*A Strange Story* (novel) 1862
*The Coming Race* (novel) 1871
**Works*. 37 vols. (dramas, essays, novels, poetry, prose, and short stories) 1873
*Pausanias the Spartan* (unfinished novel) 1876

*Library Edition
**Knebworth Edition

---

# CRITICISM

## Michael Lloyd    (essay date 1956)

[*In the following essay, Lloyd examines the aesthetic principles of* Zanoni *and* The Last Days of Pompeii.]

Mr. Hartmann in his essay on the sculptor Gibson calls to mind Bulwer-Lytton and his "idealising principle." It is Lytton whom Mr. Hartmann quotes for an epitaph on Gibson; and the artistic principles of the novelist and the sculptor have something in common. Lytton, eulogising Gibson in the Dedication to him of *Zanoni*, is eulogising himself. "I feel there is between us the bond of that secret sympathy, that magnetic chain—which unites the Everlasting Brotherhood, of whose being *Zanoni* is the type." *Zanoni* is the work offered by the "Artist in words" to the "Artist, whose ideas speak in marble," and it professes that idealising principle which he claims for both. Theirs is (says Lytton) a life, untainted by commerce, of dedication to the idealising principle in behaviour and in art; Gibson's enviably spent away from that mob whom Lytton despises. He loves *Zanoni* "not the less because it has been little understood, and superficially judged by the common herd. It was not meant for them." After all, "The common-place public scarcely understand the idealising principle, even in art. For high art is an acquired taste." Both men, despite Lytton's claim of lofty and unstained isolation, received the plaudits of their generation, and in some respects (as Mr. Hartmann says of Gibson) reflected its mentality, and chiefly its moral notions. For them art was moral; and if we wish to do more than stigmatise the mentality and the art it produced as "puritan, bourgeois and academic," it is perhaps Lytton who will best help us to understand not only its principles and its range, but the limitations of which he was himself partly aware.

"In conduct, as in art, there is an idea of the great and beautiful, by which men should exalt the hackneyed and the trite of life." The idealising principle in conduct consists in the rejection of that "worldly Prudence" which "would as often deter from the risks of Virtue as from the punishments of Vice;" and in the indulgence of "the one master talent . . . the one master passion that, rightly directed, might purify his whole being as a strong wind purifies the air."

Its process is less obscure in art. "The fact is I never have been able to satisfy myself yet with any one work which I have produced, for in my imagination there is a degree of beauty which I am unable to reach." Gibson's statement, [in B. Hartmann's "Canova, Thorvaldsen and Gibson," *English Miscellany* vi (1955)], resembles Lytton's: that the highest works of art are "the creatures of the idea in the artist's mind." On that idea the artist must fix his attention, rather than on "what he falsely calls the Natural, but which, in reality, is the Commonplace." It is a rejection of naturalism in art not unlike the rejection of the commonalty of the streets. For

> Nature is not to be copied, but *exalted* . . . The great painter, as the great author, embodies what is *possible* to *man,* it is true, but what is not *common* to *mankind.* There is truth in Hamlet . . . there is truth in the cartoons of Raffaêle; there is truth in the Apollo, the Antinoüs, and the Laocoön. But you do not meet the originals of the words, the cartoons, or the marble, in Oxford street or St. James's. All these, to return to Raffaêle, are the creatures of the idea in the artist's mind.

Lytton, like Ruskin, had never been persuaded of the artistic pedigree of the streets, and from his pages their complex vapours are banished by the deodorant of the idealising principle.

> When asked where he got his models, Guido summoned a common porter from his calling, and drew from a mean original a head of surpassing beauty. It resembled the porter, but idealised the porter to the hero. It was true, but it was not real.

Not all artists and authors, even "Raffaêle" and Shakespeare themselves, might be so content as Lytton with figures that were "true but not real." It was not the way that Murillo worked, and he got a harsh word from Ruskin [in *Stones of Venice,* 1851 and *Works,* 1902-12] in consequence. But the roots of those who work thus, disdaining the products of Nature (who does not employ the idealising principle), however far they may penetrate into earth's darker complexities, suck up a nourishment disinfected of earth's characteristic flavours.

The city of *The Last Days of Pompeii* is constructed thus. Drawn through its ruins by the competing steeds of scholarship and the imagination, Lytton unfurls again its purple awnings, replaces in their stone ledges the wine and oil jars of the vendors, sets in motion the fountains of the little court. These as he describes them are "the creatures of the idea in the artist's mind. This idea is not inborn; it has come from an intense study;" and Lytton's creatures smell of the study.

The world is one (among others) that Lytton's contemporary, Lord Leighton, painted; but across Leighton's floors of sumptuous marble, aromas blow from the authentic landscape suffused with the authentic southern light. Leighton as a youth had embraced that landscape with an ardent rapture, and in his letters writes occasionally of it with a fidelity of impression not unlike Van Gogh's. He knew the qualities of those marble floors, their colour, texture and warmth. If Lytton had ever inhaled such sensations, the idealising principle with its study, and its exaltation of nature, had drained them off. His words do not, as at their best Leighton's do, lean out to embrace the sensual origins of his perceptions; and when he comes to write of sensuality, it is with no answering sensuality or peculiar insight. This is not only because, as Mr. Hartmann quotes, "In the England of the time there existed 'a fatal horror of whatever partakes of the nude.'" It is because the idealising principle professedly disdains the nature on which it works. So Lytton writes not as a poet but as a scholar and a moralist; and his city lacks a certain flush in consequence.

The Early Victorian reconstruction of the classical south is done then lavishly, with erudition of a sort, and with (though not enough) imagination. There lingers nevertheless a sensation of cold-storage, as in the model villages of indoor exhibitions. The reconstituted villas and streets ring curiously empty. Like Leighton in his paintings, Lytton can conjure back to the baskets of street-corner girls their fruit and flowers as on the day when the ashes first smothered them; to the groups of loiterers their Tyrian purple a good deal fresher. That is their trouble. No un-idealised human figure has lived through a single un-idealised day in those museum costumes. It is not to Lytton's purpose that they should have done so; but in consequence a certain self-conscious pre-arrangement, as in films of the kind, deprives them of the promiscuous animation of groups in, for example, the neighbouring streets of Naples. Having no common business in the place, no root to suck up life from that volcanic soil, they are animated only according to the producer's preformulated designs. The complexities of life have been deliberately purged from them, leaving abstracts from the living, statuesque, enervated, over-simplified. No wonder that, as Mr. Hartmann finds Gibson's *Graces,* they "seem theatrical." They assume postures, describe gestures, impersonate qualities. The blind flower-girl is characteristic: "At every pause in the music, she gracefully waved her flower-basket round." Such commonplace functions as remain are performed gracefully and to music.

So on marble terraces before fountains accurately re-evoked, the *sortileges* of Lytton's Pompeii enact banquets at which the blood, for all their celebrated wine (an export brand of rezzina, it appears), races no more wildly than their conversation; which is almost stationary. It is no more a Pompeiian banquet than that in George Eliot's *Romola* is a symposium of quattrocento Florence. Both are the uneasy dreams of Victorian *literati* discomposed to find themselves playing host at a dinner-party in codpiece or toga. They suffer, as Mr. Hartmann says of Gibson's *Bacchus,* from "academic stiffness."

The idealising principle seeks the universal truth behind the phenomenal reality. The author, "in the divine Priesthood of the Beautiful," believes he has discovered a permanent truth of which the characters of historical periods are the temporary exponents. It may seem to us that the truth he fleshes in Pompeiian terms is not universal but Victorian, and that he offers us despite their classical decor puppets dancing to the Victorian tune. It would be strange were this not so, and the use of a historical period for a modern parable is no less characteristic of *Romola,* Pater's *Marius the Epicurean* and Gissing's *Veranilda.* Lytton has sought figures who are true but not real, and achieved Victorians who, in historical dress, adorn the discussions of their personal situations and of the questions of the 19th century with the expletives of period novels. "By Pollux, a scurvy trick!" is a hybrid as evocative as "Stuff! said the hag." Lytton fosters this dualism, deliberately mirroring in the mashers of Pompeii "the beardless

flutterers of the saloons of London." Their voices fall with a familiar cadence as by the all but authentic sea they enact the love-scenes of Daisy Ashford, or evangelise to the true faith:

> 'You are sad, you are weary. Listen then to the words of God—"Come to me!" saith He, "all ye that are heavy laden, and I will give you rest' ".
> 'I cannot now', said Apaecides, 'another time!'

For the laboriously reconstructed exhibition town is also the "New Gomorrah," "the harlot of the sea," where "in the luxuries of an unequalled climate—the imaginative refinements of a voluptuous civilisation," the rankest vices of pagan antiquity have rooted, carried hither by an Egyptian charlatan who finds here "all that his nature craved." This is precisely that Victorian paganism defined by Eustace [in *Tour through Italy,* 1813 and *Classical Tour,* 1815] and elaborated by Ruskin out of the moral attitudes of their own time. Its enticements threaten both with emasculation. Lytton brings there the lovers of *The Young Visitors,* that in them may be fought out once and for all that contest between modern virtues and moral sternness, and the antique enchantments of the pagan south. Victorian virtue is proved to have power to resist. "Clime that enervates with a soft and Circean spell," Lytton apostrophises her, " . . . Here if God meant this working-day life for a perpetual holiday, who would not sigh to dwell for ever—" God did not so mean, and for this the lovers do not sigh. It is as well for them. On such places falls the divine judgement, and in the divine judgement the Victorian puritan believes, Eustace, Ruskin, Lytton. It confirms his own judgement in rejecting a way of life that might otherwise appear to have attractions in excess of his own.

What Lytton adds in his vision of judgement is a quality absent from Gibson's classicism, but present in the Russian work which suggested the novel. The early training of Karl Brullov was academic. As a young man in Italy he asserted the freedom of painting (as distinct from sculpture) to abandon conventional beauty of form and the imitation of classical models, in favour of the variety of nature; but his work remains, nevertheless, in the tradition against whose insipidity his first major painting was a protest. *The Last Day of Pompeii,* painted on his first visit to Italy in 1823, may suggest "too vividly the premeditated and studied effects of a stage performance." [in Miliukov, *Outlines of Russian Culture,* 1942]. It is the criticism levelled against the classicism of Gibson and Lytton; but Miss Newmarch is right to draw attention to a more vigorous impulse in this quality in Brullov. She calls his work "operatic" [in *The Russian Arts,* 1916]; and the picture was stimulated by Pacini's opera, *L'ultimo Giorno di Pompei,* the rage of its day in Rome. The copyist of *The School of Athens* is apparent in Brullov's version; but its formal rhetoric is charged with a spirit alien to it, a heightened emotional tension bordering on melodrama, and, in its abrupt alternations of chiaroscuro, Caravaggiesque. To this element Lytton also proves hospitable.

*"Cette oeuvre remarquable, qui a une longueur de dix metres, renferme vingt-trois figures principales de grandeur naturelle,"* records Hoefer, and it was in Milan, as in Russia on Brullov's return, a brilliant success. Sir Walter

Scott, after an hour's absorption before it, pronounced the work "a complete epic"; and Lytton shows his respect for such pregnant taciturnity in a footnote: "When Sir Walter Scott visited Pompeii with Sir William Gell (to whom Lytton dedicates the novel), almost his only remark was the exclamation, 'The City of the Dead—the City of the Dead!'." It was the romantic view of the 20s and 30s, very different from Sir William Hamilton's acceptance of the antique world as a pattern for the present. Lytton's classical group, in the final execution of judgement on the city, invokes Brullov's invitation to terror, and its affinities are here not with the classic taste but with the gothic. The storms that portend disaster blow from the literary coast of Otranto. On the shores of the classical world are cast the gothic monsters of the deep. A witch forsakes her cave in the volcano, which she inhabits with a snake and a fox, to stalk among the draped impersonators of Phidian marble. It is the paraphernalia of the gothic novel, elevated to the apocalyptic, that Lytton uses to execute the judgements of God.

When the mountain has destroyed the city, we find the lovers reprieved; for in their breasts, unknown to them, had lain the seeds of Christianity. They are married; and writing to invite an old friend to visit them in their new home, he describes their conversion after a phase of Victorian doubt:

> My own, my more than ever beloved Ione, has also embraced the creed! . . . We know that we are united in the soul, as in the flesh, for ever and for ever! Ages may roll on, our very dust dissolved, the earth shrivelled like a scroll; but round and round the circle of eternity rolls the wheel of life—imperishable—unceasing!

For their love is an aspect not of that sensuality which is so conspicuously absent from the art of "the Early Victorian mentality," but of that religious attitude which is so conspicuously present. "Ione is by my side as I write: I lift my eyes, and meet her smile." Love

> has taken a new sentiment in our new creed . . . for mingled with religion, it partakes of religion; it is blended with pure and unworldly thoughts; it is that which we may hope to carry through eternity, and keep, therefore, white and unsullied, that we may not blush to confess it before our God.

Those who confess their love to their God in innocence had seemed to Eustace a possible product and interpretation of the south Italian landscape. To Lytton it is only despite its malignancy that they have flourished; and for their new home his lovers have removed themselves to "porticoes hallowed still by holy and venerable shades": to Athens.

The "Early Victorian mentality" is at work in that notion of a Christian marriage and the optimistic assurance of man's ultimate habitation in eternity. The stylistic naiveties, the suspect interpretation of an historical period, likewise dated, may degrade the ideas and the work into a period-piece, whose seriousness is moving chiefly when it unwittingly touches comedy. But free the idea from the dominance of a style not to our taste, and by its nature limited;

add to that optimism for the future after life, a respect for the processes of life itself, and the "Early Victorian mentality" may show itself possessed of some grandeur. The idealising principle is not jettisoned in *Zanoni*. On the contrary; but it is so modulated that the unhampered idea dominates the novel and proves itself imposing; while the artistic experience depends least on "the creatures of the idea in the artist's mind," those elements of character and plot, in which the idealising principle is at its weakest. The style is no less than before of its period (as is right), and it stamps the idea as of its period also; but if the idea has stature, that is seen to be a source of strength.

The vast spaces of eternity were in *The Last Days of Pompeii* the infinite abode of spirits. The human body might shrivel to a grain of sand, the spirit dilated to the magnitude of a denizen of all time and space. Zanoni near his death saw it thus:

> Coursing through the fields of space, he beheld the gossamer shapes, whose choral joys his spirit had so often shared. There, group upon group, they circled in the starry silence multiform in the unimaginable beauty of a being fed by ambrosial dews and serenest light. In his trance, all the universe stretched visible beyond.

Zanoni possessed the secret of endless life. He was a Rosicrucian sage who had seen the zenith of Ur; a scientist who wielded infinite power. Now, after centuries in which his eyes had been fixed on the life of this planet, he looked beyond it to the fountain of life itself:

> far up, in the farthest blue, he saw orb upon orb ripening into shape, and planets starting from the central fire to run their day of ten thousand years. For everywhere in creation is the breath of the Creator, and in every spot where the breath breathes is life.

This is the confidence of the 1840s, the assurance of a continuing life and of a boundless future beyond the grave. For Lytton still, as for Shelley, science had not stricken the human scope, but opened only the more worlds for it to inhabit. No doubt of man's own virtues yet caused him to cower before those worlds expanding to his investigation. Nevertheless the familiar human processes remained man's necessary and fruitful element; and *Zanoni* is written to expound the limitation of the sage who, with all the power of science at his disposal, has used it only to step outside them. Mejnour, Zanoni's companion Rosicrucian, has no nostalgia for the humanity from which he has sundered himself. He is no more subject to its life than to its death:

> . . . passionless and calm, sat in his cell the mystic Mejnour; living on, living ever while the world lasts, indifferent to whether his knowledge produces weal or woe; a mechanical agent of a more tender and wiser Will, that guides every spring to its inscrutable designs. Living on— living ever—as Science that cares alone for knowledge, and halts not to consider how knowledge advances happiness.

The parable is clear. Mejnour is a product of the idealising principle; and he is a dehumanised scientific intellect.

Zanoni, though he has the knowledge by which he might live forever, and the temptation to ignore the human fate, has an undissuadable inclination to humanity. It is in his blood. After centuries in which he has renounced human passions and their ties, he falls in love with a Neapolitan girl, who draws him back into the common situation. For her he loves, dies, and submits himself with faith to the peculiar life and knowledge beyond death which he believes he will share with those he loved on earth, and for whom he sacrificed himself. For it is through the human processes that wisdom and illumination are seen to lie, and Zanoni lays down one knowledge to inherit a maturer one, that which is accessible not to the learned like Mejnour, but to the simple who love and have faith: to those even, perhaps, for whom **Zanoni** "was not meant."

> I feel, at last, that through the portals of the grave lies the true initiation into the holy and the wise. Beyond those portals I await ye both, beloved pilgrims.

So he takes leave of those for whose sake he gives his life; and he exhorts Mejnour, his companion in centuries of wandering:

> Thine age survives the youth of all; and the Final Day shall find thee still the contemplater of our tombs. I go with my free-will into the land of darkness; but new suns and systems blaze around us from the grave. I go where the souls of those for whom I resign the clay shall be my co-mates through eternal youth. At last, I recognise the true ordeal and the real victory. Mejnour, cast down thy elixir; lay by thy load of years. Wherever the soul can wander, the Eternal Soul of all things protects it still!

For the human destiny Lytton had no contempt: it was sublime in this world and beyond it. This is in part what makes him, paradoxically, impatient of the intricacies of ordinary humanity; the artistic theory is a subsidiary explanation. He was more concerned with the grand design than with the details, and with the most highly evolved human figures rather than the common animal. So for all his homage to the human processes in this novel, the raw humanity of Oxford-street and St. James's unsponsored by the idealising principle remained alike outside his taste and his art.

> True art finds beauty everywhere. In the street, in the marketplace, in the hovel, it gathers food for the hive of its thoughts. In the mire of politics, Dante and Milton selected pearls for the wreath of song.

It is Lytton's limitation as a novelist that he extracts the pearl with distaste for the complex matter from which it is distilled. He wipes it too clean of that ambiguous substance; and his representation of the human scene retains therefore some of the limitations of his Pompeii. In the earlier novel he had sought to enter the human scene at a specific place and time, turning his eyes from the spirit-haunted spaces of the universe in which so select a writer naturally belongs. Yet he never gave its inhabitants the novelist's respect for individuals. They never captured his imagination for their own sake, but for some general quality they symbolised, virtue, lust, Christianity, paganism. So

it was with the city itself. By an effort of scholarship and the imagination he had raised the ghost of the city in the present, that two figurers of its own time might inhabit it for a moral test. Yet the classical world, so tangible to his predecessors, eluded his grasp.

The Naples of which he writes in **Zanoni** is supposedly the city of the 1790s; but it is not the city of Sir William Hamilton and his coterie of musicians, swimmers and scholars; still less that of Sharp and Dr. Moore, for whom the lazzarone existed. This is a contraption more wooden than the stage-set of Pompeii, a Naples where "the leechcraft has never been very skilful," where women go out at noon to shop or gossip, while men invite each other to drink a flask of Lacrima. Any of his late 18th century predecessors, with a smattering of history, eyes alert, and some words of Italian, could have told him that this is the Naples of no time.

If the contemporary representation of the city has failed, it is to Lytton an important failure:

> As Man has two lives—that of action and that of thought—so I conceive that work to be the truest representative of Humanity which faithfully delineates both, and opens some elevating glimpse into the sublimest mysteries of our being, by establishing the inevitable union that exists between the plain things of the day, in which our earthly bodies perform their allotted part, and the latent, often uncultivated, often invisible, affinities of the soul with all the powers that eternally breathe and move throughout the Universe of Spirit.

This respect of 1853 for "the plain things of the day" and the "uncultivated affinities of the soul" is a modification of the position of 1842. But if on the level of affairs Lytton's portrait of the city is wanting in veracity, it serves its purpose. A more vivacious representation might have impeded our knowledge of that other, more important city, revealed by the idealising principle, which lies behind all cities. Here it is revealed as the persistent jet of human life ineradicably ejected from this spot of ground, unquenchable as the fire within the volcano itself, and which that fire is perhaps now used to suggest. Posidonia, Sybaris, Pompeii, Naples: it has borne many names and faces, and will bear others, but its temporary identities are of little importance. That is why it is no longer adorned by the recognisable faces of a specific time scrupulously portrayed as in the earlier novel. The idealising principle has unified it with a more primitive force comparable with the timeless landscape and the mountain of fire at its gates.

To blame it, and the humanity it engenders and who will bring down judgement upon it, is no longer to the point. This globule of human and natural luxury between rock, fire and sea is but the momentary incarnation in which the human spirit is held and defined, before it escapes into the outer spaces that await it beyond death. The city is indeed the human process; the body the mechanism for the span of life. It is now a place not so much vicious as of an alarming power to concentrate and define the essence of an individual. It is like that wine they drink at its feast, from which with flushed cheeks and unsteady steps they came into the open air, which tended yet more to stimulate that glowing fever of the grape . . . every man talked, no man listened. There was something wild and fearful in the contrast between the calm beauty of the night and scene, and the hubbub and clamour . . . The wine had brought out, as it were, each man's inmost character. Some were loud and quarrelsome, others sentimental and whining; some we had hitherto thought dull, most mirthful; some we had ever regarded as discreet and taciturn, most garrulous and uproarious.

Through the human figures of *Zanoni,* among them magicians, the primal forces of good and evil are at work as before. It is melodrama, and written as melodrama, save for the scale and dignity of the moral design and the writer's exalted conviction. Now the temporary incarnation of perpetual life, which is the city, has been justly placed on an older and more permanent terrain, against which the human actor triumphantly makes his entrance into eternity:

> Afar off, Naples gleamed whitely in the last rays of the sun, and the rose-tints of the horizon melted into the azure of her glorious bay. Yet more remote, and in another part of the prospect, might be caught, dim and shadowy, and backed by the darkest foliage, the ruined pillars of the ancient Posidonia. There, in the midst of his blackened and sterile realms, rose the dismal Mount of Fire; while, on the other hand, winding through variegated plains, to which distance lent all its magic, glittered many a stream, by which Etruscan and Sybarite, Roman and Saracen, and Norman, had, at intervals of ages, pitched the invading tent. All the visions of the past—the stormy and dazzling histories of southern Italy—rushed over the artist's mind as he gazed below. And then, slowly turning to look behind, he saw the grey and mouldering walls of the castle, in which he sought the secrets that were to give to hope in the future a mightier empire than memory holds in the past.

Against the magnitude of this shore have been washed multitudinous incarnations of good and evil, each temporal, and each, when it is past, past. Pompeii and Sybaris are alike a heap of columns on a permanent landscape in which life continues. Yet for the individual a science which, like Mejnour's, concerns itself with control of this world, limits itself to a mere moment in the human progress. The issues debated by the lovers of Pompeii were of temporary significance; they themselves have passed into "the vast space of eternity." From that eminence all things created in time, the very sage himself who had seen Ur flourish and fall, seem small and brittle:

> And the moon, resting alike over the ruins of the temple of the departed Creed—over the hut of the living peasant—over the immemorial mountain-top, and the perishable herbage that clothed its sides, seemed to smile back its answer of calm disdain to the being who, perchance, might have seen the temple built, and who, in his inscrutable existence, might behold the mountain shattered at its base.

The wiser is he who abdicates from his imperviousness to life and death. Zanoni represents in conduct the antithesis of what his novel preaches in art. It is an irony that he, presented in the Dedication to Gibson as the type of the man who, like Gibson himself, has retreated from the Agora to the Cave, should in his maturer wisdom have learned to make the return journey.

*Michael Lloyd, "Bulwer-Lytton and the Idealising Principle," in* English Miscellany, *Vol. 7, 1956, pp. 25-39.*

### Keith Hollingsworth    (essay date 1963)

[*In the following excerpt, Hollingsworth discusses Bulwer-Lytton's motivations for transforming the criminal character in* Eugene Aram *into a heroic figure.*]

Bulwer's next novel, published in January 1832, was to become a storm-center of the Newgate controversy. Unlike *Paul Clifford, Eugene Aram* contained no message of social reform, and its hero was an actual murderer, whose crime was a matter of record, no matter how it might be explained. Eugene Aram had been a strange and extraordinary man, inexplicable despite being well known to history. Bulwer tried to bring him to life as the central figure in a romance and attempted a psychological character study of an unusual criminal mind.

He was led to the subject by his own interest in the abnormal, by his keen sense of the direction of popular interest, and by special circumstances which put the idea in his way. He must have read about Aram when he went through the Newgate Calendars in preparation for *Paul Clifford;* Aram's case, which had never been forgotten since his execution in 1759, appeared in these and in pamphlets.

In any such source Bulwer would have found the story of the self-taught scholar and village schoolmaster who, with a confederate, arranged a murder in such a fashion that the victim seemed to have disappeared in order to defraud creditors; who then buried the body in a cave, and continued his occupation as a gentleman usher in other places; and who was tried and executed fourteen years later, when the finding of a skeleton not that of his victim had brought suspicion upon him. The most curious feature of the case has always been the commission of a sordid crime by a man who labored passionately as a scholar. The old accounts probably exaggerate the extent and depth of Aram's scholarship, but he is said to have learned, besides Latin and Greek, French, Hebrew, Chaldee, Arabic, and Celtic; and he undertook a comparative lexicon. His best achievement was to discern the relation between Celtic and the European languages. For being the first to see it, he is still spoken of with respect. Richard Garnett wrote in the *Dictionary of National Biography* that Aram, under favorable circumstances, might have advanced the progress of comparative philology by fifty years. In the company to be found in the Newgate Calendars, he remains impressive and unique.

Attractive enough in itself, the story of Aram had a slight link with Bulwer's family history, explained in the preface to the 1840 edition of the novel. Bulwer's grandfather had employed Aram at one time as tutor to his children; and Bulwer, hearing of the connection in 1829 or 1830, collected some local traditions of the man. Former pupils of Aram, always impressed by his gentleness and benevolence, still expressed belief in his innocence, and contributed to the generally favorable character which Bulwer was to give him in the novel.

There was a third circumstance which must at least have given the novelist confidence that a book about Aram would be popular. Thomas Hood had written a serious poem, "The Dream of Eugene Aram," which appeared in his annual, *The Gem,* for 1829. This short fiction in verse shows Aram as usher at a school and takes for its climax the moment of his arrest. Troubled in mind, he tells a boy a dream about a horrible crime; when an officer comes to take him in charge, the crime is discovered to be his own. The poem was immediately popular; it was reprinted and republished and came to be known everywhere. A novelist who had already noticed Aram's story could not have failed to be impressed. Michael Sadleir, Bulwer's admirably sympathetic biographer, speaks of Bulwer's "skill in pre-judging popular taste" and his opportunism in the choice of subjects [in *Bulwer: A Panorama: Edward and Rosina, 1806-1836,* 1931].

Thus Hood and Bulwer together caused a renewal of interest in Eugene Aram; after the novel there was a spate of minor publications, and the controversy over Aram's guilt and motives, started afresh by Bulwer, continued for many years. However, the case had a considerable literature before Hood, and Bulwer required other printed sources than the short entries in the Calendars. A modern investigator, [Eric R. Watson in *Eugene Aram: His Life and Trial,* 1913], thus sums up the history of the bibliography:

> From 1759 until the publication of Hood's poem in 1829 there was a constant stream of reports of the trial. Many magazines printed accounts of it, and a multitude of pamphlets appeared. Of these pamphlets most became early out of print, but one, sold by Bristow in London, it is said, as agent for Ann Ward, of York, established itself as the standard version, and continued to be reprinted, sometimes with, sometimes without, Aram's literary remains, by a succession of Yorkshire publishers. . . . Hood's poem and Bulwer's novel appearing within a short period of one another, a remarkable revival of interest was manifested, and Aram enjoyed for a season a factitious fame, exceeding that of 1759 itself.

Bulwer must have had some of these pamphlets, and he had read what Smollett said of Aram in his continuation of Hume's history of England.

It was, therefore, a well-known story which Bulwer chose for his novel, and the record was available to any curious reader who might want to scrutinize his literary treatment of a real criminal. He had exercised on the facts, he said in his preface, "the common and fair license of writers of fiction," but he insisted that his changes were chiefly in the minor parts of the story.

Bulwer's Aram is not a schoolmaster but a morose and gloomy scholar, "one of those earnest and high-wrought enthusiasts . . . not uncommon in the last century, who were devoted to knowledge yet disdainful of its fame; who lived for nothing else than to learn." Unlike modern schoolmen, says Bulwer, Aram does not incline to the consoling hope of human perfectibility; he is a model of tenderness to individuals, but he cares nothing for society. We find him a plaintive fatalist and a pre-Darwinian evolutionist. When he goes to the highest chamber of his house for his astronomical studies, he looks out on the stars and soliloquizes thus:

> The colours of our existence were doomed before our birth—our sorrows and our crimes; —millions of ages back, when this hoary earth was peopled by other kinds, yea! ere its atoms had formed one layer of its present soil, the Eternal and the all-seeing Ruler of the universe, Destiny or God, had here fixed the moment of our birth and the limits of our career. What then is crime? What life? —Submission!

After two years' aloof residence in Grassdale, the moody stargazer yields to the friendly advances of a country gentleman of the neighborhood, Rowland Lester, and becomes acquainted with Lester's nephew, Walter, and two daughters, Ellinor and Madeline. The latter is secretly adored by her cousin Walter; heedless of him, the high-minded and romantic girl becomes infatuated with the middle-aged Aram, whose severe nobility arouses her quite remarkable capacity for hero worship. Aram resists, but gives way, and Madeline's father is pleased with the prospect of the marriage. (Madeline is happily unaware that she is in love with Manfred and Faust and with worse than these.) Aram, who is apparently a reader of Wordsworth as well as other authors, keeps her mournfully happy with his prose poems:

> If, my beautiful love, you have selected one whom the world might deem a strange choice for youth and loveliness like yours; you have, at least, selected one who can have no idol but yourself . . . how few are the lovers whom solitude does not fatigue! they rush into retirement, with souls unprepared for its stern joys and its unvarying tranquillity: they weary of each other. . . . I do not enter the temples of Nature as the stranger, but the priest: nothing can ever tire me of the lone and august altars, on which I sacrificed my youth: and now, what Nature, what Wisdom once were to me—no, no, more, immeasurably more than these—you are! Oh, Madeline! methinks there is nothing under Heaven like the feeling which puts us apart from all that agitates, and fevers, and degrades the herd of men. . . .

While Madeline, entranced by such eloquence, prepares for the wedding, the disappointed Walter Lester sets out on his travels to forget her. He searches for his father, long unheard of, and discovers evidence that the wastrel parent, under the name of Daniel Clarke, was murdered fourteen years previously by Eugene Aram. The legal machinery is set in motion, and the officers arrive with a warrant for Aram on—of course—the day of the intended marriage. Madeline steadfastly believes in Eugene's innocence; Walter, instrument of justice on behalf of a worthless father, is the bringer of sorrow to all the family. Aram is tried, speaking in Bulwer's pages part of the actual defense, and is convicted and hanged. Madeline dies heartbroken. After a long voluntary exile, Walter marries her sister Ellinor.

The facts of the case, which may be seen in Eric R. Watson's study of it, Bulwer rearranged with a romancer's facility. He removed those inconvenient persons, the wife and seven children, whom Aram deserted some few months after the crime. He changed the victim from a young married man to a practised and cold-hearted seducer. He omitted any account of the very considerable suspicion against Aram at the time of the crime. In Aram's later life, he added the Lester family, providing Aram with friends and a fiancée and the murdered man with a son to trace him. From the trial he removed all the witnesses who gave important, though circumstantial, evidence, and he thus made the conviction depend solely upon one witness, the companion Houseman, who turned king's evidence. In general, Bulwer tidied Aram up for romantic presentation, making him attractive in everything except the central fact of being a murderer. This he retained; he kept Aram morally guilty.

Despite all the matter which Bulwer thought it necessary to replace or discard, there were in the story many elements attractive to him; the substance and the legend contained the seeds of a Bulwer novel, the possibilities for popular development. First, Aram was a criminal, and the more usable for being genteel. This criminal, moreover, could be given stature. He was capable of serious treatment, Bulwer conceived, as a tragic hero in the classical tradition; but he was Romantic, he could be made a Byronic hero, and the murder could be Gothicized. Quite above these was another possibility: to analyze the ethical confusion which might lead a man to crime and to show the corruption which would follow—an intention not unlike Dostoevsky's in *Crime and Punishment*. How Bulwer supposed that all these elements could be reconciled is inexplicable. He tried, nevertheless, and added the inevitable love-story for the circulating libraries.

That Aram could, in all but rank, be dignified as a tragic hero according to Aristotle was no mean advantage to a writer like Bulwer, whose aims included intellectual distinction as well as popularity. Even if Aram's abilities had been exaggerated, they were substantial enough for the novelist's purpose. Bulwer is vague and unconvincing about the nature of Aram's genius, but his intention is clear: Aram is a man risen to intellectual if not worldly eminence who is ruined by a tragic flaw and a single crime against the moral order. Bulwer wrote in his original preface that he had tried to "impart to this Romance something of the nature of Tragedy"; and in a later preface, perhaps feeling that the classical quality had not been properly appreciated, he tried to make the point more emphatically.

The romanticizing of the hero was an equally deliberate effort. Bulwer presents Aram as a seeker of knowledge with the boundless curiosity of a Faust, a forerunner "of the intellectual spirit that broke forth when we were chil-

dren, among our countrymen." As for the Byronic, Aram's monologues, his scorn of popular interests, his nearly mystical search for the ultimate in knowledge, his loneliness and his secret guilt mark him as one of Manfred's descendants. At one of the crucial chapters the identification is suggested by an epigraph from Byron's poem: "The spirits I have raised abandon me; / The spells which I have studied baffle me."

For a character so conceived, Gothic accessories must have seemed the most appropriate ones. Up to this time, Bulwer had shown only the mildest taste for Gothic sensations; in *Eugene Aram* he supplied the deficiency and became what Mr. Sadleir calls him, inheritor of the mantle of Ann Radcliffe. Aram, in his quiet country cottage, lives in un-Gothic surroundings; but Bulwer contrives, on one splendid night-time occasion, to bring him before an improbably romantic background. Aram joins his old confederate, Houseman, at the Devil's Crag, "consecrated by many a wild tradition," in a forest "that might have reminded a German wanderer of the darkest recesses of the Hartz." The two criminals meet in a firelit cave near a roaring cataract, and they come out to find a thunderstorm in progress:

> With every instant, the lightning broke from the river chasm of the blackness that seemed suspended as in a solid substance above, brightened the whole heaven into one livid and terrific flame, and showed to the two men the faces of each other, rendered deathlike and ghastly by the glare.

The fortissimo passage does not end without a Gothic skeleton. Having escaped in the storm from four horsemen, robbers of Houseman's band, Aram comes to a gibbet, "with its ghastly tenant waving to and fro, as the winds rattled through the parched and arid bones; and the inexpressible grin of the skull fixed, as in mockery, upon his countenance."

The interesting thing about this gibbeted body (apart from the "arid" condition of the bones just after a storm) is that Bulwer did not have to invent it; he only transposed it to a fitting scene. One of the best-known pamphlets about Aram told of his discomposure at passing a gibbet after his arrest; the Gothic imagination was at work on the story before Bulwer took it over. The matter had gone this way from the start; the criminals themselves, who lacked the advantage of a castle vault, had at least buried the victim's body in a cave, an acceptable substitute. When the materials of the tale invited Gothic treatment, how could such a novelist as Bulwer decline? He did what was indicated; and he added to the Gothic an element of the homely supernatural, imitated from Scott, to whom *Eugene Aram* was dedicated. In developing the Aram story, Bulwer thus united the romance of Gothicism with the realistic factual tradition of the Newgate Calendars.

The serious problem for the novel, one which attracted Bulwer, lay in the character of Aram: how could the scholar, apparently gentle and devoted, have committed a vicious crime? On the question of motive, the materials of history provided almost nothing. Aram was reported to have admitted his guilt orally, after conviction, and to have explained that he suspected Clarke of seducing his wife. Bulwer discarded this excuse, to be free to set the psychological problem in his own terms. What he wished was to demonstrate, in Aram's reasoning, the practical fallacy in Utilitarian ethics. In *The Disowned,* the fraudulent Crauford had consciously tried to deceive another by means of Utilitarian arguments; Eugene Aram is shown deceiving himself. Disregarding any moral absolute, he balances one choice against another, considering the greatest good of the greatest number, and self-interest betrays him.

In the fictional confession, Aram describes this mental process at length. (It strikingly resembles, in outline, that of the later Raskolnikov.) Miserable under the restraints of poverty, he is approached by Houseman, a plausible outlaw whose language, when he speaks of his war against society, resembles that of Paul Clifford or of the antisocial heroes of the romantic tradition. A great discovery is within Aram's grasp, but he has not the means to complete his work. Would it not be better for mankind for him to "commit one bold wrong, and by that wrong purchase the power of good?" Aram half accepts Houseman's view that he owes nothing to society; yet he insists that he loves mankind, and rationalizes the proposed robbery and murder on the ground of social good. The problem is easier because the intended victim is an evil man, "aged with vice":

> Within myself I felt the will—the spirit that might bless mankind. I lacked the means to accomplish the will and wing the spirit. One deed supplied me with the means. Had the victim of that deed been a man moderately good . . . it might have been yet a question whether mankind would not gain more by the deed than lose. But here was one whose steps stumbled on no good act. . . .

Arousing himself for the deed, Aram mounts on wings of rhetoric: is not his aim more glorious than that of the soldier who strikes for patriotism? When the time comes, he has arrived at a high pitch of exaltation:

> I had wrapped myself above fear into a high and preternatural madness of mind. *I looked on the deed I was about to commit as a great and solemn sacrifice to knowledge, whose Priest I was.* The very silence breathed to me of a stern and awful sanctity—the repose, not of the charnel-house, but the altar.

Since these were his motives, Aram calls himself a man "bewildered by his reason rather than yielding to his vices." The outcome proves the fallacy of his reasoning and vindicates the moral order. After the murder, he finds that his noble aims have vanished:

> I occupied my thoughts, I laid up new hoards within my mind . . . but where, with the passion for wisdom still alive within me—where was that once more ardent desire . . . the desire of applying that wisdom to the service of mankind? Gone—dead—buried forever in my bosom. . . . When the deed was done, mankind seemed suddenly to have grown my foes.

He then finds himself reasoning away the validity of his former ambition—where is the good for mankind in intellectual advancement? He loves knowledge still, but as a private solace.

As for remorse, he feels it for the first time when he discovers that the murdered man belonged to the family of his betrothed; to have brought harm to them and to her is, he feels, the real evil. The murder might still be justified if it had affected only the intended victim:

> In the individual instance it was easy for me to deem that I had committed no crime. I had destroyed a man, noxious to the world; with the wealth by which *he* afflicted society I had been the means of blessing many; in the individual consequences mankind had really gained by my deed; the general consequences I had overlooked till now. . . . All my calculations were dashed to the ground at once; for what had been all the good I had proposed to do—the good I had done—compared to the anguish I now inflicted on your house? Was your father my only victim? Madeline, have I not murdered her also? . . . How incalculable—how measureless—how viewless the consequences of one crime, even when we think we have weighed them all with scales that would have turned with a hair's weight!

It is a distinctly limited ground of repentance; Aram is still weighing evils quantitatively. In the same spirit he explains his false plea of Not Guilty at the trial: he felt that he would give less pain to Madeline and her family if they could still believe in his innocence. He feels it creditable that the "struggle against truth was less for myself than for them . . . for them, a bold, a crafty, a dexterous villain I became!"

After disclosing his secret in such terms, Aram ends his confession with an appeal to the Great and Unseen Spirit and his life with the Stoic gesture of suicide.

Aram's ethical progression, as thus outlined, may contain an element of the author's reaction against Godwin as well as against Bentham. Other Godwinian youths before Bulwer had come to feel that pure reason and individual judgment might delude their follower into moral anarchy. Aram finally affirms conventional morality: one should not go beyond "the line allotted to the rest of men." But the lesson is chiefly for Benthamites. Bentham's doctrine was more capable of general misuse than Godwin's, and cheap appropriations of it were not hard to find. Aram's confession, entirely Utilitarian in principle, is intended to undercut misapplied Utilitarian ethics with a single objection. Aram, repenting, does not attribute unique importance to a man's life, nor deny the right of the private individual to kill, nor speak of the inevitable blindness of self-interest, nor consider the need of some harmony between ends and means. The sole argument is that one cannot foresee all the consequences of an act. Still expressing a calculating morality, Aram raises a practical caution against it when it is employed to condone a visible evil.

In this novel, despite its tangle of literary derivations, Bulwer laid hold of an important and original theme. He lacked the spiritual firmness to deal with it greatly, and subjected it to indignity and triviality. Overcome by his fatal inclination and talent for popularity, he subordinated his psychological theme to a commonplace romance, cheapening the whole with a plaster covering of sentiment according to current fashions. He evaded the true difficulty of analyzing Aram's motives, performing this essential task summarily in the secret autobiographical confession. He had not the capacity to execute the novel on the plane of his finest perceptions, and left us only a reminder that he might have been among the greatest of the English novelists.

Whatever Bulwer intended, and failed to do, he did not intend *Eugene Aram* as a protest against capital punishment nor even against a miscarriage of justice. He never wished to abolish the death penalty for murder; and in his novel of 1832 he did not deny, he did not question Aram's guilt. Aram, it is true, says "my hand struck—but not the *death*-blow," but this is of no legal consequence; as for the intention to murder, Bulwer inserted a footnote to emphasize that it had been present. He described Aram as morally responsible, and did not suggest that he ought to escape hanging.

Nevertheless, the tone of the book is not quite right. Although Aram never, not even at the end, seems morally heroic, it is possible to suppose at times that the author thinks him so. A writer less hasty and more subtle might have prevented this confusion, even while arousing some sympathy for the misguided criminal. Not the subject but Bulwer's failure to dissociate himself from his hero—basically a failure of imagination and of technique—became the source of contemporary objection, whenever it was sincere. First *Clifford,* then *Aram.* Bulwer had taken the side of the criminal again.

As soon as published, *Eugene Aram* was an immediate popular success; it "took Europe by storm and became one of the most abidingly popular of all Bulwer's works" [according to Sadleir]. Two individuals whose notice of the book is recorded testify—even better than the literary reviews—to its general circulation. That literate courtesan, Harriette Wilson, who had drawn Bulwer into an occasional correspondence, mentioned *Aram* as the favorite of "the boarding school miss." The other person, Pierce Egan, called upon Bulwer to present him with a curio; it was, he said, the caul of Thurtell, and Bulwer alone among literary men was worthy of possessing it.

If readers were favorable, reviewers were divided, and the author's treatment of a criminal subject was put in question at once. The *Athenaeum* found genius manifest in the book but wished it had never been written. The *Edinburgh,* noticing Bulwer's novels for the first time, found Aram incredible as a murderer for money. These reviews were balanced, and some others were entirely favorable. The *Spectator* commented upon the idealized portrait of Aram, adding: "In this we see nothing to blame: we are merely informing our readers that Mr. Bulwer's tale is far more like *Manfred* than the *Newgate Calendar,* —a compliment, certainly; though not of the kind that will contribute, in these days, to the sale of the book." The *Monthly Review* called the new book the best of Bulwer's works and found in it a fine tone of Christian philosophy. The chief attack upon it came, not surprisingly, from *Fraser's*

*Magazine.* Novelizing the *Newgate Calendar,* said Maginn, was a work suited to Bulwer's capacity, and he gleefully charged Bulwer [in *Fraser's Magazine* V (February, 1832)] with the taste for low life which Bulwer had attributed to him as MacGrawler:

> When the author of *Pelham* affects to describe refined feelings and distinguished society, he forthwith labors and becomes overstrained; but among thieves and blackguards—in the tap, the ken, the hedge-row pot-house—in the purlieus of the Minories and Whitechapel, he writes with an easy felicity of phrase that betokens an intimate acquaintance with the scenes described. . . . If the Bill is carried, and a representative given to the Tower Hamlets, let Mr. Bulwer canvass them: he will be popular and appreciated there.

The last sentence reminds us that Bulwer, besides caricaturing Maginn in *Paul Clifford,* was of the reform party in the House of Commons.

Maginn objected to Bulwer's departures from fact, to the disparities in Aram's character, and to the literary imitations evident in the novel. His last charge was this: "Finally, we dislike altogether this awakening sympathy with interesting criminals, and wasting sensibilities on the scaffold and the gaol. It is a modern, a depraved, a corrupting taste." Extraordinary crimes, such as those of Burke and Hare, induced imitation, he added; a book like this might have the same effect.

The evil of arousing a wrong sympathy with a criminal had sometimes been alleged against the newspapers. Here it was charged against a novel for probably the first time. Maginn's objections, the essence of all the criticism of Newgate fiction, were to be repeated by others—some of whom, unlike Maginn, believed what they said—against Bulwer, Ainsworth, Dickens, and lesser persons. *Eugene Aram* greatly extended its author's popularity, but it allowed a hostile critic to complain that Bulwer had shown his intellectual hero, though a thief, a liar, and a murderer, to be among the noblest of mankind.

The reader using any copy of *Aram* printed in the last hundred years may be puzzled by the strength of the attack upon the book, for he finds Eugene not guilty of murder. The change was made late; in 1840, when there was a new edition of his works, Bulwer wrote a preface for *Aram* in which he defended both the choice of subject and the treatment. In that year, the controversy over Newgate literature was lively, but he had not recently been at the center of it; with a little condescension, he set his work apart:

> The guilt of Eugene Aram is not that of a vulgar ruffian; it leads to views and considerations vitally and wholly distinct from those with which profligate knavery and brutal cruelty revolt and displease us in the literature of Newgate and the Hulks.

But in the eighteen-forties, as will appear, there was a resurgence of attacks upon Bulwer. When these had quieted, and when he was preparing *Aram* for re-issue in 1849, he made the significant changes which have been followed ever since. In the new preface for this edition, he announced that he had changed his mind about Eugene's guilt: having restudied all the evidence, he had concluded that Eugene Aram was an accomplice in the robbery but no more. In the text of the novel, Bulwer changed the substance of the criminal's confession, made his attitudes more palatable both before and after the crime, and altered some passages which had been interpreted as showing the author's admiration for the criminal. Aram looked, after all this, a different man indeed. One has to remember that from 1832 to 1849, over the whole period of attack and defense of Newgate novels, Eugene Aram was guilty of premeditated murder.

As material for the theatre, *Eugene Aram* was far more popular than *Paul Clifford,* which was dramatized in 1832 and made a melodrama in 1835. There were four stage versions of *Aram* in 1832, the year of publication; one of these was played in Edinburgh. The most successful of them was also the earliest; it was that of W. T. Moncrieff, which opened at the Surrey on February 8, 1832, not much more than a month after publication of the novel. A competing theatre had its version on stage five days later. Moncrieff's play was included in standard collections of the nineteenth century—Dick's Standard Plays, Cumberland's Minor Theatre, Lacy's Acting Editions—and in French's Acting Editions. Eric Watson, historian of the trial, records other instances of the later dramatic use of Hood's poem and Bulwer's novel.

The chief attack of the year upon *Eugene Aram* was not a review but a fictional parody, "Elizabeth Brownrigge: a Tale," which appeared in two issues of *Fraser's Magazine.* This story was once attributed to Thackeray, but it is more reasonable to accept the suggestion of Miss Miriam Thrall [in *Rebellious Fraser's,* 1934] that the authors were William Maginn and his friend J. G. Lockhart. The title came from the chief character, a woman who figures in the Newgate Calendars as a monster of cruelty. She ill-treated the girls apprenticed to her from a foundling hospital, and one of them died. Elizabeth Brownrigg was hanged September 14, 1767. Before Maginn's time, she had already served as material for parody: in the first number of the *Anti-Jacobin,* in 1797, was an "Inscription" for the door of her cell in Newgate, which read in part:

> Dost thou ask her crime?
> She whipp'd two female 'prentices to death
> And hid them in the coal-hole. For her mind
> Shap'd strictest plans of discipline. Sage
>     schemes!
> Such as Lycurgus taught, when at the shrine
> Of the Orthyan goddess he bade flog
> The little Spartans; such as erst chastised
> Our Milton when at college. For this act
> Did Brownrigg swing. Harsh laws! But time
>     shall come
> When France shall reign, and laws be all re-
>     peal'd!

The tale about her in *Fraser's* is prefaced by a long dedicatory letter addressed to the author of *Eugene Aram;* the purported author, eager for success, finds that he can achieve it by studying and imitating the works of Bulwer. "Elizabeth Brownrigge" is the result. The sarcasm is elaborate and sometimes witty, but it descends sometimes into sober diatribe. The letter parallels the preface to *Aram:* the author remarks that he has "taken a few slight liberties with the story."

> As you have omitted any mention of the wife of your Eugene, I have not thought it necessary to recall the reader's attention to the husband and sixteen children of my Elizabeth. As you have given your hero more learning and virtue than he possessed . . . I have presumed to raise the station of my heroine. . . . I have represented her in my tale as a young gentle-woman of independent fortune, a paragon of beauty, a severe and learned moral philosopher, and the Lady Bountiful of the village of Islington.

The attack is exuberant, and it makes undeniable hits. What extends it to its considerable length—its more than twenty-five thousand words seem at first to be bad editorial judgment—is that the writers make a literary game of parallels, imitating *Aram* closely at a hundred points. Some of the parallels have little satirical effect, but these contribute to the whole appearance of sedulous imitation and must have provided amusement for anyone who had just read the novel. Bulwer had prefixed a quotation, in Greek, from *Oedipus the King;* the parody uses a still apter one from *Medea,* beginning with the same "Alas, alas." Bulwer revealed that he had first begun a verse tragedy about Aram; "Brownrigge," we are told, was begun as a burletta. The damaging likeness to the novel runs through the whole of the parody: it mocks Bulwer's mannered descriptions, his rhetoric of emotion, his genteel purple passion. The young lover of Elizabeth, "who stood six feet two without his shoes, united, in the compact and slender structure of his person, the vigour of the Hercules with the elegance of the Apollo." Elizabeth has been made beautiful, too; but of course the essence of the satire (following the line of the *Anti-Jacobin* verses) lies in the conversion of the sadistic murderess into a fine-souled being who weeps at the stripes she inflicts and who explains her actions in the kind of exalted language Bulwer had put in the mouth of Aram. Some parts of the attack fall short of consistency—Elizabeth's Benthamism, surely, leaves Bulwer unscathed—but the burlesque is frequently diverting. Like Aram, Elizabeth is high-minded even in prison:

> She completed a large stock of baby-linen for the poor; she perused and commented upon the principal new publications of the day; and she composed an elaborate parallel between the characters of Socrates and Lady Jane Grey, after the manner of Plutarch.

Though "Elizabeth Brownrigge" had its origin in personal hostility, it kept on proper literary ground in exposing and exaggerating the weaknesses of Bulwer's book. It showed, to readers not aware of its authorship, only the degree of malice which makes satire possible. In this instance, personal animosity moved Maginn and Lockhart to express opinions about *Eugene Aram* which they might well have felt, though less strongly, if the book had been written by someone else.

But this entirely appropriate satire was only a visible surface over a turbulence. Despite the parody, the controversy with Bulwer was not really about the morality of the criminal theme, and the next exchange of verbal blows did not even mention it. In December 1832, the *Quarterly Review* carried a review of Morier's *Zohrab the Hostage,* commenting unfavorably on several of Bulwer's novels but saying nothing of **Eugene Aram** or Bulwer's attitude toward criminals. The tone was not improper. Bulwer, then editor of Colburn's *New Monthly Magazine,* replied in his January number with a "Letter to the Editor of the Quarterly Review." This was an open attack on Lockhart as a writer; the tone was contemptuous and angry. There was, the letter said, "no man living who possesses the same power of incorporating the narrowest sentiments in the meanest language." Michael Sadleir explains the reasons for this burst of temper, and they had nothing to do with **Paul Clifford.** The ostensible issue—the morality of Bulwer's novels—had been left behind as the quarrel progressed.

To sum up the matter, Bulwer's two novels were criticized chiefly by Maginn, with the collaboration of Lockhart, for reasons calculated to enlist the support of right-thinking people. Mr. Sadleir, sympathetic to Bulwer, calls it "Tory-cum-Grub Street" persecution. However one apportions blame in the confusion of political and personal quarreling, the critics' conviction that the novels had a dangerous tendency seems the least of their motives.

*Keith Hollingsworth, "The First Newgate Novels, 1830-34," in his* The Newgate Novel, 1830-1847: Bulwer, Ainsworth, Dickens, & Thackeray, *Wayne State University Press, 1963, pp. 65-110.*

### James C. Simmons   (essay date 1971)

[*In the essay below, Simmons details the methods of Bulwer-Lytton's documentation in his historical novels.*]

Bulwer (1803-1873) was the innovator and the foremost exponent of the new type of historical fiction based on extensive research, careful attention to factual accuracy, and the depiction of historical events and personages. His novel **Rienzi** initiated the new vogue in 1835 and his **Harold** marked its close in 1848. Of all the men and women working in historical fiction throughout this period, Bulwer displayed the most substantial talent and enjoyed the highest reputation among his contemporaries. His major historical novels represent the most scholarly and complex use of history by any Victorian novelist. He evolved the most comprehensive and articulate theory of the composition of the historical romance and he was perhaps more acutely aware than his contemporaries of the various paths open to him. He wrote in his preface to **Harold** that he had early realized there were two options available to him: "the one consists in lending to ideal personages and to an imaginary fable the additional interest to be derived from historical groupings; the other, in extracting the main interest of romantic narrative from History itself." Bulwer had taken up the first option in his first three historical romances, **The Disowned** (1828), **Devereux** (1829), and **The Last Days of Pompeii** (1834). However, he felt uneasy about the possibility of factual distortions slipping into his fictions when the historical portions were subordinated to a melodramatic narrative. And he abandoned the

method for the alternate means of using romance in the service of history, an approach he claimed to have initiated.

In his three major historical novels Bulwer was less interested in the portrayal of "mere manners" which modern scholarship and the multitude of historical romancers had already rendered familiar to the reading public. Instead he concentrated upon developing the great personages of past epochs whom he felt had been "carelessly dismissed in the long and loose record of [the] centuries." He set famous historical figures at the nucleus of his works and attempted to show how the dynamic, powerful, and continually vital makers of history went about their work.

Bulwer selected not only major historical personages for his fictions, but looked for those periods of tremendous social upheaval when the men involved were placed under the abnormal stress of cataclysmic events. He favored epochs of momentous change when an older order was giving way to a newer, and a country's history was being decisively settled for the next several hundred years. Scott, too, had frequently chosen periods of transition; but, as he made clear in his preface to *The Fortunes of Nigel,* this was for the increased possibility of picturesque development available to the novelist working in these periods. Bulwer, uninterested in picturesque contrast and juxtaposition, went to these periods of violent change for other reasons. The portrayal of historical characters at those times presented the greatest challenge to his powers as a novelist and historian. The juxtaposition of the old and the new threw the representative qualities of each period into the clearest relief for historical analysis.

Bulwer, in thus taking upon himself the task of dramatizing great and famous personages and significant moments from history, broke completely with the tradition established by Scott. The role he accepted for himself was that of historian, not novelist. His chief problem was "how to produce the greatest amount of dramatic effect at the least expense of historical truth." This difficulty was first grappled with in **Rienzi** in 1835, and the success of that "experiment" confirmed him in his belief that "the true mode of employing history in the service of romance, is to study diligently the materials as history; conform to such views of the facts as the author would adopt, if he related them in the dry character of historian." Such a method, Bulwer stressed, placed the writer under close restrictions. The chief events of the narrative are set and the characters already drawn; they cannot be tampered with by the author. Imaginative speculation is permitted only in the development of the "inner, not outer, history of man." That is, the author was free to conjecture about private passions and motivations, but this must always be speculation hedged about by close historical scholarship. In all these novels Bulwer was careful to insist that he took no liberties with the facts, but rather constructed his stories upon the real facts: "[My] boldest inventions are but deductions from the amplest evidence [I] could gather."

> For the main materials of the three Historical Romances I have composed, I consulted the original authorities of the time with a care as scrupulous as if intending to write, not a fiction,

but a history. And having formed the best judgment I could of the events and characters of the age, I adhered faithfully to what, as an Historian, I should have held to be the true course and true causes of the great political events, and the essential attributes of the principal agents.

For his three major historical novels, then, Bulwer assumed the mantle of the historian. In each case he was convinced by his own extensive investigation that a particular man or event had been misjudged by contemporary historians, and he wished to set the record straight. In *Rienzi* he was primarily concerned with salvaging the Tribune's character from the "superficial and unfair" treatment by Gibbon: "I regarded the completion of these volumes, indeed, as a kind of duty; —for having had occasion to read the original authorities from which modern historians have drawn their accounts of the life of Rienzi, I was led to believe that a very remarkable man had been superficially judged, and a very important period crudely examined." The novel, which was originally intended to be a history, was in fact the first comprehensive treatment of Rienzi to appear in England and sustained Bulwer's promise that the reader would gain "a more full and detailed account of the rise and fall of Rienzi, than in any English work of which I am aware."

In *The Last of the Barons* Bulwer undertook to explicate the complicated events of the latter half of the English fifteenth century: "I venture to think that the general reader will obtain from these pages a better notion of the important age, characterized by the decline of the feudal system, and immediately preceding that great change in society which we usually date from the accession of Henry VIII, than he could otherwise gather, without wading through a vast mass of neglected chronicles and antiquarian dissertations." Hume's judgments on the period are constantly attacked in the notes to the novel as "hasty," "inaccurate," and "more than ordinarily incorrect." The novel also contains considerable scholarly speculation regarding both the character of Richard III ("I think I shall give a new reading of Richard the Third's crimes and characters—new, but I hope not untrue") and the reasons for the sudden and decisive rupture between Edward IV and his baron Warwick in February of 1470, an aspect of their relationship that had long been obscured in histories. Bulwer's final resolution was that Edward had foolishly attempted the virtue of one of Warwick's daughters, but he did not arrive at this solution of the rupture because it was the most satisfying in terms of a romance situation. Rather he came to this conclusion only after painstaking and exhausting research into the chronicles. Since this represented an original interpretation of a crucial moment, and one at odds with the opinions of most former scholars on the period, Bulwer was careful to present his argument with an extensive annotation of sources to support his thesis. He was equally explicative in *Harold.* There he detailed the political, social, and intellectual features of the age so that the reader would understand "why England was conquered and how England survived the Conquest." And to this end he devoted much of his leisure time for almost a decade to research.

Bulwer himself traced the popularity of his historical fiction to his "faithful narration of historical facts" rather than to any fictional elements he might have employed in the composition of the novels. Confident of his research and the suppositions he drew, he stood by the validity of his historical novels as history: "Nay, [the author] ventures to believe, that whoever hereafter shall write the history of Edward IV, will not disdain to avail himself of some of the suggestions scattered throughout these volumes, and tending to throw new light upon the events of that intricate but important period." Before attempting to write, Bulwer systematically studied all available material, both ancient and modern. His general technique was to rely heavily and narrowly upon a single work for a particular section of the novel at hand, going to other sources only when some secondary circumstances, which lacked support in the main reference work, could be found elsewhere. When a particular source coincided with his own interpretation of a person or an event, Bulwer generally followed it closely. In this respect he shares in the general attitudes and practices of the literary historians of his day. Macaulay [in *Miscellaneous Essays and the Lays of Rome,* 1910], for instance, had often argued that there was no reason why, with the proper research and restraint, the formal historian could not portray a historical figure such as Elizabeth with a vividness comparable to Scott's portraiture in *Kenilworth* and "without employing a single text not authenticated by ample testimony."

Bulwer, like the literary historiographers, insisted upon the importance of imagination in breathing life into the facts of history. "Fiction," he asserted, "when aspiring to something higher than mere Romance, does not pervert, but elucidate Facts." Bulwer here echoes Carlyle's dictum [in *The Collected Works of Thomas Carlyle,* 1899], that "Stern accuracy in inquiring, bold Imagination in expounding and filling-up, these are the two pinions on which History soars." For Bulwer, as for the other literary historians, the artist in history should exercise his imagination to flesh in "the cold outlines of the rapid chronicler," achieving immediacy through color and detail. In Bulwer's historical novels the fictional element is rigidly restricted to the depiction of the "inward life" of historical personages as it determines their motives. All is worked toward a more complete understanding of the "genuine natures of the beings who actually lived [in order] to restore the warmth of the human heart to the images recalled from the grave." The purely imaginary characters, when they are introduced, are always few in number and so ordered as not to interfere with the actual historical events and motivations. Always these wholly fictitious characters are merely the passive sufferers in the panorama of history and never its active agents. Furthermore, we find that most of these minor characters exist less as fully realized individuals and more as academic abstractions. Writing as a historian and wishing to examine each age as fully as possible, Bulwer frequently set up his minor characters to embody some particular force he felt to be at work in the epoch in which he was interested. Therefore, if Nicholas in *The Last of the Barons* represents the incipient middle and commercial classes coming into prominence at the end of the fifteenth century, then we can assume that Nicholas' destiny is that of his class, for he takes his validity as a representative of a historical type rather than as an individual.

This readiness to see characters as abstractions, together with Bulwer's selection of epochs of transition, led to another characteristic feature of his historical fiction, namely the artificial balancing of characters, one against the other, the older order up against the new. This is most evident in **The Last of the Barons** where we find the dichotomy expressed chiefly in the figures of Warwick (representing the feudal order of a landed aristocracy) and Edward IV (standing for that segment of the aristocracy allied with the new commercial classes). The same division is carried out on other levels. Marmaduke, a retainer in Warwick's household, and Nicholas Alwyn, an ambitious merchant and the future mayor of London, repeat the Warwick-Edward axis. Other characters are set up, however, to illuminate various aspects of this division. Adam Warner represents the forces of modern science and knowledge incipient at this time; he is juxtaposed with Friar Bungay, who embodies medieval superstition and finally works the destruction of the scholar.

In his own day Bulwer's historical fictions were received by most critics and readers as worthy additions to the historical publications of the age. Henry Crabb Robinson, a voracious reader, worked through Bulwer's historical novels in 1843 and noted in his journal that "I could not but consider [them] as instructive as the general history of Hume." The long-hostile *Fraser's Magazine* took a kindly view of **Harold** and found that in spite of too much unassimilated history in the narrative, it still gave "a better account of the causes which led to the Norman Conquest than any book we know." Edward A. Freeman in his *History of the Norman Conquest of England* observed that **Harold** was a work "which, if the sentiment and super-natural parts be struck out, forms a narrative more accurate than most so-called histories of the time" and insisted that Bulwer's treatment of the age was superior to that of Palgrave in the latter's multi-volume studies of Saxon England. And at a number of points in his own history Freeman acknowledges debts to Bulwer's novel. Even as late as 1914 an American critic [E. G. Bell, in *Introduction to the Prose Romances, Plays, and Comedies of Edward Bulwer, Lord Lytton* 1914], could call **The Last of the Barons** "indispensable to the student of English history."

In retrospect, Bulwer's historical novels represent the major effort on the part of a select group of novelists to utilize the historical romance as a vehicle for original speculation upon historical personages and events. The others who followed his lead were somewhat less ambitious. Their fictions were closely tied to the historical researches of others. They employed the form as the readiest means of reaching a broad reading public and were content to popularize rather than initiate. The novels of Chamier, H. Martineau, Howard, Palgrave, and Macfarlane took advantage of those topics in history which were of current interest to the Victorians. Like Bulwer, they assumed the mantle of historian and wrote romances which adhered to the strict standards of accuracy laid down by their more illustrious contemporary. Together they represent an ex-

tension into the realm of historical fiction of the theories and practices of romantic historiography and, as such, their works of "light history" all share to varying degrees in the strengths and weaknesses of romantic historiography: its nationalism, partiality, hero worship, and the lack of a truly critical spirit. Like Macaulay, Carlyle, and Froude, these historian-novelists were all amateurs and men of letters, who looked upon history as an adjunct to *belles lettres,* rather than a science as did Niebuhr, Ranke, and their followers in England. These men were primarily interested in the depiction of individuals and events and they avoided the discussion of the more abstract questions of economic, political, social, and religious issues. By slighting opportunities for reflections, generalization, and the discussion of more abstract matters, these historians reduced history to a well-told tale. Behind the approach of Macaulay, Carlyle, and Froude was a firm conviction that a factual story may be, and should be, told as agreeably as a fictitious one.

Novels such as Bulwer's **Rienzi,** H. Martineau's *The Hour and the Man,* and Macfarlane's *The Camp of Refuge* realized the ultimate implications embedded within the theory and practice of romantic historiography. Their works should be of more than passing interest to students of both Victorian fiction and historiography.

*James C. Simmons, "The Novelist as Historian: An Unexplored Tract of Victorian Historiography," in* Victorian Studies, *Vol. XIV, No. 3, March, 1971, pp. 293-305.*

**John Hazard Wildman   (essay date 1974)**

[*In the following essay, Wildman emphasizes the unequivalency between Bulwer-Lytton's literary abilities and his artistic ambitions in his rendering of the legend of King Arthur.*]

In 1848 Edward Bulwer Lytton published his epic poem, **King Arthur,** in the twelve traditional books; when he brought out the 1870 edition he wrote a preface in which his loftiness of purpose towers before the reader. Solemn and Victorian, the preface announces the author's intentions and so becomes the sadly serious introduction to the most unintentionally comical poem in the language.

Lord Tennyson is not to be rivaled, Lord Lytton writes [In *The New Timon,* 1846]:

> In deference to the fame of an illustrious contemporary, I may be permitted to observe that when, in my college days, I proposed to my ambition the task of a narrative poem, having King Arthur for its hero, I could not have even guessed that the same subject would occur to a poet somewhat younger than myself, and then unknown to the Public; and though, when my work was first printed in 1848, Mr. Tennyson's 'Morte d'Arthur' had appeared, I was not aware of any intention on his part to connect it with other poems illustrating selected fables of the legendary King.

In addition, Lord Lytton's plan and purpose were completely different from those of Tennyson: "I have filled no pitcher," he remarks, "from fountains hallowed to himself."

Unlike Tennyson, Lytton eschewed Malory as a source—mainly because he wished to write "an entirely original story," but also because he wished to draw more heavily on the literature of the North. Malory's account would definitely run counter to his intentions—among other things, the problem of the guilty love of Arthur and Guenever. That situation would certainly not be appropriate to a poem in which Guenever flutters as a dove, guiding Arthur through most of the books, until she finally takes different substance as the Saxon Christian maid, Genevieve. From this point on, her marriage becomes (for the reader who retains a childhood veneration for King Arthur) a ghastly inevitability, and he experiences no surprise whatsoever, but merely a sense of morbid confirmation, when he reads near the end of the poem:

> Saxon, from Arthur they lineage date,
> Thine eagles, Arthur, from thy Saxon dove:
> The link of peace let nuptial garlands weave,
> And Cymri's queen be Saxon Genevieve!

Lord Lytton explains in his "Preface" how a difficulty set up by Malory may be solved by mental dexterity: "Enlarging on the hint in the Romance of 'Merlin'," he writes, "that there were two Guenevers 'very like each other,' I have purposely allowed to the respective wives of Lancelot and his lord—'One name, indeed, but with a varying sound'."

The question of Lancelot's chastity remains unopened in this poem. Genevieve could obviously not have been a factor; marriage to her counterpart merely suggests excessive penance.

In drawing upon the literature of the North, Lord Lytton felt that he was able to invest his poem with deep meaning and hidden seriousness:

> For the romance from which I borrow is the romance of the North—a romance, like the Northern mythology, full of typical meaning and latent import. The gigantic remains of symbol worship are visible amidst the rude fables of the Scandinavians; and what little is left to us of the earlier and more indigenous literature of the Cymrians, is characterized by a mysticism profound with fable. . . . This fondness for interior or double meaning is the most prominent attribute of the romance properly called Gothic, the feature most in common with all creations that bear the stamp of the Northern fancy . . . It unites the flying Griffin of Arabie to the Serpent of the Edda; the Persian Genius to the Scandinavian Trold; and wherever it accepts a marvel, it seeks to insinuate a type.

Among the later unions which the literature of the North sponsored, none could have more interest for the student of the biologically curious in literature than Lord Lytton's **King Arthur:** there, the Saxon dove was united to the British lion; that was the strangest marvel of all, if it were not capped by the insinuation that they would breed eagles.

The poem itself concerns Arthur's being suddenly summoned forth to a pilgrimage while he and his court are engaged in a sort of *fête champêtre*. Although others present are horrified at the apparition, Arthur knows when kings should obey and with remarkably little ado goes off. Three knights—Caradoc, Gawaine, and Lancelot—would like to go with him, but it is only after some time that Lancelot alone passes the test which allows him to proceed. Much later on Gawaine is also allowed to follow—mainly for the purpose of comic relief. He is in turn followed by a raven, who, with a disappointing lack of parallelism to the dove, does not turn into anyone at all at the end of the poem. The raven, however, continually annoys Gawaine, who has a way of being casual about extreme danger but enormously put out by trifles. A dim, faraway, retreating melancholy roar of Byron's *Don Juan* is present in the book devoted to Gawaine, just as there is a faint remembrance of Spenser in other parts. But the roar is dim indeed: it consists of a few casual rimes and a somewhat stagy insouciance about Gawaine. When the damsel leaves him, but the dog who has followed him remains true, he says to the "carle" who has taken the damsel and now wants the dog:

> "My friend," replies Gawaine, the ever bland,
> "I took thy lesson, in return take mine;
> All human ties, alas, are ropes of sand,
> My lot today tomorrow may be thine:
> But never yet the dog our bounty fed,
> Betrayed the kindness or forgot the bread."

No exception, for any breed of dog whatsoever, is provided for in this home-truth brushed with humor.

At the conclusion of his book, after four felons have felled him with clubs and he has been bound and then addressed somewhat pompously by a Viking, Gawaine's humor brims over:

> As spoke the Viking, over Gawaine's head,
> Circled the raven with triumphant caw;
> Then o'er the cliffs, still hoarse with glee, it fled.
> Thrice a deep breath the knight relieved did
>    draw,
> Fair seemed the voyage—pleasant the haven;
> "Blessed saints," he cried, "I have escaped the
>    raven!"

"As regards my employment of Humor in aid of romance," wrote Lord Lytton in his "Preface," "I need discuss neither the example of Ariosto nor the special grounds of my belief that the serious purpose of this poem is best developed by an occasionally humoristic treatment of it."

It is evident, however, that in the main the poem is overwhelmingly serious. Arthur's adventures are sufficiently complicated to justify the poem's being called a romance. They include his wandering into an idyllic land where people live close to a beautiful nature and where he escapes being forced to marry the princess only by being driven by thoughts of "Fame, Cymri, and God" to jump into a small boat and escape down one of those frequent streams of romance. The actions of the dove have also urged him to this course—not, the reader realizes at the end of the poem, for such disinterested reasons as he had supposed at the time. Ægle, the princess, threw herself to the inevitable death in the waters.

Arthur, in another episode, is allowed to see a great pageant of English history; it is described in the Argument to Book VII as "The Vision of times to be—Coeur de Lion and the age of chivalry—The Tudors—Henry VII—the restorer of the line of Arthur and the founder of civil freedom—Henry VIII and the revolution of Thought—Elizabeth and Age of Poetry—The Union of Cymrian and the Saxon, under the sway of 'Crowned Liberty'." The Tudors are given particularly benevolent roles in one of their most interesting Victorian appearances. Henry VII makes a novel visit to Arthur, who lies in a trance, and delivers himself of an unwarrantedly self-righteous speech:

> And by the corpse of Arthur kneels the king,
> And murmurs, "Father of the Tudor, hail!
> To thee nor bays, nor myrtle wreath I bring;
> But in thy Son, the Dragon-born prevail,
> And in my rule Right first deposes wrong;
> And first the weak undaunted face the strong."

Henry VIII makes a somewhat unfavorable first impression but at the end of his second stanza is triumphantly vindicated:

> He passed—Another, with a Nero's frown
> Shading the quick look of impatient eyes,
> Strides—and casts his sceptre, clattering, down
> And from the sceptre rushingly arise
> Fierce sparks; along the heath they hissing run,
> And the dull earth grows lurid as a sun.
>
> And there is heard afar the hollow crash
> Of ruin;—wind-borne, on the flames are driven:
> But where, round falling shrines, they coil and
>     flash,
> A seraph's hand extends a scroll from heaven,
> And the rude shape cries loud, "Behold, ye
>     blind,
> I, who have trampled Man, have freed the Mind!

The insinuation seems to be that Henry, after years of death, has developed a hindsight which, like occasional English legal decisions, has reversed his former foresight. Elizabeth is, naturally, the climax of this procession of Tudors in a strangely favorable light. When she walks along, "the ghosts of knighthood," joining in this frenzy of new interpretations, throw all chronology to one side, arise, and smile upon the Queen. Literature, like one of the more important universities at a centennial, has two representatives:

> With her, at either hand, two starry forms
> Glide—than herself more royal—and the glow
> Of their own lustre, each pale phantom warms
> Into the lovely life that angels know,
> And as they pass, each fairy leaves its cell,
> And GLORIANA calls on ARIEL.

The poem is strong on the side of prophecy; it can, at any time, go with the greatest ease into a solemn strain of forecasting. All of this attitude, however, seems to be based on the somewhat unfair assumption that all the world has been waiting for the nineteenth century, and all events in history take their proper perspective viewed in relationship to that enlightened age. Arthur is once told this:

> Yet from thy loins a race of kings shall rise
> Whose throne shall shadow all the seas that
>     flow;

> Whose empire, broader than the Caesar won,
> Shall clasp a realm where never sets the sun.

In the vision referred to above, a pretty little tableau is presented after the Tudors have been safely escorted away. It centers on Queen Victoria and begins with a questionable comparison:

> Mild, like all strength, sits Crowned Liberty,
> Wearing the aspect of a youthful Queen:
> And far outstretched along the unmeasured sea
> Rests the vast shadow of her throne; serene,
> From the dumb icebergs to the fiery zone,
> Rests the vast shadow of that guardian throne.

About the twentieth century, the prophetic voices, kindly despite their bluster, are mute.

So interesting have been these striking parts of the poem that the summary, like a lagging freshman theme, has gotten itself bogged down in them. It need only be said that Arthur arrives home just in time to see the Saxons invading Carduel, his capital. Genevieve, the Saxon maid turned Christian, is almost sacrificed to the pagan gods, then is not, then is almost sacrificed to the pagan gods again, and finally and eventually is not. The entire eleventh and most of the twelfth books are given over to the description of the fight. As a matter of fact, the challenging opening line of the eleventh book reads "King Crida's hosts are storming Carduel!" One begins to have dawn upon him the full revelation of why the poem has always been a failure. Circumstances and the supernatural have always been in preceding books so punctually and unfailingly predisposed to Arthur's interests that it is almost impossible to believe that any lasting harm can come to Carduel. Suspense is at a very low ebb, and Carduel's salvation in the twelfth book seems more a concern of theology and predestination than it does of drama. Again, one gets nostalgic notes of the nineteenth century, most dim and distant heard in the twentieth, when the entire situation is solved by friendship and dynastic marriage: "And dreamland sleeps round golden Carduel."

As poetry *King Arthur* is, despite its royal pretensions, of very humble origin. Occasionally there are lines that have a happy mellowness or a sudden, but subdued, grandeur. There is, for instance, this: "Rome's shadow lengthening o'er the world of man" or

> Floated a sound of laughter, musical
> As when in summer noon, melodious bees
> Cluster o'er jasmine buds, or as the fall
> Of silver bells, on the Arabian breeze;
> What time, with chiming feet in palmy shades,
> Move, round the softened Moor, his Georgian
>     maids.

or

> In linked arcades, and interwoven bowers
> Swept the long forest from that single stem:
> And, flashing through the foliage, fruits or flow-
>     ers
> In jewelled clusters, glowed from every gem
> Golconda hideth from the greed of kings,
> Or Libyan gryfons guard with drowsy wings.

But poetry of this sort is very sparingly provided in *King*

*Arthur.* Mostly, it is of the caliber of "Slow from his sight the waves the Vision bear, / And not a speck is in the purple air" or the old watered-down Miltonic Byronism of color titles: "The kingly Caesar of the Christian North," or the mere silliness of "For Heaven dawns clearest on the simple mind."

Such pairs of rimes as "wooer" and "to her," "replace" and "dais" simply serve as painful reminders that this is not Byron—as do "mind" and "rejoined" that it is not the eighteenth century; nor is characterization very successfully rendered in the phrasing of the poem. Emotions are largely conveyed through formulas too melodramatic for any but a cynic to call time-honored. The pagan priest, seized by Arthur, "thrilled with priestly wrath to feel / His sacred arm locked in a grasp of steel."

The Middle Ages is quite simply explained. It was a time "When o'er the lone yet ever-haunted ways / Went frank-eyed Knighthood with the lifted lance." Also:

> Then soul learned more than barren sense can
>     teach
> (Soul with the sense now evermore at strife);
> Wherever fancy wandered man could reach—
> And what is now called poetry was life.

(Did the future laureate note this pregnant thought?)

*King Arthur* did not thrill the Victorians. It was didactic enough, in a narrow way. It brought no blushes. But it also brought no pleasure, no escape—merely, a dreary, unexcited sort of confusion, as though one were lost in a London fog and wanted his dinner. There was none of the mellow sadness of Tennyson, none of the dim shadowiness of a King whose story had started with his leaving, whom Tennyson had always kept—even when he was on the scene—epically vague and godlike in aloofness. This other mission of King Arthur from Avalon, they rightly felt, had aborted.

*John Hazard Wildman, "Unsuccessful Return from Avalon," in* Victorian Poetry, *Vol. 12, No. 3, Autumn, 1974, pp. 291-96.*

## Allan Conrad Christensen    (essay date 1976)

[*In the excerpt below, Christensen explores Bulwer-Lytton's social views and idealist philosophy as represented in his novels.*]

Bulwer wanted his art to possess a timeless validity, and this study has generally emphasized those aspects of his work that imply his desire to appeal to the ages. Yet since he also achieved immense popularity within the context of his own age, his particular influence upon his contemporaries and immediate successors is also a matter of interest. To assess this influence fully would require one to consider the force not only of his fiction but also of his very carefully constructed plays—especially the enormously successful and frequently revived *The Lady of Lyons* (1838) and *Money* (1840). In summarizing the evidence of his influence, I shall nevertheless remain within the area of his fiction and fictional theory, which have constituted the subject of my study. His notions about the

basic duality of art—the external form as opposed to the internal soul—may also help once again to organize my discussion. For his novels demonstrated their immediate power both in the more superficial aspect of their relevance to various fads and schools and in their more fundamental adherence to his theories of ideal art.

*Pelham,* which changed the fashion in men's evening clothes in 1828, was Bulwer's first spectacular success, and in subsequent works by the so-called silver-fork novelists one discerns the first instances of his literary influence. Novels by his friend Lord Mulgrave and by Mrs. Catherine Gore (with whom after an initial misunderstanding he would also be on cordial terms) thus seem to have perpetuated his literary legend about fashionable life. Although he would insist on the independent, realistic accuracy especially of Mrs. Gore's observations, his own achievement had helped—along with novels by Ward and Lister—to make the fashionable world possible for art. *Pelham* had enforced, for example, the conventional impression of a pattern and a center—Almack's—around which an otherwise futile society could seem to circle. Certain stereotypes of social climbers, dandies, and bored women, he had also shown, could make effectively interacting central characters, while a point of view that combined affection with satire could provide such works with some complexity of interest.

Yet despite the extreme copiousness of silver-fork production, only Bulwer's novel and Disraeli's *Vivian Grey* (the first part of which had appeared in 1826) may seem to possess any enduringly significant aesthetic value. More interestingly than in the succeeding silver-fork novels, the influence of the author of *Pelham* may consequently be sought in his diffusion of a most intriguing public legend about himself. For very much like *Childe Harold* before it, *Pelham* had conveyed the impression of an identity between protagonist and author, which the author had then taken pains for some years to validate. The Pelham image, as Bulwer so successfully adumbrated it, was that of an outrageously flippant and cynical dandy aristocrat, who nevertheless had a hidden social conscience and who was utterly dedicated to noble political and aesthetic ideals. While references to it are ubiquitous in the period, the image evidently fascinated Disraeli in particular. Frequently and quite consciously, Disraeli modelled his public deportment upon Pelham's and attributed his allegedly startling social successes to his having "Pelhamized" people. In the years from 1830 to 1837, during which he struggled so hard to get into Parliament, he also submitted to the guidance of Bulwer in person. As his constant mentor, Bulwer kindly introduced him to the right people (including the woman he would marry in 1839) and enabled him to gain the social credentials required for the launching of a political career. One can also find evidence of Bulwer's influence, of course, upon most of Disraeli's novels from *The Young Duke* (1831) and onwards.

In the United States, where Bulwer's contemporary reputation was if anything even greater than in Britain, the author of *Pelham* had a notable effect upon Edgar Allan Poe. As "the most powerful influence on Poe's early prose writing," Bulwer seems to stand, in the opinion of Michael

Allen, behind Poe's frequent literary use of a persona and his general elaboration of "the fictional method of self-projection." Poe naturally drew his inspiration in this regard not only from the self-propagandizing *Pelham* but more especially from Bulwer's shorter tales, such as "Monos and Daimonos" (1830), and from the discursive *Asmodeus at Large* series (1833). And outside his art too, Poe belongs very much to the histrionic Byronic and Bulwerian tradition of the dandy who "walk[s] the paths of life," as Bulwer said, "in the garments of the stage." Emphasizing his southern gentility, Poe created his aristocratic role, which the example of Bulwer further assured him could be admirably adapted to a career of public service—in particular, as a journalist. For Bulwer had also offered Poe most striking evidence of the fact that magazine writing (which Carlyle had once termed "below street-sweeping as a trade") was now properly occupying "the first men in England." Poe dreamed for many years of editing a journal that would possess the characteristics of the *New Monthly Magazine* under Bulwer's editorship (1831-33). As described in a prospectus of 1843, Poe's journal would be resolutely independent and impartial, would endeavor to please while elevating the public taste, and, most importantly of all, would bear throughout its pages the definite, individualizing imprint of a single mind. Although successfully realized, according to Allen [in *Poe and the British Magazine Tradition*, 1969], in only a few numbers of *The Broadway Journal*, Bulwer's ideals thus continued to haunt Poe, even when he conceived of his career—still in the histrionic manner—as a lurid failure. And when Poe died, it seemed appropriate to his literary executor to publish an obituary that compared him at length to a character in Bulwer's most recent novel, *The Caxtons.* That character, Francis Vivian, is the noble, promising dandy gone bad, and his association with Poe appeared to have sufficient justice to enable it to endure for some years in the public consciousness.

*Paul Clifford* (1830) provided some of the first practical evidence of Bulwer's own commitment to noble political and social causes, and more definitely than *Pelham* it opened up a new field for the contemporary novel. While deriving from Godwin, its way of arguing on behalf of legal and penal reform appears to have made it the first important *Tendenzroman* in Britain. Bulwer followed it with *Eugene Aram* (1832), in which he advanced a thesis about criminal psychology and which remained throughout his lifetime one of his five or six most popular works. When other novelists hastened to imitate these works, though, they created not so much a school of novels with a thesis as a host of thrilling accounts of criminal life—the so-called Newgate novels. Among the most significant works to be referred thus to Bulwer's paternity are Ainsworth's best-selling *Rookwood* (1834) and *Jack Sheppard* (1839) as well as Dickens' *Oliver Twist* (and many portions of *Barnaby Rudge* and *Martin Chuzzlewit*). Later on, as Joseph I. Fradin has argued [in "The Novels of Edward Bulwer-Lytton" (Ph.D. diss., Columbia University, 1956)], the influence of *Paul Clifford* is also evident in Charles Reade's more genuinely tendentious novels—especially in "the prison scenes and reform program of *It Is Never Too Late to Mend*" (1856). Of incidental interest too is Reade's choice of the title *Masks and Faces* for a

play he subsequently turned into a novel because Godwin had once proposed the same title to Bulwer for *Paul Clifford.*

Reade's *It Is Never Too Late to Mend* derives likewise from Bulwer's treatment of crime in *Night and Morning* (1841) and *Lucretia* (1846). Fradin finds these last two works even more important, however, as forerunners of the detective story. Once called—probably inaccurately—the "earliest detective story in the English language," *Night and Morning* introduced in the character Favart the ancestor of the subsequently stereotyped "quietly menacing, ubiquitous" detective of English fiction. This novel, which has retained its peculiar power to enthrall some readers (and which contains, incidentally, an unexpectedly naughty scene in a French boarding house), surely impressed Wilkie Collins, who has more usually received credit for the invention of the English detective story. Sheridan Le Fanu was similarly influenced by Bulwer's way of plotting his stories of crime, and Fradin has noticed some startling parallels between the plots of *Lucretia* and Le Fanu's *Uncle Silas* (1864).

Still one returns to the conclusion that most of the novels following in the wake of Bulwer's criminal tales use their horrific material and the carefully contrived element of suspense towards an end that differs considerably from Bulwer's own. Whereas Bulwer subordinates everything else to his overriding desire to convey a message or establish some "metaphysical" pattern, the works of his disciples exist primarily as sensational entertainments. This fact again becomes obvious, as Fradin once more forces the point home, in connection with the supernatural fad that *Zanoni* (1842) apparently inspired. To this fad one can attribute some rather brainless works by Ainsworth and Le Fanu—as well as aspects of Collins's more satisfactory *Armadale* (1866).

Despite the extraordinary number of successors to Bulwer's early novels of fashion, crime, and the supernatural, their influence may be gauged almost more interestingly, then, with respect to the opposition they aroused. For the opposition was indeed widespread. While Bret Harte, for example, would later write a parody entitled "The Dweller of the Threshold" (1865), Bulwer's supposed responsibility for silver-fork and Newgate fiction provoked immediate and violent storms of rage. Bulwer received the greatest share of the blame for all those books that were allegedly lending glamor to high and low life and inspiring young men to become either dandies or criminals. The impression that *Pelham* merited denunciation as the very archetype of silver-fork fiction even became such a commonplace that Carlyle, who had almost surely not read the novel himself, naturally felt he could repeat it in *Sartor Resartus.* Although *Pelham* (very definitely) and its successors (rather less definitely) imply a satiric judgment of the society they treat, the satire often escaped notice, and the dandy novels were savagely parodied. At times, however, the parodies also betrayed a sneaking tendency to relish the snobberies of high life, and the dividing line between the celebrators and the satirists of the fashionable milieu is still a difficult one to draw. When the silver-fork genre had ceased properly to exist, its parodists continued

Part. VIII.

The Caxtons

There entered in the first-drawing room in my Father House in Russell St — an Elf!!! clad in white, — white — small, delicate — with curls of jet over her shoulders, — with eyes so large, — so lustrous that they shone thro' the room, as no *merely human* eyes could possibly shine; — the Elf approached — & stood facing us. — The sight was so unexpected & the apparition so strange — that we remained for some moments gazing at it in startled silence —

At length my Father, the bolder, & wiser one of the two, & more fitted to deal with the eerie things of an other world had the audacity to step close up to the little creature & bending down to examine its face said, — "What do you want, my pretty creature!"

*Manuscript page from* The Caxtons (The Earl of Lytton, The Life of Edward Bulwer, First Lord Lytton).

their ambiguous and widely appreciated efforts: "the fashionable novels seem to have taken," remarks Kathleen Tillotson [in *Novels of the Eighteen-Forties,* 1961], "a lot of killing." The efforts of the celebrators and the satirists of fashionable life finally culminated in *Vanity Fair*—whose author had been parodying the silver-fork school in general and Bulwer in particular for many years.

Thackeray had been parodying, indeed, not only Bulwer's "fashionable" poses but also—in works like "Elizabeth Brownrigge" (1832), *Catherine* (1839-40), and "George de Barnwell" (1847)—Bulwer's Newgate fiction. And because of the degree of his obsessive animosity toward Bulwer, one must actually consider Thackeray as one of the principal Victorian novelists to have been affected by Bulwer. In Bulwer's novels, he confessed in 1848 to their mutual friend Lady Blessington, "there are big words which make me furious, and a pretentious fine writing against which I can't help rebelling." Yet as Ellen Moers points out, "Thackeray's early diary testifies to the closeness with which he followed Bulwer's exclusive rise to fame, and the care with which he read *Falkland, The Disowned, Pelham, Devereux* and so on." In fact, he was constantly comparing himself jealously to Bulwer, and behind his revulsion lurked a guilty longing, not fully admitted until much later in life, to enjoy a youth like Pelham's. The complex fascination Bulwer's image of the dandy artist held for him must help to explain, then, his many contributions to the notoriously vicious campaign that *Fraser's* waged against Bulwer throughout the 1830's. It explains most importantly the *Yellowplush Papers* (1837), wherein Thackeray's protagonist is "an upside-down Pelham," as well as *Pendennis* (1848-50), which constitutes Thackeray's "serious imitation of and commentary on the fashionable novel as Bulwer and Disraeli had made it." In *The Newcomes* and *Philip* he would also employ projections of himself as commentators within the story and confess that he had learned the device from Bulwer.

Beyond the boundaries of the novel of society—high and low—and of particular social problems, Bulwer's influence operated in less controversial ways. *Ernest Maltravers* (1837) and *Alice* (1838) remained popular and quietly helped, for example, to make the usefulness of the Goethean pattern of *Bildung* clear to subsequent novelists. Although in earlier works Carlyle, Disraeli, and Bulwer himself had already employed elements of the plotting found in *Wilhelm Meister,* these two novels in particular brought the plot into an effective focus. The three-stage plot, which Bulwer would continue to use with many variations, involves the hero's rebellion and setting forth on his quest, his chastening experiences leading to his repentance, and finally his return home to discover that the object of his quest had been there all along. The pattern underlies innumerable Victorian novels, and one suspects that Bulwer, who was always recognized as an important channel for German influences, thus had some effect on many major works by Dickens, Meredith, Trollope, Eliot, and Hardy.

More easily documented, perhaps, is his influence, as Coral Lansbury has defined it, upon the novels that contributed to a certain myth about Australia. Bulwer derived from Samuel Sidney's propaganda the impression that Australia, in particular, could constitute the blessed land in which experience chastened and redeemed the hero. Hard work enabled the prodigal there to earn back the squandered patrimony, and as a new and successful man he might even hope to return to England and to harmony with himself. In a larger sense Australia was the land in which the lost soul of England—the true patrimony of Englishmen—must be recovered and nourished back to health. Given enormous popular currency in *The Caxtons* (1848-49), the Australian myth clearly influenced Dickens—for example, in his sending of Micawber (who resembles not only John Dickens but also Uncle Jack in *The Caxtons*) off to Australia. Reade's *It Is Never Too Late to Mend* likewise derives in this respect, as well as in the others I have mentioned, from Bulwer, while Henry Kingsley's Australian novel, *Geoffry Hamlyn* (1859), also owes the structure of its plot to *The Caxtons.* Since many works of literature thereafter perpetuated it, the myth came profoundly to affect the Australian consciousness of identity. It was as an author, then, rather than as Colonial Secretary that Bulwer exerted his most important influence upon Australia.

Bulwer's historical romances contributed to a related popular myth that informed the national consciousness back in Britain. As "the great disseminator of Scott's impulse in the early Victorian period," Bulwer thus seems important to Avrom Fleishman at least in part because he transmitted Scott's ambiguous myth of "the Norman yoke" on to Charles Kingsley (especially in *Hereward*), Thomas Hardy, and D. H. Lawrence. Present in both *The Last of the Barons* (1843) and *Harold* (1848), the myth amounts to an awareness of the still-enduring, rural, Saxon soul of England, which centuries of rule by an alien Norman culture have never quite extirpated. Hardy, in particular, may seem to show the evidence of Bulwer's influence here and in his own brooding sense of the large historical forces that forever reduce individual man caught in time to impotence. For his historical consciousness resulted precisely from his boyhood absorption in the romances of Bulwer—along with those of Scott, Ainsworth, and G. P. R. James—and that absorption penetrated all aspects of his mature work.

The historical works of Bulwer also have their more contemporary and timely relevance as comments upon political and social movements of the 1830's and 1840's, and some critics have found Bulwer influential in this respect too. Curtis Dahl believes Bulwer defined a new type of historical novel with present relevance, to which one can refer "Eliot's *Romola,* Shorthouse's *John Inglesant,* Thackeray's *Henry Esmond,* Reade's *The Cloister and the Hearth,* Morris's *The Dream of John Ball,* and . . . a large proportion of the historical poetry and drama of the age." As James C. Simmons has furthermore indicated [in "The Novelist as Historian: An Unexplored Tract of Victorian Historiography," *Victorian Studies* 14 (1971)], Bulwer's works influenced not only historical novelists but also professional historians, whose citations of Bulwer strengthened a prevailing impression that he was as significant an historian as Hume or Palgrave.

In another way too the historical works carried Bulwer's influence beyond the boundaries of fiction: from *The Last Days of Pompeii* (1834) and on, they in particular inspired dramatic adaptations. Most of these adaptations are, to be sure, inconsequential, but Bulwer's *Rienzi* (1835) did become the source for Wagner's third opera. And *Harold,* for which Bulwer had done the research in the library of Tennyson d'Eyncourt, provided the chief source for Tennyson's play. (In the area of historical legend and poetry, it is also worth recalling that Tennyson believed Bulwer's epic *King Arthur* of 1848 had helped at least to prepare the public taste for his *Idylls.*)

Of the remaining fictional schools one might perhaps define a novel of domestic life for the sake of the Caxton series, which in addition to *The Caxtons* includes *My Novel* (1850-53) and *What Will He Do with It?* (1857-59). But while proving that these works carried Bulwer to the zenith of his popularity, Edwin M. Eigner has also argued [in *The Nineteenth-Century Writer and His Audience,* 1969] that in them Bulwer seems to have been following rather than influentially leading the fashion. In the case, similarly, of Bulwer's contribution to the tradition of Utopian satire, evidence of his specific influence remains somewhat elusive. His *The Coming Race* (1871) apparently did have a decided influence on George Bernard Shaw, and it is clearly relevant, at least, to the entire flurry of such satires at the end of the nineteenth and the beginning of the twentieth centuries. Yet *The Coming Race* did not, it seems, have any effect on Butler's *Erewhon* (1872). Early reviewers guessed that *Erewhon* must have been written by the author of *The Coming Race,* but Butler maintained he had not yet even read Bulwer's work and resented the ascription.

Bulwer's most significant influence—to turn finally from what he considered "externals" to the "soul" of his aesthetic theory—ultimately transcended the framework of the individual schools and types of fiction. With all his prefaces, introductions, and assorted critical essays, he even became in many minds, both friendly and hostile, less the author of particular novels than the theorist and apologist for fictional "Art." His propaganda on behalf of the "metaphysical" novel may thus have implied more than just an effort to establish one fictional genre at the expense of many others. For he was seeking to define the criteria that could make novels of all sorts works not merely of entertainment but rather of high aesthetic seriousness. And although many Victorians were beginning to converge from their various quarters toward this same goal, Bulwer may deserve a special share of the credit for ensuring the success of the tendency. "After Carlyle" and—to expand Mrs. Tillotson's observation—after Bulwer, "the rift between the 'prophetic' and the merely entertaining novel widens."

The specific influence of Bulwer in this tendency to treat fiction as serious art is probably detectable in much of the critical writing of the period. K. J. Fielding has noticed, for example, Bulwer's relevance to John Forster's theory of the novel, as embodied in his articles for the Examiner. Also readily documented is the widespread attention and respect accorded in particular to Bulwer's advocacy of

"wholeness" or "unity" in fiction. Poe thus observed of *Night and Morning* that Bulwer had sacrificed everything to unity of plot, and Poe's own definition of a plot as "that in which no part can be displaced without ruin to the whole" again suggests the impact of Bulwer upon him. In worrying about how to achieve "unity" in *Vanity Fair,* Thackeray too affirmed the value of the aesthetic virtue that was linked, as Mrs. Tillotson implies, with Bulwer's name. The hostile critic W. C. Roscoe would likewise concede in 1859 the exemplary value in Bulwer's work of "the grasp of the whole design" and the way in which "he marshals all his material and concentrates his various forces on one result." But while revealing Bulwer's influence beyond the field of fiction, Matthew Arnold may provide the most interesting testimony to the force of this aspect of Bulwer's fictional theory and practice: "If I have learnt to seek in any composition for a wide sweep of interest," he wrote Bulwer in 1868, "and for a significance residing in the whole rather than in the parts, and not to give overprominence, either in my own mind or in my work, to the elaboration of details, I have certainly had before me, in your works, an example of this mode of proceeding, and have always valued it in them."

Other readers valued Bulwer's works especially for their blend of "idealized patterns of meaning" with the "appearance of reality," and it seems likely that Bulwer influenced Nathaniel Hawthorne very strongly in this area. Indeed, as John Stubbs analyzes it [in *The Pursuit of Form: A Study of Hawthorne and the Romance,* 1970], Hawthorne's entire, well-developed theory of the romance appears to derive from Bulwer—although to some extent from Scott and Cooper too. Professor Eigner's forthcoming book will tend, moreover, to show that Bulwer's theories underlie not only his own and Hawthorne's works but also those of Dickens, Emily Brontë, and Melville.

In some of these cases—and most clearly so in that of Emily Brontë—the affinity with Bulwer has probably not resulted from his specific influence. The relationship between Bulwer and Dickens, however, offers one of the most definite and important instances in literary history of two friends who profoundly and profitably influenced each other. Roughly like Goethe with respect to Schiller and Coleridge with respect to Wordsworth, Bulwer may generally have acted as the more intellectual and philosophical party in the relationship. In Bulwer's own opinion at least, Dickens was "no metaphysician" whereas he did understand "the practical part of authorship beyond my power." So their strengths operated in happily complementary fashion not only during their collaboration to produce Bulwer's *Not So Bad As We Seem* (and their other efforts on behalf of their Guild) but in all aspects of their long literary association. Their value to each other emerges with especially interesting clarity in their correspondence of 1860-62 about Bulwer's *A Strange Story,* which Dickens was publishing in *All the Year Round.*

Limiting attention, though, to Bulwer's influence upon Dickens, one may recall that Bulwer persuaded his friend to change the ending of *Great Expectations.* And while critics formerly suspected that Bulwer must have urged basely commercial considerations, it now seems clear that he had appealed to the lofty theories which he and Dickens by then held in common. For Dickens had, in fact, subscribed for many years to Bulwer's important theories: "It is indisputable," in the opinion of H. P. Sucksmith, "that many of the principles of narrative art in Bulwer's early essay ['**On Art in Fiction**'] were put into practice by Dickens from 1838 and onwards with striking success." Not only did Dickens thus repeat innumerable small motifs, details of plotting, and character types from Bulwer's novels, but he also began to use some of Bulwer's grandiose, Aristotelian vocabulary in his musings about the structure of his own novels. Sucksmith finds Dickens' application of Bulwer's notions about "reversal of fortune" and "multiple catastrophe" especially illuminating in this context. It is not surprising too, then, to observe Dickens meditating upon the technical importance of "sympathy" and of "idealised effects" which Bulwer had probably discussed with him before elaborating them in the *Caxtoniana* essays of 1862-63.

Even while elaborating his theories of a serenely ideal art, Bulwer had recognized the significance of the demonic element in life and art, and here one may observe a last important area of his influence. Melville and Poe surely responded to this aspect of his art, but it may be that Dickens, once again, best intuited the terrible beauty in his vision of revolutionary wildness and evil. Jack Lindsay has thus linked *A Tale of Two Cities* most persuasively back to *Zanoni* and the unfinished *Edwin Drood* to *A Strange Story*, and Fradin has added force to the linkages. The same two critics have also gone on to identify Bulwer as one of the major links between the Romantic believers in the energy of the Imagination and the symbolist and surrealist adventurers into the realms of the irrational.

It is perhaps only necessary to add that whatever else may be debatable the supernatural elements in Bulwer's fiction did very definitely constitute a principal influence upon Mme. Blavatsky and her theosophists. In the context, however, of Bulwer's extraordinarily pervasive influence upon the fiction, the myths, and the very conceptions of reality of his contemporaries, his contributions to theosophy may seem a distinctly minor affair.

*Allan Conrad Christensen, in his* Edward Bulwer-Lytton: The Fiction of New Regions, *The University of Georgia Press, 1976, 268 p.*

## Elliot Engel and Margaret F. King   (essay date 1981)

*[In the following excerpt, taken from an essay originally published in 1981, Engel and King define the function of the Romantic protagonist in* Eugene Aram *and other novels of the 1830s.]*

More than any other British novelist, Edward Bulwer-Lytton has been regarded as a mere literary weathercock, twirled first one way and then the other by the surface winds of popular taste. According to Edward Wagenknecht [in *Cavalcade of the English Novel: From Elizabeth to George VI*, 1943]: 'Bulwer was the most remarkable virtuoso in the history of English fiction. He could take up a line of fiction, exploit it for all it was worth, and then, just when he seemed to have written himself out, he could

turn to an entirely different kind of fiction and repeat the performance. Bulwer was very shrewd in guessing which way the cat would jump.' The fact that Bulwer's life followed the same frenzied veerings as his fiction—he was a poet, novelist, playwright, translator, editor, baronet and Member of Parliament all within a single decade—increased his vulnerability to the charge of dilletantism. The image of him as a vapid dabbler was unwittingly reinforced even by his own grandson, who once remarked: 'The range of his writing was extremely wide, and one might say that he emptied his mind into his books as fast as he filled it.' Coupled with Thackeray's brutal parodies of his fiction in *Fraser's* and Carlyle's castigations of it in *Sartor Resartus,* Bulwer's diversity has indeed diverted most modern readers and critics from his novels.

There is, of course, some justice in the fact that Bulwer has been largely ridiculed or ignored in the twentieth century. He is hardly a genius of the first order, and his humourless pretensions to such status, as reflected in his turgid, pompous prose, add a certain piquancy to the pleasures of denigrating him. On the other hand, Bulwer should not be dismissed as a mere charlatan, concocting cheap literary potions to fuel every fictional craze. Allan Christensen, in *Edward Bulwer-Lytton: The Fiction of New Regions,* has been the strongest and most recent voice in negating the image of Bulwer as a facile opportunist. Arguing that Bulwer was a dedicated artist, Christensen points to the underlying mythic or metaphysical conceptions in the novels which make their variety more apparent than real. Christensen is surely right that there is more unity than diversity among the novels, and we would argue, further, that there is an especially significant unity among those novels which he wrote from 1830 to 1837. All seven novels of this period, from *Paul Clifford* to *Ernest Maltravers* and its sequel *Alice,* try to answer the same question, perhaps the most fundamental question that early Victorian artists faced: how is the Romantic alien to function within a culture in transition, when many of the justifications for his rebellion against society are being eradicated by reform? Bulwer's fiction during the reign of William IV provides his broadest platform for addressing this issue, since in his earlier novels of the 1820s his heroes could still enjoy flaunting their disregard for society, and after 1837 he turned his enormous energies to drama and then took up a very different kind of fiction.

The Romantic protagonist, whose genius and aspirations set him at odds with a repressive society, preoccupied Bulwer from the outset of his career. His first four novels, written during the late 1820s, introduce all the Romantic prototypes which would be transmuted into his fictional heroes of the next decade: the Byronic hero, the dandy, the hero of the *bildungsroman* and the hero of the historical romance. The morbidly brooding protagonist of *Falkland,* Bulwer's first novel, has been described by Park Honan as a 'Bulwer Byronized'. Never again would Bulwer create a hero who would reject all reality beyond the terrors and the grandeur of his own ego. Indeed, Bulwer would later refer to *Falkland* as a vehicle of personal catharsis through which he purged the 'perilous stuff' of his youthful imagination. And he would point to *Pelham,* his second book, as a novel which 'put an end to Byron's Satanic mania and turned the thoughts and ambitions of young gentlemen without neckcloths, and young clerks who were sallow, from playing the Corsair, and boasting that they were villains'. In actuality, even though as a dandy Pelham out-Brummels Brummel, he is not as far removed from the Byronic rebel as Bulwer imagined him to be. As Ellen Moers notes in her study of this character type [in *The Dandy: Brummel to Beerbohm,* 1960], the dandy is 'an archetype of the human being in revolt against society', standing somewhat like the Byronic hero, 'on an isolated pedestal of self' and refusing to acknowledge any standards of dress and behaviour other than those imposed by his own will. Although Pelham was intended as an ironic under-cutting of the dandiacal pose as well as a rejection of the Byronic, the satire is so ambiguous that Pelham appeared to many readers, among them Thackeray and Carlyle, not as the deviant from a more earnest norm but rather as the norm itself.

After these two contemporary and somewhat complementary portraits of Romantic aliens, Bulwer shifted to the recent past with **The Disowned,** set in the late eighteenth century. This novel has two heroes whose characteristics reflect in part the romantic traditions which Bulwer had exploited in the novels preceding them. Clarence Linden, the young hero, is something of a dandy, and his mentor Algernon Mordaunt is, for all his philanthropic idealism, rather Byronic. But Bulwer's allegorical treatment of such characters reveals his debt to a third type of Romantic alien—the hero of the *bildungsroman* such as Goethe created in *Wilhelm Meister.* Unlike their Goethean predecessors, however, Bulwer's protagonists in **The Disowned** never move convincingly from alienation to assimilation. In **Devereux,** Bulwer's last novel of the 1820s and first historical romance, the author merges Scott's and Goethe's romantic heroes, but, once again, he departs from his models by creating a protagonist who never is absorbed into the social mainstream. By the time Devereux returns to and restores the family estate from which he was exiled, he lives almost wholly in his memories.

Bulwer's prefatory remark that Devereux is really 'a child of the nineteenth century' suggests that Bulwer's last novel of the 1820s, like the three that preceded it, is concerned with the Romantic alien's inability to merge with his society in order to find a creative but practical outlet for his genius and his energies. The largely unresolvable conflict between the Romantic alien and his culture in Bulwer's novels of the 1820s reflects in part the nature of the decade. Although weakening, the Tory obstructionism against which Byron and Shelley had raged died slowly; and the mechanistic deism of the religious establishment offered little resistance to the mechanistic materialism of an industrial economy. Added to the alienating cultural forces was Bulwer's very personal sense of alienation during this decade. In 1825 the seat in Parliament which he had hoped to gain from Hertford went instead to a friend who had intrigued for it while Bulwer was in Paris. His mother's disapproval of his marriage to Rosina Wheeler, and his subsequent refusal to accept an allowance from his mother after he married against her wishes, forced Bulwer to retire to near seclusion at Woodcot, where he had to pour all his energies into writing to support himself and

his new wife. And because Bulwer's success came first in the literary sphere rather than the political, or perhaps only because of his temperament, the influence of Byronic and German Romanticism remained strong upon him. The blatant autobiographical strains discerned by most critics in Bulwer's first four novels indicate that personal and cultural forces combined in the 1820s to keep both Bulwer's protagonists and their creator from moving effectively from Romantic self-consciousness to the earnest social consciousness of the Victorianism that began to emerge in the novels of the next decade.

As the 1830s began, Bulwer retailored his heroes to fit the changing patterns of his personal life and the cultural milieu. Many of the personal justifications for Bulwer's romantic alienation were vanishing: he had been reconciled with his mother, his allowance had been reinstated, he had settled into one niche in society as a successful novelist, and, most importantly, in 1831 he began carving out a second one as a Liberal Member of Parliament. Moreover, Regency and Tory indifference to the problems of the disadvantaged was being replaced by the social consciousness and reforming spirit of a Whig-dominated Parliament; changes could now be made by working within the system rather than attacking it from without. Therefore, the central issue which confronted Bulwer in the 1830s was whether the Romantic hero, without many of his traditional causes, was doomed to become an anachronism, or if he, like his culture, could be capable of fruitful transformation. By the end of William's reign, Bulwer had transformed his earlier prototypes of the romantic alien into the Carlylean romantic hero, who while maintaining his transcendent, anti-materialist vision is able to translate that vision into effective social action.

The transformation came gradually. Indeed, Bulwer's first two novels of this period (**Paul Clifford** and **Eugene Aram**) narrate stories of the quintessential rebel—the criminal—and in neither book can such a protagonist be effectively assimilated into his society. Nevertheless, **Paul Clifford** is considered the first *roman à thèse,* the first social problem novel, of the Victorian era. In it Bulwer merges two of his previous romantic prototypes, the dandy and the *bildungsroman* hero, and tries to invest the resultant hybrid with a strong social conscience. According to his preface, Bulwer sees **Paul Clifford** as a novel about society's warping of a young man with great potential, who turns to crime because of the brutality and bad associates he encounters when he is unjustly incarcerated. At the very end of the novel, Paul makes a stirring four-page speech in which he blames the evils of the legal and penal systems for the unsavoury directions in which his 'apprenticeship' has led him. However, little which occurs between the preface and those final pages in any way justifies classifying the novel as a *roman à thèse,* a Newgate novel or a *bildungsroman.* Bulwer does not, for example, portray Paul as brutalized or corrupted by his prison experience; instead, he warns that 'We do not intend, reader, to indicate, by broad colors and in long detail, the moral deterioration of our hero; because we have found, by experience, that such pains on our part do little more than make thee blame our stupidity instead of lauding our intention'. In actuality, more than half of the few pages devoted to Paul's imprisonment allow Paul's mentor, the roguish highwayman Augustus Tomlinson, to narrate his autobiography. Tomlinson's manners, dress and even his ennui are so reminiscent of the Regency upper class that his prison conversations with Paul could as well have been set in a drawing room. Paul is not, therefore, corrupted by a Fagin-like criminal; rather, he is dazzled by a Pelham-like dandy. And after he escapes from prison with Tomlinson, he merely exchanges his earlier associations with rakish men about town for new relationships with dandified highwaymen who have similar elegant language, dress and upper-class pretensions. After adopting the alias of 'Lovett', Paul rises to be the leader of the highwaymen because he is the dandy *par excellence:* handsome, well-tailored, clever and possessing impeccable manners.

Finding a life of crime delightful, Paul and his gang steal only from the cruel or the rich and share such an inspired devotion to their chivalric trade that any reader must find the lifestyle appealing. Viewed in the context of the entire novel, Paul's final stirring speech on social injustice seems very artificial and is clearly more fluff than substance, more nougat than Newgate. On the whole, the thrust and tone of the novel are much closer to eighteenth-century moral satire than to the earnest Victorian social-problem novels that followed. The rather frivolous social commentary implicit in Bulwer's parallels between highwaymen and Members of Parliament is much truer to the overall tenor of the novel than is Paul's reforming speech. And the society to which Paul speaks does not reform. Unable to be assimilated into an unreformed society, Paul must leave England for America where 'men who prefer labor to dependence cannot easily starve' and where 'his labors and his abilities obtained gradual but sure success; and he now enjoyed the blessings of a competence earned with the most scrupulous integrity, and spent with the most kindly benevolence.'

Despite the fact that Clifford's dandyism is far more convincing than his social activism and that the society he attempts to reform remains utterly undisturbed in its corrupt leadership and agencies, the novel still represents Bulwer's first stage in the transformation of the Romantic alien. The title character is Bulwer's first hero to engage with intensity (though without adequate motivation) in an attempt to eradicate injustice. And for the first time Bulwer creates a romantic protagonist who, by giving passionate voice to the *Zeitgeist* of the era of reform, demonstrates his potential for becoming a responsible citizen. Bulwer's analysis of Clifford's character points towards a more Victorian figure than any he had created before: 'The same temper and abilities which had in a very few years raised him in influence and popularity far above all the chivalric band with whom he was connected, when once inflamed and elevated by a higher passion, were likely to arouse his ambition from the level of his present pursuits, and reform him, ere too late, into a useful, nay, even an honorable member of society.'

*Eugene Aram,* Bulwer's next novel, at first appears as a false step in the progression from his Romantic aliens to Victorian activists, a reversion to his earlier title characters with their paralyzing yet strongly appealing self-

consciousness. Although Aram is a criminal like Paul Clifford, he is guilty of murder, a much more serious crime than Clifford's, but a crime that Bulwer portrays as a momentary aberration in an otherwise blameless life. Because of his guilty secret, Aram's alienation from society far surpasses Clifford's, from the beginning of the novel when he is virtually a hermit until the end when he is executed. Whereas Clifford's Romantic prototype is primarily the dandy, Aram is modelled on the Byronic solitary. And because his crime is not revealed to the reader until the third volume, his Byronism seems not only to explain his withdrawal from the world but also to justify that withdrawal on the basis of high-souled Romantic principles. Dubious of any one man's ability to alleviate the misery of the masses and fearing that the 'world of men' would destroy the 'wild liberty' he finds when alone in nature, Aram resists all pleas to devote his genius to public service: 'he appeared to consider the pomps of the world as shadows, and the life of his own spirit the only substance. He had built a city and a tower within the Shinar of his own heart, whence he might look forth, unscathed and unmoved, upon the deluge that broke over the rest of the earth.' Even the cabinet minister who urges Aram to enter the public sphere as his secretary praises him for the nobility of his refusal. Thus, the first two volumes of *Aram* seem not only to portray but also to applaud the Romantic hero's rejection of an active role in society in favour of cultivating the intellect and imagination through lonely communion with nature.

But the revelation of Aram's crime, while not invalidating the nobility of his character, most certainly undermines the nobility of his eschewing public service and embracing romantic retreat. Bulwer reveals in volume III that guilt and fear of public scrutiny, rather than Romantic idealism, have destroyed Aram's former ambition and his early desire to help mankind. And the burden of the crime is laid not on society but on Aram and his corrupter, Houseman. As Bulwer says in his preface: 'Here, unlike the milder guilt of Paul Clifford, the author was not to imply reform to society, nor open in this world atonement and pardon to the criminal . . . But I have invariably taken care that the crime should stand stripped of every sophistry, and hideous to the perpetrator as well as to the world.' Rather than applauding Aram's Byronism, therefore, Bulwer portrays the harm that results (both personal and social) when a Byronic hero decides to disregard the moral laws by which ordinary men are ruled.

*Eugene Aram* is Bulwer's first novel in which it is not the times which are out of joint but the man. As represented by the responsible cabinet member who tries to enlist Aram's talents in the service of the government, society is ripe for the intellect and 'sun-eyed vision' of a romantic like Aram. The sympathy with which Bulwer portrays his protagonist is not primarily designed, as Thackeray sarcastically charged, 'to show how Eugene Aram, though a thief, a liar, and a murderer, yet being intellectual was among the noblest of mankind'; rather, it underscores the tragic waste which occurs when an otherwise worthy man is ruined by his Byronic defiance of moral law and thereby rendered useless to a society eager for his contributions. The characters who can be assimilated effectively into this society are not the Byronic protagonist and his brilliant, otherworldly fiancée Madeline Lester but the less intense, less brilliant secondary characters, Walter and Ellinor Lester, who make a modest contribution to their age through public service and charitable works. Bulwer is not yet able to deflate sufficiently the wilful egotism nor the Promethean aspirations of his romantic protagonist to allow such a character to be assimilated, but in *Eugene Aram* he does acknowledge the dangers of unconstrained Byronism and creates a society in which assimilation of an equally romantic but less towering hero would be possible.

In *Godolphin,* Bulwer again portrays his protagonist as outside the sociopolitical mainstream, and, far more explicitly than in his previous novels, his central concern is to demonstrate that the fault lies with the hero instead of the times. Rather than a criminal or Byronic protagonist like Paul Clifford or Eugene Aram, Percy Godolphin is a *bildungsroman* hero whose alienation results from the influence of his early environment. Prefiguring the children of Arnold's famous simile in 'Stanzas from the Grande Chartreuse', Bulwer's hero was raised in the shadow of Godolphin Priory, a Gothic ruin that epitomizes romantic withdrawal from the world. The magnetism of the priory is evident when even the practical and politically ambitious Constance Erpingham falls temporarily under its spell, remarking, 'Methinks . . . while I look around, I feel as if I could give up my objects of life; renounce my hopes; forget to be artificial and ambitious; live in these ruins forever.' Godolphin Priory nurtures the hero's obsession with pursuing 'the Ideal, the Beautiful, and the Perfect', to the neglect of the pragmatic and the imperfect with which men committed to social and political action must grapple.

Despite the shaping influence of the priory on Godolphin, Constance Erpingham, the woman he loves, has the potential to direct his aspirations towards more practical, fruitful goals; however, her own alienation from society prevents her from exerting such a beneficial influence. In contrast to Godolphin, who recoils altogether from political action, Constance passionately pursues such action but for destructive ends. Warped like Godolphin by the experiences of her youth, she covets political power in order to keep a deathbed promise of revenge made to her father, who was ruined by political machinations earlier in the century. If Godolphin's idealism could merge with her political activism, he would be the perfect Carlylean hero, able to translate his idealism into action. But because marriage to a lord is essential to Constance's plans for vengeance, she refuses to marry Godolphin, and the embryonic influence of her practical activism upon him is aborted.

Thus, instead of having his romanticism retailored, Godolphin now has it gilded upon his soul as he withdraws from English society altogether and retreats into Italy, whose evocation of a romantic past is as narcotic in effect as Godolphin Priory. Here the sway of the 'ideal' on Godolphin is enhanced by his encounter with Volktman, an astrologer who gives quavering voice to more abstract conceptions of Imagination and Truth than even the Bulwer of the 1820s could stomach. But more damaging is his liaison with Lucilla, the astrologer's daughter, a child of

nature who will ultimately doom Godolphin when her Wordsworthian innocence curdles into a foreboding otherworldliness. The Italian countryside into which he escapes with Lucilla should be the romantic paradise he has longed for, but ironically it is a paradise without pleasure, because for all his romanticism and for all Lucilla's attractions, Godolphin still loves Constance. His relationship with Lucilla leaves him dissatisfied; his final lesson from his Italian experience seems to be the inadequacy of his romantic idealism, and he returns to Constance.

Just as Godolphin's break with Lucilla appears to represent his leaving behind an incapacitating romanticism, so his union with Constance (after the death of her first husband) would seem to herald his assimilation into English culture at a time when England could most use his talents—for the year is 1832. But Godolphin's union with Constance comes too late and is not strong enough to break the stronger union with his fatal romanticism. Constance herself finds that when the Reform Bill eliminates most of the abuses of power that ruined her father, she can finally work constructively rather than destructively within society; Godolphin, however, turns not to politics but to collecting *objets d'art,* again pursuing the Ideal, the Beautiful and the Perfect but under the most compromising circumstances since he must be subsidized by a begrudging Constance. Despite his love for her, Godolphin, unlike Carlyle's Teufelsdrockh, does not find, nor apparently desires to find, something he can work at. When at the end of the novel he finally decides to enter Parliament, it is not as a Liberal or Radical on the side of Reform, but as a Conservative, and even this gesture towards political activism is doomed. The reappearance of Lucilla, now mad, and her prediction of Godolphin's death, represent the stranglehold which Godolphin's romantic past has over him. His subsequent drowning, immediately after he has witnessed Lucilla's death, releases him from the new age which could not accommodate his lack of earnest purpose.

Although Godolphin is not assimilated into his society, his story represents a real advance in Bulwer's portrayal of the Romantic alien because Bulwer here recognizes more clearly than in any of his earlier novels the inadequacy of the purely romantic response to an age like his own. He is highly critical of Godolphin—and deliberately so, as reflected by his bizarre device of having the novel end with Constance writing Bulwer himself a letter in which she criticizes the injustice of his portrayal of Godolphin's character. In a footnote Bulwer responds to the letter by saying, '[The character of Godolphin] conveys exactly the impression that my delineation, faithful to truth, is intended to convey—the influences of our actual world on the ideal and imaginative order of mind, when that mind is without the stimulus of pursuits at once practical and ennobling.' And, as in *Eugene Aram,* Bulwer can create a Victorian activist only within the more modest dimensions of a minor character, in this case Stanforth Radclyffe, who argues the merits of public service with Godolphin, denying that men enter politics for mere vanity yet emphasizing that the huge ego of a Romantic need not be swallowed up by the philanthropy of public duty:

I see great changes are necessary: I desire, I work for these great changes. I am not blind, in the mean while, to glory. I desire, on the contrary, to obtain it; but it would only please me if it came from certain sources. I want to feel that I may realize what I attempt; and wish for that glory that comes from the permanent gratitude of my species, not that which springs from their momentary applause. Now, I am vain, very vain: vanity was, some years ago, the strongest characteristic of my nature. I do not pretend to conquer the weakness, but to turn it toward my purposes. I am vain enough to wish to shine, but the light must come from deeds I think really worthy.

Godolphin's pathetic destiny prevents him from heeding Radclyffe's advice, but the lesson will not be lost upon Bulwer's future title characters such as Rienzi and Ernest Maltravers.

By 1833, Bulwer reached an impasse in his efforts to transform the romantic idealists of his early novels into the romantic pragmatists who could guide a society open to reforming leadership. *Paul Clifford, Eugene Aram* and *Godolphin* mark an advance over Bulwer's earliest novels in that they reflect the growth of Bulwer's interest in public service; here the romantic types presented so uncritically in his novels of the 1820s undergo limited transformations which allow Bulwer to accentuate the flaws in the alienated Romantic. The dandy, for example, is metamorphosed into a highwayman with a late-blooming social conscience, the Byronic hero into a Faustian overreacher whose guilty secret is a crime of intellect rather than of passion, and the *bildungsroman* hero into a dreamy Platonist 'wandering between two worlds'—the dead world of the romantic past and the world of social activism still powerless to be born, at least in Bulwer's fiction. But in none of these transformations are the heroes' Promethean egos and aspirations sufficiently diminished for credible fusion with a Victorian milieu based on compromise between an idealized vision of one's culture as it should be and a realistic appraisal of one's culture as it is. Bulwer was still unable to portray these protagonists as finding a place in the world outside themselves, where, as Carlyle says in "The Everlasting Yea" section of *Sartor,* 'Conviction is worthless until it converts itself into conduct.'

To advance his heroes beyond the confines of their own egos, Bulwer had to turn for his setting from contemporary England to ancient Rome. His trip to Italy in 1833 did not revive his moribund marriage, as he had hoped. But it did mark an important shift in his writing career by inspiring him to write two historical novels in which the remoteness of time and place finally gave him the perspective he needed to create a romantic hero capable of significant cultural assimilation—one whose colossal self-consciousness is no longer the sole motivating force of the narrative.

In *The Last Days of Pompeii,* Bulwer's first novel to feature a hero of modest proportions, the romantic prototype is the hero of historical romance, modelled on the protagonists of Walter Scott. In light of Bulwer's repeated attacks on Scott's 'historical method' as well as on his brand of ro-

manticism, such a choice seems ironic; and indeed in other aspects Bulwer is at pains in *Pompeii* to differentiate his historical romance as markedly as possible from Scott's. His elaborate footnotes, for example, are meant to underscore the painstakingly accurate nature of Bulwer's historical research, as opposed to what he regarded as Scott's cavalier manipulation of historical fact. But Glaucus, Bulwer's protagonist, is a bloodless brother to Scott's typical hero—bland, naively romantic in his view of the world, and thoroughly decent. This decency manifests itself in the stoicism with which Glaucus endures such miseries as being framed for murder, drinking a love potion which nearly drives him insane, and awaiting death in the lion's den.

Because of his decency (and his Greek heritage), Glaucus can never be absorbed into the decadent culture of Pompeii which Bulwer pointedly parallels to decadent Regency society. But the sense of honour that alienates him from such a culture, coupled with his stoic will to persevere, are precisely the qualities which would aid in the reception of such a hero into a reforming culture like Bulwer's own. And by escaping from the labyrinth of his hero's self-consciousness, Bulwer positions himself in this novel not in his hero's mind but rather in the forum; because of this shift in vantage-point, it is Vesuvius and not the volcanic ego of any hero which casts the largest shadow over the events of the narrative. Everything in the novel is subservient to the suspense that builds with the building pressure within the volcano. Bulwer's focus on external events is intensified by his determination to dissect with impressive accuracy the customs and structure of ancient Roman society. As external events loom larger, Bulwer's preoccupation with the inner world of his hero shrinks proportionately. As a result, the mind of the protagonist and the external events of his era impinge upon each other in a way that is more Victorian than Romantic, preparing the way for a protagonist who can acknowledge the claims of a world outside that of his own idealistic vision.

With *Rienzi,* the historical novel that followed *The Last Days of Pompeii,* Bulwer finally portrays a Romantic protagonist who can move beyond alienation to social activism. The novel is set in fourteenth-century Rome, an era at least as decadent as that of Pompeii, and even more desperate for a hero. Although Rome maintains an empty pageant of popular government, the plebeians are completely at the mercy of the patricians, who, as Bulwer says, are banditti in all but name. Their contempt for church as well as state had forced the pope to flee to Avignon, depriving Rome of religious as well as secular leadership. Stepping into this void is an historical figure whose prototype differs considerably from all Bulwer's previous romantic heroes. Rienzi's personality owes practically nothing to the influence of the dandy, Byronism, the *bildungsroman* hero or the colourless young men of Scott. Rienzi is more nearly the Carlylean hero, a transcendental visionary who embodies his romantic ideals in social reform and social justice.

At the outset of the novel, Rienzi, reminiscent in some ways of Godolphin and Eugene Aram, is a dreamy scholar completely withdrawn from the world and obsessed with

Rome's romantic past. But when his brother is murdered by the patricians, Rienzi is galvanized into a patriot and a revolutionary:

> From that bloody clay [his brother's corpse] and that inward prayer, Cola di Rienzi rose a new being. But for that event, the future liberator of Rome might have been but a dreamer, a scholar, a poet; the peaceful rival of Petrarch, a man of thoughts, not deeds. But from that time, all his faculties, energies, fancies, genius, became concentrated into a single point; and patriotism, before a vision, leapt into the life and vigor of a passion, lastingly kindled, stubbornly hardened, and awfully consecrated—by revenge!

Despite the fact that revenge helps mould his desire to re-establish Rome as a true republic, Rienzi sees himself as 'the Instrument of Heaven'. As he describes in retrospect his achievement to the Holy Roman Emperor, 'I am that Rienzi to whom God gave to govern Rome, in peace, with justice, and to freedom. I curbed the nobles, I purged corruption, I amended law.' His vocation is that of Carlyle's heroes—to wrest order from chaos as he incarnates through his leadership God's will for his society.

As Rienzi's efforts towards reform progress, romantic idealism obliterates his motive of revenge. His ennobling leadership is underscored by the contrasts between him and Walter de Montreal, the bandit leader of the Grand Company who aspires to conquer Rome. Although clever, courageous and resourceful—even chivalrous in his private life—Montreal is motivated purely by the desire for power. In politics, his guiding principles spring from Machiavellian cynicism; he will turn on his allies as easily as he supports his former enemies if either shift in allegiance will advance his own ambitions. His role as Rienzi's foil culminates when Rienzi comes to arrest him:

> And there, as these two men, each so celebrated, so proud, so able, and ambitious, stood, front to front—it was literally as if the rival spirits of force and intellect, order and strife, of the falchion and the fasces—the antagonist principles by which empires are ruled and empires overthrown, had met together, incarnate and opposed.

This contrast emphasizes that romantic idealism fosters not only efficient leadership but also an altruism that safeguards the welfare of the state. As a result, while Rienzi governs Rome, the power of the patricians is checked, and the arts flourish as luxuriantly as do justice and peace.

Despite his achievements, however, Rienzi is not Bulwer's ideal romantic protagonist. His first fall from power is as precipitous as his rise, and the fall which follows his brief second ascent is fatal. None of the reforms Rienzi instituted are preserved, and Rome lapses back into the chaos generated by the struggles among banditti, patricians, mercenaries and demagogues. Most of the blame for Rienzi's failure is placed on his times—on the shortsighted selfishness with which each faction pursues its own interests, and especially on the debasement of the plebeians. Warped by its long subjugation to the patricians, the Roman populace is greedy, apathetic, capricious and insatiable in its demands for the excitement of public ceremonies. Liberty

is a mere catchword to the Roman people; they refuse either to pay taxes or bear arms. With his mind on the reforming spirit of the mid-1830s, Bulwer warns against the folly of introducing change too rapidly: 'Better one slow step in enlightenment, —which being made by the reason of a whole people, can not recede, —than these sudden flashes in the depth of a general night, which the darkness, by contrast doubly dark, swallows up everlastingly again.'

But Bulwer lays the blame for the failure of Rienzi's dream partly on the flawed dreamer himself. For the same brilliant idealism which illuminated his most inspired visions also blinded him to all of the forces that threatened to subvert his cause. Tragically unable to appreciate the dangers which surrounded him, Rienzi often lacked the prudence and judgement crucial to maintaining his position. He misjudged not only the depth of the people's baseness and the nobles' corruption but also his own manifest destiny. As a result, he falls and Rome falls with him. One reason for Rienzi's defeat, Bulwer implies, is the arena in which he chooses to fight for his vision: 'amidst a discontented nobility and a fickle populace, urged on by the danger of repose to the danger of enterprise . . . he threw himself headlong into the gulf of the rushing Time, and surrendered his lofty spirit to no other guidance than a conviction of its natural buoyancy and its heaven-directed aim.' Swept along by the tide not only of time but also of partisan politics, Rienzi finds himself awash in the very corruption he seeks to reform, even pandering to the plebeians' desire for public display and dissembling with Montreal like a fellow-Machiavel. Bulwer's apostrophes to Petrarch and direct narrative commentary suggest that literature rather than politics might have offered a more suitable forum for reform. Rienzi himself wistfully praises his friend Petrarch's choice 'To address the world, but from without the world; to persuade—to excite—to command, —for these are the aim and glory of ambition; —but to shun its tumult and toil.' In probing the reason for Rienzi's failure, Bulwer seems to move towards the conviction that society is best served when romantic idealism is translated not directly into social action but into the literature which inspires it.

For his culminating metamorphosis through which he directed his romantic outlander towards the centre of social responsibility, Bulwer required not one novel but two: *Ernest Maltravers* and its sequel *Alice.* Significantly, they were published during the first two years of Victoria's reign, when the social and political forces in flux during William's monarchy were jelling into more solid Victorianism. Together these novels narrate the maturation of a romantic hero whose lofty idealism is recast into the configuration of social commitment which his given name of 'Ernest', so quintessentially Victorian, connotes. Although the settings of these twin volumes strongly suggest novels of fashionable life, Ernest is never portrayed as a dandy, and although he suffers long spells of Byronic guilt and misanthropy, they are treated as aberrant, not normative. In these novels Bulwer is finally able either to relegate the more aristocratic, antisocial forms of romanticism to a minor role or, more often, to banish them altogether. Ernest's prototype is the *bildungsroman* hero, but Ernest's formative experiences, unlike those of his predecessor

Percy Godolphin, draw him into life's mainstream rather than maroon him outside it.

The changes in Bulwer's portrayal of the bildungsroman hero from *Godolphin* to *Ernest Maltravers* can be explained in large part by the two intervening historical novels. From his immersion in historical research, Bulwer became more conscious than in earlier novels of the impact of the times upon the hero. Moreover, Bulwer's scrutiny of the decadence of ancient and medieval Rome heightened his appreciation of his own culture—an appreciation most often voiced in *Maltravers* and *Alice* by the French Anglophile, Monsieur de Montaigne. 'Your England', he tells Ernest, 'is . . . renowned for its good sense; but it is renowned also for . . . high honesty and faith in its dealings, a warm love of justice and fair play, a general freedom from the violent crimes common on the Continent, and the energetic perseverance in enterprise once commenced, which results from a bold and healthful disposition.' The influence of the historical novels is also reflected in the characterization of Ernest, embodying the lesson Bulwer learned from creating Glaucus in *The Last Days of Pompeii:* how to scale down a romantic hero to practical proportions. That Bulwer was consciously reducing and humanizing the dimensions of his hero is evident from his description of Ernest in the preface to the 1837 edition:

> In the hero of this tale thou wilt find neither a majestic demigod, nor a fascinating demon. He is a man with the weaknesses derived from humanity, with the strength that we inherit from the soul; . . . influenced by the circumstances to which he yet struggles to be superior, and changing in character with the changes of time and fate; but never wantonly rejecting those great principles by which alone we can work out the Science of Life—a desire for the Good, a passion for the Honest, a yearning after the True.

This passage suggests a humanizing reduction not only in the romantic hero's character but also in his ideals. Ernest's pursuit of the Good, the True and the Honest has a more ethical, more Victorian orientation than Godolphin's more hedonistic pursuit of the Ideal, the Beautiful and the Perfect.

As Ernest's character reflects a lesson learned from the portrayal of Glaucus, his vocation reflects a lesson learned from the portrayal of Rienzi. Although he enters Parliament, Ernest is primarily the man of letters that Rienzi should have been. He can mix with the world without pandering to it and is not so caught up in the events of the day that he loses his perspective or his attachment to values more timeless than topical:

> But while he withdrew himself from the insipid and the idle, he took care not to become separated from the world. He formed his own society according to his tastes: took pleasure in the manly and exciting topics of the day; and sharpened his observation and widened his sphere as an author, by mixing freely and boldly with all classes as a citizen. But literature became to him as art to the artist—as his mistress to the lover—an engrossing and passionate delight. . . . From LITERATURE he imagined had come all

that makes nations enlightened and men humane. And he loved Literature the more, because her distinctions were not those of the world—because she had neither ribbons, nor stars, nor high places at her command.

Ernest is able to minister and prophesy to his culture out of his romantic idealism without being sacrificed to it, as Rienzi was.

In becoming an effective prophet, rather than a martyr or an ascetic recluse, Ernest masters a skill which eludes all his predecessors—the ability to compromise without being compromised. Paul Clifford, Eugene Aram, Percy Godolphin and Glaucus withdrew from their cultures because they refused to temper their romantic vision of what should be with at least a partial acceptance of what is; on the other hand, Rienzi was destroyed by his own people because his romantic vision of what should be blinded him to what was. By contrast, at the completion of his apprenticeship, Ernest is able to temper his Romantic vision with Victorian realism and to modify his Romantic idealism with Victorian pragmatism. In learning to compromise, a skill so central to the Victorian era that W. L. Burn has called its middle years 'the age of equipoise', Ernest must steer a course between the Scylla and Charybdis of his 'alter-egos', as Christensen calls them—Castruccio Cesarini and Lumley Ferrers. Castruccio represents the Romantic vision so turned inward upon itself that his rejection of reality leads ultimately to madness. Although a mediocre Italian poet who describes passions he has never felt, Castruccio strikes Byronic poses and exhibits an ego worthy of the most alienated of Bulwer's romantics, and in his outlandish dress he rivals Bulwer's early dandies. His romantic desire for revenge against Ernest and his egoistic naivety make Castruccio an easy dupe for Lumley Ferrers, who uses the poet as his accomplice in a scheme which, in deceiving Florence Lascelles about Ernest's true feelings for her, hastens her early death. From Castruccio's Byronic guilt, madness follows, and his withdrawal from reality is complete.

The alternative offered by Lumley Ferrers—pure pragmatic materialism—is portrayed as equally unpalatable. Where Castruccio is pathetic, Ferrers is despicable. Like Walter de Montreal in *Rienzi* Ferrers is a man of great practical gifts but no scruples. Although just as self-centred as Castruccio, he is a thoroughgoing pragmatist, manipulating and often destroying any character who can be of use to him. And he represents the threat to the public weal of a leader in whom romantic idealism and altruism are totally lacking. Like Castruccio's unadulterated romanticism, Lumley's unadulterated materialism proves fatal; ultimately he is strangled in his bed by his dupe and accomplice in Florence Lascelles's death. Just as Ernest must cultivate romanticism undistorted by Castruccio's retreat from reality, he must also seek a pragmatism unalloyed by Lumley's cynicism—and he must develop a concern for the public good untainted by the self-seeking nature of both his antagonists.

As early as halfway through *Ernest Maltravers,* the hero seems well on his way to achieving a desirable compromise between Romantic idealism and Victorian earnestness.

Unlike Bulwer's earlier heroes who resist too long the admonitions of socially responsible mentors, Ernest responds readily to those who urge him to discover his true vocation and to devote his genius to the good of his country: Monsieur de Montaigne, Lady Florence Lascelles and his guardian Frederick Cleveland. By the age of thirty Ernest has established himself both as a successful novelist and as a conscientious Member of Parliament. Yet he is miserable in both of his vocations. The sources of his misery are the flaws in his Romantic idealism, which has not yet been properly tempered to sustain the vocations he has chosen. The stress of trying to embody his Romantic vision in his writing is so great that it threatens his very life, his physician finally warning him to put his writing aside, at least temporarily. But the political career he turns to as an antidote disillusions him. His ideals of conduct are so lofty that the behaviour of his colleagues and other public figures inevitably disappoints him. Thus, unlike Bulwer's earlier Romantics, Maltravers's problem is not with entering the mainstream of society but rather with staying there. At the end of the first novel, the death of his fiancée makes him withdraw from the public sphere and remain withdrawn, first as a wanderer abroad and then as a recluse on his country estate, until the end of the second novel. During that time, he seems to regress towards the Byronic hauteur and misanthropy of many of Bulwer's earlier Romantics.

What Maltravers's romanticism lacks—the tempering element it requires if he is to resume his vocations and find them fruitful—is embodied in his first and last mentor, Alice Darvil Templeton. In an ironic reversal of *Godolphin,* Maltravers's proper soul-mate is not the politically ambitious Florence Lascelles (the counterpart of Godolphin's Constance Erpingham) but a personification of Wordsworthian Nature, like the earlier Lucilla. Unlike Lucilla, however, Alice does not tempt Ernest to withdraw still further from society. Rather, she infuses his soul with a Wordsworthian benevolence, becoming, like nature in 'Tintern Abbey', the 'anchor of [his] purest thoughts, the nurse, / The Guide, the guardian of [his] heart, and soul / Of all . . . moral being.' Ernest's discovery of Alice's constancy to him during their eighteen years apart triggers an epiphany which humanizes his romantic idealism:

> Here have I found that which shames and bankrupts the Ideal! Here have I found a virtue that, coming at once from God and Nature, has been wiser than all my false philosophy, and firmer than all my pride! . . . you, alike through the equal trials of poverty and wealth, have been destined to rise above all triumphant, —the example of the sublime moral that teaches us with what mysterious beauty and immortal holiness the Creator has endowed our human nature when hallowed by our human affections! . . . And your fidelity to my erring self has taught me ever to love, to serve, to compassionate, to respect, the community of God's creatures to which—noble and elevated though you are—you yet belong!

Alice represents not only Nature in the Wordsworthian sense but also, as Allan Christensen points out, 'Bulwer's

version of Carlyle's natural supernaturalism. Beneath the apparently arid surfaces of the external and artificial world lies a beneficent, powerfully dynamic, and fertile principle, which . . . has been subtly guiding the artist back to herself even during the years of his seeming estrangement from her.' And it is this principle which finally also equips Bulwer's Romantic alien to become a Carlylean hero:

> Maltravers once more entered upon the career so long suspended. He entered with an energy more practical and steadfast than the fitful enthusiasm of former years. And it was noticeable among those who knew him well, that, while the firmness of his mind was not impaired, the haughtiness of his temper was subdued. No longer despising Man as he is, and no longer exacting from all things the ideal of a visionary standard, he was more fitted to mix in the living World, and to minister usefully to the great objects that refine and elevate our race. His sentiments were, perhaps, less lofty, but his actions were infinitely more excellent, and his theories infinitely more wise.

If summarized and abstracted from his novels of the 1830s, Bulwer's concern with reconciling Romantic idealism with Victorian pragmatism should make him the third member of a triumvirate including Carlyle and Tennyson, who in respected works of the same decade (*Sartor Resartus* and 'Palace of Art') were preoccupied with resolving this same conflict. Yet Bulwer's fiction is never mentioned as a complement to their prose and poetry. Indeed, when Bulwer is linked with Romanticism at all, it is most often in terms similar to those of Donald Stone who labelled him the 'Dunciad-laureate' of 'second-hand Romanticism' [in *The Romantic Impulse in Victorian Fiction,* 1980]. The cause for such denigration is, of course, his style—inflated by his sense of self-importance, turgid with circumlocutions and epic similes, and risible in its bathos and bombast. Bulwer's message is so deeply buried beneath his manner (or, actually, his mannerism) that few readers wish to unearth his timely themes by separating them from the rhetorical debris. How can we take seriously an author who is capable of creating in *Paul Clifford* the following simile when he simply wishes to relate that a character desired to leave a boarding house: 'This idea, though conquered and reconquered, gradually swelled and increased at his heart, even as swelleth that hairy ball found in the stomach of some suffering heifer after its decease?' Such writing leaves the reader's stomach in much the same condition as the heifer's.

Although Bulwer's style is certainly tainted by pretentiousness and poor taste, the most noxious contaminant is his overblown Romanticism. Bulwer writes novels with the sensibility and the style of a Romantic poet, very unlike the three major novelists of the Romantic period itself, who all eschewed the impassioned style of Shelley and Byron. Peacock's style is remembered for its biting satire; Austen's, for brilliant realism; Scott's, for beguiling congeniality. Only Bulwer is remembered for bloated grandiloquence, making him a sad contrast both to his predecessors and to the two greatest Romantic novelists of the Victorian period, Charlotte and Emily Brontë. Both writers carefully moored to reality the colossal aspects of Romanticism in their fiction. For example, although Charlotte's narrator in *Jane Eyre* has an ego as titanic as any of Bulwer's heroes, it is tethered to the everyday world by a harness of deadly earnest Victorian morality. Similarly, Emily filters the Romantic passions and aspirations of Heathcliff and Cathy in *Wuthering Heights* through the mundane lens of Nelly Dean's and Lockwood's perceptions. Many of Bulwer's novels, by contrast, sound as if they were written by a Heathcliff made articulate by university education, as in the following ejaculation from *Godolphin:*

> O much-abused and highly-slandered passion!
> —Passion rather of the soul than of the heart: hateful to the pseudo-moralist, but viewed with favoring, though not undiscriminating eyes by the true philosopher: bright-winged and august AMBITION! It is well for fools to revile thee, because thou art liable, like other utilities, to abuse! The wind uproots, it scatters a thousand acorns. Ixion embraced the cloud, but from the embrace sprang a hero. Thou, too, hast thy fits of violence and storm; but without thee, life would stagnate: —thou, too embracest thy clouds; but even thy clouds have the demi-gods for their offspring!

Unfortunately, the 'passions' which prompt Bulwer's language to soar to such grandiose heights are not embodied convincingly in either Bulwer's characters or narrative personae; they have neither subjective nor objective correlatives. Because he has the grand manner without the grand matter, the image projected by Bulwer's style led to his being ridiculed as a 'lion in curl papers'. The roar of such a lion is not likely to be heeded, respected, nor even remembered.

Despite his bombastic style, Bulwer still deserves study. Even G. K. Chesterton, after characterizing Bulwer's fiction [in *The Victorian Age in Literature,* 1962] as 'mere polished melodrama', admitted that 'there was an element indefinable about Lytton, which often is in adventures; which amounts to a suspicion that there was something in him after all'. And according to Lionel Stevenson [in "Stepfathers of Victorianism," *Victorian Quarterly Review* 6 (1930)], it is only those novels written before 1838 which give Bulwer his chief significance. His merit lies partly in the fact that he was, like his heroes, a Romantic rebel, struggling against the tide of 'materialistic' realism which he saw flowing from the novels of Sir Walter Scott. In place of the pleasant, tepid romantic values which Scott transposed to the sphere of the everyday, Bulwer insisted on searing his Romanticism with highest passion. By doing so, although Bulwer could hardly stem the tide of realism, he did create in it new currents of idealized, internalized meaning which would mark a crucial divergence between the realism of Victorian fiction and that of Scott. Moreover, by his insistence on anti-realistic digressions, authorial intrusions and dramatically gratuitous subplots and characters, Bulwer may have helped delay the imposition of much more restrictive standards until nearly the twentieth century, a delay for which the Victorian novel is no doubt the richer. Finally, as this chapter has shown, Bulwer mirrored the concerns of his contemporaries and anticipated a major theme in later Victorian fiction by portraying the difficulties faced by alienated Romantics in establishing fruitful, purposive roles for themselves in a culture that both welcomed and threatened them. By successfully directing his last fictional hero of the 1830s away from solely egotistical concerns, by tempering Ernest Maltravers's idealism with an other-centred and humane regard for social issues, Bulwer prefigured similar transformations in the novels of his more gifted successors, most notably Trollope and Eliot. Thus, it seems rather unfair that Edward Bulwer-Lytton should now be viewed as merely the weathervane of Victorian fiction since he usually stirred rather than reflected the necessary winds of change by his determined, though often wrongheaded, opposition to both realism and diluted romanticism. For better or, more typically, for worse, Bulwer was always his own man.

*Elliot Engel and Margaret F. King, "Edward Bulwer-Lytton," in their* The Victorian Novel before Victoria: British Fiction during the Reign of William IV, 1830-37, *The Macmillan Press Ltd., 1984, pp. 39-60.*

### Peter W. Graham     (essay date 1981)

[*In the excerpt below, Graham considers Bulwer-Lytton's analyses of moral and social conventions in his "silver-fork" or fashionable novels.*]

Most readers aware of "silver fork" novels, those elegantly titled triple-deckers depicting the aristocratic graces and disgraces of Regency and post-Regency England, encounter them in Carlyle's *Sartor Resartus* (1833-1834), with its denunciation of the "infinite, insufferable Jew's harping and scrannel piping" of fashionable fiction, an introduction that does not encourage closer acquaintance. Other contemporaries reinforce the impression that the "silver fork" novelist's concern with realistic description of fashionable society dooms him to triviality. Hazlitt, in an essay entitled "The Dandy School" [in *Complete Works,* 1930-34], laments that

> At present, it should seem that a seat on Parnassus conveys a title to a box at the Opera, and that Helicon no longer runs water but champagne. Literature, so far from supplying us with intellectual resources to counterbalance immediate privations, is made an instrument to add to our impatience and irritability under them, and to nourish our feverish, childish admiration of external show and grandeur.

Scott, in his milder way, concurs in the first chapter of *Waverley,* where he explains that the ensuing narrative will be neither a historical romance nor a fashionable novel because "the object of my tale is more a description of men than of manners."

To be sure, many of the fashionable novels are shabby, shallow productions of poseurs who pandered to folly and pretense. These ephemera merit their consignment to back shelves and dust-bins. But other representatives of the genre deserve to be recalled from exile. Foremost among these are the works in which Edward Bulwer (not yet the genteel, intricately titled Victorian he became in his prime) portrays the far-from-prudish age of George IV.

Following the lead of the English Cantos of *Don Juan,* in which Byron determines "to show things as they really are," Bulwer's three "silver fork" novels *Pelham* (1828), *Greville* (uncompleted), and *Godolphin* (1833) prove that the genre had serious critical potential its deprecators failed to recognize, though the fact that Bulwer's ultimate verdict on the age, *England and the English* (1833) took the form of a social history rather than a novel suggests that this potential was limited. But in both his "silver fork" novels and his history, Bulwer, like Byron before him, writes as what the French call a *moraliste,* one who studies social conventions to understand society, who scrutinizes manners the better to know men.

The novel-writing *moraliste* can adopt any of several means, all of which involve the principle of contrast, for making intellectual, ethical, political, and aesthetic judgments of men and societies. He may, like Sir Walter Scott, write about the past, recent or distant. Looking backwards, he discerns what his contemporaries have gained and lost in becoming what they have become. Or he may, like the writers of good speculative fiction, extrapolate a future from present trends and thereby judge his age's circumstances and standards in light of their possible consequences. Bulwer came to use both these methods later in his career. A number of his novels, among them his most famous, *The Last Days of Pompeii* (1834), are historical; his last, *The Coming Race* (1871), speculates about the future.

In *Pelham, Greville,* and *Godolphin,* however, Bulwer's province is a minute section of the here-and-now, the Great World that the Reform Bill of 1832 would soon and substantially alter. What strategies will enable the contemporary chronicler to generate moral contrasts that will make the fashionable novel more than a compendium of trivial detail? He can rely on a technique that worked well for Voltaire in *Candide,* Fielding in the London sequences of *Tom Jones,* and Byron in *Don Juan*—the use of the "resident alien," who, living *in* a class or culture without being *of* it, sees social situations through glass of a different tint. On the other hand, he can play off a classic ideal against contemporary mores by introducing among his fashionable characters a paragon whose standards are not the world's passing ones. Bulwer combines these tactics in his "silver fork" novels. Scrutinizing the Great World, he sees a ruling class with too much power too little merited, an aristocracy whose weaknesses are those of the common herd. But Bulwer knows that human excellence, like other rarities, may be most often found among those who can best afford it; so his "silver fork" novels share a common method. Bulwer, the social assayer, places aristocratic specimens in convincing contemporary environments and records whether the sterling character be tarnished or the impure world refined. The various outcomes of this repeated experiment correspond to changes in Bulwer's perceptions of the aristocrat's role in an age of flux and of the merits of the "silver fork" novel.

*Pelham* is the first, best, and most influential of Bulwer's "silver fork" novels, and its protagonist is Bulwer's most charming and efficient aristocrat. Suave and persuasive in his fictional world, Henry Pelham changed manners and minds in the real one. His tastes in tailoring radically modified, as Beau Brummel's had done, the gentleman's standard of dress. His cheerfully rational behavior demonstrated what a public spellbound by the Byronic hero had largely forgotten, that handsome, clever, rich young men need not be melancholy misanthropes. Portraying his style-setting protagonist, Bulwer succeeds as a *moraliste* because he attaches just the right significance to details: as Pelham's epigram phrases it, "He who esteems trifles for themselves, is a trifler—he who esteems them for the conclusions to be drawn from them, or the advantage to which they can be put, is a philosopher."

Henry Pelham himself is just such a philosopher. Though he is impeccable in the mundane but exacting role of gentleman of fashion—he dresses, dines, rides, fights, converses, seduces just as contemporary decorums require—his true excellence is not so easily dated. At heart Pelham is less the Regency dandy than the *kalos kagathos* of classical Greece or the *honnête homme* of Renaissance France. Like these ancestral paragons, whether they be Achilles or Montaigne's *citoyen du monde,* Pelham is a "speaker of words and a doer of deeds," a diversely talented amateur, not a specialist as a mere dandy would inevitably be. He defies circumscription, and thereby surpasses the more limited varieties of excellence presented in some of the book's subordinate characters. Vincent, for example, is a brilliant theorizer without practical experience of the world, Gusleton a man of taste dwindled to an epicure. Sir Reginale Glanville, the book's Byronic hero, exemplifies genius and sensitivity first numbed and then killed by monomaniacal guilt and vengefulness. Pelham's mother, the dazzling Lady Frances, has insight but little inclination to look beyond her diamonds and china monsters. The need to subsist on his talents precludes Job Johnson, a low-born counterpart of Pelham, from becoming that ultimate master of detail the true philosopher. Even Ellen Glanville, the woman Pelham finds worthy of playing Millamant to his Mirabel, is limited by her sex to so passive a role that we must take Pelham's word for her superiority.

Pelham stands virtually alone in being free of the shackles imposed by profession, class, gender, temperament, and goal, but perhaps the most confining of the bonds he avoids is egocentricity. His motto is "Manage *yourself* well, and you may manage all the world," and he possesses the self-knowledge needed for this task. But his true interests lie outside himself. Pelham affirms himself a *moraliste* in a moment of candor: "I study nature rather in men than fields, and find no landscape afford [*sic*] such variety to the eye, and such subject to the contemplation, as the inequalities of the human heart." Secure in his wide-ranging competence, Pelham makes artful use of apparent frailties to test his fellow men and to distract inferiors from envying his real excellence. His most obvious characteristics—effeminacy, languor, pedantry—are misleading gestures. If Pelham takes care to adjust his "best ringlet" before making an intelligent pronouncement, he obliges his associates to choose between focusing on his surface or his substance, and by this choice to reveal their own depth or shallowness.

*Pelham* is a stronger book for its protagonist's subtly self-modulated character. It is likewise a better story and a sounder piece of social criticism because Bulwer did not yield to the temptation that seduced other young gentlemen writing fashionable novels and young writers hoping to establish their gentility by such ventures: he remained distinct from his creation. Bulwer asserted that he and Pelham had "nothing in common, except the taste for observation, and some experience in the same scenes". His moral study gains in objectivity and consistency as a result. Similarly, by having Pelham relate his own story, Bulwer doubles the efficiency of his character analysis. The narrative offers us two views of Henry Pelham—we must juxtapose the teller and the subject of the tale to form our impression of the man. Thus *Pelham*'s digressions, explanations, *bons mots,* and paradoxes are more than demonstrations of authorial cleverness. They provide clues to a reticent but articulate character who, though he tends to look beyond himself, by his manner of appraising the world enables us to appraise him.

The book's point of view and the protagonist's character offer another advantage as well. By convincing us that Pelham has the versatility to savor the varieties of worldly experience—France and England, West End and East, rogues and perfect ladies—and the wisdom to judge them, Bulwer makes us receptive to the opinions he offers through the mouth of this aristocratic philosopher. As mentioned earlier, Pelham's pronouncements on dress and deportment had considerable impact. The *moraliste*'s vision, however, must extend beyond the boudoir, the dressing-room, and the salon. Again and again Pelham makes the national contrast obvious for Englishmen of Bulwer's post-Waterloo era: he weighs British values against those prevailing in the country across the Channel, for the denizens of the Great World, once they no longer feared being subjected to the French Emperor, willingly had enslaved themselves to French tastes in dress, dance, and phrasing.

In one of several discussions of the two cultures, Pelham presents his clever friend Vincent informing a group of French aristocrats that in matters of the mind England is superior: "A man might learn to *think* sooner from your writers, but he will learn to *think justly* sooner from ours." The French man of letters, Vincent argues, is also a man of the world and therefore describes humanity in particular social settings. His more cloistered English counterpart, perhaps less urbane but more patient and profound, studies general properties of human nature, and his is the nobler enterprise because the truths it offers are not derived from observation of the ephemeral patterns we call manners and will not expire with them. Pelham, who outstays his countryman in the salon, hears the verdict on this *demi-moraliste:* "The women called him *un horreur,* and the men *un bête.* The old railed at his *mauvais gout,* and the young at his *mauvais coeur.*" Though he presents the incident without explaining it, again testing his readers' powers, Pelham implies that if national differences are great, the distance between the tactless but well-meaning guest and his suave hosts is greater.

The account of Vincent's blunder demonstrates one of Pelham's recurring points: English manners are far inferior to those prevailing on the Continent. Despite such charming exceptions as Lord Gusleton, Lady Roseville, Lady Frances, and Pelham himself, most inhabitants of the Great World cultivate a distinctively English combination of obsequiousness and insolence that with typical inconsistency they describe in a French phrase—*sang froid:*

> The English make business an enjoyment, and enjoyment a business: they are born without a smile; they rove about public places like so many easterly winds—cold, sharp, and cutting; or like a group of fogs on a frosty day, sent out of his hall by Boreas for the express purpose of *looking black at one another* . . . . They are sometimes *polite,* but invariably *uncivil* . . . they are stiff without dignity, and cringing without manners. . . . There is not another court in Europe where such systematized meanness is carried on. . . .

As he moves through so greatly deficient a Great World, Pelham finds few true peers. The mere fact that he must so carefully veil his true nature is a telling indictment of a people (Bulwer's readers included) that suffers a fool more gladly than a nonesuch. Pelham judges his society and finds it wanting but does not despair of his power to improve it. At the story's end, he retires with Ellen his wife to "fields and folios" for two years of seclusion, from which he hopes to emerge with a new goal: "instead of amusing my enemies, and the saloon, I trust yet to be useful to my friends and to mankind."

Bulwer may not have foreseen the extent of *Pelham*'s social influence when he started writing, but he soon recognized and enhanced the edifying side of the book. In the 1828 preface to the second edition, Bulwer states that

> I have not been willing that even the common-places of society should afford neither a record nor a moral; and it is therefore, from the common-places of society that the materials of this novel have been wrought. By treating trifles naturally, they may be rendered amusing, and that which adherence to *Nature* renders amusing, the same cause may also render instructive: for Nature is the source of all morals, and the enchanted well, from which not a single drop can be taken, that has not the power of curing some of our diseases.

To further his aims as a *moraliste,* Bulwer replaced the first edition's lengthy treatise on clothes, mere observation, with Pelham's famous series of maxims, elegant epigrams that begin with description but end in analysis.

Fashionable fiction, as Bulwer had come to conceive it, has a far higher purpose than its critics acknowledged. A kind of contemporary history, the "silver fork" novel can, if its material be intelligently selected and accurately presented, offer the same rewards and lessons gained from any clear and cogent historical account. Furthermore, such a novel has in its concrete and timely particulars an advantage more high-minded genres abjure: it can make serious speculation generally palatable. Bulwer's concern to make his prescription easy for his contemporary audience to swallow, a great strength in the witty and outrageous early editions, later became something readers have had cause to lament. Bulwer twice altered *Pelham,* first in 1835 after the appearance of Carlyle's criticisms in *Sartor Resartus,* second in 1840. Revising as an older writer for a more squeamish audience, Bulwer hoped to make his *mauvais fils* more responsible, less likely to offend, and more accessible to readers innocent of French; but the changes, for the most part, reduce the book's sparkle without adding to its solidity.

The mobility that led Bulwer to adapt *Pelham* for its readers enabled him throughout a long and prolific career to accommodate the varied reading tastes of his public. Even the most avid devotees of fashionable fiction could become sated with the Great World and hanker after literary low-life; consumers of rational, realistic, contemporary novels could come to hunger for melodrama, passion, and the romantic past. Accordingly, Bulwer recultivated the Gothic garden he had pruned back in *Pelham. The Disowned* (1828), a fashionable novel set in the eighteenth century, transcribes Bulwer's own adventures with the gypsies, whereas *Devereux* (1829) portrays life during the days of good Queen Anne, and *Paul Clifford* (1830) and *Eugene Aram* (1832), both "Newgate novels," focus on crime and the criminal mind.

When Bulwer returned to the Great World for his subject matter in *Greville* (begun between the composition of *The Disowned* and *Devereux*), his view of the pageant had darkened, for several possible reasons. The glamour of George IV's age of elegance was beginning to tarnish. Besides, Bulwer had gained experience in playing his own part in the revels; and the more he knew of the Great World, the less its power to dazzle him would be. Perhaps most important, worldly experience would have shown Bulwer that the rewards of a personal code like Pelham's are almost always private: when the superior individual prospers in society—particularly when society has entered a period of rapid change, as pre-Reform Bill England had done—he often prospers in spite of, rather than because of, his excellence.

Thus aristocratic excellence brings its practitioner a different lot in *Greville* than it had done in *Pelham.* With no vanity and no ambition but a haughty independence antithetical to Pelham's sociability, Greville believes that "The eternal root of *mauvais ton* is IMITATION." Unlike Pelham, who adjusts himself to every circle he enters, Greville scorns to join any coterie: " 'There is no difference between a mob at Epsom and a mob at St. Giles;' " says he, " 'the same vulgar feelings agitate each—mirth, anxiety, uproar, riot.' " Too perceptive to join in the Great World's self-venerating exclusivism, he likewise sees through the inverse delusion, worship of the common man. Greville realizes that in London society with its many gradations, the pandemic of imitation spreads from square to square, from Mayfair to Bloomsbury to Whitechapel, and thus the unfashionable many are not likely to be better bred or behaved than the modish few. Utterly without illusions in a milieu that prizes little else, Greville differs from the limited people around him in most other matters as well. Widely travelled in nations, social classes, and books, Greville has achieved at the age of twenty-five the wisdom men of fifty seldom possess in the Great

World. His house, possessions, and tastes, like his character, are large, grand, and for the most part ancient: "He had very few prettinesses of mind: he was not fond of small villas, or cabinet pictures, or books of sonnets, or very little women, or gardens of half an acre." In short, Greville is like his fashionable peers only in being bored.

Though Bulwer's son suggests that *Greville* was abandoned because its satire was becoming too personal, the title character at least is far too consistent a set of attributes ever to have lived and breathed. Instead, Greville is a *moraliste*'s gauge by which the novel's other characters unwittingly measure themselves. For instance, as they discuss Greville in the first chapter, the rake Desborough and the dupe Clavering provide necessary exposition and also reveal their respective hypocrisy and *naïveté*. Similarly the two beauties of the novel, Lady Bellingdon, the gorgeous and fanciful leader of the *ton,* and her younger sister Lady Agnes Percivale, love Greville—the former for what society imagines him, the latter (so Bulwer's outline of the unfinished novel suggests) for himself—and in their ways of loving delineate their values. Like this quartet of supporting characters, the Great World at large thinks and talks much of the man who esteems it little. Greville, unpopular yet courted, is almost universally admired for his deficiencies and disliked for his virtues. The fools of society consider him a great prize because he is inflexible and misanthropic; they think him affected for being the one man with the sense, taste, and self-sufficiency to eschew affectation and behave naturally.

*Greville*'s narrator depicts these wrong-headed beings with a mordant humor seldom found on *Pelham*'s amiably satiric pages. Botanizing among the flora of society, we encounter this taxonomy of the fashionable lady: "She is a nettle to her inferiors, and a sunflower to her betters." The *beaux esprits* who enliven drawing-rooms fare little better: "They did not possess a great deal of knowledge, but they possessed a great many books beautifully bound." In *Greville,* Bulwer's view of English society has become considerably bleaker than it had been. From the beginning of the novel, in fact, the narrator seems to peer through a cruel glass and describe with amused malice a set of not-quite-human beings who posture and grimace on the other side:

> Everyone knows that England is the most charming country in the world, especially for those who like to be amused. In that "moral air" the people are so wise that mirth would be altogether out of character. It is only in their parliaments that they stoop to levity. They there concentrate the witticisms of a whole nation in one individual, and they call that individual Sir Joseph York. In a social state they exclude the impertinence of *bons mots,* and exult in a stupendous monotony of *ennui.*
>
> Every one also is perfectly aware that the most delightful place in this brilliant country is called Hyde Park. A country retreat where a vast number of women drive about in carriages to admire the beauties of nature, while the most intellectual young men in the world make short speeches on the weather and long odds upon horses. . . .

There are one or two peculiarities in this park which are not unworthy of philosophical speculation. The English women, being proverbially the modestest ladies in the world, have, in the most conspicuous part of the Arcadian scene, erected in honor of Arthur, Duke of Wellington, proverbially the modestest man so far as ladies are concerned, an enormous statue, entirely naked. . . .

The deer in this park generally die of eating leather and oranges, and you would think by their color and consistency that the trees also died of the same complaint.

The tone set here and sustained throughout *Greville*'s completed chapters suggests Bulwer's growing disenchantment with a world he had come to see as foolish, contradictory, and unnatural. It seems that though the aristocratic philosopher may indeed exist in post-Regency society, he cannot approve of, or greatly alter, his milieu. Bulwer the *moraliste* was also finding the "silver fork" formula that had worked so well in *Pelham* a less effective vehicle for his observations on the age. In *Greville* and later *Godolphin,* Bulwer moved his fashionable novel a step closer to conventional history by replacing *Pelham*'s first-person narration with more objective third person. And, for all *Greville*'s seeming promise, Bulwer never completed the manuscript.

In *Godolphin* Bulwer stresses the cruel wastefulness of the social order that in *Greville* seemed at worst stupid and hypocritical by showing how life in the Great World thwarts potential excellence in two noble characters, the imaginative Percy Godolphin and the actively ambitious Constance Vernon. Godolphin, whom Bulwer endows with many of the opinions and attitudes, and even some of the phrases, of Greville, is, unlike that hardened and polished gentleman, drastically molded by the world he moves through. But Godolphin is the "moral antipodes" of Bulwer's other evolving aristocrat, Pelham. Whereas the talented and pleasure-loving Pelham awakens to the need of working constructively in his society, improves himself, and shapes his circumstances, the similarly situated Godolphin, "represented as possessing mental qualities of a higher and a richer nature than those to which Pelham can pretend," does nothing. His character is a fallow field, not Pelham's well-cultivated garden.

Though the qualities of such a passive protagonist must be asserted rather than demonstrated, Bulwer carefully presents the ambivalence that makes a *fainéant* of the fastidious, subtle, contemplative Godolphin. He is well born but ill provided for. Inability to transcend or embrace selfishness keeps him from becoming a philanthropist like Stainforth Radclyffe or an arch-exquisite like Augustus Saville. With the scruples to refrain from seducing the simple Lucilla, Godolphin has not moral energy enough to resist her persistent importunities; and having compromised the adoring girl, he can neither live apart from the world with her nor be happy having abandoned her. Rejected by the splendid Constance Vernon in youth, when her ambition might have kindled his talents, Godolphin weds her as Constance Countess of Erpingham, when the mere fact of alliance with her wealth, power, beauty, and

brilliance wins him the world's good opinion. Thus easily established as a man of taste and ability, he has no need or inclination to risk the ridicule of present admirers by writing books or promoting public measures and thereby provoking comparison: "Among the first in one line, why sink into the probability of being second-rate in another?" Godolphin's case shows that high rank like low can destroy gifted men: the one condition enervates genius as completely as the other exhausts it. As Godolphin comes to understand, his life is one great sin of omission: "I could sacrifice my happiness, but not my indolence; I was not ungenerous, I was inert."

Although Godolphin's failure to realize his potential is more default than defeat, Constance Vernon maneuvers effectively in the Great World; and the ways society limits her excellence clearly reveal Bulwer's sense that the time for a readjustment of standards—and institutions—had come. In *Godolphin*'s England, aristocrats are *aristoi* in name only, and Constance, whose nobility is a gift of nature rather than the inherited favor of some monarch, is obliged to waste her life and talents in gaining revenge against the high-born Tories who had betrayed and broken her father, a politician who had served their interests. As a man, or in another age, Constance could achieve direct political vengeance. The reader can easily imagine her as a Radical Whig Prime Minister forcing Reform down the throats of the Lords. Being a woman, though, Constance must submit to the same restrictions that bound the patronesses of the Regency salons. One road to power lies open. To gain a social position from which she can humiliate the snobbish aristocrats she despises, she consolidates her power through an advantageous match. With her beauty and brilliance joined to rank and riches, Constance is able to crush the old order that destroyed her father. In doing so, she personifies England's new social spirit. Under Constance's rule (not unlike the despotic control the seven Lady Patronesses held over the membership list of Almack's), birth and fortune, formerly the passports to social preeminence, now count for nothing if their possessors lack the *je ne sais quoi* that gains her sanction.

Although the motives of Constance's social revolution seem less than admirable, her despotism proves benevolent. Noble at heart, she respects excellence in others and reserves her ruthlessness for those who richly deserve destruction: "Modest merit in any rank, even insolence, if accompanied with merit, were always safe from her satire. It was the *hauteur* of foolish duchesses or purse-proud *roturiers* that she loved and scrupled not to abase." Unfortunately, Constance's selectivity cannot improve society. Her followers, who accept her verdicts without learning her principles, remain as servile as ever: "She could abase the proud, but not elevate the general tone: for one slavery she substituted another—people hugged the chains of Fashion, as before they hugged those of Titular Arrogance."

As the queen of fashion, chief intriguer of the Whig party, and counsellor to George IV, Constance achieves all (save producing a son and heir) that an ambitious woman can do in her England. Any further gratification must come obliquely, through her husband Godolphin, who has lost either the talent or the desire for greatness. Ironically, when at last Godolphin finds his self-centered life less than satisfactory and resolves to try public affairs as a tonic for middle-aged satiety, his inclinations propel him to the Tory side of the question. Though a natural cataclysm takes him out of the world before the political one can put him into Parliament, Constance has time to see that despite the achievements of her lifelong devotion to the popular cause, her power will crumble at a single act of political caprice on Godolphin's part. So fragile are the rewards of feminine ambition.

If the Great World blights Godolphin and Constance, dooming the one to inactivity, the other to undermining rather than building, Augustus Saville flourishes by living according to its values. Cold-blooded but good-tempered, sensual and philosophical, depraved yet judicious, Saville never lapses from his selfishness or impeccable style. "The very personification of a civilized and profligate life," he is Bulwer's ultimate celebration and indictment of Regency society, an individualized yet representative character who distils in his being the power of the Great World over its inhabitants. Saville confers the blessing of fashion on some acquaintances and sets others on the gambler's road to hell. His money permits the young Godolphin to run away from home; his sponsorship turns the boy into a man of the world. Saville stages for his own amusement the reunion of Godolphin and Constance amid the ruins of the Coliseum. So potent is his force that he can even contrive his own deathbed. Suiting the gesture to the moment as he always has done, the nonpareil of the old regime makes his adieux on the eve of the Reform Bill. " 'Take care of my dog—'tis a good creature;' " says the fading epicure to Godolphin,

> "and let me be quietly buried. No bad taste—no ostentation—no epitaph. I am very glad I die before the d——d Revolution that must come; I don't want to take wine with the member for Holborn Bars. I am a type of a system; I expire before the system; my death is the herald of its fall."

In another novel or at another time, the dying Saville's speech might be dismissed as the dandy's final pose, an egoist's unwillingness to allow that his world might carry on without him, but here the prophecy holds: though the Reform Bill's extension of the franchise may not have dealt the blow to England's entrenched oligarchy, it did change the constitution (and hence the complexion) of the power class.

Saville's valedictory scene shows, as do his assessments of marriages and liaisons, Constance's dissection of snobbery, and Godolphin's opinions on what lies *outside* himself, how fine a work of the *moraliste* school *Godolphin* might have been if it were less derivative. As it stands, the book contains too little of Bulwer's own intelligence and imagination. The novel's plot and allegory come, as Matthew Rosa has observed [in *The Silver Fork School,* 1936], from Goethe's *Wilhelm Meister.* The ideas on love, ambition, status, wealth, society, and women that generate specific scenes are often appropriated from La Rochefoucauld, La Bruyère, Chesterfield, and Byron, the last of whom in his turn had taken many insights from the other

three *moralistes.* This borrowing from literature in itself is no defect. What Godolphin's tale of "only yesterday" owes to life is another matter.

A good historical novel, Scott's *The Heart of Midlothian,* for instance, generally presents plausibly imagined private affairs against a backdrop of accurately described public ones. *Godolphin* takes not only its momentous matters—party warfare, Reform agitation, the death of kings, the birth of Almack's—but also the smallest details of character and incident from Regency life, as critics from the novel's earliest reviewers on have been fond of pointing out. Lord Saltream (tactfully excised from the novel in 1840) obviously represents poor, mad Lord Dudley. Constance is a glorious pastiche of the Ladies Holland, Jersey, Oxford, and Blessington, and Mrs. Norton. Vernon's death parallels Richard Brinsley Sheridan's; and Godolphin's way of life resembles that of Count D'Orsay, to whom Bulwer dedicated the revised novel. Transcribing the quirks and charms of real people, Bulwer makes a curious hybrid of *Godolphin:* with too much raw fact for a work of imagination, it is certainly no history.

Bulwer's way of framing the story implicitly acknowledges and attempts to surmount this awkwardness. He published the book anonymously (in fact, in the prefaces to the first and second editions the supposed "dying author" revels in his anonymity) and, using a device more happily employed in *Sartor Resartus,* established the author-narrator as a sort of editor or ghost writer commissioned by the widowed Constance, who, in an utterly improbable appended letter expresses her desire "that a history should be given to the world, from which lessons so deep and, I firmly believe, salutary, may be generally derived." Trusting another's talents to relay her story to the public is quite out of keeping with the pride and genius attributed to Constance; and however overcome with grief she may be supposed, a tactician of her caliber would surely not saddle a failing man with the task. But the pretext does conveniently excuse Bulwer for offering so dull a dog as his narrator. In each of Bulwer's other fashionable novels, the teller of the tale is himself a *moraliste* actively concerned to extract significance from a situation and to express the thought derived in words that delight and edify. *Godolphin*'s insights are elegant only when they appear in reported dialogue: otherwise the narrator, who prefers effusion, exclamation, and the suspense-building authorial aside to epigram, deals out facts like so many cards and leaves his readers to arrange the hands as best they can. These deficiencies of imagination and style could be expected and overlooked in a hireling doing his best to make of Constance's "Memoir" an instructive "Romance." But what the hypothetical author of *Godolphin* professes to do the real one does as well, and what might be excused in a hack is to be regretted in a *moraliste.*

Muddled though his perspective may have been in *Godolphin,* when Bulwer next scrutinizes Regency society in *England and the English* his gaze is an historian's. In some ways Bulwer's move from the fashionable novel to history is a culmination rather than an altered course, for it permits the explicit statement of general social principles implicit in the novels' case studies. *England and the English* verifies what *Godolphin* had prophesied: the change of which Constance is harbinger has come about. Reform had done to the Regency world what Vesuvius, in Bulwer's next novel, will do to Pompeii. The old aristocratic values and other less commendable offspring of social stability may persist, but beneath new surfaces.

Still, the *moraliste* tradition continues to influence Bulwer's methods in *England and the English.* Bulwer's social history is profoundly indebted to that earlier chronicle of an age in flux, La Bruyère's *Les Caractères, ou les Moeurs de ce Siècle.* Echoing the French *moraliste,* Bulwer commences *England and the English* with an acknowledgment of change. "The English of the present day," he observes, "are not the English of twenty years ago." Like La Bruyère, Bulwer expresses dissatisfaction with contemporary society and with the aristocrats who rule it. But whereas La Bruyère suggest that *honnêtes gens* and men of the court should return to the precepts of Christianity, Bulwer, a Reform Bill Radical, prescribes Bentham's "philosophy of a visible transition." The Utilitarian Bulwer is, however, not a renegade to his class. The aristocrat in him recognizes that because the people's immediate desires sometimes conflict with their ultimate needs or with moral and ethical priorities, the democratic standard of greatest happiness for the greatest number has limited applicability: "In fact, the greatest happiness principle, is an excellent general rule, but it is not an undeniable axiom."

In his introduction to *England and the English,* Standish Meacham notes that Bulwer's thoughts on the dangers of a society and a constitution with aristocratic bias come, in large measure, from James Mill's "Men and Things in 1823." Still, Bulwer vivifies the ideas as dry Utilitarian prose could not, and as social history often does not, by adopting La Bruyère's way of presenting argument through example. Bulwer's five books devoted to The English Character, Society and Manners, Education, Morality, Religion, The Intellectual Spirit of the Time, and The Political State contain much abstraction and theory, but particulars balance every generality. With the eye for trifles that proved so important in *Pelham,* Bulwer selects social detail to illustrate and enliven his arguments. In the best *moraliste* tradition, he uses *caractères* to validate his reasoning in a way that mere argumentation never could do.

In pre-Reform days, Bulwer observes, the aristocracy held virtually complete political control of England, despite the hypothetical distribution of constitutional powers among king, lords, and people. Thus England's nobles became the most politically powerful aristocracy in Europe: "Their authority has not been visible: held under popular names it has deceived the popular eye; —and deluded by the notion of a Balance of Power, the people did not see that it was one of the proprietors of the power who held the scales and regulated the weights." In like manner, England's aristocracy determines the country's social attitudes in a way that its counterparts elsewhere do not. English patricians mingle freely with the other classes. Peers marry middle-class heiresses, hunt with their country tenants, and hold open house for the local electors. As a result, those persons of intermediate position can hope to rise through matrimonial alliance or, mistaking proximity for connection, can fancy themselves on the aristocratic fringe. No one knows what he is, but everyone suspects that he can become anything:

> These mystic, shifting, and various shades of graduation; these shot-silk colours of society produce this effect: that people have no exact and fixed position—that by acquaintance alone they may rise to look down on their superiors—that while the rank gained by intellect, or by interest, is open but to few, the rank that may be obtained by fashion seems delusively to be open to all.

The fluid state of society harms the aristocrats as well as their inferiors. Pelham's sort of confidence, which presupposes a fixed social station, becomes ever harder to cultivate. Aristocratic self-sufficiency vanishes. Birth and breeding come to require, as they do in *Godolphin,* the supplementary distinction conferred by fashion. Hence the same nobleman can be affected, stupid, mean, and second-rate in town and affable, dignified, and kind in the country; for in the one place his position is unsettled and dependent on fashion, in the other securely grounded in tradition. Social uncertainty, says Bulwer, debases the aristocrat in various ways. The patrician attitude toward money becomes a hypocritical blend of respect and disdain. A nobleman springs from wealth and maintains his position by allying himself with it. At the same time, he withdraws to Almack's, White's, and Brooks's, fortresses erected to keep out the gilt-edged barbarians. Talented patricians must resort to snobbery and affected nonchalance to regain the status they lose by exercising their genius. "Byron," Bulwer shrewdly discerns, "would never have set a coronet over his bed if he had not written poetry."

*England and the English* asserts that one of political reform's most beneficial side-effects has been to overturn the social system so detrimental to the well-being of aristocrats and populace alike. A shift in social initiative corresponding to the redistribution of political power supersedes Constance's revolution:

> Fashion cannot for many years be what it has been. In political quiet, the aristocracy are the natural dictators of society, and their sentiments are the most listened to. Now, the sum of their sentiments, as we have seen, is Fashion: in agitated times, the people rise into importance, and their sentiments become the loudest and most obtrusive; the aggregate of *their* sentiments, as we have seen, is Opinion. It is *then,* that unable to lead, the aristocracy unconsciously follow the impulse, and *it becomes the fashion to be popular.*

As Mr. Saville predicted, exclusivism passes from the scene with the advent of this popular fashion. A gallery of social types goes along with it. We encounter a number of familiar figures among the *caractères* Bulwer marshals off the stage: the "metaphysical swindler" Mr. Cavendish Fitzroy, who lives elegantly on nothing a year, the "drone dandy" Lord Mute, "six feet of inanity enveloped in cloth," and the "wasp dandy" Sir Paul Snarl, out "to become a great man, by showing that he thinks *you* an exceedingly small one." Interestingly, though, these rejected characters are not the subtle depictions of pre-Reform nobility and gentility Bulwer has portrayed in his fashionable novels but the caricatures that appear in minor roles in these works and that persist in later fiction: amoral aristocrats like Dickens' Sir John Chester and Thackeray's Lord Steyne, ineffectual gentleman like George Eliot's Mr. Brooke, self-indulgent peers like Trollope's old Duke of Omnium and Beerbohm's young Duke of Dorset.

In *England and the English,* Bulwer takes leave not only of reliable old characters but of the fashionable novel as well. Totally involved in his present role of historian, he unexpectedly aligns himself with his critic Carlyle and grants no literary merits to the genre, though he admits its political utility:

> Few writers ever produced so great an effect on the political spirit of their generation as some of these novelists, who, without any other merit, unconsciously exposed the falsehood, the hypocrisy, the arrogant and vulgar insolence of patrician life. Read by all classes, in every town, in every village, these works, as I have before stated, could not but engender a mingled indignation and disgust at the parade of frivolity, the ridiculous disdain of truth, nature, and mankind, the self-consequence and absurdity, which, falsely or truly, these novels exhibited as a picture of aristocratic society. The Utilitarians railed against them, and they were effecting with unspeakable rapidity the very purposes the Utilitarians desired.

Now that Reform has ushered in a new age, Bulwer goes on to say, the vogue for this dubious sort of literature has passed:

> A description of the mere frivolities of fashion is no longer coveted; for the public mind, once settled towards an examination of the aristocracy, has pierced from the surface to the depth; it has probed the wound, and it now desires to cure.

Reasonable as Bulwer's turning toward history seems, the vehemence with which he turns against the fashionable novel needs some explaining. As the moral imperative of the preceding passage with its medical imagery echoing *Pelham*'s 1828 preface suggests, the problem lay with Bulwer's high aims for fashionable fiction. Bulwer, as we have seen, conceived of the "silver fork" novel as a fairly rigorous kind of thought experiment. He could not, for instance, justify using fashionable fiction for self-projection and wish-fulfillment or for exuberant myth-making as did Disraeli in *Vivian Grey* and *The Young Duke* respectively. Assuming that the description of "things as they really are" would edify, Bulwer the *moraliste* placed each of his paragons in a milieu whose workings were those of the actual Great World as he then saw it. This method achieved what Bulwer hoped it to do in *Pelham,* where the protagonist prospered because of his excellence and actively participated in the ordering and improving of society. But in *Greville* and *Godolphin,* it proved impossible to be both accurately descriptive and morally uplifting. To make Greville something other than a misunderstood onlooker, Godolphin more than a trifler, and Constance less than a

tough-minded subversive, Bulwer would have had either to compromise their distinctive excellences or to falsify his perceptions of the Great World. He had discovered that the moral potential of "silver fork" fiction, like the impact of the superior individual on society at large, was limited. The new democratic England taking shape needed guidance more direct than Bulwer's fashionable novels could offer. In *England and the English,* Bulwer signals his adjustment to the coming age.

Still, however Bulwer deprecates the fashionable novel in this book, we must recall that elsewhere he has proved the genre's ability to convey substance as well as surface. *Godolphin*'s account of Saville's urbanity and Constance's eminence, *Greville*'s incisive witticisms, and above all *Pelham*'s sophisticated interplay of worldliness and worthiness proclaim the young Bulwer, society entertainer though he may be, a fit inheritor of the *moraliste* tradition. In these social novels, and in *England and the English,* Bulwer accurately and intelligently presents both the sham splendors and the real graces of the Regency and post-Regency world. The charms of the stylist may divert the modern reader, but the insights of the *moraliste* should convince him, as they did Trollope, that "very much more than amusement may be obtained from Bulwer's novels."

*Peter W. Graham, "Bulwer the 'Moraliste'," in* Dickens Studies Annual, *Vol. 9, 1981, pp. 143-61.*

## B. G. Knepper (essay date 1983)

[*In the following essay, Knepper contends that* The Coming Race *is an important modern contribution to utopian literature.*]

Edward Bulwer-Lytton published his utopian novel, *The Coming Race,* in 1871, toward the end of a distinguished career in literature and government. While his reputation in both areas has diminished somewhat, the reputation of *The Coming Race* continues to grow, and its place as a classic of utopian literature seems assured. That place depends, at least in part, upon the skill with which Bulwer-Lytton kept to the modern rule for science fiction, that the advanced technology of an "other" world must be a logical extension of the implications of current scientific knowledge. His use of evolution as the basic fact of human development, of personal fields of force as the mode of mankind's next evolutionary advance, and of electricity as not only the universal structural component of matter, but also as the bridge between body and intellect, fulfills the "rule" and places his work firmly and early in the stream of modern utopian novels.

People living in the 1980s, conditioned for more than a century to think of Victorian times as dull and dowdy, find it difficult to recapture the intense excitement of living during the nineteenth century when Western culture was literally reshaping its world. Yet so it was, in politics, science, and technology (to say nothing, just now, of theology and philosophy), and, in *The Coming Race,* Bulwer-Lytton struggled to resolve the problems, the hopes, and the reservations which occupied the minds of the thinkers and theorists of his time. His task was complicated by the need to present his thinking, as Charles Dickens and

George Eliot also did, through the form of the popular novel.

In politics, then, England, as well as much of the rest of Europe, was making a stormy transition from the rule of the rich or the well-bred few to that of the common man, from oligarchy to democracy and thence, in the twentieth century, to socialism. England escaped the worst of the bloodshed which too often marked the changes on the continent, say the German revolutions of 1848, which in their turn grew out of the aborted February Revolution in France, or the ugly affair of the Commune of Paris (1871-73). Still, England had her violent moments, though perhaps none worse than the Battle of Peterloo (Manchester, 1819) which occurred when the yeomanry attacked a peaceable, if illegal, gathering of industrial workers. The massacre resulted in the death of eleven persons and the injury of some four hundred others, a negligible number by continental standards, perhaps, but quite enough to shock England into a determination to find less violent means of settling political differences. Meanwhile, political theories spawned everywhere, the Utilitarians and the Chartists building on the Reform Bill of 1832 and pointing the way toward trade-unionism and socialism, the Utilitarians eventually finding their strongest voices in John Stuart Mill and Herbert Spencer. Mill held that while the old Benthamite theory of pleasure as the central fact of human motivation was correct, it must be modified to recognize quality as well as quantity and to recognize that pleasure is a by-product of useful activity, not a goal in itself. Spencer linked utilitarian ethics to evolution. Such struggles and theories inform much of *The Coming Race,* as does the sense of eventual and inevitably violent social transition which is most powerfully expressed in the dialectic materialism of Marx and Engels.

On a lesser scale, women's rights were much debated during the nineteenth century. Mary Wollstonecraft Godwin produced her *Vindication of the Rights of Women* in 1792. The Chartists embraced the movement and, in 1851, the subject was debated in the House of Lords. In 1869, Mill's *Subjection of Women* appeared. One year later, John Bright moved a bill for women's suffrage in the House of Commons.

The ferment of ideas in the scientific world of the nineteenth century, too, caught Bulwer-Lytton's imagination and he played them off against each other constantly in *The Coming Race.* Among the controversies, perhaps none is more central than that which swirled around the subject of evolution. The earlier notion of teleological evolution, dependent upon will and purpose, demonstrable by design in nature, had been fully established before Bulwer-Lytton was born. It rested, essentially, on the authority of the studies of fossil remains as they relate to geological strata. Those remains indicate the existence of now-extinct life forms, and the teleologist argued that the progressions indicated a design and, therefore, a designer. Among the teleologists may be placed Erasmus Darwin (1731-1802), grandfather of Charles Darwin, and Jean Lamarck (1744-1829), who held that life forms are modified over long geological periods and that the modifications become hereditary, a theory which was widely held and as widely disputed. Later theorists, among them Bernard Shaw, held that purpose is demonstrable in the higher life-forms themselves without there being, necessarily, a connection with an embodied god.

Backers of teleology fought a losing battle against the mechanistic interpretations of the Darwinists who perverted Charles Darwin's theories of selection and survival of the fittest into catch-phrases, not only for biology, but for theology, political science, and even business pursuits as well. With theorists of the magnitude of Sir Charles Lyell, Herbert Spencer, and Thomas Huxley lending their support, it is little wonder that a mechanistic, hedonistic, deterministic view of life battered the teleological one and forced itself upon the consciousness of thinking men like Bulwer-Lytton, creating adherence and opposition not only between groups, but often even within individuals themselves.

Other areas of science were developing rapidly and excitingly. Electricity provides a significant example. The late eighteenth century saw the discoveries of Galvani and Volta. In the nineteenth century, Ohm, Joule, and Kirchoff broke through with discoveries which formed the basis for modern electrical technology. By 1841 Faraday had invented the electric motor, and within ten years the motor had been made practical. While power stations did not exist in Bulwer-Lytton's time, the telegraph certainly did (transatlantic cable, 1866) and medical applications were fairly common, though the X-ray was far in the future (1895).

The borderline between science and quackery in matters electrical was ill-defined. Galvani's theories about electric currents in the body, for instance, set off trains of thinking which have not yet run their course. Electrotherapy became, and remains, standard medical practice. It also became a favorite device for the charlatan. The notion that the body produces fields of force led to the marvels of electrocardiography and electroencephalography. It also led to the not quite so thoroughly demonstrated theories of the personal field of force which can influence that of another person, or which can be a factor in telepathy, or which can be the as yet evolving sixth sense. Cognates with earlier theories of astral bodies and platonic journeys of the soul were easily found and lent new support to the interest of serious investigator and fraud alike. Bulwer-Lytton was not alone in finding projections from the demonstrated to the probable to the possible both interesting and illuminating.

Technology changed the way of life of all Europe in the nineteenth century, not the least of all in England, which led the way in the Industrial Revolution. The transatlantic cable has already been mentioned, but it is a small matter compared with the changes wrought by the application of steam to mining, factories, and shipping. Steam travel began in England in 1825, and by the 1850s rail transportation was completely established throughout western Europe. Steam-powered industry, manufacturing, and shipping, land and sea, made England a world power. Still, *The Coming Race* achieves its deepest interest precisely because scientific principle is emphasized over technical application in an age obsessed with technical innovations.

To be sure, the novel is not free of imaginative technical innovations; much of its page-to-page interest depends upon them. There are power transmitters called vril-wands, housework is done by automatons, and people fly with artificial wings. A superficial reader can easily become involved with such details to the exclusion of all else. The point is that Bulwer-Lytton's interest in gimmickry and gadgetry lies in the motives of the people who develop such things and the effect of those things upon their developers. Why does one want an ultimate weapons system, and, once one has it, how does it affect the behavior of its possessor? Even granting his obvious pleasure in inventing clever, futuristic machinery, his constantly looking beyond the technology to its implications for mankind puts Bulwer-Lytton far more in the camp of Thomas Huxley, Dickens, and Shaw than, say, in that of Thomas B. Macaulay or even of H. G. Wells.

If one ignores juvenilia and begins with Bulwer-Lytton's novel *Falkland* (1827), and includes work published after his death in 1873, a conservative estimate of his literary production would include fifty-three works: twenty-six novels, nine plays, and eighteen other items. To the massiveness of this output add the great variety of kinds of writing attempted, and it is no wonder that critical estimates of its value vary so widely. Bulwer-Lytton has been seen as a serious explorer of the human condition in its many variations, as a skillful craftsman working within a well-developed critical theory, and as a clever entertainer, on the one hand, and on the other, as a hasty panderer to a vulgar public taste, as a waster of great gifts and talents, and as a crackpot in wrongheaded pursuit of the least reputable fads and notions of his time. None of these estimates is without some color of the truth; none catches the whole truth, certainly. The simple fact is that the work is too large and too various to be easily or fairly assessed in any general sense. In addition, only a small portion of the work seems likely to survive as having permanent literary value. Therefore, it seems unlikely that anyone will find it worthwhile to make a definitive study of the entire corpus. What is left, then, and what is alike possible and valuable, are studies of restricted segments of the work made from carefully limited points of view. Such examinations promise rich rewards and will go far toward establishing a sound perspective from which to view Bulwer-Lytton's achievement.

Holding to a narrow focus is, of course, always difficult and sometimes dangerous. It means, largely, that the work itself must be made the center of the critic's attention and that all other intriguing relationships must be either subordinated to it or passed over altogether. The danger is that the critic may lose the larger view, may even be betrayed into prizing narrowness for its own sake. However, if the dangers are skirted, the work comes into view on its own terms, its ideas unclouded by critical preconceptions formed by excursions into biography or by comparisons with the author's previous work. Even consideration of the work's place in literary tradition must, for the moment, be suspended. The work, like a piece of jewelry, a cathedral, or even a race horse, has a heredity and exists within a culture, but it exists, nevertheless, as an individual creation and needs, as a first thing, to be understood as one. It can then be placed easily and accurately in the larger contexts, much understanding having been gained and little lost.

My own first concern with *The Coming Race* was its relationship to Shaw's set of plays, *Back to Methuselah*. My present concern is first to examine the novel in its own right. Having done so, perhaps I can lay to rest at least one of the critical problems surrounding the novel: is *The Coming Race* a utopia or a dystopia? Does it, in short, picture a society which is the best that can be imagined, or one which is unbearably bad? This is the central problem of the story, and getting at it will go a long way toward understanding the book and, perhaps, a good part of the human dilemma as well.

Formal things first. The plot of *The Coming Race* is disarmingly simple and straightforward. In unrelieved chronological order it tells of an experience remembered, a tale carrying a warning of doom for the whole human race. The experience begins when a wealthy young American, never identified, visits an unnamed mine in an unnamed country.

Almost at once, the American's engineer-companion is devoured by "a monstrous reptile resembling . . . the crocodile or alligator, but infinitely larger."

Recovering from the shock, the traveller finds himself in an artificially lit world, on a road surrounded by fields and forests, with buildings in the distance. It is, except for the monster, a pleasant enough place: "The world without a sun was bright and warm as an Italian landscape at noon, but the air less oppressive, the heat, softer."

Approaching the buildings, Egyptian in nature, but "more ornamental and more fantastically graceful," he meets the first inhabitant; "an indescribable awe and terror" seizes him. He is confronted by a tall being, "tall as the tallest man below the height of giants," shaped like a man, "yet of another race." The creature is winged and carries a metal staff. His face is calm and beautiful, but "of a type of man distinct from our known extant races," and it "roused that instinct of danger which the sight of a tiger or serpent arouses." The traveller believes at once that this being "was endowed with forces inimical to man." However, when this godlike being places a hand upon the stranger's shoulder and touches him with the staff, all fear is replaced by "a sense of contentment, of joy, of confidence in myself and in the being before me."

The pair then enter a building, very ornate, having music in the background, birds caged everywhere, and automata for servants. The pair, along with a child, ascend by a lift to a rich apartment where, shortly, the troubled traveller is put to sleep.

When he awakens he is surrounded by more of these superior beings. In the interrogation which follows, he senses that they are trying to decide whether he should live or die. In the end, he is taken home by the one who first found him, where he is welcomed by the family—a wife, two sons, and a daughter.

At this point the plot separates into several strands and gives place in importance and interest to theoretical and

*Knebworth, Bulwer-Lytton's estate in Hertfordshire.*

philosophical constructions which are truly the guts of the story. The plot, then, continues to exist mostly to give the traveller, while under the care of several conductors, an opportunity to view various aspects of the underground culture and to compare them with their cognates in the surface culture. This technique of hanging episodes or digressions from a slender thread of plot is no invention of Bulwer-Lytton's, of course, but it allows him to present ideas from several points of view, thus deepening the perspective.

The first plot strand involves the traveller and the being who first discovered him, a minor official called Alph-Lin. Alph-Lin is the primary expositor of his culture's history, art, religion, political science, and technology. The two, while often at odds, are in many ways kindred spirits and tend to act as alter egos for each other. Ultimately Alph-Lin proves unable to protect his guest-student, but he fills the role of guide-protector as long as possible. Thus, it is not for nothing that the traveller refers to him, habitually, as "my host." Alph-Lin acts not only as the entertainer of a guest, but also as the stronger member of a symbiotic pair.

The second plot strand involves the child, Tae, son of the chief magistrate, the Tur. The superior abilities of this child underline the childishness of the traveller who is, after all, a surrogate for all "ordinary" human beings. The two actually play together, and after an initial period of

hostility this terrible child, who slays dragons with impunity, becomes a close friend of the traveller, although in some ways the relationship smacks of youthful master and exotic pet. In any case, Tae becomes yet another tutor. In the end, Tae is charged with the duty of killing the traveller, who is not only a dangerous and inferior animal, but a threat to the racial purity of the community. The child, because of his culture's religious conviction that death is only a journey to another life, has no fear of death nor any hesitation to kill any life form which he feels threatens his community. When the traveller learns of all this, he is terrified. He is also touched by Tae's willingness to accompany him in death, a wish which buys time when the child decides to ask his father's permission to kill himself as well as the stranger.

The third plot strand, and possibly the most important one, involves the girl, Zee, daughter of Alph-Lin, and the traveller. As a young female of this advanced race of subterranean giants, Zee is the more powerful of the two. In this topsy-turvy world, women are bigger and stronger than their own men, more intelligent, more aggressive, and, most importantly, more efficient users of vril, the power source which underlies all aspects of their civilization (of which, more later). Oddly, Zee is at once the feminist ideal and the caricature of all feminist ideals. While she, too, is very useful for providing a different perspective from which to measure the ideals of her race, her plot function is rather dreary: she provides the romantic pursuit which is responsible for whatever rising action there is. She is the catalyst which brings on the catastrophe, and her self-sacrifice provides the resolution. More specifically, she woos the traveller as is the custom in her culture, with all the gusto which will become the hallmark of a Shavian heroine, and expects him to display the characteristics of Shaw's womanly woman. The usual complications of the chase are present. Other young women, especially the underaged daughter of Tur, likewise aspire to the traveller's hand, a development which he finds by no means displeasing. Others, however, are horrified at the possibility of intermarriage with a surface dweller, and the traveller's fate is determined. Zee overcomes her jealousy and proposes a way out for the traveller and herself through the old love-and-honor formula. She will sacrifice honor for love and they will leave the colony to establish a version of the rose-covered cottage for themselves. The marriage will be "platonic," that is, it will be "without issue." Sensing at last the traveller's revulsion at the idea of such a marriage, Zee then decides to do the honorable thing, sacrifice her love as well. During the sleeping hours she spirits him away from the community and, using the special powers of vril, she blasts a way back into the mineshaft and restores the traveller to humanity. She blasts the shaft shut again and is heared of no more. The traveller then goes home after uttering a well-considered prophesy about the inevitable destruction of mankind, and the story is over.

The plot, then, is a tenuous thing, depending for whatever effect it may have upon a love theme and a death theme, neither of them very suspenseful. Even allowing for the attractions of fantasy, there is little in the plot itself to account for the popularity of the book in its own time. The digressions, then, as is so often the case in social satire, are more important than the plot, and that assumption will form the basis for their consideration later.

What then of style? Critics have long found this aspect of *The Coming Race* bothersome, possibly because it is to easy to misjudge the book on the basis of its none too impressive plot. However, in his recent book *Bulwer-Lytton: The Fiction of New Regions*, Allen Conrad Christensen argues on the positive side that perceptive readers have always found Bulwer-Lytton's books to have stylistic merit. He writes, "Such figures as Goethe, Carlyle, Mill, Harriet Martineau, Macaulay, Dickens, Poe, and Arnold all paid tribute at various times to the serious artistry and intellectual vigor they discerned beneath the surface of his works." This is high praise in general, though of little direct use relative to *The Coming Race* since four of the eight critics died before the novel appeared, three more were nearing the end of long careers and lives, and only one, Arnold, was still in full career. Still, if *The Coming Race* is allowed to be one of Bulwer-Lytton's better works, produced not in his dotage but at the height of his mature powers, then the evaluation is impressive. In any case, it is a refreshing change from earlier evaluations which found his style nearly beyond bearing.

Not all early statements were hostile to Bulwer-Lytton's abilities. A fairly kind estimate was written in 1858 by J.

Cordy Jeaffreson [in *Novels and Novelists; from Elizabeth to Victoria,* 1858]: "He is entitled to foremost rank amongst writers of *talent,* as distinguished from writers of genius; he is a careful and well-trained artist, deficient in creative ability."

As I have had occasion to observe elsewhere, Shaw claimed to have admired *The Coming Race* as a boy, and, in 1887, credited it with introducing the scientific method in the modern novel. Ten years later Shaw castigated Bulwer-Lytton as lazy, a man who misused literary skills to impose very slight scholarship upon the public. The kindest things he could find to say were that Bulwer-Lytton was a "romantic humbug," "insincere," and the author of "adventurous schoolboy romances." Much later, in 1944, Shaw revised his opinion and placed him among "the greatest poets and most inventive romancers."

Perhaps the strongest plea for viewing Bulwer-Lytton as a serious artist, as against a commercial boiler of pots, was made by Harold H. Watts in 1935 in an essay [in *PMLA* 50, no. I (March 1935)] entitled "Lytton's Theories of Prose Fiction." In it he traces literary theories formulated by Bulwer-Lytton in 1838 as they appear in the practice of the later novels. Watts credits Bulwer-Lytton with two notions which cast a great deal of light upon the techniques employed in *The Coming Race.* One premise is that by concentrating, in a single focus, the vicious influences of any particular error in the social system, he (the novelist) will hold up a mirror in which nations may see themselves reflected. The second is that the controlling factor of a novel is a great conception (thesis) to which all else is subordinate or incidental. The first comes close to defining the purpose of utopian literature; the second fits the catastrophic, evolutionary theme of *The Coming Race.*

On the whole, the style of *The Coming Race* is neither as unreadable as has often been suggested (see the *Dictionary of National Biography* entry as an easily available example) nor quite as skillful as its apologists would have it. Perhaps the view that Bulwer-Lytton was stuck with the tastes of contemporary popular readers, which demanded a romantic-adventure plot complete with fanciful descriptions and other fantasy, comes close to the mark. From such a plot, however, he was free to add the digressions containing the ideas for discussion that are, after all, the heart of the book. Readers are left to cope, as they can, with the puzzling ironies demanded by the genre itself.

How is it, then, that genre study should provide the best answer to the question of whether *The Coming Race* is a utopian or a dystopian work? Consider that the basic characteristic of either form is that an imagined society is compared and contrasted with an existing one. The comparison may be very overt or it may be barely implied. In times during which criticism of church or state is extremely dangerous to the writer, or simply inconvenient, the comparison may well be left to the sharpness of the reader's insight. Theoretically, a simple allegorical comparison, one to one, might be made, such as, I take it, Eugene Zamiatin did in *We,* or George Orwell in *1984.* In practice, things are not so simple and both societies are presented as, to a degree, flawed. Paradoxical as it may seem for a writer to deliberately flaw his ideal society, such flawing is quite useful. The flaws of one society can be used to highlight the flaws or virtues of the other. Moreover, if a utopia is to be convincing, it cannot present a perfect society made up of fallible human beings. No one believes in such things, suspend disbelief as much as one will. Then, too, as a human society, a new society inevitably retains some of the aspects of the old society so that in a utopia or a dystopia there must be a certain amount of trade-off and compromise; increased order and discipline is exchanged for increasing blandness, unrelieved beauty for the highlighting provided by ugliness, and so on. The result is, commonly, that the author sometimes plays the game straight with the reader and sometimes plays it ironically.

The problem is to know when to turn the text upside down and when to take it at face value. For instance, Plato's *Republic* is usually taken at face value. But should it be? How much of the *Republic* is a sneer at Sparta's mindless militarism? Is it possible that even the conception of the reluctant philosopher-king is partly a spoof? If the Greeks must wait for their utopia until such paragons are ready to hand, clearly they must wait forever. Or can one take seriously the astringent sexual puritanism of the "metallic" classes and not smile at the sexual orgy which is their reward for military prowess? Plato's book, no doubt, is to be taken straight much of the time; other parts are either ironic or impossible.

Even Sir Thomas More's *Utopia* has its moments of irony. One example must serve. The notion of prenuptial stripping of the bride and groom for the same sort of physical examination appropriate in the purchase of a horse, a thing in the case of prospective marriage partners at once sensible and outrageous, must seem ironic, unless one is to presume the subtle and urbane More lacked a sense of humor.

Jonathan Swift is an altogether tougher nut to crack. *Gulliver's Travels* poses genuinely difficult problems of interpretation. In Book I, Lilliput is England and Blefuscu is France and each is an awful place. No reasonable reader mistakes Lilliput for utopia, and if it is not dystopia, it will do as a substitute. Still, bad as it is, Lilliput has a reasonable system of education for all classes, a boast England will not be able to make with any show of truth for nearly two centuries. Nor are all Lilliputians fools and rogues. In short, with a reduction of vice and folly, and with a few reforms, Lilliput-England could at least approach the condition of a utopia. The irony in Book II is, to a degree, more subtle. Eighteenth-century Europe surely suffers from comparison with enlightened Brobdingnag, but Brobdingnag, for all its abolishing of warfare and its horror at European atrocity, is certainly not an unsullied utopian paradise. The episode about the court ladies at their toilet, or that of the ulcerous beggar, is enough to suggest that human vices and follies are magnified, along with human virtues, in the land of the giants. Book III may be passed over as an unrelieved dystopia. The Struldbruggs, monsters who age progressively but never die, are the proper emblems of ultimate awfulness. Book IV offers endless difficulties. On the surface, it presents the ultimate utopia of the Enlightenment. For the most part, institutions have faded away and only a benevolent society re-

mains, a society formed of horses. These horses, called Houyhnhnms, are contrasted with human society through Gulliver and through the wild human animals called Yahoos, some of whom the Houyhnhnms have domesticated. In Gulliver's view, mankind fails to measure up. In a sense, Houyhnhnmland is utopia, the best society that man can achieve. Had the book started with Laputa, the progression from worst to best would be clear enough. But if the land of the Houyhnhnms is indeed the earthly paradise, it is a strange one. The Houyhnhnms are docile and priggish. Their perfect society is the ultimate in dullness. Consider one of their marriage rules. Each couple is allowed to raise two, and two only, colts—one male, one female. As one colt is as good as another, a swapping custom is established to correct any failure on nature's part to make an even distribution of the sexes. The arrangement may well be humane and sensible. However, it reminds one of the tongue-in-cheek tone of the equally "sensible" arrangements of "A Modest Proposal" which proposed, "reasonably" enough, to establish cannibalism as the solution to Ireland's oversupply of paupers.

It is hardly too much to say that the extreme blandness of a perfect society is one of the most difficult points for the idealist to get over. Shaw's ultimate utopia, presented in *As Far as Thought Can Reach,* is peopled by Ancients who live forever, barring accidents, and who live a life as nearly exclusively intellectual as it is possible to imagine creatures still in the flesh to live. These Ancients explain to their young that their own intellectual experiences are so much more ecstatic than any of the children's sexual adventures that a moment of such pleasure would be more than the children could survive. Contemporary drama critics shared the scepticism of the young about this claim and pronounced adult life in A.D. 31,920, as seen by Shaw, to be unbearable, Shaw's protests of his own sincerity notwithstanding.

Recent critics tend to see *The Coming Race* as dystopian or anti-utopian. In 1965, Geoffrey Wagner described *The Coming Race* as mainly an attack on America, "the new woman," and machine technology. His perception of the satirical intention is certainly accurate, though I can hardly agree that those themes, of themselves, form the central purpose of the book, though they are certainly important elements of it. Even so, Wagner's remark that "Lytton disarms the reader with external satire, then proceeds to get down to business by pushing what seems to him topsy-turvy values *ad absurdum,*" is clearly an accurate description of Bulwer-Lytton's method. It also underlines Wagner's identification of the book as no utopia [in "A Forgotten Satire: Bulwer-Lytton's *The Coming Race.*" *Nineteenth Century Fiction* 19 (March 1965)].

In 1971, Hans Seeber published a shortened English version of his longer German article about *The Coming Race.* In it he declared that "by casting his veiled criticism of the inherent dangers of uninhibited utopianism, both political and scientific, in the form of a romance, he fathered a new variety of utopian writing, the anti-utopian novel." For Seeber, the bogeys are Utopian Socialism and scientific materialism. He credits Lytton [in "Bulwer-Lytton's Underworld: *The Coming Race* (1871)," *Moreana* 30 (1971)] as being, "in fact, the first writer to emphasize and exploit the contrast between ordinary humanity and inhuman utopian perfection, in terms of narrative treatment."

In 1979, John Weeks provided a slender introduction for a new edition of *The Coming Race.* He observed that the supermen have "little more to do than to contemplate their own perfection" and that the traveller "finds that what seemed at first to be the good life is after all indolent and boring." This language clearly seems to indicate a dystopia. Unfortunately, the thread is not pursued and Week's closing statements muddle the conception of a dystopia. They suggest, instead, that the underground people have established a utopian pattern toward which mankind is, on the whole, happily racing. "In fact," Weeks wrote, "we still haven't quite caught up with the farthest reaches of his [Bulwer-Lytton's] imagination, but we are going that way and gaining fast."

If the novel is taken as a whole and on its own terms, without modification by speculation, however well-supported, about Bulwer-Lytton's attitudes expressed elsewhere in his works about the same or similar topics, it becomes clear that proponents of both the utopian and the dystopian interpretations are right. The home truth of the book is that, take it as you will, evolution is a fact, and that mankind in its present form will be replaced by a superior species—quite likely a hostile one. Thus, the book is a dystopia for the traveller, a truth which does him little credit. He is at once terrified and bored by a world too advanced for him. He sees his own race and culture reflected in those subterranean peoples who failed to evolve and who are doomed. But never does Bulwer-Lytton present the traveller's culture as intrinsically superior to that of the undergrounders. Theirs is presented consistently as a utopia, flawed as a still evolving form must be, but in every way superior. In the end, Bulwer-Lytton does not mince matters. The traveller muses, "The more I think of a people calmly developing . . . powers surpassing our most disciplined modes of force, and *virtues* (emphasis mine) to which our life, social and political, becomes antagonistic in proportion as our civilization advances, —the more devoutly I pray that ages may elapse before there emerge into sunlight our inevitable destroyers." Just as Shaw's Ancients are unable to appreciate the joys of their terrible parents, and earlier, unevolved people died of awe and discouragement in the presence of the ancestors of the Ancients, so the traveller is unable to bear living in an advanced utopia—though looking back he wonders "how I could have rejected such a love, no matter what dangers attended it, or by what conditions it was restricted." Romantic balderdash or not, this is not the speech of a character who recalls his lover as a dystopian monster.

Acting on the premise, then, that *The Coming Race* has a dual nature, utopian in the long view, dystopian in the short, the salient features of the book may be examined freshly. The scientific theories need to be dealt with first as they underlie the social ones.

Evolution is the sine qua non of the novel. Earlier discussion distinguished between the Darwinian theory and the older, teleological sort. The distinction is basic to understanding what the work is getting at. At the time Bulwer-

Lytton wrote, the Darwinian theories were dominant and their implications were somber. They projected a world which was mechanistic with a vengeance, with the role of will and intellect reduced to the merest of nothings. Chance bound to irresistible cause and effect was everything. While all of this was largely a perversion of Darwin's own theories, it was the popularized Darwinian guff against which Browning and Tennyson, among others, revolted. If *The Coming Race* had been conceived as simply another Darwinian horror story, it would have lost none of its sense of inevitability and doom. It would also have been the unrelieved dystopia it has been so often depicted as being.

But *The Coming Race* is not an unrelieved dystopia. Repeatedly, the text makes it clear that Bulwer-Lytton's master race developed by plan, not accident, and that the mode of development included individual will and racial will plus an implied divine will as well. Consider that, immediately following a passage of the clearest survival-of-the-fittest Darwinism, Zee refers to an ancient legend which held that " 'we were driven from a region that seems to denote the world you came from, in order to perfect our condition and attain to the pure elimination of our species by the severity of the struggles our forefather underwent; and that, when our education shall become finally completed, we are destined to return to the upper world, and supplant all the inferior races now existing there.' " This passage affirms the operation of will and direction, not blind chance. Natural selection is converted from a process of accident to one of education. A second case in point revolves around the nature of vril, the substance which is the source of all the material good and power of the advanced race. The seat of vril lies in a nerve at the base of an enlarged thumb. This nerve, which develops and concentrates the vril, a substance akin to electricity, was not found either in the early ancestors of the upper race or in the contemporary "barbaric" underground races, or, by analogy, in modern human beings. It was, Zee explains, " 'slowly developed in the course of generations, commencing in the early achievements and increasing with the continuous exercise of the vril power.' " The power and skill in applying it is, thus, conceived to be hereditarily cumulative and to be the result of will and practice, not of chance. Zee adds that " 'in the course of one or two thousand years, such a nerve may possibly be engendered in those higher beings of your own race.' " As to the theory of the descent from frogs, it is indeed the amusing parody of Darwinism it is generally presumed to be. However, when the traveller asks if the theory of " 'the origin of your race in the tadpole' " is still recognized, he is put in his place by Zee. Her reply confirms the teleological position and sets the limit for human power:

> "When we know the elements out of which our bodies are composed, elements common to the humblest vegetable plants, can it signify whether the All-Wise combined those elements out of one form more than another, in order to create that in which He has placed the capacity to receive the idea of Himself, and all the varied grandeurs of intellect to which that idea gives birth? The An in reality commenced to exist as An with the donation of that capacity, and, with

that capacity, the sense to acknowledge that, however through the countless ages his race may improve in wisdom, it can never combine the elements at its command into the form of a tadpole."

Zee's father then makes the connection between physical and social evolution by remarking that his people " 'feel a reasonable assurance that whether the origins of the An [all Subterranean peoples] was a tadpole or not, he is no more likely to become a tadpole again than the institutions of the Vril-ya [the super race] are likely to relapse into the heaving quagmire and certain strife-rot of a Koom-Posh [popular democracy].' "

The final argument to be advanced here for teleology as the guiding evolutionary concept in *The Coming Race* is provided in a reflective passage by the traveller: "Perfect justice flows of necessity from perfectness of knowledge to conceive, perfectness of love to will, and perfectness of power to complete it." Besides coming down firmly on the side of will, the words are an astonishing anticipation of Shaw's conception of the prerequisites for social justice, which he articulated in *Major Barbara* and fully elaborated in *Back to Methuselah,* that social justice can occur only when love, intellect, and power are combined, eventually in supermen who will become philosopher-kings.

The scientific validity of the conception of "vril" is of secondary importance to the need in *The Coming Race* for a physical manifestation of the evolutionary process in action. In "vril," Bulwer-Lytton found a power which could be used to exploit the excitement caused by successive discoveries in electricity. While the notion of developing "vril" by a special nerve and transmitting it through a metal wand may strike a modern reader as altogether absurd and corny, it provided a simple, visible concrete object, able to represent a number of abstract notions. From the point of view of *The Coming Race*'s effectiveness as fiction, then, it hardly matters whether Bulwer-Lytton was highly learned in scientific matters or whether the names of distinguished practitioners in many fields (Faraday and Galvani, physicists; Louis Agassiz, naturalist; Lyell, geologist; Robert Owen, social scientist; Descartes, philosopher) which he scatters throughout the book are merely window dressing. Their function as a fictional artifact is to lend an aura of validity to the story as story. Their function vis-à-vis serious social theorizing is to provide apparent authority from contemporary science. The choice of electricity in the form of "vril" was an especially happy one as it provided a simple, yet comprehensive, vehicle for presenting ideas of evolutionary progress.

In the first seriously descriptive passage of *The Coming Race* concerning vril, the traveller mentions magnetism, galvanism, Faraday, mesmerism, electro-biology, and odic force as "the various forms under which the forces of matter are made manifest." He argues further that they "have one common origin . . . [and] are so directly related and mutually dependent, that they are convertible . . . into one another, and possess equivalents of power in their action." The latter point is the basis for a very complicated theory about the interrelation of all things material and spiritual. It leads to the conclusion that once life is created, it continues forever, though translated by death to a different world, and it recalls its progress from stage to stage. Vril is able to interact from one life to another so that the super-race can use it to project their wills into other animate, and even inanimate, bodies and minds and make them behave in whatever way the super-race desires. Thus vril, manipulated through a vril-staff, can power and direct automata, heal the ill, calm the overwrought, or destroy armies and cities at extreme range. So defined, vril is a universal principle which gives its users the powers of gods, at least in the old, Greek sense of gods.

As to social and political theories, *The Coming Race* contains a wealth of ideas treated in great detail. Little more than a sampling can be attempted here, leaving the reader the enormous fun of fully tracing out the details.

The effect of vril on warfare amounts to a profound social and political revolution. War becomes unthinkable in the face of overwhelming power. (Bulwer-Lytton apparently was not cynical enough to envision the twentieth-century use of "limited warfare" in the shadow of the nuclear holocaust.) Imagine a world in which not only nations but individuals possess the power to destroy multitudes at nearly any range. In such a world, strife and violence toward one's fellows must be abandoned, at whatever psychological cost.

Law, too, is a casualty to unlimited individual power in *The Coming Race.* Anarchy, however, does not result, mainly because the habit of restraint is presented as transmissible hereditarily, just as vril itself is. While the habit is being formed, restraint must be enforced by rigid custom. Dissidents have the option of migration and little else.

Class distinctions are obviously impossible to maintain. No one can exploit another through superior strength, and vril provides such an abundance of power for agriculture and such other industry as is needed, as well as the automata to run it, that economic exploitation is out of the question. Oddly enough, there are a few individuals who refuse to make even the minimum effort necessary for maintaining themselves. For these, the only suasion possible is a form of ridicule in which the community pretends that such an individual is insane and heaps luxuries upon him until shame brings him to his senses.

Even election to office brings no class privilege to the holder. As in the *Republic,* it simply brings the burden of duty with it, in those few areas in which the community must still be organized, namely light, communications, inventions, and machinery. Light is an obvious need in an underground world. Communications are restricted to other advanced communities, for the most part. Inventions, mostly in the hands of the women of the College of Sages, tend to be vril application research with occasional forays into more esoteric areas. Machinery, curiously, is in the hands of the children, girls until they are sixteen years old, boys until they are twenty. They are in charge of agriculture, housekeeping and border guarding. In the last occupation, their concern is with the possible encroachment of dangerous animals or of the barbaric nations. The children are well paid for their efforts; they earn enough in childhood to support them for the rest of their lives.

Obviously, children capable of destroying prehistoric monsters or the equivalent of modern armies suffer little from excessive parental control. Nevertheless, the family remains a strong institution. This is partly due to an ingrained reverence for life and partly to the conception of society as an extended family. In any case, families stay together until the children achieve adulthood, and the elderly are treated with respect and affection. Such treatment may be made easier with the aged who, despite average life spans of one hundred years and more, stay healthy, vigorous, and financially independent to the end. Except in sex roles and strength, the sexes are equal. While the reversal of roles and characteristics is great fun, and purportedly based on the principle that in most of the animal kingdom, most mammals aside, the female is the more powerful sex, the reversal functions more as satire than as a serious projection of a real evolutionary tendency.

At least passing mention should be made of the variety of societies extant under the Earth's surface. All of them exist under the name of An. Only a few have advanced to the possession of vril; they are known as Vril-ya. The lesser An are ranged in a progression of lesser political forms, some of which the Vril-ya have presumably passed through. These forms correspond with those in the *Republic* and to the nineteenth-century European and American models. The bottom of the heap is composed of Glek-Nas. They are democracy run wild, the anarchy which Plato contends is the inevitable tendency of universal democracy. The American Civil War and the revolutions of Europe give color to the theory. Democracy is described as Koom-Posh and is distinguished by "the government of the many, or the ascendancy of the most ignorant or hollow." The satirical intent is clear enough. But the organized anarchy of the Vril-ya must not be confused with either of the imperfect forms; it is the ideal society in which every individual is an aristocrat, a member of Plato's golden class, and a potential philosopher-king.

Leaving much unsaid about the political and social aspects of the book, especially about its extraordinarily sane and Swiftian religion, I must turn to a consideration of the characteristics it shares with other utopias and dystopias, besides what I have already done in passing. For instance, I suggest that *The Coming Race* must share honors with Francis Bacon's *The New Atlantis* as a prototype of the "scientific" utopia. Like Bulwer-Lytton, Bacon envisioned a society which combined experimental science with the creature comfort of its members. Swift's *Gulliver's Travels* received fairly extensive treatment earlier, but Book III was largely passed over. It will bear examination, however, as Bulwer-Lytton's spoofs are much in the mode of Swift's Laputa. Compare the scholars there, for instance, with their penchant for the trivial, with the College of Sages in *The Coming Race.*

H. G. Wells's *A Modern Utopia,* with its world a mirror image of the Earth, except for a population of superior people, shares several features with *The Coming Race.* For instance, each features an evolving society which places a higher value on social virtue than on hedonistic lifestyles.

Each is as much a treatise on social theory as it is a novel. They differ markedly in that Wells bases his society on an eighteenth-century norm, mankind at its best, as against Bulwer-Lytton's mankind evolved. Wells's Samurai, nevertheless, see to it that inferior specimens either do not survive or do not reproduce, a bit of genetic tinkering which raises the spectre of totalitarianism gone mad.

The similarity to Samuel Butler's *Erewhon,* which appeared one year after *The Coming Race,* has been often noted in the critical literature. The similarity seems to me to be one largely of techniques: Butler produced a dystopia, pure and simple; Bulwer-Lytton a utopia.

William Morris's *News from Nowhere* is a splendid example of another basically anarchistic society, albeit a caring one, seriously put forward as an achievable utopia. In his book, as in Bulwer-Lytton's, institutions have all but faded away, and mankind as extended family has replaced the state. Work has all but vanished, thanks to simplified needs and the development of machinery to do necessary but dull work, so that people, with more leisure than art and handicraft can satisfy, actually compete for whatever meaningful work is left. Evolution toward a super-race is no part of Morris's scheme; he is too much a perfectionist of the Shellyan mode for that. On the other hand, his earthly paradise is unmarred by the same constant, if submerged, threat of violence that Bulwer-Lytton's is.

The relationship of Shaw's work to *The Coming Race* has been glanced at in passing throughout this study. Evolution, awe, and advanced mental powers, far more sophisticated than vril, are but a few of the parallels, a matter I discussed in detail in 1971 in an article entitled "Shaw's Debt to *The Coming Race*" [in *Journal of Modern Literature* I (1971) and *MLA Abstracts*, item no. 4942 (1971)].

Finally, Aldous Huxley's *Brave New World,* as a scientific dystopia with a considerable overlay of political and social exploration, will repay comparison with *The Coming Race.* So far as I can determine, *Brave New World* is not based in theory upon teleological evolution, though it certainly implies that, freed from the mind-crushing restrictions of an inhuman, technological, totalitarian society, the human spirit would grow again.

I cannot say with any confidence that *The Coming Race* has had a profound impact upon following writers, Shaw excepted. Along with Bulwer-Lytton's other work, it has mostly languished on library shelves for a century and more. The ideas it contains and the mode of its presentation were hardly unique, even for its day, except in the way in which they were combined; the ideas were "in the air." With the recent revival of interest in his work, and the appearance of at least one new and inexpensive edition, the impact may increase. For my part, I hope it does. Wholly aside from its literary value, or the simple fact that it is fun, I count *The Coming Race* as an important item in the humanist arsenal against despair. The human spirit needs all the weapons it can muster against the hopelessness thrust at it by determinists, mechanists, and assorted totalitarians everywhere. If the human spirit can be coaxed into persisting, perhaps it may at last prevail.

*B. G. Knepper, " 'The Coming Race': Hell? or Paradise*

*Foretasted?"* in No Place Else: Explorations in Utopian and Dystopian Fiction, *Eric S. Rabkin, Martin H. Greenberg, Joseph D. Olander, eds., Southern Illinois University Press, 1983, pp. 11-32.*

## John Coates   (essay date 1984)

[*In the excerpt below, Coates addresses the social and political aspects of* Zanoni.]

*Zanoni* (1842) is a novel generally regarded as an excursion into the occult, an inferior companion of *A Strange Story* by the same author. More interesting than its "late Gothic" quality, however, is the strong political and social bias it shows, a bias which illustrates Bulwer-Lytton's ideological change during the previous ten years of his life. The views and attitudes developed in the novel are all the more interesting when one notes the many significant parallels between this aspect of *Zanoni* and Disraeli's *Coningsby* of two years later. The object of this paper will be to examine Bulwer-Lytton's views and their parallels in Disraeli's novel.

Two words seem to dominate many accounts of Bulwer-Lytton. They are unpopularity and intelligence. Michael Sadleir's authoritative account [in *Bulwer: A Panorama,* 1931] of Bulwer-Lytton's early years emphasises the degree to which it was his very intellectual superiority which drew on him the dislike of fellow writers. His immense reading accompanied a marked intellectual curiosity and a flair for grasping ideas. These qualities

> enabled him to direct his own mental forces to an extraordinary degree.

Walter Allen's comparison of Bulwer-Lytton with Aldous Huxley [in *The English Novel,* 1963] suggests the wide reading and the capacity to become conversant with ideas. It may not, however, altogether to justice to the solid seriousness Bulwer-Lytton frequently showed. He was more than the bright and entertaining purveyor of assorted snippets of reading. Several accounts of him stress the presence beneath a flamboyant or absurd exterior of a sober and scholarly mind. His grandson's biography [*The Life of Edward Bulwer First Lord Lytton,* 1913] remarks on this quality in his occult interests:

> He certainly did not study magic for the sake of writing about it; still less did he write about it without having studied it, merely for the purpose of making his readers' flesh creep.

He was far from credulous and his approach was that of a patient researcher, expecting no speedy or sensational results:

> Spirit-rappings, clairvoyance, astrology etc.
> —he investigated them all and found them all disappointingly unconvincing and unprofitable. His attitude of mind on these matters appears to have been exactly that of the members of the Psychical Research society of the present day— anxious to learn something that would extend the horizon of human knowledge and experience, yet forced to confess that nothing he had

yet witnessed really justified any definite conclusions.

The hard-headed attitude to occult phenomena is confirmed in Bulwer-Lytton's letters to his son on Victorian crazes for table-turning and other "psychic phenomena". It is worth emphasising, however, that he thought the subject well-worth investigating and it is interesting to understand why. In *Zanoni* magic and "Rosicrucianism" though strikingly evoked in themselves, are the vehicles of political and psychological insights. The sensational element in the story is subordinated to Bulwer-Lytton's philosophical intentions. This was clear to such early readers as Thomas Carlyle who wrote on February 23rd 1842 to Bulwer-Lytton:

> This book will be read and scanned far and wide; . . . it will be a liberating voice for much that lay dumb imprisoned in many human souls;. . . . it will shake old deep set errors looser in their rootings and thro' such chinks as are possible let in light on dark places very greatly in need of light.

He was perfectly correct about *Zanoni* being scanned far and wide. Bulwer-Lytton had been an international bestseller for over ten years. H.F. Chorley described him ten years before as a writer of works which are read wherever the English language penetrates, which wall the booksellers' shops in Germany and America.

About the same time George Darley remarked wryly:

> The Germans worship Bulwer—call his productions Shakespearian.

The popularity has not stood the test of time. Nevertheless Bulwer-Lytton is still given attention, rightly, as a writer with much to say about the taste of his period.

I propose to examine him instead as a man who helped to form the ideas of his age. In *Zanoni* he used the possession of his enormous and devoted public to disseminate certain ideas and attitudes, interesting and novel in themselves, and possibly important in later events. The large audience for Bulwer-Lytton's work would alone make his views phenomena of importance. They were, however, in *Zanoni* far from being merely commonplaces. Critics have frequently shown how Bulwer-Lytton continually struck out into new areas, anticipating public taste rather than relying [on] existing fashions and preoccupations to maintain his popularity. The attitude of bold experiment he often showed in the choice of style and subject is equally evident in *Zanoni,* in the area of ideas and attitudes.

Bulwer-Lytton had been immersed in reading occult and mystical literature for about seven years before the publication of *Zanoni.* It has been suggested that the reason for his interest in the uncanny was a strange incident of 1835, the spreading of a rumour of his own death. It seems, however, that the facts will bear other interpretations. The decade which saw the painful collapse of his marriage saw also a considerable shift in Bulwer-Lytton's political and social attitudes. In the early 1830s he had been markedly radical, a strong supporter of Parliamentary Reform. In his editorship of *The New Monthly* he showed an aggressively "forward-looking" attitude. The portion of *England*

*and the English* (1833) entitled "The Intellectual Spirit of the Time" provides an excellent picture of Bulwer-Lytton's own intellectual allegiances at this time. His treatment of Bentham is judicious and offers some thoughtful reservations. Bentham's philosophy is "one of the faces of truth only". Nevertheless Bulwer-Lytton firmly commits himself at this point to the spirit of rationalist criticism, of the destructive intellectual attack on institutions and attitudes of the past. The work of destruction, though drastic, is necessary and healthy, providing that new ideals and institutions can be provided to replace the old. This in fact has been done:

> What has been the influence of Bentham on his age? It has been two-fold—he has helped to destroy and he has helped to rebuild.

Unlike the eighteenth-century French philosophers, Bentham always had something to offer "if he ever annihilated a received opinion." His influence, we are to gather, is, all-in-all, highly beneficial:

> His be the merit, if while the wreck of the old vessel is still navigable, the masts of the new one, which brings relief are dimly showing above the horizon.

However modified, the tone of the essay is certainly that of a radical and legislative activist. There is a real faith in the possibility and worth of sweeping institutional change and of a wide-ranging questioning and subversion of existing values. Bentham is praised because

> he did not declaim about abuses; he went at once to their root: he did not idly penetrate the sophistries of Corruption: he smote Corruption herself. He was the very Theseus of legislative reform, —he not only pierced the labyrinth—he destroyed the monster.

I would suggest that between *England and the English* in 1833 and the publication of *Zanoni* in 1842 Bulwer-Lytton had passed an important ideological dividing line. In modern accounts of his political conversion one cannot help feeling that the man's personal unpopularity and the legend of his appalling manners still colour the picture presented:

> While continuing to write he turned his opportunistic talents to politics. . . . and changing his party became Colonial Secretary.

This account by a standard work of reference [*The Penguin Companion to Literature,* 1971], distorts a complex process. Bulwer-Lytton's motives were sincere and the conversion was very gradual. His last speech as a Liberal was in 1838 and he ceased to be a Liberal M.P. in 1841, emerging as a Tory in 1852. His ideological conversion from Benthamite reform, however, clearly antedates, and is more important than, this mere change of party-labels. It is here, I believe, that *Zanoni* is a crucial document.

There is some evidence that Bulwer-Lytton's bitter separation from his wife Rosina had a political dimension. She appears to have inherited the passionate beliefs of her mother Mrs. Wheeler. Sadleir describes mother and daughter in a somewhat prejudiced fashion but one which nevertheless suggests what Bulwer-Lytton probably felt about them:

> Mrs Wheeler obsessed with her own confused and turgid intellect had indeed set up as a sort of revolutionary sibyl. Atheism, communism of an Owenite—plus—Jacobin kind and most emphatic of all militant feminism, filled her mind with heady abstractions and her mouth with rhetoric. She talked incessantly and was the more quickly convinced of her own inspired rightness because no one interrupted her. . . . Having quarrelled with her husband the daughter hardened into a permanent replica of her mother.

The fact that Bulwer-Lytton began his investigation of occult *philosophy* in 1835, at a point when his marriage was approaching its most embittered and heart-rending point, is highly significant. Although *Zanoni* has its Gothic side, and includes effective descriptions of magical operations, it is its ideas which distinguish it. It marks a definite turning away from the philosophical radicalism Bulwer-Lytton had shared with his wife.

It is true, as Bulwer-Lytton's grandson asserted, that it was disagreement with the Liberals' attitude to the repeal of the Corn Laws in 1846, which provided the immediate reason for his change of parties. It nonetheless seems clear from his refusal of Lord Melbourne's offer of a minor government post in 1836 that he was beginning to be disillusioned with the Liberals. His deep anger over the treatment of his hero Lord Durham by the party between 1836 and 1840 certainly strengthened his disenchantment. However, ideological sympathies and intellectual biases are not completely identifiable with party-labels. This was even more true in the nineteenth century than it is now. Bulwer-Lytton's change in intellectual sympathies predates his change in party-politics.

The setting and period chosen for *Zanoni,* Naples and Paris, between 1788 and 1793, provide a frame of reference for what is partly a political statement, an exploration by Bulwer-Lytton of lines of thought foreign to his previous views. The period is crucial from a cultural point of view, the culmination of the rationalist ideals of the Enlightenment.

> Ah; at the close of the last century, the future seemed a thing tangible—it was woven up in all men's fears and hopes of the present. At the verge of that hundred years, Man, the ripest born of time, stood as at the death-bed of the Old World and beheld the New Orb, blood-red amid cloud and vapour—uncertain if a comet or a sun.

Bulwer-Lytton adopts a tone of sardonic contempt towards the voguish expression of the Enlightenment's ideals in the Paris salons just before the Revolution. In Part I, Chapter VII he presents a group of the philosophes and their admirers regaling themselves with dreams of the future:

> It was one of those petit soupers for which the capital of all the social pleasures was so renowned. . . . Vain labour for me. . . . to do

justice to the sparkling paradoxes that flew from lip to lip. The favourite theme was the superiority of the Moderns to the Ancients.

Their aspirations are shown as the wildest rhodomontade. Condorcet, who was later to kill himself to escape execution, is made to declaim a passage from his own published work:

> "And then commences the Age of Reason! Equality in instruction—equality in institutions—equality in wealth! The great impediments to knowledge are, first, the want of a common language, and next the short duration of human existence. But as to the first, when all men are brothers, why not a universal language? . . . . Life, I grant, cannot be made eternal; but it may be prolonged almost indefinitely."

Another famous historical victim of the Terror, later guillotined,

> the venerable Malesherbes sighed. Perhaps he feared the consummation might not come in time for him.

This somewhat sledge-hammer satire is, however, a minor part of **Zanoni**'s total meaning. The Parisian intellectuals are shown as transparently silly people whose nonsense could only be dangerous in the presence of other combustible matter. It is important that Bulwer-Lytton directs his attention, in this context, not at social grievances, about which comparatively little is said, but at psychological and spiritual states. The poverty of the Neapolitan peasants is graphically described and there is a suggestion of the abuses of decaying Feudalism in the nobleman who attempts to seduce Viola. However Bulwer-Lytton reminds the reader that the Ancien Régime had, in fact, greatly improved in Naples, as a result of Tanucci's reforms. Many historians have accepted that the Ancien Régime in most European states improved towards its end. It is interesting that Bulwer-Lytton should deftly touch on a point made by de Tocqueville in 1856, that revolution is not due to poverty; the paradox that France had never been so prosperous as under Louis XVI, immediately before the Revolution. Bulwer-Lytton makes it clear that the forces welling up are not derived from material conditions.

The opening chapters of **Zanoni** carefully produce indications of the deeper springs of change. It is through art, through music and painting, that part of the novel's diagnosis is made. The two characters, Viola Pisani and the Englishman Glyndon, who are to encounter the chance of spiritual development are both artists. Viola sings in the Naples Opera and Glyndon is a painter. Apart from its significance in Rosicrucian mysticism music provides Bulwer-Lytton with an excellent way of showing the emotional changes sweeping over Europe at this time. Viola's father Gaetano had for several years been writing a new sort of music,

> symphonies that excited a kind of terror in those who listened.

Wild, violent and unconventional they attempt to deal with instinctive human fears and joys through the medium of myth and legend:

> The names of his pieces will probably suggest their nature. . . . "The Feast of the Harpies", "The Witches at Benevento", "The Descent of Orpheus in Hades", "The Evil Eye", "The Eumenides".

This new choice of style and subject meets with a strong initial opposition:

> The style of the Neapolitan musician was not on the whole pleasing to ears grown nice and euphuistic in the more dulcet melodies of the day.

It is the Italy of Goldoni and the Venetian Carnival feeling the impact of the pre-romantic stirrings, common to the whole of Europe. In Viola these tendencies are deepened. She is fed on tales and legends by her peasant nurse, tales,

> perhaps as old as Greek or Etrurian fable—of demon and vampire—of the dances round the great walnut tree at Benevento, and the haunting-spell of the Evil Eye. . . . And all this fitted her to hang with a fearful joy upon her father's music.

The impulses behind the Ossian cult or the Gothic novel, the interest in the primitive or irrational in folklore, is linked in Viola with an understanding of her father's music:

> The legends and tales of Gionetta only served to make the child better understand the signification of those mysterious tones; they furnished her with words to the music.

Bulwer-Lytton is touching lightly and deftly on a European cultural phenomenon. In Glyndon the point is made clearer. He too is the creature of an age of psychological upheaval.

Bulwer-Lytton shows us that we are to see both Glyndon and Viola against the background of the time, by an interesting general reflection on that time:

> Need I remind the reader that while that was the day for polished scepticism and affected wisdom, it was the day for the most egregious credulity and the most mystical superstition—the day in which magnetism and magic found converts among the disciples of Diderot.

Five years before, Carlyle had touched on the strange growth of occultism and superstition during the 1780s in *The French Revolution*. He had used Mesmer, "an antique Egyptian hierophant in this new age" as evidence for his view of the Revolution as a *spiritual* rather than a merely social or political crisis:

> For so, under the strangest vesture, the old great truth (since no vesture can hide it) begins again to be revealed. That man is what we call a miraculous creature, with a miraculous power over men; and on the whole, with such a life in him and such a world round him as victorious Analysis . . . will never completely *name*, to say nothing of explaining.

The passage, I think, explains Carlyle's sympathy with

*Zanoni.* Bulwer-Lytton's starting-point is very similar to Carlyle's, though he is more interested in exploring the spiritual crisis in individual case-histories, and much less convinced that any good came from the Revolution as a whole,

> that hideous mockery of human aspirations.

Glyndon, as a painter, is, like Viola in music, pursuing in a confused and instinctive fashion, some deeper spiritual truth. Both of them have in their background influences which pre-dispose them to such a search. In Viola's case, it is the stories her nurse tells her and her father's music; Glyndon is influenced by

> a remote ancestor on his mother's side . . . a philosopher and alchemist.

This man's books are still extant, though rare, and some of them were in the library of Glyndon's home:

> Their platonic mysticism, their bold assertions, the high promises that might be detected through their figurative and typical phraseology made an impression on the young mind of Clarence Glyndon.

When the novel opens, he is in Naples ostensibly studying the best models of his art. As a painter he is promising, but too easily distracted from the labour involved. His attitude towards the meaning and philosophy of his art, like Viola's towards her singing, is unfocused.

It is through this question of the meaning of art that the meaning of the novel began to unfold. A fellow painter of Glyndon's and one of his acquaintances is the Frenchman Jean Nicot. He is a strong supporter of the Revolution and represents Bulwer-Lytton's attempt to probe its deeper psychological springs, to see what lies below the froth of the philosophes. The truth is an ugly one. Nicot is a highly emotional man and his emotions are disorganised and self-deceiving:

> It was also a notable contradiction in this person, who was addicted to the most extravagant excesses in every passion, whether of hate or love, implacable in revenge and insatiable in debauch, that he was in the habit of uttering the most beautiful sentiments of exalted purity and genial philosophy.

Perhaps, here, Bulwer-Lytton is slightly reminiscent of Wordsworth's view [in *The Prelude,* Book XI] of the revolutionary ethos as a place

> Where passions had the privilege to work
> And never hear the sound of their own names.

The cant of Reason, progress and philanthropy enables Nicot to indulge in all his impulses without referring them to conscience. His wish to change society stems from an unhappy and disturbed personality.

> The world was not good enough for him; he was, to use the expressive German phrase, a *world-betterer.*

As a painter Nicot is competent in execution, but Bulwer-Lytton stresses his lack of a sense of transcendent reality, as fatally limiting his art.

> His delineation of beauty was that which the eye cannot blame and the soul does acknowledge.

In fact Nicot contemptuously rejects the pursuit of the ideal in art, the attempt to render any truth beyond the senses, or above cause and effect. He tells Glyndon,

> The Italian critics and your English Reynolds have turned your head. They are so fond of their "gusto grande" and their "ideal beauty that speaks to the soul!" —soul—is there a soul?

Art, in his view, should be devoted to the state, to civic propaganda, to the presentation of political messages. His pictures sound very like those of his contemporary in reality David, and deal with

> those great Roman actions which inspire men with sentiments of liberty and valour, with the virtues of a republic.

He rejects with irritation Glyndon's suggestion that art ought to explore the sense of mystery or that

> we have a feeling as deep as love for the terrible and dark.

He will have none of this:

> "True", said Nicot, thoughtfully. "And yet that feeling is only a superstition. The nursery, with its tales of ghosts and goblins is the cradle of many of our impressions of the world."

Nicot will not look at his own emotions and his revolutionary rhetoric and Davidesque painting help him to gloss over the conflicts in his own nature and provide a simple and tidy view of the world about him. (It is interesting as a proof of the insight Bulwer-Lytton often shows and the relevance of his thought that the conflicting views of the role of art explored in *Zanoni* are very similar to those suggested in Solzhenitsyn's account in *The First Circle* of the struggles of the painter Kondrashov-Ivanov against official Soviet Art.)

It is from the temptations of Nicot's attitudes that Zanoni tries to rescue Glyndon. The role of the two sages, Zanoni and Mejnour, in the novel is an interesting one. The last survivors of an ancient brotherhood, they wish to make converts but regard this as virtually impossible because of the difficult spiritual test any initiate must pass. Zanoni acts more often as a kind of midwife of the spirit, helping individuals to achieve the best that is in them. Sometimes this is on a relatively humble level, as when he brings the gambler Cetoxa to some degree of moral stability. His real interests, however, are artistic and intellectual. He remarks to Glyndon,

> There are two avenues from the little passions and drear calamities of earth; both lead to heaven and away from hell. . . . —Art and Science.

Hence he grows involved in the lives of both Glyndon and Viola, trying to encourage each of them to discover their true selves as painter and singer, and to produce their best work. The philosophy behind this missionary work is central to Bulwer-Lytton's attitude in *Zanoni.* The real means of human improvement are not political or institutional at all. The bettering of man's condition comes through the actions of the gifted few on the intellects, opinions and morals of the many. Zanoni tells Glyndon,

> The few in every age improve the many; the many may now be as wise as the few were; but improvement is at a standstill, if you tell me the many now are as wise the few are.

The real way to change men's lives is not by changing the mechanism of the state but by acting on their minds. The social consequences of these attitudes are highly conservative ones:

> Level all conditions today, and you only smooth away all obstacles to tyranny tomorrow. The nation that aspires to *equality* is unfit for *freedom.*

Zanoni assures Glyndon that it is certainly desirable and may be possible to bring about material changes which would make men less unequal in wealth but as for removing

> disparities of the intellectual and moral (life) never! Universal equality of intelligence, of mind, of genius, of virtue! No teacher left to the world, no men wiser, better than others—were it not an impossible condition, *what a hopeless prospect for humanity!*

The denial of superior quality in intellect or excellence in life accompanies the denial of God and both are shown as leading tenets of the revolutionary ideology. Furthermore, as the episode of the philosophe who is nearly murdered for his money by his adopted son suggests, a morality based on rational self-interest may easily become the law of the jungle.

*Zanoni*'s emphasis on the importance of intellectual currents, and the growth of new ideas in human life, is accompanied by its stress on the role of the teacher. Zanoni is not a prophet or hero in Carlyle's sense. His work is conducted behind the scenes, rather than in public life; in individual cases, rather than in mass-movements. His statement to Glyndon implies that his activities stem from a conscious and consistent attitude:

> The conduct of the individual can affect but a small circle beyond himself; but the permanent good or evil that he works to others lies rather in the sentiments he can diffuse. His acts are limited and momentary, his sentiments may pervade the universe and inspire generations till the day of doom. All our virtues, all our laws are drawn from books and maxims, which are sentiments and not from deeds.

Although Zanoni is drawn to intellectual quality or artistic talent in men and women, he has not for many years of his mysteriously prolonged life, been drawn to them on an emotional level. He does not seek human involvement and is often disdainful and aloof. His vast experience has made him detached from and disenchanted with the human condition. Despite his benevolence his manners are "cold and repellent."

In his relationship with Viola, however, he cannot maintain a teacher's aloofness. Unlike the wholly intellectual Mejnour his fellow sage, he can feel love. Despite his efforts he falls in love with her. The circumstances of the time, the currents of thought and feeling at the end of the eighteenth century are highly propitious to the ideas Zanoni hopes to spread and the work he hopes to do. Viola and Glyndon, both creatures of this new time, are highly receptive to his doctrines and his personality. The first effect of Zanoni is to stimulate both of them as artists. Glyndon becomes a better painter and gains a hold over the principles of his work. Viola reaches new heights as a musician, and what is more interesting, becomes articulate. Formerly instinctive and unreflecting, she begins to write, defining her ideas and impressions for the first time.

It is at this stage that Zanoni wishes to stop his intervention. He plans that the two should marry and forward each other's work. However, an essential part of the meaning of *Zanoni* is that the spiritual thirst is a more powerful drive than romantic love. Both of his pupils are more drawn to Zanoni's secrets, his power and knowledge, than they are to each other. Zanoni, for his part, comes to love Viola. The tragedy ensues, not so much because of this, but because, for opposite reasons, they are unworthy of the spiritual knowledge they seek. Viola is too fearful and superstitious to claim it. Glyndon lacks humility and purity of heart. He boldly rushes further than his spiritual development will permit.

J.I. Fradin comments [in "The Absorbing Tyranny of Everyday Life: Bulwer-Lytton's *A Strange Story,*" *Nineteenth Century Fiction* 16 (1961-1962)] on both Bulwer-Lytton's occult interests and his aesthetic theory that

> Bulwer . . . was seeking in the deepest levels of consciousness some secret power which might transcend "the absorbing tyranny of everyday life", a power which might make whole again the world disintegrating about him

is perceptive and helpful. However, I feel that his remark on Glyndon's situation in *Zanoni* is possibly a partial misinterpretation. He says that

> we find the aspiring artist who cannot break through to the higher realms of consciousness because he fears the phantoms which . . . represent demonic evil and the unknown depths of the psyche.

Although this has much to recommend it, it does seem that at this point, Glyndon is not so much an artist as a seeker of spiritual wisdom. He has had the offer of artistic success already and refused it. Also we are told that the phantom, "the dweller of the threshold" meets all aspirants, not simply artists.

The real problem seems to be the identity of "the dweller of the threshold", however. It is indeed an obstacle to that knowledge which would "make whole" a disintegrating world. Possibly Fradin's concentration on the aesthetic theory Bulwer-Lytton developed rather later in his career leads to a certain narrowing of the meaning of *Zanoni.* The novel is concerned not so much with an artistic search, but with a spiritual quest, a quest having social and political implications.

It seems that the meaning of the horrifying being Glyndon sees in his trance is best sought in terms of the particular kind of late eighteenth-century Rosicrucianism which the novel uses rather than in parallels with Jung, interesting as these are. In his absorbing study of Bulwer-Lytton's occult fiction R.L. Wolff condemns the view [in *Strange Stories and Other Explorations in Victorian Fiction,* 1971] that *Zanoni* can fairly be called a "Rosicrucian novel". He emphasises the distinction the book draws between the imperfect glimpses of truth seen by the Rosicrucians and the perfect vision seen by Zanoni and Mejnour, survivors of the ancient "Chaldean brotherhood":

> *Zanoni* then is more properly a novel of the wisdom that the Rosicrucians did not have.

However, if we seek to study the novel in terms of the history of ideas, Wolff's distinction between Rosicrucians and "Chaldeans" seems a somewhat artificial one. It is quite true that Zanoni is made to show an attitude of patronising approval to the Rosicrucians. However, as Wolff elsewhere suggests, the reason for this lies simply in Bulwer-Lytton's wish to heighten the mysterious qualities of his novel, rather than in any serious difference between the social, moral, political or philosophical ideas of the Martinist Rosicrucians and the "Chaldeans". Wolff appears to admit the *philosophical* importance of St Martin in *Zanoni:*

> Devotee of Pascal, enemy of Voltaire, much attracted by Rousseau's sentimentalism, he seems still to deserve Bulwer's painter's praise. And what Bulwer's painter put into the footnote in *Zanoni,* we can attribute to Bulwer himself. In these passages he is telling us what kind of occultist he preferred and what kind of occultist he intends us to see in Zanoni—no vain Cabalist, no magician. For purposes of heightened mystery, Zanoni cannot of course belong to anything so recent in historic time as the order that Martines de Pasqually founded or St Martin adorned, any more than he can be a mere Rosicrucian.

Wolff seems here to have undermined his own distinction. Furthermore, the political and moral views of St Martin may be ascertained. (Indeed he has been granted mention as an important late eighteenth-century conservative thinker in a recent textbook). Those of the "Chaldeans", so far as they differ, remain unknown. Bulwer-Lytton's wish to make Zanoni a more portentous figure merely serves the purposes of fiction. Perhaps, too, it is part of the common impulse in those interested in the occult, to suggest that the wisdom they seek is especially esoteric, although those outside the circle have had partial glimpses.

I would differ from Wolff, also, in the importance he attaches to the purely *chemical* aspects of Zanoni's operations. The force which Zanoni and Mejnour control is simply "animal heat", the "Great Principle" sought by the alchemists. However, this appears to ignore the truism that alchemical terms, in their more sophisticated forms, were intended as spiritual allegories; and were extensively used as such by both Boehme and St Martin. What Zanoni offers Glyndon is essentially a mystical vision.

Wolff reads *Zanoni* very much as an occult novel and although he touched on its moral and social attitudes, does not appear to grant them always a sufficient emphasis:

> The insertion of historical scenes with footnote

references into a novel written to be awesome and mysterious damages the illusion for a modern reader, but the reader of the 1840s did not mind.

However, as Wolff again admits elsewhere, the encounter with the French Revolution is crucial to the novel's meaning. In fact, it is its political views and its analysis of the culture of a changing time which gives *Zanoni* its real importance. Essentially, I feel, Wolff's reading underestimates the seriousness and spiritual depth of the novel:

> (Bulwer had some acquaintance with "mind expanding drugs". Certainly Viola has had a convincing "bad trip".)

Bulwer's subsequent defence of the book's political attitudes in controversy with Forster implies, I would suggest, that he felt its political and moral views were more significant than this. (If the hypothesis "St Martin—Bulwer-Lytton—Disraeli" is granted, then they clearly were). Of all subjects, the Martinist Rosicrucians are, perhaps, one on which it is least wise to dogmatize. The abstruse strangeness of many of their teachings makes them difficult for a reader uninstructed in such literature, and I cannot be sure that I have understood them. There are some general points it seems safe to make, however.

Firstly, they were, as far as they were political at all, opposed to the Enlightenment and its dream of rational social progress. Both Saint-Martin and his teacher Martinez de Pasqually (or Pasqualez) are referred to in *Zanoni,* with some respect, along with Cazotte, for this reason. This is the kind of Rosicrucianism which Zanoni and Mejnour are presumably closest to. J.M. Roberts gives a useful summary of the leading doctrines of Martinism [in *The Mythology of Secret Societies,* 1974], doctrines strongly reminiscent of those of Zanoni and Mejnour:

> Their doctrinal position appears to have adopted Swedenborgian views about the relationship between this world and that of spiritual beings . . . The aim of the cult was the advancement of man's spiritual nature by "reintegration" with the world of spirits of which he had once formed part. . . . This secret brotherhood thus inherited from their ancient predecessors Eli, Enoch and Melchizidech, the task of safe-guarding God's plan for man's salvation through reintegration. Saint-Martin later gave prominence to the continued historical existence within the everyday world of persons devoted to the secret transmission of a universal religion.

The similarities between these elements in Martinism and the role of Zanoni in the novel are too obvious for comment. It is worth emphasising that it is a *spiritual* rather than an *artistic* search or initiation which is envisaged; the "reintegration" of man with something outside rather than inside himself.

Frances Yates [in *The Rosicrucian Enlightenment,* 1972] has pointed to the very close connection between the original Rosicrucianism of the early seventeenth century and the teachings of Jacob Boehme. (The point is also made by Evelyn Underhill [in *Mysticism,* 1961].) In Saint-Martin this connection with Boehme re-emerges with redoubled force. We know that he deeply reverenced Boehme, putting him second only to Christ. It is worth remembering this influence in reading *Zanoni.*

Boehme was careful to warn the merely curious [in *Personal Christianity: The Doctrines of Jacob Boehme*] from prying into holy things:

> Above all examine yourself for what purpose you desire to know the mysteries of God and whether you are prepared to employ that which will be received for the glorification of God and to the benefit of your neighbour. . . . He who has no such high purposes but merely seeks for knowledge for the gratification of self, or that he may be looked upon as something great by the world, is not fit to receive such knowledge.

Glyndon's motives, it is made clear, are thoroughly tainted by pride and self-seeking. It is because of this lack of spiritual preparation that his initiation fails and he sees Transcendent Reality in the form that he does.

The point of spiritual illumination Boehme called "the lightning flash." It came after the first three qualities of the Divine, "desire," "motion" and "anguish." The "lightning flash" might be regarded as Divine grace. It appears at the climax of the "anguish."

> But the will or the desire in the darkness cannot reach the light and therein consists the anguish and the craving for light. This anguish and craving continues until the Spirit of God enters like a flash of lightning.

Unless the aspirant is in a state of grace this will not happen and he will remain in great pain:

> Eternal unity or freedom, per se, is of infinite loveliness and mildness, but the three qualities are sharp, painful, even terrible.

It is this condition in which Glyndon, who is in a frivolous and egotistical state of mind before his initiation, finds himself. (It is, I think, no coincidence that the *fourth* part of *Zanoni* is called "the dweller of the threshold.")

The essence of the novel is that man desires spiritual enlightenment above all else, but that his moral condition prevents this. Glyndon's rashness builds for himself "a hell in heaven's despite". It is in this spiritual sphere that the reality of human life is to be found. The dream of political progress merely ends in the living hell of the Reign of Terror in Part VII.

Clearly in writing *Zanoni* Bulwer-Lytton had moved a long way from his Utilitarian position of the early 1830s. In a sense it might be considered a novel very much impregnated with the conservative and mystical tendency which gathered force in the 1840s, finding expression in such diverse phenomena as the Oxford Movement, the increasing interest in Coleridge's philosophy, in the popularity of Thomas Carlyle, and in "Young England". I would like to suggest that the political and social ideals stated and implied in *Zanoni* are more than symptomatic of the period. It is possible they may have been instrumental in the changing cultural atmosphere of the time.

Disraeli's opinion of Bulwer-Lytton had long been high.

> I have not gained much in conversation with men. Bulwer is one of the few with whom my intellect comes into collision with benefit. He is full of thought, with views at once original and just.

He wrote in 1833. He was one of Bulwer-Lytton's few friends; indeed one of the few men who could get on with him at all. *Zanoni,* of course, considerably antedates the period of their political cooperation. Their friendship, at this point, was mainly literary. It is as well to remember however, that Bulwer-Lytton was Disraeli's main contact with the literature of his day. Speaking of the 1840s Robert Blake states [in *Disraeli,* 1969]:

> The dominant figure was Carlyle at the height of his fame. It is not clear whether Disraeli ever read Carlyle. He did not read much contemporary literature apart from the works of friends like Bulwer—and very few of his friends belonged to literary circles, which he tended to despise.

*Zanoni* was published in 1842, *Coningsby* in 1844. It is not difficult to detect a striking similarity in certain leading themes and ideas in the two novels; a similarity which certainly at least suggests a reasonable possibility of some influence by Bulwer-Lytton on Disraeli at this point.

The intellectual framework of the two writers is coloured by a shared belief in the primacy of intellect and ideas over institutions or social and economic factors. Like Zanoni, Sidonia in Disraeli's novel states that intellect and ideas are the real agents of change in human affairs:

> I think that there is no error so vulgar as to believe that revolutions are occasioned by economical causes . . . I know of no period when physical comfort was more diffused in England than in 1640 . . . yet she was on the eve of the greatest and most violent changes she has yet experienced . . . The imagination of England rose against the government.

Sidonia rejects institutions:

> I do not ascribe to political institutions that paramount influence which it is the feeling of this age to attribute to them.

Like Zanoni he rejects rational self-interest as a force in the world:

> There has been an attempt to reconstruct society on the basis of material motives and calculations. It has failed. It must ultimately have failed under any circumstances . . .

The real springs of action are spiritual.

> Man is made to adore and to obey: but if you will not command him; if you give him nothing to worship; he will fashion his own divinities and find a chieftain in his own passions.

Both Zanoni the Chaldean and Sidonia the Jew are bearers of Eastern wisdom. Both deny the idea of social progress on a mass scale. Sidonia exhibits many of Zanoni's traits. He has, in particular, the same combination of interest in intellectual and artistic endeavour, and of lack of emotional involvement; the same wish to act as an impersonal spiritual midwife.

> The only human quality that interested Sidonia was intellect . . . the author, the artist, the man of science never appealed to him in vain. Often he anticipated their wants and wishes . . . but the instant they ceased to be authors, artists and philosophers, . . . the moment they were rash enough to approach intimacy and appealed to the sympathising man instead of the congenial intelligence, he saw them no more.

Both Sidonia and Zanoni possess secret sources of information; are, when they choose, fascinating conversationalists; take wide-ranging philosophical views of life; belong to ancient and mysterious bodies which are supposed to have preserved the wisdom of the past and which interfere almost unnoticed in the workings of the world. Both place the distinguished individual, the former and guider of public opinion, above representative bodies or democratic tendencies.

In both *Zanoni* and *Coningsby* there is the same stress on the value of intellect, of mind acting on mind. Speaking of such meetings when they do occur Disraeli declares:

> The tone that colours our after life is often caught in these chance colloquies, and the bent given that shapes a career.

Zanoni believes that "our sentiments may pervade the universe, and inspire generations till the day of doom." The two novels are based on the same confidence in the intellectual, expressed in the individual, as the true arena of human life. Coningsby's ruminations reflect the attitude of *Zanoni:*

> A word from his lip, a thought from his brain expressed at the right time, at the right place, might turn their hearts, might change their opinions, might influence their destiny. Nothing is great but the personal . . . You must give men new ideas, you must teach them new words, you must modify your passions.

Above all, both Bulwer-Lytton and Disraeli insist on moral goodness as the essential accompaniment of wisdom and achievement.

It would be wrong to suggest that *Zanoni* had much value as literature. A modern critic [H. Lloyd, *Bulwer-Lytton and the Idealist Principle. English Miscellany* 1956] sums up its leading defect and suggests a reason for it:

> The Naples of which he writes in *Zanoni* is supposedly the city of the 1790s; but it is not the city of Sir William Hamilton and his coterie of musicians, swimmers and scholars; still less is it that of Sharp and Dr Moore; for whom the lazzarone existed. This is a contraption more wooden than Pompeii.

The truth is that Bulwer-Lytton is more interested in ideas than in people:

> If on the level of affairs Lytton's portrait of the city is wanting in veracity, it serves its purpose. A more vivacious representation might have im-

peded our knowledge of that other more important city, which lies behind all cities.

It is not just that the novel lacks concrete and specific detail. In many places the writing is heavy and stagey.

Nevertheless, the philosophy of this novel of ideas does shine forth clearly and is of considerable interest. It represents the fruit of several years of Bulwer-Lytton's intellectual development, years when he and Disraeli often talked together. Clearly one cannot be dogmatic about an influence of this kind. Much of Disraeli's thought stems from Bolingbroke, from his own father's historical studies and from other sources. One value might be allowed to the hypothesis that he was influenced by *Zanoni*. It would throw some light on *Tancred*, the climax of the Young England Trilogy, and the weakest of the three novels. Robert Blake sums up a commonly held judgement:

> *Tancred* is the vehicle for Disraeli's own highly idiosyncratic views on race and religion . . . They really have little connection with the ideas in *Coningsby* and *Sybil*.

This verdict might be rather summary. Religion is present as a serious concern in *Coningsby* and *Sybil* and the link between political and spiritual enlightenment in Disraeli might be closer than Blake believes. It would be rash to dismiss the occult or mystical side of the Young England Trilogy as simply

> the rationalisation of his own peculiar psychological dilemma

by Disraeli. It may well have been more closely integrated, and formed more of a totality with the political and social ideas of the other two novels. The "philosophy" of *Zanoni* is such a close blend of the political and spiritual.

*John Coates, " 'Zanoni' by Bulwer-Lytton: A Discussion of Its 'Philosophy' and Its Possible Influences," in* The Durham University Journal, *n. s. Vol. XLV, No. 2, June, 1984, pp. 223-33.*

---

**James L. Campbell, Sr.   (essay date 1986)**

[*An American educator and critic, Campbell has written extensively on Victorian literature. In the following essay, he traces the novelistic development of Bulwer-Lytton's historical theories from* Devereux *to* Pausanias the Spartan.]

During Bulwer's lifetime the historical novel achieved immense prestige. Its success was due to Sir Walter Scott's Waverley novels, which determined both the historical novel's essential design and its standard performance. Scott's Victorian successors saw historical fiction as the equivalent of the epic in prose fiction, the most sublime achievement attainable in the novel. To Archibald Allison writing in *Blackwood's Magazine* in 1845, the historical novel was "a delightful and instructive species of composition" because it united "the learning of the historian with the fancy of the poet"; it taught "morality by example" and conveyed "information by giving pleasure." He went on to praise the genre for combining the charms of imagination with the treasures of research. Yet few Victorian historical novels attained many of these lofty attributes;

most were merely sensational potboilers and fussy anti-quarian costume romances.

In 1846 critic G. H. Lewes complained in the *Westminster Review* about the artistic mediocrity of historical fiction written after Scott's death. Many of these novels published in the 1840s were composed to fit a commercial formula. Lewes explained how to mix the necessary ingredients: "Sprinkle largely with love and heroism, keep up the mystery overhanging the hero's birth till the last chapter; and have a good stage villain, scheming and scowling through two volumes and a half, to be utterly exposed and defeated at last—and the historical novel is complete." This satirical recipe documents something more than a disparity between the artistic ideal and the commercial reality in historical fiction. It provides evidence of the existence of two major divisions in nineteenth-century historical fiction: the historical novel and the historical romance.

The two genres share similar outward characteristics. Each typically features actions set at least forty to sixty years in the past, real historical persons in the plot, and fairly realistic backgrounds. But the historical romance is determined by sensational and romantic plot requirements (as Lewes described) in which the action turns solely on made-up incidents. History serves only as a painted backdrop, enabling the historical romancer to justify the use of period manners, speech, and colorful costumes—hence the name costume romance. In contrast, the serious historical novel is shaped by a historical thesis, dramatizing how the forces at work in a particular period act to change public and private life. Like an academic historian, the historical novelist is concerned with historical causation, effect, and significance. He can account for social change and explain to his readers even comparatively recent changes. Andrew Sanders argues [in *The Victorian Historical Novel, 1840-1880,* 1978] that through the historical novel "the past could be seen to reflect the present, and . . . modern problems could be judged more detachedly for being considered within a historical perspective."

Bulwer had fairly well defined notions about historical fiction. While he acknowledged Scott's genius and his many contributions to the genre, Bulwer criticized him for treating his historical sources cavalierly, dwelling too much on mere picturesque effects, and having no real grandeur of artistic conception. His execution, Bulwer claimed, was superior to his conception, and Scott never seemed willing "to render palpable and immortal some definite and abstract truth." Writing in the *Monthly Chronicle* in 1838, Bulwer declared that the historical novelist must have "a perfect acquaintance" with the characteristics and spirit of the past. He should "avoid all antiquarian dissertations not essentially necessary to the conduct of his tale" as "minuteness is not accuracy." The novelist's true art, Bulwer continued, "will be evinced in the illustrations he selects, and the skill with which they are managed." Historical novelists, Bulwer advised, who follow Scott must "deeply consider all the features of the time, and select those neglected by his predecessor; —[one] would carefully note all the deficiencies of the author of *Kenilworth* [Scott], and seize at once upon the ground which [Scott] . . . omitted

to consecrate to himself." Bulwer's first attempt at historical fiction was his 1829 novel *Devereux,* which, the product of a young writer still struggling through his literary apprenticeship, proved only partially successful. Bulwer did not return again to historical fiction until 1834, when he produced his best known novel, *The Last Days of Pompeii.*

. . . . .

Both *The Last Days of Pompeii* and *Rienzi* (1835)—Bulwer's costume romance and his historical novel set respectively in ancient and medieval Italy—date in conception to the period 1832-33 and were inspired by his visit that winter to Rome and Milan. The idea for *Pompeii* originated in a painting he saw on exhibition at the Brera Gallery in Milan titled "The Last Days of Pompeii," which depicted the destruction of ancient Pompeii in 79 A.D. by the eruptions from Vesuvius. The image of Pompeii's destruction led Bulwer to Naples, where he met Sir William Gell, the respected antiquarian, who guided him in his research of Pompeii. Visiting the site of Pompeii—rediscovered in 1750 and only partially excavated in 1832-33—Bulwer witnessed the recovery of Sallust's mansion, buried for centuries beneath volcanic ash and lava. The bodies exhumed that day Bulwer brought back to life in his imagination, introducing them in his novel as Burbo, Calenus, Diomed, Julia, and Arbaces. Laying aside his incomplete manuscript of *Rienzi,* begun in Rome, Bulwer wrote nearly the whole of *Pompeii* in Naples during the winter of 1832-33.

Bentley published the completed novel in three volumes in July 1834, bringing out several additional impressions that year. Later it was reprinted in a one-volume edition in *Bentley's Standard Novels* in December 1839, as number seventy-two in the first series. Bulwer dedicated the first edition to Sir William Gell in appreciation of his assistance with the book's background sources and as a tribute to Gell's popular books on Roman antiquities. *The Last Days of Pompeii* became an immediate commercial success, creating a greater sensation with the reading public than any other novel since the publication of Sir Walter Scott's *Waverley* in 1814. James C. Simmons is probably right in his claim [in "Bulwer and Vesuvius: The Topicality of *The Last Days of Pompeii,*" *Nineteenth-Century Fiction* 24 (June 1969)] that the great popularity of Bulwer's novel was due in part to its appearance the same year as the most destructive eruption of Vesuvius in centuries. *Pompeii* has remained in print since its first appearance, becoming Bulwer's best-loved novel. It provided the subject for an opera (*Ione*), numerous stage productions, and eight film versions from as early as 1898 to as recent as 1983.

In the preface to the first edition of *Pompeii,* Bulwer set forth the book's artistic aims. Aside from his interest in the catastrophe that destroyed Pompeii, he was fascinated by the time period—"the first century of our religion and the most civilized period of Rome." From such ample materials he selected "those most attractive to the modern reader, —the customs and superstitions least unfamiliar" to the public. He preserved the symmetry of the novel by resisting the temptation to depict "the hollow but majestic civilization of Rome." Instead Bulwer confined his story to the destruction of Pompeii, focusing on the "ordinary incidents of life"—the passions, crimes, misfortunes, and reverses of its inhabitants. He gave a clue to his artistic intentions, arguing that "we understand any epoch of the world but ill if we do not examine its romance," for "there is as much truth in the poetry of life as in its prose."

Ancient Pompeii, Bulwer claimed, supplied him with the characters best suited to his subject and scene. From Pompeii's connection with the half-Grecian colony of Hercules came the idea for the characters of Glaucus and Ione, the novel's hero and heroine. The Egyptian wizard Arbaces, his base agent Calenus, and the fervent Apaecides arose from Pompeii's commercial trade with Alexandria. Olinthus, the fanatical Christian, was inspired by the early struggles of Christianity at Pompeii. And the blind slave girl Nydia was suggested to Bulwer by a friend, who speculated on the advantages a blind person might have in escaping Pompeii in the utter darkness caused by Vesuvius's eruptions. From his studies of ancient Pompeii, Bulwer strove to recreate an accurate portrait of its manners and customs set in the era of the emperor Titus. But more importantly, he sought a universal theme based on a "just representation of the human passions and the human heart" whose "elements in all ages are the same."

*The Last Days of Pompeii* is a historical costume romance; it is not shaped by a historical thesis or by any serious attempt to identify the historical forces changing public life in the Roman Empire. Romance and sensationalism, rather than historical analysis, give the book its shape and power. Its component parts—catastrophic disaster story, love and murder stories, occult thriller, revenge and fatal prophecy stories, and apology for the sectarian sternness of early Christianity—document Bulwer's artistic aims for the novel. The central action in *Pompeii* focuses on Arbaces' plots to forcibly secure Ione's love and to destroy both Glaucus and Apaecides. Arbaces frames Glaucus for Apaecides's murder, abducts Ione, and hands Glaucus over to the senate for trial. The novel reaches its dramatic climax in the famous arena scene in which Arbaces is exposed as Apaecides' murderer. At that point Vesuvius erupts, spewing forth a gigantic cloud shaped like a pine tree. Blue volcanic lightning illuminates the darkened sky, the earth trembles, and the spectators at the arena are seized with panic. All forget about Glaucus and Arbaces in their frantic efforts to escape to safety. Sallust and Glaucus go to Arbaces' villa and free Ione. En route they meet Arbaces, who demands that Ione be surrendered to him. As Glaucus resists, lightning brightens the sky, showing a large bronze statue of Augustus directly behind Arbaces. Suddenly the earth quakes and shifts, causing the statue to topple forward onto Arbaces, who is crushed beneath it. Eventually, Glaucus and Ione reach the port and safety.

Bulwer's novel closes in 89 A.D. Glaucus is married to Ione and living happily in Athens. He writes to his friend Sallust, telling him that both he and Ione have embraced Christianity, which gives a new dimension to their love for each other. Glaucus's conversion to Christianity is important because it reflects Bulwer's attitudes about both the early Christian church and the evangelical movement in nineteenth-century England. Bulwer depicts the early Christians as stern, doctrinaire, dogmatic, narrow-minded, bigoted, and joyless. They are called atheists by the Romans, who believe that the Nazarenes have rejected all deities. The Christians seem a dread sect; it is believed they always commence their religious rites by murdering a newborn child. Bulwer's narrator notes that the early Christians isolate themselves from others on religious principle, believing that non-Christians are servants of evil, false gods. Such notions lead to the separation of fathers from sons and brothers from sisters, as Christians reject their relatives who retain belief in the traditional deities.

Bulwer claims this fervor was necessary to the triumph of the early church. Its fierce zeal, fearing no danger and accepting no compromise, "inspirited its champions and sustained its martyrs." Bulwer notes that "in a dominant church the genius of the intolerance betrays its cause; in a weak and a persecuted church, the same genius mainly supports [it]. It was necessary to scorn, to loath, to abhor the creeds of other men, in order to conquer the temptations which they presented; it was necessary rigidly to believe not only the Gospel was the true faith, but the sole true faith that saved, in order to nerve the disciple to the austerity of its doctrine, and to encourage him . . . [to convert] the polytheist and the Heathen." The sectarian sternness that confines virtue and heaven to a chosen few supplies the early Christian by its very intolerance with his best instruments of success. It leads the non-Christian, Bulwer argues, to imagine that "there must be something holy in a zeal wholly foreign to his experience." But the same fervor that made "the churchman of the middle age a bigot without mercy, made the Christian of the early days a hero without fear." Bulwer's historical qualification about zeal is important. What is proper to Christian survival at Pompeii in 79 A.D. may not be laudable in England in 1834. Because of the new sectarian zeal of the Low Church faction, the strictness of the growing Sabbatarian movement, and the smugness of the new morality of the 1830s, Bulwer felt compelled to speak out against the increase of religious sectarianism and doctrinal intolerance. Like Dickens and Wilkie Collins, he opposed the more extreme manifestations of the evangelical revival that prized zeal over kindness and correct doctrine over Christian charity. To Bulwer, moderation offered the best protection against the perils of sectarian divisiveness and evangelical enthusiasm.

*Pompeii* was written expressly to please the public, though Bulwer feared its "elaborate plots and artful management" might not appeal to his female readers. The book's commercial virtues stemmed from its sensational subject, its traditional romance formulas, and its exciting narrative pace. Bulwer showed restraint in his treatment of Pompeii's destruction, effectively placing it at the novel's finale—chapters 4 through 10 in book 5, featuring nearly twenty-five pages of sustained narrative description. He wisely chose not to overemphasize the book's dramatic irony—from the start the reader knows Pompeii will be destroyed—and employed only a few hints of foreshadowing in the book. The artistic effectiveness of these descriptive scenes may have prompted Dickens to incorporate similar ones in *Barnaby Rudge* (1841), in which he vividly described the destruction of Newgate Prison during the Gordon riots. Response to *Pompeii* proved quite favorable. Isaac Disraeli wrote Bulwer that *Pompeii* was the most interesting book published in years. The poet Felicia Hemans thought the novel revealed a higher art in its conception than anything Bulwer had given the public before. It reminded her of the spirit of Goethe and of the great English dramatists of the past. And Lady Blessington believed *Pompeii* contained more true poetry than fifty epics, stamping its author as a genius par excellence. The book, she wrote Bulwer, was read and universally praised by all.

. . . . .

The resounding success of *Pompeii* encouraged Bulwer to finish the manuscript of *Rienzi,* which had been set aside in favor of other literary projects since his return from Italy. Despite a busy session in Parliament and growing discord with his wife, Bulwer completed *Rienzi; or, The Last of the Roman Tribunes* in November, enabling Saunders and Otley to publish it on 1 December 1835 in three volumes. He dedicated the novel to Alessandro Manzoni. Originally Bulwer had planned to write a nonfiction biography of Nicola di Rienzi, the remarkable fourteenth-century Italian political reformer, because he felt modern historians had judged Rienzi and his era only superficially. But he abandoned this idea, and turned the biography into a work of fiction. In his novel Bulwer took a radically different view of Rienzi's career than was found in Gibbon and Sismondi's standard histories. This was warranted, Bulwer claimed, "not less by the facts of History than [by] the laws of Fiction." In the preface to the first edition of *Rienzi,* he asserted that his biographical novel "adhered, with a greater fidelity than is customary in Romance, to all the leading events of the public life of the Roman Tribune." Alluding to Mary Russell Mitford's popular play, *Rienzi; A Tragedy* (1828), Bulwer contended that his novel presented a more comprehensive account of Rienzi's life than did any other book in English. As his novel treated the whole of Rienzi's career, he thought it belonged rather to the epic than to the dramatic school of fiction.

Bulwer described his approach to historical fiction in the preface to the 1848 edition of *Rienzi.* His novel's popular success, Bulwer said, came from his reliance on historical facts rather than fancy. Both his plot and characters closely followed historical accounts of the age. He sought to reinterpret these sources and to trace "the causes of the facts in the characters and emotions of the personages of the time." Bulwer reconstructed the inner psychological lives of actual historical characters, making *Rienzi* a "chronicle of the human heart." By such invention, Bulwer believed, he created a new harmony between character and event. He found a "completer solution of what is actual and true" by speculating on "what is natural and probable." These speculations, Bulwer argued, were not "the province of history" but belonged instead "to the philosophy of romance." In depicting the inner being, Bulwer allied himself with Thomas Carlyle's view of history. Carlyle saw history primarily as biography—as the study of the private and public worlds of the hero, who shaped great

events through the force of his personality. With respect to the protagonist, Bulwer's method departed from Scott's formula when he used an actual historical figure as the hero of his novel. Scott, in contrast, had employed fictional heroes, who, representing society and the spirit of moderation, acted as neutral observers of the contending forces of historical change. Bulwer went beyond Scott in another respect when he insisted that historical sources should play the central role in determining the historical novel's content.

*Rienzi,* unlike *Pompeii,* is a serious historical novel shaped by Bulwer's analysis of the historical forces convulsing fourteenth-century feudal Italy. The novel's controlling thesis is that Nicola di Rienzi, the book's hero, is a political genius hopelessly in advance of his time. The son of an innkeeper and washerwoman, Rienzi rises to supreme political power in Rome in 1347. He quells the violence of the feudal barons, suppresses the foreign freebooters ravaging the roads to Rome, establishes wise and just laws for the Roman people, arbitrates between princes and kings, becomes the idol of the Roman masses, acts as a special envoy of popes, and seeks to unite all Italy as a nation-state independent of the German Empire. His defeat—papal excommunication, loss of office, imprisonment, and assassination—does not stem from his character flaws (pride, insolence, and love of ostentation), but from the spirit of the age. Rienzi's brilliant political skills, powerful intellect, penetrating vision of the future, and inherent love of political moderation are out of character in an age too eager to practice guile, deception, treachery, revenge, and violence—the common political vocabulary of feudal Italy.

Rienzi fails also because he tries to raise the common people of Rome to political supremacy in order to check and moderate the rival powers of the church, the feudal barons, and the German Emperor at Prague. But lacking Rienzi's vision, the Roman people prove fickle, ignorant, and greedy because they are incapable of self-sacrifice, unable to judge events except by outward show and spectacle, and unwilling to support their own newly won political freedoms. Too long oppressed by feudal institutions, the people betray Rienzi at the moment he most needs their continued support to retain power. Rienzi, Bulwer concludes, is too much in advance of his age and too good for the base Italian people. Had he succeeded in all his plans, feudalism might have been replaced by a new era of democratic self-rule and national independence, enabling Italy to avoid nearly five hundred years of disunity and foreign domination.

In appraising Rienzi at the close of his career, Bulwer argues that he exhibits no unnecessary ostentation, indulges in no bouts of intoxicated pride, and commits no single error in policy. He is frugal, provident, watchful, and self-collected. Concentrating every thought on Rome's needs, he "indefatigably . . . inspected, ordained, and regulated all things, in the city, in the army, for peace or for war. But he was feebly supported, and those he employed were lukewarm and lethargic." Yet with all his faults, real and imputed, no single act of dark Machiavellian policy ever advances his ambition or promotes his security. Whatever

Rienzi's mistakes, Bulwer argues, "he lived and died as becomes a man who dreamed the vain but glorious dream that in a corrupt and dastardly populace he could revive the genius of the old Republic."

Bulwer also attacks modern historians—especially Gibbon and Sismondi—for their biased interpretations of Rienzi. These men, Bulwer complains, regard human beings as if they are machines. They "gauged the great, not by their merit, but [by] their success; and . . . censured or sneered at [Rienzi] . . . where they should have condemned the people." Had but half the spirit that motivated Rienzi been found in Rome, the "august republic, if not the majestic empire, of Rome, might be existing now."

Many years after the appearance of *Rienzi,* Richard Wagner told Bulwer's son, then an attaché at Vienna, that his first opera, *Rienzi* (1842), "was the direct outcome of Bulwer's romance of the same name." Of the many letters of praise Bulwer received about *Rienzi,* the most satisfying one came from Albany Fonblanque, editor of the *Examiner,* who thought Bulwer in *Rienzi* equalled Scott in his management of incident and dramatic situation.

Such praise compensated for several unfavorable reviews and charges that *Rienzi* was thinly disguised radical propaganda. These charges arose from Bulwer's expression of sympathy for Italian self-determination in the preface to the 1848 edition of *Rienzi.* He had predicted that either Naples or Sardinia might take the lead in uniting Italy. Yet he cautioned his Italian readers that in shaking off Austrian control they might find a worse prospect for freedom in the violence and bloodshed needed to separate Italy from the sway of her German Caesar. The *Conservative Magazine,* with little justice, suggested in its review that in *Rienzi* Bulwer forecast the coming role he meant to play in English politics.

. . . . .

***Leila; or, The Siege of Granada*** and ***Calderon the Courtier*** came out together in one volume under Longman's imprint in 1838. *Calderon* also appeared by itself the same year in an American edition published by Carey, Lea, and Blanchard of Philadelphia, an American publisher that specialized in reprinting English fiction. Both titles were popular with the public; each was reprinted later in Routledge's Yellowback Railway series (1855) and in Newnes's Penny Library of Famous Books (1899). Neither *Leila,* a novella, nor *Calderon,* a long short story, represents Bulwer's historical fiction at its best. Bulwer intended them as loose thematic complements to each other. Both employ Spanish settings, treat real historical events, describe the Inquisition, and feature protagonists driven by revenge and lust for power—Almamen the Enchanter and King Ferdinand in *Leila* and Roderigo Calderon and King Philip IV in *Calderon.* While each story employs one element from Sir Walter Scott's historical novel formula—a society poised on the brink of great change—neither is an example of serious historical fiction. Both are shaped by traditional romance formulas—stories about fatal destiny, changelings, forbidden love, persecuted lovers, and Byronic heroes with unsavory pasts. At the secondary level

both stories use elements taken from the eastern tale, the occult story, and the gothic romance.

In dedicating these companion tales to his old friend Marguerite, Countess Blessington, Bulwer lamented that he had not found a "More Durable Monument" on which "to Engrave A Memorial Of [their] Real Friendship." Set in 1491-92, *Leila* describes the fall of the last Moorish kingdom (at Granada) in Spain, destroyed by the machinations of Ferdinand of Aragon and his éminence grise, Tomas Torquemada. Bulwer shows little sympathy for either Spaniard and is less than enthusiastic about Ferdinand's restoration of Spanish political hegemony in old Moorish Spain. Ferdinand is drawn as the very soul of deep craft and unrelenting will, a man ruthless, cold-blooded, imperious, and haughty. Bulwer treats Queen Isabel more kindly. She is gifted and high-minded; her virtues are her own and her faults reflect the age in which she lives.

Bulwer based *Calderon the Courtier* on two literary sources: Teleforo de Trueba's *The Romance of Spain* and the elements found in Spanish comic drama. The latter, according to Bulwer, achieved its artistic power by "the prodigality of intrigue and counterintrigue upon which its interest is made to depend." Furthermore, Spanish comedy faithfully mirrored Spanish life, especially in the circle of the royal court. Here, Bulwer claimed, men "lived in a perfect labyrinth of plot and counterplot, [for] the spirit of finesse, manoeuver, subtlety, and double-dealing pervaded every family." No house remained free from internal division.

Bulwer's tale is set in the Spain of Philip III, who is a weak, indolent, and superstitious monarch. His kingdom is managed by the Duke of Lerma's political administration. But Lerma—a man mild, ostentatious, and shamefully corrupt—is easily controlled by an upstart courtier named Roderigo Calderon. Calderon's office as Philip III's secretary rests on his willingness to pursue a policy of religious persecution. The plot revolves around Calderon's rivalry with the Duke of Uzeda (Lerma's son), who schemes to supplant both his father and Calderon through his manipulation of Philip III's son, Prince Philip. But Calderon suffers defeat at the hands of his rivals. Imprisoned and tried by the Inquisition, he is found guilty, condemned to death, and publicly hanged.

A hastily written story, *Calderon* is a costume romance and romantic potboiler built only on stirring incidents and melodramatic plot fillers. Bulwer does not analyze the historical forces at work in Spain under Philip III, but focuses instead on romance. In construction *Calderon* is both superficially conceived and shoddily executed. Aside from Calderon, the protagonist, the other characters are drawn with little care or complexity. Most are pasteboard figures common to melodrama. The tale is uncharacteristic of Bulwer's writings as it does not treat his usual theme of the ideal and the real.

. . . . .

In the eight years between *Rienzi* and *The Last of the Barons,* critics attacked Bulwer for making crime appear attractive and showing undue sympathy for criminals in his

Newgate novels. He had already published three of his four Newgate romances when *The Last of the Barons* came out in February 1843, printed by Saunders and Otley in three volumes. Eight years of abuse from the critics made Bulwer sensitive about his literary reputation. While he took great pains in composing *Barons,* he was not overly sanguine that it would be judged objectively by the critics. Ill health, domestic problems, and overwork also colored his attitude, causing him to consider abandoning authorship. This mood proved but a passing one of artistic self-doubt, yet he felt so strongly that he ended the dedicatory epistle to *Barons* by observing that while the novel was his best, it would probably be the last with which he would trespass upon the public. Yet the epistle also provided ample evidence of Bulwer's continuing enthusiasm for the novel form: it contained a spirited defense of his theories about fiction. Such a commitment to the aesthetics of the novel belied any serious intention on Bulwer's part to retire from authorship.

The 1843 epistle represented Bulwer's most thoughtful views on the historical novel, a field in which he was increasingly recognized as Walter Scott's most serious and talented successor. Bulwer addressed the epistle to an unidentified critic and friend—perhaps the novelist-critic Harriet Martineau—who had long urged him to write a historical novel with an English subject. The epistle afforded Bulwer the occasion both to describe how he composed historical fiction and to take his critics to task for their cavalier approach to criticism. Historical novelists, he argued, can illustrate certain truths denied the historian and aspire "to something higher than mere romance." They can "increase the reader's practical and familiar acquaintance with the habits, the motives, and the modes of thought which constitute the true idiosyncrasy of an age."

Bulwer discovered these motives and modes of thought through a process he called "analogical hypothesis"—speculation about the psychology of actual historical personages. This speculation, if "sobered by research, and enlightened by knowledge of mankind, could clear up much that were otherwise obscure, and . . . solve the disputes and difficulties of contradictory evidence by the philosophy of the human heart."

Bulwer's use of analogical hypothesis in *Barons* gives the novel its bold controlling thesis. By reading David Hume; John Lingard; Edward Hall; Sharon Turner, the Croyland historian; Thomas Carté; Paul Rapin; Thomas Habington; and Majerus, Bulwer sought to pinpoint the exact time and specific reason Richard Nevile, the earl of Warwick, turned against Edward IV. The historical records of this era were few and badly fragmented. Hall and several other historians suggested that Warwick's sudden rebellion against Edward IV arose from private rather than public policy grievances. The king, they speculated, may have attempted to seduce Warwick's youngest daughter, Anne Nevile. Such a personal insult could explain Warwick's change of policy toward Edward IV. This motive, however, could not be proven. It was when the historical record remained unclear, Bulwer argued, that "fiction [found] its lawful province," helping by "conjecture to [connect] and clear the most broken . . . fragments of our annals."

Where the historian only hinted, Bulwer as novelist boldly used his poetic insight to interpret events. Analogical hypothesis enabled him to connect the fragments and reconstruct Warwick's motivations for his subsequent actions.

In the epistle Bulwer also expressed the view that composition was as important as method in shaping historical fiction. He took care, he affirmed, to create novels that were artistic wholes, harmonious in their parts and unified in their actions. Like paintings, literature divided its subjects into those that were familiar, picturesque, or intellectual. Bulwer believed *Barons* belonged to the last category, a class he felt would never be as popular as the other two because its merits were less obvious to the average reader. Bulwer argued that a novel should not be judged on "some prominent character" or "some striking passage," but rather on its "harmony of construction, on its fulness of design, on its ideal character, —on its essentials, in short, as a work of art." Contemporary critics, Bulwer complained, failed to use even the most elementary principles of literary art to determine the degree of failure or success in the works they undertook to judge. To Bulwer, such ignorance of the rules of art accounted for the violent fluctuations in criticism, leading "critics to condemn today and idolize tomorrow." The real distinction between low and high art, Bulwer argued, is found in the presence or absence of the ideal. He "who resigns the Dutch art [realism] for the Italian [idealism]" must remain faithful to the theory that finds "in action the movement of the grander passions or the subtler springs of conduct, seeking in repose the colouring of intellectual beauty." From such literary principles, Bulwer conceived and composed *Barons.*

Bulwer selected the reign of Edward IV (1461-70; 1471-85) for the subject of *The Last of the Barons* in order to examine a crucial era in English history, one undergoing great political and social transformation. During that period, Bulwer believed, began the policy consummated by Henry VII (1485-1509) in which the old feudal order was broken up and replaced by a new nobility allied with the growing commercial middle classes. In the fate of the hero of the age—Richard Nevile, earl of Warwick, popularly called the king-maker and the last and greatest of the feudal barons—"was involved the very principle of our existing civilization."

Bulwer envisioned two artistic aims for *Barons.* First, he wanted to describe fifteenth-century England and the passing of the age of feudalism into the age of commercialism. In particular he sought to bring into full view the characters of the principal personages of the time, their motives for public action, the state of the political factions, the condition of the people, and the great issues of the day. To this end, Bulwer made Warwick the symbol of the feudal state in conflict with Edward IV, the opposing symbol of the new commercialism. He wanted to show how a clash between Warwick, representing the past—the age of individual warlords with their personal armies and powerful family alliances—and Edward IV, exemplifying the future—the coming age of printing and steam power—ended in the defeat of the king-maker by the king. Bulwer's second aim was to reveal the character of Warwick and explain why Edward IV's staunchest supporter suddenly took up arms against him in 1470, espousing the cause of the House of Lancaster (Henry VI and Margaret of Anjou), Warwick's lifelong political enemies.

*The Last of the Barons* is a serious historical novel shaped by Bulwer's thesis that Richard Nevile turns against Edward IV because of a personal affront. Edward's assault on the virtue of Warwick's youngest daughter drives Warwick to depose Edward, force him into exile, and restore Henry VI to the English throne. But Edward IV's return to England and his sudden defeat of Warwick's armies at Barnet end in Warwick's death and Edward's restoration as king. With Warwick's demise comes the downfall of the old feudal order with its powerful baronial warlords. Bulwer argues that Edward's speedy return to the throne is fostered by the new spirit of the age. Warwick and the barons prove to be men out of step with the times. The new era favors commercialism over feudalism, middle-class traders over chivalrous knights, centralized political authority over weak monarchs controlled by baronial kingmakers, and peace at home over incessant feudal warfare. In their desire for economic prosperity, increased middle-class social mobility, and domestic tranquility, the English people restore Edward IV to power. By so doing, they ultimately endorse the subsequent Tudor despotism, which, supported by bourgeois traders, acts at the expense of the interests of the aristocracy and the peasantry. Bulwer believes that such a historical decision decreased England's chances for greater freedom of the individual. In exchanging freedom for the law and order imposed by the Tudor monarchy, England embarked upon an era of rule by regulated deceit, cold calculation, rank opportunism, lust for power, and murder honed to a political fine art—what Bulwer calls the new Italian policy.

Near the end of *Barons* Bulwer speculates on what might have occurred in England had the Lancastrian line continued and its political and social policies endured. England, Bulwer argues, might have seen the power of the monarchy limited by the strength of an aristocracy supported by the agricultural population. The great barons "would have secured and promoted liberty according to the notions of a seigneur and a Norman, by making the king but the first nobleman of the realm." Had such a policy lasted long enough to succeed, the "subsequent despotism, which changed a limited into an absolute monarchy under the Tudors, would have been prevented." Religious persecution of the Lollards (early Protestants) might have been avoided, and with it, the delayed historical revenge of the Puritans. Gradually, the political system might have changed monarchy into an aristocratic government, resting upon broad and popular political institutions. As a consequence, the commercial middle classes might have risen more slowly. And they would not have been made "the instrument for destroying [the] feudal aristocracy, and thereby establishing for a long and fearful interval the arbitrary rule of the single tyrant."

Bulwer's vision of a politically concerned aristocracy allied to a loyal and grateful peasantry—an aristocracy familiar "with the wants and grievances of that population . . . willing to satisfy the one [and] redress the

other"—speaks especially to the turbulent 1840s. In this period of economic distress and laissez-faire indifference to human suffering, many of Bulwer's contemporaries dreamt of an alliance between aristocrat and laborer, aimed in part at mitigating the horros of bourgeois industrialization. Such an alliance lay at the heart of Benjamin Disraeli's pragmatic Tory democracy and fed the idealism of Lord John Manners's Young England movement, which hoped for a revived feudal alignment of crown, church, aristocracy, town artisan, and agricultural laborer.

. . . . .

Bulwer completed his next historical novel, *Harold, the Last of the Saxon Kings,* in April 1848, composing it in less than a month. He wrote much of the novel at the home of his old parliamentary friend, Charles Tennyson D'Eyencourt, the poet's uncle, whose library at Bayon's Manor in Lincolnshire contained one of the finest private collections of early English chronicles in Britain. But the book's publication was delayed because of the tragic death of Bulwer's twenty-year-old daughter, Emily, in London on 29 April 1848, from typhus fever. Richard Bentley printed *Harold* in June 1848 in three volumes. Along with Thackeray's *Vanity Fair,* W. H. Ainsworth's *Lancashire Witches,* Anne Brontë's *Tenant of Wildfell Hall,* and Elizabeth Gaskell's *Mary Barton, Harold* became one of the most successful novels of the publishing season. Bulwer dedicated *Harold* to D'Eyencourt in appreciation of his hospitality and enthusiastic encouragement. In the dedicatory epistle to the first edition of *Harold,* Bulwer claimed he had long entertained writing a novel "on an event so important and so national [in subject] as the Norman Invasion," but he had put aside the project because he feared the ordinary reader was not familiar with the characters or events of the era.

In venturing on such new ground, Bulwer sought the proper fictional mode for his national epic, one that would "produce the greatest amount of dramatic effect at the least expense of historical truth." He wanted not to turn history into flagrant romance, but rather to extract "the natural romance of the actual history." The mode he selected—by discovery and experimentation—arose from employing romance to aid history. Bulwer based his narrative solely on authentic chronicles, constructed his plot from actual events, and described both the personalities and struggles of those who were once the living actors in the real drama. The fictitious part of the novel he confined to the inner life of his characters, which was the legitimate province of the novelist. Here he used "the agency of the passions" only so far as "they served to illustrate . . . the genuine natures of beings who had actually lived." He strove less to portray manners than to draw the great men of the age, showing their motives and policies in an event he thought the most memorable in Europe. In the preface to the third edition of *Harold,* Bulwer set forth the novel's artistic aims. He wished to acquaint readers with the imperfect fusion of the races in Saxon England, familiarize them with the contests of the parties and ambitions of the chiefs, show the strength and weakness of a kindly but ignorant church, depict a brave but turbulent aristocracy, illustrate how an energetic but disunited people lost their national liberty, and contrast these pictures with the vigorous attributes of the Norman conquerors—their energy, guile, higher knowledge, and rising spirit of chivalry. In a word, Bulwer desired his readers to understand the political and moral features of the age in order to comprehend why England was conquered and how it survived the conquest.

*Harold,* Bulwer's best historical novel, treats the closing years (1052-66) of Edward the Confessor's reign, from the return of the banished earl of Godwin and his sons to the establishment of the Norman dynasty under William I following the battle of Hastings. As a composite novel—historical novel, panoramic epic of eleventh-century Saxon England, *bildungsroman,* and romantic tale of fatal destiny and tragic love—*Harold* is shaped by Bulwer's controlling thesis that England falls victim to Norman conquest because the country is intellectually behind the times, socially backward, and politically weakened by both internal division and constant foreign invasions. Everything, Bulwer argues, is worn out in England. With a king (Edward the Confessor) enfeebled and incapacitated by superstition, a court exhausted by cabal and treachery, a church decrepit and neither learned nor brave, a nobility wearing itself away in combative rivalry yet lacking a true martial spirit, a people debilitated by slavery and materialism, and a national defense system both outdated and impotent against foreign threat, England is easily overrun by superior Norman military organization at Hastings.

By contrast, the Normans are led by an energetic and forceful warlord, who has the support of an efficient court system backed by a learned and disciplined church, as well as the aid of a fiercely effective soldiery using the latest techniques of war. Norman society, Bulwer claims, is a garrison state ruled by Spartan ruthlessness and sustained by a repressed peasantry forced to support a conquest-bent nobility. Yet despite their many flaws, the Normans represent the coming age, while the Saxons exemplify the past. In this clash between new and old, Bulwer dramatizes his theory about the nature of human progress. Drawing an analogy between human society and the natural world, he argues that all communities that advance contain, like nature, "two antagonistic powers—the one inert and resisting, the other active and encroaching." If society develops according to natural principles, then change is inevitable and society and its rulers must welcome reform. Old societies can be reborn, however, and *Harold* predicts that England will eventually absorb its Norman conquerors as it did its earlier Danish and Norwegian invaders, so that eight hundred years later Saxon notions of freedom and liberty will become the signal features of modern nineteenth-century England—a nation that need not fear social change at home or revolutions abroad (1848) because of its willingness to embrace reform and to facilitate change (the 1832 Reform Bill).

Bulwer's novel earned the respect of several important contemporary English historians. Thomas Babington Macaulay told him that "he read *Harold* too eagerly for criticism," but believed the book closer to history than romance. Francis Palgrave, the respected constitutionalist

on whose research Bulwer drew, "was delighted that his own 'dull prose' should have contributed to the book's admirable poetry." The antiquarian Thomas Wright complimented Bulwer by telling him he "was alone amongst historical novelists"; others who wrote about the past "had never really studied history" and had "perpetuated prejudices of the most vulgar kind." Several years after Bulwer's death, Lord Alfred Tennyson acknowledged his debt to Bulwer's *Harold* as the major source for his own historical verse drama about the last Saxon king. In contrast, critics writing in the major contemporary journals were less impressed by *Harold. Fraser's Magazine* approved of Bulwer's historical analysis in *Harold,* but condemned its literary style as "incoherent and unbecoming." Appraising Bulwer's novels in 1865, the *Westminster Review* found *Harold* the work of an author whose mind was commonplace. And Andrew Sanders, writing about *Harold* in 1978, felt the book's major flaw stemmed from Bulwer's technique of dispelling the wonder and strangeness of Harold's world. Bulwer, he argued, "never seems to sense that in demythologising his characters, by emphasising the validity of his own historical credentials, he diminishes both their heroism and their humanity." Such a criticism of *Harold* is just.

. . . . .

*Pausanias the Spartan,* Bulwer's last historical novel, was printed in 1876 in one volume by George Routledge and Sons. It was originally begun in 1852, but for a variety of reasons Bulwer was unable to finish it during his lifetime. His son found the manuscript—completed to the middle of the second volume with a brief two-page outline for the third volume—among his late father's papers. Deciding to publish it, he sent the manuscript to the Rev. Benjamin Hall Kennedy, professor of Greek at Cambridge University, to piece together some of its fragments and to authenticate the book's historical accuracy. Consequently, young Lytton dedicated *Pausanias* to Kennedy for his assistance.

In the dedication dated from Cintra on 5 July 1875, Lytton noted that his father planned to focus his novel on Pausanias's career following the Battle of Plataea, when the Spartan regent, as admiral of the combined Greek fleet at Byzantium, was at the summit of both his power and his public reputation. Bulwer sought to examine why as regent Pausanias proved more powerful than the Spartan king. In his novel he wanted to describe the character of a man who "was at one time the glory, and at another the terror of all Greece." His artistic aim was to depict Pausanias as a tragic hero who, driven by lust for power, by love for a woman forbidden him by his country's laws, and by a loathing for the constraints imposed on his liberty by Spartan customs, betrayed Greece to the Persians in order to rule all Hellas under the guise of making Sparta a great imperial power. Such a bold plan rested on the cooperation of others unaware of his scheme who possessed a collective authority far greater than his own. For domestic interest Bulwer employed the tragic story of Cleonice—her accidental murder by Pausanias and her reappearance as a specter haunting the repose of her guilty murderer—to achieve pathos, dark terror, and dramatic effect as well as to shape the fate of the book's misguided hero.

*Frontispiece to Bulwer's* Eugene Aram. A Tale *(1832). By Hablot K. Browne.*

Based on the portion Bulwer completed, *Pausanias* is the best of all his historical novels because he quite successfully portrays both his hero's inner life and the age in which he lives. Previously, critics complained that while Bulwer proved an accurate historian, he failed to bring his heroes fully to life. With Pausanias, unlike Glaucus, Cola di Rienzi, Warwick, and Harold, Bulwer draws a three-dimensional character and illuminates his psychological makeup.

After *Pompeii,* Bulwer's other historical novels displayed a noticeable advance in conception and method. *Pompeii* contained only the most oblique historical analysis; few of his readers recognized that in the scenes of Roman decadence Bulwer sought to portray the hedonism of the English Regency period (1807-20). Far more direct was his analysis of the forces responsible for the rise and fall of Cola di Rienzi. In *Rienzi* Bulwer put into practice his theory that good historical fiction should be founded on accurate historical reconstruction, analysis of causation, and solid interpretation. He challenged conventional accounts of fourteenth-century Italy, producing a revisionist novel that also dramatized issues current in the nineteenth-century Italian Risorgimento. The same fictional concepts were more successfully applied to *Barons* and *Harold,* which earned Bulwer the praise of contemporary histori-

ans such as Palgrave and Macaulay. In his last, unfinished historical novel, *Pausanias,* Bulwer overcame his difficulty in depicting the psychological lives of the historical personages in his story, a problem he had not fully resolved in his earlier books.

A modern critic, Lionel Stevenson, has judged Bulwer's later historical novels both "sound and scholarly" [in *The English Novel: A Panorama,* 1960]. If these novels are to be faulted, they may be criticized for being overly self-conscious about method: occasionally Bulwer interrupted his narrative to cite his sources and to acquaint his readers with contending interpretations offered by other writers. This concern for documentation infuriated contemporary critics, who accused Bulwer of parading his knowledge to no useful purpose.

Bulwer's place as a historical novelist remains secure; he was Sir Walter Scott's most important and most serious successor in the early Victorian period. Until the historical novel's return to popularity in the mid-Victorian era, no writer did more to preserve and improve upon Scott's fictional legacy than Bulwer. The other aspirants to Scott's mantle—Harrison Ainsworth, G. P. R. James, Horace Smith, John Gibson Lockhart, and Mrs. Catherine Gore—are long-forgotten today. But Bulwer's historical fiction is still read, and *Barons* and *Harold* retain their power as works of serious historical analysis. Despite their artistic flaws, his historical novels are the link between *Waverley* and *Henry Esmond;* without him the English historical novel might have expired in the 1830s and 1840s from its exploitation by romancers whose hackwork seriously undermined the genre.

*James L. Campbell, Sr., in his* Edward Bulwer-Lytton, *Twayne Publishers, 1986, 156 p.*

## Richard Bevis   (essay date 1990)

[*In the excerpt below, Bevis examines the theme of power in Bulwer-Lytton's historical play* Richelieu.]

In 1841 Edward Bulwer-Lytton described *Richelieu, The Duchess de la Vallière,* and *The Lady of Lyons,* his French history plays, as "a sort of trilogy delineating the drift of political power from 'the One Man' to 'the old provincial chivalry' to 'the People.' " In an era when the forms of power have fascinated historians and philosophers, it is surprising that this hint has not been followed up with respect to *Richelieu;* one of the most popular of Victorian plays, it has been treated lightly by twentieth-century critics. William Archer termed it "adroit" and "stagey" [in *The Old Drama and the New,* 1923], Samuel Chew "brilliant and eminently actable" [in *A Literary History of England,* 1948]: cooler and warmer versions of the same response. George Rowell praised *Richelieu's* "expert . . . use of sentiment, passion, colour, and, above all declamation" [in *The Victorian Theatre,* 1956], but pronounced it on balance "an adroit piece of costume melodrama." Words such as "adroit" and "melodramatic" have in fact dominated modern readings of the play which Michael Booth has called [in *English Melodrama,* 1965] "the last grand revival of traditional melodrama." Booth's edition of *Richelieu* [in *English Nineteenth-*

*Century Plays,* 1969] lists both its "weaknesses" and some "first-rate theatrical effects," including spectacle, rhetoric, and "melodramatic effects."

It is necessary to confront the issue of "melodrama" squarely at the outset: if ***Richelieu*** has melodramatic aspects, may we therefore condescend to it? We have been taught to regard melodrama as an inferior form, "an inappropriate and incredible modality" based on "a notoriously bourgeois aesthetic." Certainly its imaginative world is closer to the morality play or the Gothic novel than to our own, but there is more to melodrama than distressed widows and orphans, waxed moustaches and true-blue rescuers, or it would not have permeated the Victorian imagination so deeply. Does it affect us more than we care to admit, more than our antipathy to sentiment suggests it should? We have somehow to reconcile the power of the death scenes of Dickens's Little Nell and Little Jo to move us with the fact that they are quite melodramatic and, from a certain point of view, "bad writing." Are they powerful *despite* being melodramatic, or *because* they are? Daniel S. Burt points out [in *Melodrama,* 1980] that Dickens, like lesser Victorian novelists, used melodramatic effects "to dramatize a social message." Michael Booth claims that "Many of Dickens's novels can be analyzed as pure melodramas," and Paul Schlicke has shown [in *Dickens and Popular Entertainment,* 1985] how melodramatic elements are woven into three of them.

In fact, something like a critical revolution has been occurring since G. B. Shaw wrote that "A good melodrama is a more difficult thing to write than all this clever-clever comedy: one must go straight to the core of humanity to get it, and if it is only good enough, why, there you have Lear or Macbeth" and T. S. Eliot admitted, "great drama has something melodramatic in it." Sypher, in 1948, and Northrop Frye (1957) are among the last critics to attach a negative valuation to melodrama and assume that we share it; most subsequent writers have argued that it is central to human experience and not incompatible with great tragedy. Robert Heilman managed to distinguish between tragedy and melodrama (1960) without using pejorative terms. Eric Bentley in 1964 dignified melodrama as *"the Naturalism of the dream life"* and "the quintessence of drama." James L. Rosenberg asked in the same year whether melodrama might not be "perhaps the highest, rather than the most contemptible, of dramatic forms?" But it was Michael Booth's serious treatment of *English Melodrama* (1965) that brought the genre formally within the pale of academic respectability, a process ratified by Robertson Davies in *The Mirror of Nature* (1983): the last label that Sypher would have accepted for melodrama.

The *New York Literary Forum*'s issue on melodrama (1980), prefaced by Michael Kirby's "manifesto" explaining why "Structuralism accepts the artificiality of melodrama," showed that the world of professional theatre is also taking melodrama seriously. Stephen Sondheim and Christopher Bond, who collaborated on the musical *Sweeney Todd,* both hail melodrama as "larger than life." For Sondheim, the form's ability to reveal the "frightening power" inside us makes it "high theatre" and indeed "the heart of the theatrical experience": Shakespeare and Soph-

ocles are great melodramatists. Bond concedes melodrama "the capacity to passionately involve its audience." Similarly, Peter Brook has remarked that the function of melodrama is to thrill its audience into a sense of being alive. This is not the pathetic melodrama of Dickens, but something closer to the sensational melodrama of Maturin, Buckstone, G. D. Pitt, Henry Arthur Jones, and of Bulwer-Lytton when he has Richelieu emote in the moonlight coming through his Gothic casement or draw the magic circle around Julie. The house of melodrama has many rooms, and a play may visit several of them without taking up residence.

***Richelieu*** is, on occasion, splendidly melodramatic; but it is more than that. It is also a history play, though here again Bulwer-Lytton has been treated roughly by his critics, J. O. Bailey charging the play [in *British Plays of the Nineteenth Century,* 1966] with historical inaccuracies, and Ernest Reynolds citing an "excessive display of the author's learning" [in *Early Victorian Drama* (1831-1870)]. *Omnibus placere non potest.* Bulwer-Lytton himself described "historical drama" as "the concentration of historical events"—Shakespeare would surely have concurred—and provided a list of the liberties he had taken. Charles B. Qualia, who investigated Bulwer-Lytton's dramatic sources [in "French Dramatic Sources of Bulwer-Lytton's *Richelieu,*" *PMLA* 42 (March 1972)], noted that he made less use of Lemercier's *Richelieu* than of Delavigne's *Louis XI* and Hugo's *Cromwell,* and that in order to achieve some of the latter's effects he made several alterations in the historical record. One hears, I think, not only echoes of the religious nationalism of Richelieu's younger contemporary Cromwell (whom he mentions in the last scene), but also allusions to the shrewd diplomacy of Metternich, roughly Bulwer-Lytton's contemporary. Yet a reading of modern historians' accounts of Richelieu—still a controversial figure—suggests that Bulwer-Lytton has not seriously distorted the historical portrait of the man, however free his treatment of some details.

Perhaps the most serious charge against ***Richelieu***—though it is not *generally* made—is Reynolds's: that it is a "compilation [rather] than a coherent psychological study." To say this, however, is to miss the thematic principle around which the play does cohere, which is neither history nor the role of Armand Richelieu, but just what Bulwer-Lytton said it is. His service as a Reform Member of Parliament from 1831, which led to an invitation to take a government post in 1835 (he declined in order to continue writing) brought him close to the mechanisms of political power during a period in which Metternich's masterly statecraft offered a parallel with Richelieu's. The play is a sustained meditation on the nature and uses of power, returning again and again to variations on this theme; not only the famous "pen and sword" line and the part of the Cardinal but most of the major speeches and characters bear on the paradoxes of seeking or wielding different types of power.

A sense of the complexity of the word "power" is crucial here. Bertrand Russell's "the production of intended effects" [in *Power: A New Social Analysis,* 1938] will do as a starting place; the play is about how men try to produce the effects they intend. This is purposely broad, to accommodate Russell's various purposes, but too general to distinguish *Richelieu* from many other works. Alistair Buchan's "power in the sense of influence, power as distinct from force" [in *Power and Equilibrium in the 1970's*, 1973], while applicable, would also cover a great deal besides *Richelieu.* Russell, Buchan and other theorists, however, enumerate diverse subtypes of power—traditional, revolutionary, naked or pure, strategic, military, political, economic, etc. —among which are several prominent in *Richelieu.* One of the most interesting such analyses is Leonard Krieger's distinction [in *The Responsibility of Power,* 1967] between power and control (echoed by Buchan), in which generic power is distinguished from force, and political power from right; *Richelieu,* it can be argued, surveys this boundary, along which the Cardinal walks.

Russell and Bertrand de Jouvenel (like Thomas Hobbes) identify the desire for power as a fundamental constituent of human nature that may be used for good or ill. Krieger agrees but sees "the problem of power"—the tension between ethics and politics, ends and means, "responsibility by and to power"—as peculiarly modern. Russell indeed says, "There is no hope for the world unless power can be tamed . . . . " Bulwer-Lytton seems well aware of both the seriousness and the ambiguities of this discussion, and projects this awareness of the problems and potentialities of power onto his protagonist.

There are clues to the dramatist's particular concern with power in his correspondence with William Charles Macready, the original Richelieu. On 12 March 1839, five days after the opening, for example, Bulwer-Lytton was still trying to shape Macready's conception of the role (a piece of presumption deeply resented by the star). "Forgive me," wrote the author, "if I say that the *more* you come out from subdued dryness into power (which you did tonight) the more brilliant your success will be, & the more you will realize the Cardinal—." Bulwer-Lytton's *intention,* then, was precisely to produce a "coherent psychological study"—of power operating in and on and through one man—but of course only the text (and performance) can show how far he realized that aim.

What immediately becomes clear in reading or watching any version of the play is that verbal repetition of the *word* "power" in different circumstances, with the consequent accumulation of meanings, is Bulwer-Lytton's basic technique. The first scene presents the conspirators led by Baradas, who covets Richelieu's position and, beyond that, the throne itself. Baradas's value is uncomplicated: he stands for naked, revolutionary power. "Midst Richelieu's foes *I'll* find some desperate hand / To strike for vengeance," he announces, "while we stride to power." It is typical of Bulwer-Lytton's sympathetic treatment of Richelieu that he first presents a rival, reminding us of the central fact of power: *someone* will exercise it. If Louis XIII and Richelieu do not rule France, Orleans and Baradas will. Below eminence there is always ambition, a quality to which Baradas confesses in his scene-ending soliloquy, coupling it with his love for Julie de Mortemar.

> . . . my love has grown the bone

and nerve of my ambition. By the King's
Aid I will marry Julie. . . .
    . . . By the King's aid
I will be minister of France [Richelieu's
title]. . . .
· · · · · · · · · · · · · · · · · · · ·
Then, by the aid of Bouillon and the Spaniard,
I will dethrone the King. . . .

These speeches enclose the first reference to Richelieu's own power, voiced by de Mauprat, who later becomes his adherent:

> . . . Richelieu bears
> A charmed life: to all who have braved his
> power,
> One common end—the block.

The meaning of the word "power" has already begun to ramify, as it does throughout the play; here it includes both high position and the dangerous force that accompanies it.

The first appearance of Cardinal Richelieu in I. ii shows us a character as complex as the historical evidence suggests. Certainly he seems to have succumbed to one of the commonest delusions attendant on power, that of indispensability: "The King must have / No mistress but the State," he assures Joseph: "the State—that's Richelieu!" We are to remember, of course, that *"L'État, c'est moi!"* was the view associated with the most autocratic of French rulers, Louis XIV, for whose absolutism Richelieu is said to have paved the way. Throughout the scene he manipulates Julie and de Mauprat towards the marriage he has decreed for them. "Marriage and death, for one infirm old man / Through a great empire to dispense— withhold— / As the will whispers!" savors, he thinks, of divine omnipotence. A few moments earlier he has referred contemptuously to courtiers as "weak waxen minds / That flutter in the beams of gaudy Power": insect Icaruses melted by the sun. The image is appropriate to the century of the Sun King, though the power in question could as well be Richelieu's. But self-exaltation is only the hubristic side of Richelieu's highest and most altruistic quality: his ardent patriotism. "I have recreated France," he claims. Russell's treatment of the ethics of power describes a beneficent version where power is desired as a *means* to achieve the end of satisfying others' desires, and the bad effects do not outweigh the good. This is the standard by which Richelieu (and others) may be judged. "Ambitious and power-hungry" he is (as Gerhard describes the historical man), but before he leaves the stage for the first time Bulwer-Lytton's Richelieu invokes his country, not himself, as the object of his heart's desire.

His relationship with his country, however, is a psychosexual one in which libido drives ambition. (Bertrand Russell remarks that the celibacy imposed on mediaeval priests "stimulated their power impulses, as asceticism does in most cases.") Richelieu feels united, identified, with France; she is his woman, his wife (an idea picked up again in the final scene):

> France! I love thee!
> All earth shall never pluck thee from my heart!

> My mistress France—my wedded wife—sweet
>    France,
> Who shall proclaim divorce for thee and me?

are the words that conclude Act I and a soliloquy that begins "Oh, godlike power!"

The second act is dominated by Baradas as his plot gathers momentum. Compared to Richelieu's complex lucubrations and motives, the Count remains a simple character, little more than Villainous Ambition: a despot in the making. (To Bulwer-Lytton's annoyance, this was how Macready played the Cardinal.) Baradas, however, projects his own "sublime ambition" and desire for revenge onto Richelieu, whose power, he tells de Mauprat, derives from "the Fiend." This implies no moral aversion on Baradas' part: "Were Richelieu dead his power were mine . . ." In fact he aspires precisely to be "the Richelieu of the Regent Orleans," but he lacks the Cardinal's consuming (and partially redeeming) love of country; the clearly foreseen consequences of his course of action—"From the wrecks of France / I shall carve out—who knows—perchance a throne!" —do not disturb him. For Baradas power is an end, not a means: he fails Russell's most fundamental test.

In II. ii, Joseph—fearing that his master underestimates the conspirators—warns him that "their plans / Are mightier than you deem." Unmoved, Richelieu explains that policy, not force, is his strength. Seated at a desk, brandishing a pen, he utters the play's (and the author's) best-known words:

> Beneath the rule of men entirely great
> The pen is mightier than the sword.

The qualifier, usually omitted from the quotation, is essential; only *inner* greatness—intellect, integrity, literary feeling—enables an author (Bulwer-Lytton or Richelieu) to wield power superior to the force of arms. It is, however, a purely verbal stroke: Richelieu is interrupted and writes nothing. Instead he fights fire with fire. To offset the ambition of Baradas he sends François, "unnoted—young, / Ambitious," to steal the crucial despatch. Its contents will suffice to discredit the conspiracy, and, "once crush'd, / Its very ashes shall manure the soil / Of power. . . ." It is his understanding of human nature and his ability to manipulate men to his own advantage that confer strength on Richelieu; he is an author not only of words but of events.

The prospect of breaking the plot against himself and France causes Richelieu to break out in a high-strung apologue (omitted by Booth) which enlarges on the claims he made in I. ii:

> O my country,
> For thee—thee only—though men deem it
>    not—
> Are toil and terror my familiars! . . .
> . . . . . . . . . . . . . . .
> . . . No pulse in my ambition
> Whose beatings were not measured from thy
>    heart!

(Some modern historians accept this estimate of Richelieu: see Krieger and Gerhard.) Richelieu goes on to explain that even celibate priests, being "Not holier than humanity," must find something to love, and uses a classical image to describe his motives and to gloss "I have re-created France":

> Debarr'd the Actual, we but breathe a life
> To the chill Marble of the Ideal—Thus,
> In thy unseen and abstract Majesty,
> My France—my Country, I have bodied forth
> A thing to love.

Richelieu, then, plays a Platonic Pygmalion to France's Galatea; the sculptor's power is added to the author's.

The structural centre of the play, III. i, is a theatrical tour de force, set at Ruelle, Richelieu's castle, in a "Gothic Chamber"; "moonlight at the window" is "occasionally obscured" by clouds. Here Richelieu delivers his principal soliloquy, reading philosophy aloud and meditating on his means and ends. The scene resembles the opening of *Faustus,* but whereas Marlowe's approach at least *seems* dynamic, moving his protagonist forward through a series of alternatives to a new perception of himself and of the world, Bulwer-Lytton's purpose is first to complicate and then to confirm what we already know of Richelieu. The theme once again is power. Perusing a "sage and sober moralist," the Cardinal reads that "life should soar to nobler ends than power." This sets off a complicated train of reflections, sometimes aggressively *ad hominem* ("But wert thou tried?"), sometimes despairing: " . . . the Monk, the Spy, the Headsman. / And this is Power! Alas! I am not happy." Within the space of ten lines he can image himself as Prometheus, carrying "light / Which I have stolen from the angry gods," and as the patriot Lucius Junius Brutus, then fall into self-pity that he is "wasting powers that shake the thrones of earth / In contest with the insects": those "weak, waxen" courtiers again.

This tension is "resolved" by a *coup de théâtre*. Richelieu has almost talked himself into metaphysics ("Speak to me, moralist! I will heed thy counsel") when François rushes in to report on his spy mission. In a second Richelieu has flung away both the book and the ideas of renunciation it represents: "Philosophy, thou liest! / Quick—the despatch! Power—empire!" "Empire" is an interesting touch, more appropriate to Bulwer's audience than to Richelieu's divided France. In the hands of Macready (and later Edwin Booth) this visible revelation of Richelieu's values was by all accounts effective histrionics. Yet the acceptance of his own power-drive obviously does not blind the Cardinal to the dark side of power. Later in the same scene, Richelieu identifies "vanity and power" as the "tempters" of innocent women: in this case of his ward, Julie. Bulwer-Lytton anticipates modern writers such as Russell and de Jouvenel in treating power ambivalently, as something to be judged by its effects.

The arrival of the conspirators adds a new dimension to Richelieu's experience of power: he feels what it is to have lost it. First he is confronted by an angry de Mauprat, taunting him with being "powerless now / Against the sword of one resolved man." And no sooner does Richelieu win him over than he learns that his entire bodyguard has been suborned. "A retributive Power!" he exclaims, leaving the source of this retribution vague. Richelieu seems to suggest that it may be preternatural; he does not acknowledge that he is threatened by a rival *human* power.

Richelieu escapes, via "the fox's" skin, but the closing moments of the act belong to Baradas, whose star is still ascendant. Again the key passages are not in Booth. When de Beringhen observes that the would-be regent, Orleans, is "no hero," Baradas agrees—but "on his cowardice I mount to power." This ruling passion also shapes his response to the false report of Richelieu's death:

> And could he come
> To life again, he could not keep life's life—
> His power—

Baradas is there to show us how naked power, power wielded purely for its own sake, looks; he ends the act imploring "AMBITION" ("Thou dark and fallen angel") to "light us to the goal!" Though Richelieu dominates the *talk* of power in the third act, it appears to be slipping from his grasp into Baradas's, who is too blatant a villain for us to enjoy his prospects.

When Louis XIII finally appears in Act IV, we see at once why the state is in such a tumult: *"Louis le juste"* is presented as a foolish monarch and a weak man. With such a power vacuum waiting to be filled, no wonder men such as Richelieu and Baradas are striving for control. In fact, Louis's character makes so much sense of the action that we are entitled to wonder if the delay in his appearance is not a constructional fault.

Baradas is already exulting over the supposed passing of Richelieu's tyranny—"His power was like the Capitol of old— / Built on a human skull"—when the Cardinal reappears. The King is cold, however, and Richelieu does not help his cause by referring to the "fifteen years, while in these hands dwelt empire," or by his claim to have "raised aloft" Louis's throne and given him "empire." (This emphasis on *imperial* power develops late in the play.) Even Joseph thinks his master now as "powerless" as "The lackey of the ante-room," but this is only an appearance; the stripping of his secular authority has not damaged his spiritual power, "the wings of sacred Rome." Even though his "memories" of imprisoned traitors, their wives and widows, are "solemn," Richelieu engages in a power struggle for Julie with Baradas, representing Louis, before the act's end. When Baradas insists that "The country is the King"—challenging Richelieu's claim of that identity for himself in I. ii—for the first time the Cardinal falls back on his reserve strength:

> Then wakes the power which in the age of iron
> Burst forth to curb the great, and raise the low.
> Mark, where she stands! Around her form I
>     draw
> The awful circle of our solemn church!
> Set but a foot within that holy ground,
> And on thy head—yea, though it wore a
>     crown—
> I launch the curse of Rome!

There is more at work here than Catholicism, however. Russell remarks that priestly power derives from the medicine man's, and de Jouvenel adds that "Fear is the principle at the root of magical Power." Richelieu's incantation,

his great rhetorical moment, owes as much to conjuring (and, onstage, to the melodramatic effect of his red robes) as to Rome.

Baradas, whether he thinks the "awful circle" derives its potency from the Pope or the Fiend, is sufficiently impressed to fall back.

> I dare not brave you!
> I do but speak the orders of my King.
> The church, your rank, power, very word, my
>     lord,
> Suffice you for resistance: blame yourself
> If it should cost you power!

Baradas warns that the abuse of power may cost Richelieu his position; he continues to conceive of power in static, secular terms despite having just yielded to a different kind of force. Baradas will never look convincing in the fox's skin. Richelieu, and Bulwer-Lytton, on the other hand, seem as sophisticated as modern analysts about the varieties of power. Baradas fails in the play mostly because his idea of power is too simple to match the Cardinal's array of concepts and policies.

Yet Richelieu's health is now everything, because his power is personal, not institutional; if he dies, it simply evaporates. Joseph puts it succinctly at the beginning of Act Five: "His life is power; / Smite one—slay both!" His life being *identical* with power, his physical weakness is a sign, perhaps an effect, of his power's eclipse, so the crucial despatch would indeed be "medicine to Ambition's flagging heart," as Joseph says. Securing it is difficult, though, since the Governor of the Bastille is no longer impressed when bid to "Think on the Cardinal's power." A memorandum of Bulwer's, apparently dating from late 1838 and headed "Proposed alterations in Richelieu," envisions "Joseph saying at close" of V. i "that only hope is in Richelieu's last experiment at power." Subsequently, however, the author decided that only raw ambition and youthful strength could succeed theatrically in that situation, and so at scene's end he has François and de Beringhen grappling desperately (but inconclusively) for possession of the packet. *"Exeunt, struggling."* Bulwer-Lytton's memo for Act Five exhorts: "Abandon the intellectual for the terrific interest generally."

The final scene (V. ii) is a series of trials between different kinds of power. First Julie, who has nothing but the moral strength of her position, kneels before the King ("at the feet / Of power") to beg de Mauprat's life. Louis, uneasy with this kind of authority and conscious that his own interest in Julie disqualifies him as a judge, refers her to Baradas, newly created "Minister of France" in Richelieu's place. The upstart Count, raw and forceful, instead tries to use his new power to gain Julie for himself, arguing *sotto voce* that he is more worthy of her favours than de Mauprat:

> for thy sake
> I peril what he has not: fortune, power;
> All to great souls most dazzling.

Julie responds with an appeal to Louis's sense of *noblesse oblige:*

> you were born

To power—it has not flush'd you into madness,
As it doth meaner men.

Power does *not* seem to have corrupted Louis as even its prospect has Baradas, but he is—in Bulwer-Lytton's portrayal—too weak to exercise it. There is more than a hint of Pontius Pilate in the way he evades unpleasant decisions by delegating authority.

Royal redress is not forthcoming, and Baradas, ever the poor judge of character, is still breathing "ambition" in Julie's ear when Richelieu totters on for his final and most Metternichian act. He has planned as carefully as ever, and shows Louis that his knowledge of European politics is *sans pareil* in the court, but his powers are circumscribed until a bloodstained François arrives with the despatch incriminating the conspirators, at which point the intellectual indeed gives way to the terrific. As his new Minister is arrested for treason and his court crumbles around him, Louis rushes to the Lord Cardinal with "Reign, Richelieu!" In this moment of intense excitement the old master is as cool and predictable as ever:

> *Rich: (Feebly)* With absolute power?
>
> *Louis:* Most absolute! Oh, live,
> If not for me—for France!
>
> *Rich:* France!

The mere word is for him a source of strength; in a moment he is on his feet, snapping orders, condemning, reprieving, laughing.

Bailey's complaint that this revival is "melodramatic" seems to me to miss the point. Either Richelieu is not as feeble as he appeared—the fox's skin again—or he is reverting to the theme of his earlier patriotic outbursts: a mystical identity between the French body politic and the existence of Armand Richelieu. When Louis suspiciously pronounces his cure "startling" in its suddenness, the Cardinal blandly explains that "in one moment there did pass / Into this withered frame the might of France!" Although such an idea has been prepared—"What mistress like our country?" recalls the Act One soliloquy—the man's cunning is more obvious than usual, especially in the restrained way he goes on to speak of the absolute power he has just achieved. Richelieu's choice of images in his final speech (omitted by Booth) is careful; in the presence of Divine Right he is only a demi-god:

> Our glories float between the earth and heaven
> Like clouds which seem pavilions of the sun,
> And are the playthings of the casual wind;
> Still, like the cloud which drops on unseen crags
> The dews the wild flower feeds on, our ambition
> May from its airy height drop gladness down
> On unsuspected virtue;—and the flower
> May bless the cloud when it has passed away!

The play closes (in 1860 and Bailey) with this modest self-estimate of Richelieu (said by Bulwer-Lytton to be drawn from the Cardinal's own writings), which is also a neat recapitulation of the play's concern with the nature of power. It is characteristic of Richelieu as we have come to know him that, having been granted by his sovereign the power to act autonomously on behalf of French inter-

ests as he defines them, he should discourse in idealizing images that flatter Louis and subordinate himself, while defining a useful and benign role that both can play. As a concept, it shares some ground with Leonard Krieger's assertion that the qualities of the idea of power are potentiality, reciprocity and spirituality, but that political power tends to discard the notion of reciprocity: the flower will not do much for the cloud. In tone, the passage is aligned with the rosier view of Richelieu's work as "exemplary," rather than with the kind of doubts expressed by Gerhard and de Jouvenel, and suggested by Bulwer-Lytton himself in some of Richelieu's soliloquies. This is public utterance, not private revelation, and power such as Richelieu's speaks of itself circumspectly before an audience.

What Bulwer-Lytton called his "great Historical Comedy" is not unique in its concerns; *Richard II, Henry IV, Tamburlaine, Faustus,* and most history and political plays are studies in quests for power, though rarely to this extent. Nor is it without faults in plot, character and dialogue, which Bailey, Booth and the author himself have joined in pointing out. The conspiracy is an overrich mixture; too much hinges on the despatch; there is an unassimilated surplus of history; and the conclusion trails off impotently. Beyond Richelieu himself, and possibly de Mauprat, the characterization is flat: Louis is Inept, Baradas Villainous, etc. They point up the greatness of Richelieu, but also the drawbacks of the Victorian star system. The play lacks the kind of balance that Shakespeare achieved with Richard II and Bolingbroke, or Prince Hal, Hotspur and Falstaff. The dialogue, with its pauses and leaps, could be effective onstage, but has a weakness for the breathless exclamation, and the soliloquies do not transcend skillful histrionics.

My argument is simply that the play's organizing principle has not been appreciated, though it operates in every scene and major character. **Richelieu** is coherent and actable; a good director will be able to use the shadings of influence, power, ambition and control to give the action a theme-and-variations unity, and the complex discussion of power is timely. Russell remarks that we are now returning to "forms of life and thought" that are pre-eighteenth-century, before "the classic era of European equilibrium": in other words, history is bringing us back around to Richelieu's unstable world. Krieger's assertion that political power as we understand it today began in the sixteenth century provides another link. Richelieu's thought processes are eerily familiar; he would have known how to operate in the age of the *coup d'état* and the application of games theory to political intrigue. The achievement of Bulwer-Lytton is to have made this seventeenth-century statesman recognizable and pertinent in the nineteenth and twentieth without abandoning the historical basis of the character. And the political modernity of **Richelieu** is coextensive with its aesthetics, for the power claimed by the hero, that of the pen over the sword, is implicitly that of its author: the power of his rhetoric—and his melodrama—over us.

*Richard Bevis, " 'Mightier Than the Sword': The Anatomy of Power in Bulwer-Lytton's 'Richelieu',* " in Essays in Theatre, *Vol. 8, No. 2, May, 1990, pp. 95-106.*

## Park Honan (essay date 1990)

[*Honan is an American critic and specialist on Victorian literature. In the following excerpt, he asserts that Bulwer-Lytton's novels are significant for their social representation of the Victorian Age.*]

We cannot know the Victorian mind unless we know something about the career and writings of Edward Bulwer, who became Bulwer-Lytton. The trouble is that a sea of time has washed over him. His works are as strange as sea creatures in exoskeletons, with enormous tails and filaments, living in inky depths. Pull one off a library shelf and stare at its bulgy eyes and you will run away—not in fright, but in anticipation of deep boredom. Or so you and I may expect, for his reputation is low today. What are his plays but bombast? What are his novels from *Pelham* to *Kenelm Chillingly* but turgid mistakes?

In fact he could write superbly well. He charmed Dickens and had an enormous following of Victorian readers. And if Bulwer-Lytton is no longer in fashion his career is extremely significant; it begins ten years after Jane Austen's death, when England and Europe were still bemoaning Byron's loss, and runs on like a bright twisting ribbon. I want to survey that career briefly, and in the light of his first, succinct, unusually skillful and entertaining novel. Bulwer-Lytton's first novel, *Falkland,* was published in 1827 when he was nearly twenty-four and is about a seduction. Its message is simple: a good way to overcome ennui is to seduce a dazzling young woman whose M.P. husband is too busy to notice and whose child is too small to care. Lady Emily Mandeville dies of a "broken blood vessel" in her sexual excitement (presumably some other excitement would have carried her off soon anyway) and Falkland has some horrid dreams, but illicit love cures him of his gloom and sends him romping off to Spain to join a colorful democratic struggle. Yet *Falkland* had a therapeutic value for Bulwer. When he completed it in the gardens of Versailles in 1826 he had composed little else besides poetry and was recovering from a queer epistolary love affair with Lady Caroline Lamb. She had understood him: "You are like me—too fond of Lord Byron." Bulwer had been trying to live up to his own conception of Lord Byron since the age of thirteen.

He was born on May 25, 1803 to wealthy parents of old and impeccable lineage. General Bulwer, bedridden with gout, lived for a time in "hoops that suspended from his body the touch of his clothes" and died when Edward was four. From then on the boy was protected from the cries of the world. He attended four public schools briefly and came home to be pampered by his glittering mother and gently encouraged by a devoted tutor. A Byronesque attempt—*Ismael: an Oriental Tale: with Other Poems*—appeared at his mother's expense when he was seventeen. Two years later he went to Cambridge where he won some reputation for witty skill in debate, his arrogance, and for writing like Byron. Two more poetic volumes and a Chancellor's Medal opus followed. He was also reading quickly and widely, filling up ledgers with notes on English and Irish history, and walking in the long vacations. In 1824, he walked to Brocket Park and met Lady Caroline. For a few days, an affair with the most notorious of Byron's

cast-off mistresses fed gossip in London, and at Cambridge, where the arrogant young imitator was suddenly an undergraduates' laughing-stock. (Lady Caroline was known for being vain, aging, and a little nutty.) In a highly overwrought frame of mind and with a preliminary draft for *Falkland* in hand, Bulwer left Cambridge in 1825 for Paris. "I am like one of the leaves I see now before my window," he wrote to Mrs. Cunningham from Versailles, "without an aim. . . ."

Nevertheless, he took aim in *Falkland.* The hero is an ingenious composite of many romantic types (so that the little novel is a literary mosaic) and also a studied version of Bulwer's debilitating view of himself as an arch-seducer of the age. With his soft voice, his "chiselled" lip and light chestnut hair falling "in large *antique* curls," Falkland is Bulwer Byronized; plunged in Byronic ennui, he seeks the infallible Byronic cure—adultery—and then fights Byron's valorous battle, outnumbered, in a purple land. Lovelace and Werther are models for his letter writing. He has Lovelace's intensity in pursuit and Werther's hopelessness in an affair with a married woman. He is indebted to Maturin's devilish Melmoth, Plumer Ward's refined Tremaine, Rousseau of the *Confessions,* Wordsworth of the *Immortality Ode,* and at last, when he cheers his uncle's dispirited troops, to Prince Hal. Bulwer's most audacious stroke is to make him into a precocious Faust, too, a fiend-ridden "Genius" who has mastered astronomy, meteorology, and the rest of human thought and complains, like Jeremy Bentham, of the "inutility" of it all. Slabs of Gothic are lifted from Mrs. Radcliffe's novels. The scene of Lady Emily's entrapment between an unscalable cliff and the rushing tide resembles one in Scott's *The Antiquary.*

All of this ingrafting—partly acknowledged in Falkland's name-dropping—was deliberate for Bulwer. As Sir Joshua Reynolds tells Warner, a young painter in *The Disowned* (1829), "imitation, if noble and general, insures the best hope of originality," and if poor Warner and Godolphin learn it too late, their nervous breakdowns and wild drownings are instructive. (Bulwer complained in public when he thought Balzac had pillaged from *him*.)

Erasmus Falkland is murky in outline, as composites often are, but the prototype of heroes to come. His first transformation is seen in *Pelham* (1828), Bulwer's second novel, whose hero sobers up on Sauterne and soda water and is "never unpleasantly employed." Pelham is Falkland minus gloom and adultery (he resists the seductive Mme. de Perpignan and usefully solves a murder) and is also a social puppy with intellectual properties who is to be seen under other names, dourly in *Godolphin* (1833) and serenely in the late *Kenelm Chillingly* (1873). Falkland's second transformation is into Gothic villains who are intelligent, proud, mad, and murderously amorous, such as Aubrey in *Devereux* (1829) or Arbaces the Egyptian in *The Last Days of Pompeii* (1834). But his third transformation is more complex. The heroes of novels such as *Eugene Aram* (1832) and *Ernest Maltravers* (1837) and its sequel *Alice* (1838) are mental giants—very Faustlike Falklands—who pursue stupendous unknowns while suffering from "chimeras of a horrible hallucination" as Bulwer diagnosed their typical ailment. One of two things happens to them: they die violently, or they become de-Gothicized, de-Romanticized, and properly Victorianized through their experiences into models of simple piety and contentment, of a kind so badly needed by Bulwer's middle-class readers.

Perhaps the worst one can say is that their psychological problems are shallowly explored. It is just this that makes Bulwer's heroines even more easily classifiable: they are all, more or less, Lady Emily Mandevilles, nine-year-old minds in prettily bosomed bodies. Thus the question that interests us about a heroine at the outset of a Bulwer novel is whether he has decided she shall die, go crazy, or survive any ordeal intact. Insanity is the worst fate and comes on with terrible suddenness, Cassandra-like visions, and a good deal of noise:

> Then raising her voice into a wild shriek, "Beware, beware, Percy! —the rush of waters is on my ear—the splash, the gurgle! Beware! —your last hour, also, is at hand!"

> From the moment in which she uttered these words, Lucilla lapsed into her former frantic paroxysms. Shriek followed shriek; she appeared to know none around her, not even Godolphin.

Exactly what causes a heroine's death is often obscure: Madeline in *Eugene Aram* and Viola in *Zanoni* (1842) seem to expire out of sympathy with their lovers who are hanged or guillotined, and in this light Lady Emily's weak artery is a welcome detail. More impressive are the heroines who can get through anything. Alice, in the two Ernest Maltravers novels, is assaulted and pursued by her father, impregnated out of wedlock by the hero, forced to wander penniless, driven to subterfuge, and made to suffer in other ways for eighteen years until—still smiling with "dimpled lips"—she marries Ernest.

However, it is a mistake to weigh these creatures on the iron scale of realism. Particularly so, because Bulwer wished to "resort to a sort of moral or psychological distance" in portraiture, as he says in *Kenelm Chillingly* (1873). "We know that," he continues in the guise of Kenelm, "Werter and Clarissa are . . . as much remote from us in the poetic and idealized side of their natures as if they belonged to the age of Homer; and this it is that invests with charm the very pain which their fate inflicts on us." He is theorizing here half a century later, but it is significant that he alludes to the Goethe and Richardson novels that went into the making of *Falkland.* No doubt Bulwer wished to keep Erasmus and Lady Emily at a psychological distance (although the term hardly would have occurred to him in 1826). They and their literary cousins are poetic and idealized—that is, intendedly unbelievable—and if their minds so often seem stunted or darkly mysterious, their behavior and their fates do hold some charm. In his melodramatic world, even the bloodthirstiest enormities inflict no pain on us since the perpetrators and victims resemble nothing of flesh. And this is why Victorians loved him: what went on in *Lucretia* (1846) or the wilder *Night and Morning* (1841) was even worse than what went on in Birmingham's slums and yet was pleasantly innocuous from start to finish. Melodramatic characters are a

godsend if you live near tragic scenery because they invest pain with charm.

Bulwer did more than create a gallery of infantile heroines and crazy heroes, though. His lasting interest owes to his canny ability to mix seemingly incompatible appeals within one book, to his skill at construction, and to his good sense of timing and clever manipulation of nature. *Falkland* combines the Faust theme and the Byron legend, with an adultery story, Gothic terror, and military adventure.

In his next few novels, he surpassed all English predecessors in combining other traditional ingredients with Gothic. *Pelham* mixes it, not too successfully, with silver-fork wit and satire. *The Disowned* and *Devereux* were intended to be best-sellers. (Bulwer was entertaining his wife with fifteen-guinea thimbles by this time.) But they are also cool-headed experiments to see how many different kinds of novel one novel can be, and they surpass *Falkland* in this.

Morton Devereux writes his memoirs of political, philosophic, fashionable, and literary life in eighteenth-century Europe. He meets "grave Mr. Addison," "Dicky Steele," and that "very small, deformed man," Mr. Pope, as well as Dr. Swift, Bolingbroke, Mme. de Maintenon, Louis XIV, and the Czar, and in the Apennines solves a perfectly monstrous Gothic crime when he discovers his wife's slayer in the person of a monk who turns out to be his brother.

After that, Bulwer settled down to combining only two or three kinds of fiction at once. Thus *Paul Clifford* is a *roman à clef* that makes fun of a weekly magazine, the *Asinaeum,* while delivering a serious lecture in penology, and *Eugene Aram* is love idyll plus criminal case history plus terror. *Pompeii* and *Rienzi* (1835) join accurate historical reconstructions to suspense and mayhem. Novels with mythic, occult, bucolic, and Utopian interests, sensational romances and multivolumed domestic tales followed. None is dull except the latter, that is, *The Caxtons* (1849), *My Novel* (1853), and *What Will He Do With It?* (1859) or the Pisistratus Caxton books, which show only that Bulwer was bored by the countryside and was not Trollope.

He turned to the theater for lessons in construction and gave back to it in *The Lady of Lyons* (1838), *Richelieu* (1838), and *Money* (1840), the most stage-worthy of all Victorian imitations of Shakespeare. He also learned "the art of mechanical construction" from Scott's novels, and especially from Goethe's *Wilhelm Meister,* which offers the pattern of the *Bildungsroman* used in tracing so many heroic paths from youth to social conformity or a violent end. But his study of the theater accounts for the more typical structural features in his books—their vast soliloquies, four or five "acts," and catastrophes. Bulwer never tired of writing about catastrophes. In a novel, he said in his essay **"On Art in Fiction"** (1838), there ought to be a "management and combination of incidents towards the grand end." A "highly artistical" catastrophe must "revive in the consummating effect many slight details— incidents the author had but dimly shadowed out—

mysteries you had judged till then he had forgotten to clear up. . . ."

And indeed his catastrophes are large, orgiastic, sweeping, and colorful, and they clear up every mystery. *The Last Days of Pompeii* ends with a stampeding horde of thousands who are trying to toss the villain to a waiting lion in a blood-soaked amphitheater, an earthquake, billows of steam, glimmering lightnings, and a frighteningly lurid and very Gothic Vesuvius:

> Bright and gigantic through the darkness, which closed around it like the walls of hell, the mountain shone—a pile of fire! Its summit seemed riven in two; or rather, above its surface there seemed to rise two monster shapes, each confronting each, as Demons contending for a World. These were of one deep blood-red hue of fire, which lighted up the whole atmosphere far and wide; but, *below,* the nether part of the mountain was still dark and shrouded, save in three places, adown which flowed serpentine and irregular rivers of the molten lava. Darkly red through the profound gloom of their banks, they flowed slowly on, as towards the devoted city. Over the broadest there seemed to spring a cragged and stupendous arch, from which, as from the jaws of hell, gushed the sources of the sudden Phlegethon; and through the stilled air was heard the rattling of the fragments of rock, hurtling one upon another as they were borne down the fiery cataracts, darkening, for one instant, the spot where they fell, and suffused, the next, in the burnished hues of the flood along which they floated!

In this, his most famous novel, history cooperated ideally with Bulwer. Surely in *Falkland* he was already musing about its locale: "We remove the lava, and the world of a gone day is before us!" The eruption continues through four climactic chapters and pictures on a gigantic scale those horrifying gas and phosphorus flames and proscenium-rattling explosions that were entertaining hundreds from Drury Lane's accommodating ninety-foot-deep stage in the 1830s. Other historic catastrophes were comparatively timid but useful: there is the Reign of Terror in *Zanoni* and the "gory ocean" of Tewkesbury in *The Last of the Barons* (1843), for example.

In a very embryonic sense, the catastrophe is present in *Falkland,* which displays the close coordination between nature and mood and the accurate dramatic timing of cataclysms typical of Bulwer's mature work. The situation of an entrapment between a sheer cliff and high tide is used here more pointedly than in Scott: it creates the tension that precedes Emily and Erasmus's first kiss. And the evening of the seduction itself is "breathless" at first, then dark and stormy so that, at a critical moment under the oak when kisses are "like lava" and bosom is throbbing against bosom in abandonment, there is a marvelous "low roll" of thunder.

These effects are *sui generis* even in the canons of melodrama. No Hollywood producer has equaled them, I think, and Charles Dickens (whose Oliver owes to *Paul Clifford* and whose Jingler and Little Nell owe something to *Eugene Aram*) when he is writing scenes of melodramatic

content hardly seems to compete. They are partly ludicrous, of course, but never unimpressive, never really failings.

Still there are two cardinal failings that keep many of Bulwer's novels unread and out of print today. The first involves the complicated problem of his style. Oddly enough, his name is symptomatic of a grave deficiency: it lengthened little by little, to his pride, until when he was made a peer in 1866, it rumbled like one of his thunderstorms as Edward George Earle Lytton Bulwer Lytton, Baron Lytton of Knebworth. (One of his biographers reports that he savored the very sounds.) There are bits of redundant rhetoric in *Falkland,* almost none in *Pelham,* but by the time of *Devereux* strident "Bulwerese"—prose that seems to have been written by a theatrical parson brought up on *The Mysteries of Udolpho*—has set in. It is trite, tumid, inexact, archaic, and silly. Large patches of it infect all of his novels after 1829 except for *Paul Clifford* (where Fielding's style is vigorously imitated) and *The Caxtons* and *My Novel* (where Sterne's is) and the very late works.

What complicates the problem is that Bulwer could write with the conciseness of Swift and the epigrammatic smartness of Peacock. There are paragraphs in *Pelham* that glitter with the verbal irony of Oscar Wilde, as Michael Sadleir noticed, and bright epigrams in *Falkland.* Stranger still, he described his own worst faults of style perfectly in 1833 when he condemned young English novelists for writing with "an exaggerated tone and a superfluous and gratuitous assumption of energy and passion." Indeed, one is driven to the conclusion that he cared about style and composed with his own changing precepts well in mind.

In *Pelham,* a bright young friend of the hero named Vincent explains why that novel itself is so crisply written:

> For me, if I were to write a novel, I would first make myself an acute, active, and vigilant observer of men and manners. Secondly, I would, after having thus noted effects by action in the world, trace the causes by books, and meditation in my closet. It is then, and not till then, that I would study the lighter graces of style and decoration. . . .

Now, this formula might have sent the author along the trail of the comedy of manners and toward Jane Austen. Style near the outset of Bulwer's career is one of "the lighter graces" that is to subserve the accurate depiction of social behavior. But such a formula is patently unsuitable to the melodramatic novel. The "main essential of style in narrative" of *Eugene Aram*'s kind, he declares in a preface to that bloodcurdler, is rather "its harmony with the subject selected and the passions to be moved" and this leads him to write in a very different way.

Since his typical subjects tend to be idealized and unearthly, and since the "passions to be moved" in melodrama are pleasurable fright and simple awe, his language inflates with the showman's hectoring rhetoric, which asks for our delighted attention to unreal freaks and impossible horrors and descends to take in every cliché in the Gothic repertory. Thus *Aram* and *Pompeii* continue in a direction barely noticeable in *Falkland* by depending on key words such as *fierce* and *frenzy*—we read over and over of "fierce and lurid passions," "a thrilling and fierce groan," "a frenzy of jealousy," and on stereotypes such as lips that (reliably) "writhe," eyes that are "feverish," brows that are decorated with "cold drops," teeth that "grind," and so on. With Bulwer, one ought to be able to play the game and accept these, the counters of gas-lit terror, and one usually can: Gothic clichés are at least quick and vivid. His unforgivable fault is in badgering his readers in a style that is also so distended and furry it defeats its purpose, since it neither increases suspense nor prepares for thrills if it puts them into a doze, as it does.

His second cardinal fault is more serious since after all, a reader can learn to skip over swamps of Bulwerese. Philosophic pretentiousness is not so localized. It can hardly be missed in his novels because it is ingrained and pervasive: we are made aware that Bulwer, quite without qualifications, wants to be taken as a Sage. This can be felt in the author's intrusions and letters in *Falkland;* and yet his first novel interestingly points in two directions. On the one hand, it is filled with shopworn notions about nature, perception, and knowledge, but on the other it suggests a very genuine disillusionment with contemporary society. Emily's oafish husband is one of the new "Macadamized achievements," and the lovers can feel godlike because love, "even guilty Love," insulates them from the pettiness and strife of English life. Young Falkland, in fact, has seen enough to suggest that his creator has a social critic's eye and *Pelham, Greville,* and a brilliant treatise on the foibles of his countrymen, *England and the English* (1833), show that Bulwer had Thackeray-like endowments.

But an impulse to analyse society soon gave way to a willingness to placate it. Too often, from 1833 on, the Sage is only mouthing Victorian verities: "If there be anything lovely in the human heart," he writes in that very year, "it is affection!" Fortunately, however, Bulwer was not a prisoner of his deficiencies. The verve and ingenuity of *Falkland* are matched in several novels that followed it and surpassed in two perfect works. One of them is a short story, **"The Haunted and the Haunters"** (1857), a masterpiece of terror in the occult, and the other is a novel that makes a profound comment on Bulwer's melodramatic world. In *The Coming Race* (1871), an intrepid American lowers himself through a gap in the floor of a mineshaft into a lost civilization of supremely rational beings. In Vril-ya, muscular women seven feet tall study mechanics and abstract thought and woo punier but happy men. Both sexes flit about through perfumed air on detachable wings, direct automata to do the heavy work, and wield rods of such rock-shattering power that dissension and debate have become obsolete. Crime, adultery, passion, ambition, stimulants, doubts, and illusions are all missing— and so is art. Vril-ya is insufferable. The hero yearns (just as we do) for the contention and tumult of real human beings, whose very sign of life is a literature that can include such frenzied adulterers and nefarious villains and longsuffering ladies as Bulwer's.

*Falkland* would make no sense in Vril-ya. It typifies everything that is lawless, irrational, passionate, gauche, and exaggerated in Bulwer's entertainingly horrific world, since it contains in the bud his astonishing heroes and heroines, his melodramatic catastrophes, his combinations of appeal, even his imitativeness and style and philosophic pretensions, and displays his deep commitment to Romantic traditions and particularly to a Gothicism that his later novels in fact helped to preserve through the whole Victorian age.

Above all, what would mystify in Vril-ya is Bulwer's curious involvement in Byronism, the intensity of which he explained when he described how England reacted in 1824 to news of Byron's death. "We could not believe that the bright race was run," Edward Bulwer wrote later. "It was as if a part of the mechanism of the very world stood still . . . and all our worship of his genius was not half so strongly felt as our love for himself."

*Park Honan, "Bulwer," in his* Authors' Lives: On Literary Biography and the Arts of Language, *St. Martin's Press, 1990, pp. 123-33.*

---

## FURTHER READING

Brown, Andrew. "Metaphysics and Melodrama: Bulwer's *Rienzi.*" *Nineteenth-Century Fiction* 36, No. 3 (December 1981): 261-76.
> Chronicles Bulwer-Lytton's distortion of historical facts in *Rienzi.*

Campbell, James L., Sr. "Edward Bulwer-Lytton's *The Coming Race* as a Condemnation of Advanced Ideas." *Essays in Arts and Sciences* XVI (May 1987): 55-63.
> Proposes that *The Coming Race* should be grouped with later novels exploring similar themes.

Cragg, William E. "Bulwer's *Godolphin*: The Metamorphosis of the Fashionable Novel." *Studies in English Literature* 26, No. 4 (Autumn 1986): 675-90.
> Documents Bulwer-Lytton's mutability to public tastes in *Godolphin.*

Eigner, Edwin M. "Raphael in Oxford Street: Bulwer's Accommodation to the Realists." In *The Nineteenth-Century Writer and His Audience*, edited by Harold Orel and George J. Worth, pp. 61-74. Lawrence: University of Kansas Publications, 1969.
> Characterizes Bulwer-Lytton as a romantic who made concessions to realism in his later works.

Fradin, Joseph I. " 'The Absorbing Tyranny of Every-day Life': Bulwer-Lytton's *A Strange Story.*" *Nineteenth-Century Fiction* 16, No. 1 (June 1961): 1-16.
> Examines Bulwer-Lytton "as an intelligent novelist of serious intentions, if limited creative talent, attempting to record his reactions to the complex Victorian experience" in *A Strange Story.*

Rosa, Matthew Whiting. "Bulwer-Lytton." In his *The Silver-Fork School: Novels of Fashion Preceding* "Vanity Fair", pp. 74-98. Morningside Heights, N.Y.: Columbia University Press, 1936.
> Assesses *Pelham* as the most significant of the "fashionable" novels.

Shattuck, Charles H. "E.L. Bulwer and Victorian Censorship." *The Quarterly Journal of Speech* XXXIV, No. 1 (February 1948): 65-72.

> Discusses the influence of Victorian censorship upon Bulwer-Lytton's theatrical works.

Tyson, Nancy Jane. *Eugene Aram: Literary History and Typology of the Scholar Criminal.* Hamden, Conn.: Archon Books, 1983, 201 p.

> Documents the literary versions of the historical figure of Eugene Aram, including that found in Bulwer-Lytton's novel of the same name.

Wagenknecht, Edward. "From Scott to Dickens." In his *Cavalcade of the English Novel*, rev. ed., pp. 173-212. New York: Henry Holt and Company, 1954.

> Presents a general overview of the thematically diverse novels of Bulwer-Lytton.

Watts, Harold H. "Lytton's Theories of Prose Fiction." *PMLA* L, No. 1 (March 1935): 274-89.

> Critiques Bulwer-Lytton's analysis of the various components of narrative art expounded in "On Art in Fiction."

---

**Additional coverage of Bulwer-Lytton's life and career is contained in the following sources published by Gale Research: *Nineteenth-Century Literature Criticism*, Vol. 1, and *Dictionary of Literary Biography*, Vol. 21.**

# Octave Feuillet

## 1821-1890

(Also wrote under pseudonym Desiré Hasard) French novelist and dramatist.

## INTRODUCTION

One of the most popular writers in nineteenth-century France, Feuillet composed conventional, sentimental novels designed to uphold the values of the middle class, and fast-paced, well-constructed plays that catered to the tastes of Parisian audiences. His most successful works, *Le roman d'un jeune homme pauvre* (1858; *The Romance of a Poor Young Man*) and *Monsieur de Camors* (1867; *Camors; or, Life under the New Empire*), have been praised by many critics for their polished style and absorbing, if predicatable, plots.

Feuillet was born in Saint-Lô, in Normandy. In accordance with his father's wishes, Feuillet came to Paris to prepare for a diplomatic career at Louis-le-Grand College. While a student, he began to contribute literary sketches to newspapers and magazines. Soon his articles became so much in demand that Feuillet decided to devote all his efforts to writing. In 1845 he collaborated with Paul Bocage on several plays; melodramatic and unoriginal, they were judged inferior by critics and the partnership between Feuillet and Bocage eventually dissolved. Feuillet was also employed for a time as a literary assistant to the renowned novelist and playwright Alexandre Dumas *père*, but in 1851 left that post and returned to Saint-Lô. Dividing his time between the countryside and Paris, Feuillet wrote prolifically over the next three decades, producing numerous novels and plays. Public recognition followed: the Empress Eugénie so admired *The Romance of a Poor Young Man* that she appointed Feuillet her librarian at Fontainbleau, and the French Academy elected to admit Feuillet as a member in 1862. He died in Saint-Lô in 1890, one of the most respected French authors of his time.

Feuillet's works are generally romantic and didactic, often conveying a warning against the moral degradation of the aristocracy and extolling the virtues of the hard-working, pious middle class. For example, *The Romance of a Poor Young Man* features a protagonist who refuses to marry a rich young woman and destroys the proof of his claims to her fortune. The novel ends happily, however, when he inherits an even larger fortune of his own and then marries with a clear conscience. The noted critic J. Brander Matthews has pointed out that one factor which contributed to Feuillet's fame was that, in an age when scandalous novels were in vogue, Feuillet's *The Romance of a Poor Young Man* had "the choice distinction of being one of the few French novels harmless enough for perusal in young ladies' boarding-schools." Many of Feuillet's other novels and plays—among them *La petite Comtesse* (1857), *La tentation* (1860), and *Julia de Trécoeur* (1872)—also present moralistic themes aided by strong characterization

and unexpected plot twists. *Camors*, usually considered Feuillet's best novel, was described by Henry James as "one of the most highly elegant novels we have ever read," and again deals with a hero bound by "the religion of honor" who refuses to abide by the rules set out for him by a corrupt upper class.

Critics have consistently praised Feuillet's strong characterizations as well as the effective structure of his novels and dramas. Some scholars, notably George Saintsbury and Matthews, have suggested, though, that the vivid, intriguing characterizations in Feuillet's works sometimes undermine his didactic intent because negative characters are depicted as more fascinating than the positive ones. Other commentators have faulted Feuillet for blatantly tailoring his works to suit the tastes of his readers and theater-goers, with the result that, in some cases, concessions to the demands of his audience took precedence over aesthetic considerations. Nevertheless, Feuillet's writings have been admired by such notable figures as James, Saintsbury, Walter Pater, and Anatole France, the latter lauding that "composition, ordering, and . . . discretion and proportion which permit [Feuillet] to say all things, and make all things understood."

## PRINCIPAL WORKS

*La vie de Polinchinelle et ses nombreuses aventures*   (fiction)   1840
  [*Punch: His Life and Adventures,* 1946]
*\*La petite Comtesse*   (novel)   1857
*Le roman d'un jeune homme pauvre*   (novel)   1858; published in journal *Revue de Deux Mondes*
  [*The Romance of a Poor Young Man,* 1877]
*\*Bellah*   (novel)   1859
*\*La tentation*   (drama)   1860
*Rédemption*   (drama)   1861
*Histoire de Sybille*   (novel)   1862
  [*The Story of Sybille,* 1872]
*Monsieur de Camors*   (novel)   1867
  [*Camors; or, Life under the New Empire,* 1867]
*\*Julia de Trécoeur*   (novel)   1872
*Les amours de Philippe*   (novel)   1877
  [*Philippe's Love Story,* 1877]
*Le journal d'une femme*   (novel)   1878
  [*Journal of a Woman,* 1885]
*La morte*   (novel)   1886
  [*Aliette,* 1886]
*Honneur d'artiste*   (novel)   1890
  [*An Artist's Honor,* 1890]
*Théâtre complet*   (dramas)   1892-93

\*These four works were translated and published together as *Led Astray, La petite Comtesse, The Sphinx; or, Julia de Trécoeur, and Bellah* in 1873.

## CRITICISM

### Michel Levy   (essay date 1859)

[*Levy discusses the stage adaptations of two of Feuillet's works,* Le Jeune Homme Pauvre *and* Dalila, *finding both deficient in literary merit.*]

*Le Roman d'un Jeune Homme Pauvre* was first a tale in the *Revue des Deux Mondes,* which was thought well of, as being of a more moral and respectable nature than is common with French novels. Transported from the library to the stage, it has found the basis of its success entirely in the circumstance we point out. It is to the fact of French citizens being able to take their daughters, sisters, and nieces to the Vaudeville to see this new piece, that its popularity is due. There is in it a very moderate degree of talent of any kind; it has no originality whatever, and the language is of absolutely third or fourth rate quality, as to style; yet *Le Jeune Homme Pauvre* is an immense success, —a success, it must be avowed, confined exclusively to the secondary class of society, and ignored by those who lay claim to the slightest taste or discernment in literature, but which deserves emphatic notice because it characterizes certain tendencies and aptitudes of the *Bourgeoisie* in France.

From the moment M. Octave Feuillet appeared, the *Bourgeoisie* adopted him. His last two productions, *Dalila* and the *Jeune Homme Pauvre,* are as to their subjects as dissimilar as any two works by the same writer can well be; but the treatment of the subjects shows the identity of authorship, for they are treated by the same methods, and with the same want of truth and strength.

*Dalila* is the old story of an artist who is seduced and morally "made away with" by a great lady fifteen years or so older than himself, who by his desertion caused the death of a young girl to whom he is affianced. André Roswein, the presupposed "genius," is a young composer, whose first opera places him on the pinnacle of fame, and who is then and there immediately devoured by a certain Princess Leonora Falconière, the original type of which personage is now, in real flesh and blood presence, roaming through the world, from east to west, and from north to south. To begin at the beginning, the first fault of *Dalila* is its title. Dalila exists only when you presuppose Samson. One of the wittiest of Parisian critics, on the first representation of the piece, after asking where the hero is to be found, added, "I only see the jawbone of the ass, but not the hand that holds it, —*où est Samson?*" It is really too vulgar a mistake to be for ever prating about these "geniuses" who are destroyed by an unworthy love. If M. Feuillet were upon another level, intellectually speaking, he would know that they never existed. The so-called "artist" who is thus absorbed is no artist at all; he is a mere amateur, and we may be extremely sorry for the unhappy young man; but in losing him, the public loses nothing. There is, as far as *genius* goes, nothing in him to regret.

*Dalila* is altogether a mistake. It is the attempt at vice of a quiet, decorous, commonplace writer, who is desirous to see how he shall succeed in a line which is so profitable to many of his colleagues. It makes one think of some timid, consumptive, demure young gentleman, who, from being "mamma's darling" all his life, is suddenly fired with the wish to eclipse all the dandies of the fashionable world, and who plunges recklessly into pleasures and sins which as seen in him never fascinate, and against which his whole nature and aspect perpetually protest. However, the very foolishness of *Dalila* was the cause of its success. Grave fathers of families indulged for an hour or two in a peep at the abominable "great world," as they are pleased to denominate it, where Leonora Falconière is the presiding fairy, and felt at ease with an author who in the end concluded as they themselves would have done, and sent them away happy in the persuasion that beings so thoroughly of their own calibre in every respect as the hero might be ranked as "geniuses," and wept over as fallen stars.

*Le Jeune Homme Pauvre* aims, on the contrary, at being moral in the extreme, and is not in reality a whit more so than *Dalila,* because there is in it no more truth than in the latter. All the personages are little and false in the extreme, and, with vast pretence at sentimentality and romance, there is not among them all a heart that really beats, and not a drop of living blood in all their veins. The Marquis de Champcey is a ruined nobleman, —a sort of would-be Sir Charles Grandison, morally speaking, —but about as far from his model as a copy of the Transfiguration by a boarding-school young lady would be from Raphael's own immortal picture. M. de Champcey turns bailiff, or *intendant,* to a family of rich French Creoles, who are all of the feminine gender, the only man among them being a bed-ridden, paralytic grandfather, whose death forms a great feature in the drama. M. Laroque had, in his early days, exercised the respectable profession of a corsair, and in that capacity had been guilty of depriving the father of Maxime de Champcey of the greater portion of all he possessed. Hence the difficulties of the Champcey family. All this is found out on the death of old Laroque, whose will is placed by the ladies of the house in Maxime's hands. The said Maxime, on reading the papers before him, finds himself the legal possessor of the fortune of the Laroques, and burns the paper in which the repentant corsair has set this formula forth. He does this because he is in love with Marguerite Laroque, and will not disturb her peace of mind by proving to her that her father was a thief; but Maxime chooses to forget, in thus doing, that he is throwing away, as he has no right to do, the future subsistence of his young sister, for whose sake alone he has resigned himself to the acceptance of a subordinate, if not actually a menial position. Of course the whole ends by the union of Maxime and Marguerite; and a more mawkish and absurd courtship than that of these two most unreal individuals, it is barely possible to imagine. They attain to the singular combination of being wishy-washy and exaggerated at once. They whine and rant at the same time. *Le Jeune Homme Pauvre,* however, presents just that quantity of romanticism which the French *Bourgeoisie* is capable of absorbing, and it flocks even from the provinces to come and "assist" at a representation of M. Feuillet's piece.

*Michel Levy, in a review of "Dalila, et Le Roman d'un Jeune Homme Pauvre," in* The North American Review, *Vol. LXXXIX, No. CLXXXIV, July, 1859, pp. 225-28.*

## Henry James   (essay date 1868)

[*As a novelist, James is valued for his psychological acuity and complex sense of artistic form. Throughout his career, he also wrote literary criticism, in which he developed his artistic ideals and applied them to the works of others. Among the numerous dictums he formed to clarify the nature of fiction was his definition of the novel as "a direct impression of life." The quality of this impression—the degree of moral and intellectual development—and the author's ability to communicate this impression in an effective and artistic manner were the two principal criteria by which James estimated the worth of a literary work. In the following essay originally published in* The Nation *in 1868, James reviews Feuillet's* M. de Camors, *praising some of the novel's characterizations and elegant, concise style, but concluding that it is, on the whole, superficial.*]

[*Camors; or, Life under the New Empire,* the] latest novel of M. Octave Feuillet is already a year old, but we take occasion, from the recent appearance of an American translation of the work, to offer a few English comments. Let us say, to begin with, that the translation is perfectly bad; that it is equally pretentious, vulgar, and incorrect; and that we recommend no reader who has the smallest acquaintance with the French tongue to resort to it either for

entertainment or for edification. M. Octave Feuillet has been known in France for the past fifteen years as a superior writer of light works—tales, proverbs, and comedies. Those of his plays which have been acted are among the most successful of the modern French theatre, and on perusal, indeed, they exhibit a rare union of strength and elegance. A couple of years ago M. Feuillet was admitted—on the plea, we fancy, rather of his elegance than of his strength—to the French Academy. He has apparently wished to justify his election by the production of a masterpiece. In *M. de Camors* he has contributed another novel to the superior literature of his country.

One of the most interesting things about M. Feuillet's career, to our mind, is his steady improvement, or, rather, his growth, his progression. His early works treat almost wholly of fine ladies, and seem as if they were meant to be read by fine ladies—to be half-languidly perused in the depths of a satin arm-chair, between a Sèvres coffee-cup and the last number of *Le Follet,* with the corner of a velvet prayer-book peeping out beneath it. M. Feuillet has a natural delight in elegance—elegance even of the most artifical kind—and this *M. de Camors,* the ripest fruit of his genius, with all its nervous strength and energy, is one of the most highly elegant novels we have ever read. But whereas, in his first literary essays, elegance was ever the presiding spirit, she is now relegated to the second rank, and gazes serenely over the shoulders of force. M. Feuillet has gradually enlarged his foundations and introduced into his scheme of society a number of those natural factors which we find in real life to play as large a part as the artificial and conventional. Not that he has not retained, however, all his primitive arts and graces; only, they have lost their excessive perfume, and are reduced to comparative insignificance by being worn abroad in the open air of the world. The long play of *Rédemption* was much better than his short ones; *Dalila* was better still; and *Montjoie* and *M. de Camors* arc bcst of all. Nevertheless, we confess that there is not one of M. Feuillet's comedies and proverbs—"scenes," as he calls them—that we have not read with extreme delight and that we are not willing to read again. It must have been from the first an earnest of future power for the close observer that the author, in spite of the light and unsubstantial character of his materials and the superficial action of his mind, should yet be so excellent a master of dramatic form; but for this excellence—a thoroughly masculine quality—there might have been some truth in the charge that M. Feuillet was a feminine writer. But women assuredly have no turn for writing plays. A play is action, movement, decision; the female mind is contemplation, repose, suspense. In *M. de Camors* the author has simply redeemed the promise, liberally interpreted, of the strong dramatic instincts of *Le Village* and *Alix.*

In this work M. Feuillet has attempted to draw a picture of what he calls "one of the most brilliant Parisian lives of our time." He has endeavored to pull off the veil of brilliancy, and to show us his hero in all the nakedness of his moral penury. He has wished to effect a contrast between that face of a man's destiny which he presents to the world and that far other face which meets the eyes of his own soul. He has contrived for this purpose a narrative so dramatic and interesting that we shall briefly repeat its main outline. M. de Camors is the only son of the Count de Camors, who on the threshold of old age finds himself utterly disenchanted with the world. Feeling that he has come to the end of all things, and that his soul is equally indifferent to pleasure and to profit, he indites a long, didactic letter to his son and blows out his brains. This letter—an extremely clever performance—is the profession of faith of an aristocratic cynic. It declares that there are no such things as virtue and vice, and that the sole rule of life is the pursuit of agreeable physical sensations and the maintenance of a perfect equanimity. To be absolutely and consistently selfish is to come as near as possible to being happy. Wealth is essential to comfort and women are useful for pleasure. Children are an unmitigated nuisance—which, by the way, is not very civil to the count presumptive. "To be loved by women," writes the count, "to be feared by men, to be as impassible as a god before the tears of the former and the blood of the latter, to end your life in a tempest—this is the destiny which I have failed to grasp and which I bequeath to you." To cast off all natural ties, instincts, affections, sympathies, as so many shackles on his liberty; to marry only for valid reasons of interest and on no account to have children or friends, to perfect his fencing, to keep his temper, never to cry, and to laugh a little—these are the final injunctions of M. de Camors to his son. They are in many ways cold and pedantic, but they are conceived and expressed with great ingenuity. The young Count de Camors receives his father's bequest as a sacred deposit, and the story relates his attempts to apply practically these select principles. While his father has been occupied in drawing up his last will, he has been engaged in an act of supreme *rouerie* in the house of an intimate friend. So happy a start in the career of egotism is not to be thrown away, and M. de Camors says amen to the voice from beyond the grave. He forthwith prepares to enter political life, and, betaking himself with this view to a small estate in the country, presents himself as candidate for the Chamber of Deputies. In this region he meets two women—the heroines of the tale. The younger, his cousin, a poor girl in a servile position, and a great beauty, appeals to the reader's interest from the first by offering her hand in marriage to M. de Camors—an overture which he feels compelled to arrest. The young lady subsequently makes a splendid match with an old general of immense wealth. The second of M. de Camors's female friends is Mme. de Tècle, a young widow, a charming woman and an admirably-finished portrait. M. de Camors wins the love of Mme. de Tècle and returns it, but is unable, for good reasons, to obtain her hand, which he is not yet sufficient master of his emotions to abstain from soliciting. Mme. de Tècle, to whom virtue is comparatively easy, determines to stifle her passion, or at least to keep it smouldering, by means of a very odd and ingenious device. She offers to bring up her little daughter as the wife of M. de Camors, who in eight years' time, when the girl has arrived at maturity, will have reached the marrying age of a man of his society. This idea and the scene in which Mme. de Tècle unfolds it are, as we say, ingenious; delicate also, and almost poetical; but strike us as unreal, unnatural, and morbid. M. de Camors is by no means enchanted by his friend's proposi-

tion; he assents coldly and vaguely and takes his departure, thanking his stars, after all, that Mme. de Tècle had the wit to refuse him.

He becomes engaged in political life and lays the foundation of a large fortune by industrial manoeuvres. He works hard, keeps his terms with elegant dissipation, and cherishes the cold precepts of his father. After a lapse of three or four years he renews his relations with his beautiful cousin, now Mme. de Campvallar, but in so depraved (although so dramatic) a fashion that we need not enter into particulars. Mme. de Campvallar is by nature, and with a splendid feminine insolence and grace, just such an audacious and heartless soul as M. de Camors has well-nigh become by culture. The two unite their sympathies, their passions, and their lives. Finally, however, their intrigue is on the point of being discovered by the husband of Mme. de Campvallar—a *naif* and honest old warrior, the soul of purity and honor, who esteems with an almost equal warmth his wife and his wife's lover—and an exposure is averted only by the tact and presence of mind of the impenitent marquise. Her husband is concealed and listening: Camors is expected. A motive for their meeting must be improvised within the minute, and a full intelligence of the situation flashed from her eyes into those of her lover. The latter arrives radiant. The pretext is ready. Mme. de Campvallar has sworn that she will not let M. de Camors depart until he has promised to marry— whom? —Mlle. de Tècle. In this way the prayers of Mme. de Tècle are fulfilled, and a third heroine is introduced—a third, and the most charming of all. The scene just indicated is in a dramatic sense, we may add, extremely effective; and if M. Feuillet ever converts his novel into a play (as it is the fashion to do in France), here is a situation made to his hand, strong enough, by itself, to ensure the success of the piece, and admirably fitted to exhibit good acting. M. de Camors, then, marries Mlle. de Tècle and loves Mme. de Campvallar. This is well enough for the latter lady; but the other (who has a passionate childish admiration of her rival) speedily discovers the facts of the matter, and signally fails to reconcile herself to them. M. de Campvallar, whose suspicions, once dispelled, have begun once more to congregate, eventually encounters the most damning confirmation of their truth, and expires under the hideous shock. Mme. de Camors and her mother, more and more alienated from the count, and infected with the most painful impressions touching his relations to the death of M. de Campvallar, no longer conceal their open horror of his character. M. de Camors, on his own side, weary of his mistress, writhing under the scorn of his wife, whose merits he has learned to appreciate, sick of the world and of his own life, dies, without remorse and without hope.

The reader may perceive nothing in this sad story, as we have told it, to justify us in deeming it worthy of repetition; but it is certain that, told by M. Feuillet with all the energy of his great talent, it makes a very interesting tale. The author, indeed, has aimed at making it something more—at writing a work with a high moral bearing. In this we think he has signally failed. To stir the reader's moral nature, and to write with truth and eloquence the moral history of superior men and women, demand more freedom and generosity of mind than M. Feuillet seems to us to possess. Like those of most of the best French romancers, his works wear, morally, to American eyes, a decidedly thin and superficial look. Men and women, in our conception, are deeper, more substantial, more self-directing; they have, if not more virtue, at least more conscience; and when conscience comes into the game human history ceases to be a perfectly simple tale. M. Feuillet is not in the smallest degree a moralist, and, as a logical consequence, M. de Camors is a most unreal and unsubstantial character. He is at the best a well appointed fop—what the French call a *poseur.* The lesson of his life is that you cannot really prosper without principles, and that although the strict observance of "honor"—the only principle which M. de Camors recognizes—is a very fine thing in its way, there are sore straits in life from which the only issue is (M. Feuillet would say) through the portals of the Church; or, in other words, that our lives are in our own hands, and that religion is essential to happiness. This is, doubtless, very true; but somehow it is none the truer for M. Feuillet's story. To be happy, M. de Camors apparently needed only to strike a becoming attitude. When M. de Campvallar discovers him in the small hours of the night in his wife's apartment and marches on him furious, he remembers to fold his arms. Another man might have done it instinctively; but we may be sure that M. de Camors did it consciously. And so with Mme. de Campvallar. She is essentially cold, artificial, and mechanical. She is pedantically vicious. For these reasons and many others; from our inability to sympathize either with the delusions or the mortifications of his hero, M. Feuillet's book strikes us simply, as a novel, like any other. Its chief merit, we think, lies in the portraits of Mme. de Tècle and her daughter. Here, too, the author is superficial; but here, at least, he is charming. The virtues—the virtue, we may say, of these two ladies is above all things elegant, but it has a touch of the breadth and depth of nature. The work as a whole is cold and light; but it is neither vulgar nor trivial, and would amply repay perusal if only as a model of neat, compact, and elaborate dramatic writing.

*Henry James, "Octave Feuillet's 'Camors',"* in his Literary Reviews and Essays: On American, English, and French Literature, *edited by Albert Mordell, Vista House Publishers, 1957, pp. 172-78.*

### Every Saturday (essay date 1874)

[*Below, the anonymous critic surveys Feuillet's career, noting the author's ability to adapt his style to the prevailing taste of his readers.*]

To hear any one continually called the Virtuous may not only bore the public, it may end by becoming tiresome to the object of the monotonous praise. He fancies himself called upon to prove that, if he is correct, it is not for want of passions or of opportunities to be wicked; and he feels it to be due to himself to plunge into excesses for which perhaps he has very little taste. The literary career of M. Feuillet is a remarkable example of the dangers of possessing too good a character. It is probable that people who have been disappointed in *Le Sphinx,* and who do not find *M. de Camors* peculiarly edifying reading, have wondered

how M. Feuillet acquired his reputation for harmlessness. He used to be called "Le Musset des familles," and the qualification seems to promise an innocent gayety and respectable passions, which are not prominent in *Julia de Trécoeur* and *Le Sphinx.* The fact is that some years have passed since M. Feuillet deserted the pious early manner which made his books so admirably suited to adorn the drawing-room table. Yet even in his latest works we may note remains, and what are called survivals, of an early condition of stage innocence and didactic utterances. It may be worth while to trace the steps of a progress in which art has perhaps improved at the expense of morality.

The earlier successes of M. Feuillet were the deserved result of a keen eye for opportunities, and a readiness in seizing them. The Parisian public, naturally fickle, and corrupted perhaps by the constitutional monarchy of the period, was beginning to weary of the passions in tatters of the Romantic school. . . . People had ceased to be shocked at the license of the stage, but they had also ceased to care for the fevers and passions of De Musset, and had begun to suspect that something might be said on the side of common morality. This was the moment which M. Feuillet adroitly seized. He saw that he might be "all for virtue, and that sort of thing," like De Quincey's homicidal amateur, and yet be sentimental and suggestive. A wife might reclaim an erring husband, or a husband win back a wife on the point of error, by artifices which the audience appreciated, and which had the new merit of being on the side of honesty and of the family. Vice was made to hoist, in the usually quoted way, "with its own petard." Such pieces as *La Clé d'Or, La Crise, Le Cheveu Blanc,* were the successful working out of this idea. They contained all the coquetry and all the ardor of De Musset; and, after all, no one was hurt, husband and wife were made happy and the children were embraced on every side, as in the play of the *Rovers.* But there was another trait or trick of De Musset's which M. Feuillet also adapted to family use. This was the introduction of interesting sceptics, who were only too anxious to be able to believe. De Musset used to leave them in their sins; but M. Feuillet did better—he reclaimed them. To be sure, their conversion was usually the result of some happy accident which did not appear very germane to the matter of their theological difficulties. Thus the heroine of *Redemption* is an actress whose life is passed in dishevelled orgies—always good scenes on the stage—and in argument with a pious abbé. But she is brought back to the fold, not by the abbé, but by falling in love. Still, in one way or other religion and morality were reconstructed, and this was pleasing to the best sort of society.

M. Feuillet did not confine his method and his theology to the stage. Besides writing comedies and *proverbes,* he became known as the author of safe novels. Society pronounced that, unlike the tales of Feydeau and Houssaye, M. Feuillet's were romances which you could read, which you could put into the hands of young people. This was the happy result of his good sense in always making his heroes Bretons of high birth and Catholics, or with the makings of good Catholics. He chose his scenes from the life of country houses, and of excellent families who shunned the dangerous air of Paris. Persons of no birth were only introduced to be sneered at, and infidel men of science encountered painful shapes of social nemeses. Thus M. Feuillet won a large and aristocratic public, and smoothed his way to a chair among the Forty. His style was always impeccable and lively, the action of his pieces animated, his situations ingenious, his sentiments correct. And so he won the sweet voices of all the better sort of literary ladies. To be sure, some people may have thought him almost too didactic in those early days. The history of *Sybille,* for instance, begins very much in the manner of Miss Edgeworth. Sybille is an orphan, living with her grandparents, members as usual of one of the first families in Normandy. Even in her cradle Sybille is all soul. She cries for a star, and refuses to be comforted when she is prevented from riding round the lake on the back of a swan. But these early faults of character are corrected and Sybille grows up one of those angel-children, with a passion for doing good to their elders, who are frequent in fiction, and not unknown in real life. She does good to the abbé, to the village idiot, to her grandmother in Paris; she converts her governess, and wherever she goes, moral resolutions blossom in the dust of weary hearts as they do when "Pippa passes." Even Sybille, however, had once her religious doubts, and was the female Musset of the nursery. But she is reconciled to the faith by observing the courage of the abbé in a shipwreck, and after her return she becomes a little intolerant. She refuses to marry her lover because he is an unbeliever, though an unbroken series of successes might have shown her that she could convert any one. This lover, by the way, has all the women in the book sighing for him and is obliged to make a tour to Persia to cure his cousin of her hopeless affection. On his return he finds that the cousin still loves him, and as a man cannot always be in Persia, the position is becoming dangerous, when Sybille as usual rescues and reclaims the lady. But she can think of no way to bring conviction to her lover, except to die, which she does at the age of nineteen. With all her virtue there is an air of Blanche Amory and a certain staginess about Sybille; but it was a very popular staginess. Women, as Sainte-Beuve said, felt that there was a Sybille in their characters, and that in the proper circumstances they could have been all that she was. So the book was a success, though strictly speaking it was more a fantasy than a novel, and it increased M. Feuillet's deserved reputation for pleasant writing and correct opinions.

An even less equivocal success was *Le Jeune Homme Pauvre.* This was the most popular novel of its year and the shop of the bookseller who published it was besieged by carriages. The *jeune homme* of the tale finds himself ruined at the death of his father, and he has the fortitude to refuse his name to a promoter of companies, and his hand to a rich young lady whom he does not love. The faithful solicitor of his house gets him a situation as steward to a wealthy family in Brittany, and he solaces himself by keeping a voluminous journal of his experiences. If we can imagine one of Scott's most respectable young men born in the middle of our century, and relating how he was a good rider, a skilled artist, modest, brave, honest, how he leaped down from a lofty window out of regard for a lady's character, and how he was rewarded by marrying her, we

have a fair idea of this novel. The Breton scenery is prettily described, and the romantic leap from the tower of Elven made the fortune of the play founded on the story.

Soon after the publication of *Le Jeune Homme,* M. Feuillet woke one morning to find himself prematurely famous. M. Sainte-Beuve had consecrated to him one of the "Causeries de Lundi." The great critic advised his young friend to desert his religious little girls and meritorious young men, and "to plunge into the vast ocean of human nature." Now M. Feuillet had already shown, in the play called *Dalila,* that he could deal with fiery passions if he liked. There is a fisherman in one of his novels who, when he is prevented from risking his life at a shipwreck, complains that people will hold him no higher than an Englishman. M. Feuillet was perhaps afraid, that he also would become like one of those English novelists whom M. Taine sneers at (rather groundlessly) for their unceasing decency. So he took his critic's advice, plunged into the hidden depths of human nature, and brought up that very curious pearl, *M. de Camors.* Now *Camors* is a novel which we cannot imagine an English author writing. M. Feuillet is forever free from that reproach, and, like Richardson after Lovelace, no one can doubt that he can describe a consummate scoundrel. There is no modern romance which drags so wicked a hero through scenes so terrible and harrowing. Louis de Camors was a young man of good family and of good impulses. He had gone no further than ruining the happiness of his oldest friend, when his father shot himself, leaving some written advice and very little else to his son. In this curious document M. de Camors *père* advised his son to have no code but that of honor, to despise all men, and to reserve the "bloody sport of revolution" to cheer the satiety of old age. The rest of the story displays M. de Camors energetically carrying out his father's programme. He passes from sin to sin, and accumulates horror on horror's head. His last achievement is to desert his own wife for Madame de Campvallon, the wife of his greatest benefactor. This lady did not care for mere frivolous pursuits, and disdained any passion that was not grandly criminal and in the style of the sixteenth century. The sympathetic reader is desolated on finding that M. de Camors refuses to gratify her by poisoning his wife. This want of thoroughness in his character gains upon him, and he dies at last crushed by the misery of having lost even his honor. And here M. Feuillet is on his old and favorite didactic ground, "Ou un Dieu ou pas de principes," he says. This is the reiterated moral, and by this device M. Feuillet conciliates his old audience and the readers who, before he wrote *Camors,* inclined to think him dreary. His friends, also, the good people, found their natural enemies satirized. Every one could point to the wives of rich men of no rank, like Madame Bacquière and Madame Van Cuyp: "Elles jugèrent délicieux de prendre les chapeaux de leurs maris, de mettre leurs pieds dedans, et de courir en cet équipage un petit *steeple-chase* d'un bout du salon a l'autre." This sort of thing taught new people their place, and showed them what the world thought of them.

To compose a novel of modern life more terrible than *M. de Camors* seemed difficult. But M. Feuillet performed the feat, and surpassed himself, in *Julia de Trécoeur.* This story need not be analyzed. There are passions "heterocli-tal," as Sir Thomas Browne says, which are the "veniable part of things lost." We can endure them in the gravity of the Greek stage, or amid the remote fancy of the Elizabe-than drama. But they become offensive when introduced among modern surroundings, and in the environments of familiar life. In *Julia de Trécoeur* M. Feuillet has permit-ted himself the choice of such a motive. That he has pro-duced a terrible story is true enough, but when tragedy so deep is brought so near, it runs the risk of becoming in-credible and merely absurd. One scene is quite in the Eliz-abethan manner. The heroine, balanced between madness and crime, plucks wild flowers, and utters foolish tender speeches to them: "Toi, ma chère, trop maigre! toi, gentil-le, mais trop courte! toi, tu sens mauvais! —toi, tu as l'air bête!" It is like Cornelia's raving in Webster's *Vittoria Cor-rombona:* —

> You're very welcome;
> There's rosemary for you, and rue for you,
> Heart's-ease for you—I pray make much of it,
> I have left none for myself.

Clearly in *Julia de Trécoeur* we have left a long way be-hind us the domestic sentiment of *La Crise,* the elevation of *Sybille,* the complacent propriety of *Le Jeune Homme Pauvre.* M. Feuillet has advanced with the age, and has always met the demand of the day. He is a proof that it is much better for a writer to start with getting a good character, and sow his literary wild oats after his admis-sion to the Academy, than to begin with extravagant ro-mances, as M. Gautier did, and subside into innocent sto-ries like *Spirite.* Possibly if M. Feuillet had begun with *Julia de Trécoeur,* theAcademy might never have lent its sanction to his moral teaching. For even *Julia de Trécoeur* has a moral—namely, that it is a mistake to spoil children. Perhaps this original truth might have been inculcated without the use of such an awful example as Julia's. M. Feuillet must think the moral maladies of his country very terrible when he applies remedies of such peculiar and poi-sonous strength.

*"Octave Feuillet," in* Every Saturday, *Vol. 1, No. 26, June 27, 1874, pp. 710-12.*

## Albert Rhodes   (essay date 1875)

[*In the following excerpt, Rhodes explores several of Feuil-let's works, asserting that, as both novelist and playwright, "Feuillet is one of the most complete authors of his time."*]

[Feuillet] is at the same time hardy and delicate, strong and fine. As an author he has gone through several phases, the transformations of art, indicated more especially from the *Cheveu Blanc,* through *Dalila, Sibylle, Montjoie, Monsieur de Camors, Acrobate,* to the *Sphinx,* or *Julie de Trèvecoeur,* containing subtile as well as powerful cre-ations. He has shown in these feminine delicacy of every shade, an impressibility to the slightest breeze and sound, passing from the dilettante sentiment to that of intensity and passion; later on, to that of energy and force. In his violent scenes he has possessed himself, striking the right cord at the right time, never falling into errors of taste, and never ranting. By preference he uses the simplest means;

a small group, one scene, and a plain story generally suf-fice; imaginative passion does the rest. In the moving story of *Julie de Trèvecoeur,* a few persons—three in the fore-ground and two behind—in a narrow circle, set going the strongest passions, bring on a terrible climax where virtue succumbs and the liveliest sympathies are aroused for the victim, and this in one or two scenes with a few well-marked characteristics. Here, as in other of his plays, the scene opens in tranquillity, and ends in the agitation which belongs to dramatic work; the working up of these peace-ful beginnings to stormy endings shows a thorough knowl-edge of the system of contrast, without which artistic work cannot be produced.

The influence of the intellectual age in which Feuillet ap-peared may be traced in his writings. When his intelli-gence was developing into productive maturity, French society was becoming calm after the noisy years following the revolution of 1830; it abandoned itself after the storm to an indolence full of security and repose. The Romantic literature, after a hard struggle, was defeated and nearly dead; yet young people were full of its souvenirs, and the old who were still faithful to it averred that it would again live and exercise the influence which it once did. The *Her-nani* of Victor Hugo had served as one of the most fruitful causes of literary war. The echoes of the passions evoked in the novels of George Sand and the poems of Alfred de Musset were vibrating in the air. The contemporaries who had taken a part in the intellectual struggle were full of its recollections, but were no longer aggressive, a score of years after it had taken place. They who entered upon life at this time were like those who came at the close of a ban-quet; the lights were still burning, the débris of the table was there, but the guests had departed, although the echo of their songs still hung in the halls. It is probable that Feuillet felt this way, as it is indicated in his work. His early impressions are ineffaceable, but time and new influ-ences have toned them down. It is plain that he has been affected like a poet by the passion of the Romantic school, as shown in *Le Fruit Defendu* and *Alix,* which are among his first productions; the liveliest remembrance that it has left in his mind is a respect for everything which touches art; it taught him, too, a love for elegance, originality, and a disdain for the common and the vulgar. Sometimes this search after the form leads him away from simplicity; the horror of the commonplace inclines him to the artificial. Hence we find Jacques, Jean, or Pierre, the domestics, speaking a language not often heard from people in their condition. The words of one of his heroes might be applied to the author: "I have thrown myself into this extreme to avoid the natural of to-day, which appears to me trivial to the last degree; the horror of bad taste, perhaps, drives me into affectation."

M. Feuillet has a passion for the romantic—in its univer-sal sense—which probably also came to him from the early literary influences referred to. It is seen in his distaste for the real and his strong tendencies for the imaginative, in almost all that he has done. When reality appears, it is under cover of the imaginative, and is sometimes lost sight of; in his work there is a contradiction between the choice of subject and the manner of its treatment, for one is gen-erally taken from real life, and not developed after facts, but after poetic dreams. He is always occupied with graceful speech and action, and the ugly is hardly ever allowed to appear. But nature is often rude and ungainly, and to prevent it in another form is to be untrue. One can see that the continual trial in him is to merge the true in the enticing.

Among his literary characteristics may be noted a capricious fancy, a love of the niceties of language and of passionate force, accompanied throughout with a lyric murmuring which suggests a melancholy song or an autumn breeze sighing in the trees. This melancholy vein is as much a part of him as it was of Alfred de Musset. He is seldom gay, and never boisterously so, while the sadness always is nearly or remotely present. It is that inheritance which belongs to a poetic nature, the poet paying with sorrow for the divine gift. In our land we have seen such poor debtors in Poe and Hawthorne, who were exquisitely sensitive instruments which felt the jar of joyless life. But this tinge of melancholy does not color the work of Feuillet as darkly as that of the two Americans, for he has other traits which to some extent neutralize it.

He has tried to adapt an imaginative literature to the calm and morality of bourgeois life, to invest practical and honest men and women with the passion of romance. He seems to have an idea of robbing vice and dangerous passion of their seductive traits, and conferring them on people of merit; seems to have felt the power of their attraction, although he has resisted them; for his mind is, at bottom, judicious and moral. This carries him into proximity with such passions as if to enjoy the pleasure of the emotions which they inspire, but with the firm resolution to withstand them. So he often stands on the edge of the valley of poetic corruption, inhaling the perfume of its poisonous flowers and gratifying his sight with their handsome form and color. This we have seen in *La Clé d'Or, Le Cheveu Blanc,* and other of his stories and plays.

The experience of life in most writers colors their views and their work. M. Feuillet has been brought in contact with few hardships and trials, has encountered few barriers to success. His journey from the beginning has lain in pleasant places, away from the noise and struggles of the rugged highway which most of his contemporaries have been compelled to follow to arrive at the position which he enjoys. In the security of a retired life, surrounded with pleasing influences, he has seen but little of the worse side of human nature. Hence he regards humanity with a certain benevolence, is disinclined to believe in the bad man, and attenuates his evil tendencies. Therefore evil has not that power in his stories and plays which it has in real life. Badness is a malady arising from a contracted intelligence, which may be cured; it is not aggressive, is not the primary cause of the calamity which is developed in the plot. This is what he would have us believe; and man in his intentions in only blackened to the point necessary to the catastrophe of the plot, and so long as the intentions do not resolve themselves into deeds, he does not hold him guilty; in short, is disposed to let him off with a sentence as light as he can make it. As one of his contemporaries observed, often at the end, "when the time for punishing comes, his tiger becomes a young cat."

Those who read Alfred de Musset, especially *Lorenzaccio* and the *Caprices de Marianne,* will be reminded of him in some of the work of Feuillet, particularly in the dramatic proverbs and earlier plays. This influence is visible in the general composition, the characters, and even in minor details. As an illustration, one of the strongest points of resemblance is the jest—fantastic and poetic—which we find in the productions of Feuillet referred to. There are others in the passion, the scene, and the dénouement, from which the name often conferred on Feuillet arose—"the Musset de Famille"—which by one of the vagaries of popular speech is sometimes converted into "musée de famille." The title of family museum fits him as well as the other, implying as it does that the younger members of the family, as a rule, may be taken into his collection of literary curiosities without detriment to their morals. In such a name, however, there is among Frenchmen a shade of something not complimentary in the inoffensiveness it indicates, and the smile and shrug with which it is occasionally pronounced probably drove the sensitive author into such rash work as *Monsieur de Camors.*

M. Feuillet became, after two or three years, tired of hearing himself accused of mildness, *couleur de rose,* and weeping sensibility, and he took a brusque and new departure in *Monsieur de Camors.* At the time of its publication there was some gossip to the effect that the Duke de Caderousse and the Duke de Morny served as models for the hero, the author having taken the first half of each of their names; but there is little foundation for this. This plunge from the pastoral and ideal into the melodramatic and realistic, though not equal to most of his other work, had the effect of closing the mouths of those who accused him of not being able to leave the boudoir-conservatory-park sort of literature. *Monsieur Camors* was a short and quick invasion of the field of Ponson de Terrail, conducted of course with more skill than the person named could ever hope to display.

This mood is only sporadic in M. Feuillet, and after this vigorous and somewhat extravagant reply of *Monsieur Camors* to those who thought him too tame and dilettante, he returned to the kind of work which he had previously stamped with his natural characteristics.

It would be unjust to suppose that Feuillet resembles De Musset in all his work, for he has a character of his own when he leaves his first model, of which the traits are distinction and tact, and the absence of that excessiveness and hyperbole which are a part of Alfred de Musset. The idea of Feuillet is generally clear and precise, the conversation in which it is borne being full and subtile, with little or no verbiage. His analysis of sentiments is generally delicate, and never obscure. With his subtilty there is a certain depth, for few authors see their way as clearly as he in the discussion of a social problem. He is especially skilful in the affairs of the heart, is a shrewd observer, and describes clearly what he sees, and this is one of his strongest traits. By contrast, the deduction therefrom appears to be lacking in strength and grasp.

*Dalila* is up to the level of some of De Musset's work which it resembles. It is passionate, imaginative, and transpires in the land of blue skies and orange flowers, in sight of the Mediterranean, in the rays of a constant sun, terraced hillsides, marble ruins imbedded in the purple of Tyre, and crowned with the roses of Paestum; a poem in prose, beginning with light innocent gayety before a vine-clad cottage, and ending with the expiring sigh of a poet on a projecting cliff as derisive laughter and song are borne to his ear from a gala-decked bark bearing away the woman who has abandoned him for another. Here are the graceful and melancholy surroundings which usually attend the calamity in De Musset. The terminating picture of the Dalmatian swan dying on a rock in sight of her who is the cause of the death, and whose untimely gayety hastens it, in its light and shade of contrast, is equal to most of those fatal endings which the French Byron was so fond of painting. It is a dramatic story which few can read without being moved. Its name, *Dalila,* is the French one for the woman who sheared Samson of his locks and his strength; the Biblical traitor did her work with the scissors—Feuillet's with the imagination of a poet. Practical and realistic readers may find the volume indifferent, but to those of poetic feeling it possesses an irresistible charm. As may be seen on reading, it was not written for the stage, but was afterward adapted to it, and found to contain some of the highest forms of dramatic expression.

Before the production of this passionate piece of work, the author had touched rather the fine feelings of dilettante readers, and they hardly thought that he would move out of the poetic subtilties which had until then characterized him. In this rare story he changed, or rather added to, his first manner. The first was to the second as a water-color sketch is to an oil-painting which has received the sanction of official decoration in the Salon. Even his friends were surprised that the hand which had so delicately played on the strings of sublimated love should strike the chords of passion with the force which it did in this drama. In it the poet overcomes the tendency to regard humanity with leniency, and paints wickedness in strong colors; here, in short, he proves himself a master, and to my mind, *Dalila* is the work of his life.

In the *Histoire de Sibylle,* written with a proselyting aim, is given one of the most complete types of the religious novel adapted to the atmosphere of fashionable society. The author takes the woman as she is educated in a French Catholic convent, and makes her the active agent of a mystic propagandism in the drawing room. She by her zeal and religious sentimentality overcomes savants, philosophers, and Christians not within the pale of the Roman Catholic church. A virile antagonist is made to acknowledge defeat before an effeminate, graceful, and pretty conqueror. This is done adroitly, with the subtilty and taste for which the author is known, and many indifferent, indolent, and unreasoning readers—the last being much in the majority—accept the story as a fair statement of the merits of the church of Rome and of the unsoundness of the churches opposed to it. The exaggeration into which he falls, and which is perhaps permitted in the field of fiction, is corrected in another story by George Sand, "Mademoiselle de la Quintinie," where the Protestant side of the question is advocated, one novel being really a reply to the other. There is in the first a mystic love, an odor of the incense of the altar, a divine abnegation, and an angelic

surrounding, which strongly appeal to a poetic nature; in the second there is a call to the understanding and to manhood; one is a cradle for the weak and the discouraged, the other a stimulant to the man and the thinker. As in most books written to introduce an argument, both suffer artistically and fall below other work that their authors did before and since.

The same woman often appears in French drama under a different name. The "Marion Delorme" of Victor Hugo, the "Madame Mortsauf" and "La Torpille" of Balzac, the "Manon Lescaut" of the literary abbé, and the "Marguerite Gautier" of Dumas the younger, are all different portraits of the same person. Octave Feuillet has also made his Madeleine rehabilitated by love, an idea which has fructified into every shade of reproduction, and has been so much dwelt upon as to incline people to believe that it is of no uncommon occurrence. One of the oldest types of the kind in real life was that of "The Pearl," who, behind the footlights of Antioch eighteen hundred years ago, delighted the people with her beauty and her art; who, through the eloquence of a noted preacher and the birth of a new love, abandoned the flowers with which she was nightly barricaded and the admirers behind them, shook the jewels from her fingers and the dust from her feet in this gay city of the East, went to the valley of Jehoshaphat in sackcloth and ashes, and dug a hole in the side of Mount Olivet for a tenement, where she remained

*Drawing of Punch by Bertall, redrawn from a color lithograph by W. Sharp which appeared in 1850.*

repentant to the time of her death, and after a while was canonized as Saint Pelagia—the hole being shown to this day by a voluble and amiable guide, for a consideration.

M. Feuillet's Madeleine is in his play of ***Redemption,*** who hears an eloquent sermon from an abbé in Paris, and who is told by him that she will believe in the word of life when she loves. This prophecy furnishes the pivot on which the piece turns. It is a *scenario* in the lump, which finds many admirers in the French capital. As its author is held up to the young as being of inoffensive morality, it is well to give an idea of this play to show that he is not always so: Maurice is a young man of noble heart and birth, who refuses a large fortune destined for him by an aunt on account of an informality in the will, and which a notary offers to destroy. Maurice even refuses to share it with his cousin, Count Jean, who has surprised the secret of his disinterestedness. It appears Maurice had met Madeleine at the door of a convent; she was veiled, but he had recognized her. He sees her later without being seen at the house of an old Jew alchemist of whom she seeks a quick and sure poison, which she regards as a better resource against the cares of life than the divine consolation promised by the abbé. He finds her again in her room in the theatre, where he goes to rescue his cousin Jean from her dangerous wiles. He gives a portrait of her; she is a type of her dangerous class, resuming in herself seduction and perversity; he sees under this envelope of youth and grace the decrepit brain and petrified heart of an old man of evil life. She is a vampire that will ruin him in soul and body. This Maurice tells to the cousin, Madeleine listening behind a screen. As soon as Maurice retires, she appears, and writes a note. "What are you doing?" asks Count Jean. "I am inviting your cousin to supper." "Can you think of such a thing after hearing him say how he hates you?" "Foolish man, he adores me."

The perspicacity of Madeleine, it appears, is not at fault. The supper takes place; among the guests are four of her lovers, she having promised to make her choice from among them. She expects to confuse with her persiflage Maurice, who arrives late. She recognizes in him the young man of the convent, and the words expire on her lips. The repast over, she draws Jean with a glance into a boudoir, where she questions him closely about his cousin. Impatient at this catechism, where it is not a question of himself, Jean leaves her. Tired of such a life, Madeleine decides upon dying, makes her will, giving all she has to the poor, and names Maurice and the superior of the convent as her trustees. Then she desires to see the young man for the last time. She tries to justify herself before him, and not overcoming his distrust, she pours the poison into a glass of water and swallows it (a similar method is employed in the ***Sphinx***), saying, "It is death that I have swallowed: do you believe me now?" But Maurice answers, "It is not death; it is life; it is salvation; it is love. I believe you, and I love you." During the supper he had replaced the poison with an inoffensive liqueur. Thus Madeleine is saved, loved, and rehabilitated, and the prophecy is accomplished. As Maurice presses her to his arms, he says, "Regret nothing; no wife ever received before the altar greater esteem and love than I consecrate to thee before

heaven." Upon which Madeleine falls on her knees and cries, "I believe in God!"

This dénouement, as may be observed, is hardly new. The mystery of love and divine grace work wonders. The change of heart begins in the midst of an orgie, and is brought to swift conclusion in the arms of a handsome young man. It requires little reflection to teach one that heaven has had a very meagre share in the process, and that if Maurice had been a Mohammedan or a Hottentot in religion, she would have embraced his faith. M. Feuillet is probably as conscious of the weak side of his dénouement as any one else, but given his premises, he could hardly escape from his fatal conclusion; and if such objection were made, he would probably answer, "Put yourself in my place, and please tell me how you would get out of the situation in any other way and satisfy the public."

Dramatic authors generally experience difficulty in inducing a manager to undertake their plays when they are without theatrical prestige, especially in theatres like the Gymnase and the Théâtre Français, the negotiation usually involving an amount of antechamber work which is distasteful to a man of proper spirit. The manager does not believe in undiscovered genius, and to this skepticism he has been brought by a long experience; and almost the only light which guides him in selection is that of already acquired celebrity. He believes so little in it that he does not read the play of an unknown author conscientiously, and often not at all, retaining the play sometimes lest it should—one chance in a hundred—contain some feature of success, and fall into other hands; for when such an extraordinary event does occur, the manager never forgives himself. The fame of a novelist does not suffice to the director of a theatre, for he has too often seen such a one fail on the stage, notwithstanding his cleverness in storywriting. This was the case with M. Feuillet; his established reputation as a novelist did not procure, or rather would not have procured for him anything more than a polite hearing, and he adopted another mode of introduction, which was to have his second and third pieces published in the *Revue des Deux Mondes,* where they were read and praised by the public. This pointed the nose of one of the leading managers in the direction of the author's dwelling, and the positions were reversed: the manager offered terms, and the new playwright considered them.

In the character of both playwright and novelist, Octave Feuillet is one of the most complete authors of his time. There is but one other who possesses the double gift to the same degree of excellence—Alexandre Dumas.

*Albert Rhodes, "Octave Feuillet," in* The Galaxy, *Vol. XX, No. 4, October, 1875, pp. 519-29.*

**Henry James**   (essay date 1876)

[*Here, James offers a brief, laudatory review of* Un Mariage dans la Mode, *citing Feuillet's mastery of the fashionable novel genre.*]

Nothing is more striking in a clever French novel, as a general thing, than its superiority in artistic neatness and shapeliness to a clever English one. When we call an English novel clever, we usually mean that there are good things in it; we do not mean that, as a total, it is a good thing; but when we compliment a French novel, that *is* what we mean. It is the difference between a copious "Irish stew," or any dish of that respectable family, with its savory and nourishing chunks and lumps, and a scientific little *entrée,* compactly defined by the margin of its platter. M. Octave Feuillet serves us up *entrées* of the most symmetrical shape and the most spicy flavor. Putting aside Mme. Sand, it is hard to see who, among the French purveyors of more or less ingenious fiction, is more accomplished than he. There are writers who began with doing better things—Flaubert, Gustave Droz, and Victor Cherbuliez—but they have lately done worse, whereas M. Feuillet never falls below himself. He is the fashionable novelist—a gentleman or lady without a *de* to their name is, to the best of our recollection, not to be found in all his tales. He is perhaps a trifle too elegant and superfine; his imagination turns out its toes, as it were, a trifle too much; but grant him his field—the drawing-room carpet—and he is a real master. *Un Mariage dans le Monde* is the novel of the moment in France. It is of course about the conjugal aberrations of young Madame de Rias. Her husband, as the French say, "avait des torts," and Madame, in consequence, in his absence, gives a rendezvous in her garden at midnight to M. de Pontis. Another gentleman, M. de Kévern, takes a friendly interest in her, and being informed by his sister, her intimate friend, of her projected folly, writes on a sheet of paper the simple words—"you will be very unhappy to-morrow," and sends it off to her. Hereupon he settles down by the fireside to conversation and reading aloud with his sister. The evening advances, the clock strikes eleven, the door opens and admits Mme. de Rias, who flings herself into the sister's arms and asks if she can have a night's lodging. The sister assents with silent tact, and Mme. de Rias then approaches the brother, extends her hand, and utters the eloquent word—"Merci!" M. Feuillet, after a year or two, always converts his novels into plays, and we can imagine the effect of this scene upon the stage, and how the curtain will fall upon Mme. de Rias's "Merci!" amid the plaudits of effervescent French sentiment. It is quite in the taste of a scene which we remember in one of the dramas of Dumas the younger, in which a *jeune fille* has been accused of having parted with that particular attribute in virtue of which she claims this title: greatly to the distress of a gentleman who loves her, and who has been inclined to believe the charge. Sifting the matter, however, he satisfies himself of its falsity, and, delicately to indicate his change of conviction—the young lady is aware that her reputation is on trial—as he is leaving a room at the moment she enters it, he addresses her with a bow and an italicized and commendatory *"Bon soir, Mademoiselle!"* This touch, we believe, had a great sentimental success.

*Henry James, in a review of "Un Mariage dans le Monde," in* The Nation, *New York, Vol. XXII, No. 550, January 13, 1876, p. 34.*

---

**Feuillet on his inspiration:**

Nourrit, the great tenor, who sang the "Huguenots" so beautifully, lost his voice one evening, and was for some days nervously afraid that it might not come back again. Often I have had the same feeling, thinking perhaps my inspiration—which proceeds from I know not where—might fail me. Inspiration, I say, for it is nothing else. Sometimes, when reading, a line will suffice; sometimes the look of a face—often a woman's face will give birth to the nucleus of an idea, which like a nebulous small star does not yet exist. Then it embodies itself, round it the satellites group; and after due preparation the story is ready to be written. *Sybil,* which I wrote years ago, was suggested by a young woman I frequently met, and in whom I fancied a resemblance to my heroine. She has become a distinguished woman in society, and when I told her the origin of my creation, she deigned to say that she was flattered.

Although I sometimes rewrite the same page ten times, I never commence work until the plot is fully conceived and ripened to my satisfaction. The situations and conclusions are clearly outlined in my mind, and even the order of the chapters decided upon. A writer is often tempted to begin too soon. If he yields to the temptation, he soon discovers his mistake. It is a moment of supreme pleasure to the novelist, when everything is in readiness to be written down. What enjoyment he finds in the scraps of conversation he gives to his characters!

*Octave Feuillet in "An Interview with Octave Feuillet," by Le Cocy de Lantreppe,* The Critic, *July 21, 1887.*

---

### Henry James    (essay date 1877)

[*In the following review (originally published in* The Nation *in 1877) of* Les Amours de Philippe, *James congratulates Feuillet on his handling of the plot, while at the same time suggesting that the novel's action and characters are "insubstantial."*]

M. Octave Feuillet's new novel [*Les Amours de Philippe*] reaches an eighth edition within a few weeks of its appearance; and this circumstance, combined with the reputation of the author, may fairly be held to indicate that it is worth reading. M. Feuillet usually lays his hand upon an interesting fable, and his execution is always extremely neat and artistic. His defect is a too obvious desire to be what we call in English a "fashionable" novelist. He relates exclusively the joys and sorrows of the aristocracy; the loves of marquises and countesses alone appear worthy of his attention, and heroes and heroines can hope to make no figure in his pages unless they have an extraordinary number of quarterings. But there are few storytellers of our day who know how to tell their story better than M. Octave Feuillet, though we must add that it may sometimes be a question whether his story was worth telling. This one is about a young man of very ancient lineage, who is predestined by his family to a union with a young girl of a proportionate pedigree. The young girl is his cousin; he is brought up side by side with her, and, knowing that she expects to be his wife, he conceives a violent aversion to her. This rebellious sentiment is so strong that when he comes of age he declares he will never look at her again, and departs for Paris, greatly to the distress of his aristocratic father. In Paris he takes a fancy to turn playwright, and manufactures an heroic drama, with a part especially intended for a brilliant and celebrated young actress with whom he has fallen violently in love. In the portrait of Mary Gerald M. Feuillet has evidently meant to suggest the figure of an actual artist, about whom "legend" has clustered thickly—Mlle. Sarah Bernhardt—but the image is rather vague; it lacks detail, and we should have advised the author either not to go so far or to go further. Philippe, however, goes very far in the company of his young actress. She takes a fancy to his play and to his person, and, staking everything upon his drama, he mortgages his financial future on her behalf. The drama proves a colossal failure, and Mary Gerald ceases to care for a lover who has been hissed.

Philippe has a cruel awakening, but the war of 1870 breaks out in time to distract his attention. He serves in it gallantly, and on the return of peace falls in love with Mme. de Talyas, the wife of an intimate friend. This lady is a fiend incarnate and a monster of corruption, but she has charms which are so highly appreciated by Philippe that he becomes her reluctant but abject slave. Mme. de Talyas is very cleverly described by M. Feuillet, who in the portraiture of diabolical fine ladies has a very skilful touch and a very practised hand. Meanwhile Philippe's cousin and intended, the amiable Jeanne de la Roche-Ermel, is pining away at the château, deeply attached to the young man, and sorrowing over the *spretoe injuria formoe*. Mme. de Talyas has learned from Philippe that his marriage with her has been the dream of both their families, but that he has a positive repugnance to the young girl. The moment comes when she commands him, in these circumstances, to pretend to have reconciled himself to the project, in order to throw dust into the eyes of her husband. He obeys her, and the result of his obedience is that, weary of Mme. de Talyas, and disgusted at the dishonorable part he is playing, both as regards his friend, her husband, and as regards Jeanne, he falls honestly and earnestly in love with Mlle. de la Roche-Ermel. Caught in her own trap, the unscrupulous Mme. de Talyas tries first to stop the marriage, and then to bring about the death of Jeanne. At the moment when she has almost succeeded in the latter attempt Philippe comes on the scene, and seeing his fiancée in a very bad way (her rival, having invited her out to walk, has tried to push her into a lake), demands an explanation. Jeanne looks at Mme. de Talyas for a moment, and then utters one of those magnanimous fibs in which, from Victor Hugo down, French romancers delight. She says that she has by her own awkwardness slipped into the water, and that Madame has tried to save her. Madame, overwhelmed and humiliated by such generosity, retires, leaving the coast clear.

Such are the loves of Philippe, which, if they are not very pretty, are very prettily told. The faults of the tale are a certain disjointedness, the want of connection between the episode of Mary Gerald and that of Mme. de Talyas, and

the very unsubstantial and inestimable—character of the hero. The author tells us that he looked like one of the *mignons* of the court of the Valois king; and he really is hardly less contemptible. But French novelists are always addicted to making their heroes too unscrupulous first and too comfortable afterwards.

*Henry James, "Octave Feuillet's 'Les Amours de Philippe',"* in his Literary Reviews and Essays: On American, English, and French Literature, *edited by Albert Mordell, Vista House Publishers, 1957, pp. 178-80.*

## George Saintsbury  (essay date 1878)

[*Saintsbury has been called the most influential English literary historian and critic of the late nineteenth and early twentieth centuries. His studies of French literature, particularly* A History of the French Novel *(1917-19), have established him as a leading authority on such writers as Guy de Maupassant and Honoré de Balzac. Below, Saintsbury presents an overview of Feuillet's novels, praising his narrative skill but deeming his themes superficial and his characters stereotypical.*]

M. Feuillet is never eccentric, even though there be in these days a greater license of eccentricity allowed to academicians than of old. He is never abnormal or paradoxical; he does not go to the ends of the earth to catch one vagary of passion, and then laboriously elaborate its strangeness. It is not from him that we should expect the grave remark made by another writer, "Heureuse elle-même, elle trouvait naturel de faire les autres heureux," that is to say, the lady referred to was so exceedingly fond of her husband that she could not find it in her heart to be cruel to her lover. M. Feuillet, moreover, appears to be guided by something more than taste and common sense in the selection of his subjects. He proceeds distinctly upon the lines of religion and morality; he deplores the disorders which he relates as sincerely as may be; he endeavours as best he can to point out their remedies; and in his descriptions he very carefully avoids undue complaisance and undue luxuriance of language. Yet in every one of his larger novels, except *Le Roman d'un Jeune Homme Pauvre* and *Bellah,* the principal parts, or some of them, are taken by lovers whose love is unrecognised by law, and the fact of the general prevalence of such love is as much taken for granted as by Balzac himself.

The unpleasant effect which is thus produced is to my fancy much increased by a curious peculiarity of the author. I do not know whether it be a consequence of the orthodoxy upon which M. Feuillet prides himself, but in almost every case his Adams and their Eves observe strictly the traditional relationship. Eve is always the tempter, and generally speaking Adam yields in a half-hearted, remorseful, and (I fear I must say) rather currish manner. This proceeds, not so much from any intellectual conviction uncomplimentary to women, as from a kind of unacknowledged artistic predilection. The particular situation is one that M. Feuillet feels he can treat, and he treats it accordingly. It certainly produces incomparably the finest scenes in his novels, and perhaps the finest of these are those in which the temptation is unsuccessful. I should choose as M. Feuillet's masterpieces the fatal passion of Julia de Trécoeur for her step-father, and the piteous efforts of La Petite Comtesse to soften the savage breast of her learned lover. Next to these comes the scene in which M. de Camors finds his honour too weak to guarantee him against the fascinations of the Marquise de Campvallon. Varying illustrations of the same theme occur in the *Histoire de Sibylle,* where Madame Estrény and Clotilde fight for the hero; and in *Les Amours de Philippe,* where the part is played twice, once in the vicious sense by Madame de Talyas and once in the virtuous by Jeanne. Even Marguerite, in the *Roman d'un Jeune Homme Pauvre,* wayward as she is, unmistakably makes the first advances. Only *Un Mariage dans le Monde* is without this motive. But *Un Mariage dans le Monde,* like all the rest, exhibits M. Feuillet's general theory of what may be called the caducity of the feminine sex. His heroines demand in one way or other to fall, or at least to be fallen in love with. The author would apparently recommend that this weakness should be met by a sort of series of fallings in love on the part of the husband—a rather herculean task which it must be admitted has not often been attempted by those to whom it is prescribed. *Un Mariage dans le Monde* does indeed contain an instance. But the possibility of that instance is chiefly owing to the part played by the house-friend, M. de Kévern, and, as the author himself feels bound to remark, "les Kévern sont fort rares." Beyond this M. Feuillet has nothing to recommend except an improvement of feminine education, which he represents as being at a very low ebb in France. . . .

To pass to the more purely literary characteristics of M. Feuillet's work, the first thing which strikes the critical reader is its remarkably dramatic character. Nearly all French novelists have had more or less to do with the drama, and it is not to any peculiarity of M. Feuillet in this respect that I am alluding. But his purely narrative work is often much more distinguished by dramatic than by narrative peculiarities. The incident of the tree-climbing in *M. de Camors* has, I believe, struck several people in this light. So is it with the incident of Clotilde's setting her dog at the madman in *Sibylle,* and of the Jeune Homme Pauvre's solution of the difficulty at the Tower of Elven. These dramatic moments often, though not always, have little importance in the narrative as such; and from this arises a sense not exactly of incongruity, but of incompleteness. Another thing which has struck me strongly in M. Feuillet is that his execution is rarely equal to his design. No novelist introduces a subject better, no one has such a faculty of exciting expectation and engaging attention. Furthermore—and this is perhaps additional proof of his specially dramatic faculty—no one knows so well how to arrange all the accessories of his story. His descriptions are not only models of style, but models also of proportion; his by-play is excellent; his comic interludes (usually supplied by some self-indulgent old lady of the inveterate Parisian type) are capital. No one has hit off more admirably the woman of the Second Empire, whose one ambition was to be *tapageuse* in dress and in conduct, whether the *tapage* be the comparatively refined manner of la Petite Comtesse and Madame de Rias, or the mere boisterous vulgarity of Mesdames Bacquière and Van Cuyp, who run races up and down a drawing-room with their feet in their hus-

bands' hats. But with all this excellence of design and of detail the central interest is often badly preserved. When about two-thirds of the book have been read, a great disposition to yawn is apt to come over one, an incurable desire to count the remaining pages, to look at the end, to resort to any illegitimate means of finishing. The real end of *M. de Camors* is at the cruel death of the general; the real catastrophe of *Sibylle* is the dinner-party where Raoul makes his unfortunate profession of unfaith. *Bellah,* which, despite much charming description, I think quite unworthy of its author, has neither beginning nor end, properly speaking, though the beginning would have been an admirable one for a different book. It is not so with the *Roman d'un Jeune Homme Pauvre* or with *Julia de Trécoeur.* . . . Neither has the attempt at elaborate analysis of character which distinguishes *M. de Camors,* and neither comes quite up to the pathos of *La Petite Comtesse.* . . .

Were it not for the inexpressibly revolting circumstances of the catastrophe, I should call *Julia de Trécoeur* a perfect story. *Tue-la!* is one thing. For a joint society, composed of husband and lover, even though the latter be guiltless, to contemplate "la" while she kills herself, is another. It is true that suicide is the only ending dramatically possible for Julia, but the circumstances of the suicide might have been differently arranged. Again, it is not pleasant to catch a last glimpse of a heroine as she whips and forces an unfortunate horse to accompany her in her search for worlds not realised. These quite surprising blemishes are evidence of an occasional wrongheadedness at critical points which is characteristic of M. Feuillet, and of which I may have to mention some other examples. But with this single exception the story is nearly faultless. The art—difficult to reproduce in excerpts—by which Julia's succumbing to her fatal passion is depicted, is admirable, and not less admirable is that which saves Lucan from the proverbial fate of the man in whose case ladies are willing. He is virtuous without being *niais:* and his total lack of coxcombry gives him a remarkable advantage over the average French novel hero. Most remarkable of all, however, are the perfect proportion and scenic arrangements of the piece. The parts of the minor personages are adjusted to a wonderful nicety, and in no novel known to me are the character and quantity of the descriptions so excellently proportioned. In pathos of a certain kind *Julia de Trécoeur* yields among modern works of the class only to *La Petite Comtesse.*

Strikingly different in plan and in sources of interest is *Le Roman d'un Jeune Homme Pauvre,* to which must, I suppose, if comparative freedom from faults be taken as the characteristic of a masterpiece, be awarded that position among M. Feuillet's works. . . .

M. Feuillet's two latest books—for of *Julia de Trécoeur,* the *Roman d'un Jeune Homme Pauvre,* and *M. de Camors,* enough has been or will be said—are *Un Mariage dans le Monde* and *Les Amours de Philippe. Un Mariage dans le Monde* is a clever and amusing book, again illustrating the author's views on the conjugal state. The husband is vexed because his wife confuses the eighth and eighteenth centuries, the wife because her husband does not like her gaieties. The result is a tacit agreement that each shall go his and her own way. This of course means danger, and the danger is only averted by the devotion of a friend, M. de Kévern, who saves Madame de Rias from herself. The most amusing thing in the book to an English reader is the cause of the indignation with which M. de Rias's excellent mother-in-law regards him. Unfortunately the very difference of manners which makes this amusing, prevents it from being more distinctly alluded to. . . .

I have already noted in *Julia de Trécoeur* a curious instance of what may perhaps be called obliviscence on M. Feuillet's part. There are two other instances of similar false notes in his work, which are even more fatal, because, instead of occurring at the end of the book where the interest is so to speak secured and beyond danger of destruction, they occur in its course. One of these is in *M. de Camors*—the scene, to wit, in which Madame de Técle, rejecting Camors' love, proposes as a compensation that she shall educate her daughter as a wife for him. Here again the preposterous takes a touch of the revolting. The topsiturvification, to use a word which Thackeray invented under the inspiration of this very form of literature, becomes altogether too strong. From that moment the reasonable reader holds Madame de Técle responsible for Camors' future aberrations, and when they arrive he has nothing to say to her but *Tu l'as voulu.* Again in the *Histoire de Sibylle* there is a passage which rings false in a somewhat similar way. The wicked heroine Clotilde has set her cap at the hero, has failed, and to console herself has enchanted—to the utmost limits of enchantment—his scientific and impassible friend Gandrax. But she tires of Gandrax, as she does of most things, and what is the method which she takes to rid herself of this light of science? First of all she caresses her husband in his presence in a very offensive manner, and when he asks for an explanation, she informs him that she has never loved him, that his dictatorial manner is odious to her, and that he had better go. He goes, takes laudanum, and expires, gesticulating and making gruesome remarks, as if he had wished to add one more to the deathbeds of the philosophers. The reader of the scenes ought to be impressed, but he is not. He gathers from them, only the notion that M. Feuillet, unlike the Laureate's Madeline, is far from perfect in love lore. Clotilde is certainly a vulgar vixen, and her husband is an unfortunate person. But the lover has, in nautical phrase, the weather-gauge of both. He is long past the stage of being jealous of the husband, and to the lady herself he can reply that if she did not love him, so much the worse for her. In both these cases the false note is fatal to the interest of the following portions of the book.

There is yet a third charge which I must make against M. Feuillet. Skilful draughtsman as he is in many ways, he rarely—never would be perhaps a truer word—attains to the drawing of a really representative character. In *Julia de Trécoeur* and in *La Petite Comtesse* he is not far from this success, but he does not quite attain it. In his other characters he misses it altogether. It may seem a paradox, but is not so, that the portrayer of a strong individuality always at the same time, whether he knows it or not, creates a type. M. Feuillet never portrays a strong individ-

uality, and therefore he never creates a type. His most elaborate attempt at this is of course *M. de Camors.* Camors is intended to be a sort of Marlborough of private life, a man who utilises and enjoys everybody, who hates and loves nobody, who simply *exploits* the human race. It would not interfere with this conception that he fails in his plan. Failure in such a plan is pretty nearly certain, and the representation of it is moral to boot. But he not only fails, but fails ludicrously, fails so as to make his plan a mere absurdity. He has only to meet a Lescande, a Madame de Técle, a General de Campvallon, and he compromises himself at once after the fashion of a schoolboy. He is worse than the *fanfaron des vices qu'il n'a pas,* he is the *fanfaron des vices qu'il ne peut pas avoir,* a much more contemptible being. Except in his connection with Madame de Campvallon, where, guilty as he is, he is the victim of a greater and nobler viciousness than his own, he is a painful mixture of coxcomb and prig.

It is, in fact, in the choice and conception of his characters that M. Feuillet's weakness consists, just as his strength consists in the choice and conception of the framework and minor incidents of his stories. It is impossible to lay down off-hand the principle that such and such a type of character is unfitted for a hero or a heroine. If the type is rendered sufficiently faithfully and sufficiently forcibly, if it is, in Spinosian phrase, brought *sub specie aeternitatis,* that is sufficient. From this point of view, though Lord Foppington and Lady Booby are certainly not persons of much moral worth or weight, they conquer their place, a place far indeed from Hamlet and Rosalind, but in the same gallery and on the same line. M. Feuillet has contributed no single character of this kind, and the cause is clear; he has not been able to conceive any such contribution. His characters generally have indeed very singular antecedents. Their author is on the one hand strongly impressed by the society, by the prevalent tastes, and by the ordinary views of morality which he sees around him; in the second place he is desirous, and very creditably desirous, of fighting on virtue's side rather than on the side of vice; lastly he has, though fitfully and at intervals, the artistic impulse of working with a view to nothing but the goodness of the work. These motives each operating separately might have each produced something really good. His power of observation, his knowledge of what would interest his readers, his theory of the principles which ought to guide life, and his mastery of the art of writing books, are all good, but each seems to trip up the other. He tries to make his heroines fascinatingly sinful and at the same time improvingly moral. The result is that they do not fascinate and that they do not edify us. The term *honnête femme* is always on his lips when he is describing their temptations. But as one of his French critics remarks with admirable bluntness, "une honnête femme n'a pas de ces tentations." So also is it with his heroes. They stand shivering on the bank, hesitating between the "I dare not" of their honour, and the "I would" of their inclination, until when, as they always do at length, they take the plunge, we have no feeling left for them but rather wearied contempt. M. Feuillet cannot draw a strong immoral character because of his ideas of morality; he cannot draw a strong moral character because of the hankering which he feels after a certain class and kind of interest, maudlin not to say immoral; and he cannot write a book which is interesting merely as a book, because of the pre-occupations which these different motives cause him. Once and once only he has got out of his toils and worked with free hands, and the result is *La Petite Comtesse.* Again in *Julia de Trécoeur* a study of real power is produced. It has been thought by some people that the style of analytic novel-writing is after all not his forte, and that he would have done better to follow out the paths on which he entered in *Bellah* and in *Onestá.* I do not myself see in these books any promise of greater excellence than that which he has elsewhere attained. As a novelist, and it is as a novelist only that I am speaking of him, M. Feuillet seems to me to have had the thus far and no farther set before him very clearly. He has undeniable talent, talent so considerable as frequently to appear greater than it really is, and to excite astonishment that he has done no better, even in those who estimate it correctly. But he is limited. He walks over his dubious and hollow ground with dainty but uncertain step, and declines altogether to pierce to the accepted hells beneath. His vogue, such as it is, appears to be due in part no doubt to real merits of style and workmanship, but still more to his curious sentimental compound of propriety and impropriety, to his faculty of treating dubious subjects in a tone of the strictest virtue, and to his amiable weakness for excusing the sinner, and making him interesting while shaking his head very gravely over the sin. It is consoling, perhaps, to some people to meet with a teacher of undoubted morality who is so thoroughly convinced that offences must needs come, and so well skilled in making the offender amiable. To other people, however, this tone is not agreeable, and they do not find in it an excuse for the shortcomings of these novels considered as works of art.

*George Saintsbury, "Octave Feuillet," in* The Fortnightly Review, *Vol. CXXXIX, July, 1878, pp. 102-18.*

## J. Brander Matthews    (essay date 1881)

[*An American critic, playwright, and novelist, Matthews wrote extensively on world drama and served for a quarter century at Columbia University as professor of dramatic literature, the first such position at any American university. Matthews was also a founding member and president of the National Institute of Arts and Letters. In the following excerpt, Matthews discusses Feuillet's dramas, positing that they are "unhealthy" because Feuillet portrays immoral and unethical characters as virtuous.*]

Among the foremost of the French dealers in forbidden fruit, canned for export and domestic use, is M. Octave Feuillet, whose wares are well known to the public. His novels are the fine flower of the Byzantine literature of the second empire; they have been freely translated and widely read in this country. The *Romance of a Poor Young Man* has the choice distinction of being one of the few French novels harmless enough for perusal in young ladies' boarding-schools. The drama which M. Feuillet made from this novel, and of which a broadened and vulgarized version has been acted in America by Lester Wallack, is equally familiar. Two other of his plays—the *Tentation* (skilfully transmuted by Mr. Boucicault into *Led*

*Astray*) and the *Sphinx*—have been frequently shown to American play-goers. But the novels which have been translated into English, and the plays which have been acted in America are only a part of M. Feuillet's work, and they are not sufficient to give a fair idea of his qualities or his career. . . .

M. Feuillet came forward with comedies modelled on Musset's, but different from these in one important particular: Musset's heroes and heroines were a law unto themselves, —as much as to say that their loves not seldom were lawless. Now, M. Feuillet's pair of lovers had been duly married by the mayor. . . .

To the French public, . . . familiar with the most high-flown and the least lawful passion, M. Feuillet gave a new thing: he offered it the old and ever-welcome exhibition of amorous adventure, dexterously veiled by a pretence of morality. French morality is at times rather humorsome; and in one of its freaks it chose to accept M. Feuillet's pseudo-delicacy and ultra-refinement, and to close its eyes to the falsity of his ethics. The public was tired of the stormy souls in irregular situations, seen in the stories of Hugo, Dumas, George Sand, Merimée, and Musset, and it was ready for a novelty. M. Feuillet took Musset for his model, turning his morality inside out. Musset's morality was easy, to say the least; and M. Feuillet's was pretentiously paraded. His tender and glowing interiors were certified to contain only a duly married couple. Instead of the trio, —husband, wife, and lover, —almost universal in French literature, there was only a duo, in which the husband committed adultery with his own wife. It was an attempt to graft the roses and raptures of vice on the lilies and languors of virtue. By giving conjugal endearments the externals of criminal passion, M. Feuillet managed to lower marriage to the level of vulgar gallantry, and to make the reconciliation of husband and wife as interesting as the chance intrigues of a courtesan. In these boudoir dramas he outraged the sacred secrecy of wedded life; but so clever was his affectation of propriety that many respectable people did not look beneath the surface, and took him at his word. Then there were those who, having preached against the wickedness of the world, could not denounce so ingenious a writer when he declared himself their ally. Again, yet another class was pleased by these new plays, —the pretentious prudes; for there are *précieuses ridicules* now as well as two hundred years ago, though there is no Molière to put them in the pillory. Fairness requires us to admit that perhaps the author was more sincere then than we now judge from a study of his work; and if he believed in himself, why should not others believe in him? Even those who detested him were not always sharp enough to see the underlying immodesty. One of these scoffingly nicknamed him the family Musset, —the "Musset des Familles," —a slanting allusion to an eminently proper periodical publication called the "Musée des Familles." But he failed to blind so keen an observer as Sainte-Beuve, as any one can see who reads the perfidious compliments, scattered through the study of M. Feuillet's work, with which the great critic greeted *Sibylle* (a Roman Catholic *Tendenz-Romanz*), —a "novel with a purpose," written at the request of the devout and frivolous Empress, and published in 1863.

M. Feuillet followed in Musset's footsteps, not only in the form of his new ventures, but also in the mode of putting them before the public. They appeared first in the *Revue des Deux Mondes,* and then in volumes called *Scènes et Comédies* and *Scènes et Proverbes;* and, like Musset again, it was some little time before the plays thus printed and published were brought out at a regular playhouse. Although there is everywhere in M. Feuillet's work an odor of tuberoses, sweet and stifling, a few of these earlier little comedies are not open to the objection I have just urged; and in such unpretentious and simple plays, as pretty as they are petty, M. Feuillet shows at his best. The *Village* is a touching little sketch of country life. The *Fée* is an amusing attempt to import some of the quaint mystery of fairy folk-lore into this matter-of-fact nineteenth century. The *Urne* is a lively reproduction (*pastiche* is the French word) of the comedy of Marivaux and his fellows. M. Feuillet has a distinct sense of the comedy of situation, and is not lacking in Gallic lightness, although his humor has no depth and his wit no edge. In all these little plays he appears to advantage; he can handle two or three characters in the compass of a single act without overstraining his powers. Even the *Cheveu Blanc,* —a fine specimen of his new style of tickling the jaded palate of Parisians by a highly spiced dish, served with an insipid and enveloping moral sauce, —is more tolerable, because shorter, than his later and more ambitious attempts. Elegant trifling, grace, ease, and emptiness, and fine, unsubstantial talk about egotism, selfishness, and honor, —these are the characteristics of the *Scènes et Comédies;* and it is in these that M. Feuillet excels.

The three more important plays of this period of M. Feuillet's career are the *Crise, Dalila,* and *Redemption,* all of which passed through the *Revue des Deux Mondes* on their way to the stage, —the *Crise,* for one, waiting from 1848, when it appeared in the magazine, until 1854 before it got itself acted in the theatre. Seriously considered, *Redemption* is an absurd play, puerile, or at least boyish, in motive and feeble even in construction; for the prologue is useless, and the scenes are disjointed. *Dalila* is better and stronger in itself, and besides it is free from the childish endeavor to grapple with tiny hands at mighty problems which vex men's souls. In *Carnioli,* too, there is a character of force and freshness. Of these three plays, however, the *Crise* is first in interest as it was in point of time. It is the earliest of the dramas in which M. Feuillet posed as the analyst of the feminine character, and as one who had spied out all its secrets and had a balm for all its wounds. The crisis from which the play takes its title is that eventful moment in life when, according to our author, even the most honest and worthy woman, having aforetime led a reputable and humdrum life, all of a sudden has a mad desire to go to the devil headlong: it is an alleged culminating point of the feminine curiosity of knowledge of good and evil. There are plays which criticise themselves: when the story is once told, no comment is called for. The *Crise* is one of these. In the four acts there are but three characters (save a servant or two); and these three characters are the eternal trio of French fiction, —husband, wife, and lover. For ten years the husband and the wife have lived happily together. To his oldest and best friend, who is also the family physician, the husband confides that of late his wife has changed; she could not be in better health physically, but she is now, against her wont, at times restless, or irritable, or sentimental, or what not, as the whim seizes her. The doctor explains that this is the crisis in her life, —the epoch of maturity in woman, —when she longs for a bite of forbidden fruit. The husband asks for a prescription. The doctor explains that the only cure for this strange taste is for the husband to find a devoted friend who will lead the wife to the brink of the abyss, and when she shrinks back in horror she will long no more for the apples on the other side of the chasm. The husband instantly beseeches the doctor to try this experiment on his wife, and the friend reluctantly (but off-hand) consents to pretend to be the lover. Husband and lover then draw up a code, under which the lover is, if possible, to seduce the wife, —pausing before any damage is done, so that the wife may be cured by an awful warning and a narrow escape. Time passes, and the lover makes headway. The husband finds his wife's private journal and brings it to the lover, and the two men read it together to see how the wife feels. In all this playing with fire the lover and the wife kindle a flame in their own hearts. At last a guilty appointment is made. Morally, at least, the sin is committed. Just in time the husband intervenes, and, talking in parables, threatens to deprive the wife of her children should she sin. This restless and sentimental woman, be it known, has two children. So effective are these parables of the husband's that the new love fades out of the wife's heart, and she falls on her husband's neck; and then the curtain falls also, leaving in doubt the fate of the unfortunate lover.

In 1858 M. Feuillet turned his novel, the *Romance of a Poor Young Man,* into a play; and, for sufficiently obvious reasons, it is the most wholesome of his later dramas. The scene is skilfully chosen, the characters are sharply contrasted, and a dextrous use is made of our love for the heroic and self-sacrificing; so we see the play with pleasure in spite of its quick-tempered and disagreeable young woman, its high-toned and hot-headed young man, its preposterous old pirate, and its atmosphere of effeminate sentimentality. Two years later it was followed by the *Tentation,* the first comedy which M. Feuillet had written directly for acting and not for reading; and its simpler and closer structure shows the benefit of the experience gained in transferring its predecessors from the pages of a magazine to the boards of a theatre. There is bright humor and charming comedy in the courtship of the two young people; and although the two old women are somewhat farcical, even they do their share in amusing. But the main intrigue of the play is again husband, wife, and lover; and again the heroine is a lady of passionate aspirations and valetudinarian virtue; and again, when everything tends toward irretrievable mishap, the dramatist intervenes, and gives a sharp twist to plot and people; and after such a wrench the play cannot but end happily.

Any one of M. Feuillet's plays might be called *On the Brink,* and in very few of them is there an actual fall over the precipice. Here the author is lacking in intellectual seriousness; he is always ready to drop logic through a trap in his trick table. "Consequences are unpitying," says George Eliot; but M. Feuillet does not think so. However vicious any character may seem, we may be sure of his death-bed repentance, and that he will die in a state of grace and the odor of sanctity. Next to the uncleanness beneath the surface, this is M. Feuillet's worst defect; and nowhere has it done him more harm than in *Montjoye,* a comedy in five acts, brought out in 1863, three years after the *Tentation.* Taken altogether, this is perhaps M. Feuillet's best play; it is the only one of his serious pieces in which he has not mistaken violence for strength. Montjoye himself is the central figure of the picture, and indeed the only one; for all the others are merely accessory, and devised to set off the protagonist. Montjoye is a man of velvet manner and iron will, —a man who aims at success, who believes that the end justifies the means, and who bends or breaks everything to attain his end. He is a character boldly projected, although not sufficiently justified, and at the finish not self-consistent. He softens into sentiment, and so makes an effect on the audience. In criticising M. Augier, M. Zola praises the final impenitence of Maître Guérin. This final impenitence is just whatMontjoye lacks; in real life such a man would die game.

The fact is, M. Feuillet is no Frankenstein; he never creates any being he cannot control, and he makes all his creatures do his bidding at the peril of their lives. He is rather a magician, who raises good and evil spirits at will; or, to be more exact, he is a writer of fairy tales. The stories he tells are not true, and they could not happen anywhere outside of fairy land. In one of his *Scènes et Comédies* he ventured within the magic circle in a most mysterious little play called the *Fée,* in which a benevolent and sprightly little fairy plays most charming and delightful pranks, —all of them, alas! prosaically explained away before the curtain falls. Once granting that M. Feuillet is a writer of fairy tales, and it is a matter of course to find the *Belle au Bois Dormant;* and it is, perhaps, characteristic that this *Sleeping Beauty in the Wood* should be a drama rather than a comedy. The sleeping beauty is the last of a feudal line, declining into poverty and representing the past. The young prince is the head of a factory, rising in riches and thus representing the future. The beauty has an impractical and reactionary brother, and the prince has a practical and progressive sister; so the play is provided with two pairs of lovers. So far is the fairy tale followed, that, when the young prince gets into the castle, the author puts the beauty to sleep off-hand that the prince may see her so. There is much cleverness in detail as there is ingenuity in the main situation. Here frankly face to face is the conflict of old and new, past and future, irrepressible and irreconcilable; and there is no end to it. Again, M. Feuillet shows his artistic weakness. His young prince is no true man of the nineteenth century, having to do with men and machinery, and master of himself at all events; he is no true man at all. When he cannot get the woman he loves, he breaks down and moons around and weeps saltless tears. . . .

*Julie* rings false. It was a play of a kind radically opposite to that which the author had hitherto produced; and even so ingenious a writer as M. Feuillet cannot change his skin in the twinkling of an eye. In his treatment of woman M. Dumas is severe and logical to the point of brutality. Hitherto M. Feuillet had been petting and illogical to the verge of mushiness, and it was no wonder that the author of *Julie* was greeted as a literary dandy who was affecting the intense. Of a truth, morality is not a garment which an author may don and doff at will: if it be good for anything, his morality is in him, deep down in him, and cannot be torn thence.

Still more violent and forcible-feeble than *Julie* is M. Feuillet's latest play, the *Sphinx,* acted in 1874. It is hard to see in this ill-made and monstrous impossibility any trace of the neat workmanship and charming style of the family Musset. A vulgar and indigested drama like the *Sphinx* forces us to remember that the author of the *Romance of a Poor Young Man,* and of the *Sleeping Beauty in the Wood,* was first of all the author of melodramatic crudities like *Palma, ou la nuit du Vendredi-Saint.*

Such success as the *Sphinx* had was due to external accident. With M. Feuillet's usual ingenuity, he had laid his weakest scene in one of the picturesque sites of which he is fond; and the moonlit marsh of the third act did nearly as much for the *Sphinx* as the ruined tower with its lissome coat of ivy did for the *Romance of a Poor Young Man.* . . .

*Julie* and the *Sphinx,* however, are not really representative of M. Feuillet, save in minor detail; and they are artistically so inferior to his earlier plays that they seem the result of some strange freak. The best group of his dramatic works is that which includes the pieces produced between 1858 and 1865, —the *Romance of a Poor Young Man,* the *Tentation, Montjoye,* and the *Sleeping Beauty.* Although one can scarcely call these comedies strong plays, they are M. Feuillet's strongest, as they are his least offensive. They reveal his amiable talent in the most favorable light. Yet I am not sure whether some of his smaller plays, and in a painter's sense less "important," are not really better bits of work and of better workmanship. He lacks logic to construct your carefully considered edifice in five acts, and he has no breadth of style. In the space of one act he does not exhaust himself or the spectator; and he has ample marge and room enough to show off his grace, his ease, his ingenuity, his charm, and his caressing and effeminate touch. There is something feminine in the author of the *Sleeping Beauty.* Sainte Beuve remarked that M. Feuillet excelled in the women's diaries, of which he is fond, as who should say he had been a woman himself. Sustained effort is not to be expected from a writer of feminine qualities, and this is perhaps why certain of these little comedies are of greater worth than their bigger brothers. A humorous fantasy like the *Fruit Défendu,* in which, too, the humor, though not robust, is not at all what a woman could have written, or a clear-cut intaglio from life like the *Village,* a little masterpiece, —these are worth not only all the *Julies* and *Sphinxes,* but all the *Romances of Poor Young Men* and *Sleeping Beauties.* On the other hand, also, in one act are both the *Cheveu Blanc* and *Le Pour et le Contre,* the most disgusting of all his plays, in spite of their high polish and superficial decorum. To come across the *Village* in the series of M. Feuillet's plays is like a vision of the country rising before you as you stand in the overladen air of a stifling ball-room. The *Village* is one of the author's few incursions into real life. Most of his plays have their scenes laid in a world of his own much pleasanter than this work-a-day world of ours. It is a world where youth, beauty, wit, riches, titles, and idleness abound, and where there is nothing poor, or mean, or painful. Especially is there nothing like self-sacrifice. Everything has a smooth surface and a fine finish. Everybody is happy, or will be before the curtain falls. What though the fair heroine suffer for a while for her fault, —in the end all will come right, as it always does in other fairy tales.

The want of variety in the scene is to be detected also in the actions and characters of M. Feuillet's comedies, long and short. He has his favorite type of man and woman, and they reappear again and again. His men all wear dress-coats of correct cut, and white ties beyond reproach. By preference, they are men of the world, somewhat cynical, girding at society, but incapable of living out of the whirl and rush of passion; they are men

> Who tread with jaded step the weary mill,
> Grind at the wheel, and call it 'Pleasure' still,—
> Gay without mirth, fatigued without employ,
> Slaves to the joyless phantom of a Joy.

This is his favorite hero; and his favorite heroine is like unto him, save that he has greater skill in drawing women. His heroine is listless, excited, nay, feverish at times, sickly in body and soul, moved by a secret and nameless unrest, born of idle luxury. She fancies herself abandoned and lonely. "Solitude," says Balzac, "is a vacuum; and Nature abhors a vacuum in morals as in physics." The wife in the *Crise* is hysteria personified; the heroine of the *Tentation* is no better, and there are a dozen like her. One feels like prescribing cold baths and outdoor exercise for all of them. "Virtue, however solid you may think it, has need of some encouragement and of some little support," says the heroine of *Le Pour et le Contre,* —poor thing! And if her virtue is not propped and stayed, or if there come a thunder-storm, or if any other of a hundred and one accidents happen, the fragile virtue gets a fall, and there is nobody to blame.

In discussing M. Victorien Sardou, the final word is that his work is clever; so, in considering M. Octave Feuillet, the final word is that his works are unhealthy. To my mind, the author of the *Crise,* of the *Cheveu Blanc,* of the *Clef d'Or,* and of *Le Pour et le Contre,* is one of the most dangerous of modern French writers of fiction. His is an insidious immorality, parading itself in the livery of a militant virtue. His is a false art, and false art is pretty surely immoral. Summed up, his teaching is that you can touch pitch and not be defiled so long as you wear ten-button kid gloves; that you can play with fire and drop the torch so soon as the flame begins to scorch your hands; that you may handle edged tools and get off scot free; and that you can rush headlong at the precipice and pull up somehow and safely right on the brink.

*J. Brander Matthews, "The Plays of M. Octave Feuillet," in* The International Review, *Vol. XI, October, 1881, pp. 428-39.*

## The Nation   (essay date 1886)

[*In the following assessment of* La Morte, *the anonymous reviewer writes that in that novel Feuillet demonstrates a greater interest in the intellectual and spiritual issues of his time than in his previous works.*]

The exposition [in Feuillet's *La Morte*] was amusing and original. A young man, of good education, of good family, belonging, as the heroes of Octave Feuillet always do, to the "upper ten thousand," has lost his faith in revealed religion, in the supernatural; and has lost it, he thinks, for ever. He has only preserved the high sentiment of honor, the love of truth, which constitutes the "gentleman." The time comes for him to get married, and naturally he comes in contact with a girl imbued with the highest sentiments of faith, permeated, if I may say so, with religion, a pure spiritualist, a perfect Christian. The gentleman is a Parisian *par excellence;* he is worldly; she is a *provinciale,* who knows nothing of "Satan, his pomps and his works." You see at once the situation. He is perfectly honest and straightforward; he confesses his utter want of religion, his absolute rationalism; he does not affect to feel any sentiments which he does not really feel. The girl's family look upon him with fear and distrust; she also is afraid, but she hopes that love may operate the work of grace. She hesitates a moment, and then she accepts the idea of a union which may become the salvation of the man whom she loves for his frankness, his refined feelings, his culture. She cannot help hoping that marriage will transform him; that the continual spectacle of her own life, inspired and ennobled by an ardent faith, will soften his heart and make him feel the beauty and the power of her own ideal. She takes him to the altar as her lover, and she feels sure that some day or other she will bring him again to the altar as a Christian, and complete the communion of their two lives.

This is undoubtedly a very interesting situation; all the more so that it is not an uncommon one in our country, where the women receive a very religious education, and where the men are often completely imbued, not only with the philosophical ideas of the time of Voltaire, but also with the materialistic views of the Positivist school. Octave Feuillet's novel raises the whole question of the education of woman. In a highly civilized community, ought the women to receive an education based on other principles than those which form the education of men? Are they to be treated quite differently by the legislator, the moralist, and the philosopher? Are they, so to speak, two species in one? What is food for one, can it be poison for the other? . . .

In his first novels Feuillet does not exhibit such [intellectual] preoccupation; he is content to show us fine ladies and fine gentlemen, very romantic in all their notions, much absorbed by the passion of love, and living in a sort of unreal world, a world of convention, of fine language, fine manners, and preëminently fashionable. By degrees we see a higher aim developing itself in his work; his object seems to be to demonstrate how the highest social state cannot but lead to vice and crime, in the absence of a definite faith. In one of his novels, written in this new manner, *M. de Camors,* he clearly tries to prove that the religion of honor is insufficient. The father of M. de Camors traces for his son this programme of life: "To develop in all their extension the physical and intellectual gifts which chance has given to him; to make of himself the accomplished type of a civilized man of his own time; to charm women and to rule over men; to give himself all the pleasures of the mind, of the senses, of power; to subdue all the natural sentiments as the instincts of slavery; to disdain all vulgar beliefs as chimerical or hypocritical; to love nothing, to fear nothing, and respect nothing but honor." M. de Camors enters life with this programme, and whoever has read the novel knows where it leads him.

Octave Feuillet at the time of his first manner was sometimes called the "Musset des familles"—the family Musset. It may be that the slight irony contained in these words was not without influence on him. The novels of the second manner certainly show us very dreadful characters. The atmosphere is always the same—the heroes and heroines are always genteel, but it seems as if next to every angel the novelist felt the necessity of placing a devil. Some of his ladies, though they have not read Darwin and Schopenhauer, are real moral monsters; and it must be confessed that some of the "angels" are very terrestrial. What their faith may be, it is difficult to imagine; if they are to be judged by their works, their religion seems not to be incompatible with laziness, extravagance, and coquetry. It is the religion of a caste; it has gilded prayer-books and goes to the fashionable church. At times Feuillet's ladies and gentlemen make on me the impression of musk or of some other strong perfume; the air in which they move is laden with intellectual and moral incense. There is a certain sort of coarseness in all their gentility, as there is in a number of the *Vie Parisienne*. If this is spiritualism, give me a little materialism. The spiritualism of Octave Feuillet is not of the rarest quality; it is not the spiritualism of a Jansenist, or even of the pious lady of the seventeenth or the eighteenth century: it is superficial; it is the mask of a society which wishes to hide its scepticism, its love of pleasure, its egoism. Still, his novels are valuable documents for the history of our time—just as valuable as the documents of the realistic and naturalist school. They show us something different, but what they show us does exist; and Feuillet has often admirably depicted the weaknesses, the contradictions, the pretentious frivolities of a caste which, having no longer any privileges, has partly lost its sense of responsibility, and which is losing by degrees its influence in every sphere except the sphere of social vanities.

*"A Novel by Octave Feuillet," in* The Nation, *New York, Vol. XLII, No. 1082, March 25, 1886, pp. 256-57.*

### Walter Pater (essay date 1886)

[*A nineteenth-century essayist, novelist, and critic, Pater is regarded as one of the most famous proponents of aestheticism in English literature. Distinguished as the first major English writer to formulate an explicitly aesthetic philosophy of life, he advocated the "love of art for art's sake" as life's greatest offering, a belief which he exemplified in his influential* Studies in the History of the Renaissance *(1873) and elucidated in his novel* Marius the Epicurean *(1885) and other works. In the following excerpt from an essay written in 1886, Pater briefly comments on Feuillet's characterization in* La Morte.]

[In *La Morte*] M. Octave Feuillet adds two charming people to that chosen group of personages in which he loves to trace the development of the more serious elements of character amid the refinements and artifices of modern society, and which make such good company. The proper function of fictitious literature in affording us a refuge into a world slightly better—better conceived, or better finished—than the real one, is effected in most instances less through the imaginary events at which a novelist causes us to assist, than by the imaginary persons to whom he introduces us. The situations of M. Feuillet's novels are indeed of a real and intrinsic importance: —tragic crises, inherent in the general conditions of human nature itself, or which arise necessarily out of the special conditions of modern society. Still, with him, in the actual result, they become subordinate, as it is their tendency to do in real life, to the characters they help to form. Often, his most attentive reader will have forgotten the actual details of his plot; while the soul, tried, enlarged, shaped by it, remains as a well-fixed type in the memory. He may return a second or third time to *Sibylle,* or *Le Journal d'une Femme,* or *Les Amours de Philippe,* and watch, surprised afresh, the clean, dainty, word-sparing literary operation (word-sparing, yet with no loss of real grace or ease) which, sometimes in a few pages, with the perfect logic of a problem of Euclid, complicates and then unravels some moral embarrassment, really worthy of a trained dramatic expert. But the characters themselves, the agents in those difficult, revealing situations, such a reader will recognise as old acquaintances after the first reading, feeling for them as for some gifted and attractive persons he has known in the actual world—Raoul de Chalys, Henri de Lerne, Madame de Técle, Jeanne de la Roche-Ermel, Maurice de Frémeuse, many others; to whom must now be added Bernard and Aliette de Vaudricourt.

"How I love those people!" cries Mademoiselle de Courteheuse, of Madame de Sévigné and some other of her literary favourites in the days of the Grand Monarch. "What good company! What pleasure they took in high things! How much more worthy they were than the people who live now!" —What good company! That is precisely what the admirer of M. Feuillet's books feels as one by one he places them on his book-shelf, to be sought again. . . .

In a few life-like touches M. Feuillet brings out, as if it were indeed a thing of ordinary existence, the simple yet delicate life of a French country-house, the ideal life in an ideal France. . . .

A far-reaching acquaintance with, and reflection upon, the world and its ways, especially the Parisian world, has gone into the apparently slight texture of [*La Morte*]. The accomplished playwright may be recognised in the skilful touches with which M. Feuillet, unrivalled, as his regular readers know, in his power of breathing higher notes into the frivolous prattle of fashionable French life, develops the tragic germ in the elegant, youthful household.

*Walter Pater, "Feuillet's 'La Morte'," in his* Appreciations, *Macmillan and Co., 1890, pp. 228-52.*

## Anatole France   (essay date 1890)

*[France is one of the most conspicuous examples of an author who epitomized every facet of literary greatness to his own time but who lost much of his eminence to the shifting values of posterity. He embodied what are traditionally regarded as the intellectual and artistic virtues of French writing: clarity, control, perceptive judgment of wordly matters, and the Enlightenment virtues of tolerance and justice. His novels gained an intensely devoted following for their lucid appreciation of the pleasures and pains of human existence and for the tenderly ironic vantage from which it was viewed. In the following excerpt from a posthumous tribute to Feuillet originally published in* Le Temps *in 1890, France suggests that the writer's works help the reader to understand the period in which Feuillet lived.]*

During the naturalistic Terror, M. Octave Feuillet was not content to live, like Sieyès; he continued to write. It was thought that we should never see the close of that troubled period. It was believed that the rule of literary demagogy would never come to an end, that the Committee of Public Safety, directed by M. Emile Zola, and the Revolutionary Tribunal presided over by M. Paul Alexis, would operate for ever. On all the monuments of Art we read "Naturalism or Death!" And we thought that this device was eternal. All at once there came the 9th Thermidor, which we had not expected. Great days always arrive unexpectedly. They are not foreshadowed by public excitement. The 9th Thermidor which overthrew the tyranny of M. Zola was the work of the Five. They published their manifesto. And M. Zola fell to the ground, struck down by those who had obeyed him blindly the day before. . . .

In short, the naturalistic Terror is vanquished. Every one is free to write as he wishes, even in a well-bred manner, should he feel so inclined.

M. Octave Feuillet had lived through the tempest unperturbed, apparently without perceiving anything, and now and again even showing a certain consideration for M. Zola. He would readily admit: "None the less, he is very powerful. . . ." He remained the agreeable novelist that he had always been. In reading his latest work [*Honneur d'artiste*], so charming and worthy of praise, I used to admire the peaceful course of his fine talent, which is always uniform, varying as it proceeds only like the bank of a river. But it would be a great mistake to suppose that I wish to revive the quarrels of the schools over M. Octave Feuillet's new novel, and to contrast *Honneur d'artiste* with some work conceived in another frame of mind. It would be a poor way of honouring a talent which seeks to raise us above professional squabbles. M. Octave Feuillet's mind possesses a delicacy, a discretion, and a noble modesty which must find its reward in the admiration which it inspires. And further, I have neither wish nor need to decry anyone for the benefit of a writer who stands out from the rest by his singular purity, his exquisite refinement, and his graceful lucidity. . . .

M. Octave Feuillet has remained what he always was. He has not sold his soul to any devil. In his new novel he shows himself faithful to the exquisite and absolutely French art which he has exercised with pleasing authority for the last thirty years; that art of composition and deduction by which even the mere story-teller derives from Fénelon and Malebranche, and all the great classics who founded our literature on reason and good taste. It has been denied that it was necessary, or even good, to compose thus. In our day some have held that the novel should be lacking in composition and arrangement. In this respect I have heard Flaubert express pitiable ideas with magnificent enthusiasm. He used to say that we ought to cut off slices of life. This does not mean very much. If we think it well over, art consists in arrangement, and of nothing else. The only possible reply is that a good arrangement is not perceptible, that it may be taken for Nature herself. But what Flaubert did not grasp was that we can conceive Nature and things only by the way in which we arrange them. The names which we give to the world, to the cosmos, prove that we represent it to ourselves in its ordering, and that, to our minds, the universe is none other than an arrangement, an order, a composition.

To speak in the academic style of the seventeenth century, we will say that M. Octave Feuillet "has all the qualities of his art," composition, ordering, and a discretion and proportion which permit him to say all things, and make all things understood. He has also audacity, and a vigorous touch. In *Honneur d'artiste* we have found, once more, this penetrating touch, and the rapid strides when the story gathers itself up like a blood horse leaping a hedge. . . .

[When] you have read *Honneur d'artiste,* read once more M. de Maupassant's *Fort comme la mort.* I think you will enjoy comparing the two artists, the two painters, Jacques Fabrice and Olivier Bertin, who both die the victims of a cruel love. The contrast between the two natures is striking. M. Octave Feuillet delights in showing us a hero; M. de Maupassant, on the other hand, takes care that his painter shall never be a hero. For the rest, M. de Maupassant's novel is a masterpiece of its kind.

One word more, which I shall all but whisper: Certain episodes in *Honneur d'artiste* have a savour for which more than one lady reader will be secretly greedy. There is, for instance, an "up to date" marriage of a rather spicy taste. The husband goes to spend his wedding night at the club, and with a hussy. No one is awaiting his return. Madame has gone out. She comes back at eight o'clock in the morning, without offering any explanation. The husband does not insist on one: it would be *bourgeois* so to do. But he conceives a deep admiration for his wife. He thinks her a clever woman.

"*Epatant,*" he says to himself.

And on his lips it was the highest possible praise.

There is also the episode of the young girls, whose conversation among themselves is enough to make a monkey blush. If I am not mistaken the phrase is M. Feuillet's own, in a former work.

*Anatole France, "Octave Feuillet," in his* On Life & Letters, *third series, translated by D. B. Stewart, John Lane The Bodley Head Ltd., 1922, pp. 352-61.*

## Anatole France   (essay date 1890)

*[In the following excerpt from an essay originally published in 1890, France commends Feuillet for adhering to his "agreeable" style despite the pressure to write in the raw, naturalistic manner of Émile Zola prevalent in his time.]*

We have often referred . . . to the talent of Octave Feuillet. We have pointed out his art of composition, his understanding of method, and his skill in preparation. In this he was the last of the classics. He possessed secrets which to-day are lost. Some may be regretted, particularly the unity of tone, which he preserved in a masterly fashion, and which gives an incomparable harmony to his novels.

There is no need for us to recall his skill in depicting character, and hinting at situations. He had taste, a sense of proportion and tact; he was unique in being able to say anything without shocking anyone.

His art has been followed by a new one, an art which has established its position by numerous works. This is certainly not the moment to compare one form of art with another. Each generation pours its thought into the mould which best suits it. It is necessary to understand the manifestations of the most diverse arts; if Naturalism arrived, it was because it had to do so, and the critic has no duty but to explain it.

For the same reason, the Idealism of Octave Feuillet which followed on Romanticism must also be admitted. Octave Feuillet's portion was to be the poet of the Second Empire. Now that his creations are slipping back into the past, their style and character can be more readily grasped. Julia de Trécoeur, Blanche de Chelles, Julie de Cambre are all, in their fashion, true; they are women of 1855. They had the biting, brusque, uneasy, agitated, impassioned character of their period; there had been a great outburst of sensuality and of life to excess. In their refined senses lay the beginnings of neurosis.

Octave Feuillet was the exquisite revealer of a brutal, vain, and sensual world. He combined audacity and decision with grace; and he knew how to draw with a stroke the disordered mind, the debauched body. This classic writer shows us the end of a world.

He is truthful, sometimes truthful to the point of cruelty. But he is a poet; he has the poet's indulgence; he embellishes all that he touches without disfiguring it. He lovingly displays all that is left of charm and elegance, in a society without art, and where passion itself lacks eloquence. He adorns his heroes and heroines. Is he wrong? Are they any the less real for that? No, certainly not! Nature has her beauty in all times, even in sick and feverish societies. This beauty the poet discovers and reveals to us.

Feuillet's poetry is that of the Second Empire. His style is the good style of the period of Napoleon III. When the crinoline, like the pannier, possesses the charm of the past, *Julia de Trécoeur* will form part of the eternal ideal of mankind.

*Anatole France, "Octave Feuillet," in his* On Life & Letters, *third series, translated by D. B. Stewart, John Lane The Bodley Head Ltd., 1922, pp. 352-61.*

## Jane Emily Gerard   (essay date 1891)

*[In the following excerpt, Gerard commends Feuillet on the correctness and good taste of all his works.]*

No vulgar elements, no doubtful characters, are to be found in Monsieur Feuillet's books; even vice is there invariably characterised by good taste, and whenever a commandment is broken by one of these correct heroes or aristocratic heroines, it is done with perfect regard for the usages of polite society. The very last work of this distinguished artist, published shortly before his death, is characterised by the delicate workmanship we are accustomed to associate with Feuillet's name. *Honneur d'Artiste* is scarcely as vigorously written as many previous works by the same hand, but is more than sufficiently good to add to the regret we feel on realising that French literature has lost a representative which it will not be easy to replace.

*Jane Emily Gerard, in a review of "Honneur d'Artiste," in* Blackwood's Edinburgh Magazine, *Vol. CL, No. DCCCCLX, July, 1891, p. 42.*

## Mary Mian   (essay date 1946)

*[Below, Mian reviews* Punch: His Life and Times, *praising Feuillet for the realistic, sardonic quality of the title character.]*

Under the title *La Vie de Polinchinelle et ses Nombreuses Aventures,* this is a children's classic in France. It was written in 1840 by Octave Feuillet—who also produced widely popular novels and plays dealing largely with noble and neurotic ladies among the French aristocracy of the epoch. His Punch, I suspect, will live longer than any of these ladies. He has more red corpuscles.

Punch, of course, had a long and honorable history before any biography of him appeared. Feuillet sets the first appearance in Italy of Pulcinello as at the time of the visit of his own grandfather's great-uncle—roughly, 1600; scholars have traced the obstreperous little man back to the buffoons of old Latin farces. Feuillet tells of his birth and his hilarious adventures at the Italian court, and then, he says, "like all people of a liberal cast, Punch found himself drawn toward France as his natural home." There, after perilous encounters with pirate ships, robber bands and a sulphurous-tailed black cat, Punch settled down in the puppet theatres on the Champs Elysées—where we hope he may still be found.

The first translations in English of Feuillet's book appeared in Victorian days, and were sugarcoated to the taste of the times. This new one by Paul McPharlin is engagingly done in the modern idiom, and it should enable American children to give Punch his due place in the gallery of merry manikins, beside his grandchildren, Pinocchio and Mickey Mouse. What child brought up on Disney would not delight in the scene where Punch puts sneeze powder in the snuff-box of his enemy at court, Lord Boogoo-Roogoo, so that while assisting the king to retire, this lord is seized with such a spasm that he is forced to blow his nose with off-hand precision, on a monster kitchen spit?

By many small touches we would know that "Punch" was written in the free-spoken land of Voltaire. Punch found that "the wicked are always suspicious," and "among the great I found only envy and spite." When Punch left Naples, the court "felt relieved to know that its dull mind would be delivered from fear of his keen one,"but the people mourned, because Punch had played pranks on the rulers who oppressed them.

In French literature for children, from the Bibliothèque Rose of the Comtesse de Ségur to Babar, the world represented is essentially an adult one. There is none of the spirit of nostalgia for childhood which is so strong in the English Barrie and Kenneth Grahame, nor is there the spirit of rambunctious youth in revolt against its stuffy elders which we meet in Tom Sawyer or Penrod. Punch lives, disenchanted, in a world whose follies and foibles he sees with clear eyes, and learns to sharpen his wits in order to make his hard way among them. There is a tonic quality to this book, along with its healthy slapstick, good for both children and adults.

*Mary Mian, in a review of "Punch: His Life and Adventures," in* The New York Times Book Review, *July 21, 1946, p. 16.*

# FURTHER READING

McPharlin, Paul. "For Those Who Want to Know More about the Story." In *Punch: His Life and Adventures,* by Octave Feuillet, translated by Paul McPharlin, pp. 116-21. New York: A Didier Book, 1946.

> Provides background on Feuillet's life and career, focusing on *Punch*. McPharlin asserts that in Feuillet's work, "there is nothing more enduring in delight for the reader."

Tintner, Adeline R. "Octave Feuillet, *La Petite Comtesse,* and Henry James." *Revue de littérature comparée* 48, no. 2 (April-June 1974): 218-32.

> Discusses the influence of Feuillet's works on those of Henry James.

Walker, Pierre A. "The Princess Casamassima's 'Sudden Incarnation' and Octave Feuillet." *Texas Studies in Literature and Language* 31, no. 2 (Summer 1989): 257-72.

> Explores thematic and narrative connections between Henry James's novel *Princess Casamassima* and several of Feuillet's novels.

# Henry Wadsworth Longfellow

## 1807-1882

American poet, novelist, translator, dramatist, and travel writer. For additional information on Longfellow's career, see *NCLC,* Volume 2.

## INTRODUCTION

Widely admired by his contemporaries, Longfellow achieved a degree of popularity in his day that no other American poet before or since has matched. His nostalgic, inspirational verse was embraced by Americans and Europeans enduring an era of rapid social change. Shortly after his death, however, his reputation suffered a serious decline. The very characteristics which made his poetry popular—gentle simplicity and a melancholy reminiscent of German Romantics—are those that fueled the posthumous reaction against his work. Although the debate over Longfellow's literary stature continues, he is widely credited with having been instrumental in introducing European culture to the American readers of his day. Moreover, he simultaneously popularized American folk themes abroad, where his works enjoyed an immense readership.

Longfellow was born in Portland, Maine to Stephen Longfellow, a lawyer and member of the Eighteenth Congress of the United States, and Zilpah Wadsworth, whose ancestors had arrived on the *Mayflower*. In 1822 he enrolled in the newly formed Bowdoin College, of which his father was a trustee. Despite his father's wish that he study law, Longfellow preferred a literary career and began publishing poems in numerous newspapers and periodicals. Before graduation, the college offered him a professorship of modern languages, provided he first prepare himself for the post by traveling in Europe. Grateful for the opportunity to make literature his profession, he accepted and sailed for Europe. This journey greatly influenced his future work, evidenced in a unique blend of both American and foreign elements in his later writings. After three years in Europe, he returned as a professor to Bowdoin and soon published *Outre-mer; a Pilgrimage Beyond the Sea*, a book of travel sketches modeled on Washington Irving's *Sketch Book*. Longfellow later accepted a position at Harvard as the Smith Professor of Modern Languages, a post he held for eighteen years. During this time he again traveled to Europe and, in Heidelberg, discovered the works of the German Romantic poets. He subsequently incorporated much of their artistic philosophy into his work. After returning and settling in Cambridge, he developed lasting friendships with such American literary figures as Charles Sumner, Washington Allston and Nathaniel Hawthorne. Devoting himself to scholarly pursuits as well as to poetry, Longfellow published textbooks, literary essays, and numerous translations of European poets. His most ambitious translation was *The Divine Comedy of*

*Dante Alighieri*, completed late in his life and still ranked among the finest translations of Dante's work. Longfellow died in 1882.

Longfellow's first published collection of poems, *Voices of the Night*, illustrates his view that poetry should be "an instrument for improving the condition of society, and advancing the great purpose of human happiness." *Voices* is distinguished by his "Psalm of Life" and "Light of the Stars," popular inspirational pieces characterized by simple truths and maxims. The poems in this and such subsequent early collections as *Ballads and Other Poems* and *The Seaside and the Fireside* generally conclude with didactic or romanticized expressions of the poet's religious faith, balancing or, according to many critics, at times awkwardly undermining the nostalgic, melancholic reflections on life's transience that inform many of his finest poems. The longer narrative works for which Longfellow is best remembered, *Evangeline: A Tale of Acadie, The Song of Hiawatha*, and *Tales of a Wayside Inn*, address American themes and subjects, often providing vivid descriptions of the American landscape that appealed greatly to readers worldwide. *Evangeline*, written in classical dactylic hexameter and praised for both its lyrical grace and poignant storyline, relates the tale of two lovers separated during the French and Indian War. After touring America futilely in search of her exiled bridegroom, the eponymous heroine is reunited with him momentarily at his hospital deathbed. *The Song of Hiawatha*, praised upon publication as the great American epic, grafts source material from Native American mythology onto the meter and plot structure of the Finnish folk epic *Kalevala*, suggesting Longfellow's perception of a cultural and literary continuity between the Old World and the New. *Tales of a Wayside Inn*, a series of narrative poems reminiscent of Chaucer's *Canterbury Tales*, is perhaps the best example of Longfellow's versatility and mastery of the narrative form. The poems comprising this work, including one of Longfellow's most famous, "Paul Revere's Ride," are highly regarded for their plots, characterizations, and intimate atmosphere. In addition to these narrative poems, Longfellow published what he considered his masterpiece: a trilogy of dramatic poems, *The Golden Legend, The New England Tragedies,* and *The Divine Tragedy*, entitled *Christus: A Mystery*. This work treats the subject of Christianity from its beginnings through the Middle Ages to the time of the American Puritans. While acknowledging that these works contain some beautiful and effective writing, critics generally agree that Longfellow's creative gift was poetic rather than dramatic, and that the scope of this particular work was beyond his range.

During his lifetime, Longfellow was immensely popular and widely admired. He was the first American poet to gain a favorable international reputation, and his poetry was praised abroad by such eminent authors as Charles Dickens, Victor Hugo, Alfred Tennyson, and Anthony Trollope, and at home by Nathaniel Hawthorne, Ralph Waldo Emerson, James Russell Lowell, and Walt Whitman. In 1884, two years after his death, his bust was unveiled in the Poets' Corner of Westminster Abbey, making him the first American to be so honored. In the decades that followed, however, the idealism and sentimentality that characterize much of his verse fell out of favor with younger poets and critics who were beginning to embrace realism and naturalism. Longfellow's literary reputation further declined in the twentieth century with the advent of Modernism. Reviled as superficial and didactic, his poetry was largely dismissed and received little further critical attention. As Dana Gioia has noted, "Modern literary criticism on Longfellow hardly exists in the sense that it does for more overtly difficult poets like Dickinson, Stevens, or Pound. . . . The unspoken assumption, even among his advocates, has been that Longfellow's poetry requires no gloss." Some recent commentators, however, have found much to admire in Longfellow. He is often praised for his technical skill, particularly as demonstrated in his short lyrics and sonnets. He also continues to be regarded as a pioneer in adapting European literary traditions to American themes and subjects. Louis Untermeyer points out: "Longfellow may have been the poet of America's cultural adolescence. But he was more; he was also the forerunner of those who gave expression to America's maturity."

## PRINCIPAL WORKS

*Outre-mer; a Pilgrimage Beyond the Sea*. 2 vols. (travel sketches) 1833-34
*Hyperion* (novel) 1839
*Voices of the Night* (poetry) 1839
*Ballads and Other Poems* (poetry) 1842
*\*The Spanish Student* (verse drama) 1843
*The Poets and Poetry of Europe* [editor and translator] (poetry) 1845
*The Belfry of Bruges and Other Poems* (poetry) 1846
*Evangeline: A Tale of Acadie* (narrative poetry) 1847
*Kavanagh* (novel) 1849
*The Seaside and the Fireside* (poetry) 1850
*†The Golden Legend* (dramatic poetry) 1851
*The Song of Hiawatha* (narrative poetry) 1855
*The Courtship of Miles Standish, and Other Poems* (poetry) 1858
*Tales of a Wayside Inn* (narrative poetry) 1863
*The Divine Comedy of Dante Alighieri*. 3 vols. [translator] (poetry) 1865-67
*†The New England Tragedies* (dramatic poetry) 1868
*†The Divine Tragedy* (dramatic poetry) 1871
*Kéramos and Other Poems* (poetry) 1878
*Ultima Thule* (poetry) 1880
*In the Harbor: Ultima Thule, Part II* (poetry) 1882
*Michael Angelo* (narrative poetry) 1883
*The Works of Henry Wadsworth Longfellow*. 11 vols. (poetry, dramas, novels, travel sketches, and translations) 1886

\*This is the date of first publication rather than first performance.

†These were published together as *Christus: A Mystery* in 1872.

---

## CRITICISM

### Edgar Allan Poe   (essay date 1842)

[*One of the foremost American authors of the nineteenth century, Poe is widely regarded as the architect of the modern short story and the principal forerunner of aestheticism in America. In the following essay, he reviews Longfellow's verse, noting that his imagery and innovation are restricted by his moral didacticism.*]

We have said that Mr. Longfellow's conception of the aims of poesy is erroneous; and that thus, laboring at a disadvantage, he does violent wrong to his own high powers; and now the question is, what are his ideas of the aims of the muse, as we gather these ideas from the *general* tendency of his poems? It will be at once evident that, imbued with the peculiar spirit of German song (a pure conventionality) he regards the inculcation of a *moral* as essential. Here we find it necessary to repeat that we have reference only to the *general* tendency of his compositions; for there are some magnificent exceptions, where, as if by accident, he has permitted his genius to get the better of his conventional prejudice. But didacticism is the prevalent *tone* of his song. His invention, his imagery, his all, is made subservient to the elucidation of some one or more points (but rarely of more than one) which he looks upon as *truth*. And that this mode of procedure will find stern defenders should never excite surprise, so long as the world is full to overflowing with cant and conventicles. There are men who will scramble on all fours through the muddiest sloughs of vice to pick up a single apple of virtue. There are things called men who, so long as the sun rolls, will greet with snuffing huzzas every figure that takes upon itself the semblance of truth, even although the figure, in itself only a "stuffed Paddy," be as much out of place as a toga on the statue of Washington, or out of season as rabbits in the days of the dog-star.

Now with as deep a reverence for "the true" as ever inspired the bosom of mortalman, we would limit, in many respects, its modes of inculcation. We would limit to enforce them. We would not render them impotent by dissipation. The demands of truth are severe. She has no sympathy with the myrtles. All that is indispensable in song is all with which she has nothing to do. To deck her in gay robes is to render her a harlot. It is but making her a flaunting paradox to wreathe her in gems and flowers. Even in stating this our present proposition, we verify our own words—we feel the necessity, in enforcing this *truth*, of descending from metaphor. Let us then be simple and distinct. To convey "the true" we are required to dismiss from the attention all inessentials. We must be perspicuous, precise, terse. We need concentration rather than expansion of mind. We must be calm, unimpassioned, unexcited—in a word, we must be in that peculiar mood which, as nearly as possible, is the exact converse of the poetical. He must be blind indeed who cannot perceive the radical and chasmal difference between the truthful and the poetical modes of inculcation. He must be grossly wedded to conventionalisms who, in spite of this difference, shall still attempt to reconcile the obstinate oils and waters of Poetry and Truth.

Dividing the world of mind into its most obvious and immediately recognisable distinctions, we have the pure intellect, taste, and the moral sense. We place *taste* between the intellect and the moral sense, because it is just this intermediate space which, in the mind, it occupies. It is the connecting link in the triple chain.

It serves to sustain a mutual intelligence between the extremes. It appertains, in strict appreciation, to the former, but is distinguished from the latter by so faint a difference, that Aristotle has not hesitated to class some of its operations among the Virtues themselves. But the *offices* of the trio are broadly marked. Just as conscience, or the moral sense, recognises duty; just as the intellect deals with *truth;* so is it the part of taste alone to inform us of Beauty. And Poesy is the handmaiden but of Taste. Yet we would not be misunderstood. This handmaiden is not forbidden to moralise—in her own fashion. She is not forbidden to depict—but to reason and preach, of virtue. As, of this latter, conscience recognises the obligation, so intellect teaches the expediency, while taste contents herself with displaying the beauty: waging war with vice merely on the ground

of its inconsistency with fitness, harmony, proportion—in a word with το αλον [the beautiful].

An important condition of man's immortal nature is thus, plainly, the sense of the Beautiful. This it is which ministers to his delight in the manifold forms and colors and sounds and sentiments amid which he exists. And, just as the eyes of Amaryllis are repeated in the mirror, or the living lily in the lake, so is the mere *record* of these forms and colors and sounds and sentiments—so is their mere oral or written repetition a duplicate source of delight. But this repetition is not Poesy. He who shall merely sing with whatever rapture, in however harmonious strains, or with however vivid a truth of imitation, of the sights and sounds which greet him in common with all mankind—he, we say, has yet failed to prove his divine title. There is still a longing unsatisfied, which he has been impotent to fulfil. There is still a thirst unquenchable, which to allay he has shown us no crystal springs. This burning thirst belongs to the *immortal* essence of man's nature. It is equally a consequence and an indication of his perennial life. It is the desire of the moth for the star. It is not the mere appreciation of the beauty before us. It is a wild effort to reach the beauty above. It is a forethought of the loveliness to come. It is a passion to be satiated by no sublunary sights, or sounds, or sentiments, and the soul thus athirst strives to allay its fever in futile efforts at *creation*. Inspired with a prescient ecstasy of the beauty beyond the grave, it struggles by multiform novelty of combination among the things and thoughts of Time, to anticipate some portion of that loveliness whose very elements, perhaps, appertain solely to Eternity. And the result of such effort, on the part of souls fittingly constituted, is alone what mankind have agreed to denominate Poetry.

We say this with little fear of contradiction. Yet the spirit of our assertion must be more heeded than the letter. Mankind have seemed to define Poesy in a thousand, and in a thousand conflicting definitions. But the war is one only of words. Induction is as well applicable to this subject as to the most palpable and utilitarian; and by its sober processes we find that, in respect to compositions which have been really received as poems, the *imaginative*, or, more popularly, the creative portions *alone* have ensured them to be so received. Yet these works, on account of these portions, having once been so received and so named, it has happened, naturally and inevitably, that other portions totally unpoetic have not only come to be regarded by the popular voice as poetic, but have been made to serve as false standards of perfection, in the adjustment of other poetical claims. Whatever has been found in whatever has been received as a poem, has been blindly regarded as *ex statu* [according to its position] poetic. And this is a species of gross error which scarcely could have made its way into any less intangible topic. In fact that license which appertains to the Muse herself, it has been thought decorous, if not sagacious to indulge, in all examination of her character.

Poesy is thus seen to be a response—unsatisfactory it is true—but still in some measure a response, to a natural and irrepressible demand. Man being what he is, the time could never have been in which Poesy was not. Its first element is the thirst for supernal Beauty—a beauty which is not afforded the soul by any existing collocation of earth's forms—a beauty which, perhaps, *no possible* combination of these forms would fully produce. Its second element is the attempt to satisfy this thirst by *novel* combinations, *of those combinations which our predecessors, toiling in chase of the same phantom, have already set in order.* We thus clearly deduce the *novelty,* the *originality,* the *invention,* the *imagination,* or lastly the *creation* of Beauty, (for the terms as here employed are synonymous) as the essence of all Poesy. Nor is this idea so much at variance with ordinary opinion as, at first sight, it may appear. A multitude of antique dogmas on this topic will be found, when divested of extrinsic speculation, to be easily resoluble into the definition now proposed. We do nothing more than present tangibly the vague clouds of the world's idea. We recognise the idea itself floating, unsettled, indefinite, in every attempt which has yet been made to circumscribe the conception of "Poesy" in words. A striking instance of this is observable in the fact that no definition exists, in which either "the beautiful," or some one of those qualities which we have above designated synonymously with "creation," has not been pointed out is the *chief* attribute of the Muse. "Invention," however, or "imagination," is by far more commonly insisted upon. The word πoιησι itself (creation) speaks volumes upon this point. Neither will it be amiss here to mention Count Bielfeld's definition of poetry as *"L'art d'exprimer les pensées par la fiction"* ["The art of expressing ideas by means of fiction"]. With this definition (of which the philosophy is profound to a certain extent) the German terms *Dichtkunst,* the art of fiction and *Dichten,* to feign, which are used for *"poetry"* and *"to make verses,"* are in full and remarkable accordance. It is nevertheless, in the combination of the two omni-prevalent ideas that the novelty and, we believe, the force of our own proposition is to be found.

So far, we have spoken of Poesy as of an abstraction alone. As such, it is obvious that it may be applicable in various moods. The sentiment may developitself in Sculpture, in Painting, in Music, or otherwise. But our present business is with its development in words—that development to which, in practical acceptation, the world has agreed to limit the term. And at this point there is one consideration which induces us to pause. We cannot make up our minds to admit (as some have admitted) the inessentiality of rhythm. On the contrary, the universality of its use in the earliest poetical efforts of mankind would be sufficient to assure us, not merely of its congeniality with the Muse, or of its adaptation to her purposes, but of its elementary and indispensable importance. But here we must, perforce, content ourselves with mere suggestion; for this topic is of a character which would lead us too far. We have already spoken of Music as one of the moods of poetical development. It is in Music, perhaps, that the soul most nearly attains that end upon which we have commented—the creation of supernal beauty. It may be, indeed, that this august aim is here even partially or imperfectly attained, *in fact.* The *elements* of that beauty which is felt in sound, *may be* the mutual or common heritage of Earth and Heaven. In the soul's struggles at combinations it is thus not impossible that a harp may strike notes not unfamiliar to the angels. And in this view the wonder may well be less

that all attempts at defining the character or sentiment of the deeper musical impressions, has been found absolutely futile. Contenting ourselves, therefore, with the firm conviction, that music (in its modifications of rhythm and rhyme) is of so vast a moment in Poesy, as *never* to be neglected by him who is truly poetical—is of so mighty a force in furthering the great aim intended that he is mad who rejects its assistance—content with this idea we shall not pause to maintain its absolute essentiality, for the mere sake of rounding a definition. We will but add, at this point, that the highest possible development of the Poetical Sentiment is to be found in the union of song with music, in its popular sense. The old Bards and Minnesingers possessed, in the fullest perfection, the finest and truest elements of Poesy; and Thomas Moore, singing his own ballads, is but putting the final touch to their completion as poems.

To recapitulate, then, we would define in brief the Poetry of words as the *Rhythmical Creation of Beauty.* Beyond the limits of Beauty its province does not extend. Its sole arbiter is Taste. With the Intellect or with the Conscience it has only collateral relations. It has no dependence, unless incidentally, upon either Duty or *Truth.* That our definition will necessarily exclude much of what, through a supine toleration, has been hitherto ranked as poetical, is a matter which affords us not even momentary concern. We address but the thoughtful, and heed only their approval—with our own. If our suggestions are truthful, then "after many days" shall they be understood as truth, even though found in contradiction of all that has been hitherto so understood. If false shall we not be the first to bid them die?

We would reject, of course, all such matters as "Armstrong on Health," a revolting production; Pope's "Essay on Man," which may well be content with the title of an "Essay in Rhyme," "Hudibras," and other merely humorous pieces. We do not gainsay the peculiar merits of either of these latter compositions—but deny them the position held. In a notice, month before last, of [John G. C.] Brainard's Poems, we took occasion to show that the common use of a certain instrument, (rhythm) had tended, more than aught else, to confound humorous verse with poetry. The observation is now recalled to corroborate what we have just said in respect to the vast effect or force of melody in itself—an effect which could elevate into even momentary confusion with the highest efforts of mind, compositions such as are the greater number of satires or burlesques.

Of the poets who have appeared most fully instinct with the principles now developed, we may mention *Keats* as the most remarkable. He is the sole British poet who has never erred in his themes. Beauty is always his aim.

We have thus shown our ground of objection to the general *themes* of Professor Longfellow. In common with all who claim the sacred title of poet, he should limit his endeavors to the creation of novel moods of beauty, in form, in color, in sound, in sentiment; for over all this wide range has the poetry of words dominion. To what the world terms *prose* may be safely and properly left all else. The artist who doubts of his thesis, may always resolve his doubt by the single question—"might not this matter be as well or better handled in *prose?*" If it *may,* then is it no subject for the Muse. In the general acceptation of the term *Beauty* we are content to rest; being careful only to suggest that, in our peculiar views, it must be understood as inclusive of *the sublime.*

Of the pieces which constitute the present volume, there are not more than one or two thoroughly fulfilling the idea above proposed; although the volume as a whole is by no means so chargeable with didacticism as Mr. Longfellow's previous book. We would mention as poems *nearly true,* **"The Village Blacksmith," "The Wreck of the Hesperus"** and especially **"The Skeleton in Armor."** In the first-mentioned we have the *beauty* of simplemindedness as a genuine thesis; and this thesis is inimitably handled until the concluding stanza, where the spirit of legitimate poesy is aggrieved in the pointed antithetical deduction of a *moral* from what has gone before. In **"The Wreck of the Hesperus"** we have the *beauty* of child-like confidence and innocence, with that of the father's stern courage and affection. But, with slight exception, those particulars of the storm here detailed are not poetic subjects. Their thrilling *horror* belongs to prose, in which it could befar more effectively discussed, as Professor Longfellow may assure himself at any moment by experiment. There *are* points of a tempest which afford the loftiest and truest poetical themes—points in which pure beauty is found, or better still, beauty heightened into the sublime, by terror. But when we read, among other similar things, that

> The salt sea was frozen on her breast,
> The salt tears in her eyes,

we feel, if not positive disgust, at least a chilling sense of the inappropriate. In the **"Skeleton in Armor"** we find a pure and perfect thesis artistically treated. We find the beauty of bold courage and self-confidence, of love and maiden devotion, of reckless adventure, and finally of life-contemning grief. Combined with all this we have numerous points of beauty apparently insulated, but all aiding the main effect of impression. The heart is stirred, and the mind does not lament its mal-instruction. The metre is simple, sonorous, well-balanced and fully adapted to the subject. Upon the whole, there are few truer poems than this. It has but one defect—an important one. The prose remarks prefacing the narrative are really *necessary.* But every work of art should contain within itself all that is requisite for its own comprehension. And this remark is especially true of the ballad. In poems of magnitude the mind of the reader is not, at all times, enabled to include, in one comprehensive survey, the proportions and proper adjustment of the whole. He is pleased, if at all, with particular passages; and the sum of his pleasure is compounded of the sums of the pleasurable sentiments inspired by these individual passages in the progress of perusal. But, in pieces of less extent, the pleasure is *unique,* in the proper acceptation of this term—the understanding is employed, without difficulty, in the contemplation of the picture *as a whole;* and thus its effect will depend, in great measure, upon the perfection of its finish, upon the nice adaptation of its constituent parts, and especially, upon what is rightly termed by Schlegel *the unity or totality of interest.* But the practice of prefixing explanatory passages is utterly at variance with such unity. By the prefix, we are either put in possession of the subject of the poem; or some hint, historic fact, or suggestion, is thereby afforded, not included in the body of the piece, which, without the hint, is incomprehensible. In the latter case, while perusing the poem, the reader must revert, in mind at least, to the prefix, for the necessary explanation. In the former, the poem being a mere paraphrase of the prefix, the interest is divided between the prefix and the paraphrase. In either instance the totality of effect is destroyed.

Of the other original poems in the volume before us, there is none in which the aim of instruction, or *truth,* has not been too obviously substituted for the legitimate aim, *beauty.* [A] didactic moral might be happily made the *under-current* of a political theme, and, in "Burton's Magazine," some two years [ago], we treated this point at length, in a review of Moore's "Alciphron": but the moral thus conveyed is invariably an ill effect when obtruding beyond the upper current of the thesis itself. Perhaps the worst specimen of this obtrusion is given us by our poet in **"Blind Bartimeus"** and the **"Goblet of Life,"** where it will be observed that the sole interest of the upper current of meaning depends upon its relation or reference to the under. What we read upon the surface would be *vox et praeterea nihil* [a word and nothing besides] in default of the moral beneath. The Greek *finales* of **"Blind Bartimeus"** are an affectation altogether inexcusable. What the small, second-hand, Gibbonish pedantry of Byron introduced, is unworthy the imitation of Longfellow.

Of the translations we scarcely think it necessary to speak at all. We regret that our poet will persist in busying himself about such matters. *His* time might be better employed in original conception. Most of these versions are marked with the error upon which we have commented. This error is in fact, essentially Germanic. "The Luck of Edenhall," however, is a truly beautiful poem; and we say this with all that deference which the opinion of the *Democratic Review* demands. This composition appears to us *one of the very finest.* It has all the free, hearty, *obvious* movement of the true ballad-legend. The greatest force of language is combined in it with the richest imagination, acting in its most legitimate province. Upon the whole, we prefer it even to the "Sword-Song" of [Karl Theodor] Körner. The pointed moral with which it terminates is so exceedingly natural—so perfectly fluent from the incidents—that we have hardly heart to pronounce it in ill taste. We may observe of this ballad, in conclusion, that its subject is more *physical* than is usual in Germany. Its images are rich rather in physical than in moral beauty. And this tendency, in Song, is the true one. It is chiefly, if we are not mistaken—it is chiefly amid forms of physical loveliness (we use the word *forms* in its widest sense as embracing modifications of sound and color) that the soul seeks the realization of its dreams of Beauty. It is to her demand in this sense especially, that the poet, who is wise, will most frequently and most earnestly respond.

"The Children of the Lord's Supper" is, beyond doubt, a true and most beautiful poem in great part, while, in some particulars, it is too metaphysical to have any pretension to the name. In our last number, we objected, briefly, to its metre—the ordinary Latin or Greek Hexameter—dactyls and spondees at random, with a spondee in conclusion. We maintain that the Hexameter can never be introduced into our language, from the nature of that language itself. This rhythm demands, *for English ears,* a preponderance of natural spondees. Our tongue has few. Not only does the Latin and Greek, with the Swedish, and some others, abound in them; but the Greek and Roman ear had become reconciled (why or how is unknown) to the reception of artificial spondees—that is to say, spondaic words formed partly of one word and partly of another, or from an excised part of one word. In short the ancients were content to read *as they scanned,* or nearly so. It may be safely prophesied that we shall never do this; and thus we shall never admit English Hexameters. The attempt to introduce them, after the repeated failures of Sir Philip Sidney, and others, is, perhaps, somewhat discreditable to the scholarship of Professor Longfellow. The *Democratic Review,* in saying that he has triumphed over difficulties in this rhythm, has been deceived, it is evident, by the facility with which some of these verses may be read. In glancing over the poem, we do not observe a single verse which can be read, *to English ears, as a Greek Hexameter.* There are many, however, which can be well read as mere English dactylic verses; such, for example, as the well-known lines of Byron, commencing

> Know ye the / land where the / cypress and / myrtle.

These lines (although full of irregularities) are, in their perfection, formed of three dactyls and a caesura—just as if we should cut short the initial verse of the Bucolics thus—

> Tityre / tu patu / lae recu / bans—

The "myrtle," at the close of Byron's line, is a double rhyme, and must be understood as one syllable.

Now a great number of Professor Longfellow's Hexameters are merely these dactylic lines *continued for two feet.* For example—

> Whispered the / race of the / flowers and / merry on / balancing / branches.

In this example, also, "branches," which is a double ending, must be regarded as the caesura, or one syllable, of which alone it has the force.

As we have already alluded, in one or two regards, to a notice of these poems which appeared in the *Democratic Review,* we may as well here proceed with some few further comments upon the article in question—with whose general tenor we are happy to agree.

The *Review* speaks of **"Maidenhood"** as a poem, "not to be understood but at the expense of more time and trouble than a song can justly claim." We are scarcely less surprised at this opinion from Mr. Langtree than we were at the condemnation of "The Luck of Edenhall."

**"Maidenhood"** is faulty, it appears to us, only on the score of its theme, which is somewhat didactic. Its meaning seems simplicity itself. A maiden on the verge of woman-

hood, hesitating to enjoy life (for which she has a strong appetite) through a false idea of duty, is bidden to fear nothing, having purity of heart as her lion of Una.

What Mr. Langtree styles "an unfortunate peculiarity" in Mr. Longfellow, resulting from "adherence to a false system" has really been always regarded byus as one of his idiosyncratic merits. "In each poem," says the critic, "he has but one idea which, in the progress of his song is gradually unfolded, and at last reaches its full development in the concluding lines; this singleness of thought might lead a harsh critic to suspect intellectual barrenness." It leads us, individually, only to a full sense of the artistical power and knowledge of the poet. We confess that now, for the first time, we hear unity of conception objected to as a defect. But Mr. Langtree seems to have fallen into the singular error of supposing the poet to have absolutely *but one idea* in each of his ballads. Yet how "one idea" can be "gradually unfolded" without other ideas, is, to us, a mystery of mysteries. Mr. Longfellow, very properly, has but one *leading* idea which forms the basis of his poem; but to the aid and development of this one there are innumerable others, of which the rare excellence is, that all are in keeping, that none could be well omitted, that each tends to the one general effect. It is unnecessary to say another word upon this topic.

In speaking of **"Excelsior,"** Mr. Langtree (are we wrong in attributing the notice to his very forcible pen?) seems to labor under some similar misconception. "It carries along with it," says he, "a false moral which greatly diminishes its merit in our eyes. The great merit of a picture, whether made with the pencil or pen, is its *truth;* and this merit does not belong to Mr. Longfellow's sketch. Men of genius may and probably do, meet with greater difficulties in their struggles with the world than their fellow-men who are less highly gifted; but their power of overcoming obstacles is proportionably greater, and the result of their laborious suffering is not death but immortality." That the chief merit of a picture is its *truth,* is an assertion deplorably erroneous. Even in Painting, which is, more essentially than Poetry, a mimetic art, the proposition cannot be sustained. Truth is not even *the aim.* Indeed it is curious to observe how veryslight a degree of truth is sufficient to satisfy the mind, which acquiesces in the absence of numerous essentials in the thing depicted. An outline frequently stirs the spirit more pleasantly than the most elaborate picture. We need only refer to the compositions of Flaxman and of Retzsch. Here all details are omitted—nothing can be farther from *truth.* Without even color the most thrilling effects are produced. In statues we are rather pleased than disgusted with *the want of the eyeball.* The hair of the Venus de Medicis *was gilded.* Truth indeed! The grapes of Zeuxis as well as the curtain of Parrhasius were received as indisputable evidence of the truthful ability of these artists—but they are not even *classed among their pictures.* If truth is the highest aim of either Painting or Poesy, then Jan Steen was a greater artist than Angelo, and Crabbe is a more noble poet than Milton.

But we have not quoted the observation of Mr. Langtree to deny its philosophy; our design was simply to show that he has misunderstood the poet. **"Excelsior"** has not even

*The Longfellow homestead at Newbury, Mass.*

a remote tendency to the interpretation assigned it by the critic. It depicts the *earnest upward impulse of the soul—* an impulse not to be subdued even in Death. Despising danger, resisting pleasure, the youth, bearing the banner inscribed "Excelsior!" (higher still) struggles through all difficulties to an Alpine summit. Warned to be content with the elevation attained, his cry is still "Excelsior!" And, even in falling dead on its highest pinnacle, his cry is *still* "Excelsior!" There is yet an immortal height to be surmounted—an ascent in Eternity. The poet holds in view the idea of never-ending *progress.* That he is misunderstood is rather the misfortune of Mr. Langtree than the fault of Mr. Longfellow. There is an old adage about the difficulty of one's furnishing an auditor both with matter to be comprehended and brains for its comprehension.

*Edgar Allan Poe, "The American Scene: Longfellow," in his* Literary Criticism of Edgar Allan Poe, *edited by Robert L. Hough, University of Nebraska Press, 1965, pp. 116-29.*

### Anthony Trollope  (essay date 1881)

[*Trollope was a prolific and popular Victorian novelist whose works are distinguished by their humor and vivid characterizations. In the following essay, Trollope discusses the long narrative poems* Evangeline, Hiawatha, *and* The Courtship of Miles Standish, *as well as the short ballad*

"Skeleton in Armor," *praising what he describes as the "purity and pathos" of these works.*]

I not unnaturally feel disinclined to speak in public of the character and genius of Longfellow, as he is happily still among us, and as I may perhaps be allowed to call him my friend; but he stands so far aloof from the possibility of censorial severity that I think I shall hardly give offense. I certainly should abandon the idea of writing of him at all, had I aught to say which he would be hurt to hear. To criticism on his poetry he must by this time be well used. I do not remember to have seen anything more hard toward him than a parody. I, at any rate, shall not be harsh. Indeed, he gives no scope for critical severity, —never offending, never attempting to rise so high as to "o'erleap itself and fall on the other" side, never ridiculous, never magniloquent, seldom magnificent. His finer touches come so gradually upon us, that we hardly feel ourselves to be in an element above our own. Evangeline, when she finds that Gabriel is not with his father—"Gone! Is Gabriel gone?" —hardly expresses to our feelings all the pathos of her love, because we have gradually come to live among pathetic utterances. He has never received all the praise due to him, but he has thus escaped invidious remark. He had crept up to our hearts before we had learned to think that he was mastering our judgment. In this way he has escaped all hardships of criticism, and he certainly will not receive a heavy measure of it from me.

In personal contact with Longfellow, the stranger is apt

to drop the poet in the gentleman, the distinguished man of letters in the uncommonly pleasant fellow whom he has encountered. Whether this is as it ought to be I will leave my readers to decide. I do not think that poets generally make themselves so cheap, —or that distinguished men of letters do so. There is generally something which declares to you the fact that you are in the presence of a remarkable person. "This is the pleasantest man I ever met," the British stranger is inclined to say. "He is a first-class gentleman. But where is Longfellow? Where's the American poet?" And, indeed, he is not at all like his country-men in this respect, among whom, as in some other countries, the man of letters likes to claim the respect which he believes to be due to him. Motley chose to be known as Motley; so did Emerson. So also did my excellent friend Oliver Wendell Holmes, —and will do so long, let us hope. His children, his cigars, the dinner he will give you, —or more probably yourself, —are the subjects which are apt to come up with Longfellow in his conversation with you.

In speaking of Hawthorne . . . and in comparing his genius with that of others, I mentioned the purity of Longfellow, and I said that "the seraphic excellence of *Hiawatha* and *Evangeline* could have proceeded only from a mind which the world's roughness had neither toughened nor tainted." Such, to my thinking, is the peculiar nature of Longfellow's muse. But he is pure without the slightest affectation of purity. Among our own bards there are those with whom the same delicacy is their peculiar characteristic. Cowper is as pure as could be any strictest lady. But with him it amounts almost to an affectation. He rises, especially in his "Task," to great heights of poetry; —beyond, perhaps, those which, in his simplicity, Longfellow attempts. He is, too, a complete master of the melody of versification, whereas Longfellow, in the peculiar manner and methods which he has adopted, becomes sometimes almost prosaic. But a study of Longfellow's works leaves on the reader's mind a feeling that he is pure because of his nature. Cowper, on the other hand, raises a conviction that he is pure by having overcome his nature. He seems to betray a former connection with original sin. The other is simply living the life he has ever lived, in which sin has had no part. If he be seraphic, it is because he was born and bred so, and to be seraphic has come easy to him. That Cowper must have had stirring struggles with the devil in his youth, and have conquered him, is quite certain. Cowper delights in old women, as being less wicked than old men, and is pious, mad, and inspired. Longfellow takes the people as they come, and is neither pious, nor mad, nor, to the outward sense, inspired. But he is a great poet, and his poetry is perfectly pure.

He is, I think, essentially unlike his countrymen, —so much so, that, of all the poets of his day, he is the last that I should have guessed to be an American had I come across his works in ignorance of the fact. He is never loud, far-fetched, funny, or extravagant. He is unlike Bryant, Poe, Lowell, and Bret Harte. Italian poetry, which he delights to translate, —probably from the relief which he finds in having occasionally to supply words only and not ideas, —has been his model. As he is pure, so also is he graceful. But that for which you have to look, and will most surely find in his poetry, is pathos. Now a story of

love may be delightfully told, and yet not be pathetic. Look at Rosalind, where the comedy, fresh and sweet as it is, frustrates pathos; or even Juliet, where the love leaps from passion to tragedy, and never quite enters on the melancholy realm of pathos. Look at your dictionary, and you shall see that pathos is called passion. The words, indeed, from their derivation, should mean the same; but the meaning they convey to us at present is very different. No one would, I think, describe the story of *Evangeline* as one of strong passion, but no story more pathetic was ever written. A soft melancholy, which may rise indeed sometimes to tragic sorrow, but which never loses its softness and never ceases to be tender, is necessary to pathos. And such is the distinguishing characteristic of Longfellow in all his longer popular poems. Indeed, it is to be found in all that he writes, poetry as well as prose. For it we read *Evangeline* and *Hiawatha,* but it is to be found in almost all his minor poems. In the carillon of **"The Belfry of Bruges"** he hears—

> . . . or dreams he hears,
> Intermingled with the song,
> Thoughts that he has cherished long;
> Hears amid the chime and singing
> The bells of his own village ringing.

What can be more pathetic than the idea to which Thor in his challenge gives rise? —

> Thou art a God, too,
> O Galilean!
> And thus single-handed
> Unto the combat,
> Gauntlet or Gospel,
> Here I defy thee!

In singing of Nuremberg, he breaks out into pathos:

> Vanished is the ancient splendor, and before my
> dreamy eye
> Wave these mingling shapes and figures, like a
> faded tapestry.

Again:

> Then the moon in all her pride,
> Like a spirit glorified,
> Filled and overflowed the night
> With revelations of her light.

And I will quote the last lines of that well-worn song, **"Excelsior":**

> There in the twilight cold and gray,
> Lifeless, but beautiful, he lay,
> And from the sky, serene and far,
> A voice fell, like a falling star—
> 'Excelsior.'

You cannot say that any of these passages are passionate, but they will all fill you with pathos, —if your ideas as to the words be the same as mine. In this feeling, without which the man who reads much hardly passes a day of his life, Longfellow continually indulges. In the passages to which I have referred there is no charm of love, nor is there an idea of suffering; but who can read them without something of pathos coming across his heart?

I purpose in the following pages to take our poet's three

most known works and analyze them as best I may be able. I will not here give his prose works, which, charming though they be, are not as widely known as his poetry. By *Hyperion* and *Kavanagh* he has not become that Longfellow whom all readers on this side of the water delight to honor and aspire to know, but by *Evangeline, Hiawatha,* and *The Courtship of Miles Standish.* To these I will add the vision of the viking in "The Skeleton in Armor."

*Evangeline* is the story of a girl who, with all the inhabitants of the village in which she lives, is banished from her home at Grand-Pré, in Acadia. There are a few words in the poem alluding to old-fashioned British tyranny, and we are told in a short preface that when the land was given over by the French to the English, —that land which is now called Nova Scotia, —the inhabitants of Grand-Pré were supposed to have lent their aid to French rebels, and to have been driven from their homes in consequence. Seeing that they were all French, it was natural that they should have done so. It took place nearly two hundred years ago, and the poet has been, at any rate, justified in imagining the cruelty, even if it did not exist. The story begins with the description of the village:

> In the Acadian land, on the shores of the Basin of Minas,
> Distant, secluded, still, the little village of Grand-Pré
> Lay in the fruitful valley.

The poet has selected the meter of the Iliad and Æneid, and has chosen to write the work by which he will be best known to all posterity in hexameters. A friend consulted before the writing would have cautioned him of difficulties, and would have told him that their rhythm better suits the Greek or Latin language, with its closely defined prosody, than the English, which depends chiefly upon its verbal attractions, or rhymes and cadences. He would have warned the poet against the monotony of this measure when applied to English, and would have proved to him by reading a passage aloud that it falls into a sing-song melody. But, had the friend waited till the total result had been accomplished, he would not have repelled the attempt. In reading aloud, the reader has to guard against the above-named effect; but he can guard against it, and then gradually the lines assume a tranquil dignity admirably suited to the subject. Let imitators beware, lest in writing hexameters, not difficult in English, they will seem to attempt to reach Longfellow, —and will fail.

Of the Acadian village we become acquainted with six of the inhabitants. There is Benedict Bellefontaine the farmer, and his daughter Evangeline. There is Basil the blacksmith, and his son Gabriel. And there are the priest and the notary. Gabriel and Evangeline are of course in love with each other:

> Thus, at peace with God and the world, the farmer of Grand-Pré
> Lived on his sunny farm, and Evangeline governed his household.
> Many a youth, as he knelt in the church and opened his missal,
> Fixed his eyes upon her, as the saint of his deepest devotion;

. . . . .

> But, among all who came, young Gabriel only was welcome;
> Gabriel Lajeunesse, the son of Basil the blacksmith.

Thus the story of Evangeline's love is told at once, and made a fact which never for a moment leaves the reader's mind. For *Evangeline* is essentially a love-story, a story of unsuccessful love, to which is added all the charm which can be given by a true delineation of Nature in all her beauty. The blacksmith comes to visit the farmer, who is of a happy, contented mind; whereas his friend, as a politician looking deeply into things as they are, is less contented with their aspect. He gives the terrible news of the day:

> "Four days now are passed since the English ships at their anchors
> Ride in the Gaspereau's mouth, with their cannon pointed against us.
> What their design may be is unknown; but all are commanded
> On the morrow to meet in the church, where his Majesty's mandate
> Will be proclaimed as law in the land."

René Leblanc the notary then comes in to arrange preliminaries for the marriage. There is some political talk, but the business of the hour is done. There is a description of Evangeline herself, which is not only beautiful, but so wonderfully graphic as to leave an impress on the reader's mind which he never shakes off:

> Soon with a soundless step the foot of Evangeline followed.
> Up the staircase moved a luminous space in the darkness,
> Lighted less by the lamp than the shining face of the maiden.
> Silent she passed the hall, and entered the door of her chamber.

. . . . .

> Ah! she was fair, exceeding fair to behold, as she stood with
> Naked snow-white feet on the gleaming floor of her chamber!
> Little she dreamed that below, among the trees of the orchard,
> Waited her lover and watched for the gleam of her lamp and her shadow.

Then there is the part of the betrothal, where—

> Fairest of all the maids was Evangeline, Benedict's daughter!
> Noblest of all the youths was Gabriel, son of the blacksmith!

But the orders of the Englishmen come. The inhabitants of the village, one and all, are to be banished from Grand-Pré. Basil the blacksmith rebels, while Bellefontaine the farmer, with his daughter, prepare to obey the British orders:

> Meanwhile, amid the gloom, by the church Evangeline lingered.

All was silent within; and in vain at the door and
the windows
Stood she, and listened and looked, till, overcome by emotion,
"Gabriel!" cried she aloud with tremulous voice;
but no answer
Came from the graves of the dead, nor the
gloomier grave of the living.

They are all hurried down to the sea-shore, and there they
are separated. Basil and Gabriel are carried off in different
ships; while the farmer and his daughter, looking back, see
the flames and smoke rising to heaven from the ruins of
their village:

"We shall behold no more our homes in the village of Grand-Pré!"

But, alas! they are not doomed even to suffer exile together. The old father, broken-hearted, dies upon the sand,
and is buried, till in a happier time his neighbors shall return and piously place his dust in the church-yard. Then
Evangeline is carried off into the world alone.

The second part begins after the lapse of long days:

Many a weary year had passed since the burning
of Grand-Pré,
When on the falling tide the freighted vessels departed,
Bearing a nation, with all its household gods,
into exile,
Exile without an end, and without an example
in story.

. . . . .

Friendless, homeless, hopeless, they wandered
from city to city
From the cold lakes of the North to sultry
Southern savannas,—
From the bleak shores of the sea to the lands
where the Father of Waters
Seizes the hills in his hands, and drags them
down to the ocean,
Deep in their sands to bury the scattered bones
of the mammoth.

. . . . .

Long among them was seen a maiden who waited and wandered,
Lowly and meek in spirit, and patiently suffering
all things.

And so Evangeline passes on, ever looking for her lover.
We can almost see her as she wearies and fades in the
search. Life has nothing before her except the hope that
she may find her lover, —may find him who was all but
her husband. She comes upon his track again and again,
but still she misses him:

"Gabriel Lajeunesse!" said they; "O, yes! we
have seen him.
He was with Basil the blacksmith, and both have
gone to the prairies;
Coureurs-des-Bois are they, and famous hunters
and trappers."
"Gabriel Lajeunesse!" said others; "O, yes! we
have seen him.
He is a Voyageur in the lowlands of Louisiana."

The priest, her friend, was with her, and tries to console
her:

". . . O daughter! thy God thus speaketh within
thee!
Talk not of wasted affection, affection never has
wasted;
If it enrich not the heart of another, its waters,
returning
Back to their springs, like the rain, shall fill them
full of refreshment."

Hereupon the poet explains what it is he intends to do with
Evangeline, and makes his reader clearly understand the
great purpose which he has in hand:

Let me essay, O Muse! to follow the wanderer's
footsteps;—
Not through each devious path, each changeful
year of existence;
But as a traveller follows a streamlet's course
through the valley:
Far from its margin at times, and seeing the
gleam of its water
Here and there, in some open space, and at intervals only;
Then drawing nearer its banks, through sylvan
glooms that conceal it,
Though he behold it not, he can hear its continuous murmur;
Happy, at length, if he find the spot where it
reaches an outlet.

He describes the passage of his travelers onward through
forests, down rivers, and across lakes, teaching his reader
to see with the eye of his imagination the very track over
which he takes them; you smell the flowers, and you feel
the waters, and you yourself lie in your boat idle in the hot
sunshine. The gloom of the cypresses envelops you. The
sluggish movements of the lagoons almost overpower you.
The groves of orange and citron are too rich and gorgeous
for your senses. The cotton-trees nod their shadowy crests,
and the pelicans wade with their snow-white plumes. The
reader feels that nature is being described to him with singular truth. And yet Longfellow had never seen the country he paints; —has not, as I believe, seen it now. He told
me that he had never traveled through those parts of his
own continent which he had described. His traveling has
been chiefly European. But his imagination whispered to
him here what would be necessary for the adornment of
his tale. And, indeed, I think that it is mostly so when the
reader finds himself delighted by the description of places
or even of things; the word-painting is generally the effect
of imagination. Consequently, we are so often disappointed when we reach the place described. I myself cannot describe places; I enjoy the beauty and the feeling of scenic
effect, but I lack the words to render them delightful to
others. But I have some trick in depicting social scenes,
and have been often complimented on my sketch of cleri-
cal life. I am told that I must have lived in cathedral cities,
and the like, —and have, with a certain mild denial, carried off the compliments. I could not say so in my own
country, but I do not mind acknowledging to Americans
that all my clergymen have been but pastors and parsons
of the imagination. So it has been with Longfellow, and

I doubt much whether those who go southward down the Mississippi will find the scenes which he paints.

Evangeline knows that Gabriel is before her on her track, and the boatmen call on to other neighboring boatmen, but not a voice is returned:

> And when the echoes had ceased, like a sense of
>     pain was the silence.
> Then Evangeline slept; but the boatmen rowed
>     through the midnight,
> Silent at times, then singing familiar Canadian
>     boat-songs,
> Such as they sang of old on their own Acadian
>     rivers.
> And through the night were heard the mysteri-
>     ous sounds of the desert,
> Far off, indistinct, as of wave or wind in the for-
>     est,
> Mixed with the whoop of the crane and the roar
>     of the grim alligator.

But,

> Nearer and ever nearer, among the numberless
>     islands,
> Darted a light, swift boat.
>
>             . . . . .
>
> At the helm sat a youth, with countenance
>     thoughtful and careworn.
> Dark and neglected locks overshadowed his
>     brow, and a sadness
> Somewhat beyond his years on his face was legi-
>     bly written.
> Gabriel was it, who, weary with waiting, unhap-
>     py and restless,
> Sought in the Western wilds oblivion of self and
>     of sorrow.

"Angel of God," says the poet, "was there none to awaken the slumbering maiden."

> Something says in my heart that near me Gabri-
>     el wanders.
> Is it a foolish dream, an idle and vague supersti-
>     tion?
> Or has an angel passed, and revealed the truth
>     to my spirit?

Journeying on, they come upon a country homestead, in which they find Basil the blacksmith—alone. The passage begins with a description of the home of the breeder of cattle, —for to that profession has the blacksmith turned, —and of the stalwart old man as he is seen on his steed, with Spanish saddle and Spanish dress, —to which description I think my former remarks also apply. But all is picturesque, peaceful, and at the same time touched with pathos. Basil recognizes them, and tells them that Gabriel had left him only that morning. "Gone! Is Gabriel gone?" says Evangeline. Basil rejoins that his son had become weary with waiting. Of the girls of the country he would take no notice. His life had been hard to bear, and he had become a companion hard to be borne. He had gone off that very morning in his boat, and how had it been that they had not met him amid the waters? Evangeline's dream had been true, and Gabriel had been close to her while they lay that night sleeping among the reeds. But

Basil explains that, if they follow him, he will have but one day's start of them. He has gone to a Spanish town hard by, whence he will go up country to hunt the beaver. But they will catch him surely before he starts, and bring him back, oh! so willingly, to his prison. Evangeline shall rest one night, and on the morning they will again be on their journey. Basil rises to enthusiasm as he describes the charms of his new home, and the freedom, the sunny delights of the South, and the absence of Georgian tyranny. But there is no word of slavery. Alas! we fear that Basil is wrong in his outlook into the future. The joys of freedom are hardly so compatible with Southern verdure as are the "hungry winters" and "congealed rivers" and "stony ground" of the North. Basil, however, remembers himself, and the truth:

> "Only beware of the fever, my friends, beware
>     of the fever!"

They start again on their journey, and, on reaching the Spanish town, find that Gabriel had left it on the previous morning!

It is impossible to give an idea of the genius of Longfellow without insisting on the joy with which he revels among imaginary beauties of nature. It is to him a nature of his own, not requiring the sustenance of an outside world before his eyes, as was to Hawthorne the weird mysticism of a world which was only present to him in his fancy. There was nothing special in Hawthorne's personal experiences to have produced such dread ideas; and, though Longfellow has traveled in the course of an enjoyable life through scenes of much European beauty, not to that is to be attributed the luxuriance of the charm of description by which the readers of *Evangeline* are delighted. It is not necessary to produce such description that with the poet's fancy should be combined a reality of poetic scenery. Without the fancy, the scenery would be nothing. All the Alps with all their glory do not create for us a great Swiss poet. But, without the Alps or any of their glory, the classical but not particularly beautiful town of Cambridge, and the somewhat sterile region of Massachusetts, suffice, when the man comes to whom God has given the genius of Longfellow.

They pass on on their search amid various adventures, and at last they arrive at a "mission," at which dwells a priest, whose work it is to baptize, and, if possible, to teach the Indians. Here again Gabriel had been, but again had gone upon his distant journey. But, in the autumn, so says the priest, he will surely return. Evangeline declares that she will remain with him, wearing away the long day till autumn comes, and she sends Basil back with her troop of friends to their new-found home:

> Slowly, slowly, slowly the days succeeded each
>     other,—
> Days and weeks and months; and the fields of
>     maize that were springing
> Green from the ground, when a stranger she
>     came, now waving above her,
> Lifted their slender shafts.

But in the autumn he came not, nor in the winter; and in the summer she renews her search. All alone, or with companions found upon her journey, she still goes on and on, till the reader's heart is almost broken by the constancy of her purpose and its thanklessness:

> Like a phantom she came, and passed away un-
> remembered.
> Fair was she and young, when in hope began the
> long journey;
> Faded was she and old, when in disappointment
> it ended.

We seem to see her as the lines of age and sorrow come upon her during her long work. There is a persistency in the telling of the story which never wearies, —the same sort of persistency as that by which she was supported. She finds her way to Penn's city, and there, after a while, the plague also finds its way. The description is again wonderfully good:

> Wealth had no power to bribe, nor beauty to
> charm, the oppressor.

Rich and poor fall alike. And here Evangeline takes upon herself the duties of a nurse, —she by this time worn and aged, and only waiting till the Lord should release her from her troubles. And she is released. Amid the sick there is one gray old man to whose bedside she is taken, and him she finds to be her lover:

> Then there escaped from her lips a cry of such
> terrible anguish,
> That the dying heard it, and started up from
> their pillows.

On the pallet before her was stretched the form of a man whom she recognizes as Gabriel. At last they meet, —but they meet only to know each other, to die, to be buried there in the strange city, and to become a tale to be told for ever after.

*Evangeline* has taken its place among the recognized poems of the English language in such a way that it can never lose it; and she has taken her place as one of the sweetest characters in the world of letters. There is, however, but little in it but what the poet's imagination has supplied. Of Gabriel personally we know nothing, nor of Evangeline's beauty. The only description given is of her "naked snow-white feet." But of her persistency we are assured, and her innocency we cannot but take for granted. Let the reader ask himself whether he is not assured that Evangeline is pure and innocent. Then let him ask himself why? The poet has never told him so; but such has been the efficacy of the poet's song.

I can hardly myself say whether the meter has been most for him or against him. I would not have it changed; but I would hardly have recommended another attempt. One has at first to dislike it, and then one has to learn to love it. Longfellow had before tried it in "The Children of the Lord's Supper," —a poem translated from the Swedish, —and has, as I think, only partially succeeded. The difficulty consists in converting English sounds into the necessary penultimate dactyl. "Endures and stands waiting"; "I have pledged you to heaven"; —these are two, to which many could be added, which are not euphonious; and, in reading a poem in the English language produced in a meter in which the ear has become accustomed to all the soft prosody of the Latin language, the reader is at once struck and offended by a want of euphony. He returns to it in *The Courtship of Miles Standish,* and likes it somewhat better, though it has not all the softness of *Evangeline.*

*Hiawatha* I regard as Longfellow's greatest work, —greatest for continuity of purpose and success in carrying it out, though it is not that which will be best liked by the world at large. But here, again, the reader has to accustom himself to the rhythm before he can appreciate the excellence of the poem. I remember when, on its first appearance in London, it became almost an object of ridicule because of the singularity of the meter, and the continued reiteration of sounds and translations which the poet has allowed himself to adopt. He has created, too, for himself a habit of continuing his sentence without all its component parts:

> Forth went Shingebis, the diver,
> Wrestled all night with the North-Wind,
> Wrestled naked on the moorlands
> With the fierce Kabibonokka.

> On the next day of his fasting,
> By the river's brink he wandered,
> Through the Muskoday, the meadow,
> Saw the wild-rice, Mahnomonee,
> Saw the blueberry, Meenahga,
> And the strawberry, Odahmin,
> And the gooseberry, Shahbomin,
> And the grape-vine, the Bemahgut.

Repetitions such as these caught the reader's ear and eyes and produced parodies, —especially one in "Punch," which, for a time, was better known in London than *Hiawatha* itself. But *Hiawatha* has stuff in it which has enabled it to live down all such criticism, which, in regard to the author, was never other than good-natured, and has come by its own native strength to be understood and established as a great work.

The purpose of *Hiawatha* is similar to that carried out in "Orion," another poem of much power in the English language by our countryman, Horne. From some cause, which to me has ever been a mystery, "Orion" has not become popular. It contains passages to which, for description, it is difficult to find anything superior; and the thought or idea carried through the whole never flags. It is the old idea of Hercules, —of a man endowed with god-like energy, with grand desire for progress, with mental and corporeal capacities for carrying them out, but still impeded by human desires. Such was Horne's idea of Orion, as taken from the old Greek mythology; and such has been the idea—whence taken we know not—of Longfellow in describing Hiawatha, the Orion of the North American Indians. He, too, is human, but at the same time god-like, and employs himself, amid all impediments and antipathies of the human race, to conquer for them the difficulties imposed by nature. I need hardly say that there has come to the world, in these later years in which we live, another teacher, who has achieved the tasks on which the mythic Hercules, Orion, and Hiawatha spent their strength very much in vain.

*Hiawatha* is divided into twenty-two parts, of which the first two have no reference to the hero. In the first, the great god, offended by the quarrels of his people, calls them all together, over the face of the earth, by smoking his peace-pipe. They come, and obediently all profess friendship. In the second, Mudjekeewis, the West-Wind, Hiawatha's father, is chosen King of the Winds. Kabibonokka is the North-Wind, and his battle with Shingebis, the bird which will not submit to him, is ludicrously described. The four winds are named, and the fourth is in the keeping of Mudjekeewis. Then, in the third part, the birth of Hiawatha is described. Wenonah is his mother, the beautiful daughter of Nokomis:

> And Nokomis warned her often,
> Saying oft, and oft repeating,
> "O, beware of Mudjekeewis,
> Of the West-Wind, Mudjekeewis;
> Listen not to what he tells you;
> Lie not down upon the meadow,
> Stoop not down among the lilies,
> Lest the West-Wind come and harm you!"
> But she heeded not the warning,
> Heeded not those words of wisdom,
> And the West-Wind came at evening,
> Walking lightly o'er the prairie,
> Whispering to the leaves and blossoms,
> Bending low the flowers and grasses,
> Found the beautiful Wenonah,
> Lying there among the lilies,
> Wooed her with his words of sweetness,
> Wooed her with his soft caresses,
> Till she bore a son in sorrow,
> Bore a son of love and sorrow.

When he is born, his mother dies broken-hearted at the desertion of the heartless Mudjekeewis. But he is brought up by his grandmother Nokomis, and nothing can be sweeter than the story of his childhood:

> "Ewa-yea! my little owlet!
> Who is this, that lights the wigwam?
> With his great eyes lights the wigwam?
> Ewa-yea! my little owlet!"

Then, after a time, he goes forth to seek his father, who lives in an unknown country right across the world, among the Rocky Mountains. He goes so fast that he leaves the antelope behind him; indeed, he runs so quickly, that he passes the arrow as he shot it from his bow. He finds his father, and fights with him as avenging his mother. But his father is immortal and cannot be killed, and sends him home rewarded for his valor. Then we are told of Hiawatha, how he prayed and fasted in the forest:

> Not for greater skill in hunting,
> Not for greater craft in fishing,
> Not for triumphs in the battle,
> And renown among the warriors,
> But for profit of the people.

And he makes two friends, Music and Strength, —Chibiabos the musician, and Kwasind the strong man, —upon whom to depend for all his needs. He makes a boat, too, and goes a-fishing. From the birch-tree and the cedar, from the tamarack and the larch, from the fir-tree and the balsam, he took what he needed. But when his canoe was made, he had no paddles. We are told that his thoughts served him as paddles, —in which I think there is an error in the metaphor. As the poet deals with matters so palpa-

ble as a boat, he should hardly furnish it with utensils so shadowy as thoughts. He goes a-fishing with the assistance of the squirrel, and kills Mishe-Nahma, the King of Fishes.

Then we have the story of his wooing:

> "As unto the bow the cord is,
> So unto the man is woman,
> Though she bends him, she obeys him,
> Though she draws him, yet she follows,
> Useless each without the other!"

He had seen among the Dacotahs, Minnehaha, whose name is Laughing Water, the daughter of the Arrowmaker; and, in spite of the warnings of his grandmother, who thinks it safer that he should wed one of his tribe, goes off and courts her. The father gives his consent:

> And the lovely Laughing Water
> Seemed more lovely, as she stood there,
> Neither willing nor reluctant,
> As she went to Hiawatha,
> Softly took the seat beside him,
> While she said, and blushed to say it,
> "I will follow you, my husband!"

In the eleventh part, he tells of the wedding-feast, in which Chibiabos sings a song of joy and love. It is too long for insertion here, but I refer to it as a perfect expression of the feeling and melody of Longfellow's muse. I do not think that anything he has done is better than the song of Chibiabos, or more peculiarly characteristic of the man. It declares the accuracy of his ear, for he has not admitted into it a sound that grates; and the correctness of his feeling, —if I may venture to say so much of my own judgment, —for there is not a word that does not come home to me as being true to a man's admiration for a woman. Then is told the story of the son of the Evening Star, —very pretty, very graphic, very droll:

> And they laughed till all the forest
> Rang with their unseemly laughter.

Chibiabos then sings another song, and the story of the wedding is over. The second song is not equal to the first, because the poet allows himself the use of a reiterated line. Nothing is more dangerous. Now and again it has been done with wonderful effect; but it is perilously easy to miss the charm. Virgil has been very successful:

> Ducite ab urbe domum, mea carmina, ducite
>     Daphnin.

There is a sweetness and a melody in that, perhaps heightened to our ears by our imperfect familiarity with the dead language. But the sounds must be of the very softest and sweetest to admit of it. Longfellow has almost missed it in his repeated line:

> O my sweetheart, my Algonquin!

He [Hiawatha] goes out and blesses the corn-fields, carrying out his purposes of doing good to man:

> "Thus the fields shall be more fruitful,
> And the passing of your footsteps
> Draw a magic circle round them,
> So that neither blight nor mildew,

> Neither burrowing worm nor insect,
> Shall pass o'er the magic circle;
> Not the dragon-fly, Kwo-ne-she,
> Nor the spider, Subbekashe,
> Nor the grasshopper, Pah-puk-keena,
> Nor the mighty caterpillar,
> Way-muk-kwana, with the bear-skin,
> King of all the caterpillars!"

The ravens hear him, chirping and plotting together in the tops of the trees. They have their own little plans. They will get at the seed. But the watchful Hiawatha hears their scornful laughter, and determines to outwit them:

> "Kaw!" he said, "my friends the ravens!
> Kahgahgee, my King of Ravens!
> I will teach you all a lesson
> That shall not be soon forgotten!"

So he got up early and set traps for the ravens, and, of course, he catches them and slaughters them by tens and twenties. Only the king he spared, and tied him by his leg to the ridge-pole of his wigwam. There the old black bird sits struggling, vainly calling to his "people." Through the whole poem there is the same flavor of drollery. Hiawatha, in his continual battle with things evil, is always conscious of the humor of the contest, so that the reader is carried on by picturesque jest as well as pathos. But we come to the lamentation of Hiawatha for the death of his friend Chibiabos. The evil spirits league together to destroy him, and Chibiabos falls into the trap:

> Forth to hunt the deer with antlers
> All alone went Chibiabos.

But, in crossing the ice, the spirits catch him and drag him down into the water; and there they

> Drowned him in the deep abysses
> Of the lake of Gitche Gumee.

Hiawatha is inconsolable. His bard is dead. The spirit of music is fled from him:

> "He is dead, the sweet musician!"

But the medicine-men come and console him. They bring their simples and ointments, and Hiawatha yields to them:

> Thus was first made known to mortals
> All the mystery of Medamin,
> All the sacred art of healing.

I cannot tell of the wild adventures, of the tricks and gambols, of the cunning of Pau-Puk-Keewis, but must go on to the death of Kwasind, and the mischief of the Puk-Wudjies:

> "If this hateful Kwasind," said they,
> "If this great, outrageous fellow
> Goes on thus a little longer,
> Tearing everything he touches,
> Rending everything to pieces,
> Filling all the world with wonder,
> What becomes of the Puk-Wudjies?"

Then, as ever, weakness was jealous of strength, so that the Puk-Wudjies resolved to rid themselves and the world of the strong arm which did so much for them. In poetry, all strong men have been vulnerable at one point only.

Achilles was weak in his heel; Samson in his hair. Kwasind could not be touched by anything that men would do to him except on the top of his head, and there only by the cones of the fir-tree. This was a secret supposed to be known to none. But the crafty little Puk-Wudjies learned it, and gathering together a quantity of cones waited till Kwasind came floating down the river fast asleep in his boat. Then the wicked little people pelted him till he died, —

> And he sideways swayed and tumbled,
> Sideways fell into the river, —

and that was the end of Kwasind.

Then there come upon the earth all the horrors of a famine, —of famine and fever together. It is midwinter, and frost and snow cover all things. Minnehaha is starving in their wigwam, and Hiawatha can find no food for her. There is not a deer nor a rabbit in the woods:

> "Give your children food, O father!
> Give us food, or we must perish!
> Give me food for Minnehaha!"

He goes off far to the forest, but can find nothing. But he hears, or fancies that he hears, the voice of Minnehaha:

> Miles away among the mountains,
> Heard that sudden cry of anguish,
> Heard the voice of Minnehaha
> Calling to him in the darkness,
> "Hiawatha! Hiawatha!"

He hurries home, and finds her dead. Now he has lost everything. Chibiabos and Kwasind are gone; and now the best beloved of all, Minnehaha, is taken from him. In the stories that have been told to us of all those heroes who have struggled to assist their fellow-creatures, sorrow has ever been the appropriate and, as it seems to us, the only possible ending.

> "Farewell!" said he, "Minnehaha!
> Farewell, O my Laughing Water!
> All my heart is buried with you,
> All my thoughts go onward with you!
> Come not back again to labor,
> Come not back again to suffer,
> Where the Famine and the Fever
> Wear the heart and waste the body.
> Soon my task will be completed,
> Soon your footsteps I shall follow
> To the Islands of the Blessed."

I may here leave the story of Hiawatha. There are two more parts or cantos in which he is introduced to the white man, but I have done enough to describe the purport of the poem and enough also, I hope, to make all your readers aware how small a portion of it is occupied by the alliteration and repetitions to which their attention has been particularly called. The purpose has been very great, and the execution wonderfully good, mingling pathos, humor, and description in such a way as to offend none. In pathos, humor, and description it is complete, and is told in verse which never jars, at any rate on my ear. In ***Evangeline*** there is no humor, and I cannot say quite so much for the versification.

The story of Miles Standish and of John Alden is as old as the hills, but it never was told with a clearer or more deliberate purpose, nor in the telling of it were the feelings of the three persons concerned made more conspicuous. The three are all of the company of the old Pilgrim fathers who landed from the May-flower at Plymouth, and the time chosen is before the return journey of the ship to England. The persons concerned are Miles Standish the soldier, John Alden the student, and Priscilla, with whom both of them are in love. The two men are, or at least have been, fast friends; but John Alden—while he is thinking of his love, dreaming of his love, hoping that his love may be brought to love him—is desired by the soldier to go to Priscilla and, on his behalf, to ask for her hand. This he does, most mournfully, with a broken heart, but is answered by the girl, who will have nothing to say to Miles Standish, "Why don't you speak for yourself, John?"

> Into the open air John Alden, perplexed and be-
> wildered,
> Rushed like a man insane, and wandered alone
> by the sea-side;
> Paced up and down the sands, and bared his
> head to the east-wind,
> Cooling his heated brow, and the fire and fever
> within him.
> Slowly, as out of the heavens, with apocalyptical
> splendors,
> Sank the City of God, in the vision of John the
> Apostle,
> So, with its cloudy walls of chrysolite, jasper,
> and sapphire,
> Sank the broad red sun, and over its turrets up-
> lifted
> Glimmered the golden reed of the angel who
> measured the city.

These lines hardly have the pathos with which the sufferings of Evangeline are described. I do not intend to say that the story as told by Longfellow is deficient in pathos. No such story could be told by him so as to want italtogether. But the whole tale of John Alden—for he is the hero, and not Miles Standish—is narrated in the language of ordinary life, for which the Latin hexameters are hardly fitted. The history is given with great rapidity, and yet seems to include all that there is to be said. Indeed, the story as a story is admirably complete. *Evangeline* is not complete. It is vague and wandering, and given only in parts, whereas *Miles Standish* is round and finished from beginning to end. The lines I have given above have been selected as being outside the story, rather than a part of it; yet even here the meter hardly comes home to the reader as that which should have been chosen.

He meets the Captain of Plymouth, as Miles Standish is called, and tells him how he has sped in his wooing, —telling him also the question the girl had asked in reply. But the Captain becomes outrageously angry, and upbraids his friend, as he might have done in real life:

> " . . . John Alden! you have betrayed me!
> Me, Miles Standish, your friend! have supplant-
> ed, defrauded, betrayed me!"

Here I cannot but observe that the dactyls do not trip off the tongue quite so lightly as dactyls should do. Miles Standish insults his friend with bitterest words, and, going off, gives warlike advice to the elder, and people who have sent for him.

On the morrow the Mayflower is to sail on its return journey:

> Out of the sea rose the sun, and the billows re-
> joiced at his coming;
> Beautiful were his feet on the purple tops of the
> mountains;
> Beautiful on the sails of the Mayflower riding at
> anchor,
> Battered and blackened and worn by all the
> storms of the winter.
> Loosely against her masts was hanging and flap-
> ping her canvas,
> Rent by so many gales, and patched by the
> hands of the sailors.
> Suddenly from her side, as the sun rose over the
> ocean,
> Darted a puff of smoke, and floated seaward;
> anon rang
> Loud over field and forest the cannon's roar, and
> the echoes
> Heard and repeated the sound, the signal-gun of
> departure!

John Alden is so broken-hearted between the love of the girl to whom he has been so little like a lover, and the anger of the friend to whom he has been so faithful, that he resolves that he will return home in the Mayflower. But down on the sands he encounters Priscilla—

> Standing dejected among them, unconscious of
> all that was passing.
> Fixed were her eyes upon his, as if she divined
> his intention,
> Fixed with a look so sad, so reproachful, implor-
> ing, and patient,
> That with a sudden revulsion his heart recoiled
> from its purpose,
> As from the verge of a crag, where one step more
> is destruction.

He sees two hands in the clouds, one beckoning him back, and the other holding him on to the land of his adoption. He decides to stay. But, in the meantime, the impatient master of the Mayflower is glad to leave a land where there is, as he pithily remarks—

> "Short allowance of victual, and plenty of noth-
> ing but Gospel!"

The Captain is called out to fight the Indians in protection of the settlement, and this he does with all his old vigor. There is a meeting of the white men and the savages, in which, after a little discourse, the Captain murders one of the Indian leaders because he will not endure the taunts which are addressed to him. He is more unreasonable with Pecknot than he was even with John Alden. But such ways were, I suppose, apt to prevail with Indians, and Miles Standish returns to the village with the head of the chief Wattawamat, whom he had also slain in the encounter:

> Thus the first battle was fought and won by the
> stalwart Miles Standish.

Meanwhile John Alden had built himself a house, and had

made a stall close by for Raghorn, the snow-white steer which had fallen to his share when the cattle were divided, and had put up wooden bars and contrived paper window-panes, as though he were to bring his wife home. And he bethinks himself of the praises of a virtuous woman:

> How the heart of her husband doth safely trust
>   in her always,
> How all the days of her life she will do him good
>   and not evil,
> How she seeketh the wool and the flax and wor-
>   keth with gladness,
> How she layeth her hand to the spindle and hol-
>   deth the distaff,
> How she is not afraid of the snow for herself or
>   her household,
> Knowing her household are clothed with the
>   scarlet cloth of her weaving!

But, while he is discoursing with Priscilla, whom, on account of his faith to Miles Standish, he cannot marry, news is suddenly brought in that Miles Standish is dead. The Captain of Plymouth has been killed by a poisoned arrow in an encounter with the Indians. Then John Alden, in a sudden rapture of joy, clasps the motionless form of Priscilla, and, pressing her close to his heart, claims her as his own forever:

> "Those whom the Lord hath united, let no man
>   put them asunder!"

This, indeed, we are driven to confess, he does with too rapid an anxiety to be happy, considering that he has but

*Mary Potter Longfellow (1812-1835), the poet's first wife.*

that moment heard of the demise of his friend. We are told, indeed, that he does it:

> Wild with excess of sensation, the awful delight
>   of his freedom,
> Mingled with pain and regret, unconscious of
>   what he was doing.

Then there comes the wedding-day, on which Alden carries home his bride, sitting on the snow-white steer. And, in order that all things may be made to smile, Miles Standish himself comes back, the rumor of his death having been false; and he makes one pretty speech to Priscilla:

> Gravely, and after the manner of old-fashioned
>   gentry in England,
> Something of camp and of court, of town and of
>   country, commingled,
> Wishing her joy of her wedding, and loudly
>   lauding her husband.
> Then he said, with a smile: "I should have re-
>   membered the adage,—
> If you would be well served, you must serve
>   yourself; and moreover,
> No man can gather cherries in Kent at the sea-
>   son of Christmas."

I must own that **Miles Standish** is not so much to my taste as are **Evangeline** and **Hiawatha,** and, to confess the truth, I do not think that the poet gave to it the same amount of labor and thought. He has seemed to take the plot as it came to his hand, perfect in the details of the story as he found it, and has failed to elaborate it or to pare off the harshnesses, and to fit in the more delicate details with all the care that has been given to those other performances. In plot, we regard **Hiawatha** as perfect, the poem telling the story, with its purpose, in such a manner as to bring home to the reader exactly the feeling which the author intended to convey. So in **Miles Standish** is the tale well told. Judging an ordinary tale in the ordinary way, the ordinary critic would find no fault; but there lacks in it a last something of Longfellow's powers of poetry.

But the **"Skeleton in Armor,"** which is a short ballad, lacks it not at all. It is, as a ballad should be, short, concise, perfect, without a word thrown away. Of all modes of poetry the ballad seems to be the easiest; but is, I hold, the most difficult to accomplish. It must have neither beginning nor end, but must rush at once to its story, and leave off as suddenly. And the reader, or hearer, feeling that a demand is made on him for concentrated attention, will, unconsciously, forgive no weakness. In the **"Skeleton in Armor"** he is called upon to forgive none. The Skeleton begins the story of his life, and tells it all:

> "Far in the Northern Land
> By the wild Baltic strand,
> I, with my childish hand,
> Tamed the gerfalcon;
> And, with my skates fast-bound,
> Skimmed the half-frozen Sound,
> That the poor whimpering hound
> Trembled to walk on.
>
> "But when I older grew,
> Joining a corsair's crew,
> O'er the dark sea I flew
> With the marauders.

Wild was the life we led;
Many the souls that sped,
Many the hearts that bled,
By our stern orders."

Hypercriticism would perhaps find fault with the use of the French word "corsair" among those northern seas, but the poet himself would probably tell us that it had become as general in its way as the congenial term "marauders," which certainly does not offend. The viking goes on with the story of his life till he comes to its love-episode:

"Once as I told in glee
Tales of the stormy sea,
Soft eyes did gaze on me,
Burning, yet tender;
And as the white stars shine
On the dark Norway pine,
On that dark heart of mine
Fell their soft splendor."

She was a prince's child, and when he sued for her hand he was discarded.Consequently, after the manner of vikings, he runs off with her. He takes her to sea, and the father follows him. The wind fails them, and they are caught, or nearly so. But he runs the prow of his boat against his father-in-law's ship, and sends it and all that are in it to the bottom. He takes the girl home with him, —to the place he has chosen for a home, —there he builds a tower for her, and she has children; and in the course of time she dies:

"Death closed her mild blue eyes.
Under that tower she lies;
Ne'er shall the sun arise
On such another."

We believe it to be the case that Longfellow is more extensively read here in England than in his own country. At any rate, I had his own word that it was so perhaps a dozen years ago. However that may have been then, or may be now, I have no doubt that he will be equally read hereafter by all who read the English language. There is about him a clearness in his mode of telling his story, and at the same time, as I have said before, a purity and a pathos in his manner of telling it, which will insure him against oblivion.

*Anthony Trollope, "Henry Wadsworth Longfellow," in* North American Review, *Vol. CXXXII, No. 292, 1881, pp. 383-406.*

### George Saintsbury   (essay date 1907)

[*Saintsbury has been called the most influential English literary historian and critic of the late nineteenth and early twentieth centuries. As a critic of poetry and drama, he was a radical formalist who frequently asserted that subject is of little importance, and that "the so-called 'formal' part is of the essence." In the following essay, he provides an overview of Longfellow's work.*]

When the news of Longfellow's death reached London, nearly a quarter of a century ago, the evening papers published it just at the meeting time of a small private literary dining-club, of which he, Victor Hugo, and one or two

other great foreigners were members. I happened to be in the chair (or vice-chair, I forget which) that evening; and thus it fell to my lot to propose the toast of his name, with the silent honours usual in such cases. I might, I think, have claimed the office by something more than right of accident. For few people can have been "brought up" upon at least the earlier works of the poet, as far as *Hiawatha,* more than I was from childhood; and I venture to hope that still fewer have been more faithful to their bringing-up. I have met since, and I have fallen in love with, poetry of very different kinds from Longfellow's, and (in some cases) of kinds, if the word must be used, "superior" to his. But I have never felt in the least inclined, in a capital popular phrase, to "put him out of his place". Indeed, I think that he is a most excellent text for preaching the doctrine that no poet, who is a poet, ever can be put out of his place by another, with any lover of poetry who understands as well as loves. . . .

Longfellow is among the least difficult authors to read, and he should be among the easiest to criticise; though, owing to some faults of his own and more of his critics', he has not always proved so. It is certainly an unfortunate thing for a poet that his most universally known and perhaps, for a long time at any rate, his most popular poem should be one of his own worst. It is still more unfortunate (for after all, a poet cannot help the bad taste of his readers) that it should be bad of and in itself. It is most unfortunate of all that its badness should exaggerate, accentuate, and caricature certain rather too frequent characteristics of his. Now all these things are true of **"Excelsior."** The most Rhadamanthine and the most ingenious of critics could hardly strain his severity or his ingenuity in finding fault with it. The title does not mean what it ought to mean to make any sense whatever of the piece; and does mean something quite different—a blunder which is accentuated by its being used as a refrain, and by the astoundingly unlucky description of it as in "an unknown tongue". The conduct of the ungrammatical youth is that of a mere lunatic; even Alpine Clubs, which were hardly founded when Longfellow wrote, would not defend it. That of the maiden would, in the famous French phrase, "make dragoons blush". And the theology of the conclusion matches the morality of the maiden and the Latinity and common sense of the youth, by intimating divine approval of what was, on the showing of the poet, pure suicide without a purpose or an aim—unless indeed the youth knew no other way to get to Italy to effect that improvement in his Latin of which there was such urgent need. The charges, often foolishly enough brought of late, against mid-nineteenth-century "sentiment" are here amply justified. The whole thing is sheer silliness—silliness so intense that, with the accompanying want of scholarship, it would damn even an allowance of poetic expression much greater than that given here. One could but heartily wish the thing unwritten if it were not a curious literary *point de repère,* as to the way in which false taste, in poet and in readers at the same time, lashes the poet into a kind of paroxysm now and then.

But this paroxysm was never repeated. It is true, as has been said, that the worst things in it are caricatures and exaggerations of things that occur frequently in Longfellow; but these things in themselves are not despicable, and they are almost invariably accompanied by something else which redeems and transforms them. It will be, for most competent judges, something, that poets who may be called "greater", in critical slang, than he is—who are at any rate members of an extremely different school—have had a curious habit of "taking notes" from him, not in the manner which foolish people call plagiarism, but as poets take from poets. The use made by Baudelaire (not exactly an exponent of early or mid-Victorian sentiment) of **"The Psalm of Life"** in one of the finest of his poems, "Le Guignon," is unmistakable, and has not been mistaken. Yet **"The Psalm of Life"** is one of the most mixed and dangerous of Longfellow's pieces; —it has been riddled with ridicule—or rather ridicule has attempted to riddle it, and has sometimes made a hole or two. Mr. Swinburne is scarcely of the Longfellovian fellowship as that is understood by unfavourable critics: and yet some of the very finest and most characteristic verses of the Prelude to *Songs before Sunrise*—

Because man's soul is man's god still,

fall in curiously with a stanza of another of the *Voices of the Night,* **"The Light of Stars"** beginning—

The star of the unconquered will.

Those who like tracing parallel passages will have good game with Longfellow and his successors among the English-writing poets of the last seventy years. But is this because he has "imitated" others, or because others have "imitated" him in the silly sense which has been already blackmarked? Not at all. It is because to him, as to all true poets, the great commonplaces of life have presented themselves, and because he has known how to treat these commonplaces with the poetic treatment which makes them not common.

What may be said, not against but of Longfellow, with truth is that in treating these great commonplaces he is, as a rule, more indulgent to the common auditor than the greatest poets are, or than some who are not greater than he is; and that sometimes, as in **"Excelsior"** and elsewhere, this indulgence leads him astray. He is in almost all respects the opposite of his contemporary Browning, just as their other contemporary Tennyson makes up a trinity of opposites with them both. Longfellow is one of the most *automatic* of poets—to every subject that presents itself he gives, like some springs, a sort of coating of true and natural but never artificially finished poetry, varying a good deal with the quality of his subject, the fulness or slackness, concentration or dilatation of the spring itself at the moment, and other accidents. Browning is the least automatic, the most determined to submit all matters that come in his way to an apparently eccentric process of his own—a process involving sometimes (not always) a minimum of artistic expenditure, but personal and wayward to the nth. Tennyson, as little automatic as Browning, is the pure artist, never satisfied till he has brought everything to his own ideal of perfection in expression and form. It follows that Browning cannot translate at all—he can only transpose into a key of his own utterly different from the original; that Tennyson has left us but a little

translation or direct imitation, but that of curious perfection; that Longfellow almost seems to prefer translation, and while more than fairly faithful, manages always to give it a flavour of his own.

If we pass from his translations to his original verse, the same or an analogous quality confronts us. Longfellow is never startlingly felicitous; nor, on the other hand, does the sense of his felicity grow on us as we perceive more and more fully the exquisiteness of the art with which, but without artificiality, it is attained. You never have to question yourself, or him, to find out what he means; and you never are tempted almost or altogether to neglect his meaning, for the sake of the poetic supremacy with which it is conveyed. But that meaning is never contemptible—it is not so even in **"Excelsior,"** if the piece could be stripped of its absurdities of expression and ornament. It is sometimes very admirable; and it is almost invariably conveyed with less or more—not unfrequently with a very considerable "more"—of poetic treatment.

Now these are the conditions and specifications of a kind of poet who never can be too plentiful, and who, as a matter of fact, is decidedly rare. If, as some people talk with commendable gravity, poetry is a high and holy thing which ought to be cultivated like religion—that which enables the greatest number of persons to cultivate it is surely to be welcomed. If, on the other hand, as light and frivolous folk prefer to insist, poetry is one of the greatest and absolutely the most harmless of pleasures—surely again, the man who offers this in a manner that the multitude can and do appreciate, is a benefactor of his species. Nay, more, there must as surely be something not of the first-comer, something which Apollo has not given to everybody, in the man who can do this. There are so many poets who have not succeeded in giving pleasure to anybody, whether of the great vulgar or of the small, whether of the promiscuous or the fastidious feeders!

We may, however, devote a few words to this "small vulgar" itself, and beat up its quarters briefly but without much mercy. For my own part, I made up my mind long ago that the critic who pooh-poohs Longfellow's poetry is a bad critic. For one of the attributes of the critic is that he shall be, strictly by derivation and definition, a separator, a man who is able to discern the good from the bad, even though they be mixed like the heap of grain that Venus set Psyche to sort. A critic who must have his poetry sorted out for him, presented in its quiddity, "neat", to vary the metaphor, may pride himself upon his taste, but is in effect confessing his incompetence. In many cases, I fear, even the taste is not quite so genuine as it appears or would like to appear. The critics in question would too certainly at one time have adopted one current standard of poetic supremacy, at another another. At any rate, they may be left in the mire with this dilemma. If they cannot see the poetry in Longfellow because of the other things not quite so poetical which are there, they lack the first qualification of the critic, which is to know poetry when he sees it. If they cannot separate and judge it, they lack the second, which is to see it and treat it by itself. So, enough of them.

Adopting a different style of criticism ourselves, it may be well for us to survey the different divisions of the poet's verse, no one of which can be completely represented here, while large parts of it can only be represented at all by a sort of brick-of-the-house process. This last, however, is no such great misfortune, for Longfellow, in this not differing from most other poets, is by no means at his best in his longest poems, even the non-dramatic ones. Of the dramatic pieces, *The Spanish Student* and the little miracle-play inserted in *The Golden Legend* are by far the best. But of course it is open to anyone to say that neither is a *play* at all; the second being a mere clever *pastiche,* while the first is partly that, and still more a loosely told but capital story which the whim of the writer has thrown into dramatic instead of narrative form. And there is a good deal in this, though for my part I should not like *The Spanish Student* so well if it were not partly in verse, and I never read it afresh without liking it better. The *New England Tragedies,* the *Divine Tragedy* (*Christus*), and *Michael Angelo* are exposed to the same critical description, which, however, would have to take a more uncomplimentary colouring. The slight but ambitious **"Mosque of Pandora"** is by no means without merit; but it wanted another man, and above all a younger man, to write it.

Very pedantic critics of form might object to the separation of *The Golden Legend* itself from this group. To my fancy, however, it occupies a middle place between the dramatic and the purely narrative pieces. It proceeds, no doubt, as the excellent old French phrase has it, "by personages"—there are names as shoulder-headings to the different paragraphs of the verse. But in reality it is nearly as pure a narrative as the original *Der Arme Heinrich* of Hartmann von der Aue, from which it was taken. The speakers (except perhaps Elsie) have no personality—we can neglect them altogether, or at least regard them as the personages of a poem with "then said So-and-so" forming part of the verse. Often, there is no reason why there should be any "So-and-so" at all. The thing is really a sort of dreamy panorama with a certain number of cinematograph effects to enliven it—a thing that poets found out ages and ages before panoramas or cinematographs were invented or thought of. And it is (to me at least) a very delightful thing. I happen to have a fairly wide acquaintance with medieval poetry in the original tongues, and a great devotion to the Middle Ages. I do not say that Longfellow has gone very deeply into medieval sentiment. It was not his way to go very deeply, or to *appear* to go very deeply (which is perhaps a different thing), into anything. He may in parts and passages be at a disadvantage with Mr. William Morris, as he certainly is in *The Wayside Inn.* But here also his "superficiality", as it seems to some folk, has a curious quality of not being so very superficial after all. His etching is not deeply bitten; his colour is but a sort of preliminary wash. But somehow or other both are right as far as they go, and both give to the spectator an effect much more trustworthy than some far more heavily treated plates and pictures. The opening *diablerie,* and that of the scene between Prince Henry and Lucifer; the **"Tale of the Monk Felix"** and Elsie's of the Sultan's daughter; Lucifer in the church; the Prince's picture of the cathedral; Friar Claus in the cellar; the Abbess's soliloquy; the Prince and Elsie at Genoa; the voyage; the crucial scene, and the lovers' final dialogue—are things as to which I

shall respectfully ask any critic to be very sure of his criticship before he dismisses them as ordinary. We must try to make room for most of them here; and if we have to leave out any, the omission will more than justify itself should it send anyone to the original. I think I can promise that, if he has any natural taste for poetry, he will not be satisfied till he knows the whole of the poem itself. For combined variety and charm there is nothing of Longfellow's in bulk that can be compared to it.

At this point, years ago at any rate, there would have been, supposing that many people read the words which I have just written, a chorus of indignant voices, interrupting to cry, "What! do you mean to say that you prefer this second-hand medieval medley to *Evangeline?* " Certainly, I prefer it very much; and what is more, I am certain, as I by no means always am, that, whether I prefer it or not, it ought to be preferred. *Evangeline* is a pretty poem; it lends itself admirably to illustration for drawing-room-table books; it was a clever revival of an old though hopeless experiment in metre; its sentiment is not false; and it has some beautiful passages. We need not attach the slightest importance to the American criticism which says that Longfellow did not take the trouble to go west and south to get local colour for the bayous and the prairies—that he is not true to it. I think the bayous rather nice myself; and, as I am not likely ever to visit the originals, I do not care whether they are like or not. We need not attend to the grave historians who tell us (I believe quite correctly) that the Acadians, instead of being mercilessly, were rather long-suffering dealt with. These things do not matter to poetry at all. The poem, as it seems to me, suffers from two quite different defects, one of matter, one of form. The weakness in matter is twofold. In the first place, the characters, with hardly the slight exception of "Basil the Blacksmith", have no character at all. Longfellow is never very strong at this; but even Elsie in the *Legend* is far more of a person than Evangeline, and Prince Henry than Gabriel. Secondly, the pathetic conclusion is one of those "possible improbabilities" which, as all good critics have noticed from the dawn of criticism, are far worse than probable impossibilities. How did all those years pass? Of course, if Evangeline made a point of a "stern chase", if she insisted on always coming up with Gabriel (as an Irishman might say) just after he had gone somewhere else—there is nothing to say. But when she settled at Philadelphia it was different. The post may not have been very effective, and there may have been no newspapers to advertise in; but trappers wandered everywhere, and though, as I have said, it is possible, it is in the very last degree improbable that even three or four years could have passed, let alone the twenty or thirty required by the story, before Gabriel heard of her whereabouts. It is all very well to say that this is a prosaic criticism, like Mrs. Barbauld's when she told Coleridge that *The Ancient Mariner* was deficient in probability. Coleridge has brought it about that the *poetical* reader of *The Ancient Mariner* never thinks about probability: and Longfellow has not done this. He has not achieved the "suspension of disbelief ", in Coleridge's own great words.

We ought, however, to give some special attention to the form of this, which is also the form of *The Courtship of*

*Miles Standish*—the English hexameter. Longfellow had tried this earlier, in his translation of Tegnér's "Children of the Lord's Supper" and one or two other pieces. It was not surprising that so careful a student of the Germans—who had taken to the metre pretty far back in the eighteenth century—should attempt it; but the previous experiments of Coleridge might have influenced him even without this. I shall frankly say that for my part I believe this English hexameter to be a hopeless and impossible mistake, always and in every form, *as such;* —though it can be made a very effective measure by letting it follow its natural bent with us and become anapaestic. But this is not the place for a prosodic disquisition of the general kind. We must confine ourselves to the special faults or merits of Longfellow's hexameter. The defects of the whole, and of most individual lines, seem to me—in spite of some passable verses and a few effective and fairly sustained passages—to be undeniable. The chief of them, which in a way includes or excuses all or most of the others, is a quality for which French has one short and final word of three letters, *mou;* but which we cannot indicate at all exactly by "soft", and only piecemeal and inadequately by "flaccid" and others. The line lacks spring, coil and recoil, resilience and its corollary resonance. I myself think the not uncommon opinion that English has few spondees incorrect; but Longfellow is very unlucky with his, though, oddly enough, he is fond of that rather dangerous thing the spondaic ending. Usually he oscillates between almost wholly dactylic lines of a very loose, fragile, and rickety construction, and spondees of such a questionable character as

> *She in turn* related her love and all its disasters,

where it is difficult to say whether "she in"—which is little more than one syllable, or "turn-re"—which hardly any pronunciation will get into more than atrochee, is the more incompetent representative of the double-long foot. But not to spend too much time upon technical details (which could be largely multiplied, but for which we have no room), it may be said, I think, without any injustice, that, save in a few passages, the effect of the whole is monotonously slipshod, and very inferior to that even of rhythmical prose.

**The Courtship of Miles Standish** itself needs little notice; none indeed as far as the vehicle is concerned. It was naturally interesting to Americans, as dealing with the rather slender and not always pleasant materials of their early history, and to the poet and his friends as embodying a family tradition. But these things of course have nothing to do with poetic merit itself. As a story it is so slight that to criticise it as such—to point out that Priscilla is rather pert for a Puritan maiden, and that John Alden is a nincompoop or something worse—would be absurd. But if people like it they may; I suppose those who do would call it "idyllic".

Not thus to be dismissed is *Hiawatha,* though a great deal of what has been said by others about *Hiawatha,* its fidelity to authorities, the trustworthiness of these authorities, and so forth, may be dismissed with alacrity and decision. It is enough to say that the effect which the poet wished to produce—the presentation of an entirely strange civili-

sation, or half-civilisation, with imagery, diction, metre and all, adapted in strangeness—is well and even triumphantly achieved. No matter where he got the metre, and no matter whether he mixed the local colour in more senses than one. The whole is of a piece—united and congruous in effect, without gap or jar. And this is a merit which some people put highest in poetry, and which nobody can put low. Of course, the Devil's Advocate, seeing his advantage, may go on and ask whether it is not all rather *too* complete, rather *too* much of a piece—whether the unvarying and unvaried plainsong of the trochaic dimeter does not "get on the nerves" after a time, and not so very long a time; whether the constant repetition of barbaric words with their English synonyms does not overpass the effect of strange terms in poetry, and begin to produce rather that of reading a lexicon; whether Longfellow's old defect of insufficiently marked character—though Paupuk-Keewis and Iagoo, and even Nokomis, have some—is not unfortunately felt. Perhaps the poet's counsel will have to "confess and avoid" a little in this part of the matter. But on reading *Hiawatha* again, after a good many years' interval, I find that it bears the test much better than some things which I used to like when I liked it first, and which the outrage of time has, I fear, irreparably defaced for me. Perhaps it would stand shortening or thinning; but then it is fair to remember that it is, from one point of view, such a mere "bundle of episodes"—there is so very little connection running through it, except the unity of treatment spoken of above, and the presence of Hiawatha as a sort of "hero-when-wanted"—that there is no need to read it all at once. Read in batches, and at the right moment, it is very good reading, not merely for the exotic manners and unfamiliar imagery, not merely for the pleasant if not overdone music of the soft, strange, Indian names, but for other things more sheerly poetical. Indeed, as I look through the twenty-two cantos yet again, to determine what to give here, the whole being impossible, I find myself rather unexpectedly confronted with that other difficulty, what not to give, which is the selector's greatest compliment. I have given rather less than I might, with the same hope, as in the case of *The Spanish Student* and *The Golden Legend,* that the fragments will serve as baits.

Of Longfellow's *magnum opus* in a certain sense, **The Tales of a Wayside Inn,** I shall not say much. It was a little unfortunate, as I have said, in coinciding with a not wholly dissimilar attempt, Mr. William Morris's *Earthly Paradise,* which has not only much more art as a whole, but a much higher level of poetical merit in the parts. Where the contact is even closer, as in **"King Robert of Sicily,"** the contrast is especially disastrous. But read in itself, and as a frank attempt at tale-telling in verse rather than at narrative poetry, it is good pastime enough, and sometimes something very much better. The worst thing about it is its exceeding inequality. The opening story, **"Paul Revere's Ride,"** has the drawback that the excellent Paul does not seem to have run the slightest danger, though, if his friend in the belfry had been observed and caught (as he ought to have been), and hanged (as he might have been with much better right than André), it would have given some point. **"The Ballad of Carmilhan,"** again, is an imitation of the worst German manner—sham "silly sooth"; its failure being intensified by the reminder which the name gives of a very different thing in German, Hauff's most powerful and gruesome prose story. Elsewhere there are excellent things—much if not all of **"The Saga of King Olaf,"** and many smaller ones. But the distinction which I have just drawn had better be kept in mind throughout.

And so we are left with those shorter poems which, if people would only throw away mistaken traditional theories of poetry, are the real test of a poet's gift, unless he is an altogether exceptional person as well as poet, like Dante. In a short poem, the poet has only got to attend to the poetry. He can leave the story and the characters to the persons to whom they properly belong—the novelist and the dramatist. There is nothing to prevent him being as "subjective" or as "objective" as he chooses. Instead of being more or less tied to one metre, he may try a hundred in as many different poems. He has not the slightest excuse for "padding"; and his critics have no excuse for excusing him if he does pad. The immense, the legitimate, the natural charm of variety, instead of having to be painfully sought for, presents itself unsought to him, unless he is so incompetent that *ex hypothesi* he falls out of our consideration. From the stock objections of the criticaster to digressions, episodes, purple patches, etc., he is free by the very fact of the matter.

Accordingly, all Longfellow's best work is of this kind, and there is a very great deal of it. He never lost his skill at it, from the early *Voices of the Night* to the singularly beautiful introduction of *Ultima Thule.* If he made his worst slip here in **"Excelsior,"** he redeemed that slip by almost literally a hundred things that were not slips. As to the objections to "sentiment", "convention", "over-facility" and the like, I have hinted the lines of an impregnable fortification against them above, and it is not necessary to expand or emphasise these lines much. Sentiment, when it becomes (as it has rather a tendency to become) sentimentalism, is not the best of things; but it is at any rate better than the cheap and childish paradox, and much better than the banal brutality, which have been sometimes offered in its place. All conventions (except in pure "manners") are bad; but a clean and kindly convention is, at any rate, less bad than a dirty and ill-natured one. As for over-facility, that opens a very difficult critical question, which I venture to think not many of the objectors are quite learned in their craft enough to handle. For this quality is very intimately connected with that other, of adapting poetry to the general capacity, which has been noted above.

For my part, I am sorry "as a Christian" (compare Rowena's observation and Wamba's comment) for those who cannot see poetry in Longfellow's lyrics; but my sorrow in any other capacity is a good deal tempered by uncharitable doubt whether they *really* see the poetry of Poe or of Whitman, of Rossetti or of Blake. I am extremely glad, as a matter of pure humanity, that there are a large number of persons who can and do see it.

It is to be seen in various forms and ways—in description, suggestion, musical accompaniment of thought. Of the two famous poetic processes, Longfellow, no doubt, oftener adopts that of adorning and exalting the familiar

than that of seizing and making familiar the strange; but it would be unjust (the refusal is indeed at the root of all the injustice that has been done to him) to refuse him command of a certain middle way, a combination of the two nearer to the earth than to the ether, but not involving banishment from this latter. And this is what makes his companionship and guideship so valuable for those who are not exactly at home on the mountain-tops of poetry; who cannot (or cannot at first) breathe its more rarefied air. Some, of course, of his things, especially the **"Psalm of Life"** itself, are so hackneyed, so sullied by the ignoble use of cheap quotation and stale tagging of morals, that it needs the accident of fresh acquaintance, or the much rarer property of that real critical spirit which is proof against all hackneying, to enjoy them thoroughly. Others, like **"The Bridge"** for instance, pay the rather comic and unfair but very real penalty of being so indissolubly associated with their usual musical setting that the actual poetical music is, as it were, dinned out of hearing. But in late work as in early, in the unhackneyed things as in the hackneyed, there never fails for long together, or rather there is almost always present, this unpretentious and apparently easy gift of communicating something of poetical treatment, something of poetical effect, to everything, or almost everything, that is touched. It may be a happy epithet of description; it may be a musical phrase or rhythm; it may be a suggestion of thought or feeling just charmed into freedom from the merely prosaic and banal; it may even be a borrowed plume of reading freshly set in the poet's cap, a relish of out-of-the-way literature happily instilled; it may be a dozen other things tedious to particularise. But the poeticising—the disrealising and yet realising—touch is always in it, or in it so often as to obscure and cover the failures. Nay, these failures themselves, save in one or two cases, especially that gibbeted above, are themselves so modest and so little offending, that, even without the successes, they would almost escape notice. The entire absence of pretentiousness is here also a wonderful preservative. Longfellow may be sometimes insignificant, he may oftimes have the rather evanescent touch of the *improvisatore,* but he is never positively dull or offensive, rarely absurd.

Not often has a poet made a more definite promise than in the *Voices of the Night,* which, be it remembered, appeared in 1839 after a considerable apprenticeship both to speech and silence, but some years before the capital appearances of Tennyson in the *Poems* of 1842, and of Browning in *Bells and Pomegranates.* They are all given here as they were finally united by their author; and though no large handful, it is a handful of very pleasant delights. **"The Prelude"**—with its well-chosen combination of the metrical qualities of the Ballad quatrain and the Romance six—is really a remarkable fore-shadowing of Longfellow's poetical career, and the baggage he was to take with him on it: the delight in Nature; the delight in a quiet but not vulgar fancy; the delight in literature; the sympathy with humanity; the sense—rather remarkable in a person of so equable a temper, and showing itself at a time when the "browner shades" were not even near—of the passing of time and the vanity of things. And this variety shows itself at more development in what follows—the graceful **"Hymn to the Night"**; the "fine confused feeding" and "extremely valuable thoughts", as Wordsworth said of his own poems, of the **"Psalm of Life"**; the more than pretty sentiment of **"The Reaper,"** and the not less than fine bravery of **"The Light of Stars."**

For the two original ballads, **"The Skeleton in Armour"** and **"The Wreck of the Hesperus,"** I shall never shirk declaring admiration. If not the strongest of meat, they are dishes of milk very well crumbled with bread for poetical babes; and the said babes, when they grow up, will be very lucky if they find no worse food even then, and may come back to them with relish from the strong meat itself. The first *Miscellaneous Poems* sustain the note well, especially **"It is not always May"**; and **"The Goblet of Life"** is, I think, better than its **"Psalm",** a sentiment which may sound immoral, but which corresponds to the general experience of critical readers of poetry.

*The Belfry of Bruges* shows Longfellow in that peculiar character of his, the character of a poetical cicerone of foreign lands and the things appertaining to them, and the note is not monotonous. It is true that there are some weak things here which, accordingly, we do not give, it not being necessary, as in the case of **"Excelsior,"** to justify unfavourable criticism, to escape the charge of not giving the poet's most famous things. **"The Arsenal at Springfield,"** for instance, is a piece of mere claptrap, out of harmony with some of his own most spirited work, and merely an instance of a cant common at the time, though unhappily not unknown in many other times.

Of the *Songs and Sonnets,* **"Seaweed"** is peculiarly beautiful, and the famous **"The Day is Done"** is one of those which I shall not throw to the sentiment-hunting wolves. The sonnet itself was not one of Longfellow's special domains; he was not quite intense enough for it in meaning on the one hand, nor quite impeccable enough in form on the other. **"The Evening Star"** is the best of them, **"The Cross of Snow,"** for all its pathetic subject (his wife's death) and its not unhappy idea, being ruined by the *un*-blessed word "bene*dight*".

But I am letting myself be betrayed into too much particularisation. To specify the pleasant things in *The Seaside and the Fireside* and in **"Birds of Passage"** would most unjustifiably curtail the room available for those good things themselves. Let me only mention **"The Building of the Ship,"** so admirably conducted and climaxed, with its famous and justly praised political ending—one of the rare pieces of political verse which need no special prejudice in favour of their sentiments to conciliate admiration; **"Chrysaor,"** the most Browningesque thing in Longfellow; the almost adequate **"Secret of the Sea,"** and the delectable **"King Witlaf's Drinking-Horn,"** in the first parcel: the stately and noble **"Ladder of St. Augustine,"** and **"Haunted Houses,"** **"My Lost Youth,"** the once more famous **"Golden Mile-stone,"** **"Santa Filomena,"** **"Sandalphon"** (oddly suggestive and unsuggestive of a poet of the next generation who has never had his meed, Mr. O'Shaughnessy), **"Weariness,"** and many another, in the second.

Some think this kind of sampling an impertinence, but I do not believe that either good poets or good critics agree

with them. One is only performing the modest duty of an ancient apprentice, when he shouted, "What d'ye lack?" and vaunted the wares offered. If they were good wares they were none the worse, and those who were induced to buy them were the better. And these are good wares!

*George Saintsbury, "Longfellow's Poems," in his* Prefaces and Essays, *Macmillan and Co., Limited, 1933, pp. 324-44.*

---

**Margaret Fuller on Longfellow:**

Mr. Longfellow presents us not with a new product in which all the old varieties are melted into a fresh form, but rather with a tastefully arranged museum, between whose glass cases are interspersed neatly potted rose trees, geraniums, and hyacinths, grown by himself with aid of indoor heat. Still we must acquit him of being a willing or conscious plagiarist. Some objects in the collection are his own; as to the rest, he has the merit of appreciation and a rearrangement not always judicious, but the result of feeling on his part.

Such works as Mr. Longfellow's we consider injurious only if allowed to usurp the place of better things. The reason of his being overrated here is because through his works breathes the air of other lands, with whose products the public at large is but little acquainted. He will do his office, and a desirable one, of promoting a taste for the literature of these lands before his readers are aware of it. As a translator he shows the same qualities as in his own writings; what is forcible and compact he does not render adequately; grace and sentiment he appreciates and reproduces. Twenty years hence when he stands upon his own merits, he will rank as a writer of elegant if not always accurate taste, of great imitative power, and occasional felicity in an original way where his feelings are really stirred. He has touched no subject where he has not done somewhat that is pleasing, though also his poems are much marred by ambitious failings. As instances of his best manner we would mention **"The Reaper and the Flowers," "Lines to the Planet Mars," "A Gleam of Sunshine,"** and **"The Village Blacksmith."** His two ballads are excellent imitations, yet in them is no spark of fire. In **"Nuremberg"** are charming passages. Indeed, the whole poem is one of the happiest specimens of Mr. L.'s poetic feeling, taste and tact in making up a rosary of topics and images.

*Margaret Fuller, in her* Papers on Literature and Art, *1846.*

---

## Paul Elmer More   (essay date 1908)

[*More was an American critic who, along with Irving Babbitt, formulated the doctrine of New Humanism in early twentieth-century American thought. The New Humanists were strict moralists who adhered to traditional conservative values in reaction to an age of scientific innovation and artistic experimentalism. In the following essay, a centenary tribute taken from his highly esteemed* Shelburne Essays

*(1904-21), More asserts that Longfellow possessed substantial poetic gifts, and in particular praises his sonnets, but also notes that his works lack emotional depth.*]

The position of Longfellow is somewhat curious. He was, and I suppose still is, the most beloved poet of the past century, and this not only among the ignorant and half-educated, but among people of the finest culture. Men as different in temperament as Kipling and J. H. Shorthouse give credit to his wonderful knowledge of the sea, and to Shorthouse, at least, he was always "very dear." He was also one of the favourite poets of so cunning a magician in words as Lafcadio Hearn; and to such names one might add indefinitely. Yet it remains true that Longfellow has never been quite accepted by the professed critics, that they have spoken of him commonly with reservation, sometimes even with contempt. Not many, indeed, have adopted just the insolent tone of Mr. Francis Gribble, to whom Longfellow was merely a "prig," with no characteristic habit except that of "decorating his person," a "poet of the obvious and the hum-drum," a man "equally devoid of humour and of passion," whose "intellectual outfit consists of a 'storesuit' from a theological emporium." We have a right to be incensed at the tone of such writing, but, waiving this, we must still acknowledge that there has been a distinct undercurrent of protest against the poet's easy popularity. Not his the felicity he attributed to a greater name, thinking, no doubt, of the cavilling he himself endured even during his life: "O happy poet, by no critic vext!"

And this contrast between the love of so many readers for Longfellow and the hesitation of his critics is perfectly comprehensible. The critics are mainly right. Let us not blunt or pervert our taste by ignoring distinctions. In the first place, no one who has stored his mind with the work of the great poets can read Longfellow without stumbling continually over reminiscences that do not fall exactly under the head of plagiarism, but that have the effect of reducing what has been nobly and individually written to a kind of smooth commonplace. I might from my own recollection fill pages with these dulled echoes of a finer music. Let me illustrate by a few examples. Longfellow, we are told by his biographer, wrote but a single love poem (and I, for one, am ready to honour him for this reserve), that sonnet to "My morning and my evening star of love! My best and gentlest lady!" 'Tis a pretty, and, among poets, rare compliment to his wife; but somehow the taste of it grows flat, and that *best and gentlest lady* drops to something resembling the merely respectable, when we recall the most perfect of Greek epigrams, Plato's Aστηρ πριν μεν ελαμπε [The translation of the complete epigram runs: "Morning Star, that once didst shine among the living, now deceased thou showest the Evening Star among the dead." (Trans. by J. W. Mackail.)], which came to Longfellow, no doubt, through Shelley's version:

> Thou wert the morning star among the living,
> Ere thy fair light had fled;—
> Now, having died, thou art as Hesperus, giving
> New splendour to the dead.

It is not, observe, that our Longfellow has taken the precise thought of the original; there is here no charge of stealing. It is rather that his image suggests the same image used differently and more poetically by another. In the same way his complaint beginning, "Half of my life is gone, and I have let The years slip from me," inevitably forces a comparison with Milton's more resonant note: "When I consider how my light is spent Ere half my days."

Again Longfellow writes:

> God sent his Singers upon earth
> With songs of sadness and of mirth,
> That they might touch the hearts of men,
> And bring them back to heaven again—

and we remember Keats:

> Bards of Passion and of Mirth,
> Ye have left your souls on earth!
> Have ye souls in heaven, too,
> Double-lived in regions new?

Longfellow writes of the unseen dwellers in **"Haunted Houses"**:

> We meet them at the doorway, on the stair,
> Along the passages they come and go,
> Impalpable impressions on the air,
> A sense of something moving to and fro—

and the memory goes back to Thomas Hood's lines in the most ghostly of English poems:

> Those dreary stairs, where with the sounding
>     stress
> Of ev'ry step so many echoes blended,
> The mind, with dark misgivings, fear'd to guess
> How many feet ascended.
>
>                 · · · ·
>
> O'er all there hung the shadow of a fear,
> A sense of mystery the spirit daunted,
> And said, as plain as whisper in the ear,
> The place is Haunted!

But it would be tedious to multiply examples. The point, as I have said, is not that Longfellow was a plagiarist or lacked originality—greater poets than he have taken their own where they found it with a more royally predatory hand—but that these rather vague resemblances of language and metaphor so often draw our attention to the lower plane upon which his imagination moves. And here I would beg for a little indulgence. This distinction between the higher and lower planes of the imagination goes so near to the very roots of taste and criticism, it is a matter so elusive withal, that I would run the risk of an insistence which may seem like the proverbial breaking of a butterfly upon a wheel. The question turns upon that dualism, or duplicity, in human nature, often misunderstood and to-day more often ignored, the perception of which does yet in some way mark the degree of a poet's or a philosopher's initiation into the mysteries of experience. To make the point clearer, let me compare two poems which are known by heart to all, and whose effect can be tested by the impressions of memory. One is Longfellow's **"Weariness,"** of which I will quote the first and last stanzas:

> O little feet! that such long years

*Bowdoin College, 1830, where Longfellow attended college and later taught languages.*

Must wander on through hopes and fears,
Must ache and bleed beneath your load;
I, nearer to the wayside inn
Where toil shall cease and rest begin,
Am weary, thinking of your road!

. . . . .

O little souls! as pure and white
And crystalline as rays of light
Direct from heaven, their source divine;
Refracted through the mist of years,
How red my setting sun appears,
How lurid looks this soul of mine!

The other is Heine's even more familiar lyric on a some-what similar theme: "Du bist wie eine Blume," which in my translation will at least be less trite, however much of its charm may have evaporated:

So fair and fresh and pure
Even as a flower thou art;
I look on thee, and sadness
Glideth into my heart.

'T is as tho' my hands were resting
Upon thy head in prayer,
Asking that God might keep thee
So pure and fresh and fair.

Now, both of these poems have the power of touching the heart, and both have attained the noble distinction of living in the mouths of men; yet it would be uncritical to say that the impression from them is quite the same, or that their reputation is quite equal. I would not seem to be insensible to the tenderness of Longfellow's lines, but something, one feels, is still lacking to give them that penetrating, clinging appeal which belongs to Heine's even simpler song. And I think that, if we look into this difference, it will appear to depend most of all upon the greater and lesser depth of that sense of dualism which the two poets have felt and put into language. There is in Longfellow's

poem the contrast of innocent childhood and old age wearied of the world; but this contrast springs from the cumulative effect, so to speak, of time, the refracting mist of years, and beyond this the idea scarcely goes. The emotion conveyed is barely, if at all, distinguished from the sentimental pathos of daily, commonplace life. Whereas in Heine something different and, it must be said, higher, enters. It is not easy, as it never is in the case of true poetry, to define precisely where this added touch comes in—whether in the imagery of the prayer, the lingering cadence of the repeated epithets, or in some haunting vagueness of romantic irony—but one instinctively thinks more of the symbolical power of the poem than of any personal incident or emotion; and this contrast between the loveliness of youth and the satiety of age becomes a sign of a conflict inherent in the poet's own heart, nay, if you will, of the enigmatical dualism, the pathetic or terrible sense of transiency, that runs through the heart of the world.

Well, let us accept this lower position for the greater part—but not for all, as I shall attempt to show—of Longfellow's poetry. Let us admit that his peculiar popularity is due to the fact that he does not require of us any violent readjustment of our ordinary moods, that he sets our own daily thoughts and emotions to music. Is he not to be prized, and praised, for this? Like Whittier, he is the poet of the hearth and the home; yet with a difference. It is in accordance with the well-known tricks of poetic inspiration that the Quaker poet, who was never married and in his earlier years of manhood had no settled abode, should have written lovingly of the peace and protection of the home; whereas Longfellow, who knew all the intimate joys of the family, should have dwelt more on the forebodings and memories of loss. We think of Whittier's *Snow-Bound,* with its snug comforts of the hearth in a New England winter, or of his *Pennsylvania Pilgrim,* that blandest of pastoral poems; even his fancies of the future life took on this ideal of the home, as I have pointed out in another essay. But these are not the notes of Longfellow. He, rather, in a hundred various keys sings of the parting of friends; of resignation for the "one vacant chair"—

> The air is full of farewells to the dying,
> And mournings for the dead;

of the cry of David in the Chamber over the Gate for Absalom his son. Even in his child poems there often lurks a shadow of anxiety:

> I said unto myself, if I were dead,
> What would befall these children? what would
> be
> Their fate, who now are looking up to me
> For help and furtherance? Their lives, I said,
> Would be a volume wherein I have read
> But the first chapters, and no longer see
> To read the rest of their dear history,
> So full of beauty and so full of dread.

It is the treatment of these, and other such themes as these, that has made him the one poet whom you will find in almost every household, the poet who is really read and enjoyed by the people; for it is just this sentiment of facile pathos that marks the true popularity. And here, also, we discover his relation to the Teutonising and romanticising—if the word may be passed—of New England culture. From sources of German metaphysics, whether directly or indirectly, from Fichte and Schelling and Schleiermacher, Emerson brought in his transcendental philosophy; from the same romantic school came the impulse that strengthened Hawthorne in his love of the weird and the subterranean, as also his aggravated sense of solitude in the world; there Thoreau got his mystic nature cult—always, it need not be added, with differences caused by other surroundings and traditions. Longfellow brought from Germany the ideal of a world literature which should absorb the best of all lands; but more than that, he imported into Cambridge the sentimental note that runs through German letters. He gave to our poetry the romantic *Empfindsamkeit* [sensitivity], refined and qualified indeed by the purity and sweetness and strength of his own nature.

For there is about his muse, I know not what, a certain gracious sweetness, which has the power, as was said when he received his degree at Cambridge, England, "to solace the ills of life and draw men from its low cares *ad excelsiora*"—an allusion which was caught and applauded by the captious undergraduates. One might analyse the elements of this charm in part, if it were profitable. He had in the first place the rare gift of rhythm; his lines sing themselves inevitably, and there is never, except in some of his hexameters and his blank verse, any doubt about the cadence, or any feeling that the cadence does not fit the thought. Lowell was thinking of this easy rhythmical quality when he wrote of Longfellow on his sixtieth birthday:

> I need not praise the sweetness of his song,
> Where limpid verse to limpid verse succeeds
> Smooth as our Charles, when, fearing lest he
> wrong
> The new moon's mirrored skiff, he glides along,
> Full without noise, and whispers in his reeds.

And then Longfellow has the second, and still rarer, gift of interest, the power of catching the reader's attention

with the first word and holding it to the end. Personally I am not particularly fond of *Evangeline* and the other longer poems, with the exception of some of the *Tales of a Wayside Inn* and *The Golden Legend;* I think his virtue lies elsewhere. But all, or nearly all of them have at least the trick of arousing interest. So the fancy is stirred by those first words of *Evangeline,* "This is the forest primeval," and kept awake by the shifting scenes of nature and the sentimental appeal until the very close:

> While from its rocky caverns the deep-voiced
> neighbouring ocean
> Speaks, and in accents disconsolate answers the
> wail of the forest.

(Hexameters, by the way, as sonorous and rhythmical as any in the language.) Not all the great poets have this gift of interest; it is not conspicuous in Milton or Virgil or Wordsworth; it even goes at times with very inferior qualities: but always it is an immense aid in enforcing whatever other powers a writer may possess. It would not be easy to say in just what this faculty of interest resides. In Longfellow it, perhaps, depends mainly on his power of making the reader feel at once that here are his own ideas, almost his own language. Nor are the artifices of rhetoric wanting. Especially, like Lowell, our poet had a wonderful gift of metaphor. You would be surprised if you went through Longfellow and marked the copiousness, the variety, and the ingenuity of these figures. Even from memory one might bring together a long list of metaphors and similes transforming a single group of appearances, such, for example, as the phenomena of night. One might begin with the first words of the poem that follows the prelude of his first volume of collected verse:

> I heard the trailing garments of the Night
> Sweep through her marble halls.

How miraculously that too familiar image expresses the gradual hushing of the earth as twilight descends! Or, to pass from sound to vision, there is the even better stanza:

> . . . and the darkness
> Falls from the wings of Night,
> As a feather is wafted downward
> From an eagle in his flight.

Less subtle and less familiar are a dozen other metaphors of the night that might be quoted, such as the lines in *Hiawatha:*

> Where into the empty spaces
> Sinks the sun, as the flamingo
> Drops into her nest at nightfall
> In the melancholy marshes;—

or this more trivial comparison:

> In broad daylight, and at noon,
> Yesterday I saw the moon
> Sailing high, but faint and white,
> As a schoolboy's paper kite;—

or this more aerial fancy:

> As a pale phantom with a lamp
> Ascends some ruin's haunted stair,
> So glides the moon along the damp
> Mysterious chambers of the air.

These are but a few of the metaphors I might from my own memory bring together on a single theme. Most wonderful of all, perhaps, is that comparison whose beauty has grown dim to us through too much repetition:

> And the cares, that infest the day,
> Shall fold their tents, like the Arabs,
> And as silently steal away.

(And here again his art is helped by his delicate rhythmical sense. As an example of the force of little things, let the stanza be read without the word "as" in the last line, and see how flat it seems in comparison.)

Now metaphors, I know, are a dangerous rhetorical weapon, and as a rule they are used with extreme parsimony by the greatest poets; you will find a score of them in Longfellow to one in Milton. Their tendency is to substitute the diversion of fancy for the more tenacious vision of the imagination; they distract the mind ordinarily from its intense preoccupation and so lessen, while diversifying, our intellectual emotion. But they are peculiarly appropriate to such a talent as Longfellow's, as they are to Lowell's, and to them is largely due the continuance and ease of the reader's interest. And apparently they flowed into Longfellow's mind quite unbidden. There is in his published verse nothing better in its way than this simile jotted down in his diary January 29th, 1849:

> Another of Emerson's wonderful lectures. The subject *Inspiration;* the lecture itself an illustration of the theme. Emerson is like a beautiful portico, in a lovely scene of nature. We stand expectant, waiting for the High Priest to come forth; and lo, there comes a gentle wind from the portal, swelling and subsiding; and the blossoms and the vine leaves shake, and far away down the green fields the grasses bend and wave; and we ask, "When will the High Priest come forth and reveal to us the truth?" and the disciples say, "He has already gone forth, and is yonder in the meadows." "And the truth he was to reveal?" "It is Nature; nothing more."

These are the qualities of thought and manner that have at once made Longfellow the most beloved of poets and kept him from full acceptance among the critical. But there is still another aspect of his work, which is sometimes overlooked. The weakness in his genius, as in that of the New England school generally to which he belonged, was an absence of resistance. There is a significant entry in his diary, under the date March 22, 1848: "He [Lowell] says he means never to write any more poetry—at least for many years; he 'cannot write slowly enough.'" One feels this lack of the inward check in much of Longfellow; the lines flow from him too smoothly and fluently; they have not been held back long enough to be steeped in the deeper and more obstinate emotions of the breast—

> Fi, du rhythme commode,
> Comme un soulier trop grand.
>
> ["Fie on the comfortable rhythm,
> Like an oversized shoe."]

When the proper resistance came to him, it was commonly the result of some check imposed by the difficulties of form, rather than of his own artistic inhibition. Thus of all his poems, the dramas in blank verse are about the flattest, and in general his power increases with the intricacy of the rhymes employed. The rule is, of course, not without exceptions. To some readers the easy flow of the trochees in **Hiawatha** has the charm of a singing brook that bubbles over its pebbles all a summer's day. And occasionally in those free quatrains, whose secret he learned from Heine, and which seem so easy, but are really so difficult, he strikes a note that is rare enough in English. So, one sleepless night, he makes this entry in his diary: "Nahant, September 8, 1880, four o'clock in the morning," and then turns the memorandum into verse:

> Four by the clock! and yet not day;
> But the great world rolls and wheels away,
> With its cities on land and ships at sea,
> Into the dawn that is to be!
>
> Only the lamp in the anchored bark
> Sends its glimmer across the dark,
> And the heavy breathing of the sea
> Is the only sound that comes to me.

When reading these lines, it is easy to understand why Kipling reckoned Longfellow among the few poets who really knew the sea. No one who has spent much of his time on some quiet harbour of our Atlantic coast can fail to be struck by the magic evocation of that second stanza—the nightbound shore, the single light low on the water, the sleepy wash of the waves. Or, take this stanza from the poem of meditations before the flames of a driftwood fire:

> And, as their splendour flashed and failed,
> We thought of wrecks upon the main,
>
> *Of ships dismasted, that were hailed*
> *And sent no answer back again.*

Has ever any poet, in a few quiet words, expressed more perfectly the awe and mystery of the sea, the sense of that vastness where so much may happen unseen and unknown of the world?

Such triumphs Longfellow wins now and then in the least resistant metres, but his greater work, that on which his artistic fame will depend, is in the more elaborate forms, particularly in the sonnet. Professor C. E. Norton, who speaks of Longfellow with the authority of a friend and a critic, has just published a sketch of Longfellow's life, with a selection of his autobiographic poems. It is an excellent book for the occasion, but one could wish that he had, instead, brought together all the sonnets, with a study of Longfellow as an artist. For ripeness of style and imagery such a volume would stand easily at the head of American poetry, and it would show an aspect of Longfellow's genius which is obscured by the bulk of his more popular work. It would place him as a peer among the great writers of England. We should have but a slender volume—there are altogether only sixty-three of the original sonnets—but of what richness and variety of scope! Here in brief compass are all the interests of his life. His long acquaintance with books speaks in those six magnificent sonnets prefixed to the translation of *The Divine Comedy,* and in the separate sonnets on Dante, and Milton, and Keats. Was ever poet more happily celebrated than Chaucer in these lines?

> An old man in a lodge within a park;
> The chamber walls depicted all around
> With portraitures of huntsman, hawk, and
>    hound,
> And the hurt deer. He listeneth to the lark,
> Whose song comes with the sunshine through
>    the dark
> Of painted glass in leaden lattice bound;
> He listeneth and he laugheth at the sound,
> Then writeth in a book like any clerk.
> He is the poet of the dawn, who wrote
> The Canterbury Tales, and his old age
> Made beautiful with song; and as I read
> I hear the crowing cock, I hear the note
> Of lark and linnet, and from every page
> Rise odours of ploughed field or flowery mead.

And then by the side of this set the contrasted picture of Shakespeare's stage:

> A vision as of crowded city streets,
> With human life in endless overflow;
> Thunder of thoroughfares; trumpets that blow
> To battle; clamour, in obscure retreats,
> Of sailors landed from their anchored fleets;
> Tolling of bells in turrets, and below
> Voices of children, and bright flowers that throw
> O'er garden walls their intermingled sweets!

To write like this is to combine at once the function of the critic and the poet. Wordsworth may have surpassed him, but no other, I think, in this use of the sonnet.

But the literary flavour in this little book of ours would be no stronger than the other interests we associate with him. Here in the sonnets to Agassiz and Felton and Sumner, the friendships that made so large a part of his life would find expression; his tender solicitude for children speaks in **"A Shadow"** and **"To-Morrow"**; his love of nature and the sea finds here its full utterance; his reserved, yet earnest, part in the Abolition movement and the war gives pathetic dignity to **"A Nameless Grave,"** which Mr. Howells has signalised for its perfect grace and ease; his reminiscences of travel, which did so much to overcome American provincialism, give colour to **"Venice," "The River Rhone,"** and half a dozen others; the sad fortitude of his old age, as all old age is sad, breathes in this last sonnet he was to write, his farewell inscribed to **"My Books":**

> Sadly, as some old mediaeval knight
> Gazed at the arms he could no longer wield,
> The sword two-handed and the shining shield
> Suspended in the hall, and full in sight,
> While secret longings for the lost delight
> Of tourney or adventure in the field
> Came over him, and tears but half-concealed
> Trembled and fell upon his beard of white,
> So I behold these books upon their shelf,
> My ornaments and arms of other days;
> Not wholly useless, though no longer used,
> For they remind me of my former self,
> Younger and stronger, and the pleasant ways
> In which I walked, now clouded and confused.

These are but glimpses of the riches in little room that a book of Longfellow's sonnets would offer. They would set forth to unbelievers an artist of rare tact and power, and they would be the best commemoration of the sweetest character that ever revealed itself in rhymes. I know that some have professed to find a certain solemn self-complacency in Longfellow. They turn to the selections from his diary in the Life published by his brother, and point with a kind of patronising smile at such an entry as this:

> December 6. [1838. He was then in his thirty-second year.] A beautiful holy morning within me. I was softly excited, I knew not why; and wrote with peace in my heart and not without tears in my eyes, **"The Reaper and the Flowers, a Psalm of Death."**

This man takes himself too seriously, they say: he has no humour. And what then? Why, most of the great poets of the world were without humour, and have they been any the less accepted for that? Humour is well in its place, but there is no reason why we should make a fetich of it, as most of us do in these days. And as for taking his moods and inspiration overseriously, there is nothing in Longfellow's diary that in any way approaches the stupendous solemnity of Wordsworth's introductory notes to his own poems. But the best refutation of such churlish criticism is in the poems of Longfellow, especially those in the sonnet form, which from the time of Petrarch, and of Shakespeare in English, has been the chosen vehicle for poetic confession.

Turn again to that desired book of sonnets if you wish to see the mellow sweetness and the strength of Longfellow's character. I have already referred to his single love-poem, the sonnet to "My morning and my evening star," which, like most of such effusions to a man's wife, rings rather flat; but not so that other sonnet of commemoration. The story of the second Mrs. Longfellow's terrible death by fire and of her husband's efforts to save her is too well known to bear repeating, as may seem also the lines which he wrote eighteen years afterwards, and which were found in his portfolio, unpublished, after his own death:

> In the long, sleepless watches of the night,
> A gentle face—the face of one long dead—
> Looks at me from the wall, where round its head
> The night-lamp casts a halo of pale light.
> Here in this room she died; and soul more white
> Never through martyrdom of fire was led
> To its repose; nor can in books be read
> The legend of a life more benedight.
> There is a mountain in the distant West
> That, sun-defying, in its deep ravines
> Displays a cross of snow upon its side.
> Such is the cross I wear upon my breast
> These eighteen years, through all the changing
>    scenes
> And seasons, changeless since the day she died.

I think we need have no fear of the slurs of shallowness and foppery cast upon a man who carried his suffering so deep in his heart that the world was unaware of its existence. And it is pleasant to hear that the woman so honoured was worthy to be a poet's wife. She is described as having "great beauty, and a presence of dignity and distinction, the true image of a beautiful nature." Everybody knows the home over which she presided, the Craigie House, in Cambridge, that looks out from Brattle Street over which is now a park, named after the poet, to the river Charles, celebrated by him in so many songs. It had been Washington's headquarters when he was in command of the army about Boston, and Longfellow felt the ghostly presence of his great predecessor:

> Once, ah, once, within these walls,
> One whom memory oft recalls,
> The Father of his Country, dwelt,
> And yonder meadows broad and damp
> The fires of the besieging camp
> Encircled with a burning belt.
> Up and down these echoing stairs,
> Sounded his majestic tread;
> Yes, within this very room
> Sat he in those hours of gloom,
> Weary both in heart and head.

But there were other memories attached to the old mansion, which Longfellow did not put into verse. The lady who owned the house and with whom Longfellow lodged before it came into his own possession, was a personage that caused a good deal of wonder and some consternation among the pious folk of Cambridge. There are probably people still living who can recall her figure as she sat at the window reading—reading that archmocker, Voltaire, in the original French, it was believed. One of the legends about her is to the effect that she sturdily refused to allow the caterpillars on her elm-trees to be burned. "Leave them alone!" she would cry; "what are we ourselves but miserable worms!" —which would seem to be as much scriptural as Voltairian.

Here Longfellow lived a large and bountiful life, befitting one to whom fame and honour and prosperity came hand in hand, neither reluctantly nor singly. It is mainly in recognition of his character as a man and poet that his centenary has been turned all over the country into a kind of *agape;* but it is partly also because, even better than Lowell, he represents a beautiful society now passed away and almost forgotten. I was interested the other day in looking through a pamphlet just published, which contains the proceedings of the Cambridge Historical Society—an association of gentlemen and ladies formed a couple of years ago to gather and preserve local traditions. The papers are filled with memories of the little college town to which Longfellow came as a young teacher, steeped in the literatures of Europe. It would be pleasant to quote at length from the recollections of Colonel Higginson and Professor Norton; they give almost a better picture of the quaint life of the day than Lowell's essay on *Cambridge Thirty Years Ago.* Says Professor Norton in his opening address:

> So great are the changes in the town since my childhood that the aspects and conditions of those days seem more than a lifetime away. I have the happiness of passing my old age in the house in which I was born. It has always been my home; but when I was a boy, it was in the country—now it is suburban and in the heart of a city. Kirkland Street was a country road with not a single house on its southern side, but with a wide stretch quite over to Harvard Street of

marsh land and huckleberry pasture, with channels running through the thick growth of shrubs, often frozen in the winter, and on which we boys used to skate over the very site of the building in which we have met to-night. Down as far as to Inman Square, the region was solitary, while beyond Inman Square, toward Boston, was an extensive wood of pines with a dense underbrush, the haunt, as we boys used to believe, of gamblers and other bad characters from the neighbouring city, and to be swiftly hurried by if nightfall caught us near it. The whole region round my father's house was, indeed, so thinly settled that it preserved its original rural character. It was rich in wild growth, and well known to botanists as the habitat of many rare flowers; the marshes were fragrant in spring with azalea and the clethra; and through spring, summer, and autumn there was a profuse procession of the familiar flowers of New England. It was a favourite resort of birds, but there is now little left of it fit for their homes, though many of them still revisit in their migrations the noisy locality where their predecessors enjoyed a peaceful and retired abode.

> But even a greater change than that from country village to suburban town has taken place here in Old Cambridge in the last seventy years. The people have changed. In my boyhood the population was practically all of New England origin, and in large proportion Cambridge-born, and inheritors of Old Cambridge traditions. The fruitful invasion of barbarians had not begun. The foreign-born people could be counted upon the fingers. There was Rule, the excellent Scotch gardener, who was not without points of resemblance to Andrew Fairservice; there was Sweetman, the one Irish day labourer, faithful and intelligent, trained as a boy in one of the "hedge-schools" of his native Ireland, and ready to lean on his spade and put the troublesome schoolboy to a test on the Odes of Horace, or even on the *Arma virumque cano;* and at the heart of the village was the hair-cutter, Marcus Reamie, from some unknown foreign land, with his shop full, in a boy's eyes, of treasures, some of his own collecting, some of them brought from distant romantic parts of the world by his sailor son. There were doubtless other foreigners, but I do not recall them, except a few teachers of languages in the College, of whom three filled in these and later years an important place in the life of the town—Dr. Beck, Dr. Follen, and Mr. Sales. But the intermixture of foreign elements was so small as not to affect the character of the town; in fact, everybody knew not only everybody else in person, but also much of everybody's tradition, connections, and mode of life. It has been a pathetic experience for me to live all my life in one community and to find myself gradually becoming a stranger to it.

And what society was gathered together in this village among the fields and fens! Read the poems written by Longfellow on the death of his friends—on Hawthorne, Dana, Sumner, Agassiz, Felton, and I know not how many others. Or, which of our cities to-day can show any gathering of men equal to the weekly meetings of Longfellow and Lowell and Professor Norton to discuss the translation of Dante? We may, if we choose, look back upon that life as in many ways provincial; but how much of the strain and inconsequence of our would-be cosmopolitan society it lacked. One need not be a New Englander, or a Harvard man, to join heartily in honouring the poet who represents the highest and most homogeneous culture this country has yet produced.

And it is wholesome for us to read and praise Longfellow. It is not necessary to place his work as a whole beside that of the greatest poet, or to overlook his shortcomings; but I think even those shortcomings have their special value at the present hour. We are apt to take our poets rather solemnly, when we read them at all, to search for deep and complex meanings; and in the process we often lose the inward serenity and unvexed faith which it is the mission of the poet to bestow. Not the stress of our emotion or our intellectual perturbation is the measure of our understanding, but rather the depth of our response to that word of the exiled Dante, when, in the convent court, he was questioned as to what he sought—*La pace,* peace. And Longfellow knew the meaning of that word as Dante used it. In the sorrow that fell upon him after his tragic bereavement, he found solace, or at least strength, in the daily translation of *The Divine Comedy.* Every lover of poetry knows the first and finest of the sonnets he prefixed to that work:

> Oft have I seen at some cathedral door
> A labourer, pausing in the dust and heat,
> Lay down his burden, and with reverent feet
> Enter, and cross himself, and on the floor
> Kneel to repeat his paternoster o'er;
> Far off the noises of the world retreat:
> The loud vociferations of the street
> Become an undistinguishable roar.
> So, as I enter here from day to day,
> And leave my burden at this minster gate,
> Kneeling in prayer, and not ashamed to pray,
> The tumult of the time disconsolate
> To inarticulate murmurs dies away,
> While the eternal ages watch and wait.

We need have no fear of paying homage to a poet who wrote such lines as those. And he himself, if he did not, like Dante and his peers, build at the great cathedral of song, did at least add to it a fair and homely chapel, where also, to one who comes humbly and reverently, the eternal ages watch and wait.

*Paul Elmer More, "The Centenary of Longfellow," in his* Shelburne Essays on American Literature, *edited by Daniel Aaron, Harcourt Brace Jovanovich, 1963, pp. 136-54.*

## John Macy (essay date 1913)

[*Macy was an American critic and editor of the* Boston Herald *and* The Nation. *His most important work,* The Spirit of American Literature, *denounced the genteel tradition and called for realism and the use of native materials in American Literature. In the following excerpt from that study, Macy rates Longfellow's verse "of secondary quality," but adds that several of his poems, particularly his sonnets and short lyrics, are exceptional.*]

On the death of Longfellow, Whitman wrote a tribute to the other "good gray poet," which is so just and beautiful that it should be known to all who are interested in either Longfellow or Whitman.

> Longfellow in his voluminous works seems to me not only to be eminent in the style and forms of poetical expression that mark the present age (an idiosyncrasy, almost a sickness, of verbal melody), but to bring what is always dearest as poetry to the general human heart and taste, and probably must be so in the nature of things. He is certainly the sort of bard and counteractant most needed for our materialistic, self-assertive, money-worshipping Anglo-Saxon races, and especially for the present age in America—an age tyrannically regulated with reference to the manufacturer, the merchant, the financier, the politician and the day workman—for whom and among whom he comes as the poet of melody, courtesy, deference—poet of the mellow twilight of the past in Italy, Germany, Spain, and in northern Europe—poet of all sympathetic gentleness—and universal poet of women and young people. I should have to think long if I were asked to name the man who has done more, and in more valuable directions, for America.
>
> I doubt if there ever was such a fine intuitive judge and selecter of poems. His translations of many German and Scandinavian pieces are said to be better than the vernaculars. He does not urge or lash. His influence is like good drink or air. He is not tepid either, but always vital, with flavour, motion, grace. He strikes a splendid average, and does not sing exceptional passions, or humanity's jagged escapades. He is not revolutionary, brings nothing offensive or new, does not deal hard blows. On the contrary, his songs soothe and heal, or if they excite, it is a healthy and agreeable excitement. His very anger is gentle, is at second hand (as in the **'Quadroon Girl'** and the **'Witnesses'**).
>
> There is no undue element of pensiveness in Longfellow's strains. Even in the early translation, the Manrique, the movement is as of strong and steady wind or tide, holding up and buoying. Death is not avoided through his many themes, but there is something almost winning in his original verses and renderings on that dread subject—as, closing the **'Happiest Land'** dispute
>
> And then the landlord's daughter
> Up to heaven raised her hand,
> And said, 'Ye may no more contend,—
> There lies the happiest land!'
>
> To the ungracious complaint-charge of his want of racy nativity and special originality, I shall only say that America and the world may well be reverently thankful—can never be thankful enough—for any such singing-bird vouchsafed out of the centuries, without asking that the notes be different from those of other songsters; adding what I have heard Longfellow himself say, that ere the New World can be worthily original, and announce herself and her own heroes, she must be well saturated with the origi-

nality of others, and respectfully consider the heroes that lived before Agamemnon.

Longfellow is the household poet of America; the laureateship was conferred on him by popular response, immediate, spontaneous and continuous. When that is said, whatever may be added is less significant. It is a noble fate to be for many years the poet most cherished by a million hearths. The multitudinous electorate may not crown the highest poetry, but whatever it does choose and long adhere to is indubitably important in human history.

Longfellow was the first American man of letters to establish for a busy and unlearned people a visible relation between academic culture and actual literary accomplishment. During eighteen of his most productive years, when he was well known to his countrymen as the poet of their simplest sentiments, he was a teacher of modern languages and literature at Harvard College. The poet who delighted the common heart with sweet song and pleasant ballad was Professor Longfellow. As a rule professors write books which are useful only to other professors and to students obedient to academic prescription. From Professor Longfellow's study a voice reached the popular ear. This man, official tutor in an institution monastically remote from the life of the toiling many, could say in wholly intelligible verse how a common man feels who has lost a child; he knew how to touch the despair of drudgery and raise it to confidence and a sense of personal dignity. He honoured in a plain unpatronizing way the village blacksmith, and in every American village the blacksmith is a useful citizen. He had a heart for ships and shipbuilders, and he gave new meaning to the Fourth-of-July orator's figure of the "ship of state" by symbolizing it in a real ship of hewn timbers. Long poems are hard to read, and solid pages of verse repel the unaccustomed reader, but Longfellow told the stories of Evangeline, Miles Standish and Hiawatha in verse almost as easy to read as prose.

The poet-professor, who was the emissary of academic culture to the untutored, was also the ambassador of creative literature to a museum of intellectual antiquities in which Greek roots were esteemed above the flowers of living song. This poet with fine manners, dignity and delicate taste, lover of music, responsive to the contemporary songs of the nations, bore a torch of living culture among rusty grammarians and the hebraical sons of a decadent but still stupid Puritanism. His successor, Lowell, and his friend, Norton, carried the torch on, and then it went out; there came the time when the teaching of modern literature in American universities, at Harvard certainly, was divided between philologists on the one hand, men with no literary sense, who reduce Shakespeare and Milton to archaeological specimens, and, on the other hand, amiable dilettanti who illustrate the truth of Tanner's epigram: "He who can does; he who cannot teaches." Longfellow and Lowell were beneficent blunderers into that realm of degreed and gowned authority where the counting of final E's in Chaucer is supposed to be the study of poetry and the writing of a dull introduction to a superfluously new edition of Hamlet entitles a commonplace doctor of philosophy to a professorship.

Longfellow brought humane civilization to an American

university and sent academic culture to the people in his great classes beyond the college gates. To both he was the bearer of the light of contemporaneous Europe. He not only told his pupils about Dante's tomb, but read them snatches of folk-song and popularlegend. He translated modern poetry for his classes, and through his books gave America a living sense of the beauty of the Old World. A younger Harvard professor thinks that the foundations of Longfellow's fame rest almost wholly on his service in discovering to an inexperienced nation the splendours of European civilization. It was a genuine service, but it was not all nor was it the most important. His fame rests on his ability to phrase memorably ideas native to all simple minds everywhere. It is to be noted that his most cherished poems, from **"A Psalm of Life"** to the long narratives, *Evangeline* and *The Courtship of Miles Standish,* are on American subjects or on experiences common to humanity. In *Tales of a Wayside Inn,* in which are twenty-two stories, the best known is **"Paul Revere."** Nevertheless it is true that at the right moment Longfellow made America acquainted with some of the gayer beauties and the more innocent music of the old nations.

If one willing to ignore traditional evaluations, to disregard popular judgment and services that are an undeniable matter of national history, opens Longfellow for the book-in-itself, one finds him a third-rate poet. "Third-rate" is not meant quite in its contemptuous sense. The first-rate poets are Milton, Shakespeare, and Shelley whose poetry is sustained through large schemes. Less than that supreme poetry is the perfection of short poems and short passages in long poems, the perfection of Wordsworth, Keats, Tennyson, Whitman, Browning. Below that perfection Longfellow almost always falls. His best work is not unlike Gray's in its calm transparency, its pleasant meditation on religious and sentimental commonplace. His longer narratives are readable, indeed they find many readers year after year, and that alone is enough to distinguish him in a period whose poetic achievement is little more than an anthology of lyrics and fragments. But in the longer poems of the age, "The Prelude" of Wordsworth, and Browning's "The Ring and the Book," are superb lines—fragments of gold. There are few great lines in Longfellow; in *Christus* the miraculous does not happen even for a moment, except in the lines which are sentences from the English Bible turned almost word for word into metre. His verse is evenly and permanently of secondary quality. The difference between the great and the good Longfellow well knew, for he was an admirable judge; in his journal he records the opinion that Ariosto's "Orlando Furioso" is "verse rather than poetry after all."

To remind ourselves how the first-rate excels what is less than first-rate, a few examples will serve. Longfellow says in **"The Poet's Tale"**:

> And rivulets, rejoicing, rush and leap
> And wave their fluttering signals from the steep.

Wordsworth's line is:

> The cataracts blow their trumpets from the
> steep.

Somewhere in the ear is a mentor which advises that Longfellow's lines are verse and Wordsworth's is poetry.

The end of **"The Psalm of Life"** is:

> Still achieving, still pursuing,
> Learn to labour and to wait.

Multitudes have been consoled by those lines. On the field of Sebastopol a dying British soldier repeated them. Yet they are not comparable with the line so nearlike them, so far above them:

> They also serve who only stand and wait.

In a sonnet **"On Mrs. Kemble's Readings from Shakespeare"** Longfellow sings:

> O happy reader! having for thy text
> The magic book whose sibylline leaves have
>   caught
> The rarest essence of all human thought.

The lines are good, but they fail beside Wordsworth's

> Poor earthly casket of immortal verse.

It is not simply that Longfellow's ideas are commonplace. Both Wordsworth and Tennyson are commonplace and lacking in passion, but now and again some verbal wizardry works a celestial redemption of their intellectual banality.

The finest things in Longfellow are not those best known. The dear public, to whom any critic with a humane sense of the uses of literature must at times humbly bow, has honoured its poet splendidly—and missed his loftiest moments. **"A Psalm of Life"** would not disgrace a poet's juvenile volume, if it were allowed to sleep there. For some reason it does not sleep, but stirs the sentiments of the very people who may be assumed to know the Psalms of David, and knowing them can yet take seriously **"A Psalm of Life,"** "Rock of Ages," and other bad hymns! Genuine religious feeling makes the heart hospitable to very poor religious poetry. One would like to erase **"A Psalm of Life"** from every page whereon it is printed, and from every heart wherein it is remembered, and put in its place Longfellow's glorious sonnet to Milton, a sonnet which is peer of the great sonnets of Milton himself and of Wordsworth.

> I pace the sounding sea-beach and behold
> How the voluminous billows roll and run,
> Upheaving and subsiding, while the sun
> Shines through their sheeted emerald far un-
>   rolled,
> And the ninth wave, slow gathering fold by fold
> All its loose-flowing garments into one,
> Plunges upon the shore, and floods the dun
> Pale reach of sands, and changes them to gold.
> So in majestic cadence rise and fall
> The mighty undulations of thy song,
> O sightless bard, England's Maeonides!
> And ever and anon, high over all
> Uplifted, a ninth wave superb and strong,
> Floods all the soul with its melodious seas.

The six sonnets that accompany Longfellow's translation of Dante are all perfect; the first, especially, remarkable for the essential unity of its fine thought, the central metaphor, the restrainedly sonorous phrasing, is so flawless in mould and noble in content that it stands undiminished at the entrance to Dante.

> Oft have I seen at some cathedral door
> A labourer, pausing in the dust and heat,
> Lay down his burden, and with reverent feet
> Enter, and cross himself, and on the floor
> Kneel to repeat his paternoster o'er;
> Far off the noises of the world retreat;
> The loud vociferations of the street
> Become an undistinguishable roar.
> So, as I enter here from day to day,
> And leave my burden at this minster gate,
> Kneeling in prayer, and not ashamed to pray,
> The tumult of the time disconsolate
> To inarticulate murmurs dies away,
> While the eternal ages watch and wait.

That many people would not be interested in poems to poets is a conceivable reason why these masterpieces of Longfellow are less generally admired than some of his verses feeble in sentiment and unelevated by verbal inspiration. There is, however, one sonnet of his, unsurpassably lovely and poignant with a sorrow universally understood, which should have first place in the mind of every sort of reader who would care for Longfellow or any poetry. This is **"The Cross of Snow."**

> In the long, sleepless watches of the night,
> A gentle face—the face of one long dead—
> Looks at me from the wall, where round its head
> The night-lamp casts a halo of pale light.
> Here in this room she died; and soul more white
> Never through martyrdom of fire was led
> To its repose; nor can in books be read
> The legend of a life more benedight.
> There is a mountain in the distant West
> That, sun-defying, in its deep ravines
> Displays a cross of snow upon its side.
> Such is the cross I wear upon my breast
> These eighteen years, through all the changing
>   scenes
> And seasons, changeless since the day she died.

It is characteristic of Longfellow that this poem on the dreadful death of his wife should not have been published while he lived. He did not utter his more intimate passions, and this sonnet indicates that he would not rather than that he could not. His restraint is humanly admirable, but his poetry suffers because it is not charged with the heat of his soul. He is usually objective, bright and clear as prose. He seldom excites subtle sorrows or strange moods, never lights fiery passions nor disturbs the inner sources of tears for all things that are. One exceptional poem which makes its effect in a Coleridgean way, without the reader's knowing just what there is in the thought or the melody that moves him, is **"In the Churchyard at Cambridge,"** especially the first stanza.

> In the village churchyard she lies,
> Dust is in her beautiful eyes,
> No more she breathes, nor feels, nor stirs;
> At her feet and at her head
> Lies a slave to attend the dead,
> But their dust is white as hers.

Another poem which would make the fortune of a book

of "moods" by some young modern, who perhaps might be contemptuous of old Longfellow, is this:

> The tide rises, the tide falls,
> The twilight darkens, the curlew calls;
> Along the sea-sands damp and brown
> The traveller hastens toward the town,
> And the tide rises, the tide falls.
>
> Darkness settles on roofs and walls,
> But the sea, the sea in the darkness calls;
> The little waves, with their soft, white hands,
> Efface the footprints on the sands,
> And the tide rises, the tide falls.
>
> The morning breaks; the steeds in their stalls
> Stamp and neigh, as the hostler calls;
> The day returns, but nevermore
> Returns the traveller to the shore.
> And the tide rises, the tide falls.

Of Longfellow's technical gifts there is no doubt. Either because he had not a very deep nature or because his early success showed him what his audience needed, he applied his fine skill to thoughts and feelings usually not striking nor powerful, and so he became a very highly refined poet of the many. For the multitude who do not read the best poetry there is left little except the work of versifiers of limited skill of inferior literary culture, the Hemanses, Havergals, Haines Baileys and hymn writers. Longfellow devoted an accomplished artistry to a humble grade of poetry, as though a competent architect should design workmen's cottages or a true musician should prepare an evangelical hymnal.

He appeals everywhere to minds which English writers call "middle-class" and French writers call "bourgeois." It is hard to find a word that has the right connotation in America. "Common people" does not define them, and "democrat" is too valuable and excellent a word for them. Perhaps "intellectually immature" is just, but the phrase sounds snobbish and patronizing. The boys of Harrow—or was it Eton? —voted him the finest of poets. The most catholic of translators, he was translated in turn into twenty languages. He is admired by people who have the gravest troubles and the fewest troublesome ideas, who are not interested in the intensest expression of the tragedies, stresses and ecstasies of life, but who take elementary ideals deeply to heart and seek plain elementary answers to daily perplexities, who like a touch of strangeness in their poetry but do not understand it if the language is too strange.

In his journal Longfellow says of a poem he is meditating, "I must put live beating heart into it." His poetry seems passionless, without "live beating heart," as compared with the great voices of song, but three generations of simple hearts have found Longfellow a vital force in their lives.

*John Macy, "Longfellow," in his* The Spirit of American Literature, *Doubleday, Page & Company, 1913, pp. 99-110.*

### Elmer James Bailey   (essay date 1922)

[*In the following essay, originally published in 1922, Bailey examines religious thought in Longfellow's verse.*]

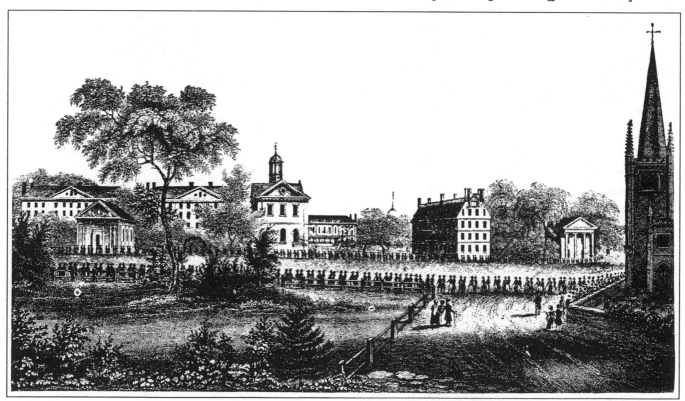

*Harvard College, 1836. Longfellow held the Smith Chair of Modern Languages from 1836-54.*

Among American poets, Longfellow is without doubt the most uniformly ethical. It is true that a noble purpose, an elevated ideal, is never lacking in our greater literature, yet Longfellow more than any other American author gives his readers the impression that his sense of goodness was innate rather than accepted, felt rather than defined. Religiously, there is a dignity in Bryant, a pathos in Poe, a loftiness in Emerson, a tenderness in Whittier, not found in Longfellow; still, if the Cambridge poet is lacking to some degree in his possession of these several qualities, he exhibits in their place, when he turns to the contemplation of the duties and conduct of life, unusual clarity of vision, steadiness of heart, and calmness of soul. Bryant interests us, because the paths which led him to confident hope are likewise open to every other man; Poe appeals to us through the very desperation with which he clung to his wavering faith that God is good; Emerson flatters us by the philosophic tone which he imparts to belief; and Whittier increases our self-respect with his insistence that the Holy Spirit finds a dwelling place in every human heart. Longfellow, however, seldom draws us in any of these ways. The religious element, so far as it finds expression in his poetry, is not evidential as in Bryant, nor romantic as in Poe, nor intellectual as in Emerson, nor intuitional as in Whittier; rather is it moralistic, vary though it may from the tacit on one hand to the openly didactic on the other.

Longfellow's frank acceptance of his moral call has unfortunately made him the victim at times of much adverse criticism and, in some places, of not a little ridicule. With the rise of the theory that art exists solely for art's sake, war was declared against all poetry which had any evident purpose beyond the giving of mere emotional pleasure. It came to be assumed that a person of real culture and true refinement of taste must therefore have outgrown the poems of Longfellow and must therefore either have left them with other playthings of youth to one's successors in the schoolroom, or have handed them pityingly on to such men and women as were dead in the sin of commonplaceness. In time, however, the reaction set in; and signs are not wanting to show that Longfellow's undeviating ethical sincerity is the very quality which assures him a permanent place in literature. It cannot be allowed, of course, that mere preaching in verse, lofty though the lesson may be, is real poetry from any point of view; still even among didactic poets, some are elected unto honor, some unto dishonor. Truth more often than not is beautiful, and so likewise is goodness; and whenever beautiful goodness and beautiful truth draw to themselves adequately beautiful expression, poetry, as Keats long ago implied, is the inevitable result.

Of Longfellow's openly didactic poems, the most frequently repeated, no doubt, is **"A Psalm of Life."** It has become so familiar, indeed, that we glance at it only to pass it over, or at most to read it without appreciation. That it is not poetry of the highest type may be admitted at the outset; yet the most jaded mind, if it can rid itself of the increment of what others have said, will have some reanswering thrill to many of its noble lines. On the whole, we do not object to being taught, if we are convinced that the teacher speaks as one having real authority. It may be well therefore to refrain from brushing aside too hastily

or contemptuously those familiar, unaffected stanzas which frankly point out that "life is real, life is earnest" and rise to a culmination hardly less than scriptural in the lines,

> Act, act in the living Present!
> Heart within and God o'erhead!

The mention of **"A Psalm of Life"** brings to mind other poems fully as well know for their like content and equal purpose. **"The Light of Stars,"** at the time of its first publication called **"A Second Psalm of Life,"** speaks the lesson, "Be resolute and calm, be self-possessed and still"; **"The Ladder of St. Augustine,"** adopting the words of the early church father, bids us rise each day upon the wrecks of yesterday; **"Excelsior,"** despite the many parodies made upon it, is still capable of enheartening the bearer of a forlorn hope; **"The Builders"** inculcates the teaching of the apostle that the body as the temple of God must be made beautiful and clean both within and without; **"The Beleaguered City"** utters the call to prayer before which the midnight phantoms of doubt depart; and **"The Castle Builder,"** addressed though it was to a child at play among his blocks, reaches a larger audience with its message,

> Build on and make thy castles high and fair,
> Rising and reaching upward to the skies;
> Listen to voices in the upper air
> Nor lose thy simple faith in mysteries.

Religiously didactic however as are many of the poems upon which Longfellow's reputation rests, it must not be hastily concluded that in them his ambition found its end. His cherished desire from the beginning of his career seems to have been to produce a noble poem upon the life and influence of Christ. Under the date of November 19, 1849, he wrote in his diary, "And now I long to try a loftier strain, and sublimer Song whose broken melodies have for so many years breathed through my soul in the better hours of life." A second entry made two months later shows that this sublimer song which the poet hoped to compose was to be dramatic in form and to bear the title of *Christus.* Yet even a decade earlier, in the very year of the publication of *Voices of the Night,* his first volume of poems, he was contemplating, we know, a poetic treatment of the heroine Elsie, who did eventually appear as the central character in *The Golden Legend.* The *Christus* in its entirety was given to the public in 1872, thus bringing to an end a work upon a religious theme which had dominated the author's life for more than thirty years. Nevertheless, the thought which had made so strong an appeal was not even then dismissed from the poet's mind. **"Judas Maccaboeus,"** which immediately followed the earlier work must, beyond a doubt, be regarded as an offshoot of the theme underlying *The Divine Tragedy;* and certainly the links binding the important posthumous fragment *Michael Angelo* to the *Christus* are neither few nor negligible. It is safe to conclude, therefore, that however varied were Longfellow's literary interests, the subject of his great religious poem was ever, in some form or another, before his mind. One critic, indeed, has gone so far as to speak of the theme of the *Christus* as "the flame by night and the pillar of cloud by day which led the poet's mind in all its onward movements." Discount this statement as we may, we can but feel that it rests upon a firm substratum of truth; and we readily agree with the same critic when he goes on to say that Longfellow's resolution "to undertake a long and elaborate poem by the holy name of Christ" was "a most rational and at the same time most satisfactory expression of the poet's personality."

Important, however, as the trilogy of the *Christus* is as an indication of ethical unity in Longfellow's literary life, it gives no far-reaching insight into the details of his religious belief. A drama, even in the case of a poet like Longfellow, can do hardly more than show the author's bias of mind or inclination of heart. The reader, whatever his suspicion, must assume that the several characters speak in their own person and utter thoughts which are often not their creator's. Still it is of value to recall that we have Longfellow's own record of a desire to show in *The Golden Legend* that "through the darkness and corruption of the Middle Ages ran a bright stream of Faith strong enough for all the exigencies of life and death." Likewise is it well not to forget that though the words of the *Finale* of the *Christus* were put into the mouth of Saint John, they were none the less the expression of Longfellow's own estimate of the essential teachings of Jesus.

> Poor, sad Humanity
> Through all the dust and heat
> Turns back with bleeding feet,
> By the weary road it came,
> Unto the simple thought
> By the great Master taught,
> And that remaineth still:
> Not he that repeateth the name,
> But he that doeth the will!

One turns unwillingly from the dramas of Longfellow, since they contain many passages of high quality, for which grandeur is often not too strong a term, and which show at times in both thought and diction an elevation which is not found elsewhere in the poet's work. With equal reluctance one must pass over with mere mention both the noble rendering of the *Divina Commedia* and the host of minor translations from various languages. Interest in the great religious poem of Dante subtended quite as great an arc in Longfellow's literary career as that marked off by his attraction to the life and abiding influence of Christ; and the mere naming of **The Good Shepherd** from the Spanish, "The Angel and the Child" from the French, "The Children of the Lord's Supper" from the Swedish, "The Statue over the Cathedral Door" from the German, and "The Soul's Complaint against the Body" from the Anglo-Saxon, recalls numbers of other translations which show Longfellow's pronounced and long-continued sympathy with the spiritual thoughts of foreign poets. Still, despite the importance of these English versions of religious poems found in other lands, one hardly dares assume that the point of view found in them was necessarily Longfellow's own. For the same reason one must all but eliminate the considerable number of longer and shorter narrative poems, despite the fact that the rejection of *Evangeline, The Song of Hiawatha, The Courtship of Miles Standish,* and *Tales of a Wayside Inn* limits one to a study of less than one-half of Longfellow's original non-dramatic poetry. Nevertheless, one is not thereby

left without a sufficient body of material to assist him in reaching very definite conclusions regarding Longfellow's most intimate religious convictions. The lyrics of which Longfellow was the author, form no inconsiderable part of his work either in amount or in value. Still further, the personal thoughts found scattered through his larger works are sure to be rediscovered in his shorter poems, sometimes merely repeated, sometimes developed at large. Finally, it is well to add, these briefer songs are so widely known and so greatly loved that in studying them one often finds himself looking not more into the poet's heart than into his own.

The attentive and reflective reader of Longfellow's shorter poems soon discovers that their author was far from being a poet of evasion as was Holmes pronouncedly in all of his earlier work, and equally as far from being sceptical as Lowell undoubtedly was at intervals. Longfellow's religious thought, moreover, was not the result of a development, as was the case with Bryant; nor did it define itself into a philosophy, as did Emerson's; neither did it take on so practical and circumstantial a form as did Whittier's. The keynote of Longfellow's religious belief was perhaps sounded when he wrote in his diary, "We have but one life here on earth and we must make that beautiful. And to do this, health and elasticity of mind are needful; and whatever endangers or impedes them must be avoided." Calmness and sweetness of spirit in full accordance with this entry were indeed the chief characteristics of Longfellow's temperament. Through the possession of some unusual and superior instinct, his soul seemed unerringly to accept or reject whatever would assist or delay its fullest development. Apparently, without resort to any book, council, or creed, as a source of authority, he took his unquestioning stand upon the three important fundamental doctrines, the goodness of God, the divinity of Christ, and the immortality of the soul. Never dealing in subtleties of logic, he seems to have assumed that like himself every one of his readers had become as a little child and therefore worthy to enter into the kingdom of Heaven.

Although Longfellow at no time turned to the Bible for authoritative substantiation of theological doctrine or religious faith, his poems abound in Scriptural allusions and quotations. All was fish to his net when he desired to express himself poetically. He laid hold upon whatever would help him to render his thought clear or his expression artistic, and made it serve those purposes alone. From the nature of the subject-matter **"Judas Maccabaeus"** was woven, warp and woof, from allusions to the Jewish Apocrypha; and Puritan stories like *The Courtship of Miles Standish* and "Giles Corey of Salem Farms," Quaker tales like **"Elizabeth"** and **"John Endicott,"** medieval pictures like **"The Vision Beautiful," "King Robert of Sicily,"** and **"The Children's Crusade,"** and scenes in the life of Christ like **"The Three Kings," "Blind Bartimeus,"** and **"The Sifting of Peter"** gained and still gain pronounced verisimilitude from their frequent allusions to incidents, characters, and teachings found in the *New Testament*. In some cases Longfellow even went so far as to transcribe into his poems long passages unchanged in diction from the King James version of the Scriptures. Perhaps the most striking, though by no means the only example of such incorporation of material is found in the eighth section of *The Divine Tragedy.* There, except that, to satisfy the demands of metre, seven unimportant words are omitted and six others equally unimportant are interpolated, the parable of the two prayers offered in the temple is transferred bodily from the eighteenth chapter of the Gospel according to Saint Luke.

> Two men went up into the temple to pray.
> The one was a self-righteous Pharisee,
> The other a Publican. And the Pharisee
> Stood and prayed thus within himself! O God,
> I thank thee that I am not as other men,
> Extortioners, unjust, adulterers,
> Or even as this Publican. I fast
> Twice in the week, and also I give tithes
> Of all that I possess! The Publican,
> Standing afar off, would not lift so much
> Even as his eyes to Heaven, but smote his breast,
> Saying: God be merciful to me a sinner!
> I tell you that this man went to his house
> More justified than the other. Every one
> That doth exalt himself shall be abased,
> And he that humbleth himself shall be exalted!

Like all poets Longfellow frequently turned to history for subject-matter; but he did not, like Bryant and Whittier, make use of it to support his religious convictions. A similar statement might be made regarding his treatment of nature. She was not to him a teacher as she was to Bryant; nor part and parcel of God as she was to Emerson; nor a symbol as she was to Whittier. To Longfellow she had objective existence, and because of her beauty was worthy of admiration; yet she seems never to have been to him a source of truth. Once indeed, writing under the influence of a German poet, Longfellow, in the early poem entitled **"Flowers,"** spoke of the blossoms of the field as a revelation of God and later on hailed them as

> Emblems of our own great resurrection,
> Emblems of the bright and better land.

Such a use of Nature, however, hardly ever recurs in the whole body of his poetry; as a rule, she had for him a message of a far different order. True, he called the songs of birds "lovely lyrics written by the hand of God" and regarded the geologist Agassiz as "summoned to read what is still unread in the manuscripts of God" and found, like Bryant, that the forest is at times a cathedral far surpassing any edifice of worship built by human hands; yet he turned to nature primarily, not for information, but for consolation, inspiration, repose. He felt the calm, majestic presence of the night, as she drew near to lay her fingers on the lips of Care and bid them complain no more; he learned from the rising of the red planet Mars, the star of the unconquered will, how sublime a thing it is to suffer and be strong; he looked upon the river moving onward without haste or noise and knew that wisdom lies in calm contentment and in perfect self-control. Plainly Nature to Longfellow, as he said in a sonnet to which he gave that very name, was not a teacher solving problems and demonstrating rules; rather was she a mentor leading mankind gently, yet not the less firmly, to the true understanding of life.

> As a fond mother when the day is o'er,

> Leads by the hand her little child to bed,
> Half willing, half reluctant to be led,
> And leaves his broken playthings on the floor,
> Still gazing at them through the open door,
> Nor wholly reassured and comforted
> By promises of others in their stead,
> Which, though more splendid, may not please
>     him more;
> So Nature deals with us, and takes away
> Our playthings one by one, and by the hand
> Leads us to rest so gently, that we go
> Scarce knowing if we wish to go or stay,
> Being too full of sleep to understand
> How far th' unknown transcends the what we
>     know.

The theological concept of the Trinity seems not to have greatly interested Longfellow. Certainly he dismissed it much more readily than Bryant to whom it persisted in presenting itself; and he gave it far less attention than Whittier whose Trinitas was the record of a real agitation of soul. That he accepted the doctrine as truth may perhaps be assumed from the couplet which stands as the fifth of his several experiments in **"Elegiac Verse,"**

> How can the Three be One? you ask me: I an-
>     swer by asking,
> Hail and snow and rain, are they not three and
>     yet one?

However much or little these lines may be assumed to prove, it is but just to admit that of the several persons in the Trinity, Longfellow in his poems only occasionally mentioned the Holy Spirit and in no place greatly developed his thought of the Father and the Son. Manifestly, he trusted in the power, the wisdom, the justice, the mercy, and the goodness of God; yet his faith seldom, if ever, found any other expression than the reiteration in one form or another that the ways of our Heavenly Father are always best. Again, although the most minute details of the life of Christ, so far as they are recorded in the Gospels, were well known to him, he was never led to dwell, in his shorter poems at least, upon his belief in the incarnation, the resurrection, and the ascension. His failure to give a precise definition of his religious faith, however, does not at any time obscure the fact that he was Christian in the fullest sense of that term. Certainly he cannot at any time be regarded as a doubter, if we will but recall his frequent insistence that Christ is eternal. Again, though we may rarely be able to place a finger upon a dogmatic statement, we find the fundamental teachings of Jesus, like a good diffused, permeating the whole of the poet's work. Turn to whatever page we will, those teachings appear, not as the pattern it is true, but rather as threads serving now as warp and now as woof in the poems of Longfellow's weaving. Thus it comes about that the poet's readers are driven to the conclusion that his faith was sound. Only on such an assumption can sincerity be postulated as one of his attributes, can real force be regarded as inherent in his frequently repeated idea, most sweetly expressed perhaps in the lines from the poem entitled **"Elegiac,"**

> In a haven of rest my heart is riding at anchor,
> Held by the chains of love, held by the anchors
>     of trust!

Upon the daily life and the spiritual state of the minister of the Gospel, Longfellow held quite decided opinions. To his mind the man who believed himself called to work in the vineyard of his Master must needs strive hourly to be perfect even as his Father in Heaven is perfect. What in Longfellow's opinion such a man should not be, is best described in **"The Birds of Killingworth."** There the parson of the town is pictured as—

> A man austere,
> The instinct of whose nature was to kill;
> The wrath of God he preached from year to
>     year,
> And read with fervor, Edwards on the Will;
> His favorite pastime was to slay the deer
> In Summer on some Adirondac hill;
> E'en now, while walking down the rural lane,
> He lopped the wayside lilies with his cane.

In contrast with this satiric presentation of a shepherd who could have been but a blind leader of the blind, one recalls the priest in *Evangeline,* that Father Felician, who stilled the strife and contention of his angry people and led them to utter the forgiving petition of their crucified Saviour. One thinks too of one of the story-tellers in the Wayside Inn, the gentle theologian who practiced the Gospel of the Golden Rule and strove "to build the universal church lofty as is the love of God and ample as the wants of man." The true pastor, Longfellow held, does not need a stately edifice wherein he and his flock may house themselveswhile he delivers his message. The surroundings are nothing, the man is all, he wrote in **"Old St. David's at Radnor,"** —

> It is not the wall of stone without
> That makes the building small or great,
> But the soul's light shining round about,
> And the faith that overcometh doubt,
> And the love that stronger is than hate.

Such light, such faith, such love, come not, in Longfellow's opinion, by chance. In the **"Hymn"** written for his brother's ordination he clearly recorded his belief that the true minister of God is divinely summoned, divinely commissioned, and divinely allowed to be the daily companion of his risen Lord.

> Christ to the young man said: "Yet one thing
>     more;
> If thou wouldst perfect be,
> Sell all thou hast and give it to the poor,
> And come and follow me!"
>
> Within this temple Christ again, unseen,
> Those sacred words hath said
> And His invisible hands today have been
> Laid on a young man's head.
>
> And evermore beside him on his way
> The unseen Christ shall move,
> That he may lean upon his arm and say,
> "Dost thou, dear Lord, approve?"

In the poem just cited Longfellow obviously expressed his belief that the minister of the Gospel must accept quite literally the words of Jesus, "Lo, I am with you always even unto the end of the world." Elsewhere, he no less plainly showed it to be his opinion that all men would do well to

make of their religion, not a theory, but a practice. In the theological sciences of dogmatics and apologetics, he had hardly even the most remote interest, far less indeed, save perhaps Whitman, than had any other American poet. Certainly in the matter of religion Longfellow seems never to have felt himself called upon to make assertions, to seek evidence, or to defend his position. Had a person approached the poet with a demand for the intellectual basis of his belief, he would no doubt have been greeted with mild surprise; and had he pressed the question, he would probably have received no further answer than "I have felt." Nevertheless, Longfellow, looking upon the ideal of Christ as that toward which every man should strive, made righteousness of life the constant burden of his message. Through the angel in *The Golden Legend,* Longfellow himself cried out to all men, —

> Be noble in every thought
> Be true in every deed!
> Let not the illusions of the senses
> Betray thee to deadly offences.
> Be strong! be good! be pure!
> The right only shall endure,
> All things else are but pretenses.

As in this passage, so elsewhere was Longfellow often formally didactic; yet his method was almost always persuasive rather than preceptive. So attractively did he clothe his thought of what constitutes the better ordering of life, so skillfully did he sound the call to duty and to the need of hourly choosing the good part which shall not be taken away, that it may not unjustly be said of him, as it was said long ago of a greater than he, "the common people heard him gladly."

In his comprehensive outlook upon the ages of a man's life, Longfellow saw not seven but seventy times seven. Judging after the manner of the spirit and not after the manner of the world, he regarded each day as hardly less than an epoch in the life of the soul. Again and again he dwelt upon the fact that the past cannot be recalled, cannot be revived. This thought is the burden of the songs in **"Keramos,"** as it is also the chief teaching of **"Morituri Salutamus."**

> Whatever hath been written shall remain,
> Nor be erased nor written o'er again;
> The unwritten only still belongs to thee:
> Take heed, and ponder well what that shall be.

The same lesson reappears in **"The Two Rivers"** where the streams of Yesterday and of Tomorrow are spoken of as making their way one to the land of darkness and dreams, the other to the land of promise and light. It recurs in *Michael Angelo,* in Valdesso's remark that "we ourselves when we commit a sin, lose Paradise as much as Adam did"; and it finds its most beautiful, though at the same time most solemn expression in **"Sundown,"**

> On the road of life one milestone more!
> In the book of life one leaf turned o'er!
> Like a red seal is the setting sun
> On the good and evil men have done,—
> Naught can today restore!

Irrevocably gone Longfellow might teach the past to be, yet he never once sounded the note of despair. He might bewail the fact that labor with what zeal we will, something still remains undone, yet he pointed out more than once the futility of sitting down to measure by any absolute standard the loss and gain in each day's life. He saw that defeat might be victory in disguise; he believed with Saint Augustine that "of our vices we can build a ladder if we will but tread beneath our feet each deed of shame"; he held that we might well fix our eyes upon the path leading to higher destinies, —

> Nor deem the irrevocable Past
> As wholly wasted, wholly vain,
> If rising on its wrecks, at last
> To something nobler we attain.

Ready though he was to admit in **"The Sifting of Peter"** that the scars of sin remain, that lost innocence returns no more, he none the less insisted that earnest souls may press through dust and heat, and refusing to accept disaster as final, may for their very failures find themselves the stronger, and become true conquerors at last. Longfellow plainly saw that there is no man but shall be tempted, tried, and sifted, no man but shall sometimes fall into sin, no man but shall some day deny his Master; still he felt that even in the hour of deepest humiliation, a man may cherish the consciousness of his unquenchable divinity and hope to build, however late, a tabernacle worthy of his Lord.

Convinced that neither in the clamor of the crowded thoroughfare nor in the shouts and plaudits of the multitude, but in ourselves alone are triumph and defeat, Longfellow laid stress upon the moulding power which exists in the performance of the duty lying nearest to one's hand. Such is the basic thought of **"The Builders,"** of **"Gaspar Becerra"** and of many another poem. What though one die unknown? Longfellow asked in substance, what though in the passing of the years one be quite forgotten? What though one's tower like Giotto's stand forever incomplete,

> No endeavor is in vain;
> Its reward is in the doing,
> And the rapture of pursuing
> Is the prize the vanquished win.

"Work is prayer," says Vittoria in speaking of the labors of Michael Angelo; and that great artist unconsciously re-echoes her thought when he rebukes the unstable Benvenuto Cellini with the words, "Have faith in nothing but in industry, and work right on through censure and applause." Pope Julius, too, in the same drama, holding that all great achievements are the natural fruits of a great character, is confident that by the excellence of the work we know the master's hand. As in these words which Longfellow placed upon the lips of three of his characters, so elsewhere did he reiterate his steady belief that success is based upon honest unappreciated daily toil, upon work hourly performed for the very work's sake. Nor, to his mind, we may conclude from another passage in *Michael Angelo,* is the structure of a noble mind ever builded upon foundations essentially different or in any way less secure.

> When anything is done,
> People see not the patient doing of it,
> Nor think how great would be the loss to man
> If it had not been done. As in a building

> Stone rests on stone, and wanting the foundation
> All would be wanting, so in human life
> Each action rests on the foregoing event,
> That made it possible, but is forgotten
> And buried in the earth.

To each hour its work, to each day its task, to each life its duty, is the great unifying principle underlying Longfellow's theory of character and conduct. Obedient himself to the call which, as he said in the **"Prelude"** to *Voices of the Night,* summoned him from the contemplation of mountain, forest, and stream to an acquaintance with the sorrows and joys dwelling within the human heart, he could well be urgent with his fellow-men that they should acquit themselves nobly in the battle of life. Exhausted at times by his own toil with book and pen, he tells us in **"Weariness,"** he could but look with pity upon the helpless infant whose little hands must learn to serve or rule, whose little feet must wander on through hopes and fears, must ache and bleed beneath their load. Nevertheless he saw clearly that those who follow us, must find hope and strength for themselves, however eager we may be to yield them aid or spare them pain. Looking back upon his early days, he might in **"My Lost Youth"** recall that "a boy's way is the wind's way and the thoughts of youth are long, long thoughts"; or safe in his manhood, he might rejoice to see the young spring forward in the race, full of hope and sublime audacity; still nothing short of well-ordered conduct, and complete self-control could meet his approval. Crowded with work as his own days always were, he recorded in the sonnet named **"Mezzo Cammin"** the deep regret that half his life was gone and that still the aspiration of his youth to build some tower of song with lofty parapet was unfulfilled. Nor, to his mind, could old age justly feel that it had earned the right to rest entirely from its labors, offering excuse in the thought that the night is come and that it is no longer day. To any who would give such reason for inactivity he spoke in **"Morituri Salutamus"** the stern, yet not the less inspiriting rebuke, —

> The night hath not yet come; we are not quite
> Cut off from labor by the failing light;
> Something remains for us to do or dare;
> Even the oldest tree some fruit may bear;
>
> . . . . .
>
> For age is opportunity no less
> Than youth itself, though in another dress;
> And as the evening twilight fades away,
> The sky is filled with stars, invisible by day.

Believing that man's chief duty from childhood to old age is to strive without ceasing after the highest good, Longfellow had little sympathy with those who would undertake to compromise with evil. He found, it is true, a certain poetic pleasure in the quaint thought that since Lucifer is permitted to live, he must therefore in a sense be God's minister working for some Good not understood by man; but he did not really believe in the existence of a personal devil, laying siege to the heart of man and tempting him to sin. Rather holding with Saint James that we are drawn away and enticed by our own desires, Longfellow recast in *The Golden Legend* a part of that apostle's message in the words,

Our lusts and passions are the downward stair
That leads the soul from a diviner air.

Again, Longfellow may have been pleased to fancy that
the memorial of a righteous act is immediately registered
in heaven, but that the book wherein our evil deeds are
written remains open for a time, that by repentance and
prayer we may erase the records from its pages; yet he had
no patience with those who like Julia, in the drama of *Michael Angelo*—

Would clothe the soul with all the Christian
    graces,
Yet not despoil the body of its gauds;
Would feed the soul with spiritual food,
Yet not deprive the body of its feasts;
Would seem angelic in the sight of God,
Yet not too saintlike in the eyes of man;
In short would lead a holy Christian life
In such a way that even one's nearest friend
Would not detect them in one circumstance
To show a change from what it was before.

This arraignment of one who would find a path however
narrow between the material and the spiritual world, of
one who would feast at once upon the fleshpots of Egypt
and the manna sent down from Heaven, was the method
chosen by Longfellow to teach the lesson that Christianity, if it is to be worth anything at all, must be first and foremost truly practical. To his mind, the Christian like the
tree in the parable is known by its fruits, —the followers
of Christ are to be adjudged profitable or unprofitable servants according as they are true doers or mere hearers of
the words of their Master.

In the last analysis, the essence of Christ's teaching is love.
Although hope is repeatedly enjoined upon us by the
Scriptures, and although we are told more than once that
if we have faith even as a grain of mustard, we have but
to command and mountains shall be removed, yet is it not
made plain that it is not so much the power springing from
hope and faith which we are to cultivate, as that arising
from love? The Law and the Prophets, it is pointed out,
hang upon just two commandments, that we love the Lord
with heart and soul and mind, and that we love our neighbors as ourselves. Still, between these two commandments
there seems to be a difference in degree, since the beloved
disciple felt called upon to ask, in his letter addressed to
the Church at large, if a man loveth not his brother whom
he hath seen, how can he love God whom he hath not
seen? This doctrine both in the emphasis laid upon the surpassing value of love and in the accent placed upon the
need of making love a practical element in one's association with one's fellows, Longfellow saw fit to present repeatedly. Disseminated through several poems, it is gathered into a single stanza near the close of **"Tegner's
Drapa,"** but is more beautifully expressed, no doubt, in
one of the *Tales of the Wayside Inn.*

The reign of violence is dead,
Or dying surely from the world;
While Love triumphant reigns instead,
And in a brighter sky o'erhead
Its blessed banners are unfurled.

. . . . .

Not to one church alone, but seven
The voice prophetic spake from heaven;
And unto each the promise came,
Diversified, but still the same.

In these words Longfellow gave expression to his understanding of Christ's frequently inculcated lesson of Love.
Elsewhere it showed other aspects. It appeared as indignant pity throughout the volume called *Poems on Slavery,*
as sympathetic freedom from prejudice in **"The Jewish
Cemetery at Newport,"** as tenderness and humility in
**"Helen of Tyre,"** and as discerning liberality in **"The Saga
of King Olaf."** Love, the reflective reader soon perceives,
is the great principle underlying the whole of Longfellow's
thought. Like faith, it was to him an evidence of things unseen. Through it he became as one of those whose creed
is, not a dead formula of words, but a daily living in the
spirit of Christ. Of such, with nothing less than inspiration, he wrote in one of the interludes of the *Tales of a
Wayside Inn,* —

The passing of their beautiful feet
Blesses the pavement of the street,
And all their looks and words repeat
Old Fuller's saying, wise and sweet,
Not as a vulture, but a dove,
The Holy Ghost came from above.

Longfellow's belief that love should be the adjusting force
of our daily conduct not only gave him peace in his outlook upon life, but made him peculiarly serene in his contemplation of death. That he grieved deeply over the loss
of those whom he loved is plainly evident in such poems
as **"Footsteps of Angels," "The Cross of Snow," "The
Chamber over the Gate,"** and **"Three Friends of Mine";**
yet never did he sorrow as those who have no hope. Even
in the earliest hours of separation from one of his children,
he could write in **"Resignation,"** —

There is no Death! What seems so is transition;
This life of mortal breath
Is but a suburb of the life Elysian,
Whose portal we call Death.

His daughter was not dead, she had but gone into a larger
school where Christ himself would be her teacher; his
friend, Parker Cleaveland, although he slept, had none the
less awakened, since God had said Amen! Members of the
companions of his early life had been carried one by one
to their graves, yet he thought of them, not as buried, but
as joined to that other band of living "called mistakenly
the dead"; Bayard Taylor lay at rest among his books, but
in some realm, some planet, some star, some vast aerial
space, he walked in peaceful gardens of delight. Palfrey
and Agassiz, Hawthorne and Summer had forgotten the
pathway to the poet's door, had left him with the sense
that something unreplaceable was gone from nature, that
summer was not summer, nor could be, since they died; yet
his trust remained unshaken and he found strength to say
in **"Auf Wiedersehen,"** —

It were a double grief, if the true-hearted,
Who loved us here, should in the farther shore
Remember us no more

Believing, in the midst of our afflictions,
That death is a beginning, not an end,

We call to them, and send
Farewells, that better might be called predic-
    tions,
Being fore-shadowings of the future, thrown
Into the vast unknown

Faith overleaps the confine of our reason,
And if by faith, as in old times was said,
Women received their dead
Raised up to life, then only for a season
Our partings are, nor shall we wait in vain
Until we meet again!

Men who like Prince Henry in the *Christus* hold tena-
ciously to earth, may regard the thought of death with terror; others who think of a book in which are written our
failings, faults, and evils, our secret sins, shortcomings and
despair, may shudder in fear; but Longfellow, believing
that they who live the life of the spirit now shall continue
to live that life hereafter, had no such dread. To him as
to his heroine Elsie in *The Golden Legend,* the grave was
but a covered bridge leading from light to light through
a brief darkness. At one time, he likened death to the lift-
ing of a latch; at another, to the chillness which precedes
the dawn, wherein we shudder for a moment ere we waken
in the broad sunshine of the other life; at still another, to
the stepping forth into the open air from a tent already luminous with light shining through its transparent walls.
In Longfellow's vision, only upon those who live unwor-
thily does Death descend as a relentless archer cruel and
swift. At times, it is true, Death to the poet, took on the
form of an unexpected guest who waiting for no man's leisure, steps in unasked and unannounced to put a stop to
all our occupations and designs; but he presents himself
more vividly, now as the Driver of the ploughshare in
whose furrow we are sown; now as the Reaper who reaps
the bearded grain at a breath and the flowers that grow between; and now as the Angel of the amaranthine wreath,
descending to whisper with a breath divine the summons
to the state of perfect peace.

Dead, in the language of every day life, our friends may
be, but the poet can think of them as never dying. Not only
does the light which a great man like Sumner leaves behind him lie for years upon the path of men; not only does
the city of Nuremberg seem famous because Durer once
trod its pavements, once breathed its air; not only do the
passion and pain of hearts that long have ceased to beat
remain to throb in hearts that are or are to be; but to Longfellow the soul of every man itself lives on, a conscious personality existent in some other sphere of activity than this
material world. Though it has forever gone from us who
yet remain in the flesh, it has but moved a little nearer "to
the Master of all music, to the Master of all singing." So
believing, Longfellow placed his own conviction upon the
lips of Preciosa in *The Spanish Student* when he caused
her to answer her own question why she should fear death,
with the thought that to die is to leave all disappointment,
care, and sorrow; all ignominy, suffering and despair, and
be at rest forever. Still Longfellow's attitude towards
death was something far greater than a reconciliation to
an inevitable change, something far more courageous than
a willingness to accept one's fate, something far more
manly than a giving way to longing for the rest which

takes the place of the painful activity of our present life.
From the beginning to the end of Longfellow's career, life
to him was real, was earnest, —death was anything but the
goal. The manly heroism of Browning's *Prospice,* the
dauntless fortitude of Tennyson's *Silent Voices* were not
wanting in the American poet. He too, as his **"Victor and
Vanquished"** plainly shows, would make a final stand, he
too would meet the last enemy of mankind in courageous,
yes, in conquering strife,

As one who long hath fled with panting breath
Before his foe, bleeding and near to fall,
I turn and set my back against the wall,
And look thee in the face, triumphant Death.
I call for aid, and no one answereth;
I am alone with thee, who conquerest all;
Yet me thy threatening form doth not appall,
For thou art but a phantom and a wraith.—
Wounded and weak, sword broken at the hilt,
With armor shattered, and without a shield,
I stand unmoved; do with me what thou wilt;
I can resist no more, but will not yield.
This is no tournament where cowards tilt;
The vanquished here is victor of the field.

*Elmer James Bailey, "Henry Wadsworth Longfellow," in
his* Religious Thought in the Greater American Poets,
1922. *Reprint by Books for Libraries Press, 1968, pp. 108-
36.*

## Alfred Kreymborg    (essay date 1929)

[*An influential poet, editor, and critic, Kreymborg is best
known as a supporter of Modernism and as founder of the
literary journal* Others, *an early publisher of experimental
verse. In the following essay, he explores the origins of
Longfellow's popularity, calling the poet "a pioneer, and the
first American to bridge the sea between European culture
and parochial barbarism."*]

From the publication of his first book of poems in 1839
to his peaceful death in Craigie House, Longfellow was the
reigning popular poet of Nineteenth Century America. At
fifty, less than twenty years after *Voices Of The Night* appeared, the prolific sentimentalist looked back upon a record of sales aggregating three hundred thousand copies.
Considering the population of the times and the average
number of readers who handle each copy of a book sold
on the stalls, one may assume that every American read
Longfellow, and most of them knew most of him by heart.
Never before or since has an American poet been endowed
by Nature with so genial a faculty for catching the fancy
of the children of all ages. The supreme ease through
which he wooed the popular heart was only equaled by the
ease through which that organ succumbed. There are
many ways of accounting for his phenomenal luck, ways
that also account for the decline in which his name is now
shrouded. Of all the poets of the New England renascence,
Longfellow is held in the greatest derision. The merest reference to his name elicits a patronizing smile or contemptuous epithet. A man who attempts the slightest praise of
the poet risks the pillory. And yet, there are still some
poems of Longfellow's worthy of incurring the risk.

In one of the five flights of his *Birds Of Passage,* he unconsciously provided the text for the rise and fall of his popularity. Characteristically, the poem is called, **"Vox Populi,"** and its events take place in the remotest regions:

> When Mazárvan the Magician
> Journeyed westward through Cathay,
> Nothing heard he but the praises
> Of Badoura on his way.
>
> But the lessening rumor ended
> When he came to Khaledan,
> There the folk were talking only
> Of Prince Camaralzaman.
>
> So it happens with the poets:
> Every province hath its own;
> Camaralzaman is famous
> Where Badoura is unknown.

Since every age and province hath its own, popular poets of to-day have interred Badoura Longfellow. The time-spirit which accepted the Cambridge poet has retreated before the latest time-spirit: an aftermath of the World War. To our bedlam speed, our science and psychology, disillusion and futility, the sweetness and light of the Victorian American are antipathetic. But any one interested in the march of our poetry must consider Longfellow carefully, for he contributed an important share to its development. In reviewing his collected poems, embracing eighteen successive volumes, one finds the best work, not in the jingles so easy to memorize, but in those mature lines in which he eschewed and escaped popularity. In relation to the collected bulk, such poems are rare, but they are available to the student catholic enough to attempt the devious and largely tedious journey through the man's long life-work. The present age, or any present age, has a tendency to look down from the fancied heights of sophistication upon the ages preceding it, and to judge them as stepping stones, or less than stepping stones. In our cocksure self-importance, we even assume we have sprung out of no-where, and possess a divine right of intelligence straight from God, or whatever successor to God we believe in—if we believe in anything beyond our narcissism. To this ego, Longfellow seems absurd and laughable, and his former vogue incomprehensible. None the less, the man was a pioneer, and the first American to bridge the sea between European culture and parochial barbarism. The latest Americans racing abroad after the latest continental culture are sailing liners not unrelated to the little ship the young Bowdoin student boarded nearly a century ago.

He first went abroad in order to learn enough languages to take charge of the department allotted to him by his alma mater—a chair he gained at twenty-two. His second trip broadened his studies and enabled him to succeed George Ticknor at Harvard in the chair of Romance Languages—a post the poet served for eighteen years. The cultures he translated for America, mostly through his own poetry, were tastefully combed for their fairer aspects. He rarely yearned beyond the virtuous and the palatable. Inside these confines, he perfected his genius for a many-faceted facility. Evil books existed for him, but only once or twice did he permit their echoes to filter into his own work. On his last trip abroad, he dined with Ruskin in Paris; the latter recorded his impression of "a quiet simple

gentlemen . . . strangely innocent and calm, caring little for things out of his own serene sphere." Naïveté was also the qualifying factor he addressed in his countrymen. He fed their ignorance on European books felt through his own, and the childlike public devoured him devotedly. The still youthful land was heaven-bent for education, and Longfellow, a teacher from his earliest conscious years, turned his didactic bent and training to the best account. His audience, like himself, believed in the goodness of life, a goodness the Quakers and Unitarians had introduced in driving out the evil-believing Calvinists. Opening with the **"Psalm Of Life,"** the poet of the people had arrived. In nine jingling verses, dripping with a larger number of clichés than any other poem in the language, Longfellow smote the heartstrings of the race. *Voices Of The Night* contained but a handful of poems in addition to the Psalm. But the Psalm was enough to gather an instantaneous public.

When the youthful professor engaged a room in Cambridge, his landlady, Mrs. Craigie, insisted on his occupying the one once honored by General Washington. Thus, the man "first in the hearts of his countrymen" was eventually followed by the man who might be termed second. In the course of a year, four editions of the *Voices* were exhausted. For more than a decade, Longfellow had given himself to the writing of two books of prose, imitative of Washington Irving. Henceforth, with the exception of one more prose effort, he would devote his spare time to poetry. The doubt he felt about himself as a poet had been swept away by public opinion. Any further inclinations of a prosaic order could be satisfied in a poetic form, since much of his future work fell into prose metrically measured. This tendency mars his longest narratives, such as *Evangeline, Hiawatha* and *Miles Standish.*

Drenched from the outset in European cultures, and in love with tender beauty, Longfellow mastered many foreign forms and metres. Of all our early poets outside of Bryant and Poe, he was the most expert in the handling of versification, and handled many more varieties than the Puritan and the esthete. When *Voices Of The Night* appeared, Poe fired the first shot accusing his successful rival of plagiarism, and emphasized the similarities between

*Craigie House, Longfellow's Cambridge residence.*

Longfellow's "Beleaguered City" and his own "Haunted Palace." Poe was by no means above suspicion on the same score. An impartial reading of the two poems shows that his charge was scarcely justified. Both poems are concerned with ghosts. Poe's are a melancholy chorus that finally "smile no more"; while Longfellow's, fleeing a church bell, are treated to an optimistic moral Poe would never have stooped to. Poe not only hated Longfellow's didacticism, but envied his popularity as compared with his own titanic misery and neglect. With the publication of Longfellow's second volume, *Ballads And Other Poems,* 1841, Poe launched an essay in which, after admitting the Professor had "written brilliant poems—by accident," he exposed the sentimentalist's weakness for obtrusive sermonizing. Curiously, the fiery Southerner paid respect to such maudlin verse as **The Village Blacksmith** and **"The Wreck Of The Hesperus,"** both of which suffer from the Professor's besetting sweet sin. These ballads are extremely childish. It is impossible to believe in the Captain's little "daughtér" and in breakers roaring "Ho! ho!" Nor can one respond to the insipid regularity of the lines to the mighty smith. This very monotony commended itself to the public: regular thought and action and dutiful goodness rewarding the day with the "night's repose." The poet did all the thinking and preaching; no effort was required of the public; hence his great audience. The day may begin "cold, and dark, and dreary," but "behind the clouds is the sun still shining." Even the melancholy poem, **"It Is Not Always May,"** lilts so jauntily as to remove the sting from the terrible truth. **"Maidenhood"** betrays an indebtedness to German sentimentality, while **"Excelsior,"** with its mounting slogan, now sounds like the caption of a transcontinental advertisement. Poe defended **"Excelsior"** against the critic, Langtree: "There is an old adage about the difficulty of one's furnishing an auditor both with matter to be comprehended and brains for its comprehension." But Longfellow did not need Poe to defend him. He had founded an organization known as The Five Of Clubs, composed of friends who fought his battles for him. Charles Sumner was one of the Five.

In the midst of the growing national upheaval which moved Whittier to action, Longfellow steeped himself in his classes and the legends of other lands. Close though he was to the rebellious Sumner, the gentle lover of lovely things removed himself, as always, from the life nearest at hand. A nostalgia for Europe and all remote things affected his writings throughout: he derived his inspiration mostly from books. After the *Ballads* had been translated into several European languages, foreigners recognized Longfellow as the outstanding representative of America. Craigie House was the haven Dickens entered on his first visit to our shores. In Longfellow, Englishmen greeted a true Victorian, and, thanks to a burly invitation from the novelist and a leave of absence from Harvard, the poet sailed for Europe a third time. Stocking his wardrobe with the latest fashions in clothes, boots and haberdashery, the dandy sailed homeward again. Moved by thoughts of Sumner, he deliberately wrote seven anti-slavery poems on shipboard. Though his worst antagonist, Margaret Fuller, hailed the sheaf as "the thinnest of all Mr. Longfellow's thin books," Hawthorne, a former classmate at Bowdoin, declared: "You have never poetized a practical subject

heretofore." Next to Whittier's war poems, Longfellow's are very insipid indeed.

Shortly after his return, in 1843, the *bonviveur* married a second time. Mrs. Craigie, the Voltairian atheist, having died two years before, the poet's affluent father-in-law gallantly bought Craigie House for Henry and Frances. The happy poet settled down in his new home, returned to his classes—which had begun to annoy him—and devoted his energies to two vast undertakings: an anthology, "The Poets And Poetry Of Europe," and a translation of sixteen cantos of the "Divina Commedia." In recognition of his first European love, Spain and the Spanish dramatists, he had already composed *The Spanish Student*—a play devoid of the requisite passion, but containing the exquisite Serenade. Further foreign indebtedness was acknowledged in *The Belfry Of Bruges.* This volume roused Poe in earnest, ably supported by the former editor of the Transcendental Dial. Longfellow remained serene, the while his friends defended him. Was he not preparing his first collected edition, to be handsomely bound and illustrated? How little Longfellow was hurt by Poe came out years later, when he turned to the doting William Winter and said: "My works seemed to give him much trouble, first and last; but Mr. Poe is dead and gone, and I am alive and still writing—and that is the end of the matter."

Margaret Fuller affected him as little. Longfellow was not in favor with his Transcendental neighbors, nor they with him. Emerson recorded an unfavorable impression of the professor's extensive wine cellar—one of the few facts which endears him to present-day radicals. He dined with the Transcendentalists—especially after the founding of *The Atlantic Monthly* in 1857, and of the Saturday Club. But he was usually a silent spectator at these functions. Meanwhile, Miss Fuller's criticism, greatly admired by Poe, was even keener than Poe's: "It does not follow, because many books are written by persons born in America that there exists an American literature. . . . Longfellow is artificial and imitative. . . . He borrows incessantly, and mixes what he borrows. . . . He is very faulty in using broken or mixed metaphors. The ethical part of his writing has a hollow, second-hand sound." She paid tribute to his "elegance, love of the beautiful, and a fancy for what is large and manly—" but concluded: "And now farewell to the handsome book, with its Preciosos and Preciosas, its Vikings and knights and cavaliers, its flowers of all climes, and wild flowers of none." But the public rapturously hailed *The Belfry* and the collected edition. Did not *The Belfry* waft them into still other climes and ages: Ghent, Nuremberg, Normandy, Chimborazo, Florence, Elsinore, old France and still older Greece? And did it not offer such lyrics as **"The Bridge," "The Day Is Done," "The Arrow And The Song,"** along with some excellent sonnets? For once in his Puritanical experience, the homebred reader could find some attachment to art for its own sake—a highly salutary need. It is also salutary to find that the author did not share the public satisfaction with his work. The following proves he was not guilty of self-esteem:

> Half of my life is gone, and I have let
> The years slip from me and have not fulfilled
> The aspiration of my youth, to build

Some tower of song with lofty parapet.

The Poe and Fuller attacks had one good effect: they caused him to turn to America for his next theme. But he chose a thing of legendry and hearsay, repeated to him by a friend of Hawthorne. The novelist left the Arcadian tale for the poet to embroider. Longfellow studied Nova Scotia, not at first hand, but through Haliburton. He visited neither Grand-Pré nor the Mississippi, but resorted to maps and records for descriptive effect—the best passages in *Evangeline.* The death of the lovers in Philadelphia came out of a walk down Spruce Street, and the technical machinery of the poem was modeled on the Greek hexameter. Out of these ingredients, the poet finished the idyl on his fortieth birthday. It met with an enormous sale, and Longfellow responded to a flattering review from Hawthorne: "This success I owe entirely to you, for being willing to forego the pleasure of writing a prose tale which many people would have taken for poetry, that I might write a poem which many people take for prose." Whether moved by modesty or conviction, the poet actually revealed the prime fault of *Evangeline.* Poe carried the criticism further by showing the absurdity of trying to copy the Greek hexameter. The spondaic rhythms of the original have no counterpart in the genus of English speech. Poe, borrowing a leaf from Coleridge's attack on prosaic portions of Wordsworth, turned certain Longfellownian hexameters into prose, and exclaimed: "There! —That is respectable prose; and it will incur no danger of ever getting its character ruined by anybody's mistaking it for verse."

While one admires the natural ease of the narrative and the fine descriptive passages, one has to accept Poe's onslaught. And the prosy movement is frequently weakened by the entrance of far-fetched similes or mixed metaphors. Longfellow's fatal facility, his absorption in bookish lore, his lack of contact with life, led him into easy lines and lines filled out by sound regardless of meaning. Here are some random images. "The pewter plates on the dresser caught and reflected the flame, as shields of armies the sunshine." "As in a church, when the chant of the choir at intervals ceases, footfalls are heard in the aisles, or words of the priest at the altar, so, in each pause of the song, with measured motion the clock clicked." "Bent like a laboring oar, that toils in the surf of the ocean, bent, but not broken, by age was the form of the notary public." Faults such as these and many more did not trouble Longfellow's public. After all, here was a beautiful story of the love of two young people loyal through the years, of their cruel separation, of the search of the girl for the boy, of the woman turned white for the man breathing his last in her arms. It sounds like nothing more than a motion picture scenario. Here are those naïve elements, led by the arm of coincidence, which move a modern audience so profoundly and often.

The poet resigned from Harvard in 1854, partly because of his tie with Sumner, which the College did not approve, but mainly because of a yearning to dedicate his remaining life to poetry. James Russell Lowell succeeded him. Longfellow, at the height of material comfort and safety, had but one rival in the field of poetic popularity: Alfred Lord Tennyson. *Evangeline* and *The Princess* had appeared during the same year, and now came *The Song Of Hiawatha* and *Idyls Of The King.* Turning once more to books for his inspiration, Longfellow decided to employ the technical scheme of the Finnish epic, *Kalevala,* with its unrhymed trochaic diameter, on an old Indian legend. Various historians, by no means noted for their fidelity to truth, supplied the principal sources of Hiawatha, and to these were added the tales of an Ojibway chief who paid visits to Craigie House—Kah-ge-go-gah-bowh. The result was a careless fusion and confusion of the Ojibway and Algonquin demigod, Manabozho, and an Iroquois chief of the sixth century, "Hiawatha." The delightful villainies of the original Manabozho were transferred, not to Hiawatha, but to the villain of the new piece: Pau-Pau-Kee-Wis. Longfellow, like his beloved Cooper, insisted on creating his heros in images of purity. Naturally, too, the hero would need a heroine to enhance the appeal of the story: the apocryphal Minnehaha. This charming girl was a concession to the sentimental white race, for the Indian is the most realistic of races. Even more glaring, positively preposterous, is the conclusion of the narrative: the entrance of the white man and his Savior as the appointed rulers of the Indian—and thus appointed by the Indian god, Gitche Manito. Hiawatha himself beholds this climax in a pictorial vision utterly without foundation in Indian psychology. Even to-day, with the scattered, depleted tribes in physical subjection to our governmental and religious systems, the traditions and prayers of the Indian persist. Hiawatha's vision is pure Longfellow and impure Indian.

Though the Indians are pardoned by Christ, it is not clear what sins they committed, unless it be that they occupied our land before the advent of our forefathers. They peacefully accept the message of the White Prophet, and gratefully resign the land to the Christians. Hiawatha departs, leaving his people to the care of their new friends and brothers. The poem met with the most enthusiastic approbation. Not alone had the poet spun a number of exotic tales, but he had done so with the full grace and sentiment of his innocent heart. To the steady lilt of the trochaic beat and feminine endings, the ears of his readers were gently captured and lulled. Not for a moment through the several thousand lines does the slightly syncopated movement vary or halt. The unfolding tale, once you submit to its hyperboles, is remarkably well handled. As always in Longfellow, description takes precedence over the plot, characterization and interplay of action. The man was too restricted to write out of any other medium but his own naïve nature. Cautious from childhood, well protected by his parents, his first wife, his second, his friends, his readers and most of his critics, the occasions he had to face life were rare. The clouds visiting his home were removed by the sun fairly soon. He loved to live with his ever-increasing library. The books he took down were generally those *en rapport* with his dulcet temperament. Small wonder that his second-hand transfiguration of Indian legendry caught the hearts of his countrymen and those of Victorian England. Longfellow won his public as easily as Hiawatha won Minnehaha. And to the praises of thepeople were added the praises of Emerson, Hawthorne and Tennyson. Added to these came the highest compliment of all: the many burlesques which persist down to the present day.

Though the national upheaval neared its crisis, Longfellow remained true to his books. Consulting volumes dealing with Plymouth and the Pilgrims, and again employing his prosy version of the Greek hexameter, he composed the serene measures of *The Courtship Of Miles Standish.* Nothing could be more prosy or worse prose than the opening lines; or the description of the captain's war-like library:

> Fixed to the opposite wall was a shelf of
> books, and among them
> Prominent three, distinguished alike for
> bulk and for binding;
> Bariffe's Artillery Guide, and the
> Commentaries of Caesar
> Out of the Latin translated by Arthur
> Goldinge of London,
> And, as if guarded by these, between them
> was standing the Bible.

This is probably the worst of the Longfellow epics, but it is graced with the first feminist in American poetry: Priscilla Alden. From his earliest down to his latest days, the poet had an eye for the ladies. Though he never permitted himself to stray beyond a courtly decorum, he seldom failed to record some pleasing impression. One may assume that Priscilla was drawn from life: she is more vivid than most of Longfellow's characters. Her historic retort to Alden—"Why don't you speak for yourself, John?" —is worthy of some up-to-date miss. Her portrait benefits from the tender humor with which the poet endows her. The scholarly John is endowed with unconscious humor, as he rushes headlong into the air and sees in the flirtatious girl, "the temptation of Satan!" Poor John is denounced by Standish as the Brutus to Miles' beloved Caesar. Determined to sail back to England, John is overtaken by the Ibsenesque Priscilla. The movie ends happily when Standish reports himself dead among the Indians and appears at the wedding in time to unite the Aldens. A week after the book appeared, twenty-five thousand copies had been sold.

Longfellow's paradisaic existence was once more interrupted by tragedy. The terrible burning to death of his wife, Frances, was a shock he never outgrew. They had been married for eighteen years—a numeral haunting his life so repeatedly that he wrote a poem about it: the beautiful sonnet, **"The Cross Of Snow."** Bryant, after the death of his wife, turned to translating Homer. Longfellow sought consolation in Dante, and went back to his translation at the time the Southern Rebellion broke out. The poet had written the first and second flights of his *Birds Of Passage,* a reversion to the lyrical forms most suited to his temperament. Among them is the jocund sketch, **"The Children's Hour,"** relating the pranks of the "blue-eyed banditti," Alice, Allegra and Edith. He dreamed more and more of the past, and in **"My Lost Youth,"** pregnant with memories of his native Portland, made use of a Lapland refrain part of which served as the title of a book by Robert Frost:

> "A boy's will is the wind's will,
> And the thoughts of youth are long, long
> thoughts."

At the height of the war, secluded in his summer home at Nahant, Longfellow began a collection of ballads and legends, connected with a Prelude, Interludes and Epilogue. For one reader at least, *Tales Of A Wayside Inn* is the poet's most enduring work. The scene is laid in the Old Horse Tavern in Sudbury, where Longfellow and a group of friends foregathered. The identity of the characters was clear to his readers, nor did he disguise them. Ole Bull, Israel Edrehi, T. W. Parsons, Luigi Monti, Daniel Treadwell and Henry Ware Wells formed the cast sitting about the "kind of old Hobgoblin Hall," the while the silent poet acted as the reporter of proceedings. Thanks to their intimacy, an intimacy he grasped realistically, the characters are delightfully differentiated; and the most attractive element is the aura of humor around them. The poet had a number of classical models to draw from: Boccaccio, Chaucer, Tennyson and others. It is to his credit that he gave free vent to the masculinity of the occasion and did not, as formerly, whitewash the tales with Puritanical restraints. Two or three are akin to Maestro Boccaccio himself. The varying measures are skillfully attuned to the type of fiction unfolded, and the interludes are rich in detail and movement. Some of the poems had already appeared; it was Longfellow's task to add new material and to give the work a dramatic sequence. **"The First Day"** was issued in 1863, The Second and Third about ten years later.

Once more the poet took his readers around the earth. It was due to this escape from the war that the poem owed its popularity. The first ballad is at once the most popular and least important: **"Paul Revere's Ride."** From this, the Student turns to a love tale, borrowing a passage from the Decameron. Then the reader is transported to **"The Legend Of Rabbi Ben Levi," "King Robert Of Sicily," "The Saga Of King Olaf," "Torquemada," "The Birds Of Killingworth."** Each of these ballads is informed with dramatic fire, the color and movement of their periods, and that clash of character required by the classic ballad monger. Longfellow had never contrived better atmosphere than the opening measures of **"Torquemada."** This poem, as well as **"King Robert,"** has genuine power and ease of narration. **"The Birds Of Killingworth"** is a contrasting allegory. The tale satirizes the instinct of killing and is partly directed against the early American Colonies. Squire, Parson and Deacon are gently ridiculed. From their midst, the Preceptor of the Academy, a lover of the "fair Almira" and a composer of sonnets, comes to the defense of birds condemned to death for living on the grain of the land:

> "Plato, anticipating the Reviewers,
> From his Republic banished without pity
> The Poets; in this little town of yours,
> You put to death, by means of a Committee,
> The ballad-singers and the Troubadours,
> The street-musicians of the heavenly city,
> The birds, who make sweet music for us all
> In our dark hours, as David did for Saul. . . ."

Then follows a plea for the birds, not excepting the crow. However—

> Men have no faith in fine-spun sentiment

Who put their trust in bullocks and in beaves—

so the troubadours are condemned. The ensuing stanza revels in a "very St. Bartholomew of Birds!" Discovering, like Herod, they have been slaughtering Innocents, the townspeople repeal the law against the birds, and lead in wagons from out of town, laden with wicker cages "full of singing birds." With the wedding of Almira and the Preceptor—a moral no reader can object to—the ballad reaches a charming cadence. **"The First Day"** is brought to a close by the sound of human "bagpipes" and the nodding of the sleepy landlord.

**"The Second Day"** opens with "a cold, uninterrupted rain" outdoors, and the inmates are reduced to plying the imprisoned hours with more tales. The reader, regaled with further circumnavigation, is conducted through Atri in Abruzzo, the city of Kandalu, Hageman in Alsace, Stralsund by the Baltic Sea, St. Castine in the Pyrenees. There is another American tale: an interpolation defending Longfellow's preference of old and foreign over new and local material. **"The Third Day"** shows no decline in imaginative power. It was written at a time when the poet, according to his critics, had waned pitifully. This part is in fact the most mature of the three. The Spanish Jew relates the incisive legend of Rajah Runjiet-Sing, who appeals to the wizardry of Solomon to help him escape Azrael, the Angel of Death. The king lifts his signet-ring and a mighty wind bears the wretched scholar to a distant, happy place:

> Then said the Angel, smiling: "If this man
> Be Rajah Runjiet-Sing of Hindostan,
> Thou hast done well to listen to his prayer;
> I was upon my way to seek him there."

The sombre blank verse pageant of the coming of Charlemagne follows. This ballad of Olger and Desiderio has terror and a swift epigrammatic climax. There is another American tale. This one has psychological searchings anticipating Edwin Arlington Robinson. Often admitting the sources of his material, Longfellow then turns to a full-bellied recital of **"The Monks Of Casal-Maggiore,"** a rollicking narrative concerning two Franciscan friars. True to the Florentine tradition, it might have graced the pages of Machiavelli. And it is made out of whole-cloth:

> "A tale that cannot boast, forsooth,
> A single rag or shred of truth . . .
> Therefore I tell it; or, maybe,
> Simply because it pleases me."

It was something for a New Englander to give way to hedonism. Whatever his didacticism, sentimental taints and derivative strains, a poet had arrived who, like his Southern antagonist, believed in beauty, and occasionally let it capture him without a Puritanic protest. An Albanian tale and a ballad in Uhlandian couplets lead to another confession of artistic faith on Longfellow's part, and a defense of his roving spirit. Poets are "birds of passage," he declaims.

> "They are not fowls in barnyards born
> To cackle o'er a grain of corn;
> And, if you shut the horizon down
> To the small limits of their town,

> What do you do but degrade your bard
> Till he at last becomes as one
> Who thinks the all-encircling sun
> Rises and sets in his back yard?"

These lines supply an excellent text on the movement toward expatriation setting in with Whistler and Henry James, and the poets, Ezra Pound and T. S. Eliot. A man who could only find his pleasures abroad and stayed at home was soon to befollowed by Americans who consigned their homes to the devil and cast their restless lot with London, Paris, or Italy.

The *Tales Of A Wayside Inn* closes appropriately with an old Puritan ballad told by the Landlord. This is the tale of Sir Christopher, Gardiner, who lived with a golden-haired lady "in the Italian manner," though he had two wives in England "whom he had carelessly left behind." Governor Winthrop, apprised of the knight's wickedness, sends bailiffs to arrest him. All they find at the country seat is "the little lady with golden hair"

> Who was gathering in the bright sunshine
> The sweet alyssum and columbine.

They arrest the girl instead and drag her in triumph before the Governor. His heart is moved by the sight of

> So fair a creature caught within
> The snares of Satan and of sin.

Unable to arrive at a better sentence, he ships her off to England to bear the other wives company. The knight is captured by an Indian and brought to the Governor. Pleading that "the colonial laws were too severe when applied to a gallant cavalier," Sir Christopher is likewise banished home. The Landlord concludes:

> Thus endeth the Rhyme of Sir Christopher,
> Knight of the Holy Sepulchre,
> The first who furnished this barren land
> With apples of Sodom and ropes of sand.

To which may be added the droll comment that Longfellow, of all poets, was the first to bring such a theme into American poetry.

Shortly after the conclusion of the war, Longfellow brought out a book of shorter poems, *Flower-De-Luce,* and the collected Household Edition in seven volumes. *Flower-De-Luce,* showing more restraint than the earlier lyrics, is distinguished for the sonnet sequence on the "Divina Commedia." The more popular poems are mere echoes of the moralizing jingles of yore. The publication of the Dante translation, in conjunction with Charles Eliot Norton's prose version, was held off until 1867, the six hundredth anniversary of the immortal Italian's birthyear. Longfellow had founded a Dante Club at his home, to which Lowell, Norton and others were invited over the best of dinners and wines. To this select circle, the new associate editor of *The Atlantic* was admitted—William Dean Howells—a youthful harbinger of the advance of the Middle-West into American literature.

Except for his life-work, *The Christus Mystery,* and the posthumous *Michael Angelo,* practically the whole of Longfellow's remaining poems were housed in the shorter forms. He never mastered the epic form of the major poets: of all his extended efforts the *Christus* is the most dismal. Though he considered it his *chef d'oeuvre* and kept it in mind over a period of thirty years, this Christian pageant of the "Apostolic, Middle and Modern Ages" is long-drawn-out and devoid of dramatic sequence or connection. The scenes are diffuse and episodic, and the best speeches, many of them long and prosaic, depend too literally on biblical or historical quotation and too little on passionate inspiration. The *Michael Angelo* is a much better dramatic poem. It is worthy of note that among the metres employed in the *Christus,* there is a dialogue in the irregular cadences of a latter-day free verse.

Volumes of shorter poems continued to appear at fairly close intervals. They added little to the poet's established reputation, though he received three thousand dollars from *The New York Ledger* for the mediocre **"Hanging Of The Crane." "The Sermon Of St. Francis," "The Three Kings," "Keramos"** and some of the sonnets are notable exceptions. In **"Moods,"** he again voiced his secret dissatisfaction with himself:

> Oh that a Song would sing itself to me
> Out of the heart of Nature, or the heart
> Of man, the child of Nature, not of Art,
> Fresh as the morning, salt as the salt sea,
> With just enough of bitterness to be
> A medicine to this sluggish mood, and start
> The life-blood in my veins, and so impart
> Healing and help in this dull lethargy!

But Longfellow was fated from the outset to find the best of himself at second hand in books. He could rarely let himself go—a restraint he shared with all Yankees, including the intoxicated Emerson. Whatever the shortcomings Longfellow brooded over, they were closed to the general public. On his last trip abroad, 1867, he had been heralded by Victorians, led by the Queen. She sent for him as the accredited minister of the whilom British Colony. With that unerring eye for colonizing countries even after they are lost, British leaders pressed momentous honors on the bashful American and his daughters. Longfellow breakfasted with Gladstone and the Duke of Argyle and lunched with Lord John Russell. And Victoria could see how anxious her attendants were to steal a glimpse of the poet so many of whose poems they had memorized. Down to this day, he is the most popular American poet in the British Empire, a fact attested by his bust in Westminster Abbey.

At home the honors continued down to his death. Though old New England was dying, under ruthless machines in the hands of youthful industrialism, the children of Cambridge proved they still loved their poet by bringing him a birthday chair hewn from the village blacksmith's chestnut tree. To them he might rightly address the lines of that occasion:

> Am I a king, that I should call my own
> This splendid ebon throne?

The final verse is prophetic of the fate into which the bulk of his work has fallen. Memorized by children at school, it is discredited as soon as they graduate:

> Only your love and your remembrance could

> Give life to this dead wood,
> And make these branches, leafless now so long,
> Blossom again in song.

This poem appeared in his last volume: *Ultima Thule.* This sheaf contains thevaliant sonnet, **"Victor And Vanquished,"** wherein the old man, fully aware of his disabilities, faces "triumphant Death."

> Wounded and weak, sword broken at the hilt,
> With armor shattered, and without a shield,
> I stand unmoved; do with me what thou wilt;
> I can resist no more, but will not yield.

To his array of published books, he addressed a sonnet as might some old knight who "gazed at the arms he could no longer wield."

His last poem, **"The Bells Of San Blas,"** shapes the thought that the past cannot be recalled:

> Out of the shadows of night
> The world rolls into light;
> It is daybreak everywhere—

a daybreak that would soon leave the author of the **"Psalm Of Life"** out of its concerns. It is unfortunate that derogatory critics of Longfellow have appropriated Emerson's speech at the poet's grave: "I cannot recall the name of our friend, but he was a good man." The old men were not intimates, nor did they admire each other with any degree of enthusiasm. But when Emerson made his comment, he was in the last stages of aphasia. Not long after Longfellow's interment in Mt. Auburn, the Concordian followed Thoreau and Hawthorne to Sleepy Hollow. The most popular and the greatest poet of the New England renascence went down together in 1882.

*Alfred Kreymborg, "The Fallen Prince of Popularity," in his* Our Singing Strength: An Outline of American Poetry (1620-1930), *Coward-McCann, Inc., 1929, pp. 97-115.*

---

**Louis Untermeyer on Longfellow:**

It is as a pioneer that Longfellow might well be given a higher rank than is usually accorded him. He was one of the first American poets to break the new earth and make it easier for those who followed to cultivate that rich soil. It was not the leader of "the genteel tradition" who dug the epical *Song of Hiawatha* out of native clay, and who invigorated history with *Evangeline, The Courtship of Miles Standish,* and **"The Ride of Paul Revere."** Longfellow may have been the poet of America's cultural adolescence. But he was more; he was also the forerunner of those who gave expression to America's maturity. If he did not deeply penetrate the local territory fertilized by his descendants, he was one of the first to explore the unexploited terrain.

*Louis Untermeyer, in his introduction to* The Poems of Henry Wadsworth Longfellow, *1943.*

**Howard Mumford Jones   (essay date 1931)**

[*A distinguished twentieth-century American critic, Jones was noted for his illuminating commentary on American culture and literature. He was awarded the Pulitzer Prize for his study of the formation of American culture in* O Strange New World *(1964), and he was also acclaimed for his critical work* The Theory of American Literature *(1948) and similar works in which he examines the relationship between America's literary and cultural development. In the following essay, Jones presents an overview of Longfellow's work, maintaining that his reputation as a simple, sentimental poet is not entirely accurate. Jones praises Longfellow's "swift and certain technique, his sense of human values, the superb skill with which he sketches in backgrounds and sets a story in motion."*]

On one level the name of Longfellow evokes memories of *Appleton's Fifth Reader,* Friday afternoon "recitations," and the false dramatics of **"The Wreck of the Hesperus."** On another, it is shrouded in that mild disdain with which recent critics of American letters have agreed to discuss most books written in this country in the nineteenth century, books characterized, they say, by vague, high aspirations, sentimentality, and the turning away from ugliness and therefore from "reality." The Longfellow legend is compounded of these attributes, and they do not arouse esthetic approval. Even the chapter in the academic *Cambridge History of American Literature* is unenthusiastic, the writer remarking with commendable caution that Longfellow's art "is worthy, to say the least, of as much praise as the similar work of his predecessors, contemporaries and successors among American poets, and is not clearly doomed to a speedier death. . . ." This is a dark saying; perhaps higher praise is not deserved; but when one compares it with the enthusiastic tributes of men like Hawthorne, one begins to wonder whether our persistent dwelling upon Longfellow's poetical defects does not point to a certain oddity in contemporary criticism.

Of course legends do not spring up without cause, and it must be confessed that there is a great deal in Longfellow to justify unkindly comment. The canonical adjective which goes with his name is "gentle"; and gentleness was the source of his weakness, as it was sometimes of his strength. I do not know how many times the word "dreams" recurs in his verses, but it is a favorite word—

> How far since then the ocean streams
> Have swept us from the land of dreams,
> That land of fiction and of truth,
> The lost Atlantis of our youth!

he writes in the dedication of *Ultima Thule,* and it was to the land of fiction and of truth, as he understood these words, that he gently returned. A quiet and sincere Christian, he was always pained at wrong and sin, always hoping the world would mend its wicked ways, but confronted with what seemed to him a moral evil, he could usually utter nothing more burning than the *Poems on Slavery,* and these do not seem to us to be of the right strength and indignation. In the didactic pieces the world remembers him by, he was perpetually telling people to be good and quiet and hopeful, to trust in a better world, to be forbearing and resigned. His were all the old-fashioned virtues,

and opening a volume to such a poem as **"Maidenhood,"** we rub our eyes in amazement:

> Maiden! with the meek, brown eyes,
> In whose orb a shadow lies,
> Like the dusk in evening skies!
>
> . . . . .
>
> Standing, with reluctant feet,
> Where the brook and river meet,
> Womanhood and childhood fleet!
>
> Gazing, with a timid glance,
> On the brooklet's swift advance,
> On the river's broad expanse!

In a world of problem children, we, whose sub-debs these lines scarcely describe, smile at the Victorian simplicity.

And then there are the more obvious and awful didactic pieces—**"The Arrow and the Song," "Excelsior," "Resignation," "A Psalm of Life,"** and the one which begins

> All are architects of Fate,
> Working in these walls of time!

and goes jigging on for thirty-four more lines with its direction to "build to-day, then, strong and sure," concluding with the pious hope that we shall some day see the "boundless reach of sky." I have even heard the name of Eddie Guest murmured in this connection. The sentiments, it must be confessed, are often similar; but as the sentiments of Mr. Guest are frequently those of the Sermon on the Mount, I presume that the question of style also enters in; and I for one, on re-reading the poet, am impressed with the fact that the style *qua* style, even in these bad pieces, is frequently lucid, compact, and excellent. In the battered **"A Psalm of Life,"** for example, one finds so admirable a quatrain as:

> Art is long, and Time is fleeting,
> And our hearts, though stout and brave,
> Still, like muffled drums, are beating
> Funeral marches to the grave.

This is not only impeccable in its handling, but we would admire, in another poem by another poet (Heinrich Heine, for example), the sudden, ghastly undertone of doom. The truth is that there are surprises in Longfellow for anybody who will read him with impartial sympathetic eyes, for the same poet who wrote **"Resignation"** (which I cheerfully surrender) was capable of unexpected grimness, as *Tales of A Wayside Inn* exists to prove. Consider, for instance, the fine reticence of the following:

> The tide rises, the tide falls,
> The twilight darkens, the curlew calls;
> Along the sea-sands damp and brown
> The traveller hastens toward the town,
> And the tide rises, the tide falls.
>
> Darkness settles on roofs and walls,
> But the sea, the sea in the darkness calls;
> *The little waves, with their soft, white hands,*
> *Efface the footprints in the sands,*
> And the tide rises, the tide falls.
>
> The morning breaks; the steeds in their stalls
> Stamp and neigh, as the hostler calls;

The day returns, but nevermore
Returns the traveller to the shore,
And the tide rises, the tide falls.

I have ventured to italicize the two lines which are the heart of this little tragedy because, when you are discussing Longfellow, you have to insist upon his virtues. But is not this fine indirection of the essence of true art?

Lucidity, gentleness, musicality—these are the essential qualities of Longfellow's poetry. They are qualities which exactly express a nature in itself gentle and clear and lovely, a nature greatly beloved in its own day, a nature with which our age has no patience because these qualities our age does not possess. The poet's soul was lucid and gentle, yet neither weak nor womanish, for Longfellow endured with dignity and calm the personal tragedies which came to him. He sought to reduce the outer world to the same condition of music which he found within—to rhythm and harmony suitable to a Christian universe created by a Christian God who, for His own purposes, permitted pain and evil to exist. Rhythm, harmony, faith, music—these were with him from the beginning to the end. If he was occasionally puzzled, it was not as a skeptic is puzzled, and though alert to the movement of thought about him in his quiet way, he endured no such doubt and loss of faith as others of his generation—perhaps because Agassiz, his principal scientific friend, was not an evolutionist. Even questionings were reduced to that dreamy state which he preferred:

Is, then, the old faith dead,
. . . and in its stead
Is some new faith proclaimed,
That we are forced to remain
Naked to sun and rain,
Unsheltered and ashamed?

. . . . .

The saints! Ah, have they grown
Forgetful of their own?
Are they asleep, or dead,
That open to the sky
Their ruined Missions lie,
No longer tenanted?

Oh, bring us back once more
The vanished days of yore,
When the world with faith was filled;

Bring back the fervid zeal,
The hearts of fire and steel,
The hands that believe and build.

So runs the last poem he ever penned, **"The Bells of San Blas,"** written in 1882, thirty-two years after *In Memoriam,* and twenty-three years after *The Origin of Species.* By 1882 most of Spencer's work had been written, and in 1883 John Fiske was to publish *The Excursions of an Evolutionist.* Across the water, French naturalism was in full swing, Ibsen and the German realists were writing, and in England, Swinburne and James Thomson had blasphemed God in their respective fashions. But whatever Huxley or Darwin or Arnold or Hardy might say, Longfellow spoke more firmly than he had spoken in **"A Psalm of Life"** forty-four years earlier:

O Bells of San Blas, in vain
Ye call back the Past again!
The Past is deaf to your prayer;
Out of the shadows of night
The world rolls into light;
It is daybreak everywhere.

Is this mere provincialism? I think not. The poet's notebooks are filled with comments upon European thought and literature; he lived in the most cultured community in America, or so the Brahmins thought; he had been abroad; he had taught foreign literatures; he numbered scientists and savants among his friends; he was the recipient of honors from learned bodies in England, Russia and Spain. It will not do to dismiss this stubborn and gentle optimism simply as an instance of the American cultural lag. Longfellow's quiet faith lies deep within; it is the later, as it is the sweeter, aspect of New England faith which thus expresses itself.

Recent fashionable attacks upon Puritanism have grossly misrepresented that belief, nor have some modern historians always been fair. The misrepresentation has a long and honorable history. For example, Matthew Arnold (in *St. Paul and Protestantism*) declares that all branches of Puritan doctrine agree that man is under a curse, and that Congregational Puritanism in particular shows "not a trace of delicacy of perception, or of philosophic thinking." This is surely an astonishing judgment, the more astonishing as one remembers that Longfellow is the product of Puritan tradition. Any definition of Puritanism large enough to cover the facts must include not merely the austerities of Calvinism, but also that simple, sweet, and gracious life out of which Longfellow developed, and which has not the slightest trace of "covenants, conditions, bargains, and parties-contractors."

The poet was no Calvinist. His brother, indeed, was a Unitarian minister, for whose ordination Longfellow wrote a hymn which, as a biographer remarks, shows "plainly the nature of the poet's Christianity."

And evermore beside him on his way
The unseen Christ shall move.

But the sense of the unseen Christ is deep-rooted in Puritan tradition, English and American; out of it spring the great passages of Puritan mysticism which are among the glories of seventeenth-century prose, and out of it spring, too, that sanity and graciousness which must be reckoned with in discussing the Puritans. Even in seventeenth-century New England, though there were fanatics, not everybody was fanatical; nor, despite the brilliant paradoxes of the modern historian, can we believe that the lives of all were dominated by the sexual repression and morbid religiosity which have been attributed to them on insufficient evidence. There is, for example, the New England village, and perhaps the best way to keep one's balance in facing this difficult subject is to remember that New England Puritanism produced the New England village, which is among the more gracious aspects of our unlovely domestic architecture. A true fanatic is not likely to be concerned with doorways and fanlights; he is content with a pillar like Simon Stylites, or a cave in the desert like a monk of the Thebaid. Doubtless many New Englanders

*Handwritten manuscript copy of the concluding stanza to "Excelsior!," which Longfellow described in 1841 as "one of the best things, if not the best, that I have written."*

strove to take the kingdom of God by violence; doubtless others sought to whip out the heretics with whips of scorpions, but that generation upon generation of them suffered from gloomy fanaticism and repressed sexuality is an assumption that simply fails to explain the facts.

A serene faith in the unseen Christ freed many a Yankee from undue introspection. Life mellowed and took on gracious ways, so that in the eighteenth-century New England which Longfellow inherited, Puritanism took its inward form in the consciousness of a divine principle of good, and its outward form in those ordered habits and deep-rooted simplicities which are traditional New England. The physical embodiment of Puritanism—the plain and beautiful houses, the gracious gardens, the shady commons—pointed to serenity within. Looking back, the poet repudiated the harshness of the past—that "tornado of fanaticism" which he portrayed in *The New England Tragedies,* but, wiser than the historians, he discerned in the Puritan colonists the fun and humor of *The Courtship of Miles Standish,* which is surely one of the astonishing historical reconstructions of American poetry. The memory of Portland clung to him, that "dear old town" where "the native air is pure and sweet" amid the "trees that

o'ershadow each well-known street, as they balance up and down," so that **"My Lost Youth,"** more than any other poem in Longfellow, shows how naturally he grew out of the beautiful life which a Puritan civilization had made possible.

A serene faith in goodness runs through his work. He sought to create for it as a solution of life a great philosophic and poetical masterpiece, the *Christus: A Mystery,* which occupies so many unread pages in his collected works. This was to be the "tower of song with lofty parapet" which, as he tells us in **"Mezzo Cammin,"** he longed to build, and on it he labored from 1849 to 1872. The theme is the unseen Christ; as Saint John tells us in the "Finale,"

> Bewildered in its search,
> Bewildered with the cry:
> Lo, here! lo, there, the Church!
> Poor, sad Humanity
> Through all the dust and heat
> Turns back with bleeding feet,
> By the weary road it came,
> Unto the simple thought
> By the great Master taught.

Even more revealing is the amusing anti-climax of the whole. Part one re-tells the gospel story; part two, *The Golden Legend* (the only successful portion) is a panorama of medieval faith; but part three, the climax, is made up of two stories of seventeenth-century Massachusetts, as though the whole creation moved to this great end! Transcendental provincialism, this, but none the less important in illuming the poet's character.

The reasons for the failure of the principal work of the poet's life arise from the inherent weakness of the poet's philosophy. It is not sufficient to say that the four dramas which make up the whole are not "dramatic," they were never intended to be so; and the intention of the whole is really epic. Nor, remembering Dante's use of vivid Florentine similes, can one believe that the story of Giles Corey was necessarily a weak closing; to illustrate modern Christianity, one time or locality, so to speak, will do as well as another. Moreover, so far as character is concerned, it is idle to say that the man who made Evangeline as familiar as Hamlet, and who stamped Miles Standish and Hiawatha upon the popular consciousness, had no mastery of character. No, the reason why *Christus* as a whole is a failure is that Longfellow did not know what he meant to do in it; and the reason he did not know what he meant to do is that Puritanism, watered into Unitarianism, had no outline and no edge, so thatconsequently the dramatic epic shaped by its spirit and philosophy had no outline and no edge. The "simple thought" which the great work was to illustrate is the practical Christianity of

> Not he that repeateth the name,
> But he that doeth the will!

but this will scarcely sustain an epic poem. There is a sense in which Unitarianism is best defined by a series of theological negatives; and it is significant that the concluding third of the trilogy portrays seventeenth-century New England, perhaps the last period in American history in which theological negatives had really a fighting force. Longfellow did not, as he might have done, bring his world drama down to the Napoleonic wars or to the Grant administration, partly because all his literary instincts pointed in another direction, and even more importantly because his mild Unitarianism was helpless before the cataclysm of a world war and the corruptions of the tragic era. Lucidity, faith, and gentleness had no practical meaning in the world of Boss Tweed.

If a Christian gentleman was thus outmoded in the era of President Grant, nothing in the development of American letters since has operated to make him once more fashionable. Strength, irony, precision, frankness—these are our praises. Indeed, to say that So-and-so writes like a gentleman would nowadays be almost to damn him. It is curious that being a gentleman and being an artist should be thought so incompatible, but as Longfellow wrote not merely like a gentleman, but also like a Christian gentleman, the lapse of years throws him more and more out of the focus of our interests. We find it a weakness that he avoided certain themes. Merely to mention sex in this connection provokes a smile. He was not, we complain, tragic or intense or sophisticated; his ethics are not sufficiently casuistical, his art not subtle enough. And because he does

not write like E. A. Robinson or Carl Sandburg or Maxwell Bodenheim, we consign him to the children.

The absence of depth in his thought and sharpness in his intellection is due in part, as I have indicated, to the vagueness of his religious philosophy, but it springs also from the peculiar circumstances under which he matured. Bowdoin College gave him the correct learning of a New England gentleman; had he gone no farther, it is possible he might have achieved at least the formal precision of the late eighteenth century. Yet as early as April, 1823, he writes home:

> I have this evening been reading a few pages in Gray's Odes. I am very much pleased with them. The 'Progress of Poesy' and the 'Ode on Eton College' are admirable. And many passages of 'The Bard,' though, I confess, quite obscure to me, seem to partake in a great degree of the sublime.

This is charming and boyish, but the tell-tale adjective is *sublime.* Already there is in him a yearning for the vast and vague.

Came then the fateful trips to Europe in 1826-1829 and 1835-1836. It is difficult for us to realize the epochal quality of these voyagers, made in the uncomfortable packets of a time when Europe was not five days, but a month or two months away. They re-made the boy who was so pleased with Gray's sublimity into the mature cosmopolitan; and if to us Longfellow's cosmopolitanism is not sophisticated, it is because we are unaware of the provincial quality of cultured America in those decades, as we are unaware of the peculiar conditions of sophisticated European thought. When Longfellow returned from his first trip abroad, the poets most in the public eye were Alsop, Halleck, Drake, Percival, Brainard, Morris, *et hoc omne genus;* when he returned the second time, *Nature* was a brand-new book, and the oration on "The American Scholar" had not yet been pronounced. Beside the provincial poets of the time, the returning Longfellow, with his talk of Göttingen and Heidelberg and Copenhagen, of Spanish bandits and the Tyrol, of Canova, Charlotte Bonaparte, von Weber, Paganini, Sydney Smith, Meyerbeer, and the advanced views of German savants, was a person of exciting information. Indeed, at a time when German was scarcely known among the literati (is it so much better known now?), Longfellow, aged nineteen, was boldly writing back: "I consider the German language and literature much more important than the Italian"; and three years later, the only American in Göttingen and delighted with the university, he was advising George Green on no account to omit studying there. It is as though a young Arkansan should write to his fundamentalist friends that they must not omit Moscow and Bolshevism.

Why, then, did not this European experience give a greater sophistication to the young professor? The truth is that Longfellow, though he found European literatures very sympathetic, acquired his cosmopolitan polish at, for him, an unfortunate time. He visited the Europe of the reaction, the medieval revival, of *Sentimentalität,* of all that Heine satirized and all that Elizabeth Barrett admired, the Europe of a dreamy and idealizing romanticism, when the key to the riddle of the universe was thought to be some-where in Germany. Art, science, and philosophy were full of vast, vague phrases. The great Goethe was speaking or-phically of a divine energy in stones and grasses, of man's longing for *"Einwirken und Einfühlen in die ganze Natur."* There was much talk of the *"Idee des Lebens"* and the *"Idee des Typus."* In England Carlyle, utterly ignorant of laboratory science, was writing transcendental phrases about light-sparkles on the Aether of Divinity and the liv-ing garment of God. The greatest speculative scientist of the age, the all-knowing Alexander von Humboldt, was to introduce his *Kosmos* with such reflections as these:

> He who can trace through by-gone times, the stream of our knowledge to its primitive sources, will learn from history how, for thousands of years, man has labored, amid the ever-recurring changes of form, to recognize the invariability of natural laws, and has thus, by the force of mind, gradually subdued a great portion of the physi-cal world to his dominion. In interrogating the history of the past, we trace the mysterious course of ideas yielding the first glimmering per-ception of the same image of a Cosmos, or har-moniously ordered whole, which, dimly shad-owed forth to the human mind in the primitive ages of the world, is now fully revealed to the maturer intellect of mankind as the result of long and laborious observation.

If such was the language of the maturer intellects, is it any wonder that European poetry was seraphic, sentimental, and diffuse? Words like Soul, the Divine, Man, Mind, Progress, Humanity were on the lips of the learned and ar-tistic. One group of French writers was calling for a return to the medieval papacy; another was hymning the throne and the altar; a third was poetizing Christianity. The Schelgels were become Catholic and mystical; formless-ness was, with the German romantics, exalted into an ideal; *Sehnsucht* and self-development were powerful words. What Longfellow brought back with him was this amorphous idealism, this vague belief in progress as a world-law (he studied Herder), this inclination to solve the poetical problem in terms of emotional moralizing as the Germans solved it. Of Richter for instance, he writes: "The most magnificent of the German prose writers. Lis-ten to his words! 'A look into a pure, loving eye; a word without falseness to a bride without falseness; and then a soft-breathing breast in which there is nothing but Para-dise, a sermon, and an evening prayer.'"

Of course, this is not all he brought back. It is pleasant to record that Cambridge found his coats, waistcoats, and neckties too gaudy; his sense of humor remained with him, even when confronting German poetry; and he at no time lost that fine control of line and meter which makes him one of the most technically gifted of American poets. And amid the strict Calvinism of Bowdoin, where first he taught, at Harvard, still rational and formal in many ways, the new culture was strange and stimulating; it is with a shock that we realize how odd and new **"A Psalm of Life"** seemed on its appearance. The poem was first read to a class studying Goethe; upon publication, we read, it was copied far and wide, not because it said an old thing, but because it was the landmark of a new culture. For the

poem is a complete denial of Calvinism, of all the theologi-cal values; it calls upon men to act in the present, and it also attacks the worship of happiness as vigorously as did Carlyle. We can not grasp at this distance the startling so-phistication of these simple and well-worn stanzas.

But however useful to the country, Longfellow's experi-ence with current European thought was such as to con-firm the general drift and tenor of his mind. If the Europe-ans had taught him to think in terms of such a world-drama as **Christus,** they had failed to teach him the neces-sity of the fundamental brain-work without which such a poem can but fail. He learned in Europe the delights of a cosmopolitan and comparative view, but the very terms of European literature were such as to confirm him in his predilection for turning books into other books. He had seen Spain, but he had not learned enough of the soul of Spain to make **The Spanish Student** anything more than a pleasant literary exercise. He delighted to translate Ger-man poetry, but the poems of Müller and Uhland and the rest, however charming, were sentimental and sweet. He was gifted with wonderful literary tact, but his flexibility as a translator was usually exercised within a relatively narrow range; indeed, only twice—in the *Coplas de Man-rique* and in certain portions of his Dante—did he ever achieve anything like the grand style. His cosmopolitan-ism was broad and genuine, but it was not deep and thor-ough, and it confirmed him in many of his natural tenden-cies.

If the dominant motif of Longfellow's poetry is thus unsat-isfactory, if Europe gave him little to strengthen him on the side of intellect, where he was weak, he is nevertheless among the greater narrative poets of American literature, and notable among those in English. The very success of his art, especially when it concerns the more familiar American stories, has dulled our appreciation of his swift and certain technique, his sense of human values, the su-perb skill with which he sketches in backgrounds and sets his story in motion. It is a genre in which he excels, a genre in which he continually improved until, in the tri-partite **Tales of a Wayside Inn,** he gave us the only successful ex-ample of the frame-story group of narratives in American letters. And while he was thus perfecting himself in the larger pieces, he was steadily improving his skill in shorter ballads. **"The Secret of the Sea,"** for example, published in 1849, is as much better than **"The Wreck of the Hesper-us"** as **"A Dutch Picture"** of 1878 is better than **"The Se-cret of the Sea."** Everybody knows what is wrong with the Hesperus poem, which requires no comment; if in **"The Secret of the Sea"** the dramatic falsities are absent, the sentimentalism remains, but **"A Dutch Picture"** is as sim-ple and homely and direct as the kind of painting from which it takes its name. Naturally his progress was not al-ways in a straight line; he never again achieved in a shorter poem the wild energy of **"The Skeleton in Armor"** of 1841, but generally speaking, Longfellow continually im-proved his practice in story-telling.

It is, of course, the fashion to sneer at **Evangeline, The Courtship of Miles Standish,** and **The Song of Hiawatha,** albeit it is a little difficult to understand the source of this contempt. **Hiawatha** has, it is true, its peculiar meter; we no longer regard the poem as a successful interpretation of the Indian; and it is quite clear that Longfellow both regularized the legends and Christianized their interpretation. But some of this criticism is surely beside the point. An author works in the light of the knowledge and artistic manner of his time; we do not complain of Chaucer that *Troilus and Criseyde* is scarcely classical in spirit, or of Mr. E. A. Robinson that no medieval knight ever talked so cleverly or so long as does his Tristram. Any one who has looked into schoolcraft must see that Longfellow honestly followed what seemed to him and his generation a safe guide; the famous meter he adopted from a Finnish folk epic, or so he thought; and if his Indians are wonderfully gentle and well-mannered, so were most of the literary Indians of his day and generation. We can scarcely complain of past poets because they lack our modern enlightenment; and for us the point should be not whether *Hiawatha* will now pass muster as an anthropological report, but whether it is successful as a poem postulated on certain literary premises. Fundamentally the question becomes one of taste; and I, for one, confess, on re-reading *Hiawatha,* that I find it remarkably good. It creates and carries its own world with it; the personages are quite as believable as the personages in, let us say, *The Eve of St. Agnes* or Morris's *The Earthly Paradise;* and the bright, simple colors of the earth, the musical Indian names, the gayety and good humor of the episodes are, after a dose of modern intellectualist verse, a positive relief. Doubtless Keats makes a more sensuous appeal; doubtless Robinson is more intense and tragic; doubtless Morris is more generous and more "poetical"; but all this is, I can not too often repeat, beside the point—it is the kind of criticism which complains of A because he does not have the qualities of B. It seems to me that Longfellow, given the materials and the age, has done wonderfully well, he has created something unique and sui generis, he has displayed the greatest literary tact, and a really superb artistic élan in carrying this small epic to a satisfactory close.

But I am even willing to surrender *Hiawatha* to the dissatisfied if in so doing I can get them to look once more, and with an impartial eye, upon *Evangeline* and *The Courtship of Miles Standish.* They are poems as soft and lovely as the paintings of the English landscape school. If we could but read these narratives for the first time, we should see, I think, how skillfully they are put together, with what deft devices the poet has knitted his plot, and how beautifully the descriptive passages are made to melt into the steady flow of the narrative—one of the most difficult feats in this kind of verse, as the relative failure of Keats in keeping his stories free of encumbrance sadly testifies. And I would particularly instance the genre paintings in both pieces—the village of Grand-Pré, for instance, as well known to most of us as *Vanity Fair,* or *David Copperfield.* Read again the opening passages of *The Courtship of Miles Standish,* and note how deftly the characters, the room, the situation are drawn—we have a complete comedy in a hundred lines. Or consider the wonderful vividness of this portrait of René Leblanc in *Evangeline;* the whole man and all his little history is made to appear before us:

> Bent like a laboring oar, that toils in the surf of the ocean,

> Bent, but not broken, by age was the form of the notary public.
> Shocks of yellow hair, like the silken floss of the maize, hung
> Over his shoulders; his forehead was high; and glasses with horn bows
> Sat astride on his nose, with a look of wisdom supernal.
> Father of twenty children was he, and more than a hundred
> Children's children rode on his knee, and heard his great watch tick.
> Four long years in the times of the war had he languished a captive,
> Suffering much in an old French fort as the friend of the English.
> Now, though warier grown, without all guile or suspicion,
> Ripe in wisdom was he, but patient, and simple, and childlike.
> He was beloved by all, and most of all by the children;
> For he told them tales of the Loup-garou in the forest,
> And of the goblin that came in the night to water the horses,
> And of the white Létiche, the ghost of a child who unchristened
> Died, and was doomed to haunt unseen the chambers of children;
> And how on Christmas eve the oxen talked in the stable,
> And how the fever was cured by a spider shut up in a nutshell,
> And of the marvelous powers of four-leaved clover and horseshoes,
> With whatsoever else was writ in the lore of the village.

How clearly a whole civilization rises up before us as we read! When our own writers of folk-novels tell us these things, we exclaim with pleasure, but when Longfellow paints pictures so exquisite, evokes with so much charm a past that has vanished, we smile because we have been told so often that he is the children's poet! I am inclined to believe that a proper appreciation of the merits of his narratives requires a riper wisdom than some of our critics yet possess.

That there are defects in both poems is clear, but they are lost in the general excellence of the pathos of the one, the geniality of the other. Perhaps the greatest fault is a certain diffuseness; the last half of *Evangeline* could, perhaps, be more condensed; the fifth and sixth sections of *The Courtship of Miles Standish* scarcely advance the narrative. But as if he recognized diffuseness as a weakness, in *Tales of A Wayside Inn,* with its charming interlinks, the poet condensed with severe economy; even the magnificent "Saga of King Olaf," long as it is, has the irony of the sagas from which it was taken. Those who do not know their Longfellow, who believe that he is merely a writer of gentle platitudes, have much to discover. There is the grim vigor of **"Kambalu"** and **"Torquemada,"** the sly humor of **"The Birds of Killingworth"** and **"Emma and Ermingard,"** the wholly successful reworking of Boccaccio in **"The Falcon of Ser Federigo,"** and the beautifully handled apologues of **"King Robert of Sicily"** and **"Azra-**

el," the last with its sardonic disillusion—in short a wide variety of good things. Not Dryden, not Morris, not Crabbe has this combination of economy of line and fertility of resource, this pellucid and restrained simplicity. The art is so great that the tales seem to tell themselves; one is not conscious, as one is with so many poetical narratives, of the continual presence of the poet at one's elbow. The work as a whole seems to me to be Longfellow's masterpiece, and I am sorry that it is so little known.

Of the numberless shorter lyrics and non-narrative pieces by Longfellow, many do not interest because they seem to us empty and trivial. In addition to this group, others which often begin well—**"Seaweed,"** the opening of which is superb, is an example—no longer please because of the rhymed moral appended to them. But there is a surprisingly large third group wherein the question of didacticism does not enter—and occasionally poems where it does—which are soft and lucent and musical, which sometimes have that captious criticism can reject. Others are more sonorous and powerful—**"Sandalphon,"** for instance, with its cunning rhymes, or the abrupt and ironic **"Jugurtha"** or, among the earlier poems, the somber **"Hymn to the Night."** In such pieces Longfellow displays a cunning and precision which is not always found in our poetry, and if they sometimes lack intensity, the perfection of style often compensates for the defect. Longfellow is almost never passionate, but the house of poetry has many mansions, and there seems to be no good reason for rejecting, as many do, the pleasure he gives us because it is not the pleasure that somebody else might give us.

And then there are the sonnets, of which he wrote or translated almost a hundred. Some critics have averred that they constitute Longfellow's real claim to greatness as a poet. Mr. Ferris Greenslet, for example, who collected them into a book, wrote stoutly that though no single sonnet of Longfellow's is among the few great sonnets, his "work in this kind is upon a more even and a higher level than any other similar body of sonnets that can readily be found." This is high praise; I am not sure it is undeserved; and the only question I would raise concerns the exact level at which we are to judge his productions. For if on the one hand he missed the grand sonnet manner of Milton and Wordsworth, he did not quite hit off that sharper, more intense, and almost colloquial manner which modern sonneteers have revived with rich and astonishing results. His sonnets have dignity and elevation, but they lack grandeur; they have ease and repose, but they do not hint of drama or tension. They are, so to speak, of the second order of one kind of sonnet-writing, without quite entering into the domain of the first order of another kind.

And yet it is a genre in which Longfellow excels. The definite form curbed his diffuseness, the intricate pattern appealed to his sense of craftsmanship, and the possibilities of the structure led him to fruitful experimentation. He thrice attempted small sonnet sequences; and in one of these, that introductory to his translation of the *Divine Comedy,* he rose to a height and dignity rare with him, and rare with most poets. He excels, too, in the sonnet of praise and portraiture; and it is a curious and important fact that in some eight or nine sonnets devoted to poets he admired,

he accomplished a feat in which Swinburne is his only rival—a combination of poetry which is fine, and of criticism which, if laudatory, is penetrating. In this form, too, he came closer to sententious philosophic utterance than he usually did, and I would cite as an instance of Longfellow at his very best, **"The Broken Oar":**

> Once upon Iceland's solitary strand
> A poet wandered with his book and pen,
> Seeking some final word, some sweet Amen,
> Wherewith to close the volume in his hand.
> The billows rolled and plunged upon the sand,
> The circling sea-gulls swept beyond his ken,
> And from the parting cloud-rack now and then
> Flashed the red sunset over sea and land.
> Then by the billows at his feet was tossed
> A broken oar; and carved thereon he read:
> "Oft was I weary, when I toiled at thee";
> And like a man, who findeth what was lost,
> He wrote the words, then lifted up his head,
> And flung his useless pen into the sea.

This has the gnomic quality of romantic poetry at its best.

And finally there is the one long poem of his in which he put such wisdom as had come to him in some seventy years of life—the **"Morituri Salutamus,"** written for the fiftieth anniversary meeting of his college class. It is a simple, unpretentious piece, written for once in rhymed pentameter; into it he introduces the inevitable literary allusion without which, for him, no poem was quite complete—this time, a long story from the *Gesta Romanorum;* he remembers all he has seen and experienced, remembers

> the endless strife,
> The discord in the harmonies of life,

remembers

> The market-place, the eager love of gain,
> Whose aim is vanity, and whose end is pain;

and seriously considers what he has to tell his ageing classmates.

> It is too late! Ah, nothing is too late
> Till the tired heart shall cease to palpitate.
> Cato learned Greek at eighty; Sophocles
> Wrote his grand Œdipus, and Simonides
> Bore off the prize of verse from his compeers,
> When each had numbered more than four-score
>     years . . .
> These are indeed exceptions; but they show
> How far the gulf-stream of our youth may flow
> Into the arctic regions of our lives,
> Where little else than life itself survives.
>
> . . . Shall we sit idly down and say
> The night hath come; it is no longer day?
> The night hath not yet come; we are not quite
> Cut off from labor by the failing light;
> Something remains for us to do or dare;
> Even the oldest tree some fruit may bear;
> Not Œdipus Coloneus, or Greek Ode,

Or tales of pilgrims that one morning rode
Out of the gateway of the Tabard Inn,
But other something, would we but begin;
For age is opportunity no less
Than youth itself, though in another dress,
And as the evening twilight fades away
The sky is filled with stars, invisible by day.

This is surely no unworthy rival of *Ulysses* and *Rabbi Ben Ezra;* here is surely the philosophic temper for which, in some sense, poetry exists; and this ripe and Senecan wisdom, these easy and colloquial lines, apparently so effortless but withal so cunning—all this, I say, is the utterance of that riper Longfellow who has been so curiously ignored.

*Howard Mumford Jones, "Longfellow," in* American Writers on American Literature, *edited by John Macy, Horace Liveright, Inc., 1931, pp. 105-24.*

## Ludwig Lewisohn   (essay date 1932)

[*Lewisohn was a German-born American novelist, editor, and critic. In the following excerpt, he derides Longfellow as a poet of unimaginative, imitative verse.*]

Far in an unimaginable future lay this world of the *Saturday Evening Post* and the *Pictorial Review,* of the dramatic theories of Brander Matthews and their practice by David Belasco, of the correspondence course and the kisses cut out of the moving-picture film, in those idyllic and aspiring days when the young Henry Wadsworth Longfellow went to Europe to fetch home learning and romance for his future students at his college in the forests of Maine. But the seeds of that future were definitely present in the young man of good Federalist antecedents who was to become the most popular of American poets. He had from time to time fleeting intuitions of what it means to be a poet. He had one early in that prelude to his first volume in which the verses are not without an agreeable and liquid cadence:

Look, then, into thine heart and write!
Yes, into Life's deep stream.

He had a clearer one much later in lines on Gaspar Becerra with their wooden trip:

O thou sculptor, painter, poet!
Take this lesson to thy heart:
That is best which lieth nearest;
Shape from that thy work of art.

Or, since he never dreamed of following this monition, perhaps the lines of neither poem express an inner experience or personal conviction but are a mere repetition of a sentiment old enough and repeated in literature often enough to have seemed to Longfellow both respectable and poetic. And that doubt sums him up—him and his kind and his intellectual descendants. The doubt has nothing to do with Longfellow's position as an educator, as an able and influential pioneer of modern language scholarship in America. As such his reputation is quite secure. But the academic critics have tried to make his services to scholarship count as poetic achievement. And that is absurd. For even in his character of a translator of verse and a transmitter of poetic culture he showed himself fundamentally unrelated to the possessors of creative vision. He was in earlier years not tempted to translate anything but the third-rate, not Goethe, not Heine, not even Schiller, not even the lyrical Uhland, but Tiedge, Müller, Mosen and Salis-Seewis. The "Coplas de Manrique" have a touch of solemn eloquence. But their content is wholly commonplace. Later he used Dante as refuge and defense from the turmoil and agony of the Civil War. And Dante, as he explained in the sonnets on the "Divina Commedia" which speak more beautifully for him than anything else—Dante was to him in truth a Cathedral at whose altar he could re-dedicate himself to the traditions of Christendom. Thus the artificer alwaystreats or leans upon the common stock of existent ideas and emotions. But since ideas and emotions do not become common and traditional until they have all but lost their edge and glow and saving power, the artificer is the comfortable repeater, safe to himself and others, of what has long been believed and approved and can no longer stir or wound or awaken. Of himself he has little to add, nor does he feel the need of addition and personal flavor, since he has no thought beyond that of edification and entertainment.

Am I slaying the thrice slain? Who, except wretched schoolchildren, now reads Longfellow? But people until but the other day read the verses of Henry van Dyke and thousands are still reading those of Robert Service. The thing to establish in America is not that Longfellow was a very small poet, but that he did not partake of the poetic character at all. For minor poets have this in common with major poets—so far as such distinctions of magnitude are not in themselves absurd—that their business and function is the transmutation of impassioned experience into intelligible personal form. Such was evidently not the business and the function of Longfellow. Twice he came near poetic speech, once in the pathetic sonnet on his dead wife, once in **"The Warning"**—"There is a poor blind Samson in this land"—when the antislavery struggle roused even him. The ballads and the moralizing lyrics are all written from without, are all lacking the organic connection with one shaken soul and are therefore outside of the soul of the world. He can fall as low as Ella Wheeler Wilcox in **"The Rainy Day"**; he can rise as high as Webster in the final lines of **"The Building of the Ship."** He never touches poetry. He borrows form and accepts content from without. The longer works are all strictly patterned upon the works of others. The plays are weary imitations of the Elizabethans; **"The Building of the Ship"** and **"Keramos"** lean almost slavishly on Schiller's "Lied von der Glocke," itself hardly a poetic masterpiece, nor has it been sufficiently observed how almost to the point of the popular and of course absurd notion of plagiarism **"The Golden Legend"** copies *Faust.* When Longfellow turned to native subjects he told pleasing or pathetic or picturesque anecdotes in forms borrowed whole. *Evangeline* and **"Miles Standish"** are imitations rather of the "Luise" of Voss than of Goethe's "Hermann und Dorothea"; for *Hiawatha* he borrowed with his most striking lapse of even the scholar's insight the measure of the Finnish folk-epic, *Kalevala.* For the *Tales of a Wayside Inn* he used a framework that is, in the good and high sense, common property. But in the elaborate **"Musician's**

Tale," "The Saga of King Olaf," he again borrowed the very measures, devices and mannerisms of the rather jejune *Frithjof's Saga* of the Swedish poet Tegner. He was really not unlike those minstrel artificers of the middle ages who borrowed freely from each other methods of dressing up a common substance and had not yet risen to the notion of expression as an individual act and therefore of literature as individual property. Doubtless this large body of narrative verse as well as certain lyrics of pleasant sentiment and easy rhythm still give pleasure to a subliterary public. But men are not contemporaries though the same decades embrace their lives. To minds concerned with the imaginative interpretation of man, of nature and of human life, Longfellow has nothing left to say.

*Ludwig Lewisohn, "The Polite Writers," in his* The Story of American Literature, *Harper & Brothers, Publishers, 1932, pp. 58-104.*

## Percy H. Boynton   (essay date 1936)

[*In the following excerpt, Boynton assess Longfellow's literary stature and provides a brief overview of his major works.*]

There is no possibility of debate as to Longfellow's immense popularity. The evidence of the number of editions in English and in other languages, the number of works in criticism, the number of titles in the British Museum catalogue, the number of poems included in scores of "Household" and "Fireside" collections, and the confidence with which booksellers stock up in anticipation of continued sales tell the story. There is a parallel between his nearly twenty years as professor of modern languages and literatures at Harvard and his achievement as a poet of the people. As a teacher it was his task to instruct in the elements of the modern languages and to make a start at acquainting Americans with the song and story of the Old World. As a poet he was largely a reteller of old tales. He had no great inventive genius; he was a man of talent, applying the same industry to his writing that he did to a somewhat impressive mastery of foreign tongues, with twenty of which he was more or less familiar. With an ambition for something less than primary eminence, he had the honesty and good sense not to pretend to inspiration. On the contrary, he was continually projecting poems and continually sitting down not to write what he had thought, but to think what he should write. He was an avid but acquiescent reader, and what his reading yielded him was literary material rather than vital ideas. He accepted and reflected the ways of his time, not modifying them in any degree. But he touched the imagination of America with his twice-told tales and he mildly stirred its milder emotions.

With such an endowment and such an ambition, he undertook early in his career to write a succession of what he called "psalms" for the people. They were brief and homely counsels of courage, faith, resolution, aspiration, industry, fidelity, human sympathy. "And thou, too, whosoe'er thou art," he wrote in **"The Light of Stars,"**

> That readest this brief psalm,
> As one by one thy hopes depart,
> Be resolute and calm.

**"The Psalm of Life,"** the most celebrated of these, is memorable for its fourth stanza:

> Art is long and Time is fleeting,
> And our hearts, though stout and brave,
> Still, like muffled drums, are beating
> Funeral marches to the grave;

but it is remembered more for the subsequent staccato appeals to ambition with its prosaic but challenging lines, "Be not like dumb, driven cattle," "Act, —act in the living present," and "Let us, then, be up and doing." **"Excelsior,"** which is balladlike in content and psalmlike in its "moral," is another homily on aspiration, vividly presented but unhappily destined to be coupled with an uproarious melody chiefly associated with high times rather than lofty sentiments. **"The Village Blacksmith"** is introduced at work and at worship, commended for his simple goodness, and applauded in an appended stanza for being so obviously good that he serves as an example for the villager and for the reader. **"The Bridge,"** in sentimental vein, develops the theme of the multitudes of sorrow-stricken who have crossed it, and the other multitudes who can see in the moonlit water a wavering symbol of divine love. As he wrote these simple lyrics, which offer little of stimulus or comfort to the modern intellectual, Longfellow was speaking as the voice of his generation in the idiom of his generation when the phrases of orthodox religion and the ethics of daily life rang true for a people who had been bred in the iteration of their cadences.

In this period of psalm-writing Longfellow as a translator was choosing sober and improving themes. The *Coplas de Manrique* is a transparently veiled Spanish homily on the vanity of human wishes; there are themes from the Spanish on "The Good Shepherd" and "The Image of God," and from Dante on "The Celestial Pilot" and "The Terrestrial Paradise." There is an Anglo-Saxon passage on "The Grave," and a German ballad in which a ribald discussion on "The Happiest Land" meets with pious reproof. In the course of this sort of writing, however, there comes "My Lady Sleeps," the serenade in *The Spanish Student,* which is as simply effective and as fortunate in its musical setting as Shelley's "Indian Serenade" or Bayard Taylor's "Bedouin Love Song." This preoccupation with other literatures inevitably had its effect on Longfellow's treatment of native themes, as in **"The Bridge,"** in which he likened the moonlight on the Charles River to a golden goblet falling into the water, a simile obviously drawn from Schiller's "König in Thule." It is an inclination, or a practice, that Longfellow admitted when, in **"Seaweed,"** he explained

> So when storms of wild emotion
> Strike the ocean
> Of the poet's soul, erelong
> From each cave and rocky fastness,
> In its vastness,
> Floats some fragment of a song.

As Longfellow came into his period of greatest productiveness, between 1845 and 1865, the play of rival interest in foreign and native themes never led him toextended treatment of his contemporary America. A story to him was a story from the past, the sources of which were in print; a ballad was what a ballad was to Bishop Percy, either a "relique" or a new tale from the past told in what purported to be the old manner. Though the prime figure in his literary vista had written "De Vulgari Eloquentia," the fund of genuine folk material, the literature of the vulgar tongue in the United States, was of no interest to him. He was not exceptional in his disregard; perhaps it is because Longfellow's present is our past that the songs and ballads of the nineteenth century are now subjects of general attention. He was certainly an orthodox member in a community of relatively high culture in America when at one and the same time he fostered thoughts of national balladry and declared that "as our character and modes of thought do not differ essentially from those of England, our literature cannot." He was right in his statement; his only error was in identifying the culture on the slopes of Beacon Hill with the culture of the whole country.

The *Tales of a Wayside Inn* in scheme, content, and literary implications are fairly representative of Longfellow and his circle. Attributing a succession of tales to a group of congenial acquaintances was an accepted device; but Chaucer and Boccaccio assembled homogeneous groups of Englishmen and Italians. Longfellow, in a land of polyglot derivations, gathered at the inn three American devotees of the past, a theologian, a scholar-bibliophile, and a poet, and with them a Norwegian musician, a Sicilian, and a Spanish Jew. Over the tales as a whole hangs an atmosphere of virtuosity such as the booklover of Bostonia might breathe in the Athenaeum Library, aware of the burying ground below and the Park Street Church beyond. It is apparent in **"Robert of Sicily"** and in **"Sir Federigo's Falcon"**—virtuosity applied to moralism. But there is a touch of cosmopolitanism in the *Wayside Tales,* too. **"The Monk of Casal-Maggiore"** is almost Boccaccian, on the safe side of ribaldry, but on its brink. And **"The Rhyme of Sir Christopher"** and his golden-haired mistress is offered without any strictures on the moral unregeneracy of the pair. **"The Birds of Killingworth,"** also, is the work of a New Englander who could look upon the Puritan past with critical detachment.

The steps toward this detachment are apparent in the four major narratives from the American past which preceded *Tales of a Wayside Inn*: Evangeline (1847), *Hiawatha* (1855), *Miles Standish* (1858), and *The New England Tragedies* (first form, 1860). The first two were the work of the scholar-poet, industrious in the collection of his data, eruditely experimental in the adoption of his measures, quite as **"The Saga of King Olaf"** was. Yet they marked in a high degree the skill in combining erudition with popular effectiveness which earned him his immense vogue. The immediate success of *Evangeline,* of which five thousand copies were sold within two months, is easy to understand. The material was fresh and the story was sentimentally appealing. The pastoral prospect at the start, the dramatic episode of the separation, the long vista of American scenes presented in Evangeline's vain search, and the final rounding out of the plot, all belong to a "best seller"; and, as it happened, there was in 1847 no widely popular novelist in the United States. The local field belonged to the author of *Evangeline* as it belonged to the authors of "Marmion" and "Don Juan" a half-century

earlier on the other side of the Atlantic. He was so free from dangerous rivalry that even his laborious employment of the exotic dactylic hexameters cost him nothing in popular esteem.

In 1854, the year of his withdrawal from Harvard, the scholar-poet hit on another American theme which drew him still farther from his own present. "I have at length hit upon a plan for a poem on the American Indians, which seems to me theright one and the only." It was again a scholar's idea: to do with the traditions of the red man what Malory had done with the Arthurian story and what Tennyson was soon to be reweaving into the "Idylls of the King." Schoolcraft's Indian researches put the material into his hands, and the Finnish epic *Kalevala* supplied the appropriate measure. *Hiawatha* appeared in 1855 and was demanded by the public in repeated reprintings.

This work of the scholar has also the elements of enduring art: a fine surface and a firm substance. It appeals to the immature as a succession of picturesque stories. Its lack of plot is no defect to the youthful reader—nothing could be more plotless than the tales of Gulliver's sojourns with the Lilliputians or the Brobdingnagians. The episodes are as vivid and circumstantial as those in *Gulliver's Travels* or *Pilgrim's Progress.* But they also deal with human types that belong to all romantic legend and all folklore: Hiawatha, the hero; Minnehaha, the spotless heroine; Chibiabos, the sweet singer, or artist; Kwasind, the strong man, or primitive force; Pau-Puk-Keewis, the mischief maker, or comic spirit. Any child will recognize them in Robin Hood, Maid Marian, Alan-a-Dale, Will Scarlet, and Friar Tuck. Again these human types are represented in the animal world of the folk tales, and natural forces are used as instruments in a supernaturally directed series of events.

Moreover, the epic note is insistent. A peace is declared among the warring tribes; Hiawatha is sent back by Mudjekeewis to live and toil among his people; he is commended by Mondamin because he prays "for advantage of the nations"; he fights the pestilence to save the people; he divides his trophies of battle with them; and he departs when the advent of the white man marks the doom of his race. So the ordering of the parts is ethnic, tracing the Indian chronicle through thestages that all peoples have traversed, from the nomad life of hunting and fishing to primitive agriculture and community life; thence to song and festival, a common religion, and a common fund of legend; and finally, in the tragic history of an oppressed people, to the decline of strength (the death of Kwasind), the passing of song (with Chibiabos), and the departure of national heroism as Hiawatha disappears into the sunset.

No other poem of Longfellow is so well harmonized in form and content. The fact of first importance is not that he derived the measure from a Finnish epic, but that this primitive epic form is the natural, unstudied way of telling a primitive story. The forms of literature that could survive only through oral transmission are simple in rhythm and built of parallel units. It was Longfellow's nice achievement to conjoin as poet and scholar,

> Legends and traditions
> With the odors of the forest,

*Chair made from the chestnut tree described in "The Village Blacksmith," presented to Longfellow by the children of Cambridge on his seventy-second birthday.*

> With the dew and damp of meadows,
> With the curling smoke of wigwams,
> With the rushing of great rivers,
> With their frequent repetitions
> And their wild reverberations,
> As of thunder in the mountains.

With *The Courtship of Miles Standish* Longfellow returned to New England, telling his first long story of his own district and people. Both *Evangeline* and *Hiawatha* were narratives that ended with themselves. The glory of the Acadians and of the Indians had departed. But *Miles Standish* was like the following *New England Tragedies* in being very much alive. For the early Puritan, Longfellow felt a respect not untinged with both repugnance and humor. For his self-righteousness, his stridency, and his arid lack of feeling for beauty he displayed an amused contempt, but for his fighting powers and his self-control he felt a good deal of admiration. Miles Standish, he explained, was stalwart, practical, even magnanimous; but he was one of the prosy, unlovable kind who banished the birds from Killingworth with costly results. The more amiable character, John Alden, one of the poet's ancestors, was like the preceptor of Killingworth in his feeling for beauty in nature and in song. *Miles Standish* is his most kindly picture of the Puritans. In *The New England Tragedies* Governor Endicott's death comes in retribution for his ways as a persecutor, and Giles Corey's sacrifice to the witchcraft fanatics is a harsh indictment of unbridled bigotry.

For the last twenty years of his life Longfellow's main pur-

suit was in sustained narrative and translation. His rendering of Dante is a scholar-poet's pre-eminent piece of American translation, at once more poetic and more scholarly than Bryant's "Iliad" or Bayard Taylor's "Faust." It was a labor of devotion, extending over many years; the fruit of his teaching as well as of his study; and, in its final form, the result of nightly counsels with his learned neighbors, Charles Eliot Norton, James Russell Lowell, and others. Age, fame, and the affectionate respect of choicest friends protected him and perhaps insulated him from the events of the day. Yet little psalms and ballads no longer contented him. Life had become an outreaching drama to which he made an approach in his cyclic *Christus; a Mystery.*

Once more his precedent was supplied him from the past. The first section, *The Divine Tragedy,* was a reworking in dramatic form of Biblical themes in the structural sequence of the medieval mystery plays. Part Two, *The Golden Legend,* used the name of the "Legenda Aurea," traditionally employed for the lives of the saints, which were later dramatized as miracle plays; and it introduced into a medieval setting an actual miracle cycle of nine units. Part Three dramatized two episodes from colonial New England. It was a monumental venture, but not a successful one. The first section is rather perfunctory. The second, medieval section is more convincing and effective; it was again the work of the scholar-poet. But the ambitious scheme was dependent upon the concluding section; and the concluding section, if it were to lead to anything definitive, demanded analysis of the modern world and an assertion of modern faith which should show that the course of Christianity had not ended in irresolution and confusion. Yet it is to irresolution and confusion that Longfellow brought it; not because it was his intention to do so, but because it was his fate. He shrank from the attempt to dramatize his own present. He really did not want to look at it. The nearest dramatic material for the culmination of his history was the tragic fanaticism of decadent Puritanism; and the best conclusion he could devise was, as a dramatist, to present it, and, as a Christian optimist, to repudiate it. The result was complete anticlimax for the chronicle as a whole, though the *New England Tragedies* in themselves are among the most vigorous of his writings.

He regarded the fragmentary and inconclusive *Christus* as a completed work. He described the completed *Michael Angelo* as "a fragment." This again is full of vitality, filled with portraits which are speaking likenesses of Renascence characters. They are confirmable and documentable, but they are also indubitably alive. The fourth act, with its great final utterance from the title character, is deeply moving. And as one reads it one can see that, in Michael Angelo, Longfellow presented his own doubts, which resulted in his own incapacity to bring the *Christus* to any definitive conclusion:

> Who knows? who knows?
> There are great truths that pitch their shining
>     tents
> Outside our walls, and though but dimly seen
> In the gray dawn, they will be manifest
> When the light widens into perfect day.
> A certain man, Copernicus by name,

Sometime professor here in Rome, has whis-
pered
It is the earth, and not the sun, that moves.
What I beheld was only in a dream,
Yet dreams sometimes anticipate events,
Being unsubstantial images of things
As yet unseen.

Writing more consciously, Longfellow continued in his latest sonnets and in his valedictory **"Bells of San Blas"** to assert the "serene faith" that has been ascribed to him. This is the poet who was the people's favorite. The thousands who never heard of Dante and Michelangelo and never opened his learned *Christus* selected and loved the poems they could understand and could respond to as good, wholesome, uncritical, unthinking, optimistic Americans. Then they turned to Tennyson, just as the same sort of Englishmen in the same period turned from Tennyson to Longfellow.

*Percy H. Boynton, "New England—Right Wing," in his* Literature in American Life: For Students of American Literature, *Ginn and Company, 1936, pp. 518-73.*

## Newton Arvin    (essay date 1961)

[*An American educator and biographer, Arvin is best known for his critically acclaimed studies of Hawthorne, Whitman, Melville, and Longfellow. In the following essay, he examines Longfellow's first five collections of short poems.*]

A reader who was familiar with Longfellow's boyhood poems, and who opened *Voices of the Night,* would have been struck very soon, surely, by the tones of a new voice:

> I heard the trailing garments of the Night
> Sweep through her marble halls!
> I saw her sable skirts all fringed with light
> From the celestial walls!

One need not share Poe's exaggerated opinion of these lines—"No poem ever opened with a beauty more august"—to be aware at once of a firmness of tone, a boldness in attack, a freshness of image, that one would have found nowhere among the juvenilia. And as this imagined reader moved through the poem, with its fine prosopopoeia of Night as a majestic, even mythic, female figure, its delicate rhythmic effects, and its language of alleviation; as he came to the last stanza—

> Peace! Peace! Orestes-like I breathe this prayer!
> Descend with broad-winged flight,
> The welcome, the thrice-prayed for, the most
> fair,
> The best-beloved Night!—

with its beautiful literary reminiscence—he would surely have felt that he was hearing the voice of a far more mature and a far more distinguishable literary artist. Not that the poem is perfect: there is a difficulty, to the visual imagination, in reconciling the "marble halls" in which Night dwells, with the "celestial walls" by the light from which her skirts are fringed. But the flaws are observable only on a second look, and one's first sense is of the sustained and hymnic character of the whole.

The poem indeed is called **"Hymn to the Night"**—Longfellow cannot not have known Novalis's "Hymns to the Night"—and the little volume is pervaded, as its title promises, by this nocturnal symbolism.

There had been an anticipation of this in one or two of the boyish poems—

> Here rest the weary oars!—soft airs
> Breathe out in the o'erarching sky;
> And Night—sweet Night—serenely wears
> A smile of peace: her noon is nigh.

But only now is the presence of Night so pervasive as to become a kind of signature:

> The night is come, but not too soon . . .
> When the hours of Day are numbered,
> And the voices of the Night
> Wake the better soul, that slumbered,
> To a holy, calm delight . . .
>     . . . That a midnight host of spectres pale
> Beleaguered the walls of Prague.

The author of these poems was always to be, in one of his roles, a poet of the Night, or the Twilight; Night was to have for him an emotional value that the day never quite had. It is not that it ever signified to him the profoundly religious meaning it had for Novalis, or the philosophical meaning it had for Hölderlin, or the bitter connotations it had for Poe. Only rarely is it the setting, as it is in **"The Beleaguered City,"** for the spectral and the menacing. Almost always it brings thoughts, as it does in **"Hymn to the Night,"** of repose, assuagement, release from care. At moments one discerns a longing for unconsciousness, even oblivion, in this poet, that runs strangely counter to other reaches of his feeling.

So strong a wish as this is seldom expressed, but one finds it explicit in such a poem as **"Curfew,"** the last poem—a kind of envoi—in *The Belfry of Bruges.* The short, heavy, two-stressed lines of **"Curfew"** have a weary and tolling music like that of the curfew-bell itself:

> Dark grow the windows,
> And quenched is the fire;
> Sound fades into silence,—
> All footsteps retire.

The closing of a book, forgetfulness of its contents, and the chilling of the hearth-stone—these follow; and then:

> Darker and darker
> The black shadows fall;
> Sleep and oblivion
> Reign over all.

It is not always, as it is here, the utter unconsciousness of sleep that is invoked, but it is almost always a release from "the cares that infest the day." This is the theme of another poem in the same volume, **"The Day is Done"**; a poem that, in its tone, its cadences, its imagery, has almost the air of a translation from the German:

> The day is done, and the darkness
> Falls from the wings of Night . . .

The poet, in his "sadness and longing"—his *Traurigkeit*

and his *Sehnsucht,* so to say—confesses that he wishes a simple lay to be read to him

> That shall soothe this restless feeling,
> And banish the thoughts of day.

The poems of the great masters resemble too much "the strains of martial music"; they suggest

> Life's endless toil and endeavor;
> And to-night I long for rest.

This piece was originally a proem to Longfellow's anthology, *The Waif,* the selections in which are mostly of the simple and undisturbing sort he calls for in **"The Day Is Done"**; but the poem has a modest authenticity of its own in its linking of Night and the thought of rest. And even when the nocturnal is absent, in these volumes, the strain of the elegiac is likely to be audible. It is audible in one of the most successful pieces in **Ballads and Other Poems,** a piece that Hawthorne understandably liked, **"The Goblet of Life."** The central metaphor here is that of the fennel that wreathes and crowns the cup of existence: bitter as its taste is, when its leaves are pressed into the waters of the cup, it imparts to them a power that, in our darkness and distress, gives "new light and strength." Much of Longfellow's misery during these years must have dictated this curiously astringent poem; the endurance, not the joy, of life is what it enforces:

> I pledge you in this cup of grief,
> Where floats the fennel's bitter leaf!
> The Battle of our Life is brief,
> The alarm,—the struggle,—the relief,
> Then sleep we side by side.

He rarely comes so close to harshness, to an almost Hardyesque harshness, as he does in this poem; but the minor key in which many of these poems are written suggests the plaintive nocturnes of some romantic composer. Nothing could be more characteristic of him, on this side, than the melancholy imagery, in **"Afternoon in February,"** of closing day, a frozen marsh, a dead river, clouds like ashes, snowfall recommencing, and a funeral train passing slowly through the meadows as one hears the dismal pealing of a funeral bell.

There is no wildness of terror or fierceness of anger in this melancholy of Longfellow's, as there is in Poe's or Melville's, and no such dull and continuous pain as he himself saw in Hawthorne's; at its most acute, it never goes beyond a bearable despondency. It could be described as romantic nostalgia of the less passionate and rebellious sort, but it is as far as possible from being a mere literary convention; it was as inherent in Longfellow's temperament as a similar vein of feeling was in, say, Heine's—without the recoil of irony. His sensibilities were tenderer, more vulnerable, more exposed to injury than most men's; and the inevitable strains of existence—bereavement, frustration, or just "causeless" dejection—told on him, especially in these years, with a sharpness that was bound to reflect itself, now and then, in his work.

There was never a time, however, when Longfellow was willing, as some greater and some lesser writers have been, to yield himself wholly to the evidence of his sensibilities

and make a coherent world-view out of his miseries. His aversion to the tragic was as temperamental as his sensitiveness to pain, and as all mankind knows, or once knew, he insisted from the outset on correcting—one might say, on contradicting—the evidence of his sensibilities by opposing to it a doctrine of earnest struggle, of courageous resolution, of cheerful and productive action. He was encouraged in this by what he had made, morally, of his reading in Goethe—

> Wer immer strebend sich bemüht
> Den können wir erlösen—
>
> Whoe'er aspires unweariedly
> Is not beyond redeeming.

but if he simplified and diluted what he found in Goethe, as he certainly did, he by no means debased or falsified it. His resolute hopefulness is quite as genuine as his melancholy, only it is the product not of spontaneous emotion but of conscious effort and self-discipline. Perhaps it is expressed most acceptably in **"The Light of Stars,"** one of the two or three better poems in **Voices of the Night.** He confesses here that in his breast, as in the night, there is no light but a cold and starry one, and especially the light of "the red planet Mars," to which he declares he is giving the first watch of the night. Mars, cold as he may be, is the planet of heroic action, and the poet is determined to accept that stern influence:

> The star of the unconquered will,
> He rises in my breast,
> Serene, and resolute, and still,
> And calm, and self-possessed.

**"The Light of Stars"** was never one of Longfellow's extravagantly popular pieces, perhaps because there is too nice a balance in it between the confession of suffering and the voice of the resisting will. There was no such balance—and no such expressive metaphor—in **"A Psalm of Life,"** or **"The Village Blacksmith,"** or **"Excelsior"**; and the slack commonplace of these inferior pieces insured their universal currency for many decades.

They had the appeal of poems that enforce "lessons"—it is Longfellow's own word—and they have repelled more exacting readers, from Poe onward, by their explicit and elementary moralizing. To Poe this meant, as we have seen, that Longfellow's conception of the aims of poetry was *"all wrong"*; that he was utterly mistaken in supposing that the Didactic was a legitimate province for the poet. Poe himself, of course, is all wrong here; there is no reason whatever why the didactic should be ruled out of serious poetry; it has an ancient and august derivation, and freely enough understood, is a powerful element in much of our contemporary verse. The real objections to Longfellow's didacticism are of another sort. One of them, as Poe was the first but not the last to point out, is that stylistically the lesson is often appended to the poem instead of being implied by it—appended with what Howells called Longfellow's "quaint doubt of the reader." Even more importantly, Longfellow's moralizing poems fail, either wholly or relatively, because he was not a moralist. His gifts were quite different from that. Nothing—to repeat—could be more sincere than his moral convictions, but they are at second hand; they were not the fruit—as Emerson's, for example, were—of solitary and independent cogitation. He lived by them, as many men have lived by truths they have learned from others; but honorable as they are, they have no intrinsic intellectual interest, and they do nothing for his poetry but enfeeble it. All this is only too evident.

Longfellow was obeying a truer instinct when he turned to the equally popular, but for him less treacherous, form of the ballad or short ballad-like poem. He had a strain of the genuine folk-poet in his make-up—in his unaffected naïveté, his simplicity of heart and mind, his love of rapid and usually pathetic story-telling, and his power of improvisation; for some of these poems were written with as little effort as a folk-singer puts into a new ballad on an old and familiar kind of subject. Hackneyed as it is, **"The Wreck of the Hesperus"** could hardly be surpassed as a literary imitation of the border ballad—for if the subject is native, the style is a perfect pastiche of the English or Scottish popular ballad, of "Sir Patrick Spens" or "The Wife of Usher's Well." It is a poem for the young, of course, without an under-feeling of any sort, but it has in it, on its boyish level, the authentic terror of the sea. So, too, has the equally familiar **"The Skeleton in Armor,"** which is a little triumph of seaworthy narrative verse; the stanza, borrowed from Drayton, plunges ahead with the speed of a vessel in a favoring wind, and the wintry imagery of Northern lands and seas is full of romantic charm—the gleam of the Northern lights, the half-frozen sound, the stars shining on the dark Norway pines, the horsemen drawing up on the white seastrand, the vessel beating to sea in a wild hurricane. The sea as both a mysterious attraction and a bitter peril is as much Longfellow's as it is Melville's, superior as Melville is in power; and a good poem like **"Sir Humphrey Gilbert"** has the presence in it of the sinister icebergs one recalls from Melville's grimmer poem, "The Berg." The "secret" in another vigorous piece, **"The Secret of the Sea"**—suggested by a Spanish ballad—is that "Only those who brave its dangers / Comprehend its mystery!"

Few poets—as so many readers, including Kipling, have felt—have had a stronger sense of the sea than Longfellow; and the best poems in *The Seaside and the Fireside,* for the most part, are the poems in the section, "By the Seaside" to which both **"Sir Humphrey Gilbert"** and **"The Secret of the Sea"** belong. The longest of these is **"The Building of the Ship."** One regrets that this poem, like some others of Longfellow's, was staled and shopworn almost from the beginning by constant use in school readers and in youthful recitation, for, flawed as it is by some of Longfellow's habitual faults—the too explicit political moral of the coda and the too facile family sentiment of one or two passages—it has, to a robust taste that can overlook these faults, a vivacity, a swiftness of movement, and a painterly concreteness of detail, as in an old-fashioned genre painting or print, that save it from simple banality. The building and the launching of a sailing-vessel—what artisan's activity could have had less of the lifelessness of a merely literary symbol for Longfellow, with his memories of a boyhood in Portland surrounded by shipyards and stocks?

To be sure, **"The Building of the Ship,"** as has often been pointed out, owes its particular form to the example of Schiller; "The Song of the Bell" was its literary model. A workmanly process is the unifying symbol in both poems, bell-casting or shipbuilding; and a master workman is the dominant figure in both. Longfellow's political moral also, the celebration of national union, is not unlike Schiller's, the celebration of civil orderliness. But if his poem is less a bravura piece than the German poem, if it is metrically less glittering, it is free from that strain of *bürgerlich* smugness, of rather crass domestic comfort-worship and political stuffiness, that hangs so heavily over Schiller's piece. Longfellow's earnest Unionism seems relatively tonic and open-aired, and even his sentimental domesticity—the love of the young workman and the Master's daughter—has a kind of innocence that keeps it inoffensive. **"The Building of the Ship,"** moreover, has a metrical animation of its own, with its hurrying lines of irregular length, its tossing rhythms, and its freely-falling rhymes.

The charm of the poem derives largely from the vividness of the tangible objects and activities in it. It is what Whitman would call a Song for Occupations, or rather for one Occupation, and it abounds in the materials of construction—the graceful model the Master builds, the timbers he assembles from a dozen regions (chestnut, elm, oak, and "The knarred and crooked cedar knees"), the keel of the ship stretched along the blocks, and its strong skeleton as it gradually emerges ("Stemson and keelson and sternson-knee"). Almost as in Whitman, one hears the sound of axes and mallets plied "with vigorous arms," and sees and smells the columns of smoke that wreathe upward from the boiling and bubbling caldron, overflowing with black tar, "heated for the sheathing." A little later one sees the rudder ready to be set in place ("With oaken brace and copper band"), the cunningly carved figurehead, the tall and tapering masts, and the slender spars. In his less intense way, Longfellow had something of Whitman's love for his "faithful solids and fluids."

He had also, what is not so characteristic of Whitman, the sense of the ghostly; "phantom" is one of his favorite words, and the ghostly is often associated for him with the idea of the sea. The lines about the future service of the figurehead have his signature all over them:

> On many a dreary and misty night,
> 'Twill be seen by the rays of the signal light,
> Speeding along through the rain and the dark,
> Like a ghost in its snow-white sark,
> The pilot of some phantom bark,
> Guiding the vessel, in its flight,
> By a path none other knows aright!

The tone of the poem as a whole is hearty and confident; it is a daylight poem; but a passage like this, conveying the sense of night and mystery, saves it from an inartistic monotony of effect. The actual building of the ship may be an emblem for Longfellow of cheerful productive effort generally, as it is also for the building of the American Union in particular; but that vigorous motive is at least momentarily counterpointed by the image of the spectral vessel in its flight. To one or two generations the poem may have been tediously familiar, but it deserves not to be wholly forgotten.

So, too, do two or three short pieces in "By the Seaside," besides those already mentioned; the group as a whole indicates how much Longfellow's art, on its own level, had matured and refined itself in the ten years since *Voices of the Night.* The least-forgotten of these poems, **"Seaweed,"** to be sure, is another flawed success. There is real enough energy in the way in which the oceanic tempest is conjured up in the opening stanzas—the Atlantic storm-wind driving the surges, laden with seaweed, upon the land, and then subsiding again until the drifting currents have found repose—but, as so often, the easy symbolism of the storm-wind as a type of the poet's wild emotion is far too heavily enforced in the succeeding stanzas; and, as someone has remarked, the seaweed itself is not a very fortunate symbol of the poet's songs. No such objection can be brought against **"Chrysaor,"** which has the kind of purity and perfection that a tiny master-work can achieve. Saintsbury thought it the most Browningesque poem of Longfellow's, though, if so, it is not the muscular but the serene Browning of whom one might be reminded. The poem enforces no reflection whatever, but simply, with a curious calm magic, summons up the image of a refulgent star rising at twilight out of the sea like the hero Chrysaor leaving the arms of his beloved Callirrhoë—"forever tender, soft, and tremulous." If the poem suggests Browning, it suggests even more strongly, with its lovely unhackneyed myth, some chastely-wrought poem in the Greek Anthology.

The star in this poem rises over a perfectly tranquil sea. The treacherous and tempestuous sea, on the other hand, lurks in the background of **"The Fire of Drift-Wood"**: the drift-wood that is burning on the hearth has come from "the wreck of stranded ships," and it is made to express, but quietly and without strain, the wreckage of the friendship that has formerly united the host and his callers. No note is forced in the poem: the scene in the parlor of the old farm-house near the port is evoked without apparent effort—the sea-breeze blowing damp and cold through the windows, the glimpses of the lighthouse and the dismantled fort beyond, the darkness of twilight gradually settling in the room until the faces fade from sight and the gloom is broken only by the voices of host and guests. They speak of an unrecallable past, of what has been but also of what might have been, and of

> The first slight swerving of the heart,
> That words are powerless to express,
> And leave it still unsaid in part,
> Or say it with too great excess.

Few poems of Longfellow's have more the character of a small drama, and one composed of materials so apparently slight and evanescent that they might seem to defy expression. The last stanza, as Howard Nemerov has said, "exactly resolves the elements of the poem, and does so without any gorgeous or spectacular fussing":

> O flames that glowed! O hearts that yearned!
> They were indeed too much akin,
> The drift-wood fire without that burned,
> The thoughts that burned and glowed within.

Much of Longfellow's shorter verse rises out of purely personal sources—out of private springs of feeling and mood—and much of it, too, rises out of his love of story

and legend. This does not mean that he was not capable of what has been called Public Speech, that he was untouched by public issues or unmoved by public wrongs. He was far from being a Shelley, a Hugo, a Whitman; but he was a representative American liberal of his generation, hopeful, humane, generous, and idealistic; and there were impersonal "political" questions that for him were productive of vivid personal emotion. **"The Building of the Ship"** is, as we have seen, a kind of political poem, and if we can recapture in imagination the ardent nationalism it expressed we shall not be surprised to learn how deeply Lincoln was affected by it when it was recited to him early in the War.

As strong as his patriotism, however, and sometimes in uneasy relation to it, was Longfellow's pacifism. There was a kind of "ambivalence" here, it is true, in his emotions. For all his personal mildness, Longfellow as a man of imagination was quite capable of being stirred and even, in a sense, pleased by the spectacle of violence; there was a strain in him of General Wadsworth or of his uncles in the Navy, and the warlike was not quite simply repellent to him. At the other pole, however, his hatred of violence, his love of the peaceful and the gentle, was even stronger and more characteristic; and he had persuaded himself wishfully, though with a benevolence one must respect, that the barbarous days of war and bloodshed were over, or that at least they were rapidly approaching their historic end.

The early forties, so long after Waterloo and our own War of 1812, were no doubt propitious to such convictions, and Longfellow made them the theme of three poems, two of which appeared in *The Belfry of Bruges* and the third in *The Seaside.* The most familiar of the three, **"The Arsenal at Springfield,"** is but half-successful if only because the anti-war theme is developed so fully indirect rhetorical terms. Yet the poem takes off from a fine simile—the burnished gunbarrels in the Arsenal rising to the ceiling like the pipes of a huge and ominous organ—and even if it is true that the comparison began by being Fanny Longfellow's, not her husband's, Longfellow knew well what to make of it. The poem has a real force, partly because the four-line stanza is managed with such easy mastery and the feminine a-rhymes are so curiously expressive here; partly too because, in his associative way, Longfellow conjures up his horrid imagery of warfare with an imaginative conviction that makes war and peace seem to be in genuine tension with each other:

> On helm and harness rings the Saxon hammer,
> Through Cimbric forests roars the Norseman's
>     song,
> And loud, amid the universal clamor,
> O'er distant deserts sounds the Tartar gong.

There is a similar tension, but in its terms a finer one, in **"The Occultation of Orion,"** another pacifist piece. Myth and astronomy together are endowed with a kind of grandeur here that one misses in the other poem; the constellation Orion is made the symbol of barbaric violence, but it is a splendid violence:

> Begirt with many a blazing star,
> Stood the great giant Algebar,

Orion, hunter of the beast!
His sword hung gleaming at his side,
And, on his arm, the lion's hide
Scattered across the midnight air
The golden radiance of his hair.

To counter this warlike metaphor Longfellow finds two metaphors of peace and harmony, the seven-stringed lyre of Pythagoras that, towering from earth to the fixed stars, symbolizes the harmonious music of the spheres, and the serene moon that, as it moves silently across the sky, "occults" or blots out—in a manner that Longfellow knew to be bad astronomy—the constellation of the great hunter:

And suddenly from his outstretched arm
Down fell the red skin of the lion
Into the river at his feet.

Peace and harmony have triumphed over violence, and the strings of the heavenly lyre, echoing a burst of angelic music, proclaim that

"Forevermore, forevermore,
The reign of violence is o'er!"

Again the theme is made explicit, but it is made so in a more dramatic and less oratorical manner than in the other poem, and it is not a fatal blemish. How fine, moreover, is the sense of radiance and harmony that, by language and imagery, Longfellow calls out in this poem!

The third of these pieces, **"Tegnér's Drapa,"** is a threnody on the Swedish poet, Esaias Tegnér, the mad bishop of Vexiö, whom Longfellow so much admired—excessively, no doubt—and whose pious poem, "The Children of the Lord's Supper," he had translated, as well as passages from his more masculine *Frithiof's Saga*. With its unrhymed lines, irregular in length, and its mythic echoes of the Prose Edda—for Longfellow identifies Tegnér with the slain god Balder—**"Tegnér's Drapa"** has a certain flavor of the archaic versification and the heathen melancholy of Icelandic poetry, but the flavor is faint at best, and after several rather fine stanzas, the poem trails off in a too-obvious and simplistic inculcation of the pacifist moral.

There is nothing comparable to **"The Occultation,"** or even to **"The Arsenal,"** in Longfellow's other contribution to the political muse, the little group of anti-slavery poems. They are too largely the product of his conscious and conscientious will, too little the product of his whole nature, to carry full conviction; and in some of them—**"The Quadroon Girl,"** for example—he falls into a deplorable vein of theatrical sentiment that betrays the unreality of his inspiration. His touch is surer when he can rely on association and picture, as in **"The Slave's Dream,"** though even this piece does not rise much above the level of good verse for school readers and recitation. Yet Longfellow's hatred of chattel slavery was as strong as any such bitter emotion could be to a man of his disposition, and two of these poems communicate it with a certain eloquence. **"The Warning,"** part of which is lifted from his old Phi Beta Kappa poem, makes rather convincing use of the figure of Samson, shorn and blinded and bound, but a menace to the temple of the commonweal; and in **"The Witnesses"** the vision of the sunken slaveships on the ocean floor, with their freight of fettered skeletons, has an even greater rhetorical force. But Longfellow had little of the Old Testament wrath in his nature that makes some things of Milton's, and even of Whittier's, vibrate with so contagious a rhetoric; and he did well never to repeat the manner of *Poems on Slavery.*

It goes without saying, now, that there is much in these five volumes that is facile and flaccid; like most minor poets who have been prolific as well as minor, Longfellow had no clear sense of the distinction between his weaknesses and his real strength. He seems to have taken as much pleasure in some of his inferior poems as in the better ones; he thought **"Maidenhood"** and **"Excelsior"** "perhaps as good as anything I have written"; and certainly he published only what he himself thought was worthy of him. His nature was so genuinely sensitive, gentle, and *gefühlvoll* that, with the best conscience in the world, he could fall a victim to the bad sentimental taste of his age; and there were subjects that normally betrayed him into the sort of false and misplaced feeling that one finds in Lydia Hunt Sigourney. One of these subjects was childhood (**"To a Child"**); he is almost always at his feeblest on this theme. Another treacherous subject for him was that of innocence or simple unstained purity (**"Maidenhood"**); one need not make light of this virtue in order to find Longfellow's celebration of it painfully wanting in moral complexity or edge. Death, too, often inspired in him a soft and second-rate emotional response, not a tragic one (**"Footsteps of Angels"**); and the fact that he shared this weakness with greater writers of the age—Dickens, Tennyson, and others—does not conduce to greater patience with him.

Both morally and artistically speaking, when such subjects are in question, there is something suspect in emotions that well up so easily as these do, and that express themselves with so little stress or struggle. In general, it was a double-natured gift that the gods bestowed on Longfellow when, as it were in his cradle, they endowed him with the talents of an improvisator. On the one hand, this gift was what enabled him, at his best, to write with a fluency, a speed, and a translucency that are appropriate to his subjects and fully expressive of them. On the other hand, when he is at his second-best or his worst, the gift was clearly a fatal one: "the weakness of his genius," as Paul Elmer More said, " . . . was an absence of resistance"; and when thoughts or feelings sprang up in him that needed to be resisted, he gave them as free a rein as the thoughts or feelings that could safely be trusted. The almost effortless rapidity with which some of his successful poems were composed did them no injury, but a similar rapidity helps to account for the failure of some others. If **"The Wreck of the Hesperus"** came into his mind not by lines but by stanzas, this, given the subject, was as it should have been; and many years later **"The Saga of King Olaf "** lost nothing of its quality through being composed, most of it, in little more than a fortnight. If, on the other hand, the dramatic poem, *Judas Maccabaeus,* on so difficult a subject, got itself written in eleven days, that fact helps to account for its disappointingness.

For these reasons, and others, one could wish away per-

## The Fire of Driftwood

We sat within the farm-house old,
Whose windows, looking o'er the bay,
Gave to the sea-breeze damp and cold
An easy entrance, night and day.

Not far away we saw the port,
The strange, old-fashioned, silent town,
The lighthouse, the dismantled fort,
The wooden houses, quaint and brown.

We sat and talked until the night,
Descending, filled the little room;
Our faces faded from the sight,
Our voices only broke the gloom.

We spake of many a vanished scene,
Of what we once had thought and said,
Of what had been, and might have been,
And who was changed, and who was dead;

And all that fills the hearts of friends,
When first they feel, with secret pain,
Their lives thenceforth have separate ends,
And never can be one again;

The first slight swerving of the heart,
That words are powerless to express,
And leave it still unsaid in part,
Or say it in too great excess.

The very tones in which we spake
Had something strange, I could but mark;
The leaves of memory seemed to make
A mournful rustling in the dark.

Oft died the words upon our lips,
As suddenly, from out the fire
Built of the wreck of stranded ships,
The flames would leap and then expire.

And, as their splendor flashed and failed,
We thought of wrecks upon the main,
Of ships dismasted, that were hailed
And sent no answer back again.

The windows, rattling in their frames,
The ocean, roaring up the beach,
The gusty blast, the bickering flames,
All mingled vaguely in our speech;

Until they made themselves a part
Of fancies floating through the brain,
The long-lost ventures of the heart,
That send no answers back again.

O flames that glowed! O hearts that yearned!
They were indeed too much akin,
The drift-wood fire without that burned,
The thoughts that burned and glowed within.

*Henry Wadsworth Longfellow, in his* Poems of Henry
Wadsworth Longfellow, *edited by Louis Untermeyer,*
*1943.*

serving in some ideal anthology of verse of the second order. There are states of feeling that remain this side of either ecstasy or despair—mournfulness, regret, elation, the simple apprehension of beauty—that Longfellow could express with a veracity that has nothing in it of falseness or the meretricious. Moods of the weather, seasons of the year, divisions of the day or night—to these external states he was delicately sensitive, and they often become the beautiful equivalents of his emotions. The physical *element* of his imagination, as Gaston Bachelard would say, was water, not fire or air, and the sea was for him a symbol that, in its allurement and its menace, had the primordial power of a symbol in a dream. He had a genius for narrative poetry—not, to be sure, of the psychological or philosophically complex sort, but in the popular and romantic sense—and he could almost always draw, to happy effect, on legend or literary tradition. His sense of form was fallible, but at his best he is an accomplished, sometimes an exquisite, craftsman, like a master in some minor art, a silversmith or a potter; and his command of his materials—language, imagery, metre, rhyme—though it is not that of a major artist, is wholly adequate to his modest purposes. It remains to be seen what he could make of larger and more ambitious forms, especially that of poetic drama.

*Newton Arvin, "Early Longfellow," in* The Massachusetts
Review, *Vol. III, No. 1, Autumn, 1961, pp. 145-57.*

### Howard Nemerov   (essay date 1963)

[*An American poet, novelist, essayist, and critic, Nemerov was awarded every major prize for poetry, including the Pulitzer Prize and the National Book Award for his* Collected Poems. *From 1988 until 1990 he held the prestigious post of poet laureate of the United States. In the following essay, he reevaluates Longfellow's waning critical reputation, claiming for some of his poems "an interest other than historical, scholarly, or biographical—an interest truly poetical, and undiminished by time."*]

Great reputation is perhaps the most curious as well as the most volatile product of civilized society; lives of great men very often remind us, Longfellow's celebrated **"Psalm"** to the contrary, what a vast deal of illusion their energy sustains around them while they live, and how perishable a commodity it proves to be after they die. William Blake put the matter with characteristic clarity:

> When Sir Joshua Reynolds died
> All Nature was degraded:
> The King drop'd a tear into the Queen's ear,
> And all his pictures faded.

But the fame of a great poet in the nineteenth century seems to us, a hundred years after, peculiarly productive of the grotesque and absurd, and of a nature extremely ready to be degraded. Here, for example, is Queen Victoria's comment on Longfellow's visit to Windsor Castle (this happened, with more or less tact, on the Fourth of July in 1868): "I noticed an unusual interest among the attendants and servants. I could scarcely credit that they so generally understood who he was. When he took leave, they concealed themselves in places from which they

haps half the poems of Longfellow's Harvard years. The rest, unequal as they may be in excellence, are worth pre-

could get a good look at him as he passed. I have since inquired among them, and am surprised and pleased to find that many of his poems are familiar to them. No other distinguished person has come here that has excited so peculiar an interest. Such poets wear a crown that is imperishable."

Alas.

And here is a description even more revealing, in my opinion, of the strangeness of this kind of fame. I am quoting an early biographer and critic, George Lowell Austin, writing in the year after the poet's death:

> It is about seven inches in height, and is broad, stout, and capacious. It holds, when filled to the brim, about five pints; has an honest handle; and is, of course, of the usual color of Wedgwood ware. . . . The jug exhibits two panels, one presenting a most admirable portrait of Mr. Longfellow, and the other the following familiar verse from the poem **'Kéramos'**:
>
> Turn, turn, my wheel! Turn round and round
> Without a pause, without a sound:
> So spins the flying world away!
> This clay, well mixed with marl and sand,
> Follows the motion of my hand;
> For some must follow, and some command,
> Though all are made of clay!
>
> One is tempted to say of the portrait, that it is one of the best, if not the best, that has been made of the poet. The remaining decorations of the jug comprise scrolls intertwined with flowers, on which are imprinted the titles of some of Mr. Longfellow's most popular poems: **The Golden Legend, Hiawatha, Evangeline, 'Psalm of Life,'** etc. As a specimen of art production, the jug is certainly one of the most beautiful and desirable, and will immensely please all lovers of Mr. Longfellow's poetry.

Alas for the jug, the specimen of art production!

Even the beard, the universal and encyclopedic beard behind which, in our childhood, half the poets of the world seemed to be hiding, is only falsely and as it were "historically" characteristic of Longfellow, who grew it only when in his fifties as a consequence of burns suffered in the fire which killed his wife; these burns made it impossible for him to shave. As simple as that!

And so it is possible, barely possible, that behind the jug, the world-renown, the official beard, there exists another poet, smaller but truer than the impressive representations of his time would allow.

It would not be quite true to say that no one nowadays reads Longfellow. A while ago, between the halves of a football game, some fifty thousand persons—I was one of them—heard great swatches of **Hiawatha** droned out over the public address system while several hundred drum majorettes twirled their batons; this was, to be sure, in Minnesota, which is Hiawatha country.

But it is probably true, as this example suggests, that Longfellow is not fashionable among literary people, is in fact regarded by them slightly, scornfully, or not at all;

and in this situation I find a problem or two, which I shall try to describe in these pages.

I am certain that the last thing Longfellow wanted was to be a problem. He was a man of very settled dispositions, and what he wanted from very early days was to be a poet—as he put it in a letter to his father, written while he was still an undergraduate at Bowdoin College, "I most eagerly aspire after future eminence in literature." In the course of a long, honorable career at teaching and writing he then achieved this eminence step by step, in a steady upward progression, until, nearing the end of his life, he was clearly one of the great poets of the world, not to America only but to England and all Europe—admired, as we have seen, by Queen Victoria and by her servants; by Saintsbury and by King Leopold of Belgium; by Baudelaire and the Princess Royal of Russia. Greater even than these, the heroine of a novel by Charles Kingsley, on her way to the Crimea to be a nurse with Florence Nightingale, took with her two books, The Bible and *Evangeline.* Longfellow's "eminence in literature," then, was in every way comparable with that attained to by his contemporaries (and acquaintances), Browning, Tennyson, and Dickens. Nothing problematic in that!

And yet—and yet. Fifty years after his death in 1882, the writer of a popular history of American literature disposes of Longfellow in a few pages of severities, breaking off in the midst to ask himself, "Am I slaying the thrice slain? Who, except wretched schoolchildren, now reads Longfel-

*Frances Appleton Longfellow (1817-1861), the poet's second wife.*

low?" And he supplies this justification for going on: "The thing to establish in America is not that Longfellow was a very small poet, but that he did not partake of the poetic character at all." (Ludwig Lewisohn, *The Story of American Literature,* first published 1932, Modern Library Edition, 1939.)

That is more or less how the matter stands at present. The world went a long way, from the schoolgirl of the seventies who unhesitatingly chose Mr. Longfellow's *Poems* as "the book that all good people loved to read," to the wretched schoolchildren of 1932, and long ways, where the world is concerned, have a trick of curving back; but it is doubtful that Longfellow will ever again achieve his past eminence. It is all very well to think of the fluctuations of the literary market as the whirligig of time brings in his revenges, but in this instance we must content ourselves with a more limited revision of judgment. Possibly, indeed, the appropriate lesson to be drawn from this history has less to do with rehabilitating Longfellow than with imposing a certain missing modesty and reasonableness upon contemporary pretensions in the same line of work.

There are at least two problems here, though they are closely related ones. First, there is the question of a violent change in literary fashion between the Victorian period and the period, if it is one, which with a prolonged optimism keeps calling itself "the modern." Second, and symptomatic of this change in literary fashion, there is an increased distance, perhaps a near-absolute separation, between what I shall have to call, having failed to find any noninvidious terms to convey my meaning, popular poetry and good poetry. Longfellow's renown, spread, like that of Browning and Tennyson, through all classes of society, suggests that for the Victorian era the two terms were very nearly synonymous, or could become synonymous, at least, in the case of these poets who were thought of, surely; as "broad" as well as "lofty" and "deep." This kind of reputation, compared with that accorded, say, Ezra Pound or William Carlos Williams on the one hand, and Edgar Guest, Ella Wheeler Wilcox, or Robert W. Service on the other, suggests the magnitude of the change, the definite nature of the separation between what have become two quite different arts, whose audiences exclude one another.

The kind of difference involved, and the tension produced, are well expressed by Cleanth Brooks and Robert Penn Warren in their influential handbook *Understanding Poetry,* where they begin a detailed and destructive analysis of Joyce Kilmer's "Trees" by writing: "This poem has been very greatly admired by a large number of people. The fact that it has been popular does not necessarily condemn it as a bad poem. But it is a bad poem." The essay which follows, brilliant as it is, cannot of course get around the difficulty that the more "objective" determinants you bring up to show that "Trees" is a bad poem, the more you must convince your readers, so far as you convince them of anything at all, that the popularity of this bad poem rests on a sentimental popular misconception of what poetry is and does; and a similar demonstration might be made, with the same justice and the same implications about popular taste, upon certain of Longfellow's "best-loved" poems.

My object in this discussion of Longfellow's work is to exhibit a poet somewhat different from the one who wrote, e. g., **"A Psalm of Life,"** *Hiawatha,* **"The Wreck of the Hesperus."** Without trying to present him, in the result, as anything like a great poet (there are fewer of these than formerly thought), I shall claim for some of his productions an interest other than historical, scholarly, or biographical—an interest truly poetical, and undiminished by time.

Longfellow was a good minor poet, at times a very good one indeed, who succumbed to the characteristic disease of minor poets especially of the nineteenth century (it would be invidious to speak of the twentieth in this connection), the fevered wish to be a major poet, accompanied quite often by the hallucination that he was. Why this kind of thing happens and goes on happening will perhaps never be altogether clear: we may remark that the ambition in itself is not blameworthy, and that knowledge, in this of all endeavors, is precisely what comes too late to be of any use; but in attempting to say why it happened to Longfellow I find that three sorts of cause become visible. These do not exist in isolation but are much interwoven, yet they may be broadly named as the encouragement of history, the encouragement of popularity, and the encouragement of literature.

1. *The Encouragement of History.* "Surely," writes Longfellow to his father, from Bowdoin College, "surely there was never a better opportunity offered for exertion of literary talent in our own country than is now offered. To be sure, most of our literary men thus far have not been profoundly so, until they have studied and entered the practice of theology, law, or medicine. I do believe that we ought to pay more attention to the opinion of philosophers, that 'nothing but nature can qualify a man for knowledge.'" In other words, America in the eighteen-twenties is thought to have so far entered civilization as to be able to support poetry; and not only so, but to support a poetry which is not merely the by-product or graceful accompaniment of the practical life of the professions, but a something in itself—a true art, and "profoundly so."

Still quite early in his career, in 1849, through the mouth of a character in his novel **Kavanagh,** Longfellow invests his wish with the questionable authority of the *Zeitgeist:* "We want a national literature commensurate with our mountains and rivers . . . a national epic that shall correspond to the size of the country . . . a national drama in which scope shall be given to our gigantic ideas and to the unparalleled activity of our people. . . . In a word, we want a national literature altogether shaggy and unshorn, that shall shake the earth, like a herd of buffaloes thundering over the prairies."

This has a pathos in the midst of its generous absurdity, "shaggy and unshorn" being perhaps the qualities we are least likely to think of in connection with Longfellow's poetry, for which, as Howard Mumford Jones has said, the canonical adjective is "gentle." Such a program for literature will sound to some like Walt Whitman, whom it anticipates, and to others like a pronouncement of the Supreme Soviet; it had been, in fact, an extremely popular idea since the formation of the Republic and it continues to be heard among us year by year, despite our extreme modernity. Though Longfellow is capable of viewing the matter with some detachment—"a man will not necessarily be a great poet because he lives near a great mountain," says another character in the same novel—the subjects he chose for the larger works of his middle period seem to show the American theme as equivocally appealing and summoning, a desire and a duty at once (*Evangeline, Hiawatha, The Courtship of Miles Standish, The New England Tragedies*), while his treatment of these—the hexameters, the measure of the *Kalevala,* the imitation Elizabethanism, a generally pervasive atmosphere of almost scholarly caution—suggests the strain attendant on becoming a great national poet and harmonizing Europe and the past with America and the future.

His solution, or one of his solutions, to this problem is quite simply to become universal and do everything, and so he writes, over a long period of time, **Christus: A Mystery,** of which the three parts, *The Divine Tragedy, The Golden Legend,* and *The New England Tragedies,* are designed to represent the theological virtues of Faith, Hope, and Charity as respectively characteristic of Antiquity, the Middle Ages, and modern times. But the connection of the parts seems, unhappily, more accidental and arbitrary than the grand design of this program would indicate, nor do the parts themselves come off so much better if considered as separate pieces. *The Golden Legend* is the most attractive, as it is the most fully imagined of the three; even so, the influence of Goethe's *Faust,* especially upon Longfellow's conception of Lucifer, is quite plain to be seen. *The Divine Tragedy* seems a mere mechanical repetition of the sources shuffled into verse, while *The New England Tragedies* sufficiently illustrate that Longfellow shared with many poets of the nineteenth century the inability as well as the desire to write dramatically.

*2. The Encouragement of Popularity.* Given the ambition of making a national literature, and given the response of all sorts of readers not only to the idea but to the productions, such as *Hiawatha* and *Evangeline,* which embodied the idea, we can scarcely blame Longfellow for accepting success as it came. His earnest sincerity, and somewhat simplistic spirit, are not in question; he was neither writing down to his audience nor posing as a prophet among the people. But he was stretching a relatively small gift over a very large frame.

This was indeed noticed, not at all uncertainly, by Edgar Allan Poe and Margaret Fuller among others. Poe, varying between a carefully limited admiration of Longfellow and a bitter resentment extending as far as a reckless and unproven charge of plagiarism, yet noted something essential: "didacticism is the prevalent tone of his song." Margaret Fuller, in an essay which Longfellow privately described as "a bilious attack," wrote an appraisal very judicious in some points, and the more damaging for the impression it gives of deep hostility straining to be fair: "Longfellow is artificial and imitative. He borrows incessantly, and mixes what he borrows, so that it does not appear at the best advantage. He is very faulty in using broken or mixed metaphors. The ethical part of his writing has a hollow, second-hand sound. He has, however, ele-

gance, a love of the beautiful, and a fancy for what is large and manly, if not a full sympathy with it. His verse breathes at times much sweetness; and if not allowed to supersede what is better, may promote a taste for good poetry. Though imitative, he is not mechanical."

But the detractors died; Longfellow and the admirers lived on, and presently the poet's fame was beyond effective question in his day: "surely," he heard from a friend, "no poet was ever so fully recognized in his lifetime as you."

An immense, a world-wide reputation must be a difficult thing to bear gracefully; it is my impression that Longfellow took it all with a beautiful modesty so far as the personal life was concerned. If he was (and he was) a trifle vain in trifles, he had never been swollen with pride, never been self-idolatrous, and was not so in the time of his greatest fame. But professionally, in the image of the poet at his work, he may have succumbed and received the enormous reverberations of his worth for the thing itself; at all events, his very success involved him in a relation with the public, a commitment to the public, to its idea of what a poet is and does, which to later judgment appears as a misfortune. The same over-encouraged ambition of an obvious fame, where largeness is taken for greatness, profundity for accuracy, importance for truth, also affected his great contemporaries Tennyson and Browning, and seems to be responsible for those large, facile gestures which we now find so oppressive in the works of those poets. The situation of Victorian poetry ought perhaps to be construed as in large part the result of a false idea (one still very common) of the poet's relation with his audience: the idea that, instead of seeking patiently the truth of the matter at hand, the poet is a repository of "values," which he affirms "in beautiful language" *pour encourager les autres.*

This is not to say that the poet, on this view of him, is insincere. But there exists a curious and even tragic tension between poetry and value. In the work of very great poets we seem to find ideas of order, harmonious articulations of our experience, inextricably involved with the poetry; these poets are admirable not because they present values (though they do) but because they become values. I mean by this simply that after a certain point in our reading we cease to judge them in the light of our experience and begin instead to judge our experience in the light of their poems.

Lesser poets, in attempting to attain this distinction, are deceived into philosophizing, or poetizing philosophically, and when time has worked a little on their poems it comes to seem as though their finest poetry escaped them by accident, when they had forgotten for some reason to conclude the poem by orienting it with explicit reference to their beliefs, their values, or when the poem had somehow evaded the censorship of "ideas." This may be one meaning of a phrase from the *Kena Upanishad* which Yeats renders so beautifully: "The living man who finds spirit, finds truth. But if he fail, he falls among fouler shapes."

This may or may not be essential among Longfellow's difficulties; I think, myself, that it is. But it is not the business of criticism to practice preventive medicine by saying

Thou Shalt Not to anyone's future; so that the poet's attempt to exceed his limitations is always necessary, and knowledge, after all the returns are in, always too late.

*3. The Encouragement of Literature.* Longfellow was from the beginning of his career as a teacher a learned and a studious man, who became accustomed to viewing the world of experience with an immediate, almost automatic reference to a wide range of books, a range much extended by his study of languages, his travels in Europe, his love of history, and his work as a translator. A few samples, drawn from among many, will show not only his scrupulousness about giving sources, but also his positive delight in doing so; the following are the opening lines of the poems in which they occur:

> Have you read in the Talmud of old . . . ?

> In Mather's Magnalia Christi,
> Of the old colonial time,
> May be found in prose the legend
> That is here set down in rhyme.

> Saint Augustine! well hast thou said . . .

Another poem, **"The Discoverer of the North Cape,"** is prefaced with the subtitle **"A Leaf from King Alfred's Orosius"**; and in his diary he notes about **"My Lost Youth"** his particular pleasure at "the bringing in of the two lines of the old Lapland song." It is also observable in this connection, about the *Tales of a Wayside Inn,* that the interludes between tales not infrequently resemble seminars in criticism and comparative literature—for example:

> "A pleasant and a winsome tale,"
> The Student said, "though somewhat pale
> And quiet in its coloring,
> As if it caught its tone and air
> From the gray suits that Quakers wear;
> Yet worthy of some German bard,
> Hebel or Voss or Eberhard,
> Who love of humble themes to sing,
> In humble verse; but no more true
> Than was the tale I told to you."

The Theologian (who had told the pleasant and winsome tale) replies "with some warmth":

> "That I deny;
> 'Tis no invention of my own,
> But something well and widely known
> To readers of a riper age,
> Writ by the skilful hand that wrote
> The Indian tale of Hobomok,
> And Philothea's classic page. . . . ."

That is, by "the folk."

Now there is nothing wrong with this in itself. Poets have always taken their stories from past literature and history and tradition. Dante and Shakespeare no less than Longfellow relied on what they read; people who believe otherwise, and think that poets write out of some simple, untutored relation with nature, are making a mistake. But the point scarcely needs to be insisted on, I hope, that when Dante read Ovid or Statius, when Shakespeare read Cinthio or Plutarch, something quite new happened; while with Longfellow, all too often, no transformation takes place in the passage from source to poem, and the result is a mere mechanical "putting into verse," a patient but routine setting down of the external facts of the matter, with nothing problematic about it, no inwardness, as though the transaction between the poet and his subject were primarily a measuring-out of feet and rhymes to be applied to something already in all essentials existing.

This doesn't by any means happen all the time, and the reference to literature is responsible for some of Longfellow's finest things as well as some of his worst; but the point here is that his love for literature, his knowledge of it, his piety toward it, may have suggested to him that the achievement of poetry was after all a simpler matter than it is generally thought to be, and may have encouraged him in a facility which by nature he already amply had.

Our attempt to find a workable relation with poets of the past is always likely to produce embarrassment at the start—and we might in charity admit that if it were possible the embarrassment would be on both sides. Words change, and the habit of speech changes. Dr. Johnson, for example, can no longer commend Dr. Levet to us by calling him "officious," because officious has ceased to mean "kind; doing good offices," which is what it meant to Dr. Johnson. In the same way, when Longfellow calls this life "a suburb of the life elysian" our dismay probably has less to do with our view of immortality than with our view of suburbs. When he continues, however, writing of his dead daughter:

> She is not dead—the child of our affection,—
> But gone unto that school
> Where she no longer needs our poor protection,
> And Christ himself doth rule,

we may have to see our difficulty, if we dislike the lines, as a difficulty of attitude, and that it is somewhat snobbish in us to refuse from Longfellow what we should gladly accept from Dante, who also speaks of heaven as a school: *nel quale é Cristo abate del collegio,* "where Christ is abbot of the college" (*Purgatorio* xxvi. 129).

It will be helpful to be as clear as possible about such distinctions, lest on the one hand we reject our poet altogether and uncritically because we do not share his beliefs, or are embarrassed by the form in which he expresses them, lest on the other hand we admire him uncritically for things he cannot truly give us. So, for example, I have seen Longfellow praised as a pioneer Imagist for the following lines:

> In broad daylight, and at noon,
> Yesterday I saw the moon
> Sailing high, but faint and white,
> As a school-boy's paper kite.
> 　　　　　—**"Daylight and Moonlight"**

Whether these lines do in fact anticipate the practice of Amy Lowell, or whether anyone ought to be praised for the anticipation, I am uncertain; but I am quite certain that this sort of imagery is uncharacteristic in Longfellow's work. Nor is he a poet of brilliant or subtle or elaborated metaphor, though there are occasional miracles of fused vision like this one:

> A memory in his heart as dim and sweet

As moonlight in a solitary street,
Where the same rays, that lift the sea, are
    thrown
Lovely but powerless upon walls of stone.
—**"Torquemada,"** from *Tales of a Wayside Inn*

His more usual practice is to limit his metaphors immediately by an application, by drawing out their meaning, by moralizing upon them; and this is of course what most offends against the taste of the present age, and makes us look with especial disfavor upon the conclusions of many of his poems as being comicallyreductive in their insistence on pointing the moral:

By the mirage uplifted, the land floats vague in
    the ether,
Ships and the shadows of ships hang in the mo-
    tionless air;
So by the art of the poet our common life is up-
    lifted,
So, transfigured, the world floats in a luminous
    haze.
                        —**"Elegiac Verse vi"**

I suppose that the attitude of many modern readers toward what is represented here would be in favor of the first two lines and against the last two; substantially the attitude of Longfellow himself in the fourth and fourteenth of these same **"Elegiac Verses":**

Let us be grateful to writers for what is left in the
    inkstand;
When to leave off is an art only attained by the
    few.

And

Great is the art of beginning, but greater the art
    is of ending;
Many a poem is marred by a superfluous verse.

Now it is certainly true that some of Longfellow's poems are spoiled for us by their endings which are so explicit and sententious; and this is especially sad in poems which otherwise attain to a considerable and convincing eloquence, such as **"The Lighthouse"** and **"The Golden Milestone."** As to the former in particular, after an achievement of the following order,

Even at this distance I can see the tides,
Upheaving, break unheard along its base,
A speechless wrath, that rises and subsides
In the white lip and tremor of the face,

it is very disappointing to be brought down to the conclusion in which the lighthouse "hails the mariner with words of love" which turn out to be platitudes.

Yet, when I consider the general question involved, of morality and statement in poetry, I am not altogether convinced of the absolute rightness of the modern attitude, or that it ought to be applied, without many reservations, to such a poet as Longfellow. He is perhaps most immediately impressive, or at any rate most accessible to us, in those relatively few poems, such as **"The Harvest Moon"** and **"Chaucer"** and **"Aftermath,"** which remain steadfastly with their minute particulars. **"Aftermath"** especially seems to me to have a very moving sort of melancholy, a music in which more is suggested than said. The aftermath

is the second mowing of the fields, in late fall; beyond this, perhaps, the poet's work in old age; and the second of the two stanzas deals with it this way:

Not the sweet, new grass with flowers
Is this harvesting of ours;
Not the upland clover bloom;
But the rowen mixed with weeds,
Tangled tufts from marsh and meads,
Where the poppy drops its seeds
In the silence and the gloom.

I shall risk saying that that is first-rate writing. It is not typical of Longfellow's style or way of concluding; yet there are more examples of the kind than people nowadays incline to acknowledge.

And in the other kind, the explicit and moralizing kind of verse, the standard idea of his being "gentle" ought not to blind us to a sometimes considerable strength. For example, in **"The Challenge,"** the "ancient Spanish legend" he begins with is a mere excuse, an occasion only, and the poem exists as a sermon on riches and poverty, as he sees

The living, in their houses,
And in their graves, the dead!
And the waters of their rivers,
And their wine, and oil, and bread!

The challenge is from the poor, who "impeach us all as traitors, / Both living and the dead," leading to this decisive and not especially gentle conclusion:

And there in the camp of famine,
In wind and cold and rain,
Christ, the great Lord of the army,
Lies dead upon the plain!

Generally, then, though Longfellow is not a poet of great dramatic powers, he does have in good measure the essential lyrical equivalent of those powers, the ability to make his moral reflections arise out of experience, emerge from the substance of the stories he tells, the images he presents. Though he is sometimes sentimental, and though it is true that "didacticism is the prevalent tone of his song," yet the substance of his teaching is often poetically just, that is, relevant to the material. Though he is more explicit about drawing the moral than is now the fashion, it may be a false romanticism in the present taste, a desire to indulge the spirit in pseudo-mysteries, which is embarrassed by plain statements and wants everything "left implicit."

This justice, indeed, is the virtue of Longfellow's poetry that I most wish to call attention to. It seems to me the constant element common to good poetry everywhere and always, and I would define this justice as the poet's acceptance of the consequences of his poem, his will to submit his will to the matter at hand, and follow where the thought will lead him. This quality will demand, no doubt, the sacrifice of incidental beauties, spectacular surprises, especially toward the end of a poem, where the consequences are most powerfully to be felt; and a poet subjected to this discipline will incline to finish his poems rather formally, definitely, explicitly, even with "a message" if that seems an appropriate result of the pressure of what has gone before. When this is properly accomplished, the reader should feel the force of the formal close as rather conventional and distant, bring the measure and the meaning to a resolution together; as in the conventional endings decreed for eighteenth-century music.

Consider in this connection **"The Fire of Drift-Wood."** The friends sitting before the fire rehearse their memories, and this naturally leads them on to think of themselves as changing in their relations with one another, and to feel "The first slight swerving of the heart, / That words are powerless to express." Then, looking into the fire, they think of the driftwood feeding it, thus of "wrecks upon the main, / Of ships dismasted, that were hailed / And sent no answer back again."

Outward and inward images come together now, in "The long lost ventures of the heart, / That send no answers back again." And the close of the poem is a very simple placing of the one against the other:

> O flames that glowed! O hearts that yearned!
> They were indeed too much akin,
> The drift-wood fire without that burned,
> The thoughts that burned and glowed within.

It is quiet, but it does its work, it exactly resolves the elements of the poem, and does so without any gorgeous or spectacular fussing.

The same is true of a much better poem, **"The Ropewalk,"** where the spinners are seen in a figure subtly involving time and fate:

> In that building, long and low,
> With its windows all a-row,
> Like the port-holes of a hulk,
> Human spiders spin and spin,
> Backward down their threads so thin
> Dropping, each a hempen bulk.

It is not going to be a "metaphysical" or conceited poem; its development will be more diffuse than that; but the quality of the world is here nevertheless a quality of thought; the wheel going round suggests that "All its spokes are in my brain."

> As the spinners to the end
> Downward go and reascend,
> Gleam the long threads in the sun;
> While within this brain of mine
> Cobwebs brighter and more fine
> By the busy wheel are spun.

In the development, which is perhaps over-extended and too catalogue-like, the rope being spun is related metaphorically to experience, as to gallows-rope and dragging anchor-cable; again the conclusion is deliberate, conventional, quiet:

> All these scenes do I behold,
> These, and many left untold,
> In that building long and low;
> While the wheel goes round and round,
> With a drowsy, dreamy sound,
> And the spinners backward go.

Here the reminder of the spinners going backward throws retrospectively a mysterious air, almost of paradox, over the details of the poem, life having been seen simulta-

neously as remembered, as lived, as spun, or fated, in the spinning of the rope.

Nor does even **"The Ropewalk,"** good as it is, define the limit of Longfellow's achievement. On the one hand, I have not touched on his humor, which is often much livelier than his present reputation allows us to believe, and shows especially well in some of the *Tales of a Wayside Inn,* e. g., **"The Monk of Casal-Maggiore," "The Cobbler of Hagenau,"** and the Landlord's final Tale of Sir Christopher Gardiner, Knight of the Holy Sepulchre,

> The first who furnished this barren land
> With apples of Sodom and ropes of sand.

On the other hand, this "gentle" and melancholy Christian poet now and then, though rarely, touches simultaneously on tragedy and greatness. **"The Chamber over the Gate,"** simple, reserved, yet, at its end, passionate quite beyond sentimentality, is a lyric poem of the first rank. And in the vast meditation *Michael Angelo,* which Longfellow left unfinished at his death, the relation of art and mortality produces, in addition to a sardonic and critical humor not felt in his poetry before, moments which have a claim to be considered the equal of the best in nineteenth century poetry:

> All things must have an end; the world itself
> Must have an end, as in a dream I saw it.
> There came a great hand out of heaven, and touched
> The earth, and stopped it in its course. The seas
> Leaped, a vast cataract, into the abyss;
> The forests and the fields slid off, and floated
> Like wooded islands in the air. The dead
> Were hurled forth from their sepulchres; the living
> Were mingled with them, and themselves were dead,—
> All being dead; and the fair, shining cities
> Dropped out like jewels from a broken crown.
> Naught but the core of the great globe remained,
> A skeleton of stone. And over it
> The wrack of matter drifted like a cloud,
> And then recoiled upon itself, and fell
> Back on the empty world, that with the weight
> Reeled, staggered, righted, and then headlong plunged
> Into the darkness, as a ship, when struck
> By a great sea, throws off the waves at first
> On either side, then settles and goes down
> Into the dark abyss, with her dead crew.

This entire scene, indeed, the meditation on the Coliseum in the fourth section of Part Three, is a study of art and life of a profound beauty rare not only for this poet but for any.

Unfashionable Longfellow is a poet of allegory rather than of symbol, of personification rather than of metaphor, of anecdote rather than myth. His ways are plain so far as he can make them so. I have tried to suggest in [this essay] what the differences and difficulties are which will make the modern reader impatient very often with this poet, but also what the rewards may be for those who, sick of the fashion, are willing to take a fresh view of the matter, and who may find, as I have found, that Longfellow, gentle as he is, maintains beneath his gentleness a fair share of that unyielding perception of reality which belongs to good poetry wherever and whenever written.

*Howard Nemerov, "On Longfellow," in his* Poetry and Fiction: Essays, *Rutgers University Press, 1963, pp. 143-58.*

## Donald Hall    (essay date 1966)

[*Hall is an American poet and critic. In the following essay, originally published in 1966, he briefly notes Longfellow's "special position" in American literature.*]

Henry Wadsworth Longfellow occupies a special position in American literature. He was universally popular in the nineteenth century, not only in the United States but in England. When Queen Victoria received him in 1868, she wrote in her diary that she "noticed an unusual interest among the attendants and servants. .. When he took leave, they concealed themselves in places from which they could get a good look at him as he passed." His fame was the product of a carefully cultivated career. One might call him the first of a long series of American poets as professional literary men. From college he had written his father, "I most eagerly aspire after future eminence in literature." He graduated at eighteen, furthered his education in Europe, and became a professor at twenty-two. By the time he was forty-seven he was able to retire from his teaching at Harvard and devote himself entirely to the writing of poetry. He lived in a splendid house on Brattle Street in Cambridge, Massachusetts, and in his elegant study wrote a massive Collected Works.

A large portion of his work is Longfellow's contribution to a myth of the country and the continent. The romantic story of **Evangeline** is an attempt to add color and texture to a part of the world that has felt the lack of a history. Longfellow's sense of history was acute. He came from a New England that tended to turn its face toward the Old, and some of his best writing happened when he saw the old world in the new. Perhaps his best lyric is his **"The Jewish Cemetery at Newport,"** with its "But ah! what once has been shall be no more!" One stanza of that poem, with its wit, intelligence, and brilliant use of poetic rhythm, shows Longfellow at his very best:

> And thus forever with reverted look
> The mystic volume of the world they read,
> Spelling it backward, like a Hebrew book,
> Till life became a Legend of the Dead.

The literary reference, to the Book of the Dead, is typical of Longfellow, and so is the delicate nostalgia, the sweet aroma of regret.

*Donald Hall, "A Note on Longfellow," in his* To Keep Moving: Essays 1959-1969, *Hobart & William Smith Colleges Press with Senaca Review, 1980, pp. 38-9.*

## Hyatt H. Waggoner    (essay date 1968)

[*Waggoner was an American educator and critic who wrote extensively on American fiction and poetry, specializing in the study of Nathaniel Hawthorne. In the following excerpt,*] *originally published in 1968, he briefly discusses some of Longfellow's better-known works.*]

Longfellow had just one thing to say, and he tried as best he could to deny it: that time is inherently and inevitably man's enemy, bringing only loss and nothingness. Longfellow is a very melancholy poet whenever he writes from the center of his sensibility. There are American poets with a sharper and more meaningful sense of tragedy, but none sadder, none with fewer resources of spirit to counter the blackness.

He did what he could to cheer himself and reassure his age by repeating the clichés about Progress and Enlightenment. But though his words of cheer convinced many and helped win him the position Oliver Wendell Holmes accorded him as "our chief singer," he himself remained unconvinced. Though even so generally perceptive a reader as his friend James Russell Lowell summed up his impression of the role Longfellow played in his age by calling his art "consoling," the Faust figure in **The Golden Legend** really speaks for Longfellow when he says:

> This life of ours is a wild aeolian harp of many
>     a joyous strain,
> But under them all there runs a loud perpetual
>     wail, as of souls in pain.

When he took his own advice and looked into his heart and wrote, he recorded the voices of the night or wrote of the sound of the sea, which reminded him of his lost youth and of the "mystery of grief and pain" found "in the very heart" of life. **Evangeline** ends with lines strangely out of tune with the message of faith proclaimed so loudly throughout the body of the poem:

> While from its rocky caverns the deep-voiced,
>     neighboring ocean
> Speaks, and in accents disconsolate answers the
>     wail of the forest.

The more he was unconvinced, the louder he needed to shout the stereotypes on which he hoped Hope might firmly rest. The last lines he wrote, a week before his death, rebuked the heart, with its vain attachment to the past, and proclaimed the triumph of Enlightenment and Liberalism in the inevitable march of Progress:

> Out of the shadows of night
> The world rolls into light;
> It is daybreak everywhere.

Everywhere but in the poet's heart perhaps. Though **"The Bells of San Blas,"** which ends with these lines, is one of Longfellow's better poems, strengthened by a dramatic interplay between the voice of the bells and the voice of the poet, who interprets the voice of the bells, yet even here the hopeful conclusion seems relatively unprepared for, tacked on. To the "me," the speaker of the poem, the bells have sung "a strange, wild melody" of decay and loss; they have spoken of an age "that is fading fast" in such a way as to "touch and search" the heart. Nothing they have said has really prepared us for the *jubilate* of the last lines. What the poem *intends* to mean is that the liberal "new faith" has happily triumphed over Catholicism. What it actually means is that it is very saddening to think of the old unenlightened times "when the world with faith was filled," but still one ought to rejoice—just why, the poem does not say.

If there is some disparity between intended and achieved moanings in **"The Bells of San Blas,"** there is absolute incoherence in Longfellow's most famous poem, **"The Psalm of Life."** It is deeply revealing of the nature of the poet's fame and of the age that honored him that this should have become his best-loved poem; for though it intends to mean that life is worth living after all, what it effectively *does* mean is that life *must* be worth living but the poet can't think why. One stanza in the poem comes through clearly and remains in the end without contradiction:

> Art is long, and Time is fleeting,
> And our hearts, though stout and brave,
> Still, like muffled drums, are beating
> Funeral marches to the grave.

Generations have been consoled by the comfort offered by the other stanzas, but the price of comfort in this case is shutting off thought. The propositions are as mixed as the metaphors. The basic exhortation is that we must "Act, —act in the living Present!" We must "trust no Future" and "let the dead Past bury its dead"; the present is all that concerns us. But three stanzas before this we have been told that our destiny is "to act, that each to-morrow / Find us farther than to-day"—in other words, to act in the present for the sake of the future. And in the stanza following we are told both that we should take comfort from the lives of those in the past and that we should live so as to guide and inspire men of the future. What then *is* the relationship of past and future to the present, of memory and hope to present action? The poem can tell us only, "Learn to labor and to wait"—labor for what, wait for what, or how this waiting is consistent with not trusting the future, it does not say.

The propositional confusion is mirrored in the metaphors. One example will suffice.

> Lives of great men all remind us
> We can make our lives sublime,
> And, departing, leave behind us
> Footprints on the sands of time;
>
> Footprints, that perhaps another,
> Sailing o'er life's solemn main,
> A forlorn and shipwrecked brother,
> Seeing, shall take heart again.

If we try to picture these images as images, what happens? How long will footprints left in sand last? Will the next tide wipe out the whole record of the past? And even if the men of the future arrive before that happens, how will they be able to *see* them while out at sea, "sailing o'er life's solemn main"? And how can the shipwrecked brother be "sailing" and *at the same time* "shipwrecked"? Either the ship has been wrecked or it has not. If not, he is sailing and can't see the footprints on the beach; if so, he is not sailing any longer but walking and being inspired.

It is relatively easy but ordinarily not worthwhile to make

fun of poor poetry. But **"A Psalm of Life"** is too bad a poem and yet too typical of the age to be simply forgotten. To the generations that grew up knowing it by heart it meant a message of courage and hope which needed no definition and discouraged inquiry into their sources and reasons—for the propositions which expressed and motivated them seemed axiomatic. Men with better minds than Longfellow settled for Activism in a time bemused by the idea of Progress. Carlyle made a doctrine of work, and Marx thought progress toward the Utopian future at once inevitable and demanding the utmost sacrifice. Only a few wondered, as did Hawthorne, Thoreau, and Melville, whether we were riding on the train or being run over, or whether the celestial railroad built by the new faith were taking us to heaven or to hell. For the many to whom Longfellow spoke effectively, it seemed best not to question the direction of the action or probe too curiously into the nature of the choices necessarily involved. It was enough to take heart and be up and doing.

That this is just what the poem meant, that such a summary does not do the poem an injustice by omitting some hint of the seriousness and difficulty of our choices, is suggested by the greater clarity with which the poet said much the same thing in **"Excelsior."** Critically, James Thurber said all that needs to be said of this poem in his satiric illustrations for it. Only a very bad poem could be so completely destroyed by a few drawings. The point enforced by the little allegory of the poem is that one must, like the youth who carried the banner with the strange device— "Excelsior," higher—go onward and upward.

Why, the voice in the poem does not say. Instead, he reports a voice from the sky which is no more informative: It merely repeats, serenely, "Excelsior." Meanwhile the dauntless young man is dead, as the old man had foreseen—

> There in the twilight cold and gray,
> Lifeless, but beautiful, he lay.

This, apparently, if the *plot* means anything, is where idealism will get you. But Longfellow, as usual when faced with the need or desire to speak hopefully, did not take his story seriously, any more than he had taken his metaphors seriously in **"A Psalm of Life."** Longfellow, we may conclude, was a very sad poet who became not simply banal but incoherent and confused when he tried to cheer himself or others. **"Excelsior"** and **"A Psalm of Life"** may well be the worst famous poems ever written.

Several of Longfellow's longer poems are better, but for the most part they are not very good, and for similar reasons. In the first place, the lack of intelligence so glaringly apparent in "A Psalm of Life" is also apparent in the longer poems, though usually not to the point of producing absurdity. Ardently admiring Goethe, Longfellow rewrites the Faust story in *The Golden Legend,* but in doing so he completely ignores Goethe's meaning: his Faust makes a pact with the Devil for no apparent reason. Or in *The Divine Tragedy* he retells the Gospel story of Christ's Passion and Resurrection in the words of the Evangelists, with a minimum of creative change and with no implied criticism or interpretation, leaving us wondering whether he has abandoned his Unitarian theology for

*Longfellow in mid-life.*

orthodoxy or is simply not interested in the meaning of the events, or supposed events, he records.

*Christus* composed of *The Divine Tragedy, The Golden Legend,* and *The New England Tragedies,* is his most ambitious poem, intended to interpret the whole development and meaning of Western history. Longfellow left the work unfinished; what remained undone was precisely those parts Longfellow would have found hardest to do, and almost certainly would have done least well: the introductory and transitional material supplying the rationale of his three-part scheme of interpretation. But we can guess what he intended. The three periods—ancient, medieval, and modern—would be characterized by the three theological virtues, hope, faith, and love, with St. Paul's order significantly reversed for the first two. The unconnected parts, as we have them and from statements outside the poems, indicate that he must have intended to say the ancient world was lifted out of its despair by the hope it found in Christ; the medieval world elaborated this hope into a mighty structure of polity and theology, all based on and expressive of its faith; and the modern world, though less hopeful and less faithful—or credulous—has

nevertheless discovered for the first time the real meaning of the hope and the faith—love.

But this is largely conjecture, resting as much on evidence outside the poems as on the faint implications of the poems themselves. Perhaps it is fortunate that the grand plan was never completed, considering the muddle Longfellow always got into when he tried to philosophize. Though the general interpretation as we have reconstructed it seems worthy enough for a long poem, a direct expression of it in philosophic verse might well have led to the kind of thinking we have in **"Excelsior"** and **"The Psalm of Life."** In a curious way then, the very lack of explicit thought in *Christus* as the poet left it contributes to whatever power the separate poems have. *The Divine Tragedy* is the least valuable of the three. As a symbolic gesture, its patchwork of quotation and paraphrase becomes a kind of liturgical re-enactment, a gesture of fidelity to which criticism is irrelevant, a genuflection. *The Golden Legend* has thought in it, but not of a sort that would helpfully advance the plan for *Christus* as a whole. The medieval world, supposedly the Age of Faith, emerges from the poem as perplexed, doubtful, torn between head and heart: a rehearsal for the nineteenth century, in short. So far as the poem works with us at all, it is only as we read the Faustian Prince Henry's meditations as Longfellow's own:

> It is the sea, it is the sea,
> In all its vague immensity,
> Fading and darkening in the distance!
> Silent, majestical, and slow,
> The white ships haunt it to and fro,
> With all their ghostly sails unfurled,
> As phantoms from another world
> Haunt the dim confines of existence!
>
> . . . . .
>
> Above the darksome sea of death
> Looms the great life that is to be,
> A land of cloud and mystery,
> A dim mirage . . .
> Leaving us in perplexity,
> And doubtful whether it has been
> A vision of the world unseen,
> Or a bright image of our own
> Against the sky in vapors thrown.

The two New England tragedies that make up the third part of *Christus* are very much better. They contain in fact some of Longfellow's best writing. Here for once he had something to say and said it well. The burden of these tales of the Puritans is the Pauline—and perfectly orthodox—idea that love is the greatest of the three theological virtues. But the Puritans betray the virtue to which they ought to be dedicated, as their persecutions of the Quakers and of the witches show. **"John Endicott"** exposes their bigotry and **"Giles Corey of the Salem Farms"** their superstitious cruelty. Both are competent, thoroughly readable narrative poems, too little known by those who continue to read anything by Longfellow. They suffer only by comparison with Hawthorne's "Endicott and the Red Cross," "The Gentle Boy," "The Man of Adamant," and "Young Goodman Brown."

*Evangeline* and *Hiawatha* were very famous in Longfellow's time and deserve a better fate than being read only by school children, as is now the case, when they are read at all. The first suffers from Longfellow's customary sentimentality and from the fact that between the opening tragedy of the dispossession and separation and the final tragedy of the reunion at death, nothing happens which is ultimately of any significance—for Evangeline or for the reader. Not enough was given in the tale as Longfellow heard it to make a long poem, but a long poem it must be. Between the high points at beginning and end the poet doggedly fills in the details of a life of almost incredible dedication and frustration, but the reader quickly foresees that the continual near-meetings will come to nothing and is tempted to skip to the end to get the suffering over with.

I have already quoted the closing lines of the poem, which record the "disconsolate" voices of the forest and the sea, but such are not the tone of the official voice of the poem. That voice records without comment the words of the priest, telling Evangeline to "have faith, and thy prayer will be answered!" Her prayer *isn't* answered, but the narrative voice seems not to notice the fact. Instead, he records, also without irony, the voice of Nature, telling Evangeline "that God was in heaven, and governed the world he created." That He was doing a rather poor job of governing in this case, from the *human* point of view, would seem obvious to the modern reader, but not, apparently, to Longfellow. Instead, he records the "inexpressible sweetness" that fills Evangeline's heart every time it seems possible that her indefatigable pursuit of her lost lover may be successful. One would think that at last the girl might have learned from disappointment not to hope.

Instead she becomes a "Sister of Mercy" carrying a taper through the night in her visits to comfort the sick among the poor and acquiring an inner light that made the recipients of her charity think they saw "Gleams of celestial light encircle her forehead with splendor." Hawthorne may have found here hints for his treatment of Hester in *The Scarlet Letter,* begun a couple of years after he read the poem; at any rate, he was, as he wrote Longfellow, much moved by it. Like Hester, Evangeline visited the sick carrying a light and seeming to be surrounded by a halo, but the distance between Hawthorne and Longfellow is measured by the essential difference between the two strikingly similar portraits. Hawthorne did not suppose, or try to get the reader to believe, that Hester's development in charity canceled the tragedy of her life. Hawthorne's portrait is drawn without the luxury of sentimentality.

*Evangeline* is a "romantic" tale in which "romantic" becomes almost a synonym for "escapist," for a refusal to take a good hard look at the facts and what they imply. Still, it has many passages of moving and authentic poetry, and for the most part the pathos does not turn into bathos. It is not difficult to see why Hawthorne was moved by it in an age less suspicious of its tender feelings than ours. With the excision of a few passages it might seem almost worthy of the fame it once had. *With* these passages, however, it must seem to most of us fatally flawed by a feature perfectly typical of Longfellow: What comes through in the poem is the terrible pathos of a life dominated by loss

and longing; the message of cheer and comfort, on the other hand, seems wholly bogus and completely unrelated to the facts as recorded.

*Hiawatha* is "romantic" in a somewhat different sense: it idealizes the Indians and is nostalgic for a simpler culture, closer to Nature; but it is not, for the most part, sentimental. The Indian legends are recorded faithfully enough to be convincing, and though Hiawatha and his associates are sometimes made to seem more like Victorian Bostonians than like Ojibways and Dacotahs, for the most part there is no necessity for making the myths more comforting than they are because they are *Indian* myths. Longfellow has been blamed for his ending, in which, as Hiawatha dies, a missionary priest brings the message of a higher and truer religion which Hiawatha then commends to his people, but only a complete relativist about religious matters ought to find this necessarily false or sentimental. It is at least true enough to history to be in a quite different category from the appliquéd moralizing of *Evangeline.*

Longfellow's generally fatal lack of intelligence, as well as the core of feeling that was all he really had to work with as a poet, are both exhibited in one of his better poems, **"The Chamber Over the Gate."** The chamber is the one in which, in the Biblical story, David wept for his son Absalom, who had died while in rebellion against his father. But Longfellow, typically, ignores all the *meaning* of his source, using only the literal scene, which supplies him his title, and the emotion of grief. His story involves no conflict of loyalties, no moral problems, no forgiveness of disloyalty. "The light goes out in our hearts" in the poem simply because of death: it could be anybody's death, for it has nothing to do with the *quality* of life. "That 't is a common grief / Bringeth but slight relief." The closing lines, from the Bible, have almost none of the meaning their original context gives them—"Would God I had died for thee, O Absalom, my son!" The grief in the poem is genuine and the poem has a valid meaning of its own, but the Biblical trappings are largely irrelevant to it.

Longfellow raided Western literature for themes and subjects, but he found very little in it but what he brought to it, a "disconsolate"—one of his favorite adjectives—sense that life was no more than a funeral march to the grave. It is partly for this reason that generally his simplest, least ambitious, most personal, and shortest lyrics are his best. Comparison with writers of more intelligence is usually fatal to him, but all too frequently he enforces the comparison by borrowing from them or imitating them. His Shakespearean dramas have all the "teachable" qualities of Shakespeare without any of the genius. The examples of Shakespeare and Goethe overwhelmed him, and the adulation so quickly won with his first volume, *Voices of the Night,* encouraged him to believe that he could at once be the Voice of the People and the bardic Voice of Truth.

His best poems seem therefore to have been written almost despite himself, without his knowing what he was doing or what they really meant. In a dozen or more short poems Longfellow is more than a merely competent story-teller and versifier. In them he writes of the "autumn within" as he thinks of his lost youth and listens to the sound of the sea. **"The Fire of Driftwood"** builds its metaphor of life as a fire without need to underscore "the secret pain" that fills the hearts of those aware of the gloom beyond the hearthside, or to add any message of comfort. **"The Tide Rises, The Tide Falls"** may seem pointless until we realize that the traveler whose footprints are effaced on the sand and who is seen no more is man, every man. Here, as in all of Longfellow's best poetry, "Sleep and oblivion/ Reign over all."

**"The Ropewalk"** is almost the only poem Longfellow ever wrote that gives us a *reason* for life's sadness, apart from the inevitability of death. (It is also one of the few in which Longfellow resisted the temptation to moralize. In it he lets his picture speak for itself, perhaps because he could not bring himself to acknowledge the full implication of what he had done.) The spinners of the rope walk backward "While the wheel goes round and round/ With a drowsy, dreamy sound" like that of "sleep and oblivion." They cannot see where they are going, and though they are laboring, nothing in the poem would tempt us to describe them as "up and doing."

**"The Jewish Cemetery at Newport"** is notable for its restrained expression of sympathy for the sufferings of the people it concerns, but it too presents men walking backward to the grave. Though it might offend the feelings of a Jew for whom Judaism is a living religion with meaning for the future, there is no anti-Semitism here, for the poem implies that the fate of the backward-looking people is really man's fate. Inevitably man looks backward to a lost youth, an age of faith, as he is swept onward by time to an alien land.

The stridency, the general irrelevance to their context, and the self-contradictory nature of Longfellow's efforts to deny this melancholy vision are the proof that the part of him able to produce successful poems remained unconvinced by the arguments he eagerly seized upon. Only when he forgot the arguments and wrote out of the recurrent, almost continuous, mood of sadness did he write really well. **"Snow-flakes"** succeeds in part just because it does not try to tell us why the snowstorm is more truly revealing of life's meaning than are the hope and promise of spring.

> This is the poem of the air,
> Slowly in silent syllables recorded;
> This is the secret of despair,
> Long in its cloudy bosom hoarded,
> Now whispered and revealed
> To wood and field.

Here Longfellow walks in the company of Emily Dickinson and Robert Frost, overshadowed but not obliterated by their presence. Like Bryant, what he found when he looked into his heart was not what the age, or he himself, wanted to confront. Bryant stopped writing, except for an occasional poem. Longfellow looked into foreign literature and wrote, as pleasanter and more likely to bring him the fame he coveted. Since he had neither Bryant's genuine concern for liberal social causes to distract him, nor Frost's cultivated toughness to help him to endure, the blackness he saw and upon occasion memorably expressed was too much for him. He retreated into the serene opulence of the public image of "our chief singer," whose

voice, as his friend Holmes also said, "wins and warms . . . kindles, softens, cheers [and] calms the wildest woe and stays the bitterest tears!" The benign confidence of the white-bearded figure on the schoolroom wall was won at a high price.

*Hyatt H. Waggoner, "Beginnings," in his* American Poets from the Puritans to the Present, *revised edition, Louisiana State University Press, 1984, pp. 3-88.*

## Cecelia Tichi   (essay date 1971)

[*Tichi is an American educator and critic. In the following essay, she argues that Longfellow imagined* Hiawatha *as "a work that would give native American (literary) materials some parity with those of Europe, and further make plausible an Indian-Euro-American cultural continuity in America."*]

The critical disesteem of Longfellow's verse hallmarks what was perhaps a certainty upon the decline of the poet's inflated reputation shortly after his death in 1882. Despite Edward Wagenknecht's sympathetic mid-twentieth-century reappraisal of Longfellow through biography, and Newton Arvin's more recent effort to establish him without apology as a minor figure in American literature, still it is quite likely that few readers yet confront a poem like *Hiawatha* with an attitude approaching disinterested openness. Howard Nemerov, for one, assures us he cannot, having "between the halves of a football game . . . heard great swatches of *Hiawatha* droned out over the public address system while several hundred drum-majorettes twirled their batons." Yet if the suggestion of Minnehaha electrically amplified seems today as bizarre as the retrospect of controversy raging over the propriety of Longfellow's unrhymed meter (adopted from the Finnish epic *Kalevala*), still there are other aspects of the poem that ought not to be obscured by current inclinations to banish it to the grade school classroom, to contemporaneous realms of *kitsch* and camp, or to the special province of the cultural historian of the nineteenth century.

For if the poem seems today beyond the pale esthetically, hedging anthropologic truth and misguidedly working, in Longfellow's terms, to "clothe the real with the ideal and make actual and common things radiant with poetic beauty," still it is possible that a significant literary motivation for the structure of *Hiawatha* has been overlooked. For more than a century since its 1855 publication criticism of the poem has focused either on the romance between Indian composite cultural hero Hiawatha and the Minnehaha of Longfellow's fictive fancy or on Longfellow's perpetuation of Henry R. Schoolcraft's ethnological error in stating that Manabozho and Hiawatha were one. Yet it seems plausible that Longfellow's design for *Hiawatha* pertains less to his softening of hard truths for the sakeof the picturesque than it does to his attitude toward cultural continuity between the old world and the new.

It was Henry James [in his *William Wetmore Story and His Friends,* 1903] who found Longfellow "interesting for nothing so much as for . . . the way in which his 'European' culture and his native kept house together." James pondered whether Longfellow's personal harmoniousness derived from "his having worked up his American consciousness to that mystic point . . . at which it could feel nothing but continuity and congruity with his European." He concluded that if "something in [Longfellow's] liberal existence . . . seemed a piece of the old world smoothly fitted into the new, so it might quite as well have been a piece of the new fitted, just as smoothly, into the old." Longfellow himself has left ample evidence of the importance he attached to evolving cultural continuity. If one may equate his position with that of his character Mr. Churchill in the passage dealing with American literary nationalism in the prose tale *Kavanagh* (1849), then Longfellow certainly anticipated a future time when the "thoughts and feelings . . . of all nations . . . finally mingle in our literature." The culmination of such mingling would be "a kind of universality" in American literature resulting from "culture and intellectual refinement" achieved "not in the growth of a day," but over centuries.

With processes of literary assimilation established in his mind as a desideratum for the growth of American literature, Longfellow appears, consciously or not, to have designed *Hiawatha* as a groundwork of native materials in a land whereon European culture could plausibly be grafted. Newton Arvin calls attention to an early (1825) essay in which Longfellow suggests that Indian materials will so engage men's imaginations that "our land will become, indeed, a classic ground."But his *Hiawatha* source materials, replete with polygamy, torture, lust, adultery, scalpings, and white men paradoxically bearing the standard of a higher civilization, yet altogether villainous—these were not in Longfellow's nineteenth century regarded as viable components of an American classicism. They did not intimate the "culture and intellectual refinement" appropriate to "mingle in our literature." Certainly they could not induce either for poet or reader the rich poetic associations Longfellow used so frequently in poems whose settings are European. Thus, if the Indian in America was to evoke qualitatively the same kind of poetic associations as historical-legendary places and personages of Europe, then it was for Longfellow to make the evocation possible by creating a work that would give native American materials some parity with those of Europe, and further make plausible an Indian-Euro-American cultural continuity in America. To do this, he structured his plot so as to reveal American Indians becoming progressively civilized up to the appearance at the end of the poem of the white Christian missionaries, presaging the Caucasian immigration and further indicating a prospective cultural suffusion of Europe into America.

Briefly considered, the plot of *Hiawatha* begins with the promise of a unified social order among tribes scattered or at enmity. The Master of Life, Gitche Manito, smokes the calumet and admonishes the tribes that

> All your strength is in your union,
> All your danger is in discord;
> Therefore be at peace henceforward,
> And as brothers live together.

He promises to send a Deliverer (Hiawatha), who later in

the poem reinforcessocial unity when he, an Ojibway, vows to marry Minnehaha of the enemy Dacotahs,

> That our tribes might be united,
> That old feuds might be forgotten,
> And old wounds be healed forever.

Still in young manhood, Hiawatha enables his people to escape the vagaries of hunting and foraging for their food. "Must our lives depend on these things?" he asks in a plaintive refrain that prefaces ritual fasting and fighting which culminate in agrarianism signalled by the arrival of Mondamin, corn. Hiawatha's next deliverance of his people is his development of picture-writing for sending messages, recording history, and communicating love. Subsequently in the poem he travels abroad

> Teaching men the use of simples
> And the antidotes for poisons,
> And the cure of all diseases.

In sum, the plot of the poem, entwined as it is with legends and romance, moves nonetheless from social unification through agrarianism and literacy to medical knowledge. Civilizing progress is marked in each step of a pattern in which the Indians increasingly master their environment. Thus in a poem structurally implying progress, Longfellow manipulates his plot to make the advent of Christianity the civilizing apotheosis of an Indian nation now prepared for it. He is not so fatuous as to suggest for the Indians a future unclouded by miseries, for surely the liquidation of Indian reservations between 1829 and 1843 with its "trail of tears" debacle of western removal beyond Missouri of the Shawnees, Delawares, and Wyandots, among others, made clear to Longfellow the fate of the Indian peoples in America. His poem **"To the Driving Cloud"** evinces his full awareness of it. Yet Christianity at the end of *Hiawatha* is the common touchstone for whites and Indians. Hiawatha's final admonishment to his people as he departs for the Land of the Hereafter is to pay heed to the missionary Black-Robe chiefs, to

> Listen to their words of wisdom,
> Listen to the truth they tell you,
> For the Master of Life has sent them
> From the land of light and morning.

From Hiawatha's view the white men in ships represent vast armed power, though even in his darker vision of tribes scattered "like the withered leaves of Autumn," he does not blame the Europeans for his peoples' fate.

It seems, moreover, that toward the end of the poem Longfellow interjects his own view in rather Whitmanesque terms within the consciousness of Hiawatha when the Indian hero recounts a vision:

> I beheld, too, in that vision,
> All the secrets of the future,
> Of the distant days that shall be.
> I beheld the westward marches
> Of the unknown, crowded nations.
> All the land was full of people,
> Restless, struggling, toiling, striving,
> Speaking many tongues, yet feeling
> But one heart-beat in their bosoms.

That "one heart-beat" of the European immigrants hints

at a cultural unity in America which, applied to belles let-tres, prefigures the ultimate "universality" Longfellow himself envisioned for American literature. If the Indians seem in the lines above too readily set aside for another social order making incursions on their lands, it might be recalled that Longfellow's *Hiawatha* deals with Indian legend, not history. He infuses the poem with just enough detail of daily life to establish a reality in which the appearance of white missionaries seems plausible. Longfellow at the end of *Hiawatha* conjoins the eternality of Indian legend with historical time. His connecting bridge, built all along, is a limited amount of anthropological detail about circumstances of eating, canoe building, etiquette, flora and fauna, etc. But having shaped the various legends in a unified work that presents the Indians as advancing in civilization, Longfellow is able at the last to suggest a continuity of cultures in America from the primitive yet dignified indigenous to the sophisticated migratory transplanted from the old world. His structural implication is that if whites are to supplant the Indians, still the latter are as he presents them worthy in their own native culture of a historic European on-grafting in America.

Possibly it was the design of Longfellow's plot structure that led him correlatively to prettify Indian life—or mercerize it, as C. F. Fiske describes the poet's sacrifice of earthiness for a surface sheen nowhere to be found in his sources. Evidence suggests that Longfellow was personally receptive to the original accounts, for his journal entry of July 31, 1854, mentions reading to his boys the Indian story of the Red Swan, a legend in which a detached scalp-figures prominently. Yet for Longfellow emphasis on the consanguinity of Indian civilization meant necessary deletion of the brutally sanguine. And if it is true that in *Hiawatha* he violated Indian myths by "insisting upon sentiments which form little or no part of Indian feeling, but which do appeal to the civilized reader," it might be suggested that Longfellow's attitude toward cultural and literary continuity between the old and new the worlds was his poetic motive for doing so.

*Cecelia Tichi, "Longfellow's Motives for the Structure of 'Hiawatha'," in* American Literature, *Vol. XLII, No. 4, January, 1971, pp. 548-53.*

## Helen Carr   (essay date 1986)

[*In the following excerpt, Carr contends that Longfellow manipulated the source material for* The Song of Hiawatha *to better fit his readers' expectations of traditional folk literature.*]

Longfellow's *The Song of Hiawatha* was the most popular poem of the nineteenth, or indeed of any century; most popular at any rate if sales are taken as a guide. Published in November 1855 both in Boston and London, it sold 4,000 copies the first day in Boston alone; 100,000 in the first two years. After 80 years a million copies had been sold, but long before then, as the poem went into numerous editions and adaptations it was hailed as the 'literary triumph' of the century. *The Song of Hiawatha* tells the story of a gentle doomed Indian in a vanished pre-colonial world, accepting and acknowledging the rightness of his

people's fate. The poem gave to its readers, especially the liberal and humanitarian, a myth which helped to make possible, for America, the acceptance of the displacement and destruction of the Indian, and for Europe, the ravages of imperialism.

But its reception was not all adulatory; not only were there those who mocked and parodied the poem, but from the beginning the question of its sources was a matter of recurrent and acrimonious debate. This relationship between Longfellow's text and its pre-text is the nexus of the racial and political problems inherent in the poem. Lévi-Strauss has said that every myth is a transformation of another myth; just as the idea of a fresh, vigorous, masculine 'American voice' was a myth for Post War expansionist America, transformed from the nineteenth century myths of the new American man, so *The Song of Hiawatha* created a myth for one culture (Euroamerican) from the myths of another (American Indian). (One could say the mythic transformations are more complex than that: although the constituent parts, the story elements, of Longfellow's myth are taken from Indian culture, the poem's structure and message is a re-formulation of other contemporary American myths about Indian-white relationships). Longfellow's reshaping of the Indian elements of his story mediates an assuaging resolution of the conflicts that lay behind American attitudes to the Indian. The finished poem was acceptable, on one level or another, to nearly all his readers, whatever the apparent differences between their view of the Indian, sympathetic, antagonistic, pitying or analytical. As Roy Harvey Pearce has said, 'he was able to create a noble savage who accommodated his readers', his culture's, and his own needs'.

Longfellow saw himself writing in the tradition of Romantic nationalism. Particularly in the earlier decades of the nineteenth century, American nationalist thought was closely patterned after European models. Nationalism was a crucial issue for Germany, Italy, the Scandinavian and Central European countries at this period, and like them Americans were much influenced by Herder and his followers' emphasis on language and traditional folk culture. Folk literature was to Herder 'the original and spontaneous expression of the national soul': a nation and its literature grew organically, in analogy with the human life cycle, from the childhood days of the primitive folk past to the maturity of civilization. What formed and enriched national literature was what Schlegel described as 'national recollections . . . and associations' going back to 'the dark ages of infant society'. For Germany and the Scandinavian countries, which had rich heritages of traditional literature like the Nibelungen Lied, the Eddas, the Sagas, this was a fruitful and rewarding focus. According to H. Mumford Jones [in his *Theory of American Literature,* 1948]; some countries - Czechoslovakia, Romania, Hungary - forged whole national folklores in an attempt to cope with their deficiency, but, happily, no such problems trouble American literary history'.

I would argue the reverse; in America, this paradigm for cultural nationalism was particularly bewildering. They shared their language with England, and the only likely candidates for 'folk' were the Indians. Walter Channing expressed the problem at some length in his 'Essay on American language and literature' in the first year of *North American Review.* 'National literature seems to be the product, the legitimate product, of a national language'. America lacked literature 'because it possesses the same language with a nation totally unlike it in almost every relation'. America would have been better off if England had taken her effete and decadent language and left them with a confused Babel of tongues. The country's only national literature is 'the oral literature of its aborigines'. The only language appropriate to the American land is the Indian's, which is

> as bold as his own unshackled conceptions, and as rapid as his step. It is now as rich as the soil on which he was nurtured, and ornamented with every blossom that blows on his path. It is now elevated and soaring, for his image is the eagle, and now precipitous and hoarse as the cataract among whose mists he is descanting.

So little Indian literature had been recorded at this stage it's unlikely that Channing's romantic enthusiasm was impeded by any actual acquaintance with the oral tradition. And his extreme and pessimistic statement of the problem seems to be unusual. Yet a national literature remained a favourite subject for Phi Beta Kappa orations, essays, and lectures, with calls to use the American landscape and the Indian as subject matter. In the first half-century of the republic, the Indian became an important symbol of the American, particularly in the period 1815-35, though present intermittently from the 'Mohawks' of the Boston Tea-Party onwards. A whole series of poems appeared on Indian subjects, with such names as *Escalala, An American Tale,* and even more dramatically, *Ma-Ka-Tai-Me-She-Kia-Kiak,* or *Black Hawk, and Scenes in the West, A National Poem in Six Cantos.* Cooper's Leather-Stocking novels were felt to do for America what Scott had done for Scotland. For twenty years after Channing's exordium east-coast literati could continue to see the Indian as noble savage and possible national symbol, even if ways of moving on from there to forge a national literature still seemed imprecise.

Yet as the westward expansion gained momentum the climate was changing. In the 1830s Catlin's 'Indian Gallery' of portraits of heroic and handsome chiefs had been a runaway success. In the 50s he went bankrupt. By 1852 an essay in the *North American Review* on Cooper's novels could say complacently:

> Civilization has a destroying as well as a creating power. It is exterminating the buffalo and the Indian, over whose fate too many lamentations real or affected have been sounded for us to renew them here.

Between 1800 and 1850 attitudes to the Indian (and the black) had in general hardened. The cult of the noble savage was only what Foucault might call a tactic in the overall ideological strategy of establishing the distance between the Euroamerican and the Indian. A national literature began to seem less desirable. The transcendentalists were rejecting ideas of nationalism for a concern with the subjective and individual, and saw American literature as the expression of liberty rather than of a national soul. As Margaret Fuller put it: 'America, if awake to the design of Heaven . . . (will) become the principal exponent . . . of the new Idea of republican liberty and justice which agitates the sleep of Europe'. James Russell Lowell in 1849 could declare: 'Mere nationality is no more nor less than so much provincialism, and will be found but a treacherous antiseptic for any poem'. There is nothing primitive about America: 'Intellectually, we were full-grown at the start'.

Lowell's view prefigures the attitudes that were to remain for the rest of the century. The fifties saw the establishment of ideas of Anglo-Saxon racial supremacy, with America as the foremost point of the evolutionary chain, a way of thinking smoothly grafted on to the still present pre-romantic paradigm of eighteenth-century American thought, the belief in Progress, with America as its crown. Race became more important than Nation: for mainstream American writers, American roots could now be claimed in England once more, while still maintaining their evolved identity. In the latter years of the century the quality of American difference was seen to be an ethical one. Whitman could be repudiated on moral grounds for a spurious Americanism, and told by Henry James: 'This democratic, liberty-loving American populace, this stern and war-tried people, is a great civilizer. It is devoted to refinement'.

The notion of a national literature had been posited on the possibility of unifying the different elements within American society. By the 1850s the belief in Anglo-Saxon superiority, and in the savage Indian as the antithesis of the civilized American, made such hoped-for unity not just unnecessary and undesirable, but impossible. The national literature debate was a version of the conflict present from the founding of the nation, between the Republican ideals of liberty and natural rights and the pragmatic, political restriction of those rights for various groups. Manifest Destiny and scientific racism politically resolved and removed this contradiction by making liberty the preserve of the highly evolved. In the same way, the development of literary Anglo-Saxonism resolved the implacable problem posed for Americans by cultural nationalism. That the latter had proved abortive was something Longfellow did not appreciate. In 1855, he remained interested in the possibility of an American literature constructed in this now out-of-date form. As his biographer, Austin, said, he lived among the Transcendentalists without being one of them, and he appears quite unaware of the changing climate of racial attitudes around him, although his close friend Louis Agassiz was an important early exponent of the theory of scientific racism. He had always had a sympathetic interest in the Indians. Even at school he had written a speech for King Philip in terms of most melancholy compassion. 'Alas the sky is overcast with dark and blustering clouds . . . our race . . . fall like withered leaves when Autumn strips the forest. Lo! I hear singing and sobbing: tis the death-song of a mighty nation, the last requiem over the grave of the fallen'. He admired Herder, and those writers who followed hisprecepts. The Scandinavian poet, Bishop Tegnér, whose *Frithiofs Saga* he reviewed for the *North American Review* in 1837, made a deep impression on him. Tegnér's poem was a model for any aspiring national poet in the Herderian tradition. Based on Scandinavian legend, this was 'an epic poem, composed of a series of ballads, each describing some event in the hero's life . . . written in the spirit of the past; in the spirit of the Old North'. Tegnér has invoked the spirit of the early Scandinavian bard, 'The sky-lark in the dawn of years/The poet of the morn'. Through the poem one can 'converse with the Genius of the Place . . . the primeval simplicity . . . solitude and stillness of this Northern Land'.

At this stage Longfellow had no knowledge of Indian legends that he could have similarly adapted, but the principles on which Tegnér had built his saga are those Longfellow was to follow when he wrote *The Song of Hiawatha.* Tegnér believed in refining the tales of the past to suit them to the civilized present: 'In the saga appears much, magnificent and heroic, which is valid for all times, and therefore both could and ought to be retained; but, in addition, one thing or another, raw, savage, barbaric, which either ought to be entirely cut out, or at least softened . . . On the one hand the poem ought not to strike too much against our more refined habits and milder way of thinking; but on the other, the national, the vigorous, the natural ought not to be sacrificed'. This version of romantic nationalism was an invaluable model for Longfellow. It fitted well with his prudish Boston gentility, and was in tune with his own concept of an American poem-not verse that was 'shaggy and unshorn' but an epic which, while drawing on native subject-matter, would prove through its civilized refinement America's cultural coming of age.

However it was not till the early 50s that Longfellow began to see the possibility of an 'Indian Edda'. He came across the work of Henry Rowe Schoolcraft, a one-time Indian agent and ethnographer, who had collected a wide range of American Indian legends, as well as information on customs and life-style. Schoolcraft himself had very contradictory attitudes towards the Indians, at one moment censoriously pointing to their indolence and vice, the next lyricising about their closeness to nature, but he saw in his material a solution to the Herderian problem of an American folk literature. In one of his publications, *Onéota,* or *Characteristics of the Red Race of America,* he included a chapter called 'A Prospective American Literature superinduced upon Indian Mythology'. Here he wrote:

> In bringing forward his collection of the historical and imaginative traditions of the Indian tribes, the writer has been aware, that he might, herein, be at the same time the medium of presenting the germs of a future mythology, which in the hands of our poets, and novelists, and fictitious writers, might admit of being formed and moulded to the purposes, of a purely vernacular literature . . . Germany has, to a great extent, reinvigorated ancient literature, and made it national and peculiar, by an appeal to her own myths and popular legends, while our writers, for the most part, are yet endeavouring to re-do, re-enact, and re-produce, what the bards and essayists of England alone have forever settled, and rendered it hopeless to eclipse. Originality

of literature, if it can be produced in the West, as the critics of Europe leave us room to think, must rely on the scenes, associations and institutions of the West.

Then in his role as natural scientist, he followed this piece of romantic nationalism with a plea for accuracy, castigating the crude versions of the Indian in the popular press, and urging fidelity to the detail of Indian life. Although this contiguity may seem surprising now, the close association of early ethnography and the cult of the picturesque lies behind it. This romance of the exotic in all its particularity finds its way too into *The Song of Hiawatha.*

When Longfellow came to write his poem he produced both the most faithful and the most faithless of the nineteenth-century versions of the Indian. He drew more than any previous writer on ethnographic and first-hand accounts of Indian life; like other previous writers on Indian themes, such as Sarah Morton and Whittier, Longfellow cited in notes added to the poem what he refers to as his 'authorities'. From its publication the doubters felt the stories were too elegant and pleasing to be aboriginal: 'too finely and fancifully touched to be of Indian origin'. This sense that such a superior poem must be essentially European soon found a particular focus. Likenesses between *Hiawatha* and the Finnish epic the *Kalevala* were noticed; accusations of plagiarism were made and indignantly denied. Longfellow, in a private letter and his journal, admitted his indebtedness to the *Kalevala* for the metre and general aim. But in public he re-iterated that the legends were genuine and aboriginal, and to be found in the writers mentioned in his notes. The controversy over the sources has revived periodically, although in this century Longfellow has mainly been criticised for his attenuation and bowdlerisation of the Indian legends, rather than for improving them. Now in general there is agreement over what the poem's sources were: for general organisation and metre the unacknowledged *Kalevala,* but for his Indian materials, as Longfellow had claimed, Schoolcraft, Catlin, Heckewelder, Tanner and other European recorders of Indian life and culture. What I want to look at here is the process by which those texts are absorbed and transformed within Longfellow's poem.

Longfellow's attempt to deal with the Indian material was bound to be problematic. One can express the difficulty in two different ways. One was the conceptual, cognitive dilemma of making sense in nineteenth-century western terms of an alien culture. Just as in the seventeenth-century de Bry could only draw Virginian Indians by giving them classical shapes, so Longfellow needed the example of the romantic cult of the folk to give him an order, a syntax for his poem. Sarah Morton's *Ouâbi* (1789) had to use a mixture of the novel of sensibility and picturesque pastoral, though she had only attempted to deal with European tales of Indian-white history, not with Indian traditional myths. Only Whittier, as far as I am aware, had before this attempted to adapt aboriginal details, though in a historical subject, and his poem Mogg Megone, had been greeted with distaste even in the more tolerant days of 1837, when he was implored to find a 'less revolting theme'. The process of reconstruction of Indian material in European terms begins in Schoolcraft's own collection;

but in his 'huge quartos, ill-digested, without any index' as Longfellow described them, he is able to leave his work heterogeneous, discontinuous, and what he called 'gross'. Secondly facing Longfellow was the political problem of dealing with the literature of a people currently dispossessed and killed with the assent of his readership. The relationship of the European-American and Indian, between settler and aboriginal, colonizer and colonized is quite different from that between bourgeoisie and peasantry of one country, problematic as that might be in its own right. Seamus Heaney has recently suggested that a similar unacknowledged rift prevented Yeats from grafting Anglo-Irish on to Celtic traditions. The relationship in each case between colonist and colonized precludes cultural continuity. This radical discontinuity underlies the whole poem, though the rupture perhaps forces itself most abruptly with the arrival of the Europeans. Even Longfellow knew something was wrong here: as he wrote to his German translator:

> What you say . . . is very true. The contact of Saga and History is too sudden. But how could I remedy it unless I made the poem very much longer? I felt the clash and concussion but could not prevent it.

In the 1850s the real westward thrust of the States was in some ways at its height; the Cherokees, whose removal in the 1830s to Kansas and Nebraska was bitterly criticized by east-coast liberals, were removed yet again, to general indifference, as the railroad went west. In the newly acquired territories of the Southwest and California the 'pacification' of the Indian was a prime objective; in California this was achieved by harshly repressive laws which were to reduce an aboriginal population of 150,000 to 17,000 by 1890. The Plains Indians had yet to be defeated. So to write as Longfellow does as if the Indians were nothing but a 'nation Scattered . . . Like the withered leaves of Autumn' reads as a premature wish fulfilment. But it's unlikely that Longfellow was consciously manipulating his material for political ends. He saw his poem as apolitical, not an apologia for the US Indian policy of the 1850s. His evasion of the political situation obfuscates contemporary injustices, but in ignoring the dubious morality and legality of the treatment of the Indians beyond the frontier, Longfellow was typical of his fellow Easterners. In addition, with the sole exception of the question of Abolition, Longfellow himself avoided thinking about current issues. In one entry to his journal he wrote: 'Dined with Agassiz to meet Emerson and others. I was amused and annoyed to see how soon the conversation drifted into politics. It was not till after dinner, in the library, that we got upon anything really interesting . . .'. Among his Boston circle Longfellow insisted on being, as far as politics were concerned, like Dickens' Mr. Skimpole, a perfect child. It is in *The Song of Hiawatha's* 'innocent' evasions, omissions and transformations, not in its intentions, that the political message lies.

How the politics enter the poem, then, is not through any direct comment on the westward movement, but in the mythic view of the Indian its narrative unquestioningly endorses. The two difficulties, the conceptual and the political, are of course inseparable: Longfellow's form repro-

duces current politically necessary preconceptions about the Indians, even when they are at total variance with his sources. These assumptions were little changed from those by which the early colonists legitimized their appropriation of land from the Indians, whom they held to be without arts, agriculture, or government, unable to make use of God's providential land, which it was encumbent on the Euroamericans to cultivate. By the nineteenth century more emphasis was laid on their childish nature and less on their association with the devil. The Indians' inevitable disappearance in the face of the white advance had come to be seen as a 'law of Nature'. These notions form the perceptual grid by which Longfellow patterns his sources. Longfellow consistently alters his material so that he infantilises, de-historicises, and, through excessive idealisation, de-humanises the Indians. Even his borrowings from the *Kalevala,* that European model for which he has been so denounced, undergo transmutation. Longfellow had, he said, pored over Indian materials for three years, but it was only when he first read the 'charming' *Kalevala* in a German translation in 1854, that he was 'able to hit on a plan for a poem on the American Indians, which seems . . . the right and the only one. It is to weave their beautiful legends together in a whole'. As Longfellow knew, the unity of the *Kalevala,* such as it is, was given to it by its editor, Elias Lönnrot, a folklorist, who, influenced by Herder, spent many years collecting Finnish runes. These oral poems from the remote peasant communities in the Karelia district tell a variety of legends about pre-Christian folk-heroes. Lönnrot had organised these into a loose, episodic epic structure (perhaps on analogy with the picaresque novel) selecting poems connected with three interrelated figures, especially the singer Väinämöinen, whose life story gives the collection its overall shape. All this Longfellow adopts, and like Lönnrot, makes the central pivot of his poem a wedding feast (not an Indian custom) at which are told other stories, ending with the coming of Christianity and the departure of the hero.

Longfellow's indebtedness to the *Kalevala's* metre was first confirmed by his German translator, Freilgarth, with whom he had read some Finnish runes in a German translation in 1842. Finnish poetry is quantitive rather than stressed, and allows apparently for many subtle modulations, so the characteristic jerkiness of **Hiawatha** is not present in the Finnish, although there in the German. Parallelisms, an important characteristic of Finnish verse, were apparent in the translation. Longfellow had read they were also present in Indian poetry-in fact they appear in rather different form-and this he used as a justification for his adoption of them, though he may also have been influenced by Herder's praise of parallelism in *The Spirit of Hebrew Poetry.* What is most striking about the resultant verse form of **Hiawatha** is its insistent naiveté, its refusal to make possible any complexities or subtleties, its efficiency in conveying the picture of a child-like Indian that was such an essential part of Longfellow's poem. As one early admirer showed, it matched the expectations of his readers:

> The measure is monotonous . . . but it is truly

Indian. It is childlike and suited to the savage ear . . . the great thing is not the pleasure the poemgives to those who know how to read it but the boldness with which you have walked lyre in hand among those poor painted children of the western forest, and learned and taught us their simple melodies. . . .

The *Kalevala* is very different from Longfellow's poem. Its unpredictability, grotesque comedy, and sometimes terrifying mythopoeic power often make it seem nearer to Longfellow's Indian sources than the bland, homogenized, melancholy *Hiawatha.* For example, Longfellow takes the idea of Minnehaha's death from the *Kalevala,* but there the comparable death of Ilmarin's wife is brought about by obstinacy and bad-temper, in a fight where she only just fails to give as good as she gets; no comparison with Minnehaha's beautiful decline. The original of Longfellow's Chibiabos, the 'sweet singer', was Lord of the Regions of Death, and elements of his myth are curiously like one of the most famous and powerful parts of the *Kalevala,* Ilmarin's visit to Tuonela, land of the dead (which Sibelius' Swan of Tuonela evokes). Yet Longfellow ignores that aspect of Chibiabos, whose story is melancholy, never disturbing. The Christian elements in the *Kalevala* have been absorbed into the myth; the virgin Marjetta conceives from a whortleberry, and when her son is crowned Väinämöinen leaves in dudgeon. No awkward inclusion of colonial history there. Longfellow took only what he needed for his pastoral threnody.

That Longfellow suppressed the influence of the *Kalevala* is just one of various hints of his anxiety about the poem's distance from its Indian sources. A similar unease lies in the erudite notes, which are often misleading (without actually being untrue), concealing more than they reveal.

This ambivalence appears at times in the very language of the poem. In the final canto Longfellow coalesces the Indian myth in which Hiawatha floats upward from his people to 'celestial regions' in his magic canoe, with the *Kalevala's* account Väinämöinen sailing off out to sea, with which Lönnrot ends. Longfellow's verse seems uncertain in which direction the boat should move, in which direction perhaps the poem is moving:

> Westward, westward Hiawatha,
> Sailed into the fiery sunset,
> Sailed into the purple vapours,
> And the people from the margin
> Watched him floating, rising, sinking,
> Till the birch canoe seemed lifted,
> High into that sea of splendor,
> Till it sank into the vapours
> Like the new moon slowly, slowly,
> Sinking in the purple distance.

This uncertainty of language is present even in the opening lines. In his 'Introduction' Longfellow follows Lönnrot more closely than anywhere else; understandably so, for Lönnrot's 'Prologue', his own work, not a rune, expresses a sentimental romanticism close to Longfellow's own, where the folk and an idyllic version of the natural world become totally identified. Here Longfellow begins: 'Should you ask me, whence these stories?' Perhaps we should.

Longfellow clearly wanted his readers to accept the authenticity of his Indian epic, yet he deals very freely with his material. One can plainly see the shifts he makes as he shapes his story to fit the form of the 'primitive', 'folk' saga, and recasts what he reads to fit the perceptual grid of the mid-nineteenth century American. I don't want to suggest that he distorts 'true' accounts of the Indians. His sources are already Euroamerican readings, with their own internal contradictions, and often Longfellow is in tune with their spirit even when he radically alters their letter. His numerous changes veil the conflicts and tensions of the historical moment present in their texts.

Schoolcraft, Longfellow's main source, provided him with the prototype for his central and subsidiary characters. Longfellow's Hiawatha is himself an amalgamation of the Algonkin Manabozho and of the Iroquoian Hiawatha. The latter was a historical figure, founder of the famous League; in Schoolcraft's account he is already confused with a mythical figure and is presented as partly supernatural, having the magic canoe and miraculous death of Longfellow's poem. Schoolcraft's description of Hiawatha bringing peace to the Five Tribes disappears from Longfellow's version. Instead peace is brought to the 'warring children' by the Gitche Manito, the Great Spirit, before Hiawatha enters the story. As to the nineteenth-century American the Indian was incapable of government, divine intervention was more appropriate. Although the story of Manabozho provides most of the incidents, his name—not sufficiently melodious - and personality (as a trickster he is undignified, half animal, anarchic, and even in Schoolcraft's expurgated version, rather lewd) play no part.

Longfellow incorporates Schoolcraft's description of farming, games, songs, picture-writing into his account. But in the original these are practised by contemporary Indians. At the end of the poem, in the prophecy of the Indians 'wandering westward' after the arrival of the white men, there is no hint that any of these skills are still practised. The assumption that the Indians had no arts or agriculture transfers all these skills to the precolombian golden age. Schoolcraft at times, in logical contradiction to his ethnographic account, denounces the Indians for refusing to farm and for remaining nomadic hunters: Longfellow's text resolves the clash.

The changes produce other effects: for example, the general elegiac air that evokes the pathos of the vanishing Indian is emphasized by such alterations as Minnehaha's death, the absence of children (which both the original Hiawatha and Manbozho have), the sad outcome of the famine and the evil consequences of the ghosts. The ending of the poem refers to Indian prophecies of the coming of the white man, but Hiawatha's suggestions that they should be welcomed is a wishful distortion of Schoolcraft's words:

> Our Indians are rather prone to regard the coming of the white man as fulfilling certain obscure prophecies of their own priests; and that they are at best, harbingers of evil to them.

Hiawatha's speech to his people recasts and reverses his source in another way. When he says his people will degenerate after the coming of the white man, who will inevitably gain power, he gives a mirror version of one of the few historical documents in Schoolcraft's work, Pontiac's message to the tribes before the rising.

---

> **It is in *The Song of Hiawatha*'s 'innocent' evasions, omissions and transformations, not in its intentions, that the political message lies.**
>
> —*Helen Carr*

---

Pontiac berates them for their decadence, urging them to regenerate themselves so they can repulse the invaders: the Master of Life says to them: 'you are wrong; I hate such conduct . . . The land on which you are, I have made for you, not for others; wherefore do you suffer the whites to dwell on your lands? Longfellow' transforms historical hostility into an anodyne, ahistorical goodwill.

A second source for the Indian material in *Hiawatha* is George Catlin's account of his western travels in the 1830s, to paint and record the Indian's way of life before

it vanished. The conception of Hiawatha as the noble and dignified leader of his people must owe far more to Catlin's admiring descriptions of the chiefs he met, than to anything in Schoolcraft. Many picturesque details, of implements, the making of the birch canoe, dishes (for the non-Indian wedding feast), food, the Indian clothes (Longfellow's Ojibwe Indians are transformed to full Plains glory) were taken from Catlin, but again Longfellow has displaced information about contemporary Indians into the mythic past. Catlin's travels only pre-date *Hiawatha* by twenty years. Although the frontier was moving all the time, much he describes was still part of Indian life. What has changed is the liberal perception of the Indian.

What Longfellow's notes tell the reader comes from Catlin is the story of the Gitchee Manito's gift of the peace pipe at the Red Pipestone Quarry. The passage from Catlin which is quoted at some length, includes the other gift in the original of the red pipe of war, suppressed in Longfellow's poetic version. As I've said, Longfellow based this section largely on Schoolcraft's account of the founding of the Iroquoian League, and this note disguises that displacement. Catlin's full text suggests a different reason why Longfellow chose to start the poem in this setting. Just before the passage in the note, Catlin wrote:

*Longfellow at the summer cottage of the Story family in Nahant, Massachusetts, 1858.*

Be not amazed if I have sought, in this distant realm, the Indian Muse, for here she dwells, and here she must be invoked - nor be offended if my narratives from this moment should savour of poetry or appear like romance.

If I catch the inspiration, I may sing (or yell) a few epistles from this famed ground before I leave it; or at least I will prose a few of its leading characteristics and mysterious legends. This place is great (not in history, for there is none of it about) in traditions, and stories, of which the western world is full and rich.

I would guess Longfellow first intended to use this setting for his own invocation of the 'Indian Muse': but in the poem as we have it he substitutes a Muse and inspiration from the vale of Tawasentha, Schoolcraft's birth place. The Muse becomes, perhaps justly enough, not the Indian traditions but their European filter. But at this moment Longfellow makes one extraordinary misapplication of his source material. He gives Schoolcraft a mellifluous, trochaic Indian name, Nawadaha. What he seems to have forgotten is that in the story as Schoolcraft tells it, Nawadaha was a tyrant (one of twins) who mercilessly oppressed the Ojibwe. When he was eventually destroyed (by having all his flesh cut off in little bits) he was found to have a heart of flint. This parapraxis is, I would argue, the most telling symptom of Longfellow's unconscious, unacknowledged guilty sense of the destructive power of the discourse in which he and Schoolcraft make known their version of the Indian.

Longfellow also drew on the works of John Heckewelder, the Moravian Brethren missionary who worked among the Pennsylvanian Delaware, and whose accounts of the gentle, honourable Delawares, as well as of the marauding, treacherous Huron, were used so extensively by Cooper in his Leatherstocking novels. Longfellow had read Heckewelder while still at school and was deeply moved by his picture of the doomed, noble Indian. He told his mother they were 'a race possessing magnanimity, generosity, benevolence, and pure religion without hypocrisy'. He re-read Heckewelder while working on *Hiawatha,* and found much on which to model his golden age. According to Heckewelder, 'they live as peaceable as any people on earth, and treat one another with the greatest respect . . . and, love their neighbours as themselves'. This biblical language, passes into the poem (Hiawatha is described as a prophet), his gentle Indian morality becoming almost a prefiguring of Christianity, a moderate-minded Unitarian John the Baptist figure. Although Heckewelder describes the ordered life of the Delawares, he never questions the assumption that the Indians have no organised government. According to Heckewelder, they are non-hierarchical and non-authoritarian, peace and justice being maintained through moral education and example. Longfellow's Hiawatha, idealised beyond Heckewelder's Indians to bloodlessness, is leader of his people by example and not by force. Longfellow's elegiac tone also owes something to Heckewelder, who wrote sadly of a way of life whose irrevocable destruction he has watched. But again, he was writing historically, not like Longfellow, in a mythic past.

Heckewelder is evoked in the notes at a curious point, quite atypical of the borrowings from him. Longfellow credits him with the words with which Mudjekewiss mocks the bear:

Hark you, Bear! you are a coward
And no brave, as you pretend:
Else you would not cry and wimper
Like a miserable woman

Like many of these notes, this may only show a readiness to mention any random point to defend the authenticity of the poem. Moyne suggests this reference hides Longfellow's particular indebtedness to the *Kalevala* at this point. It also fits well Longfellow's pervasive nineteenth century patriarchal assumptions. There is no Indian source that I can find for the lines:

As unto the bow the cord is,
So unto the man is woman,
Though she bends him, she obeys him,
Though she draws him, yet she follows
Useless each without the other.

Longfellow's Hiawatha, like a nineteenth-century American, takes for granted that he controls and dominates the natural world. Hiawatha addresses the animals as Brother as Manabozho does, but he destroys them and the forest imperialistically. Heckewelder's text refers to an Indian addressing the bear as an equal, taunting him as he would taunt a Huron, to test his courage. Heckewelder finds the incident confusing, but for Longfellow there is no doubt of man's superiority.

A fourth text that Longfellow uses is John Tanner's *Narrative of Captivity and Adventures,* which tells how he was taken from a frontier settlement at the age of nine, living with Indians till he was thirty. His captors, brutal, demoralised Indians, in what we should now call guerilla camps near the white settlers, have nothing in common with Longfellow's idealised natives, and even the kindlier, more humane Indians Tanner later joins exist in quite a different literary discourse - the captivity narrative, the antithesis of the noble savage mode. Longfellow incorporates Tanner's experience of, as a boy, growing up among these people; the highly coloured account of Tanner's adolescent hunting exploits seems to be the basis of the canto describing Hiawatha's boyhood, including the feast made to celebrate the killing of the deer. Of course Tanner used a gun, not a bow and arrow. Longfellow was apparently not anxious to draw attention to this particular borrowing, which even more than his other texts was a white version of Indianness: all he gives Tanner credit for is a reference to elm-bark cords.

The one example I have found of Longfellow's use of an unmediated Indian source is a description of picture writing which he takes from George Copway, or Kah-ge-gagah-bowh, a Christian Ojibwe chief with whom he was acquainted. In Copway's history of the Ojibwe appear the pictographs of Canto 14. Longfellow does not acknowledge this - perhaps he felt an Indian couldn't be an 'authority' or maybe a contemporary christianized Indian seemed out of place, too much part of his world to be juxtaposed with the golden age. The pictographs, like so much else, are removed from their context of contemporary Indian life, dehistoricized, but another, almost sinister adjustment here is the stress put on picture-writing as a means of recording the dead. Hiawatha invents writing to mark their gravestones, although there is nothing in any of Longfellow's sources to suggest this was an important use; it's certainly much less emphasized than its use for recording songs. But the effect is to add even more to the melancholy tone of the poem; this canto mirrors the 'neglected graveyard' of the introduction, Longfellow's analogy for his poem where the reader may 'pause . . . For a while to muse, and ponder / On a half-effaced inscription / Written with little skill of song-craft' and 'may read this rude inscription'; in the world of this poem Indian songs are transmuted into the memorial on their graves.

Although the structure of the poem is that of Hiawatha's life story, in many senses he is never allowed to reach maturity. After his marriage, his own story ends—disasters and the tales of others fill up the remainder. Even his marriage to Minnehaha is de-sexualised: after the wedding feast the only hint of consummation, the only sexual moment is when Minnehaha gives herself to the cornfield; the only fruit of their union is the flourishing corn, presented to the Europeans at the poem's end. They can have no children, because Longfellow's idealised Indians can have no progeny: they have no place in nineteenth-century America. To Hiawatha the fruit of that marriage is disease, famine and death.

The American listener, drawn into the poem in the first line ('Should you ask me, whence these legends . . .') and held there throughout ('You shall hear how Hiawatha . . .') is the emotional pivot of the poem. Changing from kindly, condescending, innocently delighted by this pastoral play, to melancholy, regretful, blameless, the listener legitimizes the necessary disappearance of the Indian from his contemporary world.

The excellence of *Hiawatha*'s sales was clearly not much marred by the critical voices of those who felt Longfellow was deceiving the public in suggesting his material was genuinely Indian: they were right, of course, though for the wrong reasons. Leaving that group aside for the moment, it is easy to see why Longfellow's poem was so successful. What made his version of the Indian so welcome was the crucial split in his poem between the idyllic past of primitive innocence, and Hiawatha's picture of the present Indians:

> I beheld our nations scattered
> All forgetful of my counsels,
> Weakened, warring with each other;
> Saw the remnants of our people
> Sweeping westward, wild and woful,
> Like the cloud-rack of a tempest,
> Like the withered leaves of Autumn.

For Longfellow's readers, there were various theories or perceptions by which they made sense of their relationship with the Indians. They might hold, like the fundamentalist Schoolcraft, that the present nomadic Indians were the degenerate ancestors of the people of Genesis, thus solving the problem of why, if all are descended from Adam, there could be such different life-styles. This view went with strong moral disapproval for the present Indians, but

allowed for a less reprehensible past. Schoolcraft had suggested that the legends he records must be corrupted, 'recent and grosser' derivations of more elevated accounts, and that the light of earlier knowledge of the truth dimly glimmered in them, so justifying Longfellow's refining transformation. This theory was by the 1850s an old-fashioned one but still powerful: Morgan felt it necessary to attack it fiercely in *Ancient Society* in 1877. The Unitarian Longfellow can have had little personal inclination to this view, but his poem proved compatible with it. Schoolcraft praised the work obsequiously, and reissued the legends in a popular edition called *The Myth of Hiawatha,* altering his text to approximate the poem better.

Others, more liberal, believed than though many present Indians were degenerate, it was as a result of the white men's treatment of them. This was the view held by Heckewelder and Catlin, who see the Indians they describe as still untarnished by frontier brutality. Although a view less prominent in the 1850s, it remained present, becoming powerful again later in the century, as the Indian Wars drew to a close and a new wave of sympathy arose for the Indians, exemplified by Helen Hunt Jackson's *A Century of Dishonor.* Longfellow's noble pre-contact Indians fused easily with this viewpoint. Those who thought in this way did not see Indians as equal. They were primitivists of a sort, seeing in the Indians' nature a rebuke to the faults of the present civilized world, but also accepting that their child-like incapacity to negotiate with the white man's world made their disappearance inevitable. As with Cooper's designation of 'red gifts' and 'white gifts', there was no doubt in the 'real world', as opposed to that of the pastoral, which was superior.

Longfellow's poem presents the modern world in terms which allow both for the primitivist sadness at loss of the tranquillity of innocence and for admiration of nineteenth century American progress:

> And the land was full of people
> Restless, struggling, toiling, starving,
> Speaking many tongues yet feeling
> But one heart beat in their bosoms.
> In the woodlands rang their axes,
> Smoked their towns in all the valleys,
> Over all the lakes and rivers
> Rushed their great canoes of thunder.

Belief in progress was fundamental to the American enterprise and to westward expansion. The Enlightenment idea of progress, based on a belief in man's natural goodness is quite compatible with primitivism: the child-like innocence of the noble savage must mature to the adult virtues of civilization. Yet, by the 1850s, for most intellectuals progress had taken on a new and racial form, one less easy to assimilate with the primitivist view point. Scientific racism held that the different races were quite distinct, possibly with different origins, and that comparative physical measurements, particularly the size of cranium definitively showed the superiority of the more highly developed white races. Longfellow's early critics were principally those who held these views. *The Boston Daily Evening Traveller* was perhaps mainly reflecting the current unpopularity of appeals to sympathy for the Indians when it said:

We cannot deny that the spirit of poesy breathes throughout the work . . . but we cannot but express a regret that our pet national poet should not have selected as the theme of his muse something higher and better than the silly legends of savage aborigines.

In practice *Hiawatha* anaesthetized American anxieties over the Indian rather than stimulating them, as Longfellow's feat in creating a best-seller from this out-of-date and unwelcome theme proved. Yet the word 'higher' suggests this paper was reflecting the growing acceptance of the concept of higher and lower races. Emerson, who accepted these latest scientific views, wrote a carefully worded, not altogether kind letter to Longfellow about the poem. After saying somewhat ambiguously that at least he always felt safe reading Longfellow's 'sweet, wholesome as maize' books, he continued:

> The danger of the Indians are, that they are really savage, have poor, small, sterile heads — no thoughts; and you must deal roundly with them and find them in brains.

It was only in the last cantos (when the Europeans arrive) that Emerson could see 'a pure gleam or two of blue sky'.

Yet, eventually, even scientific racism was able to appropriate *Hiawatha,* as an example of the white poet's power to transform even these backward savages and their ways into art. Robertson, another of Longfellow's biographers of the 1880s, insisted that 'the red man, in truth, had never been the rhapsodical, sentimental being that ignorance imagined'. Yet he marvelled at Longfellow's skill:

> It is highly improbable that the poor Red Indian will ever again receive an apotheosis so beautiful at the hand of any poet . . . Abuse and parody have now ceased; and when the Redskins themselves have died from off the face of the American continent, there will always be men and women ready to follow the poet into the primeval forest, see him make for himself a woodland flute, piping to the poor painted braves and making them dance . . . It is true that in 'Hiawatha's' pleasant numbers the Red Indian with his narrow skull and small brain is not presented to us with less embellishment than he gains in Cooper's romances; but that fact does not diminish Longfellow's credit as a poet.

*The Song of Hiawatha* could not, of course, speak to those actively engaged in displacing the Indian. was a poem for the East Coast, or at least for the bourgeois liberal or moderate conversative, not for the frontiersmen or government officials. As one Washington official testily observed, as the policy of starving out the Indian by extermination of the buffalo began:

> The idea that a handful of wild, half-naked, thieving, plundering murdering savages . . . should be dignified with the sovereign attributes of nations, enter into solemn treaties, and claim a country five hundred miles wide by one thousand miles long as theirs in fee simple, because they hunted buffalo and antelope over it, might do for beautiful reading in Cooper's novels or Longfellow's *Hiawatha,* but it is unsuited to the

intelligence and justice of this age, or the natural rights of mankind.

But the ideological positioning that underlies this—the wild hunters there, the civilized world of intelligent and just mankind here, is not very different form that of *The Song of Hiawatha,* whose consoling myth was as essential to the dispossession of the Indian as the raucous racism of the frontiersmen, or the legalistic exclusion of the Indian from natural rights in the government's bureaucratic language. Like the ethnographic texts from which it drew, *Hiawatha* provided a discourse of what Foucault calls 'assujettissement' by which these Indians become known, controlled and subject to white power.

Longfellow had produced a new version of the myth of the vanishing Indian, one that could be translated into all the various discourses that justified, more or less enthusiastically, Indian displacement. What one should criticise about the poem is not that it follows foreign models, but that it reproduces so uncritically the prejudices of its contemporary society, drifting into acceptance of its worst aspects. One might suggest that in its fusing together so many of the contradictory elements of contemporary ideology, it might be called too 'American' rather than too 'European', though this is perhaps once more to use the word 'American' in an essentialist way. *Hiawatha* was also extraordinarily successful in England, and can be seen more generally as a myth for nineteenth-century colonialism. But [F.O.] Matthiessen's suggestion that Longfellow lacked indigenous strength and was swamped by European models is clearly wrong. 'Strength' and 'vigour' are key words in this version of the American. But Longfellow's capacity for evasion, not any lack, is the problem, and what swamps him is certainly indigenous.

As William Rossetti said perceptively in 1878 [in *Lives of the Famous Poets*]:

> The sort of intelligence of which Longfellow is so conspicuous an example includes predominately 'a great susceptibility to the spirit of the age'. The man who meets the spirit of the age halfway will be adopted as a favourite child, and warmly reposited in the heart. Such has been the case with Longfellow. In sentiment, in perception, in culture, in selection, in utterance, he represents . . . the tendencies and adaptabilities of his time . . . he can enlist the sympathies of readers who approach his own level of intelligence, and can dominate a numberless multitude of those who belong to lower planes, but who share none the less his own general conceptions and aspirations. He is like a wide-spreading tree on the top of a gentle acclivity, to which the lines of all trees lower down point and converge, and of which the shadow rests upon them with kindly proximity and proximity and protection. This is popularity.

Ironically, it is perhaps because of Longfellow's perplexed and pained withdrawal from the intellectual and political debates of his day that he was so warmly welcomed by it. Longfellow had wanted to use ideals of romantic nationalism to create his American Epic. But instead of linking the white American and the Indian it placed them across an unbridgeable divide: at the end of the poem, the modern American participant-listener watches the Indians fade from sight. Longfellow had instead written a poem that met the demands of the refined and moral Anglo-Saxonism of the latter half of the century.

The tensions underlying American identity at the mid-century have to be seen in the context of the clash between the morality and idealism on which the U.S. insisted it was based, and the opportunistic barbarity of its westward progress. The Oedipal anxiety of the revolutionary state, the angst of what [D. H.] Lawrence calls the 'masterless men' was by then less powerful than the guilts stirred by its libidinous territorial drive. As Lawrence asks, 'Can you make a land virgin by killing off its aborigines?' The myth of the Virgin Land purged and purified the 'American' himself. Longfellow's feminised, de-sexualised Indians effaced the power of American desire.

*Helen Carr, "The Myth of Hiawatha," in* Literature and History, *Vol. 12, No. 1, Spring, 1986, pp. 58-78.*

---

**Van Wyck Brooks on Longfellow:**

Longfellow is to poetry what the barrel organ is to music; approached critically he simply runs on, and there is an end to the matter. But nobody dreams of criticizing Longfellow from the point of view of "mere literature": the human head and the human heart alike revolt from that. His personal sanction is rightly a traditional one, and the important thing is to see him as a beautifully typical figure and to see just what he typifies.

To Longfellow the world was a German picture-book, never detaching itself from the softly colored pages. He was a man of one continuous mood: it was that of a flaxen-haired German student on his wanderjahr along the Rhine, under the autumn sun—a sort of expurgated German student—ambling among ruined castles and reddening vines, and summoning up a thousand bright remnants of an always musical past. His was an eminently Teutonic nature of the old school, a pale-blue melting nature; and white hair and grandchildren still found him with all the confused emotion, the charming sadness, the indefinite high proposals of seventeen; —perhaps it was because they had never been opposed, never put to the test in that so innocently successful existence of his, that they persisted without one touch of disillusion, one moment of chagrin. . . . Though Longfellow had an unerring eye for the "practical application" that lurks in every shred of romance, totally unable to elude the agile moralist, the value of his moral promptings is just in proportion to the pressure behind them—and where was the pressure? His morals and ideals were, in fact, simply a part of the pretty picture-book, just as they are at seventeen: if they had not been so they would never have been laid on the shelf.

*Van Wyck Brooks, "Our Poets" (1915), in* Literature in America, *edited by Philip Rahv, 1957.*

---

## Dana Gioia    (essay date 1993)

[*Gioia is an American poet and critic. In the following essay, he traces the decline in Longfellow's literary reputation to the Modernist revision of American poetry.*]

Henry Wadsworth Longfellow was not merely the most popular American poet who ever lived but enjoyed a type of fame almost impossible to imagine by contemporary standards. His books not only sold well enough to make him rich; they sold so consistently that he eventually became the most popular living author in any genre in nineteenth-century America. His readers spanned every social class from laborers to royalty, from professors to politicians. A vast, appreciative audience read, reread, and memorized his poems. His work quickly became part of school curricula. It also entered the fabric of domestic and public life—to be recited in parlors and intoned at civic ceremonies. Many of his lines became so much a part of English that even a century and a half later people who have never read Longfellow quote him unawares: "Ships that pass in the night," "Footprints on the sands of time," "When she was good, she was very, very good," "The patter of little feet." Language remembers the poems its speakers love best, even if only as clichés.

Longfellow's fame was not limited to the United States. He was the first American poet to achieve an international reputation. England hailed him as the New World's first great bard. His admirers included Charles Dickens, William Gladstone, John Ruskin, and Anthony Trollope as well as the British royal family and their notoriously anti-American poet laureate, Alfred Tennyson. But Longfellow's fame went beyond the English-speaking world. His work traveled throughout Europe and Latin America in translation. When the playboy emperor of Brazil, Dom Pedro II, visited America, he asked to dine with Longfellow (and returned the hospitality by translating "King Robert of Sicily" into Portuguese). King Victor Emmanuel offered him a medal (which the poet declined). Charles Baudelaire adapted part of *The Song of Hiawatha* into the rhymed alexandrines of "Le Calumet de Paix." Franz Liszt set the "Prologue" of *The Golden Legend* to music. In England he eventually outsold Tennyson and Browning. Tennyson once bragged to a friend that he made two thousand pounds a year from poetry, then grumbled, "But Longfellow, alas, receives three thousand." Three years after his death Longfellow's bust was unveiled in the Poet's Corner of Westminister Abbey, the first and only time an American poet has received this honor.

Longfellow's popularity did not prevent him from receiving the esteem of literati; in his lifetime they generally regarded him as the most distinguished poet America had produced. Nathaniel Hawthorne, who held him just this side of idolatry, put him "at the head of our list of native poets." William Dean Howells considered him the one American poet who ranked with Tennyson and Browning. Even Edgar Allan Poe, his most outspoken critic, repeatedly referred to his "genius." His other admirers included Oliver Wendell Holmes, James Russell Lowell, John Greenleaf Whittier, Walt Whitman, and Abraham Lincoln. By late middle age he had become the public symbol of American cultural achievement. In 1881, the year before his death, his birthday was celebrated nationwide in schools with recitations and performances. "Surely," a friend told him, "no poet was ever so fully recognized in his lifetime as you."

Longfellow's fame was not merely literary. His poetry exercised a broad cultural influence that today seems more typical of movies or popular music than anything we might imagine possible for poetry. His poems became subjects for songs, choral work, operas, musicals, plays, paintings, symphonies, pageants, and eventually films. *Evangeline,* for instance, was adapted into an opera, a cantata, a tone poem, a song cycle, and even a touring musical burlesque show. Later, it became a movie three times—the last in 1929 starring Dolores del Rio, who sang two songs to celebrate Longfellow's arrival in talkies. **"The Village Blacksmith"** became a film at least eight times, if one counts cartoons and parodies, including John Ford's 1922 adaptation, which updated the protagonist into an auto mechanic. *The Song of Hiawatha* not only provided American artists, composers, cartoonists, and directors with a popular subject, it gave Anton Dvořák the inspiration for two movements of his "New World" symphony. It also provided the Anglo-African composer, Samuel Coleridge Taylor, with texts for three immensely popular cantatas, which until World War II were performed annually in a two-week festival at Royal Albert Hall by almost a thousand British choristers dressed as Indians. *Hiawatha's* cultural currency was so high that it was not only translated into virtually every modern European language but also into Latin. It was even recast as English prose—the way a popular movie today is "novelized" in paperback—and it eventually became a comic book. **"Paul Revere's Ride"** prompted too many adaptions to list, though Grant Wood's witty version underlines the poem's status as a national icon. Charles Ives's setting of **"The Children's Hour"** (later choreographed by Jerome Robbins for *Ives Songs*) may also have a touch of irony, but it mainly luxuriates in the poem's celebration of domesticity, for Longfellow's emotional directness appealed immensely to composers. There are over seven hundred musical settings of his work in the Bowdoin College Library.

One could go on, but I trust that by now there has been something in my catalogue of Longfellow's fame and influence to offend critics of every persuasion. Book sales and royalty figures! Patronage of kings and emperors! Comic books and movies! Dolores del Rio and red-faced English choirs! These are not valuable tokens in establishing a poet's literary merit. I offer this welter of anecdote not to argue the intrinsic worth of Longfellow's poetry, which I believe is considerable, but to make a simple point. There is something singularly odd in Longfellow's case that makes him extraordinarily difficult for contemporary critics to discuss: he is as much a part of our history as of our literature. To approach the place he occupies at the center of mid-nineteenth-century American culture a critic must cross a minefield of explosive issues; the nature of popular art, American culture's relationship to England and Europe, the social and economic assumptions of the Genteel Tradition, Christianity's place in art, the legacy of Modernism, the critical evaluation of formal and narrative poetry, the validity of didactic poetry, the literary sta-

tus of poems that require no explication, the representation of females, blacks, and Native Americans by white male authors. One could go on here as well, but this catalogue is already alarmingly long. The collective lesson it holds is that to evaluate Longfellow fairly we must first recognize the historical chasm that separates his age from our own.

If Whitman and Dickinson stand at the beginning of modern American literary consciousness, Longfellow represents the culmination of an earlier tradition. To approach him postmodern readers must make the same sort of mental adjustments they do in studying Chaucer or Milton. The necessary adjustments, however, are harder to make in Longfellow's case because, paradoxically, he—and his fellow Fireside poets—still feel so familiar. They still connect so easily to parts of American public culture. But what Longfellow connects to is *popular* culture; once we bring him into the context of contemporary high culture, especially academic literary criticism, his liberal Christian humanist assumptions seem uncomfortably dated. In intellectual discourse that valorizes indeterminacy, self-referentiality, and deconstruction, Longfellow's aesthetic has more in common with that of Virgil or Ovid than with the assumptions of Beckett or Ashbery. But unlike Virgil and Ovid, who today exist almost solely as objects of academic study, Longfellow refuses to stay in the tiny cell critics have afforded him. He can still be sighted—to the scholar's embarrassment—prowling at large in the general culture.

Although he is no longer widely taught in schools, Longfellow remains the one poet the average, nonbookish American still knows by heart—not whole poems but memorable snatches. Most English-speaking Americans can quote the openings of at least five Longfellow anthology pieces, even if they don't always know the author or title: **"The Village Blacksmith," "Paul Revere's Ride,"** *Evangeline,* **"Hiawatha's Departure,"** and **"The Arrow and the Song."** What? You don't know the last one? Yes, you do—"I shot an arrow into the air, / It fell to earth, I know not where." Most people have never read these poems. They have picked them up as part of American oral culture along with proverbs, schoolyard chants, nursery rhymes, and campfire songs. Many Americans over sixty, members of a generation that did learn Longfellow in school, can quote whole swatches of poems like **"Psalm of Life," "Excelsior,"** or **"The Wreck of the Hesperus,"** the recitation favorites of yesteryear. Few common readers will share the scholar's surprise that Wallace Stevens's wife, Elsie, preferred Longfellow's poems to her husband's.

Almost every poet has a Longfellow anecdote. Let me tell you mine. During the nearly seventeen years I worked in business, I assiduously tried to keep my after-hours literary activity a secret, but after a decade the embarrassing news leaked out. During the next few weeks various colleagues dropped into my office to ask if I really did write poetry. When I admitted my secret vice, an odd thing happened—on four separate occasions my visitors began to recite Longfellow. It was their way of letting me know poetry was OK by them. One accountant made it halfway through **"The Wreck of the Hesperus."** A senior executive intoned the opening of *Evangeline* in sonorous, if exaggerated, hexameter. No one ever quoted any other author. Longfellow was the one poet they knew by heart.

If Longfellow achieved the apogee of literary fame in his lifetime, and if his reputation still persists, however diminished, among the general public, what is the current status of his reputation among literati? The answer would have dumbfounded his contemporaries: Longfellow, if he is noted at all, is now considered a minor poet of the Genteel Tradition. If he has not yet sunk to the status of an embarrassing historical footnote like Ossian or Chatterton, he stands only marginally higher among academic critics. His long poems are unread and undiscussed; he exists precariously as the author of half a dozen short lyrics found only in the thickest anthologies. He has gradually become more a name to recognize, like William Cowper or Leigh Hunt, than an author to read. He is most definitely not an author for ambitious critics to write about. Few recent books on American poetry mention Longfellow except in passing; almost none discuss him at any length. The centenary of his death was celebrated by a single volume of scholarly papers printed, significantly, not by a university press but by the U.S. Government. So little, in fact, has been written on Longfellow recently that for years Kermit Vanderbilt and later George Hendrick made the critical dearth into a sort of running gag in successive volumes of *American Literary Scholarship.* "Increasingly rare is the scholar who braves ridicule to justify the art of Longfellow's popular rhymings," Vanderbilt characteristically quipped. The current version of nineteenth-century American poetry has no place for its once preeminent figure. Contemporary taste does not esteem the genres Longfellow favored—the ballad, idyll, pastoral romance, and moral fable—nor does it highly regard the stylistic strengths his contemporaries praised—clarity, grace, musicality, masterful versification, and memorability. These are not attributes that fit easily into the traditions of Emerson, Whitman, and Dickinson. In short, the status of Longfellow's reputation among literati is a subject less suited to a critic than an elegist.

Nowhere can the decline of Longfellow's critical reputation be measured more clearly than in his representation in serious historical anthologies. (In popular anthologies like Hazel Felleman's *Best Loved Poems of the American People* his popularity continues more or less undiminished.) The three versions of *The Oxford Book of American Verse* provide an exemplary illustration. Bliss Carman's original 1927 anthology gives more space to Longfellow than any other poet, seventeen poems spread across 37 pages. F. O. Matthiessen's considerably larger 1950 *Oxford Book of American Verse,* which ran 1,132 pages to Carman's 680, prints fourteen poems occupying 39 pages. But now Emerson, Whitman, Robinson, Frost, and Stevens have more space than he does. Longfellow consequently occupies a different position in the American canon; he is not the central nineteenth-century master but instead the greatest of the Fireside poets. By the time Richard Ellmann edited *The New Oxford Book of American Verse* in 1976, Longfellow's decline was complete. He now has only eleven poems and a little over 12 pages. Thir-

ty-five other poets have as much or more space. Even Jones Very and James Russell Lowell outrank him in the nineteenth-century canon. Overall Longfellow occupies about the same number of pages as Gary Snyder, Robert Duncan, and John Ashbery, considerably less than Denise Levertov or Galway Kinnell. How are the mighty fallen! But it is not merely the size of Longfellow's representation but its constitution that is most revealing. Ellmann includes no narrative poems in his selection (unless one considers the "Introduction" to *The Song of Hiawatha* narrative), whereas Carman and Matthiessen felt Longfellow should be represented by such narrative poems as **"Paul Revere's Ride," "The Birds of Killingworth,"** and **"The Monk of Casal-Maggiore."** Ellmann reduces him to a lyric poet. Perverse as this version of Longfellow might have seemed to a nineteenth-century reader, Ellmann merely followed the current critical consensus, which downgraded most American narrative poetry, especially Longfellow's. The third edition of *The Norton Anthology of Poetry* (1970), for example, also excluded Longfellow's narratives; it reprinted only six poems—all lyrics, three of them sonnets.

If Longfellow had been "downsized" in historical anthologies, he had become invisible in most other textbooks. The format of historical anthologies forces an editor to balance his or her individual views against the consensus of the past; no once important author, however unfashionable, is easily omitted. But the general anthologist has no similar restraints. If one examines the three leading nonhistorical college poetry textbooks—X. J. Kennedy's *An Introduction to Poetry,* John F. Nims's *Western Wind: An Introduction to Poetry,* and Laurence Perrine's *Sound and Sense,* one will find not a single poem by Longfellow, only *disjecta membra*—isolated lines used to illustrate points of rhetoric and rhythm. According to William Harmon's 1990 *Concise Columbia Book of Poetry,* no poem by Longfellow currently ranks among the top one hundred mostfrequently anthologized poems in English. Insofar as university-based readers are concerned, Longfellow has become a marginal figure.

Modern literary criticism on Longfellow hardly exists in the sense that it does for more overtly difficult poets like Dickinson, Stevens, or Pound. There is no substantial body of commentary on specific poems, no vital tradition of critical discourse that collectively sharpens our reading and challenges our preconceptions. The unspoken assumption, even among his advocates, has been that Longfellow's poetry requires no gloss. Consequently, many central aspects of his work have never been examined in any detail (the linguistic stylization and rhetoric of *Hiawatha,* for example) and misconceptions about his work abound. The best Longfellow scholarship often has a decidedly oldfashioned feel; it traces historical sources, clarifies textual problems, and connects biographical data to the poems. Such criticism addresses a small group of nineteenthcentury specialists rather than the general readership for American poetry; it implicitly ducks the issue of Longfellow's relevance to contemporary letters. On the rare occasions Longfellow criticism has spoken eloquently to a broader audience—as in essays by Horace Gregory, Howard Nemerov, and Leslie Fiedler—his champions have usually been more concerned with the general mission of keeping him, however marginally, in the canon than with examining specific features of his work. Since Longfellow's work now largely exists in a critical vacuum, one must begin any serious examination of his work with a few basic observations about the unusual nature of his poetic development and the strange combination of circumstances that brought this multitalented literary man into poetry.

The smooth progress of Longfellow's academic career has led his critics to miss how extraordinarily unusual his literary apprenticeship was among nineteenth-century American poets. He began writing verse in early adolescence—nothing odd there—publishing his first poem at thirteen in the local *Portland Gazette.* At Bowdoin College he applied himself seriously to writing and encountered immediate success. During his three years in college he published nearly forty poems. Certain of his literary vocation, Longfellow faced the obvious problem of how to make a living. His father, a successful lawyer from a family of lawyers and legislators, wanted his gifted son to study for the bar. Longfellow hoped to become a journalist, but struck a compromise with his affectionate parent: he would pursue a legal career if allowed a year of graduate study at Harvard to learn Italian and perfect his French.

At graduation Longfellow met with one of the many strokes of good luck that would characterize his literary career. The trustees of Bowdoin had decided to create a chair in the new field of Modern Languages. (It would become the fourth such program in the United States after William and Mary, Harvard, and the University of Virginia.) With extraordinary boldness and insight the trustees offered the future professorship to the eighteen-year-old Longfellow, whose talent and earnest application had impressed them, under the condition that he pursue graduate study in Europe. The improbable offer saved the young poet, who then knew only Greek, Latin, and a smattering of French, from his father's profession.

When the nineteen-year-old Longfellow boarded the Cadmus in May 1826 to sail for Havre, something significant happened—he stopped writing poems. The silence would last for the next eleven years. Most poets spend their twenties mastering their medium, usually by writing reams of verse that carry them from juvenilia into artistic maturity. Longfellow also dedicated this crucial decade to learning his craft, but in a different way from his American contemporaries: he studied European languages and literature, he translated an astonishing range of poetry—usually in its original meters, he wrote prose of every variety from fiction and memoir to grammar textbooks and literary criticism. When he returned to original poetry in late 1837 he had developed an unprecedented combination of skills for an American poet—a deep knowledge of European literature, a practical experience with dozens of poetic genres and forms from his work in translation, a trained critical mind, and an assured authorial voice developed by publishing a considerable amount of prose, most notably *Outre-Mer: A Pilgrimage Beyond the Sea* (1835), his autobiographical travelogue.

The factors that pushed Longfellow back into poetry have not been adequately explored by his biographers. His brother Samuel, who compiled the first, largely documentary biography in 1886, romantically assumed that the creative release came when the poet first moved into Craigie House, the elegant Cambridge manse that he would eventually own and occupy for the remaining forty-five years of his life. Herbert Gorham offers the more interesting theory that Longfellow's immersion in European literature during the previous ten years instilled in him an anxiety about the difficulty for an American artist to equal the Old World's tradition. Longfellow used the decade of scholarship to assimilate his influences, Gorham maintains, before his new situation in Cambridge unleashed his long-simmering imagination. Newton Arvin hardly examines the issue but implicitly assumes that Longfellow's less demanding and more congenial situation at Harvard allowed him time to rediscover poetry. There is truth in all of these observations, but certainly two other events sent Longfellow back to poetry—one tragic, the other mundane.

The tragic impetus was the sudden death of his first wife, Mary, during his second European sojourn in 1836. This trip had begun as a professional triumph for Longfellow. He had just accepted the Smith Chair in Modern Languages at Harvard, a position that not only gave him lighter duties and a larger salary than Bowdoin but also an escape from the intellectual isolation of Brunswick, Maine. Harvard's president, Joseph Quincy, had suggested that Longfellow return to Europe to perfect his German before assuming the chair. Eager to revisit Europe in his wife's company, Longfellow—against his father's advice—set sail. In Copenhagen, Mary, who was expecting their first child, took ill. They journeyed to Amsterdam where she miscarried and, after three week's confinement, seemed to recover. In Rotterdam she suddenly took ill again and died. Longfellow plunged into grief so profound that it pierced his customary reticence. "All day I am weary and sad," he confided to his diary, "and at night I cry myself to sleep like a child." When Longfellow arrived in Cambridge in December 1836 to begin his eighteen-year tenure at Harvard, he was a widower moving to a new city. He faced the external challenge of creating a new social identity and the internal struggle of redefining himself as a writer. Scholarship could not bear the psychic weight of Longfellow's grief nor adequately address his need for self-definition. Almost as soon as he returned from Europe he began composing his autobiographical *Hyperion: A Romance* (1839), and within the year he had resumed writing poetry. From this time on Professor Longfellow would be primarily an imaginative writer.

The death of Longfellow's first wife has been overshadowed by the more public and horrifying death by fire of his second wife. Longfellow wrote nothing about his first wife's death beyond a few letters and journal entries, so no adequate record exists of this crucial period. "With me," he wrote in an early letter, "all deep feelings are silent ones." But seven years after Mary's death he revisited Germany and wrote the only poem that apparently alludes to his grief, **"Mezzo Cammin."** One of Longfellow's finest poems, the sonnet lay unpublished in his papers until after his death. (Many scholars, including the editors of the

Norton anthologies, mistakenly assume that it appeared in the 1846 collection, *The Belfrey of Bruges;* the sonnet took its place there only posthumously with the publication of the *Complete Poems*). Longfellow, the most reticent of poets, seems to have considered it too personal to publish, and perhaps he also felt it was indelicate to memorialize his first wife while he courted a second, Fanny Appleton, whom he married in 1843. It is tempting to read **"Mezzo Cammin"** in an overtly autobiographical way, as describing Longfellow's despair at having wasted so much of his life and confessing the spiritual paralysis following Mary's death.

### Mezzo Cammin

Half of my life is gone, and I have let
The years slip from me and have not fulfilled
The aspiration of my youth, to build
Some tower of song with lofty parapet.
Not indolence, nor pleasure, nor the fret
Of restless passions that would not be stilled,
But sorrow, and a care that almost killed,
Kept me from what I may accomplish yet;
Though, half-way up the hill, I see the Past
Lying beneath me with its sounds and sights,—
A city in the twilight dim and vast,
With smoking roofs, soft bells, and gleaming
   lights,—

And hear above me on the autumnal blast
The cataract of Death far thundering from the
   heights.

The sonnet borrows its title from the opening line of Dante's *Inferno,* "Nel mezzo del cammin di nostra vita," which Longfellow himself later translated as "Midway upon the journey of our life." Dante uses this metaphor to describe the age of thirty-five, the halfway point in the Bible's allotted span of human life, "three-score years and ten." The precise dating of this Italian sonnet in Longfellow's papers makes it clear he composed it at thirty-five, and the sonnet's speaker is also explicitly at the midpoint in his life and presumably, like Dante, lost in a dark wood of spiritual confusion. The first quatrain specifies the speaker's particular failure—he is an artist who has not realized his youthful ambition of lyric achievement. The second quatrain also specifies the reason for his failure; it is not indolence nor dissipation nor restlessness but a nearly fatal grief to blame. Yet already the failure is significantly-qualified since his aspirations remain something the speaker "may accomplish yet." What makes this poem unusual for Longfellow is the final sestet. Rather than resolving the speaker's predicament, instead it amplifies the dilemma. The lines vividly describe how the protagonist is caught

*Longfellow (seated at center) with the group that accompanied him on his European tour of 1868-69. Standing: Samuel Longfellow (the poet's brother), Alice Longfellow (the poet's daughter), Thomas Gold Appleton, Ernest Longfellow (the poet's son), and Harriet Spelman Longfellow; at front: Mary Longfellow Greenleaf (the poet's sister), Edith Longfellow (the poet's daughter), and Anne Longfellow Pierce (the poet's sister).*

inescapably between the unrecoverable but still visible past and his distant but nonetheless inevitable death.

Few of Longfellow's poems end in such an indeterminate way. It may not have been only the poem's personal nature that led Longfellow to suppress it but also its dark and ambiguous conclusion. The sonnet, however, suggests at least two things about Longfellow in 1842 that one would not have said before his wife's death: first, he is now certain of his poetic vocation, and second, the awareness of his own mortality spurs his creative resolve.

The more mundane impetus to poetry was Longfellow's hard-earned economic security. Assuming the Smith Chair at Harvard, Longfellow had reached, at an unusually early age, the height of his profession. His years of academic toil had justified him in the eyes of his parents and the world. He now had a dependable income and was settled in a congenial spot. To a dutiful and diligent son from a middle-class family like Longfellow, these were not trivial considerations. If Longfellow eventually became the first American poet who could live off his royalties, we must not forget how economically marginal verse was in the early nineteenth century. William Cullen Bryant's *Thanatopsis and Other Poems* (1821), a volume that critics of yesteryear often cited as the first great book of American verse, earned its author $14.92 during its first five years. A charmingly symbolic sum for an American poet, but even then it wasn't much to live on. Longfellow—like Wallace Stevens and T. S. Eliot sixty years later—was essentially a bourgeois artist who needed a stable income and an orderly external routine to have the psychic freedom to create.

Whatever ambiguity existed about the young Longfellow's poetic vocation, there could be no doubt about his literary calling. When his first collection of poems, *Voices of the Night,* appeared in December 1839 the thirty-two-year-old author had already written or edited nine volumes: six small textbooks in Spanish, Italian, and French; a book of verse translation, the *Coplas de Don Jorge Manrique* (1832), which also included versions of Lope de Vega, Aldana, and Berceo; and two substantial prose works, *Outre-Mer* and *Hyperion.* He had also published a great many essays, scholarly articles, stories, and translations. Despite the demands of his academic career, Longfellow had demonstrated that he was a serious, indeed a compulsive, writer. Critics commonly fault Longfellow for not growing as a poet, as if change itself were an intrinsic sign of greatness—how many poets like Wordsworth and Swinburne or, more recently, Sexton, Lowell, and Dickey, have changed for the worse? Indeed, Longfellow's verse shows little major development across his career except for the increasing sophistication of his narrative technique and greater austerity in the late lyrics. It would, however, be more accurate to say that his early artistic growth occurred in other literary forms. The young Longfellow is found not in poetry but in *Outre-Mer, Hyperion,* and his scattered short stories. By the time he returned to poetry in his thirties—early middle age by nineteenth-century standards—he had already gone through complex, though unusual, artistic development.

*Voices of the Night* was one of the strangest debuts in American poetry. It contained nine new poems followed by seven poems rescued from Longfellow's teenage years. The bulk of the volume consisted of over twenty translations, including the lengthy "Coplas de Manrique," three substantial passages from Dante's *Purgatorio,* and diverse poems from Spanish, French, German, Danish, and Anglo-Saxon. The mixture of original and translated poems, the Greek epigraphs, the varied verse forms make the collection resemble an early volume of Ezra Pound more than anything typical of nineteenth-century America. The architecture of the volume (underscored by Longfellow's programmatic **"Prelude"**) explicitly announced the return to poetry of an author who had mastered the traditions of Europe.

In *Voices of the Night* Longfellow created an influential new archetype in American culture—the poet professor. There had been versifying professors before Longfellow, but their occupation seemed incidental to their art. Longfellow's range and erudition marked a shift in the poet's cultural role from literary amateur to professional artist; poetry was no longer a pastime but an occupation requiring a lifetime of study. A century and a half later the poet professor remains one of the four common stereotypes for the American poet that permeate both high and popular culture—the others being the bohemian vagabond (Walt Whitman, Vachel Lindsay, Allen Ginsberg), the reclusive outsider (Emily Dickinson, Robinson Jeffers, Wallace Stevens), and the self-destructive fiery genius (Edgar Allan Poe, Sylvia Plath, John Berryman, Weldon Kees). Although the New Critics despised Longfellow, these poet professors were his cultural descendants.

There is another side of Longfellow's version of the poet professor that has been decisively influential. Longfellow's public persona—articulated both in his books and in his new university position—was a figure of immense literary authority, a sensibility capable of both critical and creative activity, an intelligence embracing both "the mind of Europe" and the potential of America. If the description sounds as if it were borrowed from T. S. Eliot, the resemblance is not accidental. Longfellow was the first American poet both to define his literary identity and to build its authority by systematically assimilating European literature—not just British or classical verse but, to quote Eliot, "the whole of the literature of Europe from Homer." Although Longfellow and Eliot would have charted the high points of that tradition differently, what matters is that they shifted the poet's frame of cultural reference from Anglo-American to European literature. If this turn toward European models came in part from nationalistic assertion, it also derived from a visionary sympathy for Goethe's concept of *Weltliteratur,* the dialectic by which national literatures would gradually merge into a universal concert. Longfellow's vision of the American poet's international role was central to both Pound and Eliot, and it remains a dominant force in American poetry (locked, of course, in eternal, dialectical opposition with nativism).

Although Eliot did not take his mission directly from Longfellow, he developed it in the Harvard humanities curriculum that Longfellow helped create. Pound absorbed Longfellow's vision as part of his family heritage. Although he hated to acknowledge the connection, Pound was Longfellow's grandnephew. Rejecting his illustrious forebear's aesthetics, he nonetheless wholeheartedly embraced Longfellow's notion of the poet's education, especially the importance of learning poetry in foreign languages and mastering verse technique. Pound also shared Longfellow's conviction in the continuity of American and European culture and in the artistic integrity of poetic translation. Through Eliot and Pound the American poet's destiny as heir to European culture filtered to subsequent generations. It was the role W. H. Auden assumed in his initial American phase with ambitious long culture poems like "New Year Letter" and "For the Time Being." In a more restricted way it also shaped the intellectual identity of mid-century poets like Robert Lowell, John Berryman, Kenneth Rexroth, Weldon Kees, and Randall Jarrell, who saw themselves as mediators between American and European culture. Look, for example, at Jarrell's translations of the Brothers Grimm, Goethe, Rilke, and Chekhov. One sees a similar internationalism in the next generation, among poets as dissimilar as Robert Bly, James Wright, William Jay Smith, and Richard Wilbur— though it began to expand more noticeably beyond Eurocentric models. Although they may not have thought of their work in these terms, those poets continued a poetic tradition pioneered by Longfellow in *Voices of the Night.*

If Longfellow did not yet recognize his proper literary medium, the critics and the public did. While *Hyperion,* which had been published five months earlier, met with generally lukewarm and occasionally hostile reviews, *Voices of the Night* was an immediate success. Within weeks the first edition sold out. (There would be six printings in the first two years.) *The North American Review* claimed that Longfellow's poems—and remember there were only nine new ones plus a slight *"Envoi"*—were "among the most remarkable poetic compositions, which have ever appeared in the United States." In a letter Nathaniel Hawthorne gushed, "Nothing equal to some of them was ever written in this world, —this western world, I mean." Even while criticizing the volume on other grounds, Poe, who would make a personal mission of attacking Longfellow (sometimes anonymously or pseudonymously), singled out **"Hymn to the Night"** for extravagant praise. The poem, he predicted, would be "the greatest favorite with the public." Typically, Poe sagaciously identified the book's best poem but misjudged the public's taste. Reviewers and readers alike had already discovered their favorite—**"Psalm of Life"**—which would quickly become one of the century's most popular poems, not only in America and England but also, in translation, as far away as Russia, Iran, and China.

A scholar could compile a small anthology of apologies for this poetic chestnut. Only four years after the poet's death his brother Samuel wrote, "It has perhaps grown too familiar for us to read it as it was first read." Most of Longfellow's twentieth-century defenders—Alfred Kreymborg, Horace Gregory, Howard Nemerov, Newton Arvin, Louis Untermeyer, and others—have taken special pains to distance themselves from those "nine jingling verses, dripping with a larger number of clichés than any other

poem in the language," that, Kreymborg observed, "smote the heartstrings of the race." **"Psalm of Life,"** Longfellow's admirers have repeatedly asserted, is not the Longfellow they admire. Consequently, the poem has been banished from college anthologies and "serious" selections from the poet's work, unless, as in Cleanth Brook's and Robert Penn Warren's *Understanding Poetry* (the locus classicus of Modernist Longfellow criticism), it was used to represent what poetry should not be—a sugarcoated pill offering "truth" to readers by displaying "fine sentiments in fine language."

Surely every criticism ever aimed at **"Psalm of Life"** is, on some level, true. Yet, despite repeated assassination attempts by some of the best hit men in modern letters, this menacingly upbeat poem refuses to die. Banished from the curriculum for nearly a century, perhaps the poem is now just unfamiliar enough to show why it persists. As Daniel Littlefield, Jr., has demonstrated, the poem's popularity came *because* not *despite* its didacticism. **"Psalm of Life"** draws its identity from the colonial tradition of aphorisms in such works as *The Proverbs, The New England Primer,* and *Poor Richard's Almanack.* Kreymborg was more correct than perhaps he knew in noting that the poem contained "a larger number of clichés than any other poem in the language." If one substitutes the word *aphorism* or *proverb* for *cliché* (and one person's proverb is another's cliché), we get close to the source of the poem's most famous mental health hazard—its extraordinary memorability. By compressing the maximum number of sensible and uplifting proverbs into what is probably the most mnemonically seductive meter in English, trochaic tetrameter (the measure, for example, of Blake's "The Tyger"), and rhyming every end-stopped line, Longfellow created a masterpiece of Yankee Unitarian agitprop. **"Psalm of Life"** fails as lyric poetry because it belongs to a different genre, inspirational didactic verse. Anglo-American Modernism banished overt didacticism from high art; indeed rejecting didacticism was the first inkling of English Modernism in the 1890s. The didactic genre still exists, though in popular culture its form has shifted to prose; our contemporary equivalent is the self-help book—and poets still occasionally write them. Our **"Psalm of Life"** is *Iron John.*

The success of Longfellow's second verse collection, *Ballads and Other Poems* (1841), determined his literary future. While he would still occasionally undertake fiction and scholarly prose, he soon conceded to the wisdom of the marketplace. With the exception of his unsuccessful novel, *Kavanagh: A Tale* (1849), and the critical apparatus to his major translations, virtually all of his subsequent work would be in verse. *Ballads and Other Poems* also helped define Longfellow's poetic gifts both to himself and his public. If *Voices in the Night* revealed his mastery of the delicate lyric and his dexterity as a translator, the new volume revealed his other great strength—storytelling. Narrative poetry was the prime source of Longfellow's immense popularity. His superiority at creating compelling stories—clearly, movingly, and memorably—was his chief virtue in the eyes of his contemporaries and today it poses the chief obstacle to hisappreciation among contemporary critics. What caused such a divergence of opinion? The answer is obvious—Modernism.

Modernism declared narrative poetry at best obsolete and at worst a contradiction in terms. By prizing compression, intensity, complexity, and ellipsis, it cultivated an often hermetic aesthetic inimical to narrative poetry. Perfecting poetry's private voice, Modernism—at least American Modernism—lost the art's public voice. In many ways what we now call Modernist poetry was a collaboration between poets and critics. If there was an unmatched explosion of poetic talent between 1910 and 1940, there was also, just slightly later, an unprecedented efflorescence of critical intelligence, which developed ways of reading the challenging new verse. Among their many accomplishments the critical champions of American Modernism established the movement's genealogy in nineteenth-century literature. Three unfortunate consequences of this critical enterprise, however, were a narrow reconstruction of pre-Modernist American poetry, the development of analytical techniques that were useless in approaching verse narrative, and the identification of poetry with the lyric mode. Searching for the American precedents of Modernism, critics gradually narrowed the diverse traditions of pre-twentieth-century poetry to three-and-a-half major authors: Emerson, Dickinson, Whitman, and—reluctantly, for the Symbolist's sake—the critical half of Poe. Linking this purified canon to Modernism, the New Critics and their successors masterfully demonstrated the American genius for the lyric (in all its high culture varieties) and the non-narrative epic (the exploratory culture poem like *Leaves of Grass, The Cantos,* and *Paterson*). The simplified version of nineteenth-century American poetry that grew out of this critical tradition excludes so much interesting and enduring work that its continuing currency says less about what the era was actually like than how powerful Modernism still isin influencing our perceptions of the past.

No writers have suffered more from Modernism's revision of American poetry than Longfellow and Whittier. They represent the traditional aesthetic Modernism defined itself against. Consequently, they have been doubly damned. Not only have critics dismissed most of their poetry but their very poetic enterprise has been declared trivial—their chief genres marginalized, their prosody dismissed, their public voice deemed vulgar. The roots of the misunderstanding are too complex to examine fully here, but at its center are issues of genre, versification, and audience, all linked to the university's near monopoly over critical discourse. In a critical culture where literary merit is a function of how much discourse (in classrooms or learned journals) a poetic text can generate, their expansive and lucid poems have little to offer. William Butler Yeats observed that Longfellow's popularity came because "he tells his story or idea so that one needs nothing but his verses to understand it." Karl Keller claimed that "Whittier has been a writer to love, not to belabor." These are lethal verdicts in today's academy. But what does a reader say about a theory of poetry that has no room for Whittier's "Snow-Bound" or Longfellow's *Tales of a Wayside Inn?* There is something amiss in a literary culture that serves critics to the detriment of readers.

The mistake that most of Longfellow's advocates have made over the past half century is attempting to justify his work by Modernism's standards rather than insisting it be approached—as one would other poets separated by a significant historical gap—on its own terms. The author who emerges from this doomed defense is a gifted lyric poet, perhaps—as Richard Wilbur suggests, "the best sonneteer of his century"—but he remains a decidedly minor figure next to Browning orTennyson, Dickinson or Whitman. Once we begin to assess Longfellow on his own terms, as a master of lyric and narrative poetry, of translation and adaptation, an innovator in versification and the creator of national myths, he stands as the most versatile American poet of his century. Dickinson and Whitman surpass him in depth and intensity but no one equals his range. In his chosen field, verse narrative, he is unequalled in American poetry until E. A. Robinson and Robert Frost. His achievement in lyric poetry is less dramatic but in some ways more unusual.

Longfellow's faults as a lyric poet are too well known to belabor. His work often lacks intellectual depth. It often strays into sentimentality. His poems too often seem to begin from set conclusions rather than to discover themselves in their own imaginative process. He rarely passes up the opportunity to moralize. He is often derivative of European models. He sometimes becomes so engrossed in his metrical scheme that he loses the intensity of his poetic impulse. He rarely looks into the harsher side of reality. These are all fair criticisms, and I will add one more: Longfellow's imagination was so linear that it lacked the ability to work dialectically. His poems rarely unfold as dynamic arguments; he could not present and reconcile truly opposed points of view. This failing may partially account for the meekness that pervades so many of his poems; he could not offset his own gentle nature with a credible vision of darkness. But having catalogued Longfellow's faults, one must also point out that many of these failings are the other sides of certain virtues. The sentimentality of his worst poems comes from the same emotional directness that animates his best work. His lack of intellectual complexity is a chief strength of his popular poems and most delicate lyrics. Recognizing Longfellow's virtues amid the welter of his salient shortcomings, however, is complicated by at least two factors: he was an immensely prolific and uneven poet, most of whose work is blandly unmemorable; the cultural assumptions he made about poetry differ significantly from our own.

Longfellow's lyric poetry divides into two groups. There are the songlike poems written in a popular style, which is smooth, direct, and quick moving, and there are the crafted literary poems, which are stately, complex, and densely textured. The popular poems usually have simple syntax and they match their phrasing neatly to the line lengths. The literary poems show more complex syntax and risk stronger enjambments at the line breaks. Longfellow also differentiated the poems metrically. The popular poems usually move in stress meter, triple feet or trochees; quite often they work in a loose ballad meter with an alternating pattern of four and three stresses per line. The literary poems almost always move in rhymed iambic pentameter, a meter Longfellow used less than most major English-language poets. The popular poems often have complex, songlike stanzas with shifting line lengths and unusual rhyme schemes; they often have refrains. Longfellow, like the Elizabethan lyricists, understood that if a poet keeps the sense simple he can make the music compellingly complex. The literary poems invariably employ a standard line length and simple rhyme schemes, most often the quatrain or the sonnet. (For Longfellow, the sonnet was the quintessential high literary form.) The music, though sonorous, supports the sense rather than calls attention to itself. It is what Donald Davie might call a "chaste" style. The two types of lyric are more easily differentiated on style than subject. Longfellow dealt with serious themes in both modes, although when he wrote about overtly literary topics (**"Chaucer," "Milton," "Divina Commedia"**) he invariably used his high style.

To illustrate the difference between Longfellow's popular and high styles, hereare representative passages from two of his best-known poems, **"The Tide Rises, the Tide Falls"** (the popular style) and **"Shakespeare"** (the literary style):

> The tide rises, the tide falls,
> The twilight darkens, and the curfew calls;
> Along the sea-sands damp and brown
> The traveller hastens toward the town,
> And the tide rises, the tide falls.
>
> A vision as of crowded city streets,
> With human life in endless overflow;
> Thunder of thoroughfares; trumpets that blow
> To battle; clamor, in obscure retreats,
> Of sailors landed from their anchored fleets;
> Tolling of bells in turrets, and below
> Voices of children, and bright flowers that throw
> O'er garden walls their intermingled sweets!

In nineteenth-century lyric poetry the chief difference between the high style and the popular style was density of effect. Popular poetry strived toward a transparent texture in which local effects were subordinated to predictable general patterns of syntax and prosody. Literary poetry compressed the effects of meter, diction, metaphor, and image to achieve a richer texture; the reader was trusted to discern the general formal patterns of sound and sense through the many changes in local textural density. These two passages display different levels of poetic effect. The popular poem allows the metrical form to determine the syntax. The literary poem revels in counterpointing the two elements; it usesline breaks to syncopate the rhythm. **"The Tide Rises, the Tide Falls"** neatly balances its images, placing two images or details in each line. **"Shakespeare"** lets the images stretch or contract irregularly; there is no set syntactic pattern framing the images. The popular poem ends each stanza with a set refrain to keep the image and the mood easily focused. **"Shakespeare"** tumbles forward unpredictably. The images in the popular poem usually move forward sequentially or cyclically and rarely show dialectical opposition. The images in the literary poem are more exact, unusual, and dynamic; one never knows exactly where each new image will lead.

The two styles do not represent different stages in Longfellow's career—as they did, for example, in Yeats's case. Though the high style emerged slightly later (one first sees

it fully developed in **The Belfrey of Bruges** in 1845), the two styles essentially coexist through all of Longfellow's mature poetry. The poet saw both as valid literary modes. One aimed at the general audience, the other at the intelligentsia. A contemporary reader must, however, remember that in the nineteenth century the two modes were not seen in opposition; there was not yet a gulf between highbrow and lowbrow art. (It is surely not coincidental that the terms _highbrow_ and _lowbrow_ enter English in the second decade of the twentieth century—just as Modernism arrived in full force.) Longfellow's high style was simply a refinement of his popular mode, and the mass audience for popular poetry included the literary intelligentsia as well as common readers.

The temptation for modern critics, however, has been to assume that Longfellow's high style is naturally superior to his popular mode. His best lyric poems in the high style fit easily into contemporary notions of how genuine poetry operates. The few distinguished examples of critical analysis of specific poems—like James M. Cox's "Longfellow and His Cross of Snow"—virtually always focus on poems in the literary mode. Likewise, the handful of poems that survive in academic anthologies like **"Mezzo Cammin"** and **"The Jewish Cemetery at Newport"** (the latter surely one of the great American poems of its century), are almost inevitably products of the high style. Moreover, the fact that most of Longfellow's weakest poems are written in the popular style reinforces the scholarly prejudice toward the high style.

Although it is easier to discuss poems in the high style, since their denser verbal texture invites analysis, there is ultimately no cogent reason why Longfellow's literary poems should be categorically preferred to the best popular ones. Why should one consider **"My Lost Youth"** inferior to **"Chaucer"** because the latter has more stylistic complexity? An adequate theory of poetry leaves room to admire both. Both modes are artistically legitimate, since the test of poetry is its ability to involve and move the reader to enlightenment, consolation, or delight—not its susceptibility to critical analysis. Perhaps the real reason why the popular style appears an inferior literary medium is that its aesthetic requirements—clarity, simplicity, emotional directness, syntactic linearity, and prosodic symmetry—make it harder to write well. There is less freedom of style and subject than the high literary mode affords, and the poet faces the significant challenge of having to surprise the reader in only predictable ways. In such a transparent style every flaw and banality shows. Time is especially cruel to popular poetry; each subsequent change of attitude mercilessly exposes new imperfections.

There have probably been fewer than a dozen English-language poets who have managed to create a significant and enduring body of poetry in a popular style: Herrick, Burns, Blake, Whittier, Housman, Kipling, Stevenson, Langston Hughes, and a few others. To this select, if mostly unfashionable, company, one must add Longfellow. His many failures—and they are legion in so prolific a poet—must not blind the critic to his remarkable successes. His special gift was to bring an intense musicality and powerful atmosphere to the light texture of the popular lyric, which one sees in his best work, "My Lost Youth," "The Fire of Drift-Wood," "Snow-Flakes," "The Tide Rises, The Tide Falls," "The Ropewalk," and "Aftermath." There is even much to admire in his sentimental idylls, "The Day is Done" and "The Children's Hour," which survive a century of critical opprobrium with surprising freshness. The frank emotionalism of such poems leaves modern readers uneasy who forget the fragility of domestic happiness in an age of high infant mortality and low life expectancy. American life expectancy has doubled since Longfellow's time from approximately thirty-nine years in 1850 to seventy-five years in 1988. Medical progress has been as important as cultural trends in changing literary sensibility. (Look at how rapidly AIDS has revived a Victorian emotionalism in verse and drama.) "The Children's Hour," a poem admired by both Auden and Fiedler, was written by a man who had already watched a wife and young daughter die and would soon see his second wife suffer an excruciating death. When a literary culture loses its ability to recognize and appreciate genuine poems like "My Lost Youth" because they are too simple, it has surely traded too much of its innocence and openness for a shallow sophistication.

The issue of Longfellow's status as a major poet ultimately rests on the critical assessment of his four booklength poems—*Evangeline, A Tale of Acadie* (1847), *The Song of Hiawatha* (1855), *The Courtship of Miles Standish* (1858), and *Tales of a Wayside Inn* (1863-1873). These were the poems that earned him a preeminent position among his contemporaries, they were also the works most utterly rejected by Modernism. The long poems present a number of problems for critics, not the least of which is their proper evaluation. They are the slipperiest kind of literature to judge: they are not quite masterpieces but too good and too original to go away—like Mary Shelley's *Frankenstein* or Poe's *The Narrative of Arthur Gordon Pym*. They still command a reader's attention and linger in the memory. The poems are also troublesome for critics to discuss in a contemporary context because they bear so little relation to the subsequent tradition of longer American poems. Whereas "Song of Myself" is illuminated by the tradition it engendered, Longfellow's extended poems have little connection to twentieth-century work, not even, except tangentially, the booklength poems of Robinson and Frost. Longfellow's poems relate to earlier, mainly European traditions.

Most American long poems have been epics of self-discovery, works that consciously set out to explore and define both national and personal identities. Hence the author's autobiography eventually figures directly or indirectly in the quest. Whatever their other differences, *The Bridge, The Cantos, Paterson, A, Maximus Poems, Dream Songs, Gunslinger, The Changing Light at Sandover, History,* and *The One Day* all share the investigative dynamic of mixing personal and public mythologies. The Modernist culture epic has also been a notoriously messy genre— sprawling, discontinuous, idiosyncratic, and obscure. While each long poem has its champions, none except Whitman's, their common matrix, has been widely regarded as a success. By comparison, Longfellow's extended poems are distressingly neat and lucid: they are polished,

linear, nonautobiographical narratives. Their form is not exploratory but patterned after traditional genres— pastoral romance, folk epic, and framed tales. They are neither aimed at literary intellectuals nor—with the notable exception of *Hiawatha*—obsessed with defining national or personal identity. They are conceived as serious but popularentertainments, stories meant to enlarge the reader's humanity without deconstructing his or her moral universe.

The moral element in Longfellow's extended poems cannot be minimized. Although the poems may now seem old-fashioned in form, they remain surprisingly contemporary in their concerns. *Evangeline* depicts the personal tragedies of a displaced ethnic and religious minority driven from its homeland by an imperial power. *The Song of Hiawatha,* whatever its scholarly failings, tries to present with dignity the legends and customs of Native Americans on their own terms. *The Courtship of Miles Standish,* the least interesting of the poems, critiques the harshness and brutality of military values. *Tales of a Wayside Inn,* whose very framework celebrates multiculturalism, contains stories openly concerned with environmental sensitivity, religious tolerance, political freedom, and charity. Not the least of Longfellow's influences on American culture has been political. He helped articulate the New England liberal consciousness that eventually became mainstream American public opinion. If contemporary critics are quick to point out the internal contradictions of this ideology, it still represented the most enlightened viewpoint of its era.

There is no room here for even a minimal exploration of the poems but only a few general observations. *Evangeline* is the most poetically impressive of the longer poems. It contains passages—the prologue, the burning of Grand-Pré, the journey on the Mississippi, the description of the prairies—that are both breathtakingly beautiful and, as Longinus understood the term, sublime. The story also has a magnificent narrative sweep until the end, which reveals Longfellow's central weakness as a storyteller, his sentimentality. He lacked the tragic insight necessary to carry a painful story to its inevitable conclusion; he can only resolve it in comforting terms. That *Evangeline's* ending was, in fact, historically true does not redeem the sweet sentimentality with which the poet saturates its finale. And yet, as John Seelye has pointed out, "Evangeline does haunt us, a vague ghost adrift on the Mississippi in company with Uncle Tom and Huck Finn, those other refugee symbols of exile and disarray."

*The Song of Hiawatha* is probably the closest thing America will ever have to that European Romantic obsession, the national folk epic. This startlingly original poem was the work that made Longfellow the pre-eminently popular poet in English. It sold thirty thousand copies in its first six months in print and eventually became the most popular long American poem ever written, both at home and abroad. *Hiawatha* is also the extended poem that best displays Longfellow's two greatest gifts as a storyteller— mythmaking and narrative thrust. Like other great popular narrative artists Longfellow excelled at mythos more than logos. He could create or adapt characters that seemed to exist outside their stories. While one cannot imagine Lambert Strether outside of the particular verbal universe of *The Ambassadors,* one can easily envision Simon Legree, Count Dracula, Ebeneezer Scrooge, and Hiawatha in another medium. *Hiawatha* created a series of archetypes (some would say stereotypes) of Native American culture that have permeated the popular imagination. The most readable long narrative poem of the nineteenth century, it also displays those virtues Matthew Arnold celebrated most highly in Homer, "the rapidity of its movement, and the plainness and directness of its style." That Arnold's terms of praise sound odd to contemporary ears is one more sign of how remote our literary culture has grown from narrative poetry.

Although *The Song of Hiawatha* has received more interesting scholarly and critical attention than any other Longfellow poem, most of the analyses have been historical, biographical, anthropological, or ideological (political denunciations of *Hiawatha* have recently been the one active area of Longfellow criticism.) Consequently, the poem's specifically literary characteristics remain only half-understood. Posterity has essentially made two mutually contradictory criticisms of *Hiawatha:* first, as a narrative, its style is insufficiently naturalistic, too little, that is, like a realist novel; second, Longfellow departs too much from his mythic material and unconsciously Europeanizes his Native Americans. There is a great deal of truth in both charges, and yet they seem to miss the sheer originality of the poem, in which Longfellow tries to invent a medium in English to register the irreconcilably alien cultural material he presents. The stylistic objections to *Hiawatha,* therefore, are largely based on misconceptions of Longfellow's intentions. The most frequent criticism is of the poem's meter, the trochaic tetrameter line he borrowed from the Finnish *Kalevala,* which has seemed too artificial and formulaic to some readers. The chief advantage of this measure, however, is that it isn't naturalistic. It was an overt distancing device, as was the incorporation of dozens of Ojibway words. These devices continuously remind the listener that *Hiawatha's* mythic universe is not our world. There are many other devices of syntax, lineation, diction, and rhetoric that give the poem its distinctive style. Although more often ridiculed than understood, the style of *Hiawatha* is in its own way as original as that of Pound's *Cantos.*

The fatal flaw of *Hiawatha* is, once again, the ending—justly notorious among scholars of Native American literature—in which Hiawatha instructs his people to accept the Black-Robes and then, like Tennyson's Ulysses, sails (or rather paddles) into the sunset. Longfellow lacked the tragic vision to recognize that there could be no humane, liberal reconciliation between Native Americans and invading Europeans. The nineteenth-century poem that *Hiawatha* most resembles (but is never compared to) is Richard Wagner's libretto for *Der Ring des Nibelungen.* Wagner also recast a disparate group of pre-Christian myths into an integrated narrative, but he understood that there can be no bloodless transition from one civilization to another: a hero and a people who do not triumph are utterly destroyed. Once *Hiawatha's* narrative leaves mythic time for history it must face the tragic consequences of its mate-

rial, but tragedy was a genre beyond Longfellow's reach—perhaps even beyond the melioristic vision of Unitarian liberalism. The first twenty cantos of *Hiawatha* achieve an oddly epic grandeur, the last two dissipate in utopian social fantasy.

*Tales of a Wayside Inn* makes the most convincing case for Longfellow's narrative mastery. Here, rather than tackling an epic structure, he worked in his most congenial medium, the short tale. As Newton Arvin rightly says, "No literary undertaking could have made a happier or more fruitful use of his powers . . . his storytelling genius, his sense of narrative form, his versatility, and the opulence of his literary erudition." Roughly modeled after Boccaccio's *Decameron,* Longfellow's poem consists of a series of verse tales told by a sundry group of travelers over three days at the Red Horse Inn in Sudbury, Massachusetts. The storytellers form a diverse group—a Sicilian political refugee, a Spanish Jew, a Norwegian musician, a youthful student, a broad-minded theologian, a tender-hearted poet, the Yankee landlord—and their stories draw from all of their ethnic traditions. The narrative framework is a bit rickety, but the stories themselves, which are told in an astonishing variety of metrical forms, are, despite a few weak ones, generally splendid. The best half dozen or so tales—**"Paul Revere's Ride," "King Robert of Sicily," "The Cobbler of Hagenau," "Azrael," "The Monk of Casal-Maggiore," "The Legend Beautiful,"** and especially **"The Birds of Killingworth"**—rank among the best short American narrative poems ever written. *Tales of a Wayside Inn* is Longfellow at his most endearingly human. One senses here as in none of the other long poems his famous personal charm, warmth, and humor. When Howard Nemerov prepared a selected edition of Longfellow's poems in 1959, he ignored all of the other long poems to include nine selections from *Tales of a Wayside Inn.* Posterity may prove his strong preferences correct.

It is impossible to understand Longfellow as a poet without studying the translations that make up nearly half of his nondramatic verse. He was the first great poet-translator in American literature. In this respect, as in his cultural internationalism, he exercised a major, if unacknowledged, influence on twentieth-century poetry. By demonstrating how translation could nourish a poet's growth, he introduced a powerful imaginative dynamic into our tradition. Translation became a means for American poets both to perfect their craft and to assimilate the literature of other cultures. Longfellow also showed how translation allowed the American poet to demonstrate mastery over the European tradition and implicitly claim equal status to classic authors—a concept central both to Pound and Eliot and their descendants. Longfellow's commitment to translation was the practical extension of his assent to the ideologies of internationalism and *Weltliteratur.* He stands, therefore, at the beginning of the innovative tradition of verse translation that enlarged the possibilities of American poetry. Directly or indirectly, he is the prototype not only of Pound and Eliot but ultimately of writers as dissimilar as Kenneth Rexroth, Robert Lowell, Richard Wilbur, Robert Fitzgerald, W. S. Merwin, William Jay Smith, Elizabeth Bishop, John F. Nims, David Slavitt, and Robert Bly.

Longfellow also helped free translation from the monopoly of Greek and Latin classics that had earlier formed the bulk of serious verse translation in English. His huge body of translation consists almost entirely of poems taken from modern languages, including work by contemporary authors like Tegner and von Platen. If Longfellow helped establish a new group of "modern" masters in English such as Michaelangelo, Goethe, Gongora, Lope de Vega, and, most important, Dante, he also dared to translate minor poets—simply because their work interested or delighted him. When critics belittle Longfellow for bothering with forgotten poets like Stockman, Mahlmann, Coran, and Ducis, they forget how much easier it is to experiment with new verse forms and genres when working with congenial but unchallenging texts. Surely the reason that Longfellow made such an accomplished debut as a narrative poet in **Ballads and Other Poems** was his assimilation of the Northern European verse storytelling tradition through translating Uhland, Evald, Tegner, and various folk ballads. Likewise, his unprecedented mastery of versification grew from his attempts to recreate foreign meters in English. If some new measure worked in a translation (such as Tegner's dactylic hexameter), Longfellow would employ it for an original poem—a method of imaginative assimilation his grand nephew Pound seems to have inherited.

With some notable exceptions, however, Longfellow's translations remain more important for their influence than their abiding literary worth. He was not the equal of Dryden, Pope, or Rossetti. His theory of translation, which stressed "rendering literally the words of a foreign author" while at the same time preserving "the spirit of the original," placed restrictions on him not usually assumed by the greatest masters of verse translation. As Arvin observed, Longfellow's ideal for translation "was not paraphrase, and decidedly not 'imitation,' but what Dryden called 'metaphrase.' " Indeed Longfellow practiced a half-scholarly/half-poetic method of translation that attempts to bring over the original text *as poetry* into English with meticulous attention to its literal sense, diction, lineation, and precise versification. This formidable agenda placed enormous burdens on his poetic skill, but the results were frequently not only impressive but fascinatingly original. His translations of Virgil's First Eclogue done in fluent hexameter and Ovid's *Tristia* (III, x) in elegiac couplets remain remarkable. The challenge of recreating classical meters in English has obsessed poets for centuries, but no one ever managed to bring over the elegant rhythm of the Latin elegiac couplet more naturally than Longfellow:

> Should anyone there in Rome remember Ovid
>   the exile,
> And, without me, my name still in the city survive;
> Tell him that under stars which never set in the
>   ocean
> I am existing still, here in a barbarous land.

His best translations are astonishingly faithful to both the meaning and the music of the original. His versions of Goethe's intricately rhymed "Wanderer's Night-Songs," for example, show an uncanny fidelity to nearly every aspect of the German. But it was not merely technical skill that animated Longfellow's translations. He excelled at the form for the same reason he did at narrative; he possessed the "negative capability" of extinguishing his own personality in the authors he translated. He could recreate a poem in English while maintaining the strangeness of its beauty, as in this translation of Michelangelo's "Dante":

> What should be said of him cannot be said;
> By too great splendor is his name attended;
> To blame is easier those who him offended,
> Than reach the faintest glory round him shed.
> This man descended to the doomed and dead
> For our instruction; then to God ascended;
> Heaven opened wide to him its portals splendid,
> Who from his country's, closed against him,
>   fled.
> Ungrateful land! To its own prejudice
> Nurse of his fortunes; and this showeth well,
> That the most perfect most of grief shall see.
> Among a thousand proofs let one suffice,
> That as he exile hath no parallel,
> Ne'er walked the earth a greater man than he.

Longfellow's greatest accomplishment as a translator was his version of *The Divine Comedy* (original edition, 1867; revised text, 1870), which reflected forty years of deep involvement with the poem. Dante's position in the English-speaking world was relatively marginal until the Romantic movement, when Coleridge, Shelley, and Byron fell under his influence. The first complete English translation of *The Divine Comedy,* Henry Cary's version, did not appear until 1814, almost five centuries after the original. Longfellow's advocacy of the poem as teacher, translator, and commentator was crucial in establishing its canonical stature in America. Not the least important part of his support was putting Dante into the center of Harvard literary studies, where, through his successors, James Russell Lowell, Charles Eliot Norton, Charles Grandgent, and George Santayana, it exercised a decisive early influence on young poets like Eliot, Stevens, and cummings. Longfellow's splendidly exact and richly annotated version remained the finest verse translation for nearly three generations, until it was superseded by the Laurence Binyon and John Ciardi versions.

If translation was an essential aspect of Longfellow's vision of the new American poet whose professionalism allowed him to participate in *Weltliteratur,* so was his dedication to prosody. Longfellow was the most versatile master of versification in American literature. His range and originality in metrics remains unprecedented. Virtually all major American poets have worked primarily in iambic, syllabic, or free verse—except Longfellow, that is, who not only used almost every traditional meter known to English but also experimented with new measures, some foreign, others original to him. He explored stress meter and mixed meters, and, as Arvin observes, his accentual poems like **"The Cumberland"** prefigure Hopkins's sprung rhythm. Longfellow, like George Herbert, also habitually played with stanza shapes, inventing several new forms. Sometimes he set poems of direct and simple emotion in complex and subtle stanza forms that gave them unexpected resonance, as in the intricate stanza he invented for **"My Lost Youth"** with its shifting line lengths and unrhymed refrain. Another of Longfellow's uncelebrated contributions to English prosody was his experimentation with the unrhymed lyric, as in **"The Bells of Lynn."** He also explored free verse before Whitman, as in **"Tegner's Drapa"** (1850) and *The Golden Legend* (1851). Longfellow's *vers libre* is particularly noteworthy because it eschews the Biblical prose rhythms that characterized most free verse before the *fin de siècle*. Here are two short passages, the first from **"Tegner's Drapa,"** the second from the later *Christus* (1872):

> So perish the old Gods!
> But out of the sea of Time
> Rises a new land of song
> Fairer than the old.
> Over the meadows green
> Walk the young bards and sing.
>
> I am the voice of one
> Crying in the wilderness alone:
> Prepare ye the way of the Lord;
> Make his paths straight
> In the land that is desolate!

The diction is standard for Longfellow's age, and the second passage—like much early *vers libre*—is rhymed, but the rhythms and lineation would not be out of place in Pound's *Ripostes* half a century later. The line lengths are irregular and follow the phrasing rather than any metrical measure. The rhythm is usually rising, but Longfellow consciously disrupts the underlying iambic movement to create a looser cadence. The prosody prefigures early Modernist practices and is as innovative as anything in *Leaves of Grass.*

Today prosody is a neglected subject. Few literary critics know more than the rudiments of metrics, and, in the aftermath of the free-verse revolution, even many poets have never studied versification. The last century, however, considered prosody an essential part of literary education. Critics debated issues of versification with the vehemence our contemporaries bring to literary theory. Prosody, in fact, played an important role in Victorian literary theory. Anyone who studies the early reviews of Longfellow's books notices how much space critics devoted to discussing issues of versification. His experimentation with foreign meters, like dactylic hexamter in *Evangeline* or unrhymed trochaic tetrameter in *The Song of Hiawatha,* were hotly debated. One of his major accomplishments in the eyes of Victorian cognoscenti was his success in makingclassical hexameter work in English, something no other poet had ever been able to do with equal aplomb. (Even Matthew Arnold reluctantly admired Longfellow's success with hexameter.) Surely one reason for the drop in Longfellow's reputation has been the decline of interest among both scholars and poets in formal prosody.

The early twentieth century saw two shifts in critical attitudes toward prosody, both of which prejudiced assessments of Longfellow and his fellow Fireside poets. The first was the rise of free verse. As free verse became—through a series of misconceptions, Timothy Steele has recently argued—inextricably associated with American Modernist poetry, critics revised the nineteenth-century canon to highlight poets like Whitman, who prefigured the development, or Dickinson, who ignored many prosodic conventions. As "open form" became a mainstream concept after the Beats, it mixed with nativist sentiments to declare free verse the only true American measure and condemn formal verse as a reactionary British import. This ideology dismissed Longfellow, Whittier, and their contemporaries *en bloc.* (Whitman's supporters have often displayed a special animus toward Longfellow, since he enjoyed a huge popularity among common readers their more obstreperously democratic poet has never approached.) But the celebration of free verse would not have been so damaging had it not combined with a second shift in attitude among the surviving defenders of formal poetry—a shift that has gone undiscussed in critical literature.

Twentieth-century American poetry has gradually developed a metrical puritanism, a conviction among both poets and critics that serious formal poetry is best written (to borrow Frost's dictum) only in regular or loose iambics. Triple and trochaic meters have gradually been relegated to light verse, classical andforeign meters regarded as technical curiosities. This metrical puritanism developed as second-generation Modernists, many of whom like Yvor Winters and Allen Tate were associated with New Criticism, tried to reconcile formal metrics with Modernism. In the process of defending traditional meter

*Longfellow in 1876.*

against free verse they felt it necessary to separate the meters suitable for high art from the catchy measures of popular poetry. The tightness and subtlety of iambic meters were preferred to the intrusive and looser rhythms of triple meter or the hypnotic but inflexible trochaic measures. Consequently, whereas Longfellow or Whittier, Tennyson or Browning comfortably moved between iambic and other meters, one rarely, if ever, sees a poem in triple measure or trochees by Winters, Tate, Hart Crane, J. V. Cunningham, Robert Lowell, Richard Wilbur, Anthony Hecht, or other twentieth-century American formalists. These poets looked at the overtly musical meters favored by Whittier, Longfellow, and Poe either as vulgar concessions to popular taste or artistic misjudgments. When the free-verse prejudice against metrical poetry combined with a high art bias against noniambic verse (in an environment that down-graded all narrative poetry and popular art), who was left to defend such gems as Longfellow's **"Paul Revere's Ride"** or Whittier's "Maud Muller" and "Barbara Frietchie"? (Pound anthologized "Barbara Frietchie" in *Confucius to Cummings*—what poet today would be bold enough to do so?) Even Matthiessen, who anthologized Longfellow's narrative poems, preferred the respectable iambic ones like **"The Birds of Killingworth"** and **"The Monk of Casal-Maggiore."** If modern criticism has created a distorted version of nineteenth-century American poetry by dismissing narrative verse and popular poetry, it has produced an equally impoverished account of the era's lyric poetry by rejecting most noniambic verse. Metrical diversity was one of the chief glories of mid-nineteenth-century poetry. By privileging iambic verse, critics not only miss some of the era's greatest poems but also obscure the commitment to popular poetry shared by most of the period's best poets.

"I am a man of fortune greeting heirs," Wallace Stevens once wrote. He might have been predicting his present place in American letters. His work generated a poetic and critical tradition that sustains his central place in the canon. Longfellow's heritage, by contrast, has few claimants. His small body of lyric poems written in the high style has secured him a niche in the contemporary canon, but the traditions he most richly endowed—narrative and popular poetry—were devalued by Modernism, and his contributions to translation and scholarship have been eroded by time. His direct influence on our poetry ended with Frost, though his cultural vision of internationalism continues indirectly to shape our national literary identity. Now that Modernism itself has become a historical period along with the Genteel Tradition it helped displace, a comprehensive reassessment of our poetic canon is necessary. The task is not to reject Modernism, which was our poetry's greatest period, but to correct the blindspots and biases of its critical assumptions. A reevaluation of Longfellow will be an important part of this enterprise. How will his work be revalued in the aftermath of Modernism? If he will never regain his dominant position in nineteenth-century American poetry, he will surely reemerge as a larger and more complex figure than he has recently seemed. The continuing popularity of his work—despite nearly a century of critical scorn—proves that it still has a vitality that current critical instruments are not designed to register. "Some books are undeservedly forgotten," W.

H. Auden once wrote, "none are undeservedly remembered." Longfellow's vast influence on American culture paradoxically makes him both central and invisible; to re-evaluate his work properly will not only require capable literary critics but unprejudiced cultural critics. He can be ignored only at the cost of misreading his century. His place in American literature brings to mind Basil Bunting's poem, "On a Fly-leaf of Pound's Cantos":

> These are the Alps. What is there to say about
> them?
> They don't make sense. Fatal glaciers, crags
> cranks climb,
> jumbled boulder and weed, pasture and boulder,
> scree,
> *et l'on entend,* maybe, *le refrain joyeux at leger.*
> Who knows what the ice will have scraped on
> the rock it is smoothing?
> There they are, you will have to go a long way
> round
> if you want to avoid them.
> It takes some getting used to. There are the Alps,
> fools! Sit down and wait for them to crumble!

This tribute to Longfellow's grandnephew applies as easily to him. If Longfellow's ultimate place in American poetry is still uncertain, one thing is sure—his best work will remain a permanent part of our literature. You will have to go a long way round if you want to ignore him.

*Dana Gioia, "Longfellow in the Aftermath of Modernism,"* in The Columbia History of American Poetry, *edited by Jay Parini, Columbia University Press, 1993, pp. 64-96.*

---

## FURTHER READING

Allen, Gay Wilson. "Henry Wadsworth Longfellow." In *American Prosody*, pp.154-92. New York: American Book Company, 1935.

  Provides a detailed analysis of Longfellow's versification.

Arvin, Newton. *Longfellow: His Life and Work.* Boston: Atlantic Monthly Press, 1962, 338 p.

  Highly regarded biography containing detailed analyses of Longfellow's poems.

Bowen, Edwin W. "Longfellow Twenty Years After." *The Sewanee Review* XIII, No. 1 (January 1905): 165-76.

  Reviews Longfellow's stature as a literary figure, finding that while he "does not deserve to rank with the world's great poets," his poetry "has more in it that appeals to the human heart than does the poetry of any of his American contemporaries."

Brenner, Rica. "Henry Wadsworth Longfellow." In *Twelve American Poets Before 1900,* pp. 80-108. 1933. Reprint. Freeport, NY: Books For Libraries Press, Inc., 1968.

  Presents an overview of Longfellow's life and work.

Davidson, Gustav. "Longfellow's Angels." *Prairie Schooner* XLII, No. 3 (Fall 1968): 235-43.

  Explores the representation of angels in Longfellow's work.

Fitch, George Hamlin. "Longfellow: The Poet of the Household." In his *Great Spiritual Writers of America*, pp. 58-67. San Francisco: Paul Elder and Company, 1916.

> Praises Longfellow for the beauty of form and thought in his verse, noting "the number of striking lines he has contributed to our literature."

Fletcher, Angus. "Whitman and Longfellow: Two Types of the American Poet." *Raritan* 10, No. 4 (Spring 1991): 131-45.

> Compares Longfellow with Whitman, concluding that "these two paths in the wilderness are in fact different ways of reaching the same goals."

Gohdes, Clarence. "Longfellow." In his *American Literature in Nineteenth-Century England*, pp. 99-126. New York: Columbia University Press, 1944.

> Discusses the reception of Longellow's poetry in England.

Gorman, Herbert S. *A Victorian American: Henry Wadsworth Longfellow*. New York: George H. Doran Company, 1926, 363 p.

> Studies Longfellow in the context of the era in which he lived, calling the poet "our great Victorian." Gorman argues that "Longfellow, without being quite conscious of it, was as much English as he was American."

Higginson, Thomas Wentworth. *Henry Wadsworth Longfellow*. Boston: Houghton Mifflin Company, 1902, 336 p.

> Detailed account of Longfellow's personal and professional life, featuring numerous excerpts from correspondence and discussion of the early critical evaluation of his works.

Long, Orie William. "Henry Wadsworth Longfellow." In his *Literary Pioneers: Early American Explorers of European Culture*, pp. 159-98. Cambridge, Mass.: Harvard University Press, 1935.

> Discusses the influence of European writers, particularly Goethe, on Longfellow's art and thought.

Stedman, Edmund Clarence. "Henry Wadsworth Longfellow." In his *Poets of America*, pp. 180-224. Boston: The Riverside Press, 1885.

> Presents an overview of Longfellow's life and work.

Ullmann, S. "Composite Metaphors in Longfellow's Poetry." *Review of English Studies* 18, No. 70 (April 1942): 219-28.

> Analyzes elements of synaesthesia, "the metaphoric mingling of the various spheres of sensations," in Longfellow's verse.

Wagenknecht, Edward. *Henry Wadsworth Longfellow: Portrait of an American Humanist*. New York: Oxford University Press, 1966, 252 p.

> Concentrates on Longfellow's inner-life, social relationships, and details of his career as a scholar, professor, and man of letters.

Ward, Robert Stafford. "Longfellow's Roots in Yankee Soil." *The New England Quarterly* 41 (June 1968): 180-92.

> Examines the New England heritage of Longfellow's verse.

Wells, Henry W. "Cambridge Culture and Folk Poetry." In his *The American Way of Poetry*, pp. 44-55. New York: Columbia University Press, 1943.

> Describes Longfellow as "an ideal spokesman for the spirit of romantic sentiment pervading almost all social classes in Northern Europe and North America," but nonetheless finds his poetry derivative and lacking in feeling.

Zimmerman, Michael. "War and Peace: Longfellow's 'The Occultation of Orion.'" *American Literature* XXXVIII, No. 4 (January 1967): 540-546.

> Discusses "The Occultation of Orion." Noting that the poem possesses qualities which are uncharacteristic for a work by Longfellow, Zimmerman explains that "It is of a certain difficulty—ambiguous, paradoxical, emotionally perplexed—and it is tightly woven."

---

**Additional coverage of Longfellow's life and career is contained in the following sources published by Gale Research:** *Concise Dictionary of American Literary Biography*, 1640-1865; *Dictionary of Literary Biography*, Vols. 1, 59; *Nineteenth-Century Literature Criticism*, Vol. 2; and *Something about the Author*, Vol. 19.

# *Typee*

## Herman Melville

The following entry presents criticism of Melville's novel *Typee: A Peep at Polynesian Life* (1846). For information on Melville's complete career, see *NCLC*, Volume 3; for criticism devoted to his novels *Moby-Dick* and *Billy Budd*, see *NCLC*, Volumes 12 and 29, respectively.

## INTRODUCTION

*Typee: A Peep at Polynesian Life* (1846) was Melville's first novel. Based in part on autobiographical material, it relates the experiences of an American sailor who is held captive by the Typee, a cannibalistic tribe on the Marquesas Islands in the South Pacific. The novel thus offers an extended treatment of the theme of cultural clash between a primitive society and western civilization. Acclaimed for its wealth of factual information as well as for its entertaining narrative, *Typee* is acknowledged as an important first step in the literary career of one of America's most acclaimed writers.

In 1839, at the age of nineteen, Melville's attraction for the sea led him to sail as a cabin boy on a merchant ship bound for England. Two years later, he joined the crew of the *Acushnet*—a whaler out of New Bedford headed for the Galapagos Islands and the South Seas. Finding ship life intolerable, Melville and shipmate Richard Tobias Greene deserted in the Marquesas Islands in July 1842, and were taken in by the Typee cannibals. After a month of captivity, Melville escaped on the Australian whaler *Lucy Ann*. However, Melville deserted the *Lucy Ann* in Tahiti, following a mutiny by its crew, and was briefly imprisoned. He worked as a field hand until November 1842, when he joined the crew of the whaler *Charles and Henry* out of Nantucket. The following May, Melville was released from duty in the Hawaiian Islands; he worked there as a clerk and as a bookkeeper until August of 1844, when he returned to the United States and began writing about his experiences.

*Typee* follows the adventures of two sailors, Tom (or Tommo) and Toby, who decide to desert at Nukuheva in the Marquesas Islands because of the cruelty of their ship's captain. After they arrive on shore and travel through the island's mountainous interior, Tommo and Toby take refuge among the cannibalistic Typee natives. The men are enthusiastically welcomed by the tribe's royal leader, Mehevi, who provides them with the heavily tattooed Kory-Kory as a servant and constant companion, but prohibits them from leaving. After discovering a pile of bones and skulls, Tommo and Toby plan their escape, but a leg wound prevents Tommo from leaving. Toby does escape, however, promising to return with help. Tommo, left with only the natives for companionship, comes to appreciate many of the social customs of their unstructured society and develops close relationships with Kory-Kory and other natives. Nevertheless, after encountering tribal

customs that he perceives as barbaric, and disturbed by the prospect of being expected to eat human flesh, Tommo again determines to make his escape. Narrowly avoiding recapture, he boards the Australian whaler *Julia*, at anchor in the bay of the Typee, and begins his journey home.

Criticism of *Typee* frequently centers on Melville's contrast of primitive culture with the morals and values of western civilization. While commentators have agreed that the novel portrays western society in a negative light, some have also interpreted Tommo's escape from the island as Melville's rejection of primitive culture and, hence, his rejection of a romanticized view of the past. Additionally, scholars have examined Melville's treatment of sexual themes in *Typee*, as well as his extensive use of humor in presenting such controversial subject matter so as not to upset the moral sensibilities of his readers. The novel's autobiographical content has also received considerable attention. Early critics of the 1846 English edition, published under the title *Narrative of a Four Months Residence among the Natives of a Valley of the Marquesas Islands*, accepted the work as a factual travelogue of Melville's South Seas adventures. In America, however, most nineteenth-century critics viewed *Typee* as an imaginative work of fiction, even after Greene came forward to corroborate Melville's account. The degree to which Melville intended the work to adhere to the facts of his experiences remains a significant question among modern critics.

---

# CRITICISM

### Raymond M. Weaver    (essay date 1921)

[*In the excerpt below, Weaver lauds the originality of* Typee.]

Melville was the first competent literary artist to write with authority about the South Seas. In his day, a voyage to those distant parts was a jaunt not lightly to be undertaken. In the Pacific there were islands to be discovered, islands to be annexed, and whales to be lanced. As for the incidental savage life encountered in such enterprise, that, in Montaigne's phrase, was there to be bastardised, by applying it to the pleasures of our corrupted taste. These attractions of whaling and patriotism—with incidental rites to Priapus—had tempted more than one man away from the comfort of his muffins, and more than one returned to give an inventory of the fruits of the temptation. The knowledge that these men had of Polynesia was ridiculously slight: the regular procedure was to shoot a few cannibals, to make several marriages after the manner of Loti. The result is a monotonous series of reports of the glorious accomplishments of Christians: varied on occasions with lengthy and learned dissertations on heathendom. But they are invariably writers with insular imagination, telling us much of the writer, but never violating the heart of Polynesia.

The Missionaries, discreetly scandalised at the exploitation of unholy flesh, went valiantly forth to fight the battle of righteousness in the midst of the enemy. The missionaries came to be qualified by long first-hand contact to write intimately of the heathen: but their records are redolent with sanctity, not sympathy. The South Sea vagabonds were the best hope of letters: but they all seem to have died without dictating their memoirs. William Mariner, it is true, thanks to a mutiny at the Tongo Islands in 1805, was "several years resident in those islands:" and upon Mariner's return, Dr. John Martin spent infinite patience in recording every detail of savage life he could draw from Mariner. Dr. Martin's book is still a classic in its way: detailed, sober, and naked of literary pretensions. This book is the nearest approach to *Typee* that came out of the South Seas before Melville's time. So numerous have been the imitators of Melville, so popular has been the manner that he originated, that it is difficult at the present day to appreciate the novelty of *Typee* at the time of its appearance. When we read Mr. Frederick O'Brien we do not always remember that Mr. O'Brien is playing "sedulous ape"—there is here intended no discourtesy to Mr. O'Brien—to Melville, but that in *Typee* and *Omoo* Melville was playing "sedulous ape" to nobody. Only when *Typee* is seen against the background of *A Missionary Voyage to the Southern Pacific Ocean performed in the years 1796, 1797, 1798 in the Ship Duff* (1799) and Mariner's *Tonga* (1816) (fittingly dedicated to Sir Joseph Banks, President of the Royal Society, and companion of Captain Cook in the South Seas) can Melville's originality begin to transpire.

This originality lies partly, of course, in the novelty of Melville's experience, partly in the temperament through which this experience was refracted. Melville himself believed his only originality was his loyalty to fact. He bows himself out of the Preface "trusting that his anxious desire to speak the ungarnished truth will gain him the confidence of his readers."

When Melville's brother Gansevoort offered *Typee* for publication in England, it was accepted not as fiction but as ethnology, and was published as *Melville's Marquesas* only after Melville had vouched for its entire veracity.

Though Melville published *Typee* upright in the conviction that he had in its composition been loyal both to veracity and truth, his critics were not prone to take him at his word. And he was to learn, too, that veracity and truth are not interchangeable terms. Men do, in fact, believe pretty much what they find it most advantageous to believe. We live by prejudices, not by syllogisms. In *Typee,* Melville undertook to show from first-hand observation the obvious fact that there are two sides both to civilisation and to savagery. He was among the earliest of literary travellers to see in barbarians anything but queer folk. He intuitively understood them, caught their point of view, respected and often admired it. He measured the life of the Marquesans against that of civilisation, and wrote:

> The term 'savage' is, I conceive, often misapplied, and indeed when I consider the vices, cruelties, and enormities of every kind that spring up in the tainted atmosphere of a feverish civilisation, I am inclined to think that so far as the relative wickedness of the parties is concerned, four or five Marquesan Islanders sent to the United States as missionaries, might be quite as useful as an equal number of Americans dispatched to the Islands in a similar capacity.

Civilisation is so inured to anathema, —so reassured by it, indeed, —that Melville could write a vague and sentimental attack upon its obvious imperfections with the cool assurance that each of his readers, applying the charges to some neighbour, would approve in self-righteousness. But one ventures the "ungarnished truth" about any of the vested interests of civilisation at the peril of his peace in this world and the next. It was when Melville focussed his charge and wrote "a few passages which may be thought to bear rather hard upon a reverend order of men" with incidental reflections upon "that glorious cause which has not always been served by the proceedings of some of its advocates," that all the musketry of the soldiers of the Prince of Peace was aimed at his head. Melville himself was a man whose tolerance provoked those who sat in jealous monopoly upon warring sureties to accuse him of licence. He specifies his delight in finding in the valley of Typee that

> an unbounded liberty of conscience seemed to prevail. Those who were pleased to do so were

allowed to repose implicit faith in an ill-favoured god with a large bottle-nose and fat shapeless arms crossed upon his breast; whilst others worshipped an image which, having no likeness either in heaven or on earth, could hardly be called an idol. As the islanders always maintained a discrete reserve with regard to my own peculiar views on religion, I thought it would be excessively ill-bred in me to pry into theirs.

This boast of delicacy did not pass unnoticed by "a reverend order of men." The vitriolic rejoinder of the London Missionary Society would seem to indicate that there may be two versions of "the ungarnished truth." It should be stated, however, that the English editions of *Typee* contain strictures against the Missionaries that were omitted in the American editions. But even Melville's unsanctified critics showed an anxiety to repudiate him. Both *Typee* and *Omoo* were scouted as impertinent inventions, defying belief in their "cool sneering wit and perfect want of heart." Melville's name was suspiciously examined as being a *nom de plume* used to cover a cowardly and supercilious libel. A gentleman signing himself G. W. P. and writing in the *American Review* (1847, Vol. IV) was scandalised by Melville's habit of presenting "voluptuous pictures, and with cool deliberate art breaking off always at the right point, so as without offending decency, he may excite unchaste desire." After discovering in Melville's writing a boastful lechery, this gentleman undertakes to discountenance Melville on three scores: (1) only the impotent make amorous boasts; (2) Melville had none of Sir Epicure Mammon's wished-for elixir; (3) the beauty of Polynesian women is all myth.

Unshaken in the conviction of his loyalty to fact, Melville discovered that the essence of originality lies in reporting "the ungarnished truth."

On the subject of "originality" in literature, Melville says in *Pierre:*

> In the inferior instances of an immediate literary success, in very young writers, it would be almost invariably observable, that for that instant success they were chiefly indebted to some rich and peculiar experience in life, embodied in a book, which because, for that cause, containing original matter, the author himself, forsooth, is to be considered original; in this way, many very original books being the product of very unoriginal minds.

It is none the less true, however, that though Melville and Toby both lived among the cannibals, it was Melville, not Toby, who wrote *Typee.*

*Raymond M. Weaver, in his* Herman Melville: Mariner and Mystic, *1921. Reprint by Pageant Books, Inc. 1961, 399 p.*

---

> **Early American press review of Melville's *Typee:***
>
> Mr. Melville is brother to the Secretary of Legation in London. He was a sailor on board a whale ship, the Dolly, a fictitious name, no doubt, from which he ran away while lying in the harbor of Nukuheva, and secreted himself in a valley inhabited by a tribe called Typees, who have the reputation of being cannibals. This is the same tribe upon whom Captain Porter made his murderous onslaught, when he refitted his frigate on this island, during the last war. The island has often been visited by whalemen, but the natives appear to have made no change in their habits since they were first visited by white men, fifty years ago; and the account given of them by Mr. Melville exactly corresponds with that of Captain Porter's, which he says he has never seen.
>
> *Typee* is very pleasantly written, and apparently faithful, though it must have been done from recollection. The adventures and hair-breadth escapes are highly wrought and exciting, and the whole narrative more entertaining, not so much for the style as the facts, than Robinson Crusoe. We can honestly say of this book that it is curiously charming and charmingly instructive.
>
> National Anti-Slavery Standard *VI, No 44, 2 April 1846.*

## Richard Chase   (essay date 1949)

[*Chase is an American literary critic and the author of* The American Novel and Its Tradition *(1957), an influential examination of the romantic tradition in American fiction. In the excerpt below, originally published in his* Herman Melville: A Critical Study *(1949), he discusses* Typee *as a symbolic depiction of Tommo's withdrawal into the past.*]

The hero of *Typee* presumably suffered the same kind of alienation aboard his whaler as did Redburn aboard his merchantman. He found the crew mean-spirited and "dastardly." The captain was a vengeful "Lord of the Plank." The young hero and his companion, Toby, jumped ship in the Marquesas and fled inland. From then on the story describes another kind of alienation: the more pleasurable but more terrible alienation of one who was coddled and worshiped and at the same time inscrutably held prisoner by one's benefactors. Redburn was the young man who, though poignantly remembering the past, matured and began to accept the conditions of maturity. The young hero of *Typee* withdrew into the past, his anxieties and his pleasures were archaic, and he could finally break out of the prison of the past—his own past—only by a violent and tortured assertion of a nearly paralyzed will.

Having left the ship, the young hero and his companion fought their way into the mountainous interior of the island, painfully cutting a path through growths of yellow reeds, strong as steel rods, that thickly blocked their way. They scaled steep sunlit mountains by day and retreated into damp, wild glens by night. After much suffering from hunger and fatigue, they made a nightmarishly dangerous descent into a deep gorge which they hoped was Happar

Valley and not Typee Valley—for though the Happars were rumored to be mild and friendly, the Typees were notorious for their cannibalism. As it happened, they made the wrong choice. But, surprisingly, the Typees turned out to be ostensibly as kind and temperate as possible.

The descent into the valley of Typee was a withdrawal from the world, and the valley was, for the young hero, a sanctuary containing unknown but enticing treasures. The chief enticement, which gives its character to the whole experience, was a mild, somnolent eroticism, tinged, however, with vague intimations of "frightful contingencies." The first human beings the hero saw in the valley were a naked boy and girl, the boy's arm placed fondly about the girl's shoulders.

The young hero, who had left a fatherless family at home, was accepted into a native family, with whom he lived during his four months' stay. The family consisted of Marheyo, the patriarch who had once been a splendid warrior and now tried to make the hero happy with an abundance of touchingly foolish deeds of kindness; Tinor, the affectionate matriarch who bustled about like a benevolently officious housewife; Kory-Kory, a bizarre but endlessly thoughtful young savage who was appointed to be the hero's constant attendant; and Fayaway, a beautiful girl with whom the hero soon fell in love. There were various other young men and women in the household, but the blood relationship of all of these people was equivocal: they were not said to be brothers and sisters or sons and daughters (beyond the explicit statement that Kory-Kory was the son of Marheyo).

At first the hero was painfully ill; he had a "mysterious malady" in his leg, presumably the result of an injury sustained in the long climb over the mountains. He was overcome by dark forebodings and a profound melancholy which he recognized as being far in excess of a natural response to his physical injury and for which, therefore, he could not account. The hero's low state of spirits and his paralysis of will were, however, justified by at least two outward circumstances: the Typees might yet prove to be cannibals, and Toby, who had fled over the mountains to summon help, might have met a violent end, or so, with a placid impenetrability, the natives vaguely hinted.

But on the whole the natives were gay and kindly. They ministered to the hero's needs, and Kory-Kory carried him around on his shoulders. His body was anointed every day by the young girls of the family, and soon he was able, with the help of Kory-Kory, to bathe with the girls in an idyllic lake set enchantingly in the midst of the valley and fed with fresh waters. Gradually the hero lost all sense of time and anxiety. He sank into a pleasantly hedonistic apathy. His leg improved and he began to enjoy a sort of passive happiness, a muted and continuous erotic ecstasy. Swimming with the girls, he dove under the water and playfully tried to pull them under. Fayaway, whose blue eyes and soft tawny skin enchanted him, became his constant companion. They bathed together; they lounged long hours together in a canoe paddled by Kory-Kory; or the young hero steered the canoe while Fayaway, having slipped off her mantle, unfurled it as a sail and stood gracefully in the center of the canoe, her straight body serving

as a mast. He admired Fayaway; he admired the natives and their way of life, finding "the tranquillizing influences of beautiful scenery and the exhibition of human life under so novel and charming an aspect" a great consolation. And he admired himself; his own beloved image appealed to him with persistent eroticism. He came to feel that he was quite "the belle of the season, in the pride of her beauty and power"; and the charming, naïve natives, who reacted as surely as reflexes to his impulses, became less real external objects than extensions of his own personality. When he had first joined the household of Marheyo, Kory-Kory had insisted on feeding poi to the young hero with his own fingers. It was an appropriately symbolic act, for the hero, with a sad gaiety, was reliving his childhood in terms of the entrancingly fitting symbolic objects of which Typee Valley so expertly consisted.

But the sense of guilt and foreboding which the indulgences of his archaic emotions gave the hero could not be entirely avoided. They became sharply recrudescent when the natives insisted that he should be tattooed; it was a religious rite whose sanctions no one could do without. But Karky, the tattoo artist, with his slender instrument tipped with a shark's tooth and his small wooden mallet, aroused in the hero a deep revulsion, which proceeded far more from a fear that his body might be mutilated than from a realization that the pagan rite of tattooing would be sacrilege for a Christian. Shortly after meeting Karky, the pain in his leg returned so violently that he felt "unmanned." And this calamity was followed by the chance discovery that three tapa bundles which hung from the ridgepole of Marheyo's house contained three human heads, one of a white man, two of natives.

The hero's escape from Typee Valley was sudden and violent. An Australian whaler, in need of men, put a boat ashore, and with a terrible effort the hero limped down to the beach, eluded the hostile natives, taking advantage of a dispute among them as to whether he should be allowed to go or not, and leaving Marheyo, Kory-Kory, and Fayaway weeping in the surf, managed to fall exhausted into the boat.

In *Redburn* the young man, still a boy, learned to master the feelings aroused in him by hunger, discomfort, excrement, obscenity, cruelty, death, and alienation from his kind; and he began to see that somehow human life—personality and society—had to be based upon these things. It was an act of growing up. In *Typee* the young man performed a further act. With a great effort and much suffering, he withdrew into the recesses of his own infantile sexuality and then escaped to a higher level. He feared cannibalism in general; but specifically he feared castration. This was the real content of the nameless foreboding which he felt when he descended into Typee Valley and when he was about to escape. He did not feel this fear during the time when he was able to give himself over to the mild eroticism of the valley. To leave the archaic level of personality and civilization represented by Typee Valley was to face and suffer and overcome the fears which accompanied maturing sexuality. This figure, the hero suffering the fear of castration, became a common one in Melville's books. We can call him "the Maimed Man in the Glen"; and we shall discover him again in Ahab, in Pierre Glendinning (whose surname means "dweller in a glen"), in the "invalid Titan" of *The Confidence Man,* and in other of Melville's characters.

The hero's attachment to Fayaway cannot be regarded as a completely sexualized one. She remained a wraith of youthful erotic fantasies, as her name indicated. From the departing whaleboat the hero threw a bolt of colored cloth to Fayaway—an intolerably callous act, the reader thinks, until he begins to reflect that the young man, having taken his decisive step, now sincerely and perhaps correctly regarded Fayaway as a child or a wraith, not as a mature lover. It is by no means clear that the hero's act hurt Fayaway. . . .

The young man who had observed society in the forecastles of a merchantman and a whaler and who had seen the injustices of industrial civilization in Liverpool had begun to develop political ideas. Longing for the ideal society, where affairs are conducted with compassion and noble simplicity, he was very much impressed by the Typees. He compared Western civilization unfavorably with Typee Valley, and openly deplored the inevitable arrival of French military forces with their cruelty, corruption, and syphilis and the missionaries with their self-righteous hypocrisy. "Civilization," he decided, "does not engross all the virtues of humanity." The Typees

> deal more kindly with each other, and are more humane, than many who study essays on virtue and benevolence, and who repeat every night that beautiful prayer breathed first by the lips of the divine and gentle Jesus. I will frankly declare that after passing a few weeks in this valley of the Marquesas, I formed a higher estimate of human nature than I had ever before entertained.

In Typee the young man found mild and dignified chiefs but no police and no courts of law. There was, to be sure, an extensive system of taboo, but it was seldom oppressive and did not interfere with the harmony of daily life. The natives generally conducted themselves according to an indwelling sense of virtue and honor which kept them free of the weight of social protocol and confusion. They were, in the best sense, "carefree." Eros, far from being the malign demon that often goads and worries civilized society, conspired harmoniously with the social institutions of Typee.

Still, as the young man realized, it was part of the process of growing up to force oneself to grow beyond the Typee society. There was an unintegrated part of Typee which its bland social institutions and its benevolence either ignored or could not control: cannibalism. And cannibalism might at any moment overturn and destroy Typee society. In Typee, Eros was an emasculated god and so was its political god; he was a god who remained a child, who was content to make his social arrangements at too low a level of maturity, a god who could not face, understand, and accept the tragic realities or the larger ecstasies of human life. The tendency of Western civilization was to take cognizance of these tragic realities and to try, at least, to arrange social institutions accordingly. And so the young

man had to return to it, though he was so saddened at the thought of the undeniable advantages of Typee society.

As the author of *Mardi* intimated, "no past time is lost time." The past must be studied and understood, to keep it from playing on one its monstrous tricks of seduction. For those who could not understand their own past, or themselves as products of it, there was the danger that they would be betrayed into thinking that a reversion was really a standing in the present or a motion toward the future. In *Moby-Dick* the young man at the helm of the *Pequod* was to feel this danger one night when the crew was boiling blubber in the vats and the ship seemed to be "freighted with savages, and laden with fire, and burning a corpse, and plunging into the blackness of darkness." The young man succumbed to a momentary drowsiness and lost consciousness in an inexpressible dream. Then

> starting from a brief, standing sleep, I was horribly conscious of something fatally wrong. The jaw-bone tiller smote my side, which leaned against it; in my ears was the low hum of sails just beginning to shake in the wind. . . . I could see no compass before me to steer by . . . Nothing seemed before me but a jet gloom, now and then made ghastly by flashes of redness. Uppermost was the impression, that whatever swift, rushing thing I stood on was not so much bound for any haven ahead as rushing from all havens astern.

The young man realized, with a "stark, bewildered feeling, as of death," that in his sleep he had turned around so that he faced astern and that in letting go of the tiller he had almost brought the ship up into the wind and capsized her. He had lost his bearings, for, facing backward, he could not see the compass. Momentarily the relation of past, present, and future was confused. He feared the present and the probably disastrous future; even more he feared the past, under whose sudden influence he had turned around and almost turned the little world of the *Pequod* with him: he was gripped at this moment, as D. H. Lawrence says in his study of *Moby-Dick,* with the "horror of reversion, of undoing." In a later episode the same confusion of time is again symbolized: the *Pequod's* compass is magnetically inverted during an electric storm in the night, and the next morning finds the ship running precisely opposite to the course that had been set for her.

*Typee* was Melville's most adequately symbolized study of the past. But the memory of the past was not always accompanied by horror. In a love poem, written in later times, Melville could use such a wistful image as:

> I yearn, I yearn, reverting turn,
> My heart it streams in wake astern.

Again he could call himself and Ned Bunn (a mythical companion) "Typee-truants" who once as "pleasure-hunters broke loose"

> for our pantheistic ports:
> Marquesas and glenned isles that be
> Authentic Edens in a Pagan sea.

And with mildly sardonic wisdom he could indulge his

nostalgia for the "authentic Edens" and at the same time observe that "Adam advances.""

*Richard Chase, in his* Herman Melville: A Critical Study, *The Macmillan Company, 1949, 305 p.*

## Joseph J. Firebaugh   (essay date 1954)

[*In the following essay, Firebaugh examines Melville's use of irony and humor in* Typee.]

In all the excitement about Herman Melville, geniality has lost the day. The puzzled brow has vanquished the wreathéd smile. Confidence in Melville's profundity has kept his ingratiating humor in a sort of critical quarantine. Quarantine, fortunately, works two ways: genially, the ship rides out the period of isolation, the crew rejoicing that the pestilent critical miasma enveloping the town has not yet drifted out over the harbor—glad, too, that the ship is not unvisited by genial spirits from the shore.

Let us push our figure a little farther and swim out to the ship with these genial swarms, shunning the eye of our critical missionaries. Reveling aboard ship, "within a biscuit's toss of the merry land," let us inform our host that the land is not quite so merry as it might be, because it lacks those who find joy in the simple sailorly humor which, by altering a couple of words in a common phrase, likens a ship's biscuit to a stone. It would extend even a Herman Melville's ingenuity to maintain the present figure throughout an essay. Abandoning ship, then, let us do what we can to urge the port authorities to lift their quarantine of a certain young-animal rebelliousness which certainly may question, but will hardly threaten, constituted authority—not, at least, during the present voyage.

A salty, sailorly humor—a commonplace humor—a rather unsubtle humor—this is the first impression of the humor of *Typee*. But once we have said that it is commonplace and unsubtle, we feel how wrong we are. It is not the humor of a boy ten or twelve years old, making his first clumsy—and, to an adult, uncomfortable—essays in irony. And yet it is reminiscent of him. To that boy have been added a few years of adventure, a couple of long voyages, and, therefore, experience of forbearance and hardship and endurance—which experience, though it may have tempered the rebellious spirit, has in the process given it the double-edged blade of irony. Irony will be for the mature man a way of hacking through the over-luxuriant hollow reedy growth of life's event; for the time it is used with the clumsy uncritical lightheartedness of youth. Yet in both the irony and the manner of its use, certain depths, certain perceptions, force themselves upon our attention.

What do sailors most endure? And what, therefore, is the subject of their constant irony? Food. Food first of all. There it is, in supremely inferior quality, three times a day. On the captain's table, it may occasionally be a rooster fresh from the ship's chicken-coop, though even then it will not be a very choice rooster. "His attenuated body will be laid out upon the captain's table next Sunday, and long before night will be buried, with all the usual ceremonies, beneath that worthy individual's vest." So nearly a

corpse is this cock already, indeed, that a dinner of his flesh suggests only a funeral rite. But this spare cadaver is nothing, as food, to what the sailors endure.

> The owners, who officiate as caterers for the voyage, supply the larder with an abundance of dainties. Delicate morsels of beef and pork, cut on scientific principles from every part of the animal, and of all conceivable shapes and sizes, are carefully packed in salt, and stored away in barrels; affording a never-ending variety in their different degrees of toughness; and in the peculiarities of their saline properties. Choice old water too, decanted into stout six-barrel casks, and two pints of which is allowed every day to each soul on board; together with ample store of sea-bread, previously reduced to a state of petrifaction, with a view to preserve it either from decay or consumption in the ordinary mode, are likewise provided for the nourishment and gastronomic enjoyment of the crew.

About such ironical treatment of bad food, be it a scrawny rooster or miserable salt-beef, there is a certain mock-heroic irony—the incongruity of excessively elaborate language used to describe trivial objects of everyday vexation. The rooster is not eaten, but "buried, with all the usual ceremonies"; the "choice old water" is not poured, but "decanted into stout six-barrel casks." Polysyllabic humor is a young man's humor, for it requires sympathy—geniality—from its audience, and a certain freshness of linguistic response. Small children see the fun in long words. Unless in a convivial mood, adults often don't. Melville loves to use such words, both for their own sake and for their sheer incongruity. Sea-bread, "reduced to a state of petrifaction," provides for "nourishment and gastronomic enjoyment." Bad food always excites Melville to this ironic, polysyllabic, incongruity:

> . . . rummaging once more beneath his garment, he [Toby] produced a small handful of something so soft, pulpy, and discoloured, that for a few moments he was as much puzzled as myself to tell by what possible instrumentality such a villainous compound had become engendered in his bosom. I can only describe it as a hash of soaked bread and bits of tobacco, brought to a dough consistency by the united agency of perspiration and rain.

The "instrumentality" and "agency" of "perspiration and rain"—one ventures to suggest *precipitation*—have "engendered" more than a "villainous compound"; they combine to produce a young man's prose, a humor which only an excessive sober-sidedness will rob of its geniality.

If making a meal on a stringy rooster or a miserable hash of biscuit and tobacco excites such mock-heroics, what of that other awful taking of food, cannibalism? In dealing with it, Melville is often as genial as with biscuit or with fowl. Cannibals become "unnatural gourmands, taking it into their heads to make a convivial meal of a poor devil." Thus, before he has met the Typees; afterwards, although he is aware of "that fearful death which, under all these smiling appearances might yet menace," he is able to argue with Toby that "a more humane, gentlemanly, and amiable set of epicures do not probably exist in the Pacific." When confronted with the actual evidence of cannibalism, he abandons the humor of incongruity for sheer horror; but the horror has all along been implicit in the humor.

The ambivalence implied in the taking of nourishment, suggested in the imaginary banquet/funeral of the cock, recurs when Melville describes the slaughter of pigs for a savage banquet.

> Such is the summary style in which the Typees convert perverse-minded and rebellious hogs into the most docile and amiable pork; a morsel of which placed on the tongue melts like a soft smile from the lips of beauty.

As if it were not incongruity enough, to speak of an animal in terror of death as "perverse-minded and rebellious," or of a morsel of pork as melting "like a soft smile from the lips of beauty," Melville proceeds to greater incongruity, a virtually sacrilegious one:

> The hapless porker [—and even the most genial of us must really be excused from admiring that phrase, which smacks vilely of nineteenth-century journalism—] whose fate I have just rehearsed, was not the only one who suffered on that memorable day. Many a dismal grunt, many an imploring squeak, proclaimed what was going on throughout the whole extent of the valley: and I verily believe the first-born of every litter perished before the setting of that fatal sun.

The hideous implications of that last clause need to be stated to be believed. Prepared for by the incongruity of "imploring squeak," it coolly implies in Biblical language the cannibalism of the human race—the *methodical* cannibalism—almost indeed the unjust vengeful cannibalism of one race upon another. The point of view ironically slips from that of the pig—"imploring"—to that of the indifferent executioner—"squeak"; from that of priest—"verily"—to that of sacrificial victim—"perished." Devourer and devoured shift, change, merge; one man's meat is another man's flesh. Where is the geniality in all this? Exactly there: horror become humor and humor horror; death, life; and life, death. Awareness keeps Melville, even as a young man, from being the fool at the feast; he enjoys the food, never ignoring what he devours.

Nor does this humor imply a passive, placid acceptance of injustice. Just as awareness prevents hypocrisy at one point, so it protests indifference at another. And it does this always with an irony that denotes protest if not rebellion.

> A valiant warrior doubtless, but a prudent one too, was this same Rear-Admiral Du Petit Thouars. Four heavy, double-banked frigates and three corvettes to frighten a parcel of naked heathens into subjection.

Such ironic commentary on the treatment of the savage by the civilized—either French or missionary—is common in *Typee.* The arrogant and hypocritical exercise of power over the powerless exists also in the relationships between captain and his crew, and leads Melville's hero to desert.

I knew that our worthy captain, who felt such a paternal solicitude for the welfare of his crew, would not willingly consent that one of his best hands should encounter the perils of a sojourn among the natives of a barbarous island; and I was certain that in the event of my disappearance, his fatherly anxiety would prompt him to offer, by way of a reward, yard upon yard of gaily printed calico for my apprehension. He might even have appreciated my services at the value of a musket, in which case I felt perfectly certain that the whole population of the bay would be immediately upon my track, incited by the prospect of so magnificent a bounty.

The irony again is that of a boy—"our worthy captain" and his "fatherly anxiety." To it, however, we find added the effect of incongruity—"yard upon yard" of calico, a phrase suggesting in context a false show of lavish abundance; and anticlimax: "He might even have appreciated my services at the value of a musket," which, though the cost would be sufficiently trivial to the captain, would be "magnificent bounty" enough to set the whole population to searching for one poor powerless sailor. So the relations of venal mankind. The captain gives, but takes away even as he gives; his oration, upon allowing shore leave, is designed to rob the sailors of their pleasure in going ashore. His pettiness in the face of powerlessness Melville is able to treat with some humor: he speaks of "the holyday so auspiciously announced by the skipper."

The self-interest of the human race leads Toby and Tom to flee their ship; but self-interest follows them to the Valley of the Typees. Their fear, upon meeting a simple naked boy and girl, leads them to the most extravagantly comic conduct.

> At last they [the native couple] suffered us to approach so near to them that we were enabled to throw the cotton cloth across their shoulders, giving them to understand that we entertained the highest possible regard for them.

> The frightened pair now stood still, whilst we endeavoured to make them comprehend the nature of our wants. In doing this Toby went through with a complete series of pantomimic illustrations—opening his mouth from ear to ear, and thrusting his fingers down his throat, grinding his teeth and rolling his eyes about, till I verily believe the poor creatures took us for a couple of white cannibals who were about to make a meal of them.

The irony of mutual distrust of man for man, which Melville was to develop so fully in *The Confidence Man,* here takes a simpler form. Civilized man, in his distrust of the savage, adopts the very conduct that can only cause the savage to distrust him:

> . . . my companion broke out into a pantomimic abhorrence of Typee, and immeasurable love for the particular valley in which we were; our guides all the while gazing uneasily at one another as if at a loss to account for our conduct.

Later, when they find the truth that the tribe they have

met are Typee rather than Happar, they hypocritically make a quick change:

> In all these denunciations [of the Happars] my companion and I acquiesced, while we extolled the character of the warlike Typees. To be sure our panegyrics were somewhat laconic, consisting of repetition of that name, united with the potent adjective "Morkartee [*good*]."

The hypocrisy of the young sailors is to be sure only sensible under the circumstances. The treatment of the theme is light, deft, humorous. A skillful raconteur such as Melville could do much with the scene, re-enacting it in parlor or nursery. The serious commentary on human life is there, however, and is not the least of the elements invoking laughter. There is the same irony, the same polysyllabic humor, the same knowledge of human weakness that we have already observed. Light as the scene is, we sense its grim foundation in human fear and distrust.

Comparing and contrasting familiar with unfamiliar, a common trick of the travel books, Melville borrows for his purpose of humor by incongruity. Civilized words are applied to uncivilized situations. A medicine-man is alluded to as a "leech," that contemptuous colloquialism functioning as ironic commentary on quackery wherever found, in savagery or civilization. In describing Fayaway's becoming nudity, Melville evidently burlesques the prose of contemporary fashion-magazines:

> Fayaway—I must avow the fact—for the most part clung to the primitive and summer garb of Eden. But how becoming the costume! It showed her fine figure to the best possible advantage; and nothing could have been better adapted to her peculiar style of beauty.

Melville ridicules not only the prose of the fashion plates, but also the fashions themselves. In describing Tom's costume in Typee, he writes:

> A few folds of yellow tappa, tucked about my waist, descended to my feet in the style of a lady's petticoat, only I did not have recourse to those voluminous paddings in the rear with which our gentle dames are in the habit of augmenting the sublime rotundity of their figures.

"Sublime rotundity"—such deliberate bombast, such bland association of the ideal "sublime" with fleshly "rotundity," pushes satire by incongruity almost to its farthest extreme.

Incongruity supports Melville's primitivism; through it, he points out the advantages of savagery over civilization.

> There you might have seen a throng of young females, not filled with envyings of each other's charms, nor displaying the ridiculous affectations of gentility, nor yet moving in whalebone corsets, like so many automatons, but free, inartificially happy, and unconstrained.

Women, however, are women, wherever they may be, and Melville is not one to make them over to fit his primitivistic notions. On an occasion of crisis in Typee Valley,

> the women, who had congregated in the groves,

set up the most violent clamours, as they invariably do here as elsewhere on every occasion of excitement and alarm, with a view to tranquillizing their own minds and disturbing other people.

Nor are women's foibles the only ones satirized:

> as in all cases of hurry and confusion in every part of the world, a number of individuals kept hurrying to and fro with amazing vigour and perseverance, doing nothing themselves, and hindering others.

So Melville satirizes man: by placing civilized manners against a backdrop of primitive life to attain perspective by incongruity; and thus, by showing how certain human foibles are to be found in both civilized and primitive societies, he avoids the worst excesses of a Rousseauistic adulation of primitive man.

He is capable, moreover, of making occasional fun of both the primitivist dream and of civilized gentility, juxtaposing them with fine ironic incongruity of effect. A great native feast of raw fish is taking place:

> Let no one imagine, however, that the lovely Fayaway was in the habit of swallowing great vulgar-looking fishes: oh, no; with her beautiful small hand she would clasp a delicate, little, golden-hued love of a fish, and eat it as elegantly and as innocently as though it were a Naples biscuit. But alas! it was after all a raw fish; and all I can say is, that Fayaway ate it in a more ladylike manner than any other girl of the valley.

Lord Byron disliked to see a woman eat. This fastidious affection anticipated the gentility which Melville ridicules—ridicules by shuddering delicately himself. Beneath the delicacy, though, is the ambiguity which we have mentioned. Eating implies cannibalism, whether in Fayaway or in a civilized lady at her tea-table.

In praising women, Melville also ridicules them. Old Tinor, the type of bustling housewife, enables Melville to look both ways. She

> was, the mistress of the family, and a notable housewife, and a most industrious old lady she was. If she did not understand the art of making jellies, jams, custards, tea-cakes, and such-like trashy affairs, she was profoundly skilled in the mysteries of preparing 'amar,' 'poee-poee,' and 'kokoo,' with other substantial matters. She was a genuine busy-body; bustling about the house like a country landlady at an unexpected arrival; for ever giving the young girls tasks to perform, which the little hussies as often neglected. . . .

> To tell the truth, Kory-Kory's mother was the only industrious person in all the valley of Typee; and she could not have employed herself more actively had she been left an exceedingly muscular and destitute widow, with an inordinate supply of young children, in the bleakest part of the civilized world. There was not the slightest necessity for the greater portion of the labour performed by the old lady: but she seemed to work from some irresistible impulse.

Some persons will work wherever they are, and however

unnecessary their effort. Compulsive behavior may not have been named, but it had been observed. Primitivist that Melville often was, he saw the underlying similarities of man wherever found; and so he saw in the primitivist thesis no easy answer to the problems of man.

Sexual arrangements in Typee Valley afforded Melville a fine opportunity for perspective by incongruity. He is more completely the primitivist, more fully the rebel, in dealing with these matters than in dealing with most other subjects. His humor on this subject depends again to some degree upon verbal management. When he felt the danger that his irony would evoke anger, he seems often to have fallen back on verbal tone to convey that irony. For, as he says, "Married women, to be sure! —I know better than to offend them." He writes:

> Previously to seeing the Dancing Widows I had little idea that there were any matrimonial relations subsisting in Typee, and I should as soon have thought of a Platonic affection being cultivated between the sexes, as of the solemn connection of man and wife.

In those two words—"solemn connection"—there is as fine an ironic commentary on marriage as one might produce. For it implies the sober introspective self-assured fulfillment of early matrimony, the placid interdependence of the matrimony of middle life, the indifference of later life, the permeating happiness/unhappiness of the state in all its phases, as well as the ritualistic, institutionalized gentility of the arrangement in its economic and social status. Melville's genius was able to find just the right pair of words in which to compress all that complex of meaning. Though in such matters there is no proof, our reading does his views no violence. The young rebel knew how simultaneously to reveal and conceal his rebellion. He has, as he says, "more than one reason to believe that tedious courtships are unknown in the valley of Typee," and the deletion of that ambiguous sentence from the American edition shows that his rebellion did not go unobserved. It was sometimes more direct, although it usually kept a becoming geniality:

> As nothing stands in the way of a separation, the matrimonial yoke sits easily and lightly, and a Typee wife lives on very pleasant and sociable terms with her husbands.

Perhaps the one institution more sacred to nineteenth-century America than matrimony was religion; and although Melville is if anything more outspoken in criticizing it directly, his humorous treatment of the fact that "the penalty of the Fall presses very lightly upon the valley of Typee" employs the same methods of rebellion. Kory-kory, the hero's guardian and valet, is his guide in matters religious and moral, comparable to some contemporary orator:

> Kory-kory seemed to experience so heartfelt a desire to infuse into our minds proper views . . . that, assisted in his endeavours by the little knowledge of the language we had acquired, he actually made us comprehend a considerable part of what he said. To facilitate our correct apprehension of his meaning, he at first condensed

his ideas into the smallest possible compass. . . .

> As he continued his harangue, however, Kory-kory, in emulation of our more polished orators, began to launch out rather diffusely into other branches of his subject, enlarging probably upon the moral reflections it suggested. . . .

If through Kory-kory, the oratory of the era is ridiculed, so is the rhetoric of the Bible paraphrased and burlesqued. Kory-kory speaks of a departed chief as "paddling his way to the realms of bliss and breadfruit"; and here we have another instance of Melville's characteristic humorous thrust—as decorous in phrase as a Gift Book of the decade, as entirely suitable for the eye of a young lady; and yet, in its mockery of the phrase "milk and honey," flippantly indicative of an underlying skepticism. The skepticism is more startlingly outspoken—although still phrased with ambiguous decorum—in the passage describing a sort of native Stonehenge:

> These structures bear every indication of a very high antiquity, and Kory-kory, who was my authority in all matters of scientific research, gave me to understand that they were coeval with the creation of the world; that the great gods themselves were the builders; and that they would endure until time shall be no more. Kory-kory's prompt explanation, and his attributing the work to a divine origin, at once convinced me that neither he nor the rest of his countrymen knew anything about them.

Mehevi, in explaining the taboo to Tom, employed "a variety of most extraordinary words, which, from their amazing length and sonorousness, I have every reason to believe were of a theological nature." When they did not excite his anger, as the missionaries so often did, matters theological excited Melville's risibilities. And his laughter, though mocking, had a quiet urbanity about it remarkable in so young a man.

> They are either too lazy or too sensible to worry themselves about abstract points of religious belief. While I was among them, they never held any synods or councils to settle the principles of their faith in an ill-favoured god, with a long bottle-nose, and fat shapeless arms crossed upon his breast; whilst others worshipped an image which, having no likeness either in heaven or on earth, could hardly be called an idol. As the islanders always maintained a discreet reserve with regard to my own peculiar views on religion, I thought it would be excessively ill-bred in me to pry into theirs.

Religious tolerance, seen as a quality of gentlemanliness, brings into ironic juxtaposition two conflicting aspects of nineteenth-century culture: religiosity and gentility. Anyone who really felt this tension must have been upset by this passage. Such humor could have appealed only to persons who had some urbanity as well as some of Melville's salty rebelliousness against convention. It would require the same sort of person to appreciate Melville's mockery of the self-righteous and horrified religious man's observation of a native's abusive treatment of a god:

When one of the inferior order of natives could show such contempt for a venerable and decrepit God of the Groves, what the state of religion must be among the people in general is easily to be imagined. In truth, I regard the Typees as a back-slidden generation. They are sunk in religious sloth, and require a spiritual revival. A long prosperity of bread-fruit and cocoanuts has rendered them remiss in the performance of their higher obligations. The wood-rot malady is spreading among the idols—the fruit upon their altars is becoming offensive—the temples themselves need re-thatching—the tattooed clergy are altogether too light-hearted and lazy—and their flocks are going astray.

Such burlesque sermonizing could perhaps have deceived some and angered others; but the heartier spirits of the age were probably delighted with the utterance of polished proprieties to conceal a probing skepticism.

Much of Melville's humor, which seems to involve little or no ambiguity, appears on close scrutiny to be something more than a lively anecdote to be enacted in the nursery, as in this account of native dramatizing and ritualizing of work:

> So seldom do they ever exert themselves, that when they do work they seem determined that so meritorious an action shall not escape the observation of those around. If, for example, they have occasion to remove a stone a little distance, which perhaps might be carried by two able-bodied men, a whole swarm gather about it, and, after a vast deal of palavering, lift it up among them, every one struggling to get hold of it, and bear it off yelling and panting as if accomplishing some mighty achievement.

The same kind of primitive response to work occurs in the charming incident of Narnoo and the coconuts. When Tom asks for the coconuts, still growing on the tree, Narnoo at first "feigns astonishment at the apparent absurdity of the request"; then "the strange emotions depicted on his countenance soften down into one of humorous resignation to my will." After considerable play-acting of this sort, constructing almost an entire mock-heroic drama of difficulty realized and conquered by the ingenuity of man, Narnoo easily scampers up the tree and gets the fruit. Melville tells the incident in the historical present—a fact which may indicate that he had related it often in the homes of his friends. Our delight in this story is based, fundamentally, on the antithesis of primitive and civilized cultures. Having made of work a grim necessity, to be shunned whenever possible—retire at fifty and enjoy life!—civilized man stands lost in joy and admiration of a people who make either a convivial game or a pantomime of a necessary job of work. This humor has something paternal and patronizing about it, as when a father's heart goes out to his children, whom he sees making a game of the activity which is his daily exigency. It is this tolerance, this humanity, which makes the humor of Melville's *Typee* so rare and so delectable.

"Truth," Melville points out, "loves to be centrally located." (And there he is up to his old trick of incongruity, in taking this phrase of real-estate agents and applying it to

dialectic.) Melville knew full well that primitivism was no answer to the problems of civilized man. With becoming sailorly geniality he laughs at the primitive even while admiring it, as a father might lovingly ridicule his children's sober play. Even while laughing at it, moreover, he makes it the basis of serious reflections about his own adult and civilized sobriety. There is nothing startlingly new about making the primitive a basis for satire on civilization. A pervasive tolerant geniality however is the special contribution of Melville's humor. It suffuses his treatment both of savage custom and civilized foible. When he is genuinely angry, the humor sometimes becomes savagely ironic: the rebel in Melville sometimes conquers the humanist and the humorist. But in the main his richly tolerant humor is the palliative of his rebellion. Not that the two can be separated. A less humorous man would have been less of a rebel. Confidence takes its toll of geniality.

*Joseph J. Firebaugh, "Humorist as Rebel: The Melville of 'Typee'," in* Nineteenth Century Fiction, *Vol. 9, No. 2, September, 1954, pp. 108-120.*

## Bartlett C. Jones   (essay date 1959)

[*In the following essay, Jones finds elements of American frontier humor in* Typee.]

The question of fiction versus literal truth in Herman Melville's first novel, *Typee* (1846), has been debated for more than a century. Incredulous reactions have been ascribed to Melville's ignorance of the South Seas and his use of romantic and dramatic exaggeration; but a major obstacle to an acceptance of *Typee* as being essentially accurate remains largely unexplored. The work also employs the tall tale, braggadocio, exaggerated language, rustic figures of speech, understatement in the face of danger, and discussion of visceral responses that we associate with American frontier humor. These devices must have been difficult for nineteenth century reviewers to accept in a book purporting to state facts. When frontier humor clashed with sensibilities matured in European literary traditions, the rapport between author and reader must have suffered. And the essential truth of *Typee* would be less likely to emerge, particularly because Melville's debt to the frontier was considerable.

Before the narrator of *Typee* sets foot on shore, he passes along several tall tales concerning the prolonged duration of whaling voyages. Some sailors receive "bottled milk" when they embark and return "very respectable middle-aged gentlemen." A fanciful account of an unlucky ship buttresses Melville's contention that no whaler sails for home without a full cargo:

> I heard of one whaler, which after many years' absence was given up for lost. The last that had been heard of her was a shadowy report of her having touched at some of those unstable islands in the far Pacific, whose eccentric wanderings are carefully noted in each new edition of the South Sea charts. After a long interval, however, the Perseverance—for that was her name—was spoken somewhere in the vicinity of the ends of the earth, cruising along as leisurely as ever, her sails all bepatched and bequilted with rope-

yarns, her spars fished with old pipe staves, and her rigging knotted and spliced in every possible direction. Her crew was composed of some twenty venerable Greenwich-pensioner-looking old salts, who just managed to hobble about deck. The ends of all the running ropes, with the exception of the signal halyards and poop-down-haul, were rove through snatchblocks, and led to the capstan or windlass, so that not a yard was braced or a sail set without the assistance of machinery.

Her hull was encrusted with barnacles, which completely encased her. Three pet sharks followed in her wake, and every day came alongside to regale themselves from the contents of the cook's bucket, which were pitched over to them. A vast shoal of bonetas and albicores always kept her company.

. . . I suppose she is still regularly tacking twice in the twenty-four hours somewhere off Buggerry Island, or the Devil's-Tail Peak.

This is, perhaps, the most extreme tale in the narrative.

Braggadocio and the tall tale are blended by the helmsman who attributes animistic longing to the ship. When the captain finds fault with the way the "Dolly" was being steered, he replies:

I'm as good a helmsman as ever put hand to spoke; but none of us can steer the old lady now. We can't keep her full and bye, sir: watch her ever so close, she will fall off; and then, sir, when I put the helm down so gently and try to coax her to the work, she won't take it kindly, but will fall round off again; and it's all because she knows the land is under the lee, sir, and she won't go any more to windward.

Melville applauds the helmsman and accepts his explanation. When they reach the island, the captain tries to discourage the men from going ashore by recounting the fate, real or imagined, which other sailors had suffered at the hands of the natives. Later, a sailor exclaims:

But you don't bounce me out of my liberty, old chap, for all your yarns; for I would go ashore if every pebble on the beach was a live coal, and every stick a gridiron, and the cannibals stood ready to broil me on landing.

Melville's sympathies are entirely with the rebellious sailor and, thus, he is identified with tall tales and braggadocio before he goes ashore and his adventures begin.

The description of the flight employs exaggeration and rustic figures of speech, Toby, Melville's companion, jumps a brook "with a bound like a young roe"; they are confronted by a patch of reeds "as tough and stubborn as so many rods of steel"; and getting through them is so difficult that a "bullfrog might as well have tried to work a passage through the teeth of a comb." Another use of frontier humor, during the flight, has been pointed out in a recent book. Speaking of Melville's use of understatement, Edward H. Rosenberry says:

His understatement is not spread abroad through his pages, like the exaggeration, in little

auxiliary dabs and patches, nor does it lean so heavily on the precedents of popular humor. The character of Toby is about as close as Melville comes to the traditional understater of folklore, who gets his laughs by being casual in the teeth of terror. During the gruelling descent of the precipice into the valley of Typee, with life hanging repeatedly at the end of a vine swaying limply over the abyss, Toby comes out "in his usual dry tone" with such remarks as, "Mate, do me the kindness not to fall until I get out of your way"; or, "As soon as you have diverted yourself sufficiently, I would advise you to proceed."

Exaggeration and rustic figures of speech persist after the comrades reach the valley, but Toby's casualness in the face of danger appears only once. When the natives build a fire and begin to dance around it, the narrator asks Toby for an explanation. He replies, "Oh, nothing, getting the fire ready, I suppose." Toby goes on to say that the fire is to cook them both, that they have been fattened especially, and that he, Toby, never jokes. As four natives creep toward them, Toby gloats because his prediction seems close to fulfillment.

Much of Melville's exaggeration, while describing his stay in Typee valley, cannot be explained by the European romantic tradition or the desire to increase suspense. The hyperbole of American folk speech appears frequently. After the massaging of his leg, Melville reports that it was "much in the same condition as a rump-steak after undergoing the castigating process which precedes cooking." In praise of the bread fruit tree, the narrator says, "The autumnal tints of our American forests, glorious as they are, sink into nothing in comparison with this tree." When a native addresses him in English, Melville says that he could not have started more had he "been pierced simultaneously by three Happar spears," and upon viewing some stone terraces, he says that a "stronger feeling of awe came over me than if I had stood musing at the mighty base of the Pyramid of Cheops." Commonplace deeds of the natives are amplified in the same manner. One native, perceiving that "Tommo" wanted a hone, brings him "a huge rough mass of rock as big as a millstone" and another strikes a "sufficient number of blows to have demolished an entire drove of oxen" while killing a hog.

Some portraits of the natives, far from romanticizing them, employ quaint, even outrageous, rustic expressions. The tattooed stripes on Kory-Kory's face resemble "those country roads that go straight forward in defiance of all obstacles"; his mother, Tinor, bustles "like a country landlady at an unexpected arrival"; and one band of Typees suggests "a group of idlers gathered about the door of a village tavern, when the equipage of some distinguished traveller is brought round previous to his departure." Narmonee's desire for a clean shaven head and the females' use of green "papa" provoke Melville to fanciful, rustic humor. The natives use a shark's tooth for shaving, which is "about as well adapted to the purpose as a one-pronged fork for pitching hay." Narmonee's shaved head resembles "a stubble field after being gone over with a harrow." A native girl covered with green "papa" evokes the image of a "vegetable in an unripe state . . . that . . . ought to be placed out in the sun to ripen."

Frontier humor sometimes alluded to the functions of the human body. The reader's reaction can only be called visceral. Melville's description of the food aboard the "Dolly" is the first example of this device. Later, when the natives set a dish of steaming meat before "Tommo" and Toby, the latter maintains that they have been asked to eat baked baby or portions of a dead Happar's carcass. "Tommo" claims, "Emetics and lukewarm water! What a sensation in the abdominal regions!" The narrator delights in such revolting incidents as the eating of raw fish whole and his accidental swallowing of a half-dozen live flies. In each instance, Melville goes into detail and recounts his own physical sensations.

The sequel to *Typee,* entitled **"The Story of Toby,"** is short, running to less than fifteen pages. Many of the frontier comic devices, previously pointed out, do not appear; but Melville does pass along two tall tales, which he calls a "cock-and-bull story." One concerns a hermit, with horns in his forehead, who lived in a cave full of bones and acquired the reputation of a cannibal. The other prodigy is a boy, who was supposed to be well suited to the priesthood because he had a rooster's comb upon his head. (Are we to infer that priests are coxcombs?)

Demonstrating the rich vein of frontier humor in *Typee* serves a dual purpose. It may shed light on the incredulous response to the book and it appears relevant when dealing with Melville as an artist. Contrary to some current opinions, Melville did not turn to the frontier as an afterthought. His use of folk humor, as an element within a work of art, must be examined—whether we speak of the maturing artist or the enthusiastic beginner.

*Bartlett C. Jones, "American Frontier Humor in Melville's 'Typee',"* in New York Folklore Quarterly, *Vol. XV, No. 4, Winter, 1959, pp. 283-88.*

---

**An excerpt from *Typee:***

"Why, they are cannibals!" said Toby on one occasion when I eulogised the tribe.

"Granted," I replied, "but a more humane, gentlemanly, and amiable set of epicures do not probably exist in the Pacific."

*Herman Melville, in his* Typee, *Harcourt, Brace, and Company, 1920.*

---

**Donald E. Houghton    (essay date 1961)**

[*In the essay below, Houghton contends that the ending of* Typee *is weak and unbelievable.*]

The opening of chapter sixty-three of *Moby-Dick* shows Melville's awareness of the organic principle in art. He writes: "Out of the trunk, the branches grow; out of them, the twigs. So, in productive subjects, grow the chapters." In *Moby-Dick,* Melville put this principle into practice. It is a book in which all parts are related to the whole, and

fact and meaning are one. When we come to the great climactic ending of the book, we find not mere melodrama but a natural, inevitable fruition of everything which has come before. We have been so carefully prepared in advance for this ending and the details of the ending itself are so carefully presented that we easily follow the events, both on the literal and the philosophic levels. The ending of *Typee,* on the other hand, is quite a different matter. It appears to have been written hurriedly, and it strikes the reader as a confusing and arbitrary addition to, rather than an organic extension of, the main narrative.

Shortly before the opening of the last chapter of *Typee,* Tommo resolves to attempt to escape from the Typees, but he recognizes the extreme difficulty of his doing so: "I was continually surrounded by the savages; I could not stir from one house to another without being attended by some of them; and even during the hours devoted to slumber the slightest movement which I made seemed to attract the notice of those who shared the mats with me. In spite of these obstacles, however, I determined forthwith to make the attempt." We must also remember that in addition to being closely guarded, Tommo, suffering from a mysterious ailment in his leg, was "lame and feeble." Tommo says: "Shortly after Marnoo's visit I was reduced to such a state, that it was with extreme difficulty I could walk, even with the assistance of a spear, and Kory-Kory, as formerly, was obliged to carry me daily to the stream." This is Tommo's situation then at the opening of the last chapter of the book when he hears the rumor that Toby has arrived in a small boat to bargain for his release from the Typees. Tommo pleads with the Typees to be allowed to go to the beach to see his friend. The Typees' granting him permission to do so is the first of a series of unconvincing incidents which culminate in Tommo's escape.

The Typees, some fifty in number, take turns carrying Tommo on their backs while Tommo urges them "forward all the while with earnest entreaties." When they reach "the open space which lay between the groves and the sea," they see an English whale-boat "lying with her bow pointed from the shore, and only a few fathoms distant." The oars are manned by five natives from another part of the island. Tommo now sees that it is the friendly Karakoee, and not Toby, who has come to bargain for his release. Karakoee is standing out of the boat "near the edge of the water" and is trying unsuccessfully to buy Tommo's freedom from "several of the chiefs around him [Karakoee]." Tommo's hope is that he can somehow elude the natives who accompany him, traverse the open space between himself and the water, get by the unfriendly chiefs who surround Karahoee, get into the boat, and move away from the shore with Karahoee before the natives can act. Here is how he accomplishes this.

Tommo shouts to Karahoee to come to him, but Karakoee has troubles of his own and answers that "the islanders had threatened to pierce him [Karakoee] with their spears, if he stirred a foot towards me [Tommo]." The natives with Tommo allow him to advance further toward the boat, although they have no intention of letting him escape. He is still "surrounded by a dense throng of natives, several of whom had their hands upon me, and more than one javelin was threateningly pointed at me." Finally, thirty yards from Karakoee, the natives compel Tommo to sit down upon the ground, "while they still retained their hold upon my arms." Meanwhile, the natives at the boat not only reject the valuable prizes Karakoee offers them in exchange for Tommo's freedom but seem "bent upon driving him into the sea." Tommo interprets this aggressive behavior as "new proof of the same fixed determination of purpose they had all along manifested with regard to me. . . ." Now Tommo's situation at this point would seem to be hopeless, but not at all. Although surrounded by natives (some of whom have hold of his arm), handicapped by his bad leg, and sitting on the ground, Tommo exerts all his strength and "shaking myself free from the grasp of those who held me, I sprung upon my feet and rushed towards Karakoee."

At this crucial point Tommo does not tell us how the natives guarding him react to his sudden escape from their grasp. Instead, he abruptly shifts our attention to the natives surrounding Karakoee. When they see that Tommo has made a break in their direction, they "raise a simultaneous shout, and pressing upon Karakoee, they menaced him with furious gestures, and actually forced him into the sea." We might now reasonably expect Tommo to tell of his own arrival at the water's edge, but instead he gives us still more information about Karakoee's predicament. Karakoee, retreating from the natives who are threatening him and standing nearly to his waist in the surf, "endeavored to pacify them; but at length, fearful that they would do him some fatal violence, he beckoned to his comrades to pull in at once, and take him into the boat." Surely *now*, we think, Tommo will arrive at the boat. But no. When Tommo turns our attention from Karakoee back to himself, we find that he has apparently not moved a step from those guarding him. On the contrary, we find that at the very moment he sprang from them, they began to fight among themselves, "wounds were given, and blood flowed," and instead of his moving from *them*, everyone, except Marheyo, Kory-Kory, and Fayaway (the first reference to *her* in the chapter), has moved away from *Tommo*. Despite his earlier statement that he had "rushed" toward Karakoee, Tommo has not rushed anywhere. Now, for the second time, he decides to make a dash for the boat: "I saw that now or never was the moment." We should think so!

Once at the water's edge, Tommo will still have to face the hostile group of natives who have been giving Karakoee a bad time. Surely they will prevent Tommo from getting into the boat and leaving with Karakoee. But we find they pose no problem at all, for Melville has removed them as if by magic. Tommo says: "Clasping my hands together, I looked imploringly at Marheyo, and moved towards the now almost deserted beach." Tommo then makes it to the water, gives one parting embrace to Fayaway, and climbs into the boat. In place of the belligerent natives he has just whisked off the beach, Melville now posits a group of friendly ones, mostly women, who follow Tommo into the water. (The women are evidently more interested in Tommo's departure than in the bloody battle their men are fighting a little more than thirty yards away.) Our sense of urgency by now dissipated by Melville's arbitrary

manipulation of time, as well as events, we are not surprised that once in the boat Tommo and Karakoee do not make a quick getaway. They delay their departure further by distributing to the friendly people in the water "the articles which had been brought as my ransom." Tommo gives a musket to Kory-Kory, a roll of cotton to Marheyo, and the powderbags to the nearest young ladies. Then, as if anticipating our objections, Tommo adds: "This distribution did not occupy ten seconds, and before it was all over the boat was under full way.. .." But there is no special hurry. The natives continue to fight among themselves "until the boat was above fifty yards from the shore." Mow-Mow and six or seven other warriors then run into the surf and throw their javelins harmlessly after the boat.

As though not satisfied with this escape, Melville throws in another for good measure. About a score of natives run along the beach, swim out from a headland the boat must pass, and spread themselves "right across our course." Melville here cannot resist one last reference to cannibalism. Tommo says: "We were well aware that if they succeeded in intercepting us they would practice upon us the maneuver which has proved so fatal to many a boat's crew in these seas." But having seen how Melville extricated Tommo from his difficulties on the beach, we feel that Tommo surely can avoid capture by a few natives swimming a hundred yards from shore in "one of those chopping angry seas." Tommo strikes the nearest swimmer in the throat with a boathook, and one of the crew slashes the wrists of another who attempts to climb aboard, and in another minute the boat is out of danger. Tommo explains very briefly how he got back to a ship and home again and the book ends.

The confused ending to *Typee* may have resulted from a confusion in Melville's own mind as to what kind of book *Typee* was supposed to be—serious novel, travel book, or adventure tale. Melville probably had least in mind a serious novel. Nevertheless, *Typee* is not devoid of serious meaning, and if one wishes to look at the book as a semi-autobiographical story with serious overtones, the ending of *Typee,* however unsatisfying on a literal level, might be said to have meaning and to be related closely to the book as a whole. The escape might be viewed as a resolution of the conflict in Tommo between his desire to remain in this mindless paradise and his desire to return to civilization from which he had fled, between his enjoyment of the more obvious pleasures of the island and his revulsion at the discovery that even in Eden there is no escaping the darker side of existence. But the perfunctory way in which Melville handles the ending of *Typee* is one indication at least that he was only vaguely or unconsciously aware, if he was aware at all, of the complex symbolic meanings inherent in Tommo's situation. In any event, unlike Ishmael in *Moby-Dick,* Tommo achieves no heightened awareness as a result of what happens to him. The events he observes and participates in seem to the reader, as they no doubt seemed to Melville, more like adventures than experiences.

It is far more likely that Melville thought of *Typee* as a popular, entertaining, quasi-autobiographical travel book about an exotic, faraway place where beautiful native girls danced with voluptuous abandon and men secretly practiced cannibalism. The subtitle of *Typee, A Peep at Polynesian Life,* supports this view. But in the process of writing *Typee,* the incipient novelist in Melville kept coming to the surface, with the result that the book throughout wavers between being a semi-fictitious travel book and a semi-factual adventure story. Melville the novelist and story-teller made it extremely difficult for Melville the anthropologist and writer of romantic travel books to bring his narrative to an end after he had given us our "peep at Polynesian life." The truth is that Melville builds up considerable suspense over the fate of Tommo, especially after Tommo discovers he is not a guest but a prisoner of the Typees. Once having built up this suspense, Melville could hardly let his book end as unclimactically as a travel lecture. Since Tommo is the narrator, the reader knows from the beginning that Tommo, like Ishmael in *Moby-Dick, does* escape, and he has every reason to believe he will find out *how.* Furthermore, after the build-up of suspense, the reader would have every reason to expect that Tommo's escape from the Typees will be at least as dramatic and convincing as Melville's careful account of Tommo's escape from the ship *to* the valley of the Typees and the detailed description of life in the valley itself. But we find, in fact, that the ending of *Typee* is no such thing. Melville, of course, did add an "exciting" escape, indeed, *two* of them, but his careless, offhand presentation of these two crises suggests that his heart was not in the writing. It appears that Melville had said all he wanted to say *before* Tommo's escape, but sensing that his travel book had indeed turned into something of an adventure tale that needed a dramatic ending he tacked one on.

When the question of *Typee*'s authenticity came up after the book was published, Melville wrote to John Murray, his English publisher: "*Typee* however must at last be beleived [*sic*] on its own account—they believe [*sic*] it here now—a little touched up they say but *true.*" Whether one thinks of *Typee* as a serious book, a travel narrative, or an adventure story, it would seem much less "touched up" and much more "true" had Melville not attached such a spurious ending to an otherwise fairly believable book. In any event, the contrast between the weak ending of *Typee* (1846) and the great ending of *Moby-Dick* (1851) is further evidence of how far Melville progressed as a writer in the five years between the two books.

*Donald E. Houghton, "The Incredible Ending of Melville's 'Typee'," in* The Emerson Society Quarterly, *No. 23, I Quarter, 1961, pp. 28-31.*

## A. N. Kaul    (essay date 1963)

[*Below, Kaul explores* Typee's *depiction of the clash between the values of primitive communities and those of western civilization.*]

Even after a century *Typee* remains in some ways an angry young book. But that does not tell the whole story of its effectiveness. If this account of a brief Polynesian sojourn seems weightier than the narrative of beachcombing vagabondage in *Omoo,* the chief reason lies in the fact that its criticism of Western civilization is balanced by an alternative concept of social organization. It is a fiction which, like religion—to use Melville's own words quoted in the epigraph—presents "another world, and yet one to which we feel the tie." It is a singularly disarming if unsophisticated attempt on the part of a young writer to engage, in terms of readily available experience, a problem which is still among the profounder social problems of the West: the problem of "community lost and community to be gained" [James Baird, *Ishmael,* 1956]. It is true that in this first book Melville traveled half the circumference of the globe, and a couple of millennia backward in time, from the American civilization of the day, to discover his ideal community. In his later work he was to bridge the spatial and temporal gap between the two sides of the drama, and to give a fugitive and fleeting expression to the community theme in the contemporary world of the here and now. But this fact does not make *Typee* an exercise in literary escapism; it only places it in the American imaginative tradition of total repudiation and radical quest. In terms of the values involved, this peep at Polynesian life does not turn away from the issues that are raised; it faces them squarely.

As a work of imagination, *Typee* can be compared with two distinct kinds of fictional narrative. In the first place, there is a whole body of literature—usually of second-rate writing and no thematic pretensions—which takes the reader out of this world and into an imaginary realm where the sun always shines and the rain never falls— never at least in such a way as to remind the reader of his wet feet. The whole purpose of this literature is to induce temporary forgetfulness of life and its problems. It has nothing to do with known human and social realities; in Melville's terms, there is no recognizable tie between the world it creates for us and our own world. At the other extreme from these Shangri-las there is the serious kind of imaginary construct of which a notable example is Samuel Butler's *Erewhon.* The pretended unreality of such a realm is only a strategic device. Whether the reader is carried into it by means of a dream, an allegory, a boat, a balloon, or some other mode of literary transportation that

---

**An excerpt from *Typee:***

[The Typees] are either too lazy or too sensible to worry themselves about abstract points of religious belief. While I was among them they never held any synods or councils to settle the principles of their faith by agitating them. An unbounded liberty of conscience seemed to prevail. Those who pleased to do so were allowed to repose implicit faith in an ill-favoured god with a large bottle nose and fat shapeless arms crossed upon his breast, whilst others worshipped an image which, having no likeness either in heaven or on earth, could hardly be called an idol. As the islanders always maintained a discreet reserve with regard to my own peculiar views on religion, I thought it would be excessively ill-bred in me to pry into theirs.

*Herman Melville, in his* Typee, *Harcourt, Brace, and Company, 1920.*

---

happens to be handy, he is in truth hardly moved an inch from the reality he knows, be it of manners, morals, social institutions, or whatever it is that the writer wishes to reform. Butler's "Nowhere" is England still, but England with some of its institutions turned upside down in order to shock the reader into a concern for their abuses. For instance, consider what is perhaps the most effectively contrived inversion in Butler's satire: the Erewhon code which requires disease to be punished but which maintains that crime is an unfortunate accident for which the afflicted criminal deserves not blame but sympathy and condolence. The purpose here obviously is not to hold up the Erewhonian community as an ideal in any sense; it is merely to confront us with the recognition that crime is after all a sort of disease and that society should accordingly treat it in a more humane spirit. Such imaginary structures are thus wholly satire-determined. To revert to Melville's words, they present not another world but our own in another light.

*Typee,* needless to say, shares the impulse that lies behind both these kinds of fiction. It is full of angry, if not very artful, denunciation of civilization and its institutions. On the other hand, its portrayal of the Happy Valley is not altogether innocent of a Shangri-la-like quality of perpetual sunshine and exotic glamor. In this sense Melville was obviously exploiting simultaneously, though not without honest reservations, the taste for tropic-island bewitchment as well as the Rousseau-esque myth of aboriginal perfection. But there is more to this book than the use of these best-selling devices; there is all its seriousness. As William Ellery Sedgwick has said [in his *Herman Melville: The Tragedy of Mind,* 1944]:

> Of course it will be insisted by critics of a certain stamp that in this contrast between civilized and savage life Melville is still following "a long and ample tradition, both literary and philosophical," namely, the exaltation of the Noble Savage at the expense of his civilized opposite. True as this may be, it is not the whole truth nor the most interesting part of it. If there is a literary convention here there is the pressure of personal responses to animate it.

To this one can add that over and above the animation of personal response, there are behind *Typee* the force and confidence of an important American tradition, as also the contemporary ferment that made this an age of millennial expectations. Melville's personal formulation of it apart, preoccupation with the theme of perfect community was at this date shared by a large number of American dreamers. George Ripley, for instance, hailed the novel in the *Harbinger* for its portrayal of an "ideal society" whose perfection is based on the fact that "there is *abundance for every person,* and thus the most fruitful cause of the selfishness and crime of our enlightened and philosophic situation does not exist there. Here is the lesson which the leaders of this nineteenth century may learn from the Typee."

The most important thing about *Typee,* then, is its social theme, and this theme turns out to be the traditional American theme of a corrupt civilization at one end—one end of the globe in this case—and the dream of a simple and well-integrated community at the other. The inhabitants of the valley are not altogether the creatures of a satirical purpose. They are not Americans standing on their heads. Unlike Erewhon, Typee does not treat its criminals better. There are no criminals in Typee. Nor are there a hundred other social evils with which the civilized narrator is only too familiar. This state of affairs, as we shall see, arises primarily from the fact that life in Typee is based upon fundamentally different social principles. It exhibits an organization that makes harmony in human relations not a state of exalted virtue but simply a matter of the ordinary every-day course of things. In this connection it is worth while to note that Melville, unlike a true celebrator of the Noble Savage, is far from depicting each individual of the Polynesian tribe as a paragon of moral perfection. Like Cooper, or more like Natty Bumppo, he too distinguishes firmly between "gifts" and "nature," and points out time and again how, underneath the different and decisive customs of the country the inhabitants of the valley share the usual impulses, more developed perhaps in one direction and less in another, which belong to the common nature of humanity everywhere. If the savages offer points of contrast with civilized men, they also offer points of comparison. Mehevi at the Ti, for instance, does the honors of the house with the warmth and hospitality of an English squire; like the gentlemen of Europe the men of Typee indulge their mirth freely after the cloth is drawn and the ladies retire; the women are as lavish with cosmetics and ointments as women anywhere in the world; and, more importantly, as Melville observes in connection with a local mausoleum, both the superstitions and the faith of the Typees afford "evidence of the fact, that however ignorant man may be, he still feels within him his immortal spirit yearning after the unknown future." Nor, at the other extreme, are the savages innocent of violence and bloodshed, though such impulses are wisely channeled into carefully regulated wars.

Their physical perfection apart, Melville admires the Typees finally not for individual merit but for being a harmonious community. The principle of their social organization is their true distinction and the decisive point of contrast between them and civilized men. It is the source of their virtue and the reason for Melville's extenuation of their vice. Melville, it must be remembered, was evoking the picture of the Happy Valley across a span of unusually disillusioning experience with various forms of civilized society: civil and military, afloat as well as ashore. As Sedgwick has pointed out: "In *Typee* there are two perspectives. There is the perspective of the story proper, or of the events at the time they happened; and there is the broader perspective of the book as a whole, in which the events of the story and their circumstances are seen at a distance of four years across all the light and shadow of Melville's experience in the interim." Melville himself makes this plain when he declares that "after passing a few weeks in this valley of the Marquesas, I formed a higher estimate of human nature than I had ever before entertained. But alas! since then I have been one of the crew of a man-of-war, and the pent-up wickedness of five hundred men has nearly overturned all my previous theories."

One should accordingly refrain from looking with easy complacency upon the idealization of Typee. The over-

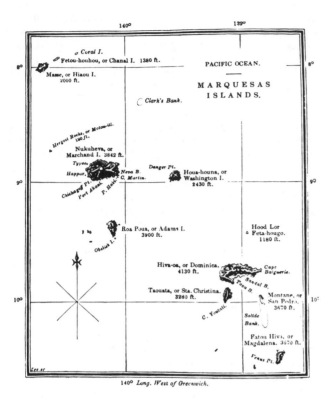

*Map from* Typee *(1846).*

drawn brightness of its image only reflects the darkness of civilized society in Melville's mind. The two images in fact mutually interpret each other. Though the valley of the Typees itself is comparatively untouched by contact with outsiders, civilization is judged in the book in terms of its effect upon other Polynesian peoples. Melville is far from claiming that the natives of these islands cannot derive immense advantage from being moved out of their Stone Age ignorance and lethargy. He is advocating not primitivism, but humanity. "Let the savages be civilised," he declares, "but civilise them with benefits, and not with evils; and let heathenism be destroyed, but not by destroying the heathen. The Anglo-Saxon hive have extirpated Paganism," he adds, pointing to the parallel in his own country, "from the greater part of the North American continent; but with it they have likewise extirpated the greater portion of the Red race."

The process of civilizing the Polynesians is spearheaded by ruthless army commanders, canting missionaries, and rapacious tradesmen, and the fruits of civilization for the natives consist of degradation and exploitation. As Melville observes with some irony about the state of affairs in the Sandwich Islands:

> Behold the glorious result! —The abominations of Paganism have given way to the pure rites of the Christian worship—the ignorant savage has been supplanted by the refined European! Look at Honolulu, the metropolis of the Sandwich Islands! —A community of disinterested merchants, and devoted self-exiled heralds of the Cross, located on the very spot that twenty years

ago was defiled by the presence of idolatry. What a subject for an eloquent Bible-meeting orator! . . . Nor until I visited Honolulu was I aware of the fact that the small remnant of the natives had been civilised into draught horses, and evangelised into beasts of burden. But so it is. They have been literally broken into the traces, and are harnessed to the vehicles of their spiritual instructors like so many dumb brutes!

Add to the destructiveness of this form of Christian-capitalist civilization the desolation caused by invading European armies and, as Melville says, who "can wonder at the deadly hatred of the Typees to all foreigners after such unprovoked atrocities? Thus it is that they whom we denominate 'savages' are made to deserve the title." It is indeed in this change from the feeling of universal love to one of distrust and hate that Melville locates the worst legacy of a corrupt civilization:

> When the inhabitants of some sequestered island first descry the "big canoe" of the European rolling through the blue waters toward their shores, they rush down to the beach in crowds, and with open arms stand ready to embrace the strangers. Fatal embrace! They fold to their bosoms the vipers whose sting is destined to poison all their joys; and the instinctive feeling of love within their breasts is soon converted into the bitterest hate.

It is against this background—the background of "the vices, cruelties, and enormities of every kind that spring up in the tained atmosphere of a feverish civilisation"—that we must regard Melville's idealization of the Typee valley. This civilization is represented more concretely, though not extensively, by the ship *Dolly,* which the narrator, presumably like other "long-haired, bare-necked youths," had been forced to join by "the united influences of Captain Marryat and hard times." In this book Melville does not dwell much either on the representative capacity of the ship or on shipboard usage. Nevertheless, it is obvious that, whether or not the sailors' expectation of adventure has been fulfilled, their poverty has remained unalleviated. As a matter of fact, the ship has only exposed them further to tyranny and inhuman neglect. In this connection one can contrast the captain of the *Dolly*—the remote and vengeful "Lord of the Plank"—with the Typee chieftain Mehevi who, though a sovereign in his own right, is so unattended by any ceremony and so close to the common inhabitants of the valley that the narrator remains for a long time unaware of his true status. It is to protest against the conditions aboard that the two sailors decide to risk falling among notorious savages rather than have any further truck with the repudiated vessel. Familiar as this gesture is in American fiction, we must notice further that the narrator and his companion Toby belong, characteristically enough, to that class of men "who never reveal their origin, never allude to home, and go rambling over the world as if pursued by some mysterious fate they cannot possibly elude."

The mysterious fate in this particular case involves a hazardous journey through certain chasms, ravines, and gorges beyond which, as the runaway sailors are convinced, lies the desired sanctuary of the Happy Valley.

The writing here is remarkable in its combination of symbolical overtones with the raciest and most straightforward narrative of physical adventure. As has been observed before, this journey constitutes a sort of descent into inferno—a Ulyssean detour to find the way home. The passage through the outlandish regions—described in chapter 7 in terms of death-like coldness, appalling darkness, and infernal torment—marks a process of dying, or a process of being born anew, or simply a necessary preparation for the different world that awaits the fugitives. When at last they view the sunny expanse of land toward which they have so painfully struggled over a period of several days, it is greeted as a revelation of Eden itself: "Had a glimpse of the gardens of Paradise been revealed to me, I could scarcely have been more ravished with the sight." *Typee* is undoubtedly a sea yarn, suitably stretched here and there as all sea yarns are, and handsomely overlaid with literary and other cliches. But it is also the first book of a great imaginative genius who started on his career at a time when his culture's experience was beginning to assume an articulate form—the form of an apprehensible and meaningful action. For all its lack of sophistication, or perhaps because of it, *Typee* captures with revealing simplicity one aspect of this action: the dialectical movement between a corrupt civilization and an ideal community, or the opposition between the dream and the reality of society in America. It is this over-all rhythm of the book which distinguishes its theme from its travel-diary method, and which constitutes its claim to serious consideration.

Having arrived in Paradise, what did Melville and Toby find there? They found sunshine and breadfruit; healthful aboriginal savages and long-haired beautiful women; nudity, dancing, and only occasional drapery of white tapa; ease and indolence, and quantities of sleep; in short, all that makes living among cannibals worth the risk. These were also the conditions that finally led Melville to despair and made him long for a speedy release from this subhuman existence. Such exotic novelties, however, do not exhaust the meaning that Melville projected into the image of Typee. He also recognized in this valley certain admirable possibilities, a social situation of which he gives a full account in chapters 17 and 27. The narrator begins in the earlier of these two chapters by saying that, having reconciled himself inwardly to an indefinite period of stay in the valley, his ailing limb seemed to heal suddenly and he entertained hope of a quick and complete recovery. "In the altered frame of mind," somewhat like Miles Coverdale after his illness at Blithedale, he now looks upon the surrounding world with fresh insight: "every object that presented itself to my notice in the valley struck me in a new light, and the opportunities I now enjoyed of observing the manners of its inmates tended to strengthen my favourable impressions." He is disposed to believe that he has found his way into the "Happy Valley" and that beyond its mountains there is "naught but a world of care and anxiety." Contrasting the Typee community with the society he has known, he is ready to extenuate even the worst abuses of the former. With regard to cannibalism, for example, he records at more than one place the horror and revulsion aroused in him by this primitive rite. This of course falls within the first of the book's two perspectives

noted by Sedgwick. But we must not forget the other, the broader perspective in which the image of Typee is flatteringly refracted through Melville's experience with civilization. In this light he argues that cannibalism—"a rather bad trait"—is practiced only on the declared enemies of the tribe, whereas in civilized societies innocent men are tortured and executed with the utmost cruelty and for no apparent reason. "The fiend-like skill we display," he concludes in a passage reminiscent of Swiftian savagery, "in the invention of all manner of death-dealing engines, the vindictiveness with which we carry on our wars, and the misery and desolation that follow in their train, are enough of themselves to distinguish the white civilised man as the most ferocious animal on the face of the earth." His "remorseless cruelty," he goes on to add, can be seen in the penal institutions of "our own favoured land"; in particular the treatment of criminals "whom we mason up in the cells of our prisons, and condemn to perpetual solitude in the very heart of our population."

In Typee, on the other hand, no one is ever brought to trial and there are no lawyers or law courts. Like America, it enjoys an abundance of natural resources, but these are universally and equally shared. Hence there are no destitute widows, no starving children, no beggars, and therefore also no "cold charities." Liberty of conscience, merely promised in the narrator's own country, prevails here without limitation or hindrance. There is neither civil nor domestic disharmony of any sort: no foreclosures of mortgages, no debts or debtors' prisons, no bolts, bars, or padlocks, no jealousies in love and no divorce. The prevailing polyandry results in no discord, and "wedlock, as known among these Typees, seems to be of a more distinct and enduring nature than is usually the case with barbarous people. A baneful promiscuous intercourse of the sexes is hereby avoided, and virtue, without being clamorously invoked, is, as it were, unconsciously practised." Of course, the Typees, like the rest of humanity, are a warring people, but their battles, unlike those of a society based upon predatory competition, are not internecine. Surely, the narrator observes,

> if our evil passions must find vent, it is far better
> to expend them on strangers and aliens, than in
> the bosom of the community in which we dwell.
> In many polished countries civil contentions, as
> well as domestic enmities, are prevalent, at the
> same time that the most atrocious foreign wars
> are waged. How much less guilty, then, are our
> islanders, who of these three sins are only
> chargeable with one, and that the least criminal!

The harmonious community life of the Typees is characterized chiefly by the absence of three institutions. In the first place, money plays no part in the social relationships of these people: "That 'root of all evil' was not to be found in the valley." Likewise, there is no repressive police machinery, and, more important than these two, no property in land. In connection with private property, Melville's narrator makes the important distinction that was being blurred by Cooper's Littlepages around the same time in the history of American fiction. In chapter 27 he makes it clear that there was no "community of goods" in Typee and that, on the contrary, "personal property" was held inviolate and was in no case encroached upon by the inhabitants. But he observes that there is a vast difference between personal property and what he calls the "investment of 'real property' " or "real estate."

> Whether the land of the valley was the joint property of its inhabitants, or whether it was parcelled out among a certain number of landed proprietors who allowed everybody to "squat" and "poach" as much as he or she pleased, I never could ascertain. At any rate, musty parchments and title deeds there were none on the island; and I am half inclined to believe that its inhabitants hold their broad valleys in fee simple from Nature herself; to have and to hold, so long as grass grows and water runs.

The question to which the narrator is led inevitably by this state of affairs is the one which was most pertinent to the fortunes of his own tradition, the tradition of a people who had sought to form a pure community in freedom from all repressive social institutions but who had found themselves developing instead into an anti-society of isolated individuals permanently warring against each other. How, he asks in more than one place, did the Typees manage, "without the aid of established law, to exhibit, in so eminent a degree, that social order which is the greatest blessing and highest pride of the social state?" If "the better principles of our nature, cannot exist unless enforced by the statute-book, how are we to account for the social condition of the Typees?" His answer is quite characteristic of the visionary cast of the whole body of imaginative literature with which I have been dealing. "Civilisation," he says, "does not engross all the virtues of humanity"; there are some natural capacities which, with its emphasis on individualism, property, and money, it has not even tried. Every man harbors a "fraternal feeling" toward other men and all human beings desire to act "in concert and good fellowship." Free from the motives which vitiate human relationships in civilized societies, the harmonious life of the Typees is based precisely upon these feelings.

> During my whole stay on the island I never witnessed a single quarrel, nor anything that in the slightest degree approached even to a dispute. The natives appeared to form one household, whose members were bound together by the ties of strong affection. The love of kindred I did not so much perceive, for it seemed blended in the general love; and where all were treated as brothers and sisters, it was hard to tell who were actually related to each other by blood.

Here, then, is Melville's image of the ideal community: the image of a sort of prelapsarian Blithedale. Like Miles Coverdale, the narrator of *Typee* also abandons the community in order to return eventually to society or civilization. The reasons for this action are quite simple. On the level of the story, it is quite natural that, after tasting of this alien Paradise, the adventurous sailor should want to go back home to his mother. Moreover, while in Typee, he cannot hope to procure medical attention for his illness. It is not true, as D. H. Lawrence seems to imply, that his diseased limb gets progressively worse in Typee and heals immediately on his return to shipboard in *Omoo*. But it is true that his illness is a projection of psychological dis-

ease, for it gets better or worse as he resigns himself to his existence in the valley or revives hopes of escape from it; and herein lies the more important motivation for the escape. To reconcile oneself to Typee is to comfort oneself falsely with an impossible primitivism. Typee is at best a picture of "community lost"—lost for good reasons—and not the image of "community to be gained." To a man of the nineteenth-century Western world, it is more than happy but also less than human. The Typees do not hunt the whale, whether we interpret that symbol in economic, technological, intellectual, psychological, or spiritual terms. However painful it may prove to be, it is a necessary part of human destiny to accept the challenge of the Leviathan. By contrast, the somnolent Typees are content to make fire by rubbing two pieces of wood for hours on end, and the movement of their inward life is characterized by similar childishness.

So Melville makes his narrator leave the Happy Valley, but neither reconciled to civilization nor in repudiation of the social values which he has observed and endorsed in Typee. The idea of community—of people forming one harmonious household—continues to be a persistent, though not equally central, theme in Melville's succeeding novels. And as for his continued denunciation of civilization, one has only to turn to *Omoo*.

*A. N. Kaul, "Herman Melville: The New-World Voyageur," in his* The American Vision: Actual and Ideal Society in Nineteenth-Century Fiction, *Yale University Press, 1963, pp. 214-79.*

### Philip Young   (essay date 1967)

[*In the following essay, Young maintains that* Typee *is a mixture of fact, fiction, and borrowed material, and explores mythic interpretations of the work.*]

> 'I'll carry you off
> To a cannibal isle . . .
> Nothing to eat but the fruit as it grows . . .
> Nothing at all but three things.'
> 'What things?'
> 'Birth, and copulation, and death.'
> 'I'd be bored.'
> 'You'd be bored.'
>
>                          Sweeney Agonistes

Nobody nowadays is going to draw much of a crowd by setting up to debate questions of literary genre; anyway the designation of *Typee* as Herman Melville's 'first novel' is pretty well established. But it should not hurt to mention the fact that a segment of autobiography crossed with travelogue is not quite what we usually have in mind when we speak of a novel. If we had not got it straight from Mr Capote that *In Cold Blood* was the first 'non-fiction novel' we might be tempted to enter *Typee* under some such curious heading. But if this should really not be called the first of Melville's novels (or 'romances'), which of his titles ought? *Mardi*, his third book? *Moby Dick*, larded with 'non-fiction', his sixth? *Pierre?*

The problem of how to classify *Typee* dogged it before it ever saw publication, and that question, which is now academic, was in the beginning crucial. 'I fear you abhor romances,' Melville wrote to his first publisher. He was perfectly correct. The Englishman John Murray, from whom travel books for his Home and Colonial Library issued endlessly, was persistently unsure of *Typee*'s credentials. Its narrative he found dramatic, and he liked the way the style kept things moving along. But he thought he detected the 'taint' of fiction, and of fiction he published none at all, not knowingly. At that, Melville was doing better overseas than he had done at home; in New York Harper's had rejected him outright—on the ground that since his story could not possibly be true it was without value, Q.E.D. Temporarily placating Murray, the author inserted three chapters of amateur anthropology, and stolidly prefaced his title, *A Peep at Polynesian Life,* with *Narrative of a Four Months' Residence among the Natives of a Valley of the Marquesas Islands.* The book was published in England in 1846; then, later the same year, in America—with *Typee* leading off.

Washington Irving, who went through most of the proofs while in London, predicted success. And a success it was; immediate and substantial, critical and popular. That little-known writer of tales, Nathaniel Hawthorne, reviewed it favourably, and so did a virtually unknown newspaperman named Walter Whitman. By 1938 some fifty-nine editions of the book in English were tallied; and that was *before* the great surge of interest that elevated Melville to the place he now occupies with James and Faulkner in a triumvirate of American novelists had really got under way. A sort of prose-Gauguin long in advance of the painter, who was to live, work, and die in the very same islands, Melville was able to summon up an air of primitive mystery, infused with broad hints (or better) of the erotic and the potentially frightening. They gave *Typee* its considerable appeal, and brought 'the man who lived among cannibals' instant fame.

Even so, sceptics and adversaries came along with the enthusiasts. Missionaries were angry; and poor Murray, though he was soon to publish *Omoo,* the sequel to *Typee,* continued to have misgivings so bothersome, that he was to ask, more than once, for 'documentary evidences' that Melville had ever so much as set foot in the Marquesas. The author could not (at any rate did not) supply them, and just as the suspicion that his bruited adventures were fictious was threatening his new-born reputation he was the beneficiary of what must have seemed an act of Providence (albeit, to the missionaries, a cruel one). Toby Greene, long-lost companion to most of his stay in the Marquesas, wrote to an unbelieving reviewer of *Typee,* revealing that he was found, and much alive, in Buffalo, New York. Further that he was 'happy to testify to the entire accuracy of the work' in those parts that involved him. To his second New York edition Melville added Greene's account of his disappearance—some compensation, at least, for the deletion of the sections on the missionaries and the French occupation of Tahiti. But even Toby was not enough for John Murray, who was feeling the pressure and asked yet again for 'evidence'. Applying a little rhetoric, Melville answered finally: 'I will give no evidence—truth is mighty and will prevail. . . .'

So, what with the energies and ingenuities of modern scholars, raking the beach for the last shell, truth has done. And so, partly because that fictional taint Murray thought he detected was incontestably present, we now call the book a novel. In particular we prize those elements which head it in the direction of one. Times, we say, have changed. In such a way that the situation is exactly reversed, to the agreeably ironic point that if our view of *Typee* had been that of its publishers one hundred and twenty years ago we might never have heard of the book. The prevalent truth today, based on a great deal of evidence Melville never supplied, is that the novel is a somewhat odd package, made up in unequal parts of fashion, fact, fancy, and felony.

The fashion of the age was, of course, for travel literature, which Murray was vigorously abetting and without which the book might never have been written, let alone published. Melville stood ready with the very mix his eventual readers favoured: romantic diversion *plus* such plain instruction in strange manners and customs, flora and fauna, and so forth, as would alleviate any guilt that vicarious cultural apostasy might provoke. Further it is unlikely that any area was so ripe for picking as the South Seas. Day-dreams of noble savages and languorous paradises could seem there both adequately alien and sufficiently plausible for most. Others, to be sure, had sailed vigorously into the region and got books out of it. But dry, unimaginative books. However green the talent, the literary discovery of the South Seas remained for a young sailor with no known prospects to make.

Of fact there was abundance. Melville had assuredly not planned a sojourn in some enchanted island when he signed on the *Acushnet,* he was lucky. Before he got home he had accumulated experience enough for five books, and he wrote them. He also began in the right place—not with his whaling adventures; rather with the relatively simple and aesthetically undemanding experience of the Marquesas. To this, real events—desertion of the ship, residence in an island valley, and departure—provided a natural form and sufficient excitement. In actuality things were pretty bad on the *Acushnet.* Poor whaling and ill health made the captain so irritable and tyrannical that two mates jumped ship at the first good chance; young Melville, sensitive and proud, thought him a brute. The *Acushnet* put into port ostensibly to avoid scurvy and to look for recruits. (It is recorded elsewhere that the natives supposed 'absolutely' that the real purpose of anchoring was 'enjoyment of female favours'.) Given the sickening possibility that home was 'several years' away for this ship, it was not completely unnatural that a young man should plan to get off it. It is virtually certain that he knew there were supposed to be cannibals in those hills, but not in all of them, and it is likely that he had heard useful things about the place from a whaling cousin, Thomas Wilson Melville, who had spent a couple of weeks there several years before, and from whom he probably took the name 'Tommo' for his personnae.

For two weeks he made plans with Toby, a friend of like inclination. Best information was that the nearest valley was inhabited by the Happa, or Happar tribe, of good repute, and the central valley by Taipis, or Typees, deplored for dietary reasons by all. On what he and Toby guessed would be their last trip ashore they took off, badly under-equipped, only to find themselves soon lost in a black, fruitless Eden, and Melville with chills and fever from a mysteriously damaged leg. They did evade the crafty *Acushnet,* which hid behind an island for twenty-four hours before sailing back in hope of catching them on the beach, but it took four days of torturous travel with one of them sick, to reach precisely the valley they had calculated to avoid. Melville watched the cuisine closely, and found nothing at fault.

No serious doubt has been thrown on his account of some other matters, either; Toby's disappearance, for instance, was probably as given in the book. It is established further that a small Australian whaler was in such need of hands as to bother with Melville's rescue; he did get aboard the *Lucy Ann,* where things were substantially worse than on the *Acushnet.* But that is another story, called **Omoo: a Narrative of Adventures in the South Seas** (1847).

Life and the travel market had put the young Melville in a most favourable position, but the exploitation of the South Seas for literary purposes required as well a little imagination and, most suitably to the times, his was then a Romantic one. He exercised it chiefly in playing up the idyllic aspects of 'Happy Valley', bringing it as close to Eden as would seem credible, while at the same time thinking to manufacture a few shudders—notably with the discovery of some shrunken heads (which do not square at all with accounts given by other visitors to the region). Probably to help his readers accept his reliability, he increased his stay, actually a bit under four weeks, to four months. Given the typography of the area in which he made it, his escape appears to have been another invention, and the melodramatic postures assumed by the prose in that episode enforce the suspicion.

Melville's fancy played not only on his own experience but on that of other writers as well; he borrowed heavily from several people, without thought of repayment. It was a common practice especially in travel literature, and no such stigma attached to it as would today. Even so, this traffic in second-hand merchandise must seem to us a curious business, particularly when writers rejected their own experience for someone else's. The famous instance in Melville is his taking the setting of Nantucket, which he had never seen, from a book on the history of that place for the opening of **Moby Dick,** though New Bedford was perfectly available to him as the port he himself had shipped out of. So with the **Peep at Polynesian Life,** as C. R. Anderson's *Melville in the South Seas* (1940) demonstrates. *Typee* is indebted to five books, and to two in particular: Captain David Porter's *Journal of a Cruise Made to the Pacific Ocean* (1815) and Charles S. Stewart's *A Visit to the South Seas* (1831). Indeed [Charles] Anderson's research has put John Murray's request for 'evidence' in a new light, for this scholar speculates that given a lively imagination and his sources Melville could have written his book 'without ever having seen the Marquesas'. The point to be made is, of course, that we do not read Melville's sources, we read him, a young man on his way to becoming a writer. But plunder the others he did, even for description of things he had certainly observed first hand, such as the bay and the physical beauty of the natives. Fayaway's 'strange blue eyes' are in one source, and in others are to be found the precedents for his accounts of native activities, including religious observances and so forth, and even some of his scenes. The memorable opening assault of the females on the *Acushnet* is to be found in Porter (poor weather on the day of its arrival, according to the ship's log, also makes one doubt that Melville personally witnessed that invasion). Thus neither his coming or his going—or his stay—appears to have been quite as his readers were asked to believe.

*Typee* is, then, questionable autobiography; the modern reader searching it instead for signs of the Melville-to-come will not be rewarded extravagantly either. As the writer himself was first to point out, his development was very rapid once begun, but slow to begin. 'From my twenty-fifth year [1844] I date my life,' he wrote to Hawthorne as he was about to finish **Moby Dick** in 1851:

> Three weeks have scarcely passed at any time between then and now, that I have not unfolded within myself. But I feel that I am now come to the inmost leaf of the bulb, and that shortly the flower must fall to the mould.

Evidence that he was still a novice in 1846 is conclusive in *Typee,* nowhere clearer than in the style, which can be distinctly amateur: 'I little thought . . . that in the space of a few weeks I should actually be a captive in the self-same valley. . . . How shall I describe the scenery that met my eye, as I looked out from this verdant recess!' Some of the conversation with Toby is so artificial that one must hope (though the purpose of it may elude him) that parody is intended: ' "You will have it to be Happar, I see, my dear fellow; pray Heaven you may find not yourself deceived," observed I. . . .' Similarly inept, at times, is the structure: 'I think I must enlighten the reader a little about the natural history of the valley,' begins Chapter 29. At other times it isn't even trying, as in Chapter 31, which starts: ' . . . I am about to string together, without any attempt at order, a few odds and ends of things not hitherto mentioned. . . .'

It will not do to exaggerate it, but some promise of a future is not *entirely* absent from this book. Melville could already be consciously amusing, as in the early passage involving the display of a royal lady's tattooed rump. And when shortly thereafter the poor mermaids are debauched aboard ship there are signs of power. The style in its light formality can be wordy, but also vigorous and spirited. Melville was already developing a knack for 'breathing life' into his prose, as we say, and that ability was to carry him a long way.

So too he was beginning to hear from his mind. Thoughtful and outspoken, *Typee* inveighs credibly against disastrous invasions of a primitive culture by Western political and religious interests; for its time it is remarkably frank, especially in its coverage of sexual matters. But most important to *Typee* is the question it implicitly poses: given the unmistakable evils of our society, is an innocent, primitive state any better? The answer seems to be that the natives are more virtuous and happy than we, but that their life cannot feed for long an intellect set in motion by a more advanced culture. However much he might wish to think so, 'civilized man' cannot content himself with a near-animal existence—eating, breeding, and (most of all by far) sleeping. As even D. H. Lawrence allowed, we 'cannot go back . . . towards the past, savage life. . . . Whatever else the South Sea islander is, he is centuries and centuries behind us. . . .' In short those islands already looked like the good place for a winter's vacation they are becoming; otherwise, eventually, a bore. Besides, Melville's Typees are emphatically *not* innocent, as Tommo's discovery of fresh human bones makes abundantly clear. This revelation is conceivably another invention: Melville needed to resolve the suspicion he had created over the matter, and to conclude that Tommo's fears were groundless would have just about wrecked the book. Whether or not his natives were in actuality cannibals is still unclear; probably they were. What is clear is that Tommo's had to be. That's what identified the work; 'Typee,' Melville explains, *means* 'cannibal' in the Marquesan dialect.

Here then began his life-long preoccupation with the shadow that falls between what appears and what is—especially with the face of evil and the various masks it hides behind. Tommo's departure is Melville's everlasting 'No' to an evil that was new to him, and to an existence that was not only mindless but eventually catastrophic to the mind. Here had already begun as well the development of what might be called his basic metaphor: of life as a voyage—a search first for a berth that would maintain a man in some tranquillity; later (and equally doomed) a quest for an intellectual haven among some fundamental truths he could believe in.

An anonymous 'old salt' is reported as having said, 'Well, *Typee* was a good story: that is the way it really was out there. But *Moby Dick! . . .* All up in the air! Crazy!' What the sailor had not detected was that even in *Typee* Melville was making a few rudimentary attempts at getting off the ground; the great symbolic, mythical powers of his masterpiece have humble origins in the Marquesas. To cite Lawrence again, Melville at his best always wrote 'from a sort of dream-self'. As an instance the critic (*Studies in Classic American Literature*) describes Tommo first entering the valley:

> Down this narrow, steep, horrible dark gorge he
> slides and struggles as we struggle in a dream,
> or in the act of birth, to emerge in the green Eden
> of the Golden Age, the valley of the cannibal
> savages.

Lawrence's 'dream-self' is a kind of mythic 'resonance' that became a full chorus in *Moby Dick.* The little matter of that bad leg (surely an emblem of inner disorder as well), for instance. Tommo half-suspects he has been bitten by a snake, and in the vague context of the first Garden the admonition of the Lord to the reptile, 'thou shalt bruise his heel', comes to mind very naturally. So might the heel of Achilles (though this is to exalt Tommo above his station) or the 'swollen foot' of Oedipus, to which the name points, or even the limp of a most contemporary mythical hero, obscurely related to Oedipus, the protago-

nist of John Barth's *Giles Goat-Boy,* who is carried pick-a-back about the campus by his brute slave Croaker precisely as Tommo is carried about the valley by his servant, the uncultivated Kory-Kory. In like fashion *Typee* corresponds roughly to several archetypal patterns, among them Joseph Campbell's hypothetical 'monomyth': a withdrawl from a troubled world into pre-history; communion if not with a deity at least with his sacred grove; and return to a different life in the awareness that civilization can't go home again either.

In a period when American critics are compulsively attuned to the mythical overtones of literary works it is no surprise that several of them should have read *Typee* 'mythically'. Nor anything peculiar (since it is the author himself who frequently remarks the parallels) in the fact that several such interpreters have seized Eden (both pre- and post-lapsarian) for a handy grip on the book. In his first work as in his last, *Billy Budd,* Melville is very mindful of the Bible story. It is he who remarks that 'the penalty of the Fall presses very lightly' on the natives, that it is not by the sweat of their brow that these men are condemned to earn their bread-fruit, that Fayaway (a convenient Eve in her affair with Tommo) wore the 'summer garb of Eden', and so on. Thus R. W. B. Lewis will find yet another American Adam in Melville's tale, another search for a lost childhood, a vanished Eden, expressing a distinctly American resistance to the whole business of growing up. At the other end of a spectrum Milton R. Stern will argue that Melville's version of the myth of Adam is an heretical inversion of the original story: the Fall in this book is not the expulsion from Eden but the fall *into* it; salvation for man cannot be found in pastoral; his only Grace lies in an escape from 'innocence', which can be accomplished only by what is forbidden, eating of the tree of knowledge.

Between and beside such views of Tommo's Eden are numerous by-paths and way-stations, but they all run out or collapse at the way the evidence of cannibalism Tommo happened on fails to accommodate itself to the story in *Genesis.* Structurally and thematically this discovery marks the conjunction of all strands of the book, but here exactly the trail is lost. Whatever the fruit of Eden, it was not human flesh that grew on that tree. Or was it?

The question now is whether, after sufficient sanity, safety and sobriety, a little speculation may not be permissible in the end. If so, the proposition would be that it is conceivable (no more is being urged) that where '*Typee* as Eden' appears to fall apart is precisely where it is most striking.

Lawrence, wild, fearless, crazy like a fox, may be summoned up one last time to remark that Melville 'might have spared himself his shudder' at the thought and sight of cannibalism among those natives:

> No doubt he had partaken of the Christian sac-
> raments many a time. 'This is my body, take and
> eat.' And surely their sacred ceremony was as
> awe-inspiring as the one Jesus substituted.

'Substituted'. Typically Lawrence doesn't explain. Drop

the bomb and let someone else pick up the pieces, that was his method (and a delight it is in the age of explication).

The pieces in this case were retrieved and reassembled by a man who was thinking of neither Lawrence or Melville but of Freud, the contemporary psychoanalytic writer, Theodor Reik. Though he did not work up his notions until 1957 (in *Myth and Guilt: the Crime and Punishment of Mankind*), they first struck him back in 1913 when he was directly associated with the master. His is, then, yet another Tale from the Vienna Woods. But he is working to our problem, and it would be foolish to dismiss without a hearing a relevant hypothesis as *it* takes the ancient story of man's first disobedience and the fruit whose mortal taste brought loss of Eden, and looks for 'reality' in it. As he notes, sexual interpretations of the tale are old as pre-Christian, new as Otto Rank, and widely held. Yet for Reik the original sin of mankind was not a sexual but a 'nutritional mistake', motivated by the wish to become God by eating a 'special kind of food'. In *Genesis* God the father appears as a tree-totem, and the origin of the grim story of its fruit lies in very primitive times when man ate his god, or despotic father, out of the wish to become that figure. ('Behold,' said the Lord after Adam had eaten, 'the man is become as one of us.') This immemorial tradition survives in the idea—fact, rather—of cannibals eating a missionary for the same, familiar reason, that they may possess the magic powers they attribute to him. In short the Biblical injunction was to abandon on pain of death the practice of eating people.

Reik also extends this reading to connect with the 'substituted' Eucharist, where the devout are united with Christ by 'incorporating' his body and blood. Thus the myth of the fall of man, and the death and redemption of Jesus as Saviour, are a single, coherent story, the early church fathers having been correct when they said that the death-bringing tree of the Fall became the life-giving tree of the Cross. Christ offered himself as atonement for an ancient crime, harking all the way back to it.

If for a moment one is willing to suspend disbelief, the problem of what this interpretation might do for *Typee* is upon him. One thought would be that we gain from such a reading of the ancient symbols a more dramatic sense of the distance in time that Tommo tumbled as he was reborn into that valley, a sharper appreciation of the millennia erased by the minutes during which he fell captive to an age when the dawn had not yet broken on western culture. Asthe natives cried 'Taboo!' and Tommo glimpsed anyway 'the disordered members of a human skeleton, the bones still fresh with moisture, and with particles of flesh clinging . . .' he saw more than he knew or we knew. He saw the heart of darkness, the leavings of Adam and Eve, evidence of what was to become man's first disobedience.

The Fall does not press lightly on *him,* so that what he saw is no more important than what he felt: the revulsion that may be said to have been the harbinger of the dawn of our history. Every bit as unwitting as Rip Van Winkle (who stumbled ignorantly into Valhalla) Tommo saw the fruit of the tree of the Garden unmasked of all *its* leaves. And though he has no way of seeing himself in such a role he is a palsied messenger come from the dead to tell us all:

not just whom we descend from but what. Which is as good a way as Melville's to leave our ailing knight, alone and palely loitering, shaken by the smiles that hold him still in thrall, haggard on a cold hill, entranced in horror.

And no birds sing. 'Birds,' writes Melville,

> —bright and beautiful birds—fly over the valley of Typee. You see them passing like spirits on the wing through the shadows of the grove. . . . Their plumage is purple and azure, crimson and white, black and gold. . . . They go sailing through the air in starry throngs; but alas! the spell of dumbness is on them all—there is not a single warbler in the valley!

*Philip Young, in an introduction to* Typee *by Herman Melville, edited by Herbert Van Thal, Cassell, 1967, pp. vii-xviii.*

### William B. Dillingham    (essay date 1972)

[*In the following excerpt, Dillingham discusses the retrospective nature of Tommo's narrative.*]

Herman Melville's first book is a peculiar combination of autobiography, fiction, and borrowings. When viewed as a novel, it may suddenly appear much like a travelogue. When approached as autobiography, it seems starkly exaggerated and fictionalized. When analyzed from the standpoint of its borrowings, it transcends them all, and the critic must face the question of why Melville borrowed what he did and why his own work is so much greater than those books he borrowed from.

*Typee* was a fit work to inaugurate the career of Herman Melville, for it, like its author, defies classification. It has its own validity as a work of art, however, and like most of Melville's books must be examined on its own terms. Always realizing that it is based on Melville's own stay among the Typees in 1842 and that he borrowed whole descriptions from such factual accounts of Polynesian life as Charles S. Stewart's *A Visit to the South Seas . . .*, Captain David Porter's *Journal of a Cruise Made to the Pacific Ocean,* and William Ellis's *Polynesian Researches,* I intend to treat *Typee* chiefly as a work of fiction. For whatever else it might be, it is an artistic creation portraying in a narrative the inner life of a hero named Tommo, who may be Herman Melville, but if so only in a recreated and synthesized form such as that which the author of a novel so often takes when he pours himself into his hero.

Tommo's journey into and out of Typee valley may have roughly paralleled Melville's own, but as D. H. Lawrence recognized a long time ago, it is also a symbolic journey which suggests the nature of experience. Lawrence's essay on *Typee* [in his *Studies in Classic American Literature,* 1923], to which many later analyses owe a great debt, discusses the book in terms of man's futile attempt to return to Eden after he has been scarred and deepened by centuries of collective experience. Though man longs to go back to primitive innocence, he cannot fit in there and he must live in his own time and place. Most modern critics have followed Lawrence's lead in thinking of Typee as Eden or Innocence. F. O. Matthiessen, for example, wrote [in his

*American Renaissance*, 1941] that Typee represents "a primitive state of innocence in which developing mankind may not remain. . . ." Ronald Mason [in his *The Spirit Above the Dust*, 1951] argued that "the key to the purpose of the book is the innocence of the Typees." William Ellery Sedgwick [in his *Herman Melville: The Tragedy of Mind*, 1944] expressed his view of *Typee* eloquently as a moment in time we all remember, a time of

> spontaneous, instinctive being, in which human consciousness is a simple and happy undertaking of rudimentary sensations and simple sensuous impressions; in which physical health and good animal spirits have a large preponderance; in which the impulses and affections of the human heart suffer no disguise nor any distortion; the phase, finally, in which as yet no painful cleavage is felt dividing a happy animality from the gentlest and most guileless impulses of the heart.

Simple, innocent, Edenic—this is unquestionably one side of Typee as it is presented in the book. James E. Miller, Jr. [in *A Reader's Guide to Herman Melville*, 1962], rightly observes, however, that "this Polynesian retreat, though a Paradise in many respects and particularly to one weary of the outrageous behavior of civilization, still falls short of the original Garden." Indeed, there is "Horror that exists not far beneath the placid surface." Just what this horror is has nowhere been better stated than by Sophia Hawthorne; in a letter to her mother she commented on "all this golden splendor and enchantment glowing before the dark refrain constantly brought as a background—the fear of being killed and eaten—the cannibalism in the olive tinted Apollos around him—the unfathomable mystery of their treatment of him" [quoted in Eleanor M. Metcalf's *Herman Melville: Cycle and Epicycle*, 1953].

As Mrs. Hawthorne seemed to discern, there are two Typees, the one evoking joy and glad animal spirits, the other fear and horror. We are aware of the beautiful green valley, but also the harsh mountains that surround it; the beauty of the people, but also their unfathomable practice of tattooing; the delightful absence of civilized dogma, but also the countless and seemingly senseless taboos; the inherent good nature of the Typees, but their unpredictability and that unfortunate ritual of eating their enemies. Why, then, is *Typee* so frequently considered a sort of idyl of the South Seas? Charles R. Anderson, for example, has written [in his *Melville in the South Seas*, 1939] that *"Typee . . .* is a wholehearted defense of the noble Savage and a eulogy of his happy life, his external beauty, and his inner purity of heart. Virtually the whole book is written in the romantic literary tradition inaugurated by Rousseau a century before." Such a view does not separate the two viewpoints of the book's narrator. The purpose and complexity of the book unfold in the two separate perspectives, and the picture of Tommo, Melville's first hero, comes into focus.

In the Preface to *Typee* the reader is in the opening sentence made aware that a period of time has elapsed since Tommo experienced the adventures he is relating: "More than three years have elapsed since the occurrence of the events recorded in this volume. The interval, with the exception of the last few months, has been chiefly spent by the author tossing about on the wide ocean." The significance of this remark goes far beyond a leisurely introduction to the narrator. It establishes the two points in time from which the experience is to be regarded—Tommo at the time of his stay with the Typees and Tommo after his escape and subsequent wanderings over the sea of life. In several other places the time lapse is underscored. In the first chapter the narrator recounts a humorous episode involving the native queen of Nukuheva "between two and three years after the adventures recorded in this volume." Several pages later he declares: "I may here state, and on my faith as an honest man, that though more than three years have elapsed since I left this same identical vessel [the *Dolly*], she still continues in the Pacific. . . ." The functioning of this dual time scheme is suggested by such sentences as the following, in which the narrator presents first his puzzled state of mind over the Typees' behavior and then indicates that he has since answered the question: "Their singular behavior almost led me to imagine that they never before had beheld a white man; but a few moments' reflection convinced me that this could not have been the case; and a more satisfactory reason for their conduct has since suggested itself to my mind."

And so the narrative goes: part of it recounting Tommo's adventures and his feelings at that time and part of it commenting on the past from the vantage point of the present. The difference that such a distinction can make is readily apparent in a consideration of Tommo's state of mind while he lived in Typee. Without distinguishing between Tommo's reconstruction of his past and his retrospective comment, it might seem that Tommo had some rough moments among the Typees and that he doubtlessly wanted to leave them, but that overall he enjoyed himself aplenty. This viewpoint is expressed, for example, on the cover of a recent paper back edition of *Typee* (Doubleday's Dolphin series): "Although his final escape was treacherous, Melville enjoyed his merry, idle days in captivity among the cannibals, where, he reported later in *Typee*, he wooed a maiden and participated in such festivities as the Feast of the Calabashes." Actually, Tommo enjoyed himself precious little.

When Tommo and his companion Toby arrive in the valley of Typee, Tommo is extremely fearful, and the question "Happar or Typee?" occurs to him repeatedly. He has heard tales of the Typees' ferocity, and he worries that he and Toby might have stumbled into the Typees' dread valley—as indeed they have—instead of having reached the friendly Happars as they had hoped. "I remained distressingly alive to all the fearful circumstances of our present situation," he writes. "Was it possible that, after all our vicissitudes, we were really in the terrible valley of Typee, and at the mercy of its inmates, a fierce and unrelenting tribe of savages?" The painful uncertainty reflected in this passage prefigures Tommo's dominant state of mind while he is in Typee. The information and misinformation which he receives about the Typees before he reaches their valley serve two functions. They set up a dramatic contrast between what Tommo expected and what he actually finds. The Typees are not half so fierce as he had heard. On the other hand, Tommo's early expectations and opinion of the Typees suggest a preconditioning of mind which he never completely overcomes. Much of his later anxiety can be accounted for in terms of this preconditioning. It is thus easier to perceive and understand Tommo's frequent state of fear while he is among the Typees if we recall with what terror he thought of them before he ever saw them.

After a week among the Typees, Tommo is still "fairly puzzled," but he begins to feel that "the horrible character imputed to these Typees appeared . . . wholly undeserved." Nevertheless he still has great apprehensions, and he quickly adds: "Notwithstanding the kind treatment we received, I was too familiar with the fickle disposition of savages not to feel anxious to withdraw from the valley, and put myself beyond the reach of that fearful death which, under all these smiling appearances, might yet menace us." He cannot think of escaping yet, however, because of some mysterious disease that has attacked his leg and made him lame. When Toby leaves the first time, Tommo becomes deeply depressed. Toby is injured by the Happars and brought back unconscious. "This incident," Tommo remarks, "threw a dark cloud over our prospects." They now realize, despondently, that there is little hope of escape. Tommo's spirits sink; his leg grows worse; and as he worries that "ere long we might be exposed to some caprice on the part of the islanders, I now gave up all hopes of recovery, and became a prey to the most gloomy thoughts. A deep dejection fell upon me. . . ." Then Toby disappears, and with that, Tommo says, "hope deserted me, and I fell a victim to despair." He feels "bitter remorse" at having come to Typee and suspects that "these treacherous savages" had "made away" with Toby. "The conduct of the islanders appeared inexplicable."

Only for brief moments can Tommo forget his troubles, as in the evening when the native girls anoint his body with "aka." But even "in the midst of so many consolatory circumstances," Tommo was "consumed by the most dismal forebodings" and he "remained a prey to the profoundest melancholy." Meanwhile his leg continued to ache and "threatened the most fatal results." Probably the word used most to describe Tommo's feelings during his stay among the Typees is "despair." He feels it frequently when he realizes that he cannot escape: "Sick at heart, I reseated myself upon the mats, and for the moment abandoned myself to despair."

As if to retain his sanity, Tommo develops a form of insensibility; then his leg improves: "Gradually I lost all knowledge of the regular recurrence of the days of the week, and sunk insensibly into that kind of apathy which ensues after some violent outbreak of despair. My limb suddenly healed, the swelling went down, the pain subsided, and I had every reason to suppose that I should soon completely recover from the affliction that had so long tormented me." Then comes the only time during his stay when he can truly enjoy himself. "Returning health and peace of mind," he writes, "gave a new interest to everything around me. I sought to diversify my time by as many enjoyments as lay within reach." His constant aide and companion, Kory-Kory, carries him daily to a small lake and watches over him while he swims and romps with the native girls. He even manages to have a rigid taboo eased so

that "the beauteous Fayaway" can paddle with him in his canoe.

His enjoyment is short-lived, however, for with the appearance and departure of Marnoo a few pages later, all his anxieties about Toby's fate and all "the most dreadful forebodings" return. A "bitter pang" shoots through him as he realizes anew that he is being kept prisoner. When Marnoo leaves, Tommo gives himself "up to the most desponding reflections." Fearing that the Typees may be aware of his great desire to escape, he determines "to make the best of a bad bargain, and to bear up manfully against whatever might betide." To allay their suspicions, he tries to "bury all regrets, and all remembrances" of his past life and fling himself "anew into all the social pleasures of the valley. . . ."

This mood is broken when he becomes deeply depressed over the prospects of being tattooed: "From the time of my casual encounter with Karky the artist, my life was one of absolute wretchedness." Then the mysterious disease of his leg returns with violence. His imagination runs wild after he sees evidence of cannibalism, and he has "horrible apprehensions" about being eaten: "My imagination ran riot in these horrid speculations, and I felt certain that the worst possible evils would befall me." After Marnoo's second visit, Tommo writes, "I was reduced to such a state, that it was with extreme difficulty I could walk. . . ." These were days, like most of his days in Typee, "of suffering and sorrow." Shortly thereafter he escapes, "but to such a state was I reduced," he says, "that three months elapsed before I recovered my health."

Such was Tommo's paradise. The question remains: if he suffered so much, physically and mentally, why do so many readers of *Typee* come away with the impression of a South Seas idyl? It is chiefly Tommo's retrospective commentary which causes that impression. In the extended recapitulation I have given above, none of that commentary was included. Tommo had an experience which was essentially negative; when he looks back over it he sometimes tells it straight—as much as it is possible to do so—but he sometimes romanticizes it. In the nearly four years after escaping from Typee, Tommo has seen much of civilization, and he has decided that the Typees, in retrospect, were not so bad after all and that his life there was more interesting than it actually was.

Tommo's retrospective comment, which frequently intrudes upon his narrative of despair, is marked by four moods. The first is nostalgia, which colors much of what he says as he remembers his stay in Typee. Tommo clearly yearns for the good old days. "In looking back to this period," he says, "and calling to remembrance the numberless proofs of kindness and respect which I received from the natives of the valley," he finds it hard to understand why he was so miserable. In the distance now, Typee seems almost like an Eden to him. Whenever passages such as the following appear in *Typee,* they suggest a mood developed over the years rather than a reflection of what Tommo felt while he lived with the natives: "The penalty of the Fall presses very lightly upon the valley of Typee. . . . Nature has planted the bread-fruit and the banana, and in her own good time she brings them to maturity, when the idle savage stretches forth his hand, and satisfies his appetite." Or

> There were none of those thousand sources of irritation that the ingenuity of civilized man has created to mar his own felicity. There were no foreclosures of mortgages, no protested notes, no bills payable, no debts of honor in Typee; no unreasonable tailors and shoemakers, perversely bent on being paid; . . . no destitute widows with their children starving on cold charities of the world; no beggars; no debtors' prisons.

Tommo makes it clear that the more he travels the world and the more he sees of humankind, the more Typee seems in retrospect an Eden. In Typee he began to have a rather high estimate of human nature, "but alas! since then I have been one of the crew of a man-of-war, and the pent-up wickedness of five hundred men has nearly overturned all my previous theories." His changing opinion could be charted perhaps in these terms: he originally maintained a very low opinion of the Typees, so low in fact that when he actually lived among them he found them strikingly unlike what he had expected, but when he left them and saw more of the world—then, they seemed positively noble by comparison. They have come to represent to him the Noble Savage, and nostalgically he looks back and praises their beauty of form and spirit, forgetting from time to time how he hated Typee when he was there. "All hail, therefore, Mehevi, King of the Cannibal Valley," he cries, "and long life and prosperity to his Typeean Majesty! May Heaven for many a year preserve him. . . . "

When the nostalgic mood is upon him, Tommo can even excuse the Typees for the aberration that horrified him most: "The reader will ere long have reason to suspect that the Typees are not free from the guilt of cannibalism; and he will then, perhaps, charge me with admiring a people against whom so odious a crime is chargeable. But this only enormity in their character is not half so horrible as it is usually described."

Nostalgia in its purest form is reflected when Tommo sighs: "In the valley of Typee ice-creams would never be rendered less acceptable by sudden frosts, nor would picnic parties be deferred on account of inauspicious snowstorms: for there day follows day in one unvarying round of summer and sunshine, and the whole year is one long tropical month of June just melting into July."

Where has the rain gone? In that tortuous journey he and Toby make through the mountains, rain falls frequently, but from the moment they reach Typee valley, rain is mentioned but once—and that time in a general comment on how showers in Typee are "intermitting and refreshing." Unless the Typees are suffering one of their rare droughts—and there is no evidence that they are—rain must have fallen during the four months Tommo lived with them. The fact that he remembers the valley as a place of constant and unvarying sunshine is further evidence of the nostalgia that sometimes distorts his retrospective vision.

Nostalgia is an emotion closely related to homesickness, and there is considerable evidence that Tommo has come to think of Typee with that feeling. Typee is in a sense a kind of home to him. From the first he thinks of Tinor and old Marheyo kindly as parental figures. He is made a part of the household, and Kory-Kory is as faithful as any brother could be. Fayaway may be more a sister than a mistress. Tommo's escape in the final chapter resembles running away from home rather than running to home. He is surrounded by his Typeean family. Together they make up a kind of domestic tableau: "Every one had left me except Marheyo, Kory-Kory, and poor dear Fayaway, who clung to me, sobbing indignantly." They know that he wishes to leave them, but they do not understand the reason. Although it pains him, old Marheyo allows his wayward "son" to leave home. In the climactic moment of the final chapter Marheyo aids Tommo in his escape: "In the midst of this tumult old Marheyo came to my side, and I shall never forget the benevolent expression of his countenance. He placed his arm upon my shoulder, and emphatically pronounced the only two English words I had taught him—'home' and 'mother.' I at once understood what he meant, and eagerly expressed my thanks to him."

It is not at all clear that Tommo actually understood Marheyo any better here than he had throughout his stay with him. The old man is even more inexplicable than the other natives. Tommo observes with wonder and incomprehension as Marheyo constructs a house that never seems to get built, sits for hours perched in a tree top, bathes at extremely odd times in a stream, or stalks through the brush with Tommo's old shoes proudly dangling from his neck. At the time of his escape Tommo thought Marheyo was telling him that he understood—that he knew Tommo wanted to return to his home and mother and that he would help him. But it seems just as likely that old Marheyo was expressing his own affection for Tommo and was trying to let him know that his home and mother were here, in Typee, and that he considered him a member of his family. Since Tommo seemed determined to run away, however, old Marheyo unselfishly helped him in whatever way he could. Tommo could not at that time have considered Typee his real home, but as he views the whole experience in retrospect, he often seems to be feeling something akin to homesickness, and ironically old Marheyo's words take on new meaning.

Tommo's second mood as he looks back is righteous anger, which characterizes that body of commentary charging various evils against civilization and voicing Tommo's thorough disapproval of missionaries. "Ill-fated people!" he cries.

> I shudder when I think of the change a few years will produce in their paradisaical abode; and probably when most destructive vices, and the worst attendances on civilization, shall have driven all peace and happiness from the valley, the magnanimous French will proclaim to the world that the Marquesas Islands have been converted to Christianity! and this the Catholic world will doubtless consider as a glorious event. Heaven help the 'Isles of the Sea!'

Such preachments against the civilized world are digressions and represent the feelings of the narrator in the *pres-*

*ent*, not his feelings or opinions while he lived with the Typees.

Tommo's anger toward the missionaries is also a reflection of his present state of mind. He apparently knew little about the work of missionaries in the South Seas until after his experience in Typee. He admits, "Not until I visited Honolulu [after Typee] was I aware of the fact that the small remnant of the natives had been civilized into draft horses, and evangelized into beasts of burden. But so it is. They have been literally broken into the traces, and are harnessed to the vehicles of their spiritual instructors like so many dumb brutes!" Thus, having lived among the Typees and then in subsequent years heard of and seen first-hand the bumbling and sometimes destructive efforts of missionaries, the narrator interrupts his reconstruction of the past to voice his present indignation at the lack of understanding manifested in missionary work among the natives. Tommo's sermonizing about the wrongs of the civilized world and the narrowness of missionaries produces the general impression of a broad-minded man living among a primitive people and appreciating as most men could not the simplicity and genuineness he finds there. As we have seen, this was far from the case.

The third mood in Tommo's retrospective narrative helps a great deal to blunt the keen sense of past recurrent suffering. It is the comfortable objectivity of the various and often extended descriptions of practically every phase of Typeean life. While Tommo is living among the Typees, he notices much but understands very little. He finds the natives unfathomable and their ways inexplicable. He is always trying to get answers to his questions, to "find out," as he puts it, "the meaning of the strange things that were going on." His failure to understand what he sees accounts for much of his frustration and agony. "I saw everything," he says, "but could comprehend nothing." All is a mystery to him. Yet it sometimes appears that he observed and understood very well, for parts of the book make up an excellent travelogue. Here is a man who in recounting his terribly depressing stay among cannibals frequently interrupts his narrative of despair to assume the stance of a tourist and to tell in a relaxed voice and in detail all about the breadfruit tree and the making of tapa. He describes a typical day in Typee valley, the ancient stone terraces, the Feast of the Calabashes, the preparation of arva, the cooking of hogs, a chief's tomb, the Typees' religious practices, the various civil institutions of Typee, matrimonial relationships among the natives, burial procedures, and a Typeean fishing party. Finally he recounts the natural history of the valley, which includes comments on dogs, cats, and various other matters. How could a traveler who noted all that so thoroughly have time to be miserable?

Again, these descriptions come from the narrator's present state of mind. They grow out of years of looking back on and reflecting and reading about the things he saw in Typee. And since there are so many of them and since they interrupt the main narrative so often, they have the effect of making his suffering seem less prolonged and intense. For example, after describing how he felt when Marnoo leaves, Tommo waits twelve chapters before telling us again what he was thinking and how he felt. During those eighty pages he tells of a few things that happened in the valley, but he spends most of the time in describing Typee and its customs.

A fourth mood is seen in the light commentary, which is often humorous. One of the most amusing episodes in the book involves Tommo's bad leg. When Mehevi first sees the situation he immediately calls for "an aged islander, who might have been taken for old Hippocrates himself." The old fellow is not as gentle as he looks, however, for he at once sets to work pinching and hammering Tommo's painfully sensitive leg with absolute vigor: "He fastened on the unfortunate limb as if it were something for which he had been long seeking, and muttering some kind of incantation continued his discipline, pounding it after a fashion that set me well nigh crazy." While this is going on, Toby frantically gestures, trying to stop Tommo's "tormentor": "To have looked at my companion . . . one would have thought that he was the deaf and dumb alphabet incarnated." When this strange form of treatment does finally end, Tommo's leg is "left much in the same condition as a rump-steak after undergoing the castigating process which precedes cooking." Now this episode is more comic than serious because of the way Tommo describes it as he views it through the film of years. It certainly was not at all amusing when it happened.

The effect produced by such incidents as the Typeean doctor's treatment of Tommo's afflicted leg is something like that which results when one listens to a talented storyteller relating with a grin anecdotes about his adventurous past. The listener may get the erroneous impression that the narrator always enjoyed himself tremendously because of his present amusement. There were moments when Tommo was mildly amused and entertained by what he saw, but the amusement and entertainment are magnified many times through the passage of years. For example, in one of those rare periods when he is able to appreciate the Typees' sheer love of life, Tommo makes a pop-gun for a child from a piece of bamboo. It causes a sensation, and Typees of all ages line up to have Tommo produce one of the marvelous toys for them. For several days sounds of the pop-guns are heard throughout the valley. Any slight annoyance that Tommo might once have felt in having to make so many toys—he finally manages to train an assistant in their manufacture—and any other disagreeable aspects of the pop-gun incident are completely lost as he reminisces about it in the most bemused terms of mock-heroism:

> Pop, Pop, Pop, Pop, now resounded all over the valley. Duels, skirmishes, pitched battles, and general engagements were to be seen on every side. Here, as you walked along a path which led through a thicket, you fell into a cunningly-laid ambush, and became a target for a body of musketeers whose tattooed limbs you could just see peeping into view through the foliage. There, you were assailed by the intrepid garrison of a house, who levelled their bamboo rifles at you from between the upright canes which composed its sides. Farther on you were fired upon by a detachment of sharpshooters, mounted upon the top of a pi-pi.

Tommo therefore narrates from two perspectives—then and now. His present moods—nostalgia, anger, objective observance, and humor—frequently intrude upon the narrative which describes his actual states of mind while he was in Typee. The result shows clearly two views of Typee and emphasizes the changing subjective quality of that entire experience for Tommo.

In a larger framework the two views of Typee suggest a fundamental concept of reality—namely, that it is ultimately unknowable. One of the most important questions to be raised after perceiving Tommo's double perspective is this: which of his views of Typee is the right one? Or, indeed, is it possible to have a true view of Typee? The past seems to become confused with the present. An experience such as Tommo's is complex and organic and does not end abruptly but undergoes transformation as it continues to be a part of his mind. The pure past, then, is irrecoverable. That warning resounds throughout **Typee,** which is very much a book about the past.

Tommo finds that lesson difficult to learn. He is the first hero Melville created and quite possibly the most naive, for he never seems to grasp the nature of the past or to realize that he cannot go back. His journey to Typee is both real and symbolic. Lawrence argued that it suggests an attempted return to the past of the race: "The heart of the Pacific is still the Stone Age; in spite of steamers. The heart of the Pacific seems like a vast vacuum in which, mirage-like, continues the life of myriads of ages back." Lawrence's argument is based on his view of Typee as a primitive Eden, which is no longer possible for modern man. The point is perceptive and interesting, but what Tommo is searching for can also be expressed in more personal and less mythic terms. If, as Lawrence states, Tommo wants to go back, it is his own past he yearns for, perhaps the joyous time of childhood. What I want to suggest here, therefore, is that Tommo's desire to leave his ship for something better is a longing for some past happy state in his experience, which he contrasts to his present restlessness.

Tommo seems to be yearning for past happier times when near the beginning he makes it clear that he cannot live in the present situation and can see no relief in the future. He feels surrounded by a crew "composed of a parcel of dastardly and mean-spirited wretches. . . ." Knowing how long whaling voyages can last, he concludes that "there was little to encourage one in looking forward to the future, especially as I had always had a presentiment that we should make an unfortunate voyage, and our experience so far had justified the expectation." His original plan of escape does not involve Typee or even the friendly Happar Valley. He merely wants to hide out in what he believes to be the lovely mountains that look down on the bay and to watch from that point ("with a cluster of plantains within easy reach") until his ship leaves. Then he plans to come down to Nukuheva and to make an "agreeable" visit with the friendly natives until a good opportunity for leaving the island presents itself.

It is a childish plan. Yet it might be expected of the Tommo who tells us early in the book that "I had made up my mind to 'run away'." He has sailed on a ship called

*Dolly,* a name that suggests the world of childhood. What he finds on board the *Dolly,* however, is opposite from the joy and innocence of childhood. The world of the *Dolly* is quite distinctly adult, with all its imperfection, and Tommo finds it intolerable. What he wants is a situation that is congenial to his own youth and naiveté. He cannot find it on the *Dolly.* He feels imprisoned and decides to run away.

Thus the basic structural pattern of the book is established—escape and return. In the beginning Tommo is depicted as a young man who cannot accept the sordidness and uncertainties of the world; he is, in a sense, a child among adults, isolated and unhappy, he would like nothing better than to go back into a time in his life when cruelty and selfishness and unhappiness were relatively unknown. In **Typee** he symbolically goes back. There he finds a situation closely resembling childhood. After his first night in the valley, he awakes and sees around him "faces in which childish delight and curiosity were vividly portrayed." As he lives among the Typees, they seem more and more like children. Even in battles with their enemies they run about making sounds that resemble "the halloos of a parcel of truant boys who had lost themselves in the woods." They seem scarcely more serious or mature in their profoundest religious affairs, for "in the celebration of many of their strange rites, they appeared merely to seek a sort of childish amusement." The chief idol is like a "doll" which the priest Kolory "alternately fondles and chides," and "the whole of these proceedings were like those of a parcel of children playing with dolls and baby houses." What little work or food gathering they do reminds Tommo of children at play. Narnee, a young chief, starts up a tree to gather coconuts, and "as if defeated in this childish attempt, he now sinks to the earth despondingly, beating his breast in well-acted despair; and then, starting to his feet all at once, and throwing back his head, raises both hands, like a school-boy about to catch a falling ball." After that exhibition he goes on to climb the tree and fling the nuts to the ground.

In every area of life the Typees are described in terms of childhood. Tommo was unhappy in the adult world, and he escaped to a child's world. But he is even more unhappy there. Once growing out of childhood, he cannot again be a part of it. In Typee his situation is reversed from that on board the *Dolly.* He is now an adult among children. The anxiety and despair which he experiences in Typee define what it means to be an adult in a child's world: he is completely alienated. He cannot communicate with the children. Their ways and their thinking are inexplicable to him, and he lives in fear because they are as unpredictable as children. All men yearn at times to return to the sunshine of childhood. In **Typee** Melville portrayed a man who got his wish. And that man could not wait to escape and return to the adult world.

If he felt imprisoned on the *Dolly,* he is many times more aware of being "hemmed in" with the Typees. Frequently Melville uses imagery that suggests Tommo's captive situation. Typee valley is hemmed in by the forbidding mountains that Tommo painfully passed through to get there. He is aware that he is also "hemmed in by hostile tribes," and cannot pass through their lands. The Typees will not even consider letting him go. He is their captive plaything. They are as mysterious to him as the mind of a child is to an adult. His opportunity for running away comes just before he is physically and psychologically destroyed by a strange and beautiful world of childlike natives.

Tommo's return to the adult world, however, does not bring him peace. After months of recovering and then years of traveling about, he once again feels hemmed in. He suffers from the absurdities of civilized dogmas which press in on him. He is surrounded by human beings who are so lacking in dignity and decency that his estimate of human nature falls considerably. After nearly four years he has to run away again. He has experienced a great deal, but maturity has not come with it. He thinks he can return to the past again, this time by recapturing it in his imagination, by calling up Typee. He sits down to write a narrative, and the reader sees what Tommo cannot—that he is the sum total of all his experience, including those years of wandering *after* he left Typee, and that he can never go back, can never remember it as it actually was, because of what he has since become. While he was on the *Dolly,* he dreamed of an Elysium of childhood; finding that Typee was not Elysium, he returned, but he was not back long before the naive dream began anew.

Separating each escape and return is a trial, a painful experience which tests the mettle of the hero and acts as a barrier preventing his returning the same way as he escaped. When Tommo and Toby run away from the *Dolly,* they must make their way through hazardous chasms and steep mountains with little food. It is almost as if they have entered a damp inferno:

> Five foaming streams, rushing through as many gorges, and swelled and turbid by the recent rains, united together in one mad plunge of nearly eighty feet, and fell with wild uproar into a deep black pool scooped out of the gloomy-looking rocks that lay piled around, and thence in one collected body dashed down a narrow sloping channel which seemed to penetrate into the very bowels of the earth. Overhead, vast roots of trees hung down from the sides of the ravine dripping with moisture, and trembling with the concussions produced by the fall. It was now sunset, and the feeble uncertain light that found its way into these caverns and woody depths heightened their strange appearance, and reminded us that in a short time we should find ourselves in utter darkness.

Here Tommo and Toby spend the first terrible night of their journey. "The accumulated horrors of that night," he says, "the deathlike coldness of the place, the appalling darkness and the dismal sense of our forlorn condition, almost unmanned me." They spend five nights chilled and wet. Tommo's injured leg and the accompanying fever nearly drive him out of his mind. During the day they alternately climb steep inclines and make their way down cavernous ravines, wandering without direction, until they finally chance upon Typee.

Although the mountain journey is the most extensively detailed trial in the book, two other experiences occur that

*Portrait of Melville's shipmate, Richard Tobias Greene, on whom the character Toby of* Typee *is based.*

must be surmounted before Tommo can make his escapes. To reach civilization again, he must kill a man, the fierce Mow-Mow. After pushing off from the land, Tommo and his rescuers encounter a group of the natives attempting to cut off their escape. As Mow-Mow swims toward the boat, Tommo painfully realizes what he must do:

> Even at the moment I felt horror at the act I was about to commit; but it was no time for pity or compunction, and with a true aim, and exerting all my strength, I dashed the boat-hook at him. It struck him just below the throat, and forced him downwards. I had no time to repeat my blow, but I saw him rise to the surface in the wake of the boat, and never shall I forget the ferocious expression of his countenance.

Tommo's other trial is only casually mentioned, but it is of great importance. After escaping Typee and living once again among civilized people, he has recently "been one of the crew of a man-of-war," he says, and that was an experience in unqualified and undiluted evil, a nightmare of concentrated wickedness. He had to go through this trial of a floating hell as a psychological preparation for writing down much of what is in *Typee.* Had he not undergone the man-of-war experience, Typee might not have looked so fine to him in retrospect and he might not have revisited it imaginatively.

These hellish experiences, which are necessary for all three escapes—the first to Typee, the second away from Typee, and third to Typee again (but this time in the imagination), act as barriers to Tommo's returning over the same route. After those terrible days in the mountains he thinks it practically impossible to go back over them. After killing Mow-Mow he has cut himself off from Typee. He can never make another actual visit there on friendly terms. Nor does he have the stomach for returning to the real and imperfect world through sailing again aboard a man-of-war. Therefore, when he escapes from Typee, it is by way of the sea, not over the mountains; when he returns to Typee, it is not by really going there but by thinking and writing about it; and when he finishes his narrative and returns once again to the outside world, the imperfect adult world, it will doubtlessly be by a different means than a man-of-war. Even if the course first traveled were not so painful, however, Tommo would still find another route to try to return by, as he explains early in the book: "There is scarcely anything when a man is in difficulties that he is more disposed to look upon with abhorrence than a right-about retrograde movement—a systematic going over of the already trodden ground; and especially if he has a love of adventure, such a course appears indescribably repulsive, so long as there remains the least hope to be derived from braving untried difficulties."

Tommo's comment about "retrograde movement" is significantly revealing. He is Melville's hero not yet mature. As Newton Arvin [in his *Herman Melville,* 1950] perceptively put it: "Not in avoiding the clash between consciousness and the unconscious, between mind and emotion, between anxious doubt and confident belief, but in confronting these antinomies head-on and, hopefully, transcending them—in that direction, as Melville intuitively saw, lay his right future as an adult person." Never-

theless, it is clear that Tommo has the makings of the kind of searching hero Melville later depicts with admiration. He is a man "in difficulties" with his surroundings as Melville's later heroes all are. He has not, however, learned enough yet about the complex and ambiguous nature of experience; his restlessness leads him backward instead of forward. Yet he knows the danger of "retrograde movement," and his backward searching is over untried routes. Like the rest of Melville's heroes he is no systematizer. He is young, but already he distrusts the dogmas and systems he sees mankind worshiping. Within him is that distinctive "love of adventure" which in a later hero develops into the preference of the "howling infinite" over the "lee shore." When Tommo realizes that there is no Typee left to him and that he must take his search to the open sea, he will then be an Ishmael.

*William B. Dillingham, in his* An Artist in the Rigging: The Early Work of Herman Melville, *University of Georgia Press, 1972, 157 p.*

## David Williams  (essay date 1975)

[*In the following essay, Williams notes differences between Melville and the narrator of* Typee, *and explores satirical aspects of the work.*]

That Herman Melville's first book, ***Typee: A Peep at Polynesian Life,*** contains elements of autobiography is indisputable, but what he made of his Marquesan excursion and captivity, if more than travelogue, is little explored. "The fact that the work is strongly autobiographical bothers some critics," observes a commentator who takes the real "memoirs" of ***Typee*** to be aesthetic rather than historical. "Although all agree that Melville stretched matters of time, setting, character, and plot to suit his narrative intentions, some fail to consider that he could also have stretched his point of view to allow an ironic relationship of author to protagonist" [Paul Witherington in *Arizona Quarterly,* XXVI (1970)]. The one reading to date which takes cogent account of this possible distance between Melville and his narrator finds the latter to be unaware of the deadening non-complexity within his primitive "Eden." Apparently recalling that John Murray accepted the manuscript for his "Colonial and Home Library" on the assurance that its narrative was "authentic," and enlarging upon D. H. Lawrence's suggestion [in his *Studies in Classic American Literature,* 1923] that Melville, as much as he wanted to, could not go back to savagery, Richard Ruland [in *Nineteenth Century Fiction* XXIII (1968)] says that "Tommo is Murray's narrator, speaking to the vast public for informative, uplifting, and escapist writing. There are, of course, long sections of ***Typee*** in which Melville and Tommo merge. Melville supports Tommo's criticism of commercialism and the fruits of missionary activity. But he understands the valley far better than Tommo does and he knows what Tommo does not: what is wrong with the life lived there and why Tommo must not stay."

"I was amused," Tommo says nevertheless for himself,

> at the appearance of four or five old women who, in a state of utter nudity, with their arms extend-

ed flatly down their sides, and holding themselves perfectly erect, were leaping stiffly into the air, like so many sticks bobbing to the surface, after being pressed perpendicularly into the water . . . They did not appear to attract the observation of the crowd around them, but I must candidly confess that, for my own part, I stared at them most pertinaciously.

When the rite is explained to him by his primitive attendant, Tommo concludes, "It was evident that Kory-Kory considered this an all-sufficient reason for so indecorous a custom; but I must say that it did not satisfy me as to its propriety." Tommo, then, is at least occasionally critical of the life lived in Typee, although, as in the present instance, he is not at all self-critical, being willing to account as piety what is his evident impropriety. Nor is Tommo seriously tempted to stay in the valley. His exaggerated fears of cannibalism, his horror of tattooing (which art has been demonstrated to be of ideal significance throughout Melville's work), and his repeated attempt to escape his kindly captors suggest that something must be wrong with Tommo. The strange malady which afflicts his leg and drives him at last to flee the valley is, in fact, part of a complex of identity which he unwittingly assumes in the larger story told by Melville. If author and protagonist tend to merge in criticizing the abuses of civilization in this primitive world, such univocality has not survived the American revised edition of 1846. This study essays, then, to re-examine the finished consistency of *Typee*'s art, to redefine in generic terms the distance between Melville and his narrator, and to identify the unrecognized objects and functions of satire in Melville's "autobiographical" work.

Ruland argues that "Tommo, like Ishmael, is conscious of himself as a story-teller. He is fully aware that he is narrating an adventure tale with a social message. The literature of the eighteenth century has not been lost on him. He emulates Swift in setting up an exotic land to berate the shortcomings of life at home." Tommo, however, berates the homeland with invective which is exacerbatingly direct. When he says, "The enormities perpetrated in the South Seas upon some of the inoffensive islanders well nigh pass belief," he speaks not at all with a satiric voice; he has assumed the pulpit. The naïve and unreflecting Gulliver, on the other hand, is a perfect vehicle for ironic satire, humane and warmhearted where the Lilliputians are petty and nasty, thoughtless and crass where the Brobdingnagians are farsighted. His early sympathy notwithstanding, as Gulliver describes the paltry foibles of Lilliput, all possible correspondence to European habits and customs escapes him; as he gives account of his dear homeland to the ideal king of Brobdingnag, he reveals his complicity in a destructive and damnable mode of thought; by the time he reaches the grand Academy of Lagado and embraces various experiments of the projectors, even offering "improvements" to some, he has lost himself in the blind folly of his race; in his last voyage to Houyhnhnm-land he seems finally to lose touch with his kind precisely by being, as he says of Captain Pocock of Bristol although disavowing it of himself or his Houyhnhnm master, "a little too positive in his own opinions, which was the cause of his destruction, as it hath been of several oth-

ers." The course of such satire seems to be progressive unreliability, a gradual falling away of the narrator from a plane where he is the unwitting spokesman for his narrator to a position where he has become the sum of every stigmatized thing. (Presumably Swift is also satirizing the satiric stance itself for its lofty purism, its divorce from the human world.) But in every case where the satire is directed against "home," it must be remembered that it is Swift, not Gulliver, who "sets up" an exotic land and regulates its reference.

Tommo seems at the outset to speak with authorial reliability; he may appear even to be "setting up an exotic land to berate the shortcomings of life" transported from home. Describing the conquest of Marquesan shores by the French, he says, "A valiant warrior doubtless, but a prudent one too, was this same Rear-Admiral Du Petit Thouars. Four heavy, double-banked frigates and three covettes to frighten a parcel of naked heathen into subjection! Sixty-eight pounders to demolish huts of cocoanut boughs, and Congreve rockets to set on fire a few canoe sheds! The clearest approximation in *Gulliver's Travels* is Gulliver's." glowing account to the king of Brobdingnag of the properties of gunpowder, but in *Typee* we are given no similar ironic dislocation of perception, only of events or circumstance (no one here defends the use of "gunpowder" on the grounds of "liberal" education, and valiance is merely imputed to, not assumed by, the Rear-Admiral). It would be, in terms of satiric technique, as if Gulliver had jeeringly approved an English invasion of Blefuscu, say, without already having done so himself. The differences here are largely those of satire and sarcasm.

Melville-Tommo displays his abhorrence of the abuses of "civilized" religion in a similarly sarcastic sentence: "Not until I visited Honolulu was I aware of the fact that the small remnant of the natives had been civilized into draught horses, and evangelized into beasts of burden." There follows an account of a New England missionary lady who, early accustomed in life to chasing cows, has gone out to great hardships of life in the South Pacific hoping to round up the souls of lost heathen. Her heavenly endeavour is assisted now by two heathen slaves yoked to her cart who permit her to do her chasing sitting down. These heathen, nominally the field white unto harvest, wait patiently like farm horses in the traces outside the church which has been built to save them. The discrepancy between missionary profession and practice may furnish another circumstantial irony, but the lack of distance between Melville and Tommo—in particular, the lack of a truly lying perspective—precludes the fulfillment of satiric form.

Both instances cited are nevertheless among the twelve lengthy passages of direct commentary omitted from the American revised edition. These omissions, totalling over twenty pages of text in the Northwestern-Newberry edition, are in every instance concerned with the declarative comparison of primitive and civilized states of being. Leon Howard [in a "Historical Note" in the 1968 Northwestern-Newberry edition of *Typee*] regards these deletions as Melville's concession to his publisher's demands for "a greater regard for the proprieties and a less blunt treatment of European civilization in the South Seas." It is at least of equal benefit, however, to judge Melville's particular revisions by aesthetic standards, according to the design of the completed work. The eight per cent reduction in the text has the effect of Herman Melville writing himself out of the script. Many of the more blatant authorial intrusions are erased and we are committed more deeply to the care of the teller of the tale. The balance of this study is intended to illustrate the artfulness of Melville's belated impulse.

The possibility has already been mentioned that Tommo as narrator is a property of John Murray's "Library." Through Tommo, Melville might well accede ironically to the tastes of a conventional middle class suspicious of fiction and starved for fact. If this is the case, then the potential for satirizing a gullible audience is almost unlimited. Consider the case of Kory-Kory making fire:

> The islander, placing the larger stick obliquely against some object, with one end elevated at an angle of forty-five degrees, mounts astride of it like an urchin about to gallop off upon a cane, and then grasping the smaller one firmly in both hands, he rubs its pointed end slowly up and down the extent of a few inches on the principal stick, until at last he makes a narrow groove in the wood, with an abrupt termination at the point furthest from him, where all the dusty particles which the friction creates are accumulated in a little heap.

> At first Kory-Kory goes to work quite leisurely, but gradually quickens his pace, and waxing warm in the employment, drives the stick furiously along the smoking channel, plying his hands to and fro with amazing rapidity, the perspiration starting from every pore. As he approaches the climax of his effort, he pants and gasps for breath, and his eyes almost start from their sockets with the violence of his exertions. This is the critical stage of the operation; all his previous labors are vain if he cannot sustain the rapidity of the movement until the reluctant spark is produced. Suddenly he stops, becomes perfectly motionless. His hands still retain their hold of the smaller stick, which is pressed convulsively against the further end of the channel among the fine powder there accumulated, as if he had just pierced through and through some little viper that was wriggling and struggling to escape from his clutches. The next moment a delicate wreath of smoke curls spirally into the air, the heap of dusty particles glows with fire, and Kory-Kory almost breathless, dismounts from his steed.

> This operation appeared to me to be the most laborious species of work performed in Typee.

Any sensitivity to diction reveals the sexual innuendo of this passage. The comedy increases when one notes that the making of fire follows hard upon a sensuous account of the "sweet nymphs" anointing Tommo's whole body with juices of the "aka." Tommo's unacknowledged desire is now immediately projected onto the matter-of-fact activity about him, but in so doing, Melville has discounted the reliability of his narrator even as he has assumed con-

trol of the reference between his "exotic land" and the readers at home (using the one to disparage the other).

The process by which Tommo is progressively revealed as a satiric *alazon* points up the total range and function of Melville's satire. Ostensibly, Tommo sets out to expose in novelistic fashion the social evils of civilization. In a number of passages retained even in the revised edition, he laments the corruption of innocence by the harbingers of civilization. One example concerns sexual wantonness:

> Our ship was now wholly given up to every species of riot and debauchery. Not the feeblest barrier was interposed between the unholy passions of the crew and their unlimited gratification. The grossest licentiousness and the most shameful inebriety prevailed, with occasional and but short-lived interruptions, through the whole period of her stay. Alas for the poor savages when exposed to the influence of these polluting examples! Unsophisticated and confiding, they are easily led into every vice, and humanity weeps over the ruin thus remorselessly inflicted upon them by their European civilizers. Thrice happy are they who, inhabiting some yet undiscovered island in the midst of the ocean, have never been brought into contaminating contact with the white man.

Somewhat like Ishmael, Tommo senses the potential evil resident in whiteness. What he fails to remember is that he is white. Tommo's pious morality recoils on him when we find out that he too has "polluted" native women with his licentious thoughts and acts.

After six months out of sight of land, the crew of the *Dolly* learn they are bound for the Marquesas. The first item on the list of Tommo's great expectations is "Naked houris." Once arrived, he spends a great deal of time swimming with a rout of vivacious girls in the lake. (This "lake," incidentally, has not been located in Marquesan geography.) He continually offers us "revealing glimpses of their forms, as, in the course of their rapid progress, they shot for an instant partly into the air."

On one level, of course, Tommo's account seems designed to titillate, though not to offend, a respectable audience. When he explains, "I was ever partial to what is termed in the 'Young Men's Own Book'—'the society of virtuous and intelligent young ladies'," his parlour euphemisms need be no more than amused protestations of his own innocence, abjurations offered less on his than on his "virtuous" readers' behalf. The type of militant piety to which he pretends, however, in the scene where he stares at the naked old women cannot originate solely in the circumstance of their being old. When the "young females" of Typee gather about Toby and him to give full play, "void of artificial restraint," to their sexual curiosity, Tommo protests that "my feelings of propriety were exceedingly shocked, for I could not but consider them as having overstepped the due limits of female decorum."

Tommo is not distressed, nevertheless, when his plan to paddle Fayaway about the lake in a canoe which is taboo to women "completely horrifie[s] Kory-Kory's notions of propriety," nor is he offended when, seized suddenly by a bewitching idea, Fayaway removes her robe and spreads it as a sail. "We American sailors pride ourselves," he says, "upon our straight clean spars, but a prettier little mast than Fayaway made was never shipped a-board of any craft." Tommo is careful, then, to observe no proprieties but those of his audience, and yet he does so with a prurience which is only aggravated by his prudery. He is quick, for example, to follow up a total glimpse of his admired "Miss Fayaway" with the assurance that he has made a dress for her out of good ship's calico: "In it she looked, I must confess, something like an opera dancer. The drapery of the latter damsel generally commences a little above the elbows, but my island beauty's began at the waist, and terminated sufficiently far above the ground to reveal the most bewitching ankle in the universe." It is this sober insistence upon conventionality, propriety, "normality" just when he has inferred or even revealed the opposite, it is the tacit desire to spy without being espied, which makes Tommo the Peeping Tom of the Typee Valley. In each of these instances, in fact, it is the narrator, and not the author, who endeavors to give us *A Peep at Polynesian Life.*

This disturbing sexuality might contribute to Tommo's satiric characterization in yet another manner. When he describes the custom in Typee of eating raw fish, Tommo exaggerates rather strangely his concern: "I grieve to state so distressing a fact, but the inhabitants of Typee were in the habit of devouring fish much in the same way that a civilized being would eat a radish . . . Raw fish! Shall I ever forget my sensations when I first saw my island beauty devour one? Oh, heavens! Fayaway, how could you ever have contracted so vile a habit?" Soon enough, however, he tells us that "the custom grew less odious in my eyes, and I soon accustomed myself to the sight." It would be surprising had he not, for the prudish Tommo seems to have hit upon a way of describing fellatio which is both expressive of his jealousy of native male competitors and is complimentary to his racial refinement: "Let no one imagine, however, that the lovely Fayaway was in the habit of swallowing great vulgar-looking fishes: oh, no; with her beautiful small hand she would clasp a delicate, little, golden-hued love of a fish, and eat it as elegantly and as innocently as though it were a Naples biscuit." Once more, Tommo appears to strain for propriety even as he reveals (for him) the opposite, except that this time the consciousness of "abnormality" is almost too much for him: "But alas! it was after all a raw fish; and all I can say is, that Fayaway ate it in a more ladylike manner than any other girl of the valley." The intense self-concern he has exhibited, not only in his sexual jealousy but in the way Fayaway's behaviour might reflect on him, begins to expose this traveller in all his crucial pride.

In contrast to the kindness, the generosity, and the devotedness of the Typees, Tommo is selfish and so egocentric that he must impose his will wherever he is. In the journey through the chaotic mountains, Toby and Tommo debate the wisdom of immediate descent to the pleasant valley below: "My companion, however, incapable of resisting the tempting prospect which the place held out of an abundant supply of food and other means of enjoyment, still clung to his own inconsiderate view of the subject, nor

could all my reasoning shake it." Toby is inconsiderate for holding opinions of his own; Tommo alone uses reason. Later Tommo's observations are the just ones, although their positions are completely reversed. Toby is denigrated for reluctance: "To the justice of these observations Toby somewhat reluctantly assented."

As a corollary of his egocentricity, Tommo furnishes many examples of his inclination toward self-aggrandizement and self-congratulation. His sense of his own generosity is badly inflated as he gives away some mouldy shoes to Marheyo. Even if he would praise his friend Toby in the descent into the valley, his language does not reach beyond himself: "I could not avoid a thousand times congratulating myself upon having such a companion in an enterprise like the present."

Most importantly, perhaps, Tommo serves as the emblem, in his reception of Marnoo, of the white man's vanity, his pride, his jealousy, and his supercilious treatment of native peoples. He says, "I made up my mind that some savage warrior of consequence, who had not yet enjoyed the honor of an audience, was desirous of paying his respects on the present occasion. So vain had I become by the lavish attention to which I had been accustomed, that I felt half inclined, as a punishment for such neglect, to give this Marnoo a cold reception." Moments later he confesses, "The conduct of the savages had prepared me to anticipate from every newcomer the same extravagant expressions of curiosity and regard." In both instances, he blames his environment for his vanity instead of the innate egocentricity which he has amply demonstrated. Melville concludes this revelation of character with devastating satiric treatment of his narrator:

> When I observed the striking devotion of the natives to him, and their temporary withdrawal of all attention from myself, I felt not a little piqued. The glory of Tommo is departed, thought I, and the sooner he removes from the valley, the better. These were my feelings at the moment, and they were prompted by that glorious principle inherent in all heroic natures—the strong-rooted determination to have the biggest share of the pudding or go without any of it.

Tommo may pass off his spiteful vanity as the excess of an heroic nature, but he does so with a metaphor drawn from child's play.

On the facing page, Melville has deliberately and skillfully contrasted Tommo's conduct with the absence of piqued pride or self-concern in the primitive mind. Kory-Kory has been left on shore while Tommo and Fayaway paddle about the lake in their infamous canoe: "Kory-Kory, who had watched our manoeuvres with admiration, now clapped his hands in transport, and shouted like a madman." It is a madness which, compared to Tommo's pose, seems heaven's sense.

Granted, then, the sexual perversion and self-conceit of Tommo, it is not difficult to see beyond the narrator's version of wickedness and folly as social diseases to the satirist's vision of evil as a disease of the intellect. The history of this diseased intellect must yet be traced in the identity of Tommo. But it should now be apparent why the young

Melville might fear misrepresentation at the hands of an unreliable narrator, and it is not unreasonable to consider his initial intrusions as a guide to authorial position. In the process, nevertheless, of making sweeping omissions, Melville has committed us more fully to the teller of his tale. It is as though he has anticipated D. H. Lawrence's slightly altered maxim (*Classic American Literature*), "Never trust the teller. Trust the tale."

The tale of *Typee* is a tale worth trusting. It has all of the literary sanction of John Milton behind it. The true response to a primitive view of the world can only be a cosmic or religious view—positively re-presenting a myth. And the myth that answers Melville's view of the Marquesan peoples is the myth of the Fall.

There is every reason to believe, from historical evidence alone, that Melville was acquainted with *Paradise Lost* before he wrote *Typee.* The internal evidence of his first literary work indicates the breadth of that acquaintance. Shortly after Satan's colossal flight across Chaos to escape the pangs of hell, the arch foe of man alights in the chaotic world outside the Garden:

> Now to th'ascent of that steep savage Hill
> Satan had journey'd on, pensive and slow;
> But further way found none, so thick entwin'd,
> As one continu'd brake, the undergrowth
> Of shrubs and tangling bushes had perplext
> All path of Man or Beast that pass'd that way,
> One Gate there only was, and that look'd East
> On th'other side: which when th'arch-felon saw
> Due entrance he disdain'd, and in contempt,
> At one slight bound high overleap'd all bound
> Of Hill or highest Wall, and sheer within
> Lights on his feet.

Tommo arrives at Nukuheva yearning for the land, having been banished from it for more than six months. Not only does he recognize the great evils of the place from which he has come, but he admits the pristine beauty of the present landscape in all its solitude, "having apparently been untenanted since the morning of the creation." In his progress through the tangled undergrowth of canes on the ascent of the steep mountain, he "further way finds none" until he employs a tool brought with him from civilization. Searching for a passage into a paradisal valley, he must avoid the only available entrance from the sea and it is with great difficulty that he at last descends the interior wall of the valley and "sheer within, lights on his feet."

One of the vehicles for expressing the movement of the Fall in *Paradise Lost* is a sustained sexual metaphor. Satan, made celibate in hell for his sexual offense of incest in Heaven, symbolically violates the garden womb, causing Adam and Eve to fall and riot in concupiscent lust. In the process, "Earth felt the wound, and . . . gave signs of woe, That all was lost" (P.L., IX, 782-84). Tommo's lame, unhealing leg which, from classical times (Oedipus), has been remarked as the sign of sexual abnormality lends support, in addition to everything else, to the idea of a symbolic violation of this other garden.

But Melville is also choosing more obvious symbols of the myth. Tommo and Toby glide through the mountain grass "much in the fashion of a couple of serpents." Tommo's innocuous diction again betrays Melville's intent when he says, "Had a glimpse of the gardens of Paradise been revealed to me I could scarcely have been more ravished with the sight." As far as Melville is concerned, Paradise has been revealed and the ravished will become the ravisher. The boy and the girl who first encounter this intruder in the garden would do well to fly his presence. The portrait Melville draws of them is hauntingly reminiscent of Adam and Eve in Milton's Paradise:

> They were a boy and girl, slender and graceful, and completely naked, with the exception of a slight girdle of bark, from which depended at opposite points two of the russet leaves of the bread-fruit tree. An arm of the boy, half screened from sight by her wild tresses, was thrown about the neck of the girl, while with the other he held one of her hands in his; and thus they stood together, their heads inclined forward, catching the faint noise we made in our progress, and with one foot in advance, as if half inclined to fly from our presence.

They do not flee, any more than Eve does, from the intruder, and yet the fact that they are not wilfully beguiled is explainable only in its satiric context.

Melville is evidently suggesting, in mythic terms, the advent of Western civilization in a primitive world. For that reason, Tommo cannot be the strong and fully evil character that the primordial Lucifer was. He is naïve, self-deceiving, and even well-intentioned at times. Perhaps that is in partial accord with Northrop Frye's theory of the displacement of myth—that it is progressively adapted to canons of plausibility. For plausibility, he argues, is gauged by the hero's powers of action; "If inferior in power or intelligence to ourselves, so that we have the sense of looking down on a scene of bondage, frustration, or absurdity, the hero belongs to the *ironic* mode."

Tommo undoubtedly belongs to the ironic mode, but the power of the myth is not impaired by his ironic status. The role the white man is cast in is that of a destroyer of innocence and youth: Tommo describes himself astride Kory-Kory's back "like the old man of the sea astride of Sinbad." Unintentionally and with even an attempt at comedy, he signals his potential role as death-dealer and devastator.

Ultimately it seems that Melville is not prepared to say much about the true primitive world, especially regarding its complicity in its fall; he is prepared only to suggest its deep-seated affinities with Eden. But he is ready, since his narrator obligingly provides his satiric focus, to say a lot about the white man. One of the trademarks of the *alazon,* says Alvin Kernan, is his tendency to reduce all things vital and spiritual to the mechanical and material. Witness Tommo's Yankee economic metaphor for the spiritual relationship between men: "Surely, thought I, they would not act thus if they meant us any harm. But why this excess of deferential kindness, or what equivalent can they imagine us capable of rendering them for it?" He distrusts the benevolence of the Typees because he is not certain what return they can possibly make on their investment.

For that same reason, he does not understand the religious

significance of the Typee beliefs. In the god Moa Artua, he sees only mercenary motives. Peeping Tommo is superseded by Doubting Thomas. He is complacent enough, however, to impose his own concepts on the Typee religion. He deprecates the carved gods of Typee in Old Testament diction, calling them "graven images." And he forces the most fantastic Christian imposition on Kolory. The priest, he says, would not be able to articulate "the creed by which he hoped to be saved." Kolory has no idea he needs to be saved and it appears that, for Melville, he would have needed no salvation had the white man not entered his world. Certainly the product of the Fall, "the sweat of thy labour," does not reach the islanders until the Europeans come, when they are "civilized into draught horses, and evangelized into beasts of burden."

The Typees do have some beliefs which are not discolored by Tommo. There is the undistorted image of their belief in immortality, recorded in the carving of the warrior heavenward bound in his canoe. There is an absence of the cult of progress in Typee, as the sympathetic depiction of Marheyo forever building his hut attests. Likewise, there is no sorrow: "There seemed to be no cares, griefs, troubles, or vexations, in all Typee. The hours tripped along as gaily as the laughing couples down a country dance." Indeed, blue devils, hypochondria, and doleful dumps never make their presence felt in this Edenic world. Never, except in Tommo, the naïve speaker, who is chronically despondent. For the white man brings his own fallen nature with him. Like Satan,

> within him Hell
> He brings, and round about him, nor from Hell
> One step no more than from himself can fly
> By change of place (*P.L.*, IV, 20-23).

The history, then, of evil as a disease of the intellect is suitably re-presented in the identity of a man who complains, "The glory of Tommo is departed," with Satan who "could not bear/Through pride that sight [*Messiah's* exaltation], and thought himself impair'd" (*P.L.*, V, 664-65). Unfortunately for Tommo (but not for Melville's satiric exposure of him) he never comes to Satan's self-recognition, "Myself am Hell" (*P.L.*, IV, 75).

By reason of the satiric plot, it is inevitably the narrator's deceitful flight from the island which concludes the chain of events leading to the fall of the Typees. The concord and unanimity witnessed by Tommo—"During my whole stay on the island I never witnessed a single quarrel, nor any thing that in the slightest degree approached even to a dispute. The natives appeared to form one household, whose members were bound together by the strong ties of affection. The love of kindred I did not so much perceive, for it seemed blended in the general love"—is now ruptured in his departure. He is responsible for the first moment of hatred in Typee. "It was at this agonizing moment, when I thought all hope was ended, that a new contest arose between the two parties who had accompanied me to the shore; blows were struck, wounds were given, and blood flowed. In the interest excited by the fray, every one had left me except Marheyo, Kory-Kory, and poor dear Fayaway, who clung to me, sobbing indignantly." Houghton's objection to this "spurious ending" seems, in

view of Melville's mythic structure, to be at least ill-considered. He says, "It appears that Melville had said all he wanted to say *before* Tommo's escape, but sensing that his travel book had indeed turned into something of an adventure tale that needed a dramatic ending he tacked one on." Such are the dangers of reading Tommo literally. For Melville had not said all he wanted to say before Tommo's escape, precisely because he was writing no simple travel book. The travel of Tommo out of the valley is the last act in the drama of the Fall. The once innocent Eden is now embroiled in civil strife, in murder, and in treachery. Tommo's betrayal of his loved ones is a fitting final expression of his Satanic role in the Garden. Fayaway, who clings to him "sobbing indignantly," knows at last she has been deceived.

For these inhabitants of Eden, the Fall is in no way fortunate. A well-meaning intruder goes away without even being sensible of the violation he has committed. He sails off philosophizing, leaving us with the certainty that all Hell shall soon follow him over the bridge spanning Chaos.

There is little doubt, in conclusion, that Melville understands the valley far better than Tommo does, and knows what Tommo does not: not what is wrong with the life lived there but what is wrong with Tommo. In the Menippean tradition of *Gulliver's Travels* (another travel book), *Typee* is a comprehensive satire which unmasks the damned and damning intellect of the Western mind itself.

*David Williams, "Peeping Tommo: 'Typee' as Satire," in* Canadian Review of American Studies, *Vol. VI, No. 1, Spring, 1975, pp. 36-49.*

---

**An excerpt from Typee:**

There was one admirable trait in the general character of the Typees which, more than any thing else, secured my admiration: it was the unanimity of feeling they displayed on every occasion. With them there hardly appeared to be any difference of opinion upon any subject whatever. They all thought and acted alike. I do not conceive that they could support a debating society for a single night; there would be nothing to dispute about; and were they to call a convention to take into consideration the state of the tribe, its session would be a remarkably short one. They showed this spirit of unanimity in every action of life: everything was done in concert and good fellowship.

*Herman Melville, in his* Typee, *Harcourt, Brace, and Company, 1920.*

---

**Michael Clark   (essay date 1978)**

[*In the following essay, Clark discusses the content and form of Tommo's narrative.*]

A balanced analysis of Herman Melville's *Typee* cannot lightly accept a simple judgment of the book, for its critical history is riddled with contradictory assertions and opinions. It has been classified as fiction, autobiography, and travel literature, with certitude on all sides, but without general agreement. We do know that the events in *Typee* have their basis in Melville's life, that Melville affirmed to his publisher, John Murray, the book to be factual, that the book was first published in Murray's series of travel literature, and that Richard Tobias Greene turned up after *Typee* was published and confirmed as true those events he had personally witnessed. Furthermore, recent critics have given carefully considered analyses of *Typee* which stress its factual nature. F.O. Matthiessen [in his *American Renaissance,* 1941], for example, has called the book a "record of experience" and, recently, Charles R. Anderson [in his *Eigo Seinen,* 1969] has pointed out the book's technical flaws and chosen to call it a "loose fictional chronicle" rather than a novel. In addition, Anderson's original study of *Typee, Melville in the South Seas,* reveals to what extent Melville's first book is rooted in the author's experience in the Pacific. And it is the facts, apparently, which have relegated *Typee* to the travel and autobiographical sections of the library shelves.

But *Typee* is much more than a factual account of Melville's sojourn in the South Seas. John Murray, with a publisher's sixth sense, detected the "taint of fiction" and Irving, hearing portions of the work read, deemed the book "exquisite" and the style "graphic." And although an early reviewer [in *The New Englander,* 4 (1846)] objected to the liberties both in morals and in facts that *Typee* presented, he nevertheless judged the book to be "not without literary merit." This initial approbation of the book's "readability" has continued with modern critics such as Richard Ruland [in *Nineteenth Century Fiction,* 23 (1968)] and Paul Witherington [in *Arizona Quarterly,* 26 (1970)] who have attempted to account for the book's final effect on the reader by examining artistic techniques such as symbolism, imagery, and structure. Granting the validity of some of their insights and, with some reservations, of their classification of *Typee* as belles-lettres, certain problems remain.

What is the relationship between literal fact and symbol? Where does fact shade into imaginary event? And at what point does imaginary reconstruction of an event become fiction? These questions have plagued critics of *Typee* since it was first published. And these questions have been raised, I think, largely because Melville has managed in his first book to do so much with the given facts. Although any report of a South Seas adventure might have had an inherent interest to the receptive, curious audience of mid-nineteenth-century America, Melville manages to transcend the bland reportage that, we might imagine, characterized the average travel book of the period, the majority of which have long since been forgotten. But whether Melville reconstituted his personal experiences with the conscious artistry that some critics have asserted is a question that will not be easily resolved. The problem has come to revolve around the question of "conscious intention." The critic often assumes that he can ascertain what exactly Melville "designed" in writing *Typee.* Yet this emphasis seems to be misplaced, for nothing we know of Melville's

writing habits suggests a "design," except in the most rudimentary sense.

I believe that any attempt to bring to bear conventional concepts of genre to the study of Melville's writings, especially of *Typee,* invites an examination of the discrepancies between the convention and Melville's work, his "botches." Perhaps, then, what is needed is not the usual prescriptive analysis but a descriptive approach to Melville's work. Instead of reading *Typee* and expecting the book to measure up to preconceived notions of genre, perhaps it is more useful to ask oneself how, in fact, the book manages to entertain. What makes the facts come alive? The emphasis in such an approach is on expression rather than on form (in the normal conception of novelistic form). For no matter how much we can argue about Melville's artistry, conscious or otherwise, there is no doubt that when he wrote *Typee,* the author possessed an acutely sensitive esthetic sensibility and that the results of that mind working on interesting personal experiences would necessarily produce a book that was both complex and expressive of the author's rich emotional life.

The major concern of this article, then, will not be on "the novel *Typee,*" but rather on the character who calls himself Tommo, who creates a work of prose from that complex, essentially unanalyzable organ, the mind. The emphasis on the narrator telling the reader about his perceptions of the world allows us to reevaluate *Typee* by the esthetic assumptions that the narrator himself, either knowingly or unknowingly, possesses. Therefore, for our purposes, the narrator is not important as a character, at least not in the normal sense of the word. As Charles Feidelson, Jr., has noted [in his *Symbolism and American Literature,* 1953], Tommo is less a character than "a capacity for perception." Furthermore, the *way* he sees is of central concern to us here. The product of his perception is not the finely conceived architectonics of the conventional fictional mode, as some critics, notably Charles R. Anderson (noted above), have cogently argued. Nevertheless, it would be incorrect to say that Melville is not concerned with form. What is obvious in *Typee,* whether the author intended it or not, is an intensely concentrated effort by Melville to find the formal components of expression which fit most closely his perceptions: the two are essentially related and are fundamentally esthetic in nature. This paper will analyze the nature of the narrator's perception by examining the basic artistic principles which Melville—like all artists, in whatever medium—uses to achieve his goal of expressing his impressions of the world: harmony, balance, centrality, and development (or progression). These elements are what esthetician Dilman Gotshalk identifies as the "chief formal principles used by the imagination of artists for the purification and enhancement of existential structure in works of art." And as I hope to show, these principles, though Melville had no reason to be conscious of them, constituted his sensibilities even at the young age of twenty-five and determined that he was much more than a writer of travel literature, in *Typee* as well as in later works.

Before examining *Typee* specifically, it will be useful both to define our terms and to justify this unusual approach.

It is especially necessary to explain our terminology since some critics have examined Melville's fiction from an esthetic approach. For example, of the four commonly accepted esthetic principles, balance has often been linked with Melville's art. But rather than being examined strictly as an esthetic principle, balance is usually considered as a quality of Melville's work that has its roots in the democratic experience, which is peculiar to American writers. Matthiessen suggests this connection when he states that Melville always retained "a firm hold on the conception of a balanced society, on the desirable relation of man to man." More recently, Beongcheon Yu also associates political equality with this esthetic principle in *Moby-Dick.*

Without denying the pertinence of the political influence, one might be more justified in saying that the relationship between politics and esthetic qualities is more complex. First, it seems that balance is not important to the writer for the same reasons that it is important to the politician or to the political ethos of the people. Thus the principle of balance, I think, has not a direct but an indirect link to the American political experience. The reasons for this are complex, but they lie in the fact that the condition of democracy makes severe demands on the writer; it separates him from traditional values but gives him nothing in return. This fact has been admirably summarized by Loren Baritz, who notes the effect on the writer of the democracy that the American Revolution produced:

> Theology was dead, politics exhausted, and philosophy inaccessible because of a relative lack of facilities and training. Creative Americans were largely forced back on their own individual resources in the antebellum period by virtue of their being Americans.

But the effects of the new democracy on American writers were more far-reaching than the post-revolutionary-war period. As late as 1916, John Dos Passos felt the unusual demands placed on the writer in America. Because the American past was predicated on the dissolution of the Old World ties, Dos Passos notes, the American artist is cut off from useful traditions and must rely on his own "glowing life within." And this "glowing life" of the American artist constitutes the basic components of man's perceptive abilities, which include not only a devotion to "balance" but also, as I hope to show, to the other form-giving qualities—harmony, centrality, and progression. These four elements need not to have been learned by Melville, for all men possess them, though artists, to be sure, are gifted with these qualities to an unusually refined degree.

This introduction will permit us to see, then, that what Melville needed to begin a writing career was not a knowledge of the developing novel genre; he needed only a mind which was open to the esthetic possibilities that life had to offer. A theory of fiction is not as necessary as is a mind which is open to experience and which can extract from experience elements which reveal the author's own unique vision of life. It is this quality, I think, which prompts Warner Berthoff [in his *The Example of Melville,* 1962] to describe Melville's narrators as possessing a "reserved freedom of response" which manifests itself in the "rhythm of their absorption and detachment." Melville's narrators have minds which seem naked of the dress of affiliations. They perceive reality directly, without any link with a political or religious ethos. This quality is much like what Melville in *Clarel* ascribed to Nathan, who, like Melville himself, did not find religious acceptance easy:

> Alone, and at Doubt's freezing pole
> He wrestled with the pristine forms
> Like the first man. By inner storms
> Held in solution, so his soul
> Ripened for hour of such control
> As shapes, concretes.

These brilliant lines, in which imagery beautifully amplifies the ideas, can be fruitfully applied to Melville's own quest for expression. The man alone confronts the chaotic experiences of his life and struggles to find the suitable "shapes" to express adequately the emotional content of those experiences.

How does one begin to analyze this person Tommo who tells us his story? Perhaps the best starting point is to identify the unusual qualities that the mind of this narrator evinces in the most trying of circumstances, cannibal captivity. For the predominant quality of the narrator's consciousness is its impressionability, whether for fear, for the unusual, or for the beautiful. His mind actively seeks to measure itself against significant experience, and his concern with beauty in general illustrates his strong esthetic bent. As we shall see, Tommo reveals a pervasive attraction for purely esthetic qualities. Thus it is tempting to accept at face value the later evaluation Melville made in *Clarel* of his younger self. Like Tommo, the young Melville was both adventurer and sensitive observer; he

> . . . supplemented Plato's theme
> With daedal life in boats and tents,
> A messmate of the elements;
> And yet, more bronzed in face than mind,
> Sensitive still and frankly kind.

How susceptible he is to the pleasing impression is manifest throughout *Typee.* A good example of this is the first sight Tommo gets of Typee valley. The vision so overwhelms him, Tommo says, that "had a glimpse of the gardens of Paradise been revealed to me I could scarcely have been more ravished with the sight." And we are led to believe that the exquisite charm of this vision plays no small part in overcoming his scruples about descending into the valley and, therefore, risking a possible encounter with cannibals. And we are told that once among the natives, his inclination to escape is effectively subverted one time by the "soothing influence" on his mind of the "beauty of the scene." Another example of his sensibilities is his description of the natives' beauty to be comparable to that of a "sculptor's model."

A more striking and sustained example of the narrator's concern with esthetic experience is manifested in his reaction to the mundane domestic activity of making tappa. A less likely example of esthetic appreciation would be difficult to find. But this practical activity is transmuted by Tommo into an enjoyable experience. After a long description of the tappa-making process, Tommo notes that the result is a cloth of "dazzling whiteness." And though the Typees prefer the relatively staid "natural tint," that does not stop the narrator from describing the esthetic possibilities of the simple cloth, to which he has at other times been exposed. "The notable wife of Kammahammaha," he notes, "used to pride herself in the skill she displayed in dyeing her tappa with contrasting colors disposed in regular figures." And then, as if to stress that he is open to every possibility of appreciation, Tommo notes that he

> was often attracted by the noise of the mallet, which, when employed in the manufacture of the cloth, produces at every stroke of its hard, heavy wood, a clear, ringing, and musical sound, capable of being heard at a great distance. When several of these implements happen to be in operation at the same time, and near one another, the effect upon the ear of a person, at a little distance, is really charming.

If making tappa is a useful art for the Typees, for Tommo it is an experience which can only be called esthetic. Surely, he is a walking art appreciation course, whose object is not a gallery of oils, but life itself.

It is obvious, then, that this finely tuned sensibility is more than receptive to esthetic experiences, even under the trying circumstances of captivity. His descriptions of his own passive susceptibility to the "beautiful" and "charming" tell us much about the esthetic nature of his consciousness. But as we have seen, the re-creation of his experiences, their transmutation into prose, reveals that his perceptions are of equal importance to the "facts" themselves. It is this shift of emphasis from object to perceiver, I think, which makes *Typee* so "readable," whereas other contemporary travel accounts did not receive the initial plaudits that *Typee* did, nor did they, for the most part, outlive their initial reception. Thus in *Typee* Melville manages to achieve what Susanne Langer calls "the illusion of life directly lived." And this "illusion" is not contingent on the use—or on the nonuse—of "facts," for as Langer, again, notes, "a slavish transcript of actual life is dim beside the word-created experiences of virtual life, as a plaster mask made directly from a living subject is a dead counterfeit compared to even the most 'conservative' portrait sculpture." In *Typee* Melville has for the most part effectively subordinated the facts to his own unique way of seeing, and he has done this by using what has been mentioned as the four formal elements of esthetic perception: centrality, development, harmony, and balance. His use of these four principles will now be examined in detail.

The first formal esthetic principle to be examined is centrality. Gotshalk defines this as the "confluence of perceptual interest to, or dominance of perceptual interest at, a point." In fiction, this center of interest is often a first-person narrator, and even if the story is about someone else (say, a Bartleby or a Gatsby), then more often than not the narrator is still the object of interest, though in a much more subtle way. With omniscient or first-person narrators, the character of central interest is usually well defined. Yet whatever complications and ambiguities that may accumulate around this concept, it is clear that in *Typee* centrality can refer only to Tommo, the narrator.

Tommo not only invites our interest, but by his rhetorical manipulation of the fictive world, he demands it. It is clear from the beginning of the book that the reader's options for "choosing sides" are woefully one-sided. The *Dolly*'s captain, for example, is "tyrannical," and "with a very few exceptions," Tommo notes, his crew "was composed of a parcel of dastardly and mean-spirited wretches, divided among themselves, and only united in enduring without resistance the unmitigated tyranny of the captain." Likewise, with certain qualifications, David Williams's article on *Typee* [in *The Canadian Review of American Studies,* 6 (Spring 1975)] is correct in pointing out that even Toby suffers by contrast to Tommo because of the latter's "self-aggrandizement and self-congratulation." But rather than criticize Tommo's delineation of the uniqueness of his own character, it seems more useful to appreciate his unceasing efforts to define his world, which is, whether in regard to self or to environment, characteristic of Melville's fiction.

Tommo is, then, a character who is intensely aware of his individuality. Indeed, his impulse to jump ship derives from the insoluble conflict of his individuality with the world. What he lacks on board ship, of course, is free expression, but, unknown to him, repression also awaits him in the Typee valley. For example, although gratification of bodily desires is never a problem in the valley, he is nevertheless restrained from free bodily movement. Note, for instance, the language he employs to describe the hindrance to his going to meet Toby, who had been rumored (falsely) to have returned: the chief who stops Tommo had an "inflexible rigidity of expression," put "his hand upon my shoulder," assumed "a tone of authority," issued an "unexpected command," made "efforts to restrain me," and "reiterated his commands still more sternly." The quick succession of inhibiting gestures and words gives an urgency to Tommo's desires for freedom. Consequently, it seems that the isolation he had felt on shipboard is not necessarily the result of "self-aggrandizement" as Williams would have us believe. Rather, it is a sign of the tragic isolation that all men participate in. And thus his shipboard alienation is mirrored in his similarly oppressed condition in Typee: "There was no one with whom I could freely converse; no one to whom I could communicate my thoughts; no one who could sympathise with my sufferings." It is this insight into a man's isolated condition on which the story's telling is predicated. Centrality, then, has to do less with egomania than with a realization that life is by nature a tragic affair.

The second esthetic principle of form that we shall examine is development. In the novel, this is the progression of the story, the plot. Generally, plot suggests a series of related actions which develop momentum because of complication. But for Melville this rather sophisticated technique was not to be discovered until *Mardi,* where it is imperfectly realized. And it would not be used with effectiveness until he came to write *Moby-Dick.* But in *Typee* the mainsprings of action are weak. The source of action, of progression, in the story lies in a more fundamental realm than action. It lies in the consciousness of existence, which devolves from the narrator's sense of tragic isolation and is given expression in the metaphor of "seeing," which is suggested in the book's subtitle: "A *Peep* at Polynesian

Life" (my italics). For the motivation for movement lies in the tension between a consciousness of a "lack" and a vision of fulfillment.

As I suggested, the word "peep" seems to have rich connotations for Melville. He seems to have associated the act of seeing with the discovery of the forbidden, of the unknown, and of the desirous, not just of physical things but also of the moral. For example, at the sexually suggestive dance scene in **Omoo** (which was cut from **Typee** because it was too risque) the narrator tells us that he and Long Ghost "had a peep at the dancers." And in a later book, Pierre's fateful encounter with Isabel (which is of momentous consequence) is preceded by Mrs. Glendinning's seemingly innocuous remark that she wants to "peep in" at the girls in the Llanyllyns's sewing circle. The act of "looking," then, has implications of moral discovery and either results from or is the cause of "curiosity," from which action becomes inevitable.

The sense of progression in Melville's fictive worlds has been admirably schematized by Charles Feidelson, Jr. For both Melville and Emerson, Feidelson says, "life was a transition from one sphere to another, each potentially including the former." And for Melville, the transition was activated by a literal and metaphoric vision. Thus Tommo's intolerable state of existence aboard the *Dolly* makes the narrator daydream of a better state, which in his mind is potentially achievable: "I straightway fell to picturing myself seated beneath a cocoa-nut tree on the brow of the mountain, with a cluster of plantains within easy reach." It matters little here that Tommo is unrealistic. His vision of a condition better than his present one (on ship as well as in Typee valley) plays no small role in his decisions to act. Likewise, his first view of Typee valley reveals "a glimpse of the gardens of Paradise" and, after some reservations, actuates Toby and Tommo to descend to the floor of the valley. Yet the vision is belied by the presence of cannibals and also by their first actual encounter with this Eden: when they attempt to feed themselves, they find the fruit "much decayed." The innate drive to penetrate to the core of existence, no matter how decayed it must inevitably prove to be, is further illustrated by the final terrifying discovery in Typee valley. At the pi-pi, Tommo's attention is captured by a vessel of wood: "prompted by a curiosity I could not repress . . . I raised one end of the cover." What he discovers in looking, of course, is evidence of cannibalism, "the last horrid revelation." But this is not the last such discovery in the Melville canon, for the endless search is the inelectuable condition of the Melvillean man, and the search is programmed to fail because the expectation which is engendered by the initial "peep" is always an ideal and as such cannot be realized.

A third principle of esthetic form that Gotshalk defines is harmony, which is qualified as possessing either complete similarity or partial similarity. Gotshalk gives an example of harmony in literature as "the repetition at a later stage of an earlier action in a drama." Another critic, De Witt Parker, calls this principle "thematic variation" in which a theme is "elaborated and embroidered" in order to make it "echo and reëcho in our minds." In any case, this princi-

ple is most difficult of the four to clearly define in fiction, though perhaps its closest parallel in the literary critic's nomenclature is symbolism. Yet to avoid the problem of determining whether Melville was consciously working in the symbolic mode, it is enough to say that the incidents which concern us are important not for the clearly defined possibilities that they open up as much as for their "resonance," their ability to create an ambience which is illustrative of other, parallel situations. Gotshalk's distinction of "complete" and "partial" harmonies will be useful to our examination of **Typee.**

An element which illustrates the principle of partial harmony is a descriptive passage at the beginning of **Typee.** While I do not think that this scene rises to the level of symbol, it does represent a rich field of allusion, innuendo, and connotation that creates an ambience particularly helpful in understanding Tommo's situation.

> There is but one solitary tenant in the chicken-coop, once a gay and dapper young cock, bearing him so bravely among the coy hens. But look at him now; there he stands, moping all the day long on that everlasting one leg of his. He turns with disgust from the mouldy corn before him, and the brackish water in his little trough. He mourns no doubt his lost companions, literally snatched from him one by one and never seen again. But his days of mourning will be few; for Mungo, our black cook, told me yesterday that the word had at last gone forth, and poor Pedro's fate was sealed. His attenuated body will be laid out upon the captain's table next Sunday, and long before night will be buried with all the usual ceremonies beneath that worthy individual's vest. Who would believe that there could be any one so cruel as to long for the decapitation of the luckless Pedro; yet the sailors pray every minute, selfish fellows, that the miserable fowl may be brought to his end.

Pedro is surely one to be pitied. And it is certainly helpful to the story that a theme of helplessness is introduced early to set the tone for Tommo's own misfortunes.

Yet a closer examination of the details of this tableau is rewarding, for there are many obvious parallels that can be drawn between Pedro and Tommo. The fact that Pedro is a "solitary tenant" does suggest the perpetual condition of Tommo (e. g., his alienation from his crewmates and his isolation in Typee valley). And like Pedro, Tommo has the use of only one good leg for much of the story. But the most striking feature of this story is the personification of the bird and, with that, the transmutation of a chicken dinner into a cannibal feast. The humor of the passage tends to disarm the reader and to distance the event from the obviously serious implication it carries for the rest of **Typee.** In particular, the passage casts the captain as a cannibal, and it implies that to Tommo, all experience (not just with savages) partakes of a life-threatening quality against which the narrator must continually battle. Thus the captain is a cannibal to Tommo, too, for he is "tyrannical" and gives a "scanty allowance" of substandard food (which again reminds us of Pedro). With only the least bit of displacement (for, after all, the cock does not escape the cannibal), the story of Pedro serves to amplify Tommo's own predicament.

"Complete harmony" is best illustrated in *Typee* by the relationship of Tommo to the character of Marnoo. This character is important to the plot of Melville's first book because by fortuitously appearing when he does, he re-awakens Tommo's latent desire to escape from captivity. But Marnoo's actual role in Tommo's escape is largely second-hand and fails to justify Tommo's extended, flattering description of him. Therefore, although it is clear that Marnoo represents some sort of ideality, it is difficult to ascertain exactly what that ideality is. And Melville, as if to stress the importance of this character, gives him for a moment the central position in the narrative. Tommo tells us, "When I observed the striking devotion of the natives to him [Marnoo], and their temporary withdrawal of all attention from myself, I felt not a little piqued." The temporary displacement of primary interest, as we shall see, is justified by thematic as well as by plot considerations.

The fact that Marnoo replaces Tommo for a short while as the center of interest in the narrative suggests the thematic identification between the two. The parallel can be seen most clearly in their respective assimilation of the artist's role. For example, there can be little doubt from the way the native is described that Melville means Marnoo's ideality to be suggestive of art and the art process. He has "natural eloquence," a "grace" in his attitudes, "striking gestures," and the changing accents of "the most accomplished orator." Furthermore, as Paul Witherington has suggested, Marnoo's tattoo of an "artu" tree may be a symbol for art. Also, the description of the native's tattooed back is clearly suggestive of an organic conception of art: "Upon his breast, arms, and legs, were exhibited an infinite variety of figures; every one of which, however, appeared to have reference to the general effect sought to be produced." Thus Marnoo not only represents the free state that Tommo in captivity longs for, but also the native seems to be "an exemplar of art" (as Witherington notes), whom Tommo wishes to approximate in his narrative, both in eloquence and in the result of organic form.

But Marnoo's ideality demands further examination. Marnoo is the one character in *Typee* who comes closest to fully integrating the totality of experience. Not only is he a noble savage, a condition which Tommo obviously admires, but also he is not restricted (as the other natives in Typee valley are) by the deadening subconsciousness of the savage state. Marnoo, like Tommo, possesses superiority over the natives because of his exposure to civilization. Tommo describes it thus: "The natural quickness of the savage had been wonderfully improved by his intercourse with the white men, and his partial knowledge of a foreign language gave him a great ascendancy over his less accomplished countrymen." He is even given a position of honor in Typee valley, and the ease with which he moves between such disparate cultures as the savage state and civilization makes Marnoo an enviable model for Tommo. It is of no little concern, then, that the "natural eloquence" and "striking gestures" that the native employs in mastering the Typees are mirrored by Tommo in his escape from

the valley, when he importunes Mow-Mow with "an eloquence of gesture." And most improbably, the savage chief is "unable to resist" these gestures, a fact which suggests that Tommo has carefully learned his lesson from the master. Of course, Tommo's escape has none of Marnoo's grace, for Tommo can never return to Typee at will—it is a one-way trip. Yet the escape permits him to attain a position where boundaries can be crossed and recrossed at will: not in the physical world but in the imaginative process of writing. Tommo's frequent, effective comparisons and contrasts between the two disparate societies are ample proof that he has attained "non-compartmentalization." So if Marnoo is a symbol for art, Tommo becomes an incarnation of that symbol in his own narration of *Typee.*

The final esthetic principle which Gotshalk notes is balance, which like harmony is actually a complex concept. On the one hand, balance is achieved by "symmetry," by the balance of similars. But it can also be achieved by "asymmetry," by the use of contrast. Obviously, the narrator of *Typee* makes much use of both types of balance. Symmetrical balance, for example, can be seen in the narrator's obvious reluctance to accept experience at face value. In fact, events often become less significant than the act of interpretation, in this case, of pairing of similars that helps us to understand not so much the event, as the narrator's attitude toward the event. An illustration of this is Tommo's comments on the "lovely damsels" with whom he shares Marheyo's household. These girls, he tells us, "instead of thrumming pianos and reading novels, like more enlightened young ladies, substituted for these employments the manufacture of a fine species of tappa." Tommo also notes that these same girls spend the majority of their time "gadding and gossiping with their acquaintances." Thus he interprets the unfamiliar activity he confronts by making references to a somewhat parallel event from a known culture. And it is this very quality of balance which attracts Tommo to praise what exists "to a certain degree"—the "equality of condition" of the general population of Typee. At the same time, this concern for balance causes him to criticize the Typees: "I could not understand why a woman should not have as much right to enter a canoe as a man."

In a similar manner, asymmetrical balance, or contrast, is an important element in Tommo's perception of life. For example, after noting that the spear in Typee is doubled as an oar, he observes that Kolory's spear "instead of terminating in a paddle at the lower end, after the general fashion of these weapons, was curved into a heathenish-looking little image." Whether this description is modeled on an actual artifact of Typee valley or whether it is a product of Melville's fertile imagination is less important, I think, than the characteristic interpretation that the narrator gives to it. The spear is, Tommo says, "emblematic" of Kolory's "double functions" of soldier-priest: "With one end in carnal combat he transfixed the enemies of his tribe; and with the other as a pastoral crook he kept in order his spiritual flock." Melville is not as subtle here as he is later in *Moby-Dick* where he describes Queequeg's hatchet-pipe, which has a similar dual purpose; yet the same rich imagination is present which takes joy in the yoking of dissimilar objects and in the irony created thereby.

Contrast, of course, is used by Melville in many other situations. It is perhaps the most noticeable principle in *Typee,* if not in all of Melville's work. He notes, for example, the incongruous nature of the peaceful and beautiful Nukuheva Bay and the "black hulls" of the French ships, whose "bristling broadsides proclaimed their warlike character." Another time, Tommo describes Admiral Du Petit Thouars standing next to a savage chief: "they stood side by side, these two extremes of the social scale." At times, the contrast between civilized and savage is to the obvious flattery of the uncivilized state (for example, the raising of children); at other times, the scale is weighted in favor of civilization (implied, for example, in the description of one of Typee's roads). The list could be extended well past the limits of interesting analysis. Suffice it to say that in any contrast, Melville was painfully aware that "Truth" resided in the never-never land, "centrally located . . . between the two extremes." The implication of this fundamental fact of life is disturbing. For every thesis, one can find an antithesis, and Melville was painfully aware that it was a moral duty not to accept either (or any) extreme. The question of how this principle applies to a relative judgment of civilization and savage life is, perhaps, the central problem in determining the implications of the esthetic consciousness of *Typee*'s narrator.

From the foregoing examples of Melville's perception, one can see the pervasive influence of the essentially esthetic form-giving qualities, all of which depend not on conscious intention but on the well developed esthetic temperament. But, finally, one must ask what this essentially esthetic vision of life means. The narrator of *Typee* is an individual sensitive enough to appreciate the innate value of the uncivilized state—and the experience there permitted him to justly evaluate the shortcomings of civilization. But whereas the state of nature offered no permanent value to the civilized mind, the civilized state he returned to was obviously too brutal for this man who felt so deeply the sources of his humanity. Therefore, after being once again a crew member of a man-of-war, he loses his faith in mankind. In essence, he enjoyed both worlds and was happy in neither. And it is for that reason that he created a third, made partly from his experiences, partly from his unique way of perceiving life, and partly from his imagination. The result, however, was wholly expressive of his self, of his own response to life.

But is *Typee* primarily a book which is a condemnation of civilzation? The cultural criticism does seem to support the critics who argue that this work is basically factual or a travel account. And the evidence that such critics as [Edgar A.] Dryden marshal makes it difficult to deny that a large part of *Typee* is devoted to criticism of Western civilization. Yet *Typee* manages to be much more. It is true that Tommo on innumerable occasions compares the state of nature favorably to civilization. For example, he likes the dress code of the Typee women better than that of civilized women. Yet overall the comparisons are not necessarily one-sided. For example (besides one or two already mentioned), a crowd of natives reminds Tommo "of

a group of idlers gathered about the door of a village tavern." Thus critics who argue that Melville is praising savage life to the detriment of civilization or vice versa, do so, too often, at the expense of the abundant contradictory evidence. Melville, through Tommo, exalts neither savagery nor civilization, except incidentally. His central concern, rather, is his own free imaginative life in its ability to draw parallels in the least likely of circumstances. The emphasis is on expression. What we have in *Typee* is a mind that refuses to be quiescent, but which like the traveler Marnoo crosses boundaries at will. But in Tommo's case, the boundaries are both of time and space and are conquered by his far-reaching imaginative vision.

It is this fact, the central role of the process of perception, that makes it less important whether to call *Typee* fact or fiction. Instead of a narrow contrast or comparison, the range of Tommo's perceptions includes all time, all space, and the emphasis falls on the act of seeing rather than on the objective world. So Tommo sees two men in the distance and they look like "Hebrew spies"; Tommo's native dress is similar to a toga of "a senator of Rome"; Marheyo looks like a "valiant Templar arrayed in a new and costly suit of armor"; and Tommo feels at one time "transported to some fairy region." These reflections, which only Tommo can make, reveal as much, if not more, about him as they do about either Typee valley or civilization. And these observations should remind us that if we want to go to Melville's Typee, a steamer or an airplane won't do.

*Michael Clark, "Melville's 'Typee': Fact, Fiction, and Esthetics," in* Arizona Quarterly, *Vol. 34, No. 4, Winter, 1978, pp. 351-70.*

**Faith Pullin   (essay date 1978)**

[*In the essay below, Pullin examines Melville's fusion of autobiographical, travelogue, and fictional elements in* Typee, *pointing out how he uses them to delineate "the basic inclinations of his thought."*]

*Typee,* Melville's first work as a professional author, is not as irrelevant to his later opus as it has usually been considered by critics. In fact, it encapsulates and prefigures the major concerns and biases of his later vision. What Melville is discovering in *Typee* is what Milton Stern has called [in *The Fine Hammered Steel of Herman Melville,* 1957], 'his relationship to the world'; his typical literary and philosophical preoccupations. *Typee* is certainly not a simple travelogue, a picaresque South Sea adventure, enjoyed, and, in some cases, endured, by a narrator whose report is largely autobiographical. It is a symbolic narrative in which Melville delineates, in however preliminary a form, the basic inclinations of his thought. In no sense is it a piece of juvenilia: Melville, in *Typee,* is the conscious craftsman; the book, as with other later works of Melville, inhabits the formal area which is only now being investigated by critics—that area where fact and fiction are so closely allied as to be indistinguishable.

Primarily, the book constitutes a rejection of primitivism. Tommo, the narrator, enters an alien, physical world but is unable to join it; his point of view is always that of the self-conscious, rational and tormented nineteenth-century thinker. Tommo observes a timeless world from the perspective of his contemporary civilization. This juxtaposition inevitably involves a consideration of the question of what civilization actually is. Melville obviously rejects the current views of his own society of the irrefutable benefits of encroaching western materialist society (a condemnation that predates Conrad's annihilation of these same values in *Heart of Darkness* and *Nostromo*). The main theme, then, of the novel, is the testing of a Rousseauistic response to experience and the rejection of that report, not simply on the part of Tommo as a 'sophisticated' representative of an advanced society, but because it is inadequate in itself. The passivity of the inhabitants of this Paradise is obviously as deeply offensive to Melville as it was to Milton. Perhaps one of the problems that Melville is grappling with in *Typee* is the idea that any kind of society is bound to be 'evil'. It's the view expressed by Conrad in a letter to Cunninghame Graham in 1899: 'Le crime est une condition nécessaire de l'existence organisée. La société est essentiellement criminelle, —ou elle n'existerait pas.' The fact that Typee is a relatively simple society in its organization and customs distracts Melville at first in his implied analysis of it. But, eventually, the simple dichotomy between idyllic Typee and evil America is found to be erroneous and irrelevant. Typee is a flawed Eden and one in which Melville's critical consciousness can find no release and no absolutes. There is no such thing as a pure state of nature: Typee offers no prospect of regenerative salvation. Neither Typee itself, nor the representative society of the *Dolly* provide any solution to the questions about the nature of human society that Melville raises in the book. Both reveal themselves as in many respects corrupt, and deeply inadequate to human needs. The limitations of life in Typee, paradoxically, come about through the very communal nature of its society. A communality that attracts Tommo but equally frustrates him, immured as he is in his solitary, individualistic consciousness. The ideal society, in this case, ought to be found on the *Dolly* since the ship provides a model of hierarchy and order and the opportunity for work (so essential to America's Puritan ethic). However, the social and legal abuses of life on that actual ship incapacitate her as any kind of model.

> In numberless instances had not only the implied but the specified conditions of the articles been violated on the part of the ship in which I served. The usage on board of her was tyrannical; the sick had been inhumanly neglected; the provisions had been doled out in scanty allowance; and her cruizes were unreasonably protracted. The captain was the author of these abuses; it was in vain to think that he would either remedy them, or alter his conduct, which was . . . arbitrary and violent in the extreme . . . , our crew was composed of a parcel of dastardly and mean-spirited wretches, divided among themselves, and only united in enduring without resistance the unmitigated tyranny of the captain.

In addition, although the atrocities often enacted on Typee are at first presented by Tommo as the natural reaction on the part of the inhabitants to European treachery,

it's clear that mutual hatred and suspicion exist between the various tribal groups themselves on the island:

> Owing to the mutual hostilities of the different tribes I have mentioned, the mountainous tracts which separate their respective territories remain altogether uninhabited; the natives invariably dwelling in the depths of the valleys, with a view of securing themselves from the predatory incursions of their enemies, who often lurk along their borders, ready to cut off any imprudent straggler, or make a descent upon the inmates of some sequestered habitation. I several times met with very aged men, who from this cause had never passed the confines of their native vale.

Tommo himself is totally individualistic at this point; he leaves the ship because he is unwilling to accept its lawlessness. Later, he escapes from Typee since he can't tolerate the suffocating luxuriousness of its life—and because he is un-free in an opposite manner from the imprisonment he experienced on the ship. He has no sense of the common good; he simply wishes to escape from situations which he has chosen but which have become oppressive to him. In this sense, Vere in *Billy Budd* is a chastened and matured Tommo, who does his duty. Tommo, on the other hand, merely uses Toby, first as a companion with whom to escape; later as someone who can rescue him from what had seemed a refuge. Toby is developed only schematically by Melville as the foil to Tommo; as someone who takes easily to the sensuous experiences in which Typee abounds, but who makes no intellectual demands on his experience. Toby's dry comments on Tommo's lack of physical expertise provide much of the humour of the entry into Typee. But the humour itself only highlights the essentially ominous quality of the experience. As has been pointed out by various critics, the question whether the first inhabitants Tommo and Toby meet are Happar (good) or Typee (bad) demonstrates Melville's characteristic sense of the ambivalent quality of experience. It is the same ambivalence that is at the centre of *The Encantadas:* 'the tortoise is both black and bright'. Tommo is, of course, engaged in an elaborate attempt at escapism. The ship is an escape from the struggle for place, position and success in his native society. As an alien, he has a spurious status on Typee but he is without the human understanding of his companions as totally as he was on the ship. This is a symbolic prefiguring of Melville's own life in which he was misunderstood and seriously undervalued by both society and family. His art was the only recompense for this, and yet the profession of writer in nineteenth-century America meant that he could not write as he wanted and succeed: 'So far as I am individually concerned, & independent of my pocket, it is my earnest desire to write those sort of books which are said to "fail" ' [6 October 1849 letter to Lemuel Shaw].

In view of the fact that, in Tommo, Melville is representing many of his own actual experiences in the South Seas, there is bound to be a large autobiographical element present in the novel; yet, Tommo stands not only for Melville but for a typical nineteenth-century intellectual / adventurer as unlike his shipmates as Melville himself obviously was. Conrad was in the same position, but his essentially sceptical response to experience, ('there are some things that do not bear too much looking into'), was deeply disturbing to Melville. In this event, the safety at which Tommo clutches in Typee is soon revealed to be deceptive and deeply ambiguous.

Throughout Melville's narrative, a factual, Crusoe-like surface covers an important symbolic substructure. The symbolic level works to support the concept of the essential ambiguity of experience and the deeply unsatisfying nature of human existence. In the beginning, the bay of Nukuheva appears as a vision of natural perfection.

> Nothing can exceed the imposing scenery of this bay. Viewed from our ship as she lay at anchor in the middle of the harbor, it presented the appearance of a vast natural amphitheatre in decay, and overgrown with vines, the deep glens that furrowed its sides appearing like enormous fissures caused by the ravages of time. Very often when lost in admiration at its beauty, I have experienced a pang of regret that a scene so enchanting should be hidden from the world in these remote seas, and seldom meet the eyes of devoted lovers of nature.

And yet, it is dangerous to take this beauty at its face value:

> I had heard too of an English vessel that many years ago, after a weary cruize, sought to enter the bay of Nukuheva, and arriving within two or three miles of the land, was met by a large canoe filled with natives, who offered to lead the way to the place of their destination. The captain, unacquainted with the localities of the island, joyfully acceded to the proposition—the canoe paddled on and the ship followed. She was soon conducted to a beautiful inlet, and dropped her anchor in its waters beneath the shadows of the lofty shore. That same night the perfidious Typees, who had thus inveigled her into their fatal bay, flocked aboard the doomed vessel by hundreds, and at a given signal murdered every soul on board.

Yet Melville's own attitude is ambivalent here. His prose operates on two distinct levels. On the one hand, he is expressing the concept of the duplicity of experience itself: on the other, he is concerned to attack the facile complacency of the view of his own century of the civilizing mission of the western, technologically advanced nations. The essentially punitive and exploitative nature of the European relationship to the South Seas is a point on which Melville insists (and develops at greater length in **Omoo**).

Melville's consideration of the nature of civilization is given visual content with the juxtaposing of the figures of the patriarch of Tior and the French admiral Du Petit Thouars. Here, Melville sets up a tableau which seems, superficially, to have an obvious meaning. But his following comment disturbs the clear reference of the picture and also disturbs the reader's common sense view of things, disorienting him. As with the factual level of the story, beneath which exists a disconcerting conceptual stratum which undercuts its apparent optimism (Tommo suffers,

but lives to tell the tale), so with this visual representation of an apparently self-evident truth:

> The admiral came forward with head uncovered and extended hand, while the old king saluted him by a stately flourish of his weapon. The next moment they stood side by side, these two extremes of the social scale, —the polished, splendid Frenchman, and the poor tattooed savage.

Melville's comment is a conventional one on the 'immeasurable distance' between the two. The Frenchman being the product of long centuries of progressive civilization and refinement, while the Marquesan 'has not advanced one step in the career of improvement'. The comment that undercuts this platitude concerns the nature of happiness, 'insensible as he is to a thousand wants, and removed from harassing cares, may not the savage be the happier man of the two?' This is the question that forms the major part of the material of the book. The answer, cumulative in nature and never explicitly stated, is that neither of them are happy, and that happiness is not a property of human life.

The isolation of Typee that Melville emphasises throughout means that it can be used as a test-case for an examination of the human condition. Activity is introduced into the narrative by the movement of Tommo's mind, by his continual speculations on the culture in which he finds himself and his (futile) attempts to adjust himself to it mentally. This offsets the static quality of the narrative. Melville's technique is highly pictorial in nature. The juxtaposition of the patriarch and the French admiral mentioned above, is set in a Douanier-Rousseau type landscape which is the reverse of realistic: 'The umbrageous shades where the interview took place—the glorious tropical vegetation around—the picturesque grouping of the mingled throng of soldiery and natives'.

The beauty of the island is always presented in visual terms. Tommo instinctively withdraws and observes; he is the detached observer whose function is to tell the story rather than to enter into it and experience it as Toby does. It is for this reason that Toby is allowed by the islanders to go—he is like them and therefore it is no conquest to convert him to their viewpoint of the desirability of purely sensual happiness. Tommo is a renegade who, in the end, lives only for escape from Eden. Not that Tommo is unresponsive to the beauty of the island, but that, finally, he is repelled by its easy luxuriance.

There are various set-pieces throughout the narrative. For instance, the scene in which the young girls swim out to welcome the *Dolly* in; and yet the immediate contact between the two worlds is, as ever, the pollution of the welcomers. The overt sexuality of the girls' dances disturbs Tommo as much as it did Melville's contemporary audience: 'The varied dances of the Marquesan girls are beautiful in the extreme, but there is an abandoned voluptuousness in their character which I dare not attempt to describe'. In many respects, *Typee* has associations with *Robinson Crusoe* in the way in which both Melville and Defoe attempt to gain the readers' confidence by the manipulation of concrete detail. And yet, in both cases, what has most deeply affected readers is, of course, the symbolic content—the manner in which the isolated individual reacts to a situation of, possibly, permanent isolation. In the case both of Tommo and Crusoe there is no genuine attempt at adaptation. As Ian Watt has pointed out, Crusoe simply seeks to re-establish the details of the society from which he has come, using objects which have conveniently been saved from the ship. Tommo isn't physically isolated (although he suffers a kind of double imprisonment, being kept against his will on an island) but he is obviously isolated psychically. In spite of the ministrations of Fayaway, he responds to the reference to 'home' and 'mother' which, naively expressed as it is, involves a recognition of the vital necessities of relating to one's own society and its emotional ties.

The early reviewers of *Typee* noted the similarity of Defoe's and Melville's methods; a reviewer in the London *Spectator* of 28 February 1846 made the following point, involving Melville's technique of heightening reality:

> Much of the book is not beyond the range of invention, especially by a person acquainted with the Islands, and with the fictions of De Foe; and we think that several things have been heightened for effect, if indeed this artistical principle does not pervade the work.

To this may be added two comments by Melville himself, from *The Confidence-Man:*

> While to all fiction is allowed some play of invention, yet, fiction based on fact should never be contradictory to it.

> And as, in real life, the proprieties will not allow people to act out themselves with that unreserve permitted to the stage; so, in books of fiction, they look not only for more entertainment, but, at bottom, even for more reality, than real life itself can show. Thus, though they want novelty, they want nature, too; but nature unfettered, exhilarated, in effect transformed.

These two views on the necessary basis of fact in fiction, combined with a heightened reality, sum up Melville's method in *Typee.* Although it was not till *The Confidence-Man* (1857) that Melville actually enunciated this theory, it is in *Typee* that he practises it; a remarkable achievement for a writer working on his first book. Melville wrote *Typee* when he was twenty-five, and was himself aware of his somewhat sudden access of intellectual—and literary—maturity. As he wrote to Hawthorne, while engaged on *Moby-Dick,* 'From my twenty-fifth year, I date my life'. The first publisher of *Typee,* John Murray, insisted on Melville's adding more factual material about life on the island to increase the authenticity of the novel; but this material did not convince contemporary reviewers. The critical controversy of the time concerning the facts of Melville's experience in the Marquesas is similar to that aroused in 1977 by Alex Haley's *Roots:* one may answer these objections in the same way, what is important is the symbolic quality of the narrative, verisimilitude is more important than mere reporting.

As an anonymous reviewer wrote in the London *Critic* in March 1846:

> The incidents, no doubt, are sometimes exaggerated, and the colouring is often overcharged, yet

> in the narrative generally there is a *raisemblance* that cannot be feigned; for the minuteness, and novelty of the details, could only have been given by one who had before him nature for his model.

What is striking about both *Typee* and *Robinson Crusoe* is the way in which the symbolic undertones are fused with the very physical quality of the narrative. Tommo describes, in close detail, and with a Defoe-like pleasure in how things are done, the manufacture of tappa:

> In the manufacture of the beautiful white tappa generally worn on the Marquesan Islands, the preliminary operation consists in gathering a certain quantity of the young branches of the cloth-tree. The exterior green bark being pulled off as worthless, there remains a slender fibrous substance, which is carefully stripped from the stick, to which it closely adheres. When a sufficient quantity of it has been collected, the various strips are enveloped in a covering of large leaves, which the natives use precisely as we do wrapping-paper, and which are secured by a few turns of a line passed round them. The package is then laid in the bed of some running stream, with a heavy stone placed over it, to prevent its being swept away. After it has remained for two or three days in this state, it is drawn out, and exposed, for a short time, to the action of the air, every distinct piece being attentively inspected, with a view of ascertaining whether it has yet been sufficiently affected by the operation. This is repeated again and again, until the desired result is obtained.

The text-book clarity of this style is in total contrast to the mixed tone of the prose in which it is embedded. Indeed, what distinguishes Melville's style in *Typee* is the very volatile changes of mood which the narrator reveals as he tells his story. For instance, the significant tableau of the indigenous ruler and the French Admiral is undercut by the humour with which Tommo mocks the scene itself and his own role in it as solemn observer: the passage ends with his memory of 'the golden-hued bunch of bananas that he held in his hand at the time, and of which I occasionally partook while making the aforesaid philosophical reflections'. The account of Kory-Kory's making fire in chapter 14 is very similar. What is presented by Melville in *Typee* is a series of animated tableaux; it is like being shown a collection of particularly rich and glamorous slides. But it is the narrator's voice that holds the attention, whether he is mocking himself and his own physical clumsiness in comparison with the more adept Toby, exclaiming at the horrors of colonialism, or responding to the perfection of the natural scene. Melville's method is one that is singularly mixed and, as such, is in line with his later works, *Mardi* (1849), *Moby-Dick* (1851) and *Pierre* (1852). There is little that is one-dimensional about *Typee;* the work has a smaller compass than those others in that it deals with a self-contained episode but it is no less rich technically. The following passage concerns an episode when the Typees hurry to sell their wares to boats on the beach:

> I could not but be entertained by the novel and animated sight which now met my view. One after another the natives crowded along the nar-

> "In Life he appears as a true Philosopher — as a wise man in the highest sense. He stands firm to his point; he goes on his way inflexibly; and while he exalts the lower to himself, while he makes the ignorant, the poor, the rich, partakers of his wisdom, of his riches, of his strength, he, on the other hand, in no wise conceals his divine origin; he dares to equal himself with God; nay, to declare that he himself is God.
>
> In this manner is he wont from youth upwards to astound his familiar friends; of these he gains a part to his own cause; irritates the rest against him; and shows to all men, who are aiming at a certain elevation in doctrine and life, what they have to look for from the world. And thus, for the nobler portion of mankind, his walk and conversation are even more instructive and purposive than his death; for to those trials every one is called, to this trial but a few."

*Inscription on the inside front cover of Melville's* New Testament and Psalms.

row path, laden with every variety of fruit. Here, you might have seen one who, after ineffectually endeavoring to persuade a surly porker to be conducted in leading strings, was obliged at last to seize the perverse animal in his arms, and carry him struggling against his naked breast, and squealing without intermission. There went two, who at a little distance might have been taken for the Hebrew spies, on their return to Moses with the goodly bunch of grapes. One trotted before the other at a distance of a couple of yards, while between them, from a pole resting on their shoulders, was suspended a huge cluster of bananas, which swayed to and fro with the rocking gait at which they proceeded. Here ran another, perspiring with his exertions, and bearing before him a quantity of cocoa-nuts, who, fearful of being too late, heeded not the fruit that dropped from his basket, and appeared solely intent upon reaching his destination, careless how many of his cocoa-nuts kept company with him.

This passage is very carefully controlled. Two initial points are made and are carried through the whole piece; these are the originality of the scene, and its vitality—the energy of the exercise being so unusual with the native people that this, in itself, produces a note of comedy. And yet, they are not of course presenting their own produce;

they have not created the abundant fruit by labour since nothing has to be cultivated on Typee. The pig becomes a recalcitrant child, refusing the 'leading strings', and incongruously clasped to the breast. The biblical allusion in the next sentence distances the scene and implicitly comments on it. The bananas themselves become animated, enlivened by their human transport system. Finally, the ultimate absurdity comes in the confusion of means and ends of the potential coconut vendor. The ironic tone here serves to maintain in the reader an appreciative, but detached, attitude. There is no attempt at involving him in the scene—quite the reverse. Nor is there any hint of anything below the surface; in fact, we are presented simply with surface and a surface of lacquered brilliance. The natives are almost ridiculed, but not quite, since they are simply exhibiting universal human traits, which can be treated with affection. And yet, as everywhere in the book, this passage is juxtaposed with, and receives its effect from, a following passage in which Tommo is deeply disturbed by the fact that Toby does not return. The ambiguous nature of all experience on the island is reinforced by this contrast. There are no answers to Tommo's questions, so he is tormented by doubt and fear: 'all their accounts were contradictory; one giving me to understand that Toby would be with me in a very short time; another that he did not know where he was; while a third, violently inveighing against him, assured me that he had stolen away, and would never come back'.

What emerges from this is that there can never be any true sociality between Tommo and the natives. The idealized Fayaway is the only person who seems capable of understanding Tommo's crippling sense of alienation, cut off, as he is, from his own culture. Fayaway seems (unconvincingly) capable of an imaginative identification that Tommo himself admits is extraordinary in someone of her age and limited experience. It is through Fayaway that Melville is able to introduce the melancholy that typifies Tommo's response to his self-inflicted predicament. That Fayaway is a fantasy figure is betrayed by the easy sentimentality with which Tommo expresses her sense of his dilemma: 'she appeared to be conscious that there were ties rudely severed, which had once bound us to our homes; that there were sisters and brothers anxiously looking forward to our return, who were, perhaps, never more to behold us'. It is more credible and, *pace* [D. H. Lawrence in his *Studies in Classic American Literature*, 1920], more moving, when the old chief Marheyo expresses his benevolent comprehension of the situation, at the time of Tommo's escape, in the words 'home' and 'mother'.

*Typee* is in some senses a comedy of manners. The first chapter sets the tone, with its episode of the Queen of Nukuheva and the French officers. This is a reported scene handled in a style of broad farce. But the naivety of the Queen is, in fact, touching rather than ridiculous; in her own terms, her behaviour is quite logical and reasonable. Melville here is employing a Swiftian type of satirical incongruity, similar to the dislocated expectations of Gulliver in various strange societies. The Queen is excited by the tattooing of an old sailor and proudly reveals her own:

the royal lady, eager to display the hieroglyphics on her own sweet form, bent forward for a moment, and turning sharply round, threw up the skirts of her mantle, and revealed a sight from which the aghast Frenchmen retreated precipitately, and tumbling into their boat, fled the scene of so shocking a catastrophe.

This passage modulates into a breezy, jocular narrative of the *Dolly* cruising on the Line.

> The man at the wheel never vexed the old lady with any superfluous steering, but comfortably adjusting his limbs at the tiller, would doze away by the hour. True to her work, the *Dolly* headed to her course, and like one of those characters who always do best when let alone, she jogged on her way like a veteran old sea-pacer as she was.

The characterization of the *Dolly* as an 'old lady' who does best left to her own devices, the total undercutting of any idea of efficiency or of the ship as a working unit; her jogging, unsuitable for a ship and her age, all combine to create the impression of successful amateur behaviour; the *Dolly* is the reverse of stylish. This passage modulates into a description of the increasingly soporific effect of the South Seas. Significantly, all thought is impossible; the crew are unable to think or act either—'Reading was out of the question; take a book in your hand, and you were asleep in an instant'. Tommo is thus put into a receptive state to respond totally to the compelling sense impressions the area provides. The passage that follows is comparable to those in **Moby-Dick** on the fascinating serenity of the Pacific.

> The sky presented a clear expanse of the most delicate blue, except along the skirts of the horizon, where you might see a thin drapery of pale clouds, which never varied their form or color. The long, measured, dirge-like swell of the Pacific came rolling along, with its surface broken by little tiny waves, sparkling in the sunshine. Every now and then a shoal of flying fish, scared from the water under the bows, would leap into the air, and fall the next moment like a shower of silver into the sea. Then you would see the superb albicore, with his glittering sides, sailing aloft, and often describing an arc in his descent, disappear on the surface of the water. Far off, the lofty jet of the whale might be seen, and nearer at hand the prowling shark, that villainous footpad of the seas, would come skulking along, and, at a wary distance, regard us with his evil eye. At times, some shapeless monster of the deep, floating on the surface, would, as we approached, sink slowly into the blue waters, and fade away from the sight. But the most impressive feature of the scene was the almost unbroken silence that reigned over sky and water. Scarcely a sound could be heard but the occasional breathing of the grampus, and the rippling at the cut-water.

What is striking here is the ominous undertone beneath the surface charm. Everything is conducted in total silence, signifying the fact that, above all, this is an inhuman scene, or rather, a scene in which humanity has no place.

The swell of the Pacific is 'dirgelike', the flying fish are scared by the passage of the ship, the prowling shark is 'villainous' and has an 'evil eye'. In spite of the humorous anthropomorphism of this, the point is made that the natural world is ambivalent and at times actively hostile.

The three passages quoted, although they span a chapter division, cohere, and typify Melville's achievement in what is by no means an apprentice work. The progress is from farcical anecdote, which nevertheless contains in itself a just appreciation of different manners and value systems (the French would have appeared equally ridiculous from a native viewpoint), to an introduction to the influence and novelty of the South Sea ethos. There follows a visual description of natural beauty, flawed by a sense of vague disquiet; and this constitutes a prefiguring of what the experience of life on Typee is to be.

Paradise itself is vitiated by the inescapable flaws of life; but a more grotesque and glaring flaw is apparent to Tommo as he arrives in the bay of Nukuheva:

> No description can do justice to its beauty; but that beauty was lost to me then, and I saw nothing but the tri-colored flag of France trailing over the stern of six vessels, whose black hulls and bristling broadsides proclaimed their warlike character.

This apparently remote retreat has already been infiltrated by Europe and taken possession of by the French. The link between the two worlds—and acceptable to neither—is the pilot who comes aboard the *Dolly*. The pilot is a disgraced English sailor, mistakenly employed by the French; his drunken antics are a suitable comment on the incongruity and ineffectuality of the Western presence in the South Seas. The immediate impact of the islanders themselves on the consciousness of Tommo causes him problems of interpretation:

> Such strange outcries and passionate gesticulations I never certainly heard or saw before. You would have thought the islanders were on the point of flying at one another's throats, whereas they were only amicably engaged in disentangling their boats.

The first event that greets the crew is the welcoming swim of the young Marquesan girls out to the *Dolly*. This, in many ways, sums up the contradictory qualities of the Western / South Sea confrontation. Again, the visual picture is totally seductive—Tommo sees the girls as mermaids 'I watched the rising and sinking of their forms, and beheld the uplifted right arm bearing above the water the girdle of tappa, and their long dark hair trailing beside them as they swam'. The arrival of the Marquesan girls signifies the entry of sexuality into the sterile ship. Tommo is fascinated, but also repelled: 'not the feeblest barrier was interposed between the unholy passions of the crew and their unlimited gratification'. There is also the sense of a mutual contamination going on: in spite of Melville's facile diatribes inveighing against the 'vice' and 'ruin' inflicted upon the 'poor savages', what comes off the page is the fear with which the Europeans respond to the unconscious sensuality and physicality of the girls.

The superiority of Western technological civilization and Melville's self-conscious mockery of it ('four heavy, double-banked frigates and three corvettes to frighten a parcel of naked heathen into subjection! Sixty-eight pounders to demolish huts of cocoa-nut boughs, and Congreve rockets to set on fire a few canoe sheds') does not alter the fact that this equipment is useless against the real dangers the island contains; dangers that threaten the very consciousness and sanity of Western man who is unable to relate to what the nineteenth century, (but not Melville) would consider a more primitive mode of existence. The incongruity of applying the European way of life to the situation here is given visual expression by the hundred French soldiers who daily take part in military exercises. These exercises take on the impact of a theatrical performance intended to dazzle the locals; but they are impressed by the meaninglessness of the ritual, rather than the power of their conquerors. It may appear at this point that Melville is following those writers who set the customs of their own society in a foreign locale, to point up their essential stupidity or wickedness. This is not Melville's intention. French customs are suitable in France. The Marquesans have their own rituals of war, which are equally contemptible to the French. What Melville is advocating is cultural separation. The evil comes from domination, from the forcing of one set of mores on a situation where they are not relevant. The question Melville is examining here is, in what does civilized behaviour consist? There is no scale of values by which societies can be measured and awarded points for civilization. Melville doesn't take the easy way out, either, and simply invert the savage / civilization dichotomy. He makes a more sophisticated response than that: 'were civilization itself to be estimated by some of its results, it would seem perhaps better for what we call the barbarous part of the world to remain unchanged'.

Although Tommo has a companion in his discovery and investigation of Typee, they are really two isolates, associated not in friendship so much as in affinity; like other Melville protagonists, Toby is a doomed, compelled wanderer: 'he was one of that class of rovers you sometimes meet at sea who never reveal their origin, never allude to home, and go rambling over the world as if pursued by some mysterious fate they cannot possibly elude'. Toby is no Sancho Panza, 'no one ever saw Toby laugh'. His speciality is a kind of dry humour which in itself comments on the real horrors of their expedition. Their entry into the 'Happy Valley' becomes a kind of Pilgrim's Progress involving, from the very start, unexpected hindrances and difficulties. The first being the thicket of reeds which proved to be 'as tough and stubborn as so many rods of steel'. The effort of breaking through this barrier nearly exhausts the couple before they have even begun their journey—Tommo describes them as 'ensnared'. Many critics have noted the frequent references to *Paradise Lost* in the entry to Typee and here Tommo and Toby, the Satanic Whitemen, are described as gliding unseen across the ridge, 'much in the fashion of a couple of serpents'. The Edenic quality of the natural scene is stated explicitly by Melville as soon as Tommo and Toby begin their attempt to descend into the valley; but it is a Paradise in which man does not figure:

> The whole landscape seemed one unbroken solitude, the interior of the island having apparently been untenanted since the morning of the creation; and as we advanced through this wilderness, our voices sounded strangely in our ears, as though human accents had never before disturbed the fearful silence of the place, interrupted only by the low murmurings of distant waterfalls.

The actual recounting of the process of traversing the terrain reveals a Defoe-like interest in factuality. The details of the descent from the ridges, the building of a shelter for the first night, impel the reader's credence and, as with Crusoe, create an admiration for human ingenuity as well as pleasure in finding out how things are done. However overtly 'philosophical' Melville becomes in his later work, he never loses his concern with real things.

The real dangers of Tommo's and Toby's situation are contrasted with the hyperbolic humour with which Toby deals with them, while Tommo maintains a condescending and incompetent calm:

> 'And what, in the name of caves and coal-holes, do you expect to find at the bottom of that gulf but a broken neck—why it looks blacker than our ship's hold, and the roar of those waterfalls down there would batter one's brains to pieces.'

> 'Oh, no, Toby,' I exclaimed, laughing; 'but there's something to be seen here, that's plain, or there would have been no path, and I am resolved to find out what it is.'

In spite of the mock-heroic quality of the description of the physical unease of their first night, Melville is surely making a serious point: the physical discomforts are dwelt on at great length and the painfulness of their experience is out of all proportion to what has caused it. Guilt at the role of interloper, and fear as to what they are to encounter obviously play a contributory part:

> I have had many a ducking in the course of my life, and in general cared little about it; but the accumulated horrors of that night, the deathlike coldness of the place, the appalling darkness and the dismal sense of our forlorn condition, almost unmanned me.

Again, it is Toby's rage and fear, however carefully controlled by irony, that express the emotional content of the situation: when Tommo wakes him up, 'poor Toby lifted up his head, and after a moment's pause said, in a husky voice, "Then shipmate, my top lights have gone out, for it appears darker now with my eyes open than it did when they were shut." Here, horror is just below the surface ('my toplights have gone out'); immediately after this, Toby comments, 'It is an insult to a man to suppose he could sleep in such an infernal place as this'. Tommo also uses laughter as a way of dealing with difficulties, 'I recommend all adventurous youths who abandon vessels in romantic islands during the rainy season to provide themselves with umbrellas'. At this point, Tommo develops the swelling in his leg which almost incapacitates him in the future. It has been observed by other commentators that the injury to Tommo's leg comes and goes according to his rejection or acceptance of life on the island. It significantly makes itself felt for the first time just before he experiences the full impact of the island's beauty:

> Had a glimpse of the gardens of Paradise been revealed to me I could scarcely have been more ravished with the sight. . . .
>
> Over all the landscape there reigned the most hushed repose, which I almost feared to break lest, like the enchanted gardens in the fairy tale, a single syllable might dissolve the spell.

Doubt is the predominant sensation on Typee. As Tommo says, 'I saw everything, but could comprehend nothing'. The very location of the valley is in doubt—when they finally manage to descend will they find themselves among the Happars or the Typees? Tommo puts the situation in all its grim reality to Toby:

> When I reminded him that it was impossible for either of us to know anything with certainty, and when I dwelt upon the horrible fate we should encounter were we rashly to descend into the valley, and discover too late the error we had committed, he replied by detailing all the evils of our present condition, and the sufferings we must undergo should we continue to remain where we then were.

The delusive quality of experience is apparent when Tommo drinks the water of the stream at the bottom of the gorge. Instead of the anticipated 'delicious sensation', the cold fluid seems to freeze him and to cause 'deathlike chills'. The appalling difficulties of their situation lead Toby to a reckless optimism; he makes himself believe that it is impossible for the inhabitants of such a lovely place to be anything else but good fellows. He rushes forward in a reckless, transcendental fervour of optimism. The nervous prose exactly parallels his inner agitation:

> Happar it is, for nothing else than Happar can it be. So glorious a valley—such forests of bread-fruit trees—such groves of cocoa-nut—such wildernesses of guava-bushes! Ah, shipmate! don't linger behind: in the name of all delightful fruits, I am dying to be at them. Come on, come on; shove ahead, there's a lively lad; never mind the rocks; kick them out of the way, as I do; and to-morrow, old fellow, take my word for it, we shall be in clover.

Although their hardships were continually overcome, the explorers gained no apparent sense of achievement from their successes. After one of the most spectacular of them, Tommo describes himself as 'cowering down to the earth under this multiplication of hardships, and abandoning himself to frightful anticipations of evil'. What seems to be implied here is that a spiritual pilgrimage is being endured by the two, of far greater intensity than the physical ills they experience, although those ills are the spur to their psychic pain.

As usual with Melville in *Typee,* a significant point in the narrative is stressed by means of a pictorial device; here, an almost emblematic use of an Adam and Eve couple, the first indigenous people that Toby and Tommo encounter:

> They were a boy and girl, slender and graceful, and completely naked, with the exception of a slight girdle of bark, from which depended at opposite points two of the russet leaves of the bread-fruit tree. An arm of the boy, half screened from sight by her wild tresses, was thrown about the neck of the girl, while with the other he held one of her hands in his; and thus they stood together, their heads inclined forward, catching the faint noise we made in our progress, and with one foot in advance, as if half inclined to fly from our presence.

Again, appearances are appallingly deceptive, since this idyllic couple, caught in a posture as if on a frieze, are later to be revealed as far from innocent; their reality is that of 'a couple of wily young things'. The reception of Tommo and Toby into the community of the Typees gives Melville scope for making use of his intense interest in craft—in the way things are done (as in the information about the techniques of whaling in *Moby-Dick*); Melville delights in knowledge almost for its own sake. He provides the reader with a sense of what it was like to be *there,* on the island. After the first welcome, Chief Mehevi provides the travellers with a calabash of poee-poee, the produce of the breadfruit tree. Melville's explanation of the difficulties involved in learning to eat this strange (to Westerners) substance is not useless pedantry but an integral part of the narrative. The reader experiences the novelty with Tommo and, like him, learns to accept the food very quickly as an ordinary element of diet. In spite of the friendly reception they have received, Tommo continues to expect that appearance and reality will prove total opposites; he goes further than this, to the extent of fearing that the greater the friendliness, the more hostility it actually conceals: 'Might it not be that beneath these fair appearances the islanders covered some perfidious design, and that their friendly reception of us might only precede some horrible catastrophe?'

As Tommo becomes more acclimatized to this society, so the factual element of the narrative becomes more prevalent. The emotional tone has been set throughout the extended approach to Typee (which takes five days). The interest of continually new experiences distracts the explorers momentarily and absorbs their attention, but beneath the surface of fact, the symbolic meaning is still intimately concerned with emotions of fear and despair. When Chief Mehevi revisits them in warrior dress, a motif is introduced that becomes of great importance at the end of the novel. This is the fact of tattooing. It had been introduced as a humorous motif early on but finally becomes a matter of fear to Tommo. He is afraid that he will be tattooed by force and that this will finally incapacitate him for rejoining his own society. And it is the tattooing of Kory-Kory (Tommo's Man Friday) that makes him into an object to Tommo; in spite of his admirable qualities, something not quite human:

> . . . the entire body of my savage valet, covered all over with representations of birds and fishes, and a variety of most unaccountable-looking creatures, suggested to me the idea of a pictorial museum of natural history, or an illustrated copy of 'Goldsmith's Animated Nature'.

Kory-Kory's father and mother take on the aspect of caricatures of common types in Western society. Again, the humour has a serious underlying purpose. Melville is making the point that human nature is universally the same. Fayaway is not disfigured by tattooing, being an unmarried girl. She, and the other girls, exhibit the same tendencies as women everywhere, but they wear flowers instead of jewels.

Following his typical method in the novel of juxtaposing idyllic and terrifying episodes, so that the interpretation of experience is always in doubt, Melville sets against the description of Tommo's first bath in the stream, the terrifying visit to the Taboo Groves. Once again, tattooing is as an index of horror—the bodies of the aged warriors there had become a dull green colour—'the hue which the tattooing gradually assumes as the individual advances in age'. Time and tattooing had destroyed any evidence of humanity in these creatures. Toby expresses the fear of Tommo also when he imagines that they have been brought there to be killed and then devoured by the cannibals (Melville points out elsewhere that cannibalism was practised by the Typees only on their enemies, dead in battle). Instead they are roused to eat in the middle of the night and then the question becomes not, are they going to be eaten, but what are they being asked to eat. 'A baked baby, by the soul of Captain Cook!' However, the Typees are revealed to have no ulterior motives but merely wish to entertain their guests in the most hospitable manner.

After the loss of Toby, Tommo is totally the prey of melancholy and depression since he must also try to disentangle the motives of his companion for not returning. 'Yes, thought I, gloomily, he has secured his own escape, and cares not what calamity may befall his unfortunate comrade.' Paradoxically, it is only when Tommo has his worst suspicions confirmed, (that he is indeed a prisoner), that he becomes at all reconciled to his situation. As he becomes more like the islanders, and refuses to speculate further about his situation, since speculation is useless, his leg begins to heal, as evidence of his psychic adjustment:

> Gradually I lost all knowledge of the regular recurrence of the days of the week, and sunk insensibly into that kind of apathy which ensues after some violent outbreak of despair. My limb suddenly healed, the swelling went down, the pain subsided, and I had every reason to suppose I should soon completely recover from the affliction that had so long tormented me.

Tommo's acceptance of his captivity gives Melville space to develop the theoretical aspect of his narrative. The intellectual structure, of which his story is an illustration, is of the relativity of the concepts of civilization and culture. The first point is the conventional one of the happier life of the Polynesian; happier, because physically comfortable and happier, because less intellectual. It is a fallacy that any society, in whatever stage of development and organization, is happy. But Melville is concerned to attack the complacent idea of the West that its mission is a civilizing one; in fact, the mission is to dominate and thereby destroy the indigenous culture. It is the superimposing of one culture upon another by force that creates chaos and breakdown. And this superimposition comes out of the arrogant belief of Civilization that her way is superior.

Will the 'voluptuous Indian be happier,' asks Melville rhetorically, if Civilization 'cultivates his mind' and 'elevates his thoughts'? Diseased, starving and dying natives answer that question mutely. To describe the actions of Civilization at home, Melville coins the phrase 'civilized barbarity'. In his investigation of the real meaning of the term 'savage', Melville brings his argument to a comic apotheosis by recommending that four or five Marquesan Islanders be sent to the United States as missionaries. For the purposes of his argument, Melville then proceeds to a panegyric on the happiness of life in Typee. However, it is essentially an external view; Tommo is unable to speak the language with any facility, and, without words, he is in no position to pontificate on the lack of cares, griefs, troubles, or vexations in Typee. Human society cannot exist without tension and conflict, and if there was no money ('that root of all evil') there must have been a barter system, which would produce its own problems. In his satirical attacks on Western civilization, Melville intends to set up the Typees as participants in an ideal society (an ideal for which he was always searching and which provides the positive against which he measures his generally negative view of human—thus saving himself from total scepticism). The ultimate statement of this position appears in chapter 27 in the following paragraph:

> During my whole stay on the island I never witnessed a single quarrel, nor anything that in the slightest degree approached even to a dispute. The natives appeared to form one household, whose members were bound together by the ties of strong affection. The love of kindred I did not so much perceive, for it seemed blended in the general love; and where all were treated as brothers and sisters, it was hard to tell who were actually related to each other by blood.

Tommo is not really qualified to make such a statement, seductive though the observation may be; he is unable to converse in any significant way with the people and he is under constant surveillance. He sees what he is permitted to see. This statement of Melville's is a rhetorical device to support his argument, not an observation that arises naturally out of the material with which he and Tommo are dealing.

The central section of the novel is a factual kernel building up density and actuality in Tommo's perception of Typee society. Chapter 20 provides documentary evidence of a typical day in the life of the Marquesans. Chapter 24 is an extended exposition, in travelogue mode, of the Feast of the Calabashes. Melville makes a straightforward attack on the authenticity of earlier accounts. *His* sources were first hand; the accounts of others are distorted, in the case of the missionaries distorted by self-seeking. Melville's ironic comment is:

> Did not the sacred character of these persons render the purity of their intentions unquestionable, I should certainly be led to suppose that they had exaggerated the evils of Paganism, in order to enhance the merit of their own disinterested labors.

Scientists are equally disingenuous in that they choose informants who tell them what they want to hear. Far from being the report of a rigorously conducted scientific investigation, the resultant book, if presented to the Marquesans themselves, 'would appear quite as wonderful to them as it does to the American public, and much more improbable'.

A focal point of this central section of the narrative is the varying reaction of Tommo and Kory-Kory to the mausoleum of the warrior chief. The effigy has a symbolic content to Tommo; perhaps because it is full of energy, of straining forward to some future goal; so different from the normal passive mode of the Marquesans, to many of whom, Tommo thinks, 'life is little else than an often interrupted and luxurious nap'. The dead chief's effigy is

> seated in the stern of a canoe, which was raised on a light frame a few inches above the level of the pi-pi. . . . The long leaves of the palmetto drooped over the eaves, and through them you saw the warrior holding his paddle with both hands in the act of rowing, leaning forward and inclining his head, as if eager to hurry on his voyage.

The chief is paddling towards heaven; to Kory-Kory heaven is a heightened version of Typee. But, in spite of the attractions of this breadfruit heaven, Kory-Kory obviously prefers the commonsense reality he presently inhabits, thus manifesting a shrewdness that Tommo admires. Kory-Kory's vision is a totally materialist one; to Tommo the image obviously means something on a poetic level; the ultimate quest, the ultimate representation of the desire for escape from the present and the real. Tommo, being a thinker, at least embryonically, can't be content with mere empiricism.

Again, this relatively sombre and reflective passage is followed, in Melville's typical manner, by a scene, on the same kind of topic, but treated in terms of broad farce. This is the episode with the god Moa Artua, who is treated by his priest as though he were a ventriloquist's dummy; the priest is a juggler who performs sleight-of-hand tricks. Tommo's comment is: 'the whole of these proceedings were like those of a parcel of children playing with dolls and baby houses'. The juxtaposition of these passages again underlines the impossibility of ever being able to interpret events and customs in Typee. Tommo responds to available images such as the chief's effigy, but is then confused and repelled by its sequel. Tommo reacts against the lack of reverence with which the islanders treat their gods, yet, in so doing, he is revealing the same lack of imagination of which the missionaries are guilty; he is imposing his own cultural values on the Typees. The section on religion is summed up with Tommo's usual mockery—a device for dealing with a topic that can't be satisfactorily assessed: 'the tattooed clergy are altogether too light-hearted and lazy—and their flocks are going astray'. Yet the emotional impact of the Typees' religion continues to be felt in the reverberations of the evocative image of the chief.

The collision of the 'civilized' and 'savage' worlds will inevitably result in the destruction of the less developed. Part of the fascination of Typee for Melville comes of

course from the fact that its existence as it is is doomed. 'Ill-fated people! I shudder when I think of the change a few years will produce in their paradisaical abode.' Melville warns that the Marquesans will suffer the same fate as the native Americans: 'The Anglo-Saxon hive have extirpated Paganism from the greater part of the North American continent; but with it they have likewise extirpated the greater portion of the Red race'.

One of the elements in Polynesian life that compels Tommo's admiration is its very communal nature; what Melville refers to as fraternal feeling. The ideal of brotherly love was one which Melville pursued all his life and, as mentioned above, the concept is one which has associated with it a high degree of optimism. Here, Tommo praises the unanimity of feeling the Typees displayed on every occasion: 'With them there hardly appeared to be any difference of opinion upon any subject whatever. They all thought and acted alike. . . . They showed this spirit of unanimity in every action of life: every thing was done in concert and good fellowship'.

However enviable this state might be in theory, it is obvious that in practice, Tommo would have found it suffocating. He is, in his actions and attitudes in the novel, an individualist par excellence. His very escape from the *Dolly* represents an inability to join his crew-mates in combined opposition to the captain; and he is to fail to join the community of Typee. It is the very isolation of Melville's protagonists, and of Melville himself, that makes society so appealing.

An oblique way of providing further evidence of the idyllic paradisial nature of life on Typee is given by Tommo's description of the birds and animals of the area; the dogs and the solitary Poe-like cat are interlopers ('it was plain enough they did not feel at home in the vale—that they wished themselves well out of it'), and are therefore offensive to Tommo. But birds, lizards and insects are totally without fear of man.

It is with the reintroduction of the question of tattooing that the emotional pattern of the novel is once more made clear, after the discursive chapters of information and observation that have given weight and balance to the actual experience, on an everyday level, of Marquesan life. The tattoo signifies Tommo's sense of the real, unbridgeable gulf between the society of nature and his own. Although Melville sums up Tommo's apprehensions with an outrageous pun 'I should be disfigured in such a manner as never more to have the *face* to return to my countrymen', this is the nub of the whole issue. To be tattooed means to be a convert to the Typees' religion. It is immediately after this that Tommo's life becomes one of 'absolute wretchedness'. His loneliness is complete: 'There was no one with whom I could freely converse; no one to whom I could communicate my thoughts; no one who could sympathise with my sufferings'.

At this point, significantly, his leg wound begins to trouble him again, stressing the fact that his adjustment to Typee has been fragile and temporary and has lasted only as long as his interest in the novelty of his new surroundings. From this point on, Tommo is desperate to escape and, as with the journey to the valley, his fear and physical unease are out of all proportion to what actually happens to him. He finally makes his escape by pretending that he still believes Toby to have returned. The determination of the Typees to retain him as a captive gives Tommo the strength to resist, since such a prospect has become terrible to him. Paradise has turned into hell, or at least, purgatory. Marheyo is the only islander equipped to understand Tommo's now frantic need to re-establish himself in his own society: 'He placed his arm upon my shoulder, and emphatically pronounced the only two English words I had taught him—'Home' and 'Mother'. I at once understood what he meant, and eagerly expressed my thanks to him'.

Critics have noted the savagery with which Tommo finally secures his escape. Even in the rescue boat, he is not safe since he is pursued by the warrior Mow-Mow. Tommo strikes him with the boat-hook in the throat. Mow-Mow's ferocious expression is the lasting impression that Tommo takes away from Typee.

Melville rounds off his story with a final diatribe against the missionaries of the Sandwich Islands. And, a sequel is appended to the main narrative. Toby miraculously reappeared and, much to Melville's delight, corroborated the main events of the story, thereby refuting those critics who had questioned its veracity; and (in the case of the British critics) the fact that *Typee* had been written by a common sailor.

Today, when literary categories are breaking down, it is easier to assess Melville's achievement in *Typee*. Is it novel or travel book; autobiography or anthropology? It is, in fact, an effective fusion of all these modes. The various devices used throughout are unified by Melville's adroit use of tone. The tall-tale, the element of broad farce, the underlying mockery, the interspersed sections of stasis and movement, whether mental agitation on Tommo's part, or actual event, the pretence of telling a simple tale, are all employed by a sophisticated literary intelligence. Melville's problem was more complex than Defoe's. His task was to deal with the fact that he had actually been in Typee personally. At times, Tommo is the narrator, at others, Melville is clearly making a direct statement to the reader. *Typee* is a seminal work of Melville's in that it initiates problems, both literary and intellectual that Melville was never really to solve, except perhaps in *Billy Budd.* Questions about the real meaning of civilization and community; the isolated, seeking life versus a reassuring, but stifling, communality. Above all, of the real meaning of human experience and its tragically ambiguous nature. What disconcerted Melville in the experience represented by *Typee* was his growing sense of the relativity of all social and cultural values.

*Faith Pullin, "Melville's 'Typee': The Failure of Eden," in* New Perspectives on Melville, *edited by Faith Pullin, The Kent State University Press, 1978, pp. 1-28.*

### Robert K. Martin   (essay date 1986)

[*Martin is an American-born Canadian critic. In the following excerpt, he discusses sexual themes in* Typee, *focusing on the conflict between Victorian mores and primitive customs.*]

### *Typee*: The Structure of the Encounters

[*Typee*] begins with two comic encounters that establish the theme of mutual incomprehension. In the one, the missionary's wife is the subject of great interest on the part of all the islanders until they attempt to look beneath her voluminous petticoats. She interprets their curiosity as a violation of her person and retreats to civilization; meanwhile the islanders are disappointed by their discovery of an ordinary woman. While Melville does not specify what they expected to find, it is possible that they expected her to be a man beneath all those layers of concealment. Whether they expected a sacred *berdache* or a divine androgyne, it is clear that they are distressed to find a mere mortal woman. The second of the encounters involves the queen, who is fascinated by a sailor's tattooing and decides to show him her own—on her ass! She does not recognize that the ass is a "taboo" part of the anatomy for the whites and so inadvertently transgresses a rule of social behavior. In each case people behave according to their own rules and are unaware how their actions will be perceived in a different social context. In part, therefore, Melville begins his novel by episodes that illustrate cultural relativism. However, they also establish a fundamental part of his social critique of Western culture: in both cases the Westerners see a sexual gesture where none is intended. In both cases they prefer concealment to display, taking display as a sign of sexual freedom. The episodes, in their comic way, make it clear that the sexual obsessions lie in the minds of the Westerners and not in the gestures of the islanders.

Throughout the novel Melville works toward the reversal of expectations. Where his audience may expect a sense of danger in the arrival on a primitive island, instead he provides a scene of generalized pleasure as the women swim out to the boat, displaying "wild grace and spirit." Melville pauses in his narrative to comment on the fate of those who unwittingly rejoice in the arrival of the visitors, and he speaks here in the editorial voice that so often steps forward to comment on the events and underscore their meaning:

> When the inhabitants of some sequestered island first descry the "big canoe" of the European rolling through the blue waters towards their shores, they rush down to the beach in crowds, and with open arms stand ready to embrace the strangers. Fatal embrace! They fold to their bosoms the vipers whose sting is destined to poison all their joys; and the instinctive feeling of love within their breasts is soon converted into the bitterest hate.

Two cultures meet here, under the symbols of the embrace and the viper, figures of love and betrayal. The horror of the Europeans' behavior is magnified by these images of an innocence abused and betrayed. And whatever hatred may finally be shown by the islanders is not laid to native malice but rather to the anger at this betrayal by those whom they have loved. It cannot pass notice here that this symbolic figure of the meeting of these two cultures recapitulates in miniature form the encounter of European and

Indian that lies at the base of American history. Melville's use indeed of the term "European" here strengthens this allusion to a prefiguration of this episode. If Americans are hated by the Indians of their land, the passage suggests, they have only their own behavior to blame.

The introductory chapters of *Typee* thus establish the social context for the inner story of the escape (or captivity) of Tom and Toby. They are important not only as a way of giving credibility but as a way of providing an interpretive structure for the story of journey, quest, and magical realm. The society from which Tom and Toby come is already identified as one of confused sexuality, moral self-righteousness, and ingratitude. Thus their departure from the ship and the "unmitigated tyranny" of the Captain is no mere adventure or personal whim; it is founded in a political and social reality. If the Captain represents the "tyranny" of Western political authority, the alternative to that authority is quickly established in terms of comradeship. Toby is presented as the first of the Dark Strangers, even though he is present on the ship, and it is he who is able to function as a guide for the passage from the world of the ship to that of the island. The description of Toby makes his symbolic role clear: "His naturally dark complexion had been deepened by exposure to the tropical sun, and a mass of jetty locks clustered about his temples, and threw a darker shade into his large black eyes." The repeated images of darkness show that Toby is already in some sense an islander. Tom's decision to flee the ship with Toby is his first commitment to the exploration of values opposed to those of Western authority. That Toby is also physically attractive suggests the way in which the erotic operates as a counterforce to the rule of conventional authority: his "remarkably prepossessing exterior" is of course the outward manifestation of an inner virtue, a kind of natural nobility that is present in all of Melville's Dark Strangers.

Melville's jocular reference to "Buggerry Island" makes it clear that he was aware of homosexual practices on shipboard (there are references to this in **White-Jacket,** as well). But it is also clear that he does not connect the reference to practices with the desire that the novel expresses for an idealized homosexuality or male friendship. Although, in the absence of the term "homosexuality," buggery and sodomy were the only terms possible to describe such activity, it seems that Melville distinguished between homosexual practices such as might occur on shipboard, frequently involving force and arising more out of necessity than out of affection, and a passionate love of men that he repeatedly described as an ideal and sought a place for. *Typee* suggests that some form of that affection might be possible, even on shipboard, although a pursuit of its fulfillment would seem to lead inevitably to escape from the ship and to the exploration of the island with a dark companion.

Tom thinks of escaping alone, but then considers the need for a friend—a "partner of my adventure," "some comrade with me," "what solace would a companion be!" When Tom and Toby have agreed to undertake an escape together, "we ratified our engagement with an affectionate wedding of palms." The repeated use of a similar metaphor in that phrase—"engagement" and "wedding"—anticipates Melville's use of the marriage metaphor to join Ishmael and Queequeg in *Moby-Dick.* There are other links to the later novel, which help to show that this early novel, although lacking much of the verbal brilliance of the later work, is not totally different in theme. The double (or triple) structure of Dark Strangers in *Typee* is replaced, of course, by the single figure of Queequeg, but the union of Tom and Toby is the first suggestion of a joining together of opposites that plays a large symbolic role in all Melville's novels. And, in anticipation of the opening of *Moby-Dick,* we first see Toby "leaning over the bulwarks, apparently plunged in a profound reverie." As a water gazer, Toby suggests, in skeletal form, the significance of the Narcissus figure that will be elaborated into one of symbolic centers of *Moby-Dick.* Here the image serves to strengthen our sense of Toby as a mirror self, a darker version of the Hero. By following Toby, then, Tom is enabled to discover something about himself.

Toby's reverie appears to have carried greater connotations for nineteenth-century readers than it may for us. As G. J. Barker-Benfield puts it, commenting on Ike Marvel's *Reveries of a Bachelor* (1850), "Reverie was commonly held to lead to masturbation, the uneconomical expenditure of male creative power." Whether or not Melville expected his readers to make this specific association (and the possibility is not remote, as will be seen in my discussion of Toby's role as a "rover"), the figure of the handsome, dark, brooding figure staring at the sea suggests a strong sensuality that is sharply contrasted to the world of work under the control of the Captain. Toby is the first manifestation of the link between the erotic and the subversive, and it is because of that link that he is able to lead the way toward the Golden Island.

The beginning of *Typee* bears a striking resemblance to Poe's *Narrative of Arthur Gordon Pym*—a vision of mixed delight and horror and a response to that vision by an "irresistible curiosity." (*Pym,* too, brings the narrator into a central relationship with a Dark Stranger, of distinctly phallic name, Dirk Peters, by means of an intermediate guide.) The mixture of delight and horror that is the response to Typee is presented as a realistic detail, but it serves equally well as a depiction of a psychic state. For the narrator, Tom, is pulled toward the images of natural beauty, lushness, and pleasure. But these cannot be attained without the commission of a crime—the abandonment of the ship. As a sailor on a whaling ship, Tom is not free; he is at the mercy of his captain. His captain, like the others in Melville's work, exercises a power of life and death over his crew and is subject to no constraints on his behavior. The tyranny of the captain, his cruelty, the inequities of social class that seem even more acute on board ship than on land, contribute to Tom's decision to leave the ship. And yet an element of terror is implicit, for the Captain warns of the fate of those who leave the ship behind. The rumor of the cannibalism of the islanders is a means of social control, as well as an externalization of the fear that must accompany such an important act of social transgression. The danger of being eaten by cannibals is the danger of losing one's body and soul—if, as seems almost certain, Melville knew *Pym,* he was familiar with the cannibalism there that marks a stage in the spiritual journey to the other, *white* side of the world. Knowing the terror, and yet almost attracted by it, the young men extend their journey to the second stage: for the journey on the ship to the South Seas is only a first, virtual frame narration; the second journey is the one that Tom and Toby take to the heart of otherness, the heart of the forbidden and appealing island.

In the virtual absence of the presentation of any world on shore, the ship takes the place of society. The ship is not a means of escaping society (as in adventure stories), but society itself. And that society is, we see, one of strict regimentation and authoritarianism. It is, in that sense, like a family, for, Melville frequently reminds us, the Captain is a father to his crew. This potential "paradise of bachelors" is spoiled by the presence of the Captain, representing the interdictions of society. The first act required, or desired, is an assertion of self and a gratification of desire, through the abandonment of authority. In order to gratify his desire, Tom must become a criminal. That this act does not seem criminal is irrelevant, as is the fact that there is no criminal intent. The rule of the Captain is absolute, from *Typee* to *Billy Budd,* and therefore natural good (as represented by Typee or by Billy) is always in conflict with social good (as represented by the Captain). Putting it another way, the gratification of desire, the search for pleasure, the Quest for the Golden Land, is always antisocial. The conflict is essential to Melville's work, for he seems to have recognized early the insight that would later be developed by Freud that personal desires must always be suppressed by society in order to provide the additional energy needed for work. The threat to society throughout Melville is the threat of play—play for its own sake. Play carries with it the notion of a self-sufficient or narcissistic eroticism, and thus it is not surprising that nineteenth-century moralists made a connection between reverie and masturbation. For it is certain that play threatens work precisely as sexuality threatens the economic structure; neither can be eliminated, but both need to be circumscribed and relegated to a restricted time of life (childhood or youth) or transformed into a new, socially useful form by making them productive rather than pleasurable in themselves. From *Typee* on, Melville recognizes that the world of play has become infinitely smaller (both historically and in individual lives) and that the "fathers" will do all they can to punish those who defect, who run away from responsibility. In *Typee* Melville has his hero make the choice for freedom and play, but he bears with him signs of his divided mind: his swollen leg, symbol of his wounded nature and also of his inability to function as "natural" man, and his constant fears that he will be eaten by the natives or that he will be tattooed. Both of these may be thought of as castration fears but are more usefully viewed as impediments to his integration into the Typee community, signs that although he has defected from the ship, he has not entirely defected from its values. The fear of being eaten, half-comic and half-horrific, seems to be largely a displacement of the fear of eating human flesh, that is, of partaking of some dark sacred meal. Tom escapes before he can commit this final transgression, the step that would appear to make him irrevocably a Typee.

Tom's companion on these adventures, Toby, has no problem with his leg and is apparently far less guilt-ridden than the narrator. Although one of the sailors, he is spiritually closer to the natives. His dark skin, "deepened by exposure," indicates that his relationship with Tom is a prelude to the relationships between Tom and the natives of Typee as well as the first indication of Melville's fundamental structure of the relationship between two young men— generally a white, European "intellectual" and a more "natural" darker Oriental or Mediterranean. Whatever the facts about the real Toby's disappearance from Typee (some of them given in Melville's "Sequel"), it is clear that the symbolic role of Toby ends once the couple has reached the interior of the island. Toby is a guide and an intermediary. His darkness signals his affinities to the natural world of Typee, and his lack of origins marks him off as someone not fixed either in the world of the ship or that of the island. "He was one of that class of rovers you sometimes meet at sea, who never reveal their origin, never allude to home, and go rambling over the world." According to John Todd, minister in Pittsfield and important religious writer on sexuality (he was Melville's apparent object of satire in "The Lightning-Rod Man"), "a roving imagination led to reverie and habitual masturbation." It seems quite likely that Melville's reference to Toby as a "rover" includes at least an association with a free sensuality. Anyone so clearly separated from the values of "home" is necessarily liberated from the associated concepts of domesticity, hence freed to the kind of unlimited masculinity that Victorian theorists saw manifested in masturbation. To "rove" was at the very least to be promiscuous and hence to be a threat to the domestic economy. The words of the well-known sea song "A-Roving" suggest that the association between "roving" and sexuality was well established:

> A-roving, a-roving
> Since roving's been my ruin,
> I'll go no more a-roving
> With you, fair maid.

Toby is in any case a free spirit. It is precisely this freedom that the novel presents as its highest value. Tommo's escape, although partly motivated by fear, is also a sign of his refusal to be "typed," to become a Typee. He too must learn to rove. The title of Melville's subsequent volume, *Omoo,* indeed, means "rover" in Polynesian, according to Melville, and indicates the extent to which Tom "becomes" Toby—or at least the hero of *Omoo,* revolting against his inadequate and incompetent captain and lingering in the South Seas, takes on many of Toby's qualities. Still later, Pip will call Queequeg a "rover" (*Moby-Dick*).

If Toby is important as a guide toward the discovery of the Golden Island, he is also important as a means for escape from the Captain. But this opposition is not only a personal one, just as the story of *Typee* should not be considered to be the story of Tom and Toby with a decorative backdrop of information about the colonization of the islands. Melville begins his novel with the encounter of two cultures, and that theme persists throughout the novel. It is the role of the Dark Strangers to help lead the Heroes of Melville's works away from the corrupt civilizations they have inhabited. By bringing Tom to Typee, the Dark Stranger allows the Hero to experience for himself a different culture and to enjoy that open embrace that first greeted the ship as it entered the harbor. Escape from the Captain means not only release into a world where play is valued but also release from a world of aggression and death. For, as the narrator puts it, "The fiend-like skill we display in the invention of all manner of death-dealing engines, the vindictiveness with which we carry on our wars, and the misery and desolation that follow in their train, are enough of themselves to distinguish the white civilized man as the most ferocious animal on the face of the earth." Although the occasion for this exclamation may be Melville's study of the effects of colonization, it is clear that his target is a larger one; it is all the crimes committed in the name of civilization by the "white civilized man" whose belief in his superior race, culture, and gender has allowed him to commit unspeakable crimes against humanity. Again and again one must remind oneself that Melville is concerned in his treatment of the South Seas with a case of virtual cultural genocide; he sees this death-blow not as an exception or a rare excess of power, but as a characteristic act of a culture based on certain values. Even in the incomplete terms of *Typee,* it is clear that Melville's purpose is to awaken the conscience of his readers to the horrors of their own society and to begin the search for an alternative.

With the help of Toby, Tom can flee the ship and begin the journey to the interior of the island. The extraordinary difficulties of this journey again remind us of *Pym* and illustrate the novel's maintenance of a romance structure of myth alongside its dense factuality. It has been pointed out that Melville's real-life journey was a relatively simple one, but the myth required an elaborate, painstaking journey. For the Golden Land must be secret, difficult of access, and enclosed. The journey there must be perilous, so that those who journey are worthy of their rare reward. Part of the evocative power of the journey in *Typee* comes from the particular forms it takes. Melville's preferred location for the Golden Land is a version of what W. H. Auden has called the "garden-island." In Auden's view, this image joins the qualities of the island, its safety and its exemption from ordinary law. It is characteristic of the garden-island that "there is no conflict between natural desire and moral duty." By introducing Tom/Tommo into the island paradise, Melville creates a conflict for his protagonist. Tommo can recognize the identity of natural desire with life on Typee, but Tom cannot escape the recollection of moral duty, or what he takes to be moral duty. For Tom/Tommo moral duty and natural desire seem irreconcilable, and so life with the Typees is ultimately impossible.

Although Tom is unable to remain there, Melville repeatedly treats Typee in terms of its superiority to "civilized" society. In every possible way he establishes the contrast between the two worlds, always to the advantage of Typee and to the disadvantage of civilization. The images are those traditionally associated with the Golden Land— lush vegetation, calm, peace, tranquility. Typee is "like the enchanted garden in the fairy tale." It is like "the gardens of Paradise." The prelapsarian implications are repeated:

"The penalty of the Fall presses very lightly upon the valley of Typee." And Melville goes on to identify specifically its unfallen nature: "I scarcely saw any piece of work performed there." The native women have "unconcealed natural graces" compared to the "stiffness, formality, and affectation" of "coronation beauties, at Westminster Abbey." Beauty and grace are not the only points of Typee's superiority; its inhabitants also demonstrate superior virtue, a trait they share with other "barbarous people," Melville asserts. "The hospitality of the wild Arab, the courage of the North American Indian, and the faithful friendships of some of the Polynesian nations, far surpass any thing of a similar kind among the polished communities of Europe." Because it is a function of his own attitude to himself and his culture, Tommo's perception of Typee is subject to radical shifts. He believes he has entered Paradise, then he feels he has fallen among cannibals; his leg swells, then his leg heals; he comes to understand something of Typee life, and then suddenly he fears for his survival (the survival of his identity much more than that of his life). This vacillation is between two extremes, neither of which can be accurate. Each of the tribes sees the other as the enemy and defines evil in terms of otherness. Are we with the good tribe or the evil tribe? Melville's point of course is that no tribe (read nation) is ever good or evil; each has its peculiar customs that may seem evil to those who do not understand them. The novel moves toward a recognition of the complexity of experience, a complexity that precludes simple categorization. Melville plays on the problem of naming in his reference to the tribal name:

> Their very name is a frightful one; for the word "Typee" in the Marquesan dialect signifies a lover of human flesh. It is rather singular that the title should have been bestowed upon them exclusively, inasmuch as the natives of all this group are irreclaimable cannibals. The name may, perhaps, have been given to denote the particular ferocity of this clan, and to convey a special stigma along with it.

This explanation of the name is one of Melville's inventions. Its fictiveness serves to stress its importance in Melville's symbolic structure. The name creates the fear; it is the category that determines our perceptions. The other tribes condemn the Typees by labeling them; newcomers cannot help meeting them with fear and hostility. The fear of cannibalism recurs in *Moby-Dick,* where it is treated with unambiguous comedy; there too Ishmael's response to Queequeg as a headhunter is based upon a label that precedes experience. In *Moby-Dick* Melville would move toward an analysis of the function of language in the establishment of systems of authority; here he begins his exploration by simply urging that true perception requires as much as possible an experience not contaminated by the preconceptions imposed by language.

There is a further ambiguity about this reference. As Paul Witherington has pointed out in a brief but fascinating comment [in *Arizona Quarterly* 26 (1970)], Melville seems to suggest a double meaning here: it is, he says, "an ambiguity that suggests either cannibalism or sensuality and, more important, the cannibalism *of* sensuality, a paradox crucial to the novel." The Typees are, indeed, lovers of flesh, and their voluptuousness evokes as much fear as their reputed cannibalism. To see the Typees correctly, one must forget one's preconceptions, which means, abandon all labels (just as *Moby-Dick* cannot be known by its etymology or library classification). By analogy, in order to see homosexuality correctly one must forget preconceptions and categories of good and evil; homosexuality is both buggery and ideal friendship. The Tom who flees at the end succumbs both to his sexual fears and to his cultural prejudices.

Because of the great difference between what the narrator reports about life on Typee and the hero's behavior, critics have often disagreed about the novel's statement on issues involving the conflict between the "primitive" and the "civilized." The early critics of the Melville revival, such as Charles Anderson [in his *Melville in the South Seas,* 1939], generally assumed that the work should be read as what Anderson calls a "brief against civilization." In this view, *Typee* is part of a Romantic tradition that makes use of a primitive culture as a way of indicting civilization. Encouraged perhaps by the primitivist spirit of the 1920s, which sought an escape from the false "progress" of Western civilization, Anderson made the classic case for the novel as a defense of the primitive: for him *Typee* is "a whole-hearted defense of the Noble Savage and a eulogy of his happy life, his external beauty, and his inward purity of heart." Hardly anyone would put the argument in quite such enthusiastic terms now, but it remains true that no statement about Typee or the Typees is critical of that society. It remains equally true that Melville used the moral superiority of the islands as a way of attacking the presumed superiority of his own society.

More recent critics, however, have frequently argued against the primitivist reading of *Typee,* although their evidence, aside from Tom's departure, is slight. Milton Stern, for instance, writes [in his *The Fine Hammered Steel of Herman Melville,* 1968], "The cliché, the flip 'philosophy' about the undressed-savage-as-happier-man-than-beribboned-admiral is relatively unimportant. It is glib and traditional, and, as it appears here, cheap and shoddy." Unfortunately, his comments do not say much more than that he does not like primitivism; he is not even able to deny its existence in the novel, merely its importance or value. It must be remembered that if primitivism seemed "traditional" in the 1950s when Stern was writing, it seemed much less so in the 1840s. The fact is that Melville's readers did not take his critique of Western society and of Christian missions lightly; their fury, and the need to excise many of these references from later editions of the book, indicate that Melville's proprimitive position was still seen as dangerously marginal. What is more, it is never "glib" since it is always clearly located in the specific observation of both the islands' virtues and, more importantly, civilization's failures. Stern believes that the conclusion of the novel indicates that primitivism is "rejected" in *Typee;* this analysis is consistent with his view that Billy Budd is a narcissist, while Nelson and Vere display "selfless circumspection." Edwin Miller, in his [1975] biography of Melville, concludes that a Rousseau-based primitivism is not actually present in Melville's works, for,

"despite the attacks upon civilization and vague statements seeming to support Rousseau's romanticism, Melville did not take the French philosopher to heart: there was too much of the puritan and the Calvinist in his nature." But the novels from *Typee* to *Moby-Dick* reveal that Melville consistently used primitive cultures as a way of criticizing a Calvinist culture (what he called "Presbyterian" in *Moby-Dick*). His statements in support of such a position, far from being "vague," are specific in their praise of natural beauty, grace, manners, the absence of violence, the absence of property-based values, and the dominance of brotherhood as fundamental concepts of human relations.

There is one clearly defined Noble Savage in *Typee,* who illustrates Melville's indebtedness to Rousseau and his appropriation of the idea of the Noble Savage for his own purposes. The Noble Savage is Marnoo, the stranger. He is, as the concept implies, a strange mixture of the savage with classical ideals of beauty. He has "matchless symmetry of form," he might have stood for the "statue of the Polynesian Apollo," he reminds Tom of "an antique bust." His striking beauty is tempered by a cheek "of a feminine softness," hinting at the androgyny that Melville associated with the realization of the ideal. Here, then, is Nature's nobleman, and Tom is immediately smitten, only to be sorely disappointed when Marnoo appears to pay him no attention: "Had the belle of the season, in the pride of her beauty and power, been cut in a place of public resort by some supercilious exquisite, she could not have felt greater indignation than I did at this unexpected slight." Marnoo is not quite as unreceptive as he at first seems. He tells the story of his life to Tom (like Toby, he has no family and no origins, he was an islander who was "carried to sea," he is another rover, and he is a man between two cultures, embodying the best of both). And he is eventually the means of Tom's escape.

The composite figure, Marnoo/Toby, represents Melville's ideal. Each of them is somewhere between civilization and savagery. Marnoo, for instance, has the Polynesian beauty (which the narrator identifies with Greek beauty), but he does not have the usual facial tattoos. He does have one very striking tattoo, though, a tree that is traced along his spine, suggesting to the narrator a "spreading vine tacked against a garden wall." Marnoo is thus identified as a life force, bearing the tree of life. He retains the original phallic power that is otherwise disappearing from the Islanders. Neither pure native nor pure civilized white, Marnoo (like his prototype Toby) points to a union of the best of both worlds, black and white, male and female, classical and romantic. His phallic potential is there as a positive force, neither destroyed as in the idols, nor grotesquely aggressive as in the adaptation of phallic energy to colonial conquest. In a fascinating passage, anticipating the black god of Queequeg, Melville discusses one of the ithyphallic idols. It is in the traditional shape, but "all its prominent points were bruised and battered, or entirely rotted away. The nose had taken its departure. . . ." Allowing for the prudishness of his readers, Melville seems to be as clear as he can be: the idol or *tiki* has lost its phallus (Poe used the nose as an elaborate phallic joke in just the same way, we recall), just as the

Typee society has lost its phallic potency. Melville then turns it all into a delightful joke, bemoaning "the wood-rot malady" as a sign of a "back-slidden generation . . . sunk in religious sloth, and requir[ing] a spiritual revival," in a wonderful parody of the language of American evangelism. Only those few rare souls, like Marnoo, who can transcend the traditional boundaries, are able to achieve the highest state in which such a revival of spiritual and erotic energy can truly take place. It is in the intermediate state, the union of civilization and savagery, rather than the victory of one or the other, that true beauty resides. Melville's vision here, as in *Moby-Dick,* is of a triumphant miscegenation in which the opposites of Western, and particularly American, history will be reconciled: in *Typee* that mystic marriage is presented in a single individual, and his relationship to the white hero/narrator is only implied. As the novels progress in time, Melville moves toward a more direct depiction of this miscegenation in terms of an actual male couple.

This theme reaches its fullest statement in the "marriage" of Ishmael and Queequeg. Queequeg is the logical conclusion of all the Dark Strangers and lovers throughout Melville's early works, and he bears with him his god, sign both of his savagery and his phallic potency (thus giving rise to all sorts of hilarious castration fears on the part of Ishmael, just as cannibalism and tattooing provide a delicious shudder in *Typee*). By his marriage to Ishmael, the South Seas are wedded to New England, primitive to Presbyterian, body to soul. But the assertion of the need for such a union runs through Melville's works. It is already present in Tommo's admiration for Marnoo and in Marnoo's part in Tommo's escape. From the patriarchal world of the ship, Tommo escapes to the matriarchal affections of Typee. But he is never free of the fear of retribution. What prevents the novel from fulfilling its dream of a union that begins the process of healing century-old wounds is what appears to be something like a Calvinist conscience on the part of Tom that makes him doubt the virtues of a society devoted to pleasure. That doubt, which seems to be deliberately attributed by Melville to his character and not merely transferred from his own consciousness, together with what seems to me Melville's inability to deal with the novel's inescapably homosexual implications, drives Tom back to the ship, abandoning the benign phallicism of a matriarchal society for the phallic aggression that comes to dominate *Moby-Dick.*

The recently discovered manuscript of parts of *Typee* reveals how fully Melville devoted himself to praise of a benign phallic world in his early drafts, even though these were later revised in the probable interests of propriety. The famous scene in chapter 14 in which Kory-Kory jealously watches as the "nymphs" anoint Tommo's body originally included a reference to "transport," later changed to "delight" (and another to "delight" replaced by the euphemistic "kindness"). This same scene included Tommo's association of his own situation with that of Captain Macheath in *The Beggar's Opera* (Melville cites the final aria, "Thus I stand like the Turk / With his doxies around"), Sardanapalus, and the Sultan. The episode is a remarkable paean to a passive receptivity, a masturbation that is ostensibly performed by the women but is certainly presided over by the spirit of Kory-Kory. It is Melville's celebration of a polymorphous and undirected sexuality that is directly related to the social order of Typee. It is one of the sources of the "sperm-squeezing" episode in *Moby-Dick.* Immediately following the scene of the anointing Melville presents the scene called "Producing Light à la Typee," another remarkably erotic passage. David Ketterer [in *Melville Society Extracts* 34 (1978)] has already called attention to the phallic imagery in this passage, but an examination of the manuscripts reveals that the original language was even more open than the version eventually published. For instance, Melville originally wrote "attains his climax" where the text now reads "approaches the climax of his effort." Thus a second masturbation, in the manuscript clearly performed for the reader's "particular gratification," follows the first scene of erotic arousal. In both cases Melville draws our attention to a self-sufficient and socially integrated sexuality that stands in sharp contrast to the Western world of shame. As Melville laughingly points out, these practices of phallic celebration would seem to be appropriately attended by a "college of vestals" were it not for "special difficulties"—presumably the lack of any virgins.

Unlike the later works, *Typee* does not indicate a Melville who was prepared to explore the meaning of male friendship in its deepest implications. He could joke about buggery, he could show ideal, handsome companions, but he could not bring the two together. It is a sign of the tentative nature of Melville's exploration of sexual issues here that a good deal of attention is given to Fayaway (the only other novel prior to *Pierre* with important women characters is the allegorical *Mardi*). This is not to say that Fayaway is a false character, merely that she is not drawn with the same passionate conviction as the male characters and that she does not fill a place in Melville's symbolic universe. Conventionally beautiful, she is "the very perfection of female grace and beauty" and every feature is "as perfectly formed as the heart or imagination of man could desire." Melville's heart is simply not in those generalized descriptions that create nothing more convincing for us than the traditional figure of romance. Still, it is important to note that Melville does give her an independence that marks her off from the heroines of more "civilized" countries. And his depiction of her sorrow at Tommo's departure does seem actually felt; there is perhaps a perception of the degree of deception involved in that romance and the inevitable need to leave such a lover behind. Are we sure that Tommo could have resisted a similar call from Marnoo? Melville, at the time of writing *Typee,* was apparently not prepared to depict the world of exclusive male friendship and sexuality that would characterize his later works. He sought to express in his first novel a work of released sexual pleasure, one in which the body could be celebrated and in which individuals could be free to explore their deeper natures. In this world, partly observed and partly imagined, Fayaway, the beautiful woman, could take her place alongside Kory-Kory, the faithful friend, and Marnoo, the handsome stranger.

The existence of such an autonomous figure as Fayaway may be one of the many indications that Melville gives in *Typee* that the society he depicts had been matriarchal at some not so distant time. The traces of matriarchal religion are evident, although power at the time of his narrative seems to reside in the men, and women are excluded from the sacred grove, and from the canoe. One of the novel's striking scenes has Tommo and Fayaway violate the taboo by sailing together, one of Melville's few deliberate violations of likely historical accuracy. The scene serves to emphasize Melville's use of the novel to explore a critique of social organization and sexual convention. Melville notices the existence of a system of polyandry, and he is perceptive enough to see its implications. He begins his discussion of marriage customs by noting that the unit is normally composed of two men and one woman. After a young couple has been formed, an older man comes along and carries them off to his house. "This disinterested and generous-hearted fellow," Melville remarks facetiously, "now weds the young couple—marrying damsel and love at the same time—and all three henceforth live together as harmoniously as so many turtles." The description of apparently bisexual men may be colored by Melville's own tastes, but he moves quickly to see the larger social implications, for this "plurality of husbands" "speaks volumes for the gentle disposition of the male population." Melville concludes on something of a comic note by suggesting the possibility of male harems, but concluding of American men, "we are scarcely amiable and forbearing enough to submit to it." Despite the joking tone, Melville's references make it clear that he recognizes the arbitrariness of male domination—and the mere suggestion of the opposite patterns of female domination, so feared by men, should be enough to display its foolishness and intolerable nature. Melville is radical enough to suggest that the aggressive behavior of men is related to the Western concept of marriage. The acquisition of a bride becomes the first step in the development of a system of private property and of the defense of that private property by force if necessary. On Typee, on the other hand, private ownership of anything other than personal articles does not seem to exist. Land is apparently held "in fee simple from Nature herself" until, of course, the colonists seize it. When men are not competing for the ownership of women, Melville suggests, they are free to develop friendships among themselves, friendships like those of Polynesia described in **Typee** and **Omoo**.

Melville's myth of the Golden Land is intricately tied up with his notion of male friendship. Toby was not, apparently, the mere random companion Melville tries to depict. Melville thought enough of the real Toby, Richard Tobias Greene, to keep a daguerreotype of him until his death, where it was found among his possessions. Late in his life he wrote a very moving poem to Toby, now called (in an amusing erotic pun) Ned Bunn, in which he recalls their journey to "Marquesas and glenned isles that be / Authentic Edens in a pagansea." He recognizes that their world has passed with time and that tourists now take the place of the earlier voyagers, but he still recalls with pleasure the Paradise they one knew:

> But we, in anchor-watches calm,
> The Indian Psyche's languor won,
> And, musing, breathed primeval balm
> From Edens ere yet overrun;

> Marvelling mild if mortal twice,
> Here and hereafter, touch a Paradise.

The sense of Paradise lost here is double, of course, for he has lost not only the Paradise that all men lose, the paradise that the Bible calls Eden, but also the paradise of male friendship that he knew with Ned/Toby. Many people have the sense that growing older involves a sense of loss, but when growth implies the abandonment of a potential for deep affection, as Melville felt in his own life, the sense of loss is particularly acute. The South Seas were for Melville at least three things, in ascending order of abstraction: the place I was with Ned, the place where male friendship is recognized and institutionalized, and the place where we all lived once, where there was plenty to eat, warmth and sunshine, happiness and harmony. These ideas are inseparable for an understanding of Melville's first novel. They are the elements that enable Melville to transform his material from social satire into a vision, if still somewhat fogged, of an alternate world that may come to replace the rule of Captains, colonial governors, and missionaries.

Fact or fiction? Defense of innocence or rejection of the primitive? Like Melville's later work, *Typee* evades easy definition. The "facts" of *Typee* provide a basis for Melville's critique of society and a justification for his violation of Victorian taboos. Its "fictions" enable Melville to make his own use of this material and to turn an apparent travel narrative into the symbolic exposition of a spiritual autobiography. Although Melville's narrator does not have the ability to deal fully with the sexuality of the tale he himself relates, he does make a giant step forward when he comes to recognize the impossibility of judging by appearances. There can be no answer to the good/evil dilemma of Typee, since the dilemma itself is false. There is only experience. By bearing in mind, however, that innocence stands, among other things, for homosexuality (although a homosexuality that is itself in some sense "innocent"), one can understand Melville's problem and the confusion of his critics. *Typee* is a work that proposes the superiority of a "savage" morality over a "civilized" one, but one that must simultaneously stay free of all definitions. Tommo does not finally reject the Typees; he flees them. Melville had not yet developed the ironic distance that would enable him to handle his narratives of a younger, more naive self. There are times when Melville seems like James Baldwin's David [in his *Giovanni's Room,* 1956], spending his life, "having run so far, so hard, across the ocean even, only to find myself brought up short before the bulldog in my own backyard." Typee was a Paradise that evoked both desire and fear—a fear even that desire might be fulfilled—and that could only achieve its purity when seen from afar, in the long retrospect of Melville's life. The "enviable isles" of the early novels became those of the later poems, the islands of memory, purified by time and washed free of fear. They could finally only be attained in death. That, of course, would be the story, and the burden, of *Billy Budd*.

The sense of *Typee*'s incompleteness that many readers feel comes from the inadequate resolution of the novel's own inner dynamics. There are, as we have seen, two journeys involved: the journey on board ship (the childhood world of the "Dolly") and the journey from the ship to the interior of the island. Since the novel effectively ends with the return of Tom to the ship, it is clear that the second of these is the real "plot" of the novel; and yet the novel encompasses both. But the two plots are inherently opposed, since one is undertaken under the rule of the Captain, and the other is undertaken in opposition to the Captain. As Toby acts as the guide to the island, one is led to expect that Marnoo will act as a second guide to the spiritual center of the island. But Tom, along with Melville perhaps, was unable to follow him into that "sacred grove," which seems to involve partaking of human flesh: the sexual taboos were too strong, and so the novel is strangely aborted. Fear brings us back to our beginnings. But the book's inner logic holds that Tom must continue his journey on the island. If Melville could not yet present a hero capable of doing that, he could at least move to a position where the hero might be appraised for the nature of his behavior. Melville is too close to Tom to know what to make of his deepest feelings.

*Robert K. Martin, in his* Hero, Captain, and Stranger: Male Friendship, Social Critique, and Literary Form in the Sea Novels of Herman Melville, *The University of North Carolina Press, 1986, 144 p.*

## Bruce L. Grenberg  (essay date 1989)

[*In the excerpt below, Grenberg examines the conflict between primitive social values and civilized society in* Typee, *contending that Melville's novel fails to resolve these issues.*]

In light of the sharply divided religious and cultural commitments of the reading public in the 1840s, we are not surprised by its mixed reaction to *Typee.* The religious and moral watchdogs of both England and America could scarce do anything but castigate "An apotheosis of barbarism" [quoted in Jay Leyda's *Melville Log,* 1951] and scorn Melville's "habits of gross and shameless familiarity not to say unblushing licentiousness, with a tribe of debased and filthy savages of Marquesas. . . ." On the other hand, more Romantic spirits could rejoice at finding "Mr. Melville's book . . . full of things strange and queer to the ears of Broadway and Chestnut Street," and rise occasionally to outright hyperbole: "Enviable Herman! A happier dog it is impossible to imagine than Herman in the Typee valley." Even more predictable, from our vantage point, were the countless statements to the general effect that Mr. Melville ought to "learn the worth of the morality taught by the Christian missionary, before he ventures to criticize his motives, or to disparage his work."

For those interested in understanding *Typee* as a work of art, the most significant result of this contemporary criticism of the novel is that both factions, however opposed in judgment, were in agreement that *Typee* was a simple, polarized narrative that lauded the simple native life and attacked the values of Christian civilization. Although in our relatively sophisticated age we tend to react against evangelism and zeal and find Melville's licentiousness rather tame, we persist in seeing *Typee* as a book of polarized and polarizing values. We in our own form of high morality speak of Melville's "social consciousness" and alternately speak of his romanticism, primitivism, or self-liberation. But this prevailing view of the novel, whether expressed in nineteenth- or twentieth-century terms, is simplistic, and expresses more our reductive critical mentality than Melville's creative mentality.

To cast significant doubt upon this neatly categorized critical vision of *Typee* is easy enough. Although one thrust of the book presents the Typee natives as pure, innocent children of nature facing destruction by the corrupt power of frigate-Christianity, a counterthrust of approximately equal force asserts the natural corruption of flesh-eating, idol-worshipping, whimsically violent and ignorant savages whose only possible redemption lies in the saving force of culture and benign Christianity. One can also point to a first-person, controlling narrator who simultaneously lauds the native life and plots an escape from it every waking moment, a narrator who "goes native," but with all the nicety of a proper Christian gentleman. Or, to cap Melville's apparent "confusion," one might examine the whole *Typee-Omoo* sequence of Tommo's adventures, wherein he deserts one ship because of its uncivilized conditions, finds "paradise" with a blue-eyed Marquesan, flees this haven for another unknown ship, mutinies, etc., etc.

By looking at *Typee* in this fashion it is true that we have replaced simple bivalence with ambiguity. But for all the book's complexity it would be wrong to conclude that Melville was merely confused. Although Melville's experiences in the Marquesas and the Sandwich Islands, on the *Acushnet* and the *United States,* were traumatically, startlingly inconsistent with his intellectual and emotional expectations, in *Typee* and *Omoo* Melville attempts to assimilate and comprehend that disjunctive experience, to square his experience with his cultural, familial, and personal mold, in short, to order and unify the disparate elements of his highly varied life.

In a real sense we have asked the wrong questions of *Typee.* The true issue is not which culture will prevail— the answer to that is self-evident. Nor should we ask of the novel which culture Melville "favors"—for there is, properly speaking, no answer to that question at all. Christian, Western culture and heathen, Polynesian naturism do form the poles of Melville's experience and mentality in *Typee,* but rather than play one against the other, Melville sets himself the task of wedding the two and putting them to rest in harmonious felicity.

That *Typee* is, in fact, a "problem" novel is indicated by Melville's total disregard for convincing motivation. Tommo jumps ship largely because of bad food and little prospect of a good voyage: Melville doesn't even tell us why Toby leaves. This same sense of irrational, totally arbitrary action pervades the sailors' descent into the Typee valley, the primary, critical action that determines the whole course of the narrative. As the narrative progresses, not only are we at a loss to explain the narrator's contradictory impulses to remain and to flee, but we are also unable to determine the motives of the Typees in treating Tommo alternately as a recovered child and as an untrustworthy prisoner.

Neither in the beginning, through the middle, nor at the end does Melville provide clear or even adequate motivation for what is going on. One might casually attribute this failure to first-book inexperience, and undoubtedly this plays a part in the whole truth. But this *ex nihilo* quality in the tale also suggests the character of unresolved essential conflict, and by examining the book in this light, one finds a number of otherwise obdurate difficulties at least partially explained. *Typee* is romance, not literal dream, but the terms of its conflicts are elemental to Melville's developing mind and yield something like a paradigm of Melville's artistic concerns in the novels that follow in such rapid succession.

One finds abundant evidence in *Typee* pointing toward an "easy" interpretation. Almost everyone reading the book for the first time would unhesitatingly agree that the primary thrust of the tale is toward a romantic praise of the free, uncomplicated life of the savage in nature—a praise expressed largely in contrast to a pervading criticism of restrictive, unintegrated civilized life. The evidence for such generalization is so rife that it scarcely bears repetition, let alone refutation. One thinks immediately of the portrait of the "patriarch-sovereign of Timor" and the "polished, splendid Frenchman," Du Petit Thouars. Or one recalls perhaps the most glaring example of Melville's cultural comparisons—his disquisition on the contract-free, coinless society of Typee in contrast to the "thousand sources of irritation that the ingenuity of civilized man has created to mar his own felicity," the hydra-heads of the monster Money. Evidence of this movement in the book can be found, in fact, on almost every page.

However strong this evidence appears in itself, there are qualifying and opposing ideas in the book which are represented with equal force. Not merely incongruities of narrative and thought, but radical antinomies of mind insinuate the book and shape its meaning and form. Even granting that Melville probably included the anecdote of Kory-Kory's laborious fire-making (Chapter 14) as comic interlude or even "filler," the sketch sounds a discordant note in the purportedly unrelieved felicity of savage life. And there are other, more significant, values at odds with the overall pattern of development. One suspects a double edge to Tommo's seeming praise, that "the minds of these simple savages, unoccupied by matters of graver moment, were capable of deriving the utmost delight from circumstances which would have passed unnoticed in more intelligent communities," for within that verdant recess Tommo frequently falls prey to a "deep dejection . . . , which neither the friendly remonstrance of my companion, the devoted attentions of Kory-Kory, nor all the soothing influences of Fayaway could remove." Not unqualified ecstasy, but an inconclusive alternation of delight and woe is the result of Tommo's being "cut off . . . from all intercourse with the civilized world."

Ultimately, Tommo's disorienting experience forces him to rethink the suppositions of Western culture. His radical isolation from his informing culture, however eagerly sought, creates in him an ambivalent attitude, a sense of "eager uncertainty," toward all the factors of his experience. As a result, the events, characters, and ideas of his narrative are fraught with radically opposing values and implications. The simplicity of the Typees is also seen as narrowness: "The little space in which some of these clans pass away their days would seem almost incredible." Unanimity of brotherly feeling among the tribe, whereby "there hardly appeared to be any difference of opinion upon any subject whatever," and due to which "they all thought and acted alike," can and does become oppressive to the man who not many years earlier had dearly loved an argument for its own sake. And the most piercing anomaly in terms of our response to plot and theme is Tommo's categorical assertion that "the continual happiness, which . . . appeared to prevail in the valley, sprung principally from that all-pervading sensation which Rousseau has told us he at one time experienced, the mere buoyant sense of a healthful physical existence"—a most strange apology by the Tommo who remains semi-invalid throughout his residence in nature and recovers only upon his return to civilization and a "quack" physician.

But these numerous and important contradictions do not constitute the deepest conflict in the book. Beneath the contradictions lurk yet deeper oppositions that defy resolution. These are seen most clearly in Melville's attitude toward the Marquesans (especially Fayaway—the first of Melville's markedly synecdochal characters) and in his attitude toward religion, both the Marquesan and Christian.

Melville's description of the noble Marquesans emphasizes, above all, "the European cast of their features," and, indeed, the people Melville chooses to typify the ideal state of nature are, in reality, "European natives." The fairest of all these autogenous hybrids is Fayaway—whose Polynesian hair "flowed in natural ringlets over her shoulders," whose "strange blue eyes" seemed "most placid yet unfathomable," whose "soft and delicate hands" can only be compared to those of a "countess," and whose feet "were as diminutive and fairly shaped as those which peep from beneath the skirts of a Lima lady's dress." At this level of ambiguous expression, the erstwhile contrasts between native and civilized characteristics are transformed into comparisons and analogues. And at this point we begin to suspect that Tommo's allegiance lies with neither native nor with civilized culture, but with some ideal realm not yet seen by land or sea.

If we examine in its totality Tommo's attitudes toward religion in *Typee,* we find a similar, persistent inability to fasten upon any realistic option and a concomitant yearning for some ideal fusion of possibilities. Tommo in the most overt fashion attacks the Christianity of the missions which forces itself upon alien cultures and spells the long, painful death of those cultures. Thus, Tommo argues on the one hand that the Marquesans (and all Polynesians) would be better off left to themselves, where a natural democracy might operate, and where "common sense law" might prevail, impelled by an "indwelling . . . universally diffused perception of what is *just* and *noble*. . . ." On the other hand, he can, and does, assert: "let the savages be civilized, but civilize them with benefits, and not with evils; and let heathenism be destroyed, but not by destroying the heathen." However attractive this statement of benevolent conversion might be to Tommo, and to us, it is precisely such an ideal accommodation of the two cultures that Melville in *Typee* and *Omoo* depicts as impossible. And yet it is equally clear in these books that this is the *only* solution that Tommo would find acceptable.

If Christianity falters in *Typee,* the primitive religion of the Typees, the only stated alternative, never enters the race. However strongly Tommo is drawn to the Typees, he is immediately and irrevocably appalled by the heart of their culture—the religion of Taboo. Tommo's journey into the "solemn twilight" and "cathedral-like gloom" of the Taboo groves is redolent of Goodman Brown's penetration into the Satanic forest.

And Melville repeatedly links the Typees' highest religious expression directly with their most inhuman, revolting practice—cannibalism. His description of the Taboo groves is immediately followed by "Midnight Misgivings," and although at the time these misgivings are groundless, they point ahead to the "Mysterious Feast" of Chapter 32, which, structurally, precipitates Tommo's flight from the valley. His horror at the Typees' desire to tattoo him is heightened by his discovery that "the whole system of tattooing was . . . connected with their religion. . . ." What Tommo instinctively fears in the Typees' religion, and indeed in their whole culture, is revealed in his spontaneous revulsion at the idea of being tattooed: "I now felt convinced that in some luckless hour I should be disfigured in such a manner as never more to have the *face* to return to my countrymen, even should an opportunity offer." He fears, in short, for his identity, both self-defined and as it is defined by the opinion of his civilized culture.

Although Tommo's sympathies, perspectives, and ideas seem intractably tangled in careless contradiction, certain basic lines of force control the book in its totality. Out of the inconsistency, contradiction, and paradox operating in plot, character, and theme, there is clearly discernible a powerful impetus toward an accommodating comprehensiveness. If Matthew Arnold's "Stanzas from the Grande Chartreuse" offers a gloss upon Melville's specifically religious quandary, a more complete analogue to the totality of *Typee* (and *Omoo*) is found in Marvell's "The Garden." Like the speaker in Marvell's poem, Melville's protagonist retreats, at least momentarily, to a pseudo-Paradise, wherein he too can exclaim:

> What wond'rous Life is this I lead!
> Ripe Apples drop about my head;
> The Luscious Clusters of the Vine
> Upon my Mouth do crush their Wine;
> The Nectaren, and curious Peach,
> Into my hands themselves do reach;
> Stumbling on Melons, as I pass,
> Insnar'd with Flow'rs, I fall on grass.

But for Melville, as for Marvell, mere sensuous delight is not enough; the mind and soul must enter and, through apprehension, transcend mere experience:

> Mean while the Mind, from pleasure less,
> Withdraws into its happiness:
> The Mind, that Ocean where each kind
> Does streight its own resemblance find;
> Yet it creates, transcending these,

> Far other Worlds and other Seas,
> Annihilating all that's made
> To a green Thought in a green Shade.

This "creative annihilation" of manifold sensuous experience into a green unity of the soul and all its apprehensions is the ultimate goal of Tommo in *Typee*. But whereas for Marvell the statement becomes attainment, for Tommo the statement merely serves as a bitter reflection upon the recalcitrant terms of his own dilemma. The radically discordant elements of his experience refuse to be annihilated into a unity.

The basic ambiguities and ambivalences in *Typee* constitute, as it were, the prolegomena to the ambiguities and ambivalences in the next five novels. On the one hand, all experience, no matter how various or contradictory, has prima facie value as actuality. And Melville depicts the human response to this reality as immediate, playing over the texture of reality as a Typee might fondle a string of beads, a paddle, his own tattoos, a cocoa-nut, or his woman. Compelled toward freshness, contrast, even contradiction, this force, as Melville depicts it, is essentially expansive and "multilinear," projecting the self into each object of experience, thrusting it toward an infinity that is accretionary in process, an infinity to be attained only in the exhaustion of all possible experience. The other force operating in the self is essentially restrictive and "curvilinear." Assimilative of completed experience, it is synthetic in process and impels one toward a unity deriving from necessary experience. Beginning with *Typee,* Melville depicts the self's determined, even desperate, efforts to square this multiplicity with this drive to unity.

Neither force, as Melville defines it, is intrinsically self-defeating or even debilitating. Even together, although opposed radically, they do, in fact, provide the motive power to Melville's art through *Moby-Dick.* Yet there is in their conjunction an inherent instability that causes Melville problem after problem and that, ultimately, leads to the collapse of his grand intention in *Moby-Dick* and *Pierre.* In the early works we see Melville working out to a clearer and clearer definition, the tragic terms of a high and noble mind that has set for itself an impossible task.

One scarcely is tempted to call *Typee* a tragedy, yet in its quality as a "problem" narrative we see the incipient forms of *Mardi* and *Moby-Dick,* which certainly are tragedies. Tommo, like Faust, is trapped by his own inability to say "Enough!" Each experience is sought, yet none is satisfying. The individual elements of his experience remain disappointingly discrete—native and civilized, heathen and Christian—so that not even compromise is possible. Melville offers no possibility for a positive interaction of the two cultures, nor does he suggest any kind of "suburbanite" civilized primitivism: there is no Walden Pond in Polynesia. Nukuheva and Tahiti, as border environments where one might have civilized trappings yet commune with nature, are, in fact, the targets of Melville's most scornful attack. Tommo demands the best of possible worlds; he requires an ideal, composite reality that will include all the good and exclude all the bad features of his real experience. The closest Tommo ever gets to his "green thought in a green shade" is in Chapter 7, when he treats us to a fairly conventional description of the unspoiled beauty of Polynesia, viewed as "the gardens of Paradise." There is, however, another prospect that Tommo finds even more impressive. In Chapter 6, Melville provides the first of several Pisgah visions in his fiction when Tommo stands atop "what seemed to be the highest land on the island" and looks down upon "the lonely bay of Nukuheva, dotted here and there with the black hulls of the vessels composing the French squadron." Tommo exclaims that it was "altogether the loveliest view I ever beheld, and were I to live a hundred years, I should never forget the feeling of admiration which I then experienced."

Significantly, both descriptions are of distant perspectives. Tommo's eye is able to comprehend the whole without concern for distracting detail. Yet even to Tommo, the scene first cited is fragile to the point of appearing hallucinatory (he has just talked about his fever), and he fears that the harsh reality of a spoken word might shatter it. The second passage cited gives the sense of an "objective," real scene, although of ideal composition. Even the heretofore hated French frigates have aesthetic value here, and the significance of the scene lies in its evocation of the desired ideal composition of the two cultures: for at least this one fleeting instance civilization and nature are integrated in Tommo's experience. Tommo's experience of this harmony once in the book is critical in defining all that he would like to achieve, yet there is a pervasive dramatic irony here, for ultimately this momentary concord is set

*Melville's gravestone, Woodlawn Cemetery, the Bronx, New York.*

against his persistent failure to achieve a lasting reconciliation of his conflicting impulses.

*Typee* remains, then, an open-ended, unresolved "problem" narrative, and it does little more than broach the problems that are to persist in Melville's fiction for the next four years. In view of Melville's central conception of the human dilemma in *Typee,* it is little wonder that he should be persistently torn between the urge to push narrative to a conclusion and the compulsion to dwell upon any and all interesting, however unassimilable, factors. What is clear in *Typee,* becomes clearer in *Mardi,* and is almost miraculously hidden in *Moby-Dick,* is Melville's inability or unwillingness to give dominant control to plot, to place any fetters upon the impetus to express direct intuitions without regard for form or overall effect. The friction in his early novels between narrative plot and thematic structure but reflects Melville's desire to capture humanity's conflicting, even self-negating, desires to find some intrinsic unity in experience and, at the same time, to explore what appears as endless possibility.

*Typee* is a particularly good place to begin an examination of this difficult problem, because in this first book the lines of conflict are drawn clearly. The plot of Tommo's adventures is simple. Dissatisfied with life aboard ship, he strikes out on a straight line at the earliest possible opportunity— that is, when the ship touches land. This rectilinear movement is soon deflected by the actualities of terrain and disorientation, but does, in fact, finally lead to the paradise of the Typee valley and Fayaway. Viewed in terms of its own implications, Tommo's flight should end here. He "should" settle in the valley of beauty and abundance beyond belief with the fairest maiden of the land and, if compelled to write for some inexplicable reason, should send his MS out to be found in a bottle, if at all. Strangely enough, not only did Melville not remain in his Typee valley, but he does not even allow his fictional self to remain. Instead, he writes surely one of the strangest endings to a novel in all nineteenth-century literature.

The ending of the novel has provoked considerable commentary but relatively little controversy. The prevailing critical view is that Tommo's striking of Mow-Mow represents a violent rejection of primitivism in favor of civilization. But Tommo takes leave of the Typees with a blow *and an embrace.* When Tommo embraces Fayaway, gives gifts to Kory-Kory and Marheyo, and almost simultaneously strikes out at Mow-Mow, he aptly symbolizes his almost perfect ambivalence. Weeping fondly over an impossible present and past, he sets out in desperate search of "some other world." The emphatic ambiguity of *Typee*'s ending emphasizes and derives from Melville's difficulty in containing the book's complex thought structure and resolving its conflicts through the agency of narrative. Faced with the series of contrary alternatives that arise out of his views on civilized and primitive life, Christianity and Taboo, enthusiasm and restraint, the physical and the mental life, Tommo is unable to arrive at any clear-cut choice. Strictly speaking, he finds it equally unsatisfactory either to leave or to remain in the Typee valley. And, in fact, the relationship between *Typee*'s plot and its thematic structure might be described as an uneasy suspension. Tommo's headlong descent into the valley and his precipitate rush to the beach are direct lines of movement, but during the whole central portion of the book, from the tenth to the last chapter, plot movement is suspended by Melville's explorations into the realm of meanings and values.

Such persistent inquiry into meaning and value does not lead inevitably to plot suspension; in such sprawling, thoughtful books as *Middlemarch* or *The Brothers Karamazov,* plot moves not only in spite of, but also through, complex thought structures. But as Melville conceives humanity the compulsion to synthesize and the like compulsion to extend to new experience lead necessarily to a radical impasse of thought. Working essentially disjunctive forms of thought (either/or), Melville inverts the Ramean dialectic and arrives not at answers—but questions. Because Tommo's highly varied experience refuses to be contained by any single available dogma or principle, all dogmas and principles are found wanting, and he is left in a state of unsatisfied yearning for wholeness.

Hence, however dissatisfying Tommo's reluctant escape from the Typees might appear on the surface, in one sense it does adequately reflect Melville's correct intuition that the questions raised by *Typee* have not been answered and that continued exploration is necessary. Whatever practical reasons prompted Melville to write *Omoo* and *Mardi,* there is little question that in essence they are continuations of the themes, ideas, and questions first brought to light in *Typee.*

*Bruce L. Grenberg, in his* Some Other World to Find: Quest and Negation in the Works of Herman Melville, *University of Illinois Press, 1989, 240 p.*

---

**An excerpt from *Typee*:**

Fayaway—I must avow the fact—for the most part clung to the primitive and summer garb of Eden. But how becoming the costume! It showed her fine figure to the best possible advantage; and nothing could have been better adapted to her peculiar style of beauty.

*Herman Melville, in his* Typee, *Harcourt, Brace, and Company, 1920.*

---

## Peter J. Bellis   (essay date 1990)

[*In the following excerpt, Bellis discusses the role of the human body in* Typee, *contending that Melville reveals the "intersection between white and native cultures" in the person of Tommo, who confronts tattooing, cannibalism, and the native remedies for his infected leg.*]

Tommo, the narrator of *Typee,* introduces his reader to the Marquesans through a pair of anecdotes. In both cases, the contrast between white and native cultures turns on their different views of the body and its relation to the self. Melville presents these as merely "amusing inci-

dent[s]," but behind his comic tone lie issues that will become central to his text.

In the first of these episodes, a group of natives encounters a white woman for the first time, in the person of a missionary's wife. At first they admire this "new divinity," but "becoming familiar with its charming aspect, and jealous of the folds which encircled its form, they sought to pierce the sacred veil of calico in which it was enshrined." For Europeans, be they missionaries or military men, the body is an essentially private and interior space, a "shrine" whose limits cannot be pierced without putting the self at risk. Clothing reinforces this by converting the body's "exterior," the skin, into an interior; the body's outline may be represented or suggested by the "veil" of clothing, but it is not to be directly revealed.

For the Marquesans, on the other hand, the body has no special privilege or private status:

> [The lady's] sex once ascertained, their idolatry was changed into contempt; and there was no end to the contumely showered upon her by the savages, who were exasperated at the deception which they conceived had been practised upon them. . . . she was stripped of her garments, and given to understand that she could no longer carry on her deceits with impunity.

To the natives, clothing that obscures the form of the body is a "deceit"; representing instead of revealing the body is withholding, and thus *mis*-representing, the self. For them, the human body is the basis of a shared, communal identity; to hide one's body from view is to deny a primary social bond. Since they do not regard an individual's body as something private, a unique and inalienable attribute of the self alone, they cannot understand the Western desire to withhold it from public scrutiny.

In the second of Tommo's anecdotes, it is the body's *surface* that comes into question. The king and queen of Nukuheva are ushered onto an American ship by a group of French officers, who have dressed them in European clothing befitting their "elevated station." There is, however, "one slight blemish" in the king's appearance, "a broad patch of tattooing" across his face that makes him look "as if he wore a huge pair of goggles." The natives adorn themselves not by covering the body but by marking it directly, permanently altering it. Unlike a pair of goggles, a tattoo does not remain external to and detachable from the body; it becomes an inseparable part of the body.

The queen's legs, visible below the hem of her dress, are also "embellished with spiral tattooing"; Western clothes cannot fully conceal these tattoos or the view of the body they suggest. Neither can "civilized" conventions prevent a "shocking . . . catastrophe," as the queen, much to the "consternation" of the French, shows her delight in one of the sailors' tattoos—"all at once the royal lady, eager to display the hieroglyphics on her own sweet form, bent forward for a moment, and turning sharply round, threw up the skirts of her mantle, and revealed a sight from which the aghast Frenchmen retreated precipitately." The term "hieroglyphics" is a telling slip on Melville's part, for the Marquesans have no written language, not even a pictographic one. It is only from the European perspective that tattoos take on the status of signs, inscriptions independent of the body that bears them. It is for Westerners that the tattooed body becomes a text, a signifying object deprived of its link to an interior and private self. For the Marquesans, the body does not yield a self-knowledge distinct from one's public identity; it thus need not be withheld or preserved from external alteration. It may be embellished, and thus changed, with the embellishments becoming part of an undivided, essentially public or social self.

In beginning with these examples, Melville's narrator indicates the importance of bodily identity in *Typee.* He positions his text squarely between these opposing cultural views, in a way that outraged Melville's American publishers, who cut both passages from their "revised edition" of the novel. But in the events of the narrative, it is Tommo's body, not his text, that is the point of intersection between white and native cultures, and he finds himself forced to defend it as the privileged and private ground of identity. If his identity is to remain the same—if he is to remain himself—he believes that his body must retain its spatial integrity, its "wholeness." If a part of the body is lost or its surface marked (tattooed), this will create a visible discontinuity in its appearance, marking it as no longer in its original state, no longer self-identical. And a temporal discontinuity in the form of the body in turn implies a fundamental discontinuity within the self; Tommo will no longer be able to know or recognize himself. He may undergo an external change of costume among the Typees, but a tattoo would be a far more radical change, one that would threaten his very identity.

The desire to preserve the body, and thus the self, from external change or discontinuity is the point from which Melville begins his consideration of bodily identity. The narrators/protagonists of *Typee* and *White-Jacket* both regard threats to the shape or surface of their bodies as threats to their sense of self. But where *Typee* places such threats outside the limits of Western culture, *White-Jacket* locates them at the heart of "civilized" order. In *Mardi* and *Moby-Dick,* this interiorizing movement shifts from the cultural level to that of the body itself, as Melville sketches the disastrous philosophical and psychological consequences of the marking or loss of a part of the body. Even if the body could be preserved from external violation, he concludes, it is always already divided, differing from and within itself over time—the internally corrupt and self-consuming body is the nightmare image that haunts *Redburn* and leads Melville from defense to critique and finally to abandonment of the notion of bodily identity.

As should be clear by now, I take Melville to be speaking primarily of bodies *as bodies,* as literal, physical objects rather than symbolic ones. In so doing, I am departing from a long line of critics—from Richard Chase and Newton Arvin in the late 1940's through Michael Rogin and Neal Tolchin in the 1980's—who have sought the symbolic or psychological "meaning" of Tommo's leg injury, for example, or of White-Jacket's garment. Instead, I am aligning myself with readers like Sharon Cameron, who [in her *The Corporeal Self,* 1981] has emphasized the brute

literalness of the "disembodiments" of *Moby-Dick.* She and I stake out the same territory, if you will, but we approach it from opposite directions: in Cameron's reading, birth itself is a disembodiment, a cutting away of the self from nurturing mother and world; the body exists only as a fragment, incomplete as long as it is withheld from relations with others. She sees Melville and his characters as struggling to overcome that incompletion through fantasies of fusion with or incorporation of both external objects and other persons. I, on the other hand, approach *Moby-Dick* not in isolation, but as a culmination and critique of Melville's earlier work. From my perspective, the yearning to transcend the limits of the body appears only as a *response* to the breaching of those limits, to the loss of Melville's earlier faith in the bodily self as an integral and independent unit. The line between self and other remains, for him, an essential demarcation.

Tommo's first fear is of a fate far worse than tattooing, for the Typees are notorious cannibals; indeed, the very word "Typee" means "a lover of human flesh." "The thought of voluntarily throwing ourselves into the hands of these cruel savages, seemed to me an act of mere madness," he says. Tommo conflates "selves" and bodies here; his "panic" comes from the recognition of his body as a physical object, one that may be possessed by—fall into the hands of—another.

Cannibalism is a particularly terrifying form of death because it involves the complete destruction of the body—both its fragmentation and its absorption into another body. Both Christian burial and native ritual designate a space belonging to the body, and the coffin suggests, and symbolically preserves, the body's shape. But cannibalism's intent is to destroy the spatial integrity of the body, to obliterate its *difference from* other bodies by literally making it part of them.

Even before Tommo enters the Typee valley, he is thus conscious of his body as a crucial but vulnerable determinant of his identity. By the time he and Toby make their descent from the mountains, one of Tommo's legs has become painfully swollen—he "half suspect[s]" that he has been bitten by a snake, even though the islands are supposedly free of them. It is after this wound, this reminder of his "fall" into embodiment, that he first glimpses a landscape he compares to "the gardens of Paradise." This symbolic estrangement from his surroundings is soon internalized; twenty-four hours later, "I could not look at the limb which had pained me so violently . . . without experiencing a sense of alarm." Tommo's body may *look* as if it remains a continuous whole, but he feels it as sharply divided: the pain makes his leg seem something alien, something other than the "me" on which "it" is inflicting pain. Proprioceptive self-consciousness is no longer coextensive with the body; Tommo now finds his perceiving "self" defined *in opposition* to part of his body—this is what produces his "sense of alarm."

Once among the Typees, Tommo feels immobilized by his injury, "cut off . . . from all intercourse with the civilized world." "It was idle for me to think of moving from the place," he laments. At first, his native attendant Kory-Kory carries him about, like a "porter" shouldering a "trunk." His body is reduced to the status of an object without motive power, and Tommo is thereby returned to a state of childlike dependence—he is shown how to eat and wash himself as if he were indeed "a forward, inexperienced child."

The Typees' "medical practice" only reinforces this split between body and self, treating Tommo's leg almost as a separate object. A native "leech" begins by "manipulating" the leg, and then, "on the supposition probably that the complaint had deprived the leg of all sensation, began to pinch and hammer it in such a manner that I absolutely roared with the pain." The "old wizard" acts as if Tommo's leg were no longer connected to the rest of his body, and continues his "treatment" despite Tommo's pleas and screams. The "patient" has to be held down, like "a struggling child in a dentist's chair," until this "torture" has run its course. The healing Tommo desires becomes a torture he cannot prevent; he cannot control either the pain in his leg or what others may do to increase or diminish it. The only link between mind and leg is a pain that cannot even be verbalized: he can only "roar" helplessly. "My unfortunate limb," Tommo concludes, "was now left much in the same condition as a rump-steak after undergoing the castigating process that precedes cooking." It is now simply a piece of flesh to him—that Tommo can compare a part of his own body to edible meat suggests a drastic alienation from it, to say the least.

What is for Tommo an *internal* "disorder," a dual rupture of both the body's space and the link between body and self, the natives seem to treat only *externally,* with "poundings" followed by the application of "herbal remedies"—the "doctor" leaves the leg "swathed in leafy bandages." These "mild applications" can, however, only "soothe the pain," diminishing Tommo's awareness of his body. And insofar as they do so, they also diminish his sense of himself as a white man from outside the valley.

When ships are sighted approaching the bay, Tommo's reaction is immediate and physical: "It sent a thrill of joy through my whole frame." He is prevented from going to the beach, however, and gradually sinks into a state of "apathy," losing track of time and giving up all hope of escape. It is at this point that "My limb suddenly healed, the swelling went down, the pain subsided." This "healing" takes place because he has begun "to bury all regrets, all remembrances of my previous existence"—because he no longer tries to preserve the connection between his present existence in the valley and his past outside it. In forgetting his earlier life, Tommo enacts a metaphorical suicide and "burial" of his former self.

With this act of self-forgetting, Tommo also becomes less fearful of the Typees' cannibalism, but this threat is soon replaced by that of tattooing. All the natives are tattooed in some manner; not even "the beauteous form of Fayaway was altogether free from the hideous blemish." The most extreme form of tattooing is represented by the old guardians of the Ti,

> on whose decrepit forms time and tattooing seemed to have obliterated every trace of humanity. Owing to the continued operation of this latter process, which only terminates among the warriors of the island after all the figures sketched upon their limbs in youth have been blended together . . . the bodies of these men were of a uniform dull green color.

When the tattooing process is complete, the shape and color of the body are completely obliterated, and with them "every trace of humanity"—these "repulsive-looking creatures" have become "fixtures," both immobile and apparently unconscious of events around them. The unmarked human form is, for Tommo, the ground of individual and human identity. Tattooing, whether partial or complete, means that the body is no longer in its original state; the body, and thus the self, is now something other—something less—than itself.

Tommo compares the tattoo artist Karky to a "stone-cutter," a "dentist," and an "army surgeon," implying that he breaks off, removes, or excises part of the body. He later speaks of Karky as an "artist," filled "with all a painter's enthusiasm" at the prospect of working on Tommo's white skin. But even if the artist "adds to" the body, he nevertheless treats it as an object, and would have others do so as well—as a two-dimensional surface whose only value is as the ground for his designs. Karky wishes to "distinguish *himself* in his profession" (my emphasis), but he would so by making his "client" no longer distinguishable in the same way—as the same person—he was before.

In Tommo's image, the tattoo "artist" treats the skin as a painter treats the surface of a canvas, denying its inseparable link to the rest of the body and to the self. But tattooing in fact works by puncturing the skin, breaking into the space of the body and inserting an alien substance, the dye. The tattoo is at once "on" and "in" the body, external and internal to it. Tattooing introduces into/onto the body some*thing* distinct from the self, violating both its spatial integrity and its exclusive relation to the self. The body as a "whole" is thereby distinguished from the self, and this, in Melville's terms, is a radical self-alienation:"What an object he would have made of me!" Tommo exclaims.

Karky wishes to inscribe a set of "parallel bands which were to encircle my countenance," a design like one that Tommo has earlier compared to "the grated bars of a prison window." This tattoo will destroy the relation between self and body, imprisoning its bearer in a body, behind a face, that has become alien to him. As Karky traces the design across Tommo's face with his finger, "the flesh fairly crawled upon my bones"—his body turns against itself, its component parts separating in revulsion.

"Horrified at the bare thought of being rendered hideous for life," Tommo tries to escape from Karky. "This incident opened my eyes to a new danger," he says, the possibility that "I should be disfigured in such a manner as never more to have the *face* to return to my countrymen." A tattooed face is a particularly traumatic disfigurement, for the face is the part of the body's surface that is revealed in identifying oneself to others. The face is also a part of the body that cannot be seen except in a reflected, mediated fashion—Tommo will not be able to see his tattooed face except as the face of another, or as the effect of his transformation is reflected in another's facial expression.

He will always be known—and, in a literal sense, *seen*—as "a 'man who lived among the cannibals.' " The tattoo that inscribes his entry into Typee society will be reinscribed by every white man's glance, marking him as estranged from his own "civilized" world.

Tommo often speaks of the natives' "physical strength and beauty," but his emphasis is on the unmarked, "natural" body and the absence of any "natural deformit[ies]" or "blemishes" among the Typees. He links their physical health to a natural morality, a "sort of tacit common-sense law which . . . has its precepts graven on every breast." The echo here is of St. Paul's distinction between the letter written "in tables of stone" and the Spirit written "in fleshy tables of the heart" (2 Cor 3:3). If God's spiritual Law is written on the human breast (for the skin is continuous with the body as a whole, and thus with the heart), man's marking of the body must therefore be like the letter that Paul says "killeth" (2 Cor 3:6). Tommo often calls a tattoo a "blemish," and his choice of words is instructive: it is those with "blemishes" whom the Old Testament prohibits from "coming nigh" to make an offering to the Lord (Lev 21:16–24). A tattoo will be "the utter ruin of my 'face divine,' " he says.

"From the time of my casual encounter with Karky the artist, my life was one of absolute wretchedness," Tommo laments. This new threat makes him more keenly aware of his "state of captivity," of the external constraints that separate him from civilization, and it is at this point that his "painful malady," "after having almost completely subsided—began again to show itself, and with symptoms as violent as ever. This added calamity nearly unmanned me." The consciousness of his outward vulnerability is internalized in his wounded leg, which Tommo associates with the loss of a defining physical and psychological characteristic, an "unmanning."

A different set of "fearful apprehensions" now begins to "consume" him, as he discovers more evidence of the Typees' cannibalism—three shrunken heads, including that of a white man. "I shuddered at the idea of the subsequent fate his inanimate body might have met with. . . . Was I destined to perish like him—like him, perhaps, to be devoured, and my head to be preserved as a fearful memento of the event?" Such a "preservation" of the body in fragmented, diminished form is only a further desecration, a parody of preservation. A week later, Tommo finds the bones of an enemy warrior, the remains of a cannibal feast.

Given his redoubled sense of physical danger, Tommo is now determined to escape, regardless of his physical weakness. When ships enter the harbor, he leaps up, "insensible to the pain that had before distracted me," and goes down to the beach in spite of the natives' opposition. He clambers into a boat and, in fighting off his pursuers, dashes a boat hook at one of them—wounding or scarring him in the process. He has seen the natives' wish to tattoo him only as a desire to do violence to his body. The violence of tattooing is for them only secondary, however; here Tommo inflicts violence for its own sake, with no thought of the scars or marks it will leave. The contrast is a paradigmatic one, symbolizing the violence inherent in the

Western drive to "civilize" native cultures, the violence on which the very notion of "civilization" is constructed.

*Peter J. Bellis, in his* No Mysteries Out of Ourselves: Identity and Textual Form in the Novels of Herman Melville, *University of Pennsylvania Press, 1990, 222 p.*

---

# FURTHER READING

Anderson, Charles Roberts. *Melville in the South Seas.* 1939. Reprint. New York: Dover Publications, 1966, 514 p.
> Important biographical and critical study of Melville's experiences in the South Seas and the novels they inspired.

Bergman, David. "Cannibals and Queers: Man-Eating." In his *Gaiety Transfigured: Gay Self-Representation in American Literature*, pp. 139-62. Madison: University of Wisconsin Press, 1991.
> Discusses the connected themes of homosexuality and cannibalism in *Typee* and other works of literature.

Dryden, Edgar. "Portraits of the Artist as a Young Man: Narrative Form in Melville's Early Novels." In his *Melville's Thematics of Form: The Great Art of Telling the Truth*, pp. 31-80. Baltimore: The John Hopkins Press, 1968.
> Examines the function of Melville's "author-hero" narrator in *Typee*.

Duban, James. "The Nature of True Virtue: *Typee* through *Mardi.*" In his *Melville's Major Fiction: Politics, Theology, and Imagination*, pp. 3-36. DeKalb: Northern Illinois University Press, 1983.
> Explores the theme of morality and virtue in *Typee*, concluding that Melville reveals "the moral inconsistencies and general harm which result from the misguided effort of civilization to rehabilitate so-called primitive and barbarous societies."

Joswick, Thomas P. "*Typee*: The Quest for Origin." *Criticism* XVII, No. 4 (Fall 1975): 335-54.
> Discusses *Typee* as it relates to the myths of human origins.

Mushabac, Jane. "Embarkations." In her *Melville's Humor: A Critical Study*, pp. 37-78. Hamden, Conn.: Archon Books, 1981.
> Examines the function of humor in *Typee*, concluding that Melville's "humorous vision is a love story of men passing their time together in this life."

Ruland, Richard. "Melville and the Fortunate Fall: *Typee* as Eden." *Nineteenth Century Fiction* 23, No. 3 (December 1968): 312-23.
> Explores Tommo's description of Typee society, suggesting that his escape reveals Melville's ambivalence toward an idyllic vision of man's past.

Samson, John. "*Typee*: Perception and Preconception in Polynesia." In his *White Lies: Melville's Narratives of Facts*, pp. 22-56. Ithaca, N.Y.: Cornell University Press, 1989.
> Examines how Melville blends autobiographical material with fiction in *Typee* to create "an account of the collective fiction that is the white culture's history and a

plea for a tolerant, relativistic perception . . . of historical reality."

Stanton, Robert. "*Typee* and Milton: Paradise Well Lost." *Modern Language Notes* LXXIV, No. 5 (May 1959): 407-11.
> Compares the setting of *Typee* with that of Milton's Eden.

Sweeney, Gerard M. "Melville's Smoky Humor: Fire-Lighting in *Typee*." *Arizona Quarterly* 34, No. 4 (Winter 1978): 371-76.
> Discusses Melville's use of bawdy humor in the thinly disguised masturbatory scene in which Kory-Kory lights a fire.

Tanselle, G. Thomas. "The First Review of *Typee*." *American Literature* XXXIV, No. 4 (January 1963): 567-71.
> Presents excerpts from favorable 1846 reviews of *Typee* that appeared in New York's *Weekly News*.

Weidman, Bette S. "*Typee* and *Omoo*: A Diverging Pair." In *A Companion to Melville Studies*, edited by John Bryant, pp. 85-121. New York: Greenwood Press, 1986.
> Offers an overview of *Typee* and *Omoo*, discussing Melville's literary style and purpose, manuscript and publication information, the place of these novels in Melville studies, and the criticism engendered by these works.

Witherington, Paul. "The Art of Melville's *Typee*." *Arizona Quarterly* 26, No. 2 (Summer 1970): 136-50.
> Examines *Typee* as an experimental novel, focusing on its complex structure and Melville's "trying out of narrative rhythm, symbolism, narrative focus, and setting."

---

Additional coverage of Melville's life and career is contained in the following sources published by Gale Research: *Concise Dictionary of Literary Biography 1640-1865*; *DISCovering Authors*; *Dictionary of Literary Biography*, Vols. 3, 74; *Nineteenth-Century Literature Criticism*, Vols. 3, 12, 29; *Something about the Author*, Vol. 59; *Short Story Criticism*, Vol. 1; and *World Literature Criticism*.

# Motoori Norinaga

## 1730-1801

(Born Ozu Norinaga) Japanese classical scholar, literary theorist, and poet.

### INTRODUCTION

Motoori was Japan's first prominent literary theorist and the most influential of the Japanese national learning, or *kokugaku*, scholars. His commentaries on the classics of Japanese literature, including studies of the *Kojiki* (*The Record of Ancient Matters*) and Lady Murasaki's *Genji monogatari* (*The Tale of Genji*), contributed to the revival of interest in the "ancient Way"—a concept integral to the restoration of Japan's idealized past. Motoori sought to remove foreign (especially Chinese) influences from the study of literature; he rebelled against Buddhist and Confucian didacticism, basing his literary theory instead on a rigorous anti-intellectualism and on his concept of *mono no aware* (literally, "a deep feeling over things"), the apprehension of which, Motoori contended, would ennoble the Japanese and bring about a resurgence of their ancient values and purity.

Motoori was born in Matsuzaka in the Ise province to a merchant, Ozu Sadatoshi, and his wife, Okatsu. His father's death in 1740 left the family business in the hands of Motoori's elder half-brother, Sadaharu, who supported Okatsu and her children. After Sadaharu's death in 1751, Okatsu arranged that Motoori, who had shown no inclination for business, be sent to Kyoto to study medicine and classical Chinese and Japanese literature. He remained in Kyoto for five years; while there, he changed his family name, adopting that of his ancestor, the samurai Motoori Takehide, and began writing his first essay on poetry, *Ashiwake obune* (c. 1756; *A Little Boat Breaking a Path Through the Reeds*). In 1763, he met the eminent scholar Kamo no Mabuchi, who was to become his mentor. Mabuchi encouraged him to undertake a study of the *Kojiki*, which led Motoori to write the *Kojiki den*, the product of more than three decades of research and thought. He completed the work in 1798, three years before his death at the age of seventy-one.

Although he wrote on various topics and composed poetry, most of Motoori's works are commentaries on ancient literature or expositions of his literary theory. His *Ashiwake obune*, an essay on the difficulty of writing verse, adumbrates his notion of great poetry as arising from a sensitivity to the beauty and sadness of all things. Motoori developed this concept, called *mono no aware*, in two later works: *Shibun yōryō* (1763), his first study of the eleventh-century novel *Genji monogatari*; and *Isonokami sasamegoto* (1763), a comparative analysis of Chinese and Japanese poetry. In the former, Motoori argues that *mono no aware* defines the theme and tone of the novel, which he holds up as a masterpiece of literature. In the latter, he discusses *mono no aware* both as the object of poetry and as a moral

principal. Motoori believed that through the study of the past one could recover the lost sensibilities of ancient Japan, and to this end he devoted considerable effort to the composition of the *Kojiki den*. Published posthumously in 1822, the work contains his elucidation of the *Kojiki*, a classical text that records Japan's mythological history. He also wrote on related topics, as in his discourse on government, the *Tamakushige* (1786; *The Jeweled Comb-Box*); his *Tamakatsuma* (1801), a collection of essays containing his views on politics, economics, and religion; and his *Uiyamabumi* (1798), a guidebook for students of literature. In addition, Motoori presented his philosophical outlook in such works as *Naobi no mitama* (1771), which outlines his belief in the pervasive power of supernatural forces and beings.

Criticism of Motoori's work has focused primarily on the value of his literary commentaries and on the influence of his thought. Although he did produce many short poems, these works have elicited little commentary by scholars, who generally regard his verse as negligible. However, much attention has been devoted to Motoori's theory of literature. Described as modern, humanistic, and anti-rational, his theory mingles ethical and aesthetic concerns and incorporates his belief in humanity's innate moral qualities and in the limits of human knowledge. Critics have also noted that Motoori's studies of ancient Japanese literature and culture evince a strongly nationalist attitude, leading John S. Brownlee to call his ideas "the fountainhead of modern Japanese nationalist thought." Despite these political reverberations in his writings, however, the greater portion of critical commentary has centered on the lasting value of Motoori's scholarship, literary insight, and understanding of Japan's ancient past.

# PRINCIPAL WORKS

*Ashiwake obune*  (essay)  c. 1756
*Isonokami sasamegoto*  (essay)  1763
*Shibun yōryō*  (criticism)  1763
*Naobi no mitama*  (essay)  1771
*Kuzubana*  (essay)  1780
*Tamaboko hyakushu*  (poetry)  1786
*Tamakushige*  (essay)  1786
  [*The Jeweled Comb-Box* published in journal *Monumenta Nipponica*, 1988]
*\*Kojiki den*  (criticism)  1798
*Uiyamabumi*  (essay)  1798
  [*Uiyamabumi* published in journal *Monumenta Nipponica*, 1987]
*Tamakatsuma*  (essays)  1801

*This work was not published in its entirety until 1822.

# CRITICISM

## Makoto Ueda   (essay date 1967)

[*Ueda is a Japanese-born American scholar, translator, editor, and critic of Japanese literature. In the following essay, he examines Motoori's literary theory, elucidating the key concept of* mono no aware.]

What would a Shintoist theory of literature be like? Beyond doubt Motoori Norinaga (1730-1801) was the best qualified person to answer the question, for he was not only a great philosopher whose work marked the peak of the Shinto revival in the eighteenth century, but also a devoted scholar in literature who wrote a number of textual and critical studies on Japanese classics. A literary theory formulated by a philosopher-scholar, rather than by a poet, novelist, or playwright, is rare in Japan, too. Gifted with sharp intellect, Norinaga consciously made an effort to construct a theory of literature consistent within itself and with the whole system of his philosophy. The result is a remarkably methodical poetics covering all aspects of literary writing and giving them a center of reference. He was indeed the first major literary *theorist* in Japan, in the stricter sense of the word.

With all his keen intellect, however, Norinaga's philosophy is characterized by its rigorous anti-intellectualism. Perhaps precisely because he had such a logical, penetrating mind he became so painfully aware of the limitations of that mind. "A mind is limited, however wise the man may be," he writes in a typical passage. "The mind is such a tiny thing and can know nothing that lies beyond its borders." One often meditates, for instance, on the wonders of heaven and earth—whether the earth is hanging in the sky, or is placed on something else. Any attempt to explain it in rational terms would be an act of haughty arrogance as well as of pitiful ignorance. The universe is full of mysteries, man's life abounds in irrationalities, and one would better accept all this as lying beyond the realm of human knowledge. Norinaga criticizes Buddhist and Confucian philosophers for that reason; they pretend to know the unknowable, they try to rationalize the irrational.

Norinaga's distrust of discursive reason has another basis: intellect cannot create. Intellect is a dissecting power, not a creative energy. The limitations of human knowledge arise partly from that fact; a mind can never completely know something it is unable to create. Norinaga tries to substantiate this contention by referring to the act of procreation. The wisest philosopher, the most enlightened scholar, or the most skillful artisan cannot concoct a living human being. But an ordinary man and woman, "with no toiling mind, with no helping tool, and with no painstaking effort," can produce a baby. The whole act, as Norinaga sees it, is "not even worthy of description; it is awkward, effeminate, and more senseless than child's play." Yet it can do what the best of human minds cannot. Man's mind is not capable of explaining the most "awkward" of his own acts; how could one expect it to explain profound mysteries that lie between heaven and earth?

Not to explain the mysteries, but to make them metaphysically comprehensible, Norinaga inevitably brings in the concept of gods, who, naturally, are omniscient, creative, and irrational from man's point of view. For a Classicist such as Norinaga, gods lay conveniently at hand—the gods in Shintoism. Shinto gods, as described in *The Record of Ancient Matters (Kojiki), The Chronicles of Japan,* and other early Japanese writings, are indeed omniscient, creative, and irrational. They are the creators and manipulators of all things in nature. The gods use people, animals, and plants as men use tools. And the gods do not necessarily make good use of their mighty power, because there are evil gods as well as benevolent ones. Furthermore, evil gods may sometimes do good deeds, and good gods evil. To think of all gods as benevolent and merciful is no more than man's wishful thinking. For gods are, after all, as temperamental and irrational as human beings; they are as susceptible to wrath as human beings. In fact, gods themselves sprang from the same source as men, animals, and all other objects in the universe. This source is the Holy Spirit of the God of Creation. The gods are more powerful than men because they rank higher in the scheme of the Holy Spirit, just as men rule over animals and birds because of their higher rank in the same scheme.

The fact that Shinto gods, ranking higher in the hierarchy of things, can manipulate men, does not necessarily mean that men are devoid of free will. Men, indeed, are under the control of the gods, but they are free within their status and ability allotted by the God of Creation. Again it is like animals and birds having their own free lives, although men, more high-ranking and powerful, can catch, tame, or kill them. Each man, therefore, must repudiate determinist ethics and try to do his best within the realm where he is free. Norinaga is quite insistent on this. "If a person should think he could leave everything to divine will and become irresponsible for his conduct," he says, "he would be making a grave mistake. It is each man's responsibility to do his best within his power." The God of Creation has given each man an ability to perform good deeds out of his own free will; if he fails to do so, he fails to fulfill his god-given capacity and is inferior to birds and insects. Instances of such failure occur frequently in modern times, as man, over-confident of his rational mind, has lost sight of the God of Creation above him and of the Holy Spirit within him. To correct this deplorable modern trend is simple: man has only to break through his hard, man-made surface of rational and didactic thinking and to return to his inner true heart given by the Holy Spirit. To return to the true heart is the very basis of ethics; in fact, that must be the purpose of life for all men, since it is the only way by which man can know the Creator.

How can one return to his inborn true heart, the heart devoid of all superficialities? Here literature comes in. A work of literature can and should penetrate through all the barriers of artificial thinking, finally reaching the innermost part of the human heart. It purifies a human soul by discarding all the impure elements that surround it; the soul is thereby liberated from man-made fetters. The *mono no aware,* Norinaga's famous term describing the essence of literature, can be understood as a principle of such self-emancipation.

In defining *mono no aware,* Norinaga begins with an etymological analysis of the word. According to Norinaga, *aware* consists of two interjections, *a* and *hare,* both of which are used when one's heart is greatly moved. One cries out, for example, "*A,* how beautiful the moon is!" or "*A,* what a pitiful thing this is!" or "*Hare,* how lovely the flowers are!" or "*Hare,* what a good child you are!" *Aware,* which combines these two interjections, is primarily a word describing a deeply moved heart, a heart filled with intense emotion. The emotion could be joy, happiness, wonder, horror, hatred, love, grief, anger, jealousy, or anything else. It may be said, however, that two of the emotions, love and grief, tend to dominate, since they are the most heart-engaging emotions. "Human feelings are deepest in love," says Norinaga. "The most profound and touching instances of *mono no aware* are therefore most frequently observed in love affairs." This is why there have been so many love poems and love stories written since ancient times. Grief, on the other hand, is an even more universal feeling than love; frequently love itself turns into grief. Man faces grief more often than happiness, because he is imperfect, weak, and easily hurt; besides, grief, being always painful, penetrates deeper into the heart. "Man feels more deeply when his wish is thwarted," Norinaga observes. "Therefore, one commonly equates *aware* with grief nowadays." In any case, the feeling of *aware* emerges when the heart is deeply and genuinely moved in the face of some external event.

How can one distinguish deep and genuine feelings from shallow and impure ones? Here our attention must be shifted to the fact that *aware* is modified by *mono* in the phrase *mono no aware (no* is a modifying particle). *Mono* literally means "thing(s)"; so *mono no aware* would mean "a deep feeling over things." Norinaga explains the meaning of "things": "*mono,*" he says, "is a word which is added when one speaks in broad terms." *Mono,* in other words, generalizes the meaning of *aware.* "A deep feeling" cannot be any feeling out of personal idiosyncrasy, but must be a feeling that emerges from any man under the same circumstances. A sad thing is sad to any sensitive person; if there is anyone who fails to feel sad, he is heartless, or, in Norinaga's idiom, he does not know *mono no aware.* Looking at cherry blossoms in full bloom, one is always moved by their beauty; if there is anyone who is not, he does not know *mono no aware.* Emphasizing the universality of *mono no aware,* Norinaga cites a practical example, too. Keeping a household, one would always want to cut down unnecessary expenses; if there is a housewife who would not, she is lacking in *mono no aware.* Norinaga sums up his idea of *mono no aware* in a short passage: "A person who has a heart capable of understanding things would always experience the feeling that the occasion calls for, though he does not try to do so. Those who find themselves otherwise do not know how to respond to things; they do not have a heart capable of feeling what it should." A deep, genuine feeling is something that springs spontaneously from the heart, from the pure, sensitive heart. *Mono no aware,* though a universal human feeling in origin, is an elevated, purified feeling for the modern man who has lost his natural sensibility. Herein lies an explanation for the ennobling effect of *mono no aware* on the modern man, and for the function of literature in the modern world.

Why is it that many men in modern times have lost their nature-given faculty of feeling genuinely? Because, Norinaga answers, a number of social, moral, and religious codes have besieged the human heart. The Bushidō, or Japanese chivalry, has consistently taught that a warrior should think lightly of his life; this has suppressed a free play of his genuine feelings, for what man would not value his life? Confucianism has always forced many so-called virtues upon the conduct of men, so much so that nowadays men are the captives of didactic ideas. Buddhism rejects *mono no aware,* too; in fact, it aims at the unhuman, precisely the opposite of human feelings. It renounces grief over death, love between men and women, and anything else that is human. But here lies the weakness of Buddhism, for no man can be completely unhuman. As Norinaga says, even the most holy priest cannot but be moved at the sight of beautiful cherry blossoms, or of a lovely lady he happens to meet in the street. "If there is a priest who has no such feeling," Norinaga writes, "he is more heartless than birds and insects—he is, we should say, no better than a rock or a tree." This is a view diametrically opposed to that of the medieval Japanese. Norinaga's view is that a man, even a Buddhist priest, cannot but be a man with human feelings. Norinaga goes on to prove it by saying that so many famous priests in the past composed poems on the beauty of blossoms, or even on the beauty of women. He goes so far as to contend that priests compose more love poems than laymen because their desires are more deeply suppressed. Norinaga is in no sense criticizing the verse-writing of priests here; he is simply trying to show the purging effect of *mono no aware* in literature.

Through the idea of *mono no aware* Norinaga can also explain the motive for writing a poem or a story, which Tsurayuki disposed of as a mere expressive instinct. Norinaga takes an example of a man depressed for some personal reason. "If the man has a wife who knows *mono no aware,*" he says, "he will be consoled by talking with her. Even when he will not talk, the wife will see into his heart and treat him fittingly, sharing his grief and giving him solace." A man who is moved with a heart-rending emotion will speak it out, hoping, consciously or unconsciously, that the emotion will be shared by other men. The listeners, if they know *mono no aware,* will be able to understand his feeling and share it with him. To know that his feeling is shared by someone else is itself a great pleasure and solace to the man. One writes a poem or a story for this reason. Norinaga says: "If a person leaves his feelings unexpressed within his heart, they will get tangled more and more until they become unbearable to him. But if he writes them out in poetry or prose according to the occasion and sends it to a friend who has a similar mind, his anguish will be emptied and his melancholy consoled." About the motive of reading a poem or a story, Norinaga has this to say: "When reading, for instance, of a man worried over something and buried in deep gloom, one is often struck with the feeling of realness. This is because one has understood the man's heart and knows *mono no aware.* And one has been able to understand the man's heart because one has read all about the circumstances that caused his melancholy." *Mono no aware,* primarily a feeling that can be shared deep in the heart of everyone, gives a motive to both writers and readers.

Because of this communicative function, *mono no aware* becomes an important principle both aesthetic and moral. A man lacking in genuine feeling cannot distinguish beauty from ugliness, good from evil. Imagine a man looking up at the sky. If he lacks the capacity for feeling deeply, the sky will have no meaning to him. But, as Norinaga says, "If he knows *mono no aware,* the sky will look sad or gay, depending upon his state of mind at the time." This is so even with an insentient object like the sky; his feelings will be aroused more when the object is a human being. For instance, reading the account of Kashiwagi's adultery in *The Tale of Genji,* those who cannot feel deeply will have no sympathy with Kashiwagi; those who are confined within Confucian morality will no doubt loathe the adulterer. But look at Prince Genji, who knows *mono no aware.* He takes pity on Kashiwagi, and in spite of the fact that he is the very victim of that incident. Norinaga observes: "A good person, because he knows *mono no aware,* can understand how unbearable the feeling of love could be. So he does not bitterly censure a man who has erred on this account." An evil person is the one who cannot sympathize with others because he cannot feel with others.

"A person who is insistent on his own feelings alone and who vigorously attacks what other people say," Norinaga remarks, "is an egoist who does not know *mono no aware.*" *Mono no aware* is an opposite of egoism; it enables one to feel with others, to understand others.

*Mono no aware* has now become a mode of perception. To feel is to perceive and to know—to know in the broadest sense; for to feel with a person or a thing means to know the person or the thing thoroughly. Norinaga explains this: "Living in this world, a person sees, hears, and meets all kinds of events. If he takes them into his heart and feels the hearts of the events within it, then one may say the person knows the hearts of the events, the cores of the facts—he knows *mono no aware.*" A person cannot really feel unless he knows what it is that makes him feel. Only those who know the heart of a grieving man can feel the grief with him; only those who know the cause of the joy can feel happy with the joyous person. "Therefore," Norinaga says, "when a man understands the heart of a joyous or sorrowful event, he can be said to know *mono no aware.* The man who does not know the heart will feel nothing—neither joy nor sorrow." Sometimes a man who does not understand the heart pretends to feel happy or sad. "Such is what we call a superficial feeling," Norinaga says. "In truth the man does not know *mono no aware.*"

Knowing or understanding, as Norinaga uses the term, is primarily intuitive. A man who knows *mono no aware* does not have to objectively examine an event; instantaneously he takes it into his heart, feels it, and understands it. In fact, *mono no aware* is so spontaneous that the man feels it with or without his voluntary will. When a man with a capacity for feeling deeply hears or reads about a sad event, then "an uncontrollable feeling spontaneously arises in his heart, and he feels sad even if he does not want to." "Feelings," Norinaga says elsewhere, too, "cannot be controlled by the man, though they are his own." *Mono no aware* penetrates into the heart deeper than reason or will, than Confucian teachings of good and evil. This explains why a scrupulous man at times feels tempted to break a commandment, or in fact does so. *Mono no aware* is more deeply rooted in the human heart and hence more valid in its application than Confucian or Buddhist teachings. And this is why a literary work filled with ethically repugnant incidents may deeply move the reader's heart.

If, then, *mono no aware* is a mode of cognition more intuitive, far-reaching, and valid than others, what would ultimate human reality be like as seen through it? Norinaga answers that it is foolish, effeminate, and weak. "All human feelings," he says, "are quite foolish in their true, natural state. People try hard to trim, modify, and improve them so that they may appear wise, but as a result they gain only some decorated feelings, and not true natural ones." The innermost human heart is as foolish and weak as a woman's or a child's. Any feeling that is manly, discreet, and righteous is not a true human feeling; it is artificial, it is made up by reading books, by conforming to social norms, by adhering to Buddhist or Confucian disciplines—in brief, by suppressing one's heart in one way or another. "The original, natural heart of man," Norinaga writes, "is most straightforward, senseless, poor, and unsightly." Such effeminate feelings are manifested more often in women than in men, because women are "poorer in controlling their emotions and hence more apt to reveal their true hearts." If her beloved child were to die, a mother would shed tears profusely and appear almost insane with grief, while the father might look calm and even indifferent, without dropping a tear. But this is so only because the father has hidden his natural feelings in fear of appearing unmanly; his heart is as grief-ridden as the mother's. To take another example, a warrior is expected to sacrifice his life for the sake of his lord and his country. Yet, when he lies dying in the battlefield, would he not wish to see once more his beloved wife and children, or his aging father and mother? Is it not true that the manliest soldier, as fearless as a devil, feels sorrow during the last moments of his life? "Such is," Norinaga concludes, "the true nature of the human heart common to millions of men, common to saints as well as to ordinary men. . . . If there should be anyone who has no such feeling, he would be inferior to beasts and birds, or to trees and rocks. Who in the world would not feel sad as he lies dying?"

Such effeminate feelings, as they are rooted in the human heart deeper than any other, are most moving when they are expressed straightforwardly. A direct expression of them is more powerfully appealing than rhetoric or logical persuasion. Norinaga illustrates this point by telling a story of a man determined to kill two captives. An onlooker, taking pity on the victims, tries to dissuade the man, lecturing to him how evil it is to kill a fellow man. The capturer, while a bit moved, is not quite convinced. Then one of the captives, like a brave soldier, speaks out and tells how lightly he thinks of his life and how worried he is about the future of the pitiless murderer. His capturer, angered at this, immediately kills him. In contrast, the other captive is weeping, wailing, and pleading; again and again he cries out the same words: "Please spare my life." The murderer is finally moved and saves his life. A literary work is expected to do what this second captive has done—that is, to speak out the true human heart, which is foolish, effeminate, and weak. A good work of literature has a strong appeal for this reason. That, indeed, is the justification of literature. "Poetry," Norinaga declares, "has its prime aim in presenting the natural ways of the foolish human heart." And here is Norinaga's definition of literature: "Poetry or the novel does not concern itself with good or evil, wisdom or stupidity. It only describes in detail what man truly feels in his natural self, from which we learn what the innermost part of the human heart is like. It is through a work of literature that we learn what true human feelings are, that we learn *mono no aware*."

In this connection it is interesting to observe how totally the poetic spirit, the central idea in medieval Japanese aesthetics, has been transformed by Norinaga. According to Norinaga's definition, "the poetic spirit in modern times lies in expressing the senseless, foolish feelings of the true heart in some interesting, attractive way." In contrast with medieval aestheticians and with Bashō, who insisted on the suppression of human feelings, Norinaga maintains that the poetic spirit consists in the very expression of the true human heart as it is freed from all its external restrictions. Even a human desire, that archenemy of medieval

Japanese aestheticians, is admitted into the poetic spirit by Norinaga, with a proviso. "There are poems that draw on desires, too," he says, "if the desires involve feelings." If the desire is nothing more than "a heart that only wishes to possess something"—if it is nothing more than greed or avarice—then it has no place in poetry. But if the desire generates feelings, it may very well become the source for poetic creation. "Love," Norinaga observes, "springs originally out of desire, but it involves deep feelings." Thus love is frequently dealt with in a poem or a story.

A literary work, then, is an honest expression of foolish but true human feelings as they naturally are in the innermost part of the heart. To use Norinaga's simile, it is like "showing the kitchen and bedrooms to the guest, rather than receiving him in the parlor." In another of his metaphors, poetry is a "tool that cleans up a dusty heart." A question here is why Norinaga did not take a liking to the contemporary novels, which were certainly more realistic than early court novels, or to the Haiku, which dealt with the life of common men more substantially than early poetry. It is a relevant question, because we know Norinaga had a broad view of poetry, so broad as to include not only linked verse and the Haiku but also the Nō, ditties, comic poetry, the puppet theater, and popular songs. His answer is that a straightforward expression of the human heart as it is does not necessarily produce a good work of literature; in fact, a realistic description of a modern man's feelings often results in a meager work. This is because man no longer has a pure heart in the modern age. Norinaga elaborates: "In discussing the nature of poetry, one would assume that the poem is an expression of natural feelings. But with the passing of time men's hearts have grown more and more false, less and less pure. In modern times, therefore, the essence of verse-writing lies in adorning words and making the poem beautiful. . . . It is not that poetry has declined in modern times. It is rather that men's hearts have deteriorated with time." According to Norinaga, some contemporary poems and novels are good works of literature in that they are faithful representations of human reality, but they are not the very best because they represent an inferior kind of human reality. This could not be helped; the fault lies not with the poet or novelist, but with the age. For this reason Norinaga encourages the student of poetry to express his true feelings as they are, and not to decorate and hence falsify his feelings. "A modern poet should express his heart as it is," he says. "One might try to compose a simple poem in an ancient fashion, thinking that contemporary poetry has swerved from what poetry should be. But this is to misinterpret the ideal of poetry." The honest expression of a degenerate heart is a lesser evil than the contrived expression of a pretentious heart.

Though extremely difficult, there is a way for a modern man to attain a true heart, and thereby a good poem. This is by delving into good poems of ancient times and by learning the language in which they are written. A modern poet should not try to imitate the feelings of ancient masters; this would be a falsification of his feelings. Instead, he should try to learn their poetic language and make it his own. "Then his heart would be gradually transformed by ancient poetry and books," Norinaga says, "until it becomes at one with an ancient master's heart. Thereupon he can freely express his own feelings." As against the traditionally held view that one should attain a true heart in order to write a good poem, Norinaga is arguing that a true heart can be attained only through good poetry, for, according to him, no thought or feeling exists without the language. Words are the organizers of the human mind; they give form to the formless. In writing a poem, therefore, one should first seek words, and not feelings. "Feelings are not to be sought; they are something that naturally arises," Norinaga says. "To be sought are words. This is why I say the first principle of verse-writing is to arrange the words in good order."

---

**"Poetry," Norinaga declares, "has its prime aim in presenting the natural ways of the foolish human heart."**

*—Makoto Ueda*

---

Norinaga has repeatedly emphasized the importance of artistic expression in literary writing. About lyric poetry in particular, he once declared: "Poetry is an art of language, in which the artist expresses his feelings in an appropriate way. If one should speak out his feelings as they are, there would be no poetry at all—or, at best, the worst kind of poetry." By "an appropriate way" Norinaga means "such a way that words are neither too many nor too few, that they flow smoothly and sound pleasant." Poetry must have art, that is, "the words must be well regulated, neat, and orderly." This might seem a contradiction to Norinaga's definition of poetry as a simple, straightforward expression of true human feelings. It is no contradiction, however, because in Norinaga's opinion a direct expression of deeply felt emotion is always regulated, neat, and orderly. Norinaga illustrates this by taking an example in the way in which a man weeps on a sad occasion. When the sorrow is not deep the man only sobs spasmodically. If it is a truly deep grief he wails, with a steady voice that has certain rhythmical patterns. "When the grief is intense," Norinaga concludes, "the man's voice would have a regulated flow without his conscious intention." Likewise, the words of a man in deep grief are naturally regulated and have artistic qualities in themselves; if a man speaks in a plain language, one can see his grief is shallow. "True poetry," Norinaga asserts, "has its essence in those words that are naturally artistic as they have spouted out of a deeply moved heart." Here is also a reason why the Classicist Norinaga preferred the poetry of Tsurayuki's time to that of more ancient times; the very earliest poems, he thought, were "so extremely simple that they often looked crude, unrefined, and shabby."

What is true of poetry is true of prose works, too. One of Norinaga's sharp perceptions was that poetry and the novel were the same in essence. "There is no art of poetry apart from the art of the novel," he once said, "nor is there any art of the novel apart from the art of poetry. Poetry

and the novel have precisely the same aim." The aim is, of course, to express true human feelings as the heart is deeply moved. Norinaga defines the novel almost in the same terms as poetry. "People have various feelings at various occasions in life," he says. "The novel describes those things which stir especially deep feelings. It reveals *mono no aware* in doing so." Like the poet, the novelist is inextricably involved in various life-feelings, so much so that he cannot contain them within himself. These feelings, poured into the novel, would move anyone who reads it.

The difference between the novel and poetry is suggested by the word "describe," which Norinaga used in the above definition. Elsewhere he uses the words "describe in minute detail" in explaining the essence of the novel. He writes of the author of *The Tale of Genji*:

> The novelist, with a heart exceedingly sensitive to *mono no aware,* penetrated all kinds of events and all types of people in the world as she saw or heard about them. Each time her heart readily responded, and the responses gradually accumulated in her, until she could not contain them in herself. Thereupon she set out to describe them in minute detail, making use of fictional characters she created. Things that she approved of or disagreed with, things that she thought hateful—she put them all into the minds and words of those characters, thereby having her obsessed heart cleansed.

Whereas the poem directly presents feelings in a rhythmical language, the novel "describes them in minute detail." In this respect the novelist finds it convenient to have fictional characters into whom he can pour his feelings; even the most odious things he can say through a fictional character. Through fictional persons and fictional situations, the novelist can describe the ultimate of joy, grief, love, or anger, as well as hatred. In this way he can describe "what a good man's heart is like, what an evil man's heart is like"; in brief, he can show "the details of the innermost human heart." In depicting a good man the novelist can gather all the attributes of benevolent men in the world; in presenting a malignant person he can pile up all the world's evils in that character. The novelist can present his idea or feeling through his selective creation of fictional characters and situations. A tragic hero, said Aristotle, must be a man of high social status. Norinaga in effect says the same. "When one responds to the sight of a man suffering from a disaster," he writes, "it makes a great difference whether the victim is a noble courtier or a lowly person. One's sympathy would be especially deep upon seeing a noble person crushed under a disaster." A novelist who wishes to describe the sorrow of life would create a nobleman in deep grief; the reader would feel the sorrow more deeply that way. Fictionalization is a necessary and effective scheme for the novel, which must, unlike poetry, describe. Poetry presents feelings, but the novel describes the circumstances that have prompted the feelings.

For this reason a poet living in the modern degenerate age should learn the purer feelings of early poets by reading classics of fiction such as *The Tale of Genji*. The student of verse-writing will make a far greater progress if he reads not only Classical poetry but also the novels of Classical times, because in this way he will come to know the soil in which that poetry took its roots. To a person who has not read the novels, the titles of Classical poems would sound strange, as if coming from some remote land. For those who are well acquainted with Classical novels, reading an ancient poem would be like listening to an intimate friend, whereas the poem would seem to be a total stranger's words to those who have not read them. In this respect poetry and the novel complement one another.

All of these arguments of Norinaga's about the nature of a literary work make sufficiently clear his view on the use of literature. It goes without saying that he rejects both a Confucian and a Buddhist view; sometimes he seems too emotionally insistent in his rejection, no doubt because the age he lived in was so overwhelmingly in favor of didactic literature. "Poetry is feelings spoken out in an appropriate way," he says in one passage. "A poet utters whatever is in his heart, good or bad. Why should he be blamed for speaking out his amorous feeling? If his poem is good, why shouldn't it deserve high praise?" "Confucianism has its own aim," he says in another passage. "Buddhism has its own aim. The novel has its own aim. If one should mix them up and build up an argument thereon, that will be a fallacious argument indeed." Confucianism and Buddhism would condemn a maiden who, taking pity on a man desperately in love with her, secretly meets him without her parents' permission. Yet literature would approve of her; in fact there are numerous literary works describing such a maiden. This is because "novels are not concerned with the moral acceptability of her deed; they simply admire her *mono no aware.*" It is like admiring a beautiful lotus flower blooming in a muddy pool. The externals surrounding it may be dirty, but that does not change the quality of its beauty. A novel may describe adulterous love, but this is all for "making the flower of *mono no aware* bloom." Morally evil as it may be, it is aesthetically most beautiful. Many moralist scholars who condemned *The Tale of Genji* on ethical grounds are completely in the wrong.

According to Norinaga, then, literature is independent of all didactic purposefulness; in no case does it make usefulness its prime aim. This does not imply literature is useless; on the contrary literature can be, and usually is, greatly useful, without aiming to be so. Norinaga explains this by an apt metaphor. "Trees have no intention of helping men when they grow large," he says. "But if a tall tree stands in the forest, men may cut it down and make excellent lumber out of it. They may use the lumber for various purposes—for making a big thing or a small thing, for doing a good thing or an evil thing." A literary work grows naturally out of a man's heart; though it may be used by various men for various purposes, it is primarily not intended to be so.

After admitting that the usefulness of literature is only incidental, Norinaga goes on to explain the three ways in which literature can be useful. First, literature can give the pleasure of emotional purgation; secondly, it can nourish *mono no aware*; and thirdly, it can help attain the ultimate of Shintoism. . . . The first use stems from Norinaga's definition of literature as emotional expression. A person

can purge his obsession by expressing it in words; he feels consoled as he expects, consciously or unconsciously, his worry to be shared by others. The same can be said of a person who hears or reads about the life of someone else. "As the reader reads about someone's life resembling his own," Norinaga says, "he comes to realize that his sorrows are not only his own, whereupon he feels consoled." Literature communicates human feelings, and the communication is a solace both to the one who initiates the communication and to the one who receives it.

The communicative function of literature leads to the second use of literature: a literary work nourishes man's sensitivity to true human feelings. "Novels describe the various ways in which things happen and people feel," Norinaga says. "Therefore the reader, without special effort, comes to know how things happen in the world, and how people behave and feel on various occasions." Literature is knowledge—it is informative of true human feelings. "It records human feelings as they are," Norinaga says, "and shows to the reader what they are like." It describes, for instance, how a parent feels toward his child. A son, reading a work of literature, may realize how dear a father's love is; then he will realize, too, why he should be kind to his father. Literature, by simply describing true feelings of a father toward his son, in effect teaches the importance of filial piety. "There is nothing better than poetry," Norinaga declares, "to make one familiar with human feelings and with the true cause of an event, or to soften a man's heart and nourish kindness in it." A work of literature is not a sermon, but it teaches the basis of ethics; it teaches *mono no aware*, how men generally feel and why one should be kind, tolerant, and sympathetic toward others. It teaches, in brief, what the universal true heart is like—the heart that has been buried underneath the contemporary social and moral norms.

Now one can easily see the third and most important use of literature as conceived by Norinaga. Through literature, and only through literature, man can return to his innermost self—the self that is energetic and creative as bestowed by the God of Creation. "Make it your habit to write poetry, to read old tales, and to learn thereby about the poetic spirit of the ancients," Norinaga advises. "This will be an immense help not only for those studying the art of poetry but also for those trying to attain the ancient ways of the gods." A person who writes good poetry or who reads good works of literature can, without knowing it, purge all modern rational thoughts that have suppressed his heart, or all medieval Buddhist ideas that have tried to reduce his humanity. Literature helps one to approach Shinto gods, who are more truly human than modern men, and Shintoism, in turn, helps one to understand a work of literature, which probes all areas of the human mind, rational and irrational, conscious and subconscious. "Unlike Confucianism or Buddhism, Shintoism does not indulge in any of the noisy debates over Good and Evil, or over Right and Wrong," Norinaga says. "It is all-inclusive, bountiful, and gracious—exactly what poetry aims at." In short, literature helps one to return to basic humanity, as Shintoism does.

All in all, it may be said that Norinaga's theory of literature is a remarkably modern, humanistic one. Ironically enough, this is so because he derived his theory from Shintoism, a religion now generally considered obsolete and dead. The truth is that Shintoism is humanistic in its basic view of the world and of man; its cosmos is ruled by anthropomorphic gods; men are derived from and can eventually become gods. In insisting that men should know the ways of ancient gods, Norinaga is actually saying, as some romantic primitivists did, that men should return to their true unsophisticated selves so well expressed by primitive people who were unspoiled by the evils of civilization. This aim would most effectively be attained through literature, for literature is capable of expressing human feelings without the process of abstraction or generalization. Human feelings, in their original form, are all pre-moral and may look foolish or senseless in the light of modern rational and ethical ideas. By reading works of literature one comes to learn about those basic human feelings that lie deeper than rational and didactic thoughts; one comes to know *mono no aware*. Literature does not aim to teach; it simply presents or describes inmost human feelings. But in its presentation or description it shows how weak and foolish men really are, and therefore how necessary it is for them to understand, sympathize, and help each other. Through works of literature man comes to know who he really is, where he stands in the scheme of things, and what he is expected to do in his present existence.

*Makoto Ueda, "Shintoism and the Theory of Literature: Norinaga on the Art of Writing," in his* Literary and Art Theories in Japan, *The Press of Western Reserve University, 1967, pp. 196-213.*

## Donald Keene  (essay date 1976)

[*Keene is one of the foremost American translators and critics of Japanese literature. In the excerpt below, he assesses Motoori's importance to Japanese literature.*]

Motoori Norinaga (1730-1801) was certainly one of the greatest Japanese scholars, perhaps the greatest. His writings covered three main areas—literature, philology, and Shinto thought—though he himself would probably not have recognized distinctions among these different aspects of the Way. His essays on literature in particular are of genuine, abiding value, and not merely of historical interest or, like so much poetic criticism of the past, intriguing because of occasional flashes of understanding. Motoori's analyses of Japanese poetry or of *The Tale of Genji* are not only valid, but anticipate arguments still being advanced. His writings are colored by his conviction of the supreme importance of Japanese poetry and prose, but they display an erudition and a sensitivity that accord perfectly with his subjects.

Motoori is most celebrated for his reconstruction of the *Kojiki,* a task that engaged him from about 1764 to the completion in 1798. Other scholars, notably Kamo no Mabuchi, had tried to decipher the songs and prose, but Motoori obtained little assistance from his predecessors. His task was to restore the original pronunciations of the text, basing his work on the known vocabulary of the time, as revealed in phonetically transcribed materials. Motoori

also studied the *Manyōshū* with great care, in the manner of his teacher, but his chief concern was to master its vocabulary and syntax, rather than to capture its spirit. His primary interest in reconstructing the *Kojiki* text, for that matter, was not literary. Although he amply demonstrated in his discussions of *The Tale of Genji* how profoundly literature moved him, his studies of *Kojiki* were conceived of in terms of an investigation into the Way of ancient Japan. The *Kojiki* was not only a sacred text, but contained the most reliable information on how the Japanese behaved before being infected with Chinese ideas. No amount of time was too great to devote to so important a task, and Motoori's reconstruction of the *Kojiki* pronunciations was so successful that they have been retained to this day with only minor modifications.

The third aspect of Motoori's activity, the establishment and proclamation of the Way of Japan, was closely linked with his *Kojiki* studies. The purely Japanese virtues—worship of the gods and of their descendant, the emperor—were contrasted with the superficial, meretricious reasoning of the Chinese and of Japanese infatuated with Chinese thought. A detailed examination of Motoori's political and theological views does not lie within the scope of [this essay], but it should not be forgotten that even when Motoori wrote literary criticism of the greatest acumen, these nationalistic conceptions were never far from his mind.

Motoori spent most of his life in the small commercial city of Matsuzaka, near Ise. As a young man he studied medicine in Kyoto and profited from the opportunity to pursue his earlier interest in Japanese literature. His decision to take up medicine, like his changing of his surname from the plebeian Ozu to Motoori in 1752, probably indicated a desire to escape from the chōnin class of his father, a wealthy cotton merchant who had died in 1740. After his return to Matsuzaka in 1757 Motoori set himself up as a physician and practiced this profession even while deeply involved in kokugaku studies. Most educated Japanese enjoyed traveling, but Motoori rarely left Matsuzaka, apparently too absorbed in his work to leave his books.

Motoori's first published work, *Ashiwake Obune (A Little Boat Breaking a Path Through the Reeds)*, seems to have been written during his stay in Kyoto. This essay is an honest attempt to confront the real problems involved in composing poetry, and not, like so many similar books, a mere restatement of platitudes. One event during Motoori's stay in Kyoto made this essay possible, a meeting with Keichū, which inspired Motoori to search for the truth about poetry and to make of himself "a little boat breaking a path through the reeds," the implied meaning of the title. He was resolved to brush aside the encumbrances hindering his boat and sail directly to the heart of poetry. Motoori wrote of Keichū with the deepest respect, but he easily surpassed his master, thanks perhaps to the methodology of Ogyū Sorai which he learned (along with medicine) from his teacher Hori Keizan (1688-1757).

*Ashiwake Obune* fairly bubbles over with ideas. It is written in question-and-answer form, and covers a wide range of topics. In 1763 Motoori wrote an expanded and far more systematic version of this essay, but most of the basic ideas that would remain characteristic of Motoori's writings on literature were present in his first work.

***Ashiwake Obune*** opens with a statement and question:

> The *uta* is a Way for assisting the government of the country. It must not be thought of as a plaything to be toyed with idly. That is why one finds statements to this effect in the preface to the *Kokinshū*. What do you think of this opinion?

The questioner reveals a Confucian attitude toward literature and brings to mind the controversy over . . . [Kada no Arimaro's] statement that the uta (waka poetry) was of no help in promoting good government. Motoori's answer to the question shows familiarity with Arimaro's arguments, but he introduced a distinctive note:

> Answer. This is incorrect. The basic function of the uta is not to assist the government, nor is it intended to improve the person. It is the outward expression of thoughts in the mind, and nothing else. Undoubtedly some poems do assist the government, and others serve as a lesson to people. Some poems also are harmful to the country and others do damage to the person. These effects surely depend on the particular poem produced by the mind of a particular person. A poem can be used for evil or for good; it can be used to express excitement, depression, grief, joy, or any other mood. . . . And if, moreover, it is wondered why there are so few poems with a didactic message and so many about love, it is because that is the area in which the true nature of poetry is naturally expressed. No emotion is as powerful as love, and it is precisely because every single person desires to be successful in love that there are so many poems on the subject. Few sages in the world are so given to improving themselves and obtaining the good that they think exclusively about didactic matters; that is why there are so few didactic poems.

Motoori believed that the importance of poetry consisted in being the vehicle for man's deepest emotions. Like Arimaro, he considered the *Shin Kokinshū* to be the supreme collection of Japanese poetry, not merely because of the exquisite polish of the diction, but because its poets best expressed their sensitivity to the world.

The key expression in Motoori's aesthetic judgments was *mono no aware*. The word *aware* was found in the *Manyōshū* as an expression of wonder or awe. Motoori defined the word in terms of this original meaning:

> When we speak of knowing *mono no aware* we refer to the cry of wonder that comes to our lips when our mind is moved by the realization that something we have seen, heard or touched is *aware*. Even in our common speech today people say *aa* or *hare*. When they have been impressed by the sight of the moon or the cherry blossoms they will say, "*Aa*, what splendid blossoms!" or "*Hare*, what a lovely moon!" *Aware* is the combination of the two cries of *aa* and *hare*.

But the simple exclamation of wonder or delight was of less importance to Motoori than the act of "knowing" *mono no aware*. It is not that a person merely exclaims "Ahh" blankly before some sight of nature; he must distinguish it by means of his senses and emotions.

> One is moved because one has recognized *mono no aware*. This means, for example, if something joyous makes us feel happy, it is because we have recognized the joyful nature of the thing.

Such an act of cognition, by the senses rather than the intellect, revealed to Motoori the essential meaning of literature.

Motoori's "teacher," Kamo no Mabuchi, had unreservedly admired the masculinity of the *Manyōshū* and earlier poetry, but although Motoori devoted many years of his life to elucidating the *Kojiki*, the rugged simplicity of its songs clearly did not please him as much as poetry that stemmed from a sense of *mono no aware*. In ***Ashiwake Obune*** he presents the question:

> Why, if we imitate poetry that reveals the beauty and truth of feelings of people in the past, should we not adopt the ancient manner of the *Nihongi* and the *Manyōshū*, rather than take as our only model the *Kokinshū*, which is rather ornamented and artificial?

To this he replies:

> The *Nihongi* and *Manyōshū* poems are so extremely plain and simple that many are actually clumsy, provincial, and ugly.

This opinion was expressed before Motoori had come in contact with Mabuchi's teachings, and does not reflect his later preferences, but even in his maturity Motoori could never accept masculinity as the ideal in poetry. Instead, he proclaimed femininity and frailty as the essence of literature:

> When I speak of human feelings I mean those that are frail, like those of children and women. Those that are masculine, correct and severe, do not belong to the domain of human feelings.

Motoori means that women and children openly express feelings that men are obliged by their social position to control or conceal.

> The true feelings of people are awkward and untidy. Supposing a beloved child dies—surely there would be no difference in the depth of the grief of the father and mother. But the father would try to pretend this was not so, even as the mother, overcome by lamentations, is blinded by her tears. Why should this be the case? The mother, unable to conceal her true feelings, expresses them exactly as they are. The father unavoidably must worry about how he appears in others' eyes, and he will control or suppress his emotions for fear people will think him softhearted. He will not shed a single tear, nor will he reveal on his face the terrible grief he feels in his heart, but will present a picture of noble resignation. The mother's appearance will be unseemly, distraught and disheveled. But this is what is meant by showing feelings as they actually are. The father's appearance is indeed masculine and severe, and it is admirable that he

manages somehow not to appear distraught, but these are not his true feelings. . . . One may see, then, that the real appearance of human emotions is frail, untidy, and foolish. And since poetry is something that describes feelings, it is fitting that it should accord with the feelings and also be untidy, clumsy, and frail.

Motoori believed that poetry was the product of deep emotions, expressed in a manner that might have seemed unmanly or indecorous to Mabuchi. The sensitive person, when overcome by feelings of *aware,* naturally and inevitably expresses himself in poetry.

> The man who "knows *mono no aware*" may attempt when he encounters something that is *aware* not to think about it, but he cannot prevent himself from feeling the *aware.* It is like a man with good hearing who, though he tries not to hear the thunder, hears it and is afraid. . . . The words that naturally burst forth when the poet is unable to resist *aware* inevitably multiply and become decorated, and eventually form themselves into a poem.

It may be wondered why a man, having relieved his feelings by expressing in poetry his intimations of *aware*—"the pity of things," as one translator put it—should still find it necessary to show his poem to other people. Motoori answered this:

> A poem is not merely something composed to describe one's feelings when one cannot bear any longer the *mono no aware.* When the feelings are extremely deep, one's heart still feels dissatisfied and unresigned, even after having composed a poem. In order to feel comfort one must read the poem to someone else. If the other person hearing the poem finds it has *aware,* this greatly comforts the poet. . . . Even though reading one's poem to someone else brings no material advantage either to the listener or the poet, it is quite natural that the poet feel compelled to read it aloud to another person; and since this is the intent of poetry, it is a most basic principle and not an accident that poems must be heard by others. Someone who does not understand this might say that a true poem describes one's emotions exactly as they are, whether good or bad, and it has nothing to do with whether or not people hear it. Such an argument sounds plausible, but it betrays ignorance of the true meaning of poetry.

Motoori's description of the poetic process suggests Murasaki Shikibu's famous statement on how a writer comes to compose novels:

> It is a matter of his being so moved by things both good and bad, which he has heard and seen happening to men and women that he cannot keep it all to himself but wants to commit it to writing and make it known to other people—even to those of later generations.

A poem, then, originates as a moment of emotional awareness so intense that it cannot be stifled. The emotion finds expression naturally in the traditional poetic forms, and must then be recited to others in order to satisfy an inner

necessity. But no matter how sincere a poet may be, he must clothe his emotions in appropriate language. Even in ancient times poets sought heightened expression for their thoughts, but it was easier then, before words and thoughts had become debased, to write a beautiful poem using ordinary, daily words. Today, however, the poet must study the *Kokinshū, Gosenshū,* and *Shūishū* for their language, but the highest achievement in the poetic art is the *Shin Kokinshū.* No age has produced such magnificent poetry as that of the *Shin Kokinshū,* and this collection is particularly valid for modern men because the emotions described and the language employed are still meaningful; men can no longer hope to imitate the innocence and simplicity of the *Manyōshū* or earlier poetry.

Although Motoori's researches on the *Kojiki* are his most impressive scholarly monument, his writings on *The Tale of Genji* are even more likely to excite our admiration. His love for the work is unmistakable, and it was not philological or ideological. He considered it the supreme masterpiece of literary beauty and the embodiment of *mono no aware.* The medieval commentaries on *The Tale of Genji* had been moral interpretations, whether Buddhist or Confucian; the Nō play *Genji Kuyō* portrays Murasaki Shikibu suffering the torments of hell for having written a novel containing fabrications. Even in the Tokugawa period such men as Kada no Azumamaro or the Confucian scholar Kumazawa Banzan (1619-91) had discussed *The Tale of Genji* in terms of its success in inculcating the principle of "encouraging virtue and chastising vice." Motoori dismissed such interpretations with contempt, declaring that they were responsible for the general inability of readers to understand the true nature of the work:

> It is simply a tale of human life which leaves aside and does not profess to take up at all the question of good and bad, and which dwells only upon the goodness of those who are aware of the sorrow of human existence (*mono no aware*). The purpose of *The Tale of Genji* may be likened to the man who, loving the lotus flower, must collect and store muddy and foul water in order to plant and cultivate the flower. The impure mud of illicit love affairs described in the tale is there not for the purpose of being admired but for the purpose of nurturing the flower of the awareness of the sorrow of human existence.

This for Motoori was the meaning of this great novel. He contrasted it with the didacticism of Chinese literature which, "stripped of its surface ornamentation and polish is totally inept when it comes to describing real emotions." *The Tale of Genji* is a supreme artistic creation because it captures man's deepest feelings directly, without moralizing over them or attempting to rationalize.

The reason for reading *The Tale of Genji* was not to absorb a moral lesson painlessly, as had often been claimed, nor was it simply to kill time. It was necessary in order to cultivate one's sensitivity to *mono no aware,* and beyond *mono no aware* was the Way.

> Every man must be aware of the essence of beauty. If he fails to know it, he will not understand *mono no aware* and will be without feelings. The way to learn the essence of beauty is to compose

poetry and read novels carefully. Moreover, when one has absorbed the elegance of feeling of the men of the past and, in general, the elegance of the whole world of long ago, it will serve as a ladder for learning the ancient Way.

This Way, unlike that of the Confucianists, was not an attempt to systematize knowledge or to reduce it to logical patterns. As Yoshikawa Kōjirō put it, for Motoori "reality was infinitely complex, mysterious and marvelous. It was impossible to explain it with human knowledge because human knowledge was limited." Ultimately, one reaches the stage of wonder at the work of the gods, the stage where one can only cry out, *"Aware!"*

The ancient works that describe how the gods created the world, the *Kojiki* and *Chronicles of Japan,* are neither systematic nor didactic. There was no need to teach moral principles in an age when people always acted with sincerity and directness. A knowledge of these two works—not only their meaning but their language—can give people of modern times the same outlook on the world of the ancients. It was the function of the scholar to elucidate the Way in the hopes that someday it might be adopted by the ruler as the principle for governing the nation:

> The scholar should consider that his task is to investigate and elucidate the Way; he should not attempt to put it into practice himself. Then, after he has studied and elucidated the ancient Way and taught its general principles and written them down in books, a day will surely come, even if it takes five hundred years or one thousand years, when the Ruler will adopt and practice it, and promulgate it to the nation. The scholar must wait for that time.

Motoori's reconstruction of the *Kojiki* was a supreme act of "investigating and elucidating the Way." Each phrase of the original was subjected to the utmost scrutiny. Sources were cited for the pronunciations adopted, geographical and historical background material was supplied, and Motoori's own comments interspersed, making **Kojiki Den** less a commentary than a presentation of Motoori's total understanding of the past. Even an apparently simple section in the *Kojiki* often elicited an imposing display of information: for example, a passage in forty-two characters that merely states how the emperor Ōjin ordered the construction of certain waterways and storehouses was provided with six pages of minute annotations. The display of erudition is overwhelming.

Motoori also wrote many waka. Unlike most other waka poets of his day, he recognized the existence of other forms of poetry; early in his career he was even ready to admit that haikai or Jōruri might be better suited to contemporary men than the waka. Later he decided that, since all varieties of Japanese poetry were essentially branches of the same art, it was foolish to devote oneself to minor offshoots rather than to the core, the waka. When Kamo no Mabuchi, who always insisted on the importance of a kokugaku scholar's composing poetry, accepted Motoori as his disciple, he asked him to submit some poems. Motoori's waka, in the *Shin Kokinshū* style, displeased Mabuchi exceedingly. About one, an inoffensive description of cherry blossoms falling at an old temple, Mabuchi

wrote, "This is not even a poem." About another, on cherry blossoms "burying the moss," he merely commented, "Disgusting." Mabuchi declared, "If you like this style of poetry, you should give up your studies of the *Manyōshū.*"

Motoori dutifully began to compose verse in the *Manyōshū* style, but late in life he wrote, "If a man today writes in the old style of the *Manyōshū,* it will not be his own true feelings but a fabrication written in imitation of the *Manyōshū.*" He undoubtedly considered his own poems in this style a fabrication, and that was why he advocated the *Shin Kokinshū* style which permitted him to write from the heart. But whatever style he adopted, his poetry was undistinguished. There is not much to choose between his hackneyed descriptions of cherry blossoms and his Shinto poems, like the following one, phrased in archaic language:

> *kusuwashiki*
> *kotowari shirazute*
> *Karahito no*
> *mono no kotowari*
> *toku ga hakanasa*

> How vain it is
> For the men of China
> To discuss the reason of things
> When they know not the reason
> Of the miraculous!

Despite his failings as a poet, Motoori was unquestionably the greatest of the kokugaku scholars. Yet, paradoxically, he disliked the word *kokugaku* and even attacked it, declaring that Japanese learning should simply be called "learning" without the qualifying adjective "national." The objection is typical of Motoori, yet as he himself was aware, the purity of language and thought he advocated represented a special development. Motoori's knowledge and sensitivity gave to the Japanese learning first advocated by Azumamaro, Keichū, and Mabuchi a dignity commensurate with their high purpose, and established it as a rival to the Confucian and Buddhist thought that had long been dominant.

*Donald Keene, "Waka Poetry: Kokugaku and the Waka,"* in his World within Walls: Japanese Literature of the Pre-Modern Era, 1600-1867, *Holt, Rinehart and Winston, 1976, pp. 300-33.*

### Yoshikawa Kōjirō    (essay date 1983)

*[In the following excerpt from a work originally published in Japanese in 1975, Yoshikawa discusses Motoori's philosophy.]*

Reality, according to Norinaga, is infinitely complex, mysterious, and bizarre. It is beyond man's knowledge, which is but limited. The mystery of reality can be found anywhere around us with just a little reflection. For instance, "Does the *terra* on which we live hang from the firmament or does it rest on matter? In any event it is most mysterious." Further, "Just reflect on oneself. Is it not strange that we see things with our eyes, hear with our ears, utter words with our mouth, walk with our legs, and manage a myriad of things with our hands? Equally wondrous are the facts that birds and insects fly in the air and trees and grasses put forth flowers and bear fruit." How can all these phenomena be explained by human knowledge?

Any attempt to generalize this complex reality with human knowledge and to explicate and regulate it by deriving what appear to be laws therefrom invariably leads to fallacy. This is because man's intellect is limited whereas reality is infinitely complex. What appear to be laws do not apply to every aspect of reality, and therefore application of any law accompanies compulsion or coercion. Such teachings of foreign origin as Confucianism and Buddhism have, Norinaga maintains, all fallen into such fallacies.

We cannot deny the existence of deities. We cannot but believe the existence of transcendental beings since all the wonders of reality are attributable to the creation of the universe by deities. All realities exist as they were willed by the deities. "Everything whatsoever in this world, the seasonal changes, rain and wind, a myriad of fortunes and misfortunes that fall upon the nation and individuals are all deeds of deities." Both nature and human affairs are but results of divine decree.

According to Norinaga, the works that describe the process of creation of the universe by deities most correctly are the *Kojiki* and the *Nihon shoki,* the classics written in Japan. Particularly accurate in delineation is the former. It was written not on the basis of human knowledge, at least of that of individuals. It records intact the tradition transmitted from the age of the deities. Since "nothing pretentious is added," the descriptions there are most reliable. It describes only the deeds of deities and gives no principles. What are given there, however, are prototypes of all realities of later ages and therefore the book provides an explanation to those realities.

> Yononaka no
> aru omobuki wa
> nanigoto mo
> Kamiyo no ato wo
> tazunete shirayu
>
> (Whatever exists in this world can be understood
> by tracing it back to the age of the deities)

Though the *Kojiki* gives no principles, one should not make light of it since "while it appears shallow outwardly, it is fathomless in its content, containing things profound and subtle which are beyond the reach of man's knowledge."

This world, Norinaga asserts, is filled not only with good and happiness but also with evil and misery. This is the will of the deities as there are both good and evil deities. Good (*yogoto*) invariably involves evil (*magagoto*) and evil invariably involves good. Hence, good and evil are interchangeable. This correlation between good and evil in reality exists also in its prototype, i.e. the intercourse among deities described in the *Kojiki.* The auspicious event that the two deities, Izanagi and Izanami, gave birth to the various islands constituting Japan through sexual intercourse (*mito no maguwai*) ends in the death of the female deity, Izanami, a misfortune caused by finally giving birth to the Deity of Fire. This, however, is followed again by an aus-

picious event when three deities of noble character, with Amaterasu Ōmikami—equated by Norinaga with the sun shining brightly even today in the firmament—as the elder sister, were born when the male deity performed his ablutions at Tachibana no Odo on his way back from visiting the female deity in Hades (*Yomi no kuni*). This, according to Norinaga, is nothing other than the prototype of the phenomenon in reality that good and evil or fortune and misfortune occur perpetually in succession.

Evil, however, cannot after all conquer good. A pristine illustration of this in the *Kojiki* is, according to Norinaga, the tradition that when the female deity in Hades insisted on killing a thousand souls a day, the male deity retorted by proposing to give birth to one thousand and five hundred lives.

Furthermore, in the interplay of good and evil man invariably detests evil and aspires to do what is good. He is inclined so by nature and not under compulsion through education, as this is again the will of the deities. Izanagi's ablutions at Tachibana no Odo, to begin with, which are a pristine exemplar of such conduct, were done of his own accord and not under compulsion. "Since human beings were thus created by the spirit of Musubi no Kami (the deity who gives birth to all beings) so as to detest evil and do what is good, they know for themselves what they should do without being taught."

Not only human beings but also animals know how to live from birth. This is because they are innately equipped by the will of the deities with the means to live as what they are born to be. "All creatures whatsoever living in this world down to birds and insects inherently know how to act since they are ordained to act so by virtue of the divine spirit of Musubi no Kami." This is all the moreso with man who is the lord of all creatures. If he could not acquire this power without having it forced on him by education, he would be inferior to the beasts. For this very reason, Norinaga holds, there were no such terms as morals or ethics meaning compulsion by laws in ancient Japan. True, there was the word *michi* (the way), but it denoted only the path on the ground. Nevertheless, insofar as the term *michi* is used today to denote the fundamental truth that man and animals exist by virtue of heavenly will, man must realize that he is living within the purview of and supported by that truth of *michi.* "Man, insofar as he is man, must have knowledge of the Way." "Particularly, it is not proper for those pursuing learning in whatever field or those learned enough to read books to make light of this truth by showing no interest in the Way and without making any effort to acquire knowledge of the true meaning of the deities' grace." In short, man has to be a philosopher.

One should strive to materialize the Way by translating the philosophy thus attained into practice. True, everything in this world is created by the will of the deities, but this does not mean that man may idle away, relying on divine will. "It is a serious mistake if anyone thinks that he had better entrust everything in the deities' hands and not meddle in things, leaving them to take their own course no matter whether it be good or bad." "It is the way of man to strive to the best of his ability." However, it is beyond human power to judge whether his efforts will be rewarded or not, as the will of both good and evil deities is involved. One should of course avoid compulsion, but to "abandon oneself to fate is also against the Way of man."

The textbooks for attaining and practising the Way are the *Kojiki* and the *Nihon shoki*. Out of these two works the former, because of its mode of verbal expression (*monoii no sama*), transmits the deeds of the deities more faithfully than the latter which is written in Chinese (*kanbun*).

However, there is one thing extremely important in approaching the Way. One will invariably fail if he snatches at these two classics unpremeditatedly in ardent desire to know the Way "since the two works do not explain the Way concretely as the Confucian and Buddhist works do, although the various deeds of the deities described therein no doubt point to the Way." "Beginners would not be able to appreciate the Way just by reading the two classics no matter how hard they try." They would not only fail to appreciate the Way but would also fall into fallacy unintentionally or contort the passages from their original meaning. Those who are accustomed to the Confucian and Buddhist methods of acquiring the knowledge of man through books which present principles try to read the two classics in the same fashion, namely as works presenting principles instead of primeval models, and the principles they try to read in perforce are those of Confucianism and Buddhism.

The conventional exegetic works on the two classics such as the *Shaku nihongi* and the *Nihongi shiki* as well as the views of the so-called "Shintō scholars" (*Shintōka*) with the exception of Keichū (1640-1701) (greatly respected by Norinaga) and Kamo no Mabuchi (1697-1769) (Norinaga's direct teacher) have all fallen into this error. When Norinaga asserts that this erroneous interpretation, which had originated historically from Buddhism, has been furthered in the past one hundred and fifty years by Confucianism, he probably had in his mind Yamasaki Ansai's (1618-1682) Suika Shintō. In short, if one tries to seek for a philosophical system straightforwardly with an attempt to become a philosopher, he will invariably fall into an error.

Norinaga proposes a method to avoid such an error. To approach the essence of things through one's emotions is a prerequisite to attaining philosophy. In Norinaga's own words it is "to appreciate the emotion of things" (*mono-no-aware wo shiru*). Further, the best way of training in this emotional approach is, again in Norinaga's own words, "to acquire the sense of elegance" (*miyabi no omomuki wo shiru*) by reading classical tales and poetry, which are exemplars of the language of emotion, and to compose *waka*, representative style of poetry in Japan. One can attain the Way or truth by reading the works expounding the Way only after preparing himself through such a method.

What underlies this view of Norinaga's is his contention that the mode of verbal expression (*monoii no sama*), particularly that in emotional language, directly reflects one's mind and is therefore an important factor in the reality of man. What is set as another premise is that man's emo-

tions are the most important among the various functions of the human mind, and that human mind can after all be reduced to emotion. This may be proved by the fact that Norinaga frequently maintains in his works on poetics that emotion is shared by all beings including animals. "All beings whatsoever have emotion." "Because of emotion they are moved by what they experience." The cry of the animals is an expression of their feelings and so is man's composing poetry. Particularly what man feels are complex and profound because of his ascendency over all other beings and of his keen mind. "Man's feelings are more variegated than those of birds and beasts since the range of his activities is wider and therefore he has more chances to encounter things." "Thus, he feels joy, sorrow, anger, delight, pleasure, fun, fear, anxiety, affection, enmity, yearning, and compassion."

Why, then, are man's feelings so variegated? It is because man perceives the essence of things through emotional intuition, which is nothing other than to "appreciate the emotion of things" (*mono-no-aware wo shiru*). "For instance, man is delighted when encountering things delightful as he perceives through intuition what makes those things delightful. He feels sorrow when encountering things sorrowful as he perceives what makes those things sorrowful. To perceive on various occasions the essence of joy and sorrow is to appreciate *mono-no-aware*."

The reality surrounding us that offers a chance for us to feel *mono-no-aware* is the beautiful nature such as the moon and flowers.

> The difference between appreciating and not appreciating *mono-no-aware* comes from whether one is touched in heart when he sees beautiful flowers or the silvery moon. Our heart is moved by the beauty of the moon and flowers because we perceive the very essence of their beauty. Without that we will not be moved even by viewing beautiful flowers and the silvery moon. Such people are said to lack the sense of appreciating *mono-no-aware*.

This applies not only to nature but to all realities. A person who "perceives the elegance or the beauty of not only the moon and flowers but also of all beings" and is stirred in the depth of his heart, "feeling what is joyful as joyful, what is interesting as interesting, what is sorrowful as sorrowful, and what is lovable as lovable" has the sense to "appreciate *mono-no-aware*." Hence, it is one of the first prerequisites for man to appreciate *mono-no-aware*. "Those who possess the sense of appreciating *mono-no-aware* are said to be people of sensitive mind (*kokoro aru hito*) and those without such sense are stolid people (*kokoro naki hito*)."

Furthermore, it is the nature of man to feel an impulse to convey the profound emotions stirred within him to others. He is not content just with a monologue. "Man cannot help telling others what has profoundly touched his mind," and the means of conveying his feelings is nothing other than *waka* poetry. People who are not able to convey their feelings through *waka* are imperfect, inferior even to animals. "Even birds and insects on occasion chirp songs with a tune of their own. Is it not shameful for man not to be able to compose a single *waka?* It is indeed despicable to think that one can get by without being able to compose a *waka.*" In short, man has to be literary-minded, or more precisely, a poet. "Every man has to have the sense to appreciate elegance (*miyabi no omomuki*). Without this one will not be able to appreciate *mono-no-aware.*" In other words he will be nothing more than a stolid person (*kokoro naki hito*) who is unable to perceive the essence of things through emotion.

Norinaga holds that it is only after attaining the basic requirements of man, that is, to become a man of sensitive mind capable of perceiving *mono-no-aware* or equipped with the 'sense of elegance,' that one can approach the Way or philosophy. This method, according to Norinaga, was cultivated by his teacher, Kamo no Mabuchi. He states by quoting Mabuchi's words as follows: "If one wishes to appreciate the ancient Way, he should first read the poetry of antiquity, try to compose verses in the archaic style himself, and next study ancient prose and learn to write in the same style. After mastering the ancient language in this manner he should peruse the *Kojiki* and *Nihon shoki.*" "Without a knowledge of the ancient language one will not be able to understand the ancient meaning of the words; without a knowledge of the ancient meaning he will not be able to appreciate the ancient Way."

Why did Mabuchi give prominence, as a step to attaining the Way, to the *Man'yōshū,* which at first glance seems unrelated to the Way? Norinaga responds by stating that poetic literature expresses flexibility and delicacy, which are also the features of the Way. "The Way of the deities had not even a particle of the artificial discussions on good and evil or rights and wrongs often found in Confucianism and Buddhism. It is opulent, magnanimous, and refined, the characteristics most befittingly expressed by *waka.*"

The fact that poetical literature is by nature flexible and delicate led Norinaga to attach importance to amatory odes which are particularly delicate. "Since love, above all other passions, is most penetrating, heartrending, and irresistible, it is natural that there are numerous verses full of pathos particularly among amatory *waka.*"

The most heartrending among the amatory *waka,* Norinaga holds, are those on illicit love. Everyone knows without being taught that such a love is against morality. Precisely because of that it stirs man's emotion. "Almost everyone knows what is good, what is evil, and what is inexcusable. Even a child knows that it is evil to seduce a married woman." Nevertheless, this type of lust, even knowing that it is an evil, is so deeply rooted and uncontrollable that one is apt to be wholly overtaken with it.

According to Norinaga, *waka* is independent of and unrelated to politics or morality.

> *Waka,* by nature, is not for assisting politics nor for regulating one's life. It is nothing other than an expression of what one feels in his mind. Indeed, among the odes there might be some that would be serviceable to politics or afford moral lessons, but at the same time there might be those injurious to the government or disastrous

to man's morality. This is because poetry flows out naturally from the composer's mind.

Norinaga's contention that *waka,* a literary genre based on emotion, treasures flexibility, leads him to the conclusion that man's emotions are by nature effeminate and frail. "Almost every man, no matter how intelligent he may be, is not much different from women and children if we search into the depth of his mind. All beings are thus effeminate and frail," and it is sheer bluster to pretend not to be so.

This can be proved in daily life by the fact that while mothers grieve bitterly over the death of a child, fathers tend to hide their tears, patching up appearances. In this case mothers are more honest than fathers. The fact that "men, though feeling grief or compassion at the bottom of their hearts, cunningly conceal their true feelings by suppressing their emotion and keep up appearances before the public eye" is "attributable to the temperament of the samurai class in recent ages and also to the arguments of the Chinese Confucians," which are far removed from human feelings. True, it is the way of a devoted samurai to lay down his life for his country, "but would he not feel sorrowful facing death when he thinks of his wife, children, and his aged parents?" "There is nothing more sorrowful in this world than death." That is why the *Kojiki,* which gives the primeval prototypes of human conduct, relates, "Even Izanagi, the great god who created the country and all other beings and established the Way for the world, mourned over the death of the goddess, Izanami, by shedding tears like a child." Pretending not to be sad is an unnatural custom advocated by Confucianism and Buddhism.

In this connection Norinaga's affirmation of unrepressed emotion leads him to asimilar affirmation of unfettered desires, frequently deriding the conventional views on human desire, particularly the negative attitude of the Confucians. In Norinaga's view desire is also part of man's nature, decreed by the deities. "Man, by nature, earnestly desires to eat delicacies, to wear fine clothes, to live in a luxurious house, to possess valuables, to be respected by others, and to enjoy longevity." "It is because of those erroneous views that many people pretend not to be desirous of all these things, regarding them perforce as something evil, something that should not be desired." This applies also to carnal desire. "Is it not true that people revered as masters (*sensei*) or holy priests (*shōnin*) overtly praise the beauty of the moon and flowers but pass by a nice-looking woman indifferently as if she had not caught his sight?" "If one is to appreciate the beauty of nature, why should he not appreciate the beauty of women?" Any person who does not feel so "must be said to be devoid of human feelings." Moreover, Confucian scholars pretend not to be desirous of money while having a craving for books, but is it not that they can buy books only because they have money? It was for his affirmation of desires that Norinaga detested living in the mountain woods where there is hardly anything to stimulate one's earthly desires.

Norinaga, who treasures flexibility as the essence of emotion, does not adhere only to the archaic style as that of the *Man'yōshū* in the field of *waka.* He holds that the *waka*

*A late nineteenth-century depiction of the Shinto gods Izanagi and Izanami.*

former has many points yet to be desired when compared with the latter."

Norinaga uses a metaphor to explain the difference between the *Man'yōshū* and the works of later ages: "The archaic style of *waka* is like white refined clothes whereas that of later ages is like a robe dyed in varied colors such as crimson and violet." Both white robes and colored dresses have a value of their own. What is important is the propriety of the color.

Norinaga further asserts that if anyone thinks that dyed robes are not genuine since they are artificial, he must not forget that *waka* is also artificial. "*Waka,* though a means to express one's feelings, is different from ordinary language in that it is accompanied by embellishment and beautiful musical tune. It has been so even from the ages of the deities." It is precisely because of this artificiality that *waka* can convey profound feelings and thereby move man's heart and even that of the spirits.

This is evidenced, Norinaga insists, by everyday experience. A cry evoked by deep sorrow, for instance, has a tone of its own. "One merely weeps when the grief is not so bitter, but when he cries aloud from deep sorrow, his voice bears an expression which excites profound compassion in those who hear it." The same can be said of *waka*. "It is again far from falsehood. Through its embellished words it can convey reality and therefore moves the reader." This view of Norinaga's on the *waka* of later ages is closely related to his contention that artificiality is also due to the will of the deities, another pillar of his philosophy.

There was a criticism of his views in his day that they were close to those of Lao-tzu and Chuang-tzu even though Norinaga himself had felt repulsion against Chinese Confucianism. To this Norinaga responds by saying that the followers of Lao-tzu all detested artificiality, but that what they prized is contrary to nature. What they regarded as nature is far from nature in its truest sense or from the Way or *michi* propounded by Norinaga. "If it is proper to leave things to take their natural course, it is nothing but nature to leave artifice as artifice. To detest artifice is nothing other than compulsion which is contrary to nature."

Norinaga's esteem for the *waka* of later ages or for the artifice therein is a manifestation of his progressive view of history, which is another pillar of his philosophy. As a reason for his esteem he states, "Among varied things there are cases in which those of later ages are superior to those of antiquity. Hence, it is erroneous to deny things of later ages sweepingly." Elsewhere, after stating, "There are cases in which things of later ages are superior to those of earlier ages among a variety of things," he gives the following example: mandarine oranges (*tachibana*) which were much treasured in antiquity must have been far inferior in taste to the tangerines of his days. From this he concludes, "There are a multitude of things which did not exist in antiquity but are available today and things which were inferior in quality in antiquity but are now of superb quality. Judging from this, how can one say that there will in the future not be anything superior to what we have

of the later ages, particularly the *Kokinshū* and the *Shin-kokinshū,* should be valued for acquiring the 'sense of elegance' (*miyabi no omomuki*). While the verses in the *Man'yōshū* are often too naive and simple, reflecting the character of the ancient ages, those in the *Kokinshū* and the *Shin-kokinshū* deal with more complex subjects and are therefore more intricate in emotion. For this reason Norinaga places the zenith of Japanese *waka* in the ages of the latter two works. "Taking a survey through the history from antiquity up to the present age, it might duly be said that *waka* reached the stage of completion with the compilation of the *Kokinshū,* but it is perhaps more appropriate to regard the *Shin-kokinshū* as the peak since the

today?" As shall be mentioned later, Norinaga regards learning as a typical case of this.

Norinaga's view that one can better appreciate the elegance (*miyabi no omomuki*) of archaic *waka* by composing verses modeled after them rather than by just reading them passively derives not only from his view mentioned previously that man should be poetic-minded in expressing things, but also from his contention that one's own experience best reflects reality. "There is difference in the depth of perceiving things depending on whether they are conceived as matters concerning oneself or not. Things not concerning oneself never impress one so profoundly as those concerning oneself." This is to say that an object is never fully appreciated insofar as it is viewed merely as an object. It can be thoroughly appreciated only by experiencing it for oneself. "The same can be said of poetry. Archaic-style poetry, being something remote from us, cannot be fully mastered no matter how hard we ponder over it. However, we shall come to appreciate it if we compose verses in that style ourselves since we give our mind particularly to things we experience ourselves."

*Waka* literature is thus esteemed by Norinaga as a source for appreciating elegance or *miyabi no omomuki,* but another source equally valued by him is fictional literature such as the *Genji monogatari.* Norinaga explains this by saying that tales or *monogatari* generally provide the reader with something entertaining "by depicting all sorts of events of this world, i.e. good, evil, phenomenal, ludicrous, and pitiable events," and at the same time show the reader the psychology and the way of behavior of man when he confronts such events. They instruct the reader that "man thinks so and so when seeing or hearing about such and such things, feels so and so when confronting such and such events, and that while the mind and conduct of good people are so and so, those of malicious people are so and so." In short, the experiences of the characters in the tales become at once those of the reader.

The greatest benefit of tales, however, is, Norinaga holds, that they serve as a source for appreciating the value and the working of emotion, namely *mono-no-aware.* This is precisely why affairs between the two sexes tend to be their central theme. "This is because there is nothing more deep-rooted in the human mind than love." Particularly heartrending is the emotion or *aware* of the several cases of illicit love treated in the *Genji monogatari.* To regard that work as a mere didactic story, a view which prevailed prior to Norinaga, is, according to him, to use a cherry tree, which is properly for viewing its blossoms, for firewood. It is not that firewood is unnecessary for life, but for that purpose there are other trees.

Norinaga further discusses the value of "appreciating the emotion of things" as, "This applies also to the way of governing oneself, one's family, and one's country." Moreover, he asserts that fiction delineates the various aspects of human life far better than historical works, quoting the dialogue between Genji and Tamakatsura in the "Hotaru" chapter of the *Genji monogatari.* Lastly Norinaga attributes the fact that the *Genji monogatari* deals only with the life of aristocrats and not that of the populace, though *monogatari* tales are generally expected to cover "all sorts

of things," to the conditions of the age in which the tale was written.

The foregoing are only part of Norinaga's interpretations of Mabuchi's view that it is a prerequisite for "appreciating the Way" to read and compose *waka* and to read *monogatari* literature. What is more important is Norinaga's contention that the mode of verbal expression directly reflects the workings of one's mind and that for that reason it should be regarded as important as a source for studying man's nature. It is on the basis of this thought that he gives the above-mentioned evidences to Mabuchi's theory that the ancient meaning (*koi*) and therefore the ancient Way (*kodō*) is appreciated only by mastering the ancient language (*kogen*).

This view of Norinaga's is most important. It is commonly thought that verbal expression is a means to convey a fact and that what is important is the fact conveyed rather than the expression. Norinaga's view was different from this. The fact conveyed is indeed important, but the mode of verbal expression which conveys the fact is also in itself a fact equally important as an object, i.e. the fact conveyed by the language, since it directly reflects the psychology of the speaker who is at once the subject who conveys the fact to others. In short, how to express was regarded as equally important as what to express. Moreover, he maintained that it is advisable to depend on verbal expression for the study of the ancient ages whose state of affairs is not so clear to us today.

Norinaga first gives a general view.

> In most cases there is coherence and community among the language (*kotoba*), deed (*waza*), and mind (*kokoro*) of an individual. For instance, a man of judicious mind also speaks and acts judiciously while a man of stupid mind speaks and acts stupidly. Furthermore, men think, speak, and act in a manly manner whereas women think, speak, and act in a womanly manner.

This principle, Norinaga maintains, is applicable to appreciating the ancient spirit. "The differences among ages are similar to this. People of antiquity, of the medieval ages, and of the recent ages spoke and acted in their respective-manner coherent with their mind." Hence, it is essential to grasp the mind, language, and deeds of the ancients as factors closely interrelated in order to appreciate the Way of the ancient ages.

What, then, is important as the language of antiquity? It is, according to Norinaga, nothing other than *waka* since "the language in which the ancients spoke has been transmitted to this day through *waka.*" More correctly they are the verses in the *Kojiki, Nihon shoki,* and *Man'yōshū.* The very fact that Norinaga gives poetry as an exemplar of archaic language is nothing else but an indication of his deference to the language that gives heed to the mode of verbal expression and of his contention that the mode of verbal expression is closely linked with man's mind and deeds.

Moreover, his contention that the *Man'yōshū* is far superior to the *Nihon shoki* and the *Kojiki* as a source for appreciating archaic language not only in that it contains more verses but also in that the *Shoki* is written in pure *kanbun* and the *Kojiki* has not completely extricated itself from the *kanbun* style may be construed to mean that the *Man'yōshū* is more appropriate than the other two works as a source for studying the mode of expression of the archaic language.

As regards the "deeds" or *waza* of the ancients, Norinaga states, "The deeds [of the ancients] have been transmitted through the chronicles," namely the *Kojiki* and the *Nihon shoki,* but "since those chronicles describe events through words, they, too, are within the confines of language." Though Norinaga alludes here to the aspect of language as a means of transmitting historical facts, which are in themselves objective, his assertion that the historical facts are after all language shows that he gave prominence to language or *kotoba* among the three factors, the mind (*kokoro*), language (*kotoba*), and deeds (*waza*) or at least between the latter two.

Finally, as for the mind or *kokoro,* Norinaga's words "the state of one's mind can be discerned through *waka*" derive in part from his contention mentioned above that the flexible and delicate feelings treated in *waka* accord with the flexibility and delicacy of the Way, the norm of the human mind. However, judging from his words which he adds as a conclusion "Since language, deeds, and mind are coherent with one another, it is through archaic language and *waka* that people of later ages can acquire knowledge of the ancients' thought and deeds and thereby understand the conditions of the world in which they lived," it is indisputably evident that he valued language most among the three factors, the mode of expression in particular.

Similar discussions appear frequently in other works. "Since one's intention and deeds are conveyed by language, the most important thing in a book is the language in which it is written." Norinaga's contention here is that books are after all language. Further, "Since man's mode of life and thinking can be inferred from his way of expression, all events of antiquity are also discernible by clarifying the ancient language." Here the words "the way of expression" (*monoii no sama*) indicate most clearly Norinaga's thought that the study of the mode of expression is the basis for elucidating history and man's nature. Thus Norinaga, whose thought was founded on his esteem for reality, may be said to have started from regarding verbal expression as the most basic reality of man.

This view of Norinaga's, when viewed from the methodological standpoint, probably made the historians and philosophers of his day who were concerned merely about the facts conveyed by language realize the defects of their method, and further provided a firm ground for the scholarship of his day which had been engaged in annotating ancient works as its main task. Moreover, his views are most suggestive even to us today in the methodological aspect. As a matter of fact he wrote his principal exegetic works such as the **Kojiki-den** on the basis of this theory, and they all won great success as works analysing the mind or *kokoro* and pursuing the deeds or *waza* of the ancients through the study of the ancient language.

As a proof of the validity of his method, which, according

to Norinaga, enables the reader to approach the Way by training himself to appreciate "the emotion of things" and the "sense of elegance," he points out the failures of his contemporaries who did not follow this method.

> "Surveying the state of people engaged in learning, most of those who pursue the Way or the principles [i.e. those who aspire to become philosophers] are engrossed merely in arguments of Chinese origin, disregarding *waka* as mere idleness. Since they do not bother to open and read anthologies and hence have no knowledge of the delicate feelings of the ancients, they fail to appreciate also the Way of antiquity which they profess to seek."

On the contrary, those who simply adore the elegance (*miyabi*) of antiquity without giving any thought to the Way, the principle of the world, are, according to Norinaga, mere dilettantes. "If one adores antiquity, he should give primary thought to and clearly appreciate the Way, the root of ancient culture. Those who neglect this and become immersed merely in minor details cannot be said to be true lovers of antiquity. In such a case, even if they compose *waka,* it would be sheer idleness."

To appreciate the Way does not necessarily mean to practise the Way. While the former is a task of learning, the latter is that of politics. The very fact that both the ruler and the ruled exist in the form of the sovereign and subjects is also a decree of the deities. If it is the duty of the ruler to govern in accordance with the Way, it is the duty of the ruled including those engaged in learning to submissively follow the ruler. "The Way is to be practised and disseminated throughout the country by the ruler. It is audacious and against the Way for a commoner to reform the government for the reason that the existing rule is incompatible with the Way. Commoners should submissively follow the dictates of the ruler no matter whether they are good or evil." Norinaga himself practised this. "Since I myself have thought thus, I have endeavored not to put the Way into practice but to pursue and clarify it."

The topmost ruler in Japan, in Norinaga's view, is the imperial family, the descendants of Amaterasu Ōmikami, the Sun Goddess, and today they are assisted by the family founded by Azumateru-kamu Mioya no Mikoto, namely Tokugawa Ieyasu, who revered the imperial family. This situation should not be changed.

A ruler or *kami* "holds a high position, rules a province or a district, governs a multitude of people, is respected by the populace, and leads an opulent and pleasant life" whereas the ruled or the *shimo* are "to eat plentifully, be freed from hunger, wear clothes enough to keep warm, and live peacefully in a decent house." All these are of course "the favors of the emperor, one's ancestors, and of his parents" but basically "the gifts of the deities." Hence, one should not be negligent in revering the deities, presuming upon their mercy. Though there might be occasions in which one's prayers are not answered, he should not forget that the greater part of his life is due to heavenly grace. To bear a grudge against the deities just for the reason that a small portion of his desires were not granted is tantamount to reproaching a person who kindly spared ninety-nine *ryō* instead of the the requested sum of one hundred *ryō.*

Norinaga, however, does not mean to say that everything should be laid in the hands of the deities as stated earlier in this [essay]. His advice to those in charge of government is chiefly to carry out reform not too hastily. "It is not advisable to abolish a long-standing practice all of a sudden even though it is deemed incompatible with the Way" since "all things including the rise and fall or prosperity and decline of things depend on the will of the deities, and one cannot change them just by human power." Also in the **Hihon Tamakushige,** a memorial written at the request of the Lord of Kishū, he advises several reforms to be effected in the spirit stated above, adding each time that the reforms should be made with the greatest circumspection.

This, however, does not apply to learning. "It is absurd in learning to adhere blindly to things old without discussing their rights and wrongs." It was precisely for this reason, Norinaga maintains, that he modified without hesitation the points he thought impertinent in the views of his master, Mabuchi. He also advises his own students to correct his views whenever they find them inappropriate. What is important, he asserts, is not the teacher but the Way or truth.

Norinaga, however, maintains that the only works which correctly discuss the Way at present are his, particularly the **Kojiki-den.** The works of other writers are imbued with erroneous views. Among the works on poetics those by Keichū are recommendable, but they fail to deal with the Way. Even the works of Mabuchi, Norinaga's master, fall short in dealing with the Way. "There is no other work aside from Norinaga's for grasping instantly the general meaning of the Way." "My works contain everything that has come into my mind while studying the classics, and there is nothing that has been left out."

Norinaga's views given above and his methodology based on those views were in most cases advanced as a result of his aversion to Confucianism, particularly the officially authorized Neo-Confucianism of Chu Hsi, which had been dominant from the early Tokugawa period up to his days. What Norinaga disliked about Confucianism was that it advocates an ideal community replete with only good and happiness as a world of Sages. "Confucianism, however, preaches the materialization of a world of only good by sweeping out the dirt from every nook and corner of society, which is something that can never be realized." Moreover, it presses on man morals impossible to put into practice. "To use a metaphor, the Sages urge man to jump across a ditch of one *jō* [3.3 yards] in width. However, none of the tens of millions of people can jump as much as the Sages teach. All they can jump across is a ditch three or four feet wide." What the Sages teach is like the statement of virtues of a medicine which is never so efficacious as is stated.

Moreover, the Confucianists attempt to explain reality with such principles as the Heavenly Decree (*tenmei*), Heavenly Way (*tendō*), Yin and Yang (*inyō*), and the Five Elements (*gogyō*) as the basis of their unrealistic moral teachings, and asa consequence they often fall into contradiction. This is because they try to reason out every aspect of reality with man's limited knowledge. For instance, the Heavenly Way, according to them, is said to bring happiness to the virtuous and misfortune to the wicked, but Confucius and his descendants, who were men of highest virtue, cannot be said to have lived a happy life. In the first place, the so-called Sages, setting aside Confucius, such as King T'ang of the Yin and King Wu of the Chou, were all usurpers who seized the throne from the preceding dynasty and constructed their theory only to justify their usurpation. The Confucian theories thus formulated deviate from truth all the more because they excel in argument. Particularly, when the Neo-Confucianists after the Sung dynasty denied human desire as sheer lust, they forgot that human desire was also an ordination of heaven.

Norinaga's aversion to Confucianism started already while he was studying it in his youth under Hori Keizan (1688-1757) in Kyoto. In the **Ashiwake obune,** a work on poetics probably written around that time, he asserts the superiority of Japanese *waka,* comparing it with Chinese poetry. Further, he attributes the superiority of Japanese poetry over Chinese poetry to the fact that the former has the particles, *te, ni, wo, wa,* which the latter lacks. Nevertheless he frequently avails himself of Chinese classics as a source in his discussions, and the tone of his criticism toward Chinese poetry at this stage which states that it might have reality to the Chinese though it does not to the Japanese who are foreigners is as yet not so severe as that of his later view.

Norinaga's repulsion against Confucianism intensified and became decisive after returning to his native town, Matsusaka, at the age of twenty-eight and devoting himself to the study of National Learning or *kokugaku* while practising pediatrics for the rest of his life. His critical attitude toward Chinese civilization as a whole became conspicuous after writing the **Naobi no mitama** at the age of forty-two as an introduction to his life work, the **Kojiki-den,** and further coming to write the **Kuzubana** as a refutation to a criticism on the **Naobi no mitama** by a Confucian scholar named Ichikawa Tamon, styled Kakumei (1740-1795). There he attributes the errors of the Chinese to their ignorance of the Way of the deities described in the *Kojiki.*

Norinaga's thought formed on the basis of his criticism toward Confucianism, however, may be regarded as having evolved from the views of some Confucian scholars preceding him, particularly those of the anti-Chu Hsi school. The stream of thought to reject Sung Neo-Confucianism propounded by Chu Hsi and his followers as a dogmatic view which forces people with rigor and to lay stress on human emotions and desire started with Itō Jinsai in the seventeenth century and became more conspicuous with Ogyū Sorai in the early eighteenth century. Furthermore, it was an important factor in Sorai's thought that man should be literary before being philosophical and that the mode of verbal expression is the basis for understanding man. Moreover, a quest for transcendent being is also found in Sorai's thought.

It is possible to say that Norinaga's esteem for the *Kojiki* was a leap which marked a new step in the development of his thought and that it was in the deities described in that work that he discovered what was needed in the type of philosophy that presupposes the existence of a transcendental being. This leap in his thought seems to have weighed on his mind. The following answer to Ichikawa Tamon's criticism seems to have been made in connection with this problem: "Do you mean to say that I, although believing at the bottom of my heart that there is no such thing as a deity, assert the existence of deities in defense of the classics of our country? If that is your contention, I have many things to say."

Norinaga's method of expounding his views through annotations as evidenced in his life work, the *Kojiki-den,* is again in line with the method employed by Jinsai and Sorai, who also set forth their views through the comments in their respective works, the *Rongo kogi* and the *Rongo-chō.* This method of giving one's thoughts through the annotations in exegetic works is typically Confucian in the fullest sense of the term even though Norinaga himself refused to admit that he was a successor of Jinsai and Sorai.

---

**Masao Maruyama discusses Motoori's view of the ancient Way:**

According to Norinaga in *Naobi no mitama,* the way of life of the ancient Japanese, who were free of all normative restrictions and lived in accordance with "the true spirit [*magokoro*] they were born with" and "went through life tranquilly and happily," was as such the Way of the Gods. And the creation of the foundations of this Way of the Gods could be ascribed to the imperial ancestor gods: "What is the Way of the Gods? It is not the natural way of heaven and earth [this should be understood and not be confused with the views of the Chinese Taoists, added Norinaga], nor is it a way made by man. This Way was originated by the Gods Izanagi and Izanami in accordance with the spirit of the august deity Takami-musubi-no-kami, and was received, preserved, and handed down by the Sun Goddess, Amaterasu." In later ages, Norinaga argued in *Kuzubana,* the true or inborn spirit was obscured by the Chinese spirit, and the Way of the Gods was prevented from revealing itself in all its purity by the many norms "created by the sages . . . on the basis of their own private intellect." Of this turn of events, he observed in *Tamakushige,* "it is commonly said that it is the natural course of things for the conditions of society and the spirit of the people to change in this way with the changing times. However, these are not natural developments but are also *brought about by the actions of the gods.*" This decline was directly the work of the evil god, Magatsubi. But even an evil god is a god. Magatsubi, too, descends from the "spirit" (*mitama*) of the two gods, Takamimusubi and Kamimusubi, so man is helpless in the face of his actions.

*Masao Maruyama in his* Studies in the Intellectual History of Tokugawa Japan, *translated by Mikiso Hane, Princeton University Press, 1974.*

---

The fact that he was particularly susceptible to "the emotion of things" or *mono-no-aware* since he lived a life as a physician born of mercenary stock in the social system strictly divided into the four classes and because his family, which had once enjoyed wealth, was on the wane just like the Tokugawa shogunate in his days was presumably not unrelated to the formation of his thought.

What we have seen above is merely a digest of Norinaga's thought, and insofar as it is a digest, it would not comply with Norinaga's intention. Norinaga himself states at the end of the *Naobi no mitama* in which he himself summarizes his thought and method, ". . . Hence, although it is against the Way to discuss about it to this extent. . . ." Presumably Norinaga, who valued the "mode of verbal expression" (*monoii no sama*), means to say that his thought lies in each of the words he employs or more precisely in the tone of the words he utters. He would also have hoped that his thought be traced minutely through his detailed analysis of the archaic words he made in the *Kojiki-den* and other works. A thinker who never aspired to set forth his thought in the form of thought; a philosopher who never desired to present his philosophy in the form of philosophy—that was Motoori Norinaga.

*Yoshikawa Kōjirō, in his* Jinsai, Sorai, Norinaga: Three Classical Philologists of Mid-Tokugawa Japan, *The Tōhō Gakkai, 1983, 299 p.*

### John S. Brownlee   (essay date 1988)

[*In the following essay, Brownlee discusses* Tamakushige, *a discourse in which Motoori espouses Japanese nationalism.*]

Motoori Norinaga, 1730-1801, first wrote *Tamakushige, The Jeweled Comb-Box,* in 1786, with no apparent intention of publishing the essay. In the following year he composed *Hihon Tamakushige, The Jeweled Comb-Box: The Treasured Book,* in response to a wide-ranging request by Tokugawa Harusada, 1728-1789, the daimyo of Kii, for general advice on current problems in his domain. This second essay was then redrafted as a fuller version of *Tamakushige* to better illustrate Norinaga's teachings and was finally published in 1789. . . . The shorter essay, *Hihon Tamakushige,* appeared posthumously in 1851.

Tokugawa Harusada requested the advice of scholars because, as a result of the Temmei famine, the country was suffering from inflation and violence in the form of peasant protests and riots. When a daimyo asked for advice in such circumstances, he usually received learned tracts from Confucian scholars, offering counsel on politics and administration, stressing the correct postures for officials in positions of responsibility, and justifying their views by references to their preferred Chinese texts. Harusada may have read *Tamakushige* with some surprise, for the essay denounces Chinese thought as remote and fruitless, and claims that Confucian theories were of no practical use regarding the administration of Japan. *Tamakushige* was the first tract to base government on the Ancient Way of Japan, as found in the classical histories *Kojiki* and *Nihon Shoki,* rather than on the Chinese classics.

Norinaga was born in the small town of Matsuzaka in Ise province. In 1752, when he was twenty-two years old, he went to Kyoto to study Chinese medicine in order to become a physician and support his family as the head of the house. He also began to study Japanese literature and his interest was aroused by *Hyakunin Isshu Kaikanshō* by the priest-scholar Keichū, 1640-1701. Returning to Matsuzaka after five years of study, Norinaga set up practice as a physician, and the income from his medical practice eventually provided him with the leisure to develop his growing interest in Japanese studies.

The turning point in his life came in 1763 when he met Kamo no Mabuchi, 1697-1769, the leading scholar of ancient Japanese literature, who stopped for a single night at an inn in Matsuzaka. The 67-year-old Mabuchi and 34-year-old Norinaga passed the entire night in learned discussion. Mabuchi encouraged the younger man in his desire to study *Kojiki,* saying that it was essential to shed the Chinese influence and study the true mind of the ancient Japanese. This was feasible through a philological study of *Kojiki,* the earliest classic writing of Japan with the least Chinese influence in thought and style of expression.

For the rest of his life Norinaga constantly referred to the methods and aims of his master, Mabuchi, and this relationship sustained him even after Mabuchi's death in 1769, as he produced original works on Japanese language and literature. He progressed beyond the literary studies of his predecessors and sought to articulate the meaning of the Way by an exhaustive study of the texts dealing with the mythological and ancient periods of Japanese history. He spent thirty-four years writing **Kojikiden,** a monumental study of *Kojiki* that was completed in 1798.

When Norinaga wrote **Tamakushige,** he had already established a pattern of teaching, lecturing in cycles on the classics and *Genji Monogatari* at his residence in Matsuzaka. He experienced at first hand the contemporary social and economic problems, for they adversely affected his own life and activities. His career as physician and scholar suffered from the deterioration of social conditions, the details of which he noted in his diary. Income declined, students could not afford to continue their studies, and Norinaga was sometimes obliged to suspend lectures. Thus his suggestions in **Tamakushige** were, in his own mind, urgent and to the point. It may be doubted, however, whether Harusada found much in the essay to help him restore peace and prosperity to his domain.

*Nationalism in the Thought of Norinaga*

In denouncing Chinese theories of government and society, Norinaga joined one of the major trends of thought in the Tokugawa period. There had been a marked increase of intellectual activity with the social stability resulting from the founding of the Tokugawa bakufu in 1603. With official encouragement, the samurai elite turned from warfare to scholarship and administration, and a new era of intellectual history began in Japan. For the first time the discipline of systematic philosophy was widely practiced, both in the Chu Hsi school of Confucianism supported by the bakufu, and in the numerous domain schools and independent academies. This philoso-

phy posed difficulties for Japanese thinkers because it was based on Chinese texts, accepted the truth of Chinese assumptions, and employed basic concepts of Chinese metaphysics and epistemology, all of which required adaptation to the conditions of Japanese history and society.

The effort to make this adaptation was one of the main trends of Confucian thought in Japan, and it resulted in original developments such as the Sorai school, with which Norinaga was well acquainted. yet the Japanese adaptation of Chinese Confucianism remained unacceptable to many scholars precisely because of its Chinese origins. Some sought a specifically Japanese basis for thought, and Norinaga's predecessors in this endeavor are well known. Kada no Azumamaro, 1669-1736, was the first to seek explicit recognition of independent Japanese thought, while Kamo no Mabuchi developed such ideas further, delving deeply into the Japanese classics, especially *Man'yōshū,* to search for the Japanese Way. His approach was philological: as he told Norinaga, the ancient Japanese Way was to be found in the ancient words. Norinaga enlarged the scope of his teacher's studies beyond literature into history and philosophy. His philosophical range included epistemology, metaphysics, aesthetics, and ethics, although the divisions were not clearly marked in Tokugawa times and scholars broadly tackled all issues.

In method, Norinaga was the equal of the Confucian philosophers of the day, and this was important for the credibility of his position. Ogyū Sorai, 1666-1728, rejected the accumulated interpretations of centuries of Chinese philosophical study in favor of a return to the ancient texts as the basis for determining the Way of the Former Kings. Similarly Norinaga based his ideas upon a profound study of ancient Japanese works, and his multi-volume commentary of *Kojiki* will never be equaled.

Norinaga's nationalistic stance is found throughout his writings. He constantly criticized Chinese thought, and held up Japanese concepts as correct and superior. In his essay **Uiyamabumi,** 1798, he lamented that people assume 'studies' means 'Chinese studies', while studies of his own land are labeled 'Japanese studies'. This should not be, claimed Norinaga: 'studies' in general should refer to the studies of a person's native land, and it is the studies of foreign countries that should be distinguished, as in 'Chinese studies'. Similarly, in **Tamakushige,** Norinaga pointed out that the fact that the Sun Goddess was born in Japan demonstrates the country's superiority vis-à-vis other nations. He even went on to say that Japanese rice is by far the best in the world, yet another indication of Japan's blessed superiority. Of Norinaga's extreme belief in his country's divinely bestowed uniqueness there can be no doubt.

*Myths and Rationalism*

Throughout his writings Norinaga emphasized the weak and limited nature of human intellect—it cannot extend to the great principles of life and the universe, and these mysteries must remain forever unfathomed. Not only is intellect limited, it is uncreative. In an astonishing passage in **Tamakatsuma,** a miscellany begun in 1793, Norinaga observed that human intellect can never produce a human being, whereas an ordinary man and woman, with no special thought and without the aid of any instruments, can create a baby. Yet, as he pointed out repeatedly and heatedly, in China the custom was to understand everything on the basis of ideas generated by human intellect. These ideas, he complained, have no basis in reality. Such fundamental Chinese concepts as yin and yang, the five elements, the trigrams, and so forth, were nothing but false constructs of conceited intellect. Hence it was no accident that China displayed a disordered political history, in contrast to Japan's stable succession of emperors.

Norinaga saw the need to expose the inadequacies of Chinese philosophy in order to lay a correct foundation for Japanese political thought. This is why *Tamakushige,* his discourse on government, contains an extended discussion of the Land of the Dead as understood in a myth found in *Kojiki* and *Nihon Shoki.* This discourse is not a digression, as it may appear at first sight, for its purpose is to put forward an independent Japanese version of human destiny and at the same time refute the grievous errors that arise from using ideas generated by human intellect. In Chinese thought, both Confucianist and Buddhist teachings about the fate of human beings after death were wrong, Norinaga claimed, and these errors had been transmitted to Japan. The Chinese believed in the existence of various heavens and hells, and they held that a person's destiny is determined by his own moral behavior during life. Under these delusions, people faced their end with false attitudes, seeing visions of the buddhas, hearing music, and smelling fragrant perfumes. They composed deathbed poems expressing resignation, acceptance, or even joy at the prospect of death.

All of this, Norinaga maintained, was wrong. Death is, and should be, a matter for sorrow. Everyone, rich or poor, high or low, good or evil, must go to the Land of the Dead and remain there, forever separated from family and parents. This truth about death cannot be understood from intellectual reasoning; it is known only from a tale about the Land of the Dead that has been transmitted from the Age of the Gods. The deity Izanagi descended into the Land of the Death in search of his departed wife, the deity Izanami. The place was dark and gloomy, and the deities there were ugly, selfish, and aggressive.

According to Norinaga, this singular tale, transmitted in Japan alone, contained the truth. Of course, it was easier to accept the plausible rationalizations about death held in Chinese traditions than to face the grim reality of the Land of the Dead. Everyone naturally prefers the paradises of Buddhism; unfortunately these heavens do not exist.

Norinaga developed his belief in the literal existence and continuing activities of the deities into the basis for his whole philosophy. In ancient times, he wrote, some of the gods were visible, and some invisible. In modern times, they are mostly invisible, but they are known through their activities; the Sun Goddess, the most important of all, is of course visible, for she is seen daily by everyone. The activities of these deities neatly solved, for Norinaga, the perennial problem of evil in the world, because evil results from the activities of the wicked deities. In his view, the explanation for good and evil lay plainly in the tales

transmitted from the Age of the Gods. It is only necessary to read them and understand what they say, and not try to explain away their meaning by the exercise of intellect. Norinaga maintained faith in the ultimate triumph of good, although he could cite no authority to support this view. The records of the Age of the Gods describe the activities of the good and evil deities, but say nothing about the final victory of the good deities.

Thus Norinaga's interpretation of the tale about the Land of the Dead was completely literal, as was also his general approach to the entire body of myths recorded in *Kojiki* and *Nihon Shoki.* He knew where he stood, and he understood the implications of his position. Unlike his nationalist tendencies regarding the superiority of Japan, an outlook generally shared in one form or other by most Tokugawa intellectuals, Norinaga's insistence on the literal interpretation of the ancient myths was by no means uncritically accepted. Alternative positions, advocating rationalization of the myths, had been clearly delineated in Tokugawa Japan and had put Norinaga on the defensive.

*Opposing Schools of Thought*

The current Neo-Confucianism viewed history fundamentally as a record of facts. In China, the purpose of compiling the facts into historical works was to demonstrate virtue and evil in rulers, thereby presenting a guide for administrators. Behind this lay the belief that Heaven countenances the continuing rule of virtuous rulers only, and that this principle accounts for the rise and fall of dynasties in China. Bad rulers fell, by the ordinance of Heaven, to be replaced by good ones. Neo-Confucians believed that this truth was clearly demonstrated by an objective and dispassionate review of the events of history; there was no need to twist or distort the facts.

When this attitude toward history was transferred to Japan, an adaptation obviously had to be made for the fact that there had never been a change of imperial dynasty, and historians conveniently transferred the burden of praise and opprobrium to lesser figures, such as regents and shoguns. A dispassionate and indeed critical attitude toward the facts of history was displayed by Hayashi Razan, 1583-1657, who was an adviser to Tokugawa Ieyasu and initial author of *Honchō Tsugan,* a work that greatly influenced the even more critical Arai Hakuseki, 1657-1725. The most important application of Razan's thought appears in his *Jimmu Tennō Ron.* According to *Kojiki,* Emperor Jimmu descended from heavenly ancestors, inaugurated his rule of Japan in 660 B.C., and moved eastward, subduing resistance along the way. Well acquainted with Chinese sources, Razan supported the suggestion that the imperial house had in fact been founded as an offshoot of a Chinese ruling family by Wu Taibo, a member of the house of Zhou. The records tell that Wu left China in the thirteenth century B.C., which, with a certain amount of juggling, might correspond to the heavenly descent of Emperor Jimmu. Although the story of Wu Taibo was well known in Japan, this was the first time that a prominent scholar had used it to present a rational interpretation of the historical basis of the Jimmu myth.

An even more challenging position to Norinaga's teachings had been adopted by Arai Hakuseki, who offered, in his *Koshitsū,* a reinterpretation of ancient history that was far-reaching in its implications. Hakuseki accepted as substantially true the narratives presented in *Kojiki* and *Nihon Shoki,* but he made a vital transposition for the purpose of better understanding: the acts recorded in the ancient books were not those of gods, but of men. He stated his fundamental insight thus: 'What are called the gods are human beings.' Hakuseki's respect for the great shrines such as Ise and Atsuta was not thereby diminished, because he sought not to destroy the myths but to find their true and hidden meaning. He maintained that inexact knowledge of the uses of Chinese characters had brought about a misunderstanding of the way the ancients viewed human heroes. The ancient people revered their outstanding men and called them beautiful. But reading about them in the way that the characters subsequently came to be understood, later generations believed that the ancients worshipped gods rather than respected human beings.

In addition to viewing the ancient gods as heroes rather than deities, Hakuseki sought to rationalize other aspects of the myths. He devoted much energy to a study of place names mentioned in the myths, submitting them to an analysis of language usage. He suggested, for example, that the Plain of High Heaven, Takamagahara, was merely a place in Hitachi province. He also rationalized the acts of the gods, for example, proposing that the tales about the birth of Japan were merely myths representing the historical act of people opening up new land to agricultural use in ancient times.

Tokugawa-period rationalization was so strong that it influenced even scholars for whom the myths of the Age of the Gods were essential. *Dai-Nihon Shi* was a major work of loyalist history, and hence it was necessarily based on the ancient myths. But the sponsor of the work, Tokugawa Mitsukuni, 1628-1701, admitted, 'The matters of the Age of the Gods are all strange, and hard to include in the chronicle of Emperor Jimmu.' Accordingly the work did not begin with the founding of Japan by the gods, but with the inauguration of imperial rule by Jimmu. However, it did concede the main point of the Age of the Gods by listing Jimmu's descent from the Sun Goddess. Asaka Tampaku, 1656-1737, one of the scholars who worked on *Dai-Nihon Shi,* was even more emphatic and declared, 'The events of the Age of the Gods are far-fetched and insignificant, and should be disregarded.'

*Conclusion*

It is ironic that belief in the activity of the gods led Norinaga to adopt a conservative social philosophy that differed hardly at all from that of his Confucian adversaries. Since everything that exists is in accord with the will of the gods, including the evil gods, then it is harmful and contrary to the divine will to attempt to make reforms. Evil practices and customs are brought about by evil gods. It is important, he said, that inferiors should respect their superiors, and each man should do what he is naturally equipped to do: obey his lord, be dutiful to his parents, and work hard at the family enterprise. These are the things that lie within the powers of humans; the larger issues of war and

peace, famine and plague, are the doings of the gods; their causes cannot be comprehended, let alone remedied.

Norinaga grappled unsuccessfully in **Tamakushige** with the general question of what constitutes the sphere of divine activity, and what humans ought to attempt. He introduced the concept of a sacred sphere and a secular sphere, based on a covenant made in the Age of the Gods between the Sun Goddess and her representative, the deity Takami Musubi, on the one hand, and the deity Ōkuninushi on the other, regarding the respective jurisdictions of the succession of emperors and Ōkuninushi. According to this agreement, secular matters involved all the affairs regularly carried out by organized government, and Norinaga believed that the Tokugawa government of the day was correctly performing its proper functions. But he proceeded to destroy this distinction between the sacred and the profane spheres by observing that since the agreement was made between two deities, both spheres must ultimately be considered sacred. He never managed to repair the damage that this observation made to his entire political philosophy. In his defense it may be noted that the thrust of Confucian thought was to connect, rather than separate, the divine and human arenas, and that no equivalent of the Western problem of free will existed in East Asian philosophy.

We are not told the reaction of Tokugawa Harusada to **Tamakushige.** Concerned about the political management of economic problems, he was doubtless seeking practical advice to remedy the unstable situation obtaining in his fief. Instead, he may well have been puzzled by Norinaga's insistence on the will of the gods and the need to reject Chinese thought, and by his lengthy disquisition on the Land of the Dead. The essay ends up saying nothing more helpful than that the government was in good order, and everyone ought to perform his time-honored duties. Perhaps Norinaga had misunderstood the request?

In the light of hindsight, modern scholars have paid tribute to the originality and pertinence of Norinaga's ideas. Ōkubo Tadashi, for example, notes that Norinaga generated a new approach, quite different from that of Sorai, who largely concentrated on the techniques to be exercised by those in authority. Norinaga noted in his diary the conditions of the ordinary people's daily life and spoke essentially for them. He believed in the same things as they did, for Shinto is the heritage of all the Japanese people, and he brought those beliefs to bear on political discussion for the first time. For this reason, Ōkubo considers **Tamakushige** a classic deserving careful reading.

There exists yet another aspect of Norinaga's teachings, not generally articulated. His ideas constitute the fountainhead of modern Japanese nationalistic thought. Norinaga forcefully propounded the uniqueness and superiority of Japan because of the nation's divine origins and the unbroken imperial succession. The only thing that is missing is Japan's special mission to generate harmony throughout Asia. Although a long period of historical development, full of contingencies, lay between Norinaga and the Japanese imperialists of the twentieth century, it is difficult to deny that there is a connection.

But it would be unfair to blame Norinaga for what happened to his ideas after his death. Instead, we may appreciate his ability to penetrate to the central values of Japanese national life and articulate them so clearly. More than this, we should separate his ideas from their subsequent political development, and observe the output of a brilliant and systematic mind in a purely scholarly endeavor. His work on *Kojiki,* for example, will never be equaled. But the basis for his thought—literal belief in the myths from the Age of the Gods, and outright espousal of the irrational— is widely unacceptable among modern intellectuals who are likely to encounter his work. A single reading of *Kojiki* and *Nihon Shoki* is enough to realize that Norinaga's belief in the literal truth of the myths contained in those two records was questionable for an educated man of the eighteenth century. For this reason it is important that his works be introduced in translation, that he may have his day in court and display the excellent nature of his reasoning, if only we are permitted to disallow his premises.

*John S. Brownlee, "The Jeweled Comb-Box: Motoori Norinaga's 'Tamakushige',"* in Monumenta Nipponica, *Vol. 43, No. 1, Spring, 1988, pp. 35-61.*

---

# FURTHER READING

Matsumoto, Shigeru. *Motoori Norinaga, 1730-1801.* Cambridge, Mass.: Harvard University Press, 1970, 261 p.

Biographical and psychological study of Motoori.

Nishimura, Sey. "First Steps into the Mountains: Motoori Norinaga's *Uiyamabumi.*" *Monumenta Nipponica* 42, No. 4 (Winter 1987): 449-93.

Discusses Motoori's guidebook for students of literature. A translation of the work follows the essay.

# Friedrich Schlegel

## 1772-1829

(Full name Karl Friedrich August Schlegel) German critic, essayist, and novelist.

## INTRODUCTION

Considered the founder of modern literary scholarship, Schlegel is primarily known as an early proponent of German Romantic literature, the main theoretician of Romantic irony, and the co-founder, along with his brother August Wilhelm, of the influential journal *Das Athenäum*. The two brothers were important members of the Jena circle, a group associated with the University of Jena that included such Romantic writers as Ludwig Tieck, Friedrich Schleiermacher, and Novalis. Schlegel is noted for his paradoxical manner of writing and his enigmatic "fragments"—condensed, aphoristic essays and reviews in which he expressed many of his most important critical ideas. Although he was regarded as a literary eccentric due to this unconventional approach to criticism, his abstruse aesthetic theories came to embody the literary program of the Romantics. Schlegel applied these theories to his novel *Lucinde*, an experimental work which foreshadowed the development of the modern novel.

Schlegel was born in Hanover, the son of Johann Adolf Schlegel, a noted hymn writer and fabulist, and the nephew of the dramatist and critic Johann Elias Schlegel. Although his family had planned for him a career in banking, Friedrich decided to follow his elder brother August Wilhelm to Göttingen University, becoming an authority on the literature and culture of ancient Greece. Moving to Leipzig in 1791, he established friendships with the poet Novalis and with Caroline Böhmer, a political revolutionary and gifted thinker whose radical views greatly influenced his philosophy of history and literature. In 1798 Friedrich and his brother launched the landmark journal *Athenäum*. Although lasting only three years and having a readership of less than 1,200, the journal became the main voice of the early German Romantic movement and established Friedrich Schlegel as one of the movement's most innovative and insightful theorists. In 1799, Schlegel wrote his only novel, *Lucinde*, loosely based on his affair with his then mistress and future wife, Dorothea Veit, the daughter of philosopher Moses Mendelssohn. *Lucinde*'s frank sexual content scandalized the German literary world, and Schlegel was considered so obscene that in certain towns he was denied permission to stay overnight. In 1802 he settled in Paris, hoping to study Oriental philosophy and languages and support himself by lecturing on German literature. During his stay he started his second journal, *Europa*, which lasted only four issues. At this time he also developed an interest in Catholicism. This religious curiosity intensified upon his return to Germany in 1804, and four years later he announced his official conversion to Catholicism. By then Schlegel had grown con-

servative: to the dismay of his friends and fellow Romantics, he renounced the radical social views and artistic experimentalism he championed in his youth. Schlegel continued to produce scholarly works in his later years, publishing *Uber die Sprache und Weisheit der Indier*, a study of the language and philosophy of India, as well as *Geschichte der alten und neuen Literatur*, a survey of the history of literature, and *Philosophie der Geschichte*, a series of lectures on the history of thought, religion, and political institutions. He died in Dresden of a stroke in 1829.

Schlegel's early works reflect his classical training. The essays collected in *Die Griechen und Römer* and *Geschichte der Poesie der Griechen und Römer* are conventional treatises which trace European literary history, emphasizing the intellectual and social circumstances in which classical literature was produced. In these essays, Schlegel contrasted ancient and modern poetry, asserting his preference for the former. While Schlegel felt an affinity for classical poetry, he also attempted to understand modern literature. Schlegel's philosophy undergoes a change in emphasis in the essays and fragments written for the *Athenäum*. In these works he praises modern, post-classical poetry precisely because it is characterized by incessant revision, a "restless longing for the new, the piquant, and the striking." In his exploration of the differences between classical and modern poetry, Schlegel hoped to forge a synthesis of the two; he labeled this hybrid literature "romantic" (*romantisch*), and defined it in *Athenäum Fragment 116* as "a progressive, universal poetry. . . . It tries to and should mix and fuse poetry and prose, inspiration and criticism. . . . The romantic kind of poetry is still in the state of becoming; that, in fact, is its real essence: that it should forever be becoming and never be perfected." In *Gespräch über die Poesie*, a four-part treatise on the nature of poetry presented in the form of a Socratic dialogue, Schlegel suggests that the novel (*roman*) is the new genre destined to embody this poetic ideal. His own attempt at the novel, *Lucinde*, is a mixture of various genres. Its radical structure combines a fragmentary narrative with letters, fantasies, allegories, dialogues, and essays, and follows virtually no chronological order. Although containing little plot, the novel essentially depicts the emotional growth of Julius, a semi-autobiographical figure, through a series of relationships; ultimately, he finds both physical and spiritual gratification with Lucinde, a character reminiscent of Dorothea Veit.

During his lifetime and throughout the nineteenth century, Schlegel's position as a critic was overshadowed by that of his older brother August Wilhelm, an influential theoretician of aesthetics and translator of Shakespeare. This subdued recognition stemmed in part from his conversion to Catholicism, which prevented him from republishing his works in predominantly Protestant Germany, as well as from the fragmentary, esoteric style that characterizes much of his prose. Modern commentators, however, note that the basic concepts behind the elder Schlegel's literary criticism were in fact adaptations of Friedrich's ideas. The *Athenäum Fragments* and *Gespräch über die Poesie* are generally regarded as Schlegel's most important contributions to the history of criticism. The theories developed in these texts greatly impressed his contemporaries and became a manifesto for Jena Romanticism. Critics also credit the *Fragments* for introducing the concept of irony into modern literary discussion. According to Schlegel, it was by exploring the concept of irony, the "form of the paradox" as he defined it, that a poet gained insight and achieved a "feeling for the universe." Of his later writings, *Uber die Sprache und Weisheit der Indier* is seen as an inaugurating document in the field of Indic philology. *Geschichte der alten und neuen Literatur* and *Philosophie der Geschichte* are widely admired, and have prompted René Wellek to call Schlegel "one of the greatest critics of history."

---

# PRINCIPAL WORKS

*Die Griechen und Römer* (criticism) 1797
*Lyceums-Fragmente* (essays) 1797
  [*Lyceum Fragments* published in *Friedrich Schlegel's* Lucinde *and the Fragments*, 1971]

*Athenäums-Fragmente* (essays) 1798
  [*Athenäum Fragments* published in *Friedrich Schlegel's* Lucinde *and the Fragments*, 1971]
*Geschichte der Poesie der Griechen und Römer* (criticism) 1798
"Uber Goethes *Meister*" (essay) 1798
*Lucinde: Ein Roman* (novel) 1799
  [*Lucinde* published in *Friedrich Schlegel's* Lucinde *and the Fragments*, 1971]
*Gespräch über die Poesie* (dialogues) 1800
  [*Dialogue on Poetry* published in *Dialogue on Poetry and Literary Aphorisms*, 1968]
*Ideen* (essays) 1800
  [*Ideas* published in *Friedrich Schlegel's* Lucinde *and the Fragments*, 1971]
"Uber die Unverständlichkeit" (essay) 1800
  ["On Incomprehensibility" published in *Friedrich Schlegel's* Lucinde *and the Fragments*, 1971]
*Alacros: Ein traverspiel in zwei Aufzügen* (drama) 1802
*Uber die Sprache und Weisheit der Indier* (essay) 1808
  ["On the Language and Wisdom of the Indians" published in *The Aesthetic and Miscellaneous Works of Friedrich von Schlegel*, 1849]
*Geschichte der alten und neuen Literatur*. 2 Vols. (lectures) 1812
  [*Lectures on the History of Literature, Ancient and Modern*, 1818]
*Sämmtliche Werke*. 10 vols. (criticism, essays, lectures, drama) 1822-25
*Philosophie des Lebens* (lectures) 1827
  [*The Philosophy of Life and Philosophy of Language in a Course of Lectures*, 1847]
*Philosophie der Geschichte* (lecture) 1828
  [*Philosophy of History*, 1835]
*Friedrich Schlegel 1794-1802: Seine prosaischen Jugenschriften*. 2 vols. (essays, criticism, novel) 1882
*Literary Notebooks 1797-1801* (notebooks) 1957
*Kritische Friedrich Schlegel-Ausgabe*. 24 vols. (essays, criticism, novel, drama, lectures) 1958–

---

# CRITICISM

## *The Westminster Review* (essay date 1825)

[*In the following essay, the critic appraises Schlegel's Collected Works (1823-24), concluding that his writings are "interesting and valuable." The critic notes, however, that Schlegel's religious and political views resulted in a biased assessment of world literature.*]

Frederick Schlegel is the brother of Augustus William Schlegel, well known in England as the translator of Shakespeare, as the friend of Madame de Stael, and as one of the greatest linguists and philologists of the day. Frederick was born at Hanover, in the year 1772, and, although intended for a merchant, received an excellent education. On being sent, in his sixteenth year, into a counting-house at Leipsic, the contrast between his previous pursuits and the monotony of his new life, made the former doubly precious to him, and he felt that powerful disinclination to trade which has been experienced by so many young men who have aspired to fame, and which is so well described by Goethe in his *Wilhelm Meister*. He almost immediately gave up business in disgust, and returned to study. Just then literature and science were, in Germany, at full flood. Wieland and Herder were not long past the meridian of their splendor, and Goethe and Schiller were contending, like brothers more than rivals, for the palm of glory. Wolf had reduced philology to a science; and Schelling and Fichte had risen, from the instructions of Kant, equal to their master. All these great men had a commanding influence over the youth of that period, and among them Novalis, Tieck and the Schlegels were particularly distinguished. Frederick Schlegel, at first, devoted himself more particularly to the study of every thing connected with ancient Greece; afterwards he was deeply interested by the writings of Goethe and Fichte. In some of the sentiments he then entertained, we find more evidence of enthusiasm than of good sense.

It was not long before he tried his powers as an author. He published, in 1797, the first part of a very remarkable work, though it has never been completed, under the title of **Griechen und Roemer**; and in 1798 he published **Die Poesie der Griechen und Roemer.** In 1797 his brother Augustus William, himself, and Tieck originated a periodical work called the *Athenaum;* his articles in it were distinguished by bold and original paradoxes. It was very soon evident, that he loved notoriety more than truth, and cared little about the correctness of a thought, if it were only striking. At this period, top, he wrote **Lucinde** a romance, which was, in form and spirit, a copy of the *Fiametta* of Boccacio. The author seems to have thought the world might be amused by a history of his amours, and by exaggerated pictures of sensual enjoyment ending in madness. In this he was mistaken; his book was more decried and condemned then read, and the second part has never been published.

Schlegel, like many others, prepared the way, by sensuality, for disgust and bigotry. An ill-regulated imagination, a passion for distinction, and a sort of wild enthusiasm for the age of chivalry, had at that period led many able men from the paths of simplicity and truth. Winkelman forsook Protestantism for Papacy out of mere motives of worldly interest; but, subsequently, several poets, authors, and artists, turned Catholics because the Protestant mode of worship was too formal, and unfavourable to the fine arts and to poetry. Frederick Schlegel was one of these. In 1802, he and his wife both renounced the Protestant heresy, and sought consolation in the bosom of the Catholic church; and from that time to the present he has been enlisted in the ranks of those who see no salvation for mankind, either here or hereafter, but through the instrumentality of a legitimate monarchy and an infallible hierarchy.

All his writings, since this change, have been dictated by some narrow and unfounded theory. That he has a great command of language cannot be denied; and his translation of the Latin poetry of the middle ages, his *Lothar,* and his *Maller,* are quite admirable for their style, but are poor in matter and in thought. In 1808, when he went to Vien-

na, he appeared to have caught something of the general feelings which then prevailed in Germany, and to entertain a proper sense of the injuries his country suffered by the oppression of Napoleon. In 1809, he accompanied count Stadion to Bavaria, and gave himself the trouble to assume the character of a liberal; but it was evident to those who could appreciate him, that like all apostates, he hated the religion he had forsaken; and that his only object was, to obtain consideration and preferment by supporting the opinions of the Austrian oligarchy. When the campaign had been decided in favour of Buonaparte, he returned to Vienna, and was more closely united than ever with Gentz, and more patronized by Metternich. Here, being no longer required by his patrons to fan the weak and lambent flame of German patriotism, he resumed his old studies, and wrote lectures on modern history, and those lectures on literature, which are to be more immediately the object of our remarks. His doctrines and opinions were so pleasing to prince Metternich that he sent him to Frankfort as a counsellor of legation. But, by this time, a change of circumstances made this crafty diplomatist sensible that it was time to repress that ardour in favour of freedom which he had endeavoured to rouse when the object was to overthrow Buonaparte; and Schlegel was recalled to Vienna that he might, by his writings in the Quarterly Review—(*Jahrbücher der Litteratur*), and John Bull (*Concordia*), of Vienna, oppose the growing love of the Austrians for freedom and independence. He has ever since continued to labour in this his vocation with a success greatly, we believe, to the satisfaction of his employers, and the regret of all men who have at heart the amelioration of mankind.

We have been induced to give this short sketch of Schlegel's life, that we might enable our readers duly to appreciate some of his writings. His work on ancient and modern literature has been translated into English, and may be expected to have some influence in England. Schlegel, however unsound in his judgment, is unquestionably a man of considerable talent and great acquirements. He is an eloquent writer and an acute reasoner, and if not a sound is a very ingenious critic; he is well acquainted with the languages, poetry, and philosophy, both of the ancient and modern world; and he has acquired considerable reputation by his writings. But a wish to justify his own apostacy and his present political opinions have given a tendency to his labours, against which it is necessary to warn the reader. His eloquence and his acuteness are both directed to prove, by the circumstances of civil and literary history, that the principle of an absolute monarchy, united with hierarchy, is of divine origin.

This is just the sort of jesuitical book which appears to convince the understanding while it only strengthens prejudice. That patriotism and a due sense of religion are virtuous emotions few men doubt; and on these, says Schlegel, must every national literature be founded. A perversion of terms, a cunning misapplication of names which stand for some emotions that are dear to the hearts and cherish the best associations of man, is precisely one of the means by which designing men in all ages have triumphed over the plain and unsuspecting understandings of the great mass of mankind. What emotion is supposed to be more sacred than a love of country. It is the love of home, of the endearments of infancy, of our friends and kindred, it is the love of all we have ever learnt to respect or have enjoyed through the brightest days of our existence. Those, however, who wish to obtain or preserve political power, have artfully applied the name of this engrossing and delightful sentiment to a narrow obedience to their political systems, and to a reverence for the institutions by which their power is secured. They conjure up the sentiment by the word, and they seek to invest erroneous and absurd institutions with all the security which can be derived from the strongest and most permanent affections of the heart and mind. No where has this cunning system been, of late, more systematically acted on than in Austria. For a long time the government of that country succeeded in checking the influx of improvement by mere negative measures. The people were surrounded by a wall of moral prohibitions, which the emperor Joseph, the French revolution, and the war for freedom, burst through in several places. It has since been found that the old mounds would be quite insufficient to check the flood of knowledge, and it was resolved so to divert and spread the stream, that it might be completely under the guidance of those whose only object is, to make every thing subservient to their own power. Gentz, a literary man, has the credit of having recommended to prince Metternich an extension of the old system, of perverting what could not be stopped. Werner, Kollin, Adam Müller, Haller, Schlegel, and others, all men of talent, but of weak judgment, who had forsaken the plainness of Protestantism for the gauds of Popery, and unpaid liberalism for the bounties of a court, were severally invited to Vienna, and were ennobled and caressed, that they might employ their ingenuity in turning the desire of knowledge in the people to the account of their rulers. Doubts and inquiries were to be answered with eloquence, but eloquence glozing over fraud; and the strong emotions which circumstances had excited were not to be suppressed, but directed to some vague chimeras beyond the government and the church. Too well have they succeeded, and the glowing spirit of enthusiasm finding no nutritive food, grew sick with disappointment, and has, at length, apparently ended in more servile submission, and in swelling that licentiousness which has so long distinguished the Austrian capital and people.

It is in this point of view that Schlegel's literary history calls for our notice. It is a fair specimen of the mode employed, under the direction of the governments of Germany, to beguile men into error by pretending to teach them truth, and to amuse them with a vain parade of trifling or useless knowledge. Schlegel has the art of appearing disinterested, and writes without passion, though he never loses sight of the main object of his labours. He pretends to take a calm view of his whole subject; his apparent impartiality acquires the confidence of his reader, which he abuses by omitting to notice those authors whose writings make against his theory, whatever it happens to be, or by only noticing the errors which they, in common with other men, may have committed. Authors, whose writings are favourable to his views, are, on the other hand, praised beyond measure, and their errors justified or defended. All his observations, however general they may appear, are made to bear on present times and circumstances, and ex-

pressly intended to impose on the minds of his readers those opinions which the Austrian government is peculiarly desirous of circulating.

We agree with him, for example, that philosophy must be one of the subjects treated of in literary history, of which, as it relates to the mind, it is the most important part. We fully agree with him, too, that literature would lose very much, if those who are favoured by fortune and called by birth to the highest offices of the state, were to neglect the improvement of the mind, and only devote themselves to their public duties; leaving the cultivation of the arts and sciences wholly to those who are excluded by circumstances from the high offices of the state, and the actual business of the nation. But we do not agree in the conclusion which he draws from this circumstance, namely, that a class of nobles are the natural instructors of mankind, and that other men are destined to receive the impress of their character, and the form of their civilization, from them. It is, we believe, quite necessary, wherever a nobility is in the exclusive possession of the government and the higher officers of state, that such a doctrine should be taught; for knowledge and civilization, which do not flow from them, will unquestionably soon destroy their privileged existence. They who will have or keep power must have superior knowledge; and any *class* of men can only have this by excluding others from the acquisition. Certainly a society takes the most effectual means of limiting its own power, when it will suffer only one small portion of its members to seek knowledge, and when they and all the rest are limited in their inquiries by a necessity of avoiding every thing which might, by a remote possibility, lead to the diminution of certain pre-established privileges. If Mr. Schlegel's deduction were correct, Hungary or Poland should have outstripped Holland and England; Turkey should have been the furthest advanced, and the United States of North America the most backward, in knowledge, power, and improvement.

Having thus pointed out the general principle which has guided the pen of the author, we shall be brief in our notice of some individual lectures. In the first he describes the poetry of the Greeks up to the time of Socrates, and in the second, their literature and philosophy during the latter part of their career, including the Alexandrian school. Here he remarks very appropriately, "our present modes of thought, and our knowledge, are so closely derived from the ancients, that it is difficult to treat of literature without beginning with them. It is also preferable to begin with the Greeks, because their mental culture seems to have sprung and grown up entirely among themselves, and to be almost independent of the civilization of other nations." Poor Homer must be made to advocate modern priestcraft. According to our author he had some presentiment of a higher, if not of a revealed religion, while Hesiod is described as supporting in opposition to Homer a sort of materialism. Hesiod, therefore, the less national, the less successful poet, was the type of the French philosophers, and Homer, who will be eternally read and admired, owed much of his success to his writings being in accord with the national feelings, and from foreseeing, as it were, the religious principles which were afterwards to guide the world.

If Mr. Schlegel fails in making Homer a very useful auxiliary in the cause of the hierarchy, he does him ample justice as a poet. But the writings of Homer have, in this respect, been so long duly appreciated, that it seems hardly necessary to repeat Mr. Schlegel's remarks, particularly as we see in them nothing very new or very profound.

Pindar was accused by the ancients of being too much attached to the Persians. The manner in which he is defended by Schlegel shows that this critic thinks even a want of patriotism is a virtue, if it is lost in admiration of a foreign monarch and of a civilizing nobility. "The reproach made to Pindar," he says, "may be easily explained. It is evident, from his poems, that he disliked the dominion of the people, which even at that time had occasioned several contentions in Greece, and seemed likely to lead to still greater confusion. Among the Doric tribes, also, the power of the nobility was great, and there was a strong attachment to the monarchical form of government. In the ancient world this and the dominion of a higher order of nobility, never appeared in a more splendid and favourable point of view than in the Persian empire; which, however individual monarchs might have abused their power, was founded on high-minded thoughts and pure and noble manners." Pindar, therefore, had the great merit, in the eyes of Mr. Schlegel, of hating democracy and loving kingly power. Any man may have the same partialities, but, in general, we look for them only among those who have been *born* the subjects of a monarch, who are paid like Mr. Schlegel for entertaining them, or who being ambitious and wanting abilities to attain honourable distinction where competition is entirely free, are ready to barter mind and heart, and sacrifice thought and sentiment, for the poor nicknames and collars with which a Tzar or a Kaiser designates, as a huntsman does his dogs, the miserable slaves who yelp down the imperial prey.

We pass over all Schlegel's remarks on the other Greek poets, historians, and philosophers, which are both correct and well-expressed, regretting merely that a man who has displayed such powers should have perverted them to so mischievous a purpose. Of Demosthenes, Schlegel says not a word; and why? because his powerful eloquence was directed against a monarch. If this sort of emasculation of mind goes on for a few years in Austria, we shall expect to find the history of Germany re-written, and the rude members of the House of Hapsburg all transformed into Bayards or Grandisons. In the same spirit Schlegel, when treating of the literature of Rome, has omitted to mention Catullus, who was guilty of failing in respect for the emperor; and has endeavoured to gain for Virgil the reputation of a national poet, because he reverenced his sovereign as a God—*et erit mihi semper deus.* We were somewhat surprised that the author should do justice to Tacitus, but of him he says—"Of the Latin authors there is only one more whom it is necessary to mention, Tacitus. The profound sense of this author, who is full of thought, and the brevity and strength of his style which is admirably adapted to his matter, appears the more inimitable, as various authors have attempted in vain to imitate him. In these three authors the Latin language is found in its greatest purity and perfection: in Caesar, with unadorned simplicity and grandeur; in Livy, with all the pomp and ornament of oratorical perfection, but, without exaggeration, and beautifully and nobly formed; in Tacitus, with depth, strength, and art, full of the ancient dignity of old Rome."

In writing the history of the literature of the Romans, we expected that the author would have described the progress of their jurisprudence; particularly as he subsequently takes occasion to refer much of what is good in modern civilization to the influence of the Roman laws. Up to the time of the Twelve Tables, or rather to the time of the law named after Publius, the Romans had no written laws, and were governed by a code which was known only to the priests. In the second period of the Roman history, or under the aristocracy, the form of proceeding was still regulated by this common law; but the laws themselves were written and acted on to the very letter. Under the emperors both law and justice became more scientific, or rather theoretical, and allowed the utmost latitude to arbitrary decisions; they were, in fact, mere names or algebraical signs, which were explained according to the fancy of the judge. That this system could have contributed to the progress of European civilization, as contended for by Mr. Schlegel, is impossible. We should rather say that the Roman and Ecclesiastical laws had impeded and perverted the development of the national institutions, at least of Germany, and checked its freedom by introducing learned subtleties and artificial distinctions. These two branches of law have, we honestly believe, done more injury to the progress of mankind, than the eruptions and devastations of the Huns and the Goths.

We shall devote a few words to some parts of the sixth, seventh, and eight lectures, in which Mr. Schlegel discusses the literature of the middle ages, and particularly of Germany. He mentions Theodorick, Charlemagne, and our own Alfred, as having been the chief promoters of the literature of their respective people. But before their time Ulphilas had translated the Bible from the Greek into Gothic, though his version was prose. The northern languages and literature were earlier cultivated, therefore, than the author supposes; and *Beowulf,* a poem of the third and fourth centuries, in a northern tongue, is a decisive proof of the high antiquity of the literature of the Germans. Mr. Schlegel supposes that the Germans on the borders of the Baltic, derived their Runic characters from the Phoenicians, who came there to trade. According to tradition, however, they were invented by *Teut,* which seems to mean, that the Runic characters were invented by the Teutschen (Germans). Runa signifies, sometimes poetry, sometimes written characters, and sometimes magic. But as religion, magic, and poetry, are among all people originally one and the same, the Runic characters must have been the first religious writing of the Germans, and were probably nearly coeval with their spoken language.

The author assumes, as unquestioned, the genuineness of the ancient Edda; we are disposed, however, to believe, that a considerable part of it was written at later periods. The travels of Thor are undoubtedly an invention of aftertimes. That the Edda, however, in its original form, existed before the poems of Ossian, or earlier than ninth century is quite certain, from the poem of Beowulf, and from other Anglo-Saxon poems of the seventh century, in which Christian heroes frequently receive the name of Baldus.

We quite agree with Schlegel in his estimate of the Nibelungenlied, who assigns it one of the first places among the epicpoems of modern Europe. We are indebted, unquestionably, to the Goths for the original poem, as well as for the heroic poems relating to the same period which Charlemagne caused to be collected. We regret, therefore, with our author that the Gothic tongue is now entirely lost. As far as we can judge from Ulphilas's Bible, it was rich, clear, varied, flexible, and harmonious. The author of the Nibelungen will remain like the author of the Iliad, for even unknown. It is, in fact, a poem of the people, in which the traditions of their heroes were handed down from father to son; it was altered in its language as the language of the people changed, and occasionally new matter was added to it; though the marrow and pith remains as it was anciently dictated by the manners of the people, and has never undergone the pruning of a court or a critic-trained poet. The assertion of our author that Heinrick von Offerdingen was the latest person who had re-written the Nibelungen, is one of those numerous assertions which, without any foundation, are made for the sole purpose of conferring honour on Austria. If we were to hazard a conjecture on this point, we should say the latest version of the Nibelungen was made by some poet who dwelt in Switzerland. At least, the best manuscripts have been found there, and there was preserved longest, and even up to our own times in Haslithal and in Avers, the dialect in which this version is written.

According to Schlegel it was under Frederick 1st in the twelfth century, that the German muse first tuned her lyre to any fine harmony, and she sank again into slumber or inactivity at the beginning of the fourteenth century. He designates the reigns of the Saxon line of emperors, as the period when the civilization of the old Germans was highest.

The ninth lecture is on Italian literature; and, as might be expected from the different views of the poets, and the different subjects which they treat, he places Tasso above Dante. We can pardon Schlegel, though we think it an error, for preferring the Gierusalemma Liberata of Tasso to the Orlando of Ariosto; but we can only attribute to a gross prejudice his opinion, that the latter scarcely deserves the name of a poet. There can be no apology, no excuse for a man of any depth of mind placing the Gierusalemma above the Inferno. The great merit of Tasso consists in his very polished language, which is, perhaps, however, almost too refined, and in particular episodes and passages in which he seems to have embodied the warm feelings of his own tender and impassioned heart. Clorinda's death and his description of the charms of Armida, may be mentioned as examples of what we mean; and their effect is powerful, but the whole poem wants force and evenskill, in handling the subject, which is perplexed, and its unity destroyed, by his introduction of mythological Christian-heathens. The story is on the whole inartificially constructed, and its parts are united in a very cumbrous and slovenly manner. Dante was the first, when his native

language was yet unformed and unpolished, to recognise the treasures of antiquity, and to bring them again into common circulation. He was the first to polish the poetical language of the Italians, and perhaps the only poet who, in the same degree, has united the beauties of classical literature with the romantic spirit of the northern nations. He not only polished the language of his country, but he adopted an admirable subject, and invented a form in which to treat it beautifully adapted to its nature. With Schlegel's admiration of Shakspeare, we should be quite at a loss to account for the preference he gives to Tasso above Dante, could it not be explained by his aversion to the political and religious opinions of this great man. Schlegel is, by office, an admirer of the papal power, and Dante did what he could to diminish it. For a similar reason he censures Machiavelli, though he acknowledges his excellence as an historian. Machiavelli's works on Livy, and his not dying in the orthodox catholic faith, were quite sufficient to influence Mr. Schlegel's opinion.

The manner in which this apostate German speaks, in his fifteenth lecture, of his great countryman, Luther, is a good specimen of the whole work. We scarcely know which most to admire in it; the nonsense of the first part, or the cunning, with which, at the conclusion, Luther is made out to be a very wicked, but a very great man. The whole passage is admirably adapted to a lecture-room in the Austrian capital; but Mr. Schlegel intended his work should be read in all ages and countries. "There were, so to speak," he says,

> in the mighty soul of this man, so richly endowed by God and nature, two opposing principles, contending for the mastery over him. In all his writings, there is a contest betwixt light and darkness, betwixt an immovably firm faith, and his own untamed passions, betwixt God and himself. The judgment of men, both then and now, could not be other than different, and even opposite, as to the side which he chose, and the use which he made of his extraordinary powers. As far as I am concerned, I must say, both of his writings and his life, that they make no other impression on me than that of pity, which we always feel, when we see how a great and sublime spirit is ruined and destroyed by its own guilt.

That Schlegel, and all the tribe of mystics and enthusiasts, to which he belongs, should hate Luther, is not at all surprising. They might have forgiven his exposure of the errors of papacy, but they can never pardon his thorough contempt and hatred for all sorts of cant. He was the representative of a class of men, who, in all their feelings and thoughts, are the very antipodes of the mystics. Though powerful, his understanding was plain; theirs is weak and confused; they encourage melancholy and build their power and their influence entirely on some shadowy fears; he loved God in loving the world; his mind was full of ardent hope, and more than any other religious reformer we know, he taught men, both by his example and his precepts, that their own happiness should be their first care. It is for his plain, honest, and homely way of looking both at religion, and the affairs of life, that he is hated by the Catholic mystics of Austria. There was a contest in the mind of Luther, but it was between the errors he had been taught, and the truths which nature and reason dictated. No man ever struggled more earnestly and seriously to obtain truth, and if he was not completely successful, it must be attributed to his education and to the age in which he lived, and not to any defect in his powerful and well-organized mind. As an author, and the creator of German prose, the great reformer deserves the respect of all his countrymen. Even at this period, when the language has been so extensively cultivated, we may admire in Luther's German Bible, the spirit of the translator, the strength, dignity, and grace of the language, the flexibility and skill with which he adapts his words to the matter, from the most simple narration to the most sublime prophecy, as well as the harmony of his periods which gratify the ear and assist the memory. Besides doing injustice to Luther, Schlegel has neglected to mention the great opponent of Erasmus, Ulrich Von Hutten. He was certainly one of the most gifted men of that period, and one of the most popular writers, and ought, therefore, to have a conspicuous place in every work in which it is pretended to give a mere outline of German literature. Mr. Schlegel best knows why he was guilty of the omission.

As our chief object in this paper has been, to point out the political bearing of Mr. Schlegel's literary history, we do not think it necessary to follow him in his discussions on the literature of the rest of the world. In treating of English, French, and Spanish authors, his political prejudices have not so much scope. Yet even here we find an unmeasured praise of Spanish and Portuguese literature, dictated by his feelings as a Catholic.

We close our remarks on a book, which, possessing many excellencies, and teaching many truths, aims principally at introducing into the mind, under cover of an artful eloquence, the principles of slavery; and at perpetuating the dominion of bigotry and despotism undisguised and unashamed. Mr. Schlegel stands forward, the unblushing advocate of the debasing principles of the Austrian government; and makes even his literary discussions the means of perverting the minds of the rising generation.

Although such is our honest opinion of Mr. Schlegel's Lectures, they are too valuable in a literary point of view, to be neglected by the reader who can profit by the ingenuity and originality of many of his critical remarks; and who, at the same time, has acuteness enough to detect the error when he deduces consequences which cannot justly be derived from his premises, or who is vigilant, enough to be always on his guard against the effect of insidious propositions, which are likely though, from their apparent harmlessness, and sometimes from their novelty and ingenuity, to gain admission into the mind of a too easy reader. Our observations may, perhaps, neutralize the latent poison of the work, and render it as innoxious, as it is, in many parts, interesting and valuable.

*"Schlegel's 'Lectures on Literature'," in* Westminster Review, *Vol. III, No. VI, April, 1825, pp. 321-33.*

## Heinrich Heine   (essay date 1835)

[*One of the most prominent literary figures in nineteenth-century Europe and in the history of his native Germany,*

*Heine is remembered for his poetry—characterized by passionate lyricism and wry irony—as well as for his distinctive commentaries on politics, art, literature, and society. In the following excerpt, originally published in 1835, he praises Schlegel for his "profound mind" and his translations of Sanskrit, but faults him for living in the past and interpreting literature in "the interests of Catholicism."*]

With the conscientiousness which I have strictly prescribed for myself, I must mention here that several Frenchmen have complained that my criticism of the Schlegels, especially Mr. August Wilhelm, has been much too harsh. I believe, however, that such a complaint would not occur if people here were better acquainted with the history of German literature. Many Frenchmen know Mr. A. W. Schlegel only from the book [*De l'Allemagne*] by Madame de Staël, his noble patroness. Most of them know only his name, and his name rings in their memory like something venerably famous, such as, for example, the name Osiris, about whom they also know only that he is a peculiar freak of a god who was worshipped in Egypt. About the other points of similarity between Mr. A. W. Schlegel and Osiris they know absolutely nothing.

Since I was once a student of the elder Schlegel at the university, one might think I owed him a certain forbearance. But did Mr. A. W. Schlegel spare old [Gottfried August] Bürger, his literary father? No, and he acted according to custom and tradition. For in literature, as in the forests of the North American Indians, fathers are killed by their sons as soon as they have become old and feeble. . . .

[Friedrich] Schlegel was more important than Mr. August Wilhelm, and indeed the latter lived only on his brother's ideas and understood only the art of developing these ideas. Fr. Schlegel was a man of profound mind. He recognized all the glories of the past, and the felt all the sufferings of the present. But he did not understand the sacredness of these sufferings and the necessity of them for the future salvation of the world. He saw the sun going down and gazed sadly at the spot of its setting and lamented the nocturnal darkness that he saw approaching; and he did not notice that a new dawn was gleaming from the opposite direction. Fr. Schlegel once called the historian "a prophet in retrospect." This expression is the best description of Schlegel himself. He hated the present, the future frightened him, and his inspired, prophetic gaze penetrated only into the past, which he loved.

Poor Fr. Schlegel, he did not see in the sufferings of our time the sufferings of rebirth but the agony of dying, and from fear of death he fled to the tottering ruins of the Catholic Church. Afterall, it was the most suitable refuge for a man of his temperament. He had enjoyed considerable cheerful abandon in his life, but he considered this sinful, a sin which required subsequent expiation, and the author of *Lucinde* had of necessity to become a Catholic.

*Lucinde* is a novel, and except for his poems and an adaptation of a Spanish play, *Alarkos,* it is the only original work Fr. Schlegel left behind. In its day there was no lack of eulogists of the novel. The present Right Reverend Mr. Schleiermacher published enthusiastic letters about *Lucinde.* There was not even any lack of critics who praised this work and prophesied confidently that it would one day be considered the best book in German literature. The authorities should have arrested these people, just as in Russia the prophets who prophesy a public catastrophe are locked up until their prophecy has been fulfilled. No, the gods have preserved our literature from such a misfortune. Schlegel's novel was soon generally condemned because of its dissolute inanity and is now forgotten. Lucinde is the name of the heroine, a sensual, witty woman or, rather, a mixture of sensuality and wit. Her worst fault is simply that she is not a woman but an unpleasant combination of two abstractions, wit and sensuality. May the Blessed Virgin forgive the author for having written this book; the Muses will never forgive him.

A similar novel called *Florentin* is mistakenly attributed to the late Schlegel. They say this book is by his wife, a daughter of the famous Moses Mendelssohn, whom he took away from her first husband and who went over with him to the Roman Catholic Church.

I believe that Fr. Schlegel was serious about Catholicism. I do not believe this of many of his friends. In such matters it is very difficult to ascertain the truth. Religion and hypocrisy are twin sisters, and the two look so alike that sometimes they cannot be distinguished. The same figure, clothing, and speech. Except that the second of the two sisters drawls out the words somewhat more melodiously and repeats the little word "love" more often. —I am speaking of Germany; in France the one sister has died, and we see the other still in deepest mourning.

After the appearance of Madame de Staël's *De l'Allemagne* Fr. Schlegel presented the public with two more large works, which are perhaps his best and in any case deserve very laudatory mention. They are his ***Wisdom and Language of India*** and his ***Lectures on the History of Literature*** With the former book he not only introduced the study of Sanskrit into Germany but also founded it. He became for Germany what William Jones was for England. He had learned Sanskrit with great ingenuity, and the few fragments which he gives in this book are skillfully translated. With his profound powers of intuition he recognized perfectly the significance of the Indian epic meter, the *sloka,* which flows along as broad as the clear and sacred river, the Ganges. In contrast how petty Mr. A. W. Schlegel shows himself to be when he translates a few fragments from Sanskrit into hexameters and does not know how to praise himself enough for not letting any trochees slip in and for whittling out so many clear little metric art works in alexandrines. Fr. Schlegel's work on India has certainly been translated into French, and I can spare myself further praise. My only criticism is the ulterior motive behind the book. It was written in the interests of Catholicism. These people had rediscovered in the Indian poems not merely the mysteries of Catholicism, but the whole Catholic hierarchy as well and its struggles with secular authority. In the *Mahabharata* and in the *Ramayana* they saw, as it were, an elephantine Middle Ages. As a matter of fact, when in the latter epic King Visvamitra quarrels with the priest Vasistha, this quarrel concerns the same interests about which the Emperor quarreled with the Pope, although here in Europe the point in dispute was

called investiture and there in India it was called the cow Sabala.

The same fault can be found with Schlegel's lectures on literature. Friedrich Schlegel surveys the entire literature from an elevated point of view, but this elevated point of view is nonetheless always the belfry of a Catholic church. And with everything Schlegel says you hear these bells ringing; sometimes you even hear the croaking of the church ravens that flutter around him. To me the whole book is redolent of the incense of high mass, and I seem to detect nothing but tonsured ideas peeking out of its most beautiful passages. Yet in spite of these defects I know of no better book in this field. Only by combining Herder's works of a similar kind could one get a better survey of the literature of all peoples. For Herder did not sit in judgment on the various nations like a literary grand inquisitor, condemning or absolving them according to the degree of their faith. No, Herder viewed all mankind as a mighty harp in the hand of the great master, each nation seemed to him one string of this giant harp turned to its special note, and he understood the universal harmony of the harp's various tones.

Fr. Schlegel died in the summer of 1829, as a result of gastronomical intemperance, it was said. He was fifty-seven years old. His death caused one of the most repulsive literary scandals. His friends, the party of the clergy, whose headquarters were in Munich, were annoyed at the discourteous manner in which the liberal press had discussed the death, so they defamed and abused and insulted the German liberals. Yet they could not say of any of them "that he had seduced the wife of an intimate friend and for a long time afterward lived from the alms of the wronged husband."

*Heinrich Heine, "The Romantic School," translated by Helen Mustard, in his* The Romantic School and Other Essays, *edited by Jost Hermand and Robert C. Holub, Continuum, 1985, pp. 1-127.*

### Søren Kierkegaard   (essay date 1841)

[*One of the most influential nineteenth-century philosophers, Kierkegaard is esteemed for his studies in religious reform, social criticism, psychology, and communication. His insistence that the individual must acknowledge the importance of faith and the limitations of reason, and accept personal responsibility for determinations of truth and appropriate courses of action has become a central component of the philosophy of Existentialism in the twentieth century. In the following excerpt, originally published in 1841, Kierkegaard criticizes the portrayal of love in* Lucinde *for being "immoral" and "cowardly."*]

Friedrich Schlegel's celebrated novel ***Lucinde,*** which became the gospel of the Young Germany and the system for its *Rehabilitation des Fleisches* [rehabilitation of the material], and which was an abomination to Hegel, will here be the object of investigation. This discussion is not without difficulties, however, for ***Lucinde,*** as everyone knows, is a very obscene book, and by including certain passages for closer examination I shall be incurring the risk of making it impossible for even the purest reader to come away wholly unscathed. I shall therefore be as provident and sparing as possible.

In order not to do Schlegel an injustice one must recall the numerous errors which have crept into the many relationships in life, and in particular which have been relentless in making love as tame, well-behaved, sluggish and apathetic, as utilitarian and serviceable as any other domesticated animal, in short, as unerotic as possible. To this extent one must be extremely beholden to Schlegel should he succeed in finding a solution. But alas, the only climate he discovers in which love can thrive is even worse, not a climate somewhat further south in relation to our northern climate, but an ideal climate that exists nowhere. Accordingly, it is not only the tame ducks and geese of a domesticated love which beat their wings and utter a terrifying cry when they hear the wild birds of love whistling by overhead. No, it is every more deeply poetic person, whose longings are too strong to be bound by romantic cobwebs, whose demands on life are too great to be satisfied through writing a novel, who here, precisely on behalf of poetry, must lay down his protest and endeavour to show that it was not a solution Friedrich Schlegel discovered but a delusion he strayed into, must endeavour to show that to live is something different from to dream. When we consider more closely what Schlegel opposed with his irony, it will surely not be denied that there both was and is much in the ingress, progress, and egress of marriage deserving such a correction, and which makes it natural for the subject to seek to emancipate himself from such things. There is an extremely constricted seriousness, a purposiveness, a wretched teleology worshipped by many like an idol, which demands every infinite pursuit as its rightful sacrifice. Love is thus nothing in and through itself, but only becomes something through the purpose whereby it is accommodated to that pettiness whose success creates such a furore in the private theatre of the family. 'To have purposes, to carry out purposes, to interweave purposes artfully with purposes into a new purpose: this ridiculous habit is so deeply rooted in the foolish nature of godlike man that if once he wishes to move freely without any purpose, on the inner stream of ever flowing images and feelings, he must actually resolve to do it and make it a set purpose. . . . It is, to be sure, a different matter with people who love in the ordinary way. The man loves in his wife only the race, the woman in her husband only the degree of his natural qualities and social position, and both love in their children only their own creation and property. . . . Oh, it is true, my friend, man is by nature a most serious animal. There is a moral prudishness, a straitjacket in which no rational human being can move. In God's name let it be sundered! There is, on the other hand, the moonlit kind of theatre marriages of an overwrought romanticism for which nature, at least, has no purpose, and whose barren breezes and impotent embraces profit a Christian state no more than a pagan one. Against all these let irony rage! But it is not merely against untruths such as these that Schlegel directs his attack. There is a Christian view of marriage which, at the very hour of the nuptials, has had the audacity to proclaim the curse even before it pronounces the benediction. There is a Christian view that places all things under sin, that recognizes no exception, spares nothing, not the child in the womb nor the most beautiful among women. There is a seriousness in this view too high to be grasped by the harassed toilers of prosaic daily life, too severe to be mocked by marital improvisors. —Thus those times are now past when mankind lived so happily and innocently without sorrow and tribulation, when everything was so like man, when the gods themselves set the fashion and sometimes laid aside their heavenly dignity in order to steal the love of some earthly woman; when one who quietly, furtively sneaked away to a rendezvous could fear or flatter himself by finding a god among his rivals; those times when the sky arched itself proudly and beautifully over happy love like a friendly witness, or with quiet gravity concealed it in the solemn peace of the night; when everything lived only for love, and everything was in turn only a myth about love for the happy lovers. But there lies the difficulty, and it is from this perspective that one must evaluate the efforts of Schlegel and all earlier and later romanticism: *those times are past,* and still the longing of romanticism draws back to them. But in so doing it undertakes no *peregrinationes sacras* [sacred pilgrimage] but *profanus* [secular pilgrimage]. Were it possible to reconstruct a bygone age, one must reconstruct it in its purity, hence Hellenism in all its naïveté. But this is what romanticism refuses to do. It is not properly Hellenism it reconstructs, but an unknown continent it discovers. But what is more, its enjoyments are refined to a high degree; for it does not merely seek to enjoy naïvely, but in this enjoyment desires to become conscious of the destruction of the given ethic. This is just the point of its enjoyment, as it were, that it smiles at the ethic under which it believes others groan, and in this lies the free play of ironic arbitrariness. Christianity by means of the spirit has established a dissension between the spirit and the flesh, and either the spirit must negate the flesh or the flesh negate the spirit. Romanticism desires the latter, and is different from Hellenism in that along with the enjoyment of the flesh it also enjoys the negation of spirit. This it claims is to live poetically. I trust it will become apparent, however, that poetry is precisely what it misses, for true inward infinity proceeds only from resignation, and only this inward infinity is in truth infinite and in truth poetic.

Schlegel's *Lucinde* seeks to suspend the established ethic, or as Erdmann not infelicitously expresses it: 'All moral determinations are mere sport, and it is accidental to the lover whether marriage is monogamous or whether *en quatre,* etc. Were it possible to imagine that the whole of *Lucinde* were merely a caprice, an arbitrarily fashioned child of whim and fancy gesticulating with both her legs like the little Wilhelmine without a care for her dress or the world's judgment; were it but a light-headed whimsicality that found pleasure in setting everything on its head, in turning everything upside down; were it merely a witty irony over the total ethic identified with custom and use: who then would be so ridiculous as not to laugh at it who would be such a distempered grouch that he could not even gloat over it? But this is not the case. Quite the contrary, *Lucinde* has a most doctrinaire character and a certain melancholy seriousness pervading it which seems to derive from the fact that its hero has arrived at this glorious knowledge of the truth so late that a part of his life has gone unutilized. The audacity which this novel so often reverts to, which it clamours for, as it were, is therefore not a momentary whimsical suspension of that which is objectively valid, so that the expression 'audacity' as used here would itself have been capricious in using so strong an expression with deliberate abandon. No, this audacity is just what one calls audacity, but which is so amiable and interesting that ethics, modesty, and decency, which at first glance have some attraction, seem rather insignificant entities by comparison. Surely everyone who has read *Lucinde* will agree that it does have such a doctrinaire character. But should anyone wish to deny it, I must then ask him to explain how the Young Germany could have been so completely mistaken about it; and should he succeed in answering this, I shall then remind him that it is well known that Schlegel later became a Catholic and as such discovered the Reformation to have been the second fall of man, a fact which sufficiently shows that *Lucinde* was seriously intended.

*Lucinde* seeks to abrogate all ethics, not simply in the sense of custom and usage, but that ethical totality which is the validity of mind, the dominion of the spirit over the flesh. Hence it corresponds fully to what we have . . . designated as the special pursuit of irony: to cancel all actuality and set in its place an actuality that is no actuality. In the first place, therefore, it is quite in order that the girl, or rather, the wife in whose arms Julian finds repose, that Lucinde 'was also one of those who have a decided inclination for the romantic, and who do not live in the ordinary world but in one self-created and self-conceived,' one of those, therefore, who properly have no other actuality than the sensual; quite in order, secondly, that it is one of Julian's great tasks to bring before his imagination an eternal embrace—presumably as the only true actuality.

If we consider *Lucinde* as such a catechism of love, it requires of its disciples 'what Diderot calls the perception of the flesh,' 'a rare gift,' and pledges them to develop it into that higher sense of artistic voluptuousness. Naturally, Julian appears as priest in this worship 'not without unction,' that is, as one 'to whom the spirit itself spake through a voice from heaven, saying: "Thou art my beloved son in whom I am well pleased" '; as one who cries out to himself and others: 'Consecrate thyself and proclaim that only nature is venerable and only health agreeable.' What it seeks is a naked sensuality in which the spirit is a negated moment; what it opposes is a spirituality in which sensuality is an assimilated moment. To this extent it is incorrect when it takes as its ideal the little two-year-old Wilhelmine, 'for her years the most clever [geistreichste] person of her time,' since in her sensuality the spirit is not negated because it is not yet present. It desires nakedness altogether and so despises the northern coldness, and it seeks to ridicule that narrowmindedness unable to tolerate nakedness. However, I shall not concern myself any further whether this is a narrowmindedness, or whether the veil of attire is still not a beautiful image of how all sensuality ought to be, since when sensuality is intellectually mastered it is never naked. Instead, I shall merely call attention to the fact that the world still forgives Archimedes for running stark naked through the streets of Syracuse, and this surely not because of the mild southern climate, but because his spiritual exaltation, his 'eureka, eureka' was a sufficient attire.

The confusion and disorder that *Lucinde* seeks to introduce into the established order [Bestaaende] it illustrates itself by means of the most perfect confusion in its design and structure. At the very outset Julian explains that along with the other conventions of reason and ethics he has also dispensed with chronology. He then adds: 'For me and for this book, for my love of it and for its internal formation, there is no purpose more purposive than that right at the start I begin by abolishing what we call order, keep myself entirely aloof from it, and appropriate to myself in word and deed the right to a charming confusion.' With this he seeks to attain what is truly poetical, and as he renounces all understanding and allows the phantasy alone to rule, it may well be possible for him and the reader, should the latter wish to do likewise, to let the imagination maintain this confusion [Mellemhverandre] in a single perpetually moving image. —In spite of this confusion, however, I shall endeavour to bring a kind of order into my presentation and let the whole consolidate itself at one definite point.

Julian, the hero of this novel, is no Don Juan (who by his sensual genius casts a spell over everything like a sorcerer; who steps forth with an immediate authority showing himself lord and ruler, an authority which words cannot describe but of which some representation may be had from a few imperious bars of Mozart; a being who does not seduce but by whom all would like to be seduced, and were their innocence restored to them would desire nothing more than to be seduced again; a daemon who has no past, no history of development, but springs forth at once fully endowed like Minerva), but a personality ensnared in reflection who develops only successively. In the 'Apprenticeship of Manhood' we learn more of his history. 'To play faro with the appearance of the most violent passion, and yet to be distracted and absent-minded; to venture everything in a heated instant and as soon as it is lost to turn away indifferently: this was just one of the vicious habits by which Julian fulminated away his youth.' The author thinks that by this single characteristic he has adequately portrayed Julian's life. In this we fully agree. Julian is a young man who, intensely torn asunder within, has by this very sundering acquired a living idea of that sorcery which in a few moments is able to make a man many, many years older; a young man who by this very sundering is in apparent possession of an enormous power, just as surely as the excitement of desperation produce athletic prowess; a young man who long ago had already begun the grand finale, but who nevertheless flourishes the goblet with a certain dignity and grace, with an air of intellectual ease in the world, and now summons all his strength in a single breath in order by a brilliant exit to cast a glorifying nimbus over a life which has had no value and leaves no bereavement behind; a young man who has long been familiar with the thought of suicide, but whose stormy soul has begrudged him time to reach a decision. Surely love must be that which shall save him! After having been on the verge of seducing a young and innocent girl (a fairy-tale, however, which has no further significance for him, since she was obviously too innocent to satisfy his thirst for knowledge), he discovers in Lisette the very teacher he needs, an instructress who has long been initiated into the nocturnal mysteries of love, and whose public instruction Julian tries in vain to restrict to a private instruction for himself alone.

The portrait of Lisette is perhaps the most accomplished in the whole novel, and the author has treated her with a visible partiality and spared nothing in order to cast a poetic glow over her. As a child she was more melancholy [*tungsindig*] than light-minded [*letsindig*], but even then she had been daemonically excited by sensuality. Later she had been an actress, but only for a short time, and she always poked fun at her lack of talent and at all the boredom she had endured. Finally, she had offered herself completely to the service of sensuality. Next to independence she had an immense love for money, which she nevertheless knew how to use with taste. Her favours she allowed to be repaid sometimes by sums of money, sometimes by the satisfaction of a whimsical infatuation for some particular person. Her boudoir was open and wholly without conventional furniture, for on every side there were large, expensive mirrors, and alternating with these superb paintings by Correggio and Titian. In place of chairs she had genuine oriental carpets and some groups of marble in half life-size. Here she often sat Turkish fashion the whole day long, alone, her hands folded idly in her lap, for she despised all womanly tasks. She refreshed herself from time to time with sweet-scented perfumes, and had stories, travelogues, and fairy-tales read to her by her jockey, a plastically fair youth whom she had seduced in his fourteenth year. But she paid little heed to what was read, except when there was something ridiculous or some platitude which she, too, found true; for she esteemed nothing but reality, had no sense for anything else, and found all poetry ridiculous. Such is Schlegel's portrayal of a life, which, however corrupt it may be, nevertheless seems to put forward the claim to be poetical. The thing particularly prominent here is the exclusive indolence which bothers about nothing, which cannot be bothered with working but despises every womanly pursuit, which cannot be bothered with occupying the mind but merely lets it be occupied, which dissolves and exhausts every power of the soul in enervating enjoyments and causes consciousness itself to evaporate in a nauseous twilight. But enjoyment it was nonetheless, and surely to enjoy is to live poetically. The author seems also to want to find something poetical in the fact that Lisette did not always consider only money when distributing her favours. At such moments he seems to want to illuminate her wretched love with a reflection of that devotion belonging to innocent love, as if it were more poetical to be a slave to one's caprice than to money. So there she sits in this luxurious room with external consciousness slipping away from her, the huge mirrors reflecting her image from every angle produce the only consciousness she has remaining. When referring to her own person she usually called herself 'Lisette', and often said that were she able to write she would then treat her story as though it were another's, altogether preferring to speak of herself in third person. This, evidently, was not because her earthly exploits were as world historical as a Caesar's, so that her life was not her own because it belonged to the world. It was simply because the weight of this *vita ante acta* [previous life] was too heavy for her to bear. To come to herself concerning it, to allow its menacing shapes to pass judgment upon her, this would indeed be too serious

to be poetical. But to allow this wretched life to dissolve itself in indefinite contours, to stare at it as though it were something indifferent to her, this she liked to do. She might grieve over this lost and unhappy girl, she might offer her a tear, perhaps, but that this girl was herself she wanted to forget. But it is weak to seek to forget, although on occasion there may be stirring in this an energy foreshadowing something better. But to seek to relive oneself poetically in such a way that remorse can have no sting because it concerns another, all the while allowing enjoyment to become intensified through a secret complicity, this is a most effeminate cowardice. Throughout the whole of *Lucinde,* however, it is this lapsing into an aesthetic stupor which appears as the designation for what it is to live poetically, and which, since it lulls the deeper ego into a somnambulant state, permits the arbitrary ego free latitude in ironic self-satisfaction.

But let us examine this more closely. There have been many attempts to show that such books as *Lucinde* are immoral, and there have been frequent cries of shame and ignominy over them. But so long as the author is allowed overtly to claim and the reader covertly to believe that such works are poetical, there is not much to be gained by this, and this so much the less since man has as great a claim on the poetical as the moral has claim on him. Be it therefore said, as it shall also be shown, that they are not only immoral but unpoetical, and this because they are irreligious. Let it be said first and last that every man can live poetically who in truth desires to. If we next inquire what poetry is, we might answer with the general characterization that poetry is victory over the world. It is through a negation of the imperfect actuality that poetry opens up a higher actuality, expands and transfigures the imperfect into the perfect, and thereby softens and mitigates that deep pain which would darken and obscure all things. To this extent poetry is a kind of reconciliation, though not the true reconciliation; it does not reconcile me with the actuality in which I live, for no transubstantiation of the given actuality occurs. Instead, it reconciles me with the given actuality by giving me another actuality, a higher and more perfect. Indeed, the greater the opposition, so much the more imperfect is the reconciliation, so that it often becomes no reconciliation at all but rather animosity. Only the religious, therefore, is capable of effecting the true reconciliation, for it renders actuality infinite for me. The poetical may well be a sort of victory over actuality, but the process whereby it is rendered infinite is more like an abandonment of, than a continuation in, actuality. To live poetically is therefore to live infinitely. But infinity may be either an external or an internal infinity. The person who would have an infinitely poetical enjoyment also has an infinitely poetical enjoyment also has an infinity before him, but it is an external infinity. When I enjoy I am constantly outside myself in the 'other'. But such an infinity must cancel itself. Only if I am not outside myself in what I enjoy but in myself, only then is my enjoyment infinite, for it is inwardly infinite. He who enjoys poetically, were he to enjoy the whole world, would still lack one enjoyment: he does not enjoy himself. To enjoy oneself (naturally not in a Stoic or egotistical sense, for here again there is no true infinity, but in a religious sense) is alone the true infinity.

If after these considerations we return to the claim that to live poetically is the same as to enjoy (and this opposition between poetic actuality and the given actuality, precisely because our age is so deeply penetrated by reflection, must exhibit itself in a much deeper form than it has ever before appeared in the world; for previously the poetic development went hand in hand with the given actuality, but now it is in truth a matter of to be or not to be, now one is not satisfied to live poetically once in a while, but demands that the whole of life should be poetic), then it readily appears that this utterly fails to secure the highest enjoyment, the true happiness wherein the subject no longer dreams but possesses himself in infinite clarity, is absolutely transparent to himself. This is only possible for the religious individual who does not have his infinity outside himself but within himself. To revenge oneself is accordingly a poetic enjoyment, and the pagans believed that the gods had reserved all vengeance unto themselves because it was sweet. But though I were to have my revenge absolutely sated, though I were a god in the pagan sense before whom all things trembled and whose fiery anger were able to consume everything, still, I would in revenge merely be enjoying myself egotistically, my enjoyment would be merely an external infinity. To this extent the simplest human being who did not permit his vengeance to rage but mastered his anger was much nearer to having overcome the world, and only he enjoyed himself in truth, only he possessed inward infinity, only he lived poetically. If from this standpoint we would consider the life set forth in *Lucinde* as a poetic life, then we might allow it every possible enjoyment—but the right to use one predicate in describing it will surely not be denied us: it is an infinitely cowardly life. And provided one will not claim that to be cowardly is to live poetically, it might well be possible for this poetic life to exhibit itself rather unpoetically, that is to say, wholly unpoetically. For to live poetically cannot mean to remain obscure to oneself, to work oneself up into a disgusting suggestiveness, but to become clear and transparent to oneself, not in finite and egotistical satisfaction, but in one's absolute and eternal validity. And if this be not possible for every human being then life is madness, in which case it is a matchless foolhardiness for the individual—though he be the most gifted who has ever lived in the world—to delude himself in thinking that what was denied all others was reserved for him alone. Either to be a human being is absolute, or the whole of life is nonsense—despair the only thing awaiting everyone not so demented, not so uncharitable and haughty, not so desperate as to believe himself the chosen one. Hence one should not restrict himself to reciting certain moralisms against the whole tendency after *Lucinde,* which, often with much talent and often enchantingly enough, has taken it upon itself not to lead but to lead astray. One must not allow it to deceive itself and others that it is poetic, or that it is through this way that one attains what every human being has an imperative demand for—to live poetically.

But let us return to Julian and Lisette. Lisette ends her life as she began it, fulfilling what Julian never had enough time to resolve, and through the act of suicide seeks to attain the goal of all her aspirations—to be rid of her self. However, she preserves her aesthetic tact to the very end, and the last words which, according to her servant, she

pronounced in a shrill voice: 'Lisette must die, must die now! An inexorable fate requires it!' must be regarded as a kind of dramatic silliness quite natural for one who had formerly been an actress on the stage and who subsequently became one in life as well. —Now the death of Lisette must naturally have made an impression on Julian. I shall let Schlegel speak for himself, however, lest anyone think I distort. 'The first effect of the death of Lisette was that Julian idolized her memory with fanatical veneration.' Yet not even this event was sufficient to develop Julian: 'This exception to what Julian regarded as ordinary among the female sex (the average woman, according to Julian, did not possess the same "high energy" as Lisette) was too unique, and the circumstances in which he found her too sordid for him to acquire true perspective through this.'

Julian, after withdrawing in loneliness for a time, is again allowed by Schlegel to come into contact with society, and in a more intellectual relation to certain of this life's feminine members once more runs through several love affairs, until he finally discovers in Lucinde the unity of all these discrete moments, discovers as much sensuousness as cleverness [*Aandrighed*]. But as this love affair has no deeper foundation than intellectual sensuousness, as it embraces no moment of resignation, in other words, since it is no marriage, and as it asserts the view that passivity and vegetating constitute perfection; so here again the ethical integrity is negated. Accordingly, this love affair can acquire no content, can achieve no history in a deeper sense; and so their amusements can only be the same *en deux* as those with which Julian had formerly occupied his loneliness, namely, in considering what some clever lady would say or reply on some piquant occasion. It is a love without real content, and the eternity so often mentioned is none other than what might be called the eternal pleasure instant, an infinity without infinity and as such unpoetic. One can hardly refrain from smiling, therefore, when such a frail and fragile love fancies itself able to withstand the storms of life, fancies itself in possession of a strength sufficient to look upon 'the harshest whim of chance as an excellent jest and a frolicsome caprice.' For this love is not at home in the actual world, but belongs to an imaginary world where the lovers are themselves lords over storms and hurricanes. Moreover, as everything in this alliance is calculated in terms of enjoyment, so naturally it conceives its relation to the generation deriving its existence [*Tilvaerelse*] from it equally egotistically: 'Thus the religion of love weaves our love ever more closely and firmly together, for the child doubles the happiness of its gentle parents like an echo.' Occasionally, one comes across parents who with foolish seriousness wish to see their children well settled as soon as possible, perhaps even to see them well settled in the grave. Julian and Lucinde, on the other hand, seem to want to keep their offspring always at the same age as the little Wilhelmine so as to derive amusement from them.

Now what is problematic about *Lucinde* and the whole tendency connected with it is that although beginning with the freedom and constitutive authority of the ego, it does not go on to arrive at a still higher aspect of mind but instead at sensuality, and consequently at its opposite. Ethics imply a relation of mind to mind, but as the ego seeks a higher freedom, seeks to negate ethical mind, it thereby succumbs to the law of the flesh and the appetites. But as this sensuality is not naïve, it follows that the same arbitrariness that established sensuality in its supposed privileges may at the next moment pass over to assert an abstract and eccentric aspect of mind. These vibrations may be conceived partly as the play of the irony of the world with the individual, partly as an attempt by the individual to mimic the irony of the world.

*Søren Kierkegaard, "Irony after Fichte," in his* The Concept of Irony, *translated by Lee M. Capel, 1841. Reprint by Collins, 1966, pp. 257-344.*

## *Blackwood's Edinburgh Magazine*   (essay date 1843)

[*In the following review of* Gechichte der alten und neuen Literatur (History of Ancient and Modern Literature) *the critic summarizes Schlegel's ideology, contending that he was as much a philosopher as a literary critic.*]

"I would not have you pin your faith too closely to these Schlegels," said Fichte one day at Berlin to Varnhagen Von Ense, or one of his friends, in his own peculiar, cutting, commanding style—"I would not have you pin your faith to these Schlegels. I know them well. The elder brother wants depth, and the younger clearness. One good thing they both have—that is, hatred of mediocrity; but they have also both a great jealousy of the highest excellence; and, therefore, where they can neither be great themselves nor deny greatness in others, they, out of sheer desperation, fall into an outrageous strain of eulogizing. Thus they have bepraised Goethe, and thus they have bepraised me." Some people, from pride, don't like to be praised at all; and all sensible people, from propriety, don't like to be praised extravagantly: whether from pride or from propriety, or from a mixture of both, philosopher Fichte seemed to have held in very small account the patronage with which he was favoured at the hands of the twin aesthetical dictators, the Castor and Pollux of romantic criticism; and, strange enough also, poet Goethe, who had worship enough in his day, and is said to have been somewhat fond of the homage, chimes in to the same tune thus:

> The Schlegels, with all their fine natural gifts, have been unhappy men their life long, both the one and the other; they wished both to be and do something more than nature had given them capacity for; and accordingly they have been the means of bringing about not a little harm both in art and literature. From their false principles in the fine arts—principles which, however much trumpeted and gospeled about, were in fact egotism united with weakness—our German artists have not yet recovered, and are filling the exhibitions, as we see, with pictures which nobody will buy. Frederick, the younger of these Dioscouri, choked himself at last with the eternal chewing of moral and religious absurdities, which, in his uncomfortable passage through life, he had collected together from all quarters, and was eager to hawk about with the solemn air of a preacher to every body: he accordingly betook himself, as a last refuge, to Ca-

tholicism, and drew after him, as a companion to his own views, a man of very fair but falsely overwrought talent—Adam Müller.

As for their Sanscrit studies again, that was at bottom only a *pis aller*. They were clear-sighted enough to perceive that neither Greek nor Latin offered any thing brilliant enough for them; they accordingly threw themselves into the far East; and in this direction, unquestionably, the talent of Augustus William manifests itself in the most honourable way. All that, and more, time will show. Schiller never loved them: hated them rather; and I think it peeps out of our correspondence how I did my best, in our Weimar circles at least, to keep this dislike from coming to an open difference. In the great revolution which they actually effected, I had the luck to get off with a whole skin, (*sie liessen mich noth dürftig stehen,*) to the great annoyance of their romantic brother Novalis, who wished to have me *simpliciter* deleted. 'Twas a lucky thing for me, in the midst of this critical hubbub, that I was always too busy with myself to take much note of what others were saying about me.

Schiller had good reason to be angry with them. With their aesthetical denunciations and critical club-law, it was a comparatively cheap matter for them to knock him down in a fashion; but Schiller had no weapons that could prostrate them. He said to me on one occasion, displeased with my universal toleration even for what I did not like. "Kotzebue, with his frivolous fertility, is more respectable in my eyes than that barren generation, who, though always limping themselves, are never content with bawling out to those who have legs—Stop!"

That there is some truth in these severe remarks, the paltry personal squibs in the *Leipzig Almanach* for 1832, which called them forth, with regard to Augustus Schlegel at least, sufficiently show: but there is a general truth involved in them also, which the worthy fraternity of us who, in this paper age, wield the critical pen, would do well to take seriously to heart; and it is this, that great poets and philosophers have a natural aversion as much to be praised and patronized, as to be rated and railed at by great critics; and very justly so. For as a priest is a profane person, who makes use of his sacred office mainly to show his gods about, (so to speak,) that people may stare at them, and worship him; so a critic who forgets his inferior position in reference to creative genius, so far as to assume the air of legislation and dictatorship, when explanation and commentary are the utmost he can achieve, has himself only to blame, if, after his noisy trumpet has blared itself out, he reaps only ridicule from the really witty, and reproof from the substantially wise. Not that a true philosopher or poet shrinks from, and does not rather invite, true criticism. The evil is not in the deed, but in the manner of doing it. Here, as in all moral matters, the tone of the thing is the soul of the thing. And in this view, the blame which Fichte and Goethe attach to the Schlegels, amounts substantially to this, not that in their critical vocation the romantic brothers wanted either learning or judgment generally, but that they were too ambitious, too pretenceful, too dictatorial; that they must needs talk on all subjects, and always as if they were the masters and the lions, when they were only the servants and the exhibitors; that they made a serious business of that which is often best done when it is done accidentally, viz. discussing what our neighbours are about, instead of doing something ourselves; and that they attempted to raise up an independent literary reputation, nay, and even to found a new poetical school, upon mere criticism—an attempt which, with all due respect for Aristarchus and the Alexandrians, is, and remains, a literary impossibility.

But was Frederick Schlegel merely a critic? No! He was a philosopher also, and not a vulgar one; and herein lies the foundation of his fame. His criticism, also, was thoroughly and characteristically a philosophical criticism; and herein mainly, along with its vastness of erudition and comprehensiveness of view, lies the foundation of its fame. To understand the criticism thoroughly, one must first understand the philosophy. Will the *un*philosophical English reader have patience with us for a few minutes while we endeavour to throw off a short sketch of the philosophy of Frederick Schlegel? If the philosophical system of a transcendental German and *Viennese* Romanist, can have small intrinsic practical value to a British Protestant, it may extrinsically be of use even to him as putting into his hands the key to one of the most intellectual, useful, and popular books of modern times—*The history of ancient and modern literature,* by Frederick Von Schlegel; —a book, moreover, which is not merely "a great national possession of the Germans," as by one of themselves it has been proudly designated, but has also, through the classical translation of Mr Lockhart, been made the peculiar property of English literature.

In the first chapter of his *Philosophie des Lebens,* the Viennese lecturer states very clearly the catholic and comprehensive ground which all philosophy must take that would save itself from dangerous error. The philosopher must start from the complete living totality of man, formed as he is, not of flesh merely, a Falstaff—or of spirit merely, a Simon Pillarman and Total Abstinence Saint—but of both flesh and spirit, body and soul, in his healthy and normal condition. For this reason clearly—true philosophy is not merely sense-derived and material like the French philosophy of Helvetius, nor altogether ideal like that of Plotinus, and the pious old mathematical visionaries at Alexandria; but it stands on mother earth, like old Antaeus drinking strength therefrom, and filches fire at the same time, Prometheus-like, from heaven, feeding men with hopes—not, as Aeschylus says, altogether "blind," but only blinking. Don't court, therefore, if you would philosophize wisely, too intimate an acquaintance with your brute brother, the baboon—a creature, whose nature speculative naturalists have most cunningly set forth by the theory, that it is a parody which the devil, in a fit of ill-humour, made upon God's noblest work, man; and don't hope, on the other hand, as many great saints and sages have done, by prayer and fasting, or by study and meditation, to work yourself up to a god, and jump bodily out of your human skin. Assume as the first postulate, and lay it down as the last proposition of your "philosophy of life," that a man is neither a brute, nor a god, nor an angel, but simply and sheerly a man. Furthermore,

as man is not only a very comprehensive and complex, but also, (to appearance at least,) in many points, a very contrary and contradictory creature, see that you take the *whole* man along with you into your metaphysical chamber; for if there be one paper that has a bearing in the case amissing out of your green bag, (which has happened only too often,) the evidence will be imperfect, and the sentence false or partial—shake your wig as you please. Remember, that though you may be a very subtle logician, the soul of man is not all made up of logic; remember that reason, (*Vernunft,*) the purest that Kant ever criticized withal, is not the proper vital soul in man; is not the creative and productive faculty in intellect at all, but is merely the tool of that which, in philosophers no less than in poets, is the proper inventive power, imagination, as Wordsworth phrases it: Schlegel's word is *fantasie.* Remember that in more cases than academic dignities may be willing to admit, the heart (where a man has one) is the only safe guide, the only legitimate ruler of the head; and that a mere metaphysician, and solitary speculator, however properly trimmed,

> One to whose smooth-rubb'd soul can
>     cling
> Nor form nor feeling, great nor small;
> A reasoning, self-sufficing thing,
> An intellectual all-in-all,

may write very famous books, profound even to unintelligibility, but can never be a philosopher. Therefore reject Hegel, "that merely thinking, on a barren heath speculating, self-sufficient, self-satisfied little Ego;" and consider Kant as weighed in the balance and found wanting on his own showing: for if that critical portal of pure reason had indeed been sufficient, as it gave itself out to be, for all the purposes of a human philosophy, what need was there of the "practical back-door" which, at the categorical command of conscience, was afterwards laid open to all men in the "Metaphysic of Ethics?" As little will you allow your philosophical need to be satisfied with any thing you can get from Schelling; for however well it sounds to "throw yourself from the transcendental emptiness of ideal reason into the warm embrace of living and luxuriant nature," here also you will find yourself haunted by the intellectual phantom of absolute identity, (say absolute inanity,) or in its best phasis a "pantheizing deification of nature." Strange enough as it may seem, the true philosophy is to be found any where rather than among philosophers. Each philosopher builds up a reasoned system of a part of existence; but life is based upon God-given instincts and emotions, with which reason has nothing to do; and nature contains many things which it is not given to mortal brain to comprehend, much less to systematize. True philosophy is not to be found in any intellectual system, much less in any of the Aristotelian quality, where the emotional element in man is excluded or subordinated; but in a living experience. To know philosophy, therefore, first know life. To learn to philosophize, learn to live; and live not partially, but with the full outspread vitality of human reason. You go to college, and, as if you were made altogether of head, expect some Peter Abelard forthwith, by academic disputation, to *reason* you into manhood; but neither manhood nor any vital whole ever was learned by reasoning.

Pray, therefore, to the Author of all good, in the first place, that you may *be* something rather than that you may *know* something. Get yourself planted in God's garden, and learn to grow. Woo the sun of life, which is love, and the breeze which is enthusiasm, an impulse from that same creative Spirit, which, brooding upon the primeval waters, out of void brought fulness, and out of chaos a world.

Such, shortly, so far as we can gather, is the main scope, popularly stated, of Frederick Schlegel's philosophy, as it is delivered in his two first lectures on the philosophy of life, the first being titled, "Of the thinking soul, or the central point of consciousness;" and the second, "Of the loving soul, or the central point of moral life." The healthy-toned reader, who has been exercised in speculations of this kind, will feel at once that there is much that is noble in all this, and much that is true; but not a little also, when examined in detail, of that sublime-sounding sweep of despotic generality, (so inherent a vice of German literature,) which delights to confound the differences, rather than to discriminate the characters, of things; much that seems only too justly to warrant that oracular sentence of the stern Fichte with which we set out, *"The younger brother wants clearness;"* much that, when applied to practice, and consistently followed out in that grand style of consistency which belongs to a real German philosopher, becomes what we in English call Puseyism and Popery, and what Goethe in German called a *"chewing the cud of moral and religious absurdities."* But we have neither space nor inclination, in this place, to make an analysis of the Schlegelian philosophy, or to set forth how much of it is true and how much of it is false. Our intention was merely to sketch a rapid outline, in as popular phrase as philosophy would allow itself to be clothed in; to finish which outline without extraneous remark, with the reader's permission, we now proceed.

If man be not, according to Aristotle's phrase, a ζωον λογικον in his highest faculty, a *ratiocinative,* but rather an emotional and imaginative animal; and if to start from, as to end, in mere reason, be in human psychology a gross one-sidedness, much more in theology is such a procedure erroneous, and altogether perverse. If not the smallest poem of a small poet ever came to him from mere reason, but from something deeper and more vital, much less are the strong pulsations of pure emotion, the deep seated convictions of religious faith in the inner man, to be spoke of as things that mere reason can either assert or deny; and in fact we see, when we look narrowly into the great philosophical systems that have been projected by scheming reasoners in France and Germany, each man out of his own brain, that they all end either in materialism and atheism on the one hand, or in idealism and pantheism on the other. All our philosophers have stopped short of that one living, personal, moral God, on whose existence alone humanity can confidently repose—who alone can give to the trembling arch of human speculation that keystone which it demands. The idea of God, in fact, is not a thing that individual reason has first to strike out, so to speak, by the collision or combination of ideas, the collocation of proofs, and the concatenation of arguments. It is a living growth rather of our whole nature, a primary instinct of all moral beings, a necessary postulate of healthy humanity, which is given and received as our life and our breath is, and admits not of being reasoned into any soul that has it not already from other sources. And as no philosopher of Greek or German times that history tells of, ever succeeded yet in inventing a satisfactory theology, or establishing a religion in which men could find solace to their souls, therefore it is clear that that satisfactory Christian theology and Christian religion which we have, and not only that, but all the glimpses of great theological truth that are found twinkling through the darkness of a widespread superstition, came originally from God by common revelation, and not from man by private reasoning. The knowledge of God and a living theology is, in fact, a simple science of experience like any other, only of a peculiar quality and higher in degree. All true human knowledge in moral matters rests on experience, internal or external, higher or lower, on tradition, on language as the bearer of tradition, on revelation; while that false, monstrous, and unconditioned science to which the pride of human reason has always aspired, which would grasp at every thing at once by one despotic clutch, and by a violent bound of logic bestride and beride the All, is, and remains, an oscillating abortion that always would be something, and always can be nothing. A living, personal, moral God, the faith of nations, the watchword of tradition, the cry of nature, the demand of mind, received not invented, existing in the soul not reasoned into it—this is the gravitating point of the moral world, the only intelligible centre of any world; from which whatsoever is centrifugal errs, and to which whatsoever is opposed is the devil.

Not private speculation, therefore, or famous philosophies of any kind, but the living spiritual man, and the totality of the living flow of sacred tradition on which he is borne, and with which he is encompassed, are the two grand sources of "the philosophy of life." Let us follow these principles, now, into a few of their widespread streams and multiform historical branchings. First, the Bible clearly indicates what the profoundest study of the earliest and most venerable literatures confirms, that man was not created at first in a brutish state, crawling with a slow and painful progress out of the dull slime of a half organic state into apehood, and from apehood painfully into manhood; but he was created perfect in the image of God, and has fallen from his primeval glory. This is to be understood not only of the state of man before the Fall as recorded in the two first chapters of Genesis; but every thing in the Bible, and the early traditions of famous peoples, warrants us to believe, that the first ages of men before the Flood, were spiritually enlightened from one great common source of extraordinary aboriginal revelation; so that the earliest ages of the world were not the most infantine and ignorant to a comprehensive survey, as modern conceit so fondly imagines, but the most gigantic and the most enlightened. That beautiful but material and debasing heathenism, with which our Greek and Latin education has made us so familiar, is only a defaced fragment of the venerable whole which preceded it, that old and true heathenism of the holy aboriginal fathers of our race. "There were giants on the earth in those days." We read this; but who believes it? We ought seriously to consider what it means, and adopt it *bona fide* into our living faith of man, and

*August Wilhelm Schlegel, Friedrich's brother and co-founder of the* Athenäum. *Painting by August Tischbein, 1793.*

man's history. Like the landscape of some Alpine country, where the primeval granite Titans, protruding their huge shoulders every where above us and around, make us feel how petty and how weak a thing is man; so ought our imagination to picture the inhabitants of the world before the Flood. Nobility precedes baseness always, and truth is more ancient than error. Antediluvian man—antediluvian nature, is to be imaged as nobler in every respect, more sublime and more pure than postdiluvian man, and postdiluvian nature. But mighty energies, when abused, produce mighty corruptions; hence the gigantic scale of the sins into which the antediluvian men fell; and the terrible precipitation of humanity which followed. This is a point of primary importance, in every attempt to understand how to estimate the value of that world-famous Greek philosophy, which is commonly represented as the crown and the glory of the ancient world. All that Pythagoras and Plato ever wrote of noble and elevating truths, are merely flashes of that primeval light, in the full flood of which, man, in his more perfect antediluvian state, delighted to dwell; and it is remarkable in the case of Pythagoras, Anaxagoras, Thales, and so many other of the Greek philosophers, that the further we trace them

back, we come nearer to the divine truth, which, in the systems of Epicurus, Aristipus, Zeno, or the shallow or cold philosophers of later origin, altogether disappears. Pythagoras and Plato were indeed divinely gifted with a scientific presentiment of the great truths of Christianity soon to be revealed, or say rather restored to the world; while Aristotle, on the other hand, is to be regarded as the father of those unhappy academical schismatics from the Great Church of living humanity, who allowed the ministrant faculty of reason to assume an unlawful supremacy over the higher powers of intellect, and gave birth to that voracious despotism of barren dialectics, in the middle ages commonly called the scholastic philosophy. The Greek philosophy, however, even its noblest Avatar, Plato, much less in the case of a Zeno or an Aristotle, was never able to achieve that which must be the practically proposed end of all higher philosophy that is in earnest; viz. the coming out of the narrow sphere of the school and the palaestra, uniting itself with actual life, and embodying itself completely in the shape of that which we call a church. This Platonism could not do. Christianity did it. Revelation did it. God Incarnate did it. Now once again came humanity forth, fresh from the bosom of the divine creativeness, conquering and to conquer. There was no Aristotle and Plato—no Abelard and Bernard here—reason carping at imagination, and imagination despising reason. But once, if but once in four thousand years, man appeared in all the might of his living completeness. Love walked hand in hand with knowledge, and both were identified in life. The spirit of divine peace brooded in the inner sanctuary of the heart, while the outer man was mailed for the sternest warfare. Such was pure Christianity, so long as it lasted—for the celestial plant was condemned to grow in a terrestrial atmosphere; and there, alas! it it could only grow with a stunted likeness of itself. It was more than stunted also—it was tainted; for are not all things tainted here? Do we not live in a tainted atmosphere? do we not live in a time out of joint? Does not the whole creation literally groan? Too manifestly it does, however natural philosophers may affect to speak of the book of nature, as if it were the clear and uncorrupted text of the living book of God. Not only man, but the whole environment of external nature, which belongs to him, has been deranged by the Fall. In such a world as this, wherein whose will not believe a devil cannot believe a God, it was impossible for Christianity to remain in that state of blissful vital harmony with itself with which it set out. It became divided. Extravagant developments of ambitious, monopolizing faculties became manifest on every side. Self-sufficing Pelagianism and Arianism, here; self-confounding Gnosticism and Manichaeism there. Then came those two great strifes and divisions of the middle ages—the one, that old dualism of the inner man, the ever-repeated strife between reason and imagination, to which we have so often alluded—the other, a no less serious strife of the outward machinery of life, the strife between the spiritual and the temporal powers, between the Pope and the Emperor. This was bad enough; that the two vicars of God on earth should not know to keep the peace among themselves, when the keeping of the peace among others was the very end and aim of the appointment. But worse times were coming. For in the middle ages, notwithstanding the rank evils of barren scholasticism, secular-minded popes, and intrusive emperors, there was still a church, a common Christian religion, a common faith of all Christians; but now, since that anarchical and rebellious movement, commonly called the Reformation, but more fitly termed the revolution, the overturning and overthrowing of the religion of Christendom, we have no more a mere internal strife and division to vex us, but there is an entire separation and divorce of one part of the Christian church (so called) from the main mother institution. The abode of peace has become the camp of war and the arena of battles; that dogmatical theology of the Christian church, which, if it be not the infallible pure mathematics of the moral world, has been deceiving men for 1800 years, and is a liar—that theology is now publicly discussed and denied, scorned and scouted by men who do not blush to call themselves Christians; there is no universal peace any longer to be found in that region where it is the instinct of humanity, before all things, to seek repose; the only religious peace which the present age recognizes, is that of which the Indian talks, when he says of certain epochs of the world's history, *Brahma sleeps!* Those who sleep and are indifferent in spiritual matters find peace; but those who are alive and awake must beat the wind, and battle, belike, with much useless loss of strength, before they can arrive even at that first postulate of all healthy thinking—there is a God. *"Ueber Gott werd ich nie streiten,"* said Herder. "About God I will never dispute." Yet look at German rationalism, look at Protestant theology—what do you see there? Reason usurping the mastery in each individual, without control of the higher faculties of the soul, and of those institutions in life by which those faculties are represented; and, as one man's reason is as good as another's, thence arises war of each self-asserted despotism against that which happens to be next it, and of all against all—a spiritual anarchy, which threatens the entire dissolution of the moral world, and from which there is no refuge but in recurring to the old traditionary faith of a revolted humanity, no redemption but in the venerable repository of those traditions—the one and indivisible holy Catholic church of Christ, of whom, as the inner and eternal keystone is God, so the outer and temporal is the Pope.


Such is a general outline of the philosophy of Frederick Schlegel—a philosophy belonging to the class theological and supernatural, to the genus Christian, to the species sacerdotal and Popish. Now, without stopping here to blame its sublime generalities and beautiful confusions, on the one hand, or to praise its elevated tendency, its catholic and reconciling tone on the other, we shall merely call attention, in a single sentence, physiologically, to its main and distinguishing character. It was, in fact, (in spirit and tendency, though not in outward accomplishment,) to German literature twenty years ago what Puseyism is now to the English church—it was a bold and grand attempt to get rid of those vexing doubts and disputes on the most important subjects that will ever disquiet minds of a certain constitution, so long as they have nothing to lean on but their own judgment; and as Protestantism, when consistently carried out, summarily throws a man back on his individual opinion, and subjects the vastest and most momentous questions to the scrutiny of reason and the tor-

ture of doubt, therefore Schlegel in literary Germany, and Pusey in ecclesiastical England, were equally forced, if they would not lose Christianity altogether, to renounce Protestantism, and to base their philosophy upon sacerdotal authority and ecclesiastical tradition. That Schlegel became a Romanist at Cologne, and Dr Pusey an Anglo-Catholic at Oxford, does not affect the kinship. Both, to escape from the anarchy of Protestant individualism, (as it was felt by them,) were obliged to assert not merely Christianity, but a hierarchy—not merely the Bible, but an authoritative interpretation of the Bible; and both found, or seemed to find, that authoritative interpretation and exorcism of doubt there, where alone in their circumstances, and intellectually constituted as they were, it was to be found. Dr Pusey did not become a Papist like Frederick Schlegel, for two plain reasons—first, because he was an Englishman; second, because he was an English churchman. The authority which he sought for lay at his door; why should he travel to Rome for it? Archbishop Laud had taught apostolical succession before—Dr Pusey might teach it again. But this convenient prop of Popery without the Pope, was not prepared for Frederick Schlegel. There was no Episcopal church, no Oxford in Germany, into whose bosom he could throw himself, and find relief from the agony of religious doubt. He was a German, moreover, and a philosopher. To his searching eye and circumspective wariness, the general basis of tradition which might satisfy a Pusey, though sufficiently broad, did not appear sure enough. To his lofty architectural imagination a hierarchical aristocracy, untopped by hierarchical monarch, did not appear sufficiently sublime. To his all-comprehending and all-combining historical sympathies, a Christian priesthood, with Cyprian, Augustine, and Jerome, but without Hildebrand, Innocent, and Boniface, would have presented the appearance of a fair landscape, with a black yawning chasm in the middle, into which whoever looked shuddered. Therefore Frederick Schlegel; spurning all half measures, inglorious compromises, and vain attempts to reconcile the irreconcilable, vaulted himself at once, with a bold leap, into the central point of sacerdotal Christianity. The obstacles that would have deterred ordinary minds had no effect on him. All points of detail were sunk in the overwhelming importance of the general question. Transubstantiation or consubstantiation, conception, maculate or immaculate, were a matter of small moment with him. What he wanted was a divinely commissioned church with sacred mysteries—a spiritual house of refuge from the weary battle of intellectual east winds, blasting and barren, with which he saw Protestant Germany desolated. This house of refuge he found in Cologne, in Vienna; and having once made up his mind that spiritual unity and peace were to be found only in the one mother church of Christendom, not being one of those half characters who, "making *I dare not* wait upon *I would,*" are continually weaving a net of paltry external *no's* to entangle the progress of every grand decided *yes* of the inner man, Schlegel did not for a moment hesitate to make his thought a deed, and publicly profess his return to Romanism in the face of enlightened and "ultra-Protestant" Germany. To do this certainly required some moral courage; and no just judge of human actions will refuse to sympathize with the motive of this one, however little he may feel himself at liberty to agree with the result.

But Frederick Schlegel, a well informed writer has said, "became Romanist in a way peculiar to himself, and had in no sense given up his right of private judgment." We have not been able to see, from a careful perusal of his works, (in all of which there is more or less of theology,) that there is any foundation for this assertion of Varnhagen. Frederick Schlegel, the German, was as honest and stout a Romanist in this nineteenth century as any Spanish Ferdinand Catholicus in the fifteenth. Freedom of speculation indeed, within certain known limits, and spirituality of creed above what the meagre charity of some Protestants may conceive possible in a Papist, we do find in this man; but these good qualities a St Bernard, a Dante, a Savonarola, a Fénélon, had exhibited in the Romish Church before Schlegel, and others as great may exhibit them again. Freedom of thought, however, in the sense in which it is understood by Protestants, was the very thing which Schlegel, Göres, Adam Müller, and so many others, did give up when they entered the Catholic Church. They felt as Wordsworth did when he wrote his beautiful ode to "Duty;" they had more liberty than they knew how to use—

Me this uncharter'd freedom tires;
I feel the weight of chance desires;
My hopes no more must change their
    name—
I long for a repose that ever is the same.

And if it seem strange to any one that Frederick Schlegel, the learned, the profound, the comprehensive, should believe in Transubstantiation, let him look at a broader aspect of history than that of German books, and ask himself—Did Isabella of Castile—the gentle, the noble, the generous—establish the Inquisition, or allow Ximenes to establish it? In a world which surrounds us on all sides with apparent contradictions, he who admits a real one now and then into his faith, or into his practice, is neither a fool nor a monster.

In his political opinions, Schlegel maintained the same grand consistency that characterizes his religious philosophy. He had more sense, however, and more of the spirit of Christian fraternity in him than, for the sake of absolutism, to become a Turk or a Russian; nay, from some passages in the *Concordia*—a political journal, published by him and his friend Adam Müller, in 1820, and quoted by Mr Robertson—it would almost appear that he would have preferred a monarchy limited by states, conceived in the spirit of the middle ages, to the almost absolute from of monarchical government, under whose protection he lived and lectured at Vienna. To some such constitution as that which now exists in Sweden, for instance, we think he would have had no objections. At the same time, it is certain he gave great offence to the constitutional party in Germany, by the anti-popular tone of his writings generally, more perhaps than by any special absolutist abuses which he had publicly patronized. He was, indeed, a decided enemy to the modern system of representative constitutions, and popular checks; a king by divine right according to the idea of our English nonjurors, was as necessary a corner-stone to his political, as a pope by apostolical succession to his ecclesiastical edifice. And as no confessed corruption of the church, represented as it might be by the

monstrous brutality of a Borgia, or the military madness of a Julius, was, in his view, sufficient to authorize any hasty Luther to make a profane bonfire of a papal bull; any hot Henry to usurp the trade of manufacturing creeds; so no "sacred right of insurrection," no unflinching patriotic opposition, no claim of rights, (by petitioners having *swords* in their hands,) are admissible in his system of a Christian state. And as for the British constitution, and "the glorious Revolution of 1688," this latter, indeed, is one of the best of a bad kind, and that boasted constitution as an example of a house divided against itself, and yet *not* falling, is a perfect miracle of dynamical art, a lucky accident of politics, scarcely to be looked for again in the history of social development, much less to be eagerly sought after and ignorantly imitated. Nay, rather, if we look at this boasted constitution a little more narrowly, and instruct ourselves as to its practical working, what do we see?

> Historical experience, the great teacher of political science, manifestly shows that in these dynamical states, which exist by the cunningly devised balance and counter-balance of different powers, what is called governing is, in truth, a continual strife and contention between the Ministry and the Opposition, who seem to delight in nothing so much as in tugging and tearing the state and its resources to pieces between them, while the hallowed freedom of the hereditary monarch seems to serve only as an old tree, under whose shades the contending parties may the more comfortably choose their ground, and fight out their battles. *(Philosophie des Lebens)*

It is but too manifest, indeed, according to Schlegel's projection of the universe, that all constitutionalism is, properly speaking, a sort of political Protestantism, a fretful fever of the social body, having its origin (like the religious epidemic of the sixteenth century) in the private conceit of the individual, growing by violence and strife, and ending in dissolution. This is the ever-repeated refrain of his political discourses; puerile enough, it may be, to our rude hearing in Britain, but very grateful to polite and patriotic ears at Vienna, when the cannon of Wagram was yet sounding in audible echo beneath their towers. The propounder of such philosophy had not only the common necessity of all philosophers to pile up his political in majestic consistency with his ecclesiastical creed, but he had also to pay back the mad French liberalism with something more mad if possible, and more despotic. And if also Danton, and Mirabeau, and Robespierre, and other terrible Avatars of the destroying Siva in Paris, had raised his naturally romantic temperament a little into the febrile and delirious now and then, what wonder? Shall the devil walk the public streets at noon day, and men not be afraid?

We said that Frederick Schlegel's philosophy, political and religious, but chiefly religious, was the grand key to his popular work on the history of literature. We may illustrate this now by a few instances. In the first place, the "many-sided" Goethe seems to be as little profound as he is charitable, when he sees nothing in the Sanscrit studies of the romantic brothers but a *pis aller,* and a vulgar ambition to bring forward something new, and make German men stare. We do not answer for the elder brother; but

Frederick certainly made the cruise to the east, as Columbus did to the west, from a romantic spirit of adventure. He was not pleased with the old world—he wished to find a new world more to his mind; and, beyond the Indus, he found it. The Hindoos to him were the Greeks of the aboriginal world—"*diese Griechen der Urwelt*"—and so much better and more divine than the western Greeks, as the aboriginal world was better and more divine than that which came after it. If imagination was the prime, the creative faculty in man, here, in the holy Eddas, it had sat throned for thousands of years as high as the Himalayas. If repose was sought for, and rest to the soul from the toil and turmoil of religious wars in Europe, here, in the secret meditations of pious Yooges, waiting to be absorbed into the bosom of Brahma, surely peace was to be found. Take another matter. Why did Frederick Schlegel make so much talk of the middle ages? Why were the times, so dark to others, instinct to him with a steady solar effluence, in comparison of which the boasted enlightenment of these latter days was but as the busy exhibition of squibs by impertinent boys, the uncertain trembling of fire-flies in a dusky twilight? The middle ages were historically the glory of Germany; and those who had lived to see and to feel the Confederation of the Rhine, and the Protectorate of Napoleon, did not require the particular predilections of a Schlegel to carry them back with eager reaction to the days of the Henries, the Othos, and the Fredericks, when to be the German emperor was to be the greatest man in Europe, after the Pope. But to Schlegel the middle ages were something more. The glory of Germany to the patriot, they were the glory of Europe to the thinker. Modern wits have laughed at the enthusiasm of the Crusades. Did they weep over the perfidy of the partition of Poland? Do they really trust themselves to persuade a generous mind that the principle of mutual jealousy and mere selfishness, the meagre inspiration of the so-called balance of power in modern politics, is, according to any norm of nobility in action, a more laudable motive for a public war, than a holy zeal against those who were at once the enemies of Christ, and (as future events but too clearly showed) the enemies of Europe? Modern wits sneer at the scholastic drivelling or the cloudy mistiness of the writers of the middle ages. Did they ever blush for the impious baseness of Helvetius, for the portentous scaffolding of notional skeletons in Hegel? But, alas! we talk of we know not what. What spectacle does modern life present equal to that of St Bernard, the pious monk of Clairvaux, the feeble, emaciated thinker, brooding, with his dove-like eyes, ("*oculos columbinos,*") over the wild motions of the twelfth century, and by the calm might of divine love, guiding the sceptre of the secular king, and the crosier of the spiritual pontiff alike? Was that a weak or a dark age, when the strength of mind and the light of love could triumph so signally over brute force, and that natural selfishness of public motive which has achieved its cold, glittering triumphs in the lives of so many modern heroes and heroines—a Louis, a Frederick, a Catharine, a Napoleon? But indeed here, as elsewhere, we see that the modern world has fallen altogether into a practical atheism by the idolatry of mere reason; whereas all true greatness comes not down from the head, but up from the heart of man. In which greatness of the heart, the Bernards and the Barba-

rossas of the middle ages excelled; and therefore they were better than we.

It is by no means necessary for the admirer of Schlegel to maintain that all this eulogium of the twelfth century, or this depreciation of the times we live in, is just and well-merited. Nothing is more cheap than to praise a pretty village perched far away amid the blue skies, and to rail at the sharp edges and corners of things that fret against our ribs. Let it be admitted that there is not a little of artistical decoration, and a great deal of optical illusion, in the matter; still there is some truth, some great truth, that lay in comparative neglect till Schlegel brought it into prominency. This is genuine literary merit; it is that sort of discovery, so to speak, which makes criticism original. And it was not merely with the bringing forward of new materials, but by throwing new lights on the old, that Frederick Schlegel enriched aesthetical science. If the criticism of the nineteenth century may justly boast of a more catholic sympathy, of a wider flight, of a more comprehensive view, and more various feast than that which it superseded, it owes this, with something that belongs to the spirit of the age generally, chiefly to the special captainship of Frederick Schlegel. If the grand spirit of combination and comprehension which distinguishes the *Lectures on Ancient and Modern Literature,* be that quality which mainly distinguishes the so called Romantic from the Classical school of aesthetics, then let us profess ourselves Romanticists by all means immediately; for the one seems to include the other as the genus does the species. The beauty of Frederick Schlegel is, that his romance arches over every thing like a sky, and excludes nothing; he delights indeed to override every thing despotically, with one dominant theological and ecclesiastical idea, and now and then, of course, gives rather a rough jog to whatever thing may stand in his way; but generally he seeks about with cautious, conscientious care to find room for every thing; and for a wholesale dealer in denunciation (as in some views we cannot choose but call him) is really the most kind, considerate, and charitable Aristarchus that ever wielded a pen. Hear what Varnhagen Von Ense says on this point—

> The inward character of this man, the fundamental impulses of his nature, the merit or the result of his intellectual activity, have as yet found none to describe them in such a manner as he has often succeeded in describing others. It is not every body's business to attempt an anatomy and re-combination of this kind. One must have courage, coolness, profound study, wide sympathies, and a free comprehensiveness, to keep a steady footing and a clear eye in the midst of this gigantic, rolling conglomeration of contradictions, eccentricities, and singularities of all kinds. Here every sort of demon and devil, genius and ghost, Lucinde and Charlemagne, Alarcos, Maria, Plato, Spinoza and Bonald, Goethe consecrated and Goethe condemned, revolution and hierarchy, reel about restlessly, come together, and, what is the strangest thing of all, do *not* clash. For Schlegel, however many Protean shapes he might assume, never cast away any thing that had ever formed a substantial element in his intellectual existence, but

found an *advocatus Dei* to plead always with a certain reputable eloquence even for the most unmannerly of them; and with good reason too, for in his all-appropriating and curiously combining soul, there did exist a living connexion between the most apparently contradictory of his ideas. To point out this connexion, to trace the secret thread of unity through the most distant extremes, to mark the delicate shade of transition from one phasis of intellectual development to another, to remove, at every doubtful point, the veil and to expose the substance, that were a problem for the sagacity of no common critic.

We take the hint. It is not every Byron that finds a Goethe to take him to pieces and build him up again, and peruse him and admire him, as Cuvier did the Mammoth. Those who feel an inward vocation to do so by Schlegel may yet do so in Germany; if there be any in these busy times, even there, who may have leisure to applaud such a work. To us in Britain it may suffice to have essayed to exhibit the fruit and the final results, without attempting curiously to dissect the growth of Schlegel's criticism.

The outward fates of this great critic's life may be found, like every thing else, in the famous "Conversations Lexicon;" but as very few readers of these remarks, or students of the history of ancient and modern literature, may be in a condition to refer to that most useful Cyclopaedia of literary reference, we may here sketch the main lines of Schlegel's biography from the sources supplied by Mr Robertson, in the preface to his excellent translation of the *Lectures on the philosophy of history.* Whatever we take from a different source will be distinctly noted.

The brothers Schlegel belonged to what Frederick in his lectures calls the third generation of modern German literature. The whole period from 1750 to 1800, being divided into three generations, the first comprehends all those whose period of greatest activity falls into the first decade, from 1750 to 1760, and thereabout. Its chief heroes are Wieland, Klopstock, and Lessing. These men of course were all born before the year 1730. The second generation extends from 1770 to 1790, and thereabouts, and presents a development, which stands to the first in the relation of summer to spring—Goethe and Schiller are the two names by which it will be sent down to posterity. Of these the one was born in 1749, and the other in 1759. Then follows that third generation to which Schlegel himself belongs, and which is more generally known in literary history as the era of the Romantic school—a school answering both in chronology, and in many points of character also, to what we call the Lake school in England. Coleridge, Wordsworth, and Southey, are contemporaries of Tieck, Novalis, and the Schlegels. Their political contemporaries are Napoleon and Wellington. The event which gave a direction to their literary development, no less decidedly than it did to the political history of Europe, was the French Revolution. Accordingly, we find that all these great European characters—for so they all are more or less—made the all important passage from youth into manhood during the ferment of the years that followed that ominous date, 1789. This coincidence explains the celebrity of the famous biographical year 1769—Walter Scott was born in that year, Wellington and Napoleon, as every body

knows—and the elder Aristarchus of the Romantic school, *the* translator of Shakspeare, Augustus William Von Schlegel, was born in 1767. At Hanover, five years later, was born his brother Frederick, that is to say, in May 1772, and our Coleridge in the same year—and to carry on the parallel for another year, Ludwig Tieck, Henry Steffens, and Novalis, were all born in 1773. These dates are curious; when taken along with the great fact of the age—the French Revolution—they may serve to that family likeness which we have noted in characterizing the Romanticists in Germany and the Lake school in England. When Coleridge here was dreaming of America and Pantisocracy, Frederick Schlegel was studying Plato, and scheming republics there. In the first years of his literary career, Schlegel devoted himself chiefly to classical literature; and between 1794 and 1797 published several works on Greek and Roman poetry and philosophy, the substance of which was afterwards concentrated into the four first lectures on the history of literature. About this time he appears to have lived chiefly by his literary excertions—a method of obtaining a livelihood very precarious, (as those know best who have tried it,) and to men of a turn of mind more philosophical than popular, even in philosophical Germany, exceedingly irksome. Schlegel felt this as deeply as poor Coleridge—"to live by literature," says he, in one of those letters to Rahel from which we have just quoted—"is to me *je länger je unerträglicher*—the longer I try it the more intolerable." Happily, to keep him from absolute starvation, he married the daughter of Moses Mendelsohn, the Jewish philosopher, who, it appears, had a few pence in her pocket, but not many; and between these, and the produce of his own pen, which could move with equal facility in French as in German, he managed not merely to keep himself and his wife alive, but to transport himself to Paris in the year 1802, and remain there for a year or two, laying the foundation for that oriental evangel which, in 1808, he proclaimed to his countrymen in the little book, *Ueber die Sprache und Weisheit der Indier.* Meanwhile, in the year 1805, he had returned from France to his own Germany—alas, then about to be *one* Germany no more! And while the sun of Austerlitz was rising brightly on the then Emperor of France, and soon to be protector of the Rhine, the future secretary of the Archduke Charles, and literary evangelist of Prince Metternich, was prostrating himself before the three holy kings, and swearing fealty to the shade of Charlemagne in Catholic Cologne. There were some men in those days base enough to impeach the purity of Schlegel's motives in the public profession thus made of the old Romish faith. Such men, wherever they are to be found now or then, ought to be whipped out of the world. If mere worldly motives could have had any influence on such a mind, the gates of Berlin were as open to him as the gates of Vienna. As it was, not wishing to expatriate himself, like Winkelmann, he had nowhere to go to but Vienna; in those days, indeed, mere patriotism and Teutonic feeling, (in which the Romantic school was never deficient,) independently altogether of Popery, could lead him nowhere else. To Vienna, accordingly, he went; and Vienna is not a place—whatever Napoleon, after Mack's affair, might say of the "stupid Austrians"—where a man like Schlegel will ever be neglected. Prince Metternich and the Archduke Charles had eyes in their head; and with the latter, therefore, we find the great Sanscrit scholar marching to share the glory of Aspern and the honour of Wagram; while the former afterwards decorated him with what of courtly remuneration, in the shape of titles and pensions, it is the policy alike and the privilege of politicians to bestow on poets and philosophers who can do them service. Nay, with some diplomatic missions and messages to Frankfurt also, we find the Romantic philosopher entrusted; and even in the great European Congress of Vienna in 1815, he appears exhibiting himself, in no undignified position, alongside of Gentz, Cardinal Gonsalvi, and the Prince of Benevento. We are not to imagine, however, from this, either that the comprehensive philosopher of history had any peculiar talent for practical diplomacy, or that he is to be regarded as a thorough Austrian in politics. For the nice practical problems of diplomacy, he was perhaps the very worst man in the world; and what Varnhagen states in the place just referred to, that Schlegel was, what we should call in England, far too much of a high churchman for Prince Metternich, is only too manifest from the well-known ecclesiastical policy of the Austrian government, contrasted as it is with the ultramontane and Guelphic views propounded by the Viennese lecturer in his philosophy of the eleventh and twelfth centuries. Frederick Schlegel wished to see the state, with relation to the church, in the attitude that Frederick Barbarossa assumed before Alexander III. at Venice—kneeling, and holding the stirrup.

> An emperor tramples where an emperor knelt.

Joseph II., in his estimation, had inverted the poles of the moral world, making the state supreme, and the church subordinate—that degrading position, which the Non-intrusionists picture to themselves when they talk of Erastianism, and which Schlegel would have denominated simply—Protestantism.

During his long residence at Vienna, from 1806 to 1828, Schlegel delivered four courses of public lectures in the following order: —One-and-twenty lectures on Modern History, delivered in the year 1810; sixteen lectures on Ancient and Modern Literature, delivered in the spring of 1812; fifteen lectures on the Philosophy of Life, delivered in 1827; and lastly, eighteen lectures on the Philosophy of History, delivered in 1828. Of these, the Philosophy of Life contains the theory, as the lectures on literature and on history do the application, of Schlegel's catholic and combining system of human intellect, and, altogether, they form a complete and consistent body of Schlegelism. Three works more speculatively complete, and more practically useful in their way, the production of one consistent architectural mind, are, in the history of literature, not easily to be found.

Towards the close of the year 1828, Schlegel repaired to Dresden, a city endeared to him by the recollections of enthusiastic juvenile studies. Here he delivered nine lectures **Ueber die Philosophie der Sprache, und des Worts,** on the Philosophy of Language, a work which the present writer laments much that he has not seen, as it is manifest that the prominency given in Schlegel's Philosophy of Life

above sketched to living experience and primeval tradition, must, along with his various accomplishments as a linguist, have eminently fitted him for developing systematically the high significance of human speech. On Sunday the 11th January 1829, he was engaged in composing a lecture which was to be delivered on the following Wednesday, and had just come to the significant words— *"Das ganz vollendete und voll-kommene Verstehen selbst, aber"*—"The perfect and complete understanding of things, however"—when the mortal palsy suddenly seized his hand, and before one o'clock on the same night he had ceased to philosophize. The words with which his pen ended its long and laborious career, are characteristic enough, both of the general imperfection of human knowledge, and of the particular quality of Schlegel's mind. The Germans have a proverb: —*"Alles wäre gut wäre kein* Aber *dabei"*—"Every thing would be good were it not for an Aber—for a However—for a But." This is the general human vice that lies in that significant Aber. But Schlegel's part in it is a virtue—one of his greatest virtues—a conscientious anxiety never to state a general proposition in philosophy, without, at the same time, stating in what various ways the eternal truth comes to be limited and modified in practice. Great, indeed, is the virtue of a Schlegelian Aber. Had it not been for that, he would have had his place long ago among the vulgar herds of erudite and intellectual dogmatists.

Heinrich Steffens, a well-known literary and scientific character in Germany, in his personal memoirs recently published, describes Frederick Schlegel, at Jena in 1798, as

> a remarkable man, slenderly built, but with beautiful regular features, and a very intellectual expression—(*im höchsten Grade gisntreich.*) In his manner there was something remarkably calm and cool, almost phlegmatic. He spoke with great slowness and deliberation, but often with much point, and a great deal of reflective wit.

He was thus a thorough German in his temperament; so at least as Englishmen and Frenchmen, of a more nimble blood, delight to picture the Rhenish Teut, not always in the most complimentary contrast with themselves. As it is, his merit shines forth only so much the more, that being a German of the Germans, he should by one small work, more of a combining than of a creative character, have achieved an European reputation and popularity with a certain sphere, that bids fair to last for a generation or two, at least, even in this book-making age. Such an earnest devotedness of research; such a gigantic capacity of appropriation; such a kingly faculty of comprehension, will rarely be found united in one individual. The multifarious truths which the noble industry of such a spirit either evolved wisely or happily disposed, will long continue to be received as a welcome legacy by our studious youth; and as for his errors in a literary point of view, and with reference to British use, practically considered, they are the mere breadth of fantastic colouring, which, being removed, does not destroy the drawing.

*"Frederick Schlegel," in* Blackwood's Edinburgh Maga-

zine, *Vol. LIV, No. CCCXXXI, September, 1843, pp. 311-24.*

### George Brandes    (essay date 1906)

[*Brandes was a Danish literary critic and biographer. In his major critical work,* Hovedstromniger i det 19de Aarhundredes Litteratur *(1872-90;* Main Currents in Nineteenth-Century Literature), *Brandes viewed French, German, and English literary movements as a series of reactions against eighteenth-century thought. In the following excerpt from that work, he reads* Lucinde *as a manifesto for Romanticism.*]

At the University of Jena, in June 1801, a young candidate for the degree of doctor stood on the rostrum delivering his thesis. Everything possible was done to put him out and annoy him; the unprecedented step was taken of providing opponents. One of these, a somewhat inept young man, desiring to distinguish himself, began: "*In tractaiu tuo erotico Lucinda dixisti,*" &c., &c. To this the candidate shortly responded by calling his opponent a fool. A regular uproar ensued, and one of the professors indignantly declared that it was thirty years since the platform of the school of philosophy had been profaned by such disgraceful behaviour. The candidate retorted that it was thirty years since any one had been so disgracefully treated. This candidate was Friedrich Schlegel, in those days so much dreaded on account of his terrible opinions that he was sometimes refused permission to spend a night in a town. In a rescript from the *Universitets-Kuratorium* of the Electorate of Hanover to the Pro-Rector of Göttingen, dated September 26, 1800, we read: "Should the Professor's brother, Friedrich Schlegel, notorious for the immoral tendency of his writings, come to Göttingen, purposing to stay there for any time, this is not to be permitted; you will be so good as to intimate to him that he must leave the town."

Somewhat harsh justice this—and all the to-do was on account of *Lucinde*!

It is not the creative power displayed in it which makes *Lucinde* one of the most important works of the Romantic School, for, in spite of all the "fleshly" talk in the book, there is no flesh and blood in it, no real body. Neither is it depth of thought. There is more philosophy in the few paradoxical pages written by Schopenhauer under the title *Metaphysik der Liebe* than in pretentious *Lucinde* from beginning to end. It is not even a bacchantic joy in nature, in life. If we compare it with Heinse's *Ardinghello,* a book glowing with genuine Southern joy of life, we see clearly how anaemic and theoretic *Lucinde* is. It is as a manifesto and programme that the book is valuable. Its main idea is to proclaim the unity and harmony of life as revealed to us most clearly and most comprehensibly in the passion of love, which gives a sensual expression to the spiritual emotion, and spiritualises the sensual pleasure. What it aims at depicting is the transformation of real life into poetry, into art, into Schiller's "play" of powers, into a dreamy, imaginative existence, with every longing satisfied, a life in which man, acting with no aim, living for no purpose, is initiated into the mysteries of nature, "under-

stands the plaint of the nightingale, the smile of the new-born babe, and all that is mysteriously revealed in the hieroglyphics of flowers and stars."

This book is totally misunderstood by those who, like Kierkegaard, arm themselves with a whole set of dogmatic principles, and fall upon it, exclaiming: "What it aims at is the unmitigated sensuality which excludes the element of spirituality; what it combats is the spirituality which includes an element of sensuality." One can scarcely realise the blindness implied by such an utterance—but there are no better blinders than those provided by orthodoxy. Nor is it possible really to understand *Lucinde* so long as, like Gutzkow, we only see in it a vindication of the doctrine of free love, or, like Schleiermacher, a protest against incorporeal spirituality, a denunciation of the affected foolishness that denies and explains away flesh and blood. The fundamental idea of the book is the Romantic doctrine of the *identity of life and poetry.* This serious thought, however, is presented in a form expressly calculated to win the laurels of notoriety. Our admiration is aroused by the bold, defiant tone of the author's challenge, by the courage, born of conviction, with which he exposes himself to personal insult, and to public, ill-natured discussion of his private life. Worthy of admiration, too, is the skill with which the different views and watchwords of Romanticism are collected and presented to us in small compass; for all the various tendencies of the movement, developed by so many different individuals, are to be seen in this one book, spreading fanwise from a centre. But we are disgusted by the artistic impotence to which the so-called novel, in reality a mere sketch, bears witness, by its many beginnings that end in nothing, and by all the feeble self-worship which seeks to disguise barrenness by producing an artificial and unhealthy heat in which to hatch its unfertile eggs. Caroline Schlegel has preserved for us the following biting epigram, written soon after the book came out—

> Der Pedantismus bat die Phantasie
> Um einen Kuss, sie wies ihn an die Sünde;
> Frech, ohne Kraft, umarmt er die,
> Und sie genas mit einem todten Kinde,
> Genannt Lucinde.

> [Pedantry asked Fancy for a kiss; she sent him to Sin; audaciously but impotently he embraces Sin; she bears him a dead child, by name Lucinde.]

Beyond considering the word "sin" inappropriate—for *Lucinde* only sins against good taste and true poetry—I have no fault to find with this cruel satire.

At the very core of *Lucinde* we have once again subjectivity, self-absorption, in the form of an arbitrariness which may develop into anything—revolution, effrontery, bigotry, reaction—because it is not from the beginning associated with anything that is a power, because the Ego does not act in the service of an idea which could give to its endeavour stability and value; it acts neither in the service of civil nor of intellectual liberty. This arbitrariness or lawlessness, which, in the domain of art, becomes the Friedrich Schlegelian "irony," the artist's attitude of aloofness from his subject, his free play with it (resulting, as far as poetry is concerned, in the dictatorship of pure form, which mocks at its own substance and destroys its own illusions), becomes in the domain of real life an irony which is the dominant feature in the characters and lives of the gifted few, the aristocracy of intellect. This irony is a riddle to the profane, who "lack the sense of it." It is "the freest of all licences," because by its means a man sets himself outside of and above himself; yet it is also the most subject to law, being, we are told, unqualified and inevitable. It is a perpetual self-parody, incomprehensible to "the harmonious vulgar" (*harmonisch Platten*—the name bestowed by the Romanticists on those who live contentedly in a trivial, common-place harmony), who mistake its earnest for jest and its jest for earnest.

It is not merely in name that this irony bears a fundamental resemblance to Kierkegaard's, which also aristocratically "chooses to be misunderstood." The Ego of genius is the truth, if not in the sense in which Kierkegaard would have us understand his proposition, "Subjectivity is the truth," still in the sense that the Ego has every externally valid commandment and prohibition in its power; and, to the astonishment and scandal of the world, invariably expresses itself in paradoxes. Irony is "divine audacity." In audacity thus comprehended there are endless possibilities. It is freedom from prejudice, yet it suggests the possibility of the most audacious defence of all possible kinds of prejudices. It is more easily attainable, we are told, by woman than by man. "Like the feminine garb, the feminine intellect has this advantage over the masculine, that its possessor by a single daring movement can rise above all the prejudices of civilisation and bourgeois conventionality, at once transporting herself into the state of innocence and the lap of Nature." The lap of Nature! There is an echo of Rousseau's voice even in this wanton tirade. We seem to hear the trumpet-call of revolution; what we really hear is only the proclamation of reaction. Rousseau desired to return to the state of nature, when men roamed naked through the pathless forests and lived upon acorns. Schelling wished to turn the course of evolution back to the primeval ages, to the days before man had fallen. Schlegel blows revolutionary melodies on the great romantic "wonder-horn." But, as we read in *Des Knaben Wunderhorn:* "Es blies ein Jäger wohl in sein Horn—Und Alles was er blies, das war verlorn" ["A hunter blew into his horn, and all that he blew the wind carried away "].

The result is not intellectual emancipation, but simply a refinement of pleasure. The whole wide domain of love is transformed into the domain of art. As Romantic poetry is poetry to the second power, poetry about poetry, refined and chastened poetry, so the love of the Romanticists is refined and chastened love, "the art of love." The different degrees of the higher sensuality are described and classified. I refer the reader to *Lucinde,* which does not, like *Ardinghello,* present us with voluptuous descriptions, but merely with dry, pedantic theory, the empty framework of which it is left to the reader's experience and imagination to fill. Romantic audacity is, in one of its aspects, idleness, the indolence of genius. Idleness is described as "the life-atmosphere of innocence and inspiration." In its highest expression it is pure passivity, the life of the plant. "The highest, most perfect life is a life of pure vegetation."

The Romanticists return to nature to such good purpose that they revert to the plant. Passive enjoyment of the eternally enduring moment would be their idea of perfection. "I meditated seriously," says Julius to Lucinde, "upon the possibility of an eternal embrace." As genius, which is independent of toil and trouble, and voluptuous enjoyment, which in itself is passive bliss, have nothing to do with aim, action, or utility, so idleness, *dolce far niente,* comes to be regarded as the best that life can offer, and purpose, which leads to systematic action, is denounced as ridiculous and philistine. The principal utterance to this effect in *Lucinde* is the following: "*Industry and utility* are the angels of death with the flaming swords, who stand in the way of man's return to Paradise." Yes, that is exactly what they are! Industry and utility bar the way back to all the Paradises which lie behind us. Therefore we hold them sacred! Utility is one of the main forms of good; and what is industry but the renunciation of distracting pleasures, the enthusiasm, the power, whereby this good is attained!

*Return* to perfection is, in art, a return to the lawlessness of genius, to the stage at which the artist may do one thing, or may do another which is exactly the opposite. In life it is the retrogression of idleness, for he who is idle goes back, back to passive pleasure. In philosophy it is the return to intuitive beliefs, beliefs to which Schlegel applies the name of religion; which religion in its turn leads back to Catholicism. As far as nature and history are concerned, it is retrogression towards the conditions of the primeval Paradise. Thus it is the central idea of Romanticism itself—retrogression—which explains how it was that even the heaven-storming *Lucinde,* like all the other heaven-stormers of the Romanticists, had not the slightest practical outcome.

In *Lucinde,* then, as in a nutshell, are to be found all the theories which, later in the history of Romanticism, are developed and illustrated by examples. In such an essay as that on the Instinct of Change by the Aesthete in Kierkegaard's *Enten-Eller* ("Either-Or") idleness is systematised. "Never adopt any calling or profession. By so doing a man becomes simply one of the mob, a tiny bolt in the great machinery of the state; he ceases to be master. . . . But though we hold aloof from all regular callings, we ought not to be inactive, but to attach great importance to occupation which is identical with idleness. . . . The whole secret lies in the independence, the absence of restraint. We are apt to believe that there is no art in acting unrestrained by any law; in reality the most careful calculation is required, if we are not to go astray, but to obtain enjoyment from it. . . ."

Idleness, lawlessness, enjoyment! This is the three-leaved clover which grows all over the Romanticist's field. In such a book as Eichendorff's *Das Leben eines Taugenichts* ("Life of a Ne'er-do-Well") idleness is idealised and exalted in the person of the hero. And purposelessness is another important item, which must on no account be overlooked. It is another designation for the genius of Romanticism. "To have a purpose, to act according to that purpose, artificially to combine purpose with purpose, and thereby create new purposes, is a bad habit, which has become so deeply rooted in the foolish nature of godlike man, that he is obliged, when for once it is his desire to float aimlessly upon the stream of constantly changing images and emotions, to do even this of settled purpose. . . . It is very certain, my friend, that man is by nature a serious animal." (Julius to Lucinde.)

On the subject of this utterance, even that orthodox Christian, Kierkegaard, says:

> In order not to misjudge Schlegel, we must bear in mind the perverted ideas which had insinuated themselves into men's minds in regard to many of the relations of life, and which had specially and indefatigably striven to make love as tame, well broken-in, heavy, sluggish, useful, and obedient, as any other domestic animal—in short, as unerotic as possible. . . . There is a very narrow-minded morality, a policy of expediency, a futile teleology, which many men worship as an idol, an idol that claims every infinite aspiration as its legitimate offering. Love is considered nothing in itself; it only acquires importance from the purpose it is made to serve in the paltry play which holds the stage of family life.

It is perhaps admissible to conclude that what Kierkegaard says about "the tame, well broken-in, sluggish, and useful domestic animal, love," found its most apt application in Germany, which at that time was undoubtedly the home of the old-fashioned womanliness. The satirical sallies in Tieck's comedies occasionally point in the same direction. In his *Däumling* ("Hop-o'-my-thumb") a husband complains of his wife's craze for knitting, which gives him no peace; a complaint which, perhaps, can only be understood in Germany, where to this day ladies are to be seen knitting even in places of public entertainment—at the concerts on the Brühlsche Terrasse in Dresden, for example. Herr Semmelziege says: —

> Des Hauses Sorge nahm zu sehr den Sinn ihr ein,
> Die Sauberkeit, das Porzellan, die Wäsche gar:
> Wenn ich ihr wohl von meiner ew'gen Liebe sprach,
> Nahm sie der Bürste vielbehaartes Brett zur Hand,
> Um meinem Rock die Fäden abzukehren still.
>
> . . . . .
>
> Doch hätt' ich gern geduldet Alles, ausser Eins:
> Dass, wo sie stand, und wo sie ging, auswärts, im Haus,
> Auch im Concert, wenn Tongewirr die Schöpfung schuf,
>
> . . . . .
>
> Da zaspelnd, haspelnd, heftig rauschend, nimmer still,
> Ellnbogen fliegend, schlagend Seiten und Geripp,
> Sie immerdar den Strickstrumpf eifrig handgehabt.
>
> [Her mind was occupied with household cares—
> The washing, and the china, and the cook:
> Did I begin to speak of endless love,
> She took the bristled clothes-brush in her hand,
> And calmly turned me round and brushed my coat.

> . . . . .
>
> All this I bore quite placidly, but not
> That, sitting, standing, everywhere we went,
> Yes, even at concerts, when sweet strains beguiled,
>
> . . . . .
>
> Entwining, clicking, rustling, never still,
> Her elbows flying, thumping on her side,
> Her knitting-needles vigorously she plied.]

The most comical part of this satire is the passage which, whether intentionally or unintentionally on the author's part, reads like a parody of the well-known Roman Elegy in which Goethe drums the hexameter measure, "leise mit fingernder Hand," upon his mistress's back: —

> Einst als des Thorus heilig Lager uns umfing,
> Am Himmel glanzvoll prangte Lunas keuscher Schein,
> Der goldnen Aphrodite Gab' erwünschend mir,
> Von silberweissen Armen ich umflochten lag.
> Schon denkend, welch ein Wunderkind so holder Nacht,
> Welch Vaterlandserretter, kraftgepanzert, soll
> Dem zarten Leib entspriessen nach der Horen Tanz,
> Fühl' ich am Rücken hinter mir gar sanften Schlag:
> Da wähn ich, Liebsgekose neckt die Schulter mir,
> Und lächle fromm die süsse Braut und sinnig an:
> Bald naht mir der Enttäuschung grauser Höllenschmerz
> Das Strickzeug tanzt auf meinem Rücken thätig fort;
> Ja, stand das Werk just in der Ferse Beugung, wo
> Der Kundigste, ob vielem Zählen, selber pfuscht.

> [The sacred hymeneal couch had received us; Luna's chaste beams illumined our chamber. Encircled by white arms I lay, praying for Aphrodite's favour, dreaming of the marvellous child that needs must be the offspring of a night like this, the mighty hero who in fulness of time shall see the light. Soft taps upon my shoulder rouse me from my dream;' tis my sweet bride caressing me; I thank her silently, with tender, meaning smile. One moment later, and my heart is torn by hellish pangs of disillusionment; it is her knitting that is dancing on my back; worse still—she is at the turning of the heel, that point when the most skilful, despite their counting, often blunder.]

When the cult of the useful is carried as far as this, we can understand advocacy of purposelessness.

But purposelessness and idleness are inseparable. "Only Italians," we are told, "know how to walk, and only Orientals how to lie; and where has the mind developed with more refinement and sweetness than in India? And in every clime it is idleness which distinguishes the noble from the simple, and which is, therefore, the essence of nobility."

This last assertion is outrageous, but its very audacity is significant. It shows the attitude of Romanticism towards the masses. To have the means to do nothing is, in its estimation, the true patent of nobility. Its heroes are those who cultivate the unremunerative arts, and are supported by others—kings and knights like those in Fouqué's and Ingemann's books, artists and poets like those in Tieck's and Novalis's. It separates itself from humanity, will do nothing for it, but only for the favoured few. The hero and heroine in *Lucinde* are the gifted artist and the woman of genius; it is not the ordinary union, but the "nature-marriage" or the "art-marriage" (*Naturehe, Kunstehe*) for which our interest is claimed. Observe how Julius at once asks Lucinde whether her child, if a girl, shall be trained as a portrait or as a landscape painter. Only as a member of the fraternity of artists do her parents take any interest in her. Only authors and artists have part and lot in the poetry of life.

It is not difficult to understand how it was that *Lucinde* was barren of any social results. But though the book had no practical outcome, though it was too feeble to effect any kind of reform, there was, nevertheless, something practical underlying it.

Let us cast a glance at the principal characters. They stand out in strong relief upon a background of the profoundest scorn for all the prose of real life and all the conventions of society. The book is in no wise ashamed of its erotic theories; in its conscious purity it feels itself elevated above the judgment of the vulgar: "It is not only the kingly eagle which dares to scorn the screaming of the ravens; the swan, too, is proud, and pays as little heed. Its only care is that its white wings shall not lose their brightness; its only desire, to cling, unruffled, to Leda's breast, and breathe forth all that is mortal in it in song."

The image is pretty and daring, but is it true? The story of Leda and the swan has been treated in so many ways.

Julius is a pessimistic (*zerrissener*) young man, an artist, of course. We are told in the *Lehrjahre der Männlichkeit,* the chapter containing what Flaubert has called *l'éducation sentimentale,* that it was strikingly characteristic of him that he could play faro with apparently passionate eagerness, and yet in reality be absent-minded and careless; he would dare everything in the heat of the moment, and as soon as he had lost would turn indifferently away. Such a trait may not excite our admiration, but it at all events produces a pretty distinct impression of a pleasure-loving, *blasé* young man, who, feeling no powerful impulse towards action, seeks for excitement while leading a life of careless, coldly despairing idleness. The history of his development is indicated, as is often the case with quite young men, simply by a succession of female names.

Of the women in question we have only very slight sketches, like the pencil-drawings in an album. One of these introductory portraits is rather more elaborated than the rest, that of a *dame aux camélias* sunk in Oriental indolence, who, like the original *dame aux camélias,* is raised above her position by a true passion, and dies when she is neither understood nor believed. She dies by her own hand, makes a brilliant exit from life, and seems to us, as she is described sitting in her boudoir with her hands in her lap, surrounded by great mirrors and inhaling perfumes, like a living image of the aesthetic stupor of self-contemplation and self-absorption, which was the final development of Romanticism. After passing through numbers of erotic experiences, all equally and exceedingly repulsive, Julius finally makes the acquaintance of his feminine counterpart, Lucinde, whose impression is never effaced. "In her he met a youthful artist" (Of course!), "who, like himself, passionately worshipped beauty and loved nature and solitude. In her landscapes one felt a fresh breath of real air. She painted not to gain a living or to perfect herself in an art" (On no account any purpose or utility!) "but simply for pleasure" (Dilettantism and irony!). "Her productions were slight water-colour sketches. She had lacked the patience and industry required to learn oil-painting." (No industry!) . . . "Lucinde had a decided leaning towards the romantic" (Of course she had; she is romance incarnate!). "She was one of those who do not live in the ordinary world, but in one created by themselves. . . . With courageous determination she had broken with all conventions, cast off all bonds, and lived in perfect freedom and independence." From the time when Julius meets her, his art too becomes more fervid and inspired. He paints the nude "in a flood of vitalising light;" his figures "were like animated plants in human shapes."

With Julius and Lucinde life flows on smoothly and melodiously, "like a beautiful song," in perpetually aroused and satisfied longing. The action passes, as it were, in a studio where the easel stands close to the alcove. Lucinde becomes a mother, and their union is now the "marriage of nature" (*die Naturehe*). "What united us before was love and passion. Now nature has united us more closely." The birth of the child gives the parents "civic rights in the state of nature" (probably Rousseau's), the only civic rights they seem to have valued. The Romanticists were as indifferent to social and political rights as Kierkegaard's hero, who was of opinion that we ought to be glad that there are some who care to rule, thereby freeing the rest of us from the task.

*George Brandes, "Social Endeavours of the Romanticists: Lucinde" and "Romantic Purposelessness," in his* Main Currents in Nineteenth Century Literature: The Romantic School in Germany, Vol. II, *William Heinemann, 1906, pp. 69-74, 75-80.*

### Howard E. Hugo   (essay date 1948)

[*In the following essay, Hugo presents a detailed examination of Schlegel's Romantic dialogue* Gespräch über die Poesie, *calling the treatise "an essay rich in suggestiveness for critics of all times by virtue of its brilliant insights into the nature of aesthetics."*]

"Mettons le marteau dans les théories, les poétiques et les systèmes. Jetons bas ce vieux plâtrage, qui masque la façade de l'art!" cries [Victor] Hugo in the *Préface de Cromwell;* it is Tashtego's hand with a hammer, nailing a red flag to the masthead, that we last see in the great novel of American Romanticism, *Moby Dick;* it was the hammer along with the sickle that was to be the emblem of the political party whose doctrines were based on Marx's tract of 1848. The hammer, with its connotations as an instrument of violent destruction and equally vigorous rebuilding, is perhaps the most appropriate symbol for the Romantic movement; and the literary treatises of Romanticism reflect a tendency to destroy the ideology of the immediate past, in order to make room for the outlook of the present. If this may be taken to be a distinguishing characteristic of the Romantic manifesto, certainly Friedrich Schlegel's **Gespräch über die Poesie** must be seen as a model, indeed the *fons et origo,* for much of the writing that was to follow.

Schlegel's work was written and first appeared in 1800. A curious, uneven essay, conceived in the form of a dialogue between seven young intellectuals whose names are reminiscent of a seventeenth-century pastoral [Amalia, Camilla, Markus, Ludoviko, Antonio, Andrea, and Lothario], it nevertheless is one of the significant documents in the development of European Romanticism; and with it are to be found, albeit often in rudimentary form, many of the ideas we consider unique to the movement. Naturally one of the chief dangers in an examination of such a brilliant essay is that the critic, who already has certain *a priori* concepts, is too apt to see significance, when none exists, in the chance phrase—particularly when it is lifted out of context. Therefore, the chief endeavor in this brief discussion of Schlegel's work, will be to discover the nature of his thought within the limits that Schlegel himself establishes. What is his definition of "classical"? Against what elements in the period we now call Neo-Classic is he rebelling? What does he mean by *Poesie?* These and other similar questions must be the subject of any inquiry whose aim is true criticism—that is to say, understanding. If, from our vantage point in history, his answers occasionally seem erroneous or imperfect, the very existence of the questions he poses can be revealing insofar as they illuminate certain aspects of the age. What is important to see, is that we have here one of the first examples of the type of criticism now associated with all aesthetic *avant-gardes:* documents whose primary interest is in the shape of things

to come, where the writer considers himself not merely the wielder of the blue-pencil, but rather—in the words of Shelley—"the hierophant of the unapprehended inspiration." This shift in the conception of the critic himself, so important in our own day, was an insight peculiar to Romanticism—indeed, I would venture to say, to German Romanticism. And if this speculation be granted, then the major portion of our gratitude must go to Friedrich Schlegel.

The first section of the **Gespräch** is actually a short introduction, where Schlegel discusses directly with the reader—without using the framework of a fictitious dialogue—the identity of *Poesie* with metaphysics. Here an idea which is later expanded at some length, is initially presented: *Poesie* is universal, a necessary ingredient of the ego; it is the very stuff of reality, and the physical universe—in a metaphor used by Schlegel—is itself a kind of divine poetry. Perhaps it would be clarifying, and legitimate in view of Schlegel's admitted affiliation with German Idealism, to borrow the Kantian distinction between the phenomenal and the numinal: *Poesie* belongs to the region of the numinal—the locus of pure Idea—which manifests itself through the world of phenomena. In any case, the *new* poetry will not be merely sensuous, the substance without the spirit.

> Unermeßlich und unerschöpflich ist die Welt
> der Poesie wie der Reichthum der belebenden
> Natur an Gewächsen, Thieren und Bildungen
> jeglicher Art, Gestalt und Farbe.

*Poesie* and *Natur* are made one. What then is the mission of the individual poet, in this cosmic scheme? He too creates his own *Poesie,* limited in scope by the human finitude of the poet; he must exist in a state of unceasing activity, ever widening his poetic insights and capabilities.

There follows the first dialogue—to the modern reader, a somewhat flimsy vehicle in which to propound complicated ideas. Incidentally, it may be noted that Schlegel's employment of the dialogue seems scarcely for traditional Socratic reasons, since his young *literati,* comprising what one might call the first Romantic *avant-garde,* are in wonderful agreement throughout their discussions. This dubious intellectual drama is evident in the four principal parts of the work, when Andrea, Ludoviko, Antonio, and Markus each read prepared speeches. We find that Camilla praises a play she has just seen, and her conversational opening leads to a brief survey of "die sogenannten classischen Dichter der Engländer." Schlegel's use of the term "classical" is frankly derogatory, when he speaks of Pope and Dryden as two apostles of false poetry, representatives of "eine moderne Krankheit, durch die jede Nation hindurch müsse, wie die Kinder durch die Pocken"—a sickness epidemic in France and England. At the request of the *cénacle,* Andrea reads his paper, **"Die Epochen der Dichtkunst,"** which is the author's systematic exposition of the history of culture from the Greeks to his own era.

Knowledge of art and of general culture, says Schlegel, is only obtained via history.

> Es ist aller Kunst wesentlich eigen, sich an das
> Gebildete anzuschließen, und darum steigt die

Geschichte von Geschlecht zu Geschlecht, von Stufe zu Stufe immer höher ins Altherthum zurück, bis zur ersten ursprünglichen Quelle.

For us Europeans, the sole, original, and primitive "spring" is Hellas, just as was Homer for the Greeks of the post-Heroic age. The epic, Schlegel continues, was the great art form and the parent of all the *genres* that followed; thus he describes the decay of the epic plant which has left behind the seeds from which grow new species, purveyors of new beauty. This notion of the iambic and elegiac, as well as comedy and tragedy, all evolving out of the epic was rather a literary commonplace in Schlegel's day. The sense of decay and rebirth, the feeling that one cycle must terminate as a necessary pre-condition for the creation of another, even the metaphor of the organism that must die in order that new generations may come to life, (the legend of the phoenix rising again out of its own ashes is used later in Schlegel's work)—these are the qualities of his thought that mark it as looking toward the future rather than back to the past.

In his praise of the Greek poetry of the Heroic age, Schlegel stays within the tradition of the great eighteenth-century Hellenists. Winckelmann, almost a half-century earlier, had described the perfection of Greek art which possessed "eine edle Einfalt und eine stille Größe"; indeed, he had advised the modern artist to imitate Greek models directly as a short-cut to excellence rather than turn to nature itself, since the modern eye had lost its earlier ability to view nature with clarity and understanding. It is when Schlegel demonstrates his complete historicity, that he takes his point of departure from Winckelmann. Greek poetry of the *goldne Zeitalter* was canonic and perfect, Schlegel says: hence it is the model *in spirit* for all succeeding poetry. It was the product of a genuine, wholesome outlook; it arose out of a real need and not out of a desire for servile imitation; it was "eins und untheilbar durch das festliche Leben freyer Menschen und durch die heilige Kraft der alten Götter"; it was—to return to his original definition of the highest *Poesie*—the poetry of an age that best realized the union of ideality and reality. But because we are caught up in the ceaseless flow of history and the ideals of one age can never act, in their particularity, as the standards for another, we cannot hope to re-attain the pristine purity of ancient Greece. Thus in a few paragraphs Schlegel overthrows the whole Renaissance and Neo-Classic theory of imitation. The art of the great age of Greece is still retained as the *sine qua non;* there is no perfection than that which defies repetition. It is a revolutionary shift, however, when the attempt to duplicate the external forms of an earlier historical epoch is abandoned, and there is instead a turning toward a more metaphysical inquiry into the conditions that make perfection possible. The attitude of the seventeenth and eighteenth-century thinkers was based essentially on a rational outlook, a belief in the analytic and orderly processes of reason. Schlegel is forced to take recourse to ontological rather than logical concepts; and if one finds confusion in his ideas, it is wise to remember his being the herald of a *Weltanschauung* still in a stage of early formulation. Succeeding thinkers like Hegel and Schopenhauer were to postulate and qualify the terms that Schlegel was seeking—

terms that with him find only a partial and tentative expression.

By his canonization of the great age of Greece, in effect he rewrites the history of culture. For a brief moment in history, "great" tragedy and comedy enter on the heels of the epic; although comedy, having evolved from the Iambic and a *parody* of the epic, suffers from an intrinsic weakness.

Alles, was noch folgt, bis auf unsre Zeiten, ist Überbleibsel, Nachhall, einzelne Ahndung, Annäherung, Rückkehr zu jenem höchsten Olymp der Poesie.

The Alexandrian school is mere empty virtuosity; the art of Rome—and here Schlegel was one of the first to differentiate between Greek and Roman culture—owes its poorness to the original sin of Alexandrian imitation. The so-called Golden or Augustan age is completely revaluated; no product of a genuine, indigenous *Zeitgeist,* it is dismissed as the shallow imitation of a shallow imitation. The sole *forte* of the Romans was satire, says Schlegel. Unfortunately they strove to transcend this limited *genre,* and failure was inevitable.

The *Cinquocento* in Italy, the ages of Louis XIV in France and Queen Anne in England, the Aufklärung in Germany—"jedes folgende war leerer und schlechter noch als das vorhergehende, und was sich die Deutschen zuletzt als golden eingebildet haben, verbietet die Würde dieser Darstellung näher zu bezeichnen." It is as if he saw the Alexandrian tradition as another race of Tantalus, and each culture that partook of the original misconception produced nothing but relatively worthless art. There was "kein classisches Werk in so langer Zeit:" the word "classical" again describes poetry that is unique to its own age, poetry that pursues its own ideal and rests solely on its own cultural environment.

The descent of the wild Gothic-German races to the shores of the Mediterranean led to the first manifestation of valid art in modern times. The impact of Arabian and Oriental culture upon the Northerners gave rise to the romance, and finally Dante appeared as the triumphal synthesis—the poet whose work was also the product of a genuine mythology, the Roman Catholic Church. The germ for the concept of the North and the South each creating distinct and separate literatures, an idea later expanded by such writers as Mme. de Staël and Sismondi, is planted here; what is equally significant is Schlegel's assertion that at least part of the greatness of Dante was concomitant with the poet's dependence upon the Christian myth. Schlegel's historicity makes him tacitly attribute equal value to both Greek and Christian mythology, just as later in the **Gespräch** he expresses similar admiration for the mythology of the East.

Shakespeare and Cervantes: these are the two poets who best embody for Schlegel the recapturing of the nature of true *Poesie.* The canonic aspect of their genius makes them literally incomparable, as was Homer. The Spanish writer reached the pinnacle of his achievement in *Don Quixote,* where he conceived a new form for the vehicle of his unique expression; while it is the history plays of Shakespeare that represent the acme of his greatness.

The cycle of true *Poesie* followed by a period of decadent Alexandrianism returns after Shakespeare and Cervantes, although strictly speaking it is less the recurrence of a cycle than it is the reassertion of the original post-Homeric tradition: all European Neo-Classicism continues in the same unhappy line of the Augustan *goldne Zeitalter.* There is the same feeling of the bulk of the responsibility for the modern *falsche Poesie* resting with the French, that is apparent in Goethe's remark thirty years before: "Französgen, was willst du mit der griechischen Rüstung, sie ist dir zu gros und zu schweer." Again the time belongs to the skillful *virtuosi* rather than to the real poets; again the misconceived quest is to recreate the alien forms of a so-called Golden Age.

> Aus oberflächlichen Abstractionen und Räsonnements, aus dem misverstandenen Altherthum und dem mittelmäßigen Talent entstand in Frankreich ein umfassendes und zusammenhängendes System von falscher Poesie, welches auf einer gleich falschen Theorie der Dichtkunst ruhete . . .

Schlegel interjects a note of hope into this dismal literary scene when he says that Winckelmann and Goethe have prepared the way, (and we are reminded of his own desire to become the Winckelmann of his generation); it will be the mission of the modern critic to act as the seer, the *vates,* for the poets of the future, to find the genuine poetic tradition, and to unite the modern *Poesie* and modern philosophy—that is, Idealism—in a glorious synthesis. And this mission, adds Schlegel in a statement mirroring the increasing awareness of race and of nation, will be reserved for the Germans.

**"Die Epochen der Dichtkunst"** is followed once more by a short dialogue between the young men and their "bluestocking" girls. Schlegel touches briefly upon the subject of French false poetry, but the main concern is with the nature of *Poesie* itself, as at the start of the *Gespräche.* There is much insistence on the inward and subjective elements, the identity of poetry with metaphysics and the whole structure of the universe, and the ignoring of external aspects which he considers as mere rhetoric—"et tout le reste est littérature." All the forward-looking qualities that are so much a part of Romanticism, perhaps best incarnate in the title of Wagner's *Die Kunstwerk der Zukunft,* give Schlegel's writing the dynamic vigor, the trumpet-call-to-action tone, that characterize the manifesto. Winter is over and spring is here, cries Ludoviko. He concludes, "Ich lebe nicht in Hoffnung sondern in Zuversicht der Morgenröthe der neuen Poesie;" and he then reads his paper to the little group. This is the portion of Schlegel's work that may well contain the most important of his intellectual contributions, not only to the body of thought of the Romantic movement, but to the history of aesthetics as a whole. Certainly **"Die Rede über Mythologie und symbolische Anschauung"** holds the most interest for the modern reader who is aware of the paramount concern in our own day with the place of the symbol and the myth in literature.

In **"Die Epochen der Dichtkunst"** when Schlegel was discussing the merits of Greek *Poesie,* it was a greatness he defined in terms of a relation of art to men and the gods: "eine und untheilbar durch das festliche Leben freyer Menschen und durch die heilige Kraft der alten Götter." In short, the prerequisites for true as against false poetry are that it be the creation of free men, and that it arise within the framework of a mythology—in other words, within an ordered universe. In this section the idea stated *en passant* is expanded.

What is the cause of the defective condition of modern poetry? Must the twin mysteries of the soul and of love—the proper subjects of great art—remain unexplained in modern *Poesie?* And Schlegel regretfully concludes that they must, at least until we discover our own mythology and build our own symbols.

> Es fehlt . . . unsrer Poesie an einem Mittelpunkt, wie es die Mythologie für die Alten war . . . Wir haben keine Mythologie.

The Greeks were able to create their symbols out of the purely sensuous since their gods were closer to mere natural manifestations; "Die neue Mythologie muß . . . aus der tiefsten des Geistes herausgebildet werden." With the moderns, says Schlegel, the locus of the new mythology will be "in dem großen Phänomen des Zeitalters, im Idealismus!" This alone can be the basis for a new art which will partake of the same canonic, absolute quality as did Greek culture. The result will be a genuine rebirth of spirit—similar to the Greek in that both would be *Dinge-ansich,* with a deep and inward resemblance, and not merely a superficial parallelism of forms.

Schlegel emphasizes that the mythology of the future will be manifest in poetry rather than in philosophy, and stresses once more his earlier identification of *Poesie* with the cosmic structure: Spinoza and the new physics are both seen as necessary—but only partial—ingredients in the new outlook. This is an important distinction, lest one think that he saw the coming *Poesie* to be simply the vehicle for the concepts of *Idealismus.* The *real* Golden Age will arrive when *Naturphilosophie* and mythology are synthesized. In any case—and again we are struck by the revolutionary cast of his mind—the old divinities are dead: "Die neuen Götter haben den Herrlichen vom hohen Thron der Wissenschaft herabgestürzt."

Despite the confusion and the vagueness that mark this section of the *Gespräch,* the more one considers the radical ideas advanced by Schlegel, the more one is amazed by the keenness of his insights. Western philosophy may be viewed as a series of footnotes to Plato, says Whitehead; it is tempting to make a similar assertion about Romanticism and Friedrich Schlegel. "The new gods have thrown the glorious ones down from the high throne of knowledge": Novalis and Chateaubriand tried to demonstrate the validity of the Christian myth in modern art; Heine was to attack them and their followers in *Uber Deutschland,* Nietzsche's *Also Sprach Zarathustra* appeared eighty-five years after Schlegel's work, and the twilight of the gods was celebrated with still more passion and fire. If it is felt that Romantic literature failed to live up to Schlegel's great expectations—and perhaps no literature ever could live up to such demands—still, the falling-off of the actual from the ideal is no indictment of his originality and brilliance. The answers that Schlegel gives to the problems that he poses are inconclusive and unsatisfying, but it is sufficient that he was cognizant of the questions; for it may well be that we search for absolute answers where none *can* exist.

The dialogue that bridges this essay and the next, the **"Brief über den Roman,"** is actually not much more than an extended footnote to the previous section. Schlegel in the person of Lothario underscores the notion that all art is symbolic:

> Alle heiligen Spiele der Kunst sind nur ferne Nachbildungen von dem unendlichen Spiele der Welt, dem ewig sich selbst bildenden Kunstwerk.

Artistic creativity and the interplay of spirit and matter are seen as parallel processes.

There is also a short recapitulation of Schlegel's idea, that Dante's greatness was principally a function of the poet's dependence on Christian mythology. That Schlegel could postulate Christianity as a mythology alongside the Greek and Oriental systems is itself a departure from orthodox critical thought of the period toward a completely historical outlook. No judgment of comparative values is made; the sole criterion is whether or not an author is faithful to the mythological "climate of opinion" of his time.

Antonio reads the **"Brief über den Roman"** after the group has raised the question of the relation of the past excellence of the epic to the possible future of the novel.

**"Der Brief über den Roman"** is of less philosophic import than the preceding section about mythology, since Schlegel is more concerned with the validity of a literary form than with a metaphysical concept. At the same time it is significant that he sees the novel as a serious and important art-form, and more than that, as *the* new form to embody the new *Poesie*. It is nowhere more apparent than here that Schlegel's main interest was less with contemporary literature than with the art of the future; it is this forward-looking quality, what might almost be called the discovery of the future tense in criticism, that was the distinctive feature of Romantic manifestos and the aesthetics they propounded. Schlegel, like so many of the critics after him, saw his own age as an interim period and the writers in it as figures of transition. Hence the focus of his thought is less descriptive—in the traditional sense of the critic examining contemporary literature within a given frame of reference—than it is normative, with the critic resolving present artistic imperfections into a future synthesis.

Antonio commences with a rebuttal of one of his friends who had attacked the novels of Friedrich Richter, (Jean Paul). Antonio grants that they are a hodge-podge of French influence and bad sentimentality; still, "solche Grotesken und Bekenntnisse noch die einzigen romantischen Erzeugnisse unsers unromantischen Zeitalters sind." He admits that the novels of their age and the preceding century are mostly weak and mere "arabesques," but one must remember that they are all *Naturprodukte* and hence contain positive elements. Perhaps the form is as yet un-

disciplined, but at least the novel *per se* does not share in the tradition of false Alexandrian *Poesie*. It is rather a spontaneous, indigenous product of its period; in short, it is *Romantic*.

The dichotomy arises between the actual state of the novel, whose poverty Schlegel is forced to admit, and the novel in its ideality. It is potentially a valid vehicle for true *Poesie* even though the productions of the present may show no promise. The best proof of Schlegel's faith in the novel is his comparison between it and the epic, and the statement that "der Roman habe am meisten Verwandtschaft mit der erzählenden ja mit der epischen Gattung." The novel is not regarded as the modern imitation of the epic, or even the continuation of the epic line; there are formal parallels, but nevertheless each form—the epic in ancient Greece, the novel in the modern period—is the unique and genuine expression of its *Zeitalter*.

A possible ambiguity appears when Schlegel attempts to differentiate between "modern" and "romantic." Evidently he felt that his immediate age was not completely *romantisch,* even as the great era of Greek poetry was exclusively *classisch;* but all the positive elements of his contemporary literature—the true as opposed to the false *Poesie*—were romantic. It is obvious that part of the identification he makes between "Roman" and "romantisch" is etymological, implicitly if not explicitly: "Ein Roman ist ein romantisches Buch", and the present-day novels are "die einzigen romantischen Naturprodukte unsers Zeitalters." Is "romantic" for Schlegel an attribute of the art of certain periods, his own for instance? Does he go as far as Stendhal who exclaims, in capital letters, "Tous les grands écrivains ont été romantiques de leur temps"? Does "romantic" have the same absolute and canonic meaning for Schlegel as did the term "classic", when applied to the true *Poesie* of Greece? The last essay in the *Gespräch*—**"Versuch über den verschiedenen Styl in Goethe's früheren und späteren Werken"**—does not provide us with any neat answers to these questions. Insofar as Schlegel saw in Goethe the most prominent poet of the day, and the writer who was most likely to produce the representative *Poesie* in the immediate future, Schlegel's comments and his critical approach to Goethe are more illuminating than any additional theorizing would be.

Schlegel is less interested in any single work of Goethe's than he is in the poet's development: the critic, he says, must seek the whole man behind the individual creative product, since the isolated work of art is incomprehensible when viewed outside of the context of the creative personality. Here we have, in essence, the theoretical justification for the biographical-historical approach of the nineteenth-century; from the work we move to a study of the artist and his personality, and thence from the artist to a consideration of the external forces acting upon him.

Schlegel sees the first period of Goethe's writing as a conflict between objectivity and subjectivity, with the triumph of the latter in *Werther* and *Götz von Berlichingen*. This is the early stage; Goethe's art progresses in a dynamic fashion to a higher plane, and the manifestation of the new spirit is *Wilhelm Meisters Lehrjahre,* (which appeared four years before the *Gespräch*). The book was for Schlegel a partial fulfillment of his critical demands; in this opinion he was seconded by Novalis, who stated that "ein Roman muβ durch und durch Poesie sein," and who found *Wilhelm Meister* the most satisfactory novel to answer his requirements.

Schlegel sets forth "die Vereinigung des Antiken und des Modernen" as the great question tormenting our age. Are these periods in a fundamental, irreconcilable antagonism? Goethe the man, as well as *Wilhelm Meister,* are actual demonstrations that a synthesis—albeit incomplete—is possible.

> Diese groβe Combination [i. e., the antique and the modern in Goethe] eröffnet eine ganz endlose Aussicht auf das, was die höchste Aufgabe aller Dichtkunst zu seyn scheint, die Harmonie des Classischen und des Romantischen.

The antique-classical and the modern-romantic each exhibit the necessary qualifications for high art: fidelity to the true spirit of the age, the employment alone of artforms that have emerged out of this same *Zeitgeist,* and finally a unity that can exist only when a literary generation abandons slavish imitation and a concomitant false mythology.

When does the emulation of the *spirit* of ancient Greece—a "good" thing—become a servile and Alexandrian *Epigonentum?* We sense that Schlegel is aware of the problem and is trying to resolve it to his own satisfaction. After all, it would be legitimate to see French seventeenth-century tragedy, using Schlegel's own terms, as the happy union of true classical spirit with modern native French culture; yet French Neo-classicism was anathema to him, as it was to most of the Romantic critics who came in his wake. Despite his attempts to obtain historical catholicity of taste, where all literature is assessed according to the degree to which it expresses its age, Schlegel is forced to make affirmations and condemnations when he is faced with the spectre of historical relativism. His distinction between a spiritual emulation and a shallow imitation of Greece, his notion of the canonic nature of the art of certain epochs—both these are ideas which must be seen as Schlegel's answer to the problem of understanding versus judgment. They are also two concepts singled out of a host of others, which afford us adequate testimony of his place as a great critic and aesthetician.

The *Gespräch über die Poesie* remains not only as a document important for a comprehension of the course of Romanticism, but also as an essay rich in suggestiveness for critics of all times, by virtue of its brilliant insights into the nature of aesthetics.

*Howard E. Hugo, "An Examination of Friedrich Schlegel's Gespräch über die Poesie'," in* Monatshefte, *Vol. XL, No. 1, January, 1948, pp. 221-31.*

## Victor Lange   (essay date 1955)

[*Lange is a German-born American educator and critic. In the following essay, he traces the development of Schlegel's literary theories.*]

Few European writers have been so ceaselessly and so brilliantly concerned with the large philosophical assumptions as well as the specific means and purposes of literary criticism as was Friedrich Schlegel, and among them there is none whose achievement is more elusive and more difficult to assess. Schlegel's work reflects an extraordinary rich and complicated if not always attractive mind; it is abundant and varied, but its total impression is diffuse and disjointed and lacking in continuity of intellectual development. Its impulses are often more astounding than its conclusions, and in its peremptory and oracular manner it tends to be challenging rather than lucid. "Most of your writings," commented his friend Novalis, "lead me into Cimmerian darkness"; and when Byron turned to some of Schlegel's later and uncommonly sober lectures, they seemed always to carry him to the verge of meaning, but "lo! he goes down like sunset, or melts like a rainbow, leaving a rather rich confusion."

The chance of obtaining a reliable view of Schlegel's performance is, for us, made doubly difficult by the fact that many of his major writings are today not easily obtained; with the exception of his aphorisms and a few essays, they have seldom if ever been reissued, and much material, probably of decisive importance for a total appraisal, has remained unpublished. Little wonder, then, that there exists as yet no study, either biographical or critical, that would adequately portray this awkward and eccentric figure, and that would assign to him a just place in the history of modern literary criticism.

If one were to begin a discussion of Schlegel's work by determining his position at the onset of his career within the tradition of European thinking, one would be struck by the remarkable balance with which he maintains himself between two main sources of modern intellectual history—the reappraisal of the classical heritage as it was represented in Germany by Winckelmann, and the new manner of perceiving the relationship of the critic and historian to his object which was most amply argued in the earlier works of Herder. Winckelmann and Herder, more than any other two native thinkers, determined the evolution of German classicism, the kind of cultural philosophy that Goethe, Schiller, and Humboldt represent and that is best described as a modern form of humanism—to distinguish it from the orthodox form of classicism that we know in France and early eighteenth-century England. This German form of classicism, Henri Peyre has quite properly insisted, is in fact not a belated local excrescence of the classicism of Racine or Dryden, but a preliminary phase of the emerging romantic sensibility. In this process of shifting the ideas of the classical world into the focus of the new organic philosophies that the late eighteenth century had formulated, Friedrich Schlegel is one of the most sensitive agents.

He began, slowly and tentatively, with a series of writings on the ancient world and its specific excellences. **"Vom Wert des Studiums der Griechen und Römer"** (1794) and **"Über das Studium der griechischen Poesie"** (written 1794, published three years later) are his first two pieces of independent analysis; they deal not merely with individual ancient poets or with types of writing, but with the special intellectual situation that produced them. These essays are, in a strictly academic sense, as speculative and as dubious as that dithyrambic account of classical attitudes that the young Nietzsche offered less than a century later; but if this seems, in both, a defect of scholarly detachment, it points as well to their common concern with the uses of antiquity for an interpretation of the present.

Schlegel, like Nietzsche, sets off the body of classical literature against the character of his age, in order to contrast, without the maudlin self-pity of Rousseau or the melancholy pathos of Gibbon, the special intellectual assumptions of classical and modern literature. What interested him, as it had only a few years earlier preoccupied Herder, was to obtain a clear insight into the complex human situation of the moderns, against the background of the simple, the natural, proportions of the·human being which the Greeks seemed to him to have represented. But Schlegel's first studies in classical poetry differ in emphasis from the cultural speculations of Herder and his contemporaries (even from those of Schiller and Goethe); they are distinguished by their single-minded attention, from the very beginning, to the evidences of changing sensibility in the mainstream of European literature. This is to say that he was then, as he was throughout his career, first and foremost preoccupied not so much with the large historical judgment as with the literary document itself, with its properties, its forms, and its spiritual context. Literature, poetry, was for him the most clearly articulated and therefore the most telling expression of the human energy; it was the central achievement of a given culture. If, by his first writings, he hoped to become, in Herder's words, the Winckelmann of Greek poetry, he meant to establish, in the realm of poetry, that delicate balance between categorical reverence for the example of the Greeks and an awareness of the particular perspectives from which his or any other modern period might exercise this respect.

The influence of Winckelmann and Herder upon Schlegel was important and even decisive; yet his emerging view of the antithesis between "classical" and "modern" owes as much to his reading of Kant. And it coincides, though perhaps without Schlegel's being fully aware of it at the time, with the typological categories in Schiller's essay, "Über naive und sentimentalische Dichtung." In the terms of these familiar philosophical antecedents, Schlegel assumes a disparity between idea and appearance that is resolvable in the creation of beauty. In beauty, chaos may become cosmos, and cosmosis the ultimate creative order adequate to the human potentialities. To represent this free playing and "disinterested" state of order in beauty is the purpose of all classical art. Modern poetry, on the other hand, does not aim, in Schlegel's early view (as in Schiller's), at the creation of an objective beauty with a validity, an aesthetic existence in itself; it represents rather, and makes available for analysis, the tensions of life which are bound to remain irreconcilable. Modern art creates not beauty but what Schlegel in the **"Studium"** essay, adopting the terminology of Herder and Kant, calls the "interesting"—a reflected image of the fundamental discrepancies of life, of the discrepancies between emotion and intelligence, between nature and speculation, between individual impulse and a transcending order.

*Dorothea Veit, wife of Schlegel and inspiration for* Lucinde. *Oil painting by Anton Graff, 1790.*

The tragedy of the Greeks (the "aesthetic" tragedy) projected a vision of ideal harmony; modern ("philosophical") tragedy offers in its greatest and most characteristic specimens—and Schlegel had, of course, *Hamlet* in mind—a "maximum of spiritual despair." "There is no more perfect representation of the unresolvable disharmony of the human mind—the true subject matter of philosophical tragedy—than the infinite discrepancies between thought and action in Hamlet's character." "Philosophical" tragedy disturbs without resorting to a vision of relief, it unsettles without catharsis; indeed, its main object is to produce in the audience a philosophical state of doubt and unrest. The modern poet—this is Schlegel's central if not altogether original thesis—recognizes the inevitable alienation of the mind vis-à-vis nature and does not, and cannot, in his work transcend a situation which in its essence is tragic; his main effort must, therefore, be directed not at aesthetic reconciliation, but at making the inescapable conflicts between nature and mind articulate and transparent.

Schlegel's attitude in outlining these differing intellectual resources is, even in his early writings, not unequivocally partial to the classical temper; he is remarkably objective in his analysis of the modern situation and one would not suspect from the extraordinarily lively and impressive account of Shakespeare's demonic heroism that this magnificent capacity of the moderns for the rendering of, as he says, "the colossal dissonance between man and his fate" appears to him but a passing crisis of taste—which is overcome by a sort of dialectic synthesis in the neoclassical productions of Goethe, who had, particularly in *Werther*, proved his modern sensibility but who had also experienced the corrective discipline of a profound insight into the nature of Greek feeling. Early in 1794, Schlegel wrote to his brother, "The problem of our poetry seems to me the fusing of the essentially modern with the essentially classical; Goethe is the first in an entirely new phase of the history of art to have begun approaching this goal . . ." It is not the least important aspect of Schlegel's **"Studium"** essay that it provides the first congenial and positive interpretation in German criticism of the turn in Goethe's career from the mood of the Storm and Stress to that of *Iphigenie* and *Tasso.*

As yet, Schlegel had no term by which to describe this new, supramodern attitude; where he uses the term "romantic" in these first essays, he refers to the gothic, if subtle, fantasies of "that great barbarian intermezzo" of which the monumental work of Dante is the most sublime specimen. It was only after reading *Wilhelm Meister* that he defined Goethe's neoclassical synthesis as "romantic." What interests us here is Schlegel's conviction that it is the eminently critical disposition of the modern poet that should enable him, as it had Goethe, to transcend the limitation of his tragic involvement in life. The modern poet, Schlegel had argued in the **"Studium"** essay, finds himself increasingly divorced from his surrounding society; he becomes an "isolated egotist" who, because of his ever more acute perception of the paradox of existing forms of faith, must turn either to a sentimental kind of formalism or to the appealing devices of parody. His medium is prose. As he becomes more and more conscious of the force upon his own writing of the accumulated body of past literary theory, he will tend to produce didactic, essayistic or, as Schlegel calls it, "philosophical" writing. In his efforts at rendering faithfully the characteristic or "interesting" phenomena of life, he will feel compelled to engage, poetically speaking, in "chemical experiments, in the arbitrary separation and reassembling of the primary art forms." By his modern perspicacity he will inevitably break up the seeming unity of nature and dissolve its organization into elementary particles.

In the **"Studium"** essay the analytical state of mind appears as a destructive if inescapable condition of the modern poet; but after 1794, as Schlegel shifts his philosophical allegiance from Kant to Fichte, the ability of the modern mind to accept this capacity of the reflective intelligence with radical self-consciousness evolves into perhaps his most positive advantage. And if, for the earliest Schlegel, it was the *poet* who neutralizes the tension of the moderns by his recall of the compensating image of the Greeks, so it is in the essays and aphorisms written after 1796 the *critic* who must represent the modern detachment as the projection of his unique sensibility and insight.

Almost as soon as the **"Studium"** essay was published, Schlegel, in one of his first critical fragments, seemed inclined to disavow it. It is "but a mannered hymn in prose to the objective element in poetry; its worst feature seems to me the total lack of that indispensable quality of irony." "Irony"—this is from now on the term which indicates the specific—romantic—mode of creative procedure. It expresses, as another aphorism puts it, "the clear con-

sciousness of eternal agility, of the infinite abundance of chaos." As early as 1794, in the essay **"Vom ästhetischen Werte der griechischen Komödie,"** he had defended Aristophanes' frequent suspension of the dramatic illusion: "This," he said, "is not clumsiness but deliberate calculation; indeed, it is an expression of the most intense vitality. For life at its most incandescent creates as it destroys, and if it cannot destroy an object outside itself, it must turn upon itself, its own creations." Fichte's *Wissenschaftslehre* of 1794 reinforced Schlegel's notion of the chance of the creative individual to maintain himself suspended between the antitheses of life, and, thus mirroring rather than mastering them, to transcend the modern sense of disharmony and limitation. In the work of art, that chance of freedom, that "magic idealism," as Novalis called it, enables the imagination to create its own coherent world of meaning.

We need not pursue the question of the philosophical validity of this concept of irony which many of Schlegel's contemporaries found more striking than productive. Schiller—for various reasons eager to express his distaste for Schlegel—complained to Goethe of the barrenness of Schlegel's critical vocabulary, its "sachlose Wortstrenge"; Hegel, in a celebrated passage, felt in its radical subjectivism something like "satanic impertinence." Schlegel's conception of irony, he argues, is purely formal and lacks philosophical substance; it bypasses the problem of understanding, "die denkende Vernunft," and remains on an elusively speculative, even histrionic level; it seems to dispose, haughtily and with windy notions, "verblasene Vorstellungen," of the puzzling relationship between concreteness and abstraction. Valid though Hegel's criticism may be in terms of his own philosophy, it misses the point of Schlegel's intention in the use of the term "ironic." Schlegel was not concerned with defining substance but with the possibility of creating a mode of preception adequate to its assumed infinity.

What matters for our present consideration of Schlegel's principles of literary criticism is this: that the ironic attitude which qualifies the *poet* to produce a construct of specific aesthetic validity enables the *critic,* not merely to recognize and judge this construct, but to perform a function that comprises and indeed transcends that of the poet. The critic illuminates the original exercise of the poet in a recreative process and on a level where, as Schlegel says, he has brought himself to an understanding of understanding.

It is perhaps useful, before we examine more precisely Schlegel's definition of the critic, to remind ourselves of some of the preliminaries of the critical process which Schlegel enumerates in various contexts. There are many kinds of criticism, but no adequate theory of poetry has as yet been formulated: "What you may find in existing treatises on aesthetics concerning poetry and its form is just about sufficient to explain the principles of watchmaking. Nowhere will you find the slightest conception of the higher form of art, or an adequate conception of poetry."

The most disarming form of criticism is that which Schlegel describes in the *Lyceum Fragment 57* as characteristic of the mystic-minded amateurs of art who would deplore any sort of criticism as vivisection, as destructive of all enjoyment; if they were logical, the most telling judgment of even a remarkable work would be "potztausend." Only slightly more useful is what Schlegel calls the micrological sort of criticism, a procedure without profile or consequence, which provides a bare Linnean classification of the parts of an organic whole. Nor must criticism be content with a sentimental account of biographical niceties.

The immediate objective of the critic is the elucidation of a human product, and criticism must therefore in some sense be directed towards the maker of this product. One must know how to distinguish the poet from his work, he states peremptorily in one of his Vienna lectures. Yet there is in Schlegel none of the psychological curiosity about the poetic process that is so prominent in the contemporaneous English critics. He is not to any serious degree interested in a theory of composition, such as Coleridge offers us, and seldom enters into a discussion of the difference between feeling and understanding or of the state of mind in which the poet moves towards fancy and imagination. He is concerned with the artist neither as an abstraction nor as a physiologically distinct species, but as a configuration of a total interplay of cultural forces. The larger essays which he devotes to Jacobi or Lessing, to Boccaccio or Cervantes or Goethe, are therefore, ultimately, attempts at crystallizing a particular type of cultural insight.

What makes his critical procedure of special interest to us is that it is always the literary document as an autonomous "construct" from which he proceeds. It is striking to find this ostensibly speculative critic insisting again and again upon the primary importance of craftsmanship. The first requirement of a work of art is for Schlegel a clear purpose and a distinctness of means that alone creates shape and self-sufficiency. The poet's imagination must not be poured into some sort of chaotic poetic effusion—"eine chaotische Überhauptpoesie"—but must be used to produce a work of definite form and type. Why, he asks, in one of the **Athenaeum Fragments,** should it be so absurd to compare an author to a manufacturer? He regrets the absence in modern literary life of academies of poetry, he admires Lessing for his infinite skill of construction in which instinct and design are perfectly blended. "A thoroughly developed poetic action is a self-contained whole, a technical world of its own." These are the observations of a perceptive reader whose sense of detail, of rhythm and cadence, of what he calls the fragrance of the text, should disarm those who are inclined to find Schlegel insensitive to the concrete realities of a poem. It is well, on the other hand, to recognize that Schlegel accepts, without any uncertainty, the given character of such a thing as a poetic structure. His attention is not therefore, in a generic sense, directed to the question: "What is a poem?" He is preoccupied almost exclusively with the requirements of the critic.

The ideal critic, as Schlegel puts it, is in fact a reader who commands a multiplicity of perspectives, who ruminates, "ein Leser der wiederkäut," who should have more than one stomach. Like the poet, he must have ceased to be involved in what he writes about, and, beyond merely recollecting emotion in tranquillity, he should have transcended the idea he wishes to express: "as long as the artist is in a state of enthusiasm and inventiveness he is, for pur-

poses of communication, in an illiberal state of mind." The critic must share in that ironic attitude which is the productive,the philosophical element of the poet himself; this is the meaning of that often quoted but much misunderstood maxim, "Poetry can only be criticized by poetry." Generations of critics have felt justified in deriving from this deceptively simple fragment the license for impressionistic and sentimental self-indulgence. What Schlegel actually envisages is the critic who is congenial to the poet in the sense that both are equally engaged in dealing with that "dim analogue of creation." What the poet constructs, the critic, favored over the poet in that he is twice removed from nature, must reconstruct; and, as he offers a mirror image of the mirror image, he surpasses the poem itself.

Criticism thus transcends poetry; this is a logical consequence of the earlier statement that the critic must be occupied with the understanding of understanding. Hence also Schlegel's not merely facetious designation of his elaborate essay on Goethe's *Wilhelm Meister* as the "Übermeister." This peculiarly rich review has become one of the key documents of German romantic criticism. It rests, as a matter of fact, upon a definition of the term "romantic" that is here for the first time distinct and explicit. "Romantic," as we have seen, Schlegel used in his early essays only loosely as the antithesis of "modern"; after about 1797, and under the influence of Schleiermacher and Wackenroder, it assumed more and more a connotation of irrationality, mysticism, religious fervor, and mediaeval Christianity. In the review of *Wilhelm Meister* (1798) and in a number of simultaneous aphorisms, notably that unfathomable (and therefore recklessly quoted) **Athenaeum Fragment 116,** "romantic" is identified with the special quality of Goethe's "Roman," in which life seems to Schlegel thoroughly spiritualized and this spiritualized life in turn represented with what he regards as the ultimate in poetic irony and mobility.

> Romantic poetry [this is the beginning of the canonical aphorism] is poetry progressively universal. Its purpose is not merely to reunite all separate (or specific) forms of poetry and to bring poetry in touch again with philosophy and rhetoric. It aims as well at mixing and blending poetry and prose, inspiration and criticism, it must identify life and poetry and in turn make life and society poetic; it must infuse a poetic quality into wit, and charge and saturate the forms of art with the substance of culture [Bildungsstoff].

These are the first three crowded sentences of a long passage which ends with the categorical statement that "romantic poetry cannot be exhaustively defined in any one system of theory," and that "only a divining sort of criticism might venture to approach its ideal. Romantic poetry is infinite in scope; it alone springs from a sense of freedom: indeed, it is its first axiom, that the freedom, the free-playing will [die Willkür] of the poet can tolerate no law above itself."

One cannot fail to be struck by the characteristically dynamic vocabulary of this passage; it speaks of uniting and separating, of fusing and mixing, of identifying, charging, and saturating. Thisis, of course, indicative of the place of Schlegel's criticism, and romantic criticism in general, in the tradition of the Christian and Neoplatonic theory of creation, of its belief in the subordinate importance of the vessel, as compared to the creative, the divine energy that may reside in it.

If we apply the consequences of this insight to the purposes of romantic criticism—and Schlegel's review of *Wilhelm Meister* is a most telling example—we recognize that it is, in the end, not so much the objective reality of the poem that occupies the critic as the critical act that plays upon the poem and illuminates it as a nearly inexhaustible system of refractions and responses. Goethe scholars have sometimes noted with disapproval the almost total disregard in Schlegel's review of what a more positivistic-minded criticism would describe as Goethe's "actual" intentions. But the critic's relationship to a poem is, for Schlegel, not that of an expositor of more or less concealed but nevertheless discoverable and perhaps objective meanings; it is rather that of an intelligent artist in his own right who, by virtue of his receptive sensibility and his close attention to the suggestive poetic detail, is in a position to elucidate, to manipulate, and, on a level of further intellectual differentiation, to reassemble the primary symbols of the poet.

If, then, it is the business of the critic to produce an object of a specific sort of meaning, different from though dependent upon that of the poet, this task is performed most superbly by one who is critic and poet at once. The definition of this supreme form of criticism is contained in the passage in the *Wilhelm Meister* review which is devoted to an appraisal of Goethe's use, in the novel, of a critique of *Hamlet*. The details of Goethe's conception of *Hamlet* need not occupy us here. Wilhelm, it will be recalled, analyzes the play with a view to a more effective reorganization of its parts; and, as Schlegel reflects upon the legitimacy of this—characteristically romantic—purpose, he comes to the following important conclusions:

> Goethe's view of *Hamlet* as it is here presented is not so much criticism as poetry. Indeed, what else but a poem could result, when a poet contemplates and represents a poetic production? Yet the reason for calling this passage poetry is not that the poet's view transcends the limits of the poem by advancing all sorts of insights and assertions. Every piece of criticism must do that—because every poetic work of whatever kind holds more than it conveys and aims at more than it realizes. It is, rather, a matter of purpose and procedure.

There is an essential difference, Schlegel continues, between analytical criticism and "poetic criticism." The first simply states, "like an inscription," what the object is, what its "place" in the world is or should be; it requires no more than a dedicated and undivided human being who will focus his attention for as long as necessary upon the poem. If he wishes to communicate what he has perceived, he may produce a piece of discursive criticism which Schlegel here, and in the title of his own collection of essays, calls a "Charakteristik." But the poetic critic must do more; he must, in a sense, repeat the original performance, re-imagine the original imagery, and then extend and re-form the poem. What distinguishes the poetic critic from the "ordinary" critic is his respect—and this is one of Schlegel's most important notions—for the special character which any part of the work of art derives from its poetic context. The poetic critic will recognize the "members," the units of a work of art, only insofar as they exist in an aesthetic context; he will never dissect the work into its "original" (i. e., prepoetic) elements, elements which, even though they are by themselves perfectly valid and "living" universals, are yet "dead" apart from the total poetic purpose.

From the *Wilhelm Meister* review, Goethe emerges as the supreme example of the "critical poet," and, as Schlegel understood the term, the "poetic critic." He is the prototype of the "modern" poet exactly by virtue of his critical awareness. "The distinguishing feature of modern literature is its precise relationship to criticism and theory and the dominant influence of the latter." This critical sense, argues Schlegel, enabled Goethe to evolve the literary form that is most adequate to the situation with which the modern poet has to deal. This form is the novel, and to a definition of its specific "romantic" possibilities Schlegel devotes an extraordinary amount of critical labor and enthusiasm. The three most extensive discussions of this form, apart from dozens of scattered aphorisms, occur in the essay on *Wilhelm Meister*, in one section of the ***Gespräch über die Poesie*** which first appeared in 1800, and in a review of Goethe's *Works* published in 1808.

Before we examine Schlegel's notions of the novel, we may inquire into his view of literary genres in general. They are not for him, of course, normative categories either in the sense of Lessing's modified classicist theory or in the more liberal understanding of Goethe's "natural forms" that evolve in analogy to natural organisms. Schlegel regards them as barely more than projections of historical, psychological, or sociological conditions which have no compelling permanency. When, as in his theory of tragedy or comedy, he recognizes a certain continuity of the genre, he bases this in the main on the technical requirements of dramatic or theatrical practice and not on any sort of continuity of human characterological or metaphysical issues. Yet, literary forms are in one way or another related to the given structure of any particular society or community. All the more reason, then, for Schlegel, to investigate the special qualities of the contemporary idiom. Those forms which he finds appropriate to his own taste and time and which are congenial, above all, to the reflective, ironic temper of the modern mind are the fragment, the dialogue (das Gespräch), the rhapsody, the arabesque, the ironic comedy, and the speculative, satirical, or polemical aphorism. All these are "mixed" forms ("All pure, classical forms," he says in ***Lyceum Fragment 60***, "are now absurd"); their essential purpose is not the conveying of private feelings, but the establishment, through what Schlegel calls infinite or "elliptical" discourse, of a community of opinion and perception. The lyrical soliloquy, so indicative of a later and different sort of nineteenth-century romanticism, is for Schlegel an enviable but certainly a primitive and inferior manner.

Unlike these forms, which have at least a sporadic historical character in common, the form of the novel is radically new and certainly without a continuous history. The novel (der Roman) represents for Schlegel the most significant invention of the modern analytical sensibility. It is related by its philosophical and discursive purpose not to the classical epic but to the didactic poem, whose greatest single specimen is the *Divine Comedy.* Its only genuine antecedent is Cervantes' masterpiece. But, since the subsequent history of fiction, with the possible exception of the ironic writings of Swift, Sterne, and Jean Paul, was in a variety of ways concerned with providing merely realistic entertainment, Schlegel can maintain that the novel is not a consistent art form; it is not, in a strict sense, a genre—there are only single conspicuous instances of the kind of philosophical—or poetic—fiction that Schlegel had in mind.

The novel is the equivalent of the Socratic dialogue; it aims at "integrating intellectual, moral, and social beliefs on the level of poetry," and a sufficient theory of the novel would therefore represent the keystone of a modern philosophy of art. There is something extraordinarily appealing for us in Schlegel's reflections upon the ingredients of fiction. They do not represent merely the novelist's sense of character or of incident; the novel is not a psychological portrait but a series of "allegorical arabesques" which are to evoke, primarily, our sense of the discrepancies and disproportions of life, our sense of what Schlegel calls the grotesque or the fantastic. "It is not the dramatic continuity of a narrative plot that provides the unity of the novel," he remarks in **Gespräch über die Poesie;** "what gives it coherence is the central intellectual perspective." This central intellectual perspective must mobilize every individual poetic device. Here, indeed, Schlegel offers us another facet of the romantic intent; fiction must represent the ironic, that is, the "sentimental" attitude in a fantastic form, and the fantastic form is the autonomous reality of the dream so characteristic of the novels of Jean Paul.

It must also strike us as curiously appropriate to our own view of fiction when we find Schlegel insisting upon the synthetic, the "mixed" character of fiction, that is to say, upon its intellectual range and mobility, its marshalling of possibly heterogeneous devices which, held together not by any psychological consistency of character but by the roving and synoptic power of its author's poetic intelligence, create a "compendium, an encyclopedia of the total spiritual life of an individual." At the same time, however oblique the narrative perspective may be, there should be nothing in the romantic narrative that is not in detail concrete, realistic, experienced, even autobiographical. But whatever the measure of "reality" which Schlegel admits and demands in the novel, it can be justified only within the transcending framework of a belief in the universal spirituality of life. "Realism" has, in this sense, for Schlegel a scholastic connotation; it is not an antecedent but a consequence of a poetic act. "No poetry—no reality"—this is the formula offered in one of the *Athenaeum* aphorisms.

The form of the novel, then, with its intricate and varied possibilities of statement seemed to Schlegel the supremely

"romantic" mode, and it is perfectly in keeping with its broad definition that such works as *Hamlet* or Lessing's *Nathan* should appear closer to "fiction" than, in a strict sense, to the drama. The novel is equalled and perhaps surpassed in its suitability for the romantic intention only by a sort of allegorical fantasy which Schlegel, in passing, calls the poetic fairy tale or parable, "das poetische Märchen." This form, which his friend Novalis regarded as the epitome of poetry, does not merely interest or mobilize or involve the imagination (I am paraphrasing **Athenaeum Fragment 429**), it fascinates and enchants the mind by its quality of the bizarre, its deliberate association of speculation, poetry, and action. In the novel and fairy tale, so immensely attractive to Schlegel, the poetic experience is wholly subordinated to the philosophical, the constructive intention; these forms are, to use a Fichtean term, altogether "posited."

The practice of art, as we have seen, is for Schlegel a form of discourse which represents and, on the critical level, reassesses by "enthusiastic abstraction" the elements of experience and points implicitly to their present disjointedness and disunity. The accumulative force of this discourse, infinite in scope, offers an ever more certain prospect of a possible synthesis of belief. "Das Gespräch bannt als Form alle Einseitigkeit." The representation of this "synthetic" form of belief Schlegel and the romantic group call the new mythology. It is most elaborately set forth in Schelling's *Philosophie der Kunst* of 1802-03. Since this is perhaps the most consequential of all romantic insights, we must touch at least briefly upon its form and place in Schlegel's thinking.

> The modern poets are compelled to produce everything from within [Schlegel writes in **Gespräch über die Poesie**], and many have done it magnificently; but each of them had to do it alone, each work was a fresh beginning from nothing. Our modern poetry lacks the center that their mythology supplied for the ancients; this is, in fact, the main difference between the ancient poets and the modern—that we have no mythology. But let me add that we are not far from having one, or rather, that it is time we should make a serious effort to produce one.

This is, historically speaking, a familiar argument; Schlegel himself must have come across it in Herder's third collection of *Fragmente* (1767) and his "Iduna" (1796), where almost the entire range of related problems is first indicated. But what distinguishes Schlegel's thinking from Herder's is that, certainly at this time, he rejects any temptation to resort to a mere re-creation of past mythological substance. "Let us study ancient mythology," this was Herder's challenge, "in the spirit of poetic heuristics—in order to become inventors ourselves"; to Schlegel, neither the ancient mythology nor the Christian nor, indeed, the Oriental is in substance repeatable; they correspond to an as yet coherent empirical reality which, in the differentiated and speculative modern world, is impossible to achieve. What is needed is a new "synthetic" mythology which reflects the diversity of modern thinking. Unlike its ancient counterpart, it cannot hope to be merely a figurative rendering of states of mind fundamentally in harmony with its sustaining world. "The new mythology must, on the contrary, be newly created from the profoundest resources of the mind."

In his **"Rede über die Mythologie"** Schlegel refers to three sources from which the new mythology might be drawn: the idealistic philosophy of Fichte, the abstract and image-less thinking of Spinoza, and the emerging interest in the special sort of natural science which his own friends J. W. Ritter and Henrik Steffens had advanced. This new synthetic mythology or, in Schelling's celebrated phrase, "this great mythological poem" is in the making.

However orphic Schlegel's language may seem as he elaborates this vision, it is clear that he sees in the issue of the new mythology the condition of all modern poetry. With its emphasis upon the metaphorical nature of all incidents of reality and upon the constructive role of the philosopher-poet, it gives to poetry an extreme degree of intellectual and spiritual transparency. "Mythology," he insists, "is the core and center of all poetry." The appropriate manner of modern poetry is not the pragmatic, the confined, the explicit or what he calls the "exoteric" manner (exoteric is, significantly enough, the mode of the drama, for which Schlegel had little interest and which, compared to other modes, he recognized as merely "psychological" and private and therefore exhausted and inadequate); the appropriate manner is "esoteric," the manner of philosophical poetry which, like *Wilhelm Meister* or Novalis' *Ofterdingen,* offers a contrived and aesthetically specific world of meaning, held together by figures and incidents constructed according to a supranatural logic. Poetic forms such as the novel, the parable, the fairy tale, or the didactic poem all contribute to this new tactical purpose of myth making. Indeed, myth, fairy tale, and that "universe" which is established in the work of fiction are all analogous: "every novel should be constructed in the manner of a fairy tale—every true mythology is so by definition." Especially in the light of subsequent literary history, we must not underrate the importance of Schlegel's preoccupation with this whole matter of the synthetic creation of a new mythology.

In his later writings—for instance, in the essay *Über die Sprache und Weisheit der Inder* (1808) that was to be of great consequence for the subsequent study of comparative mythology by men such as Creuzer, Görres, or Bachofen—Schlegel greatly elaborates his views of the nature and importance of myth.

At the time of the **"Rede über die Mythologie"** he was prepared to maintain that the corollary of his arguments was an inevitable and ever more exclusive concern with issues of poetic form and method rather than with an objective content. Yet it was, in the end, not he but the poets and critics of the later nineteenth century who fully accepted the consequences of this "formalist" conclusion. Only a decade later, Schlegel himself disavowed this earlier emphasis upon the primacy of formal resources in the poet, together with his faith in a new secular mythology. "We have been predominantly interested in theories of poetic form," he writes in 1812. "There exists as yet no theory of the adequate content—although as far as the effect of poetry upon life is concerned, this would be infinitely more important." This sounds very different indeed from

the language of the *Gespräch über die Poesie;* but by 1812, we must not forget, Schlegel had in nearly all respects changed the direction of this thinking; even though he did not revert to classicism, he had become a Catholic in religion, and royalist in politics.

If it is the ultimate task of the romantic effort to establish a new mythology, the role of the poet and that of the critic have become still more closely related; and we may therefore finally ask two crucial questions: What criteria does Schlegel recognize as to the quality, the excellence, of a given poem; and secondly, what is his gauge of the reliability of the critical judgment?

Both questions depend for their answer upon the acceptance of a kind of sanction that transcends the individual poet or critic. A poem, Schlegel insists, exercises a constant and unique sort of power by virtue of being an inexhaustible and continually challenging product. The critic, confronted by a poem, must above all determine whether or not it possesses this power, whether it displays the imaginative complexity and ironic self-consciousness upon which a poetic structure depends, whether, indeed, it *is* a poem. The criteria for this procedure of critical identification are, as Schlegel himself admits, elusive enough. If we go beyond mere impressionistic statements of taste, we must recognize that what determines the critic's reliability is not any sort of faithfulness to an objective property of the poem; no poem has only one meaning. Its meaning changes with each critical act that is brought to bear upon it. Criticism is effective and valid, therefore, only in proportion to the degree to which it can establish, and subsequently maintain, the meaning of a poem, first in a given historical situation and eventually in the total tradition of poetry. The history of a poem, that is to say, the history of its intellectual vitality, is the only dependable indication of its value or its greatness.

There exists for Schlegel no categorical distinction between literary criticism and literary history. Neither mode, he warns in a review of Adam Müller's *Vorlesungen über die deutsche Wissenschaft und Literatur,* must be pursued by itself; for as no poem, no single work of art, can be assessed by itself but depends for its rank upon the total canon of poetry, so a given performance of literary criticism can derive its validity only from an awareness of its place in the tradition of judgment. To be conscious of this interdependence of the individual critical act and the perspectives of history is the distinction of only the rarest critics—a distinction which even Lessing, that most admired among Schlegel's predecessors, did not attain. Dilthey, in his essay on the origins of hermeneutics, emphasizes the importance in Schlegel's thinking, of the interplay of various critical objectives:

> Die Begriffe, welche [ihn] in seinen glänzenden Arbeiten über griechische Poesie, Goethe, Boccaccio leiteten, waren die der inneren Form des Werkes, der Entwicklungsgeschichte des Schriftstellers und des in sich gegliederten Ganzen der Literatur. Und hinter solchen einzelnen Leistungen einer nachkonstruierenden philologischen Kunst lag für ihn der Plan einer Wissenschaft der Kritik, einer ars critica, welche

auf eine Theorie des produktiven literarischen Vermögens gegründet sein sollte.

As for Schlegel himself, he hoped that his *Geschichte der alten und neuen Literatur,* those sixteen lectures which he delivered in Vienna in 1812, might point the way towards the kind of "critical" literary history that would never lose sight of the specific individuality of the work of art, but would yet recognize the binding nature of tradition. These, together with his brother's Berlin and Vienna lectures and Adam Müller's *Vorlesungen,* are the most influential documents of the German romantics' conception of literary history. They offer principles of judgment and a synoptic scheme of world literature from Greek and Oriental beginnings to the height of the idealistic faith that remained exemplary throughout the literary historiography of the nineteenth century.

But these lectures, and this must be said in conclusion, however energetic their intellectual grasp, reveal a bias of historical thinking that is of much importance for our estimate of Schlegel's criticism. His faith in the universal presence, the identity, of the spirit and his indifference, therefore, to the concrete circumstances of time and space restricted the effectiveness of his method. He was not lacking in respect for historical fact, but of far greater importance to him was the act of judging. If the recognized it to be one of the primary duties of the critic to understand the variety of historical and aesthetic phenomena without prejudice or sentimentality, he was at the same time possessed by a burning desire to recognize and proclaim the examples of greatness. This is, perhaps, in any critic, one of the unresolvable incongruities of purpose. In Schlegel it created a tension which, for better or for worse, remained a characteristic element of his work from the days of his admiration for Winckelmann to his fanatical devotion in later life to the faith of the Church. It was one of the reasons, I suspect, why his influence upon subsequent literary theory was never so great as that of his more single-minded brother, August Wilhelm. Yet, Friedrich Schlegel's work continues to exercise its strong appeal, not least because it reflects a rare awareness of the precariousness of the critic's task. "I have expressed," Schlegel concludes in his last aphorism, "a few ideas that point to the center; I have greeted the dawn in my way, from my point of view. Let anyone who knows the road do likewise in his way and from his point of view."

*Victor Lange, "Friedrich Schlegel's Literary Criticism," in* Comparative Literature, *Vol. VII, No. 4, Fall, 1955, pp. 289-305.*

## René Wellek   (essay date 1955)

[*Wellek's* A History of Modern Criticism, *from which the essay below has been taken, is a comprehensive study of literary critics of the last three centuries. Wellek's critical method, as demonstrated in* A History *and outlined in his* Theory of Literature (1949), *is one of describing, analyzing, and evaluating a work solely in terms of the problems it poses for itself and how the writer solves them. For Wellek, biographical, historical, and psychological information is incidental. In the following excerpt, he examines the key concepts in Schlegel's criticism, including myth, irony, the romantic, and the novel. Wellek considers Schlegel to be the originator of hermeneutics and "one of the greatest critics of history."*]

Friedrich Schlegel (1772-1829)—five years younger than his brother August Wilhelm (1767-1845)—was the more original and seminal mind of the two. His critical activity and effect precedes, to a large degree, that of August Wilhelm. It is admittedly difficult to decide questions of priority with exactness in the case of two intimate brothers and friends, but there seems little doubt that the initiative was almost always Friedrich's. However, August Wilhelm developed distinct critical theories of his own and cannot be described as a mere echo of his brother, even though he served as codifier and popularizer of Friedrich's doctrines. One can hardly deny the greater effectiveness of August Wilhelm's expositions, especially outside of Germany. His Vienna *Lectures on Dramatic Art and Literature,* which were delivered 1808-09 and published 1809-11, affected the course of critical thought very widely, especially after they had been translated into French (1814), English (1815), and Italian (1817). It is also true that Friedrich Schlegel was far less influential outside of Germany, since his conversion to Roman Catholicism in 1808 prevented him from republishing most of his early writings and on the whole limited the appeal of his later work to the definitely conservative and Catholic world of the Restoration period. *The Lectures on Ancient and Modern Literature,* translated into English by J. G. Lockhart in 1815, was the only book of Friedrich's which attracted international attention.

The early writings of Friedrich Schlegel, however, are of the greatest significance both for the history of romanticism and a general history of criticism. In close proximity to Schiller (whom he came to hate) Friedrich renewed the debate on ancients and moderns and developed from it the theory of the romantic which in his brother's version spread, literally, around the world. But Friedrich was not merely the propagandist of a catchword, the writer of literary manifestoes which would give him purely historical importance; he was also the author of a critical theory which anticipates many of the most urgent interests of our own time. In Friedrich's theory of the romantic there were contained and implied theories of irony and myth in literature and the novel which are pertinent even today. Moreover, Friedrich Schlegel reflected on the theories of criticism, interpretation, and literary history so fruitfully that he can be claimed as the originator of hermeneutics, the theory of "understanding" which was later formulated by Schleiermacher and Boeckh and thus influenced the whole long line of German theoreticians of methodology. These are solid claims to fame, to which we must add Friedrich's pioneering work in Indic philology and philosophy and his wide-ranging historical and practical criticism of Goethe and Lessing, Homer, Camões, Boccaccio, and many other writers of almost all ages and nations.

Friedrich Schlegel started out as a classical philologist. His ambition was to become the "Winckelmann of Greek poetry," and all his early publications, which include two books, are devoted to this plan. But Friedrich Schlegel's studies of Greek poetry were not, of course, antiquarian contributions to literary history (though they display an astonishing learning for so young a man). As such they would necessarily be obsolete today and merit only mention in a history of classical scholarship. Rather, he conceived of literary history as so closely integrated with criticism that the history of Greek literature appeared to him both the nourishing soil and the proving ground of an aesthetic. Greek literature, in these early writings, was considered uniquely suitable to such a purpose, for Friedrich Schlegel not only saw the Greek works as eternal models of perfection, as archetypes of poetry, but also thought of Greek literary history as natural, spontaneous, undisturbed by outside interference, and complete in itself. Greek culture is called "throughout original and national, a whole complete in itself, which merely by internal evolution reached its highest summit and, in a complete cycle, then sank back into itself." Greek poetry thus contains a complete collection of examples of all the different genres and contains them in a natural order of evolution. It serves both as a theory of genres and as a picture of the whole cycle of the organic evolution of an art, as a kind of laboratory for theory, as "the eternal natural history of taste and art." This evolution is conceived on the analogy of biological evolution, in terms of growth, proliferation, blossoming, maturing, hardening, and final dissolution, an analogy which during the 19th century received a great deal of impetus from Darwinian evolutionism and led to such curiosities of literary history as Brunetière's evolutionary histories or John Addington Symonds' *Shakspere's Predecessors in the Drama*. Though this Greek evolution must be thought of as somehow necessary and fated and the table of genres as complete, Friedrich Schlegel did not succumb to the relativistic implications of his theory. When he said over and over again that the "best theory of art is its history" he did not mean the usual 19th-century historical relativism which is still crippling our present-day literary scholarship. He did not give up the task of evaluation or hide behind neutral history. In these early writings Friedrich Schlegel found his standard in the prescriptive nature, the ideal model of the great Greek classics; and late in his life he came to impose more and more religious criteria derived from his Christian philosophy. But in his middle stage, which clearly is the most interesting today, he recognized that the Greeks cannot command the unique position he had claimed for them and that his theory of the relation between history and criticism must be extended to the whole of literature without idolatry of any one nation or age. He saw that the whole history of the arts and sciences forms an order, one whole, or as he came to call it, an "organism" or an "encyclopedia," and that this order is the "source of objective laws for all positive criticism." For Schlegel literature thus forms "a great completely coherent and evenly organized whole comprehending in its unity many worlds of art and itself forming a single work of art." T. S. Eliot in "Tradition and the Individual Talent" has said substantially the same. But Schlegel—differing from the unhistorical Eliot—can say that he is "disgusted with every theory which is not historical" and that the "completion of every science is often nothing but the philosophical result of its history." Schlegel thus rejects both unhistorical theorizing and historical

relativism. He recognizes that the result of Herder's universal tolerance is the denial of any general standard of evaluation, in effect the abdication of criticism. The method of Herder to "contemplate every flower of art, without evaluation, only according to place, time, and kind, would finally lead to the result that everything must be as it is and was." Also, in later years Friedrich Schlegel rejected Adam Müller's similar concept of "mediating" (*vermittelnd*) criticism, since it abolishes the difference between the good and the bad and amounts to saying, "Providence orders everything for the best, and everything had to come about as it did according to the philosophy, so dear to our contemporaries, of King Gorboduc: 'All that is, is.' " But the critical view cannot be simply absorbed by the historical because books are not "original creatures." These protests against historical relativism are timely even today and were timely especially in Germany, where in the later 19th century historical relativism destroyed criticism more thoroughly than in any other country.

Beyond formulating convincingly the relation between history and criticism and stressing the aim of criticism as the "ascertaining of the value and nonvalue of poetic works of art," Schlegel made many fruitful suggestions concerning the nature of critical procedure and interpretation. It is obvious that he derives from the tradition of philology. He always stresses the share of philology in critical practice: "one cannot read out of pure philosophy or poetry without philology." Philology means to him the love of words, the detailed attention to the text, "reading," interpretation. A critic, he can say wittily, "is a reader who chews his cud. He should have more than one stomach." Reading or interpretation is always understood to be the right combination of micrology and attention to the whole. "One should exercise the art of reading both very slowly in a constant analysis of the detail and more quickly, in one swoop, for a survey of the whole." One should not merely be sensitive to beautiful passages but be able to seize the impression of the whole, since "the first condition of all understanding, and hence also of the understanding of a work of art, is an intuition of the whole."

Schlegel wants the critic to "spy on what [the poet] wanted to hide from our sight or at least did not want to show at first: on the author's secret intentions, which he pursues in silence and of which we can never assume too many in a genius." We should uncover the deeply hidden, the unfathomable, and understand an author even better than he understood himself. These are dangerous and paradoxical theories, with a measure of truth which has been exploited by much modern criticism far beyond Friedrich Schlegel's dreams. Mostly, though, Schlegel suggests sound and sober principles of interpretation. He repeats the commonplaces of the historical spirit, the necessity of sympathetic entry into remote times and countries, and he always stresses that one must know all the writings of an author in order to grasp their common spirit. In "art history," he understands, "one mass explains and illuminates the other. It is impossible to understand a part by itself." The construction and knowledge of the whole (of art and poetry) is the one and essential condition of all criticism. History and criticism are one. Every artist illuminates every other artist: together they form an order.

Schlegel attempts to describe what is needed in good criticism: "(1) a kind of geography of a world of art; (2) a spiritual and aesthetic architectonics of the work, its nature, its tone; and finally (3) its psychological genesis, its motivation by laws and conditions of human nature." He speaks constantly of the whole: the spirit, the tone, the general impression. Mostly he thinks of criticism as a "reconstructive" process. The critic must "reconstruct, perceive, and characterize the more subtle peculiarities of a whole. . . . One can say that one has understood a work and a mind only if one can reconstruct its course and structure. This profound understanding, if expressed in definite words, is called characterization and is the actual business and inner essence of criticism." Yet Schlegel has no use for the psychology of the reader, and he is strongest in his condemnation of the British psychological critics like Kames. He makes the sensible distinction between "fantastics" (i. e. the theory of creation, of imagination) and "pathetics" (a theory of the psychology of the reader, of the effects of poetry), but comes then to the conclusion that "not much is gained for criticism so long as one wants only to explain the aesthetic sense in general, instead of thoroughly exercising, applying, and forming it." He therefore rightly remarks that "almost all judgments on art are either too general or too specific. The critics should look for the golden mean here in their own productions, not in the works of the poets."

Schlegel recognizes also the dangers of what we might call exclamatory criticism. "If many mystical lovers of art who consider all criticism dissection and every dissection a destruction of enjoyment were to think consistently, 'I'll be damned!' would be the best judgment on the greatest work. There are critics who do not say more, though at much greater length." In general he describes the aim of criticism as "to give us a reflection of the work, to communicate its peculiar spirit, to present the pure impression in such a way that the presentation itself verifies the artistic citizenship of its author: not merely a poem about a poem, in order to dazzle for a moment; not merely the impression which a work has made yesterday or makes today on this or that person; but the impression which it should always make on all educated people." This recognizes the universal appeal any critical judgment makes, a claim which Schlegel apparently found excessive at times: he would say merely that the "finished view of a work is always a critical fact" and that it can make no other claims than its "invitation to everybody to seize his own impression just as purely and to define it just as strictly" as the critic himself. At times, however, he can embrace the fallacy of "creative" criticism. "Poetry can only be criticized by poetry. A judgment on art which is not itself a work of art, either in its matter, as presentation of a necessary impression in its genesis, or in its beautiful form and a liberal tone in the spirit of old Roman satire, has no citizens' rights in the realm of art." But possibly the subclauses limit the demand of the main clause: actually a work of criticism is artistic to Schlegel if it is a precise reproduction of an impression or if it simply has the satirical polemical tone, the verve he loved and admired in himself and others.

"Polemics" is one of Friedrich Schlegel's favorite words and concepts. One of the functions of criticism is negative,

the removal of the false, the making of room for the better, and this is polemics as practiced by writers like Lessing. "Polemics" is only the observe side of "productive" criticism, by which Schlegel means something much more practical and useful than "creative" criticism. He means criticism which we might possibly better call "incitory" or "anticipatory," criticism which is not the "commentary on an existing, completed, even exhausted literature" but the *organon* of a literature which is just beginning to form itself. It is thus a criticism which is not merely explanatory and conservative but productive—at least indirectly so, by guidance, command, or instigation. His own criticism was surely "productive" in his great years, when he stimulated a whole emerging literature and helped to give it direction. Instigating, directing, "producing" a new literature will always be one of the tasks of criticism which cannot be reduced—as is fashionable today—to the preservation and winnowing of tradition. But "creative" criticism, the production of another work of art, is an aberration, a needless duplication of a work of art, a blurring of necessary distinctions.

Schlegel's actual standards of evaluation and conception of poetry changed at least twice in his career: about 1796, when he abandoned his "Graecomania"—apparently under the impact largely of Schiller's treatise on *Naive and Sentimental Poetry*—and, more slowly and gradually, after 1801, when he moved toward a purely religious-conception which finally led him to his conversion in 1808. But long before, poetry had become subordinated in his mind to philosophy and religion. In the early writings on Greek poetry, especially **"Über das Studium der griechischen Poesie,"** which, we must remember, was finished before Schlegel could have read Schiller's treatise, Schlegel expounds a view of the contrast between the ancients and the moderns which in many ways is very similar to Schiller's. It derives, of course, from Winckelmann, from Schiller's *Letters on Aesthetic Education,* and from Goethe, yet it is elaborated with sharp distinctiveness and dogmatic assertiveness. The ideal of poetry is Greek poetry which is objective, "disinterested" (in the Kantian sense), perfect in form, impersonal, pure in its genres, and free from merely didactic and moralistic considerations. But more important than this rehearsal of the familiar traits of Winckelmannian "classicity" is Schlegel's negative characterization of the moderns.

Modern poetry is artificial, "interesting" (i. e. not disinterested, involved in the author's personal ends), "characteristic," "mannered" (in Goethe's sense, which contrasts subjective manner with objective style), impure in its mixing and confusion of genres, impure in its admixture of the didactic and philosophical, impure in its inclusion of even the ugly and the monstrous, and anarchic in its rejection of laws. Modern literature has "the terrible and yet fruitless desire to spread itself into the infinite, the eager thirst to penetrate the individual." Against the closed cycle of antiquity there stands the moderns' system of infinite progression, their unsatisfied "yearning" (*Sehnsucht*), a word which later became one of the shibboleths of romanticism. Even Shakespeare, though he is called the "summit of modern poetry," is never totally beautiful. He is mannered throughout, even though his manner is the greatest. Goethe alone affords hope for a return to objective art, to classical beauty, though Schlegel recognizes that he is still in between the interesting and the beautiful, the mannered and the objective. Schlegel, of course, conceives of the hoped-for German classicism not as actual imitation of the ancients but as a rebirth of an objective philosophy of art. No individual Greek writer, nor even less, of course, Greek theory and criticism, can become the model and authority. Schlegel always had a low opinion of Aristotle's *Poetics.*

**"Über das Studium der griechischen Poesie,"** then, contains the germ of the theory of the romantic. What was needed was only to change the minus signs into plus signs in front of the characterization of the moderns. Schlegel even in that treatise admits the necessity of the modern situation and praises many modern authors. He must have recognized that his dream and ideal, the harmony and objectivity of Greek poetry, is completely contrary to the actual bent of his own mind and the trend of the times. His reading of Schiller's treatise on *Naive and Sentimental Poetry* strengthened (as Schlegel acknowledged) this recognition and speeded up his change of heart or possibly, rather, his change of front. Fortified by Schiller's defense of the "sentimental," Schlegel, in the preface to **Die Griechen und Römer** (1797), which included the hitherto unprinted **"Über das Studium,"** takes an intermediate position admitting the provisional aesthetic value of the "interesting." The conversion to the modern is complete when in the same year (1797) Schlegel surprisingly calls his essay, **"Über das Studium,"** "a mannered prose hymn on the objective in poetry." A year later comes the famous "fragment" (No. 116) of the *Athenaeum* which defines romantic poetry as "progressive universal poetry." This fragment has been quoted over and over again and has been made the key for the interpretation of the whole of romanticism. But one should recognize that it is only one of his deliberately mystifying pronouncements and that in it Schlegel uses the term "romantic" in a highly idiosyncratic way which he himself very soon abandoned. The use of the term in this fragment had actually no influence on its establishment as a contrast to classical. Schlegel adopted the term in preference to "modern" or "interesting" because it had no pejorative or strictly chronological connotations and because at this time he was clearly playing with its etymological affinity with the *Roman,* the novel. The fragment in the *Athenaeum* wavers bewilderingly between a characterization of a poetry of the future and a novel of the future. The mission of romantic poetry is not only to "reunite the separate genres of poetry, to put poetry in touch with philosophy and rhetoric . . . it should combine poetry and prose, genius and criticism, the poetry of art and the poetry of nature. . . . Romantic poetry is still becoming: indeed its real essence is that it is always only becoming and never completed . . . . Romantic poetry is the only kind which is more than a kind; it is, so to speak, poetry itself: in a certain sense all poetry is or should be romantic." This is a program, a claim, a "vista toward a limitless growing classicity," as he says paradoxically; something so all-inclusive, all-embracing, and vague that the whole fragment assumes concrete meaning only if we think of his aspiration for the romantic novel to embrace all genres and of his earlier speculations which contrasted the cyclical course of Greek poetry with the unlimited perfectibility of the moderns.

In the **Gespräch über die Poesie** (1800) Schlegel returns to the old meaning of the term romantic. In his sketch of the **"Epochs of Poetry"** which is part of the **Gespräch,** Shakespeare is characterized as laying the "romantic foundations of modern drama." In the speech on mythology, another part of the piece, Cervantes and Shakespeare are referred to as belonging to "romantic poetry." Thus "romantic" is not simply identical with Schiller's "sentimental," since Shakespeare is romantic in Schlegel and naive in Schiller. Schiller considers the immediate relation to reality, the imitation of nature, as naive, while Schlegel sees a romantic trait in the avidity for the fullness of life. The terms clearly overlap on many points; Schlegel, however, draws a further contrast between the romantic and the modern. They differ, according to him, as a painting by Raphael or Correggio differs from a fashionable copper engraving. Lessing's *Emilia Galotti* is called "unutterably modern" and "not in the least romantic," while Shakespeare is the "real center and core of romantic imagination." The romantic thus can be found rather in the Renaissance and the Middle Ages, "in that age of knights, of love and fairy tales, whence the thing and the word are derived." But then the romantic is said to be not a genre but an element of poetry, which may dominate or recede more or less yet must never be totally absent. All poetry, Schlegel concludes illogically, must be romantic. These passages contain the essential distinctions of the romantic from the classical and the modern (i. e. pseudo-classical). But Friedrich Schlegel does not consider his own age romantic: he singles out the novels of Jean Paul as the "only romantic products of an unromantic age." Nor does he expressly contrast the classical and the romantic (though he alludes to their possible union). The most influential formulations of the great dichotomy belong only to his brother, August Wilhelm, even though all its elements are in Friedrich Schlegel.

Schlegel's poetic ideal takes on much more concrete meaning if we examine his demands for irony, myth, and the mysterious, his conception of the novel, in fact his whole new hierarchy of genres. He does not call irony "romantic irony." All the early passages using the term comment on the irony of Socrates, on his "sublime urbanity," without any particular modern application. Only the review of *Wilhelm Meister* (1798) and the **Gespräch über die Poesie** (1800) give it a meaning in the context of modern literature. Irony is, in part, associated with Schiller's play-concept of art, the Kantian view of art as free activity. We demand irony, "we demand that the events, the people, in brief the whole play of life, should really be conceived and represented as play." Irony is associated with paradox. It is "a form of paradox. Paradox is what is at the same time good and great." Irony is his recognition of the fact that the world in its essence is paradoxical and that an ambivalent attitude alone can grasp its contradictory totality. For Schlegel irony is the struggle between the absolute and the relative, the simultaneous consciousness of the impossibility and the necessity of a complete account of reality. The writer must thus feel ambivalent toward his work: he stands above and apart from it and manipulates it almost playfully. "In order to be able to describe an object well," Schlegel can say, "one must have ceased to be interested in it . . . as long as the artist invents and is inspired he remains at least for communication in an illiberal frame of mind." Thus art demands the "liberal frame of mind," the power of the artist to raise himself above his own "highest." "Irony is a clear consciousness of the infinitely full chaos," of the dark and inexplicable world, but it is also highly self-conscious, for irony is self-parody, "transcendental buffoonery" which "rises above one's art, virtue, and genius." Irony is thus associated with "transcendental poetry," with the "poetry of poetry" which Schlegel finds in Pindar, Dante, and Goethe. Irony to Schlegel is objectivity, complete superiority, detachment, manipulation of the subject matter. Schlegel praises *Wilhelm Meister* for the irony with which the hero is portrayed by Goethe, who seems to "smile down from the heights of his spirit upon his masterwork"; and he looks for similar attitudes in Aristophanes, Cervantes, Shakespeare, Swift, Sterne, and Jean Paul.

There is no evidence that Schlegel found irony in the constant interference of the author in his work, in the deliberate breaking of the illusion. Only in one fragment (No. 42 of the *Lyceum*) is there an allusion to the Italian *buffo* which might be so interpreted. But Schlegel speaks there of poetry in general, not of the drama, and the reference to the buffo means only that the ironic author always smiles at his imperfect medium just as the buffo laughs at his comic role. There is no recommendation of very old devices of art: the playwright on the stage, the play within the play, the author appearing in his own novel, which became such particular favorites of Tieck and Brentano, E. T. A. Hoffmann and Heine, and came to be known as "romantic irony." At the time that Schlegel formulated his ideas on irony he did not know Tieck's comedies and he never considered them realizations of his ideals. Goethe, Shakespeare, and Cervantes, not his fellow romanticists, were his ironists.

Still, Schlegel's theory easily lent itself to a subjectivist interpretation; in his own novel *Lucinde* he certainly exemplified extreme subjectivism, playing with illusion, moral and artistic irresponsibility. There is no contradiction between these two attitudes, and in dialectical thinking one extreme easily passes into the other.

Friedrich Schlegel introduced the term irony into modern literary discussion. Before, there are only adumbrations in Hamann. Schlegel's use of the term differs from the earlier purely rhetorical meaning and from the view of tragic irony in Sophocles which was developed early in the 19th century by Connop Thirlwall. Schlegel's concept was taken up by Solger, in whom it first assumed a central position for critical theory and for whom all art becomes irony. Hegel and later Kierkegaard criticized Schlegel's concept, utterly mistaking it as a consequence of his adherence to the Fichtean philosophy of ego, as sheer opportunism, artistic and moral frivolity. But in the actual texts there is no justification for such disparagement. One must realize, moreover, that irony for Schlegel is only one element of modern self-consciousness and is combined with very different requirements.

Among these, Friedrich Schlegel's demand for a new myth, an ironical, self-consciously elaborated, philosophical myth, is the most striking. In the speech on mythology, which also forms a part of the *Gespräch über die Poesie* (1800), Schlegel develops the thesis—familiar today and still relevant—that modern literature lacks the support, the mother-soil, of myth. Classical and Christian mythology had been used throughout the course of modern literature, and Germans preceding Schlegel, especially Herder and Klopstock, had loudly called for the revival of Teutonic mythology, a return to the sources of folk imagination. But Schlegel suggests a new and different mythology which would derive a new system of relationships, a "hieroglyphical expression of surrounding nature," from the new idealistic philosophy (Fichte) and the new physics (Schelling's *Naturphilosophie*). The exact nature of the new mythology is left vague in this manifesto. Schlegel suggests as further sources the pantheism of Spinoza and the Orient, especially India, a hint which he later pursued systematically in his own Indic studies. But Schlegel apparently does not mean by myth merely a new cosmology or an exploitation of philosophical concepts; he thinks of it, rather, as a system of correspondences and symbols. Myth is an analogue of the "wit of romantic poetry," as it is exemplified in the works of Cervantes and Shakespeare, which are full of "artfully arranged confusion, charming symmetry of contrasts, marvelous eternal alternation of enthusiasm and irony." Myth is something he calls "an indirect mythology," a new world view which abolishes the course of logical reason and returns us to the "beautiful confusion of imagination, the original chaos of human nature, for which I do not as yet know any more beautiful symbol than the colorful milling throng of the ancient Gods." However obscurely this is phrased, the sense becomes clear if we see the passage in the light of the other pronouncements on irony and the romantic. "Idealism" (i. e. Fichtean philosophy) means free play; life as play and all art as symbolic. Schlegel does not yet use the distinction between allegory and symbol drawn by Goethe and Schelling. He thus can say, "All beauty is allegory" and "Because it is inexpressible, one can express the highest only allegorically." Art, therefore, is myth, symbolism, even "divine magic."

More light is thrown on Schlegel's conception of poetry by several recently published fragments on beauty. Schlegel distinguishes there between multiplicity, unity, and totality in beauty. The triad is derived from Kant's table of the categories of quantity, which he interprets as plenty, richness, and life in a work of art; harmony, organization; and perfection or divinity. The first two criteria are the well-known requirements of unity and variety, local texture and general structure, or whatever we may call them today. The third category is clearly the same as the mythic or the infinite of other passages. At times, Schlegel has in mind simply the cosmic quality of art which was familiar to Schiller and Kant. The "infinite" is the morally sublime, the assertion of man's moral freedom, his resistance to suffering in tragedy; but mostly, with increasing emphasis and frequency, poetry becomes a part of divine creation, a smaller parallel to the work of art which is nature. "All holy plays of art are only distant imitations of the infinite play of the world, of the eternally self-creating work of art"—so runs an early passage formulated in a pantheistic terminology. But soon we get phrases like "Art is a visible appearance of God's Kingdom on earth," and "Only that can be beautiful which has a relation to the infinite and divine," or poetry "is nothing else than a pure expression of the inner eternal word of God." Poetry becomes more and more identified with philosophy and religion. Philosophy and poetry are proclaimed different forms of religion and the union of philosophy and poetry is envisaged as an ultimate aim. In effect, poetry is pronounced, at first, to be "only another expression of the same transcendental view of things, differing only in its form" from idealistic philosophy. After Schlegel's conversion, poetry for him forms, along with history, mythology, language, science, and art, only one of the rays of the single light of higher knowledge, revelation. Poetry thus loses more and more of its specific meaning and becomes confused and amalgamated with religion, philosophy, and the whole universe itself. Even before this, the *Gespräch über die Poesie* (1800) had spoken of the "formless and unconscious poetry which stirs in plants, shines in light, smiles in a child, glistens in the flower of youth, glows in the loving breast of women." But then one of the interlocutors could still ask mockingly: "Is then everything poetry?" But later if someone had asked Schlegel whether everything good and beautiful is religion, he would have received a roundly affirmative answer. One must recognize how influential this cosmic extension of the meaning of poetry (with its antecedents and parallels in Plato and Shelley) became during the 19th century. It was a development detrimental to the establishment of a genuine theory of literature.

Schlegel's many speculations about particular genres proved more fruitful than his mystical generalities on the significance of poetry. In his early writings on Greek literature he is most interested in the theory of genres because the development of Greek literature presented him with a survey of the main genres. He did not get to the discussion of tragedy in detail but in connection with Homer devoted long arguments to the epic. He violently rejected Aristotle's approximation of the epic and tragedy and argued, using Wolf's theories about the gradual composition of the Homeric poems, for a theory of the epic in which each larger or smaller member has, like the whole, its own life and internal unity. An epic thus has a different structure from that of a drama: it not only begins *in mediis rebus* but also ends there. It is always both a continuation and the beginning of something else. The events in the epic are not free actions or necessary decisions of fate but contingent, chance events, for everything marvelous is contingent. The affinity to some of the contemporary discussions between Schiller and Goethe is clear, but Schlegel's contrast between the almost atomistic epic and the unified drama, the epic as a series of chance events and the tragedy of fate and inexorable necessity, seems exaggerated and scholastic in its rigidity.

The novel is later discussed by Schlegel with much greater originality and suggestiveness, in close relation with his theories of the romantic, myth, and irony and with actual contemporary practice. His **"Letter on the Novel"** (which is also a part of the *Gespräch über die Poesie*) presents a program, a history, and an implied defense of his own attempt at a novel, the unlucky *Lucinde* (1799). Schlegel has no patience with realistic art, though he is full of avid lust for life in its variety and fullness. He condemns the realistic novel of the English, including even Fielding. He admires Swift, Sterne, and Diderot. *Jacques le Fataliste* is superior to Sterne, as it is free from sentimental admixtures. Jean Paul also excels Sterne in that his "imagination is much more diseased, and hence much odder and much more fantastic." But all these recent novelists seem to him only preparatory to an understanding of the "divine wit," the imagination of an Ariosto, a Cervantes, and a Shakespeare. The novel is thus not grouped with the epic at all, for the epic (he still thinks mostly of Homer) is impersonal, objective, and heroic, while the novel in his sense expresses a subjective mood and allows indulgence in an author's humor which would be quite out of place in an epic. By a novel, a *Roman,* Schlegel means the "ironic, fantastic, romantic" art of Cervantes, Sterne, Diderot, Jean Paul, and his own *Lucinde.* The realistic novel, he would admit, tells us (as does Fanny Burney's Cecilia) how people get bored in London or (as Fielding) how a country squire curses. But in novels he loves the "arabesque" (a term derived from Goethe), the play of imagination, the irony, and the subjective. Thus, Rousseau's *Confessions* are called a better novel than *La Nouvelle Héloïse.* His own *Lucinde* consisted of such arabesques, or what the century called "rhapsodies," and of highly personal erotic confessions. Novalis' *Heinrich von Ofterdingen* combines the novel and the myth. In the **"Letter on the Novel"** Goethe's *Wilhelm Meister* has lost its earlier central position and is praised only for attempting the impossible ideal of uniting classical and romantic.

The romantic, irony, and myth are all combined in this all-embracing genre, the *Roman,* which contains narration, song, and other forms. The old hierarchy of genres is overthrown. Drama and epic are dethroned, the novel exalted. But it is a very peculiar novel: Thomas Mann's ironic myths, Joyce, or Kafka would come nearer to a fulfillment of his prophecy than the realistic novel of the 19th century. Schlegel even saw the consequences of writing novels "out of psychology": "It seems very inconsistent and pusillanimous to want to shy away even from the slowest and most detailed analysis of unnatural lusts, most gruesome tortures, revolting infamy, and disgusting sensual and spiritual impotence." But he could hardly have endorsed his mock proposal, as nothing was further from his taste than plodding, "lifelike" art.

In the early writings on Greek poetry, tragedy is considered the summit of Greek and presumably of all literature. Sophocles, especially, is so completely identified with the highest beauty, the harmony of the whole, that praise could hardly go higher. Greek tragedy is interpreted as a necessary strife between mankind and fate, but that strife is resolved in harmony and mankind is victorious even though physically defeated. Hercules, in the *Trachiniae,* though dying, "wings upward at last, free." Shakespeare, on the other hand, the example of modern, "interesting," or "philosophical" tragedy, centers his art around character rather than fate. The total impression of *Hamlet* is a maximum of despair. Its end result is the "eternal colossal dissonance which divides mankind and fate forever." During the fruitful middle years Schlegel's interest in tragedy receded in favor of the novel. It re-emerges in the *History of Ancient and Modern Literature* (1812), where, in the context of the discussion of Calderón, a new three-type or three-stage theory of tragedy is expounded. A purely picturesque art of depiction is the lowest stage. The second is the characterization of the whole, "where the world and life in its full variety, in its contradictions and odd complications, where man and his existence, this involved riddle, is depicted as such a riddle." Shakespeare is the greatest master of this stage. But beyond it there arises a third stage, in which the dramatist not only expounds but solves the riddle of existence and shows how "the Eternal arises from the earthly catastrophe." This threefold distinction is explained by a further and different classification of three kinds of catastrophes in tragedy, which are compared to the *Inferno, Purgatorio,* and *Paradiso.* The hero may perish completely, like Macbeth or Wallenstein or Faust (in the German legend, for Schlegel could not yet know Goethe's happy ending). The second kind of solution is that of reconciliation, as at the end of the *Oresteia* or in *Oedipus at Colonus.* The third and highest stage is that of spiritual transfiguration of the hero, for which the Christian endings of Calderón's plays are Schlegel's example and the justification of the exalted position which he now ascribes to Calderón.

On the whole, Schlegel obviously holds to the doctrine of the distinction and even purity of genres. In his early writings he severely condemned the mixing of genres as a modern disease, and even later he praised Lessing for showing that each work "should be only excellent in its genus and species, as otherwise it would become an unsubstantial thing in general." He condemns pedantic classifications but obviously agrees with the interlocutors in his *Gespräch über die Poesie* who argue that the "imagination of the poet must not pour itself into a chaotic poetry in general, but every work must have its completely distinct character according to form and genre." A theory of genres would be a specific theory of poetry. This point of view is somewhat modified, in the later revised version, when another interlocutor admits that the "essential form of poetry lies in its distinct genres and their theory," but not the "essence of poetry itself, which is alone ceaselessly inventive and creative, eternal imagination." When Schlegel recommended the romantic novel he rather formulated the principles of a new inclusive genre than advocated the mingling of the old ones.

Moreover, in discussing Lessing's *Laokoon* Schlegel does not favor an actual union of the arts. He sensibly criticizes Lessing for ignoring the differences between sculpture and painting and argues that each art should try to overcome the limitations of its material. Just because sculpture uses so heavy and dead a material as stone, it should try to make it alive and living. Just because music is so fluid and flowing, it must attempt to express the permanent, to "build a proud temple out of the eternal relations of harmony" and leave "the whole firm as a monument in the soul of the listener." The poet also uses sound which occurs successively in time, but at the end of a poem the "whole must stand clearly like a picture in one presenta-

tion before the eyes of the listener or even reader." Poetry is the universal art, and thus there can be poems which are written wholly in the spirit of painting and others which are musical, or even both simultaneously. Several works of Cervantes and Tieck are referred to without specification, and some poems of the ancients and Goethe are given as examples of poems that draw something from sculpture. Descriptive poetry in the 18th-century sense is, however, condemned, not because it tried to achieve the effects of painting in poetry but because it was atomistic, concerned only with particulars. "This is the death of all feeling for art, which first of all and primarily is based on a view of the whole." The way is open here for the picture poems of the romanticists, the musical songs in words, the sculpturesque poetry of Keats, Landor, and Gautier. But no union of the arts, no absorption of one art by another, is advocated, and poetry keeps its central position as the most universal of the arts.

The creative act is thought of by Schlegel as a combination of the conscious and subconscious, of "instinct" and "intention." However, in the *Gespräch* there are passages which speculate on the possibility of schools of poetry. Even the hope is expressed that poetry which had been a "tale of heroes, and then a game of the knights, and finally the handicraft of burghers would become a thorough science of true scholars and the honest art of inventive poets." Though this might sound like a recommendation for sheer academicism, for art as a craft (and has been interpreted as such), it surely cannot be taken literally in the light of all of Schlegel's other writings. His concept of poetry is far too closely related to that of Schelling and Novalis, who actually use the term "unconscious." The idea of a "school" is merely a paradoxical formula for Schlegel's desire for collective art, the social art of the future, for the whole romantic ideal of "symphilosophizing." His school is a *côterie,* a *cénacle,* not a *Singschule* in the style of the *Meistersänger.* Also in his allusions to the role of the artist in society Schlegel is only apparently contradictory. He can call him an "isolated egoist" and suggest that "even in its outward customs the manner of life of artists should be thoroughly distinct from that of other people. They are Brahmins, a higher caste, ennobled not by birth but by free self-dedication." This attitude best suited his own manner of life, his pride, his hatred of the German *Philister* and the cultural representatives of the Berlin Enlightenment, and his ever present desire to *épater le bourgeois,* so prominent in his paradoxes and witty formulas. But Schlegel opposed the purely individual isolated artist, what he called the "Stubenluft," of earlier German literature. At a period when his liberalism was at his height, in a defense of the German revolutionary Georg Forster, Schlegel praised him as a "social" writer who lived up to his ideal of the total man. In describing Lessing's position in German literature he dwelt on the loneliness, the single-handedness of his struggle more than on anything else. Schlegel's whole conception of polemical criticism, of an "encyclopedia," presupposes teamwork, some kind of association, a group of friends, or possibly a class of clerics, an élite. When the flood of enthusiasm for folk poetry was at its highest in Germany, Schlegel did not share it, though he admired ancient mythic poetry. He even wrote a satirical review of a collection of German folk songs in which he parodied Goethe's review of *Des Knaben Wunderhorn,* and in the ***History of Ancient and Modern Literature*** he considered folk poetry as valuable only as a survival of ancient heroic poetry. He even calls it a proof of the dissolution of real national poetry. "It is not always the right condition that poetry, which should inspire, keep alive and further develop the spirit of a whole nation, be left to the people alone." The emphasis is now laid on poetry as an expression of a nation and its peculiar character: national literature should be based on its legends, its history, its myth, and should appeal to the whole nation. But when Schlegel praises Spanish literature as the "most national" of all, he pulls himself up and declares that he is far from "considering the national point of view as the only one from which the value, in world history, of a literature should be judged." The overriding value is now religion, revelation.

Schlegel never shared the latecomer's prophecy of the extinction of poetry, precisely because he never conceived of it as an isolated skill. Poetry, he believed with Herder, is the mother-tongue of the human race, a natural function of man. He rejected the view that poetry is only "the symbolic child's language of mankind in its youth." It is to him an activity of the human mind which cannot disappear, rather to be perfected in the future than perfect in the past. Man, he feels, is gaining rather than losing in the strength and sensitivity of his feeling, in true aesthetic vital force. Schlegel has no patience with the worship of a golden age of poetry, and the golden ages of the French and English seem to him not golden or poetic at all. He rejects, at least for modern times, the idea of a cycle, of growth and decay, quoting the example of Calderón as that of a sudden rebirth in an age of apparent total decadence, of a phoenix rising out of its own ashes. He believed, even in his Catholic years, in perfectibility, in the open structure of modern literature, in its great civilizing role. He could not otherwise have been a leader of a group, the herald of an "aesthetic revolution" in Germany. After all, romantic poetry, modern poetry, was for him "progressive universal poetry."

We shall glance only briefly at Friedrich Schlegel's achievements as a literary historian, scholar, and practical critic. Literary history was his earliest ambition, fulfilled by his fragmentary history of Greek poetry. A brief sketch, the **"Epochs of Poetry,"** takes a central position in the ***Gespräch,*** and later in life he considered the ***History of Ancient and Modern Literature*** (delivered in 1812, published in 1815) the culmination of his literary career. Heine, in his malicious account of the Schlegels, suggested that "Friedrich Schlegel there surveyed the whole of literature from an elevated point of view, but that elevation is always the bell tower of a Catholic church." But this is grossly exaggerated. The book, one must admit, is in many ways disappointing with respect to literary criticism. It attempts, rather, a general survey of the intellectual, religious, philosophical, and literary history of mankind on a scale which is small for the tremendous scope of its ambition. It includes a philosophy of history which predicts the ultimate victory of Roman Catholicism over the forces of the Enlightenment and all other forms of secularism. Literary history and criticism is thus crowded out by unc-

tuous exhortations, philosophical and religious reflections, and speculations on the history of language which today are totally obsolete. But in spite of these long stretches of irrelevancy the book contains much literary criticism and history in the strict sense, and most of it, based in large part on Schlegel's earlier researches and reflections, represents his most considered and systematic view of many authors and problems.

We have sufficiently discussed Schlegel's early views of the history of Greek poetry, its cyclical rise and fall, its explication of the sequence of genres, and the theory of the epic and tragedy he elicits from Homer and Sophocles. In spite of his glorification of Greek classical beauty, even his early conception of the Greeks had some original features which were later developed by him in much greater fullness. He apparently was one of the first to sense the dark background or underground of Greek life, the element which Nietzsche exalted seventy years later as "Dionysian." Schlegel emphasizes that we should consider the "Greek orgies and mysteries not as foreign stains and chance aberrations but as an essential part of ancient culture, as a necessary step in the gradual development of the Greek spirit." With the appreciation of the Orphic in Greek poetry and in the mysteries goes Schlegel's exaltation of Aristophanes, which was then a comparative novelty. A very early paper is devoted to the **"Aesthetic Value of Greek Comedy,"** which is seen in its joy, sublime freedom, and unlimited autonomy. The social purpose and the realistic detail of the old comedy are completely ignored. Aristophanes seems to anticipate romantic irony. Even in Sophocles Schlegel finds fused the "divine drunkeness of Dionysus, the deep inventiveness of Athene, the quiet serenity of Apollo." But with Schlegel's turn toward the romantic and Christian his sight was sharpened for the nonclassical elements in the Greeks. He sees the ancient Greeks now as less unique in the context of the ancient Orient. He stresses in Aeschylus the "struggle between the old chaos and the idea of law and harmonious order," and he condemns Greek naturalism and materialism much more strongly and sees it now everywhere. In this he goes along with the development of German classical studies of his time: he shares, though moderately, in the attacks on the glorification of the Greeks by the medieval enthusiasts among his contemporaries and by those who saw the limitations of Greek civilization from the point of view of Christianity. He sympathizes with the new interest in Greek myth and its symbolist interpretation introduced by Creuzer. He also looks for anticipations of the Christian spirit among the Greeks and finds them in Sophocles, who has an "intuition of the divine," whose tragedies end in reconciliation and a hint of transfiguration.

With his shift to the romantic Schlegel's concrete interest in the Middle Ages grew considerably. Here the stimulation of his brother was probably decisive. He devoted some research in the Paris libraries to manuscripts of Provençal poetry in preparation for an edition which never materialized and laboriously read through the scarce minor works of Boccaccio. The piece which he devoted to a characterization of Boccaccio (1801) has pioneering value and some critical interest, for Schlegel suggests there an aesthetic of the *novella* in which he sees the presentation of a subjective mood and view in an indirect and symbolic manner. Schlegel belongs also to the early German admirers of Dante (following his brother). He sees in him a proof of the artificial character of the oldest modern poetry, as Dante's poem is contrived in its structure according to scholastic concepts and thus contrasts with Homer's naturally growing work. Without knowing it Schlegel here contradicts Vico, who had seen in Dante the Italian Homer, the representative of a heroic age. Also in the *History* Schlegel admits that in Dante poetry and Christianity are not in complete harmony and that the *Divine Comedy* is, at least in places, only a theological didactic poem.

The revival of Nordic and Old Germanic studies in Germany, in which his brother and his friend Tieck took a prominent part, turned Schlegel's attention also to the Nordic Middle Ages. He wrote elaborately on Ossian (expressing grave doubts of its authenticity and speculating on its date), on the *Edda,* and more sketchily on the *Nibelungenlied* and Wolfram von Eschenbach. In the *History* Schlegel characterizes the German *Minnesang,* trying to differentiate it from the Provençal courtly lyric. Later he more and more stressed the value for modern poetry of national history, legends, and memories, and these memories were, for the Nordic nations, mostly medieval. He also argues against the term "Dark Ages" and gives a favorable account of medieval civilization, stressing the survival of antiquity, the beginnings of the Renaissance as early as the times of Charlemagne, the advantages of chivalry, courtly love, the beauties of Gothic architecture, and so forth. But one cannot say that his medievalism is extreme or exclusive like that of many of his contemporaries. One has also the definite impression that his acquaintance with the actual literature was limited and that he did not overrate its artistic value. Strangely enough he rated Chaucer below Hans Sachs and shows little concrete knowledge of Old French literature, though he had encouraged and supervised his wife's German version of the Old French Merlin romance.

The Renaissance (not yet called so) is much more fully in his mind. It is to him *the* romantic age. His admiration for Shakespeare, Cervantes, and Camões is almost unbounded. French literature of the Renaissance, however, is almost completely ignored (with the exception of meager remarks on Montaigne and Rabelais) and Italian literature is rated curiously low. Schlegel considers Tasso a subjective sentimentalist, unsuccessful in the heroic epic, and he definitely prefers Camões to Ariosto. Machiavelli, though treated with respect, is singled out as a strange un-Christian anomaly. Surprising and even odd is the praise for Guarini's *Pastor Fido* as "permeated with the spirit of antiquity, great and noble, even in its form, like the drama of the Greeks." Shakespeare attracted Schlegel very early, especially *Hamlet,* which at that time he saw as a philosophical tragedy (a contradiction according to his theory), a tragedy of despair, of the disproportion between thinking and acting powers. Schlegel's Hamlet clearly is a development of Goethe's in the direction of Coleridge's philosophical prince. With his brother, Friedrich was one of the first critics to stress that Shakespeare was a "most purposeful artist" (1797), but his concrete discussions of

Shakespeare seem quite divided in purpose and conception. He shows the then prevalent German interest in Shakespeare's histories as a national myth and can express the preposterous opinion that *Henry V* is the "summit of Shakespeare's power." He also shares Tieck's and his brother's uncritical predilection for the apocrypha. *Locrine* especially is considered by him as important for an understanding of Shakespeare, apparently in contrast to the sonnets and poems, which for Schlegel are a proof of the sweetness of Shakespeare's personality and hence, surprisingly, a proof of Shakespeare's own immense remoteness from the stage. It is strange that Schlegel, with all his interest in the fantastic and idyllic Shakespeare, the Italian Shakespeare one might say, could still come to the conclusion that Shakespeare is basically an "old Nordic and not a Christian poet," and can even speak of his feeling as "generally Nordic and truly German." German here means, of course, Germanic as it was used at that time, but Schlegel also claims that only the German critics have understood Shakespeare and that he is peculiarly theirs. Schlegel was caught in the general wave of German nationalism during the Napoleonic era and was enticed by the current North and South contrast which, in the case of the English Shakespeare, was complicated by a violent antipathy for the commercial, utilitarian, and materialistic England of the 18th century which made Shakespeare appear a lonely survivor of an almost prehistoric Nordic age.

No literature elicited as much admiration and interest from Friedrich in his later years as Spanish literature. Cervantes especially is to him a romantic, poetic writer in spite of his satire against chivalry. *Don Quixote* is the model of the novel, fantastic, poetic, humorous. The *Novelas, Galatea,* the play *Numancia,* and even *Persiles* are also highly admired. The Spanish medieval romances are the most beautiful he knows, and in later years Calderón rises in his estimation to the highest position among all dramatists, being "preeminently Christian and therefore the most romantic of all." Schlegel, besides, took an intense interest in Camões. The *Lusiads* is praised as the greatest heroic poem of modern times, right after Homer, by far exceeding Ariosto in color and fullness of imagination. A special article elaborates this praise in a lyrical description of the contents, coupled with a comparative disparagement of Virgil and Tasso.

French tragedy and literature in general was the pet aversion of the German romanticists and the main polemical butt of his brother. Friedrich's early writings are full of violent invectives. French tragedy is called a mere "empty formality without power, charm, and substance; even its form is an absurd barbaric mechanism, without internal vital principle and natural organization." The French are considered a nation "without poetry," and the so-called classics of the French and English are dismissed as not even worthy of mention in a history of art. But this violence abated considerably with time, his stay in France, and his turn to Catholicism. In the *History,* though there is still no sympathy shown for neoclassical theory, Corneille's *Cid* and Racine's *Athalie* are praised very warmly. Surprisingly, even Voltaire's *Alzire* finds favor in Schlegel's eyes, though otherwise Voltaire is one of the villains of his *History.* Schlegel, moreover, does not endorse his brother's attack on Molière; the praise for Bossuet is very generous for obvious reasons, while Pascal is mainly characterized as a sophistical enemy of Schlegel's friends, the Jesuits. Rousseau, though Schlegel considers him merely a negative force without positive creed, is exalted as the greatest French author of the 18th century.

English literature outside Shakespeare interested Friedrich Schlegel (possibly for linguistic reasons) least. Praise and appreciation of Milton is very limited and the influence of his Latinized vocabulary is called unfortunate. The Christian theme of *Paradise Lost* is considered to erect insuperable barriers to success. Richardson is mildly appreciated, as well as Sterne, but in general the English of the 18th century are attacked as the representatives of the modern spirit, "modern" meaning secular and commercial. Gibbon especially is singled out for frequent ridicule; the *Memoirs* is considered an "immensely comic book." Gibbon merely loved the material magnificence of the Romans and might as well have written on the Turks. The English 18th-century critics are mercilessly dismissed: "there is not the most modest hint of a sense for poetry in Harris, Home [Lord Kames], and Johnson."

There is comparatively little criticism of contemporary foreign literature in Friedrich Schlegel: the *History* shows Schlegel's sympathetic awareness of the French Catholic revival, De Bonald, Lammenais, and Joseph de Maistre. Schlegel wrote a warmly appreciative review (1820) of Lamartine, especially of the first volume of the *Méditations,* which fitted into a scheme for contrasting Lamartine the poet of faith with Byron the poet of despair. Still, Byron, though condemned as the poet of negation, is, as was usual on the Continent at that time, grossly overrated. Lucifer in *Cain* is, for instance, preferred to Goethe's Mephistopheles. Among more recent English writers Schlegel praises only Burke for political reasons and gives a very critical account of Scott's poetry as a mere "mosaic of isolated fragments of romantic legend."

One feature of the *History* should be singled out for particular praise. Schlegel tries to pay some attention to the minor nations of Northern and Eastern Europe. In a spirit of tolerant nationalism he insists that every nation has a right to its language and peculiar literature. He refers to the existence at least of Russian and medieval Czech literature and shows some awareness of the revival of Hungarian literature, even mentioning one author, Kisfaludy.

Naturally, Schlegel's main efforts in practical criticism were devoted to German literature. Considering his general outlook, one must admire his generous appreciation of Luther, even in the *History.* The praise of Optiz is unusual for the time and setting, and Schlegel shares the extravagant admiration of his friends for Jakob Böhme. Some of the most detailed criticism Schlegel wrote was devoted to Lessing, his great favorite among the older German authors. As Lessing is usually considered the representative author of the German Enlightenment and can hardly be divorced from the rationalistic Protestant tradition, this sympathy seems surprising at first. It cooled considerably after the conversion, yet in his most romantic years Schlegel wrote an enthusiastic article and edited a three-volume anthology with introductions, one of them on the "Char-

acter of Protestants." Part of Schlegel's sympathy must be explained by his desire to capture the great palladium of the Enlightenment for himself and his friends: to show that Lessing is by no means the ordinary rationalist, that especially the *Education of the Human Race* points toward a new religion. Schlegel quite frankly surrenders Lessing's claim to greatness as a poet and dramatist and is interested primarily in his character, his "great free style of life," his open-mindedness, and the strength of his unpopular opinions even more than in his prose style, his "mixture of literature, polemics, wit, and philosophy." Lessing's fragmentary form, his "combinatory spirit," is for Schlegel the model and the justification of his own fragments, many of which he quoted as "iron filings" in the article on Lessing. His anthology is, in part, made up of snippets: the antiquarian or theological context is dropped in order to isolate the passages which Schlegel felt to be of contemporary import and to reveal Lessing's spirit rather than his opinions. One must recognize that posterity has, on the whole, endorsed Schlegel's view: the position of Lessing the poet has decreased and that of the thinker has increased, just as Schlegel himself desired.

The relations of Friedrich Schlegel to Goethe and Schiller underwent such changes and were so complicated by personal clashes, literary politics, and even the background influence of women that a complete exposition hardly belongs in a history of criticism. Still, Friedrich Schlegel was also a serious critic of Schiller and Goethe, and thus his opinions need attention in our context. At first, Schlegel admired Schiller, and undoubtedly his early aesthetic writings were profoundly influenced by Schiller's. **"Über das Studium der griechischen Poesie"** contains praise of Schiller's lyric poetry—which is compared to Pindar—the power of his feeling, the nobility of his mind, the dignity of his language, his "chest and voice"—indeed, praise so extravagant that Schlegel has been suspected of irony or insincerity. The change was certainly marked very soon when Schlegel reviewed Schiller's *Musenalmanach,* and there slyly ridiculed Schiller's poem "Die Würde der Frauen," suggesting it should be read backwards stanza by stanza. The feminist in Schlegel simply could not tolerate Schiller's middle-class ideal of women. In "Die Ideale" Schlegel sees the "convulsion of despair," an "almost sublime excess," and even suggests that "the health of the imagination once disrupted is incurable." That Schlegel did not like Schiller's epigrams (*Xenien*), some of which were directed against him, is not surprising, but he made a tactical mistake when he pointed out that Schiller's periodical *Die Horen* published mostly translations. Schiller then broke with August Wilhelm, who had supplied a majority of these translations and had been very glad to get paid for them. After this break the Schlegels adopted a policy of public silence toward Schiller, partly in order not to endanger their good relations with Goethe. But privately Schlegel voiced the most unfavorable opinions of everything that Schiller published and even his most personal notes show that he considered him merely a "rhetorical sentimentalist," a "poetical philosopher but not a philosophical poet." Even the aesthetic writings are roundly condemned. But with the years—after the personal animosities faded and Schiller died—Schlegel came to a much more favorable appreciation of Schiller's works.

The *History* recognizes that Schiller was the "real founder of the German drama," that he was "through and through a dramatist," and that his "passionate rhetoric" was essential to it. Even his philosophical preparations for poetry are defended, and the possibility of the philosophical lyric is illustrated from Schiller's example. Schlegel seems to have recognized that he himself belonged to Schiller's generation: he sees him passing from the modern to the romantic and once groups him with Jean Paul, Tieck, Novalis, and himself.

The relation to Goethe developed differently and found much fuller public expression in detailed discussions of Goethe's works. It is difficult to realize today that Goethe, after the great success of *Werther,* had fallen into comparative oblivion in the 80's and that the Schlegels did very much to rebuild his fame on quite different grounds. The initiative there belongs to August Wilhelm, but Friedrich also played an important role. Friedrich Schlegel printed, as a fragment of his forthcoming book **"Über das Studium der griechischen Poesie,"** a piece on Goethe (1796) in which he hails him as the "dawn of true poetry and pure beauty." Goethe opens a vista toward a new stage of aesthetic culture. His works are the "irrefutable proof that the objective is possible and that the hope of beauty is not a vain illusion of reason." Friedrich even claims that *Faust,* when finished, will probably far excel *Hamlet.* Very soon afterward, however, the ratio is strangely defined in favor of *Hamlet* as something like 100:7. But it would be hard to think of higher praise than that Friedrich heaped on Goethe's idyll "Alexis und Dora," and he never wrote better and more appreciative criticism than the essay on *Wilhelm Meister* (1798) and the **"Essay on the Different Styles of Goethe's Early and Late Works,"** included in the *Gespräch* (1800). The review of *Wilhelm Meister* is justly famous, as it succeeds in defining the attitude of the author, the general impression and the particular character of each part, and the main characters of the action. Schlegel also puts his finger on the break in the book (which he did not know was caused by Goethe's rewriting and incorporation of the *Theatrical Mission*), though he prefers the later parts with their mysteries and philosophies to the earlier realistic sections that seem so much more alive today. The attempt to survey Goethe's whole artistic development is also highly successful in its somewhat schematic distinction of three stages, represented by *Goetz von Berlichingen, Tasso,* and *Hermann und Dorothea* respectively. Schlegel's sense of style is remarkable if one considers how clearly he arranges works whose dates of composition were unknown to him and how well he ranks Goethe's works according to their importance.

But apart from these public pronouncements Schlegel's private notes show increasing misgivings about Goethe and a slow but decided turning away from complete adoration. Very early Schlegel notes that "Goethe is without the word of God," and *Meister* is considered "imperfect, because it is not mystic enough." Goethe's works are even called "much more similar to mechanical works of art than the ancients, Shakespeare, and the romantics. . . . Goethe's works have no unity, no totality: only here and there is there a faint beginning." But nothing of this appeared in public, and as late as 1802 Goethe went far out

*Johann Wolfgang von Goethe, a principal subject of Schlegel's criticism. From an oil painting by Heinrich Kolbe, c. 1822-26.*

of his way to produce Schlegel's play **Alarcos.** Friedrich's first public criticisms of Goethe were directed against the neoclassicism of his views on art propounded in the *Propyläen,* but the formal pronouncements continued to be very favorable and respectful. Among them the review of four volumes of Goethe's works (1808) is the most elaborate. It is most vocal in its praise of Goethe's lyrics and lyrical romances, with discriminating remarks on individual poems. Much that Goethe wrote in classical meters is especially admired and classed together as the outline of a great didactic cycle. *Wilhelm Meister* is again reviewed, with a difference. Schlegel now defends it against his friend Novalis' famous saying that *Meister* is a novel directed against poetry. He even recants his theory of the romantic novel. The novel is now called "no real genre . . . every novel . . . that is really poetic forms an individual in itself." But there are reservations, blaming Goethe for the way he scattered his energies in mere sketches, outlines, fragments, and minor experimental works. The treatment in the *History* is very perfunctory and hurried. *Meister* is now ranked below *Faust, Iphigenie, Tasso,* and *Egmont,* which (with the best lyrics) will preserve Goethe's fame; and Goethe is called the Shakespeare of his age. But in conclusion it is suggested that to his way of thinking Goethe should be called rather a German Voltaire: a malicious comparison if one considers the context of the times and Voltaire's reputation among the public Schlegel was addressing. The private notes show that this classification had been long in Schlegel's mind and that his resentment of Goethe's paganism and supposed enmity to

Christianity went so far that he spoke in private letters of his "meanness." Whatever one may think about the convolutions of Schlegel's opinions and their often very personal motivations, one must recognize that he suggested many important critical views of the works of both Goethe and Schiller. Considering his close analysis of *Wilhelm Meister* and many poems, Saintsbury's judgment that he "blenches at the book—still more at the passage and the phrase" seems strange, to say the least. It is probably suggested by a reading of the *History* which, in its very scope, demanded large generalizations, wide vistas, and sweeping opinions. But there is a place for such synthesis, of which Friedrich Schlegel, after all, was an early pioneer. His brief history of recent German literature there included is remarkable, even if one considers only such a feature, in recent times hailed as a great discovery, as its division according to three generations: those who matured in the 50's and 60's of the 18th century, Klopstock, Lessing, Wieland, etc.; those who entered literature in the 70's, such as Goethe and Herder; and a third generation appearing late in the 80's and early 90's, with which he classed himself.

One cannot say that Schlegel was a systematic critic of his own friends and contemporaries, but he has written an excellent impressionistic characterization of Jean Paul, of his "piquant lack of taste," his "attractive clumsiness"; one of Tieck, of whom, in spite of personal friendship, he was not uncritical; and has pronounced on many other of his German contemporaries. His high regard for the tawdry and hollow Zacharias Werner must be classed as an aberration caused by his sympathy for a fellow convert.

One aspect of Schlegel's criticism deserves special emphasis: its form. His early works were conventional treatises written in an abstract expository style. In his late writings, such as the *History,* Schlegel returned again to formal exposition and rotund periods. But in his middle period he developed forms which were, at least in Germany, new in criticism. The "Charakteristik" is the critical essay on a single author or book in which Schlegel applies a vocabulary of criticism which mingles abstract definitions or approximations with impressionistic and even lyrical passages. Impressionism became a doubtful blessing of criticism in the course of the 19th century when it degenerated into the purple patches of Pater and Oscar Wilde, but at the time, Schlegel's evocations must have struck readers as something novel and welcome compared to the formalism of the treatises on aesthetics or the cut-and-dried report of the conventional book review. Besides the "Charakteristik," Schlegel discovered the "fragment," the aphorism, as a vehicle for criticism. It was not, of course, a totally new discovery—Lichtenberg and Chamfort are his masters—but he quite definitely and consciously used the fragment in order to indulge in the mere unsupported pronouncement, the metaphorical surprising analogy, the oracular and even mystifying statement, and witty paradox. At its best he can open, with a glimpse, wide vistas; at its worst he can note down pretentious witticisms and even trivialities. But one must be literal-minded indeed not to recognize that Schlegel was engaged in warfare, that he wanted and needed attention at the price of paradox and offense, and that he loved the grandiose, mysterious, and

irrational too much to suppress it. The most concentrated masterpiece of Schlegel's criticism, **Gespräch über die Poesie,** is a Platonic dialogue in a very free form, with interspersed lectures and papers read aloud by the interlocutors. It seems the right medium for Schlegel, neither too formal nor too informal, too short to be merely mystifying nor too long to be misty and nebulous, as he can become at his worst. But with all due reservations Friedrich Schlegel seems—if we think only of what he said on criticism, myth, irony, the romantic, and the novel—one of the greatest critics of history.

*René Wellek, "Friedrich Schlegel," in his* A History of Modern Criticism: 1750-1950, The Romantic Age, *Yale University Press, 1955, pp. 5-35.*

## Ernst Behler   (essay date 1968)

[*Behler is a German-born educator and critic. In the following essay, he discusses Schlegel's definition of Romanticism.*]

The definition of Romanticism has always been the despair of the literary historian. It is inherent in the nature of designations of epochs to arouse suspicion that such categorizing suffocates the abundance of life and art in the formula of a concept. For this reason such designations continue to remain the favorite subject of nominalistic scepticism. This reservation is especially applicable to the term "European Romanticism", comprising a movement which had as its device, multiplicity, and as its virtue, formlessness, extending itself to all fields of the intellectual world—literature and poetry, music and painting, philosophy and science, politics and religion—and also manifesting itself in a variety of national peculiarities. Thus Romanticism has always been considered as an exemplary model of the superiority of reality over endeavors to define, of the inability to comprehend life by means of a concept.

Nevertheless, critics have untiringly expended their energies on this enigmatic phenomenon for more than a century. When limited to the ventures to fathom Romanticism as a literary movement, two approaches appear to be especially fruitful among the numerous books concerning *Die Wesensbestimmung der Romantik, The Meaning of Romanticism,* and *Les définitions du romantisme.*

The first approach is of an etymological nature. It consists in the attempt to reveal the essence of the matter through the history of the word "Romantic". Studies of this kind demonstrate that the term "Romantic" was used during the 17th and early 18th centuries, presumably first in England. It served to illustrate fantastic qualities of landscape and painting, adventurous and exotic features, and also sentimental experiences of love. During this period of time in France, England, and then in Germany, "Romantic" also appeared as a literary category emphasizing certain characteristics of post-classical literature in the works of Ariosto, Tasso, Shakespeare, and Dante, as well as in those of Cervantes and Calderon. Later the word came into vogue among contemporary literary critics as a designation for that new kind of literature that manifested itself in various European countries at the beginning of the 19th century. This meaning is now to be explored by analyzing the different contents which were poured into the formula "Romanticism" by the manifold representatives of this movement.

The second approach to the meaning of Romanticism is of a critical nature. Here, one is no longer concerned with the meaning of the word, but solely with the matter itself, that is, with the literature, the poetry, and the programmatical writings of this movement. The comparative study of these works has as its goal the demonstration of that which is common to all the Romantic authors, regardless of its relation to their own definition of Romanticism. This assumption appears to be all the more necessary in view of the amazing fact that most of the authors whom we today call Romantic poets did not consider themselves to be Romantics. This applies to the Schlegel brothers, to Novalis and Brentano, as well as to Madame de Staël and Chateaubriand, and also to Coleridge, Wordsworth, Keats, Shelley, and Lord Byron.

To be sure, the term "Romantic" belongs to the critical vocabulary of the Schlegel brothers, Madame de Staël, Coleridge, and numerous other authors of the time. It was indeed a favorite expression for the German critics, as is exemplified in Novalis' aphorism beginning with the well-known postulate: "The world must be romanticized." Having been influenced by the contemporary meaning of the word, many a critic and historian has been seduced into thinking that these authors were referring to themselves when employing the concept "Romantic".

Upon closer consideration, however, one soon discovers that the term "Romantic" in that period was by no means used to designate the literary movement which we today call by that name. When August Wilhelm Schlegel speaks of the Romantic era of European literature, he unmistakably refers to the works of the modern European nations, more specifically, to the literary productions of Dante, Ariosto, Tasso, Camoes, Cervantes, Calderon, and Shakespeare. According to August Wilhelm Schlegel, these authors have initiated a poetic style standing in contrast to classical literature and deriving from inspirations provided by medieval chivalry, love, honor, and the Christian religion. His younger brother Friedrich Schlegel also bestowed a typological meaning upon the term "Romantic", as is evidenced by his famous statement: "According to my point of view and usage, Romantic is that which presents a sentimental content in a fantastic form." He did not, however, find the "actual center, the core of Romantic imagination" in his own epoch, which he called an "un-Romantic era", but in Shakespeare and in the post-medieval period of European literature. "This is where I look for and find the Romantic", Schlegel says, "in the older Moderns, in Shakespeare, Cervantes, in Italian poetry, in that age of knights, love, and fairy tales in which both the thing itself and the word for it originated." Novalis conceived of the Romantic as a poet of fairy tales who poetizes reality, whereby, however, only one aspect of his own poetic mission finds fulfillment. Similarly, Coleridge says that his subject in the composition of the *Lyrical Ballads* consisted of "persons and characters supernatural, or at least romantic", while it was left to Wordsworth

"to give the charm of novelty to things of every day, and to excite a feeling analogous to the supernatural by awakening the mind's attention from the lethargy of custom, and directing it to the loveliness and the wonders of the world before us". Without any hesitation, we would call this second endeavor Romantic, yet Coleridge does not do so. In fact, he contrasts it to what he visualizes as being Romantic. As late as 1814, Madame de Staël, like Schlegel, specified Romantic poetry as having its origin "in the songs of the minnesinger" and in the ideals of knighthood and Christianity.

Thus the etymological approach to the meaning of Romanticism ends in an impasse. This method may indeed lead to manifold andinteresting applications of the word by the Romantic authors, but concepts thus determined unfortunately have the disadvantage of not referring to that epoch in which our discussion centers.

Only in the second decade of the 19th century, do the beginnings of the present usage of "Romantic" become evident. Then, representatives of the new literary movement were polemically labeled by their adversaries—the traditional neoclassicists and newly developing realists—with this term that formerly had signified post-medieval literature. The best-known example of this metamorphosis of meaning in Heinrich Heine's satirical study of 1833 on *The Romantic School* of Germany. Ten years earlier in his pamphlet "Racine and Shakespeare", Stendhal had courageously revealed himself to be a Romantic, presumably the first author to have done so. In the hands of this great satirist, however, the designation was chiefly a means to ridicule the opposing school of neoclassicism. For him the Romantic attitude meant primarily poetic originality, rebellion against the yoke of neoclassical rules. "All great writers were the Romantics of their day" according to Stendhal, whereas the neoclassicists were "those who, a century after the death of the great writers, copy them instead of opening their eyes and imitating nature". This led to the ironical consequence that the idols of neoclassicism, Molière and Racine, were the Romantics of their era just as Homer was in his time.

In view of this failure of the etymological approach, we must ask ourselves what the Romantics themselves attempted and how their literary program can be defined. This question shall now be answered by Friedrich Schlegel.

At first glance this endeavour appears to be a considerable limitation of the topic. Friedrich Schlegel was a German author who, compared to his brother August Wilhelm Schlegel, had only a modest influence on Western literature. Because of his ill-famed aphorisms, he was considered to be a literary eccentric even in his native country. His reputation is that of an author who reveled in expressing ideas gained through piercing reflection in a paradoxical manner. Confronted with this tendency to aphoristic style and deliberate literary abstruseness, August Wilhelm Schlegel remarked goodnaturedly: "He succeeds with aphorisms better than with articles and with self-coined words better than with aphorisms. In the final analysis, his entire genius might be reduced to mystical terminology."

How can one possibly demonstrate the original idea of Romanticism through this individualistic author?

Nevertheless, one must concede that with Friedrich Schlegel we are at the roots of the program of European Romanticism. As René Wellek has shown in his well-known article ["The Concept of Romanticism"], the European concept of Romanticism may chiefly be derived from two books: from Madame de Staël's *De l' Allemagne* of 1814, called the "Bible of Romanticism", and from August Wilhelm Schlegel's lectures on the *History of Dramatic Art and Literature* of 1813, referred to by Prague's Josef Körner as the "message of German Romanticism toEurope". The after-effects of these works can easily be seen in Victor Hugo's "Preface to Cromwell" and in Stendhal's "Racine and Shakespeare"; they are also to be found in Coleridge, Edgar Allan Poe, and in the main figures of Romanticism in Mediterranean and Slavonic Europe.

Heinrich Heine had surmised, however, that Madame de Staël chose August Wilhelm Schlegel as an experienced guide when out of enthusiasm for Romanticism she penetrated the intricate jungle of German literature and philosophy. If one were able to prove a dependence of the French authoress—as many critics contend—then one could assume this to be the case with even greater conviction on the part of August Wilhelm Schlegel. Those parts of his work that are of primary interest to us are often nothing but re-formulations of ideas formerly expressed by his younger brother in the paradoxical style of his aphorisms. With good reason basic concepts of August Wilhelm Schlegel's literary criticism have been considered popularized adaptions of the thought of his more subtle younger brother.

Thus with Friedrich Schlegel we are the beginning of a process of translation extending to August Wilhelm Schlegel, to Madame de Staël, and directly into the Romantic movement. Admittedly, the end of this chain might differ considerably from its beginning; however, Friedrich Schlegel is the source from whence the multiple ideas which we today consider as "Romantic" originated.

Friedrich Schlegel's literary program has been the subject of various studies. With respect to origins and impulses of his theory, two hypotheses may be distinguished. The first establishes a close relationship between Schlegel's concept of literature and the genre of the novel, and the second derives his ideas from philosophical reflections, from a new world view. It may also be said that according to the first interpretation, Goethe was Schlegel's model, while according to the second, Schiller provided the stimulus.

The first hypothesis was originally formulated by Rudolf Haym, who in his *Romantic School* of 1870 said: "Schlegel, always ready for new constructions and new formulas, drew the doctrine from *Wilhelm Meister's Apprenticeship* that the genuine novel constitutes a non plus ultra, a sum of everything poetic. He consequently gave this poetic ideal the name Romantic poetry." According to this view, Romantic poetry equals "Romanpoesie", the poetry of the novel.

Of course, many objections may be raised against this theory. First of all, the concept "Romantic" seems to be used in an ambiguous manner. Secondly, Goethe's *Wilhelm Meister* is granted too important a position for Schlegel's literary theory. Finally, the genre of the novel assumes a pre-eminence which cannot be justified. *Wilhelm Meister's Apprenticeship* appeared in 1796 and thus could not have influenced the inceptions of Schlegel's literary theory dating back to 1794. Nevertheless, these early concepts dominate his later program formulated in 1797. The genre of the novel, on the otherhand, was given primary importance by Schlegel for only a short period of time. In the third volume of the *Athenaeum,* he says already: "Only through religion can logic develop into philosophy, only from this source stems that which makes philosophy more than science. And without religion we will have only novels, or the triviality today called 'belles lettres' instead of an eternally rich and infinite poetry."

The central idea of Schlegel's poetics obviously cannot be reduced to a genre favored during this or that period of his life. It seems to possess a significance which surpasses transitory evaluations; in other words, it makes an absolute demand. Schlegel calls this nucleus "the absolute maximum of poetry", a formula first discovered in his unpublished manuscripts by Hans Eichner, who joined it, however, to the former theory of the novel. Thus the task remains to work out what Schlegel understood by the absolute ideal of literature.

At this point the second hypothesis becomes interesting. Arthur O. Lovejoy [in *Essays in the History of Ideas,* 1960] first developed this interpretation in opposition to Rudolf Haym. He emphasized that Friedrich Schlegel was an ardent admirer of classical literature at the beginning of his literary career, that he wanted to demonstrate classical aesthetics to be an "absolute norm of art", and in doing so, considered himself to be the "Winckelmann of Greek poetry". Under the influence of Schiller's praise of the sentimental poet, however, Schlegel converted to modern, Romantic poetry. From now on, that which he had rejected in his classical period was elevated to his highest ideal.

Lovejoy has the merit of having brought into view the manifold ingredients of Schlegel's literary program. During the course of his development, Schlegel passes through two aesthetics, alternately endowed with the highest attributes. These are the aesthetics of nature and art, of life and spirit, of naïveté and sentimentality, of antiquity and modernity, of Classicism and Romanticism. Lovejoy has also shown that Schlegel based these two aesthetics on different philosophies of history. The classical theory of aesthetics is founded on Herder's cyclical, organic view of history, whereas modern aesthetics builds upon Kant's idea of an infinite progression. The conclusion drawn from these insights is impaired, however, by Lovejoy's contention that Schlegel had sacrificed one aesthetical system for the other, that he had evolved from a Classicist to a Romantic.

In reality, Schlegel's literary theory must be seen as an attempt to unite these two antagonistic aesthetics, to find a synthesis of the antique and the modern, the Classical and the Romantic. This was indeed his way of bringing "poetry to the highest ideal possible on earth".

The inspirations for this undertaking date back to the year 1795, that is, to a period during which Schlegel was primarily occupied with laying the foundations for a history of Greek and Roman literature. On February 27, 1794, he wrote to his brother: "The problem of our poetry seems to be the synthesis of the essentially modern and the essentially antique." Thus even his scholarly studies of classical antiquity served the primary purpose of establishing the program for a new literary epoch.

His treatise **"On the Study of Greek Poetry,"** completed in 1795 and published in 1797, is the first comprehensive manifestation of this intention. The title is misleading, however, since the topic is by no means limited to classical poetry. In fact, Schlegel deals with the whole of European literature in order to "detect the path of this aesthetic culture", to divine "the meaning of the preceding history of literature", and to open "a great perspective of the future". The study centers about the idea that European literary history is determined by two predominant ideals. The first had been promoted by the ancients, who achieved "beauty in itself" in uniform perfection and undisturbed harmony in their works. The moderns, on the other hand, gave preference to the "restless longing for the new, the piquant, and the striking". At this time Schlegel concentrated the advantages of the Classicists into the term "the objective". In order to define the characteristic feature of modern literature through a similarly expressive formulation in contrast to the "genuinely beautiful" of ancient poetry, he coined the phrase "the interesting".

By means of this distinction between objective and interesting literature, Schlegel had established concepts similar to Schiller's dichotomy of naïve and sentimental poetry. Whereas Schiller's categories are of an ahistorical, typological nature, however, Schlegel's terms also reveal the literary historian.

Schlegel was of the opinion that these two epochs of European literary history belonged to the past. Whereas objective or classical literature had reached its apex in Sophocles and had disintegrated thereafter, interesting or modern poetry had reached its climax in Shakespeare, only to degenerate in the hands of his epigones. A third ideal and a new impetus in Europe's history was now demonstrated by Goethe, who unified the achievements of the objective and the interesting, of Classicism and Romanticism. This Greek in a sentimental age was able to clothe an antique spirit in a modern garment and to surround modern individuality with a classical aura. Through Goethe's example, Schlegel depicted a "new level of the aesthetic culture", carrying European literature to that decisive point from whence, "if left to itself, it could not degenerate, but could only be hindered in its progress through external forces".

This program of uniting the "essentially modern with the essentially antique" clearly anticipates the leading ideas of the aphorisms of the *Athenaeum* of 1798. The major task of both texts is to synthesize nature and art, the real and the ideal, to develop naïveté into deliberation and arbitrariness into instinct. These thoughts also suggest the message of the **Dialogue on Poetry** of 1799. In the concluding portions of this essay, one of the interlocutors praises Goe-

the for having presented classic content in modern form, and he adds: "This great combination opens an entirely new and unlimited perspective on what seems to be the ultimate goal of all literature, the harmony of the Classical and the Romantic."

The path of European literature is thus marked by three stages for Schlegel. Literary history moves forward in a dialectical process which can be illustrated by the well-known scheme—thesis, antithesis, and synthesis. The first epoch is that of Classical literature, its highest achievement being the disinterested objective beauty of the Attic drama. The next significant step in this progression is found in the flowering of Romantic literature, the ideal of which embodies interesting, subjective beauty, manifesting itself most conspicuously on Shakespeare's stage. Now a third epoch may be expected, combining the excellence of Classicism with the virtues of Romanticism. It was precisely this climax of European literature that Schlegel tried to further in his programmatical writings.

Schlegel had published only parts of his literary works. The aphorisms of the *Athenaeum,* for example, constitute a selection from literary and philosophical notebooks containing thousands of fragments. The distinction between Classicism and Romanticism is also a predominant theme of these manuscripts, especially in those dating from 1797.

Generally speaking, these reflections may be characterized as having established an extreme opposition of literary styles, the greatest antimony of intellectual culture. Schlegel tries to propose a complete antithesis of literary values in order to produce the highest ideal of poetry through the reconciliation of these polarities. As is now known, the most comprehensive antimony of Europe's literary culture consisted for him in the contrast of the antique and the modern, usually rendered in these aphorisms by the terms "Classical" and "Progressive".

Schlegel obviously did not cenceive of these terms only as historical categories designating certain epochs. He also used them in a typological sense for genuine literary styles which may also be called perfection and completion (Classic) and imperfection and striving (Progressive). Indeed, Schlegel renders the Classical by words such as "limitation", "abstraction", "noble", "uniformity and naturalness", whereas the Progressive is expressed by phrases such as "expanse", "universality", "confusion, awkwardness, inconsequence", and "mixture of elements".

To quote from these notes at random, Schlegel says: "The Classical is necessarily self-restraint", or "The Classical is systematic formation". Concerning the contrasts of Classical and Progressive style, one comes across a statement such as: "The Classical genres have only unity, the Progressive ones, only totality", or "The Classical is fixed, synthetical, the Progressive is fluid, analytical". This original antimony of literary ideals is paraphrased in these notebooks by means of many other complementary terms, contrasting the "systematical" with the "fluid", the "correct" with the "intuitive", "instinct and deliberation", "consequence and caprice", poetry and philosophy, art and science.

From these numerous dichotomies, there also arises the

theory of Romantic style, which like the "Progressive" is constructed in opposition to the Classical. As has been previously mentioned, Schlegel did not employ the word in our contemporary meaning. To begin with, the Romantic is distilled from the most prominent representatives of post-medieval literature and is thus an essential element of modern literature. As such, it embodies the "erotic", the "mystically marvelous", the "elegiac, idyllic, and sentimental", the "absolutely arbitrary", the witty and capricious, which exhibits itself, for instance, in the transplantation of modern forms into antique surroundings, in the "intermingling of all genres of poetry and prose", or in the interlacing of nature and art, poetry and science, of "fantasy, sentimentality, and mimicry".

Owing to this technique observed in modern authors, works obtain a "Romantic coloring", they are "Romanticized", appear to be "Romantically piquant", and display a "Romantic beauty like the adornments and finery of ladies". It is in this connotation that Schlegel speaks of a "Romantic seriousness" in *Don Quixote,* of a "charming, Romantic tastelessness in Novalis", of Romantic geniality manifesting itself in "natural artificiality and in arbitrary naturalness". Furthermore, he speaks of "Romantic roguery and vulgarity", of "Romantic thrashings and witty smut in Cervantes", which are "beautiful to the point of perfection". He finds a "treatment of the remote in *Persiles",* which is "very Romantic" because as in Cervantes, "it transfigures a thing into mild reflection".

Yet the Romantic is not entirely synonymous with the Modern, since its scope is not limited to an epoch. Schlegel says: "The Romantic remains eternally new—the Modern changes with the fashion." Furthermore, he sees a definite tendency toward the Romantic even in Homer. He calls Virgil, Horace, and Ovid "Romantic figures", and among "Romantic genres of the ancients", he emphasizes "Socratic dialogues, memorabilia, symposia, idylls, elegies, satires, conversations of the Gods, Plutarchic biographies, and annals". Thus like the Classical, the Romantic is an essential element of literature having an eternal value which necessitates its integration with the Classical into the new ideal of literature.

Schlegel's task, in a word, arose out of a "plurality of imperatives". In his *History of Criticism* George Saintsbury said: "Ancient without Modern is a stumbling block, Modern without Ancient is foolishness utter and irremediable." Similarly, Schlegel recognized that mere Classicism is "regressive", mere Progression, however, fruitless, and that "productive power already constitutes limitation". This dialectical interrelationship of Classicism and Progression finds expression in the postulate: "Everything ancient is renewed through the study of the Classical, and everything modern should be ancient, that is, Classical, and becomes ancient, that is, outdated and antiquated." In a more precise phrase, Schlegel demands: "All Romantic studies should be made Classical; all Classical studies should be romanticized."

This endeavor is most clearly expressed in a series of aphorisms of 1797 which Schlegel entitled *On the Basis of Aesthetics.* A typical example of the antinomical thought process of this aesthetic ideal is the aphorism stating: "Thesis:

There should be models. Antithesis: There should be no models; art must progress eternally. Antimony of the Classical and the Progressive." Previously, Schlegel had set up as "antithetical laws of the pure aesthetic" the following: "(1) Every genre must necessarily be; i. e., distinct, limited, classical. (2) Every genre must be limited."

If one were to search for a more basic designation for these antitheses, sprouting up in hundreds of aphorisms, no terms would be more appropriate than those with which Schlegel labels two highest values of the literary work of art. They form indeed the focal points of his theory of poetry. These are the postulates of "infinite unity" and "infinite abundance" which are united in the absolute demand that a perfect work of art must present "infinite abundance in infinite unity".

One easily realizes that the term "infinite unity" comprises the features of the Classical style; that is, shape, form, and structure. "Infinite abundance", on the other hand, represents the peculiarities of that poetic style otherwise called Romantic or Progressive. The latter concept is of special interest because "infinite abundance" stands in the closest relationship to the "genuinely creative faculty within man", that is, to imagination. Schlegel says: "The essence of imagination is the perception of infinite abundance. Imagination is a supernatural faculty, is always revelation, enthusiasm, and inspiration. —Intoxication, dream, and wit all belong to imagination." In a fragment of 1804 he says: "The presentiment of infinite abundance is combined with rapture, with a dissolution of the limited ego."

Schlegel was of course fully aware of the fact that the postulates of "infinite unity" and "infinite abundance", especially if taken absolutely, mutually exclude each other. In his Paris lectures on European literature of 1803, he states: "An infinite unity which is simultaneously infinite abundance and variety is naturally in innermost conflict with itself, a conflict which finally resolves itself into harmony, but nevertheless exists in the present state." Yet this paradox proclaims the highest demand of poetry in an impressive way. In more moderate formulations but also without the paradoxical charm of the Romantic, these two postulates have again and again been recognized by critics as the ultimate criteria of poetry. Even in our time they are evident in T. S. Eliot, or they appear in René Wellek's *Theory of Literature,* where he states with regard to the evaluation of a literary work: "Our criterion is inclusiveness: 'imaginative integration' and 'amount (and diversity) of material integrated'."

Here again, the goal of Schlegel's attempt at synthesis becomes paramount. It is the "absolute work of art", the "highest maximum of poetry", an idea which anticipated basic tendencies of modern literature.

For a certain period of time, Schlegel considered the novel to be the best vehicle for the realization of this poetic ideal. This preference for the novel, however, has to be taken with a grain of salt. Schlegel never referred to a historically realized form of this genre, but sketched the blueprint for a novel superseding even Goethe's highly esteemed *Wilhelm Meister.* "A perfect novel should be a Romantic work of art far greater than *Wilhelm Meister",* he said, "more modern and more classical, more philosophical and more ethical and poetic, more political, more liberal, more universal, more social". Furthermore, Schlegel abandoned the novel as the embodiment of the literary ideal as early as 1800. With his **"Speech concerning Mythology"** he recognized symbolic poetry as the very climax of literature and took a position similar to that of Novalis. Thus the highest maximum of poetry should be rendered by that term which Schlegel coined himself for the phenomenon of "infinite abundance in infinite unity". This term has recently been expounded by Karl Konrad Polheim as the culmination of Schlegel's aesthetic, but again brought into too close a tie with the theory of the novel. This is the concept of the arabesque.

With this program Schlegel revealed deep insights into the essence of literature, insights by no means limited to his own literary movement. In his endeavor to unite the two antithetical aesthetics of nature and art, of Classicism and Romanticism, he parallels similar efforts made by Schiller. Simultaneously, Schlegel anticipates an important theme of 19th century literature reflected in Friedrich Nietzsche, Thomas Mann, and André Gide, and manifesting itself as an antagonism of two fundamental aesthetics; namely, nature and culture, life and decadence, Vitalism and Puritanism. Finally, his postulate to produce an absolute work of art, the highest maximum of poetry, is applicable to all great poetry and brings this critic into accordance with the great authors of history.

In conclusion, we must now discuss the question as to which artist is equal to the enormous task here outlined, what qualities of the intellect he must possess in order to fulfill this "plurality of imperatives".

This problem includes the complex theme of the mental attitude of the modern author. In his attempt at a solution, Schlegel was able to draw inspirations from a philosopher who had recently taken the act of absolute creation, of the voluntary active deed ("Tathandlung") of the ego as a basis for new reflections upon human freedom. This philosopher was Fichte. With new vigor he had penetrated the depths of subjectivity and had also shown the objective world in a new light, namely, as a non-ego posited by the ego and standing in an indissoluble interdependence with the ego.

The reality surrounding the ego thus assumed a shifting double meaning. Reality could be viewed as influencing and limiting the ego, but only as long as the ego "did not reflect upon this relationship and did not reach the conclusion that the ego itself posited this limiting non-ego". If the ego, however, concentrates on this relationship, then it becomes cognizant of the fact that "this interdependent action between the ego and the non-ego . . . is an action of the ego with itself". According to this point of view, the "foundations of ideality and reality" coincide within the ego. Fichte called this aspect of his *Science of Knowledge* "transcendental", and according to him philosophy should always remain faithful to the transcendental interpretation of the world. "This discipline", Fichte admits, "derives all consciousness from that which is independent of all consciousness . . . but as soon as one reflects upon this fact, that which is independent of consciousness is re-

vealed to be a product of the ego's cognitive power". Through his famous act of philosophical reflection, Fichte thus proved reality, which he called the non-ego, to be the product of a spiritual power which he called the ego.

This philosophical position has always elicited legitimate doubt. Schlegel had an ingenious idea, however, while studying Fichte's *Science of Knowledge*. He recognized that this absolute creation of reality, this expression of the ego in the non-ego, and the limiting reactive influence of the non-ego upon the ego, applies to at least one type of individual whose goal is indeed absolute creation—the modern author.

With Fichte's "transcendental" concept Schlegel also found an appropriate phrase to expose the special relationship existing between an artist and his work. "In analogy to the artificial language of philosophy", he coined the term "transcendental poetry" for that poetic act of creation place in the alternation of creative emergence and the limiting recession of the artist's ego, in which process the author expresses both himself and his work.

For this "transcendental" attitude of the artist, no word is more appropriate than irony. Schlegel indeed said: "Irony dominates in transcendental poetry". This type of irony which we today call "Romantic irony" applies chiefly to the relationship between an artist and his creation. Georg Lukács saw this most clearly when in his *Theory of the Novel,* he considered Romantic irony in the "Age of Subjectivity", in a "world without God", as the "only possible foundation for a genuine and total creation".

Schlegel rendered this aspect of irony in the aphorisms of the *Athenaeum* by complementary terms that at first glance appear to be somewhat eccentric. In aphorism 51, for instance, he called irony a "constant alternation between self-creation and self-destruction". A similar and recurrent formulation of the same phenomenon is the phrase "developed to the point of irony", whereby Schlegel understood the highest perfection, a perfection, however,which just because of its utmost achievement leads to self-criticism and thus shifts to its contrary. In this context Schlegel defined deliberation and arbitrariness as naïveté "up to the point of irony" or the naïve as a refinement "up to the point of irony". Schlegel therefore found two antagonistic powers within the creative process: creative enthusiasm counteracted by special irony.

This idea of poetry had already been exposed in his early treatises on Classical literature. Like Nietzsche, Schlegel derived the origins of Greek poetry from a Dionysiac phenomenon, from a super-individual and intoxicating experience which evokes both bliss and horror. Poetic imagination is first inspired by an "intuition of infinity", by a "living image of incomprehensible omnipotence" which discharges itself in "solemn joyfulness", in "orgiastic dances", in a "blissful rapture" surrounded by music. "Demonic possession and higher inspiration" formed the origin of poetry for Schlegel. Herein he could refer to Plato who had taught in *Ion* that poets derive their beautiful products not through art and clearsightedness, but through divine inspiration, and who in his *Laws* had related the old myth that the poet sitting on the tripod of the

Muses is out of his mind and willingly lets his words flow from the fountain of his lips.

In these early studies Schlegel held the opinion that this effervescent poetic enthusiasm might turn against itself. "The most intense passion", he says, "is eager to wound itself, if only to act and to discharge its excessive power." His work **"On the Aesthetic Value of Greek Comedy"** of 1794 presents irony as a destructive reaction against the primordial Dionysian ecstasy of poetic enthusiasm. He says here: "This self-infliction is not inaptitude, but deliberate impetuousness, overflowing vitality, and often has a positive, stimulating effect, since illusion can never be fully destroyed. Intense agility must act, even destroy; if it does not find an external object, it reacts against a beloved one, against itself, its own creation. This agility then injures in order to provoke, not to destroy." Later however, in the language of the *Athenaeum,* permeated by Fichte's subjective and reflective philosophy, this original stimulus of the poet appeared as "self-creation". Accordingly, the counteracting and limiting scepticism toward one's own productive capability was labeled "self-destruction".

The most important aspect of this theory for an understanding of the poetic process is the assumption that in the poet's mind, the creative strivings are counteracted by the scepticism of irony. More specifically, the function of irony does not reside so much in the destruction of creative production, but rather in a mediating position between enthusiasm and scepticism. Schlegel defined irony as a "constant alternation between self-creation and self-destruction" or as the "form of the paradox", as a shifting between opposite poles. This idea is expressed in aphorism 53 of the *Athenaeum* stating: "It is equally fatal to the spirit to have a system and not to have a system. Thus one must come to the decision to combine both."

The result obtained from the ironical hovering above self-creation and self-destruction was formulated by Schlegel as "self-restraint". Indeed, the function of irony could find no better expression. For Wilhelm Dilthey [in his *Leben Schleiermachers,* 1870] Schlegel's early concepts of irony embrace the "aesthetic and moral atmosphere of Pantheism; they are related to that which Goethe called resignation, and which Schleiermacher's *Speeches on Religion* referred to as melancholy".

With this concept of irony Schlegel's literary program finds a unified structure. Irony depicts that attitude of the mind which allows the artist to mediate between two opposing aesthetical systems, to be equally receptive to the imperatives of Romantic enthusiasm and Classical restraint, and thereby to promote that which constitutes the central motivation for Schlegel's literary theory. This was the endeavor to "constantly expand the scope of poetry and to approximate poetry to the highest ideal possible on earth".

*Ernst Behler, "The Origins of the Romantic Literary Theory," in* Colloquia Germanica, *1968, pp. 109-26.*

## Paul de Man   (essay date 1969)

[*A major influence on recent American literary criticism and theory, de Man gained attention in part through his association with the critical movement known as deconstruction. Many of his writings have focused on European Romanticism, a period which, according to Jonathan Culler, de Man believed to contain "the boldest, most self-conscious writing of the Western tradition." In the following excerpt, de Man briefly discusses Schlegel's theory of Romantic irony, arguing that it is characterized by an endless process of self-destruction and self-invention and is not a vehicle for reconciliation or unity.*]

Far from being a return to the world, the irony to the second power or "irony of irony" that all true irony at once has to engender asserts and maintains its fictional character by stating the continued impossibility of reconciling the world of fiction with the actual world. Well before Baudelaire and [E. T. A.] Hoffmann, Friedrich Schlegel knew this very well when he defined *irony,* in a note from 1797, as *"eine permanente Parekbase."* Parabasis is understood here as what is called in English criticism the "self-conscious narrator," the author's intrusion that disrupts the fictional illusion. Schlegel makes clear, however, that the effect of this intrusion is not a heightened realism, an affirmation of the priority of a historical over a fictional act, but that it has the very opposite aim and effect: it serves to prevent the all too readily mystified reader from confusing fact and fiction and from forgetting the essential negativity of the fiction. The problem is familiar to students of point of view in a fictional narrative, in the distinction they have learned to make between the persona of the author and the persona of the fictional narrator. The moment when this difference is asserted is precisely the moment when the author does not return to the world. He asserts instead the ironic necessity of not becoming the dupe of his own irony and discovers that there is no way back from his fictional self to his actual self.

It is also at this point that the link between irony and the novel becomes apparent. For it is at this same point that the temporal structure of irony begins to emerge. [Jean] Starobinski's error in seeing irony as a preliminary movement toward a recovered unity, as a reconciliation of the self with the world by means of art, is a common (and morally admirable) mistake. In temporal terms it makes irony into the prefiguration of a future recovery, fiction into the promise of a future happiness that, for the time being, exists only ideally. Commentators of Friedrich Schlegel have read him in the same way. To quote one of the best among them, this is how Peter Szondi [in *Satz und Gegensatz,* 1964] describes the function of the ironic consciousness in Schlegel:

> The subject of romantic irony is the isolated, alienated man who has become the object of his own reflection and whose consciousness has deprived him of his ability to act. He nostalgically aspires toward unity and infinity; the world appears to him divided and finite. What he calls irony is his attempt to bear up under his critical predicament, to change his situation by achieving distance toward it. In an ever-expanding act of reflection he tries to establish a point of view beyond himself and to resolve the tension between himself and the world on the level of fiction [*des Scheins*]. He cannot overcome the neg-

ativity of his situation by means of an act in which the reconciliation of finite achievement with infinite longing could take place; through prefiguration of a future unity, *in which he believes,* the negative is described as temporary [*vorlaüfig*] and, by the same token, it is kept in check and reversed. This reversal makes it appear tolerable and allows the subject to dwell in the subjective region of fiction. Because irony designates and checks the power of negativity, it becomes itself, although originally conceived as the overcoming of negativity, the power of the negative. Irony allows for fulfillment only in the past and in the future; it measures whatever it encounters in the present by the yardstick of infinity and thus destroys it. The knowledge of his own impotence prevents the ironist from respecting his achievements: therein resides his danger. Making this assumption about himself, he closes off the way to his fulfillment. Each achievement becomes in turn inadequate and finally leads into a void: therein resides his tragedy.

Every word in this admirable quotation is right from the point of view of the mystified self, but wrong from the point of view of the ironist. Szondi has to posit the belief in a reconciliation between the ideal and the real as the result of an action or the activity of the mind. But it is precisely this assumption that the ironist denies. Friedrich Schlegel is altogether clear on this. The dialectic of self-destruction and self-invention which for him, as for Baudelaire, characterizes the ironic mind is an endless process that leads to no synthesis. The positive name he gives to the infinity of this process is freedom, the unwillingness of the mind to accept any stage in its progression as definitive, since this would stop what he calls its "infinite agility." In temporal terms it designates the fact that irony engenders a temporal sequence of acts of consciousness which is endless. Contrary to Szondi's assertion, irony is not temporary (*vorlaüfig*) but repetitive, the recurrence of a self-escalating act of consciousness. Schlegel at times speaks of this endless process in exhilarating terms, understandably enough, since he is describing the freedom of a self-engendering invention. "(Die romantische Poesie)," he writes—and by this term he specifically designates a poetry of irony—

> kann . . . am meisten zwischen dem Dargestellten und dem Darstellenden, frei von allem realen und idealen Interesse, auf den Flügeln der poetischen Reflexion in der Mitte schweben, diese Reflexion immer wieder potenzieren und wie in einer endlosen Reihe von Spiegeln vervielfachen. . . . Die romantische Dichtart ist noch in Werden; ja das ist ihr eigentliches Wesen, daß sie ewig nur werden, nie vollendet sein kann. . . . Nur eine divinatorische Kritik dürfte es wagen, ihr Ideal charakterisieren zu wollen. Sie allein ist unendlich, wie sie allein frei ist, und das als ihr erstes Gesetz anerkennt, daß die Willkür des Dichters kein Gesetz über sich leide.

But this same endless process, here stated from the positive viewpoint of the poetic self engaged in its own development, appears as something very close to Baudelaire's lucid madness when a slightly older Friedrich Schlegel describes it from a more personal point of view. The passage is from the curious essay in which he took leave from the readers of the *Athenäum;* written in 1798 and revised for the 1800 publication, it is entitled, ironically enough, **"Über die Ünverständlichkeit."** It evokes, in the language of criticism, the same experience of *"vertige de l'hyperbole"* that the spectacle of the pantomime awakened in Baudelaire. Schlegel has described various kinds of irony and finally comes to what he calls "the irony of irony."

> . . . Im allgemeinen ist das wohl die gründlichste Ironie der Ironie, daß man sie doch eben auch überdrüssig wird, wenn sie uns überall und immer wieder geboten wird. Was wir aber hier zunächst unter Ironie der Ironie verstanden wissen wollen, das entsteht auf mehr als einem Wege. Wenn man ohne Ironie von der Ironie redet, wie es soeben der Fall war; wenn man mit Ironie von einer Ironie redet, ohne zu merken, daß man sich zu eben der Zeit in einer andren viel auffalenderen Ironie befindet; wenn man nicht wieder aus der Ironie herauskommen kann, wie es in diesem Versuch über die Unverständlichkeit zu sein scheint; wenn die Ironie Manier wird, und so den Dichter gleichsam wieder ironiert; wenn man Ironie zu einem überflüssigen Taschenbuche versprochen hat, ohne seinen Vorrat vorher zu überschlagen und nun wider Willen Ironie machen muß, wie ein Schauspielkunstler der Leibschmerzen hat; wenn die Ironie wild wird, und sich gar nicht mehr regieren läßt.

> Welche Götter werden uns von allen diesen Ironien erretten können? das einzige wäre, wenn sich eine Ironie fände, welche die Eigenschaft hätte, alle jene großen und kleinen Ironien zu verschlucken und zu verschlingen, daß nichts mehr davon zu sehen wäre, und ich muß gestehen, daß ich eben dazu in der meinigen eine merkliche Disposition fühle. Aber auch das würde nur auf kurze Zeit helfen können. Ich fürchte . . . es würde bald eine neue Generation von kleinen Ironien entstehn: denn wahrlich die Gestirne deuten auf phantastisch. Und gesetzt es blieb auch während eines langen Zeitraums alles ruhig, so wäre doch nicht zu trauen. Mit der Ironie ist durchaus nicht zu scherzen. Sie kann unglaublich lange nachwirken. . . .

Our description seems to have reached a provisional conclusion. The act of irony, as we now understand it, reveals the existence of a temporality that is definitely not organic, in that it relates to its source only in terms of distance and difference and allows for no end, for no totality. Irony divides the flow of temporal experience into a past that is pure mystification and a future that remains harassed forever by a relapse within the inauthentic. It can know this inauthenticity but can never overcome it. It can only restate and repeat it on an increasingly conscious level, but it remains endlessly caught in the impossibility of making this knowledge applicable to the empirical world. It dissolves in the narrowing spiral of a linguistic sign that becomes more and more remote from its meaning, and it can find no escape from this spiral. The temporal void that it reveals is the same void we encountered when we found allegory always implying an unreachable anteriority. Allegory and irony are thus linked in their common discovery of a truly temporal predicament. They are also linked in their common de-mystification of an organic world postulated in a symbolic mode of analogical correspondences or in a mimetic mode of representation in which fiction and reality could coincide. It is especially against the latter mystification that irony is directed: the regression in critical insight found in the transition from an allegorical to a symbolic theory of poetry would find its historical equivalent in the regression from the eighteenth-century ironic novel, based on what Friedrich Schlegel called *"Parekbase,"* to nineteenth-century realism.

This conclusion is dangerously satisfying and highly vulnerable to irony in that it rescues a coherent historical picture at the expense of stated human incoherence. Things cannot be left to rest at the point we have reached. More clearly even than allegory, the rhetorical mode of irony takes us back to the predicament of the conscious subject; this consciousness is clearly an unhappy one that strives to move beyond and outside itself. Schlegel's rhetorical question "What gods will be able to rescue us from all these ironies?" can also be taken quite literally. For the later Friedrich Schlegel, as for Kierkegaard, the solution could only be a leap out of language into faith.

*Paul de Man, "The Rhetoric of Temporality," in* Interpretation: Theory and Practice, *edited by Charles S. Singleton, The Johns Hopkins Press, 1969, pp. 173-209.*

## Hans Eichner   (essay date 1970)

[*Eichner is an Austrian-born educator and critic who has written extensively on Friedrich Schlegel. In the following essay, he examines Schlegel's periodical* Europa, *his Paris lectures on literature, and his contributions to the journal* Concordia.]

The two years Schlegel spent in Paris present a puzzle to his biographer. His Paris notebooks are crowded with titles of plays, novels, and romances he was planning to write—dozens of titles, which he kept changing and rearranging, grouping and regrouping in patterns of four, eight, and sixteen. On reading these pages with their countless repetitions and contradictions, one gets the impression of a mind obsessed. Yet in other ways, these years were extremely productive.

While the *Athenäum* had been a biannual publication, his new periodical, *Europa,* was planned, more ambitiously, as a quarterly. Schlegel had counted on substantial contributions from his friends in Germany, but was soon short of copy, and by the time the fourth and last issue of *Europa* appeared, eighteen months later than planned, he had had to write a full third of the periodical himself.

*Europa* opens with an account of Friedrich's journey to Paris, **"Reise nach Frankreich,"** which vividly illustrates the extent to which the extravagant hopes for a better future that he had entertained around 1799 had been dashed. Leaving Germany had aroused his patriotism, but the two poems he wrote on the occasion celebrate the past rather than the present and are accompanied by sad reflec-

tions on "what the Germans had been once" (in the Middle Ages), "what they could be," and what they were now. The rather superficial characterization of the French that follows gives them credit for gaiety, *esprit,* and scientific ability, but denies them all talent for music, poetry, and painting.

The rest of the essay strikes a note of mysticism that reflects Schlegel's study of Böhme, to whose writings Tieck had introduced him. Europe, we are told, does not have the unity commonly ascribed to it, but is rent by a dichotomy of North and South. Such dichotomies are a characteristic feature of the European civilization, which has been vitiated, from its beginnings, by an unnatural separation of Poetry and Philosophy (i. e., of man's imaginative and his reasoning powers). This separation is responsible for the Europeans' "total incapacity for religion" and the "complete atrophy" of their "higher faculties." In modern Europe, man has sunk to his lowest depths—a fact from which it does not follow that he must soon rise again. On the contrary: if Europe is to see better times, its broken spirit must be restored by the healing influence of Asia, particularly India, where the faculties of the human mind have remained integrated and which is therefore the home and eternal source of religion. The East (Asia) and the North (Northern Europe) are the "visible poles of the Good Principle" on earth.

It can hardly be claimed that these speculations formed an auspicious beginning for Schlegel's new journalistic venture. His second contribution to his periodical, an essay with the title "Literatur" and largely devoted to pressing the claims of philosophic Idealism, was equally unlikely to gain him new friends. Idealism is said to be "the center and the basis of German literature; no physics comprehending the whole of nature is possible without it, and higher poetry, being a different expression of the same transcendental view, differs from Idealism only in its form." The essay provides an attractive and interesting summary of the activities of the Romantic circle, but was bound to strike Schlegel's readers as one-sided and written in the interest of his own faction.

Schlegel's last contribution to the first issue of *Europa* was a description of paintings in the Louvre—the first of a series of five articles on this form of art. It is this series that represents the main achievement of Schlegel's periodical.

In the absence of techniques for a reasonably accurate reproduction of paintings, descriptions were the only means available at that time for acquainting art lovers abroad with the collections in Paris, which had been recently enriched by numerous paintings sent home by the French armies from their campaigns in Italy and the Low Countries. Schlegel thus had the incentive, but also the handicap of writing about works of art for a public that was denied all direct experience of them. In response to this task, he developed considerable descriptive powers, but inevitably tended to emphasize what he called the "poetry" or the "spirit" of the paintings rather than their form.

No doubt, such a method is open to the objection that it pays least attention to those features of paintings that give them their characteristic pictorial value; it would, for instance, be totally incapable of dealing with abstract art. But this is an objection Schlegel would not have entertained. In his view, it was the function of painting to "glorify religion and to reveal its mysteries even more beautifully and clearly than can be done in words," so that the value of a painting lay not in its sensuous qualities, nor in its "charm and beauty," but in its symbolic meaning, in the signification of the divine, without which a picture "does not deserve to be called a work of art."

To a certain extent, of course, this had already been said by Wackenroder; but Schlegel was more consistent, and hence more radical, in his conclusions. Wackenroder still felt—like the classicists—that the high Renaissance represented the supreme achievement in European painting (though, of course, he did not use the *term* "Renaissance" and thought of this period as belonging to the Middle Ages). Schlegel's scale of values was different. According to him, it had been the early Italian painters who had been most loyal to the true, religious function of art. The young Raphael, who was still inspired by loving piety, had risen to the greatest height; subsequently, misled by the splendors of antiquity and by the example of Michelangelo, he had strayed from the "pious path of love." With Raphael, Michelangelo, Titian, Correggio, and Giulio Romano, the "decay of art" had begun; Titian, Correggio, and their contemporaries were the "last painters" worthy of that name.

Linked with early Italian painting in Schlegel's mind was what he called the "old German school" of Van Eyck, Dürer, and Holbein, as well as such painters as Altdorfer and Memling, who were then almost completely unknown. Here, as in so many other ways, Schlegel's writings on art must be seen in relation to their own day, if their importance is to be realized. French and German painting, art criticism, and art instruction were dominated by classicism: Art students were supposed to learn painting from the study of plaster casts of Greek and Roman sculptures and to demonstrate what they had learned in this way by painting scenes from the Homeric epics. No less a figure than Goethe supported these sterile and misguided practices with all his energy and authority. Thus, Schlegel's new doctrines, one-sided as they may seem to us, had a wholesome and liberating influence. Goethe was furious, and it was Schlegel's new theory of art, not of poetry, that put an end to the tacit alliance that had so long existed between the great poet and the Romantics. But the young generation thrilled to the new teachings, and Schlegel had the satisfaction of seeing his and Wackenroder's theories put into practice by a whole group of painters, the *Lucasbund,* which included such artists as Overbeck, Pforr, Cornelius, Schadow, and Schlegel's stepsons Johannes and Philipp Veit.

While the first three issues of *Europa* had appeared, reasonably promptly, in 1803, the fourth and last was delayed till 1805; first the publisher and then Schlegel himself had lost interest in the quarterly, which sold badly and so proved a poor investment. Schlegel's attempts at finding suitable employment—among other things, he had dreamed of founding an Academy of German Writers in Paris—also failed. He now produced a Lessing anthology

in three volumes, to which he himself contributed five essays. But though a good deal of thought had gone into this publication—Schlegel's selection of extracts from Lessing's writings is stimulating, and his own contributions would merit detailed discussion . . . —it did not catch on, and a substantial part of the first and only printing was still unsold six years later. Thus, Schlegel would have been in dire straits indeed if he had not been helped out by a fortunate accident. In the fall of 1803, the sons of a wealthy German businessman, Sulpiz and Melchior Boisserée, were touring France, accompanied by a friend, J. B. Bertram. Having been appreciative readers of *Europa,* the three travelers called on Schlegel, and their visit had important results: the Boisserées and their friend decided to stay in Paris as Dorothea's paying guests and engaged Friedrich to lecture to them on European literature.

The text of these lectures has been preserved and shows that Schlegel's views on European literature had undergone no fundamental change since 1800; in fact, the most informative passage on the *Roman* and on romantic poetry reads, in part at least, like a paraphrase of *Athenäums-Fragment 116:*

> The concept of the *Roman* as established by Boccaccio and Cervantes is that of a *romantic book,* a romantic composition in which all forms and genres are mingled and intertwined . . . There are historical, rhetorical and dialogic passages; all these styles . . . are mixed and combined with one another in the most significant and artful ways. Poetry of every kind, —lyrical, epic, didactic poetry and romances (*Romanzen*)—are scattered throughout the whole work . . . The *Roman* is a poem consisting of poems, a whole tissue of poems . . . Such a poetic composition . . . makes possible a much more artful poetic structure (*Verschlingung von Poesie*) than the epic or the drama, in which at least unity of tone prevails. . . . Here, where the poet may entirely abandon himself to his fanciful caprice, the outpourings of his own moods, his playful humor, where no unity of tone prevents his being serious and jesting in turn, monotony is almost impossible. The *Roman* is the most original, the most characteristic, and the most perfect form of romantic poetry . . .

There are, however, changes in detail. Since 1800, Schlegel had added Calderón and Camoens to his canon of great romantic poets and had studied the Provençal manuscripts which—as yet undiscovered by the French—gathered dust in the *Bibliothèque Nationale.* Above all, there is nothing in these lectures that corresponds to the theories of the **"Rede über die Mythologie."** The religious convictions that form the background to these lectures are Christian rather than pantheistic. . . .

. . . .

In the winter of 1815/16, Schlegel had begun to make plans for a new periodical, his fourth and last; but when, almost two years later, he announced his intentions in a prospectus, the project was vetoed by Metternich. Schlegel's retirement from government service enabled him, however, to revive his plans and to produce six issues of what was intended to be a monthly, the first five appearing more or less on time from August through December, 1820, while the sixth was not published till April, 1823. In Frankfort, Schlegel had decided to call his periodical *Concordia*, this title being intended to express the hope that his new venture might help to promote concord between the various branches of Christendom and bridge the schism caused by the Reformation. Accordingly, he had counted on the cooperation of such Protestant authors as A. W. Schlegel and Schleiermacher. When his plans finally materialized, he retained the old title, but his intentions had changed. As he explained in the very first sentence of his new periodical, its purpose was to provide an analysis of the "total moral condition of our age" by a "considerable number of scholars and scientifically trained men in Austria and the rest of *Catholic* Germany"—though he was cautious enough to add that he would "everywhere show the greatest respect for the thoroughly learned, truly Christian and pious Protestants."

Schlegel himself contributed two major essays, **"Signatur des Zeitalters"** and **"Von der Seele,"** an interesting discussion of the religious poetry of Lamartine—who is celebrated as the greatest living French poet—and some minor pieces. There is little in **"Von der Seele"** that Schlegel did not say again in greater detail in his lectures of 1827 and 1828; but the other essay, **"Signatur des Zeitalters,"** which, with its 150 pages, dominates the whole periodical, is so vivid an expression of the political position Schlegel had now reached that a brief discussion of it will be useful.

Schlegel begins by deploring that, while external peace had been achieved with the defeat of Napoleon, inner discord, party strife, and personal unhappiness prevailed throughout Europe. The origins of this spiritual malaise, according to Schlegel, were not to be found exclusively in the "false theories and pernicious systems of the eighteenth century"; indeed, the French Revolution had only been "a particular symptom, a partial outbreak, a first crisis" of a far more fundamental disease—the "religious, moral and political unbelief of the age." Faith and love were only aroused and preserved by faith and love, and hence the disease could only be healed by positive teachings, not by polemics. Such polemics were, however, the dominant mode of political expression; in fact, it was the curse of the age that nothing was considered dispassionately, everything becoming immediately a matter of party strife and faction.

A "limitless striving" for the chimeras of "absolute unity and absolute liberty" poisoned the atmosphere, the former leading to the deductive philosophical systems that denied a personal god, the latter leading to the general and no less pernicious clamor for parliamentary systems along British or American lines—a veritable "English sickness." But pernicious extremism was to be found among the protagonists of the right as well as the wrong ideas, among the "ultras" as well as the liberals. They both shared the common error of promoting the concept of a "purely mathematical, merely mechanical and machine-like" state that—whether it be the absolutism of a Louis XIV or that of an elected government—rode roughshod over the sacred claims of "Christian private and family life" and the rights of the Church bestowed on it by God.

The true ideal was the very opposite; it was the Christian, "organic" state. Just as an organism consists of cells that are combined into a living whole dependent on them while they are dependent on it, so the organic state, according to Schlegel, consisted of "minor centers" forming a living whole around the major center, the monarch. These minor centers—the basis and substance of the state—are the "corporations," i. e., the Family, the Church (fully realized only in its Catholic form), the Guilds (comprising the trades, business, and industry), and the School (comprising the world of learning, education, and science): "This theory of the eternal and essential, original corporations, the Church and the School, the Family and the Guild throws the best, and indeed the only proper, light on the nature and the purpose of the State, if these are to be taken and understood in a positive sense."

This concept of the state, Schlegel insisted, was totally different from the purely negative concept according to which its sole purpose was to safeguard "property and persons." Insofar as the state could be regarded independently of its "natural organs," the corporations, its role was indeed only the maintenance of "external peace," while "inner and spiritual peace" was to be maintained by the Church. In fact, Schlegel laid down that it was best to "govern as little as possible" (though to govern decisively when necessary). Moreover, such a state was essentially conservative; for it was one of its basic principles to "allow continued existence and the maintenance of its legitimate possessions to everything that exists already." Yet, through the corporations, the state had a clearly defined positive function as well; for, while constitutional monarchies on the British pattern had a king who was a ruler in name only, so that they were the battleground of party strife, the government of an organic state would have a genuine monarch with real and very substantial powers. It could, consequently, be above the parties, which it ought to "ignore completely, . . . leave to their own nullity and regard as non-existent," while the monarch—the "principal support, solid center and coping-stone of the whole"—performed an essential role in keeping the powers of the separate corporations in check, maintaining their balance, and ensuring their "living harmony and cooperation."

Evidently, Schlegel no longer quite adhered to the views he had proclaimed in his Vienna lectures on history and literature. The concept of the ethnic state, which, in spite of his federalist views, had been so important to him during the Napoleonic wars, had by now receded into the background. In fact, he now deplored the "national hatred" and the "unlimited national vanity" displayed by so many nations during the last two decades and cherished the fond hope that the days of chauvinism were over. Moreover, throughout the **"Signatur des Zeitalters"** and in the most marked contrast to his lectures of 1810, he almost studiously avoided comment on the role the nobility was to play in his ideal state. But his basic model was still, as it had been for so many years, the Holy Roman Empire: "Perhaps never in the whole course of world history," he now wrote, "had a greater, organically more comprehensive, free idea of comparable vitality been realized in political life than the idea of the old German Christian Catholic empire as it existed . . . from King Conrad I to Charles V." To sum up, then, however vigorously he himself might have protested against this way of putting it, the way forward for Schlegel was still, or once again, the way back into an irretrievable past.

A similar spirit of conservatism and an even greater fusion of theological and political considerations characterize the articles contributed to the *Concordia* by other writers, particularly those by Schlegel's friend Bucholtz and by three major representatives of the final, Catholic stage of the Romantic movement, Franz von Baader, Zacharias Werner, and Adam Müller. Müller, whose writings considerably influenced the historical school of political economy, presented a theory of national finance "systematically set forth on a theological foundation," defending, among other things, and in complete agreement with Schlegel, the institution of feudal servitude. His article provoked readers to complain to Metternich, who bitterly told Gentz "that he was being deserted on all sides, that those on whom he had most relied were straying into eccentric byways, and that he was offered absurd suggestions instead of concrete assistance."

*Hans Eichner, in his* Friedrich Schlegel, *Twayne Publishers, Inc., 1970, 176 p.*

---

**An excerpt from *Lucinde***

How could distance make us more distant, since for us the present is, as it were, too present? We have to lessen and cool the consuming fire with playful good humor, and therefore the wittiest of all the shapes and situations of happiness is for us also the loveliest. One above all is wittiest and most beautiful: when we exchange roles and in childish high spirits compete to see who can mimic the other more convincingly, whether you are better at imitating the protective intensity of the man, or I the appealing devotion of the woman. But are you aware that this sweet game still has quite other attractions for me than its own—and not simply the voluptuousness of exhaustion or the anticipation of revenge? I see here a wonderful, deeply meaningful allegory of the development of man and woman to full and complete humanity. There is much in it—and what is in it certainly doesn't rise up as quickly as I do when I am overcome by you. . . .

That was my dithyrambic fantasy on the loveliest situation in the most beautiful world!

*Friedrich Schlegel,* Lucinde, *in Friedrich Schlegel's* Lucinde *and the* Fragments, *trans. by Peter Firchow, 1971.*

---

**Peter Firchow** (essay date 1971)

[*Firchow is an American educator and critic. In the following essay, he discusses Schlegel's philosophy and works, concentrating on the form and function of* Lucinde.]

*Lucinde* is an unusual book written at a time of unusual books and unusual events. In 1799, the year of its publication, the French Revolution was taking its first militant steps into Empire, and a new literary and philosophical movement, as yet unnamed, was also preparing to march against the old establishment. For Napoleon, it was supposedly a struggle of the liberal French armies against the restrictive forces of the conservative world; for the Romantics, as they came later to be called, it was a war against the rational, neoclassic conception of art and life, symbolized by the French authors and philosophers of the seventeenth century. Though *Lucinde,* unlike, say, Wordsworth and Coleridge's *Lyrical Ballads* of 1798, represents only a small battle in this great Romantic war, the novel is nevertheless noteworthy for its intensity, and for the lessons in strategy it provides, because its leader was one of the most famous, brilliant, and aggressive strategists the whole movement possessed.

When *Lucinde* was first published, most of its public realized that it was an unusual novel, but only in the sense that it was unusually bad. Still, the book was not wholly without enthusiastic admirers, even quite eminent ones. For example, Friedrich Schleiermacher, Schlegel's old friend and former roommate, was moved to publish in 1800 a collection of fictional letters, *Confidential Letters on Schlegel's Lucinde,* in which most of the prevalent hostile attitudes toward the novel were taken up and refuted. And another friend, the philosopher Fichte, declared in September 1799 that *Lucinde* was one of the greatest productions of genius he knew, and that he was about to embark on his third reading of it. But these and some few other favorable reactions were not enough to stem the tidal wave of hostile criticism that threatened to inundate the book completely. Friends and philosophers might console Schlegel, but they could not rescue his book from general condemnation.

The hostile contemporary reception of a literary work of merit is, of course, no unusual occurrence; on the contrary, it is one of the clichés of literary history. What one generation rejects, the next accepts; what one generation throws into the garbage pail, the next places on the dining-room table. As Kierkegaard perceived, one's generation and the public are not merely often, but usually, wrong.

The cliché, however, has not held completely true in this particular instance. Although, in Germany at any rate, the public in the twentieth century has at last given wide acceptance to *Lucinde,* the critics have been more slow and grudging in their approval. The reasons for this critical hesitancy are complex, but the very fact of the hesitancy probably indicates how much ahead of its time *Lucinde* actually was.

At the very beginning it appeared almost as if *Lucinde* was meant to be taken out of time entirely, as if, in fact, the novel would be completely forgotten. Friedrich Schlegel himself may have been partly responsible for this temporary oblivion. When in 1823 he came to edit and publish his complete works, he omitted *Lucinde* altogether. By that time Schlegel, grown old, Catholic, and conservative, no longer approved of his period of youthful radicalism and exuberance. But what the aging Schlegel perhaps wished to eradicate from the memory of mankind was resurrected six years after his death by an artist and critic who was still young, exuberant, and radical. In 1835, Karl Gutzkow issued the second edition of *Lucinde,* and it soon became one of the basic texts of the Young Germany movement of which he was a leader.

The second edition of *Lucinde* forced a smaller re-enactment of the original battle of 1799. Ironically, the most notable hostile critical reaction came from Heinrich Heine, himself a quasi member of the Young Germany movement, as well as a sometime Romantic. In his extended essay "The Romantic School" (1836), Heine discusses the career of Schlegel and gives a brief analysis of his novel. He begins by asserting that *Lucinde* is "ludicrously Romantic," and he concludes—alluding to Schlegel's Catholicism—with the remark that, though the Mother of God may be able to forgive Schlegel for having written it, the Muses never will. Six years later, another writer of considerable reputation, Kierkegaard, made an even sharper attack on the novel, charging that it denies the spirit for the sake of the flesh, that it aims at naked sensuality, and, finally, that it attempts to eliminate all morality.

Succeeding nineteenth-century critics by and large mirror these condemnations of Heine's and Kierkegaard's, usually with more scholarship if less wit. Rudolf Haym, the author of a long work bearing the same title as Heine's essay—and, though first published in 1870, probably still the most comprehensive study of the early Romantic movement in Germany—calls *Lucinde* an "aesthetic monstrosity"; his contemporary, Wilhelm Dilthey, in his biography of Schleiermacher, considers it self-evident that this novel is "morally as well as poetically formless and contemptible."

It is only with the coming of the twentieth century that more liberal and favorable critical views began to be expressed, most significantly by Josef Körner, Paul Kluckhohn, Wolfgang Paulsen, K. K. Polheim, and Hans Eichner. However, even these views have not been able to prevail wholly, in part perhaps because they themselves have often been halfheartedly maintained. Josef Körner, for example, though tracing the origins of *Lucinde* with a good deal of sympathy and scholarship, still comes to the conclusion that Schlegel did not achieve in it what he had hoped, and that such form as *Lucinde* displays is ultimately due to chance. Wolfgang Paulsen, who is even more overtly sympathetic and who expends much ingenuity in an attempt to prove that *Lucinde* is not formless, nevertheless feels compelled to assert that the third part of the novel is undeveloped and incompetent. Only Paul Kluckhohn, in his study of eighteenth-century and Romantic conceptions of love, Hans Eichner, in his introduction to the recent critical edition of *Lucinde,* and K. K. Polheim in his afterword to the Reclam edition of the novel, evaluate it in anything like a wholly positive way. But even these favorable or ambiguously favorable modern criticisms are balanced by others that are almost unambigu-

ously unfavorable. The novelist Ricarda Huch, for example, does not even bother to disguise her contempt; for her *Lucinde* is an artistic miscarriage, formless, pretentious, and dull.

The question that naturally arises out of this brief and partial review of *Lucinde's* critical reputation is, why should anyone bother to read this novel? If past and present critics have been so nearly unanimous in their condemnation of it, what is it then that makes this book so unusual? One answer, perhaps, is contained implicitly in the question itself. For surely a book must be unusual when, after all the charges that have been leveled against it, it still insists upon being read. And *Lucinde* does insist on being read: today it is probably the best known and most popular novel to come out of the German Romantic movement.

The primary reason for its continued vitality is not far to seek. *Lucinde* was the cause of one of the most notorious literary scandals of the early nineteenth century, for it was thought to be a pornographic novel. Pornography, as modern literature so amply testifies, is usually a profitable commodity—but in this respect as well *Lucinde* was unusual, since its first edition definitely did not sell well. Nevertheless, the reputation of being a dirty book, fostered by numerous more or less puritanical critics, has stayed with *Lucinde* to the present day and has no doubt increased its readership. A recent German edition, for example, is copiously illustrated with woodcuts of nude figures in various positions. But, as is so often the case, the illustrations have very little to do with the text. *Lucinde's* reputation for frank sensuality has been greatly exaggerated; by present-day standards, it is very mild indeed. There are no four-letter words and hardly any graphic description of any sort (let alone sexual). Like the traditional Hollywood movie, there is a fade-out at all the crucial moments, and, for the rest, the sexuality is kept very vague and, to use one of Schlegel's favorite words, allegorical. No doubt *Lucinde* has been a disappointment to many of its readers.

Basically, there are two reasons why the virtually innocent *Lucinde* got such a wicked reputation. The first of these can be traced to the social and hypocritical phenomenon of a double morality, a dichotomy which *Lucinde* was designed to attack. It is highly probable that that mythical entity, the average reader of the late eighteenth and early nineteenth centuries, was not significantly more moral than the average reader of the twentieth century. As an examination of even a small city like Weimar will testify, the moral behavior of the upper (and, therefore, reading) classes was open to considerable censure from a Victorian point of view (as Thackeray did censure it later). Furthermore, any good bibliography of the period will quickly prove that there was no lack of genuine pornography, and that any dearth in the German supply could easily be supplemented from the French. No doubt many a German reader savored his curious and erotic little volume in private while he condemned *Lucinde* in public for overstepping the bounds of decency. And he could do so without any real sense of contradiction because ordinary pornography was thought of as nothing more than an amusing and stimulating trifle—it was usually unpretentious and did not presume to be taken seriously. But *Lucinde* clearly presumed to be taken seriously, both as a work of art and as an attempt to revise the existing code of moral and social conduct. Most pornography was published either pseudonymously or anonymously. Not *Lucinde*: its title page boldly proclaimed that it was written by one of Germany's foremost literary critics. What by contemporary standards should have been a private concern, an anonymous, naughty triviality, had become a matter of excited public discussion. Thatis one reason why the publication of *Lucinde* constituted a scandal. What is acceptable in private is not always acceptable in public.

A further cause can be traced to an even more serious breach of this distinction between private and public morality. Schlegel presumed to use recognizably real people and events as the models for his fictional characters and actions. To anyone who knew anything of the lives of Schlegel and his then mistress, Dorothea Veit, it was obvious that Julius was a thinly disguised Schlegel and Lucinde a thinly clad Dorothea. Schlegel had violated another, even more inviolable social taboo: he had admitted the public into his own bedroom. And not merely admitted, but welcomed it in. That was not just scandalous; it was unheard of.

Since *Lucinde* is partially and consciously an autobiographical novel—and a roman à clef—it is obvious that to understand and appreciate it as fully as possible, one needs to know something of the life and thinking of the author, enough, at any rate, to make the relationship of *Dichtung* to *Wahrheit* comprehensible.

Friedrich Schlegel was born in Hanover on March 10, 1772, the youngest son of a Lutheran pastor, Johann Adolf Schlegel. His parents had originally intended him for a business career and had apprenticed him to a Leipzig banker. But in 1790 Schlegel, unhappy with this life, persuaded his parents to allow him to study law at Göttingen, where his brother, August Wilhelm (1767-1845), was pursuing classical studies under the famous philologist Christian Gottlob Heyne. It was at Göttingen, one can safely say, that Schlegel's intellectual life took its rise; and it was there as well that the two brothers began to forge the intellectual alliance which was later to exercise such an enormous influence on the course of German and European literature. With the elder brother initially providing the guiding hand, they undertook together extensive aesthetic and philosophical studies which contributed to Friedrich's deepening interest in Plato, Winckelmann, and the Dutch philosopher Hemsterhuis.

Around Easter 1791, Schlegel left Göttingen for Leipzig, where at first he continued to study law, but gradually began to devote most of his attention to art history, philosophy, and literature. It was during this period of his life (1791-1793) that he met Friedrich von Hardenberg, later to become famous under the pseudonym "Novalis," as well as one of Schiller's patrons, Christian Gottfried Körner, and Schiller himself. But despite these new friends and acquaintances, his closest intellectual ties were still to his brother, who was now in Amsterdam. The brothers maintained an intensive and searching correspondence, and Friedrich confided to August Wilhelm the various stages of a progressively more serious spiritual cri-

sis. The cause of this crisis—portrayed in *Lucinde* in the section entitled "Apprenticeship for Manhood"—seems primarily to have been Schlegel's growing inability to reconcile his idealism with the reality he saw about him. Secondarily, it may also have been the result of a kind of—possibly sexually induced—self-disgust, complicated by considerable financial difficulties. August Wilhelm (who seems to be the distant friend to whom Julius holds out his arms in the "Apprenticeship") was able to help him with money, but Friedrich's moods of depression were partly relieved only when, in the spring of 1793, he decided to give up law and devote himself entirely to the study of philosophy and literature. A more complete recovery followed shortly afterwards, when, in the summer of the same year, he undertook to act as a kind of guardian to his brother's mistress (and later wife), Caroline Boehmer, who was staying in a village near Dresden. Caroline—Julius's first great love in the "Apprenticeship"—was one of the most intelligent, exciting, and charming women of the age, and was obviously good social and emotional medicine for the moody Schlegel.

About this time Schlegel began to devote himself to an intensive study of Greek literature. Inspired by the example of Winckelmann and influenced by the brilliant criticism of Johann Gottfried Herder, he had great hopes of doing for Greek literature what Winckelmann had done for Greek art. That he was never able to realize these hopes can be accounted for in part by his need to supplement his meager income through rapid and frequent publication, and in part (if one may judge by his later performance) by his chronic inability to complete any of his major literary undertakings—*Lucinde* included.

In the essays from this early period (1794-1795), Schlegel is, though with considerable qualifications, a classicist. In discussing the literary achievement of classical antiquity, he generally adheres to the neoclassic party line, repeating, for example, the old cliché that the value of the ancients lies in their striving for the typical, the universal, and the beautiful. He deviates, however, from neoclassical convention in his attempts to contrast the direction and practice of modern literature with that of the ancient. And, in so doing, Schlegel begins to reveal an unseemly interest in modern literature which was eventually to move him to a critical position in many respects quite the reverse of the classic.

This interest in modern literature grew more apparent in the following two years (1796-1797). Though still largely adhering to the neoclassic critical principles, Schlegel during this time wrote almost solely on modern subjects. Publishing chiefly in Reichardt's journals (first *Deutschland,* later *Lyceum der schönen Künste*), Schlegel wrote extensive review essays on Schiller's *Musenalmanach auf das Jahr 1796* (an annual poetical almanac) and on Schiller's journal, *Die Horen* ("The Hours"), as well as three further essays, on F. H. Jacobi's novel *Woldemar,* on Georg Forster, and on Lessing. These essays began to bring him something approaching national fame and, in certain circles, notoriety.

Reputation, despite Shakespeare, is usually paid for: in Schlegel's case, the price was Schiller's enmity. Schiller, who had been rather annoyed by Schlegel during the few encounters he had had with him, was enraged by his biting reviews of his work and responded by severing all personal contact with him and by including several satirical lashes at him in his and Goethe's series of epigrams, the *Xenien.* Schlegel did not respond to the personal element in these attacks; he merely wrote an unfavorable review of Schiller's journal, the *Musenalmanach,* in which the *Xenien* had been published. And he probably acted wisely in not doing so, for, although he had irredeemably lost any chance of gaining Schiller's favor, his reputation was not so secure that he could afford to offend the Weimarian Jove, Goethe.

During these years, Schlegel was groping toward a way of defining the essentially "modern" in modern literature. In his earlier writings, particularly **"On the Study of Greek Poetry"** (written 1795; published 1797), Schlegel had contrasted modern with ancient literature and had arrived at the conclusion that modern literature was concerned primarily not with the beautiful but with what he called the "interesting," meaning thereby that the modern writer was prepared to sacrifice beauty to a didactic, philosophic interest. Furthermore, the modern writer generally was more realistic, more devoted to portraying individual rather than general nature: he was, in Schlegel's terminology, "characteristic." The modern writer also, unlike the ancient, strove for originality and gave free play to his imagination, and, in doing so, developed an individualistic mannerism; consequently his works were, to Schlegel, "fantastic," "individual," and "mannered."

---

**Disappointing as *Lucinde* may be initially, it will repay close reading and study, for the novel illustrates, perhaps better than any other work of fiction to come out of the German Romantic movement, the relation between Romantic theory and practice.**

**—*Peter Firchow***

---

The causes for these differences Schlegel saw as residing ultimately in the differences between ancient and modern civilization. Greek civilization seemed to him "natural"— that is, primarily instinctual—whereas modern civilization was "artificial," or rationally controlled. However, as a consequence of its instinctuality or sense-orientation, Greek civilization was cyclical: it could and did achieve perfection, but only an instinctual perfection, limited and finite. Modern civilization, on the other hand, being controlled by reason, could and did err, because reason errs. Nonetheless, reason could by its very nature always find its way back to the right track, and therefore opened up the possibility of an eventual perfection *without limits.* But because this was a process or a kind of dialectic, no modern work of art was perfect, though every modern work of art was on the way to perfection. Ancient civilization

and art, in other words, were static and perfect; modern civilization and art were progressive and imperfect.

Schlegel's ostensible reason for writing these early classicist essays was to bring about a reform of modern literature whose tendencies toward the "interesting" he found deplorable. Though he clearly recognized that, given the inherent character of modern civilization, it was impossible and even undesirable to reshape modern literature according to the model of the ancient, he still hoped for a kind of fusion of modern progressivism with the ancient ideals of beauty and calm repose, a fusion whose beginnings he already thought to perceive in Goethe. Schlegel's classicism, then, did not advocate a servile imitation of ancient practice and rules, but a revivification of modern literature by an incorporation of classical ideals.

Though the analysis of modern literature contained in these early critical writings already adumbrates the later doctrine which came to be known as Romanticism, Schlegel was not yet prepared to take the decisive step. This step—or, rather, leap—could be taken only after he had determined to his satisfaction not merely what was modern, but what was *essentially* modern. What Schlegel wanted to do, beginning with the fall of 1796, was to find a concept and a word that would enable him to distinguish what he considered the false tendencies in modern literature (e. g., French pseudo-classicism and Richardsonian realism) from those which were true and good. In the course of the following year, Schlegel gradually formulated a theory which would allow him to do this.

In July 1797, Schlegel had moved from Jena to Berlin. There he entered into an intellectual society centered on the salons of Rahel Levin and Henriette Herz, and frequented by men like Schleiermacher (the Antonio of the section in *Lucinde* entitled "Julius to Antonio") and Ludwig Tieck. It was at this time that Schlegel also read the aphorisms of Chamfort which had been the subject of a recent and favorable review by his brother. It was this reading of Chamfort that gave Schlegel the idea of writing aphorisms or, as he called them, "fragments" of his own. Schlegel by this single stroke managed not only to turn his greatest weakness, his chronic fragmentariness, into his greatest literary virtue, but also to lay the foundation for his immortality—which, however, has also, perhaps with a certain poetic justice, been fragmentary. It was these fragments which, of all Schlegel's writings, made the greatest impression on his contemporaries, and it is for these—and for *Lucinde*—that he is chiefly remembered.

During the brief period between 1797 and 1800, Schlegel published three collections of these aphoristic dicta, the first two under the rubric *Fragments,* the third with the title **Ideas.** This last collection, first published in 1800 but the direct result of thought and work reaching back to 1798, is particularly interesting for *Lucinde,* because here, as in the novel, Schlegel is primarily concerned with working out the theoretical and practical aspects of his new religion. In fact, the **Ideas** can perhaps best be seen (and understood) as a fragmentary mirror of *Lucinde,* though not a broken one; it clearly reflects his increasing religious awareness and his desire to be the prophet of what he terms the "religion of man and artist." To be sure, the

*Ideas* is also interesting in itself; it is perhaps the most finished, the most polished of all his collections of fragments. But at the same time it is probably also the most incomprehensible, since it is the best specimen of what Schlegel in a subsequent moment of ironic inspiration called "the dialect of the fragments." Perhaps for this reason, it did not make and has not left behind much of an impression. And the very fact that Schlegel published no more fragments thereafter indicates that they may have been a kind of dead end: the *Ideas* did not lead to further ideas.

This is not true of the *Lyceum Fragments* (1797), and certainly not true of the second and largest collection, the *Athenaeum Fragments* (1798). The real impact was made by this latter series: the *Lyceum Fragments* served only as an appetizer to this much richer intellectual repast. The *Athenaeum Fragments,* like its contemporary across the Channel, the Lyrical Ballads, constitutes a landmark in the development of modern literature; and, rather curiously and possibly significantly, it is also a joint production, with one author doing the lion's share of the work. In the case of the *Athenaeum Fragments* it was Friedrich who was definitely responsible for most of the fragments, and for the most important ones, with his brother, August Wilhelm, a very distant second, and Schleiermacher and Novalis bringing up the rear with only a very few contributions. Still, though the work is largely Friedrich's, the very notion of a shared creation, of a collaborated work of art, gives us an idea of how fresh (in a double sense) the fragments were, how much against the usual conceptions of what a literary work should be like; and in this the fragments of course resemble *Lucinde.* No wonder then that at least one reader thought they had been written by a madman.

The choice of the word "fragments" to describe his new work indicates that Schlegel was attempting to differentiate his kind of aphorism from those of his predecessors, notably Chamfort. And in fact he saw himself quite consciously as the "restorer of the epigrammatic genre." This boast holds less true of the *Lyceum Fragments* in which the fragments, like Chamfort's, tend to be brief and self-contained, very much in the manner of traditional aphorisms. The *Athenaeum Fragments,* however, as Hans Eichner has suggested, is unusual in that it forms a unit in a way most collections of aphorisms do not; and in that a number of the fragments refer back and forth to each other, and indeed often become comprehensible only when seen in their mutual relations. Also, it seems clear that although the *Athenaeum Fragments* does cover a great deal of rather variegated territory (moral, political, philosophical, historical), it is nonetheless primarily literary. And it is in this last respect that it is possibly most unusual, for never before had there been such a curious form of criticism. Indeed, one of Schlegel's own definitions for his fragments was "condensed essays and reviews," and certainly a large number of the fragments are just that. And even more certainly the impression they made at the time and have left behind is very definitely literary. (For Schlegel and his friends, we should remember, the distinction between works of literature and works of philosophy was by no means as strict as it is today.) More specifically, it was Schlegel's proclamation here of the doc-

trine of Romanticism that gave the fragments and himself immortality.

But before we turn to the ticklish problem of Romanticism, a few more words on the fragments are in order. One of these should probably be a word of warning: the fragments are often extremely difficult—not merely to translate, but simply to understand. It should be remembered that even his own brother objected to the difficult terminology of the *Athenaeum Fragments,* and that one of his best friends and closest intellectual associates, Schleiermacher, complained to him about the incomprehensibility of the *Ideas.* It should also be recalled that Schlegel replied to these charges in his essay **"On Incomprehensibility,"** where he rests his defense largely on the contention that the fragments are incomprehensible because they are ironic. In any case, the passage of time, the acceptance of "Romantic" or nonrational modes of thought, the labors of critics and intellectual historians, have rendered the obstacles somewhat less formidable, but Schlegel nonetheless was probably right when he predicted in one of his fragments (*Ideas, 135*) that no one would ever "probe entirely" the intention of his work, or when he proclaimed in another fragment which appears in the manuscript but which he apparently lacked the courage to print (*Ideas, 129a*): "You are not really supposed to understand me, but I want very much for you to listen to me." It is possible that part of this attitude may simply be the result of putting a good (or bad) face on a bad (or good) show, but certainly that is not the whole explanation. That is, this "sublime impudence," as he called it, does not mean that Schlegel is merely mocking his readers in the manner of Dada or Pop-Camp; not at all. It means rather, that Schlegel was here relying to some extent at least on inspiration rather than rhetoric; and he probably would have been among the first to agree that he too was incapable of fully probing his own intention.

It is possible that something like this perception may lurk behind the name Schlegel chose for his petite and plentiful progeny. For surely one of the reasons why the fragments are fragmentary, ruins and not complete edifices, is that Schlegel wants us to intuit what might have been but never was, wants us to take the fragment and make of it a whole, take the ruin and reconstruct the edifice. Another reason they are fragments clearly derives from the fact that they are literally fragments, or at least that a good many of them are. That is, they are bits and pieces which Schlegel extracted from his notebooks, from the jottings of years, from his grand attempt to build a system of literature which would put order into the criticism and understanding of the classics. This great work was, as we have seen, never completed; only the blueprint of the vast system and a great many abandoned building materials and some unfinished structures remain, and from these Schlegel decided to salvage the fragments. So we can see that the fragments, despite their form and, to use Goethe's image for them, despite their waspishness, are not in revolt against the idea of systems; Schlegel was too much of a disciple of Kant to do that. No, the fragments are not against systems, they are a substitute for one, a brilliant substitute, for unlike a fully formulated system they need exclude nothing because it is contradictory, or even self-contradictory; they can and do bring the entire noisy federation of literary and philosophical quarrels under one roof.

It was the **Athenaeum Fragments** and the new, revolutionary doctrine it unsystematically but powerfully proclaimed that provided the critical base for the creative activity of the writers who now began to gather around Schlegel and his brother. This group, formed early in 1798, included besides the Schlegel brothers, Tieck, Schleiermacher, and, somewhat later, Novalis. They were the nucleus of what in the nineteenth century came to be known as the early Romantic movement (*Frühromantik*), a nucleus which, through the pages of its "official" journal, the *Athenaeum* (edited and largely written by the two Schlegels), exploded over Germany, destroying as best it could the old neoclassical precepts.

This new doctrine, Romanticism, was Schlegel's answer to the question of what was essentially or ideally modern, the question which had occupied him since the last of his classicist essays. It was an answer that derived ultimately from a new emphasis on and understanding of the function of the novel. In fact, it was the novel, that distinctively modern genre, which gave the name to the new movement. Out of the German (originally French) word for novel, *Roman,* Schlegel constructed his all-important adjective, romantisch.

*Novalis (pseudonym of Friedrich von Hardenberg), poet and friend of Schlegel's. Oil portrait by Franz Gareis.*

The most concise, and for that reason probably most enigmatic, statement of Schlegel's new doctrine is contained in the famous **Athenaeum Fragment 116,** but Schlegel also elaborated it more fully elsewhere, particularly in his review of Goethe's *Wilhelm Meister* (1798) and in the section entitled **"Letter on the Novel"** in his **Dialogue on Poetry** (1799). These three works form the basic texts, the manifestos of the Romantic movement in Germany. In brief, they advocate what Schlegel termed a "progressive, universal poetry." The novel is progressive, as we have seen, because it belongs to a civilization which is progressive, but it is also universal because it contains within itself all things. The perfect novel is a perfect mixture of all previous genres, a fusion and confusion of epic, dramatic, lyric, critical, and philosophic elements. Since, however, such a perfect union is humanly impossible, the perfect novel is unattainable, is something which one can only approximate, never achieve. Romantic poetry is therefore inherently progressive, or in the words of fragment 116, "the romantic kind of poetry is still in the state of becoming; that, in fact, is its real essence: that it should forever be becoming and never be finished."

The novel, though the most perfect expression of romantic art, was not its only manifestation. Although Schlegel had based his concept on the word novel (*Roman*), he also made use of other existing connotations of *romantisch,* connotations referring back to the medieval romances and to the literature of the Middle Ages as a whole. Indeed, Schlegel saw the novel as a return to and a development of this medieval tradition. It was this sense of the word *romantic* that enabled Schlegel, for example, to consider Shakespeare as a romantic writer par excellence, though, to be sure, Shakespeare also qualified by virtue of his anti-classic mixture of tragedy and comedy, as well as by his irony.

But once Schlegel broadened the application of his term *romantic* in this way, it was inevitable that he should lose control over it. Soon he began to discover all sorts of "romantic" traits in even the most classical writers, and in the end only the Greek tragedians were excluded. So, by a curious process of irony, his earlier attempt to make modern literature classic had ended by making almost all literature romantic.

Schlegel's intense preoccupation with literary theory, particularly with the theory of the novel, quite naturally led him to the idea of putting his new doctrine into practice. As early as 1794, Schlegel had toyed with the idea of writing a novel and it is even possible that he may have written portions of one. When, in the late fall of 1798, Schlegel began seriously to work on **Lucinde** he may have made use of some of the materials for this earlier novel, but whether or not he did so does not really matter. For the plot of **Lucinde** is the least important thing about it, since it has practically no plot; and whatever shape the earlier novel may have had, it did not resemble **Lucinde's.** The classicist Schlegel of 1794 would hardly have been capable of producing the kind of "formless" novel that **Lucinde** is. Only Schlegel's new Romantic doctrine can account for it.

The impetus to write **Lucinde** was, however, not wholly theoretical. The very fact that the title character is a woman who bears a striking resemblance to Schlegel's then mistress, Dorothea Veit, shows that the novel is an expression not merely of Schlegel's theory, but also of his life. Schlegel had met Dorothea at Henriette Herz's salon soon after his arrival in July 1797. Dorothea was not a particularly attractive woman, and she was almost eight years older than Schlegel, but she more than made up for these defects by her charm, vivacity, and intelligence. The daughter of a well-known philosopher and friend of Lessing's, Moses Mendelssohn, she had been given what for a woman of her time was an extraordinarily good education. At the age of eighteen, however, her parents arranged a marriage for her to the banker Simon Veit, a man considerably older than herself and hardly the sort either to understand or to share her intellectual and artistic interests. By the time she met Schlegel, she had borne Veit four sons (only two of whom survived infancy), but even these were not sufficient to reconcile her to her unhappy marriage.

A physical and spiritual love at first sight seems to have seized both Schlegel and Dorothea. Except for Caroline (his brother's wife from 1796 to 1803), Schlegel had never met a woman of such brilliance and charm: Dorothea was completely overwhelmed by Schlegel's intellectual superiority, which she was to acknowledge for the rest of his life, and which she was to venerate for the rest of her own. In 1798 Dorothea separated from her husband and after her divorce lived with Schlegel. Though Schlegel and Dorothea did not marry until 1804, the main reason for the delay does not seem to have been a desire to shock the bourgeoisie. Rather, it seems to have been Dorothea's wish to retain some legal influence on the lives of her children, which she could not have done had she married Schlegel at once.

From the very beginning of their relationship, Schlegel assumed the role of the enthusiastic spiritual and intellectual leader, and Dorothea that of the equally enthusiastic follower. Under his inducement and supervision, Dorothea undertook a whole series of translations and adaptations, and even wrote a novel of her own, *Florentin* (1801). Just before their marriage, Dorothea left Judaism to become a Protestant and when, in 1808, Schlegel converted to Catholicism, Dorothea did likewise. For the rest of her life, Dorothea remained a sincere and dedicated Catholic, determined and successful in converting members of her family to her new religion.

The further details of Schlegel's and Dorothea's life need not be given here, since they do not contribute to any fuller understanding of *Lucinde.* It is enough to know that the later Schlegel, after converting to Catholicism, was quite a different man from the earlier one. To be sure, he was still interested in literature and philosophy, but as he became Catholic, he also became conservative, and his thinking and criticism reflected that change. The radical younger Schlegel gradually merged and disappeared into the middle-aged propagandist and *Hofsekretär* in Metternich's conservative Austrian empire. As with so many other Romantics, Schlegel's Romanticism led to the Church and to an uncritical self-immolation at its altars.

As might be expected from the outline of Schlegel's criti-

cal theories on the novel given in the preceding section, *Lucinde* is a mixture of many things. This mixture may, on a first and even second reading, seem confusing, and there is perhaps no real consolation in knowing that it was meant to be so. But disappointing as *Lucinde* may be initially, it will repay close reading and study, for the novel illustrates, perhaps better than any other work of fiction to come out of the German Romantic movement, the relation between Romantic theory and practice. It belongs, after all, to that highly unusual category of literature: a work of art of major importance by a critic of major importance.

The master key to the mystery of *Lucinde* is the recognition that it is first and foremost a religious book. At the time Schlegel was writing this novel, he became convinced of the necessity of a new religion and of his fitness to be its prophet. This "religion" was, of course, not to be a rigidly structured one; that would have gone too much against the grain of his critical thinking, as well as his personality. It was to be, rather, more in the nature of a new mythology, a new morality, and a new philosophy. *Lucinde* represents the first installment (the "erster Teil," as the original title page has it) of this new vision; it is not so much a novel in the conventional, traditional sense as it is a fusing together of fictionalized philosophy, figurative morality, and allegorical religion.

There are numerous and continual references in *Lucinde* to support the contention that this is a religious book: references to Julius as a priest, Lucinde as a priestess, to both being purified, to his being anointed, to her being, at least in a vision, beatified. Indeed, the "Apprenticeship for Manhood," the longest single block of the novel, is concerned with the delineation of an increasingly intense spiritual crisis from which Julius is finally saved by Lucinde and by what Lucinde represents. The question which this whole section of the novel faces and attempts to resolve is the question of what and why one should believe, and how, in consequence, one is to act.

The religion of which Julius and Lucinde are priest and priestess is the religion of love. Though in the abstract this may seem rather trite, in practice it is not so. For from this religion there follow certain rules of behavior which attack not merely the usual conceptions of morality, but also the customary sentimentalities of love. There are two main dogmas in this religion—at least as it is fragmentarily presented here—which, in turn, form the two main themes of the novel: the love of man for man, or friendship; and the love of man for woman, or passionate love. Friendship, it is made amply clear in the course of the novel, is possible only among men, for in Schlegel's conception, women are wholly passionate and consequently incapable of Platonic disinterestedness. But if woman's passionate nature is her weakness, it is also her strength, for unquestionably the love of woman is more significant and important for Schlegel than the love of man. It is not by accident that the title of the novel is identical with the name of its female rather than its male protagonist; at the center of Schlegel's new religion stands, quite unmistakably, the feminine ideal. Lucinde—a name derived from the Latin *lux,* meaning light—is Julius's illumination.

Ironically, however, her light is not the light of day; it is, instead, as we can see from the section entitled "Yearning and Peace," the light of night, the light of the pale moon and stars. Lucinde, like Diana, is a priestess of the night, and, like Diana's symbol, the moon, her illumination is indirect and by reflection, as the moon reflects the light of the sun. The moon and the woman are mirrors, are passive, and the man who loves a woman truly sees his own light and his own image reflected in her; he loves himself, Narcissus-like, in her. The love of woman leads, consequently, to a fuller awareness of the self.

It is in this sense that *Lucinde* is what H. A. Korff calls it: the most complete formulation of the Romantic ideal of marriage, and hence a most revolutionary work. Unquestionably, one of Schlegel's most important objectives in this novel is to define man's relation to woman, and, in doing so, implicitly to contrast it with the attitude of the Enlightenment. This attitude—which Schlegel had attacked explicitly in his extended review of F. H. Jacobi's *Woldemar*—was that sexual love and intellectual love do not mix, that, as in Jacobi's novel, a man must not sleep with the woman he loves, that he must not defile "true" love by carnal lust. It is this ridiculous attitude that Schlegel attempts to explode in this fragmentary anti-*Woldemar,* though, to be sure, his zeal sometimes carries him too far in the other direction, as for example in Julius's assertion that disinterested love between man and woman is quite impossible. Essentially, however, Schlegel's attitude toward love anticipates that of D. H. Lawrence: it is both—and must be both—a spiritual and a sexual union, but not a narrow, exclusive one, not a perverse institution designed to restrict experience, but an organic means for exploring it more broadly and deeply.

Still, for Schlegel, as for most of his contemporaries, woman is the symbol of passivity, a symbol which is obviously derived from woman's sexual role. But unlike his contemporaries, or, for that matter, traditional Western attitudes, Schlegel does not find this passivity inferior to the male's activity. Quite the reverse: Schlegel turns upside down the usual concept which makes passivity weakness and activity strength; for him, it is passivity which is to be idealized, not activity.

For Schlegel passivity is, however, not merely sexual, or more accurately, not exclusively sexual. Indeed, in the second section of the novel, entitled "A Dithyrambic Fantasy on the Loveliest Situation in the World," it is precisely the reversal of roles in sexual intercourse which Schlegel sees as the "loveliest situation." Passivity is for Schlegel not merely a feminine but a universal attitude; it is the preference of the unconscious to the conscious, of the imagination to the rational faculty. It is only through man's submission to nature that man can fulfill himself most completely. Carlyle was later to make much of this idea.

Though woman is for Julius (and Schlegel) the most obvious and most important symbol and manifestation of nature's principle of passivity, she is not the only one. The plant and the night also occupy places of considerable importance in Schlegel's symbology. The plant represents passivity and unconsciousness par excellence, since it instinctually obeys the mandates of nature and does not need to discover rules by which to develop itself. Nature has taken care of all that already. The plant grows, blossoms, and withers in harmony with the seasons and the course of nature; it does not rebel against dying because it cannot be conscious of rebellion. It exists for nothing but itself; it is its own achievement and purpose. Mankind, on the other hand—at least perverted, conventional mankind—rebels against nature and makes its own rules. Man attempts to live according to ideals and purposes outside himself and outside of nature. He seeks to impose his own consciousness upon nature. According to Schlegel, this is man's perversion. Man must be dis-educated from such falseness, and brought back to an awareness that he can achieve perfection only in passivity, or, as Julius remarks, in a state of *"pure vegetating."* Man must live like a plant; he must be passive and purposeless.

Though the identification of man with plant occurs sporadically throughout the novel, it is made most emphatic in the section entitled "Idyll of Idleness." Toward the end of this section, Schlegel also extends this identification and the active-passive distinction on which it is based into a further distinction which in its phrasing is evocative of Nietzsche's later dichotomy of Dionysian and Apollonian. This distinction is introduced by a vision in which Julius imagines himself in a theater. On the stage, there is a figure of a bound Prometheus in the act of creating men, while in the background are seen the shapes of Hercules, Hebe, Venus, and Cupid. Prometheus is helped as well as controlled in his task by a number of creatures who resemble little devils. The audience is made up of the men Prometheus has created and continues to create. They display no individual traits whatsoever; they are like the products of an assembly line.

This vision is intelligible only in terms of Schlegel's principle of passivity. Here Schlegel is making a distinction between two types of creation: the Promethean and the Herculean. Prometheus rebelled against the gods (against nature) in bringing fire to mankind and in creating mankind unnaturally, that is, mechanically and not organically. Prometheus's perversion of nature makes him a prisoner of the Satanic creatures—and Satan, of course, was also a rebel against God—a prisoner, in other words, of a rebellious, perverted morality; and he is forced to create man, whether he wants to or not, in accordance with the stultifying demands of this morality. Hercules, on the other hand, does not create mankind in this mechanical and immoral fashion. His creation is organic; he could keep "fifty girls busy during a night." Hercules creates through love and passion—he is accompanied by the stimuli of Hebe, Venus, and Cupid. And, as a consequence, their fates differ: Prometheus is bound, Hercules free; Prometheus was brought down from the divine to the human, whereas Hercules was deified. Consequently, if man is to become god he must work through nature, not against it.

A further symbol of passivity in the novel is the night. Lucinde is called the "priestess of the night," and it is apparent that she holds her office because it is the night which—at least in relation to the day—is passive. The night is the time of rest, of dreams rather than thought, but also of love and passion. For true passivity, according to Schlegel, does not mean inactivity, boredom, or laziness; it means, rather, a passivity in relation to nature, a passivity which in turn makes man really and naturally creative. The word passion, in German ("Leidenschaft," from "leiden," to suffer) as in English (from the Latin "pati," to suffer), is derived from the same concept, that of suffering, of passivity, of being done to rather than doing; but, again both in English and German, the word passion denotes an emotional force of great power. Stated differently, passion is something which cannot be consciously willed, but only triggered by nature; and once released, it possesses enormous energy. Consequently, the truly creative and energetic man is one who is passive and in accordance with nature; he does not obey the arbitrary rules of reason or man, but succumbs instead to divine inspiration. The true artist lets his work of art grow as a plant grows, naturally and for itself alone.

It is this perception which explains a good deal of the curious and otherwise inexplicable form of *Lucinde.* As Julius remarks in speaking of this "poem of truth," this is the reason why he resolves never "to prune its living fullness of superfluous leaves and branches"; he wants to let it grow naturally and unhindered. It is for the same reason that he asserts at the beginning of the novel his "incontestable right to confusion" in matters of form. He will not be bound by man-made rules; he will only be bound by the rules of nature and by the impulse of his inspiration. The much criticized formlessness of *Lucinde* is therefore not a blunder on Schlegel's part: it is an integral and necessary element of the principle which infuses the work as a whole.

This does not mean, however, that *Lucinde* has no form or shape. It means only that it has its own shape, just as every flower and fruit has a shape, but not the same shape every other flower or fruit does. *Lucinde* is formless only when the concept of form is considered in a neoclassic, Aristotelian sense. Looked at for itself, it reveals its own form.

*Lucinde* is a novel which is very much aware of itself, so much so in fact that at times it makes criticisms of itself and its structure. Indeed, at the end of one of the first sections of the novel, the "Allegory of Impudence," the author speculates upon the reception which this "mad little book" would enjoy "should it ever be found, perhaps printed, and even read." The interruptions, the lack of artful transitions, the chaotic confusion of proper time sequence, all these are not the result of inartistic insensitivity, but carefully planned occurrences. For example, in the first part of the novel, the letter from Julius to Lucinde is interrupted just when Julius wants to begin relating the history of his life, something which he is therefore able to do only later in the novel. This interruption is blamed on an "unkind chance" which, since it is not further explained at this point, could mean virtually anything. But this supposedly unkind chance is really not so unkind after all, for it allows Schlegel to draw the reader's attention to the connection between the novel's formal construction and its theme, and to warn him that, though chance has interrupted him, chance has also provided him with further opportunities, particularly the opportunity to mold chance, and let it carry him beyond the limitations of any

kind of orderly, rational plan. Thus chance, which at first seems merely arbitrary, becomes the ordering principle of nature, becomes the inspiration which will convey to the work a wholeness more real and organic than any man-made principles could impose.

This self-consciousness, and the formal peculiarities which accompany it, must also be seen, if they are to be properly understood, in relation to the persona of the novel. For, despite the fact that this is demonstrably in part an autobiographical novel, it is not irrelevant to introduce the concept of the persona, that is, of a speaker in the novel who is distinct from its real author. After all the subtitle of *Lucinde* is "Confessions of a Blunderer," and on at least one occasion an explicit reference is made to the fact that the novel is being written in the mask of a blunderer. Consequently, at least some of the apparent "blunders" of the novel are to be seen not as the faults of Schlegel, but as those of his mask, Julius.

The concept of the persona is one which interested Schlegel a great deal. It was this concept, in fact, that shaped his ideas of irony and wit, ideas of paramount importance for *Lucinde.* Schlegel traced the technique of the persona to what he believed were its origins in ancient Greek comedy, specifically to the device of the "parabasis," that is, a speech in the name of the poet delivered to the audience in the middle of the play. Schlegel perceived that this technique of interruption—or what Brecht was later to call the alienation effect—was essentially the same method practiced by the personae or narrators of Cervantes, Diderot, Sterne, and Jean Paul, all novelists whom Schlegel admired. The interruptive method of *Lucinde* seems clearly modeled on the novels of particularly the last two of these authors.

In Schlegel's mind, the idea of interruption or parabasis was intimately connected with the idea of irony. Indeed, in one of his fragments he states that "irony is a permanent parabasis." In other words, irony consists of a continual self-consciousness of the work itself, of an awareness of the work of art as a fiction and as an imitation of reality at one and the same time. In this respect, the irony of a work of art corresponds to the ironic attitude which Schlegel saw as mandatory in actual life. Only through irony could man achieve simultaneously a closeness to reality and a distance from it. Only the ironic attitude enabled man to commit himself wholly to finite reality and at the same time made him realize that the finite is trivial when viewed from the perspective of eternity.

Schlegel's conception of wit is related to his understanding of irony. When he uses the word "wit" he is not using it primarily in the present-day sense of joking or punning; for him wit is rather—as it was for most of the eighteenth century—the capacity to discover similarities and to form ideas: wit in the sense of intelligence rather than of simple humor. Perhaps the closest modern synonym for wit in this older sense is "serendipity." It is through wit that truth is divined, not rationally understood. Wit is not reason: reason comprehends mechanically and laboriously, wit perceives immediately and through inspiration.

From this idea of wit or serendipity, it follows that a work of art should not be ordered by reason but by wit. It should not possess a rational, conventional form, but a natural and, as Schlegel calls it, "witty form." In one of his fragments, Schlegel states that every novel must have "chaos and eros" and that it must combine a "fantastic form" with a "sentimental plot." But this idea of a "fantastic" form does not mean that the author is to follow any and every whim which happens to strike him; rather, he is, according to the **Dialogue on Poetry,** to follow a "cultivated arbitrariness" and construct his work according to an "artistically ordered confusion." Schlegel—despite his occasionally striking similarities to the surrealists—is not an advocate of automatic writing. Again and again he refers to the right and duty of the author to select and order his materials. For example, after the first interruption in the opening section of **Lucinde,** the narrator, Julius, explains to us why he has *chosen* to insert the "Dithyrambic Fantasy" in this particular place. Sterne's Tristram and Fielding's narrators in *Joseph Andrews* and *Tom Jones* had earlier done much the same thing.

As might be expected, in **Lucinde** Schlegel does not adhere to the usual practice of parceling his materials into chapters of roughly equal length. Rather, the novel is divided into thirteen sections (each prefaced by some kind of descriptive title) of greatly varying length. The longest of these, the "Apprenticeship for Manhood," is almost wholly narrative and occupies virtually the entire middle third of the novel. Its length and central placement fairly clearly indicate that it is to represent the focal core of the novel. Though the relatively formal conventionality of this section presents few structural problems, the remaining twelve non-narrative sections pose questions which are at times hard to explain—for example, what is the point of their order of sequence, how do they relate to the central section and to each other? In theory, at least, an answer to these questions should not be difficult, since, if **Lucinde** does indeed possess its vaunted natural or "organic" form, it ought to be possible to show how all the separate parts form a unified whole.

It is easy enough to demonstrate that **Lucinde** displays a kind of formal symmetry: the central section, the "Apprenticeship," is preceded and followed by six short sections. But the fact of this symmetry is certainly not sufficient to allow us to claim unity for the novel as a whole; unity does not consist of such a strictly external ordering. Still, the fact that there is symmetry does give us an indication that there is some kind of ordering sense present in **Lucinde;** if nothing more, it suggests that the first six sections are a preparation for the central section, and that the last six represent either some sort of further growth of the ideas contained in the central section or a denouement of the action of that section.

One way of getting at the function of the opening six parts of the novel is to investigate the function of the central part. On the most obvious level, it is a story, narrating, as the title suggests, the growth of the protagonist's mind. But the presentation of this process of maturation is curious. Though obviously a story, it does not, for example, really focus on character analysis or plot development. The characters, including even Julius, are only rudimen-

tarily described and the narrative line is virtually without suspense. The focus throughout this section seems to be elsewhere: not on analysis, but on a simple description of Julius's life and the events which lead him first into and then out of his spiritual crisis. It seems to follow necessarily, therefore, that if this section is to achieve full meaning and impact, it must be placed within a context which will give it such significance. That is precisely what the preceding and following short sections do.

In a very rough way, the structure of **Lucinde** works as follows. The first six parts of the novel provide us with a picture of what Julius is, the central part shows us how he came to be what he is, and the last six parts adumbrate the further directions of his growth. This ordering corresponds more or less to the way we would normally approach any object in nature: first we observe what it is; then we inquire how it came to be what it is; and, lastly, we speculate upon what it will become. Seen from this point of view, the form of **Lucinde** is definitely natural and organic.

The first sections serve not only to give us some notion of the character of the persona, Julius, but also to prepare us for the unorthodox formal and thematic qualities of the novel. The first part, the letter from Julius to Lucinde, symbolically suggests several of the themes which will occupy the novel: its setting in a garden indicates the importance of nature; its expression of passionate love for Lucinde (as girl, woman, and mother) strikes a note which will be picked up repeatedly later on; its dichotomy of illusion and reality prepares us for subsequent fantasies and allegories—all of them, significantly, products of the imagination; and, finally, its emphasis upon confusion in nature and art warns us to expect further innovations in the structure of the novel.

The next three sections explore some of the thematic implications of the first part, particularly those relating to love and sexual passion. Almost necessarily—considering the time when this novel was published—they are also concerned with conventional attitudes and reactions toward sex and the literary expression of sexual matters. "A Dithyrambic Fantasy on the Loveliest Situation in the World" is, like some of the later sections, a veiled and semihumorous description of sexual intercourse, which begins to suggest the extremely important place of woman in this novel. "A Description of Little Wilhelmine" continues this focus upon women, and begins, by means of a rather playful allegory, to make a distinction between conventional morality and the morality of nature. This distinction is developed more fully in the following section, the "Allegory of Impudence." Indeed, here Schlegel describes figuratively and in brief the process which Julius is to undergo explicitly and directly in the main section of the novel. This process is one in which Julius learns to reject the old, conventional moral code and to accept the new, unconventional one. The religious framework within which this spiritual transformation is cast indicates further that this is not an ordinary process, but one of great significance: it is not merely a change of moral systems, but a religious conversion.

"An Idyll of Idleness" defines in greater detail the nature

and principles of this new religion, emphasizing particularly the importance of the principle of passivity. Next to the gods Wit, Impudence, and Fantasy, it now admits into the Schlegelian pantheon the god Hercules as a deity subsidiary to the demiurge Nature. And it further establishes Julius as a prophet worthy—or one who has now become worthy—of proclaiming the new religion.

The following section, "Fidelity and Playfulness," consisting entirely of dialogue between Julius and Lucinde, demonstrates the practice of this new religion. Its rituals, we now see, are few and simple. Essentially there appear to be two which are important: the first a purification/confession, the removal of all misunderstandings between the lovers; and the second a consummation, sexual intercourse—or, to use Julius's phrase, "appeasing the offended gods." To a lesser extent, this section also serves as an occasion to discuss other implications of the new religion, particularly those having to do with social behavior. These implications are also, as might be expected, sexual.

It is at this point that Schlegel inserts the main segment of the novel, "Apprenticeship for Manhood," and it is an apt point, because now that we have been properly instructed in the nature and practice of the new religion, it should be made apparent to us as well how this religion came to be, and how Julius was converted to it. This is in essence what this section does. We see Julius at the beginning moving into a mood of spiritual despair in which everything loses meaning for him; then we watch him move gradually out of this despair as a result of his encounters with and loves for various women. And we see him, finally, gain peace spiritually and physically in his love for Lucinde, a love which releases within him his latent creative energies. Julius has rejected the values of conventional society, those unnatural and destructive values, and accepted in their place the values of nature, which are creative and constructive, and which convey to him for the first time a sense of the organic wholeness of his being. In discovering his love for Lucinde, Julius has discovered, as Schlegel says at the end of the third-person narrative, "the most beautiful religion."

The last two or three pages of this section form a transition from the "Apprenticeship" proper to the shorter sections which follow. These pages are narrated in the first person and apparently represent the viewpoint of an older Julius looking back upon the experiences which he has recorded. Julius here observes that there is something in these experiences which can be communicated not by means of a story but only through symbols. It is this attempt at symbolic communciation which shapes much of the following sections. And, further, these later sections concern themselves with a Julius who is moving into and speculating about his future.

The section which immediately follows the main one corresponds in function roughly to the earlier "Allegory of Impudence." Its title, "Metamorphoses," explicitly reveals that it is concerned with change, specifically a change in Julius's character and outlook. It sums up, symbolically, the transformation that Julius has undergone in the "Apprenticeship": one here described as a metamor-

phosis from the egoism of Narcissus to the duality of Pygmalion, from the self-sufficiency of one life to the self-sufficiency of two lives. The point which this section makes is the same as that of the preceding one: man can realize the wholeness of his own being only through the love of another, not by himself alone.

The first of the following "Two Letters" reveals Julius moving to a point beyond the one reached at the end of the "Apprenticeship for Manhood." The fact that Lucinde is about to have a baby forces Julius to new realizations about the nature of human existence. He reaches a new stage of awareness: he now knows the metamorphosis described in the preceding section is not final, but only one in a progressive (perhaps infinite) series. Faced with the prospect of fatherhood, Julius discovers within himself not only a new esteem for parental responsibility and useful, domestic objects, but also the knowledge that the union of two bodies and spirits is not final and complete. A more complete union, a greater wholeness, can only be achieved through the creation of new life. And in creating new life, Julius and Lucinde act in accordance with the dictates of nature. For nature demands that every plant bear fruit. Now it becomes clear to Julius that his love for Lucinde and her love for him is something which exists not simply for itself alone: it leads, rather, to a fuller love of all things. What illuminates them, illuminates the world as well.

The second letter consists almost wholly of a vision induced by a report of Lucinde's severe and, as Julius thinks, fatal illness. In this vision, he imagines what the course of his future life would be if he were compelled to live it without Lucinde. This produces two new realizations: the first that, though it is possible for him to exist without Lucinde, a meaningful and satisfying life would be impossible without her. Though his love for Lucinde may, as the first letter showed, lead to further loves, without Lucinde there can be no love at all—except the love of death. This forms the basis for his second realization: that in certain circumstances, death can be meaningful and beautiful, that it can be a transformation devoutly to be wished, for it re-establishes the possibility of union.

The next section, "A Reflection," is an elaborate pun based on a confusion of philosophical and sexual imagery and terminology. The "reflection" in other words, is not merely a mental but also a sexual action. But Schlegel's intention here is not merely humorous. For him, the sexual act is symbolic of the action of nature and the universe. Sexual union is, after all, the union of opposites, just as in certain philosophical systems, particularly those of Hegel, Fichte, and Schelling, the motive principle of the universe is a fusion of opposites. Beneath the humor, there is definitely a level at which Schlegel is attempting to demonstrate symbolically that man and woman cannot exist for themselves alone, but can find wholeness as well as individuality only in each other. "A Reflection" serves, then, the function of generalizing upon Julius's experiences and his new awareness: out of these he has constructed a philosophy and religion which are valid not merely for himself but for all mankind.

The following section reverts once more to the form of letters, though this time they are directed not at Lucinde, but at a friend, Antonio. Both letters are concerned with the question of friendship and serve as a kind of definition of what friendship among men should be. This is a problem which had earlier concerned Julius in the "Apprenticeship for Manhood," but here it is elaborated not only more fully but also from a somewhat different point of view. It is appropriate that a discussion of friendship should be inserted at this point because it represents a different manifestation, or new transformation, of love. It is a further means of achieving the unity of one's being.

Julius's treatment of the idea of friendship seems at times to suggest that this word is being used as a synonym for homosexuality, but it would be unwise to make such an identification too hastily. In "Fidelity and Playfulness" as well as elsewhere in the novel, Julius had already observed that friendship was impossible among women because women, passionate by nature, were incapable of a purely intellectual relationship. This disqualification of women is based upon a dichotomy of the intellect and passion. For a woman, love must be a mixture of intellect and passion; for a man it may be either. Friendship, therefore, it would appear, is not a bodily, but a spiritual thing. What seems quite clear, however, is that for Julius friendship functions as a further fulfillment of his being; it represents another stage of growth. Friendship—at least true friendship—is a different kind of union, a different kind of transformation from that which he experienced in his love for Lucinde. It is one more way of penetrating into the heart of nature.

"Yearning and Peace," which follows, not merely acts as a kind of balance to the earlier "Fidelity and Playfulness" (both consist almost wholly of dialogue), but also furthers the idea of the growth or expansion of love. The underlying notion of this section, that peace can only be found in yearning and yearning only in peace, echoes the earlier idea proposed in "Reflection," the idea of a union of opposites. And, in both instances, this union of opposites is indicative of a process, a series of transformations, a state of becoming, not of being. Furthermore, here the growth or transformation of love is not merely suggested in general philosophic and symbolic terms but concretely realized. Julius and Lucinde are no longer the only members of the new religion: Julius dreams of his Juliane (probably Caroline), and Lucinde of her Guido. The union which originally comprised only Julius and Lucinde is expanding into a far more comprehensive one.

The final section of the novel, "Dalliance of the Imagination," represents both a summation of Julius's growth and an indication of further transformations. It also, as the title indicates, reasserts the importance of the imagination—the imagination which has created this novel—as a kind of ultimate weapon for achieving union with nature and the infinite. It is through the imagination that man transforms himself most fully and can see himself finally achieve the fullest awareness of his being and the most complete closeness to nature. In the end, it is the imagination which perceives, unifies, creates, and, through its anointed priest, reveals.

*Lucinde* is a fragment. The novel, as it was first published in 1799, represents only a part of the whole novel Schlegel

intended to write, and indeed only a part of what Schlegel did write. The continuation, as he planned it, was to be primarily in the form of poems with relatively brief connecting prose passages. For various reasons which need not concern us here, Schlegel never brought himself to putting all the pieces of this second part together and publishing it, though he did publish separately many of the poems which he had written for the continuation. The prose passages, however, were not published during his lifetime; more than a century was to pass before Josef Körner brought them once again to light.

*Lucinde,* as is apparent from Schlegel's notebooks and from the novel itself, was intended, even in its projected complete form, to be only a part of a more grandiose plan. This larger plan envisioned the writing of four novels (the immortal Four Novels of the "Allegory of Impudence"), which would incorporate the whole of Schlegel's new religion and philosophy. But, as with almost all of Schlegel's grandiose plans, this one was doomed never to come to fruition. With Schlegel, as with Julius, it seems that the greater his plans, the smaller were the chances of their ever being realized.

Still, the form of the projected continuation of the novel and the place the completed *Lucinde* was to occupy in Schlegel's tetralogy do permit us to see the fragmentary novel in proper perspective. *Lucinde,* we can reasonably surmise, was planned as one of the four gospels in Schlegel's new religion; each further gospel was to present another aspect of this religion until, with the last, St. Friedrich's evangelical work would have been accomplished. It is this idea of a progressively more complete revelation which also accounts for the mixture of formal techniques in *Lucinde:* letters, allegories, puns, symbols, fantasies, visions, dialogues, autobiography, prose poetry, and—in the unpublished continuation—rhymed poems. This mixture of forms represents an attempt to reflect formally the profusion and confusion of nature, the wealth of different forms which inhabit the universe. *Lucinde,* in other words, represents an attempt to portray not only thematically but also formally a spiritual and intellectual growth and union. The intellectual and spiritual transformations are accompanied by formal ones. This structural and thematic pattern, of course, matches exactly the one proposed by Schlegel in his fragment 116 with its doctrine of a progressive and universal poetry. And, ironically, in its incompleteness, *Lucinde* matches another part of this doctrine as well: for since it is incomplete, *Lucinde* can never *be* a novel, but must forever be attempting to *become* one.

*Peter Firchow, in an introduction to* Friedrich Schlegel's "Lucinde" and the Fragmants, *translated by Peter Firchow, University of Minnesota Press, 1971, pp. 3-39.*

### Loisa C. Nygaard    (essay date 1980)

[*In the following essay, Nygaard examines the unconventional time-structure in* Lucinde, *contending that, through its unusual form, "the novel represents perhaps the most radical Romantic attempt to create a new mythology."*]

We tend not to expect much from a critic turned author, and Friedrich Schlegel's *Lucinde* seems to fulfill our worst expectations. Since the time of its first appearance, it has been widely attacked and condemned by reader and critic alike, both for the moral reprehensibleness of its content (a bold depiction of sexual love outside the bounds of marriage), and for the aesthetic inadequacies of its unusual form. The list of its detractors is a distinguished one, including Schiller, Hegel, Kierkegaard, Rudolf Haym, Wilhelm Dilthey, Friedrich Gundolf and Georg Lukács. Despite this general consensus as to the literary value of *Lucinde,* however, it has not been consigned to the oblivion many declare it richly deserves: its importance as a document of early Romanticism—and its author's stature as one of Germany's greatest literary critics and theorists—have guaranteed it a continuing audience. Understandably enough, those who have concerned themselves with the novel have tended to study it as a reflection of early Romantic ideas and attitudes, or as an embodiment of its author's theories. The unfortunate result of such a focus of attention has been that the unique form of the novel has been largely neglected, even though it is both inherently interesting, and of theoretical importance as a foreshadowing of developments in the modern novel. It is only in recent years that a few critics, spurred by the obvious affinities between Schlegel's innovative techniques and recent experiments in fiction, have begun to examine more closely the structure of this novel.

K. K. Polheim observes in an article on *Lucinde* that this work is not an isolated phenomenon, but belongs to a tradition in the novel that embraces the works of Cervantes, Diderot and Sterne, and reemerges in the twentieth century with the novels of Mann, Joyce and others. Even within the context of this tradition, however, *Lucinde* represents one of the most radical departures. It is composed of a central narrative section (entitled "Lehrjahre der Männlichkeit"), which is surrounded on each side by six shorter sections made up of a mixture of letters, essays, dreams, reflections and small allegories. The essayistic and reflective elements are not integrated into the plot—indeed, with the exception of the "Lehrjahre" section, the novel has no plot to speak of—nor are they simply presented as reflections of the hero upon his own experiences. They tend to take on independent status, and even come to dominate the discourse of the novel. Another striking characteristic of this work is that, again with the exception of the "Lehrjahre der Männlichkeit", the narrative follows no discernable type of chronological ordering. Since this peculiar feature lies at the root of most of *Lucinde*'s deviations from novelistic conventions accepted in its day, it provides an excellent starting point for a study of the form of this work.

The absence of a conventional temporal structure becomes evident upon even the most cursory examination of *Lucinde.* With the continuing exception of the "Lehrjahre" section, there is no clear order among events in the novel. In fact, the sequence of events is so vague and jumbled that there is no good reason why the young "Wilhelmine" of the third chapter ("Charakteristik der kleinen Wilhelmine") could not be the child promised to Julius and Lucinde in the ninth. Within the narrative itself there are frequent and apparently random shifts between past and present tense; and even where the tense remains constant, the narrator's temporal perspective on events often

changes. In her discussion of *Lucinde* in a book on the structure of the Romantic novel, Esther Hudgins gives an excellent description of the confusion these shifts create at the beginning of the novel:

> Das Buch scheint in gut epischer Tradition in der Mitte, mit einem Brief an die Geliebte, anzufangen. Die Zeitbestimmung wird aber sofort schwankend, da die als Erinnerung erscheinende Verbindung mit der Geliebten plötzlich als 'schöner Traum', der noch in der Zukunft zu realisieren ist, bezeichnet wird. Da in der erklärenden Nachschrift zu dem einleitenden 'Gemisch von den verschiedentsten Erinnerungen und Sehnsuchten' die Berichtform zum Präsens übergeht, erscheint hier die Erzählgegenwart erreicht. Zu Beginn des zweiten Teils des Eingangskapitels wird diese Bestimmung aber wieder unsicher, da der Erzähler den vorausgegangenen Briefteil als ein unterbrochenes Selbstgespräch bestimmt, dessen Fortsetzung den genauen Plan zur Geschichte bereits einschloß. Es muß sich, demnach, im Widerspruch zu der Einleitung, doch um einen Rückblick handeln. [*Nicht—Epische Strokturen des Romantuschen Romans,* 1975]

In the face of so much flux and ambiguity, we must assume that Schlegel deliberately set out to confuse his readers, and this is exactly the conclusion Hudgins arrives at: "die Absicht ist offenbar: durch diese komplizierte Verwirrung die Zeitorientierung des Lesers unmöglich zu machen".

What possible justification could exist for such a deliberate obfuscation of temporal sequence? The narrator of the novel himself offers a partial explanation of his narrative technique:

> Für mich und für diese Schrift, für meine Liebe zu ihr und für ihre Bildung in sich, ist aber kein Zweck zweckmäßiger, als der, daß ich gleich anfangs das was wir Ordnung nennen vernichte, weit von ihr entferne und mir das Recht einer reizenden Verwirrung deutlich zueigne und durch die Tat behaupte. Dies ist um so nötiger, da der Stoff, den unser Leben und Lieben meinem Geiste und meiner Feder gibt, so unaufhaltsam progressiv und so unbiegsam systematisch ist. Wäre es nun auch die Form, so würde dieser in seiner Art einzige Brief dadurch eine unerträgliche Einheit und Einerleiheit erhalten und nicht mehr können, was er doch will und soll: das schönste Chaos von erhabnen Harmonien und interessanten Genüssen nachbilden und ergänzen.

But this "explanation" is itself in need of interpretation. The narrator seems to be making the paradoxical statement that *because* the substance of his life is "progressiv", temporally ordered, the form of his work must be chaotic. He is clearly asserting his freedom from the laws of external reality, the laws of succession and causality, but to what end? H. A. Korff [in *Geist der Goethezeit,* 1940] concluded that Schlegel's main purpose was to "épater le bourgeois". Given Schlegel's iconoclasic tendencies as a young man, this answer undoubtedly holds a lot of truth, but one would like to think there was more behind the author's innovative approach than a desire to shock.

Perhaps we can gain a more satisfying understanding of the temporal form of *Lucinde* if we consider the attitude toward time reflected in the narrative itself. That time in its broadest sense is indeed an important concern of the narrator's is a fact easily overlooked, since he seldom refers explicitly to "time" as such. He is not concerned with time in the abstract, as a successive flow of discrete instants, or with time as measured by the clock. Instead, he is addressing himself to the problems time and change create in the lives of men, and to the ways these problems can be resolved, the amorphous flow of events ordered and fashioned into a coherent whole. Though this complex of issues is a familiar one, no term exists that defines it precisely. It goes beyond our usual conception of "time", and in many ways reflects the kinds of problems confronted on a larger scale in the study of human history—problems such as how to organize events and how to go about establishing connections between them. However, because the narrator of this novel is dealing with these issues on an intimate and personal level, far removed from the vast arena conjured up by the word "history", the more flexible term "time" seems to be a better designation for this thematic complex in the novel.

The narrator's attitude toward time (in this broad sense) is most clearly delineated in the section that Schlegel himself referred to as "der historische Teil", in the "Lehrjahre der Männlichkeit". The "Lehrjahre" describe the progression of the hero Julius from a state of Romantic "Zerrissenheit" to a mature acceptance of life and its responsibilities. At the opening, the hero's "Zerrissenheit", and the confusion and unhappiness it entails, are to a large extent the result of his inability to deal with the flow of time in his life. He has no overview over his experiences, no sense of the necessary interrelationships between past, present, and future. A gambler, he is willing to risk his future well-being on the turn of a card. He has no conception of the natural development of events, but expects "in jedem Augenblick, es müsse ihm etwas Außerordentliches begegnen". Memories from the past seem just as real to him as the present. The narrator emphasizes his hero's total lack of any sense of continuity among the events and elements of his life when he remarks:

> alles was er liebte und mit Liebe dachte, war abgerissen und einzeln. Sein Dasein war in seiner Fantasie eine Masse von Bruchstücken ohne Zusammenhang; jedes für sich Eins und Alles, und das andre was in der Wirklichkeit daneben stand und damit verbunden war, für ihn gleichgültig und so gut wie gar nicht vorhanden.

Time for Julius is a destructive, divisive element which separates his life into discrete blocks having no meaningful relationship to each other. Because his life has no goal or direction, because he can perceive no purpose or underlying pattern to his existence, he has no way of coming to terms with the fragmentary nature of his own experience. Nevertheless, he tries again and again to find some comfortable mode of existence in time, some sort of compromise solution to the problems it presents. Each successive state in his development reflects a stage in this process, as a brief look at the overall pattern of the "Lehrjahre" will reveal.

Julius's first attempt to resolve the tensions created in his life by time and change follows a predictable and familiar pattern: he tries to flee back into the past, to return to the happy time of childhood when he was whole and free from his current tensions and anxieties. He tries to effect this return through his love for a very young girl, a "Jugendfreundin": "Er gedachte an ein edles Mädchen, mit dem er in ruhigen glücklichen Zeiten der frischen Jugend aus reiner kindlicher Zuneigung freundlich und fröhlich getändelt hatte.. Daß sie kaum reif und noch an der Grenze der Kindheit war, reizte sein Verlangen nur um so unwiderstehlicher." This attempt to recapture the past, like all such attempts, naturally fails. Julius decides to leave his native city forever, symbolically turning his back upon his past and everything it represents.

The nature of his next attempt to come to terms with time is also reflected in his relationship with a woman, in this case a courtesan who calls herself "Lisette". She, like himself, has turned her back on the past, and lives only for the present and future. The narrator tells us: "Sie schien ganz sorgenlos nur in der Gegenwart zu leben und war doch immer auf die Zukunft bedacht"—a statement from which any mention of the past is notably absent. Lisette is so alienated from her own past that whenever she talks about it, she always refers to herself in the third person: "Auch wenn sie erzählte, nannte sie sich nur Lisette, und sagte oft, wenn sie schreiben könnte, wollte sie ihre eigne Geschichte schreiben, aber so als ob es ein andrer wäre." She has no appreciation for the time-arts, literature and music, but has a passionate interest in the atemporal arts of sculpture and painting. Because of her ability to cut herself off from the past, to continually start over, she maintains a certain naiveté even in the midst of her depravity. But her love for Julius is her downfall: it is a complete experience that involves her whole being, and reminds her of her youth and lost innocence. When Julius deserts her, her feelings of guilt and worthlessness overwhelm her, and she commits suicide. Thus the past proves inescapable.

After this experience, Julius understandably enough gives up women, and confines himself to male friendships. This period of life is restless and unproductive. He has ceased in his attempts to find any sort of coherence among his experiences and, as the narrator tells us, lives only for the present moment:

> .. die Wut der Unbefriedigung zerstückte seine Erinnerung, er hatte nie weniger eine Ansicht vom Ganzen seines Ich. Er lebte nur in der *Gegenwart,* an der er mit durstigen Lippen hing, und vertiefte sich ohne Ende in jeden unendlich kleinen und doch unergründlichen Teil der ungeheuren Zeit, als müsse es nun in diesem endlich zu finden sein, was er schon so lange suche (my emphasis).

At this point, when Julius in on the verge of disintegration, he meets the woman "die seinen Geist zum erstenmal ganz und in der Mitte traf". The various fragmented elements of his existence seem to come together for him: "Die Vergötterung seiner erhabenen Freundin wurde für seinen Geist ein fester Mittelpunkt und Boden einer neuen Welt." However, he still does not manage to achieve an integrated existence in time, for his relationship to her is incomplete. As the wife of a close friend, this woman must forever remain out of his reach, like some unobtainable ideal. Thus, during this period of his life, the hero lives in the past and future, but has no sense of the present, for the central fact of the present remains the nonpossession of this woman:

> Seine Kraft und seine Jugend weihte er der erhabenen künstlerischen Arbeit und Begeisterung. Er vergaß sein Zeitalter und bildete sich nach den Helden der Vorwelt, deren Ruinen er mit Anbetung liebte. Auch für ihn selbst *gab es keine Gegenwart,* denn er lebte nur in der Zukunft und in der Hoffnung, dereinst in ewiges Werk zu vollenden zum Denkmal seiner Tugend und seiner Würde (my emphasis).

Over the years, Julius drifts apart from this woman, though he never forgets her. The next important stage of his career is his relationship to a kindly woman whom he loves as a sister. She offers him the example of a unified and coherent existence in time, one in which there is a close organic connection between past, present and future:

> Alles was sie unternahm, atmete den Geist freundlicher Ordnung, und wie von selbst entwickelte sich die gegenwärtige Tätigkeit allmählich aus der vorigen und bezog sich still auf die künftige. In dieser Anschauung begriff es Julius klar, daß es keine andre Tugend gebe als Konsequenz.

The harmony of her existence finds its source in her warm heart and loving nature. She does not represent "ängstliche Ordnung", but a Romantic synthetic wholeness: the narrator describes her conversation as "eine reizende Verwirrung von einzelnen Einfällen und allgemeiner Teilnahme, von fortgesetzter Aufmerksamkeit und plötzlicher Zerstreuung".

With this example of an ordered existence before him, Julius meets and falls in love with Lucinde, and all the various elements of his existence at last fall together for him. Lucinde means everything to him that his previous love had, and in addition offers him the present enjoyment of a rich sensual relationship. As Julius did for Lisette, Lucinde revives the past for Julius: "Auch er erinnerte sich an die Vergangenheit und sein Leben ward ihm, indem er es ihr erzählte, zum erstenmal zu einer gebildeten Geschichte." A few pages later, the narrator gives a more extended description of the new wholeness Julius has found in his life:

> Wie seine Kunst sich vollendete und ihm von selbst in ihr gelang, was er zuvor durch kein Streben und Arbeiten erringen konnte: so ward ihm auch sein Leben zum Kunstwerk, ohne daß er eigentlich wahrnam, wie es geschah. Es ward Licht in seinem Innern, er sah und übersah alle Massen seines Lebens und den Gliederbau des Ganzen klar und richtig, weil er in der Mitte stand. Er fühlte, daß er diese Einheit nie verlieren könne, das Rätsel seines Daseins war

gelöst, er hatte das Wort gefunden, und alles schien ihm dazu vorherbestimmt und von den frühsten Zeiten darauf angelegt, daß er es in der Liebe finden sollte, zu der er sich aus jugendlichem Unverstand ganz ungeschickt geglaubt hatte.

His love for Lucinde offers him a center from which to organize his experiences. From his present perspective, his past had a goal and purpose: to prepare him for this love. From apparently aimless wandering, these experiences have been transformed into "Lehrjahre". The present moment now has content and value, and he can look with confidence into the future. His life as he now perceives it has unity and structure, like a work of art.

In the course of his "Lehrjahre", Julius has tried out many partial and inadequate solutions to the problems time presented in his life, attempting first to flee into the past, then to live only for the present moment, and finally to forget the present and live in memory of the past and anticipation of the future. But through his love for Lucinde, he at last achieves an integrated existence in time, and henceforth always perceives past, present and future as intimately connected parts of an organic whole. This is evident in the images he uses to refer to time in the sections which precede and succeed the "Lehrjahre der Männlichkeit", all of which describe the period after he has fallen in love with Lucinde. He explains in "Dithyrambische Fantasie über die schönste Situation" that once the development of the universal spirit is finished, and the pattern of history complete, we will see the essential oneness of past and future:

> Was wir ein Leben nennen, ist für den ganzen, ewigen innern Menschen nur ein einziger Gedanke, ein unteilbares Gefühl. Auch für ihn gibts solche Augenblicke des tiefsten und vollsten Bewußtseins, wo ihm alle die Leben einfallen, sich anders mischen und trennen. Wir beide werden noch einst in Einem Geiste anschauen, daß wir Blüten Einer Pflanze oder Blätter Einer Blume sind, und mit Lächeln werden wir dann wissen, daß was wir jetzt nur Hoffnung nennen, eigentlich Erinnerung war.

He describes this same unity in natural images of the succession of the generations in "Zwei Briefe":

> Im endlosen Wechsel neuer Gestalten flicht die bildende Zeit den Kranz der Ewigkeit, und heilig ist der Mensch, den das Glück berührt, daß er Früchte trägt und gesund ist. Wir sind nicht etwa taube Blüten unter den Wesen, die Götter wollen uns nicht ausschließen aus der großen Verkettung aller wirkenden Dinge. . . .

Julius is directly linked to the natural pattern of birth, death and renewal that he here refers to as the substance of eternity through his love for Lucinde and the promise of children their relationship brings.

The organic view of time implied by these images is not peculiar to ***Lucinde,*** but characterizes all of Schlegel's thinking. As Klaus Briegleb remarks in his book on Schlegel's thought [*Ästhetische Sittlichkeit,* 1962]:

> Die philosophische Erfahrung, die Friedrich

Schlegels wissenschaftlicher Maxime zugrundeliegt, sieht Anfang, Gegenwart, und Zukunft . . . der Geschichte im Bilde Einer Wahrheit. Aus der Einheit des Anfangs entfaltet sich die Fülle des Lebens, die heilige Fülle genannt wird, weil sie aus den Wurzeln ihres Ursprungs lebt, auf ihn zurückdeutet.

This same attitude toward time is also found in the work of other early Romantic writers, notably Novalis.

Surprisingly enough, it is in the sections that relate to the period *after* Julius has arrived at a perception of time as an organic continuum that his narrative becomes chaotic and disjointed. The temporal form of these sections does not seem to correspond to the new view of time that informs them. But the chaotic time-structure of these latter sections is not meant to indicate disintegration and confusion—quite the contrary. It is one more sign that the hero perceives time as a unified whole, so that ordinary time distinctions no longer have any significance. Everything flows together for him into a cohesive mass, an extended present that embraces both past and future. This extended present could perhaps best be defined by reference to one of Novalis's fragments:

Die gewöhnliche Gegenwart verknüpft Vergangenheit und Zukunft durch Beschränkung. Es entsteht Kontiguität, durch Erstarrung Krystallisazion. Es giebt aber eine geistige Gegenwart, die beyde durch Auflösung identifizirt, und diese Mischung ist das Element, die Atmosphäre des Dichters.

The whole novel is narrated from the standpoint of this extended present, even the "Lehrjahre" section—for though it describes past events, it describes only those events and those aspects of events which led up to this present and are important from this standpoint. This explains why the "Lehrjahre" section may seem so unsatisfying as narration: the episodes are not fleshed out, not described for their own sake, but are schematically presented in their relationship to the ultimate development of the hero. This section is indeed, as Henriette Herz remarked, more "Romanenextrakt" than "Roman". Thus, the whole of *Lucinde* represents a unique attempt to depict a present moment in novel form: in this work, past and future do not exist in their own right, but only as extensions of this moment. Several features of the novel's narrative technique can be referred to its efforts to portray an extended present. The narrator of *Lucinde* does his best to ensure that we perceive everything (with the exception of the "Lehrjahre") as present and immediate. The vignettes, little allegories and encounters between Julius and Lucinde are described as if they were taking place before our very eyes. He deliberately uses forms—the letter, allegory, essayistic reflection, fictional dialogue—that hover in time, and have no specific time referent. The sense we have that the novel is portraying one extended moment is further strengthened by the frequent recurrence of thematic patterns and motifs, and the continual reversion to previous situations and ideas in essayistic reflections. The narrator himself makes it clear in a letter to Antonio that he is trying to tell a story which concentrates on the present. After

reproaching Antonio for misunderstanding him, he remarks:

Freilich ist meine eigene Nachlässigkeit an allem schuld. Vielleicht war's auch Eigensinn, *daß ich die ganze Gegenwart mit Dir teilen wollte, und Dich über Vergangenheit und Zukunft doch nicht belehrte.* Ich weiß nicht, es widerstand meinem Gefühl, auch hielt ich's für überflüssig, denn ich traute Dir in der Tat unendlich viel Verstand zu (my emphasis).

For the narrator, the story of past and future is "überflüssig" because both are contained in and implied by the story of the present.

The description of the temporal stance of the narrator given in this brief passage contains the key to many of the more unusual characteristics of *Lucinde.* As we have seen, the narrator's substitution of an extended present for a linear time continuum explains the apparently confused time sequence of the novel. It also helps explain the heavy emphasis placed in this work on essayistic and reflective elements. In discussing the novel as genre in *Das Sprachliche Kunstwerk,* Wolfgang Kayser distinguishes between "Vordergrundsgeschehen", the central story in a novel, and "epischer Vorgang", which he himself defines as "die Ausweitung, das Hinstellen der Menschen und Geschehnisse des Vordergrundes in einen weiten gefüllten Raum, in eine größere Welt". A conventional novel gains this epic breadth by weaving together a background of subplots, secondary characters and the like to provide a framework for the main events. The absence of such epic elements in *Lucinde* has frequently been remarked. But a typical epic extension into space and time would have required the narrator of this novel to follow a more normal chronological ordering, and would have abrogated the unique experiment in fiction he is attempting here. The narrator instead creates a broader context for the main action by extending his work into the timeless realm of thought and abstract ideas. The reflections and intellectual speculations that accompany the action in *Lucinde* become the equivalent of the "epischer Vorgang" Kayser describes.

However, in seeking the "epic" qualities of this novel in the reflective and essayistic elements, we are certainly approaching, if not passing beyond, the limits of what could safely be called "epic". The concept of the "epic" inevitably involves extension in time. In avowedly trying to relate the present without at the same time telling the story of past and future, the narrator of this novel is violating the essentially temporal nature of the novel form, and is trying to transcend the boundaries Lessing had laid down between the plastic arts on the one hand and literature and music on the other. Schlegel, who was a great admirer of Lessing's and who was also fascinated by genre theory, was undoubtedly aware of the outrageousness of what he was attempting here. We will have to probe further to discover if there was more to his experiment than a delight in his own iconoclasm.

Though commentators on *Lucinde* have ignored the important passage on the novel's temporal perspective quoted above from Julius's letter to Antonio, and have thus failed to remark the emphasis on the present in the novel, many have sensed a certain timeless quality in the narrative. [Hans] Eichner very perceptively comments [in "Einleitung" to the *Kritische Friedrich Schlegel Ausgabe,* Vol. V, 1967]:

> Wenn Schlegel aber seine Philosophie der Liebe.. in einem Roman darstellen wollte, so konnte es kein Roman der üblichen Art sein. Schlegels Thema war ja keine Liebes*geschichte,* sondern ein Zustand, zu dessen Wesen die Unwandelbarkeit gehört, —kein äußerlicher Vorgang, der erzählt, d. h. chronologisch entfaltet werden konnte, sondern etwas rein Innerliches, das in immer wieder erneuten Ansätzen und Vorstößen gleichsam eingekreist werden mußte. Daher die Form der *Lucinde*. . . .

Esther Hudgins similarly remarks: "Die *Lucinde* ist nicht primär auf die Darstellung einer Begebenheit hin angelegt, sondern nähert sich mit ihren Reflexionen, Träumen und allegorischen Darstellungen oft der Beschreibung eines Bewußtseinszustandes."

As these statements attest, most critics who have noted the atemporality of the narrative have regarded it as an aspect of the novel's concern with mental states and inward experiences, a side-effect of its attempt to portray something "rein Innerliches". It is very tempting to follow the lead of these critics, and to use the novel's apparent subjectivity to explain its unusual approach to temporal order. For the treatment of time in *Lucinde,* though it is far removed from our usual methods of organizing events, recalls the way the human consciousness actually experiences time. The frequent and sudden shifts in the novel from the past to present or future, its close juxtaposition of incidents widely separated in time, could be explained by reference to the mind's freedom to move at will from concern with the present to memory or anticipation, and its ability arbitrarily to link otherwise unrelated incidents. In resorting to such explanations for the form of the novel, we would be working in terms of the familiar distinction between "objective" and "subjective" time, between the rigid linear progression of events in the outside world which can be quantified and measured, and the fluid and malleable flow of events as experienced by the individual consciousness. The narrator of *Lucinde* sometimes seems to be thinking in terms of a similar distinction. He continually emphasizes that his experience of time as an organic unity is an inner experience: it is, for example, "mit dem Auge seines Geistes" that he sees all the various stages of Lucinde's development collapsed in a sequence of atemporal images. In the second of the "Zwei Briefe", he discusses the possible disjunction between a subjective experience of duration and actual time lapse: "Jeder einzeln Atom der ewigen Zeit kann eine Welt von Freude fassen, aber sich auch zu einem unermeßlichen Abgrund von Leiden und Schrecken öffnen." However, when he tries to give more precise definition to this distinction in the very last section of the novel ("Tändeleien der Fantasie"), he does not simply contrast time as it is perceived by the mind with time as it exists in the outside world. Instead, he distinguishes between different internal modes of perceiving time, between the ways different human faculties

define temporal relationships. Only reason makes distinctions between past, present and future: it brings before the spirit "Erinnerung an ehemalige Zwecke oder Aussichten auf künftige", and it is able "den hohlen kalten Täuschungen [past and future] einen Anstrich von Farbe und eine flüchtige Hitze zu geben". Imagination, or "Fantasie", however, embraces all elements of time into a rich and harmonious present:

> Alte wohlbekannte Gefühle tönen aus der Tiefe der Vergangenheit und Zukunft. Leise nur berühren sie den lauschenden Geist und schnell verlieren sie sich wieder in den Hintergrund verstummter Musik und dunkler Liebe. Alles liebt und lebt, klaget und freut sich in schöner Verwirrung.

The temporal order of this novel is clearly not the order of time as perceived by the reason, a progressive flow of discrete instants, but the order of time as perceived by the imagination, an harmonious totality captured in an immediate present. And this imaginative view of time is not just "time as perceived by the individual consciousness" or "subjective time", but represents a whole new way of experiencing and relating to time.

The complex view of time underlying the distinctions the narrator is making here must be attributed largely to the influence of Immanuel Kant. As Schlegel's fragments, notebooks and letters attest, he was very familiar with Kant's writings, though he frequently criticized and perhaps even more often misunderstood them. In his *Kritik der reinen Vernunft,* Kant offered a radical redefinition of the nature of time. He denied that it was an aspect of ultimate reality, a set of relationships among "things in themselves", and instead defined it as a *form* within which the human mind perceives the external world. According to Kant, time cannot be separated from human consciousness and consequently has no "objective" existence:

> Die Zeit ist nicht etwas, was für sich selbst bestünde oder den Dingen als objektive Bestimmung anhinge, mithin übrig bliebe, wenn man von allen subjektiven bedingungen der Anschauung derselben abstrahiert.. Die Zeit ist nichts anders als die Form des innern Sinnes, d. i. des Anschauens unserer selbst und unsers innern Zustandes. Denn die Zeit kann keine Bestimmung äußerer Erscheinungen sein; sie gehöret weder zu einer Gestalt oder Lage u. s. w., dagegen bestimmt sie das Verhältnis der Vorstellungen in unserm innern Zustande.. Die Zeit ist also lediglich eine subjektive Bedingung unserer (menschlichen) Anschauung.. und an sich, außer dem Subjekte, nichts.

Space was likewise defined as an "Anschauungsform", and cause and effect and other similar relations among phenomena as categories used by our consciousness to organize experience.

Though Schlegel was later to object to many aspects of Kant's concept of time, Kant's ideas had a decisive influence on the development of his own thinking. Schlegel and his fellow early Romantics frequently abused and distorted Kant's philosophy, just as they did that of Fichte, Spinoza and any other philosopher to whom they gave their attention, but many of their most interesting ideas grew out of their misinterpretations. Kant's revelation that many phenomena which had formerly been regarded as aspects of external reality were in truth aspects of human consciousness led them to the rather dubious conclusions that the given "Anschauungsformen" were not fixed and immutable, that there were different possible ways of perceiving the world, and that if one could succeed in transforming man's perceptions, one could possibly transform his reality. These assumptions underlie Novalis's famous dictum: "Es liegt nur an der Schwäche unsrer Organe und der Selbstberührung, daß wir uns nicht in einer Feenwelt erblicken." When Schlegel talks about the organs of perception, he makes an even more radical claim: "Die Augen sind der einzige Theil des menschlichen Leibes, die der Mensch sich selbst macht." This statement suggests that we ourselves create the modes in which we perceive the world.

I have indulged in this digression on Kant and his influence because it is in this context that the treatment of time in *Lucinde* becomes most interesting. We observed earlier in regard to the narrator's handling of time that he seemed to be deliberately setting out to confuse his reader. He accomplishes this by working against the reader's conventional expectations of the novel as genre, and by rendering totally useless his usual methods of ordering events. But this destruction of familiar patterns of organization also has a positive aspect: it enables the narrator to go one step further to suggest new ways of establishing relationships among events. Having used his much vaunted "Verwirrungsrecht" to thoroughly bewilder his audience, he can then use the form of his work to restructure their experience of time. Through the temporal form of the novel he can offer them new modes of perceiving time, new "eyes" through which to observe their world.

We can discern the direction in which the author is trying to mold his reader's perception of time if we reconsider the basic characteristics of the temporal form of the novel. The timeless present which the narrator chooses as his temporal medium, his abandonment of a conventional ordering among events, his cavalier treatment of the laws of sequence and distortion of duration—all these characteristics recall qualities of the treatment of time in *myth*. The narrator of *Lucinde* is not content with relating the process through which he found a new coherence among his own experiences in time; the temporal form of his work encourages the reader to discover for himself a new synthetic mode of perceiving time as a unified whole. Thus through the *form* of his work the narrator brings his audience closer to an experience of time which parallels that offered in mythology. In this context it is striking that when Schlegel in his **"Rede über die Mythologie"** explicitly relates mythology to Romantic literature, he does so in terms of the *structure* of the two, and in terms which recall those used in the passage quoted above from *Lucinde* which defines the imaginative concept of time underlying the temporal form of the narrative:

> Da finde ich nun eine große Ähnlichkeit mit jenem großen Witz der romantischen Poesie, der nicht in einzelnen Einfällen, sondern in der Konstruktion des Ganzen sich zeigt, und den

> unser Freund uns schon so oft an den Werken des Cervantes und des Shakespeare entwickelt hat. Ja diese künstlich geordnete Verwirrung, diese reizende Symmetrie von Widersprüchen, dieser, wunderbare ewige Wechsel von Enthusiasmus und Ironie, der selbst in den kleinsten Gliedern des Ganzen lebt, scheinen mir schon selbst eine indirekte Mythologie zu sein.. Denn das ist der Anfang aller Poesie, den Gang und die Gesetze der vernünftig denkenden Vernunft aufzuheben und uns wieder in die schöne Verwirrung der Fantasie, in das ursprüngliche Chaos der menschlichen Natur zu versetzen, für das ich kein schöneres Symbol bis jetzt kenne, als das bunte Gewimmel der alten Götter.

Through the time structure of his novel, the author of *Lucinde* is seeking to recapture the structure of myth, and to encourage the emergence of a new type of consciousness which is capable of perceiving the world as an integrated and complexly interrelated whole.

In his **"Rede über die Mythologie"**, Schlegel asserted that what modern literature most needed was a new mythology—a cry since echoed by many poets and authors:

> Es fehlt, behaupte ich, unsrer Poesie an einem Mittelpunkt, wie es die Mythologie für die der Alten war, und alles Wesentliche, worin die moderne Dichtkunst der antiken nachsteht, läßt sich indie Worte zusammenfassen: Wir haben keine Mythologie. Aber setze ich hinzu, wir sind nahe daran eine zu erhalten, oder vielmehr es wird Zeit, daß wir ernsthaft dazu mitwirken sollen, eine hervorzubringen.

However, critics have agreed that Schlegel's own efforts to produce such a mythology—like similar efforts on the part of his fellow Romantics—were a failure. And anyone who looks closely at the use of mythological patterns and figures in *Lucinde,* at the references to Hercules and the "Sataniken" in "Idylle über den Müßiggang" or to Narcissus and Ganymede in "Metamorphosen", must agree that this novel represents a very inadequate start toward the creation of a new mythology. However, to consider only such references is perhaps to restrict too narrowly one's range of vision. Schlegel observed in the **"Rede"** that there are many ways of reaching the goal of creating a new mythology, and explicitly stated in a later revised version of this essay: "Das Wesentliche der Mythologie aber liegt nicht in den einzelnen Gestalten, Bildern oder Sinnbildern, sondern in der lebendigen Naturanschauung, welche allen diesen zum Grunde liegt." As we have seen, *Lucinde* seeks to evoke this "lebendige Naturanschauung" by reorganizing its audience's experience of reality. Thus, the novel represents perhaps the most radical Romantic attempt to create a new mythology, not through its content, by interweaving mythological references or creating new mythological figures, but through its *form,* by recapturing the synthetic perception of reality which for the Romantics was the essence of myth.

*Loisa C. Nygaard, "Time in Friedrich Schlegel's 'Lucinde'," in* Colloquia Germanica, *Vol. 13, No. 4, 1980, pp. 334-49.*

## Raymond Immerwahr    (essay date 1980)

[*In the following essay, Immerwahr discusses Schlegel's philosophy of Greek literature and culture and his ideal of "Classical-Romantic synthesis" as presented in* Uber das Studium der Griechischen Poesie *and the fragments from the periodicals* Athenäum *and* Lyceum.]

The tendency of several generations of scholars to divide Friedrich Schlegel's early critical development into a Classicist period from 1794 through 1796 and a Romantic period beginning in 1797 may be traced partly to the edition which they used, partly to the writings upon which they concentrated. Jacob Minor's edition of the critical prose writings up to 1802 is divided into two volumes: The first consists of writings originating over a period from 1794 to 1798 and is devoted to ancient literature. The second volume comprises utterances dating from the period 1796 to 1802 devoted to literature from the Middle Ages to the eighteenth century, a span of cultural history which Schlegel sometimes calls modern but which he regards preeminently as the Romantic Age. It must be pointed out in this connection that Schlegel's early writings use 'romantic' primarily as a concept of cultural history, though not without typological associations, and there is as yet little differentiation of 'romantic' and 'modern.' Later the 'modern' comes to mean those currents of the sixteenth to eighteenth centuries, such as neo-Classicism, Rationalism, and unimaginative realism, which have deviated from the true character of the Romantic Age.

Scholars could disregard the substantial chronological overlap between Minor's two volumes because their attention was concentrated upon polemically charged utterances in which Schlegel seemed first to fight valiantly on one side of a revived *Querelle des anciens et des modernes* and then to leap over to the opposite side. The pro-Classicist polemics are concentrated in Minor's first volume and were all written, or at least begun, between 1794 and 1796. The anti-Classicist pronouncements date from 1797; their arguments for the literature of the Romantic Age set the tone for the great programmatic manifestoes of the *Athenäum* (1798-1800), that journal published by Friedrich and August Wilhelm Schlegel which erected the platform of the German Romantic Movement. The purport of the documents on which attention was concentrated in the first volume of Minor's edition seemed to be the establishment of ancient classicism as a normative model for all ages, no matter how hard their author had to work to withstand the attraction he felt for the poetic literature of the Romantic Age. The second volume appeared to acclaim once and for all Romantic literature from Dante to Sterne and Goethe, occasional fond glances back to ancient literature notwithstanding.

The distortion of Schlegel's complex view of ancient and Romantic literature could not be corrected until late in the 1950s, when the new *Kritische Ausgabe* began to appear. The superior completeness of this edition for all periods and aspects of Schlegel's development makes it more difficult to divide Schlegel's most fruitful critical writings into diametrically opposed periods. The new edition has also focused attention on Schlegel's striving for a synthesis of the Classical and the Romantic, which its editor-in-chief,

Ernst Behler, especially pointed out in a separate article. Schlegel's application of Romantic principles to ancient literature had already been recognized in the excellent studies by August Emmersleben and Werner Mettler. This problem is also dealt with in an important contribution by Richard Brinkmann. But Schlegel's intellectual development has been obscured by the tendency of some monographs to explain all its phases in terms of a single formula. Most recently the introduction to Volume VIII of the *Kritische Ausgabe* has demonstrated a dialectic reciprocity throughout Schlegel's critical and philosophical thought between a concentration and cyclical movement which he associates with the Classical and the unlimited expansiveness and progression which he attributes to the Romantic.

I shall attempt here to identify the qualities that Schlegel admired in ancient literature, to clarify his concept of the Classical, and to draw attention to formulations of his ideal of a Classical-Romantic synthesis in representative utterances during the period covered by Minor's two volumes as well as in some later pronouncements. This will enable us to view Schlegel's brief engagement in the controversy over the relative merits of the ancient and the modern from the perspective of his more enduring interests and aspirations.

We must first of all distinguish the writings of Friedrich Schlegel which treat ancient literature for its own sake from those which contrast it with modern literature. The lengthy treatise **"Ueber das Studium der Griechischen Poesie"** (hereafter called **"Studium-Aufsatz"**) falls into the second category. It actually deals more with Romantic than with ancient literature but is concerned precisely with the need of the moderns to study and emulate the ancient Greeks. It had precursors in an essay **"Ueber die Grenzen des Schönen,"** written in 1794, and one **"Vom Wert des Studiums der Griechen und Römer,"** dating from 1795 to 1796. The two essays first named especially projected the discord of Schlegel's own subjective experience upon the cultural history of the entire Christian era, emphasizing in contrast the harmony achieved by the ancient Greeks. Schlegel rests this contrast upon two sets of laws apparently derived from Kant's *Kritik der Urteilskraft* and from such writings of Schiller as *Über Anmut und Würde,* the one set being the natural laws controlling human destiny and the other the laws of man's free will.

There has been much debate over the influence of another treatise by Schiller, *Über naive und sentimentalische Dichtung,* on the polarities of the **"Studium-Aufsatz"** and over the question whether Schiller's concept of the 'sentimental' made Schlegel more receptive to the 'romantic.' Schlegel read Schiller's work with great interest and reported its impact on him in a letter to August Wilhelm written 15 January 1796, immediately after he had sent off his own manuscript to August Wilhelm. Schlegel's treatise argues that among the ancient Greeks the harmony between nature and human volition enabled their culture to develop spontaneously and organically to an ideal realization of this harmony in Sophocles, from which, however, it inexorably declined to the decadence and barbarism of Alexandria and the late Roman Empire. In the post-antique world the human will is at odds with nature. The human intellect struggles to resolve the conflict but cannot reconcile the fullness and vitality of nature with the unity and harmony essential to art, or rather it can only aspire toward a gradual approximation of this ideal. Precisely in this endless process of working toward an ever higher degree of harmony with nature the modern artistic intellect can profitably emulate the ideal briefly consummated in ancient Greece.

This contrast of a rise and fall of culture among the ancients with the slow, uneven, but unlimited advance possible for the moderns remained a permanent feature of Schlegel's critical thought, even though he later abandoned or forgot the Kantian underproppings and drastically modified his concept of emulating the ancient Greeks. The philosophical framework and, even more, the polemical tone of the **"Studium-Aufsatz"** were needed to fight off the increasing fascination that such writers as Dante, Shakespeare, and Goethe were exerting upon Schlegel in 1795 and 1796, when that essay was written. The essay itself, and especially the preface, which was written later, far from being a confident championing of the ancients against the moderns, are an agonized, at times even desperate, effort to reconcile the grandeur of Dante, the beauty, depth, and richness of Shakespeare, and the exciting promise of Goethe, with the ideal of Classical harmony achieved by the Greeks. As Richard Brinkmann puts it, "Von vornherein geht es in dieser Schrift ganz entschieden um die moderne Literatur und bis zum Schluβ grundsätzlich um nichts anderes." In the preface Schlegel does mention the impression made upon him by *Über naive und sentimentalische Dichtung* and struggles even more intensely to justify his interest in Romantic poetry, but he cannot give up the general argument of the body of his essay or its advocacy of the emulation of the ancients by the moderns. Brinkmann calls Schlegel's position in the **"Studium-Aufsatz"** "ein eigentümliches Gemisch von kantischen Gedanken in der Umbildung durch Schiller," incorporating as well ideas derived from Fichte.

When Schlegel discussed Greek literature and culture without direct reference to the moderns, he emphasized not so much an abstract ideal of perfection as qualities and tendencies that he was later to acclaim as Romantic in the programmatic utterances of the *Athenäum* and would try to exemplify in his novel *Lucinde.* Let us consider first the essay **"Vom ästhetischen Werthe der Griechischen Komödie."** It exalts the work of Aristophanes as a rhapsodic hymn to Dionysian joy, a manifestation of exuberant vitality, an expression of the universal love which animates all life. As regards form, Schlegel emphasizes the freedom of Aristophanic comedy from all rules and limitations, its control by caprice and whimsy, and its mischievous transgression of the limits of decorum, plausibility, and theatrical illusion. Aristophanes is mentioned favorably several times in the *Athenäum*. The private Paris-Cologne lectures of 1803-1804 and the public Vienna lectures of 1812 present the same viewpoint from a more scholarly perspective, emphasizing the local cultural and social background, the relation of Aristophanic to the lost Doric comedies, the formal function of the parabasis, and especially, as in the case of the *Athenäum* references, Aristo-

phanic wit. In this way Aristophanes is brought closer to Shakespeare and Cervantes, as the latter are discussed in the *Gespräch über die Poesie.* The Paris-Cologne lectures even find Tieck's *Zerbino* comparable to Aristophanic comedy. The concept of an all-pervading vital force expressed in the early essay on Greek comedy was to become the underlying principle of Schlegel's *Gespräch über die Poesie* and indeed of all of his philosophical and religious thought for the remainder of his career. The rejection of dramatic form and illusion anticipates the most radical aphoristic *Fragmente* and some aspects of their concept of irony.

An essay **"Ueber die weiblichen Charaktere in den griechischen Dichtern"** and its more famous sequel of 1797, **"Ueber die Diotima,"** anticipate another central theme of Schlegel's novel *Lucinde,* an ideal of feminine temperament and education and of woman's role in society devoid of sexual bias. The qualities to be emphasized in woman and man alike are the universal human ones, and both sexes should aspire toward a common humanity. The Diotima in question is mentioned in Plato's *Symposium*. She, as well as a number of ancient Greek poetesses and literary characters, are cited as evidence against the belief that woman had a subordinate role in Greek culture generally. Schlegel concedes this, with some qualifications, as far as Athens was concerned but marshals evidence against it for ancient Greek culture elsewhere. His characterization of Plato's Diotima, whom he conjectures to be a member of a Pythagorean female order, is modeled on the contemporary personality of Caroline Böhmer, the later wife of his brother August Wilhelm, a woman to whom he again erects a memorial in a figure of the novel *Lucinde.* The tradition of relating Plato's Diotima to a modern woman admired or loved by a northern European author was begun by Hemsterhuis, who applied this name to the Princess Gallitzin. Although Schlegel applied the name Diotima to Caroline Böhmer in personal correspondence, the reflection of Caroline-Diotima appears in *Lucinde* in two seemingly different figures, one unnamed, one called Juliane. This tradition culminates in Hölderlin's Diotima, Suzette Gontard, in numerous poems and the novel *Hyperion.*

These important essays of Schlegel's early period as well as some other, later studies of Greek literature in the first volume of the Minor edition and elsewhere, which we shall consider a little later, give no support to the notion that the "Classicist" writings of the young Schlegel were at variance with the principles of the *Athenäum* period. We have observed one source of this notion in the tortured argument of the **"Studium-Aufsatz."** The complementary idea that Schlegel turned sharply away from his admiration of ancient literature and his affirmation of the Classical principle in 1797 is based on certain of the **"Kritische Fragmente"** published that year in the *Lyceum.* The extreme example is No. 60: "Alle klassischen Dichtarten in ihrer strengen Reinheit sind jetzt lächerlich." Another, No. 7, directly attacks the one-sidedness of the **"Studium-Aufsatz"** and in doing so might seem to reject the Classical ideal drawn from ancient Greek literature as well. Read carefully, neither of these *Fragmente* deprecates either ancient literature or the classical ideal. The important word in No. 60 is "jetzt." The strict separation of categories associated with (and appropriate for) ancient literature is ridiculously inappropriate for modern literature. No. 7 points to the one-sidedness of the **"Studium-Aufsatz"** and its complete lack of "der uņentbehrlichen Ironie" but can still take pride in that essay's "zuversichtliche Voraussetzung, daβ die Poesie unendlich viel wert sei."

The laborious theoretical argument and polemical tone of the **"Studium-Aufsatz"** and its somewhat impudent repudiation in these two *Fragmente* mark out the gradual development of a crisis in Schlegel's critical values which reached a feverish peak in 1795 and 1796, before these *Fragmente* were written for the *Lyceum*. Their impudent tone is in part in expression of the kind of euphoric relief that is characteristic of early convalescence, in part an element of the new hyperbolic style that Schlegel was to cultivate for the next four years, particularly in the **Athenäum-Fragmente** of 1798. The **"Studium-Aufsatz"** had been an engagement fought, not on one side of the *Querelle des anciens et des modernes,* but on both sides, essentially, as indicated in the quotation above from Richard Brinkmann, a struggle for and against modern literature. These two **Lyceum-Fragmente** do not mean that Schlegel has turned renegade but that he has recognized the futility and senselessness of the conflict. He is now free to justify his admiration for Dante, Boccaccio, Ariosto, Shakespeare, Cervantes, Sterne, Diderot, and Goethe without any sense of disloyalty to Homer, Pindar, Aeschylus, Sophocles, and Aristophanes. He can, moreover, recognize further affinities between ancient and modern literature and give a truly universal and timeless significance to the Classical ideal. The fact that he has in no way turned against ancient literature or the Classical is substantiated by other *Fragmente* in the *Lyceum* series. One of them, No. 84, even supports the positive aspects of the antithesis developed in the **"Studium-Aufsatz:"** "Aus dem, was die Modernen wollen, muβ man lernen, was die Poesie werden soll; aus dem, was die Alten tun, was sie sein muβ."

Even before the publication of these **"Kritische Fragmente,"** Schlegel had begun to apply the term 'klassisch' to modern writers. An earlier issue of the 1797 volume of the *Lyceum* contains his essay on the recently deceased Georg Forster, subtitled "Fragment einer Charakteristik der deutschen Klassiker." As one of these, Forster (who had lost favor for sympathizing with the French Revolution) should be recognized as a benefactor of the German nation. In this essay and the one entitled **"Über Lessing"** appearing in the same issue of the *Lyceum* as the **"Kritische Fragmente,"** the concept 'Classical' is associated with the principle of unending progressive development, which had previously been reserved for the 'Romantic.' "Jeder Pulsschlag seines [Forsters] immer tätigen Wesens strebt *vorwärts.*" Within a few lines *Nathan der Weise* is termed "das Werk [Lessings] . . . welches . . . eigentlich das *klassische* ist" and found to be "vom schwebenden Geist Gottes unverkennbar durchglüht und überhaucht." This is the same spirit that Schlegel had recognized in Aristophanic comedy in 1794; it is that very spirit which "in der romantischen Poesie überall unsichtbar sichtbar schweben [muβ]" according to a central pronouncement of the **Gespräch über die Poesie** published in 1800.

Schlegel's writings from 1798 on contain abundant examples of ancient literature to which he attributes Romantic qualities, modern works which he calls Classical, and formulations of the ideal synthesis. His first contribution to the *Athenäum,* a critical commentary to August Wilhelm Schlegel's translations of three "Elegien aus dem Griechischen," stresses precisely elements common to ancient and romantic poets alike. In a fragmentary elegy by Hermesianax of Colophon (late fourth century B.C.) Friedrich sees that combination of intense passion, tender feeling, and cultivated sensuality that he would shortly try to achieve in his own **Lucinde.** He describes the elegy in terms of polarities familiar to us from his *Fragmente:* It is a "Gemisch von Liebe und Witz, von schmachtender Hingegebenheit und geselliger Besonnenheit." "Es istihm [dem Elegiker] freylich der heiligste Ernst . . . : aber er lächelt dann auch wieder über seinen Gegenstand, über sich selbst, und die an seinem Stoff verübte Willkühr. . . . Er weiβ um seine Kunst, und über sie spottend gefällt er sich doch mit ihr und zeigt sie gern." Here one is especially reminded of Schlegel's eulogy of the irony in Goethe's *Wilhelm Meisters Lehrjahre.* In an elegy by Kallimachos he sees "ein so seltsames Gemisch von Willkühr und Nothwendigkeit, von Zufall und Absicht," particularly suited to this category. The commentary to A. W. Schlegel's translations of "Idyllen aus dem Griechischen," also dating from 1798 but published in 1800 in the third volume of the *Athenäum* (216-32) is in the same spirit. Schlegel attributes to the idylls a unity that is at once "sociable" and "subjective" (like that of the *Athenäum* itself ). In the poet Bion he finds naïveté, roguishness, and a sweet inwardness.

Friedrich Schlegel's closest approach to a consecutive presentation of the organic development of ancient Greek literature prior to the turn of the century, an unfinished **Geschichte der Poesie der Griechen und Römer,** was begun at the time of the **Lyceum-Fragmente** and published in 1798, the year the first volume of the *Athenäum* appeared. The greatest part of this work is devoted to the Homeric epics. Schlegel's evaluation of them is still fresh and illuminating to the lay reader of the twentieth century. In the course of his exposition he defines the 'Classical' in an organic sense, much as in the case of Forster: "Classisch ist ein Gedicht schon, wenn es nur für irgend eine entschiedne Stufe der natürlichen Bildung, . . . das vollkommenste seiner ächten Art ist." But the concept of ancient Classical literature presented here incorporates the mystic, the rapturous, even the orgiastic, as one side of a polarity between orphic mysticism and "gnomic" self-restraint.

Friedrich Schlegel conceived his programmatic journal, the *Athenäum,* as an organic fusion of the work of its several contributors and of artistic and intellectual disciplines, both of which elements he epitomized in the Greek prefix Syn- (Sym-). Such a multifaceted synthesis is, in particular, the animating principle of the long series of *Fragmente* in the first volume, the greater part of which were his own work. Some of his best-known *Fragmente* apply this principle precisely to the concepts of the 'Classical' and the 'Romantic' in association with the theme of irony introduced in the **Lyceum-Fragmente. Athenäum-**

*Fragment 51* defines the naïve as "was bis zur Ironie, oder bis zum steten Wechsel von Selbstschöpfung und Selbstvernichtung natürlich, individuell oder klassisch ist, oder scheint" and concludes with the example of Homer. The most famous *Fragment* of all, No. 116, gives a new meaning to the theme of the **"Studium-Aufsatz,"** that the Classical quality of ancient literature is to serve as an ideal for the endless progression of Romantic poetry: "Sie ist der höchsten und der allseitigsten Bildung fähig; nicht bloß von innen heraus, sondern auch von außen hinein; indem sie jedem, was ein Ganzes in ihren Produkten sein soll, alle Teile ähnlich organisiert, wodurch ihr die Aussicht auf eine grenzenlos wachsende Klassizität eröffnetwird." In other words, Schlegel has transformed the seemingly sharp differentiation of his earlier argument into a complete synthesis. Similarly, No. 149 insists—in express contradiction of Winckelmann—that the discipline of Classical studies must start with a determination "der absoluten Identität des Antiken und Modernen, die war, ist oder sein wird." Precisely because the Classical is "das . . . schlechthin Ewige" (No. 404), Schlegel can acclaim Dante, Shakespeare, and Goethe as "der große Dreiklang der modernen Poesie, der innerste und allerheiligste Kreis unter allen engern und weitern Sphären der kritischen Auswahl der Klassiker der neuern Dichtkunst" (No. 247).

The first contribution presented in the great critical symposium in the third volume of the *Athenäum*, the **Gespräch über die Poesie,** is a historical survey of the **"Epochen der Dichtkunst."** It applies the principle of unified form developing organically out of chaos and several polarities typical of this journal to categories, periods, and individual authors of Greek and Roman literature. On the question of emulating models from ancient literature, this essay affirms the need to trace the continuity of literature and culture from the present back to antiquity but rejects the slavish imitation of ancient models and the application of patterns and rules derived from them that were attempted in the reigns of Augustus in Rome and Louis XIV in France, by the Italian *Cinquecentisti,* and in eighteenth-century England and Germany. The very use of this Italian term implies Schlegel's rejection of the concept of a Renaissance, a revival of Classical antiquity, as advocated particularly by Italian humanists in the sixteenth century. It is because of his rejection of any such *rinascimento* that he avoids the term 'Renaissance' itself. The great artistic and literary creation of the Renaissance is for him simply a continuation, even a flowering, of the Romantic Middle Ages. The sense in which ancient Classicism may properly be emulated by the moderns is explained in the Paris-Cologne lectures of 1803-4. The universality and ideality of ancient Greek literature can never be imitated because it is always inseparably fused with particular characteristics growing out of regional societies and traditions. We can best emulate the ancients, first by being true to our own national and regional traditions, then by adopting their practice of compiling "eine kleine Auswahl der besten Werke unserer eigenen Sprache und Nation" as a model for continuous study. Schlegel is referring to the ancients' own application of the term 'Classical' in a collection of early Greek lyric poetry known as *Delectus Classicorum.* The poems in this collection were not chosen for their "correctness" or flawlessness—the qualities deemed

Classical in the eighteenth century—but for originality, vigor, and genius.

In other writings of the Paris-Cologne period we find examples of the synthesis of Classical and Romantic values in two modern writers: The *Lusiades* of Camoëns is "das einzige was noch neben Homer ein episches Gedicht genannt zu werden verdient" and the only modern work to treat ancient mythology in a romantic spirit. Lessing "wollte die wahrhaft auf Einsicht gegründete Nachbildung und Wiederbelebung [des Altertums] herbeiführen." He therefore directed the attention of his countrymen to the rich treasures of English, Italian, and Spanish literatures as a kind of *Delectus Classicorum* of the modern age.

The lectures and critical writings to which I have just referred date from the period when Friedrich Schlegel was turning toward a Catholic Christian view of the history of culture and the significance of art. During this period as well as after the formal conversion of 1808, his ideal synthesis of the Classical and the Romantic has a new Christian orientation. This introduces a concern for the justification of ancient and Renaissance sensuality in terms of Christian ethics and a pervading reference to a primal divine revelation, obscured but never wholly forgotten in all ancient and Oriental mythology, art, and literature. His

*Friedrich Schleiermacher, prominent theologian and member of the Jena circle.*

description of the early fifteenth-century Martyrdom of Saint Agatha by Del Piombo in the journal *Europa* makes it clear that "die Würde und der große Sinn des klassischen Altertums" is wholly appropriate to a Christian, Romantic work. Where the art and mythology of the ancients and the Renaissance, however sensual, express such a feeling for the dignity of nature as the source of earthly grace and beauty, they reflect an image of that original revelation. Schlegel's need to justify from a Christian standpoint the portrayal of fleshly beauty appears especially urgent in the lengthy additions introduced for the text of the **Sämmtliche Werke** (Wien, 1822-25), dating from late in his Viennese Catholic period. They stress the necessity of the portrayal but add some qualifications regarding the manner in which it is to be accomplished:

> Es kann schwerlich jemand für einen vollendeten Maler gelten, der nicht auch den nackten Körper und die blühende Karnation darzustellen versteht. . . . Nicht mit großen Massen nackter Schönheit soll der Maler seinen Raum anfüllen . . . ; sondern in der blühenden Lieblichkeit, sittsam enthüllter, nur sparsam angebrachter Reize, an weiblichen, kindlichen oder jugendlichen Gestalten, liegt der wahre Zauber der Anmut in Gemälden. . . . Wo es also der Gegenstand erfordert, darf der Maler alles darstellen, was wesentlich zu diesem gehört.

At the pinnacle of ancient Greek culture Schlegel finds sensuality still associated with a feeling for the Divine spirit animating natural phenomena. Only when fleshly beauty came to be prized for its own sake did ancient art and literature sink into decadence. But in Schlegel's eyes even the lascivious sensuality of the late ancient world was no more detrimental to art than the fanatical asceticism of the early Christians. His aesthetic ideal, that "klare besonnene Schönheit" of the Periclean age, is an equilibrium of these two extremes. The dynamic synthesis of the Classic-Romantic polarity is consummated in the tragedies of Sophocles no less than in the epic of Camoëns.

With his new Christian orientation Schlegel becomes more alert to romantic elements in ancient mythology, literature, and culture. Criticizing the attempt to recapture Homeric verse in German hexameters by such translators as J. H. Voss, he points to the sounder example of Medieval romantic poets, who confined themselves to the Homeric content, "der im höchsten Grade romantisch ist." Indeed, under other circumstances and with a differently constituted language, Homer himself might have given it a rhymed Romantic form. The abduction of a princess as the cause of a long war is in conformity to the spirit of a heroic age, "die in so manchen Stücken an die christliche Heldenzeit, und das Rittertum des Mittelalters erinnert." Elsewhere Schlegel conjectures that the pre-Aristophanic comedy of the Dorians may have been more like modern Romantic comedy (e. g., Shakespeare). "Wirklich scheint sie, nach den Fragmenten zu urteilen, mit dem Charakter der Heiterkeit und Freudigkeit etwas sehr Romantisches gehabt zu haben."

Two themes from Schlegel's early "Classicist" phase of 1794-96 which return in the 1812 lectures are the ideal of the dignity and cultural stature of womanhood and the

contrasting principles of ancient cyclical versus modern endlessly progressive development. He no longer attempts to present evidence against the inferior status of woman among the Greeks generally but sees the seclusion and segregation of Greek women as a foreign, "Asiatic" element marring Greek manners and customs and leading to the ultimate decay of the civilization. He does, however, point to the recognition of the natural rights and dignity of women in Sparta, among the Dorians generally, and in the life style of the Pythagoreans. The contrast of cyclical de-

---

### *Athenäum-Fragment No. 116*

Romantic poetry is a progressive, universal poetry. Its aim isn't merely to reunite all the separate species of poetry and put poetry in touch with philosophy and rhetoric. It tries to and should mix and fuse poetry and prose, inspiration and criticism, the poetry of art and the poetry of nature; and make poetry lively and sociable, and life and society poetical; poeticize wit and fill and saturate the forms of art with every kind of good, solid matter for instruction, and animate them with the pulsations of humor. It embraces everything that is purely poetic, from the greatest systems of art, containing within themselves still further systems, to the sigh, the kiss that the poetizing child breathes forth in artless song. It can so lose itself in what it describes that one might believe it exists only to characterize poetical individuals of all sorts; and yet there still is no form so fit for expressing the entire spirit of an author: so that many artists who started out to write only a novel ended up by providing us with a portrait of themselves. It alone can become, like the epic, a mirror of the whole circumambient world, an image of the age. And it can also—more than any other form—hover at the midpoint between the portrayed and the portrayer, free of all real and ideal self-interest, on the wings of poetic reflection, and can raise that reflection again and again to a higher power, can multiply it in an endless succession of mirrors. It is capable of the highest and most variegated refinement, not only from within outwards, but also from without inwards; capable in that it organizes—for everything that seeks a wholeness in its effects—the parts along similar lines, so that it opens up a perspective upon an infinitely increasing classicism. Romantic poetry is in the arts what wit is in philosophy, and what society and sociability, friendship and love are in life. Other kinds of poetry are finished and are now capable of being fully analyzed. The romantic kind of poetry is still in the state of becoming; that, in fact, is its real essence: that it should forever be becoming and never be perfected. It can be exhausted by no theory and only a divinatory criticism would dare try to characterize its ideal. It alone is infinite, just as it alone is free; and it recognizes as its first commandment that the will of the poet can tolerate no law above itself. The romantic kind of poetry is the only one that is more than a kind, that is, as it were, poetry itself: for in a certain sense all poetry is or should be romantic.

*Friedrich Schlegel,* Athenäum-Fragment No. 116, *in* Friedrich Schlegel's *Lucinde* and the Fragments, *trans. by Peter Firchow, 1971.*

velopment and infinite progression appears in a new, Christian Romantic guise. Greek culture has its origins in a Titanic age of wild natural energy and depth and ends in a debilitated rational civilization. It is characterized throughout its course by a nostalgic yearning for the Titanic past. The endlessly progressive course of modern Christian poetry is oriented "vielmehr nach der Zukunft him . . . , so weit dieselbe durch Ahndung des Göttlichen in Sinnbildern erreicht werden mag."

*Raymond Immerwahr, "Classicist Values in the Critical Thought of Friedrich Schlegel," in JEGP, Vol. LXXIX, No. 3, July, 1980, pp. 376-89.*

### Phillipe Lacoue-Labarthe and Jean-Luc Nancy (essay date 1980)

[*In the following essay, Lacoue-Labarthe and Nancy consider Schlegel's attempt to construct a definition of literature and Romanticism in his* Gespräch über die Poesie (Dialogue on Poetry) *and* Athenaeum-Fragment No. 116.]

What then, is the question?

Quite simply, it is *the* question: "What is literature?"

In Romanticism's own terms, and especially in those peculiar to the very well-known [*Athenaeum-Fragment 116*] (on which from all indications, the *Lessons* [by August W. Schlegel] and the *Conversation* [*Gespräch über die Poesie*] are, after all, the commentary) a certain question arises: "What is Romantic poetry?" To be more precise: "What is the Romantic genre?" Consequently, this question is nothing less than what, in condensed form, we called the question of the "literary genre."

In any case, the important thing is that the question be precisely *this* question. That is to say that first of all, the question must persist and be maintained—and obviously, that we must wait for the answer. It does not only mean that Romanticism is, strictly speaking, the locus at which this question appears, nor even that Romanticism inaugurates the era of literature. Nor does it only mean that, as a result, Romanticism can find no other definition than that of the perpetual introversion of the question, "what is Romanticism," or "what is literature?" It means rather that Romanticism, as such, dates literature as its constant auto-implication, and as the ever-repeated asking of its own question. It means therefore that there is and can be no answer either to the Romantic question or to the question of Romanticism. Or at least, that the answer could only be interminably deferred, a constantly deceptive answer which always recalls the question (if only by denying that it is still necessary to ask the question). This is why Romanticism, which comes into being at a given moment, the moment of its question, will always be more than just an "era," or, on the other hand, why, even now, it has not stopped in-completing the era it began. And this is something of which Romanticism was perfectly conscious: "The genre of Romantic poetry is still in the process of becoming; it is its true essence to be always only becoming and never to be capable of completing itself." (*Athenaeum-Fragment 116*: "Die romantische Dichtart ist noch im

Werden; ja das ist ihr eigentliches Wesen, daβ sie ewig nur werden, nie vollendet sein kann.")

Romanticism finds itself in an impossible situation where it cannot answer the very question with which it is confused, or in which it is entirely caught up. This inherent impossibility within Romanticism is, of course, the reason why the question is actually an empty one, and why, under the rubric of Romanticism or of literature (or of "Poetry," "*Dichtung*," "Art," "Religion," etc.), the question only comes to bear on something indistinct and indeterminate, something that indefinitely recedes as one gets closer to it. It is something susceptible to being called (almost) any name, but not able to tolerate any one of these names: it is an unnameable thing without shape or form—in the end, this something is "nothing." Romanticism (literature) is that which has no essence, not even in its inessentiality. And this, after all, is perhaps the reason why the question is never really asked, or else, why it is asked an incalculable number of times—and why the Romantic texts, in their fragmentation or even in their dispersion, are only the interminable answer (always approximate, neither here nor there) to the question that is really unformable, *i. e.,* always too quickly, too lightly and too easily formulated, just as if the "thing" worked all by itself.

Moveover, neither the fragments (for "form"), nor religion, for example (for "contents"), unless it be *vice versa,* could adequately answer or ask the question of literature (of Romanticism), since, in any case, all of these only came to be by removing what they had sought to enclose; or, to state it another way, they were only the *Darstellung* of what was refused to every presentation in itself, in the exact ratio of its will to appear. "Literature" did not start to devote itself just yesterday to swerving from the truth. If one notived that the term "mystical" designated the specular itself for Schlegel, it remains nevertheless clear that, quite understandably, he signalled thereby the negative theology of Jacob Boehme. This was necessary then, as it will always be, if one dares to say "another turn." And in many ways, this is what the *Conversation* represents here.

There are two reasons for this, the first one being, of course, the fact that the *Conversation,* once again, seems to attack the question head on. It has to do quite openly with "poetry" (literature); of all the texts that appeared in the *Athenaeum,* it is the only essay of any depth devoted to poetry. Or at least, it is the most ambitious of them. Most importantly, it is auto-referential by its own method of exposition, its *Darstellung:* it is a dialogue, and that fact alone is sufficient to bring to the fore the same question of literature, brought into play here until the time that it becomes witness to its own impossibility. But we know all too well that this question will never be brought into play except by means of the "formalist" inversion, by the endless interreflection (*miseen-abyme*) that is inseparably specular and speculative. And it is not quite certain that, in this interreflection, the question is always capable of losing that very thing (what thing?) it claimed was the question.

But here it is necessary to de-compose.

And to note, first of all, that the dialogue, no more than the letter or the aphorism, is not a stranger to fragmentation. Moreover, it will be recalled that this was unequivocally announced in **Athenaeum-Fragment 77**: "A dialogue is a chain or a crown of fragments. An exchange of letters is a dialogue on a greater scale, and memorabilia are a system of fragments." ("Ein Dialog ist eine Kette, oder ein Kranz von Fragmenten. Ein Briefwechsel ist ein Dialog in vergrössertem Maβstabe, und Memorabilien sind ein System von Fragmente.") We have spoken of the "necessity of fragmentation." The words could not be more appropriate when they refer to the **Ideas** and to the **Letter to Dorothea.**

On the whole, Friedrich never yielded one bit on this early demand of Romanticism. If we may make a conjecture, he would even rather have "increased" its role (—think, for example, of the fact that the **Conversation** itself does not fail to contain a letter). As we shall see momentarily, this is doubtless the explanation for the rather singular fashion in which he conceives and creates dialogue, not at all comparable to that of August (who had strongly encouraged him along this line), nor to that of Novalis (whom Friedrich in turn, with his usual strategy, had more or less encouraged to follow the same path).

The essentially fragmentary nature of the dialogue has at least one consequence (among many others which we cannot examine here): the dialogue, no more than the fragment, does not properly constitute a genre. This is the reason why, in fact, the dialogue, like the fragment, is a privileged battlefield for the question of genre as such. But let us not be too hasty.

The fact that the dialogue is not a genre means first of all (by means of an equivalency to which we are already accustomed) not that the dialogue lacks something vis-á-vis genre, but rather that it can, by definition, contain all genres. The dialogue is the "non-genre," or the "genre" that is a mixture of genres. The dialogue thus takes us back not only to its own origin (*i. e.,* for Schlegel, a Platonic one), but also to the Roman satire, and, in general, to all the late literature of the Alexandrine era in which all the forms of ancient poetry, including philosophy, of course, came together, reflecting each other, thereby fulfilling themselves. From this fact is also issued the very tight link forged between dialogue (and the fragment as well, but in a more immediate manner for the former) and the spirit of society (the social, the urban[e]), the *Witz,* great culture, popularity, lively intellectualism, virtuosity, etc.: in short, all those values and qualities that Romanticism took from the tradition of the Enlightenment and from English or French moral philosophy, qualities which, by the way, the dialogue had not failed preferentially to cultivate.

We are now in well-charted territory. This also explains how the dialogue, by perpetuating the necessity of fragmentation, allows for the appearance of several contradictions, which no genre (or "genre") theretofore used by Schlegel in the *Athenaeum* had permitted. In distinction from the letter in particular, which was based quite emphatically on the opposition between writing and speech (that is to say as well, as we have mentioned, between mas-

culinity and femininity), and which, because of that, carried to its most acute point the problem of popularity. The dialogue (and we are not twisting things around in order to state matters in this fashion) is actually in the position of a relief (*relève*) inasmuch as, in the **Conversation,** it is explicitly given as the transcription (a more or less exact one, to which point we shall return) of real conversations. Moreover, to see women, in fact, oppose the spontaneous practice of simple conversation (though it be brilliant) and call rather for reports, that is, for the reading of written texts, is not one of the lesser paradoxes of this text. This exchange of roles is revealing as well, and we shall soon see, in the most minute fictional creation of the **Conversation,** that the male protagonists' observation of this female injunction allows the dialogue's author to realize the wish he had previously expressed in the **Letter to Dorothea,** and to write, by mixing styles and genres (thus including the "letter" itself ) these little essays whose number he hoped to increase. He no longer feared the proliferation of "projects" in which the rapid change of subject inherent in a lively conversation was cause for worry, and which essays were a necessary step to be taken on the road to true popularity. In this way, the dialogue, once and for all, attained the position of what we have called the "moral genre of the fragment," and, if it does not wholly fulfill this (we shall see why), it actually only misses the mark by very little. From this point on, the reader is not astonished when, under the rubric of "didascalic genre," or, what comes to the same thing, under the rubric of the "reciprocal transfers between poetry and philosophy,"he finds that one of the reports especially insists on the gnomic aphorisms (and the philosophical dialogues). Nor is he astonished when he finds that one of its substitutes (in this case, the "letter") refers, with the intercalation of Rousseau, to the tradition of the confession, or to that of "subjective literature" in general. The dialogue is, above all, the "genre of the Subject."

And paradoxically, this brings the dialogue back to its origin, that is to say, to Plato. In fact, all the themes that we have briefly outlined above interweave and intersect around what fragment 42 of the *Lyceum* calls "the exalted urbanity of the Socratic muse" ("die erhabne Urbanität der sokratischen Muse"). For modern metaphysics, it follows once again that Socrates (the person and the character) has always represented the projected incarnation or prototype of the Subject itself. For Schlegel, at least, the reason is that Socrates (*i. e.,* Plato's Socrates; the Socrates in Plato's works) is, in a wholly privileged way, what could be termed the ironic subject; in other words, Socrates is the locus at which the very exchange that defines irony ("logical beauty," [*"logische Schönheit"*] according to **Lyceum 42**) operates both figuratively and in practice. This is the exchange of form and truth, or, in what amounts to the same thing, of poetry and philosophy. Socrates is thus made the subject "genre" whereby—and wherein—literature begins (and begins with all the power of reflection, because irony is that as well: the very power of infinite reflection or reflexivity, which is another way of saying specularity). In a rigorous argument, Socrates would thus be called the formal or figurative Subject (the exemplary Subject) and would thereby be considered to be the eponymous "genre" of literature, that is, philosophy.

Consequently, this is a "genre" beyond all genres, including a theory of this very "beyond": in other words, it is a general theory of genres, and of itself as well.

It is precisely at this point that the novel is called into question.

But it is necessary to be patient a little longer in order to unfold these matters in a methodical fashion, hoping of course that they are in fact unfoldable. There are actually three elements that are put into play; to put it efficaciously: the name, the author, the reflection. This in turn supposes three questions: that of genre, of subject, and finally of theory, questions which are inextricably linked with one another. As is always the case in Romanticism, there is no privileged position that might afford a bird's eye view; there is no fixed point (*ancrage*) beginning at which one might categorize (*arrimer*); and thus arrange, if not organize, a system. This is the reason why fragment 42 of the *Lyceum,* always in the name of irony, proffers the dialogue as a pure and simple substitute for the system. "Wherever people philosophize, not only in a systematic fashion, but also in either oral or written dialogues, irony must be both demanded and used" (". . . denn überall wo in mündlichen oder geschriebenen Gesprächen, und nur nicht ganz systematisch philosophiert, soll man Ironie leisten und fordern . . .").

However, in order to see a bit more clearly, ironically or not, one must resolutely begin with this platitude: the **Conversation,** deliberately (it re-marks on this at least twice) takes the Platonic dialogue as a model. And it is not just any dialogue, but rather the one which, more than any other, by its agonistic nature, connotes the social: that is to say, the *Symposium.* This does not mean, of course, that the **Conversation** presupposes a fictional symposium. Unlike Hemsterhuis, for example, who pushed the cult of genre (or of "genre") to the point at which he claimed to have been able to retranscribe a Platonic dialogue that he had miraculously "discovered," Schlegel only copied the model's structure, that of a dialogue with intercalated reports or "discourses," in an appropriate format. More precisely, as we shall soon understand, the only thing that interests him is the complexity of the structure of something like the *Symposium:* that is to say, that, the question is not at all of a dialogue, but rather of a story including, or recalling, a dialogue, which in turn, contains intercalated discourses.

We know that, since antiquity, this type of structure has been the reason for the true originality of the Platonic mode of writing. It is this structure as well that we in fact find in varying degrees of complexity in most of the major dialogues of Plato, from the *Republic* to the *Sophist,* and including the *Theaetetus.* We know too that this very structure was not only "reflected" on and condemned by Plato in the *Republic* (in the light of the epic structure, and under the name, if name it be, of a mixed diegesis, that is to say, of a mixture of pure story and of "mimetic" or dramatic form). But also it is this structure which proved to be of great consternation to Aristotle in his attempt at creating a taxonomy in the *Poetics.* This was so much the case that he was forced to yield and leave a blank, or anonymous space—for lack of a common term, a concept lacking for a single genre (between prose and poetry, according to Diogenes Laertius), in which he could have placed the mimes of Sophon and Xenarch, the *Sokratikoi Logoi,* and didactic poems, such as those of Empedocles. Added to that and thereby giving justice to the inventor of this "art without a name" is the fact that Plato's condemnation of "genre" (or the "self-criticism," as it were, of Plato) devolved upon the general putting into question (*mise-en-cause*) of mimesis, that is to say, as far as writing is concerned, the putting into question of "apocryptia," of the dissimulation and the dispersion of the author (or of the subject of discourse) behind the figures (characters or narrators) of dialogical narration. For Schlegel, this mimetic power had always been the lot (or appanage) of the genius, and particularly, of the great writer. We therefore understand that, in the aftermath of the Greeks that Romanticism would wish itself to be, the Platonic dialogue appears as the very model of the union of the poetic and of the philosophical, and consequently, as the original matrix of the *novel,* that is, of that thing for which the Moderns had finally found a name.

> **Lyceum 26:** "Novels are the Socratic dialogues of our time." ("Die Romane sind die sokratischen Dialoge unserer Zeit.")
>
> **Athenaeum 252:** "A philosophy of poetry in general . . . would hover between a unification and separation of philosophy and poetry, of praxis and poetry, of poetry in general and the various genres and species. . . . A philosophy of the novel, whose first foundations are seen in Plato's political theory, would be the keystone . . ." ("Eine philosophie der Poesie überhaupt . . . würde zwischen Vereinigung und Trennung der Philosophie und der Poesie, der Praxis und der Poesie, der Poesie überhaupt und der Gattungen und Arten schweben. . . . Eine Philosophie des Romans, deren erste Grundlinien Platos politische Kunstlehre enthält, wäre der Schluβstein.")

This is actually what the **Conversation** proposes.

Or at least, it is what allows for the explanation of its own *Darstellung,* or, in other words, its own method of fictional creation.

Irony, of course, is both its rule and its principle.

First of all, that which constitutes order in the **Conversation,** or, in other terms, the fiction-making (*mise-en-fiction*)—in order not to say incorrectly, the staging (*mise-en-scène*)—is ironic in a strict sense, and down to the smallest detail. Here it would be necessary to take the time to dissect carefully the "fabrication" of the text. Failing that, we shall be satisfied to point out two major characteristics, which are, by the way, practically inseparable.

The first one is obviously (if we do not forget that we are still in the realm of the "necessity of fragmentation") the reunion, as if "through the looking glass," of the group itself, and, as if by mere chance, in its most "critical" phase—that is to say, the phase that, in the fall of 1799, began with the last great meeting at Jena, where all the members of the "alliance," except Schleiermacher, had a reunion. In fact, many people have spoken a bit too rashly about the *Conversation,* for it is not very difficult to illuminate the identities of the protagonists of the *Conversation:* the whole *Athenaeum* is there, everyone with his own preoccupations (from the "new mythology" to the "characteristic of Goethe"), his quirks of tongue and mind (particularly evident in the "reports" where Friedrich gives free rein to his genius at pastiche and to his virtuosity). There are the salient features of each one's character or personality (from good humor to guarded caution, from playfulness to rivalry or to quick retorts). And the simple interrelations of everyone within the group show, like an open book, the seeds of the group's impending dissolution. It is doubtless correct to emphasize the fact that, whatever the "realism" of the *Conversation,* it is basically only the author of the text who speaks or gives his theoretical views. That, by the way, is the second major characteristic of this "fiction-making" to which we shall return momentarily. But it is obvious that the latter characteristic does not preclude the former; on the contrary, that is precisely the logic of mimetic behavior where the more the differences (that is to say, the dissimulation) are accentuated, the more the identity is reinforced, and *vice versa.* Schlegel was less aware than any other member of the group of this fact, Schlegel, who had made a career as a virtuoso, and who recognized in this principle (which is, from at least one point of view, the principle of the self-constitution of the Subject) the basis of the power of the novel. . . . That is why it is hardly valid not to see in the two women's roles in the *Conversation*—Amalia and Camilla—Caroline and Dorothea respectively. As for the men's roles, one can see the philosopher of the meeting, and the author of the *Discourse on Mythology,* Schelling, in Ludoviko; in Lothario, whose pseudonym is borrowed from Goethe and who, in this case, represents the poet who always announces a work to come, we see Novalis. In Marcus, the Goethe "specialist" obsessed by the problems of the theater, is Tieck; in Andrea, the philologist who begins the series of reports with his recapitulation of the history of literature (the *Eras of Poetry*), can be seen August. Finally, giving every man his due, in Antonio (which, in *Lucinde,* was Schleiermacher's pseudonym, for he was the one who knew about sailing), we see Friedrich himself, or "himself," whose prestation is at the center of the *Conversation* (this **"Letter on the Novel,"** which is precisely not a report, which was not even supposed to have been divulged, and which actually re-marks, this time on the literary level, all that is at stake in the *Letter to Dorothea*). This prestation, which is a proposition for a "theory of the novel," is actually the keystone of this "philosophy of poetry" that actually determines the extent of the former.

Nevertheless, the **"Letter on the Novel"** does not occupy the center of the text. For that to be the case, it would be necessary, at least if we follow the series of reports, for Marcus's essay on Goethe's styles to have been followed by Lothario's reading of the work, which, from the beginning, he has attempted to create, and for which, at the end, he settles for a repeated promise.

The "theory of the novel" would be the center of the *Conversation,* were it not for the absence of the work—the "poem," the *"Dichtung"* (for at the moment, the genre matters little). In which case, again as a result of irony, the re-mark would be doubly impeccable: first, by the author, or "novelist," insofar as he projects himself and disperses himself in the multiplicity of characters or "personalities" he creates (and we know he does this in order to reassure himself of his power); that would be the second characteristic of the "fiction-making" of which, we spoke earlier. But it would also be the re-mark (and this time a new step is taken, marking a greater degree of complexity in the *Darstellung,* in the broadest sense) of the "fiction-making" itself—that is to say the Platonizing, if not really Platonic, re-mark of the infinite power of introversion that is characteristic of "literary" mimesis.

This, however, is not the case. Certainly, there are allusions to the "fabrication" of the *Conversation* which subtly "reflects" itself (Schlegel is a master in underhanded manipulation, and in any case the Platonic model is the *law*). Just as the *Conversation* would be the transcription of real conversations, in the beginning of the text there is a short passage on the division between truth and fiction; in the same way, the first discussion, during which the rules of play for this modern "symposium" are adopted, is concerned with—and this comes as no surprise—the theater, and precisely with the *theater* (which, according to Plato, was the purely mimetic genre) and not with the novel. Similarly, Lothario's missing work, which places the *Conversation* in a state of disequilibrium, or more precisely, puts it off-center, should have been a tragedy. Here, the power of irony is at a disadvantage. That is to say as well that it is reinforced. For there is nothing in the whole work left to chance or to quick improvisation; for you can't judge a book by its cover.

That nothing is left to chance means exactly that the **"Letter on the Novel"** cannot be at the center of the *Conversation* because the *Conversation is not itself a novel.* To put it another way, borrowing a formula from the self-same **"Letter on the Novel,"** with the proviso that the terms be inverted: only a novel is equal to the task of containing its own reflection and of including the theory of its own "genre." Once more, with the terms in their correct order: there can be no theory of the novel that is not a novel. And neither the *Conversation* nor the **"Letter on the Novel"** contained in it is a novel. But *Lucinde* could very well be a novel, unless, in this game of funhouse mirrors (*cette fausse mise-en-abyme*) which is the ultimate ironic barb, the incomplete aspect of *Lucinde* (upon which the **"Letter"** offers much commentary) is sought and reflected; unless the dialogue is the form of renunciation, the *Darstellung* of the impossibility of self-constitution, and that the parody of Plato (or the multiple pastiche, already present, of the Romantic "style") is the admission of the insufficiency and failure of the work; unless, quite possibly, it is the "out of work quotient" (*l'indice du désoeuvrement*). In which case, beyond, (or rather aside from) the question of literature there would be a sort of uncanny writing secretly at work in this apparatus. But where then would the difference go, and would irony still be able to control such an ob-literation of the mark (*un tel démarquage*)?

This is perhaps the basic reason why the *Conversation* is never quite able to define or delimit the Romantic genre, that is to say, the literary genre—and most certainly not, though we often think in this fashion, in (or like) the novel. This does not mean that the novel is not the "genre" that was obstinately sought for by Romantic theory; the contrary is the case. But it means rather that the inability to be defined or delimited is probably part of the essential nature of this genre. Without a doubt, genre is the completed, differentiated, and identifiable product of an engenderment or of a generation; even in German, where the etymology of the word is completely different, *Gattung* is not unrelated to congregation in general, indeed, to marriage. However, the process of generation or of assembly obviously presupposes interpenetration and confusion; that is to say, a *mixture* (*gattieren,* in German, means "to mix"). This would seem to be precisely what the Romantics sought as the very essence of literature: union, in the satire (another name for mixture) or in the novel (or even in the Platonic dialogue), the union of poetry and philosophy, the confusion of all the genres that had previously been delimited by ancient poetics, the interpenetration of the old and the new, etc. But is that sufficient to define the nature of the mixture? What is, in fact, the nature of the fusion or union? And, all told, what is a genre? Or to be more precise, Genre?

The answer is quite simple and well-known to us besides. Simple and unfathomable: Genre is "more than a genre" ("Die romantische Dichtart ist die einzige, die mehr als Art . . ." *Athenaeum-Fragment 116*). It is an Individual and an organic Whole capable of self-engenderment (*Athenaeum-Fragment 426*); it is a World, the absolute *Organon*. In other words: generation is dissolution (*Auflösung*) in the sense of Kant's intussusception, that is to say, that the idealist step in the properly speculative sense of the term, has in fact been taken. Not only is there dissolution like decomposition or resolution, but also, beyond a simple chemism (again, *Athenaeum-Fragment 426*), there is a dissolution like organicism itself or like the process of auto-formation. This is actually a far cry from being able to delimit a genre, but is completely equivalent to Genre *in toto* (in the absolute), in the dissolution of all limits and the making absolute of all individuality. The literary Genre is Literature itself, the *Literary Absolute* (*L'Absolu littéraire*); it is "true literature," Schlegel would say several years later, that is to say, literature that is not "one genre or another, willing to content itself, as if by whimsy, with a specific formation, but rather that literature is a great totality, with complex connections and organization, which encompasses in its unity many worlds of art—it is a unitary work of art" (". . . so daß nicht etwa nur diese oder jene Gattung, wie es das Glück will, zu einiger Bildung gelangen, sondern daß vielmehr die Literatur selbst ein Großes durchaus zusammenhängendes und gleich organisiertes, in ihrer Einheit viele Kunstwelten umfassendes Ganzes und einiges Kunstwerk sei . . . "). Re-read fragment 116, or look at the *Essence of Criticism:*

> Romantic poetry . . . should not only unite the divers genres of poetry and make poetry, philosophy and rhetoric join together. It intends to, and has to, both mix and meld poetry and prose, genius and criticism, artistic and natural poetry, poetic life and society, poeticize the *Witz,* fill to the brim all the various forms of art with basic cultural materials, and inspire them with flashes of humor. Romantic poetry includes everything poetic from the largest system of art, itself containing other systems, down to the breath or kiss that the child-poet exhales in an artless song. . . . It is more than adequate to the greatest and most universal formation . . . ; for each whole that its products should form, it adopts a similar organization of its parts, and is thereby given to a perspective that allows for a limitless classificatory system. . . . Other poetic genres are complete and can now be fully dissected. . . . Only Romantic poetry is infinite as only it is free. . . . The genre of Romantic poetry is the only one that is more than a genre: it is, in a way, the very art of poetry: in a certain sense, all poetry is or should be Romantic.

> Just as one must look to mythology for the origin and common source of all poetic genres, it is equally true that . . . poetry is the tallest cyme of all, found in the flower from which, once perfect (*sich vollendet*), the spirit of all the arts and sciences is resolved (*sich auflöst*).

It is understandable then, how in this situation, Literature, or Poetry, the "Romantic genre," insofar as the thing exists at all, is always sought for as a kind of "beyond" of literature itself. In actuality, this is what prohibits the *Conversation* from producing the promised concept. The process as such of absolutization or infinitization *exceeds,* in all senses of the word, the theoretical or philosophical power in general of which it is, after all, the fulfillment. The "auto" movement, if it can be called that—auto-formation, auto-organization, auto-dissolution, etc. —is always in a state of excess with itself. In a certain way, this is also what fragment 116 marks: "The genre of Romantic poetry is still in the process of becoming, and it is its proper essence that it is always only becoming, and that it is never capable of completing itself. No theory can exhaust it, and only a clairvoyant sort of criticism could dare to characterize its ideal." ("Die romantische Dichtart ist noch im Werden; ja das ist ihr eigentliches Wesen daß sie ewig nur werden, nie vollendet sein kann. Sie kann durch keine Theorie erschopft werden, und nur eine divinatorische Kritik dürfte es wagen, ihr Ideal charakterisieren zu wollen.").

*Philippe Lacoue-Labarthe and Jean-Luc Nancy, "Genre," in* Glyph 7— Textual Studies—The Strasbourg Colloquium: Genre, *edited by Samuel Weber, The Johns Hopkins University Press, 1980, pp. 1-14.*

### Eric A. Blackall    (essay date 1983)

[*Blackall was an English-born American educator and critic who has written extensively on German literature. In the following essay, he analyzes Schlegel's theory of the novel as formulated in his* Gespräch über die Poesie (Dialogue on Poetry), *and discusses the theory's application to* Lucinde.]

Friedrich Schlegel (1772-1829), the younger of two brothers famous in the annals of criticism, began his literary career with the publication of several essays on Greek poetry, the most important of which, entitled **"Über das Studium der griechischen Poesie"** [**"On the Study of Greek Po-**

etry"], appeared in 1797. This essay contrasts Greek poetry as idealizing and objective with modern poetry, which is individual and characterizing [*charakteristisch*]. On the whole the essay avers that modern poetry is inferior to Greek poetry, but it also testifies to Schlegel's concern with and interest in modern poetry. What was lacking, however, at this early point in his career was a true system of poetics adequate to account for modern poetry. This he worked out in the various notebooks he kept, in the Fragments that he published between 1797 and 1800, and in the ***Gespräch über die Poesie*** [***Dialogue on Poetry***] of 1800.

In order to understand Friedrich Schlegel's pronouncements on the novel as a poetic form, we must first examine his conception of poetry. The central statement is to be found in the 116th of the Fragments that he published in the programmatic critical journal *Das Athenäum,* edited by himself and his brother August Wilhelm, in 1798. Beginning with the definition of romantic poetry as "progressive universal poetry" [*eine progressive Universalpoesie*], Schlegel develops first what he means here by "universal": poetry is to reunite the separate genres and reestablish contact with philosophy and rhetoric, embrace all that is poetic whether artistically articulated or not, combine poetry and prose, enthusiasm and critical stance, and maintain a free equipoise between what is represented and the representing agent, each mirroring the other to a higher and higher power, in mutual and continual reflection. He then explains that by "progressive" he means that poetry is not established as a given, but is and will always be in process of developing itself, can never be completely realized, and cannot be characterized by theory or critically analyzed—only "divinatory criticism" can describe what it is and what it is out after.

In speaking of articulated and unarticulated poetry I am paraphrasing what I believe Schlegel to mean in this passage by the terms *Kunstpoesie* and *Naturpoesie*. Romantic poetry, he says, is to combine both, and he goes on to make a distinction between artistic "systems" and "the sigh, the kiss which a child breathes out in artless song." Schlegel writes "das dichtende Kind," meaning that the child is thereby making poetry. There is, Schlegel said elsewhere, a poetry in all of us. Each of us has his own individual poetry, and it is up to each of us to develop it. More than that, poetry is in all nature. Without this "formless and unconscious poetry in the stirring of plants, the gleaming of light, the smiles of a child, the shimmering blossoms of youth, the glowing love of women, there would be no poetry of words." This *Naturpoesie* is the divine spark within us, and it would seem that Schlegel means by it a striving outward in joyous response to the world around us, and the intimation of the eternal. To be a poet, one must have this sense, which is a kind of religious urge, an individual view or experience of the infinite. "The life and force of poetry consists in going out of oneself, detaching a piece of religion, and then returning with it and making it a part of oneself. It is just the same with philosophy."

This conception of poetry is to be what animates the *Roman,* which word we would normally translate as "novel." Hans Eichner, the distinguished editor of Frie-

drich Schlegel, asserts [in "Friedrich Schlegel's Theory of Romantic Poetry," *PMLA* LXXI, 1956], however, that Schlegel uses the word to mean a work of romantic poetry and not to designate a particular genre. He points out that the word had a somewhat wider connotation in the late eighteenth century, and quotes from a section of Herder's *Humanitätsbriefe,* which says that the representative genre of postclassical poetry was "der Roman," that it originated in the confusion and mixture of genres in the late Middle Ages, and that it was used by Shakespeare to present a great breadth of subject matter and to convey a great expanse of time and place, so that in each of his dramas there was a perfect "philosophical novel." The use of this same form to contain a vast range and variety of material was testified to, said Herder, by the development of the English novel during the eighteenth century. We know that Schlegel read this work on its appearance in 1796, for he reviewed it, albeit perfunctorily and without referring to this passage. Eichner points out that three ideas basic to Schlegel's concept of the *Roman* are present here: its predominant place in modern literature, the central position of Shakespeare in its development, and the designation of variety of content—and of form—as its overriding characteristic.

It is true that Schlegel in various places affirmed that Shakespeare was the link between the modern *Roman* and the Middle Ages, that he termed Dante's *Divine Comedy* a "Roman," and that he made a notation for himself to the effect that Shakespeare's tragedies were a mixture of classical tragedy and *Roman*. His brother August Wilhelm asserted in his famous Berlin lectures of 1803-1804 that all modern drama should be judged on the principle of the *Roman*. But would it not seem that Herder and both the Schlegels were all using the word *Roman* in the manner that we English speakers would use the term "romance"? This makes better sense, both as regards the Middle Ages and with respect to Shakespeare, or Dante—or *Don Quixote,* heralded by Friedrich Schlegel quite early as a seminal work and as the "only completely romantic *Roman.*" It is clear that Schlegel recognized that a romance could be in prose or in verse, or preferably in both. The term could therefore be applied to Ariosto as well as to *Jacques le fataliste* or the plays of Shakespeare which, as he asserted, were either rooted in romances or were romances. And it is used consistently to mean "romance" throughout the Boccaccio essay of 1801, for Schlegel recognized that many early romances were in fact collections of novellas that together made up a romance. His specification of what constituted the form of romance, as distinct from its content, was to be refined progressively, resulting in a broadening out of the concept *Roman* to include novels that would not normally be termed romances (such as Diderot's *La Religieuse*) and in various attempts at a typology of the *Roman*.

When Schlegel made his famous statement "Der Roman ist ein romantisches Buch," he was therefore thinking primarily, it would seem, of the romance rather than the novel—a distinction, as we have noted above, that German is unable to make—but he was also implying that to satisfy the demands of romantic poetry all novels should be romances. He was at the same time distinguishing the novel from other poetic forms by his use of the word "Buch," implying both something to be read (hence not a drama) and something extensive (hence not a poem or a novella). As he himself said, the statement is not so tautological as it might at first sight appear. We should add that it is proscriptive as well as descriptive. The statement occurs in the **"Brief über den Roman"** [**"Letter on the Novel"**], published in the *Athenäum* in 1800 as the third main section of the *Gespräch über die Poesie.* During the preceding three years Schlegel had been consistently preoccupied with a specification of the concept, as his notebooks amply show. Let us therefore first follow the progress of his thinking through these private notebooks before turning to his published statements on the subject, the most important of which are the essay on *Wilhelm Meister* (1798), the **"Brief über den Roman,"** and his Vienna lectures of 1812. In what follows I shall use the word "novel" when Schlegel uses the word *Roman*.

In his earliest surviving notebook, which belongs to the years 1797 and 1798, Schlegel traced the origins of the novel to mixed forms of the later Middle Ages. He also observed that "most novels are just compendia of individuality." The notion of the novel as compendium was to be taken up again in one of his earliest published fragments, which states that "many of the best novels are compendia, encyclopedias of the whole intellectual life of an individual of genius; works of that nature, even though in quite a different form, like [Lessing's drama] *Nathan the Wise,* acquire thereby something of the quality of a novel. And every man who is cultured and self-cultivating has within himself a novel, though he need not express it in writing." It is therefore unnecessary for anyone to write more than one novel, he says—assuming, we would add, that the novel is of this postulated ideal type. We note the stress here on inner life and the individual, rather than on the depiction of outer reality. The novel, he says, again in this earliest notebook, tends naturally toward digressions—especially to what the ancients called *parekbasis,* where the author speaks directly to the reader—or at least the "philosophical" novel does, and he discredits "empirical" novels that depend too exclusively on external plot. In a first attempt at categorization Schlegel distinguishes four types of novels. There are "poetic" novels, either "fantastic" or "sentimental," and "prose" novels, either "philosophical" or "psychological." All of these he calls "imperfect" novels. A perfect novel would presumably be a combination of all four. It should, he said elsewhere, like all poetry, combine the "fantastic," the "sentimental" and the "mimic."

Some explanation of these terms would seem to be desirable before we proceed further, for Schlegel uses them in a very particular sense. By "mimic" he means what we would be more likely to call "mimetic," that is to say "realistic," the representation of the real stuff of the finite world of human experience—persons, events, places, times. By "fantastic" he means the opposite of this; unreal material, fantasy, purely imaginative worlds. By "sentimental" he most definitely does not mean sentimentality in the normal sense, and expressly says so in the **"Brief über den Roman":** he is using this term to mean material in which feeling predominates, real and not affected or ex-

cessive feeling, and "spiritual" rather than sensual feeling. Schiller had used the term *sentimentalisch* to denote poetry of reflection in which the person of the poet is very much present as a constitutive factor. Schlegel uses *sentimental* in the same general sense but specifies it to mean involvement in the sense of a meeting between mind and world that arises from an urge outward, the source of which, as he says in the **"Brief über den Roman,"** is ultimately some form of love.

The "sentimental" novel is characterized as epic in material, elegiac in spirit, and idyllic in form, here taking up Schiller's contrast of elegiac and idyllic in his essay "On Naive and Sentimental Poetry" as two modes of "sentimental" or reflective poetry. By a "philosophical" novel Schlegel means one primarily concerned with a thesis or philosophy, with ideas or philosophies; by a "psychological" novel he means one centrally concerned with character, though also with the interaction of character and events. A "psychological" novel is declared to be essentially analytical, its greatest power residing in its "unshakable coldness." The "fantastic" novel is for the senses and the imagination, the "psychological" novel for the intellect, and the "philosophical" novel for the reason. There should be "no love" in the psychological novel—by which Schlegel probably means none from the author, cold objectivity. Everything is clearly accounted for and worked out in the psychological novel, whereas in the philosophical novel everything should be "boldly touched on, brilliantly flung out [*genialisch hingeworfen*], like lightning and storm—almost caricature—everything extreme and eccentric," in other words not elaborately developed, not integrated into a causal structure, but moving from one flash of an idea to the next. The psychological novel has clear protagonists around which the other characters arrange themselves in graduated importance, but in the philosophical novel there should be no main character and no completely passive ones, for all the characters together make up the novel. There should be interplay of wit in the philosophical novel, says Schlegel. A philosophical novel, he suggested, should always have a dunderhead [*Dummkopf*] and a clown [*Narr*] in it, a dunderhead presumably being one who is unwittingly foolish and a clown one who consciously propagates folly. He seems to be thinking of a sort of philosophical dialogue such as is to be found in several novels of the eighteenth century, and the dialogues of Plato were obviously also very much in his mind, for in one of the earliest published fragments he expressly stated: "Novels are the socratic dialogues of our time. *Savoir vivre* has fled the halls of academic philosophy and taken refuge in this liberal form." The Fragment I have just quoted was published in 1797. In the previous year Schlegel reviewed a famous philosophical novel of the eighteenth century which had just come out in a revised edition, Jacobi's *Woldemar,* a pretentious [and bad] novel that claimed to be dealing with serious ethical topics but did so clumsily and superficially. Schlegel rightly remarked that the book had no philosophical unity despite its claims to philosophic intentions, for its "philosophy" was merely a distillate of Jacobi's own personality, and the characters, situations, and emotions were woefully poorly used to demonstrate any ideas whatsoever.

Schlegel was not satisfied with his nomenclature for the two types of prose novel, and later in the notebooks we find him using "critical" for "psychological" novel, and then using "mimic" and "political" and finally "ethical" as categories of prose novels. It is not always easy to understand the implications of this changing terminology, but by "political novel" he would seem to mean one dealing with the life of a nation, or larger community, whereas the "mimic" novel would be concerned with an individual person's experiences (for instance Don Quixote's) and the "absolute mimic novel" would be biographical. In Dante, he says, the *Inferno* is predominantly mimic, the *Purgatorio* sentimental, and the *Paradiso* fantastic.

The purpose of the ethical novel is to poeticize life [*das Leben zu poetisiren*]. It would therefore seem to be synonymous with his concept of what a romantic novel should be. In one fragment, expressed in mathematical symbols, he draws a distinction between the poetic novel as "ethos taken to the power of infinity" [*unendlich potenziert*], the philosophical novel as "ethos taken to its infinite root" [*unendlich radiziert*], and the ethical novel as "both." Relevant is also this entry in the notebooks: "In the ethical novel the greatest cohesion, flow, no gaps or jumps; conversations, dreams, letters, recollection. Fine loquaciousness. —*Confessions* [presumably Rousseau's] belong to the romantic novel." And this: "In every ethical novel an absolute chaos of character [*ein absolutes Chaos von Charakter*] necessary: but preferably only inward and in all [*besser aber nur innerlich und in allen*]." Faced with such a cryptic utterance as this last, we must never forget that it is a jotting in a notebook and does not represent a considered formulation. Nevertheless it seems to be trying to say something important. Interpretation hings on the two key words *Chaos* and *Charakter*. The former is used by Schlegel (and others of the German Romantics) to denote not muddle but unity, "chaos" in the sense of the chaos of Genesis, prior to the creation of the world and its dichotomies, and to the emergence of consciousness. The "chaos" that the Romantics *sought* was a harking back to a unity lost in the modern world. Another entry in these notebooks describes the form of the desired novel as "a formed, artificial chaos" [*ein gebildetes künstliches Chaos*], artificial in the sense of something constructed by art, formed in art. But what does Schlegel mean by "absolute chaos *of character*"? Is he referring to the general character of the work? Does he mean "character of chaos"? Or is he referring to the characters, the personages in the novel, as the concluding dative plural *in allen* might suggest? If we look through the notebooks, we find that Schlegel uses *Charakter* in both these senses. Leaving aside the possibility that Eichner in his deciphering may have misread *in allem* as *in allen,* which in view of his general meticulousness seems to me unlikely, we are left with the impression that in this particular statement Schlegel has moved from the sense of "general character" to that of "the characters," who of course are part of the general character. The concept of "chaos," as Schlegel understands it, is therefore not incompatible with "cohesion," for it implies a unitary although manifold whole. Digressions and "fine loquaciousness" are part of the cohesion, and Schlegel praises Sterne's loquaciousness as "good because it springs from the endless variety of self-contemplation" [*aus der unendlichen Mannichfaltigkeit der Selbstanschauung*].

Perhaps the best way to get at these distinctions is to look at some of Schlegel's examples, though here again he is not always consistent. But Ariosto's is a "fantastic" romance, Tasso's is "sentimental," *Jacques le fataliste* is a "philosophical" novel, *La Religieuse* a "psychological" one. *The Tempest* and *A Midsummer Night's Dream* are "fantastic," *Romeo and Juliet* and *Hamlet* are "both sentimental and philosophical," but the "philosophical" predominates in *Hamlet* and the "sentimental" in *Romeo and Juliet.* Eventually Schlegel's categorizations in the notebooks seem to reduce themselves to the triadic "fantastic sentimental mimic" as a typology of the novel in which, as Eichner has pointed out, the mimic represents the ideal of fullness of life, the fantastic means the free play of fancy, and the sentimental embodies love. One might add that the mimic and the fantastic represent outer finitude and inner infinitude respectively, and the sentimental a mediating power reaching out and drawing back in, the force of what is called in the **116th Athenäum Fragment** "poetic reflection."

There are in these notebooks various comments on *Wilhelm Meister* which imply that Schlegel thought it was tending toward what a romantic novel should be without completely getting there. He wished for a greater range of style and topics. It provided a "philosophy of the universe," but it was not "mystical" enough, though it was poetic, at least in its form. But the true form of a novel should be "elliptical," he says, if it is to be an "absolute" book and have "mystical" character, "mythological character," "personality." By "elliptical" Schlegel means having two centers. Mysticism was for him a philosophy that, in contrast to empiricism, recognized the existence of the supernatural and infinite, and posited as its basis an Absolute involving a tension out of which a philosophic system was dialectically evolved. The "elliptical" form that Schlegel desired for the novel implies such an opposition within a cohesive whole. Hence the image of the two centers, which probably also implied that a novel should move simultaneously on two planes, one of which should be transcendental. His remark to the effect that *Wilhelm Meister* was not mystical enough would in that case seem to mean that the transcendental dimension was not sufficiently developed to satisfy him completely. These remarks are elaborated further in the *Wilhelm Meister* essay of 1798. For instance the "poetic" nature of the form is there shown to lie in its progressiveness, in which each book of the novel takes up what has been achieved in the previous book and also contains the germ of the following book, so that the whole has progressive "organic" form. The phrase "philosophy of the universe" has been significantly modified to "sense of the universe," for this is obviously not a "philosophical" novel in Schlegel's use of that term. And the novel's cohesion—"no gaps or jumps; conversations, dreams, letters, recollection"—is described as a "magic hovering between forwards and backwards," with the image of the theater predominating (even the Beautiful Soul lives "theatrically," he rightly says), an apprenticeship in learning how to live according to one's nature.

The *Fragmente* published in the *Athenäum,* also in 1798, contain expansions and reformulations of some of the germinal ideas in the notebooks. Schlegel here discredits those novels where everything revolves around a hero who is the author's spoilt darling. The constitution of a novel should definitely be republican, he says. This seems intended to apply to all novels, whereas in the notebooks the point had been made only with regard to "philosophical" novels. He now repeatedly talks of the union of philosophy and poetry in a novel, which may well mean that he was by now moving away from the acceptance of a purely "philosophical" novel. If a novel is to teach anything, he says, the lesson must emerge from the whole, not from individual parts. We can also observe in the ***Athenäum Fragments*** a further development of his notion of *parekbasis,* a development that leads him to the important concept of the arabesque as a mode of romantic form. He admires what he calls the "arabesques" fashioned from old tales in Tieck's *Franz Sternbalds Wanderungen* and considers them an important part of the richness of that truly romantic novel. He also admires its "sense of irony," representing the reflexiveness that he had advocated in the 116th Fragment, to which we referred at the beginning of this chapter. On Jean Paul Richter, perhaps the most famous novelist of the day apart from Goethe, he is ambivalent. He admires his grotesque humor, for this constitutes his poetry. But he also considers the arabesques (or digressions) of *Siebenkäs* "leaden" and the prose of the novel either heavy or sentimental (in the bad sense). He seems to have as yet no understanding of the poetic force of Jean Paul's cohesive discordance and purposeful disjunctiveness. . . . He is, however, feeling his way in these Fragments toward a validation of the grotesque as a poetic mode, or at least as a poetic element, and in this he is working outward from his reading of Jean Paul as he previously worked outward from his reading of Cervantes and *Wilhelm Meister.*

The full florescence of all these germinal ideas is attained in the ***Gespräch über die Poesie,*** published in the *Athenäum* in 1800, and especially in that section of it entitled **"Brief über den Roman."** This is the third of the four main sections of the work, the sections being linked with each other by dialogues between fictive interlocutors. The introduction justifies the dialogue form. Every human being has his own poetry, and each such "poetry" is different from all the others, whereas reason is one and the same in all of us. Reason therefore unites men in their likeness to each other, poetry unites them in their differences. Each of us has a longing to develop his own poetry, and does so by experiencing the poetry of others. This "poetry" means individuality, an innermost power of self-development, connected more with the imagination than with the reason, a "self-made unreason" [*selbstgemachte Unvernunft*], self-expanding from the desire produced by what it has already attained, the primal urge for expansion in man, the desire to embrace more and more of the inexhaustible world of poetry, individuality striving to realize itself by extending beyond itself by its own powers. Poetry is therefore the transcendence of individual bounds by the assertion of individual power, the progressive assimilation of the created "poem" of the universe by our own poetic power. By means of the dialogue form of this work Schlegel aims at presenting the different "poetries" of individuals who can connect because of a common "center" [*Mittelpunkt*], namely poetry itself. For poetry, thus conceived, is born of the spirit of love (in its desire to embrace other poetries) and leads naturally to communion with others. In fact life should be the continuous expansion of one's poetry toward ever greater comprehensiveness, total comprehensiveness being attainable only in death.

The first main section of the dialogue is a contribution read by one of the characters on **"Epochs of Poetry,"** a historical survey from the Greeks to the present, with interesting comments on the mixture of genres in Ariosto and assertion of the prime importance of Cervantes and Shakespeare. This leads to a conversation in which demands for a theoretical delimitation of genres are raised on the one hand and countered on the other by assertions that this is useless, that it does not produce poetry, and that poetry is indivisible. The second "paper" read is addressed to the reasons for the decline of poetry since the times of Shakespeare and Cervantes, attested by the previous speaker, and declares that the reason for this is that modern poetry lacks a center such as mythology provided for the ancients, and hence the modern poet has to create such a center from inside his own work, an individual center and not one shared by the communality. Another solution to the problem would be the creation of a new mythology, which the speaker considers thoroughly possible. From his remarks it is clear that he, and Schlegel, consider mythology to be the organizing of the disparate "chaos" of experience into a meaningful and therefore "harmonious" whole. ("Only that confusion from which a world can spring, is [a true] chaos," Schlegel said elsewhere.) Greek mythology achieved this, and it is apparent that the Romantics have the same aspirations for poetry. This speaker reiterates the point, already made several times by Schlegel, that poetry should fuse with philosophy, especially with idealist philosophy, which was also a search for a center, and with recent natural philosophy or "physics," which was also working toward a "mythological" conception of nature. The difference between the old and the new mythology would be that the latter would proceed from the intellect whereas the former had evolved from the imagination playing on sensory experience. But though its roots would be in idealism, the new mythology should produce a new "realism"—by which he means a new understanding of the real world, of reality as opposed to ideas—and "this new realism, because it is of idealist origin and must float [*schweben*] above idealist ground, so to speak, will manifest itself as poetry which is based on the harmony of ideas and reality." All mythology is the hieroglyphic expression of surrounding nature as transfigured by human imagination and love. It is a securing in terms accessible to our minds and senses of that which otherwise evades the comprehension of our consciousness. It is "all connection and transformation." The "wit" [*Witz*] of romantic poetry—the power that connects and transforms imaginatively—is therefore a sort of indirect mythology. We find it in Cervantes and Shakespeare, and . . .

> Yes indeed, that artfully ordered confusion, the attractive symmetry of contradictions, the wondrous constant alternation of enthusiasm and

irony operating even in the smallest elements of the whole, seem to me to be a sort of indirect mythology. The organization is the same and the arabesque is certainly the oldest, original form of human fancy. Neither such wit nor any mythology can exist without some such original, [which is] primal and unreproducible, essentially indissoluble, in all of whose transformations its original nature and strength shimmer through, and the glint of reversals and dislocations, of the simple and the stupid, is visible in its unreflective depths. For all poetry begins by disrupting the process and laws of rationally thinking reason and transporting us back into the beauteous confusion of fancy, the original chaos of human nature for which I would know of no better symbol so far evolved than the motley throng of the ancient gods.

The speaker then calls for a revivification of this old mythology transfused by the spirit of Spinoza and by the new insights provided by physics. He also advocates the investigation of other mythologies.

Spinoza and physics? The speaker goes on to refer to the "dynamic paradoxes" of physics, meaning presumably its revelation of the polar oppositions and contrary motions in nature. And Spinoza? Presumably because his whole philosophy was based on a concept of substance which was primal, unitary, and eternal, rejecting Descartes's distinction between extended substance, thinking substance, and God, and asserting that all substance was God. Earlier Schlegel had said that it was difficult to understand how one could be a poet and not revere Spinoza because his philosophy embodied the alpha and omega of all fancy [*Fantasie*], the basic ground and general state on which all individual imagination rests and from which it breaks forth separately. His philosophy provided the general foundation for every individual kind of "mysticism," which, as we have seen, is for Schlegel closely allied to poetry. Mysticism, in contrast to empiricism, posited an Absolute, and Spinoza's "God" was of course such an Absolute.

The third main section, the **"Brief über den Roman,"** begins with a defense of the novels of Jean Paul Richter. Charges brought against these were on the one hand that they were muddled and had no perceptible plot, and on the other hand that they were too subjective. The speaker, Antonio, asserts that such combinations of the grotesque and the confessional were the only truly romantic products of an unromantic age, and then proceeds to a spirited defense of Sterne as "arabesque" in form, and of *Jacques le fataliste* as an arabesque without Sterne's "sentimental admixtures" [*sentimentale Beimischungen*]. He vindicates the arabesque as a literary form where the fantastic (or fanciful) can find expression in an age that is not naturally inclined toward the fantastic. If one can appreciate Swift, Sterne, and Diderot, then one is well on the way toward an appreciation of the divine wit and fancy of Ariosto, Cervantes, and Shakespeare. He places Jean Paul above Sterne because his fancy is "sicklier" [*kränklicher*] and therefore weirder and more fantastic. He is much wittier than Sterne, and because of this even his "sentimental aspect" is "lifted above the sphere of English sensibility"

[*durch diesen Vorzug erhebt sich selbst seine Sentimentalität in der Erscheinung über die Sphäre der engländischen Empfindsamkeit*].

There then follows the famous definition of romanticism as "that which portrays a sentimental subject in fantastic form" [*was uns einen sentimentalen Stoff in einer fantastischen Form darstellt*], and Schlegel's explanation, already quoted above, that by "sentimental" he does not mean tearfulness or flabby, comforting moralizing, but that which is imbued with feeling [*Gefühl*] appealing to our minds, not our senses [*nicht ein sinnliches, sondern das geistige*]. The contrast is therefore between real feeling appealing to the mind, and simulated feeling delighting the senses. There is also the contrast between "sentimental," meaning real feeling, and "fantastic," meaning the product of the imagination, the fictive. In a romantic work the two are to merge, for this "sentimental" urge is a form of love, a hieroglyphic of eternal love, a striving from the real toward a realm attainable only in the imagination. "Only imagination [*Fantasie*] can grasp the mystery of this [eternal] love and present it as a mystery, and this mysterious quality is the source of the fantastic in the form of all poetic representation." Since the Infinite reveals itself only indirectly in the reality of the finite world, it is necessarily only to be comprehended by that faculty of the fancy which Schlegel calls "wit" [*Witz*].

Schlegel uses the term *Witz* to designate the faculty of perceiving similarities and of making connections. This was a usage current in the eighteenth century, and is ultimately based on Locke's distinction between wit as the perception of likenesses and judgment as the observation of differences. The Enlightenment was not, however, entirely satisfied with this distinction. It was pointed out by several thinkers, for example by the influential German philosopher Christian Wolff, that judgment was a necessary part of wit, for wit proceeded from a combination of perspicacity and imagination, and was really the discovery of *hidden* likenesses. Schlegel seems to be using the term in this extended sense of establishing connections that normally escape the logical operations of the reason, connections between seemingly disparate and quite unconnected things, connections perceived or fabricated by this faculty of the human mind or spirit. It is a "combinatory" force, divinatory, even prophetic at times, the product of inspiration, emitting flashes of insight, related to genius, and therefore opposed to systematic reasoning. Since the connections established by *Witz* may sometimes be highly personal, even eccentric, the term often has the added connotation of producing something "witty," or being witty, ingeniously or amusingly formulated. In referring to Jean Paul as being wittier than Sterne, Schlegel is using the term in both these senses. One result of this is that in romantic poetry there is not, and cannot be, any greater validity given to visible truth than to fiction or semblance, no poetic distinction between the historically attested and the imaginary. Hence its combination of the confessional or real with the arabesque or imaginary.

The novel is not a specific genre: it is a "romantic book," and should ideally embrace all genres. If a particular novel does not do so, the reason lies in its individual character.

What was best in the best novels so far, was the more or less veiled confessional element, "the fruit of his [the novelist's] experience, the quintessence of his individuality." The "arabesque" element usually only makes itself felt in the endings when "bankrupts regain funds and credit, poor suckers get to eat, pleasant rogues turn honest and fallen women turn virtuous again"—in other words in the contrived fictions with which novels are often brought to a close. It is clear from the tone that Schlegel is not satisfied with these forced finalities: the *Confessions* of Rousseau and Gibbon's *Autobiography,* he says, are better novels than *La Nouvelle Héloïse.*

The final section of the **Gespräch** is an essay comparing the style of Goethe's earlier and later works, praising the progressivity of his production to date and pointing to the centrality of *Faust,* at this time still a fragment, though a published fragment. *Götz von Berlichingen* with its manifold richness and its "formless" form seems to Schlegel less dated than *Werther,* and he notes with approbation the harmonious portrayal of disharmony in *Torquato Tasso* and its mysterious ending, the dissonances presented in *Egmont,* and the progressive nature of *Wilhelm Meister* from an artist-novel to a much broader conception, combining a modern sensibility with antique spirit. All these works are described as if they were novels, and all of them are interpreted romantically.

References to Cervantes are constant throughout the **Gespräch über die Poesie,** and it is clear that *Don Quixote* has become a touchstone for Schlegel in evaluating novels. It was, as he had said, the nearest approximation to his ideal of the romantic novel. It had the self-reflexiveness that he so much desired, for in Part Two the novel "returns into itself, working down to its very depths with unfathomable understanding," creating from within itself a central point of reference during the process of its own evolution. In his Paris lectures of 1803-1804 to the brothers Boisserée he called Cervantes the "most profound, most inventive, most artistic of all novelists," and linked him with Boccaccio as the progenitors of the modern novel, now categorized as "a romantic book . . . in which all forms and genres are mingled and intertwined," a form that makes possible the most manifold complexity, the "primal, most individual and most perfect form of romantic poetry," as exemplified by *all three* of Cervantes's larger works (that is to say, *Don Quixote, Galatea,* and *Persiles*). In the twelfth of the Vienna lectures of 1812 he contrasts the poetic portrayal of life in *Don Quixote* with the prosaic representation of life in later novels. But in no age, he says, is life unfavorable to or unsuitable for poetic presentation. A poet can give new illumination to what seems banal or unpoetic by what Schlegel calls "the higher transformation of things in a magic mirror" in which past, present, and future appear and time becomes the eternal fullness of time. In eighteenth-century France, he remarks in the fourteenth of these lectures, the novel became a favorite vehicle for the expression of ideas and emotions that did not easily fit into "the old forms" of literature. Thus Voltaire, Rousseau, and Diderot each made of the novel something personal to him, and different, Voltaire making it the perfect vehicle for his wit, Rousseau for his own particular rhetoric, and Diderot to indulge his caprice [*Muth-*

*willen*]. The English novelists of the time were more concerned with the prose rendering of events culled from everyday life, and Richardson, for all his gifts, proved that on such lines the novel could not become a poetic form. And Jean Paul, he says in the sixteenth of these lectures, portrayed in his own peculiar way the rich variety of a chaotic and dissonant age, but with wit and feeling and a style that corresponded in its own dissonance and motley colorfulness exactly to the very world that it described. In neither of these two sets of lectures was Schlegel largely concerned with the novel, but what he said there indicates that his concept of what a novel should be had not radically changed from what he had sketched in those early notebooks and developed in the published fragments and the **Gespräch über die Poesie.** The great difference between the notebooks and the **Gespräch** is that in the latter he has abandoned all attempts at a typology of the novel. Another significant development is the greater stress on form, culminating in the concept of the arabesque as the expression of *Witz,* and the reiteration in even stronger terms that a novel should cultivate a mixture of modes and styles to present poetically a fusion of the real and the fanciful, in which the categories of rational observation are displaced and superseded by wider vistas and deeper premonitions, and the stuff of life imaginatively transfigured to capture that eternal, primal unity which our fragmented experience of the finite world reflects, a unity that embraced and contained variety.

In a section of the notebooks headed "Von der Schönheit in der Dichtkunst" [On Beauty in Poetry] Schlegel asserts that beauty has three constituent components: oneness, multiplicity, and wholeness (or: unity, variety, and totality). These, as Eichner has pointed out, are Kantian categories (of quantity), but applied here to the work of art to mean coherence, breadth, and the fusion of finite and infinite. The wholeness of poetry is the expression of a dialectical interplay between unity and variety, the two key concepts of all Schlegel's philosophizing. The search for absolute unity is the predominant characteristic of philosophy, particularly of idealist philosophy which, for instance in Kant, becomes the analysis by the mind of itself. And yet Kant had revealed the limitations of the reason and denied the possibility of our knowing any unitary Absolute. Fichte had posited such an Absolute in his concept of the Ego, but the world, nature in all its variety, was, as non-Ego, opposed to the free activity of the Ego. Schlegel rejects this, because the plenitude of nature is for him a necessary concomitant to that unity striven for by the mind—and the prime task of poetry is to embody this interplay in its totality. Hence his affection for Spinoza, whose concept of substance posited an identity, not an opposition, of absolute unity and absolute variety. And recent discoveries in the physical sciences (oxygen, electricity, galvanism) with their assertion of a unitary life-force in the multiplicity of natural phenomena seemed to him to be tending in the same direction. Basically he was concerned with evolving a philosophical system that should combine the absolute unity of substance with the absolute variety of its manifestations, persistence with change, Being with Becoming. Ernst Behler asserts that by interpreting change as motivated by striving and longing, and by asserting that the absolute unity is this same force, which he called "love" and saw therefore as a manifestation of the divine, Schlegel was working his way toward some kind of solution, though he never was able to express this in an articulated philosophical system. Nor did he need to, we may add; for the true expression of all these ideas was for him poetry, which was to combine absolute unity with absolute variety. Behler suggests that irony and wit can be seen as the manifestation of the tension between these two basic concepts of unity and variety. Both irony and wit are functions of the free play of the mind. Freedom was the key concept for Fichte, as also for Schlegel. Irony is for Schlegel "constant self-parody" of the mind, and consciousness of the "infinitely full chaos" of the world (and all experience). In an article of 1803 he expressly states that the novel is the genre preeminently suited to dissolving the opposition of poetry to reality by poeticizing the real, and it therefore should always show a tendency toward mythology. As an example he cites Novalis's *Heinrich von Ofterdingen.* By the exercise of caprice, *Willkür,* the poet displays his absolute freedom in digressions, in arabesques, in "artistically arranged confusion." Wit, *Witz,* Schlegel defined, in an essay on Lessing of 1804, as "the innermost mingling and interpenetration of reason and fancy," as the freedom of the mind operating with plenitude of thoughts.

In 1794 Friedrich Schlegel had contemplated writing a novel of his own, of which a plan is preserved, but he did not get down to writing it until the winter of 1798. The plan indicates that the novel was to be concerned with two characters who together constitute a whole—a man cultured and basically pure, but ingenuous and enthusiastic, who is to develop through love, friendship, and worldly experience into a coordinated human being, and a woman of enthusiasm and high culture who preserved femininity (in contrast to a secondary female character of rich culture who does not), the whole to be elevated but easy and joyful in tone. *Lucinde,* published in 1799, represents the development of this plan, but the focus is more on love and friendship than on worldly experience. Indeed it seems to say that the only educative experience is love. We have already noticed the central position that Schlegel accorded to love in his literary theory. Love means for him not merely the great transfiguring force in human experience, but also the experience in which above all others the inner and outer world become one. Thereby it becomes in romantic thinking (for we shall find similar statements about love in others of the German Romantics) the Absolute in which all that is individual is contained and sustained, the one primal force and the one life force, the infinite in the finite, that which gives man the sense of unity with the universe. As regards form, this means that the individual personages of a poetic work become metamorphoses of this one central force, and that persons and world become one.

For Friedrich Schlegel love in our finite individual experience combines both the sensual and the spiritual, and any attempt to divide the two or devalue the one in favor of the other is deprecated. This is the theme of *Lucinde,* and it grew to a certain extent out of his own personal experience. For in July 1797 he met Dorothea Veit, his future wife, and was swept off his feet by her combination of intelligence and sensuality. Four years earlier he had en-

countered Caroline Böhmer, later to become his brother's wife and still later the wife of the philosopher Schelling, who had a similar combination of qualities, as history was indeed to show. In an essay **"On Diotima"** (published in 1795), he was already attacking conventional ideals of masculinity and femininity in society (masterful aggressiveness and selfless devotion) and asserting that in the full life neither such extreme can have any place but both must merge and enrich each other. And that is love.

The form of *Lucinde* is as unconventional as its content. Being concerned with reflections rather than events, with inner rather than external experience, it has no "story" as such and therefore eschews any attempt at chronological narration, except in the seventh section, which is entitled [Apprenticeship to Manliness], "Lehrjahre der Männlichkeit" a *Bildungsroman* in miniature that traces the development of the "hero" Julius up to the point where the novel begins. This is flanked on either side by six shorter sections, reflections in various literary forms on the theme of love, arabesques surrounding the central "confessional" narrative. Quite early on in the book the hero Julius, who is also the fictive author of the novel, claims to have discarded a progressively unfolding narration as unsuited to the subject and chosen instead to give us discrete fragments he has written at various times without order—"a strange mixture of different memories and longings."

The first section is a letter from Julius to Lucinde and announces the theme: their love is a mingling of spirituality and sensuality; wit and delight characterize their embraces, which are "romantic confusion" and can be described only in "a charming confusion" [*einer reizenden Verwirrung*]. The work has already become self-reflexive, in that Julius is here describing the novel in which he figures. Straight progression would falsify the subject, and indeed nothing of the kind is given us. We progress therefore nonprogressively to a "Dithyrambic Fantasia on the Most Beautiful Situation," which restates the theme of the first section around the witty idea that the reversal of roles in the love act is an allegory of the perfection of masculine and feminine into full, whole humanity. The metaphor is somewhat shocking, or was in 1799, so the third section, the "Portrait of Little Wilhelmina," leads up to an attack on false modesty; Wilhelmina kicks her legs immodestly in the air, is unabashedly sensual and yet at the same time very intelligent, is impelled by fancy rather than intellect [*Verstand*],and in that is like a poet. This, says Julius—Schlegel, is a portrait of the ideal he has before him as he writes (more self-reflexiveness). Wilhelmina is the novel itself. We are then given, as the fourth section, an "Allegorie von der Frechheit" [Allegory of Insolence], which is a jocular allegory of how *Lucinde* came to be written, or might have been (but surely wasn't). The poet stands within a "chaos" of beautiful flowers, is jumped at by what seems to be a monster but turns out to be a frog, and is then told by Wit, *der Witz,* the creative force *per se,* that this "monster" is public opinion. Since the poet turns it on its back and then deems it to be nothing but a frog, he implies that he does not care a fig about public opinion. Wit then shows him four young men at a crossroads, representing the four novels that he could be about to write, all faced with the choice between modesty [*Delikatesse*] or insolence [*Frechheit*]. One of the novels (obviously the about-to-be-written or being-written **Lucinde**) chooses the latter, and *Witz,* his creative mind, approves of the choice. (Don't worry, dear reader. You are not getting any more confused than Schlegel intends you to be!) The poet now feels a new power within him, sees the world as a "carnival of lust and love" but then dissolves it in a flash and hears the words: "Destroy and Create, One and All," and the admonition that it is time for him to proclaim the sanctity of nature and health. There follows a rhetoric of love, interspersed with comments on the reactions the novel is likely to provoke among its readers.

Having attacked modesty and prudery and defended insolence, the novel now demolishes useful occupation and defends laziness in an "Idyll of Indolence." Love has no purpose but itself. The general busyness of most human beings is really based on an antipathy to the world, which can be understood only in leisurely reflection. A parable at the end of this section contrasts Prometheus, as representing the ethic of work and enlightenment, with Hercules, the goal of whose labors was to enjoy fifty girls in one night, an activity of "noble indolence." He got to Olympus, but Prometheus didn't. The sixth section, "Treue und Scherz"—"Devotion and Diversion" might be the appropriate translation—is a dialogue between the lovers during love-making, simultaneously serious and joking, for, we are told, "society is chaos that can achieve form [*Bildung*] and harmony only through wit, for it one does not joke and play with the elements of passion they coagulate into thick lumps and darken everything."

The first six arabesques have been cast in a variety of forms such as Schlegel required of a novel: letter, fantasia, portrait, allegory, rhetorical excursus, idyll, and dialogue. The "Apprenticeship to Manliness" which follows is a third-person narration tracing the successive stages of Julius's sensual-spiritual development up to the point of his meeting with Lucinde. The progression is from emotion-without-a-target through a succession of sexual experiences involving an innocent girl, a society lady, a prostitute, a soul-friend, a sister-figure, an educated girl who recoils from the act, and finally Lucinde, a free-living artist, in whom he finds love, himself, and the impulse to art—so that he can now look back on his narration, self-reflexively, as a work of art. He realizes that his narration has involved transformation of experience by his present state of mind; and this realization leads to the first of the second set of arabesques, the eighth section, "Metamorphoses," concerned with metamorphoses of the loving mind. It begins with a parable of the union of external and internal worlds in love, and emphasizes the fact that full love is not elevation from the mortal to the immortal but a complete union of the two. In its description of the three successive stages of objectlessness, narcissism, and mutuality, this section is a metaphorical recapitulation of the apprenticeship narrated in nonmetaphorical terms in the preceding section, an interpretation in poetry of its prose.

The ninth section consists of two "letters" from Julius to Lucinde. The first begins by his expression of joy at her impending motherhood, which he views as a sign from the gods that their love is part of the great chain of all living things. The letter has an arabesque form and consists of a series of disconnected fragments dealing with aspects of the love-relationship, reaching its climax in a passage that relates their love to the general life-force of the universe, returning thereby to the tone of the beginning of the letter, which therefore has something of a circular form. The second letter expresses his anguish at Lucinde's illness, his relief at her recovery, and yet his satisfaction at being able to see pain as an image of the eternal dissonance of the universe and therefore interpret it meaningfully. Lucinde, he says, had become the mediator between his "fragmented self and indivisible, eternal humanity," as he contemplated the possibility of her death and subsequently her return to life. This second letter is a continuous statement, not broken into fragments, not circular but progressive, progressing toward the assertion that what he has experienced is the thought of dissolution in freedom and the fact of re-establishment in hope. We note that in these two letters the "action," if one may call it such, has proceeded beyond the point at which the novel started. In contrast to the seriousness of these reflections, section 10 is a parodic reflection in the vocabulary of Fichte on sexual powers in humans and other forms of life. It ends with the observation that Nature seeks an eternal circle of experiments, each of which is completely new, but is in its individual separateness likewise an image of the ultimate inseparable Individuality, what Fichte calls the "absolute Ego" and what Novalis . . . calls the "personality of the Universal."

The eleventh section consists of two letters from Julius to a friend named Antonio. The first of these explains that their friendship had declined because Antonio is too ready with negative criticism to encourage frankness, the essential basis for any friendship. What is friendship? The second letter distinguishes between "external" [*äusserlich*] friendship, which takes in more and more persons, and "inner" [*ganz innerlich*] friendship, which depends on the sympathy and symmetry of minds, demands repose and humble reverence for the "divinity" of the other. This leads over to the twelfth section, which is entitled "Sehnsucht und Ruhe"[Longing and Repose], a lyrical dialogue between Julius and Lucinde on the curious fact that in repose one experiences deep longing. Repose is here interpreted as *undisturbed* longing, its image is Night, Lucinde is priestess of the Night, and the mood of the dialogue moves close to Novalis's *Hymns to Night* and the second act of Wagner's *Tristan and Isolde,* both of which authors were familiar with Schlegel's novel. To die in the ecstasy of love is a serious note to strike in a novel that Schlegel himself had described, albeit proleptically, as "light-hearted" [*leichtfertig*], and indeed this second set of arabesques, even including the Fichte parody, has become increasingly serious. So Schlegel rounds it all off with some "Tändeleien der Fantasie" [Dallyings of Fancy], asserting that there is something to be said in favor of letting the fancy float on a stream of images and feelings without further purpose—delighting in play and resulting in a motley dance of life, without ulterior motives. We end therefore with a paean to the imagination and a degrading of the *Verstand*—the intellect always concerned with purpose and intent—just as we had begun with praise of imaginative confusion and a rejection of logical consequentiality.

*Lucinde* cannot be treated as an illustration of the ideas expressed in the *Gespräch über die Poesie,* because the latter was not worked out until after Schlegel stopped writing the novel. The title page of *Lucinde* indicates that what was published was only the first part of a novel. Its appearance was greeted with general consternation, although some persons, notably the philosopher Schleiermacher, spoke up in its defense. Its ethical message was misconstrued, even by writers as acute as Hegel and Kierkegaard. Kierkegaard did realize that Schlegel was reacting against prevalent eighteenth-century notions that love was either sensual or spiritual, but he did not appreciate that Schlegel was arguing (indirectly, for there is not much argument in the book) for a fusion of the two as the nature of true love. That Schlegel did not get his message across to most readers was largely owing to the fact that the sensual occupies much more space in the book than the spiritual. In short his moral failure was due to some degree of aesthetic failure. Nevertheless the novel is a fascinating experiment, in its use of arabesques, its combination of genres, its irony, and its self-reflexiveness.

*Eric A. Blackall, "The Novel as Romantic Book: Friedrich Schlegel," in his* The Novels of the German Romantics, *Cornell, 1983, pp. 21-43.*

## Cathy Comstock   (essay date 1987)

[*In the following essay, Comstock examines the role of irony as it relates to incomprehensibility in Schlegel's essay "Über die Unverständlichkeit" ("On Incomprehensibility").*]

In his parting essay to the readers of the *Athenaeum,* **"Über die Unverständlichkeit" ["On Incomprehensibility"]**, Friedrich Schlegel purports to answer the many "complaints of incomprehensibility"which had been directed at the *Athenaeum* journal, and proffers his "firm resolve really to be comprehensible, at least this time." The series of digressions and deflations which follow, however, soon lead one to suspect that **"Über die Unverständlichkeit"** is meant not as a clarification, but a demonstration of incomprehensibility. This dramatization of the value of uncertainty is made possible through the "transcendental buffoonery" [transzendentale Buffonerie] of irony, the same culprit declared "unquestionably" responsible for "a great part of the incomprehensibility of the *Athenaeum.*" The crucial role that irony enacts in all of Schlegel's critical theory is given its fullest display in this essay, which emphasizes process rather than concept, playfulness rather than clarity.

For Schlegel, the elusive movement of irony is "absolutely necessary" for two important and paradoxical reasons. First, the evasion of linear analysis made possible through irony protects the ineffable from the disintegrating influence of rational investigation, thereby preserving the mystery essential to art and religion, to life itself, which he sees as founded on a "point of strength that must be left in the dark" [Punkte, der im Dunkeln gelassen werden muβ]. At the same time that it enforces this defensive distance between the real and the ideal, irony, in appropriately contradictory fashion, makes the experience of the absolute

accessible through its own mirroring of the "infinite play" of the sublime. The experience of irony offered us in **"Über die Unverständlichkeit"** moves us closer to essential truth, in other words, by stepping back, by showing us, through its own unwillingness to be bound to certain meaning, that the split between form and essence inherent to our temporal condition is not lamentable but valuable.

In recent critical commentary, there has been a great deal of interest in—and disagreement about—the role of irony for the romantics in general and Schlegel in particular. This subject has induced some "remarkable cases of critical vertigo," perhaps because of its problematic position in regard to what are often seen as the two central and opposing concerns of romantic aesthetics: a quest for transcendent truth and a loyalty to the conditions of existential reality. In view of this potential clash of interests, Schlegel's repeated championing of irony might seem surprising, since the difficulties of achieving an art of essence would appear to be highlighted by irony, as a trope which especially emphasizes the division and deferment of the linguistic realm.

Critics have generally framed irony's relation to the rift between the ideal and the real by aligning it with one side or the other, viewing it as moving toward either an eventual recuperation of the ideal or the demystification of any such hope. Analysts of the first inclination, such as Peter Szondi [in *Satz und Gegensatz,* 1964] see Schlegelian irony as promising a "recovered unity" in which the disturbing gap between the absolute and the relative will finally be closed. [In *The Shape of German Romanticism,* 1979] Marshall Brown describes this state as "a utopian future that is unrealizable in fact, but toward which irony nonetheless tends." When considered in the light of Schlegel's writings and especially **"Über die Unverständlichkeit,"** several problems with this approach arise. Most noticeably, this view, which presents the split between ideal and real as a wound to be healed, is in direct opposition to Schlegel's own statement that irony is "absolutely necessary" for its ability to arouse "a feeling of indissoluble antagonism between the absolute and the relative." In addition, in Szondi's analysis, the orientation of irony toward a "future unity" is associated with a hopeless and finally despairing attachment to the ideal. The romantic ironist is characterized as "the isolated, alienated man," who "nostalgically aspires toward unity and infinity," and hence finds that "each finite achievement becomes in turn inadequate and finally leads into a void: therein lies his tragedy." Again, this picture simply does not correspond to the celebratory tone of Schlegel's own prose, which suggests not tragic frustration, but the good-humored exuberance one would expect from his fondness for a "transcendental buffoonery" styled after "an averagely gifted Italian *buffo.*"

Focusing on irony's deconstructive tendencies, Paul de Man and Tilottama Rajan view romantic irony not as an inadequate vehicle to a recovered unity, but as the deliberate de-mystification of that illusion. For Rajan, the "self-irony" of many romantic texts indicates an insistent awareness of the gap between existence and essence and shows itself in a clash between "the poetry of experience" and a "Utopian narrative of Romantic desire." For de Man [in *Interpretation: Theory and Practice,* ed. by Charles Singleton, 1969], Schlegelian irony is emphatically opposed to any possible "reconciliation between the ideal and the real": "Friedrich Schlegel is altogether clear on this. The dialectic of self-destruction and self-invention which for him . . . characterizes the ironic mind is an endless process that leads to no synthesis."

Surprisingly, these two very different approaches to the aims of irony culminate in a similar conclusion as to its effects. Like Szondi, Rajan and de Man see irony as a force of frustration that eventually leads to despair or dismissal. Rajan characterizes the romantics as turning away from "pure irony," "that radical irony which makes it impossible to turn back to illusions." Even de Man, who notes Schlegel's initial view of irony as a liberating influence, an "exhilarating," "self-escalating act of consciousness," sees it finally as too much the mode of demystification for Schlegel to tolerate:

> The rhetorical mode of irony takes us back to the predicament of the conscious subject; this consciousness is clearly an unhappy one that strives to move beyond and outside itself. . . . For the later Friedrich Schlegel . . . the solution could only be a leap out of language into faith.

Such a dismal view of the ironic perspective underrates, however, the positive process generated by its "absolute infinite negativity." Irony makes possible an alternation of "creation and de-creation," as Anne Mellor describes it [in *English Romantic Irony,* 1980], which can potentially free us from our finite concerns in order that we may take part in a more essential reality, "the fertile chaos" at the heart of existence:

> A skeptical awareness of the limitations of one's knowledge is necessary, Schlegel felt, to detach imagination from an excessive commitment to its own finite creations. . . . By doing so, irony can free the imagination to discover or create ever-new relationships, to participate once again in the fertile chaos of life. . . .

While de Man also sees Schlegelian irony as constituted by an ongoing exchange of invention and destruction, in his view this process spirals into the nothingness of "a linguistic sign that becomes more and more remote from its meaning," until it finally reveals an inescapable "temporal void." I would agree with Mellor, however, that for Schlegel irony leads not to the abyss but to the ineffable, to an "unstructured openness" which affords a "sacred participation in the process of life." In this view the conflict between skepticism and transcendence leads not to frustration but to a higher understanding: "The romantic ironist . . . deconstructs his own texts with the expectation that such deconstruction is a way of keeping in contact with a greater creative power."

One aspect of Mellor's analysis acts, perhaps, to limit it, in ways which a different reading of **"Über die Unverständlichkeit"** highlights. Mellor's discussion treats irony primarily as a concept, that of "philosophical irony," rather than as linguistic figure. This is not a surprising emphasis, since Schlegel's writings are often read primarily as meta-

physical philosophy, and hence are most often construed in terms of a coherent set of concepts. As Janice Haney-Peritz points out [in *Studies in Romanticism* 22, 1983], however, such an approach implies a delimiting clarity of conceptualization which Schlegel's discourse, with its open-endedness of form and formulation, does not encourage. By avoiding the confounding effects of irony as trope in Schlegel's work, Mellor grants her model a stability which enables her to apply it to a wide range of texts, and finally to hold it up as a therapeutic technique which "can potentially free individuals and even entire cultures from totalitarian modes of behavior," and bring us "pleasure, psychic health, and intellectual freedom." As appealing as such a picture may be, it is purchased at the cost of attention to Schlegel's own prose, and especially **"Über die Unverständlichkeit,"** which undermines clarity of concept in general and Utopian states in particular, emphasizing instead the rapid and unpredictable movement of linguistic figure. It is, of course, this continual displacement of meaning which de Man sees as revealing a "void" at the heart of existence.

Yet, paradoxically, **"Über die Unverständlichkeit"** points to this gap between language and stable meaning as a void not to be a-voided, even from the viewpoint of a redemptive humanism, since it is that uncertain distance which allows for the potentially transformative impact of Schlegelian irony. Incomprehensibility is the surprising common denominator between the sacred and the profane, the ineluctable and the linguistic, because for Schlegel the "eternal agility" of irony figures forth the "infinitely abundant chaos" of the divine itself. Close regard of the prose of **"Über die Unverständlichkeit"** thus becomes crucial to our understanding, since it is through experience rather than explanation that its ironic language promotes our appreciation of that mysterious movement which for Schlegel constitutes "the infinite play of the universe."

The unflattering but easily recognizable symptoms of irony are described for us in the essay, when Schlegel admiringly quotes an earlier fragment in this regard:

> 'Es ist ein sehr gutes Zeichen, wenn die harmonisch Platten gar nicht wissen, wie sie diese stete Selbstparodie zu nehmen haben, den Scherz gerade für Ernst und den Ernst für Scherz halten.'

> [It is a very good sign when the harmonious bores are at a loss about how they should react to this continuous self-parody, when they fluctuate endlessly between belief and disbelief until they get dizzy and take what is meant as a joke seriously and what is meant seriously as a joke.]

Our exposure to this unusual learning process starts early in the piece. As though to give us fair warning of the experience ahead, the narrator mentions an earlier resolution he had once made to himself:

> Nun ist es ganz eigen an mir, daß ich den Unverstand durchaus nicht leiden kann, auch den Unverstand der Unverständigen, noch weniger aber den Unverstand der Verständigen. Daher hatte ich schon vor langer Zeit den Entschluß gefaßt, mich mit dem Leser in ein Gespräch über diese

Materie zu versetzen, und vor seinen eignen Augen, gleichsam ihm ins Gesicht, einen andern neuen Leser nach meinem Sinne ze konstruieren . . .

[Now, it is a peculiarity of mine that I absolutely detest incomprehension, not only the incomprehension of the uncomprehending but even more the incomprehension of the comprehending. For this reason, I made a resolution quite some time ago to have a talk with my reader, and then create before his eyes—in spite of him as it were—another new reader to my own liking . . .]

This plan, in the digressive manner typical of the essay, is dropped without further specification. But the process of creating a new reader is not. Instead, the narrator sets about shaping us more to his own liking, encouraging our enlightened comprehension of incomprehensibility by tossing us into the midst of it, at the very point that he is promising to meet our conventional expectations:

Ich wollte zeigen, daß man die reinste und gediegenste Unverständlichkeit gerade aus der Wissenschaft und aus der Kunst erhält, die ganz eigentlich aufs Verständigen und Verständlichmachen ausgehn, aus der Philosophie und

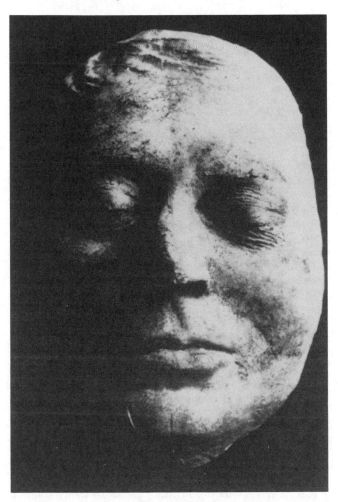

*Schlegel's death mask.*

Philologie; und damit das ganze Geschäft sich nicht in einem gar zu handgreiflichen Zirkel herumdrehen möchte, so hatte ich mir fest vorgenommen, dieses eine Mal wenigstens gewiß verständlich zu sein.

[I wanted to show that the purest and most genuine incomprehension emanates precisely from science and the arts—which by their very nature aim at comprehension and at making comprehensible—and from philosophy and philology; and so that the whole business shouldn't turn around in too palpable a circle I had made a firm resolve really to be comprehensible, at least this time.]

Even as we are promised the comprehensible, we may haplessly suspect that we are "taking what is meant as a joke seriously and what is meant seriously as a joke," in our uncertainty as to when the narrator is being ironic. Is he poking fun at his inability to be "comprehensible," or our misapprehensions of that notion? We could assume that his desire not to turn "in too palpable a circle" implies that he will be avoiding his old ways of obfuscation and trodding the reformed path of a more literal style of prose. But the first half of the sentence complicates the promise of the second. Since the penitent resolve "really to be comprehensible" follows upon the assertion that the "purest and most genuine incomprehension" proceeds from just such a linear approach, to attempt that scientific clarity would mean that he was making true comprehension impossible, and hence failing in his effort "to be comprehensible." Thus, in vowing not to be circular he has managed to be so, and to cast doubt as well on any desire for him to do otherwise.

After this dizzying introduction, the narrator enters into a series of subjects tenuously connected by the ground they provide for a survey of the foibles of the "Critical Age." This section, looked at in combination with a counter vision of the "new age" presented at the end of the essay, has the rough shape of a satiric dismissal of the opposition and its attitudes, as though to clear the way for the promotion of a superior viewpoint. Yet the experience of both these passages belies that expectation, for any coherent sense of rhetorical aims is continually set askew by unclassifiable ironic signals. This section revolves around a subject which is a likely target for Schlegel's satiric prowess, a concept obviously antithetical to the approach of the essay: a "real language" aimed at ending "all understandable misunderstandings" by establishing a set, one-to-one correspondence between word and thought. But even this subject, which does undergo considerable ridicule along the way, is introduced to us in a manner which makes it very difficult to determine the narrator's attitude toward it, due to unaccountable fluctuations in tone:

Ich wollte auf das hindeuten was die größten Denker jeder Zeit (freilich nur sehr dunkel) geahndet haben . . . ; ich meine eine reelle Sprache, daß wir aufhören möchten mit Worten zu kramen, und schauen alles Wirkens Kraft und Samen. Die große Raserei einer solchen Kabbala, wo gelehrt werden sollte, wie des Menschen Geist sich selbst verwandeln . . . ein dergleichen Mysterium durfte ich nun nicht . . .

naiv und nackt darstellen. . . . Ich muβte demnach auf ein populäres Medium denken, um den heiligen, zarten, flüchtigen, luftigen, duftigen gleichsam imponderablen Gedanken chemisch zu binden.

[I wanted to focus attention on what the greatest thinkers of every age have divined (only very darkly, to be sure) . . . : I mean by this a real language, so that we can stop rummaging about for words and pay attention to the power and source of all activity. The great frenzy of such a Cabala where one would be taught the way the human spirit can transform itself . . . I simply could not portray a mystery like this . . . naively and nakedly. . . . Consequently I had to think of some popular medium to bond chemically the holy, delicate, fleeting, airy, fragrant, and, as it were, imponderable thought.]

The excessive flourish of the contention that the "greatest thinkers of every age have divined" this possibility, in combination with the sudden condescension of the comment that they have done so "only very darkly, to be sure," alerts us to a satirical thrust, but not to its target: is it those "greatest thinkers," the over-assured narrator, or the hope for a "real language" itself? The flat naivete of "real" ["reelle"], and the narrator's earlier doubt about making language "comprehensible" might incline us toward the last. But that conjecture is disallowed by the description which follows, associating "real language" with the "power and source of all activity." The narrator then turns once again to disband all the impact of the preceding eloquence: "Consequently I had to think of some popular medium to bond chemically the holy, delicate, fleeting, airy, fragrant, and, as it were, imponderable thought." The pseudo-scientific diction, the contrast between the mechanical nature of the bonding and the elusive fragility and profundity of that which it would bind, all serve to make obvious fun of the endeavor to confine either word or thought to a stable alignment.

At this point, the narrator does shift into a virtuoso display of sarcasm, which is unambiguously pointed at the specious assumptions underlying this kind of pragmatic approach. The reductiveness of such a strategy is first reflected, with wily economy, in the narrator's protestation of his pleasure at the "progress" of the age:

Zugleich hatte ich mit innigem Vergnügen die Progressen unsrer Nation bemerkt; und was soll ich erst von dem Zeitalter sagen? Dasselbe Zeitalter, in welchem auch wir zu laben die Ehre haben; das Zeitalter, welches, um alles mit einem Worte zu sagen, den bescheidnen aber vielsagenden Namen des kritischen Zeitaltersverdient, so daβ nun bald alles kritisiert sein wird, auβer das Zeitalter selbst, und daβ alles immer kritischer und kristischer wird . . .

[At the same time, I noted with sincere pleasure the progress of our country—not to speak of our age! The same age in which we too have the honor to live; the age that, to wrap it all up in a word, deserves the highly suggestive name of the Critical Age, so that soon now everything is going to be criticized, except the age itself and

everything becomes continually more and more critical . . . ]

For those rationalist contemporaries who would have him package meaning in comprehensible parcels, he offers his counter compliment to the age, by "wrapping it all up in a word." The fallacies of such a goal-oriented approach are expanded upon in his next seeming digression as well, through the juxtaposition of "real language" and the "glorious prospect" of alchemy held forth by Girtanner, a scientist of the time:

Nur ganz kürzlich wurde dieser Gedanke einer reellen Sprache mir von neuem erregt, und eine glorreiche Aussicht öffnete sich dem innern Auge. Im neunzehnten Jahrhundert, versichert uns Girtanner, im neunzehnten Jahrhundert wird man Gold machen können; und ist es nicht schon mehr als Vermutung, daβ das neunzehnte Jahrhundert nun bald seinen Anfang nehmen wird? . . . Wie gern werden nun alle Künstler sich entschlieβen den kleinen unbedeutenden Überrest vom achtzehnten Jahrhundert noch zu hungern, und diese groβe Pflicht künftig nicht mehr mit betrübtem Herzen erfüllen; denn sie wissen, daβ teils noch sie selbst in eigner Person, teils aber auch und desto gewisser ihre Nachkommen in kurzem werden Gold machen können.

[Only a very short while ago this thought of a real language occurred to me again and a glorious prospect opened up before my mind's eye. In the nineteenth century, so Girtanner assures us, in the nineteenth century man will be able to make gold; and isn't it now more than mere conjecture that the nineteenth century is going to begin?. . . . How gladly all artists will now resolve to go on being hungry for the slight, insignificant remainder of the eighteenth century, and in future no longer fulfill this sacred duty with an aggrieved heart; for they know that in part they themselves, and in part also (and all the more certainly) their descendants will shortly be able to make gold.]

The futility of any project which seeks to objectify and hence "capture" the ideal, whether in the form of fixed meaning or a literally golden age, is succinctly summarized in the closing remarks on Girtanner's chances for success:

Aber alles das sind nur Hirngespinste oder Ideale: denn Girtanner ist gestorben, und ist demnach für jetzt so weit davon entfernt Gold machen zu können, daβ man vielmehr mit aller Kunst nur so viel Eisen aus ihm wird machen können, als nötig wäre, sein Andenken durch eine kleine Schaumünze zu verewigen.

[But all these things are merely chimeras or ideals: for Girtanner is dead and consequently for the moment so far removed from being able to make gold that one might extract with all possible artistry only so much iron out of him as might be necessary to immortalize his memory by way of a little medallion.]

We are not allowed the satisfactions of this satiric finale for long, however. With a disconcerting "Furthermore," we are led into a discussion which does not join clearly to that which went before, except perhaps to undermine indirectly its belligerent approach. A parody of all strategies of attack is hinted at in the narrator's excessive admiration for the way a critic has attacked the attackers of the *Athenaeum:*

> Überdem haben sich die Klagen über die Unverständlichkeit so ausschließlich gegen das *Athenaeum* gerichtet, es ist so oft und so vielseitig geschehen, daß die Deduktion am besten eben da ihren Anfang wird nehmen können, wo uns eigentlich der Schuh drückt.

> Schon hat ein scharfsinniger Kunstrichter . . . das *Athenaeum* gegen diese Vorwürfe freundschaftlich verteidigt, und dabei das berüchtigte Fragment von den drei Tendenzen zum Beispiel gewählt. Ein überaus glücklicher Gedanke! Gerade so muß man die Sache angreifen.

> [Furthermore, the complaints of incomprehensibility have been directed so exclusively and so frequently and variously at the *Athenaeum* that my deduction might start off most appropriately right at the spot where the shoe actually hurts.

> A penetrating critic . . . has already been good enough to defend the *Athenaeum* against these attacks and in so doing has used as an example the notorious fragment about the three tendencies. What a marvelous idea! This is just the way one should attack the problem.]

We are left to wonder, if we can extricate ourselves from the momentum of his transition, what connection is being made, or what alternative proposed to the methods of the "Critical Age." But this teasing digressiveness is crucial to the approach of the essay, as is the frequent difficulty of deciding when the speaker is being "serious" and when not. The unexplained detours and mysterious vacillations in tone distinguish the delinquent playfulness of this use of irony from a more coherent, systematic form, such as we would associate with satire, which encourages a reconstruction of the "right" meaning in response to surface incongruities, a superior "truth" to replace that which has been dissolved. Given this convention, when Schlegel deflates certain positivistic notions, he risks the likelihood of repeating the very procedures he criticizes, by transfering to himself the oppressive authority he has opposed. As Jonathan Culler has written [in *Structuralist Poetics: Structuralism, Linguistics and the Study of Literature,* 1975],

> It is . . . extremely difficult to undermine or criticize the stereotype without having recourse to another stereotype, which is that of irony itself. As Roland Barthes asks, "How can one deflate stupidity without declaring oneself intelligent?" How can the ironist criticize one point of view or attitude for being excessively limited without asserting the completeness and truth of his own?

It is just this self-justifying closure which the ironic irresolution of the essay avoids. By disrupting our attempts to construct a unified aim for the irony, by turning away from a subject just as we are starting to make "sense" of

it, by intermingling the terminology of opposing camps, the speaker keeps our perception of his ends uncertain, and hence continually open to new understandings. In this section, for instance, the mechanical concept of "real language," with its chemical bonding and a mission to "wrap" meaning up, is interwoven with a discourse of transformation and mystery, concerned with "the great frenzy of . . . a Cabala where one could be taught the way the human spirit can transform itself." And, while the narrator dismisses the deceased Girtanner's scheme with acid satire, that attack is first diffused by the sudden shift in subject, and then actually turned against the narrator's own projection of the nineteenth century, an oft-quoted Utopian vision which closes the essay.

Before we come to that ending, however, we are presented with a passage crucial to our reception of **"Über die Unverständlichkeit."** With surprising directness, the speaker finally addresses the subject of the essay, the value of comprehensibility. As though to signal our serious attention to this complex and profound matter, the style is more straightforwardly explanatory and enthusiastic than at any other point. Yet, while the speaker seems sincerely eager to impress upon us the reasons that incomprehensibility is of essential importance, his discussion is marked even here by an ironic indirection that forces us to seek out rather than merely to accept his contentions:

> Aber ist denn die Unverständlichkeit etwas so durchaus Verwerfliches und Schlechtes? —Mich dünkt das Heil der Familien und der Nationen beruhet auf ihr; wenn mich nicht alles trügt, Staaten und Systeme, die künstlichsten Werke der Menschen, oft so künstlich, daß man die Weisheit des Schöpfers nicht genug darin bewundern kann. . . . Ja das Köstlichste was der Mensch hat, die innere Zufriedenheit selbst hängt, wie jeder leicht wissen kann, irgendwo zuletzt an einem solchen Punkte, der im Dunkeln gelassen werden muß, dafür aber auch das Ganze trägt und hält, und diese Kraft in demselben Augenblicke verlieren würde, wo man ihn in Verstand auflösen wollte. Wahrlich, es würde euch bange werden, wenn die ganze Welt, wie ihr es fodert, einmal im Ernst durchaus verständlich würde. Und is sie selbst diese unendliche Welt nicht durch den Verstand aus der Unverständlichkeit oder dem Chaos gebildet?

> [Is comprehensibility really something so unmitigatedly contemptible and evil? Methinks the salvation of families and nations rests upon it. If I am not wholly deceived, then states and systems, the most artificial productions of man, are often so artificial that one simply can't admire the wisdom of their creator enough. . . . Yes, even man's most precious possession, his own inner happiness, depends in the last analysis, as anybody can easily verify, on some such point of strength that must be left in the dark, but that nonetheless shores up and supports the whole burden and would crumble the moment one subjected it to rational analysis. Verily, it would fare badly with you if, as you demand, the whole world were ever to become wholly comprehensible in earnest. And isn't this entire, unending

world constructed by the understanding out of incomprehensibility and chaos?]

In some ways, this is a fairly open declaration of the need for incomprehensibility, which is equated clearly with the fertile "chaos" out of which "this entire, unending world" is constructed. But at the same time, another important reason for its value is cast in a form so enigmatically ironic that its significance can easily slip by us without some extended contemplation. Directly after proclaiming that the "salvation of families and nations" may depend upon incomprehensibility, the speaker comments, "If I am not wholly deceived, then states and systems, the most artificial productions of man, are often so artificial that one simply can't admire the wisdom of their creator enough." In an effort to determine the relevance of this remark, we might assume that since "states and systems" are rational, hierarchical constructions, they are mentioned merely for sarcastic contrast, a conclusion also suggested by "künstlichsten" ["artificial"], which connotes the false and overly mannered, and by the arch protestation that "one simply can't admire the wisdom of their creator enough." Yet the unexplained shift from a purely positive rhetoric inclines one to question the exact significance of the comment, especially since the supercilious humility of the introductory phrase, "If I am not wholly deceived," implies that the speaker is far from deluded, and about to offer us a profound insight as to the relationship between the artificial and the "salvation of families and nations."

The connection, it seems, is based on disconnection: the artificial does indeed have its value, a value which derives not from a misguided attempt to incorporate the natural and essential, but from its open proclamation of its distance from that ideal. This gap between the relative and the absolute is of utmost importance, since it protects that mysterious essence which "shores up and supports the whole burden and would crumble the moment one subjected it to rational analysis," and hence must be "left in the dark" in order to thrive. This suggestion implies in turn the reason that ironic discourse is necessary to the preservation of that hidden "point of strength": irony too, with its playful resistance to being "bonded" to the "imponderable," flaunts its artifice and thus insists upon the separation of form and essence, the "indissoluble antagonism between the absolute and the relative." Irony can do so, in addition, with a sense of humor and self-reflexivity which emphasizes the freedom rather than the loss, the pleasure rather than the despair of such a condition.

The passage which follows, the compromised Utopian vision mentioned earlier, dramatizes vividly the dynamics of such strategic indecipherability. Here the speaker offers us a compelling picture of a transformed nineteenth century, a time when "understanding itself will be understood," in a manner which remorselessly entangles the earnest and the ironic. The lyrical endorsement which initiates the passage shows at first only a small sign of the disruption to come:

> Ein andrer Trostgrund gegen die anerkannte Unverständlichkeit des *Athenaeums* liegt schon in der Anerkennung selbst, weil uns eben diese auch belehrte, das Übel werde vorübergehend

sein. Die neue Zeit kündigt sich an als eine schnellfüβige, sohlenbeflügelte; . . . Lange hat es gewetterleuchtet am Horizont der Poesie; in eine mächtige Wolke war alle Gewitterkraft des Himmels zusammengedrängt; . . . bald aber wird nicht mehr von einem einzelnen Gewitter die Rede sein, sondern es wird der ganze Himmel in einer Flamme brennen und dann werden euch alle eure kleinen Blitzableiter nicht mehr helfen.

[Another consolation for the acknowledged incomprehensibility of the *Athenaeum* lies in the very fact of this acknowledgement, precisely because this has taught us that the evil was a passing one. The new age reveals itself as a nimble and quick-footed one. . . . For a long time now there has been lightning on the horizon of poetry; the whole thunderous power of the heavens had gathered together in a mighty cloud; . . . But soon it won't be simply a matter of one thunderstorm, the whole sky will burn with a single flame and then all your lightning rods won't help you.]

While we might question the description of the *Athenaeum* as an "evil," and no more than a "passing one," at that, the lofty enthusiasm which follows encourages us to ignore those doubts; we can easily assume, for instance, that the evil will pass not because incomprehensibility will cease to exist, but because this "nimble and quick-footed" age will cease to regard it as a problem.

But in the midst of this rhapsodic forecast, those earlier hints of dissidence are magnified to a degree that cannot be ignored:

> Dann nimmt das neunzehnte Jahrhundert in der Tat seinen Anfang, und dann wird auch jenes kleine Rätsel von der Unverständlichkeit des *Athenaeums* gelöst sein. Welche Katastrophe! Dann wird es Leser geben die lesen können. Im neunzehnten Jahrhundert wird jeder die *Fragmente* mit vielem Behagen und Vergnügen in den Verdauungsstunden genieβen können, und auch zu den härtesten unverdaulichsten keinen Nuβknacker bedürfen. Im neunzehnten Jahrhundert wird jeder Mensch, jeder Leser die **Lucinde** unschuldig, die *Genoveva* protestantisch und die didaktsichen *Elegien* von A. W. Schlegel fast gar zu leicht und durchsichtig finden.

[Then the nineteenth century will indeed make a beginning of it and then the little riddle of the incomprehensibility of the *Athenaeum* will also be solved. What a catastrophe! Then there will be readers who will know how to read. In the nineteenth century everyone will be able to savor the fragments with much gratification and pleasure in the after-dinner hours and not need a nutcracker for even the hardest and most indigestible ones. In the nineteenth century every human being, every reader will find **Lucinde** innocent, *Genoveva* Protestant, and A. W. Schlegel's didactic *Elegies* almost too simple and transparent.]

The glorious vision of the expansive understanding of the new age suddenly becomes as much parody as prophecy.

The reference to the solving of the "little riddle of the incomprehensibility of the *Athenaeum*" reiterates the earlier idea that its evil was a passing one, but does so now with an overwrought humility which casts doubt on the nature of that solution. At the same time, the Utopian qualities of this vision, which sounds more and more absurdly comprehensive—"In the nineteenth century everyone will be able to savor the fragments . . . In the nineteenth century every human being, every reader will find *Lucinde* innocent . . ."—evokes an earlier prediction of the time to come: "In the nineteenth century, so Girtanner assures us, in the nineteenth century man will be able to make gold. . . ."

The ironic acrobatics become especially pronounced with the injection of "What a catastrophe!" a double-edged exclamation which opens up the rest of the passage to opposing interpretations as well. Since "readers who know how to read" should be far from a catastrophic occurrence, we might decide that this response is part of a good-humored mocking of the author himself, who will now be deprived of the fun of scandalizing his formerly conservative readers with his inexplicable writings. But since that phrase also echoes the earlier critical tone taken toward Girtanner, who sought the "beautiful and great in this catastrophe" of Utopian alchemy, we could take the interjection more straightforwardly, and look for the negative aspects of these new readers, already suggested by the dubious description of the *Athenaeum* as a "little riddle." We don't have to look far to meet with the suspect description of these new and improved readers as after-dinner consumers of the "simple and transparent," nibbling on romantic art like snacks: "In the nineteenth century everyone will be able to savor the fragments with much gratification and pleasure in the after-dinner hours and not need a nutcracker for even the hardest and most indigestible ones." The image of the nutcracker especially suggests that these nineteenth-century readers bear an unfortunate resemblance to their eighteenth-century predecessors, for it implies a continued devotion to "real language," bound to its kernel of meaning like a nut to its shell. While the fact that they do "not need a nutcracker for even the hardest and most indigestible ones," could be a sign of their willingness not to try to reduce the incomprehensible to clarity, it could also indicate that they are merely more smug about their ability to "crack" the code by themselves. As though to insure the impossibility of settling on a single interpretation, the German verb "genieβen," translated here as "savor"—"In the nineteenth century everyone will be able to savor the fragments with much gratification and pleasure"—means "to eat and drink" as well as "to enjoy"; it hence suggests on the one hand a prolonged and appreciative contemplation of the fragments, and on the other, an insensitive, gluttonous consumption, a conclusion further hinted at by the great "gratification and pleasure" which they derive from this activity.

This alternation—or cohabitation, we might say—of vision and sarcasm, which becomes most unpredictable when we would ordinarily expect an essay to be most conclusive, exemplifies the role of irony in Schlegel's theory. Irony, as he wrote in *Athenaeum-Fragment 121*, "perfects" a concept not by refining or clarifying it, but by

transforming it into movement, an on-going creative process motivated by our inability to settle on a unilateral truth:

> Eine Idee ist ein bis zur Ironie vollendeter Begriff, eine absolute Synthesis absoluter Antithesen, der stete sich selbst erzeugende Wechsel zwei streitender Gedanken.
>
> [An idea is a concept perfected to the point of irony, an absolute synthesis of absolute antitheses, the continual self-creating interchange of two conflicting thoughts.]

Since the narrator speaks in this essay of his resolve to shape a new reader before our eyes, without defining that concept, the action of **"Über die Unverständlichkeit"** itself could serve as our model. Thus we might hypothesize a reading experience aimed not at ending the engagement but extending it, as the narrator imagines the greatest writers and readers doing: "I have a suspicion that some of the most conscious artists of earlier times are still carrying on ironically, hundreds of years after their deaths, with their most faithful followers and admirers" [Einige der absichtlichsten Künstler der vorigen Zeit habe ich in Verdacht, daβ sie noch Jahrhunderte nach ihrem Tode mit ihren gläubigsten Verehrern und Anhängern Ironie treiben].

A devotion to the perpetual motion of irony, the "truly transcendental buffoonery . . . which rises infinitely above all limitations" [wirklich transzendentale Buffonerie . . . welche . . . über alles Bedingte unendlich erhebt], reappears throughout Schlegel's writing. Its importance to his view of art is expanded upon by his writings on religion as well. For most of his commentators, Schlegel's increasing interest in the spiritual in later years indicates that he eventually turns away from irony and its centrifugal energies, in search of a " 'firm basis' " of meaning. As Behler and Struc put it [in their introduction to *Friedrich Schlegel, Dialogue on Poetry and Literary Aphorisms,* 1968],

> Schlegel turned away from his early position of irony and subjectivism to a more objective . . . attitude. . . . Schlegel is no longer content with the ironical affirmation of the modern artist's subjectivity, but looks for a "matrix," a "firm basis." Many critics have seen in this demand . . . the first symptom of Schlegel's later conversion to Catholicism.

This view is paralleled in de Man's contention that for the later Friedrich Schlegel it was necessary to "leap out of language into faith." Even Mellor, who characterizes Schlegelian irony as affording a "sacred participation in the process of life," sees it as antithetical to the spiritual, and hence pictures Schlegel as succumbing to a need for "refuge" in the "calmer certainties of an ordered universe." To characterize Schlegel's interest in Catholicism as representing a rejection of irony and a desire for "calmer certainties," however, is to neglect his own writings, both early and late, which suggest, as we have seen in **"Über die Unverständlichkeit,"** that irony does not violate mystical meaning, but supports it. One index of this compatibility is Schlegel's willingness to discuss mysticism in irreverently ironic terms, as in **Athenaeum-Fragment 398:**

> Der Mystizismus ist die mäßigste und wohlfeil-ste aller philosophischen Rasereien. Man darf ihm nur einen einzigen absoluten Widerspruch kreditieren, er weiß alle Bedürfnisse damit zu bestreiten und kann noch großen Luxus treiben.

> [Mysticism is the cheapest and most moderate of all philosophical ravings. Only credit one of its absolute contradictions, and you will thereby supply all its needs and even allow it to live in the lap of luxury.]

A more direct endorsement comes in a work as late as the **Dialogue of Poetry,** written in 1800 but revised in 1832, in which the play of irony is equated both with romantic art and with the eternal, self-creating movement of the universe:

> Jedes Gedicht soll eigentlich romantisch. . . . Auch machen wir diese Foderung überall, ohne eben den Namen zu gebrauchen. Selbst in ganz populären Arten wie z. B. im Schauspiel, fodern wir Ironie; wir fodern, daß die Begebenheiten, die Menschen, kurz das ganze Spiel des Lebens wirklich auch als Spiel genommen und darges-tellt sei. . . . Alle heiligen Spiele der Kunst sind nur ferne Nachbildungen von dem unendlichen Spiele der Welt, dem ewig sich selbst bildengen Kunstwerk.

> [Every poem should actually be romantic. . . . We make this demand everywhere, without using the name. Even in the quite popular genres, as for instance the drama, we demand irony; we demand that events, men, in short the play of life, be taken as play and be represented as such. . . . All the sacred plays of art are only a remote imitation of the infinite play of the uni-verse, the work of art which eternally creates it-self anew.]

The connection of irony to the sacred and the sublime is suggested as well in the aphorisms on religion to be found in the last set of critical fragments, the **Ideen,** known for their mystical orientation. These associate irony with the mystery central to both art and religion, by profering its characteristic qualities of play and contradiction as the necessary, even the highest attributes of religion. Here we are told that "Morality without a sense for paradox is vul-gar" [Moralität ohne Sinn für Paradoxie ist gemein], and, even more unconventionally, that religion will not attain its greatest potential until it develops these qualities more fully, for it is at present "a variety of poetry which, unsure of its own lovely playfulness, takes itself too seriously and too one-sidedly" [eine Abart von Poesie zu halten, die ihr eignes schönes Spiel verkennend sich selbst zu ernsthaft und einseitig nimmt].

We might conjecture, then, that Schlegel's love of irony and its effervescent self-destruction does not give way to the desire for a more direct route to the truth. Rather, irony helps to make the immanent accessible through its own incomprehensibility, which short-circuits the aggres-sively linear quality of our search for the essential, and en-courages our engagement with mystery through experi-ence rather than quest. For Schlegel, the sublime, the "in-finite play of the universe," is not something one under-stands but participates in, a complex experience drama-tized through irony, which doesn't "say" truth but allows for it. This "transcendental buffoonery" thus invites us to realize in ourselves as well as our language the happy asset of an "eternal agility." It is this ongoing involvement which **"Über die Unverständlichkeit"** offers us, by aban-doning stability of meaning and leading us into "the irony of irony," until, as the narrator wryly confesses, "One can't disentangle oneself from irony any more, as seems to be happening in this essay on incomprehensibility" [Man nicht wieder aus der Ironie herauskommen kann, wie es in diesem Versuch über die Unverständlichkeit zu sein scheint . . .].

*Cathy Comstock, " 'Transcendental Buffoonery': Irony as Process in Schlegel's 'Über die Unverständlichkeit'," in* Studies in Romanticism, *Vol. 26, No. 3, Fall, 1987, pp. 445-64.*

---

# FURTHER READING

Campbell, T. M. "Friedrich Schlegel's Apostasy and the *Europa*." *Modern Language Notes* XLI, No. 2 (February 1926): 86-96.
> Contends that the journal *Europa,* which Schlegel edited from 1803-5, provides the first indication of a shift in Schlegel's philosophy from an aesthetic to a religious orientation.

Eichner, Hans. "Friedrich Schlegel's Theory of Romantic Poetry." *PMLA* LXXI, No. 5 (December 1956): 1018-41.
> Discusses the terminology Schlegel used to discuss his theory of Romantic poetry.

Finlay, Marike. "An Ironic Twist of a Semiotics of Narrative: Friedrich Schlegel's *Roman*." *Canadian Review of Compara-tive Literature* 11, No. 4 (December 1984): 559-595.
> Develops a semiotic analysis of *Lucinde.*

Higonnet, Margaret R. "Organic Unity and Interpretative Boundaries: Friedrich Schlegel's Theories and Their Appli-cation in His Critique of Lessing." *Studies in Romanticism* 19, No. 2 (Summer 1980): 163-92.
> Asserts that "Schlegel's views on the problems of herme-neutics find their fullest and most systematic treatment in his several commentaries on [Gotthold] Lessing."

——. "Writing from the Feminine: *Lucinde* and *Adolphe.*" In *Annales Benjamin Constant 5,* edited by Etienne Hof-mann, pp. 17-35. Lausanne: Organe de l'Association Benja-min Constant, 1985.
> Examines the depiction of women in Schlegel's *Lucinde* and Benjamin Constant's *Adolphe.*

Hughes, Glyn Tegai. "Profusion and Order: The Brothers Schlegel." In his *Romantic German Literature,* pp. 41-60. New York: Holmes and Meier Publishers, Inc., 1979.
> Includes an overview of Schlegel's life and work, and as-sesses the legacy of his theories of Romantic literature.

Immerwahr, Raymond. "The Subjectivity or Objectivity of

Friedrich Schlegel's Poetic Irony." *The Germanic Review* XXVI (October, 1951): 173-91.

Examines Schlegel's aphorisms on irony.

Kayser, Wolfgang. "The Grotesque in the Age of Romanticism." In *The Grotesque in Art and Literature,* translated by Ulrich Weisstein, pp. 48-99. Bloomington: Indiana University Press, 1963.

Contains an analysis of Schlegel's use of the terms "grotesque" and "arabesque" in his literary criticism.

Koerner, Konrad. "Friedrich Schlegel and the Emergence of a Historical-Comparative Grammar." *Lingua E Stile* XXII, No. 3 (September 1987): 341-65.

Discusses Schlegel's contribution to linguistics, focusing on *Uber die Sprache und Weisheit der Indier* (*On the Language and Wisdom of India*).

Littlejohns, Richard. "The 'Bekenntnisse Eines Ungeschickten': A Re-Examination of Emancipatory Ideas in Friedrich Schlegel's *Lucinde.*" *The Modern Language Review* 72, No. 3 (July 1977): 605-14.

Discusses aspects of female emancipation in *Lucinde,* contending "the current view that *Lucinde* is primarily a statement of advanced social doctrines is as much a distortion of the novel as the allegation in the nineteenth century that it is the pornographic work of a libertine."

Lovejoy, Arthur O. "On the Meaning of 'Romantic' in Early German Romanticism." In his *Essays in the History of Ideas,* pp. 183-206. Baltimore: Johns Hopkins Press, 1948.

Analyzes various meanings of the term "romantic" (*romantisch*) in Schlegel's criticism.

Monroe, Jonathan B. "*Universalpoesie* as Fragment: Friedrich Schlegel and the Prose Poem." In his *A Poverty of Objects: The Prose and the Politics of Genre,* pp. 45-71. Ithaca, N. Y.: Cornell University Press, 1987.

Discusses Schlegel's theories on the relationship between poetry and prose as set forth in his *Athenäum-Fragments* and *Literary Notebooks.*

Prawer, S. S. "In Pursuit of First Principles." *Times Literary Supplement,* No. 3887 (10 September 1976): 1100-01.

Reviews two volumes of Schlegel's *Kritische Ausgabe* relating to his literary criticism and writings on philosophy and religion. Prawer notes Schlegel's wide range of interests, as well as his attempt to find underlying principles linking disparate texts, but also points out that many of his contributions to literature "turn out to be lackluster by the standards their author himself set in the essays he wrote for the *Athenäum.*"

Review of *The Philosophy of History: In a Course of Lectures,* by Friedrich Schlegel. *Southern Quarterly Review* III, No. VI (April 1843): 263-317.

Reviews Schlegel's *Philosophy of History,* calling it "vague, fantastical and unsatisfactory, —there is a constant straining towards some invisible end, —a continual groping amid fogs, and clouds, and darkness, for something which the writer supposes to be latent there, but which remains wholly untangible to him."

Weltman, J. "The Religion of Friedrich Schlegel." *Modern Language Review* XXXI, No. 4 (October 1936): 539-44.

Argues that Schlegel's conversion to Catholicism did not represent a dramatic alteration of his philosophy; rather, it was the logical culmination of his belief that "religion, mythology, and Catholicism are practically identical."

Wessell, Leonard P., Jr. "The Antinomic Structure of Friedrich Schlegel's 'Romanticism'." *Studies in Romanticism* 12, No. 3 (Summer 1973): 648-69.

Investigates the philosophical foundations of Schlegel's theory of Romanticism, which, Wessell notes, is a synthesis of classical and modern elements.

---

Additional coverage of Schlegel's life and career is contained in the following sources published by Gale Research: *Dictionary of Literary Biography,* Vol. 90.

# Nineteenth-Century Literature Criticism

Cumulative Indexes
Volumes 1-45

# How to Use This Index

## The main references

---

Calvino, Italo
1923-1985.....CLC 5, 8, 11, 22, 33, 39,
73; SSC 3

---

**list all author entries in the following Gale Literary Criticism series:**

*BLC = Black Literature Criticism*
*CLC = Contemporary Literary Criticism*
*CLR = Children's Literature Review*
*CMLC = Classical and Medieval Literature Criticism*
*DA = DISCovering Authors*
*DC = Drama Criticism*
*HLC = Hispanic Literature Criticism*
*LC = Literature Criticism from 1400 to 1800*
*NCLC = Nineteenth-Century Literature Criticism*
*PC = Poetry Criticism*
*SSC = Short Story Criticism*
*TCLC = Twentieth-Century Literary Criticism*
*WLC = World Literature Criticism, 1500 to the Present*

## The cross-references

---

See also CANR 23; CA 85-88;
obituary CA 116

---

**list all author entries in the following Gale biographical and literary sources:**

*AAYA = Authors & Artists for Young Adults*
*AITN = Authors in the News*
*BEST = Bestsellers*
*BW = Black Writers*
*CA = Contemporary Authors*
*CAAS = Contemporary Authors Autobiography Series*
*CABS = Contemporary Authors Bibliographical Series*
*CANR = Contemporary Authors New Revision Series*
*CAP = Contemporary Authors Permanent Series*
*CDALB = Concise Dictionary of American Literary Biography*
*CDBLB = Concise Dictionary of British Literary Biography*
*DLB = Dictionary of Literary Biography*
*DLBD = Dictionary of Literary Biography Documentary Series*
*DLBY = Dictionary of Literary Biography Yearbook*
*HW = Hispanic Writers*
*JRDA = Junior DISCovering Authors*
*MAICYA = Major Authors and Illustrators for Children and Young Adults*
*MTCW = Major 20th-Century Writers*
*SAAS = Something about the Author Autobiography Series*
*SATA = Something about the Author*
*YABC = Yesterday's Authors of Books for Children*

**Antoine, Marc**
See Proust, (Valentin-Louis-George-Eugene-)
Marcel

**Antoninus, Brother**
See Everson, William (Oliver)

**Antonioni, Michelangelo** 1912- ..... **CLC 20**
See also CA 73-76

**Antschel, Paul** 1920-1970...... **CLC 10, 19**
See also Celan, Paul
See also CA 85-88; CANR 33; MTCW

**Anwar, Chairil** 1922-1949 ....... **TCLC 22**
See also CA 121

**Apollinaire, Guillaume** .. **TCLC 3, 8, 51; PC 7**
See also Kostrowitzki, Wilhelm Apollinaris
de

**Appelfeld, Aharon** 1932- ...... **CLC 23, 47**
See also CA 112; 133

**Apple, Max (Isaac)** 1941-........ **CLC 9, 33**
See also CA 81-84; CANR 19; DLB 130

**Appleman, Philip (Dean)** 1926- ..... **CLC 51**
See also CA 13-16R; CAAS 18; CANR 6,
29

**Appleton, Lawrence**
See Lovecraft, H(oward) P(hillips)

**Apteryx**
See Eliot, T(homas) S(tearns)

**Apuleius, (Lucius Madaurensis)**
125(?)-175(?) ................ **CMLC 1**

**Aquin, Hubert** 1929-1977......... **CLC 15**
See also CA 105; DLB 53

**Aragon, Louis** 1897-1982........ **CLC 3, 22**
See also CA 69-72; 108; CANR 28;
DLB 72; MTCW

**Arany, Janos** 1817-1882........ **NCLC 34**

**Arbuthnot, John** 1667-1735......... **LC 1**
See also DLB 101

**Archer, Herbert Winslow**
See Mencken, H(enry) L(ouis)

**Archer, Jeffrey (Howard)** 1940- .... **CLC 28**
See also BEST 89:3; CA 77-80; CANR 22

**Archer, Jules** 1915- .............. **CLC 12**
See also CA 9-12R; CANR 6; SAAS 5;
SATA 4

**Archer, Lee**
See Ellison, Harlan

**Arden, John** 1930- .......... **CLC 6, 13, 15**
See also CA 13-16R; CAAS 4; CANR 31;
DLB 13; MTCW

**Arenas, Reinaldo**
1943-1990 ............. **CLC 41; HLC**
See also CA 124; 128; 133; HW

**Arendt, Hannah** 1906-1975 ........ **CLC 66**
See also CA 17-20R; 61-64; CANR 26;
MTCW

**Aretino, Pietro** 1492-1556 .......... **LC 12**

**Arghezi, Tudor**................... **CLC 80**
See also Theodorescu, Ion N.

**Arguedas, Jose Maria**
1911-1969 ............... **CLC 10, 18**
See also CA 89-92; DLB 113; HW

**Argueta, Manlio** 1936-............ **CLC 31**
See also CA 131; HW

**Ariosto, Ludovico** 1474-1533........ **LC 6**

**Aristides**
See Epstein, Joseph

**Aristophanes**
450B.C.-385B.C.... **CMLC 4; DA; DC 2**

**Arlt, Roberto (Godofredo Christophersen)**
1900-1942 ............. **TCLC 29; HLC**
See also CA 123; 131; HW

**Armah, Ayi Kwei** 1939-.... **CLC 5, 33; BLC**
See also BW 1; CA 61-64; CANR 21;
DLB 117; MTCW

**Armatrading, Joan** 1950-......... **CLC 17**
See also CA 114

**Arnette, Robert**
See Silverberg, Robert

**Arnim, Achim von (Ludwig Joachim von**
**Arnim)** 1781-1831 .......... **NCLC 5**
See also DLB 90

**Arnim, Bettina von** 1785-1859.... **NCLC 38**
See also DLB 90

**Arnold, Matthew**
1822-1888 ..... **NCLC 6, 29; DA; PC 5;**
**WLC**
See also CDBLB 1832-1890; DLB 32, 57

**Arnold, Thomas** 1795-1842 ..... **NCLC 18**
See also DLB 55

**Arnow, Harriette (Louisa) Simpson**
1908-1986 .............. **CLC 2, 7, 18**
See also CA 9-12R; 118; CANR 14; DLB 6;
MTCW; SATA 42, 47

**Arp, Hans**
See Arp, Jean

**Arp, Jean** 1887-1966............... **CLC 5**
See also CA 81-84; 25-28R; CANR 42

**Arrabal**
See Arrabal, Fernando

**Arrabal, Fernando** 1932- ... **CLC 2, 9, 18, 58**
See also CA 9-12R; CANR 15

**Arrick, Fran**..................... **CLC 30**

**Artaud, Antonin** 1896-1948 ..... **TCLC 3, 36**
See also CA 104

**Arthur, Ruth M(abel)** 1905-1979.... **CLC 12**
See also CA 9-12R; 85-88; CANR 4;
SATA 7, 26

**Artsybashev, Mikhail (Petrovich)**
1878-1927 ................. **TCLC 31**

**Arundel, Honor (Morfydd)**
1919-1973 ................. **CLC 17**
See also CA 21-22; 41-44R; CAP 2;
SATA 4, 24

**Asch, Sholem** 1880-1957 ......... **TCLC 3**
See also CA 105

**Ash, Shalom**
See Asch, Sholem

**Ashbery, John (Lawrence)**
1927- ...... **CLC 2, 3, 4, 6, 9, 13, 15, 25,**
**41, 77**
See also CA 5-8R; CANR 9, 37; DLB 5;
DLBY 81; MTCW

**Ashdown, Clifford**
See Freeman, R(ichard) Austin

**Ashe, Gordon**
See Creasey, John

**Ashton-Warner, Sylvia (Constance)**
1908-1984 .................. **CLC 19**
See also CA 69-72; 112; CANR 29; MTCW

**Asimov, Isaac**
1920-1992 ...... **CLC 1, 3, 9, 19, 26, 76**
See also BEST 90:2; CA 1-4R; 137;
CANR 2, 19, 36; CLR 12; DLB 8;
DLBY 92; JRDA; MAICYA; MTCW;
SATA 1, 26, 74

**Astley, Thea (Beatrice May)**
1925- ...................... **CLC 41**
See also CA 65-68; CANR 11, 43

**Aston, James**
See White, T(erence) H(anbury)

**Asturias, Miguel Angel**
1899-1974 ........ **CLC 3, 8, 13; HLC**
See also CA 25-28; 49-52; CANR 32;
CAP 2; DLB 113; HW; MTCW

**Atares, Carlos Saura**
See Saura (Atares), Carlos

**Atheling, William**
See Pound, Ezra (Weston Loomis)

**Atheling, William, Jr.**
See Blish, James (Benjamin)

**Atherton, Gertrude (Franklin Horn)**
1857-1948 .................. **TCLC 2**
See also CA 104; DLB 9, 78

**Atherton, Lucius**
See Masters, Edgar Lee

**Atkins, Jack**
See Harris, Mark

**Atticus**
See Fleming, Ian (Lancaster)

**Atwood, Margaret (Eleanor)**
1939- ..... **CLC 2, 3, 4, 8, 13, 15, 25, 44;**
**DA; PC 8; SSC 2; WLC**
See also AAYA 12; BEST 89:2; CA 49-52;
CANR 3, 24, 33; DLB 53; MTCW;
SATA 50

**Aubigny, Pierre d'**
See Mencken, H(enry) L(ouis)

**Aubin, Penelope** 1685-1731(?) ........ **LC 9**
See also DLB 39

**Auchincloss, Louis (Stanton)**
1917- ............. **CLC 4, 6, 9, 18, 45**
See also CA 1-4R; CANR 6, 29; DLB 2;
DLBY 80; MTCW

**Auden, W(ystan) H(ugh)**
1907-1973 ...... **CLC 1, 2, 3, 4, 6, 9, 11,**
**14, 43; DA; PC 1; WLC**
See also CA 9-12R; 45-48; CANR 5;
CDBLB 1914-1945; DLB 10, 20; MTCW

**Audiberti, Jacques** 1900-1965 ...... **CLC 38**
See also CA 25-28R

**Auel, Jean M(arie)** 1936-.......... **CLC 31**
See also AAYA 7; BEST 90:4; CA 103;
CANR 21

**Auerbach, Erich** 1892-1957 ....... **TCLC 43**
See also CA 118

**Augier, Emile** 1820-1889 ........ **NCLC 31**

**August, John**
See De Voto, Bernard (Augustine)

**Augustine, St.** 354-430 .......... **CMLC 6**

**Aurelius**
See Bourne, Randolph S(illiman)

**Austen, Jane**
  1775-1817 .... **NCLC 1, 13, 19, 33; DA;
      WLC**
  See also CDBLB 1789-1832; DLB 116

**Auster, Paul** 1947- .............. **CLC 47**
  See also CA 69-72; CANR 23

**Austin, Frank**
  See Faust, Frederick (Schiller)

**Austin, Mary (Hunter)**
  1868-1934 ................. **TCLC 25**
  See also CA 109; DLB 9, 78

**Autran Dourado, Waldomiro**
  See Dourado, (Waldomiro Freitas) Autran

**Averroes** 1126-1198 ............. **CMLC 7**
  See also DLB 115

**Avison, Margaret** 1918- .......... **CLC 2, 4**
  See also CA 17-20R; DLB 53; MTCW

**Axton, David**
  See Koontz, Dean R(ay)

**Ayckbourn, Alan**
  1939- ........... **CLC 5, 8, 18, 33, 74**
  See also CA 21-24R; CANR 31; DLB 13;
      MTCW

**Aydy, Catherine**
  See Tennant, Emma (Christina)

**Ayme, Marcel (Andre)** 1902-1967... **CLC 11**
  See also CA 89-92; CLR 25; DLB 72

**Ayrton, Michael** 1921-1975 ........ **CLC 7**
  See also CA 5-8R; 61-64; CANR 9, 21

**Azorin** ......................... **CLC 11**
  See also Martinez Ruiz, Jose

**Azuela, Mariano**
  1873-1952 ............. **TCLC 3; HLC**
  See also CA 104; 131; HW; MTCW

**Baastad, Babbis Friis**
  See Friis-Baastad, Babbis Ellinor

**Bab**
  See Gilbert, W(illiam) S(chwenck)

**Babbis, Eleanor**
  See Friis-Baastad, Babbis Ellinor

**Babel, Isaak (Emmanuilovich)**
  1894-1941(?) .............. **TCLC 2, 13**
  See also CA 104

**Babits, Mihaly** 1883-1941 ....... **TCLC 14**
  See also CA 114

**Babur** 1483-1530 ................. **LC 18**

**Bacchelli, Riccardo** 1891-1985 ..... **CLC 19**
  See also CA 29-32R; 117

**Bach, Richard (David)** 1936- ....... **CLC 14**
  See also AITN 1; BEST 89:2; CA 9-12R;
      CANR 18; MTCW; SATA 13

**Bachman, Richard**
  See King, Stephen (Edwin)

**Bachmann, Ingeborg** 1926-1973..... **CLC 69**
  See also CA 93-96; 45-48; DLB 85

**Bacon, Francis** 1561-1626 ......... **LC 18**
  See also CDBLB Before 1660

**Bacovia, George** ................. **TCLC 24**
  See also Vasiliu, Gheorghe

**Badanes, Jerome** 1937- ........... **CLC 59**

**Bagehot, Walter** 1826-1877 ...... **NCLC 10**
  See also DLB 55

**Bagnold, Enid** 1889-1981 .......... **CLC 25**
  See also CA 5-8R; 103; CANR 5, 40;
      DLB 13; MAICYA; SATA 1, 25

**Bagrjana, Elisaveta**
  See Belcheva, Elisaveta

**Bagryana, Elisaveta**
  See Belcheva, Elisaveta

**Bailey, Paul** 1937- .............. **CLC 45**
  See also CA 21-24R; CANR 16; DLB 14

**Baillie, Joanna** 1762-1851 ....... **NCLC 2**
  See also DLB 93

**Bainbridge, Beryl (Margaret)**
  1933- .... **CLC 4, 5, 8, 10, 14, 18, 22, 62**
  See also CA 21-24R; CANR 24; DLB 14;
      MTCW

**Baker, Elliott** 1922- .............. **CLC 8**
  See also CA 45-48; CANR 2

**Baker, Nicholson** 1957- ........... **CLC 61**
  See also CA 135

**Baker, Ray Stannard** 1870-1946... **TCLC 47**
  See also CA 118

**Baker, Russell (Wayne)** 1925- ...... **CLC 31**
  See also BEST 89:4; CA 57-60; CANR 11,
      41; MTCW

**Bakhtin, M.**
  See Bakhtin, Mikhail Mikhailovich

**Bakhtin, M. M.**
  See Bakhtin, Mikhail Mikhailovich

**Bakhtin, Mikhail**
  See Bakhtin, Mikhail Mikhailovich

**Bakhtin, Mikhail Mikhailovich**
  1895-1975 .................. **CLC 83**
  See also CA 128; 113

**Bakshi, Ralph** 1938(?)- ........... **CLC 26**
  See also CA 112; 138

**Bakunin, Mikhail (Alexandrovich)**
  1814-1876 ................. **NCLC 25**

**Baldwin, James (Arthur)**
  1924-1987 ...... **CLC 1, 2, 3, 4, 5, 8, 13,
      15, 17, 42, 50, 67; BLC; DA; DC 1;
      SSC 10; WLC**
  See also AAYA 4; BW 1; CA 1-4R; 124;
      CABS 1; CANR 3, 24;
      CDALB 1941-1968; DLB 2, 7, 33;
      DLBY 87; MTCW; SATA 9, 54

**Ballard, J(ames) G(raham)**
  1930- ........ **CLC 3, 6, 14, 36; SSC 1**
  See also AAYA 3; CA 5-8R; CANR 15, 39;
      DLB 14; MTCW

**Balmont, Konstantin (Dmitriyevich)**
  1867-1943 ................. **TCLC 11**
  See also CA 109

**Balzac, Honore de**
  1799-1850 .... **NCLC 5, 35; DA; SSC 5;
      WLC**
  See also DLB 119

**Bambara, Toni Cade**
  1939- .............. **CLC 19; BLC; DA**
  See also AAYA 5; BW 2; CA 29-32R;
      CANR 24; DLB 38; MTCW

**Bamdad, A.**
  See Shamlu, Ahmad

**Banat, D. R.**
  See Bradbury, Ray (Douglas)

**Bancroft, Laura**
  See Baum, L(yman) Frank

**Banim, John** 1798-1842 ......... **NCLC 13**
  See also DLB 116

**Banim, Michael** 1796-1874 ...... **NCLC 13**

**Banks, Iain**
  See Banks, Iain M(enzies)

**Banks, Iain M(enzies)** 1954- ....... **CLC 34**
  See also CA 123; 128

**Banks, Lynne Reid** .............. **CLC 23**
  See also Reid Banks, Lynne
  See also AAYA 6

**Banks, Russell** 1940- .......... **CLC 37, 72**
  See also CA 65-68; CAAS 15; CANR 19;
      DLB 130

**Banville, John** 1945- .............. **CLC 46**
  See also CA 117; 128; DLB 14

**Banville, Theodore (Faullain) de**
  1832-1891 ................. **NCLC 9**

**Baraka, Amiri**
  1934- ........ **CLC 1, 2, 3, 5, 10, 14, 33;
      BLC; DA; PC 4**
  See also Jones, LeRoi
  See also BW 2; CA 21-24R; CABS 3;
      CANR 27, 38; CDALB 1941-1968;
      DLB 5, 7, 16, 38; DLBD 8; MTCW

**Barbellion, W. N. P.** .............. **TCLC 24**
  See also Cummings, Bruce F(rederick)

**Barbera, Jack** 1945- .............. **CLC 44**
  See also CA 110

**Barbey d'Aurevilly, Jules Amedee**
  1808-1889 ................. **NCLC 1**
  See also DLB 119

**Barbusse, Henri** 1873-1935 ........ **TCLC 5**
  See also CA 105; DLB 65

**Barclay, Bill**
  See Moorcock, Michael (John)

**Barclay, William Ewert**
  See Moorcock, Michael (John)

**Barea, Arturo** 1897-1957 ........ **TCLC 14**
  See also CA 111

**Barfoot, Joan** 1946- .............. **CLC 18**
  See also CA 105

**Baring, Maurice** 1874-1945 ........ **TCLC 8**
  See also CA 105; DLB 34

**Barker, Clive** 1952- .............. **CLC 52**
  See also AAYA 10; BEST 90:3; CA 121;
      129; MTCW

**Barker, George Granville**
  1913-1991 ................. **CLC 8, 48**
  See also CA 9-12R; 135; CANR 7, 38;
      DLB 20; MTCW

**Barker, Harley Granville**
  See Granville-Barker, Harley
  See also DLB 10

**Barker, Howard** 1946- ............ **CLC 37**
  See also CA 102; DLB 13

**Barker, Pat** 1943- ................ **CLC 32**
  See also CA 117; 122

**Barlow, Joel** 1754-1812 ......... **NCLC 23**
  See also DLB 37

**Barnard, Mary (Ethel)** 1909- ....... **CLC 48**
  See also CA 21-22; CAP 2

**Betjeman, John**
1906-1984 . . . . . . . **CLC 2, 6, 10, 34, 43**
See also CA 9-12R; 112; CANR 33;
CDBLB 1945-1960; DLB 20; DLBY 84;
MTCW

**Bettelheim, Bruno** 1903-1990 . . . . . . **CLC 79**
See also CA 81-84; 131; CANR 23; MTCW

**Betti, Ugo** 1892-1953 . . . . . . . . . . . . . **TCLC 5**
See also CA 104

**Betts, Doris (Waugh)** 1932- . . . . **CLC 3, 6, 28**
See also CA 13-16R; CANR 9; DLBY 82

**Bevan, Alistair**
See Roberts, Keith (John Kingston)

**Beynon, John**
See Harris, John (Wyndham Parkes Lucas)
Beynon

**Bialik, Chaim Nachman**
1873-1934 . . . . . . . . . . . . . . . . **TCLC 25**

**Bickerstaff, Isaac**
See Swift, Jonathan

**Bidart, Frank** 1939- . . . . . . . . . . . . . . **CLC 33**
See also CA 140

**Bienek, Horst** 1930- . . . . . . . . . . . . **CLC 7, 11**
See also CA 73-76; DLB 75

**Bierce, Ambrose (Gwinett)**
1842-1914(?) . . . . . . . **TCLC 1, 7, 44; DA;**
**SSC 9; WLC**
See also CA 104; 139; CDALB 1865-1917;
DLB 11, 12, 23, 71, 74

**Billings, Josh**
See Shaw, Henry Wheeler

**Billington, (Lady) Rachel (Mary)**
1942- . . . . . . . . . . . . . . . . . . . . **CLC 43**
See also AITN 2; CA 33-36R; CANR 44

**Binyon, T(imothy) J(ohn)** 1936- . . . . **CLC 34**
See also CA 111; CANR 28

**Bioy Casares, Adolfo**
1914- . . . . . . . . . . . . **CLC 4, 8, 13; HLC**
See also CA 29-32R; CANR 19, 43;
DLB 113; HW; MTCW

**Bird, C.**
See Ellison, Harlan

**Bird, Cordwainer**
See Ellison, Harlan

**Bird, Robert Montgomery**
1806-1854 . . . . . . . . . . . . . . . . . **NCLC 1**

**Birney, (Alfred) Earle**
1904- . . . . . . . . . . . . . . . **CLC 1, 4, 6, 11**
See also CA 1-4R; CANR 5, 20; DLB 88;
MTCW

**Bishop, Elizabeth**
1911-1979 . . . . . . **CLC 1, 4, 9, 13, 15, 32;**
**DA; PC 3**
See also CA 5-8R; 89-92; CABS 2;
CANR 26; CDALB 1968-1988; DLB 5;
MTCW; SATA 24

**Bishop, John** 1935- . . . . . . . . . . . . . . **CLC 10**
See also CA 105

**Bissett, Bill** 1939- . . . . . . . . . . . . . . **CLC 18**
See also CA 69-72; CAAS 19; CANR 15;
DLB 53; MTCW

**Bitov, Andrei (Georgievich)** 1937- . . . **CLC 57**
See also CA 142

**Biyidi, Alexandre** 1932-
See Beti, Mongo
See also BW 1; CA 114; 124; MTCW

**Bjarme, Brynjolf**
See Ibsen, Henrik (Johan)

**Bjornson, Bjornstjerne (Martinius)**
1832-1910 . . . . . . . . . . . . . . **TCLC 7, 37**
See also CA 104

**Black, Robert**
See Holdstock, Robert P.

**Blackburn, Paul** 1926-1971 . . . . . . **CLC 9, 43**
See also CA 81-84; 33-36R; CANR 34;
DLB 16; DLBY 81

**Black Elk** 1863-1950 . . . . . . . . . . . . **TCLC 33**
See also CA 144

**Black Hobart**
See Sanders, (James) Ed(ward)

**Blacklin, Malcolm**
See Chambers, Aidan

**Blackmore, R(ichard) D(oddridge)**
1825-1900 . . . . . . . . . . . . . . . . **TCLC 27**
See also CA 120; DLB 18

**Blackmur, R(ichard) P(almer)**
1904-1965 . . . . . . . . . . . . . . . . **CLC 2, 24**
See also CA 11-12; 25-28R; CAP 1; DLB 63

**Black Tarantula, The**
See Acker, Kathy

**Blackwood, Algernon (Henry)**
1869-1951 . . . . . . . . . . . . . . . . . **TCLC 5**
See also CA 105

**Blackwood, Caroline** 1931- . . . . . . . **CLC 6, 9**
See also CA 85-88; CANR 32; DLB 14;
MTCW

**Blade, Alexander**
See Hamilton, Edmond; Silverberg, Robert

**Blaga, Lucian** 1895-1961 . . . . . . . . . **CLC 75**

**Blair, Eric (Arthur)** 1903-1950
See Orwell, George
See also CA 104; 132; DA; MTCW;
SATA 29

**Blais, Marie-Claire**
1939- . . . . . . . . . . . . **CLC 2, 4, 6, 13, 22**
See also CA 21-24R; CAAS 4; CANR 38;
DLB 53; MTCW

**Blaise, Clark** 1940- . . . . . . . . . . . . . . **CLC 29**
See also AITN 2; CA 53-56; CAAS 3;
CANR 5; DLB 53

**Blake, Nicholas**
See Day Lewis, C(ecil)
See also DLB 77

**Blake, William**
1757-1827 . . . . . **NCLC 13, 37; DA; WLC**
See also CDBLB 1789-1832; DLB 93;
MAICYA; SATA 30

**Blasco Ibanez, Vicente**
1867-1928 . . . . . . . . . . . . . . . . **TCLC 12**
See also CA 110; 131; HW; MTCW

**Blatty, William Peter** 1928- . . . . . . . . **CLC 2**
See also CA 5-8R; CANR 9

**Bleeck, Oliver**
See Thomas, Ross (Elmore)

**Blessing, Lee** 1949- . . . . . . . . . . . . . . **CLC 54**

**Blish, James (Benjamin)**
1921-1975 . . . . . . . . . . . . . . . . . **CLC 14**
See also CA 1-4R; 57-60; CANR 3; DLB 8;
MTCW; SATA 66

**Bliss, Reginald**
See Wells, H(erbert) G(eorge)

**Blixen, Karen (Christentze Dinesen)**
1885-1962
See Dinesen, Isak
See also CA 25-28; CANR 22; CAP 2;
MTCW; SATA 44

**Bloch, Robert (Albert)** 1917- . . . . . . . **CLC 33**
See also CA 5-8R; CANR 5; DLB 44;
SATA 12

**Blok, Alexander (Alexandrovich)**
1880-1921 . . . . . . . . . . . . . . . . . **TCLC 5**
See also CA 104

**Blom, Jan**
See Breytenbach, Breyten

**Bloom, Harold** 1930- . . . . . . . . . . . . . **CLC 24**
See also CA 13-16R; CANR 39; DLB 67

**Bloomfield, Aurelius**
See Bourne, Randolph S(illiman)

**Blount, Roy (Alton), Jr.** 1941- . . . . . **CLC 38**
See also CA 53-56; CANR 10, 28; MTCW

**Bloy, Leon** 1846-1917 . . . . . . . . . . . . **TCLC 22**
See also CA 121; DLB 123

**Blume, Judy (Sussman)** 1938- . . . **CLC 12, 30**
See also AAYA 3; CA 29-32R; CANR 13,
37; CLR 2, 15; DLB 52; JRDA;
MAICYA; MTCW; SATA 2, 31

**Blunden, Edmund (Charles)**
1896-1974 . . . . . . . . . . . . . . . . **CLC 2, 56**
See also CA 17-18; 45-48; CAP 2; DLB 20,
100; MTCW

**Bly, Robert (Elwood)**
1926- . . . . . . . . . . **CLC 1, 2, 5, 10, 15, 38**
See also CA 5-8R; CANR 41; DLB 5;
MTCW

**Bobette**
See Simenon, Georges (Jacques Christian)

**Boccaccio, Giovanni**
1313-1375 . . . . . . . . . . **CMLC 13; SSC 10**

**Bochco, Steven** 1943- . . . . . . . . . . . . . **CLC 35**
See also AAYA 11; CA 124; 138

**Bodenheim, Maxwell** 1892-1954 . . . **TCLC 44**
See also CA 110; DLB 9, 45

**Bodker, Cecil** 1927- . . . . . . . . . . . . . . **CLC 21**
See also CA 73-76; CANR 13, 44; CLR 23;
MAICYA; SATA 14

**Boell, Heinrich (Theodor)** 1917-1985
See Boll, Heinrich (Theodor)
See also CA 21-24R; 116; CANR 24; DA;
DLB 69; DLBY 85; MTCW

**Boerne, Alfred**
See Doeblin, Alfred

**Bogan, Louise** 1897-1970 . . . . . **CLC 4, 39, 46**
See also CA 73-76; 25-28R; CANR 33;
DLB 45; MTCW

**Bogarde, Dirk** . . . . . . . . . . . . . . . . . . **CLC 19**
See also Van Den Bogarde, Derek Jules
Gaspard Ulric Niven
See also DLB 14

**Bogosian, Eric** 1953- . . . . . . . . . . . . . **CLC 45**
See also CA 138

Braverman, Kate  1950-  . . . . . . . . . .  **CLC 67**
See also CA 89-92

Brecht, Bertolt
1898-1956  . . . . . .  **TCLC 1, 6, 13, 35; DA;**
**DC 3; WLC**
See also CA 104; 133; DLB 56, 124; MTCW

Brecht, Eugen Berthold Friedrich
See Brecht, Bertolt

Bremer, Fredrika  1801-1865  . . . . .  **NCLC 11**

Brennan, Christopher John
1870-1932  . . . . . . . . . . . . . . . . .  **TCLC 17**
See also CA 117

Brennan, Maeve  1917-  . . . . . . . . . . . . .  **CLC 5**
See also CA 81-84

Brentano, Clemens (Maria)
1778-1842  . . . . . . . . . . . . . . . . . .  **NCLC 1**

Brent of Bin Bin
See Franklin, (Stella Maraia Sarah) Miles

Brenton, Howard  1942-  . . . . . . . . . .  **CLC 31**
See also CA 69-72; CANR 33; DLB 13;
MTCW

Breslin, James  1930-
See Breslin, Jimmy
See also CA 73-76; CANR 31; MTCW

Breslin, Jimmy  . . . . . . . . . . . . . . .  **CLC 4, 43**
See also Breslin, James
See also AITN 1

Bresson, Robert  1907-  . . . . . . . . . . . .  **CLC 16**
See also CA 110

Breton, Andre  1896-1966 . . .  **CLC 2, 9, 15, 54**
See also CA 19-20; 25-28R; CANR 40;
CAP 2; DLB 65; MTCW

Breytenbach, Breyten  1939(?)-  . .  **CLC 23, 37**
See also CA 113; 129

Bridgers, Sue Ellen  1942-  . . . . . . . . .  **CLC 26**
See also AAYA 8; CA 65-68; CANR 11,
36, CLR 18; DLB 52; JRDA; MAICYA;
SAAS 1; SATA 22

Bridges, Robert (Seymour)
1844-1930  . . . . . . . . . . . . . . . . . .  **TCLC 1**
See also CA 104; CDBLB 1890-1914;
DLB 19, 98

Bridie, James. . . . . . . . . . . . . . . . . . . .  **TCLC 3**
See also Mavor, Osborne Henry
See also DLB 10

Brin, David  1950-. . . . . . . . . . . . . . .  **CLC 34**
See also CA 102; CANR 24; SATA 65

Brink, Andre (Philippus)
1935-. . . . . . . . . . . . . . . . . . . . .  **CLC 18, 36**
See also CA 104; CANR 39; MTCW

Brinsmead, H(esba) F(ay)  1922-  . . . .  **CLC 21**
See also CA 21-24R; CANR 10; MAICYA;
SAAS 5; SATA 18

Brittain, Vera (Mary)
1893(?)-1970 . . . . . . . . . . . . . . . .  **CLC 23**
See also CA 13-16; 25-28R; CAP 1; MTCW

Broch, Hermann  1886-1951. . . . . . .  **TCLC 20**
See also CA 117; DLB 85, 124

Brock, Rose
See Hansen, Joseph

Brodkey, Harold  1930-. . . . . . . . . . .  **CLC 56**
See also CA 111; DLB 130

Brodsky, Iosif Alexandrovich  1940-
See Brodsky, Joseph
See also AITN 1; CA 41-44R; CANR 37;
MTCW

Brodsky, Joseph . .  **CLC 4, 6, 13, 36, 50; PC 9**
See also Brodsky, Iosif Alexandrovich

Brodsky, Michael Mark  1948-  . . . . .  **CLC 19**
See also CA 102; CANR 18, 41

Bromell, Henry  1947-. . . . . . . . . . . . . .  **CLC 5**
See also CA 53-56; CANR 9

Bromfield, Louis (Brucker)
1896-1956 . . . . . . . . . . . . . . . . . .  **TCLC 11**
See also CA 107; DLB 4, 9, 86

Broner, E(sther) M(asserman)
1930-. . . . . . . . . . . . . . . . . . . . . . .  **CLC 19**
See also CA 17-20R; CANR 8, 25; DLB 28

Bronk, William  1918-. . . . . . . . . . . . .  **CLC 10**
See also CA 89-92; CANR 23

Bronstein, Lev Davidovich
See Trotsky, Leon

Bronte, Anne  1820-1849. . . . . . . . .  **NCLC 4**
See also DLB 21

Bronte, Charlotte
1816-1855 . . .  **NCLC 3, 8, 33; DA; WLC**
See also CDBLB 1832-1890; DLB 21

Bronte, (Jane) Emily
1818-1848 . . . .  **NCLC 16, 35; DA; PC 8;**
**WLC**
See also CDBLB 1832-1890; DLB 21, 32

Brooke, Frances  1724-1789 . . . . . . . . .  **LC 6**
See also DLB 39, 99

Brooke, Henry  1703(?)-1783 . . . . . . . . .  **LC 1**
See also DLB 39

Brooke, Rupert (Chawner)
1887-1915 . . . . . . .  **TCLC 2, 7; DA; WLC**
See also CA 104; 132; CDBLB 1914-1945;
DLB 19; MTCW

Brooke-Haven, P.
See Wodehouse, P(elham) G(renville)

Brooke-Rose, Christine  1926-  . . . . . .  **CLC 40**
See also CA 13-16R; DLB 14

Brookner, Anita  1928-. . . . . .  **CLC 32, 34, 51**
See also CA 114; 120; CANR 37; DLBY 87;
MTCW

Brooks, Cleanth  1906-. . . . . . . . . . . .  **CLC 24**
See also CA 17-20R; CANR 33, 35;
DLB 63; MTCW

Brooks, George
See Baum, L(yman) Frank

Brooks, Gwendolyn
1917-  . . . . . .  **CLC 1, 2, 4, 5, 15, 49; BLC;**
**DA; PC 7; WLC**
See also AITN 1; BW 2; CA 1-4R;
CANR 1, 27; CDALB 1941-1968;
CLR 27; DLB 5, 76; MTCW; SATA 6

Brooks, Mel. . . . . . . . . . . . . . . . . . . . .  **CLC 12**
See also Kaminsky, Melvin
See also DLB 26

Brooks, Peter  1938-. . . . . . . . . . . . . .  **CLC 34**
See also CA 45-48; CANR 1

Brooks, Van Wyck  1886-1963. . . . . .  **CLC 29**
See also CA 1-4R; CANR 6; DLB 45, 63,
103

Brophy, Brigid (Antonia)
1929-. . . . . . . . . . . . . . . . . .  **CLC 6, 11, 29**
See also CA 5-8R; CAAS 4; CANR 25;
DLB 14; MTCW

Brosman, Catharine Savage  1934-. . . .  **CLC 9**
See also CA 61-64; CANR 21

Brother Antoninus
See Everson, William (Oliver)

Broughton, T(homas) Alan  1936-  . . .  **CLC 19**
See also CA 45-48; CANR 2, 23

Broumas, Olga  1949-. . . . . . . . . .  **CLC 10, 73**
See also CA 85-88; CANR 20

Brown, Charles Brockden
1771-1810 . . . . . . . . . . . . . . . .  **NCLC 22**
See also CDALB 1640-1865; DLB 37, 59,
73

Brown, Christy  1932-1981. . . . . . . .  **CLC 63**
See also CA 105; 104; DLB 14

Brown, Claude  1937-  . . . . . . . .  **CLC 30; BLC**
See also AAYA 7; BW 1; CA 73-76

Brown, Dee (Alexander)  1908-  . .  **CLC 18, 47**
See also CA 13-16R; CAAS 6; CANR 11;
DLBY 80; MTCW; SATA 5

Brown, George
See Wertmueller, Lina

Brown, George Douglas
1869-1902 . . . . . . . . . . . . . . . .  **TCLC 28**

Brown, George Mackay  1921-. . . .  **CLC 5, 48**
See also CA 21-24R; CAAS 6; CANR 12,
37; DLB 14, 27, 139; MTCW; SATA 35

Brown, (William) Larry  1951-. . . . . .  **CLC 73**
See also CA 130; 134

Brown, Moses
See Barrett, William (Christopher)

Brown, Rita Mae  1944-. . . . .  **CLC 18, 43, 79**
See also CA 45-48; CANR 2, 11, 35;
MTCW

Brown, Roderick (Langmere) Haig-
See Haig-Brown, Roderick (Langmere)

Brown, Rosellen  1939-. . . . . . . . . . . .  **CLC 32**
See also CA 77-80; CAAS 10; CANR 14, 44

Brown, Sterling Allen
1901-1989 . . . . . . . . .  **CLC 1, 23, 59; BLC**
See also BW 1; CA 85-88; 127; CANR 26;
DLB 48, 51, 63; MTCW

Brown, Will
See Ainsworth, William Harrison

Brown, William Wells
1813-1884 . . . . . . . .  **NCLC 2; BLC; DC 1**
See also DLB 3, 50

Browne, (Clyde) Jackson  1948(?)-. . .  **CLC 21**
See also CA 120

Browning, Elizabeth Barrett
1806-1861 . . . . .  **NCLC 1, 16; DA; PC 6;**
**WLC**
See also CDBLB 1832-1890; DLB 32

Browning, Robert
1812-1889 . . . . . . . .  **NCLC 19; DA; PC 2**
See also CDBLB 1832-1890; DLB 32;
YABC 1

Browning, Tod  1882-1962 . . . . . . . . .  **CLC 16**
See also CA 141; 117

Bruccoli, Matthew J(oseph)  1931- . .  **CLC 34**
See also CA 9-12R; CANR 7; DLB 103

Bruce, Lenny . . . . . . . . . . . . . . . . . . . CLC 21
See also Schneider, Leonard Alfred

Bruin, John
See Brutus, Dennis

Brulls, Christian
See Simenon, Georges (Jacques Christian)

Brunner, John (Kilian Houston)
1934- . . . . . . . . . . . . . . . . . . . . CLC 8, 10
See also CA 1-4R; CAAS 8; CANR 2, 37;
MTCW

Brutus, Dennis 1924- . . . . . . . . CLC 43; BLC
See also BW 2; CA 49-52; CAAS 14;
CANR 2, 27, 42; DLB 117

Bryan, C(ourtlandt) D(ixon) B(arnes)
1936- . . . . . . . . . . . . . . . . . . . . . . CLC 29
See also CA 73-76; CANR 13

Bryan, Michael
See Moore, Brian

Bryant, William Cullen
1794-1878 . . . . . . . . . . . . . . NCLC 6; DA
See also CDALB 1640-1865; DLB 3, 43, 59

Bryusov, Valery Yakovlevich
1873-1924 . . . . . . . . . . . . . . . . . . TCLC 10
See also CA 107

Buchan, John 1875-1940 . . . . . . . . TCLC 41
See also CA 108; DLB 34, 70; YABC 2

Buchanan, George 1506-1582 . . . . . . . LC 4

Buchheim, Lothar-Guenther 1918- . . . CLC 6
See also CA 85-88

Buchner, (Karl) Georg
1813-1837 . . . . . . . . . . . . . . . . . NCLC 26

Buchwald, Art(hur) 1925- . . . . . . . . . CLC 33
See also AITN 1; CA 5-8R; CANR 21;
MTCW; SATA 10

Buck, Pearl S(ydenstricker)
1892-1973 . . . . . . . . . CLC 7, 11, 18; DA
See also AITN 1; CA 1-4R; 41-44R;
CANR 1, 34; DLB 9, 102; MTCW;
SATA 1, 25

Buckler, Ernest 1908-1984 . . . . . . . . CLC 13
See also CA 11-12; 114; CAP 1; DLB 68;
SATA 47

Buckley, Vincent (Thomas)
1925-1988 . . . . . . . . . . . . . . . . . . CLC 57
See also CA 101

Buckley, William F(rank), Jr.
1925- . . . . . . . . . . . . . . . . . CLC 7, 18, 37
See also AITN 1; CA 1-4R; CANR 1, 24;
DLB 137; DLBY 80; MTCW

Buechner, (Carl) Frederick
1926- . . . . . . . . . . . . . . . . CLC 2, 4, 6, 9
See also CA 13-16R; CANR 11, 39;
DLBY 80; MTCW

Buell, John (Edward) 1927- . . . . . . . . CLC 10
See also CA 1-4R; DLB 53

Buero Vallejo, Antonio 1916- . . . CLC 15, 46
See also CA 106; CANR 24; HW; MTCW

Bufalino, Gesualdo 1920(?)- . . . . . . . . CLC 74

Bugayev, Boris Nikolayevich 1880-1934
See Bely, Andrey
See also CA 104

Bukowski, Charles
1920-1994 . . . . . . . . CLC 2, 5, 9, 41, 82
See also CA 17-20R; 144; CANR 40;
DLB 5, 130; MTCW

Bulgakov, Mikhail (Afanas'evich)
1891-1940 . . . . . . . . . . . . . . TCLC 2, 16
See also CA 105

Bulgya, Alexander Alexandrovich
1901-1956 . . . . . . . . . . . . . . . . . TCLC 53
See also Fadeyev, Alexander
See also CA 117

Bullins, Ed 1935- . . . . . . . . CLC 1, 5, 7; BLC
See also BW 2; CA 49-52; CAAS 16;
CANR 24; DLB 7, 38; MTCW

Bulwer-Lytton, Edward (George Earle Lytton)
1803-1873 . . . . . . . . . . . . . . NCLC 1, 45
See also DLB 21

Bunin, Ivan Alexeyevich
1870-1953 . . . . . . . . . . . . TCLC 6; SSC 5
See also CA 104

Bunting, Basil 1900-1985 . . . . CLC 10, 39, 47
See also CA 53-56; 115; CANR 7; DLB 20

Bunuel, Luis 1900-1983 . . CLC 16, 80; HLC
See also CA 101; 110; CANR 32; HW

Bunyan, John 1628-1688 . . LC 4; DA; WLC
See also CDBLB 1660-1789; DLB 39

Burford, Eleanor
See Hibbert, Eleanor Alice Burford

Burgess, Anthony
CLC 1, 2, 4, 5, 8, 10, 13, 15, 22, 40, 62,
81
See also Wilson, John (Anthony) Burgess
See also AITN 1; CDBLB 1960 to Present;
DLB 14

Burke, Edmund
1729(?)-1797 . . . . . . . . LC 7; DA; WLC
See also DLB 104

Burke, Kenneth (Duva)
1897-1993 . . . . . . . . . . . . . . . CLC 2, 24
See also CA 5-8R; 143; CANR 39; DLB 45,
63; MTCW

Burke, Leda
See Garnett, David

Burke, Ralph
See Silverberg, Robert

Burney, Fanny 1752-1840 . . . . . . . NCLC 12
See also DLB 39

Burns, Robert
1759-1796 . . . . . . LC 3; DA; PC 6; WLC
See also CDBLB 1789-1832; DLB 109

Burns, Tex
See L'Amour, Louis (Dearborn)

Burnshaw, Stanley 1906- . . . . . CLC 3, 13, 44
See also CA 9-12R; DLB 48

Burr, Anne 1937- . . . . . . . . . . . . . . . . CLC 6
See also CA 25-28R

Burroughs, Edgar Rice
1875-1950 . . . . . . . . . . . . . . TCLC 2, 32
See also AAYA 11; CA 104; 132; DLB 8;
MTCW; SATA 41

Burroughs, William S(eward)
1914- . . . . . . . CLC 1, 2, 5, 15, 22, 42, 75;
DA; WLC
See also AITN 2; CA 9-12R; CANR 20;
DLB 2, 8, 16; DLBY 81; MTCW

Burton, Richard F. 1821-1890 . . . . NCLC 42
See also DLB 55

Busch, Frederick 1941- . . . CLC 7, 10, 18, 47
See also CA 33-36R; CAAS 1; DLB 6

Bush, Ronald 1946- . . . . . . . . . . . . . CLC 34
See also CA 136

Bustos, F(rancisco)
See Borges, Jorge Luis

Bustos Domecq, H(onorio)
See Bioy Casares, Adolfo; Borges, Jorge
Luis

Butler, Octavia E(stelle) 1947- . . . . . CLC 38
See also BW 2; CA 73-76; CANR 12, 24,
38; DLB 33; MTCW

Butler, Robert Olen (Jr.) 1945- . . . . . CLC 81
See also CA 112

Butler, Samuel 1612-1680 . . . . . . . . . LC 16
See also DLB 101, 126

Butler, Samuel
1835-1902 . . . . . . TCLC 1, 33; DA; WLC
See also CA 104; CDBLB 1890-1914;
DLB 18, 57

Butler, Walter C.
See Faust, Frederick (Schiller)

Butor, Michel (Marie Francois)
1926- . . . . . . . . . . . . . CLC 1, 3, 8, 11, 15
See also CA 9-12R; CANR 33; DLB 83;
MTCW

Buzo, Alexander (John) 1944- . . . . . . CLC 61
See also CA 97-100; CANR 17, 39

Buzzati, Dino 1906-1972 . . . . . . . . . . CLC 36
See also CA 33-36R

Byars, Betsy (Cromer) 1928- . . . . . . . CLC 35
See also CA 33-36R; CANR 18, 36; CLR 1,
16; DLB 52; JRDA; MAICYA; MTCW;
SAAS 1; SATA 4, 46

Byatt, A(ntonia) S(usan Drabble)
1936- . . . . . . . . . . . . . . . . . . . CLC 19, 65
See also CA 13-16R; CANR 13, 33;
DLB 14; MTCW

Byrne, David 1952- . . . . . . . . . . . . . . CLC 26
See also CA 127

Byrne, John Keyes 1926- . . . . . . . . . . CLC 19
See also Leonard, Hugh
See also CA 102

Byron, George Gordon (Noel)
1788-1824 . . . . . . NCLC 2, 12; DA; WLC
See also CDBLB 1789-1832; DLB 96, 110

C.3.3.
See Wilde, Oscar (Fingal O'Flahertie Wills)

Caballero, Fernan 1796-1877 . . . . . NCLC 10

Cabell, James Branch 1879-1958 . . . TCLC 6
See also CA 105; DLB 9, 78

Cable, George Washington
1844-1925 . . . . . . . . . . . TCLC 4; SSC 4
See also CA 104; DLB 12, 74

Cabral de Melo Neto, Joao 1920- . . . CLC 76

Cabrera Infante, G(uillermo)
1929- . . . . . . . . . . . . CLC 5, 25, 45; HLC
See also CA 85-88; CANR 29; DLB 113;
HW; MTCW

Cade, Toni
See Bambara, Toni Cade

Cadmus
See Buchan, John

Caedmon fl. 658-680 . . . . . . . . . . . . CMLC 7

Caeiro, Alberto
See Pessoa, Fernando (Antonio Nogueira)

**Cage, John (Milton, Jr.)** 1912- ..... **CLC 41**
See also CA 13-16R; CANR 9

**Cain, G.**
See Cabrera Infante, G(uillermo)

**Cain, Guillermo**
See Cabrera Infante, G(uillermo)

**Cain, James M(allahan)**
1892-1977 ............. **CLC 3, 11, 28**
See also AITN 1; CA 17-20R; 73-76;
CANR 8, 34; MTCW

**Caine, Mark**
See Raphael, Frederic (Michael)

**Calasso, Roberto** 1941- .......... **CLC 81**
See also CA 143

**Calderon de la Barca, Pedro**
1600-1681 .............. **LC 23; DC 3**

**Caldwell, Erskine (Preston)**
1903-1987 ........ **CLC 1, 8, 14, 50, 60**
See also AITN 1; CA 1-4R; 121; CAAS 1;
CANR 2, 33; DLB 9, 86; MTCW

**Caldwell, (Janet Miriam) Taylor (Holland)**
1900-1985 .............. **CLC 2, 28, 39**
See also CA 5-8R; 116; CANR 5

**Calhoun, John Caldwell**
1782-1850 ................. **NCLC 15**
See also DLB 3

**Calisher, Hortense**
1911- ........ **CLC 2, 4, 8, 38; SSC 15**
See also CA 1-4R; CANR 1, 22; DLB 2;
MTCW

**Callaghan, Morley Edward**
1903-1990 .......... **CLC 3, 14, 41, 65**
See also CA 9-12R; 132; CANR 33;
DLB 68; MTCW

**Calvino, Italo**
1923-1985 ..... **CLC 5, 8, 11, 22, 33, 39,
73; SSC 3**
See also CA 85-88; 116; CANR 23; MTCW

**Cameron, Carey** 1952- ............ **CLC 59**
See also CA 135

**Cameron, Peter** 1959- ............. **CLC 44**
See also CA 125

**Campana, Dino** 1885-1932 ........ **TCLC 20**
See also CA 117; DLB 114

**Campbell, John W(ood, Jr.)**
1910-1971 ................... **CLC 32**
See also CA 21-22; 29-32R; CANR 34;
CAP 2; DLB 8; MTCW

**Campbell, Joseph** 1904-1987 ....... **CLC 69**
See also AAYA 3; BEST 89:2; CA 1-4R;
124; CANR 3, 28; MTCW

**Campbell, (John) Ramsey** 1946- .... **CLC 42**
See also CA 57-60; CANR 7

**Campbell, (Ignatius) Roy (Dunnachie)**
1901-1957 .................. **TCLC 5**
See also CA 104; DLB 20

**Campbell, Thomas** 1777-1844 .... **NCLC 19**
See also DLB 93

**Campbell, Wilfred** ................. **TCLC 9**
See also Campbell, William

**Campbell, William** 1858(?)-1918
See Campbell, Wilfred
See also CA 106; DLB 92

**Campos, Alvaro de**
See Pessoa, Fernando (Antonio Nogueira)

**Camus, Albert**
1913-1960 .... **CLC 1, 2, 4, 9, 11, 14, 32,
63, 69; DA; DC 2; SSC 9; WLC**
See also CA 89-92; DLB 72; MTCW

**Canby, Vincent** 1924- ............. **CLC 13**
See also CA 81-84

**Cancale**
See Desnos, Robert

**Canetti, Elias** 1905- ...... **CLC 3, 14, 25, 75**
See also CA 21-24R; CANR 23; DLB 85,
124; MTCW

**Canin, Ethan** 1960- .............. **CLC 55**
See also CA 131; 135

**Cannon, Curt**
See Hunter, Evan

**Cape, Judith**
See Page, P(atricia) K(athleen)

**Capek, Karel**
1890-1938 ..... **TCLC 6, 37; DA; DC 1;
WLC**
See also CA 104; 140

**Capote, Truman**
1924-1984 ...... **CLC 1, 3, 8, 13, 19, 34,
38, 58; DA; SSC 2; WLC**
See also CA 5-8R; 113; CANR 18;
CDALB 1941-1968; DLB 2; DLBY 80,
84; MTCW

**Capra, Frank** 1897-1991 .......... **CLC 16**
See also CA 61-64; 135

**Caputo, Philip** 1941- ............. **CLC 32**
See also CA 73-76; CANR 40

**Card, Orson Scott** 1951- .... **CLC 44, 47, 50**
See also AAYA 11; CA 102; CANR 27;
MTCW

**Cardenal (Martinez), Ernesto**
1925- ................. **CLC 31; HLC**
See also CA 49-52; CANR 2, 32; HW;
MTCW

**Carducci, Giosue** 1835-1907 ...... **TCLC 32**

**Carew, Thomas** 1595(?)-1640 ........ **LC 13**
See also DLB 126

**Carey, Ernestine Gilbreth** 1908- .... **CLC 17**
See also CA 5-8R; SATA 2

**Carey, Peter** 1943- ............. **CLC 40, 55**
See also CA 123; 127; MTCW

**Carleton, William** 1794-1869 ...... **NCLC 3**

**Carlisle, Henry (Coffin)** 1926- ...... **CLC 33**
See also CA 13-16R; CANR 15

**Carlsen, Chris**
See Holdstock, Robert P.

**Carlson, Ron(ald F.)** 1947- ........ **CLC 54**
See also CA 105; CANR 27

**Carlyle, Thomas** 1795-1881 .. **NCLC 22; DA**
See also CDBLB 1789-1832; DLB 55

**Carman, (William) Bliss**
1861-1929 ................. **TCLC 7**
See also CA 104; DLB 92

**Carnegie, Dale** 1888-1955 ........ **TCLC 53**

**Carossa, Hans** 1878-1956 ........ **TCLC 48**
See also DLB 66

**Carpenter, Don(ald Richard)**
1931- ..................... **CLC 41**
See also CA 45-48; CANR 1

**Carpentier (y Valmont), Alejo**
1904-1980 ....... **CLC 8, 11, 38; HLC**
See also CA 65-68; 97-100; CANR 11;
DLB 113; HW

**Carr, Emily** 1871-1945 .......... **TCLC 32**
See also DLB 68

**Carr, John Dickson** 1906-1977 ...... **CLC 3**
See also CA 49-52; 69-72; CANR 3, 33;
MTCW

**Carr, Philippa**
See Hibbert, Eleanor Alice Burford

**Carr, Virginia Spencer** 1929- ...... **CLC 34**
See also CA 61-64; DLB 111

**Carrier, Roch** 1937- ............ **CLC 13, 78**
See also CA 130; DLB 53

**Carroll, James P.** 1943(?)- ......... **CLC 38**
See also CA 81-84

**Carroll, Jim** 1951- .............. **CLC 35**
See also CA 45-48; CANR 42

**Carroll, Lewis** ............. **NCLC 2; WLC**
See also Dodgson, Charles Lutwidge
See also CDBLB 1832-1890; CLR 2, 18;
DLB 18; JRDA

**Carroll, Paul Vincent** 1900-1968.... **CLC 10**
See also CA 9-12R; 25-28R; DLB 10

**Carruth, Hayden** 1921- .... **CLC 4, 7, 10, 18**
See also CA 9-12R; CANR 4, 38; DLB 5;
MTCW; SATA 47

**Carson, Rachel Louise** 1907-1964... **CLC 71**
See also CA 77-80; CANR 35; MTCW;
SATA 23

**Carter, Angela (Olive)**
1940-1992 ...... **CLC 5, 41, 76; SSC 13**
See also CA 53-56; 136; CANR 12, 36;
DLB 14; MTCW; SATA 66;
SATA-Obit 70

**Carter, Nick**
See Smith, Martin Cruz

**Carver, Raymond**
1938-1988 ... **CLC 22, 36, 53, 55; SSC 8**
See also CA 33-36R; 126; CANR 17, 34;
DLB 130; DLBY 84, 88; MTCW

**Cary, (Arthur) Joyce (Lunel)**
1888-1957 ............... **TCLC 1, 29**
See also CA 104; CDBLB 1914-1945;
DLB 15, 100

**Casanova de Seingalt, Giovanni Jacopo**
1725-1798 ................... **LC 13**

**Casares, Adolfo Bioy**
See Bioy Casares, Adolfo

**Casely-Hayford, J(oseph) E(phraim)**
1866-1930 ............. **TCLC 24; BLC**
See also BW 2; CA 123

**Casey, John (Dudley)** 1939- ........ **CLC 59**
See also BEST 90:2; CA 69-72; CANR 23

**Casey, Michael** 1947- .............. **CLC 2**
See also CA 65-68; DLB 5

**Casey, Patrick**
See Thurman, Wallace (Henry)

**Casey, Warren (Peter)** 1935-1988 ... **CLC 12**
See also CA 101; 127

**Casona, Alejandro** ................. **CLC 49**
See also Alvarez, Alejandro Rodriguez

Cassavetes, John  1929-1989....... **CLC 20**
See also CA 85-88; 127

Cassill, R(onald) V(erlin)  1919-... **CLC 4, 23**
See also CA 9-12R; CAAS 1; CANR 7;
DLB 6

Cassity, (Allen) Turner  1929- .... **CLC 6, 42**
See also CA 17-20R; CAAS 8; CANR 11;
DLB 105

Castaneda, Carlos  1931(?)-........ **CLC 12**
See also CA 25-28R; CANR 32; HW;
MTCW

Castedo, Elena  1937- ............. **CLC 65**
See also CA 132

Castedo-Ellerman, Elena
See Castedo, Elena

Castellanos, Rosario
1925-1974 ............. **CLC 66; HLC**
See also CA 131; 53-56; DLB 113; HW

Castelvetro, Lodovico  1505-1571..... **LC 12**

Castiglione, Baldassare  1478-1529 ... **LC 12**

Castle, Robert
See Hamilton, Edmond

Castro, Guillen de  1569-1631........ **LC 19**

Castro, Rosalia de  1837-1885 ..... **NCLC 3**

Cather, Willa
See Cather, Willa Sibert

Cather, Willa Sibert
1873-1947 ....... **TCLC 1, 11, 31; DA;**
**SSC 2; WLC**
See also CA 104; 128; CDALB 1865-1917;
DLB 9, 54, 78; DLBD 1; MTCW;
SATA 30

Catton, (Charles) Bruce
1899-1978 ................... **CLC 35**
See also AITN 1; CA 5-8R; 81-84;
CANR 7; DLB 17; SATA 2, 24

Cauldwell, Frank
See King, Francis (Henry)

Caunitz, William J.  1933-......... **CLC 34**
See also BEST 89:3; CA 125; 130

Causley, Charles (Stanley)  1917-..... **CLC 7**
See also CA 9-12R; CANR 5, 35; CLR 30;
DLB 27; MTCW; SATA 3, 66

Caute, David  1936-............... **CLC 29**
See also CA 1-4R; CAAS 4; CANR 1, 33;
DLB 14

Cavafy, C(onstantine) P(eter)...... **TCLC 2, 7**
See also Kavafis, Konstantinos Petrou

Cavallo, Evelyn
See Spark, Muriel (Sarah)

Cavanna, Betty ................... **CLC 12**
See also Harrison, Elizabeth Cavanna
See also JRDA; MAICYA; SAAS 4;
SATA 1, 30

Caxton, William  1421(?)-1491(?)..... **LC 17**

Cayrol, Jean  1911-............... **CLC 11**
See also CA 89-92; DLB 83

Cela, Camilo Jose
1916- ............ **CLC 4, 13, 59; HLC**
See also BEST 90:2; CA 21-24R; CAAS 10;
CANR 21, 32; DLBY 89; HW; MTCW

Celan, Paul ................... **CLC 53, 82**
See also Antschel, Paul
See also DLB 69

Celine, Louis-Ferdinand
............. **CLC 1, 3, 4, 7, 9, 15, 47**
See also Destouches, Louis-Ferdinand
See also DLB 72

Cellini, Benvenuto  1500-1571 ....... **LC 7**

Cendrars, Blaise
See Sauser-Hall, Frederic

Cernuda (y Bidon), Luis
1902-1963 ................... **CLC 54**
See also CA 131; 89-92; DLB 134; HW

Cervantes (Saavedra), Miguel de
1547-1616 ...... **LC 6, 23; DA; SSC 12;**
**WLC**

Cesaire, Aime (Fernand)
1913- ............... **CLC 19, 32; BLC**
See also BW 2; CA 65-68; CANR 24, 43;
MTCW

Chabon, Michael  1965(?)- ......... **CLC 55**
See also CA 139

Chabrol, Claude  1930- ............. **CLC 16**
See also CA 110

Challans, Mary  1905-1983
See Renault, Mary
See also CA 81-84; 111; SATA 23, 36

Challis, George
See Faust, Frederick (Schiller)

Chambers, Aidan  1934- ........... **CLC 35**
See also CA 25-28R; CANR 12, 31; JRDA;
MAICYA; SAAS 12; SATA 1, 69

Chambers, James  1948-
See Cliff, Jimmy
See also CA 124

Chambers, Jessie
See Lawrence, D(avid) H(erbert Richards)

Chambers, Robert W.  1865-1933... **TCLC 41**

Chandler, Raymond (Thornton)
1888-1959 ................. **TCLC 1, 7**
See also CA 104; 129; CDALB 1929-1941;
DLBD 6; MTCW

Chang, Jung  1952-............... **CLC 71**
See also CA 142

Channing, William Ellery
1780-1842 ................. **NCLC 17**
See also DLB 1, 59

Chaplin, Charles Spencer
1889-1977 ................. **CLC 16**
See also Chaplin, Charlie
See also CA 81-84; 73-76

Chaplin, Charlie
See Chaplin, Charles Spencer
See also DLB 44

Chapman, George  1559(?)-1634...... **LC 22**
See also DLB 62, 121

Chapman, Graham  1941-1989 ...... **CLC 21**
See also Monty Python
See also CA 116; 129; CANR 35

Chapman, John Jay  1862-1933 ..... **TCLC 7**
See also CA 104

Chapman, Walker
See Silverberg, Robert

Chappell, Fred (Davis)  1936-.... **CLC 40, 78**
See also CA 5-8R; CAAS 4; CANR 8, 33;
DLB 6, 105

Char, Rene(-Emile)
1907-1988 ........... **CLC 9, 11, 14, 55**
See also CA 13-16R; 124; CANR 32;
MTCW

Charby, Jay
See Ellison, Harlan

Chardin, Pierre Teilhard de
See Teilhard de Chardin, (Marie Joseph)
Pierre

Charles I  1600-1649............... **LC 13**

Charyn, Jerome  1937- ........ **CLC 5, 8, 18**
See also CA 5-8R; CAAS 1; CANR 7;
DLBY 83; MTCW

Chase, Mary (Coyle)  1907-1981 ...... **DC 1**
See also CA 77-80; 105; SATA 17, 29

Chase, Mary Ellen  1887-1973....... **CLC 2**
See also CA 13-16; 41-44R; CAP 1;
SATA 10

Chase, Nicholas
See Hyde, Anthony

Chateaubriand, Francois Rene de
1768-1848 ................. **NCLC 3**
See also DLB 119

Chatterje, Sarat Chandra  1876-1936(?)
See Chatterji, Saratchandra
See also CA 109

Chatterji, Bankim Chandra
1838-1894 ................. **NCLC 19**

Chatterji, Saratchandra ........... **TCLC 13**
See also Chatterje, Sarat Chandra

Chatterton, Thomas  1752-1770 ....... **LC 3**
See also DLB 109

Chatwin, (Charles) Bruce
1940-1989 ........... **CLC 28, 57, 59**
See also AAYA 4; BEST 90:1; CA 85-88;
127

Chaucer, Daniel
See Ford, Ford Madox

Chaucer, Geoffrey
1340(?)-1400 ............. **LC 17; DA**
See also CDBLB Before 1660

Chaviaras, Strates  1935-
See Haviaras, Stratis
See also CA 105

Chayefsky, Paddy ................. **CLC 23**
See also Chayefsky, Sidney
See also DLB 7, 44; DLBY 81

Chayefsky, Sidney  1923-1981
See Chayefsky, Paddy
See also CA 9-12R; 104; CANR 18

Chedid, Andree  1920-............. **CLC 47**

Cheever, John
1912-1982 ...... **CLC 3, 7, 8, 11, 15, 25,**
**64; DA; SSC 1; WLC**
See also CA 5-8R; 106; CABS 1; CANR 5,
27; CDALB 1941-1968; DLB 2, 102;
DLBY 80, 82; MTCW

Cheever, Susan  1943-.......... **CLC 18, 48**
See also CA 103; CANR 27; DLBY 82

Chekhonte, Antosha
See Chekhov, Anton (Pavlovich)

Chekhov, Anton (Pavlovich)
1860-1904 ........ **TCLC 3, 10, 31; DA;**
**SSC 2; WLC**
See also CA 104; 124

Chernyshevsky, Nikolay Gavrilovich
1828-1889 .................. NCLC 1

Cherry, Carolyn Janice  1942-
See Cherryh, C. J.
See also CA 65-68; CANR 10

Cherryh, C. J. .................... CLC 35
See also Cherry, Carolyn Janice
See also DLBY 80

Chesnutt, Charles W(addell)
1858-1932 .... TCLC 5, 39; BLC; SSC 7
See also BW 1; CA 106; 125; DLB 12, 50,
78; MTCW

Chester, Alfred  1929(?)-1971 ....... CLC 49
See also CA 33-36R; DLB 130

Chesterton, G(ilbert) K(eith)
1874-1936 ......... TCLC 1, 6; SSC 1
See also CA 104; 132; CDBLB 1914-1945;
DLB 10, 19, 34, 70, 98; MTCW;
SATA 27

Chiang Pin-chin  1904-1986
See Ding Ling
See also CA 118

Ch'ien Chung-shu  1910- .......... CLC 22
See also CA 130; MTCW

Child, L. Maria
See Child, Lydia Maria

Child, Lydia Maria  1802-1880 .... NCLC 6
See also DLB 1, 74; SATA 67

Child, Mrs.
See Child, Lydia Maria

Child, Philip  1898-1978 ........ CLC 19, 68
See also CA 13-14; CAP 1; SATA 47

Childress, Alice
1920- ......... CLC 12, 15; BLC; DC 4
See also AAYA 8; BW 2; CA 45-48;
CANR 3, 27; CLR 14; DLB 7, 38; JRDA;
MAICYA; MTCW; SATA 7, 48

Chislett, (Margaret) Anne  1943- ... CLC 34

Chitty, Thomas Willes  1926- ....... CLC 11
See also Hinde, Thomas
See also CA 5-8R

Chomette, Rene Lucien  1898-1981 .. CLC 20
See also Clair, Rene
See also CA 103

Chopin, Kate ....... TCLC 5, 14; DA; SSC 8
See also Chopin, Katherine
See also CDALB 1865-1917; DLB 12, 78

Chopin, Katherine  1851-1904
See Chopin, Kate
See also CA 104; 122

Chretien de Troyes
c. 12th cent. - .............. CMLC 10

Christie
See Ichikawa, Kon

Christie, Agatha (Mary Clarissa)
1890-1976 ...... CLC 1, 6, 8, 12, 39, 48
See also AAYA 9; AITN 1, 2; CA 17-20R;
61-64; CANR 10, 37; CDBLB 1914-1945;
DLB 13, 77; MTCW; SATA 36

Christie, (Ann) Philippa
See Pearce, Philippa
See also CA 5-8R; CANR 4

Christine de Pizan  1365(?)-1431(?) .... LC 9

Chubb, Elmer
See Masters, Edgar Lee

Chulkov, Mikhail Dmitrievich
1743-1792 .................... LC 2

Churchill, Caryl  1938- ........ CLC 31, 55
See also CA 102; CANR 22; DLB 13;
MTCW

Churchill, Charles  1731-1764 ........ LC 3
See also DLB 109

Chute, Carolyn  1947- ............. CLC 39
See also CA 123

Ciardi, John (Anthony)
1916-1986 ............. CLC 10, 40, 44
See also CA 5-8R; 118; CAAS 2; CANR 5,
33; CLR 19; DLB 5; DLBY 86;
MAICYA; MTCW; SATA 1, 46, 65

Cicero, Marcus Tullius
106B.C.-43B.C. .............. CMLC 3

Cimino, Michael  1943- ............ CLC 16
See also CA 105

Cioran, E(mil) M.  1911- .......... CLC 64
See also CA 25-28R

Cisneros, Sandra  1954- ...... CLC 69; HLC
See also AAYA 9; CA 131; DLB 122; HW

Clair, Rene ...................... CLC 20
See also Chomette, Rene Lucien

Clampitt, Amy  1920- ............. CLC 32
See also CA 110; CANR 29; DLB 105

Clancy, Thomas L., Jr.  1947-
See Clancy, Tom
See also CA 125; 131; MTCW

Clancy, Tom ..................... CLC 45
See also Clancy, Thomas L., Jr.
See also AAYA 9; BEST 89:1, 90:1

Clare, John  1793-1864 ........... NCLC 9
See also DLB 55, 96

Clarin
See Alas (y Urena), Leopoldo (Enrique
Garcia)

Clark, Al C.
See Goines, Donald

Clark, (Robert) Brian  1932- ........ CLC 29
See also CA 41-44R

Clark, Curt
See Westlake, Donald E(dwin)

Clark, Eleanor  1913- ........... CLC 5, 19
See also CA 9-12R; CANR 41; DLB 6

Clark, J. P.
See Clark, John Pepper
See also DLB 117

Clark, John Pepper  1935- .... CLC 38; BLC
See also Clark, J. P.
See also BW 1; CA 65-68; CANR 16

Clark, M. R.
See Clark, Mavis Thorpe

Clark, Mavis Thorpe  1909- ........ CLC 12
See also CA 57-60; CANR 8, 37; CLR 30;
MAICYA; SAAS 5; SATA 8, 74

Clark, Walter Van Tilburg
1909-1971 ................... CLC 28
See also CA 9-12R; 33-36R; DLB 9;
SATA 8

Clarke, Arthur C(harles)
1917- ...... CLC 1, 4, 13, 18, 35; SSC 3
See also AAYA 4; CA 1-4R; CANR 2, 28;
JRDA; MAICYA; MTCW; SATA 13, 70

Clarke, Austin  1896-1974 ........ CLC 6, 9
See also CA 29-32; 49-52; CAP 2; DLB 10,
20

Clarke, Austin C(hesterfield)
1934- ................. CLC 8, 53; BLC
See also BW 1; CA 25-28R; CAAS 16;
CANR 14, 32; DLB 53, 125

Clarke, Gillian  1937- ............. CLC 61
See also CA 106; DLB 40

Clarke, Marcus (Andrew Hislop)
1846-1881 ................. NCLC 19

Clarke, Shirley  1925- ............. CLC 16

Clash, The ...................... CLC 30
See also Headon, (Nicky) Topper; Jones,
Mick; Simonon, Paul; Strummer, Joe

Claudel, Paul (Louis Charles Marie)
1868-1955 ............... TCLC 2, 10
See also CA 104

Clavell, James (duMaresq)
1925- ................. CLC 6, 25
See also CA 25-28R; CANR 26; MTCW

Cleaver, (Leroy) Eldridge
1935- ................. CLC 30; BLC
See also BW 1; CA 21-24R; CANR 16

Cleese, John (Marwood)  1939- ..... CLC 21
See also Monty Python
See also CA 112; 116; CANR 35; MTCW

Cleishbotham, Jebediah
See Scott, Walter

Cleland, John  1710-1789 ........... LC 2
See also DLB 39

Clemens, Samuel Langhorne  1835-1910
See Twain, Mark
See also CA 104; 135; CDALB 1865-1917;
DA; DLB 11, 12, 23, 64, 74; JRDA;
MAICYA; YABC 2

Cleophil
See Congreve, William

Clerihew, E.
See Bentley, E(dmund) C(lerihew)

Clerk, N. W.
See Lewis, C(live) S(taples)

Cliff, Jimmy ...................... CLC 21
See also Chambers, James

Clifton, (Thelma) Lucille
1936- ............... CLC 19, 66; BLC
See also BW 2; CA 49-52; CANR 2, 24, 42;
CLR 5; DLB 5, 41; MAICYA; MTCW;
SATA 20, 69

Clinton, Dirk
See Silverberg, Robert

Clough, Arthur Hugh  1819-1861 .. NCLC 27
See also DLB 32

Clutha, Janet Paterson Frame  1924-
See Frame, Janet
See also CA 1-4R; CANR 2, 36; MTCW

Clyne, Terence
See Blatty, William Peter

Cobalt, Martin
See Mayne, William (James Carter)

Coburn, D(onald) L(ee)  1938- ...... CLC 10
See also CA 89-92

**Cocteau, Jean (Maurice Eugene Clement)**
1889-1963 .... **CLC 1, 8, 15, 16, 43; DA; WLC**
See also CA 25-28; CANR 40; CAP 2;
DLB 65; MTCW

**Codrescu, Andrei** 1946- ........... **CLC 46**
See also CA 33-36R; CAAS 19; CANR 13, 34

**Coe, Max**
See Bourne, Randolph S(illiman)

**Coe, Tucker**
See Westlake, Donald E(dwin)

**Coetzee, J(ohn) M(ichael)**
1940- ................. **CLC 23, 33, 66**
See also CA 77-80; CANR 41; MTCW

**Coffey, Brian**
See Koontz, Dean R(ay)

**Cohen, Arthur A(llen)**
1928-1986 ................. **CLC 7, 31**
See also CA 1-4R; 120; CANR 1, 17, 42;
DLB 28

**Cohen, Leonard (Norman)**
1934- ......................... **CLC 3, 38**
See also CA 21-24R; CANR 14; DLB 53;
MTCW

**Cohen, Matt** 1942- ............... **CLC 19**
See also CA 61-64; CAAS 18; CANR 40;
DLB 53

**Cohen-Solal, Annie** 19(?)- ........ **CLC 50**

**Colegate, Isabel** 1931- ........... **CLC 36**
See also CA 17-20R; CANR 8, 22; DLB 14;
MTCW

**Coleman, Emmett**
See Reed, Ishmael

**Coleridge, Samuel Taylor**
1772-1834 ........ **NCLC 9; DA; WLC**
See also CDBLB 1789-1832; DLB 93, 107

**Coleridge, Sara** 1802-1852 ....... **NCLC 31**

**Coles, Don** 1928- ............... **CLC 46**
See also CA 115; CANR 38

**Colette, (Sidonie-Gabrielle)**
1873-1954 ...... **TCLC 1, 5, 16; SSC 10**
See also CA 104; 131; DLB 65; MTCW

**Collett, (Jacobine) Camilla (Wergeland)**
1813-1895 ................ **NCLC 22**

**Collier, Christopher** 1930- ......... **CLC 30**
See also CA 33-36R; CANR 13, 33; JRDA;
MAICYA; SATA 16, 70

**Collier, James L(incoln)** 1928- ..... **CLC 30**
See also CA 9-12R; CANR 4, 33; JRDA;
MAICYA; SATA 8, 70

**Collier, Jeremy** 1650-1726 .......... **LC 6**

**Collins, Hunt**
See Hunter, Evan

**Collins, Linda** 1931- .............. **CLC 44**
See also CA 125

**Collins, (William) Wilkie**
1824-1889 ............... **NCLC 1, 18**
See also CDBLB 1832-1890; DLB 18, 70

**Collins, William** 1721-1759 ......... **LC 4**
See also DLB 109

**Colman, George**
See Glassco, John

**Colt, Winchester Remington**
See Hubbard, L(afayette) Ron(ald)

**Colter, Cyrus** 1910- .............. **CLC 58**
See also BW 1; CA 65-68; CANR 10;
DLB 33

**Colton, James**
See Hansen, Joseph

**Colum, Padraic** 1881-1972........ **CLC 28**
See also CA 73-76; 33-36R; CANR 35;
MAICYA; MTCW; SATA 15

**Colvin, James**
See Moorcock, Michael (John)

**Colwin, Laurie (E.)**
1944-1992 ............. **CLC 5, 13, 23**
See also CA 89-92; 139; CANR 20;
DLBY 80; MTCW

**Comfort, Alex(ander)** 1920-........ **CLC 7**
See also CA 1-4R; CANR 1

**Comfort, Montgomery**
See Campbell, (John) Ramsey

**Compton-Burnett, I(vy)**
1884(?)-1969 ...... **CLC 1, 3, 10, 15, 34**
See also CA 1-4R; 25-28R; CANR 4;
DLB 36; MTCW

**Comstock, Anthony** 1844-1915 .... **TCLC 13**
See also CA 110

**Conan Doyle, Arthur**
See Doyle, Arthur Conan

**Conde, Maryse** 1937-............. **CLC 52**
See also Boucolon, Maryse
See also BW 2

**Condon, Richard (Thomas)**
1915- ............ **CLC 4, 6, 8, 10, 45**
See also BEST 90:3; CA 1-4R; CAAS 1;
CANR 2, 23; MTCW

**Congreve, William**
1670-1729 ... **LC 5, 21; DA; DC 2; WLC**
See also CDBLB 1660-1789; DLB 39, 84

**Connell, Evan S(helby), Jr.**
1924- ................. **CLC 4, 6, 45**
See also AAYA 7; CA 1-4R; CAAS 2;
CANR 2, 39; DLB 2; DLBY 81; MTCW

**Connelly, Marc(us Cook)**
1890-1980 ................... **CLC 7**
See also CA 85-88; 102; CANR 30; DLB 7;
DLBY 80; SATA 25

**Connor, Ralph.................... TCLC 31**
See also Gordon, Charles William
See also DLB 92

**Conrad, Joseph**
1857-1924 ....... **TCLC 1, 6, 13, 25, 43;
DA; SSC 9; WLC**
See also CA 104; 131; CDBLB 1890-1914;
DLB 10, 34, 98; MTCW; SATA 27

**Conrad, Robert Arnold**
See Hart, Moss

**Conroy, Pat** 1945-............. **CLC 30, 74**
See also AAYA 8; AITN 1; CA 85-88;
CANR 24; DLB 6; MTCW

**Constant (de Rebecque), (Henri) Benjamin**
1767-1830 ................. **NCLC 6**
See also DLB 119

**Conybeare, Charles Augustus**
See Eliot, T(homas) S(tearns)

**Cook, Michael** 1933- ............. **CLC 58**
See also CA 93-96; DLB 53

**Cook, Robin** 1940-............... **CLC 14**
See also BEST 90:2; CA 108; 111;
CANR 41

**Cook, Roy**
See Silverberg, Robert

**Cooke, Elizabeth** 1948- ........... **CLC 55**
See also CA 129

**Cooke, John Esten** 1830-1886..... **NCLC 5**
See also DLB 3

**Cooke, John Estes**
See Baum, L(yman) Frank

**Cooke, M. E.**
See Creasey, John

**Cooke, Margaret**
See Creasey, John

**Cooney, Ray .................... CLC 62**

**Cooper, Henry St. John**
See Creasey, John

**Cooper, J. California................ CLC 56**
See also AAYA 12; BW 1; CA 125

**Cooper, James Fenimore**
1789-1851 ............... **NCLC 1, 27**
See also CDALB 1640-1865; DLB 3;
SATA 19

**Coover, Robert (Lowell)**
1932- ..... **CLC 3, 7, 15, 32, 46; SSC 15**
See also CA 45-48; CANR 3, 37; DLB 2;
DLBY 81; MTCW

**Copeland, Stewart (Armstrong)**
1952- ..................... **CLC 26**
See also Police, The

**Coppard, A(lfred) E(dgar)**
1878-1957................ **TCLC 5**
See also CA 114; YABC 1

**Coppee, Francois** 1842-1908 ...... **TCLC 25**

**Coppola, Francis Ford** 1939-....... **CLC 16**
See also CA 77-80; CANR 40; DLB 44

**Corbiere, Tristan** 1845-1875 ..... **NCLC 43**

**Corcoran, Barbara** 1911-.......... **CLC 17**
See also CA 21-24R; CAAS 2; CANR 11,
28; DLB 52; JRDA; SATA 3, 77

**Cordelier, Maurice**
See Giraudoux, (Hippolyte) Jean

**Corelli, Marie** 1855-1924........ **TCLC 51**
See also Mackay, Mary
See also DLB 34

**Corman, Cid..................... CLC 9**
See also Corman, Sidney
See also CAAS 2; DLB 5

**Corman, Sidney** 1924-
See Corman, Cid
See also CA 85-88; CANR 44

**Cormier, Robert (Edmund)**
1925- ............... **CLC 12, 30; DA**
See also AAYA 3; CA 1-4R; CANR 5, 23;
CDALB 1968-1988; CLR 12; DLB 52;
JRDA; MAICYA; MTCW; SATA 10, 45

**Corn, Alfred (DeWitt III)** 1943-.... **CLC 33**
See also CA 104; DLB 120; DLBY 80

**Cornwell, David (John Moore)**
1931- . . . . . . . . . . . . . . . . . . . . CLC 9, 15
See also le Carre, John
See also CA 5-8R; CANR 13, 33; MTCW

**Corrigan, Kevin** . . . . . . . . . . . . . . . . CLC 55

**Corso, (Nunzio) Gregory** 1930-. . . CLC 1, 11
See also CA 5-8R; CANR 41; DLB 5, 16;
MTCW

**Cortazar, Julio**
1914-1984 . . . . . . CLC 2, 3, 5, 10, 13, 15,
33, 34; HLC; SSC 7
See also CA 21-24R; CANR 12, 32;
DLB 113; HW; MTCW

**Corwin, Cecil**
See Kornbluth, C(yril) M.

**Cosic, Dobrica** 1921- . . . . . . . . . . . . . CLC 14
See also CA 122; 138

**Costain, Thomas B(ertram)**
1885-1965 . . . . . . . . . . . . . . . . . . . CLC 30
See also CA 5-8R; 25-28R; DLB 9

**Costantini, Humberto**
1924(?)-1987 . . . . . . . . . . . . . . . . . CLC 49
See also CA 131; 122; HW

**Costello, Elvis** 1955-. . . . . . . . . . . . . . CLC 21

**Cotter, Joseph Seamon Sr.**
1861-1949 . . . . . . . . . . . . . TCLC 28; BLC
See also BW 1; CA 124; DLB 50

**Couch, Arthur Thomas Quiller**
See Quiller-Couch, Arthur Thomas

**Coulton, James**
See Hansen, Joseph

**Couperus, Louis (Marie Anne)**
1863-1923 . . . . . . . . . . . . . . . . . TCLC 15
See also CA 115

**Court, Wesli**
See Turco, Lewis (Putnam)

**Courtenay, Bryce** 1933-. . . . . . . . . . . CLC 59
See also CA 138

**Courtney, Robert**
See Ellison, Harlan

**Cousteau, Jacques-Yves** 1910-. . . . . . CLC 30
See also CA 65-68; CANR 15; MTCW;
SATA 38

**Coward, Noel (Peirce)**
1899-1973 . . . . . . . . . . . . CLC 1, 9, 29, 51
See also AITN 1; CA 17-18; 41-44R;
CANR 35; CAP 2; CDBLB 1914-1945;
DLB 10; MTCW

**Cowley, Malcolm** 1898-1989 . . . . . . . CLC 39
See also CA 5-8R; 128; CANR 3; DLB 4,
48; DLBY 81, 89; MTCW

**Cowper, William** 1731-1800. . . . . . . NCLC 8
See also DLB 104, 109

**Cox, William Trevor** 1928- . . . CLC 9, 14, 71
See also Trevor, William
See also CA 9-12R; CANR 4, 37; DLB 14;
MTCW

**Cozzens, James Gould**
1903-1978 . . . . . . . . . . . . . . CLC 1, 4, 11
See also CA 9-12R; 81-84; CANR 19;
CDALB 1941-1968; DLB 9; DLBD 2;
DLBY 84; MTCW

**Crabbe, George** 1754-1832. . . . . . . NCLC 26
See also DLB 93

**Craig, A. A.**
See Anderson, Poul (William)

**Craik, Dinah Maria (Mulock)**
1826-1887 . . . . . . . . . . . . . . . . NCLC 38
See also DLB 35; MAICYA; SATA 34

**Cram, Ralph Adams** 1863-1942. . . . TCLC 45

**Crane, (Harold) Hart**
1899-1932 . . . . . . . TCLC 2, 5; DA; PC 3;
WLC
See also CA 104; 127; CDALB 1917-1929;
DLB 4, 48; MTCW

**Crane, R(onald) S(almon)**
1886-1967 . . . . . . . . . . . . . . . . . . CLC 27
See also CA 85-88; DLB 63

**Crane, Stephen (Townley)**
1871-1900 . . . . . . . TCLC 11, 17, 32; DA;
SSC 7; WLC
See also CA 109; 140; CDALB 1865-1917;
DLB 12, 54, 78; YABC 2

**Crase, Douglas** 1944-. . . . . . . . . . . . . CLC 58
See also CA 106

**Crashaw, Richard** 1612(?)-1649. . . . . . LC 24
See also DLB 126

**Craven, Margaret** 1901-1980. . . . . . CLC 17
See also CA 103

**Crawford, F(rancis) Marion**
1854-1909 . . . . . . . . . . . . . . . . TCLC 10
See also CA 107; DLB 71

**Crawford, Isabella Valancy**
1850-1887 . . . . . . . . . . . . . . . . NCLC 12
See also DLB 92

**Crayon, Geoffrey**
See Irving, Washington

**Creasey, John** 1908-1973. . . . . . . . . CLC 11
See also CA 5-8R; 41-44R; CANR 8;
DLB 77; MTCW

**Crebillon, Claude Prosper Jolyot de (fils)**
1707-1777 . . . . . . . . . . . . . . . . . . . LC 1

**Credo**
See Creasey, John

**Creeley, Robert (White)**
1926- . . . . . CLC 1, 2, 4, 8, 11, 15, 36, 78
See also CA 1-4R; CAAS 10; CANR 23, 43;
DLB 5, 16; MTCW

**Crews, Harry (Eugene)**
1935- . . . . . . . . . . . . . . . . CLC 6, 23, 49
See also AITN 1; CA 25-28R; CANR 20;
DLB 6; MTCW

**Crichton, (John) Michael**
1942- . . . . . . . . . . . . . . . . . . CLC 2, 6, 54
See also AAYA 10; AITN 2; CA 25-28R;
CANR 13, 40; DLBY 81; JRDA;
MTCW; SATA 9

**Crispin, Edmund** . . . . . . . . . . . . . . . . CLC 22
See also Montgomery, (Robert) Bruce
See also DLB 87

**Cristofer, Michael** 1945(?)- . . . . . . . . CLC 28
See also CA 110; DLB 7

**Croce, Benedetto** 1866-1952 . . . . . . TCLC 37
See also CA 120

**Crockett, David** 1786-1836 . . . . . . . NCLC 8
See also DLB 3, 11

**Crockett, Davy**
See Crockett, David

**Croker, John Wilson** 1780-1857 . . NCLC 10
See also DLB 110

**Crommelynck, Fernand** 1885-1970 . . CLC 75
See also CA 89-92

**Cronin, A(rchibald) J(oseph)**
1896-1981 . . . . . . . . . . . . . . . . . . CLC 32
See also CA 1-4R; 102; CANR 5; SATA 25,
47

**Cross, Amanda**
See Heilbrun, Carolyn G(old)

**Crothers, Rachel** 1878(?)-1958. . . . . TCLC 19
See also CA 113; DLB 7

**Croves, Hal**
See Traven, B.

**Crowfield, Christopher**
See Stowe, Harriet (Elizabeth) Beecher

**Crowley, Aleister**. . . . . . . . . . . . . . . . TCLC 7
See also Crowley, Edward Alexander

**Crowley, Edward Alexander** 1875-1947
See Crowley, Aleister
See also CA 104

**Crowley, John** 1942-. . . . . . . . . . . . . . CLC 57
See also CA 61-64; CANR 43; DLBY 82;
SATA 65

**Crud**
See Crumb, R(obert)

**Crumarums**
See Crumb, R(obert)

**Crumb, R(obert)** 1943-. . . . . . . . . . . . CLC 17
See also CA 106

**Crumbum**
See Crumb, R(obert)

**Crumski**
See Crumb, R(obert)

**Crum the Bum**
See Crumb, R(obert)

**Crunk**
See Crumb, R(obert)

**Crustt**
See Crumb, R(obert)

**Cryer, Gretchen (Kiger)** 1935-. . . . . . CLC 21
See also CA 114; 123

**Csath, Geza** 1887-1919. . . . . . . . . . . TCLC 13
See also CA 111

**Cudlip, David** 1933-. . . . . . . . . . . . . . CLC 34

**Cullen, Countee**
1903-1946 . . . . . . TCLC 4, 37; BLC; DA
See also BW 1; CA 108; 124;
CDALB 1917-1929; DLB 4, 48, 51;
MTCW; SATA 18

**Cum, R.**
See Crumb, R(obert)

**Cummings, Bruce F(rederick)** 1889-1919
See Barbellion, W. N. P.
See also CA 123

**Cummings, E(dward) E(stlin)**
1894-1962 . . . . . . CLC 1, 3, 8, 12, 15, 68;
DA; PC 5; WLC 2
See also CA 73-76; CANR 31;
CDALB 1929-1941; DLB 4, 48; MTCW

**Cunha, Euclides (Rodrigues Pimenta) da**
1866-1909 . . . . . . . . . . . . . . . . TCLC 24
See also CA 123

Deighton, Len .............. CLC 4, 7, 22, 46
See also Deighton, Leonard Cyril
See also AAYA 6; BEST 89:2;
CDBLB 1960 to Present; DLB 87

Deighton, Leonard Cyril 1929-
See Deighton, Len
See also CA 9-12R; CANR 19, 33; MTCW

Dekker, Thomas 1572(?)-1632...... LC 22
See also CDBLB Before 1660; DLB 62

de la Mare, Walter (John)
1873-1956 .. TCLC 4, 53; SSC 14; WLC
See also CDBLB 1914-1945; CLR 23;
DLB 19; SATA 16

Delaney, Franey
See O'Hara, John (Henry)

Delaney, Shelagh 1939-........... CLC 29
See also CA 17-20R; CANR 30;
CDBLB 1960 to Present; DLB 13;
MTCW

Delany, Mary (Granville Pendarves)
1700-1788 ................... LC 12

Delany, Samuel R(ay, Jr.)
1942- ............. CLC 8, 14, 38; BLC
See also BW 2; CA 81-84; CANR 27, 43;
DLB 8, 33; MTCW

De La Ramee, (Marie) Louise 1839-1908
See Ouida
See also SATA 20

de la Roche, Mazo 1879-1961...... CLC 14
See also CA 85-88; CANR 30; DLB 68;
SATA 64

Delbanco, Nicholas (Franklin)
1942- ..................... CLC 6, 13
See also CA 17-20R; CAAS 2; CANR 29;
DLB 6

del Castillo, Michel 1933-......... CLC 38
See also CA 109

Deledda, Grazia (Cosima)
1875(?)-1936 ............... TCLC 23
See also CA 123

Delibes, Miguel ................. CLC 8, 18
See also Delibes Setien, Miguel

Delibes Setien, Miguel 1920-
See Delibes, Miguel
See also CA 45-48; CANR 1, 32; HW;
MTCW

DeLillo, Don
1936- ..... CLC 8, 10, 13, 27, 39, 54, 76
See also BEST 89:1; CA 81-84; CANR 21;
DLB 6; MTCW

de Lisser, H. G.
See De Lisser, Herbert George
See also DLB 117

De Lisser, Herbert George
1878-1944 ................. TCLC 12
See also de Lisser, H. G.
See also BW 2; CA 109

Deloria, Vine (Victor), Jr. 1933-.... CLC 21
See also CA 53-56; CANR 5, 20; MTCW;
SATA 21

Del Vecchio, John M(ichael)
1947- ..................... CLC 29
See also CA 110; DLBD 9

de Man, Paul (Adolph Michel)
1919-1983 ................. CLC 55
See also CA 128; 111; DLB 67; MTCW

De Marinis, Rick 1934-........... CLC 54
See also CA 57-60; CANR 9, 25

Demby, William 1922-....... CLC 53; BLC
See also BW 1; CA 81-84; DLB 33

Demijohn, Thom
See Disch, Thomas M(ichael)

de Montherlant, Henry (Milon)
See Montherlant, Henry (Milon) de

Demosthenes 384B.C.-322B.C. ... CMLC 13

de Natale, Francine
See Malzberg, Barry N(athaniel)

Denby, Edwin (Orr) 1903-1983..... CLC 48
See also CA 138; 110

Denis, Julio
See Cortazar, Julio

Denmark, Harrison
See Zelazny, Roger (Joseph)

Dennis, John 1658-1734........... LC 11
See also DLB 101

Dennis, Nigel (Forbes) 1912-1989.... CLC 8
See also CA 25-28R; 129; DLB 13, 15;
MTCW

De Palma, Brian (Russell) 1940-.... CLC 20
See also CA 109

De Quincey, Thomas 1785-1859 ... NCLC 4
See also CDBLB 1789-1832; DLB 110

Deren, Eleanora 1908(?)-1961
See Deren, Maya
See also CA 111

Deren, Maya ..................... CLC 16
See also Deren, Eleanora

Derleth, August (William)
1909-1971 ................... CLC 31
See also CA 1-4R; 29-32R; CANR 4;
DLB 9; SATA 5

de Routisie, Albert
See Aragon, Louis

Derrida, Jacques 1930-........... CLC 24
See also CA 124; 127

Derry Down Derry
See Lear, Edward

Dersonnes, Jacques
See Simenon, Georges (Jacques Christian)

Desai, Anita 1937-........... CLC 19, 37
See also CA 81-84; CANR 33; MTCW;
SATA 63

de Saint-Luc, Jean
See Glassco, John

de Saint Roman, Arnaud
See Aragon, Louis

Descartes, Rene 1596-1650 ........ LC 20

De Sica, Vittorio 1901(?)-1974 ..... CLC 20
See also CA 117

Desnos, Robert 1900-1945........ TCLC 22
See also CA 121

Destouches, Louis-Ferdinand
1894-1961 ................. CLC 9, 15
See also Celine, Louis-Ferdinand
See also CA 85-88; CANR 28; MTCW

Deutsch, Babette 1895-1982 ....... CLC 18
See also CA 1-4R; 108; CANR 4; DLB 45;
SATA 1, 33

Devenant, William 1606-1649 ....... LC 13

Devkota, Laxmiprasad
1909-1959 ................. TCLC 23
See also CA 123

De Voto, Bernard (Augustine)
1897-1955 ................. TCLC 29
See also CA 113; DLB 9

De Vries, Peter
1910-1993 .... CLC 1, 2, 3, 7, 10, 28, 46
See also CA 17-20R; 142; CANR 41;
DLB 6; DLBY 82; MTCW

Dexter, Martin
See Faust, Frederick (Schiller)

Dexter, Pete 1943-........... CLC 34, 55
See also BEST 89:2; CA 127; 131; MTCW

Diamano, Silmang
See Senghor, Leopold Sedar

Diamond, Neil 1941- ............. CLC 30
See also CA 108

di Bassetto, Corno
See Shaw, George Bernard

Dick, Philip K(indred)
1928-1982 ............. CLC 10, 30, 72
See also CA 49-52; 106; CANR 2, 16;
DLB 8; MTCW

Dickens, Charles (John Huffam)
1812-1870 ..... NCLC 3, 8, 18, 26; DA;
WLC
See also CDBLB 1832-1890; DLB 21, 55,
70; JRDA; MAICYA; SATA 15

Dickey, James (Lafayette)
1923-........ CLC 1, 2, 4, 7, 10, 15, 47
See also AITN 1, 2; CA 9-12R; CABS 2;
CANR 10; CDALB 1968-1988; DLB 5;
DLBD 7; DLBY 82, 93; MTCW

Dickey, William 1928-......... CLC 3, 28
See also CA 9-12R; CANR 24; DLB 5

Dickinson, Charles 1951-.......... CLC 49
See also CA 128

Dickinson, Emily (Elizabeth)
1830-1886 .. NCLC 21; DA; PC 1; WLC
See also CDALB 1865-1917; DLB 1;
SATA 29

Dickinson, Peter (Malcolm)
1927-................... CLC 12, 35
See also AAYA 9; CA 41-44R; CANR 31;
CLR 29; DLB 87; JRDA; MAICYA;
SATA 5, 62

Dickson, Carr
See Carr, John Dickson

Dickson, Carter
See Carr, John Dickson

Didion, Joan 1934-..... CLC 1, 3, 8, 14, 32
See also AITN 1; CA 5-8R; CANR 14;
CDALB 1968-1988; DLB 2; DLBY 81,
86; MTCW

Dietrich, Robert
See Hunt, E(verette) Howard, Jr.

Dillard, Annie `1945-........... CLC 9, 60
See also AAYA 6; CA 49-52; CANR 3, 43;
DLBY 80; MTCW; SATA 10

Dillard, R(ichard) H(enry) W(ilde)
1937-..................... CLC 5
See also CA 21-24R; CAAS 7; CANR 10;
DLB 5

**Drummond de Andrade, Carlos**
1902-1987 ................... **CLC 18**
See also Andrade, Carlos Drummond de
See also CA 132; 123

**Drury, Allen (Stuart)** 1918- ........ **CLC 37**
See also CA 57-60; CANR 18

**Dryden, John**
1631-1700 ... **LC 3, 21; DA; DC 3; WLC**
See also CDBLB 1660-1789; DLB 80, 101,
131

**Duberman, Martin** 1930- .......... **CLC 8**
See also CA 1-4R; CANR 2

**Dubie, Norman (Evans)** 1945- ...... **CLC 36**
See also CA 69-72; CANR 12; DLB 120

**Du Bois, W(illiam) E(dward) B(urghardt)**
1868-1963 ...... **CLC 1, 2, 13, 64; BLC;**
                                      **DA; WLC**
See also BW 1; CA 85-88; CANR 34;
CDALB 1865-1917; DLB 47, 50, 91;
MTCW; SATA 42

**Dubus, Andre** 1936- ... **CLC 13, 36; SSC 15**
See also CA 21-24R; CANR 17; DLB 130

**Duca Minimo**
See D'Annunzio, Gabriele

**Ducharme, Rejean** 1941- .......... **CLC 74**
See also DLB 60

**Duclos, Charles Pinot** 1704-1772 ..... **LC 1**

**Dudek, Louis** 1918- .......... **CLC 11, 19**
See also CA 45-48; CAAS 14; CANR 1;
DLB 88

**Duerrenmatt, Friedrich**
.............. **CLC 1, 4, 8, 11, 15, 43**
See also Duerrenmatt, Friedrich
See also DLB 69, 124

**Duerrenmatt, Friedrich**
1921-1990 ...... **CLC 1, 4, 8, 11, 15, 43**
See also Duerrenmatt, Friedrich
See also CA 17-20R; CANR 33; DLB 69,
124; MTCW

**Duffy, Bruce** (?)- ................. **CLC 50**

**Duffy, Maureen** 1933- ............ **CLC 37**
See also CA 25-28R; CANR 33; DLB 14;
MTCW

**Dugan, Alan** 1923- .............. **CLC 2, 6**
See also CA 81-84; DLB 5

**du Gard, Roger Martin**
See Martin du Gard, Roger

**Duhamel, Georges** 1884-1966 ....... **CLC 8**
See also CA 81-84; 25-28R; CANR 35;
DLB 65; MTCW

**Dujardin, Edouard (Emile Louis)**
1861-1949 .................. **TCLC 13**
See also CA 109; DLB 123

**Dumas, Alexandre (Davy de la Pailleterie)**
1802-1870 ........ **NCLC 11; DA; WLC**
See also DLB 119; SATA 18

**Dumas, Alexandre**
1824-1895 ............. **NCLC 9; DC 1**

**Dumas, Claudine**
See Malzberg, Barry N(athaniel)

**Dumas, Henry L.** 1934-1968 ..... **CLC 6, 62**
See also BW 1; CA 85-88; DLB 41

**du Maurier, Daphne**
1907-1989 ............. **CLC 6, 11, 59**
See also CA 5-8R; 128; CANR 6; MTCW;
SATA 27, 60

**Dunbar, Paul Laurence**
1872-1906 ...... **TCLC 2, 12; BLC; DA;**
                                **PC 5; SSC 8; WLC**
See also BW 1; CA 104; 124;
CDALB 1865-1917; DLB 50, 54, 78;
SATA 34

**Dunbar, William** 1460(?)-1530(?) .... **LC 20**

**Duncan, Lois** 1934- ............... **CLC 26**
See also AAYA 4; CA 1-4R; CANR 2, 23,
36; CLR 29; JRDA; MAICYA; SAAS 2;
SATA 1, 36, 75

**Duncan, Robert (Edward)**
1919-1988 .... **CLC 1, 2, 4, 7, 15, 41, 55;**
                                                    **PC 2**
See also CA 9-12R; 124; CANR 28; DLB 5,
16; MTCW

**Dunlap, William** 1766-1839 ....... **NCLC 2**
See also DLB 30, 37, 59

**Dunn, Douglas (Eaglesham)**
1942- ..................... **CLC 6, 40**
See also CA 45-48; CANR 2, 33; DLB 40;
MTCW

**Dunn, Katherine (Karen)** 1945- ..... **CLC 71**
See also CA 33-36R

**Dunn, Stephen** 1939- ............ **CLC 36**
See also CA 33-36R; CANR 12; DLB 105

**Dunne, Finley Peter** 1867-1936.... **TCLC 28**
See also CA 108; DLB 11, 23

**Dunne, John Gregory** 1932- ........ **CLC 28**
See also CA 25-28R; CANR 14; DLBY 80

**Dunsany, Edward John Moreton Drax**
**Plunkett** 1878-1957
See Dunsany, Lord; Lord Dunsany
See also CA 104; DLB 10

**Dunsany, Lord**.................... **TCLC 2**
See also Dunsany, Edward John Moreton
Drax Plunkett
See also DLB 77

**du Perry, Jean**
See Simenon, Georges (Jacques Christian)

**Durang, Christopher (Ferdinand)**
1949- .................... **CLC 27, 38**
See also CA 105

**Duras, Marguerite**
1914- ...... **CLC 3, 6, 11, 20, 34, 40, 68**
See also CA 25-28R; DLB 83; MTCW

**Durban, (Rosa) Pam** 1947- ........ **CLC 39**
See also CA 123

**Durcan, Paul** 1944- ............ **CLC 43, 70**
See also CA 134

**Durrell, Lawrence (George)**
1912-1990 .... **CLC 1, 4, 6, 8, 13, 27, 41**
See also CA 9-12R; 132; CANR 40;
CDBLB 1945-1960; DLB 15, 27;
DLBY 90; MTCW

**Dutt, Toru** 1856-1877.......... **NCLC 29**

**Dwight, Timothy** 1752-1817...... **NCLC 13**
See also DLB 37

**Dworkin, Andrea** 1946- ........... **CLC 43**
See also CA 77-80; CANR 16, 39; MTCW

**Dwyer, Deanna**
See Koontz, Dean R(ay)

**Dwyer, K. R.**
See Koontz, Dean R(ay)

**Dylan, Bob** 1941- ...... **CLC 3, 4, 6, 12, 77**
See also CA 41-44R; DLB 16

**Eagleton, Terence (Francis)** 1943-
See Eagleton, Terry
See also CA 57-60; CANR 7, 23; MTCW

**Eagleton, Terry** .................... **CLC 63**
See also Eagleton, Terence (Francis)

**Early, Jack**
See Scoppettone, Sandra

**East, Michael**
See West, Morris L(anglo)

**Eastaway, Edward**
See Thomas, (Philip) Edward

**Eastlake, William (Derry)** 1917- ..... **CLC 8**
See also CA 5-8R; CAAS 1; CANR 5;
DLB 6

**Eberhart, Richard (Ghormley)**
1904- ............... **CLC 3, 11, 19, 56**
See also CA 1-4R; CANR 2;
CDALB 1941-1968; DLB 48; MTCW

**Eberstadt, Fernanda** 1960- ........ **CLC 39**
See also CA 136

**Echegaray (y Eizaguirre), Jose (Maria Waldo)**
1832-1916 ................... **TCLC 4**
See also CA 104; CANR 32; HW; MTCW

**Echeverria, (Jose) Esteban (Antonino)**
1805-1851 ................. **NCLC 18**

**Echo**
See Proust, (Valentin-Louis-George-Eugene-)
Marcel

**Eckert, Allan W.** 1931- ........... **CLC 17**
See also CA 13-16R; CANR 14; SATA 27,
29

**Eckhart, Meister** 1260(?)-1328(?) .. **CMLC 9**
See also DLB 115

**Eckmar, F. R.**
See de Hartog, Jan

**Eco, Umberto** 1932- ........... **CLC 28, 60**
See also BEST 90:1; CA 77-80; CANR 12,
33; MTCW

**Eddison, E(ric) R(ucker)**
1882-1945 ................. **TCLC 15**
See also CA 109

**Edel, (Joseph) Leon** 1907- ...... **CLC 29, 34**
See also CA 1-4R; CANR 1, 22; DLB 103

**Eden, Emily** 1797-1869 ........ **NCLC 10**

**Edgar, David** 1948- .............. **CLC 42**
See also CA 57-60; CANR 12; DLB 13;
MTCW

**Edgerton, Clyde (Carlyle)** 1944- .... **CLC 39**
See also CA 118; 134

**Edgeworth, Maria** 1767-1849...... **NCLC 1**
See also DLB 116; SATA 21

**Edmonds, Paul**
See Kuttner, Henry

**Edmonds, Walter D(umaux)** 1903- ... **CLC 35**
See also CA 5-8R; CANR 2; DLB 9;
MAICYA; SAAS 4; SATA 1, 27

**Edmondson, Wallace**
See Ellison, Harlan

Edson, Russell.................. CLC 13
See also CA 33-36R

Edwards, G(erald) B(asil)
1899-1976................. CLC 25
See also CA 110

Edwards, Gus 1939-.............. CLC 43
See also CA 108

Edwards, Jonathan 1703-1758.... LC 7; DA
See also DLB 24

Efron, Marina Ivanovna Tsvetaeva
See Tsvetaeva (Efron), Marina (Ivanovna)

Ehle, John (Marsden, Jr.) 1925-.... CLC 27
See also CA 9-12R

Ehrenbourg, Ilya (Grigoryevich)
See Ehrenburg, Ilya (Grigoryevich)

Ehrenburg, Ilya (Grigoryevich)
1891-1967............. CLC 18, 34, 62
See also CA 102; 25-28R

Ehrenburg, Ilyo (Grigoryevich)
See Ehrenburg, Ilya (Grigoryevich)

Eich, Guenter 1907-1972.......... CLC 15
See also CA 111; 93-96; DLB 69, 124

Eichendorff, Joseph Freiherr von
1788-1857.................. NCLC 8
See also DLB 90

Eigner, Larry...................... CLC 9
See also Eigner, Laurence (Joel)
See also DLB 5

Eigner, Laurence (Joel) 1927-
See Eigner, Larry
See also CA 9-12R; CANR 6

Eiseley, Loren Corey 1907-1977..... CLC 7
See also AAYA 5; CA 1-4R; 73-76;
CANR 6

Eisenstadt, Jill 1963-............. CLC 50
See also CA 140

Eisner, Simon
See Kornbluth, C(yril) M.

Ekeloef, (Bengt) Gunnar
1907-1968................ CLC 27
See also Ekelof, (Bengt) Gunnar
See also CA 123; 25-28R

Ekelof, (Bengt) Gunnar............. CLC 27
See also Ekeloef, (Bengt) Gunnar

Ekwensi, C. O. D.
See Ekwensi, Cyprian (Odiatu Duaka)

Ekwensi, Cyprian (Odiatu Duaka)
1921-................... CLC 4; BLC
See also BW 2; CA 29-32R; CANR 18, 42;
DLB 117; MTCW; SATA 66

Elaine........................ TCLC 18
See also Leverson, Ada

El Crummo
See Crumb, R(obert)

Elia
See Lamb, Charles

Eliade, Mircea 1907-1986......... CLC 19
See also CA 65-68; 119; CANR 30; MTCW

Eliot, A. D.
See Jewett, (Theodora) Sarah Orne

Eliot, Alice
See Jewett, (Theodora) Sarah Orne

Eliot, Dan
See Silverberg, Robert

Eliot, George
1819-1880.... NCLC 4, 13, 23, 41; DA;
WLC
See also CDBLB 1832-1890; DLB 21, 35, 55

Eliot, John 1604-1690.............. LC 5
See also DLB 24

Eliot, T(homas) S(tearns)
1888-1965..... CLC 1, 2, 3, 6, 9, 10, 13,
15, 24, 34, 41, 55, 57; DA; PC 5; WLC 2
See also CA 5-8R; 25-28R; CANR 41;
CDALB 1929-1941; DLB 7, 10, 45, 63;
DLBY 88; MTCW

Elizabeth 1866-1941.............. TCLC 41

Elkin, Stanley L(awrence)
1930-... CLC 4, 6, 9, 14, 27, 51; SSC 12
See also CA 9-12R; CANR 8; DLB 2, 28;
DLBY 80; MTCW

Elledge, Scott.................... CLC 34

Elliott, Don
See Silverberg, Robert

Elliott, George P(aul) 1918-1980..... CLC 2
See also CA 1-4R; 97-100; CANR 2

Elliott, Janice 1931-............... CLC 47
See also CA 13-16R; CANR 8, 29; DLB 14

Elliott, Sumner Locke 1917-1991... CLC 38
See also CA 5-8R; 134; CANR 2, 21

Elliott, William
See Bradbury, Ray (Douglas)

Ellis, A. E........................ CLC 7

Ellis, Alice Thomas................ CLC 40
See also Haycraft, Anna

Ellis, Bret Easton 1964-........ CLC 39, 71
See also AAYA 2; CA 118; 123

Ellis, (Henry) Havelock
1859-1939.................. TCLC 14
See also CA 109

Ellis, Landon
See Ellison, Harlan

Ellis, Trey 1962-................. CLC 55

Ellison, Harlan
1934-.......... CLC 1, 13, 42; SSC 14
See also CA 5-8R; CANR 5; DLB 8;
MTCW

Ellison, Ralph (Waldo)
1914-...... CLC 1, 3, 11, 54; BLC; DA;
WLC
See also BW 1; CA 9-12R; CANR 24;
CDALB 1941-1968; DLB 2, 76; MTCW

Ellmann, Lucy (Elizabeth) 1956-.... CLC 61
See also CA 128

Ellmann, Richard (David)
1918-1987.................. CLC 50
See also BEST 89:2; CA 1-4R; 122;
CANR 2, 28; DLB 103; DLBY 87;
MTCW

Elman, Richard 1934-............. CLC 19
See also CA 17-20R; CAAS 3

Elron
See Hubbard, L(afayette) Ron(ald)

Eluard, Paul.................. TCLC 7, 41
See also Grindel, Eugene

Elyot, Sir Thomas 1490(?)-1546..... LC 11

Elytis, Odysseus 1911-......... CLC 15, 49
See also CA 102; MTCW

Emecheta, (Florence Onye) Buchi
1944-............... CLC 14, 48; BLC
See also BW 2; CA 81-84; CANR 27;
DLB 117; MTCW; SATA 66

Emerson, Ralph Waldo
1803-1882...... NCLC 1, 38; DA; WLC
See also CDALB 1640-1865; DLB 1, 59, 73

Eminescu, Mihail 1850-1889..... NCLC 33

Empson, William
1906-1984........ CLC 3, 8, 19, 33, 34
See also CA 17-20R; 112; CANR 31;
DLB 20; MTCW

Enchi Fumiko (Ueda) 1905-1986.... CLC 31
See also CA 129; 121

Ende, Michael (Andreas Helmuth)
1929-........................ CLC 31
See also CA 118; 124; CANR 36; CLR 14;
DLB 75; MAICYA; SATA 42, 61

Endo, Shusaku 1923-..... CLC 7, 14, 19, 54
See also CA 29-32R; CANR 21; MTCW

Engel, Marian 1933-1985.......... CLC 36
See also CA 25-28R; CANR 12; DLB 53

Engelhardt, Frederick
See Hubbard, L(afayette) Ron(ald)

Enright, D(ennis) J(oseph)
1920-.................... CLC 4, 8, 31
See also CA 1-4R; CANR 1, 42; DLB 27;
SATA 25

Enzensberger, Hans Magnus
1929-........................ CLC 43
See also CA 116; 119

Ephron, Nora 1941-............ CLC 17, 31
See also AITN 2; CA 65-68; CANR 12, 39

Epsilon
See Betjeman, John

Epstein, Daniel Mark 1948-........ CLC 7
See also CA 49-52; CANR 2

Epstein, Jacob 1956-.............. CLC 19
See also CA 114

Epstein, Joseph 1937-............. CLC 39
See also CA 112; 119

Epstein, Leslie 1938-.............. CLC 27
See also CA 73-76; CAAS 12; CANR 23

Equiano, Olaudah
1745(?)-1797............. LC 16; BLC
See also DLB 37, 50

Erasmus, Desiderius 1469(?)-1536.... LC 16

Erdman, Paul E(mil) 1932-........ CLC 25
See also AITN 1; CA 61-64; CANR 13, 43

Erdrich, Louise 1954-.......... CLC 39, 54
See also AAYA 10; BEST 89:1; CA 114;
CANR 41; MTCW

Erenburg, Ilya (Grigoryevich)
See Ehrenburg, Ilya (Grigoryevich)

Erickson, Stephen Michael 1950-
See Erickson, Steve
See also CA 129

Erickson, Steve.................... CLC 64
See also Erickson, Stephen Michael

Ericson, Walter
See Fast, Howard (Melvin)

Eriksson, Buntel
See Bergman, (Ernst) Ingmar

Ferlinghetti, Lawrence (Monsanto)
1919(?)- . . . . . . . . CLC 2, 6, 10, 27; PC 1
See also CA 5-8R; CANR 3, 41;
CDALB 1941-1968; DLB 5, 16; MTCW

Fernandez, Vicente Garcia Huidobro
See Huidobro Fernandez, Vicente Garcia

Ferrer, Gabriel (Francisco Victor) Miro
See Miro (Ferrer), Gabriel (Francisco
Victor)

Ferrier, Susan (Edmonstone)
1782-1854 . . . . . . . . . . . . . . . . . NCLC 8
See also DLB 116

Ferrigno, Robert 1948(?)- . . . . . . . . . CLC 65
See also CA 140

Feuchtwanger, Lion 1884-1958 . . . . . TCLC 3
See also CA 104; DLB 66

Feuillet, Octave 1821-1890 . . . . . . NCLC 45

Feydeau, Georges (Leon Jules Marie)
1862-1921 . . . . . . . . . . . . . . . . . TCLC 22
See also CA 113

Ficino, Marsilio 1433-1499 . . . . . . . . LC 12

Fiedeler, Hans
See Doeblin, Alfred

Fiedler, Leslie A(aron)
1917- . . . . . . . . . . . . . . . . . CLC 4, 13, 24
See also CA 9-12R; CANR 7; DLB 28, 67;
MTCW

Field, Andrew 1938- . . . . . . . . . . . . . CLC 44
See also CA 97-100; CANR 25

Field, Eugene 1850-1895 . . . . . . . . . NCLC 3
See also DLB 23, 42, 140; MAICYA;
SATA 16

Field, Gans T.
See Wellman, Manly Wade

Field, Michael . . . . . . . . . . . . . . . . . TCLC 43

Field, Peter
See Hobson, Laura Z(ametkin)

Fielding, Henry
1707-1754 . . . . . . . . . . . LC 1; DA; WLC
See also CDBLB 1660-1789; DLB 39, 84,
101

Fielding, Sarah 1710-1768 . . . . . . . . . . . LC 1
See also DLB 39

Fierstein, Harvey (Forbes) 1954- . . . CLC 33
See also CA 123; 129

Figes, Eva 1932- . . . . . . . . . . . . . . . . CLC 31
See also CA 53-56; CANR 4, 44; DLB 14

Finch, Robert (Duer Claydon)
1900- . . . . . . . . . . . . . . . . . . . . . . CLC 18
See also CA 57-60; CANR 9, 24; DLB 88

Findley, Timothy 1930- . . . . . . . . . . CLC 27
See also CA 25-28R; CANR 12, 42;
DLB 53

Fink, William
See Mencken, H(enry) L(ouis)

Firbank, Louis 1942-
See Reed, Lou
See also CA 117

Firbank, (Arthur Annesley) Ronald
1886-1926 . . . . . . . . . . . . . . . . . TCLC 1
See also CA 104; DLB 36

Fisher, M(ary) F(rances) K(ennedy)
1908-1992 . . . . . . . . . . . . . . . . . CLC 76
See also CA 77-80; 138; CANR 44

Fisher, Roy 1930- . . . . . . . . . . . . . . . CLC 25
See also CA 81-84; CAAS 10; CANR 16;
DLB 40

Fisher, Rudolph
1897-1934 . . . . . . . . . . . . . TCLC 11; BLC
See also BW 1; CA 107; 124; DLB 51, 102

Fisher, Vardis (Alvero) 1895-1968. . . . CLC 7
See also CA 5-8R; 25-28R; DLB 9

Fiske, Tarleton
See Bloch, Robert (Albert)

Fitch, Clarke
See Sinclair, Upton (Beall)

Fitch, John IV
See Cormier, Robert (Edmund)

Fitgerald, Penelope 1916- . . . . . . . . CLC 61

Fitzgerald, Captain Hugh
See Baum, L(yman) Frank

FitzGerald, Edward 1809-1883 . . . . NCLC 9
See also DLB 32

Fitzgerald, F(rancis) Scott (Key)
1896-1940 . . . . . . TCLC 1, 6, 14, 28; DA;
SSC 6; WLC
See also AITN 1; CA 110; 123;
CDALB 1917-1929; DLB 4, 9, 86;
DLBD 1; DLBY 81; MTCW

Fitzgerald, Penelope 1916- . . . . . . CLC 19, 51
See also CA 85-88; CAAS 10; DLB 14

Fitzgerald, Robert (Stuart)
1910-1985 . . . . . . . . . . . . . . . . . CLC 39
See also CA 1-4R; 114; CANR 1; DLBY 80

FitzGerald, Robert D(avid)
1902-1987 . . . . . . . . . . . . . . . . . CLC 19
See also CA 17-20R

Fitzgerald, Zelda (Sayre)
1900-1948 . . . . . . . . . . . . . . . . . TCLC 52
See also CA 117; 126; DLBY 84

Flanagan, Thomas (James Bonner)
1923- . . . . . . . . . . . . . . . . . . CLC 25, 52
See also CA 108; DLBY 80; MTCW

Flaubert, Gustave
1821-1880 . . . . . . . . NCLC 2, 10, 19; DA;
SSC 11; WLC
See also DLB 119

Flecker, (Herman) James Elroy
1884-1915 . . . . . . . . . . . . . . . . . TCLC 43
See also CA 109; DLB 10, 19

Fleming, Ian (Lancaster)
1908-1964 . . . . . . . . . . . . . . . . CLC 3, 30
See also CA 5-8R; CDBLB 1945-1960;
DLB 87; MTCW; SATA 9

Fleming, Thomas (James) 1927- . . . . CLC 37
See also CA 5-8R; CANR 10; SATA 8

Fletcher, John Gould 1886-1950 . . . TCLC 35
See also CA 107; DLB 4, 45

Fleur, Paul
See Pohl, Frederik

Flooglebuckle, Al
See Spiegelman, Art

Flying Officer X
See Bates, H(erbert) E(rnest)

Fo, Dario 1926- . . . . . . . . . . . . . . . . CLC 32
See also CA 116; 128; MTCW

Fogarty, Jonathan Titulescu Esq.
See Farrell, James T(homas)

Folke, Will
See Bloch, Robert (Albert)

Follett, Ken(neth Martin) 1949- . . . . CLC 18
See also AAYA 6; BEST 89:4; CA 81-84;
CANR 13, 33; DLB 87; DLBY 81;
MTCW

Fontane, Theodor 1819-1898 . . . . . NCLC 26
See also DLB 129

Foote, Horton 1916- . . . . . . . . . . . . . CLC 51
See also CA 73-76; CANR 34; DLB 26

Foote, Shelby 1916- . . . . . . . . . . . . . CLC 75
See also CA 5-8R; CANR 3; DLB 2, 17

Forbes, Esther 1891-1967. . . . . . . . . CLC 12
See also CA 13-14; 25-28R; CAP 1;
CLR 27; DLB 22; JRDA; MAICYA;
SATA 2

Forche, Carolyn (Louise)
1950- . . . . . . . . . . . . . . . . . . . CLC 25, 83
See also CA 109; 117; DLB 5

Ford, Elbur
See Hibbert, Eleanor Alice Burford

Ford, Ford Madox
1873-1939 . . . . . . . . . . . . TCLC 1, 15, 39
See also CA 104; 132; CDBLB 1914-1945;
DLB 34, 98; MTCW

Ford, John 1895-1973. . . . . . . . . . . . CLC 16
See also CA 45-48

Ford, Richard 1944- . . . . . . . . . . . . . CLC 46
See also CA 69-72; CANR 11

Ford, Webster
See Masters, Edgar Lee

Foreman, Richard 1937-. . . . . . . . . . CLC 50
See also CA 65-68; CANR 32

Forester, C(ecil) S(cott)
1899-1966 . . . . . . . . . . . . . . . . . CLC 35
See also CA 73-76; 25-28R; SATA 13

Forez
See Mauriac, Francois (Charles)

Forman, James Douglas 1932-. . . . . . CLC 21
See also CA 9-12R; CANR 4, 19, 42;
JRDA; MAICYA; SATA 8, 70

Fornes, Maria Irene 1930-. . . . . . . CLC 39, 61
See also CA 25-28R; CANR 28; DLB 7;
HW; MTCW

Forrest, Leon 1937- . . . . . . . . . . . . . . CLC 4
See also BW 2; CA 89-92; CAAS 7;
CANR 25; DLB 33

Forster, E(dward) M(organ)
1879-1970 . . . . . CLC 1, 2, 3, 4, 9, 10, 13,
15, 22, 45, 77; DA; WLC
See also AAYA 2; CA 13-14; 25-28R;
CAP 1; CDBLB 1914-1945; DLB 34, 98;
DLBD 10; MTCW; SATA 57

Forster, John 1812-1876 . . . . . . . . NCLC 11

Forsyth, Frederick 1938-. . . . . . . CLC 2, 5, 36
See also BEST 89:4; CA 85-88; CANR 38;
DLB 87; MTCW

Forten, Charlotte L. . . . . . . . . TCLC 16; BLC
See also Grimke, Charlotte L(ottie) Forten
See also DLB 50

Foscolo, Ugo 1778-1827. . . . . . . . . NCLC 8

Fosse, Bob . . . . . . . . . . . . . . . . . . . . CLC 20
See also Fosse, Robert Louis

**Fosse, Robert Louis** 1927-1987
  See Fosse, Bob
  See also CA 110; 123

**Foster, Stephen Collins**
  1826-1864 ................. NCLC 26

**Foucault, Michel**
  1926-1984 ............. CLC 31, 34, 69
  See also CA 105; 113; CANR 34; MTCW

**Fouque, Friedrich (Heinrich Karl) de la Motte**
  1777-1843 .................. NCLC 2
  See also DLB 90

**Fournier, Henri Alban** 1886-1914
  See Alain-Fournier
  See also CA 104

**Fournier, Pierre** 1916- ............ CLC 11
  See also Gascar, Pierre
  See also CA 89-92; CANR 16, 40

**Fowles, John**
  1926- .... CLC 1, 2, 3, 4, 6, 9, 10, 15, 33
  See also CA 5-8R; CANR 25; CDBLB 1960
    to Present; DLB 14, 139; MTCW;
    SATA 22

**Fox, Paula** 1923- ................. CLC 2, 8
  See also AAYA 3; CA 73-76; CANR 20,
    36; CLR 1; DLB 52; JRDA; MAICYA;
    MTCW; SATA 17, 60

**Fox, William Price (Jr.)** 1926- ..... CLC 22
  See also CA 17-20R; CAAS 19; CANR 11;
    DLB 2; DLBY 81

**Foxe, John** 1516(?)-1587 ........... LC 14

**Frame, Janet** .......... CLC 2, 3, 6, 22, 66
  See also Clutha, Janet Paterson Frame

**France, Anatole** .................. TCLC 9
  See also Thibault, Jacques Anatole Francois
  See also DLB 123

**Francis, Claude** 19(?)- ............ CLC 50

**Francis, Dick** 1920- ......... CLC 2, 22, 42
  See also AAYA 5; BEST 89:3; CA 5-8R;
    CANR 9, 42; CDBLB 1960 to Present;
    DLB 87; MTCW

**Francis, Robert (Churchill)**
  1901-1987 ................... CLC 15
  See also CA 1-4R; 123; CANR 1

**Frank, Anne(lies Marie)**
  1929-1945 ......... TCLC 17; DA; WLC
  See also AAYA 12; CA 113; 133; MTCW;
    SATA 42

**Frank, Elizabeth** 1945- ............ CLC 39
  See also CA 121; 126

**Franklin, Benjamin**
  See Hasek, Jaroslav (Matej Frantisek)

**Franklin, Benjamin** 1706-1790... LC 25; DA
  See also CDALB 1640-1865; DLB 24, 43,
    73

**Franklin, (Stella Maraia Sarah) Miles**
  1879-1954 ................... TCLC 7
  See also CA 104

**Fraser, (Lady) Antonia (Pakenham)**
  1932- ....................... CLC 32
  See also CA 85-88; CANR 44; MTCW;
    SATA 32

**Fraser, George MacDonald** 1925- .... CLC 7
  See also CA 45-48; CANR 2

**Fraser, Sylvia** 1935- .............. CLC 64
  See also CA 45-48; CANR 1, 16

**Frayn, Michael** 1933- ...... CLC 3, 7, 31, 47
  See also CA 5-8R; CANR 30; DLB 13, 14;
    MTCW

**Fraze, Candida (Merrill)** 1945- ..... CLC 50
  See also CA 126

**Frazer, J(ames) G(eorge)**
  1854-1941 ................. TCLC 32
  See also CA 118

**Frazer, Robert Caine**
  See Creasey, John

**Frazer, Sir James George**
  See Frazer, J(ames) G(eorge)

**Frazier, Ian** 1951- ................ CLC 46
  See also CA 130

**Frederic, Harold** 1856-1898 ...... NCLC 10
  See also DLB 12, 23

**Frederick, John**
  See Faust, Frederick (Schiller)

**Frederick the Great** 1712-1786 ...... LC 14

**Fredro, Aleksander** 1793-1876 ..... NCLC 8

**Freeling, Nicolas** 1927- ........... CLC 38
  See also CA 49-52; CAAS 12; CANR 1, 17;
    DLB 87

**Freeman, Douglas Southall**
  1886-1953 ................. TCLC 11
  See also CA 109; DLB 17

**Freeman, Judith** 1946- ............ CLC 55

**Freeman, Mary Eleanor Wilkins**
  1852-1930 ............. TCLC 9; SSC 1
  See also CA 106; DLB 12, 78

**Freeman, R(ichard) Austin**
  1862-1943 ................. TCLC 21
  See also CA 113; DLB 70

**French, Marilyn** 1929- ...... CLC 10, 18, 60
  See also CA 69-72; CANR 3, 31; MTCW

**French, Paul**
  See Asimov, Isaac

**Freneau, Philip Morin** 1752-1832 .. NCLC 1
  See also DLB 37, 43

**Freud, Sigmund** 1856-1939 ....... TCLC 52
  See also CA 115; 133; MTCW

**Friedan, Betty (Naomi)** 1921- ...... CLC 74
  See also CA 65-68; CANR 18; MTCW

**Friedman, B(ernard) H(arper)**
  1926- ....................... CLC 7
  See also CA 1-4R; CANR 3

**Friedman, Bruce Jay** 1930-.... CLC 3, 5, 56
  See also CA 9-12R; CANR 25; DLB 2, 28

**Friel, Brian** 1929- ........... CLC 5, 42, 59
  See also CA 21-24R; CANR 33; DLB 13;
    MTCW

**Friis-Baastad, Babbis Ellinor**
  1921-1970 ................... CLC 12
  See also CA 17-20R; 134; SATA 7

**Frisch, Max (Rudolf)**
  1911-1991 ..... CLC 3, 9, 14, 18, 32, 44
  See also CA 85-88; 134; CANR 32;
    DLB 69, 124; MTCW

**Fromentin, Eugene (Samuel Auguste)**
  1820-1876 ................. NCLC 10
  See also DLB 123

**Frost, Frederick**
  See Faust, Frederick (Schiller)

**Frost, Robert (Lee)**
  1874-1963 .... CLC 1, 3, 4, 9, 10, 13, 15,
            26, 34, 44; DA; PC 1; WLC
  See also CA 89-92; CANR 33;
    CDALB 1917-1929; DLB 54; DLBD 7;
    MTCW; SATA 14

**Froude, James Anthony**
  1818-1894 ................. NCLC 43
  See also DLB 18, 57

**Froy, Herald**
  See Waterhouse, Keith (Spencer)

**Fry, Christopher** 1907- ....... CLC 2, 10, 14
  See also CA 17-20R; CANR 9, 30; DLB 13;
    MTCW; SATA 66

**Frye, (Herman) Northrop**
  1912-1991 ................. CLC 24, 70
  See also CA 5-8R; 133; CANR 8, 37;
    DLB 67, 68; MTCW

**Fuchs, Daniel** 1909-1993 ........ CLC 8, 22
  See also CA 81-84; 142; CAAS 5;
    CANR 40; DLB 9, 26, 28; DLBY 93

**Fuchs, Daniel** 1934- .............. CLC 34
  See also CA 37-40R; CANR 14

**Fuentes, Carlos**
  1928- ...... CLC 3, 8, 10, 13, 22, 41, 60;
            DA; HLC; WLC
  See also AAYA 4; AITN 2; CA 69-72;
    CANR 10, 32; DLB 113; HW; MTCW

**Fuentes, Gregorio Lopez y**
  See Lopez y Fuentes, Gregorio

**Fugard, (Harold) Athol**
  1932- .... CLC 5, 9, 14, 25, 40, 80; DC 3
  See also CA 85-88; CANR 32; MTCW

**Fugard, Sheila** 1932- .............. CLC 48
  See also CA 125

**Fuller, Charles (H., Jr.)**
  1939- ............. CLC 25; BLC; DC 1
  See also BW 2; CA 108; 112; DLB 38;
    MTCW

**Fuller, John (Leopold)** 1937- ....... CLC 62
  See also CA 21-24R; CANR 9, 44; DLB 40

**Fuller, Margaret** ................. NCLC 5
  See also Ossoli, Sarah Margaret (Fuller
    marchesa d')

**Fuller, Roy (Broadbent)**
  1912-1991 ................. CLC 4, 28
  See also CA 5-8R; 135; CAAS 10; DLB 15,
    20

**Fulton, Alice** 1952- ............... CLC 52
  See also CA 116

**Furphy, Joseph** 1843-1912 ....... TCLC 25

**Fussell, Paul** 1924- ............... CLC 74
  See also BEST 90:1; CA 17-20R; CANR 8,
    21, 35; MTCW

**Futabatei, Shimei** 1864-1909 ...... TCLC 44

**Futrelle, Jacques** 1875-1912 ...... TCLC 19
  See also CA 113

**G. B. S.**
  See Shaw, George Bernard

**Gaboriau, Emile** 1835-1873 ...... NCLC 14

**Gadda, Carlo Emilio** 1893-1973 .... CLC 11
  See also CA 89-92

**Gaddis, William**
1922- ........ **CLC 1, 3, 6, 8, 10, 19, 43**
See also CA 17-20R; CANR 21; DLB 2;
MTCW

**Gaines, Ernest J(ames)**
1933- ............. **CLC 3, 11, 18; BLC**
See also AITN 1; BW 2; CA 9-12R;
CANR 6, 24, 42; CDALB 1968-1988;
DLB 2, 33; DLBY 80; MTCW

**Gaitskill, Mary** 1954-............. **CLC 69**
See also CA 128

**Galdos, Benito Perez**
See Perez Galdos, Benito

**Gale, Zona** 1874-1938 ............ **TCLC 7**
See also CA 105; DLB 9, 78

**Galeano, Eduardo (Hughes)** 1940-... **CLC 72**
See also CA 29-32R; CANR 13, 32; HW

**Galiano, Juan Valera y Alcala**
See Valera y Alcala-Galiano, Juan

**Gallagher, Tess** 1943-.... **CLC 18, 63; PC 9**
See also CA 106; DLB 120

**Gallant, Mavis**
1922- ........... **CLC 7, 18, 38; SSC 5**
See also CA 69-72; CANR 29; DLB 53;
MTCW

**Gallant, Roy A(rthur)** 1924- ....... **CLC 17**
See also CA 5-8R; CANR 4, 29; CLR 30;
MAICYA; SATA 4, 68

**Gallico, Paul (William)** 1897-1976 ... **CLC 2**
See also AITN 1; CA 5-8R; 69-72;
CANR 23; DLB 9; MAICYA; SATA 13

**Gallup, Ralph**
See Whitemore, Hugh (John)

**Galsworthy, John**
1867-1933 .... **TCLC 1, 45; DA; WLC 2**
See also CA 104; 141; CDBLB 1890-1914;
DLB 10, 34, 98

**Galt, John** 1779-1839............ **NCLC 1**
See also DLB 99, 116

**Galvin, James** 1951-.............. **CLC 38**
See also CA 108; CANR 26

**Gamboa, Federico** 1864-1939...... **TCLC 36**

**Gann, Ernest Kellogg** 1910-1991.... **CLC 23**
See also AITN 1; CA 1-4R; 136; CANR 1

**Garcia, Cristina** 1958- ............ **CLC 76**
See also CA 141

**Garcia Lorca, Federico**
1898-1936 ........ **TCLC 1, 7, 49; DA;**
**DC 2; HLC; PC 3; WLC**
See also CA 104; 131; DLB 108; HW;
MTCW

**Garcia Marquez, Gabriel (Jose)**
1928- .... **CLC 2, 3, 8, 10, 15, 27, 47, 55;**
**DA; HLC; SSC 8; WLC**
See also Marquez, Gabriel (Jose) Garcia
See also AAYA 3; BEST 89:1, 90:4;
CA 33-36R; CANR 10, 28; DLB 113;
HW; MTCW

**Gard, Janice**
See Latham, Jean Lee

**Gard, Roger Martin du**
See Martin du Gard, Roger

**Gardam, Jane** 1928-.............. **CLC 43**
See also CA 49-52; CANR 2, 18, 33;
CLR 12; DLB 14; MAICYA; MTCW;
SAAS 9; SATA 28, 39, 76

**Gardner, Herb**.................... **CLC 44**

**Gardner, John (Champlin), Jr.**
1933-1982 ..... **CLC 2, 3, 5, 7, 8, 10, 18,**
**28, 34; SSC 7**
See also AITN 1; CA 65-68; 107;
CANR 33; DLB 2; DLBY 82; MTCW;
SATA 31, 40

**Gardner, John (Edmund)** 1926-..... **CLC 30**
See also CA 103; CANR 15; MTCW

**Gardner, Noel**
See Kuttner, Henry

**Gardons, S. S.**
See Snodgrass, W(illiam) D(e Witt)

**Garfield, Leon** 1921-.............. **CLC 12**
See also AAYA 8; CA 17-20R; CANR 38,
41; CLR 21; JRDA; MAICYA; SATA 1,
32, 76

**Garland, (Hannibal) Hamlin**
1860-1940 .................. **TCLC 3**
See also CA 104; DLB 12, 71, 78

**Garneau, (Hector de) Saint-Denys**
1912-1943 ................. **TCLC 13**
See also CA 111; DLB 88

**Garner, Alan** 1934-.............. **CLC 17**
See also CA 73-76; CANR 15; CLR 20;
MAICYA; MTCW; SATA 18, 69

**Garner, Hugh** 1913-1979 ......... **CLC 13**
See also CA 69-72; CANR 31; DLB 68

**Garnett, David** 1892-1981 ......... **CLC 3**
See also CA 5-8R; 103; CANR 17; DLB 34

**Garos, Stephanie**
See Katz, Steve

**Garrett, George (Palmer)**
1929- .................. **CLC 3, 11, 51**
See also CA 1-4R; CAAS 5; CANR 1, 42;
DLB 2, 5, 130; DLBY 83

**Garrick, David** 1717-1779 .......... **LC 15**
See also DLB 84

**Garrigue, Jean** 1914-1972 ........ **CLC 2, 8**
See also CA 5-8R; 37-40R; CANR 20

**Garrison, Frederick**
See Sinclair, Upton (Beall)

**Garth, Will**
See Hamilton, Edmond; Kuttner, Henry

**Garvey, Marcus (Moziah, Jr.)**
1887-1940 ............. **TCLC 41; BLC**
See also BW 1; CA 120; 124

**Gary, Romain** .................... **CLC 25**
See also Kacew, Romain
See also DLB 83

**Gascar, Pierre** .................... **CLC 11**
See also Fournier, Pierre

**Gascoyne, David (Emery)** 1916- .... **CLC 45**
See also CA 65-68; CANR 10, 28; DLB 20;
MTCW

**Gaskell, Elizabeth Cleghorn**
1810-1865 .................. **NCLC 5**
See also CDBLB 1832-1890; DLB 21

**Gass, William H(oward)**
1924- ... **CLC 1, 2, 8, 11, 15, 39; SSC 12**
See also CA 17-20R; CANR 30; DLB 2;
MTCW

**Gasset, Jose Ortega y**
See Ortega y Gasset, Jose

**Gautier, Theophile** 1811-1872 ..... **NCLC 1**
See also DLB 119

**Gawsworth, John**
See Bates, H(erbert) E(rnest)

**Gaye, Marvin (Penze)** 1939-1984 ... **CLC 26**
See also CA 112

**Gebler, Carlo (Ernest)** 1954-....... **CLC 39**
See also CA 119; 133

**Gee, Maggie (Mary)** 1948-........ **CLC 57**
See also CA 130

**Gee, Maurice (Gough)** 1931-....... **CLC 29**
See also CA 97-100; SATA 46

**Gelbart, Larry (Simon)** 1923- ... **CLC 21, 61**
See also CA 73-76

**Gelber, Jack** 1932-........ **CLC 1, 6, 14, 79**
See also CA 1-4R; CANR 2; DLB 7

**Gellhorn, Martha (Ellis)** 1908- .. **CLC 14, 60**
See also CA 77-80; CANR 44; DLBY 82

**Genet, Jean**
1910-1986 ... **CLC 1, 2, 5, 10, 14, 44, 46**
See also CA 13-16R; CANR 18; DLB 72;
DLBY 86; MTCW

**Gent, Peter** 1942-................. **CLC 29**
See also AITN 1; CA 89-92; DLBY 82

**Gentlewoman in New England, A**
See Bradstreet, Anne

**Gentlewoman in Those Parts, A**
See Bradstreet, Anne

**George, Jean Craighead** 1919-...... **CLC 35**
See also AAYA 8; CA 5-8R; CANR 25;
CLR 1; DLB 52; JRDA; MAICYA;
SATA 2, 68

**George, Stefan (Anton)**
1868-1933 ............... **TCLC 2, 14**
See also CA 104

**Georges, Georges Martin**
See Simenon, Georges (Jacques Christian)

**Gerhardi, William Alexander**
See Gerhardie, William Alexander

**Gerhardie, William Alexander**
1895-1977 ................... **CLC 5**
See also CA 25-28R; 73-76; CANR 18;
DLB 36

**Gerstler, Amy** 1956-.............. **CLC 70**

**Gertler, T.** ...................... **CLC 34**
See also CA 116; 121

**Ghalib** 1797-1869 .............. **NCLC 39**

**Ghelderode, Michel de**
1898-1962 ................. **CLC 6, 11**
See also CA 85-88; CANR 40

**Ghiselin, Brewster** 1903- .......... **CLC 23**
See also CA 13-16R; CAAS 10; CANR 13

**Ghose, Zulfikar** 1935-............. **CLC 42**
See also CA 65-68

**Ghosh, Amitav** 1956- ............. **CLC 44**

**Giacosa, Giuseppe** 1847-1906 ...... **TCLC 7**
See also CA 104

**Gibb, Lee**
  See Waterhouse, Keith (Spencer)

**Gibbon, Lewis Grassic** ............. **TCLC 4**
  See also Mitchell, James Leslie

**Gibbons, Kaye** 1960- ........... **CLC 50**

**Gibran, Kahlil**
  1883-1931 .......... **TCLC 1, 9; PC 9**
  See also CA 104

**Gibson, William** 1914- ........ **CLC 23; DA**
  See also CA 9-12R; CANR 9, 42; DLB 7;
  SATA 66

**Gibson, William (Ford)** 1948- ... **CLC 39, 63**
  See also AAYA 12; CA 126; 133

**Gide, Andre (Paul Guillaume)**
  1869-1951 ....... **TCLC 5, 12, 36; DA;**
                                    **SSC 13; WLC**
  See also CA 104; 124; DLB 65; MTCW

**Gifford, Barry (Colby)** 1946- ....... **CLC 34**
  See also CA 65-68; CANR 9, 30, 40

**Gilbert, W(illiam) S(chwenck)**
  1836-1911 ................. **TCLC 3**
  See also CA 104; SATA 36

**Gilbreth, Frank B., Jr.** 1911- ...... **CLC 17**
  See also CA 9-12R; SATA 2

**Gilchrist, Ellen** 1935- ... **CLC 34, 48; SSC 14**
  See also CA 113; 116; CANR 41; DLB 130;
  MTCW

**Giles, Molly** 1942- ............... **CLC 39**
  See also CA 126

**Gill, Patrick**
  See Creasey, John

**Gilliam, Terry (Vance)** 1940- ....... **CLC 21**
  See also Monty Python
  See also CA 108; 113; CANR 35

**Gillian, Jerry**
  See Gilliam, Terry (Vance)

**Gilliatt, Penelope (Ann Douglass)**
  1932-1993 ........... **CLC 2, 10, 13, 53**
  See also AITN 2; CA 13-16R; 141; DLB 14

**Gilman, Charlotte (Anna) Perkins (Stetson)**
  1860-1935 ....... **TCLC 9, 37; SSC 13**
  See also CA 106

**Gilmour, David** 1949- ............. **CLC 35**
  See also Pink Floyd
  See also CA 138

**Gilpin, William** 1724-1804 ...... **NCLC 30**

**Gilray, J. D.**
  See Mencken, H(enry) L(ouis)

**Gilroy, Frank D(aniel)** 1925- ........ **CLC 2**
  See also CA 81-84; CANR 32; DLB 7

**Ginsberg, Allen**
  1926- ...... **CLC 1, 2, 3, 4, 6, 13, 36, 69;**
                                    **DA; PC 4; WLC 3**
  See also AITN 1; CA 1-4R; CANR 2, 41;
  CDALB 1941-1968; DLB 5, 16; MTCW

**Ginzburg, Natalia**
  1916-1991 .......... **CLC 5, 11, 54, 70**
  See also CA 85-88; 135; CANR 33; MTCW

**Giono, Jean** 1895-1970 ......... **CLC 4, 11**
  See also CA 45-48; 29-32R; CANR 2, 35;
  DLB 72; MTCW

**Giovanni, Nikki**
  1943- ...... **CLC 2, 4, 19, 64; BLC; DA**
  See also AITN 1; BW 2; CA 29-32R;
  CAAS 6; CANR 18, 41; CLR 6; DLB 5,
  41; MAICYA; MTCW; SATA 24

**Giovene, Andrea** 1904- ............. **CLC 7**
  See also CA 85-88

**Gippius, Zinaida (Nikolayevna)** 1869-1945
  See Hippius, Zinaida
  See also CA 106

**Giraudoux, (Hippolyte) Jean**
  1882-1944 ................. **TCLC 2, 7**
  See also CA 104; DLB 65

**Gironella, Jose Maria** 1917- ....... **CLC 11**
  See also CA 101

**Gissing, George (Robert)**
  1857-1903 ............ **TCLC 3, 24, 47**
  See also CA 105; DLB 18, 135

**Giurlani, Aldo**
  See Palazzeschi, Aldo

**Gladkov, Fyodor (Vasilyevich)**
  1883-1958 ................. **TCLC 27**

**Glanville, Brian (Lester)** 1931- ...... **CLC 6**
  See also CA 5-8R; CAAS 9; CANR 3;
  DLB 15, 139; SATA 42

**Glasgow, Ellen (Anderson Gholson)**
  1873(?)-1945 ............... **TCLC 2, 7**
  See also CA 104; DLB 9, 12

**Glassco, John** 1909-1981 ........... **CLC 9**
  See also CA 13-16R; 102; CANR 15;
  DLB 68

**Glasscock, Amnesia**
  See Steinbeck, John (Ernst)

**Glasser, Ronald J.** 1940(?)- ........ **CLC 37**

**Glassman, Joyce**
  See Johnson, Joyce

**Glendinning, Victoria** 1937- ........ **CLC 50**
  See also CA 120; 127

**Glissant, Edouard** 1928- ........ **CLC 10, 68**

**Gloag, Julian** 1930- ............... **CLC 40**
  See also AITN 1; CA 65-68; CANR 10

**Glowacki, Aleksander** 1845-1912
  See Prus, Boleslaw

**Gluck, Louise (Elisabeth)**
  1943- ............... **CLC 7, 22, 44, 81**
  See also Glueck, Louise
  See also CA 33-36R; CANR 40; DLB 5

**Glueck, Louise** .................. **CLC 7, 22**
  See also Gluck, Louise (Elisabeth)
  See also DLB 5

**Gobineau, Joseph Arthur (Comte) de**
  1816-1882 ................. **NCLC 17**
  See also DLB 123

**Godard, Jean-Luc** 1930- ........... **CLC 20**
  See also CA 93-96

**Godden, (Margaret) Rumer** 1907- ... **CLC 53**
  See also AAYA 6; CA 5-8R; CANR 4, 27,
  36; CLR 20; MAICYA; SAAS 12;
  SATA 3, 36

**Godoy Alcayaga, Lucila** 1889-1957
  See Mistral, Gabriela
  See also BW 2; CA 104; 131; HW; MTCW

**Godwin, Gail (Kathleen)**
  1937- ............. **CLC 5, 8, 22, 31, 69**
  See also CA 29-32R; CANR 15, 43; DLB 6;
  MTCW

**Godwin, William** 1756-1836 ...... **NCLC 14**
  See also CDBLB 1789-1832; DLB 39, 104,
  142

**Goethe, Johann Wolfgang von**
  1749-1832 ........ **NCLC 4, 22, 34; DA;**
                                    **PC 5; WLC 3**
  See also DLB 94

**Gogarty, Oliver St. John**
  1878-1957 ................. **TCLC 15**
  See also CA 109; DLB 15, 19

**Gogol, Nikolai (Vasilyevich)**
  1809-1852 ........ **NCLC 5, 15, 31; DA;**
                                    **DC 1; SSC 4; WLC**

**Goines, Donald**
  1937(?)-1974 ............ **CLC 80; BLC**
  See also AITN 1; BW 1; CA 124; 114;
  DLB 33

**Gold, Herbert** 1924- ....... **CLC 4, 7, 14, 42**
  See also CA 9-12R; CANR 17; DLB 2;
  DLBY 81

**Goldbarth, Albert** 1948- ......... **CLC 5, 38**
  See also CA 53-56; CANR 6, 40; DLB 120

**Goldberg, Anatol** 1910-1982 ....... **CLC 34**
  See also CA 131; 117

**Goldemberg, Isaac** 1945- .......... **CLC 52**
  See also CA 69-72; CAAS 12; CANR 11,
  32; HW

**Golden Silver**
  See Storm, Hyemeyohsts

**Golding, William (Gerald)**
  1911-1993 .... **CLC 1, 2, 3, 8, 10, 17, 27,**
                                    **58, 81; DA; WLC**
  See also AAYA 5; CA 5-8R; 141;
  CANR 13, 33; CDBLB 1945-1960;
  DLB 15, 100; MTCW

**Goldman, Emma** 1869-1940 ....... **TCLC 13**
  See also CA 110

**Goldman, Francisco** 1955- .......... **CLC 76**

**Goldman, William (W.)** 1931- .... **CLC 1, 48**
  See also CA 9-12R; CANR 29; DLB 44

**Goldmann, Lucien** 1913-1970 ....... **CLC 24**
  See also CA 25-28; CAP 2

**Goldoni, Carlo** 1707-1793 .......... **LC 4**

**Goldsberry, Steven** 1949- .......... **CLC 34**
  See also CA 131

**Goldsmith, Oliver**
  1728-1774 ........... **LC 2; DA; WLC**
  See also CDBLB 1660-1789; DLB 39, 89,
  104, 109, 142; SATA 26

**Goldsmith, Peter**
  See Priestley, J(ohn) B(oynton)

**Gombrowicz, Witold**
  1904-1969 ........... **CLC 4, 7, 11, 49**
  See also CA 19-20; 25-28R; CAP 2

**Gomez de la Serna, Ramon**
  1888-1963 .................. **CLC 9**
  See also CA 116; HW

**Goncharov, Ivan Alexandrovich**
  1812-1891 ................. **NCLC 1**

Goncourt, Edmond (Louis Antoine Huot) de
1822-1896 . . . . . . . . . . . . . . . . NCLC 7
See also DLB 123

Goncourt, Jules (Alfred Huot) de
1830-1870 . . . . . . . . . . . . . . . . NCLC 7
See also DLB 123

Gontier, Fernande 19(?)- . . . . . . . . . CLC 50

Goodman, Paul 1911-1972 . . . . CLC 1, 2, 4, 7
See also CA 19-20; 37-40R; CANR 34;
CAP 2; DLB 130; MTCW

Gordimer, Nadine
1923- . . . . CLC 3, 5, 7, 10, 18, 33, 51, 70;
DA
See also CA 5-8R; CANR 3, 28; MTCW

Gordon, Adam Lindsay
1833-1870 . . . . . . . . . . . . . . . NCLC 21

Gordon, Caroline
1895-1981 . . . CLC 6, 13, 29, 83; SSC 15
See also CA 11-12; 103; CANR 36; CAP 1;
DLB 4, 9, 102; DLBY 81; MTCW

Gordon, Charles William 1860-1937
See Connor, Ralph
See also CA 109

Gordon, Mary (Catherine)
1949- . . . . . . . . . . . . . . . . . CLC 13, 22
See also CA 102; CANR 44; DLB 6;
DLBY 81; MTCW

Gordon, Sol 1923- . . . . . . . . . . . . . . . CLC 26
See also CA 53-56; CANR 4; SATA 11

Gordone, Charles 1925- . . . . . . . . . . CLC 1, 4
See also BW 1; CA 93-96; DLB 7; MTCW

Gorenko, Anna Andreevna
See Akhmatova, Anna

Gorky, Maxim . . . . . . . . . . . . . TCLC 8; WLC
See also Peshkov, Alexei Maximovich

Goryan, Sirak
See Saroyan, William

Gosse, Edmund (William)
1849-1928 . . . . . . . . . . . . . . . TCLC 28
See also CA 117; DLB 57

Gotlieb, Phyllis Fay (Bloom)
1926- . . . . . . . . . . . . . . . . . . . CLC 18
See also CA 13-16R; CANR 7; DLB 88

Gottesman, S. D.
See Kornbluth, C(yril) M.; Pohl, Frederik

Gottfried von Strassburg
fl. c. 1210- . . . . . . . . . . . . . . . CMLC 10
See also DLB 138

Gould, Lois . . . . . . . . . . . . . . . . . CLC 4, 10
See also CA 77-80; CANR 29; MTCW

Gourmont, Remy de 1858-1915 . . . . TCLC 17
See also CA 109

Govier, Katherine 1948- . . . . . . . . . . CLC 51
See also CA 101; CANR 18, 40

Goyen, (Charles) William
1915-1983 . . . . . . . . . . . . CLC 5, 8, 14, 40
See also AITN 2; CA 5-8R; 110; CANR 6;
DLB 2; DLBY 83

Goytisolo, Juan
1931- . . . . . . . . . . . . CLC 5, 10, 23; HLC
See also CA 85-88; CANR 32; HW; MTCW

Gozzi, (Conte) Carlo 1720-1806 . . NCLC 23

Grabbe, Christian Dietrich
1801-1836 . . . . . . . . . . . . . . . . NCLC 2
See also DLB 133

Grace, Patricia 1937- . . . . . . . . . . . . CLC 56

Gracian y Morales, Baltasar
1601-1658 . . . . . . . . . . . . . . . . . LC 15

Gracq, Julien . . . . . . . . . . . . . . . . CLC 11, 48
See also Poirier, Louis
See also DLB 83

Grade, Chaim 1910-1982 . . . . . . . . . CLC 10
See also CA 93-96; 107

Graduate of Oxford, A
See Ruskin, John

Graham, John
See Phillips, David Graham

Graham, Jorie 1951- . . . . . . . . . . . . . CLC 48
See also CA 111; DLB 120

Graham, R(obert) B(ontine) Cunninghame
See Cunninghame Graham, R(obert)
B(ontine)
See also DLB 98, 135

Graham, Robert
See Haldeman, Joe (William)

Graham, Tom
See Lewis, (Harry) Sinclair

Graham, W(illiam) S(ydney)
1918-1986 . . . . . . . . . . . . . . . . CLC 29
See also CA 73-76; 118; DLB 20

Graham, Winston (Mawdsley)
1910- . . . . . . . . . . . . . . . . . . . CLC 23
See also CA 49-52; CANR 2, 22; DLB 77

Grant, Skeeter
See Spiegelman, Art

Granville-Barker, Harley
1877-1946 . . . . . . . . . . . . . . . . TCLC 2
See also Barker, Harley Granville
See also CA 104

Grass, Guenter (Wilhelm)
1927- . . . . . CLC 1, 2, 4, 6, 11, 15, 22, 32,
49; DA; WLC
See also CA 13-16R; CANR 20; DLB 75,
124; MTCW

Gratton, Thomas
See Hulme, T(homas) E(rnest)

Grau, Shirley Ann
1929- . . . . . . . . . . . . . CLC 4, 9; SSC 15
See also CA 89-92; CANR 22; DLB 2;
MTCW

Gravel, Fern
See Hall, James Norman

Graver, Elizabeth 1964- . . . . . . . . . . CLC 70
See also CA 135

Graves, Richard Perceval 1945- . . . . CLC 44
See also CA 65-68; CANR 9, 26

Graves, Robert (von Ranke)
1895-1985 . . . . . . CLC 1, 2, 6, 11, 39, 44,
45; PC 6
See also CA 5-8R; 117; CANR 5, 36;
CDBLB 1914-1945; DLB 20, 100;
DLBY 85; MTCW; SATA 45

Gray, Alasdair 1934- . . . . . . . . . . . . . CLC 41
See also CA 126; MTCW

Gray, Amlin 1946- . . . . . . . . . . . . . . CLC 29
See also CA 138

Gray, Francine du Plessix 1930- . . . . CLC 22
See also BEST 90:3; CA 61-64; CAAS 2;
CANR 11, 33; MTCW

Gray, John (Henry) 1866-1934 . . . . TCLC 19
See also CA 119

Gray, Simon (James Holliday)
1936- . . . . . . . . . . . . . . . . CLC 9, 14, 36
See also AITN 1; CA 21-24R; CAAS 3;
CANR 32; DLB 13; MTCW

Gray, Spalding 1941- . . . . . . . . . . . . . CLC 49
See also CA 128

Gray, Thomas
1716-1771 . . . . . . LC 4; DA; PC 2; WLC
See also CDBLB 1660-1789; DLB 109

Grayson, David
See Baker, Ray Stannard

Grayson, Richard (A.) 1951- . . . . . . . CLC 38
See also CA 85-88; CANR 14, 31

Greeley, Andrew M(oran) 1928- . . . . CLC 28
See also CA 5-8R; CAAS 7; CANR 7, 43;
MTCW

Green, Brian
See Card, Orson Scott

Green, Hannah
See Greenberg, Joanne (Goldenberg)

Green, Hannah . . . . . . . . . . . . . . . . . CLC 3
See also CA 73-76

Green, Henry . . . . . . . . . . . . . . . . CLC 2, 13
See also Yorke, Henry Vincent
See also DLB 15

Green, Julian (Hartridge) 1900-
See Green, Julien
See also CA 21-24R; CANR 33; DLB 4, 72;
MTCW

Green, Julien . . . . . . . . . . . . . . . CLC 3, 11, 77
See also Green, Julian (Hartridge)

Green, Paul (Eliot) 1894-1981 . . . . . . CLC 25
See also AITN 1; CA 5-8R; 103; CANR 3;
DLB 7, 9; DLBY 81

Greenberg, Ivan 1908-1973
See Rahv, Philip
See also CA 85-88

Greenberg, Joanne (Goldenberg)
1932- . . . . . . . . . . . . . . . . . . CLC 7, 30
See also AAYA 12; CA 5-8R; CANR 14,
32; SATA 25

Greenberg, Richard 1959(?)- . . . . . . . CLC 57
See also CA 138

Greene, Bette 1934- . . . . . . . . . . . . . . CLC 30
See also AAYA 7; CA 53-56; CANR 4;
CLR 2; JRDA; MAICYA; SAAS 16;
SATA 8

Greene, Gael . . . . . . . . . . . . . . . . . . . CLC 8
See also CA 13-16R; CANR 10

Greene, Graham
1904-1991 . . . . CLC 1, 3, 6, 9, 14, 18, 27,
37, 70, 72; DA; WLC
See also AITN 2; CA 13-16R; 133;
CANR 35; CDBLB 1945-1960; DLB 13,
15, 77, 100; DLBY 91; MTCW; SATA 20

Greer, Richard
See Silverberg, Robert

Greer, Richard
See Silverberg, Robert

**Gregor, Arthur** 1923- .............. CLC 9
See also CA 25-28R; CAAS 10; CANR 11;
SATA 36

**Gregor, Lee**
See Pohl, Frederik

**Gregory, Isabella Augusta (Persse)**
1852-1932 .................. TCLC 1
See also CA 104; DLB 10

**Gregory, J. Dennis**
See Williams, John A(lfred)

**Grendon, Stephen**
See Derleth, August (William)

**Grenville, Kate** 1950- ............. CLC 61
See also CA 118

**Grenville, Pelham**
See Wodehouse, P(elham) G(renville)

**Greve, Felix Paul (Berthold Friedrich)**
1879-1948
See Grove, Frederick Philip
See also CA 104; 141

**Grey, Zane** 1872-1939 ............ TCLC 6
See also CA 104; 132; DLB 9; MTCW

**Grieg, (Johan) Nordahl (Brun)**
1902-1943 .................. TCLC 10
See also CA 107

**Grieve, C(hristopher) M(urray)**
1892-1978 ............... CLC 11, 19
See also MacDiarmid, Hugh
See also CA 5-8R; 85-88; CANR 33;
MTCW

**Griffin, Gerald** 1803-1840 ........ NCLC 7

**Griffin, John Howard** 1920-1980.... CLC 68
See also AITN 1; CA 1-4R; 101; CANR 2

**Griffin, Peter** ..................... CLC 39

**Griffiths, Trevor** 1935- ......... CLC 13, 52
See also CA 97-100; DLB 13

**Grigson, Geoffrey (Edward Harvey)**
1905-1985 ................. CLC 7, 39
See also CA 25-28R; 118; CANR 20, 33;
DLB 27; MTCW

**Grillparzer, Franz** 1791-1872...... NCLC 1
See also DLB 133

**Grimble, Reverend Charles James**
See Eliot, T(homas) S(tearns)

**Grimke, Charlotte L(ottie) Forten**
1837(?)-1914
See Forten, Charlotte L.
See also BW 1; CA 117; 124

**Grimm, Jacob Ludwig Karl**
1785-1863 ................. NCLC 3
See also DLB 90; MAICYA; SATA 22

**Grimm, Wilhelm Karl** 1786-1859 .. NCLC 3
See also DLB 90; MAICYA; SATA 22

**Grimmelshausen, Johann Jakob Christoffel**
von 1621-1676 ................. LC 6

**Grindel, Eugene** 1895-1952
See Eluard, Paul
See also CA 104

**Grossman, David** 1954- ........... CLC 67
See also CA 138

**Grossman, Vasily (Semenovich)**
1905-1964 .................. CLC 41
See also CA 124; 130; MTCW

**Grove, Frederick Philip** ............ TCLC 4
See also Greve, Felix Paul (Berthold
Friedrich)
See also DLB 92

**Grubb**
See Crumb, R(obert)

**Grumbach, Doris (Isaac)**
1918- .................. CLC 13, 22, 64
See also CA 5-8R; CAAS 2; CANR 9, 42

**Grundtvig, Nicolai Frederik Severin**
1783-1872 .................. NCLC 1

**Grunge**
See Crumb, R(obert)

**Grunwald, Lisa** 1959- ............. CLC 44
See also CA 120

**Guare, John** 1938- ....... CLC 8, 14, 29, 67
See also CA 73-76; CANR 21; DLB 7;
MTCW

**Gudjonsson, Halldor Kiljan** 1902-
See Laxness, Halldor
See also CA 103

**Guenter, Erich**
See Eich, Guenter

**Guest, Barbara** 1920- ............. CLC 34
See also CA 25-28R; CANR 11, 44; DLB 5

**Guest, Judith (Ann)** 1936- ....... CLC 8, 30
See also AAYA 7; CA 77-80; CANR 15;
MTCW

**Guild, Nicholas M.** 1944- ......... CLC 33
See also CA 93-96

**Guillemin, Jacques**
See Sartre, Jean-Paul

**Guillen, Jorge** 1893-1984.......... CLC 11
See also CA 89-92; 112; DLB 108; HW

**Guillen (y Batista), Nicolas (Cristobal)**
1902-1989 ..... CLC 48, 79; BLC; HLC
See also BW 2; CA 116; 125; 129; HW

**Guillevic, (Eugene)** 1907-.......... CLC 33
See also CA 93-96

**Guillois**
See Desnos, Robert

**Guiney, Louise Imogen**
1861-1920 .................. TCLC 41
See also DLB 54

**Guiraldes, Ricardo (Guillermo)**
1886-1927 .................. TCLC 39
See also CA 131; HW; MTCW

**Gunn, Bill** ....................... CLC 5
See also Gunn, William Harrison
See also DLB 38

**Gunn, Thom(son William)**
1929- ........... CLC 3, 6, 18, 32, 81
See also CA 17-20R; CANR 9, 33;
CDBLB 1960 to Present; DLB 27;
MTCW

**Gunn, William Harrison** 1934(?)-1989
See Gunn, Bill
See also AITN 1; BW 1; CA 13-16R; 128;
CANR 12, 25

**Gunnars, Kristjana** 1948-.......... CLC 69
See also CA 113; DLB 60

**Gurganus, Allan** 1947-............ CLC 70
See also BEST 90:1; CA 135

**Gurney, A(lbert) R(amsdell), Jr.**
1930- ................. CLC 32, 50, 54
See also CA 77-80; CANR 32

**Gurney, Ivor (Bertie)** 1890-1937... TCLC 33

**Gurney, Peter**
See Gurney, A(lbert) R(amsdell), Jr.

**Gustafson, Ralph (Barker)** 1909-.... CLC 36
See also CA 21-24R; CANR 8; DLB 88

**Gut, Gom**
See Simenon, Georges (Jacques Christian)

**Guthrie, A(lfred) B(ertram), Jr.**
1901-1991 .................. CLC 23
See also CA 57-60; 134; CANR 24; DLB 6;
SATA 62; SATA-Obit 67

**Guthrie, Isobel**
See Grieve, C(hristopher) M(urray)

**Guthrie, Woodrow Wilson** 1912-1967
See Guthrie, Woody
See also CA 113; 93-96

**Guthrie, Woody** ................... CLC 35
See also Guthrie, Woodrow Wilson

**Guy, Rosa (Cuthbert)** 1928-........ CLC 26
See also AAYA 4; BW 2; CA 17-20R;
CANR 14, 34; CLR 13; DLB 33; JRDA;
MAICYA; SATA 14, 62

**Gwendolyn**
See Bennett, (Enoch) Arnold

**H. D.** ........ CLC 3, 8, 14, 31, 34, 73; PC 5
See also Doolittle, Hilda

**Haavikko, Paavo Juhani**
1931- .................. CLC 18, 34
See also CA 106

**Habbema, Koos**
See Heijermans, Herman

**Hacker, Marilyn** 1942- .... CLC 5, 9, 23, 72
See also CA 77-80; DLB 120

**Haggard, H(enry) Rider**
1856-1925 .................. TCLC 11
See also CA 108; DLB 70; SATA 16

**Haig, Fenil**
See Ford, Ford Madox

**Haig-Brown, Roderick (Langmere)**
1908-1976 .................. CLC 21
See also CA 5-8R; 69-72; CANR 4, 38;
CLR 31; DLB 88; MAICYA; SATA 12

**Hailey, Arthur** 1920- .............. CLC 5
See also AITN 2; BEST 90:3; CA 1-4R;
CANR 2, 36; DLB 88; DLBY 82; MTCW

**Hailey, Elizabeth Forsythe** 1938-... CLC 40
See also CA 93-96; CAAS 1; CANR 15

**Haines, John (Meade)** 1924-....... CLC 58
See also CA 17-20R; CANR 13, 34; DLB 5

**Haldeman, Joe (William)** 1943-..... CLC 61
See also CA 53-56; CANR 6; DLB 8

**Haley, Alex(ander Murray Palmer)**
1921-1992 .... CLC 8, 12, 76; BLC; DA
See also BW 2; CA 77-80; 136; DLB 38;
MTCW

**Haliburton, Thomas Chandler**
1796-1865 ................. NCLC 15
See also DLB 11, 99

**Hatteras, Amelia**
See Mencken, H(enry) L(ouis)

**Hatteras, Owen** . . . . . . . . . . . . . . . . **TCLC 18**
See also Mencken, H(enry) L(ouis); Nathan, George Jean

**Hauptmann, Gerhart (Johann Robert)**
1862-1946 . . . . . . . . . . . . . . . . . **TCLC 4**
See also CA 104; DLB 66, 118

**Havel, Vaclav** 1936- . . . . . . . . **CLC 25, 58, 65**
See also CA 104; CANR 36; MTCW

**Haviaras, Stratis** . . . . . . . . . . . . . . . **CLC 33**
See also Chaviaras, Strates

**Hawes, Stephen** 1475(?)-1523(?) . . . . . **LC 17**

**Hawkes, John (Clendennin Burne, Jr.)**
1925- . . . . . . **CLC 1, 2, 3, 4, 7, 9, 14, 15, 27, 49**
See also CA 1-4R; CANR 2; DLB 2, 7; DLBY 80; MTCW

**Hawking, S. W.**
See Hawking, Stephen W(illiam)

**Hawking, Stephen W(illiam)**
1942- . . . . . . . . . . . . . . . . . . . . **CLC 63**
See also BEST 89:1; CA 126; 129

**Hawthorne, Julian** 1846-1934 . . . . . **TCLC 25**

**Hawthorne, Nathaniel**
1804-1864 . . . . . . **NCLC 39; DA; SSC 3; WLC**
See also CDALB 1640-1865; DLB 1, 74; YABC 2

**Haxton, Josephine Ayres** 1921- . . . . **CLC 73**
See also CA 115; CANR 41

**Hayascca y Eizaguirrc, Jorge**
See Echegaray (y Eizaguirre), Jose (Maria Waldo)

**Hayashi Fumiko** 1904-1951 . . . . . . . **TCLC 27**

**Haycraft, Anna**
See Ellis, Alice Thomas
See also CA 122

**Hayden, Robert E(arl)**
1913-1980 . . . . . . **CLC 5, 9, 14, 37; BLC; DA; PC 6**
See also BW 1; CA 69-72; 97-100; CABS 2; CANR 24; CDALB 1941-1968; DLB 5, 76; MTCW; SATA 19, 26

**Hayford, J(oseph) E(phraim) Casely**
See Casely-Hayford, J(oseph) E(phraim)

**Hayman, Ronald** 1932- . . . . . . . . . . . **CLC 44**
See also CA 25-28R; CANR 18

**Haywood, Eliza (Fowler)**
1693(?)-1756 . . . . . . . . . . . . . . . . **LC 1**

**Hazlitt, William** 1778-1830 . . . . . . **NCLC 29**
See also DLB 110

**Hazzard, Shirley** 1931- . . . . . . . . . . . **CLC 18**
See also CA 9-12R; CANR 4; DLBY 82; MTCW

**Head, Bessie** 1937-1986 . . . **CLC 25, 67; BLC**
See also BW 2; CA 29-32R; 119; CANR 25; DLB 117; MTCW

**Headon, (Nicky) Topper** 1956(?)- . . . **CLC 30**
See also Clash, The

**Heaney, Seamus (Justin)**
1939- . . . . . . . . **CLC 5, 7, 14, 25, 37, 74**
See also CA 85-88; CANR 25; CDBLB 1960 to Present; DLB 40; MTCW

**Hearn, (Patricio) Lafcadio (Tessima Carlos)**
1850-1904 . . . . . . . . . . . . . . . . . . **TCLC 9**
See also CA 105; DLB 12, 78

**Hearne, Vicki** 1946- . . . . . . . . . . . . . . **CLC 56**
See also CA 139

**Hearon, Shelby** 1931- . . . . . . . . . . . . . **CLC 63**
See also AITN 2; CA 25-28R; CANR 18

**Heat-Moon, William Least** . . . . . . . . . **CLC 29**
See also Trogdon, William (Lewis)
See also AAYA 9

**Hebbel, Friedrich** 1813-1863 . . . . . **NCLC 43**
See also DLB 129

**Hebert, Anne** 1916- . . . . . . . . . **CLC 4, 13, 29**
See also CA 85-88; DLB 68; MTCW

**Hecht, Anthony (Evan)**
1923- . . . . . . . . . . . . . . . . . **CLC 8, 13, 19**
See also CA 9-12R; CANR 6; DLB 5

**Hecht, Ben** 1894-1964 . . . . . . . . . . . . **CLC 8**
See also CA 85-88; DLB 7, 9, 25, 26, 28, 86

**Hedayat, Sadeq** 1903-1951 . . . . . . . **TCLC 21**
See also CA 120

**Heidegger, Martin** 1889-1976 . . . . . . **CLC 24**
See also CA 81-84; 65-68; CANR 34; MTCW

**Heidenstam, (Carl Gustaf) Verner von**
1859-1940 . . . . . . . . . . . . . . . . . . **TCLC 5**
See also CA 104

**Heifner, Jack** 1946- . . . . . . . . . . . . . . **CLC 11**
See also CA 105

**Heijermans, Herman** 1864-1924 . . . **TCLC 24**
See also CA 123

**Heilbrun, Carolyn G(old)** 1926- . . . . . **CLC 25**
See also CA 45-48; CANR 1, 28

**Heine, Heinrich** 1797-1856 . . . . . . . **NCLC 4**
See also DLB 90

**Heinemann, Larry (Curtiss)** 1944- . . **CLC 50**
See also CA 110; CANR 31; DLBD 9

**Heiney, Donald (William)**
1921-1993 . . . . . . . . . . . . . . . . . . **CLC 9**
See also CA 1-4R; 142; CANR 3

**Heinlein, Robert A(nson)**
1907-1988 . . . . **CLC 1, 3, 8, 14, 26, 55**
See also CA 1-4R; 125; CANR 1, 20; DLB 8; JRDA; MAICYA; MTCW; SATA 9, 56, 69

**Helforth, John**
See Doolittle, Hilda

**Hellenhofferu, Vojtech Kapristian z**
See Hasek, Jaroslav (Matej Frantisek)

**Heller, Joseph**
1923- . . . . **CLC 1, 3, 5, 8, 11, 36, 63; DA; WLC**
See also AITN 1; CA 5-8R; CABS 1; CANR 8, 42; DLB 2, 28; DLBY 80; MTCW

**Hellman, Lillian (Florence)**
1906-1984 . . . . . . **CLC 2, 4, 8, 14, 18, 34, 44, 52; DC 1**
See also AITN 1, 2; CA 13-16R; 112; CANR 33; DLB 7; DLBY 84; MTCW

**Helprin, Mark** 1947- . . . . . **CLC 7, 10, 22, 32**
See also CA 81-84; DLBY 85; MTCW

**Helyar, Jane Penelope Josephine** 1933-
See Poole, Josephine
See also CA 21-24R; CANR 10, 26

**Hemans, Felicia** 1793-1835 . . . . . . **NCLC 29**
See also DLB 96

**Hemingway, Ernest (Miller)**
1899-1961 . . . . **CLC 1, 3, 6, 8, 10, 13, 19, 30, 34, 39, 41, 44, 50, 61, 80; DA; SSC 1; WLC**
See also CA 77-80; CANR 34; CDALB 1917-1929; DLB 4, 9, 102; DLBD 1; DLBY 81, 87; MTCW

**Hempel, Amy** 1951- . . . . . . . . . . . . . **CLC 39**
See also CA 118; 137

**Henderson, F. C.**
See Mencken, H(enry) L(ouis)

**Henderson, Sylvia**
See Ashton-Warner, Sylvia (Constance)

**Henley, Beth** . . . . . . . . . . . . . . . . . . . **CLC 23**
See also Henley, Elizabeth Becker
See also CABS 3; DLBY 86

**Henley, Elizabeth Becker** 1952-
See Henley, Beth
See also CA 107; CANR 32; MTCW

**Henley, William Ernest**
1849-1903 . . . . . . . . . . . . . . . . . . **TCLC 8**
See also CA 105; DLB 19

**Hennissart, Martha**
See Lathen, Emma
See also CA 85-88

**Henry, O.** . . . . . . . . **TCLC 1, 19; SSC 5; WLC**
See also Porter, William Sydney

**Henry, Patrick** 1736-1799 . . . . . . . . . . **LC 25**

**Henryson, Robert** 1430(?)-1506(?) . . . . **LC 20**

**Henry VIII** 1491-1547 . . . . . . . . . . . . **LC 10**

**Henschke, Alfred**
See Klabund

**Hentoff, Nat(han Irving)** 1925- . . . . . **CLC 26**
See also AAYA 4; CA 1-4R; CAAS 6; CANR 5, 25; CLR 1; JRDA; MAICYA; SATA 27, 42, 69

**Heppenstall, (John) Rayner**
1911-1981 . . . . . . . . . . . . . . . . . . **CLC 10**
See also CA 1-4R; 103; CANR 29

**Herbert, Frank (Patrick)**
1920-1986 . . . . . . . . . . **CLC 12, 23, 35, 44**
See also CA 53-56; 118; CANR 5, 43; DLB 8; MTCW; SATA 9, 37, 47

**Herbert, George** 1593-1633 . . . . **LC 24; PC 4**
See also CDBLB Before 1660; DLB 126

**Herbert, Zbigniew** 1924- . . . . . . . . **CLC 9, 43**
See also CA 89-92; CANR 36; MTCW

**Herbst, Josephine (Frey)**
1897-1969 . . . . . . . . . . . . . . . . . . **CLC 34**
See also CA 5-8R; 25-28R; DLB 9

**Hergesheimer, Joseph**
1880-1954 . . . . . . . . . . . . . . . . . **TCLC 11**
See also CA 109; DLB 102, 9

**Herlihy, James Leo** 1927-1993 . . . . . . **CLC 6**
See also CA 1-4R; 143; CANR 2

**Hermogenes** fl. c. 175- . . . . . . . . . . **CMLC 6**

**Hernandez, Jose** 1834-1886 . . . . . . **NCLC 17**

**Herrick, Robert**
1591-1674 . . . . . . . . . . **LC 13; DA; PC 9**
See also DLB 126

**Herring, Guilles**
See Somerville, Edith

**Hollander, John** 1929- ...... **CLC 2, 5, 8, 14**
See also CA 1-4R; CANR 1; DLB 5;
SATA 13

**Hollander, Paul**
See Silverberg, Robert

**Holleran, Andrew** 1943(?)- ........ **CLC 38**
See also CA 144

**Hollinghurst, Alan** 1954- ......... **CLC 55**
See also CA 114

**Hollis, Jim**
See Summers, Hollis (Spurgeon, Jr.)

**Holmes, John**
See Souster, (Holmes) Raymond

**Holmes, John Clellon** 1926-1988.... **CLC 56**
See also CA 9-12R; 125; CANR 4; DLB 16

**Holmes, Oliver Wendell**
1809-1894 ................. **NCLC 14**
See also CDALB 1640-1865; DLB 1;
SATA 34

**Holmes, Raymond**
See Souster, (Holmes) Raymond

**Holt, Victoria**
See Hibbert, Eleanor Alice Burford

**Holub, Miroslav** 1923- ............. **CLC 4**
See also CA 21-24R; CANR 10

**Homer** c. 8th cent. B.C.- ..... **CMLC 1; DA**

**Honig, Edwin** 1919- ............. **CLC 33**
See also CA 5-8R; CAAS 8; CANR 4;
DLB 5

**Hood, Hugh (John Blagdon)**
1928- ................ **CLC 15, 28**
See also CA 49-52; CAAS 17; CANR 1, 33;
DLB 53

**Hood, Thomas** 1799-1845........ **NCLC 16**
See also DLB 96

**Hooker, (Peter) Jeremy** 1941- ...... **CLC 43**
See also CA 77-80; CANR 22; DLB 40

**Hope, A(lec) D(erwent)** 1907- .... **CLC 3, 51**
See also CA 21-24R; CANR 33; MTCW

**Hope, Brian**
See Creasey, John

**Hope, Christopher (David Tully)**
1944- ...................... **CLC 52**
See also CA 106; SATA 62

**Hopkins, Gerard Manley**
1844-1889 ........ **NCLC 17; DA; WLC**
See also CDBLB 1890-1914; DLB 35, 57

**Hopkins, John (Richard)** 1931- ...... **CLC 4**
See also CA 85-88

**Hopkins, Pauline Elizabeth**
1859-1930 ............. **TCLC 28; BLC**
See also BW 2; CA 141; DLB 50

**Hopkinson, Francis** 1737-1791 ...... **LC 25**
See also DLB 31

**Hopley-Woolrich, Cornell George** 1903-1968
See Woolrich, Cornell
See also CA 13-14; CAP 1

**Horatio**
See Proust, (Valentin-Louis-George-Eugene-)
Marcel

**Horgan, Paul** 1903- ............. **CLC 9, 53**
See also CA 13-16R; CANR 9, 35;
DLB 102; DLBY 85; MTCW; SATA 13

**Horn, Peter**
See Kuttner, Henry

**Hornem, Horace Esq.**
See Byron, George Gordon (Noel)

**Horovitz, Israel** 1939- ............ **CLC 56**
See also CA 33-36R; DLB 7

**Horvath, Odon von**
See Horvath, Oedoen von
See also DLB 85, 124

**Horvath, Oedoen von** 1901-1938... **TCLC 45**
See also Horvath, Odon von
See also CA 118

**Horwitz, Julius** 1920-1986........ **CLC 14**
See also CA 9-12R; 119; CANR 12

**Hospital, Janette Turner** 1942- ..... **CLC 42**
See also CA 108

**Hostos, E. M. de**
See Hostos (y Bonilla), Eugenio Maria de

**Hostos, Eugenio M. de**
See Hostos (y Bonilla), Eugenio Maria de

**Hostos, Eugenio Maria**
See Hostos (y Bonilla), Eugenio Maria de

**Hostos (y Bonilla), Eugenio Maria de**
1839-1903 ................. **TCLC 24**
See also CA 123; 131; HW

**Houdini**
See Lovecraft, H(oward) P(hillips)

**Hougan, Carolyn** 1943- ........... **CLC 34**
See also CA 139

**Household, Geoffrey (Edward West)**
1900-1988 .................. **CLC 11**
See also CA 77-80; 126; DLB 87; SATA 14,
59

**Housman, A(lfred) E(dward)**
1859-1936 ...... **TCLC 1, 10; DA; PC 2**
See also CA 104; 125; DLB 19; MTCW

**Housman, Laurence** 1865-1959 ..... **TCLC 7**
See also CA 106; DLB 10; SATA 25

**Howard, Elizabeth Jane** 1923- ... **CLC 7, 29**
See also CA 5-8R; CANR 8

**Howard, Maureen** 1930- ..... **CLC 5, 14, 46**
See also CA 53-56; CANR 31; DLBY 83;
MTCW

**Howard, Richard** 1929- ...... **CLC 7, 10, 47**
See also AITN 1; CA 85-88; CANR 25;
DLB 5

**Howard, Robert Ervin** 1906-1936... **TCLC 8**
See also CA 105

**Howard, Warren F.**
See Pohl, Frederik

**Howe, Fanny** 1940- .............. **CLC 47**
See also CA 117; SATA 52

**Howe, Julia Ward** 1819-1910 ..... **TCLC 21**
See also CA 117; DLB 1

**Howe, Susan** 1937- ................ **CLC 72**
See also DLB 120

**Howe, Tina** 1937- ................ **CLC 48**
See also CA 109

**Howell, James** 1594(?)-1666 ........ **LC 13**

**Howells, W. D.**
See Howells, William Dean

**Howells, William D.**
See Howells, William Dean

**Howells, William Dean**
1837-1920 ........... **TCLC 7, 17, 41**
See also CA 104; 134; CDALB 1865-1917;
DLB 12, 64, 74, 79

**Howes, Barbara** 1914- ............ **CLC 15**
See also CA 9-12R; CAAS 3; SATA 5

**Hrabal, Bohumil** 1914- ........ **CLC 13, 67**
See also CA 106; CAAS 12

**Hsun, Lu** ...................... **TCLC 3**
See also Shu-Jen, Chou

**Hubbard, L(afayette) Ron(ald)**
1911-1986 .................. **CLC 43**
See also CA 77-80; 118; CANR 22

**Huch, Ricarda (Octavia)**
1864-1947 .................. **TCLC 13**
See also CA 111; DLB 66

**Huddle, David** 1942- ............. **CLC 49**
See also CA 57-60; DLB 130

**Hudson, Jeffrey**
See Crichton, (John) Michael

**Hudson, W(illiam) H(enry)**
1841-1922 .................. **TCLC 29**
See also CA 115; DLB 98; SATA 35

**Hueffer, Ford Madox**
See Ford, Ford Madox

**Hughart, Barry** 1934- ............. **CLC 39**
See also CA 137

**Hughes, Colin**
See Creasey, John

**Hughes, David (John)** 1930- ....... **CLC 48**
See also CA 116; 129; DLB 14

**Hughes, (James) Langston**
1902-1967 ..... **CLC 1, 5, 10, 15, 35, 44;**
**BLC; DA; DC 3; PC 1; SSC 6; WLC**
See also AAYA 12; BW 1; CA 1-4R;
25-28R; CANR 1, 34; CDALB 1929-1941;
CLR 17; DLB 4, 7, 48, 51, 86; JRDA;
MAICYA; MTCW; SATA 4, 33

**Hughes, Richard (Arthur Warren)**
1900-1976 ................. **CLC 1, 11**
See also CA 5-8R; 65-68; CANR 4;
DLB 15; MTCW; SATA 8, 25

**Hughes, Ted**
1930- ........ **CLC 2, 4, 9, 14, 37; PC 7**
See also CA 1-4R; CANR 1, 33; CLR 3;
DLB 40; MAICYA; MTCW; SATA 27,
49

**Hugo, Richard F(ranklin)**
1923-1982 ............. **CLC 6, 18, 32**
See also CA 49-52; 108; CANR 3; DLB 5

**Hugo, Victor (Marie)**
1802-1885 .. **NCLC 3, 10, 21; DA; WLC**
See also DLB 119; SATA 47

**Huidobro, Vicente**
See Huidobro Fernandez, Vicente Garcia

**Huidobro Fernandez, Vicente Garcia**
1893-1948 ................. **TCLC 31**
See also CA 131; HW

**Hulme, Keri** 1947- .............. **CLC 39**
See also CA 125

**Hulme, T(homas) E(rnest)**
1883-1917 ................. **TCLC 21**
See also CA 117; DLB 19

**Hume, David** 1711-1776............ **LC 7**
See also DLB 104

**James, Andrew**
See Kirkup, James

**James, C(yril) L(ionel) R(obert)**
1901-1989 . . . . . . . . . . . . . . . . . **CLC 33**
See also BW 2; CA 117; 125; 128; DLB 125;
MTCW

**James, Daniel (Lewis)** 1911-1988
See Santiago, Danny
See also CA 125

**James, Dynely**
See Mayne, William (James Carter)

**James, Henry**
1843-1916 . . . . . . **TCLC 2, 11, 24, 40, 47;**
**DA; SSC 8; WLC**
See also CA 104; 132; CDALB 1865-1917;
DLB 12, 71, 74; MTCW

**James, Montague (Rhodes)**
1862-1936 . . . . . . . . . . . . . . . . . **TCLC 6**
See also CA 104

**James, P. D.** . . . . . . . . . . . . . . . . **CLC 18, 46**
See also White, Phyllis Dorothy James
See also BEST 90:2; CDBLB 1960 to
Present; DLB 87

**James, Philip**
See Moorcock, Michael (John)

**James, William** 1842-1910 . . . . . **TCLC 15, 32**
See also CA 109

**James I** 1394-1437 . . . . . . . . . . . . . . . . **LC 20**

**Jameson, Anna** 1794-1860 . . . . . . . **NCLC 43**
See also DLB 99

**Jami, Nur al-Din 'Abd al-Rahman**
1414-1492 . . . . . . . . . . . . . . . . . . . **LC 9**

**Jandl, Ernst** 1925- . . . . . . . . . . . . . . . **CLC 34**

**Janowitz, Tama** 1957- . . . . . . . . . . . . **CLC 43**
See also CA 106

**Jarrell, Randall**
1914-1965 . . . . . . . **CLC 1, 2, 6, 9, 13, 49**
See also CA 5-8R; 25-28R; CABS 2,
CANR 6, 34; CDALB 1941-1968; CLR 6;
DLB 48, 52; MAICYA; MTCW; SATA 7

**Jarry, Alfred** 1873-1907 . . . . . . . **TCLC 2, 14**
See also CA 104

**Jarvis, E. K.**
See Bloch, Robert (Albert); Ellison, Harlan;
Silverberg, Robert

**Jeake, Samuel, Jr.**
See Aiken, Conrad (Potter)

**Jean Paul** 1763-1825 . . . . . . . . . . . **NCLC 7**

**Jeffers, (John) Robinson**
1887-1962 . . . . **CLC 2, 3, 11, 15, 54; DA;**
**WLC**
See also CA 85-88; CANR 35;
CDALB 1917-1929; DLB 45; MTCW

**Jefferson, Janet**
See Mencken, H(enry) L(ouis)

**Jefferson, Thomas** 1743-1826 . . . . **NCLC 11**
See also CDALB 1640-1865; DLB 31

**Jeffrey, Francis** 1773-1850 . . . . . . . **NCLC 33**
See also DLB 107

**Jelakowitch, Ivan**
See Heijermans, Herman

**Jellicoe, (Patricia) Ann** 1927- . . . . . . **CLC 27**
See also CA 85-88; DLB 13

**Jen, Gish** . . . . . . . . . . . . . . . . . . . . **CLC 70**
See also Jen, Lillian

**Jen, Lillian** 1956(?)-
See Jen, Gish
See also CA 135

**Jenkins, (John) Robin** 1912- . . . . . . . **CLC 52**
See also CA 1-4R; CANR 1; DLB 14

**Jennings, Elizabeth (Joan)**
1926- . . . . . . . . . . . . . . . . . . . . **CLC 5, 14**
See also CA 61-64; CAAS 5; CANR 8, 39;
DLB 27; MTCW; SATA 66

**Jennings, Waylon** 1937- . . . . . . . . . . **CLC 21**

**Jensen, Johannes V.** 1873-1950 . . . . **TCLC 41**

**Jensen, Laura (Linnea)** 1948- . . . . . . **CLC 37**
See also CA 103

**Jerome, Jerome K(lapka)**
1859-1927 . . . . . . . . . . . . . . . . . **TCLC 23**
See also CA 119; DLB 10, 34, 135

**Jerrold, Douglas William**
1803-1857 . . . . . . . . . . . . . . . . . **NCLC 2**

**Jewett, (Theodora) Sarah Orne**
1849-1909 . . . . . . . . **TCLC 1, 22; SSC 6**
See also CA 108; 127; DLB 12, 74;
SATA 15

**Jewsbury, Geraldine (Endsor)**
1812-1880 . . . . . . . . . . . . . . . . . **NCLC 22**
See also DLB 21

**Jhabvala, Ruth Prawer**
1927- . . . . . . . . . . . . . . . . **CLC 4, 8, 29**
See also CA 1-4R; CANR 2, 29; DLB 139;
MTCW

**Jiles, Paulette** 1943- . . . . . . . . . . . **CLC 13, 58**
See also CA 101

**Jimenez (Mantecon), Juan Ramon**
1881-1958 . . . . . . . . **TCLC 4; HLC; PC 7**
See also CA 104; 131; DLB 134; HW;
MTCW

**Jimenez, Ramon**
See Jimenez (Mantecon), Juan Ramon

**Jimenez Mantecon, Juan**
See Jimenez (Mantecon), Juan Ramon

**Joel, Billy** . . . . . . . . . . . . . . . . . . . . **CLC 26**
See also Joel, William Martin

**Joel, William Martin** 1949-
See Joel, Billy
See also CA 108

**John of the Cross, St.** 1542-1591 . . . . **LC 18**

**Johnson, B(ryan) S(tanley William)**
1933-1973 . . . . . . . . . . . . . . . . **CLC 6, 9**
See also CA 9-12R; 53-56; CANR 9;
DLB 14, 40

**Johnson, Benj. F. of Boo**
See Riley, James Whitcomb

**Johnson, Benjamin F. of Boo**
See Riley, James Whitcomb

**Johnson, Charles (Richard)**
1948- . . . . . . . . . . . . . **CLC 7, 51, 65; BLC**
See also BW 2; CA 116; CAAS 18;
CANR 42; DLB 33

**Johnson, Denis** 1949- . . . . . . . . . . . . **CLC 52**
See also CA 117; 121; DLB 120

**Johnson, Diane** 1934- . . . . . . . **CLC 5, 13, 48**
See also CA 41-44R; CANR 17, 40;
DLBY 80; MTCW

**Johnson, Eyvind (Olof Verner)**
1900-1976 . . . . . . . . . . . . . . . . . **CLC 14**
See also CA 73-76; 69-72; CANR 34

**Johnson, J. R.**
See James, C(yril) L(ionel) R(obert)

**Johnson, James Weldon**
1871-1938 . . . . . . . . . . **TCLC 3, 19; BLC**
See also BW 1; CA 104; 125;
CDALB 1917-1929; CLR 32; DLB 51;
MTCW; SATA 31

**Johnson, Joyce** 1935- . . . . . . . . . . . . **CLC 58**
See also CA 125; 129

**Johnson, Lionel (Pigot)**
1867-1902 . . . . . . . . . . . . . . . . . **TCLC 19**
See also CA 117; DLB 19

**Johnson, Mel**
See Malzberg, Barry N(athaniel)

**Johnson, Pamela Hansford**
1912-1981 . . . . . . . . . . . . . . **CLC 1, 7, 27**
See also CA 1-4R; 104; CANR 2, 28;
DLB 15; MTCW

**Johnson, Samuel**
1709-1784 . . . . . . . . . . **LC 15; DA; WLC**
See also CDBLB 1660-1789; DLB 39, 95,
104, 142

**Johnson, Uwe**
1934-1984 . . . . . . . . . . **CLC 5, 10, 15, 40**
See also CA 1-4R; 112; CANR 1, 39;
DLB 75; MTCW

**Johnston, George (Benson)** 1913- . . . **CLC 51**
See also CA 1-4R; CANR 5, 20; DLB 88

**Johnston, Jennifer** 1930- . . . . . . . . . . **CLC 7**
See also CA 85-88; DLB 14

**Jolley, (Monica) Elizabeth** 1923- . . . **CLC 46**
See also CA 127; CAAS 13

**Jones, Arthur Llewellyn** 1863-1947
See Machen, Arthur
See also CA 104

**Jones, D(ouglas) G(ordon)** 1929- . . . . **CLC 10**
See also CA 29-32R; CANR 13; DLB 53

**Jones, David (Michael)**
1895-1974 . . . . . . . . . **CLC 2, 4, 7, 13, 42**
See also CA 9-12R; 53-56; CANR 28;
CDBLB 1945-1960; DLB 20, 100; MTCW

**Jones, David Robert** 1947-
See Bowie, David
See also CA 103

**Jones, Diana Wynne** 1934- . . . . . . . . **CLC 26**
See also AAYA 12; CA 49-52; CANR 4,
26; CLR 23; JRDA; MAICYA; SAAS 7;
SATA 9, 70

**Jones, Edward P.** 1950- . . . . . . . . . . **CLC 76**
See also BW 2; CA 142

**Jones, Gayl** 1949- . . . . . . . . . **CLC 6, 9; BLC**
See also BW 2; CA 77-80; CANR 27;
DLB 33; MTCW

**Jones, James** 1921-1977 . . . . **CLC 1, 3, 10, 39**
See also AITN 1, 2; CA 1-4R; 69-72;
CANR 6; DLB 2; MTCW

**Jones, John J.**
See Lovecraft, H(oward) P(hillips)

**Jones, LeRoi** . . . . . . . . **CLC 1, 2, 3, 5, 10, 14**
See also Baraka, Amiri

**Jones, Louis B.** . . . . . . . . . . . . . . . . . **CLC 65**
See also CA 141

Jones, Madison (Percy, Jr.) 1925- ... **CLC 4**
See also CA 13-16R; CAAS 11; CANR 7

Jones, Mervyn 1922- ......... **CLC 10, 52**
See also CA 45-48; CAAS 5; CANR 1;
MTCW

Jones, Mick 1956(?)- ............. **CLC 30**
See also Clash, The

Jones, Nettie (Pearl) 1941- ........ **CLC 34**
See also BW 2; CA 137

Jones, Preston 1936-1979 ......... **CLC 10**
See also CA 73-76; 89-92; DLB 7

Jones, Robert F(rancis) 1934- ....... **CLC 7**
See also CA 49-52; CANR 2

Jones, Rod 1953- ................ **CLC 50**
See also CA 128

Jones, Terence Graham Parry
1942- ...................... **CLC 21**
See also Jones, Terry; Monty Python
See also CA 112; 116; CANR 35; SATA 51

Jones, Terry
See Jones, Terence Graham Parry
See also SATA 67

Jones, Thom 1945(?)- ............. **CLC 81**

Jong, Erica 1942- ...... **CLC 4, 6, 8, 18, 83**
See also AITN 1; BEST 90:2; CA 73-76;
CANR 26; DLB 2, 5, 28; MTCW

Jonson, Ben(jamin)
1572(?)-1637 .... **LC 6; DA; DC 4; WLC**
See also CDBLB Before 1660; DLB 62, 121

Jordan, June 1936- .......... **CLC 5, 11, 23**
See also AAYA 2; BW 2; CA 33-36R;
CANR 25; CLR 10; DLB 38; MAICYA;
MTCW; SATA 4

Jordan, Pat(rick M.) 1941- ........ **CLC 37**
See also CA 33-36R

Jorgensen, Ivar
See Ellison, Harlan

Jorgenson, Ivar
See Silverberg, Robert

Josephus, Flavius c. 37-100 ..... **CMLC 13**

Josipovici, Gabriel 1940- ........ **CLC 6, 43**
See also CA 37-40R; CAAS 8; DLB 14

Joubert, Joseph 1754-1824 ....... **NCLC 9**

Jouve, Pierre Jean 1887-1976 ..... **CLC 47**
See also CA 65-68

Joyce, James (Augustine Aloysius)
1882-1941 ...... **TCLC 3, 8, 16, 35; DA;
SSC 3; WLC**
See also CA 104; 126; CDBLB 1914-1945;
DLB 10, 19, 36; MTCW

Jozsef, Attila 1905-1937.......... **TCLC 22**
See also CA 116

Juana Ines de la Cruz 1651(?)-1695 ... **LC 5**

Judd, Cyril
See Kornbluth, C(yril) M.; Pohl, Frederik

Julian of Norwich 1342(?)-1416(?) .... **LC 6**

Just, Ward (Swift) 1935- ........ **CLC 4, 27**
See also CA 25-28R; CANR 32

Justice, Donald (Rodney) 1925- .. **CLC 6, 19**
See also CA 5-8R; CANR 26; DLBY 83

Juvenal c. 55-c. 127 ............. **CMLC 8**

Juvenis
See Bourne, Randolph S(illiman)

Kacew, Romain 1914-1980
See Gary, Romain
See also CA 108; 102

Kadare, Ismail 1936- ............. **CLC 52**

Kadohata, Cynthia................. **CLC 59**
See also CA 140

Kafka, Franz
1883-1924 .... **TCLC 2, 6, 13, 29, 47, 53;
DA; SSC 5; WLC**
See also CA 105; 126; DLB 81; MTCW

Kahn, Roger 1927- ............... **CLC 30**
See also CA 25-28R; CANR 44; SATA 37

Kain, Saul
See Sassoon, Siegfried (Lorraine)

Kaiser, Georg 1878-1945 .......... **TCLC 9**
See also CA 106; DLB 124

Kaletski, Alexander 1946- ........ **CLC 39**
See also CA 118; 143

Kalidasa fl. c. 400- .............. **CMLC 9**

Kallman, Chester (Simon)
1921-1975 ................. **CLC 2**
See also CA 45-48; 53-56; CANR 3

Kaminsky, Melvin 1926-
See Brooks, Mel
See also CA 65-68; CANR 16

Kaminsky, Stuart M(elvin) 1934- ... **CLC 59**
See also CA 73-76; CANR 29

Kane, Paul
See Simon, Paul

Kane, Wilson
See Bloch, Robert (Albert)

Kanin, Garson 1912-............. **CLC 22**
See also AITN 1; CA 5-8R; CANR 7;
DLB 7

Kaniuk, Yoram 1930- ............. **CLC 19**
See also CA 134

Kant, Immanuel 1724-1804 ...... **NCLC 27**
See also DLB 94

Kantor, MacKinlay 1904-1977 ...... **CLC 7**
See also CA 61-64; 73-76; DLB 9, 102

Kaplan, David Michael 1946- ...... **CLC 50**

Kaplan, James 1951- ............. **CLC 59**
See also CA 135

Karageorge, Michael
See Anderson, Poul (William)

Karamzin, Nikolai Mikhailovich
1766-1826 .................. **NCLC 3**

Karapanou, Margarita 1946- ....... **CLC 13**
See also CA 101

Karinthy, Frigyes 1887-1938 ...... **TCLC 47**

Karl, Frederick R(obert) 1927- ..... **CLC 34**
See also CA 5-8R; CANR 3, 44

Kastel, Warren
See Silverberg, Robert

Kataev, Evgeny Petrovich 1903-1942
See Petrov, Evgeny
See also CA 120

Kataphusin
See Ruskin, John

Katz, Steve 1935- ................ **CLC 47**
See also CA 25-28R; CAAS 14; CANR 12;
DLBY 83

Kauffman, Janet 1945-............ **CLC 42**
See also CA 117; CANR 43; DLBY 86

Kaufman, Bob (Garnell)
1925-1986 ................. **CLC 49**
See also BW 1; CA 41-44R; 118; CANR 22;
DLB 16, 41

Kaufman, George S. 1889-1961..... **CLC 38**
See also CA 108; 93-96; DLB 7

Kaufman, Sue .................. **CLC 3, 8**
See also Barondess, Sue K(aufman)

Kavafis, Konstantinos Petrou 1863-1933
See Cavafy, C(onstantine) P(eter)
See also CA 104

Kavan, Anna 1901-1968 ...... **CLC 5, 13, 82**
See also CA 5-8R; CANR 6; MTCW

Kavanagh, Dan
See Barnes, Julian

Kavanagh, Patrick (Joseph)
1904-1967 .................. **CLC 22**
See also CA 123; 25-28R; DLB 15, 20;
MTCW

Kawabata, Yasunari
1899-1972 ............. **CLC 2, 5, 9, 18**
See also CA 93-96; 33-36R

Kaye, M(ary) M(argaret) 1909-..... **CLC 28**
See also CA 89-92; CANR 24; MTCW;
SATA 62

Kaye, Mollie
See Kaye, M(ary) M(argaret)

Kaye-Smith, Sheila 1887-1956..... **TCLC 20**
See also CA 118; DLB 36

Kaymor, Patrice Maguilene
See Senghor, Leopold Sedar

Kazan, Elia 1909-........... **CLC 6, 16, 63**
See also CA 21-24R; CANR 32

Kazantzakis, Nikos
1883(?)-1957 .......... **TCLC 2, 5, 33**
See also CA 105; 132; MTCW

Kazin, Alfred 1915- ........... **CLC 34, 38**
See also CA 1-4R; CAAS 7; CANR 1;
DLB 67

Keane, Mary Nesta (Skrine) 1904-
See Keane, Molly
See also CA 108; 114

Keane, Molly.................. **CLC 31**
See also Keane, Mary Nesta (Skrine)

Keates, Jonathan 19(?)- ........... **CLC 34**

Keaton, Buster 1895-1966 ........ **CLC 20**

Keats, John
1795-1821 ... **NCLC 8; DA; PC 1; WLC**
See also CDBLB 1789-1832; DLB 96, 110

Keene, Donald 1922- ............. **CLC 34**
See also CA 1-4R; CANR 5

Keillor, Garrison.................. **CLC 40**
See also Keillor, Gary (Edward)
See also AAYA 2; BEST 89:3; DLBY 87;
SATA 58

Keillor, Gary (Edward) 1942-
See Keillor, Garrison
See also CA 111; 117; CANR 36; MTCW

Keith, Michael
See Hubbard, L(afayette) Ron(ald)

Keller, Gottfried 1819-1890 ....... **NCLC 2**
See also DLB 129

**Kellerman, Jonathan** 1949- ........ **CLC 44**
See also BEST 90:1; CA 106; CANR 29

**Kelley, William Melvin** 1937- ...... **CLC 22**
See also BW 1; CA 77-80; CANR 27;
DLB 33

**Kellogg, Marjorie** 1922- ........... **CLC 2**
See also CA 81-84

**Kellow, Kathleen**
See Hibbert, Eleanor Alice Burford

**Kelly, M(ilton) T(erry)** 1947- ...... **CLC 55**
See also CA 97-100; CANR 19, 43

**Kelman, James** 1946- ............ **CLC 58**

**Kemal, Yashar** 1923- .......... **CLC 14, 29**
See also CA 89-92; CANR 44

**Kemble, Fanny** 1809-1893 ....... **NCLC 18**
See also DLB 32

**Kemelman, Harry** 1908- ........... **CLC 2**
See also AITN 1; CA 9-12R; CANR 6;
DLB 28

**Kempe, Margery** 1373(?)-1440(?) ..... **LC 6**

**Kempis, Thomas a** 1380-1471 ....... **LC 11**

**Kendall, Henry** 1839-1882....... **NCLC 12**

**Keneally, Thomas (Michael)**
1935- ...... **CLC 5, 8, 10, 14, 19, 27, 43**
See also CA 85-88; CANR 10; MTCW

**Kennedy, Adrienne (Lita)**
1931- ................... **CLC 66; BLC**
See also BW 2; CA 103; CABS 3;
CANR 26; DLB 38

**Kennedy, John Pendleton**
1795-1870 ................. **NCLC 2**
See also DLB 3

**Kennedy, Joseph Charles** 1929- ...... **CLC 8**
See also Kennedy, X. J.
See also CA 1-4R; CANR 4, 30, 40;
SATA 14

**Kennedy, William** 1928-... **CLC 6, 28, 34, 53**
See also AAYA 1; CA 85-88; CANR 14,
31; DLBY 85; MTCW; SATA 57

**Kennedy, X. J.**.................... **CLC 42**
See also Kennedy, Joseph Charles
See also CAAS 9; CLR 27; DLB 5

**Kent, Kelvin**
See Kuttner, Henry

**Kenton, Maxwell**
See Southern, Terry

**Kenyon, Robert O.**
See Kuttner, Henry

**Kerouac, Jack** ..... **CLC 1, 2, 3, 5, 14, 29, 61**
See also Kerouac, Jean-Louis Lebris de
See also CDALB 1941-1968; DLB 2, 16;
DLBD 3

**Kerouac, Jean-Louis Lebris de** 1922-1969
See Kerouac, Jack
See also AITN 1; CA 5-8R; 25-28R;
CANR 26; DA; MTCW; WLC

**Kerr, Jean** 1923-................. **CLC 22**
See also CA 5-8R; CANR 7

**Kerr, M. E.**................... **CLC 12, 35**
See also Meaker, Marijane (Agnes)
See also AAYA 2; CLR 29; SAAS 1

**Kerr, Robert** ................... **CLC 55**

**Kerrigan, (Thomas) Anthony**
1918- ..................... **CLC 4, 6**
See also CA 49-52; CAAS 11; CANR 4

**Kerry, Lois**
See Duncan, Lois

**Kesey, Ken (Elton)**
1935- ...... **CLC 1, 3, 6, 11, 46, 64; DA;**
                                              **WLC**
See also CA 1-4R; CANR 22, 38;
CDALB 1968-1988; DLB 2, 16; MTCW;
SATA 66

**Kesselring, Joseph (Otto)**
1902-1967 ................... **CLC 45**

**Kessler, Jascha (Frederick)** 1929-.... **CLC 4**
See also CA 17-20R; CANR 8

**Kettelkamp, Larry (Dale)** 1933- .... **CLC 12**
See also CA 29-32R; CANR 16; SAAS 3;
SATA 2

**Keyber, Conny**
See Fielding, Henry

**Keyes, Daniel** 1927- .......... **CLC 80; DA**
See also CA 17-20R; CANR 10, 26;
SATA 37

**Khayyam, Omar**
1048-1131 ............ **CMLC 11; PC 8**

**Kherdian, David** 1931-........... **CLC 6, 9**
See also CA 21-24R; CAAS 2; CANR 39;
CLR 24; JRDA; MAICYA; SATA 16, 74

**Khlebnikov, Velimir** .............. **TCLC 20**
See also Khlebnikov, Viktor Vladimirovich

**Khlebnikov, Viktor Vladimirovich** 1885-1922
See Khlebnikov, Velimir
See also CA 117

**Khodasevich, Vladislav (Felitsianovich)**
1886-1939 ................. **TCLC 15**
See also CA 115

**Kielland, Alexander Lange**
1849-1906 ................. **TCLC 5**
See also CA 104

**Kiely, Benedict** 1919-.......... **CLC 23, 43**
See also CA 1-4R; CANR 2; DLB 15

**Kienzle, William X(avier)** 1928- .... **CLC 25**
See also CA 93-96; CAAS 1; CANR 9, 31;
MTCW

**Kierkegaard, Soren** 1813-1855.... **NCLC 34**

**Killens, John Oliver** 1916-1987..... **CLC 10**
See also BW 2; CA 77-80; 123; CAAS 2;
CANR 26; DLB 33

**Killigrew, Anne** 1660-1685.......... **LC 4**
See also DLB 131

**Kim**
See Simenon, Georges (Jacques Christian)

**Kincaid, Jamaica** 1949-... **CLC 43, 68; BLC**
See also BW 2; CA 125

**King, Francis (Henry)** 1923-..... **CLC 8, 53**
See also CA 1-4R; CANR 1, 33; DLB 15,
139; MTCW

**King, Martin Luther, Jr.**
1929-1968 ......... **CLC 83; BLC; DA**
See also BW 2; CA 25-28; CANR 27, 44;
CAP 2; MTCW; SATA 14

**King, Stephen (Edwin)**
1947- ............. **CLC 12, 26, 37, 61**
See also AAYA 1; BEST 90:1; CA 61-64;
CANR 1, 30; DLBY 80; JRDA; MTCW;
SATA 9, 55

**King, Steve**
See King, Stephen (Edwin)

**Kingman, Lee**.................... **CLC 17**
See also Natti, (Mary) Lee
See also SAAS 3; SATA 1, 67

**Kingsley, Charles** 1819-1875 ..... **NCLC 35**
See also DLB 21, 32; YABC 2

**Kingsley, Sidney** 1906-............ **CLC 44**
See also CA 85-88; DLB 7

**Kingsolver, Barbara** 1955-...... **CLC 55, 81**
See also CA 129; 134

**Kingston, Maxine (Ting Ting) Hong**
1940- ................ **CLC 12, 19, 58**
See also AAYA 8; CA 69-72; CANR 13,
38; DLBY 80; MTCW; SATA 53

**Kinnell, Galway**
1927- ........... **CLC 1, 2, 3, 5, 13, 29**
See also CA 9-12R; CANR 10, 34; DLB 5;
DLBY 87; MTCW

**Kinsella, Thomas** 1928- ......... **CLC 4, 19**
See also CA 17-20R; CANR 15; DLB 27;
MTCW

**Kinsella, W(illiam) P(atrick)**
1935- .................... **CLC 27, 43**
See also AAYA 7; CA 97-100; CAAS 7;
CANR 21, 35; MTCW

**Kipling, (Joseph) Rudyard**
1865-1936 ...... **TCLC 8, 17; DA; PC 3;**
                                       **SSC 5; WLC**
See also CA 105; 120; CANR 33;
CDBLB 1890-1914; DLB 19, 34, 141;
MAICYA; MTCW; YABC 2

**Kirkup, James** 1918- .............. **CLC 1**
See also CA 1-4R; CAAS 4; CANR 2;
DLB 27; SATA 12

**Kirkwood, James** 1930(?)-1989 ...... **CLC 9**
See also AITN 2; CA 1-4R; 128; CANR 6,
40

**Kis, Danilo** 1935-1989 ........... **CLC 57**
See also CA 109; 118; 129; MTCW

**Kivi, Aleksis** 1834-1872 ........ **NCLC 30**

**Kizer, Carolyn (Ashley)**
1925- ................. **CLC 15, 39, 80**
See also CA 65-68; CAAS 5; CANR 24;
DLB 5

**Klabund** 1890-1928............ **TCLC 44**
See also DLB 66

**Klappert, Peter** 1942-............ **CLC 57**
See also CA 33-36R; DLB 5

**Klein, A(braham) M(oses)**
1909-1972 ................... **CLC 19**
See also CA 101; 37-40R; DLB 68

**Klein, Norma** 1938-1989 .......... **CLC 30**
See also AAYA 2; CA 41-44R; 128;
CANR 15, 37; CLR 2, 19; JRDA;
MAICYA; SAAS 1; SATA 7, 57

**Klein, T(heodore) E(ibon) D(onald)**
1947- ...................... **CLC 34**
See also CA 119; CANR 44

Kleist, Heinrich von
    1777-1811 . . . . . . . . . . . . . . **NCLC 2, 37**
    See also DLB 90

Klima, Ivan   1931- . . . . . . . . . . . . . . **CLC 56**
    See also CA 25-28R; CANR 17

Klimentov, Andrei Platonovich   1899-1951
    See Platonov, Andrei
    See also CA 108

Klinger, Friedrich Maximilian von
    1752-1831 . . . . . . . . . . . . . . . . . **NCLC 1**
    See also DLB 94

Klopstock, Friedrich Gottlieb
    1724-1803 . . . . . . . . . . . . . . . . **NCLC 11**
    See also DLB 97

Knebel, Fletcher   1911-1993 . . . . . . . . **CLC 14**
    See also AITN 1; CA 1-4R; 140; CAAS 3;
    CANR 1, 36; SATA 36; SATA-Obit 75

Knickerbocker, Diedrich
    See Irving, Washington

Knight, Etheridge
    1931-1991 . . . . . . . . . . . . . . **CLC 40; BLC**
    See also BW 1; CA 21-24R; 133; CANR 23;
    DLB 41

Knight, Sarah Kemble   1666-1727 . . . . . **LC 7**
    See also DLB 24

Knowles, John
    1926- . . . . . . . . . . . **CLC 1, 4, 10, 26; DA**
    See also AAYA 10; CA 17-20R; CANR 40;
    CDALB 1968-1988; DLB 6; MTCW;
    SATA 8

Knox, Calvin M.
    See Silverberg, Robert

Knye, Cassandra
    See Disch, Thomas M(ichael)

Koch, C(hristopher) J(ohn)   1932- . . . **CLC 42**
    See also CA 127

Koch, Christopher
    See Koch, C(hristopher) J(ohn)

Koch, Kenneth   1925- . . . . . . . . **CLC 5, 8, 44**
    See also CA 1-4R; CANR 6, 36; DLB 5;
    SATA 65

Kochanowski, Jan   1530-1584 . . . . . . . **LC 10**

Kock, Charles Paul de
    1794-1871 . . . . . . . . . . . . . . . . **NCLC 16**

Koda Shigeyuki   1867-1947
    See Rohan, Koda
    See also CA 121

Koestler, Arthur
    1905-1983 . . . . . . . **CLC 1, 3, 6, 8, 15, 33**
    See also CA 1-4R; 109; CANR 1, 33;
    CDBLB 1945-1960; DLBY 83; MTCW

Kogawa, Joy Nozomi   1935- . . . . . . . **CLC 78**
    See also CA 101; CANR 19

Kohout, Pavel   1928- . . . . . . . . . . . . . **CLC 13**
    See also CA 45-48; CANR 3

Koizumi, Yakumo
    See Hearn, (Patricio) Lafcadio (Tessima
    Carlos)

Kolmar, Gertrud   1894-1943 . . . . . . **TCLC 40**

Konrad, George
    See Konrad, Gyoergy

Konrad, Gyoergy   1933- . . . . . . **CLC 4, 10, 73**
    See also CA 85-88

Konwicki, Tadeusz   1926- . . . . . **CLC 8, 28, 54**
    See also CA 101; CAAS 9; CANR 39;
    MTCW

Koontz, Dean R(ay)   1945- . . . . . . . . . **CLC 78**
    See also AAYA 9; BEST 89:3, 90:2;
    CA 108; CANR 19, 36; MTCW

Kopit, Arthur (Lee)   1937- . . . . **CLC 1, 18, 33**
    See also AITN 1; CA 81-84; CABS 3;
    DLB 7; MTCW

Kops, Bernard   1926- . . . . . . . . . . . . . . **CLC 4**
    See also CA 5-8R; DLB 13

Kornbluth, C(yril) M.   1923-1958 . . . . **TCLC 8**
    See also CA 105; DLB 8

Korolenko, V. G.
    See Korolenko, Vladimir Galaktionovich

Korolenko, Vladimir
    See Korolenko, Vladimir Galaktionovich

Korolenko, Vladimir G.
    See Korolenko, Vladimir Galaktionovich

Korolenko, Vladimir Galaktionovich
    1853-1921 . . . . . . . . . . . . . . . . **TCLC 22**
    See also CA 121

Kosinski, Jerzy (Nikodem)
    1933-1991 . . . . **CLC 1, 2, 3, 6, 10, 15, 53,
                       70**
    See also CA 17-20R; 134; CANR 9; DLB 2;
    DLBY 82; MTCW

Kostelanetz, Richard (Cory)   1940- . . **CLC 28**
    See also CA 13-16R; CAAS 8; CANR 38

Kostrowitzki, Wilhelm Apollinaris de
    1880-1918
    See Apollinaire, Guillaume
    See also CA 104

Kotlowitz, Robert   1924- . . . . . . . . . . . **CLC 4**
    See also CA 33-36R; CANR 36

Kotzebue, August (Friedrich Ferdinand) von
    1761-1819 . . . . . . . . . . . . . . . . **NCLC 25**
    See also DLB 94

Kotzwinkle, William   1938- . . . **CLC 5, 14, 35**
    See also CA 45-48; CANR 3, 44; CLR 6;
    MAICYA; SATA 24, 70

Kozol, Jonathan   1936- . . . . . . . . . . . **CLC 17**
    See also CA 61-64; CANR 16

Kozoll, Michael   1940(?)- . . . . . . . . . **CLC 35**

Kramer, Kathryn   19(?)- . . . . . . . . . . **CLC 34**

Kramer, Larry   1935- . . . . . . . . . . . . . **CLC 42**
    See also CA 124; 126

Krasicki, Ignacy   1735-1801 . . . . . . . **NCLC 8**

Krasinski, Zygmunt   1812-1859 . . . . **NCLC 4**

Kraus, Karl   1874-1936 . . . . . . . . . . . **TCLC 5**
    See also CA 104; DLB 118

Kreve (Mickevicius), Vincas
    1882-1954 . . . . . . . . . . . . . . . . **TCLC 27**

Kristeva, Julia   1941- . . . . . . . . . . . . **CLC 77**

Kristofferson, Kris   1936- . . . . . . . . . **CLC 26**
    See also CA 104

Krizanc, John   1956- . . . . . . . . . . . . . **CLC 57**

Krleza, Miroslav   1893-1981 . . . . . . . . **CLC 8**
    See also CA 97-100; 105

Kroetsch, Robert   1927- . . . . . . **CLC 5, 23, 57**
    See also CA 17-20R; CANR 8, 38; DLB 53;
    MTCW

Kroetz, Franz
    See Kroetz, Franz Xaver

Kroetz, Franz Xaver   1946- . . . . . . . . **CLC 41**
    See also CA 130

Kroker, Arthur   1945- . . . . . . . . . . . . **CLC 77**

Kropotkin, Peter (Aleksieevich)
    1842-1921 . . . . . . . . . . . . . . . . **TCLC 36**
    See also CA 119

Krotkov, Yuri   1917- . . . . . . . . . . . . . **CLC 19**
    See also CA 102

Krumb
    See Crumb, R(obert)

Krumgold, Joseph (Quincy)
    1908-1980 . . . . . . . . . . . . . . . . . **CLC 12**
    See also CA 9-12R; 101; CANR 7;
    MAICYA; SATA 1, 23, 48

Krumwitz
    See Crumb, R(obert)

Krutch, Joseph Wood   1893-1970 . . . . **CLC 24**
    See also CA 1-4R; 25-28R; CANR 4;
    DLB 63

Krutzch, Gus
    See Eliot, T(homas) S(tearns)

Krylov, Ivan Andreevich
    1768(?)-1844 . . . . . . . . . . . . . . . **NCLC 1**

Kubin, Alfred   1877-1959 . . . . . . . . **TCLC 23**
    See also CA 112; DLB 81

Kubrick, Stanley   1928- . . . . . . . . . . . **CLC 16**
    See also CA 81-84; CANR 33; DLB 26

Kumin, Maxine (Winokur)
    1925- . . . . . . . . . . . . . . . **CLC 5, 13, 28**
    See also AITN 2; CA 1-4R; CAAS 8;
    CANR 1, 21; DLB 5; MTCW; SATA 12

Kundera, Milan
    1929- . . . . . . . . . . **CLC 4, 9, 19, 32, 68**
    See also AAYA 2; CA 85-88; CANR 19;
    MTCW

Kunitz, Stanley (Jasspon)
    1905- . . . . . . . . . . . . . . . . **CLC 6, 11, 14**
    See also CA 41-44R; CANR 26; DLB 48;
    MTCW

Kunze, Reiner   1933- . . . . . . . . . . . . . **CLC 10**
    See also CA 93-96; DLB 75

Kuprin, Aleksandr Ivanovich
    1870-1938 . . . . . . . . . . . . . . . . . **TCLC 5**
    See also CA 104

Kureishi, Hanif   1954(?)- . . . . . . . . . . **CLC 64**
    See also CA 139

Kurosawa, Akira   1910- . . . . . . . . . . . **CLC 16**
    See also AAYA 11; CA 101

Kushner, Tony   1957(?)- . . . . . . . . . . . **CLC 81**
    See also CA 144

Kuttner, Henry   1915-1958 . . . . . . . **TCLC 10**
    See also CA 107; DLB 8

Kuzma, Greg   1944- . . . . . . . . . . . . . . . **CLC 7**
    See also CA 33-36R

Kuzmin, Mikhail   1872(?)-1936 . . . . **TCLC 40**

Kyd, Thomas   1558-1594 . . . . . . **LC 22; DC 3**
    See also DLB 62

Kyprianos, Iossif
    See Samarakis, Antonis

La Bruyere, Jean de   1645-1696 . . . . . **LC 17**

**Lacan, Jacques (Marie Emile)**
1901-1981 .................. **CLC 75**
See also CA 121; 104

**Laclos, Pierre Ambroise Francois Choderlos de** 1741-1803 .............. **NCLC 4**

**Lacolere, Francois**
See Aragon, Louis

**La Colere, Francois**
See Aragon, Louis

**La Deshabilleuse**
See Simenon, Georges (Jacques Christian)

**Lady Gregory**
See Gregory, Isabella Augusta (Persse)

**Lady of Quality, A**
See Bagnold, Enid

**La Fayette, Marie (Madelaine Pioche de la Vergne Comtes** 1634-1693 ...... **LC 2**

**Lafayette, Rene**
See Hubbard, L(afayette) Ron(ald)

**Laforgue, Jules** 1860-1887 ....... **NCLC 5**

**Lagerkvist, Paer (Fabian)**
1891-1974 .......... **CLC 7, 10, 13, 54**
See also Lagerkvist, Par
See also CA 85-88; 49-52; MTCW

**Lagerkvist, Par**
See Lagerkvist, Paer (Fabian)
See also SSC 12

**Lagerloef, Selma (Ottiliana Lovisa)**
1858-1940 ............... **TCLC 4, 36**
See also Lagerlof, Selma (Ottiliana Lovisa)
See also CA 108; CLR 7; SATA 15

**Lagerlof, Selma (Ottiliana Lovisa)**
See Lagerloef, Selma (Ottiliana Lovisa)
See also CLR 7; SATA 15

**La Guma, (Justin) Alex(ander)**
1925-1985 .................... **CLC 19**
See also BW 1; CA 49-52; 118; CANR 25; DLB 117; MTCW

**Laidlaw, A. K.**
See Grieve, C(hristopher) M(urray)

**Lainez, Manuel Mujica**
See Mujica Lainez, Manuel
See also HW

**Lamartine, Alphonse (Marie Louis Prat) de**
1790-1869 .................. **NCLC 11**

**Lamb, Charles**
1775-1834 ....... **NCLC 10; DA; WLC**
See also CDBLB 1789-1832; DLB 93, 107; SATA 17

**Lamb, Lady Caroline** 1785-1828 .. **NCLC 38**
See also DLB 116

**Lamming, George (William)**
1927- .............. **CLC 2, 4, 66; BLC**
See also BW 2; CA 85-88; CANR 26; DLB 125; MTCW

**L'Amour, Louis (Dearborn)**
1908-1988 ............... **CLC 25, 55**
See also AITN 2; BEST 89:2; CA 1-4R; 125; CANR 3, 25, 40; DLBY 80; MTCW

**Lampedusa, Giuseppe (Tomasi) di** ... **TCLC 13**
See also Tomasi di Lampedusa, Giuseppe

**Lampman, Archibald** 1861-1899 .. **NCLC 25**
See also DLB 92

**Lancaster, Bruce** 1896-1963 ....... **CLC 36**
See also CA 9-10; CAP 1; SATA 9

**Landau, Mark Alexandrovich**
See Aldanov, Mark (Alexandrovich)

**Landau-Aldanov, Mark Alexandrovich**
See Aldanov, Mark (Alexandrovich)

**Landis, John** 1950- .............. **CLC 26**
See also CA 112; 122

**Landolfi, Tommaso** 1908-1979 ... **CLC 11, 49**
See also CA 127; 117

**Landon, Letitia Elizabeth**
1802-1838 ................ **NCLC 15**
See also DLB 96

**Landor, Walter Savage**
1775-1864 ................ **NCLC 14**
See also DLB 93, 107

**Landwirth, Heinz** 1927-
See Lind, Jakov
See also CA 9-12R; CANR 7

**Lane, Patrick** 1939- .............. **CLC 25**
See also CA 97-100; DLB 53

**Lang, Andrew** 1844-1912 ......... **TCLC 16**
See also CA 114; 137; DLB 98, 141; MAICYA; SATA 16

**Lang, Fritz** 1890-1976 ............ **CLC 20**
See also CA 77-80; 69-72; CANR 30

**Lange, John**
See Crichton, (John) Michael

**Langer, Elinor** 1939- .............. **CLC 34**
See also CA 121

**Langland, William**
1330(?)-1400(?) ............ **LC 19; DA**

**Langstaff, Launcelot**
See Irving, Washington

**Lanier, Sidney** 1842-1881 ........ **NCLC 6**
See also DLB 64; MAICYA; SATA 18

**Lanyer, Aemilia** 1569-1645 ......... **LC 10**

**Lao Tzu** ....................... **CMLC 7**

**Lapine, James (Elliot)** 1949- ....... **CLC 39**
See also CA 123; 130

**Larbaud, Valery (Nicolas)**
1881-1957 ................. **TCLC 9**
See also CA 106

**Lardner, Ring**
See Lardner, Ring(gold) W(ilmer)

**Lardner, Ring W., Jr.**
See Lardner, Ring(gold) W(ilmer)

**Lardner, Ring(gold) W(ilmer)**
1885-1933 ............... **TCLC 2, 14**
See also CA 104; 131; CDALB 1917-1929; DLB 11, 25, 86; MTCW

**Laredo, Betty**
See Codrescu, Andrei

**Larkin, Maia**
See Wojciechowska, Maia (Teresa)

**Larkin, Philip (Arthur)**
1922-1985 .... **CLC 3, 5, 8, 9, 13, 18, 33, 39, 64**
See also CA 5-8R; 117; CANR 24; CDBLB 1960 to Present; DLB 27; MTCW

**Larra (y Sanchez de Castro), Mariano Jose de**
1809-1837 ................ **NCLC 17**

**Larsen, Eric** 1941- ............... **CLC 55**
See also CA 132

**Larsen, Nella** 1891-1964 ..... **CLC 37; BLC**
See also BW 1; CA 125; DLB 51

**Larson, Charles R(aymond)** 1938-... **CLC 31**
See also CA 53-56; CANR 4

**Latham, Jean Lee** 1902-.......... **CLC 12**
See also AITN 1; CA 5-8R; CANR 7; MAICYA; SATA 2, 68

**Latham, Mavis**
See Clark, Mavis Thorpe

**Lathen, Emma** .................... **CLC 2**
See also Hennissart, Martha; Latsis, Mary J(ane)

**Lathrop, Francis**
See Leiber, Fritz (Reuter, Jr.)

**Latsis, Mary J(ane)**
See Lathen, Emma
See also CA 85-88

**Lattimore, Richmond (Alexander)**
1906-1984 .................... **CLC 3**
See also CA 1-4R; 112; CANR 1

**Laughlin, James** 1914- ............ **CLC 49**
See also CA 21-24R; CANR 9; DLB 48

**Laurence, (Jean) Margaret (Wemyss)**
1926-1987 .. **CLC 3, 6, 13, 50, 62; SSC 7**
See also CA 5-8R; 121; CANR 33; DLB 53; MTCW; SATA 50

**Laurent, Antoine** 1952- ........... **CLC 50**

**Lauscher, Hermann**
See Hesse, Hermann

**Lautreamont, Comte de**
1846-1870 ......... **NCLC 12; SSC 14**

**Laverty, Donald**
See Blish, James (Benjamin)

**Lavin, Mary** 1912- ...... **CLC 4, 18; SSC 4**
See also CA 9-12R; CANR 33; DLB 15; MTCW

**Lavond, Paul Dennis**
See Kornbluth, C(yril) M.; Pohl, Frederik

**Lawler, Raymond Evenor** 1922- .... **CLC 58**
See also CA 103

**Lawrence, D(avid) H(erbert Richards)**
1885-1930 ....... **TCLC 2, 9, 16, 33, 48; DA; SSC 4; WLC**
See also CA 104; 121; CDBLB 1914-1945; DLB 10, 19, 36, 98; MTCW

**Lawrence, T(homas) E(dward)**
1888-1935 ................. **TCLC 18**
See also Dale, Colin
See also CA 115

**Lawrence of Arabia**
See Lawrence, T(homas) E(dward)

**Lawson, Henry (Archibald Hertzberg)**
1867-1922 ................. **TCLC 27**
See also CA 120

**Lawton, Dennis**
See Faust, Frederick (Schiller)

**Laxness, Halldor** ................. **CLC 25**
See also Gudjonsson, Halldor Kiljan

**Layamon** fl. c. 1200-............ **CMLC 10**

**Laye, Camara** 1928-1980 ... **CLC 4, 38; BLC**
See also BW 1; CA 85-88; 97-100; CANR 25; MTCW

**MacDonald, George** 1824-1905 . . . . . **TCLC 9**
See also CA 106; 137; DLB 18; MAICYA;
SATA 33

**Macdonald, John**
See Millar, Kenneth

**MacDonald, John D(ann)**
1916-1986 . . . . . . . . . . . . . **CLC 3, 27, 44**
See also CA 1-4R; 121; CANR 1, 19;
DLB 8; DLBY 86; MTCW

**Macdonald, John Ross**
See Millar, Kenneth

**Macdonald, Ross** . . . . . **CLC 1, 2, 3, 14, 34, 41**
See also Millar, Kenneth
See also DLBD 6

**MacDougal, John**
See Blish, James (Benjamin)

**MacEwen, Gwendolyn (Margaret)**
1941-1987 . . . . . . . . . . . . . . . **CLC 13, 55**
See also CA 9-12R; 124; CANR 7, 22;
DLB 53; SATA 50, 55

**Machado (y Ruiz), Antonio**
1875-1939 . . . . . . . . . . . . . . . . . . **TCLC 3**
See also CA 104; DLB 108

**Machado de Assis, Joaquim Maria**
1839-1908 . . . . . . . . . . . . . **TCLC 10; BLC**
See also CA 107

**Machen, Arthur** . . . . . . . . . . . . . . . . . . **TCLC 4**
See also Jones, Arthur Llewellyn
See also DLB 36

**Machiavelli, Niccolo** 1469-1527 . . **LC 8; DA**

**MacInnes, Colin** 1914-1976 . . . . . . **CLC 4, 23**
See also CA 69-72; 65-68; CANR 21;
DLB 14; MTCW

**MacInnes, Helen (Clark)**
1907-1985 . . . . . . . . . . . . . . . **CLC 27, 39**
See also CA 1-4R; 117; CANR 1, 28;
DLB 87; MTCW; SATA 22, 44

**Mackay, Mary** 1855-1924
See Corelli, Marie
See also CA 118

**Mackenzie, Compton (Edward Montague)**
1883-1972 . . . . . . . . . . . . . . . . . . **CLC 18**
See also CA 21-22; 37-40R; CAP 2;
DLB 34, 100

**Mackenzie, Henry** 1745-1831 . . . . **NCLC 41**
See also DLB 39

**Mackintosh, Elizabeth** 1896(?)-1952
See Tey, Josephine
See also CA 110

**MacLaren, James**
See Grieve, C(hristopher) M(urray)

**Mac Laverty, Bernard** 1942- . . . . . . . **CLC 31**
See also CA 116; 118; CANR 43

**MacLean, Alistair (Stuart)**
1922-1987 . . . . . . . . . . **CLC 3, 13, 50, 63**
See also CA 57-60; 121; CANR 28; MTCW;
SATA 23, 50

**Maclean, Norman (Fitzroy)**
1902-1990 . . . . . . . . . . . **CLC 78; SSC 13**
See also CA 102; 132

**MacLeish, Archibald**
1892-1982 . . . . . . . . . . . **CLC 3, 8, 14, 68**
See also CA 9-12R; 106; CANR 33; DLB 4,
7, 45; DLBY 82; MTCW

**MacLennan, (John) Hugh**
1907-1990 . . . . . . . . . . . . . . . . **CLC 2, 14**
See also CA 5-8R; 142; CANR 33; DLB 68;
MTCW

**MacLeod, Alistair** 1936- . . . . . . . . . **CLC 56**
See also CA 123; DLB 60

**MacNeice, (Frederick) Louis**
1907-1963 . . . . . . . . . . . **CLC 1, 4, 10, 53**
See also CA 85-88; DLB 10, 20; MTCW

**MacNeill, Dand**
See Fraser, George MacDonald

**Macpherson, (Jean) Jay** 1931- . . . . . . **CLC 14**
See also CA 5-8R; DLB 53

**MacShane, Frank** 1927- . . . . . . . . . . **CLC 39**
See also CA 9-12R; CANR 3, 33; DLB 111

**Macumber, Mari**
See Sandoz, Mari(e Susette)

**Madach, Imre** 1823-1864 . . . . . . . **NCLC 19**

**Madden, (Jerry) David** 1933- . . . . **CLC 5, 15**
See also CA 1-4R; CAAS 3; CANR 4;
DLB 6; MTCW

**Maddern, Al(an)**
See Ellison, Harlan

**Madhubuti, Haki R.**
1942- . . . . . . . . . **CLC 6, 73; BLC; PC 5**
See also Lee, Don L.
See also BW 2; CA 73-76; CANR 24;
DLB 5, 41; DLBD 8

**Madow, Pauline (Reichberg)** . . . . . . . . **CLC 1**
See also CA 9-12R

**Maepenn, Hugh**
See Kuttner, Henry

**Maepenn, K. H.**
See Kuttner, Henry

**Maeterlinck, Maurice** 1862-1949 . . . **TCLC 3**
See also CA 104; 136; SATA 66

**Maginn, William** 1794-1842 . . . . . . **NCLC 8**
See also DLB 110

**Mahapatra, Jayanta** 1928- . . . . . . . . **CLC 33**
See also CA 73-76; CAAS 9; CANR 15, 33

**Mahfouz, Naguib (Abdel Aziz Al-Sabilgi)**
1911(?)-
See Mahfuz, Najib
See also BEST 89:2; CA 128; MTCW

**Mahfuz, Najib** . . . . . . . . . . . . . . . **CLC 52, 55**
See also Mahfouz, Naguib (Abdel Aziz
Al-Sabilgi)
See also DLBY 88

**Mahon, Derek** 1941- . . . . . . . . . . . . . **CLC 27**
See also CA 113; 128; DLB 40

**Mailer, Norman**
1923- . . . . . . **CLC 1, 2, 3, 4, 5, 8, 11, 14,
28, 39, 74; DA**
See also AITN 2; CA 9-12R; CABS 1;
CANR 28; CDALB 1968-1988; DLB 2,
16, 28; DLBD 3; DLBY 80, 83; MTCW

**Maillet, Antonine** 1929- . . . . . . . . . . **CLC 54**
See also CA 115; 120; DLB 60

**Mais, Roger** 1905-1955 . . . . . . . . . . **TCLC 8**
See also BW 1; CA 105; 124; DLB 125;
MTCW

**Maistre, Joseph de** 1753-1821 . . . . **NCLC 37**

**Maitland, Sara (Louise)** 1950- . . . . . . **CLC 49**
See also CA 69-72; CANR 13

**Major, Clarence**
1936- . . . . . . . . . . . . **CLC 3, 19, 48; BLC**
See also BW 2; CA 21-24R; CAAS 6;
CANR 13, 25; DLB 33

**Major, Kevin (Gerald)** 1949- . . . . . . . **CLC 26**
See also CA 97-100; CANR 21, 38;
CLR 11; DLB 60; JRDA; MAICYA;
SATA 32

**Maki, James**
See Ozu, Yasujiro

**Malabaila, Damiano**
See Levi, Primo

**Malamud, Bernard**
1914-1986 . . . . . . **CLC 1, 2, 3, 5, 8, 9, 11,
18, 27, 44, 78; DA; SSC 15; WLC**
See also CA 5-8R; 118; CABS 1; CANR 28;
CDALB 1941-1968; DLB 2, 28;
DLBY 80, 86; MTCW

**Malaparte, Curzio** 1898-1957 . . . . . **TCLC 52**

**Malcolm, Dan**
See Silverberg, Robert

**Malcolm X** . . . . . . . . . . . . . . . . . **CLC 82; BLC**
See also Little, Malcolm

**Malherbe, Francois de** 1555-1628 . . . . . **LC 5**

**Mallarme, Stephane**
1842-1898 . . . . . . . . . . **NCLC 4, 41; PC 4**

**Mallet-Joris, Francoise** 1930- . . . . . . **CLC 11**
See also CA 65-68; CANR 17; DLB 83

**Malley, Ern**
See McAuley, James Phillip

**Mallowan, Agatha Christie**
See Christie, Agatha (Mary Clarissa)

**Maloff, Saul** 1922- . . . . . . . . . . . . . . . **CLC 5**
See also CA 33-36R

**Malone, Louis**
See MacNeice, (Frederick) Louis

**Malone, Michael (Christopher)**
1942- . . . . . . . . . . . . . . . . . . . . . . **CLC 43**
See also CA 77-80; CANR 14, 32

**Malory, (Sir) Thomas**
1410(?)-1471(?) . . . . . . . . . . . **LC 11; DA**
See also CDBLB Before 1660; SATA 33, 59

**Malouf, (George Joseph) David**
1934- . . . . . . . . . . . . . . . . . . . . . . **CLC 28**
See also CA 124

**Malraux, (Georges-)Andre**
1901-1976 . . . . . . **CLC 1, 4, 9, 13, 15, 57**
See also CA 21-22; 69-72; CANR 34;
CAP 2; DLB 72; MTCW

**Malzberg, Barry N(athaniel)** 1939- . . . **CLC 7**
See also CA 61-64; CAAS 4; CANR 16;
DLB 8

**Mamet, David (Alan)**
1947- . . . . . . . . . **CLC 9, 15, 34, 46; DC 4**
See also AAYA 3; CA 81-84; CABS 3;
CANR 15, 41; DLB 7; MTCW

**Mamoulian, Rouben (Zachary)**
1897-1987 . . . . . . . . . . . . . . . . . . **CLC 16**
See also CA 25-28R; 124

**Mandelstam, Osip (Emilievich)**
1891(?)-1938(?) . . . . . . . . . . . . **TCLC 2, 6**
See also CA 104

**Mander, (Mary) Jane** 1877-1949 . . . **TCLC 31**

**Masters, Edgar Lee**
1868-1950 ..... **TCLC 2, 25; DA; PC 1**
See also CA 104; 133; CDALB 1865-1917;
DLB 54; MTCW

**Masters, Hilary** 1928- ........... **CLC 48**
See also CA 25-28R; CANR 13

**Mastrosimone, William** 19(?)- ...... **CLC 36**

**Mathe, Albert**
See Camus, Albert

**Matheson, Richard Burton** 1926- ... **CLC 37**
See also CA 97-100; DLB 8, 44

**Mathews, Harry** 1930- ......... **CLC 6, 52**
See also CA 21-24R; CAAS 6; CANR 18,
40

**Mathias, Roland (Glyn)** 1915- ...... **CLC 45**
See also CA 97-100; CANR 19, 41; DLB 27

**Matsuo Basho** 1644-1694 ........... **PC 3**

**Mattheson, Rodney**
See Creasey, John

**Matthews, Greg** 1949- ........... **CLC 45**
See also CA 135

**Matthews, William** 1942- ......... **CLC 40**
See also CA 29-32R; CAAS 18; CANR 12;
DLB 5

**Matthias, John (Edward)** 1941- ...... **CLC 9**
See also CA 33-36R

**Matthiessen, Peter**
1927- ........... **CLC 5, 7, 11, 32, 64**
See also AAYA 6; BEST 90:4; CA 9-12R;
CANR 21; DLB 6; MTCW; SATA 27

**Maturin, Charles Robert**
1780(?)-1824 ............... **NCLC 6**

**Matute (Ausejo), Ana Maria**
1925- ...................... **CLC 11**
See also CA 89-92; MTCW

**Maugham, W. S.**
See Maugham, W(illiam) Somerset

**Maugham, W(illiam) Somerset**
1874-1965 ...... **CLC 1, 11, 15, 67; DA;**
**SSC 8; WLC**
See also CA 5-8R; 25-28R; CANR 40;
CDBLB 1914-1945; DLB 10, 36, 77, 100;
MTCW; SATA 54

**Maugham, William Somerset**
See Maugham, W(illiam) Somerset

**Maupassant, (Henri Rene Albert) Guy de**
1850-1893 .... **NCLC 1, 42; DA; SSC 1;**
**WLC**
See also DLB 123

**Maurhut, Richard**
See Traven, B.

**Mauriac, Claude** 1914- ............ **CLC 9**
See also CA 89-92; DLB 83

**Mauriac, Francois (Charles)**
1885-1970 .......... **CLC 4, 9, 56**
See also CA 25-28; CAP 2; DLB 65;
MTCW

**Mavor, Osborne Henry** 1888-1951
See Bridie, James
See also CA 104

**Maxwell, William (Keepers, Jr.)**
1908- ...................... **CLC 19**
See also CA 93-96; DLBY 80

**May, Elaine** 1932- .............. **CLC 16**
See also CA 124; 142; DLB 44

**Mayakovski, Vladimir (Vladimirovich)**
1893-1930 ............... **TCLC 4, 18**
See also CA 104

**Mayhew, Henry** 1812-1887 ...... **NCLC 31**
See also DLB 18, 55

**Maynard, Joyce** 1953- ........... **CLC 23**
See also CA 111; 129

**Mayne, William (James Carter)**
1928- ...................... **CLC 12**
See also CA 9-12R; CANR 37; CLR 25;
JRDA; MAICYA; SAAS 11; SATA 6, 68

**Mayo, Jim**
See L'Amour, Louis (Dearborn)

**Maysles, Albert** 1926- ............ **CLC 16**
See also CA 29-32R

**Maysles, David** 1932- ............. **CLC 16**

**Mazer, Norma Fox** 1931- ......... **CLC 26**
See also AAYA 5; CA 69-72; CANR 12,
32; CLR 23; JRDA; MAICYA; SAAS 1;
SATA 24, 67

**Mazzini, Guiseppe** 1805-1872 .... **NCLC 34**

**McAuley, James Phillip**
1917-1976 .................. **CLC 45**
See also CA 97-100

**McBain, Ed**
See Hunter, Evan

**McBrien, William Augustine**
1930- ...................... **CLC 44**
See also CA 107

**McCaffrey, Anne (Inez)** 1926- ...... **CLC 17**
See also AAYA 6; AITN 2; BEST 89:2;
CA 25-28R; CANR 15, 35; DLB 8;
JRDA; MAICYA; MTCW; SAAS 11;
SATA 8, 70

**McCann, Arthur**
See Campbell, John W(ood, Jr.)

**McCann, Edson**
See Pohl, Frederik

**McCarthy, Charles, Jr.** 1933-
See McCarthy, Cormac
See also CANR 42

**McCarthy, Cormac** .............. **CLC 4, 57**
See also McCarthy, Charles, Jr.
See also DLB 6

**McCarthy, Mary (Therese)**
1912-1989 ... **CLC 1, 3, 5, 14, 24, 39, 59**
See also CA 5-8R; 129; CANR 16; DLB 2;
DLBY 81; MTCW

**McCartney, (James) Paul**
1942- ................... **CLC 12, 35**

**McCauley, Stephen (D.)** 1955- ..... **CLC 50**
See also CA 141

**McClure, Michael (Thomas)**
1932- ...................... **CLC 6, 10**
See also CA 21-24R; CANR 17; DLB 16

**McCorkle, Jill (Collins)** 1958- ..... **CLC 51**
See also CA 121; DLBY 87

**McCourt, James** 1941- ............ **CLC 5**
See also CA 57-60

**McCoy, Horace (Stanley)**
1897-1955 ................. **TCLC 28**
See also CA 108; DLB 9

**McCrae, John** 1872-1918 ........ **TCLC 12**
See also CA 109; DLB 92

**McCreigh, James**
See Pohl, Frederik

**McCullers, (Lula) Carson (Smith)**
1917-1967 .... **CLC 1, 4, 10, 12, 48; DA;**
**SSC 9; WLC**
See also CA 5-8R; 25-28R; CABS 1, 3;
CANR 18; CDALB 1941-1968; DLB 2, 7;
MTCW; SATA 27

**McCulloch, John Tyler**
See Burroughs, Edgar Rice

**McCullough, Colleen** 1938(?)- ...... **CLC 27**
See also CA 81-84; CANR 17; MTCW

**McElroy, Joseph** 1930- ......... **CLC 5, 47**
See also CA 17-20R

**McEwan, Ian (Russell)** 1948- ... **CLC 13, 66**
See also BEST 90:4; CA 61-64; CANR 14,
41; DLB 14; MTCW

**McFadden, David** 1940- .......... **CLC 48**
See also CA 104; DLB 60

**McFarland, Dennis** 1950- ......... **CLC 65**

**McGahern, John** 1934- ........ **CLC 5, 9, 48**
See also CA 17-20R; CANR 29; DLB 14;
MTCW

**McGinley, Patrick (Anthony)**
1937- ...................... **CLC 41**
See also CA 120; 127

**McGinley, Phyllis** 1905-1978 ...... **CLC 14**
See also CA 9-12R; 77-80; CANR 19;
DLB 11, 48; SATA 2, 24, 44

**McGinniss, Joe** 1942- ............. **CLC 32**
See also AITN 2; BEST 89:2; CA 25-28R;
CANR 26

**McGivern, Maureen Daly**
See Daly, Maureen

**McGrath, Patrick** 1950- ........... **CLC 55**
See also CA 136

**McGrath, Thomas (Matthew)**
1916-1990 ............... **CLC 28, 59**
See also CA 9-12R; 132; CANR 6, 33;
MTCW; SATA 41; SATA-Obit 66

**McGuane, Thomas (Francis III)**
1939- ............... **CLC 3, 7, 18, 45**
See also AITN 2; CA 49-52; CANR 5, 24;
DLB 2; DLBY 80; MTCW

**McGuckian, Medbh** 1950- ......... **CLC 48**
See also CA 143; DLB 40

**McHale, Tom** 1942(?)-1982 ....... **CLC 3, 5**
See also AITN 1; CA 77-80; 106

**McIlvanney, William** 1936- ........ **CLC 42**
See also CA 25-28R; DLB 14

**McIlwraith, Maureen Mollie Hunter**
See Hunter, Mollie
See also SATA 2

**McInerney, Jay** 1955- ............ **CLC 34**
See also CA 116; 123

**McIntyre, Vonda N(eel)** 1948- ..... **CLC 18**
See also CA 81-84; CANR 17, 34; MTCW

**McKay, Claude** ..... **TCLC 7, 41; BLC; PC 2**
See also McKay, Festus Claudius
See also DLB 4, 45, 51, 117

**McKay, Festus Claudius**　1889-1948
　See McKay, Claude
　See also BW 1; CA 104; 124; DA; MTCW;
　　WLC

**McKuen, Rod**　1933-. . . . . . . . . . . . **CLC 1, 3**
　See also AITN 1; CA 41-44R; CANR 40

**McLoughlin, R. B.**
　See Mencken, H(enry) L(ouis)

**McLuhan, (Herbert) Marshall**
　　1911-1980. . . . . . . . . . . . . . . **CLC 37, 83**
　See also CA 9-12R; 102; CANR 12, 34;
　　DLB 88; MTCW

**McMillan, Terry (L.)**　1951-. . . . . **CLC 50, 61**
　See also CA 140

**McMurtry, Larry (Jeff)**
　　1936-. . . . . . . . . **CLC 2, 3, 7, 11, 27, 44**
　See also AITN 2; BEST 89:2; CA 5-8R;
　　CANR 19, 43; CDALB 1968-1988;
　　DLB 2; DLBY 80, 87; MTCW

**McNally, T. M.**　1961-. . . . . . . . . . . **CLC 82**

**McNally, Terrence**　1939-. . . . . . **CLC 4, 7, 41**
　See also CA 45-48; CANR 2; DLB 7

**McNamer, Deirdre**　1950-. . . . . . . . . **CLC 70**

**McNeile, Herman Cyril**　1888-1937
　See Sapper
　See also DLB 77

**McPhee, John (Angus)**　1931-. . . . . . **CLC 36**
　See also BEST 90:1; CA 65-68; CANR 20;
　　MTCW

**McPherson, James Alan**
　　1943-. . . . . . . . . . . . . . . . . . . **CLC 19, 77**
　See also BW; CA 25-28R; CAAS 17;
　　CANR 24; DLB 38; MTCW

**McPherson, William (Alexander)**
　　1933-. . . . . . . . . . . . . . . . . . . . . **CLC 34**
　See also CA 69-72; CANR 28

**McSweeney, Kerry**. . . . . . . . . . . . . . **CLC 34**

**Mead, Margaret**　1901-1978. . . . . . . . **CLC 37**
　See also AITN 1; CA 1-4R; 81-84;
　　CANR 4; MTCW; SATA 20

**Meaker, Marijane (Agnes)**　1927-
　See Kerr, M. E.
　See also CA 107; CANR 37; JRDA;
　　MAICYA; MTCW; SATA 20, 61

**Medoff, Mark (Howard)**　1940-. . . **CLC 6, 23**
　See also AITN 1; CA 53-56; CANR 5;
　　DLB 7

**Medvedev, P. N.**
　See Bakhtin, Mikhail Mikhailovich

**Meged, Aharon**
　See Megged, Aharon

**Meged, Aron**
　See Megged, Aharon

**Megged, Aharon**　1920-. . . . . . . . . . . . **CLC 9**
　See also CA 49-52; CAAS 13; CANR 1

**Mehta, Ved (Parkash)**　1934-. . . . . . . **CLC 37**
　See also CA 1-4R; CANR 2, 23; MTCW

**Melanter**
　See Blackmore, R(ichard) D(oddridge)

**Melikow, Loris**
　See Hofmannsthal, Hugo von

**Melmoth, Sebastian**
　See Wilde, Oscar (Fingal O'Flahertie Wills)

**Meltzer, Milton**　1915-. . . . . . . . . . . **CLC 26**
　See also AAYA 8; CA 13-16R; CANR 38;
　　CLR 13; DLB 61; JRDA; MAICYA;
　　SAAS 1; SATA 1, 50

**Melville, Herman**
　　1819-1891. . . . **NCLC 3, 12, 29, 45; DA;
　　　　　　　　　　　　　　　SSC 1; WLC**
　See also CDALB 1640-1865; DLB 3, 74;
　　SATA 59

**Menander**
　　c. 342B.C.-c. 292B.C.. . . . **CMLC 9; DC 3**

**Mencken, H(enry) L(ouis)**
　　1880-1956. . . . . . . . . . . . . . . . . **TCLC 13**
　See also Hatteras, Owen
　See also CA 105; 125; CDALB 1917-1929;
　　DLB 11, 29, 63, 137; MTCW

**Mercer, David**　1928-1980. . . . . . . . . . **CLC 5**
　See also CA 9-12R; 102; CANR 23;
　　DLB 13; MTCW

**Merchant, Paul**
　See Ellison, Harlan

**Meredith, George**　1828-1909. . . **TCLC 17, 43**
　See also CA 117; CDBLB 1832-1890;
　　DLB 18, 35, 57

**Meredith, William (Morris)**
　　1919-. . . . . . . . . . . . . . **CLC 4, 13, 22, 55**
　See also CA 9-12R; CAAS 14; CANR 6, 40;
　　DLB 5

**Merezhkovsky, Dmitry Sergeyevich**
　　1865-1941. . . . . . . . . . . . . . . . . **TCLC 29**

**Merimee, Prosper**
　　1803-1870. . . . . . . . . . . . **NCLC 6; SSC 7**
　See also DLB 119

**Merkin, Daphne**　1954-. . . . . . . . . . . **CLC 44**
　See also CA 123

**Merlin, Arthur**
　See Blish, James (Benjamin)

**Merrill, James (Ingram)**
　　1926-. . . . . . . . **CLC 2, 3, 6, 8, 13, 18, 34**
　See also CA 13-16R; CANR 10; DLB 5;
　　DLBY 85; MTCW

**Merriman, Alex**
　See Silverberg, Robert

**Merritt, E. B.**
　See Waddington, Miriam

**Merton, Thomas**
　　1915-1968. . . . . . . . **CLC 1, 3, 11, 34, 83**
　See also CA 5-8R; 25-28R; CANR 22;
　　DLB 48; DLBY 81; MTCW

**Merwin, W(illiam) S(tanley)**
　　1927-. . . . . . **CLC 1, 2, 3, 5, 8, 13, 18, 45**
　See also CA 13-16R; CANR 15; DLB 5;
　　MTCW

**Metcalf, John**　1938-. . . . . . . . . . . . . **CLC 37**
　See also CA 113; DLB 60

**Metcalf, Suzanne**
　See Baum, L(yman) Frank

**Mew, Charlotte (Mary)**
　　1870-1928. . . . . . . . . . . . . . . . . . **TCLC 8**
　See also CA 105; DLB 19, 135

**Mewshaw, Michael**　1943-. . . . . . . . . . **CLC 9**
　See also CA 53-56; CANR 7; DLBY 80

**Meyer, June**
　See Jordan, June

**Meyer, Lynn**
　See Slavitt, David R(ytman)

**Meyer-Meyrink, Gustav**　1868-1932
　See Meyrink, Gustav
　See also CA 117

**Meyers, Jeffrey**　1939-. . . . . . . . . . . **CLC 39**
　See also CA 73-76; DLB 111

**Meynell, Alice (Christina Gertrude Thompson)**
　　1847-1922. . . . . . . . . . . . . . . . . . **TCLC 6**
　See also CA 104; DLB 19, 98

**Meyrink, Gustav**. . . . . . . . . . . . . . . **TCLC 21**
　See also Meyer-Meyrink, Gustav
　See also DLB 81

**Michaels, Leonard**　1933-. . . . . . . . **CLC 6, 25**
　See also CA 61-64; CANR 21; DLB 130;
　　MTCW

**Michaux, Henri**　1899-1984. . . . . . **CLC 8, 19**
　See also CA 85-88; 114

**Michelangelo**　1475-1564. . . . . . . . . . . **LC 12**

**Michelet, Jules**　1798-1874. . . . . . **NCLC 31**

**Michener, James A(lbert)**
　　1907(?)-. . . . . . . . . . **CLC 1, 5, 11, 29, 60**
　See also AITN 1; BEST 90:1; CA 5-8R;
　　CANR 21; DLB 6; MTCW

**Mickiewicz, Adam**　1798-1855. . . . . **NCLC 3**

**Middleton, Christopher**　1926-. . . . . . **CLC 13**
　See also CA 13-16R; CANR 29; DLB 40

**Middleton, Stanley**　1919-. . . . . . . . **CLC 7, 38**
　See also CA 25-28R; CANR 21; DLB 14

**Migueis, Jose Rodrigues**　1901-. . . . . **CLC 10**

**Mikszath, Kalman**　1847-1910. . . . . **TCLC 31**

**Miles, Josephine**
　　1911-1985. . . . . . . . **CLC 1, 2, 14, 34, 39**
　See also CA 1-4R; 116; CANR 2; DLB 48

**Militant**
　See Sandburg, Carl (August)

**Mill, John Stuart**　1806-1873. . . . . **NCLC 11**
　See also CDBLB 1832-1890; DLB 55

**Millar, Kenneth**　1915-1983. . . . . . . . **CLC 14**
　See also Macdonald, Ross
　See also CA 9-12R; 110; CANR 16; DLB 2;
　　DLBD 6; DLBY 83; MTCW

**Millay, E. Vincent**
　See Millay, Edna St. Vincent

**Millay, Edna St. Vincent**
　　1892-1950. . . . . . **TCLC 4, 49; DA; PC 6**
　See also CA 104; 130; CDALB 1917-1929;
　　DLB 45; MTCW

**Miller, Arthur**
　　1915-. . . . **CLC 1, 2, 6, 10, 15, 26, 47, 78;
　　　　　　　　　　　　　　　DA; DC 1; WLC**
　See also AITN 1; CA 1-4R; CABS 3;
　　CANR 2, 30; CDALB 1941-1968; DLB 7;
　　MTCW

**Miller, Henry (Valentine)**
　　1891-1980. . . . . . **CLC 1, 2, 4, 9, 14, 43;
　　　　　　　　　　　　　　　DA; WLC**
　See also CA 9-12R; 97-100; CANR 33;
　　CDALB 1929-1941; DLB 4, 9; DLBY 80;
　　MTCW

**Miller, Jason**　1939(?)-. . . . . . . . . . . . . **CLC 2**
　See also AITN 1; CA 73-76; DLB 7

**Miller, Sue**　1943-. . . . . . . . . . . . . . . **CLC 44**
　See also BEST 90:3; CA 139

Miller, Walter M(ichael, Jr.)
1923- ..................... **CLC 4, 30**
See also CA 85-88; DLB 8

Millett, Kate 1934-............. **CLC 67**
See also AITN 1; CA 73-76; CANR 32;
MTCW

Millhauser, Steven 1943-....... **CLC 21, 54**
See also CA 110; 111; DLB 2

Millin, Sarah Gertrude 1889-1968 .. **CLC 49**
See also CA 102; 93-96

Milne, A(lan) A(lexander)
1882-1956 ................... **TCLC 6**
See also CA 104; 133; CLR 1, 26; DLB 10,
77, 100; MAICYA; MTCW; YABC 1

Milner, Ron(ald) 1938-....... **CLC 56; BLC**
See also AITN 1; BW; CA 73-76;
CANR 24; DLB 38; MTCW

Milosz, Czeslaw
1911- ... **CLC 5, 11, 22, 31, 56, 82; PC 8**
See also CA 81-84; CANR 23; MTCW

Milton, John 1608-1674... **LC 9; DA; WLC**
See also CDBLB 1660-1789; DLB 131

Minehaha, Cornelius
See Wedekind, (Benjamin) Frank(lin)

Miner, Valerie 1947- ............. **CLC 40**
See also CA 97-100

Minimo, Duca
See D'Annunzio, Gabriele

Minot, Susan 1956- ............. **CLC 44**
See also CA 134

Minus, Ed 1938-................. **CLC 39**

Miranda, Javier
See Bioy Casares, Adolfo

Miro (Ferrer), Gabriel (Francisco Victor)
1879-1930 ................... **TCLC 5**
See also CA 104

Mishima, Yukio
....... **CLC 2, 4, 6, 9, 27; DC 1; SSC 4**
See also Hiraoka, Kimitake

Mistral, Frederic 1830-1914 ..... **TCLC 51**
See also CA 122

Mistral, Gabriela............ **TCLC 2; HLC**
See also Godoy Alcayaga, Lucila

Mistry, Rohinton 1952-........... **CLC 71**
See also CA 141

Mitchell, Clyde
See Ellison, Harlan; Silverberg, Robert

Mitchell, James Leslie 1901-1935
See Gibbon, Lewis Grassic
See also CA 104; DLB 15

Mitchell, Joni 1943-............. **CLC 12**
See also CA 112

Mitchell, Margaret (Munnerlyn)
1900-1949 ................. **TCLC 11**
See also CA 109; 125; DLB 9; MTCW

Mitchell, Peggy
See Mitchell, Margaret (Munnerlyn)

Mitchell, S(ilas) Weir 1829-1914 .. **TCLC 36**

Mitchell, W(illiam) O(rmond)
1914-....................... **CLC 25**
See also CA 77-80; CANR 15, 43; DLB 88

Mitford, Mary Russell 1787-1855.. **NCLC 4**
See also DLB 110, 116

Mitford, Nancy 1904-1973........ **CLC 44**
See also CA 9-12R

Miyamoto, Yuriko 1899-1951 ..... **TCLC 37**

Mo, Timothy (Peter) 1950(?)-..... **CLC 46**
See also CA 117; MTCW

Modarressi, Taghi (M.) 1931-...... **CLC 44**
See also CA 121; 134

Modiano, Patrick (Jean) 1945-..... **CLC 18**
See also CA 85-88; CANR 17, 40; DLB 83

Moerck, Paal
See Roelvaag, O(le) E(dvart)

Mofolo, Thomas (Mokopu)
1875(?)-1948 ........... **TCLC 22; BLC**
See also CA 121

Mohr, Nicholasa 1935-...... **CLC 12; HLC**
See also AAYA 8; CA 49-52; CANR 1, 32;
CLR 22; HW; JRDA; SAAS 8; SATA 8

Mojtabai, A(nn) G(race)
1938-................ **CLC 5, 9, 15, 29**
See also CA 85-88

Moliere 1622-1673 ...... **LC 10; DA; WLC**

Molin, Charles
See Mayne, William (James Carter)

Molnar, Ferenc 1878-1952....... **TCLC 20**
See also CA 109

Momaday, N(avarre) Scott
1934-................. **CLC 2, 19; DA**
See also AAYA 11; CA 25-28R; CANR 14,
34; MTCW; SATA 30, 48

Monette, Paul 1945-............. **CLC 82**
See also CA 139

Monroe, Harriet 1860-1936...... **TCLC 12**
See also CA 109; DLB 54, 91

Monroe, Lyle
See Heinlein, Robert A(nson)

Montagu, Elizabeth 1917-........ **NCLC 7**
See also CA 9-12R

Montagu, Mary (Pierrepont) Wortley
1689-1762 ................... **LC 9**
See also DLB 95, 101

Montagu, W. H.
See Coleridge, Samuel Taylor

Montague, John (Patrick)
1929-................... **CLC 13, 46**
See also CA 9-12R; CANR 9; DLB 40;
MTCW

Montaigne, Michel (Eyquem) de
1533-1592 .......... **LC 8; DA; WLC**

Montale, Eugenio 1896-1981... **CLC 7, 9, 18**
See also CA 17-20R; 104; CANR 30;
DLB 114; MTCW

Montesquieu, Charles-Louis de Secondat
1689-1755 ................... **LC 7**

Montgomery, (Robert) Bruce 1921-1978
See Crispin, Edmund
See also CA 104

Montgomery, L(ucy) M(aud)
1874-1942 ................... **TCLC 51**
See also AAYA 12; CA 108; 137; CLR 8;
DLB 92; JRDA; MAICYA; YABC 1

Montgomery, Marion H., Jr. 1925-.. **CLC 7**
See also AITN 1; CA 1-4R; CANR 3;
DLB 6

Montgomery, Max
See Davenport, Guy (Mattison, Jr.)

Montherlant, Henry (Milon) de
1896-1972 ............. **CLC 8, 19**
See also CA 85-88; 37-40R; DLB 72;
MTCW

Monty Python................... **CLC 21**
See also Chapman, Graham; Cleese, John
(Marwood); Gilliam, Terry (Vance); Idle,
Eric; Jones, Terence Graham Parry; Palin,
Michael (Edward)
See also AAYA 7

Moodie, Susanna (Strickland)
1803-1885 ............. **NCLC 14**
See also DLB 99

Mooney, Edward 1951-........... **CLC 25**
See also CA 130

Mooney, Ted
See Mooney, Edward

Moorcock, Michael (John)
1939-................. **CLC 5, 27, 58**
See also CA 45-48; CAAS 5; CANR 2, 17,
38; DLB 14; MTCW

Moore, Brian
1921-......... **CLC 1, 3, 5, 7, 8, 19, 32**
See also CA 1-4R; CANR 1, 25, 42; MTCW

Moore, Edward
See Muir, Edwin

Moore, George Augustus
1852-1933 ................. **TCLC 7**
See also CA 104; DLB 10, 18, 57, 135

Moore, Lorrie .............. **CLC 39, 45, 68**
See also Moore, Marie Lorena

Moore, Marianne (Craig)
1887-1972 .... **CLC 1, 2, 4, 8, 10, 13, 19,
47; DA; PC 4**
See also CA 1-4R; 33-36R; CANR 3;
CDALB 1929-1941; DLB 45; DLBD 7;
MTCW; SATA 20

Moore, Marie Lorena 1957-
See Moore, Lorrie
See also CA 116; CANR 39

Moore, Thomas 1779-1852........ **NCLC 6**
See also DLB 96

Morand, Paul 1888-1976.......... **CLC 41**
See also CA 69-72; DLB 65

Morante, Elsa 1918-1985........ **CLC 8, 47**
See also CA 85-88; 117; CANR 35; MTCW

Moravia, Alberto....... **CLC 2, 7, 11, 27, 46**
See also Pincherle, Alberto

More, Hannah 1745-1833 ....... **NCLC 27**
See also DLB 107, 109, 116

More, Henry 1614-1687............. **LC 9**
See also DLB 126

More, Sir Thomas 1478-1535 ....... **LC 10**

Moreas, Jean.................... **TCLC 18**
See also Papadiamantopoulos, Johannes

Morgan, Berry 1919-............. **CLC 6**
See also CA 49-52; DLB 6

Morgan, Claire
See Highsmith, (Mary) Patricia

Morgan, Edwin (George) 1920-..... **CLC 31**
See also CA 5-8R; CANR 3, 43; DLB 27

Nabokov, Vladimir (Vladimirovich)
1899-1977 ..... **CLC 1, 2, 3, 6, 8, 11, 15,
23, 44, 46, 64; DA; SSC 11; WLC**
See also CA 5-8R; 69-72; CANR 20;
CDALB 1941-1968; DLB 2; DLBD 3;
DLBY 80, 91; MTCW

Nagai Kafu...................... **TCLC 51**
See also Nagai Sokichi

Nagai Sokichi   1879-1959
See Nagai Kafu
See also CA 117

Nagy, Laszlo   1925-1978............ **CLC 7**
See also CA 129; 112

Naipaul, Shiva(dhar Srinivasa)
1945-1985 ............... **CLC 32, 39**
See also CA 110; 112; 116; CANR 33;
DLBY 85; MTCW

Naipaul, V(idiadhar) S(urajprasad)
1932- ....... **CLC 4, 7, 9, 13, 18, 37**
See also CA 1-4R; CANR 1, 33;
CDBLB 1960 to Present; DLB 125;
DLBY 85; MTCW

Nakos, Lilika   1899(?)- ............ **CLC 29**

Narayan, R(asipuram) K(rishnaswami)
1906- ............ **CLC 7, 28, 47**
See also CA 81-84; CANR 33; MTCW;
SATA 62

Nash, (Frediric) Ogden   1902-1971 .. **CLC 23**
See also CA 13-14; 29-32R; CANR 34;
CAP 1; DLB 11; MAICYA; MTCW;
SATA 2, 46

Nathan, Daniel
See Dannay, Frederic

Nathan, George Jean   1882-1958 ... **TCLC 18**
See also Hatteras, Owen
See also CA 114; DLB 137

Natsume, Kinnosuke   1867-1916
See Natsume, Soseki
See also CA 104

Natsume, Soseki .............. **TCLC 2, 10**
See also Natsume, Kinnosuke

Natti, (Mary) Lee   1919-
See Kingman, Lee
See also CA 5-8R; CANR 2

Naylor, Gloria
1950- ........... **CLC 28, 52; BLC; DA**
See also AAYA 6; BW; CA 107; CANR 27;
MTCW

Neihardt, John Gneisenau
1881-1973 ................... **CLC 32**
See also CA 13-14; CAP 1; DLB 9, 54

Nekrasov, Nikolai Alekseevich
1821-1878 ................. **NCLC 11**

Nelligan, Emile   1879-1941....... **TCLC 14**
See also CA 114; DLB 92

Nelson, Willie   1933-.............. **CLC 17**
See also CA 107

Nemerov, Howard (Stanley)
1920-1991 ............. **CLC 2, 6, 9, 36**
See also CA 1-4R; 134; CABS 2; CANR 1,
27; DLB 6; DLBY 83; MTCW

Neruda, Pablo
1904-1973 ..... **CLC 1, 2, 5, 7, 9, 28, 62;
DA; HLC; PC 4; WLC**
See also CA 19-20; 45-48; CAP 2; HW;
MTCW

Nerval, Gerard de   1808-1855...... **NCLC 1**

Nervo, (Jose) Amado (Ruiz de)
1870-1919 .................. **TCLC 11**
See also CA 109; 131; HW

Nessi, Pio Baroja y
See Baroja (y Nessi), Pio

Nestroy, Johann   1801-1862...... **NCLC 42**
See also DLB 133

Neufeld, John (Arthur)   1938- ...... **CLC 17**
See also AAYA 11; CA 25-28R; CANR 11,
37; MAICYA; SAAS 3; SATA 6

Neville, Emily Cheney   1919-....... **CLC 12**
See also CA 5-8R; CANR 3, 37; JRDA;
MAICYA; SAAS 2; SATA 1

Newbound, Bernard Slade   1930-
See Slade, Bernard
See also CA 81-84

Newby, P(ercy) H(oward)
1918- .................... **CLC 2, 13**
See also CA 5-8R; CANR 32; DLB 15;
MTCW

Newlove, Donald   1928- ............ **CLC 6**
See also CA 29-32R; CANR 25

Newlove, John (Herbert)   1938-..... **CLC 14**
See also CA 21-24R; CANR 9, 25

Newman, Charles   1938-.......... **CLC 2, 8**
See also CA 21-24R

Newman, Edwin (Harold)   1919- .... **CLC 14**
See also AITN 1; CA 69-72; CANR 5

Newman, John Henry
1801-1890 ................. **NCLC 38**
See also DLB 18, 32, 55

Newton, Suzanne   1936-........... **CLC 35**
See also CA 41-44R; CANR 14; JRDA;
SATA 5, 77

Nexo, Martin Andersen
1869-1954 ................. **TCLC 43**

Nezval, Vitezslav   1900-1958 ...... **TCLC 44**
See also CA 123

Ng, Fae Myenne   1957(?)-.......... **CLC 81**

Ngema, Mbongeni   1955- .......... **CLC 57**
See also CA 143

Ngugi, James T(hiong'o)........ **CLC 3, 7, 13**
See also Ngugi wa Thiong'o

Ngugi wa Thiong'o   1938-..... **CLC 36; BLC**
See also Ngugi, James T(hiong'o)
See also BW; CA 81-84; CANR 27;
DLB 125; MTCW

Nichol, B(arrie) P(hillip)
1944-1988 ................... **CLC 18**
See also CA 53-56; DLB 53; SATA 66

Nichols, John (Treadwell)   1940-.... **CLC 38**
See also CA 9-12R; CAAS 2; CANR 6;
DLBY 82

Nichols, Leigh
See Koontz, Dean R(ay)

Nichols, Peter (Richard)
1927- ...................**CLC 5, 36, 65**
See also CA 104; CANR 33; DLB 13;
MTCW

Nicolas, F. R. E.
See Freeling, Nicolas

Niedecker, Lorine   1903-1970.... **CLC 10, 42**
See also CA 25-28; CAP 2; DLB 48

Nietzsche, Friedrich (Wilhelm)
1844-1900 .............. **TCLC 10, 18**
See also CA 107; 121; DLB 129

Nievo, Ippolito   1831-1861 ....... **NCLC 22**

Nightingale, Anne Redmon   1943-
See Redmon, Anne
See also CA 103

Nik.T.O.
See Annensky, Innokenty Fyodorovich

Nin, Anais
1903-1977 ...... **CLC 1, 4, 8, 11, 14, 60;
SSC 10**
See also AITN 2; CA 13-16R; 69-72;
CANR 22; DLB 2, 4; MTCW

Nissenson, Hugh   1933-........... **CLC 4, 9**
See also CA 17-20R; CANR 27; DLB 28

Niven, Larry ..................... **CLC 8**
See also Niven, Laurence Van Cott
See also DLB 8

Niven, Laurence Van Cott   1938-
See Niven, Larry
See also CA 21-24R; CAAS 12; CANR 14,
44; MTCW

Nixon, Agnes Eckhardt   1927-...... **CLC 21**
See also CA 110

Nizan, Paul   1905-1940........... **TCLC 40**
See also DLB 72

Nkosi, Lewis   1936-.......... **CLC 45; BLC**
See also BW; CA 65-68; CANR 27

Nodier, (Jean) Charles (Emmanuel)
1780-1844 ................. **NCLC 19**
See also DLB 119

Nolan, Christopher   1965-.......... **CLC 58**
See also CA 111

Norden, Charles
See Durrell, Lawrence (George)

Nordhoff, Charles (Bernard)
1887-1947 ................. **TCLC 23**
See also CA 108; DLB 9; SATA 23

Norfolk, Lawrence   1963-.......... **CLC 76**
See also CA 144

Norman, Marsha   1947- ........... **CLC 28**
See also CA 105; CABS 3; CANR 41;
DLBY 84

Norris, Benjamin Franklin, Jr.
1870-1902 ................. **TCLC 24**
See also Norris, Frank
See also CA 110

Norris, Frank
See Norris, Benjamin Franklin, Jr.
See also CDALB 1865-1917; DLB 12, 71

Norris, Leslie   1921- .............. **CLC 14**
See also CA 11-12; CANR 14; CAP 1;
DLB 27

North, Andrew
See Norton, Andre

North, Anthony
See Koontz, Dean R(ay)

North, Captain George
See Stevenson, Robert Louis (Balfour)

North, Milou
See Erdrich, Louise

Northrup, B. A.
See Hubbard, L(afayette) Ron(ald)

**Paulding, James Kirke** 1778-1860.. **NCLC 2**
See also DLB 3, 59, 74

**Paulin, Thomas Neilson** 1949-
See Paulin, Tom
See also CA 123; 128

**Paulin, Tom**................ **CLC 37**
See also Paulin, Thomas Neilson
See also DLB 40

**Paustovsky, Konstantin (Georgievich)**
1892-1968 ................. **CLC 40**
See also CA 93-96; 25-28R

**Pavese, Cesare** 1908-1950 ........ **TCLC 3**
See also CA 104; DLB 128

**Pavic, Milorad** 1929-............. **CLC 60**
See also CA 136

**Payne, Alan**
See Jakes, John (William)

**Paz, Gil**
See Lugones, Leopoldo

**Paz, Octavio**
1914- ....... **CLC 3, 4, 6, 10, 19, 51, 65;**
**DA; HLC; PC 1; WLC**
See also CA 73-76; CANR 32; DLBY 90;
HW; MTCW

**Peacock, Molly** 1947-............. **CLC 60**
See also CA 103; DLB 120

**Peacock, Thomas Love**
1785-1866 ................. **NCLC 22**
See also DLB 96, 116

**Peake, Mervyn** 1911-1968...... **CLC 7, 54**
See also CA 5-8R; 25-28R; CANR 3;
DLB 15; MTCW; SATA 23

**Pearce, Philippa** ................. **CLC 21**
See also Christie, (Ann) Philippa
See also CLR 9; MAICYA; SATA 1, 67

**Pearl, Eric**
See Elman, Richard

**Pearson, T(homas) R(eid)** 1956- .... **CLC 39**
See also CA 120; 130

**Peck, Dale** 1968(?)- .............. **CLC 81**

**Peck, John** 1941- ................. **CLC 3**
See also CA 49-52; CANR 3

**Peck, Richard (Wayne)** 1934- ...... **CLC 21**
See also AAYA 1; CA 85-88; CANR 19,
38; JRDA; MAICYA; SAAS 2; SATA 18,
55

**Peck, Robert Newton** 1928-.... **CLC 17; DA**
See also AAYA 3; CA 81-84; CANR 31;
JRDA; MAICYA; SAAS 1; SATA 21, 62

**Peckinpah, (David) Sam(uel)**
1925-1984 ................. **CLC 20**
See also CA 109; 114

**Pedersen, Knut** 1859-1952
See Hamsun, Knut
See also CA 104; 119; MTCW

**Peeslake, Gaffer**
See Durrell, Lawrence (George)

**Peguy, Charles Pierre**
1873-1914 ................. **TCLC 10**
See also CA 107

**Pena, Ramon del Valle y**
See Valle-Inclan, Ramon (Maria) del

**Pendennis, Arthur Esquir**
See Thackeray, William Makepeace

**Penn, William** 1644-1718.......... **LC 25**
See also DLB 24

**Pepys, Samuel**
1633-1703 ........... **LC 11; DA; WLC**
See also CDBLB 1660-1789; DLB 101

**Percy, Walker**
1916-1990 .... **CLC 2, 3, 6, 8, 14, 18, 47,**
**65**
See also CA 1-4R; 131; CANR 1, 23;
DLB 2; DLBY 80, 90; MTCW

**Perec, Georges** 1936-1982 ........ **CLC 56**
See also CA 141; DLB 83

**Pereda (y Sanchez de Porrua), Jose Maria de**
1833-1906 ................. **TCLC 16**
See also CA 117

**Pereda y Porrua, Jose Maria de**
See Pereda (y Sanchez de Porrua), Jose
Maria de

**Peregoy, George Weems**
See Mencken, H(enry) L(ouis)

**Perelman, S(idney) J(oseph)**
1904-1979 ... **CLC 3, 5, 9, 15, 23, 44, 49**
See also AITN 1, 2; CA 73-76; 89-92;
CANR 18; DLB 11, 44; MTCW

**Peret, Benjamin** 1899-1959 ....... **TCLC 20**
See also CA 117

**Peretz, Isaac Loeb** 1851(?)-1915... **TCLC 16**
See also CA 109

**Peretz, Yitzkhok Leibush**
See Peretz, Isaac Loeb

**Perez Galdos, Benito** 1843-1920 ... **TCLC 27**
See also CA 125; HW

**Perrault, Charles** 1628-1703 ......... **LC 2**
See also MAICYA; SATA 25

**Perry, Brighton**
See Sherwood, Robert E(mmet)

**Perse, St.-John** .............. **CLC 4, 11, 46**
See also Leger, (Marie-Rene Auguste) Alexis
Saint-Leger

**Peseenz, Tulio F.**
See Lopez y Fuentes, Gregorio

**Pesetsky, Bette** 1932-............. **CLC 28**
See also CA 133; DLB 130

**Peshkov, Alexei Maximovich** 1868-1936
See Gorky, Maxim
See also CA 105; 141; DA

**Pessoa, Fernando (Antonio Nogueira)**
1888-1935 ............ **TCLC 27; HLC**
See also CA 125

**Peterkin, Julia Mood** 1880-1961.... **CLC 31**
See also CA 102; DLB 9

**Peters, Joan K.** 1945-............. **CLC 39**

**Peters, Robert L(ouis)** 1924-........ **CLC 7**
See also CA 13-16R; CAAS 8; DLB 105

**Petofi, Sandor** 1823-1849........ **NCLC 21**

**Petrakis, Harry Mark** 1923-........ **CLC 3**
See also CA 9-12R; CANR 4, 30

**Petrarch** 1304-1374................. **PC 8**

**Petrov, Evgeny** ................. **TCLC 21**
See also Kataev, Evgeny Petrovich

**Petry, Ann (Lane)** 1908- ...... **CLC 1, 7, 18**
See also BW; CA 5-8R; CAAS 6; CANR 4;
CLR 12; DLB 76; JRDA; MAICYA;
MTCW; SATA 5

**Petursson, Halligrimur** 1614-1674 .... **LC 8**

**Philipson, Morris H.** 1926-........ **CLC 53**
See also CA 1-4R; CANR 4

**Phillips, David Graham**
1867-1911 ................. **TCLC 44**
See also CA 108; DLB 9, 12

**Phillips, Jack**
See Sandburg, Carl (August)

**Phillips, Jayne Anne** 1952- ..... **CLC 15, 33**
See also CA 101; CANR 24; DLBY 80;
MTCW

**Phillips, Richard**
See Dick, Philip K(indred)

**Phillips, Robert (Schaeffer)** 1938-... **CLC 28**
See also CA 17-20R; CAAS 13; CANR 8;
DLB 105

**Phillips, Ward**
See Lovecraft, H(oward) P(hillips)

**Piccolo, Lucio** 1901-1969.......... **CLC 13**
See also CA 97-100; DLB 114

**Pickthall, Marjorie L(owry) C(hristie)**
1883-1922 ................. **TCLC 21**
See also CA 107; DLB 92

**Pico della Mirandola, Giovanni**
1463-1494 ................. **LC 15**

**Piercy, Marge**
1936- ........ **CLC 3, 6, 14, 18, 27, 62**
See also CA 21-24R; CAAS 1; CANR 13,
43; DLB 120; MTCW

**Piers, Robert**
See Anthony, Piers

**Pieyre de Mandiargues, Andre** 1909-1991
See Mandiargues, Andre Pieyre de
See also CA 103; 136; CANR 22

**Pilnyak, Boris** ................... **TCLC 23**
See also Vogau, Boris Andreyevich

**Pincherle, Alberto** 1907-1990 ... **CLC 11, 18**
See also Moravia, Alberto
See also CA 25-28R; 132; CANR 33;
MTCW

**Pinckney, Darryl** 1953-........... **CLC 76**
See also CA 143

**Pindar** 518B.C.-446B.C.......... **CMLC 12**

**Pineda, Cecile** 1942-.............. **CLC 39**
See also CA 118

**Pinero, Arthur Wing** 1855-1934 ... **TCLC 32**
See also CA 110; DLB 10

**Pinero, Miguel (Antonio Gomez)**
1946-1988 ................. **CLC 4, 55**
See also CA 61-64; 125; CANR 29; HW

**Pinget, Robert** 1919- ........ **CLC 7, 13, 37**
See also CA 85-88; DLB 83

**Pink Floyd**...................... **CLC 35**
See also Barrett, (Roger) Syd; Gilmour,
David; Mason, Nick; Waters, Roger;
Wright, Rick

**Pinkney, Edward** 1802-1828 ..... **NCLC 31**

**Pinkwater, Daniel Manus** 1941-.... **CLC 35**
See also Pinkwater, Manus
See also AAYA 1; CA 29-32R; CANR 12,
38; CLR 4; JRDA; MAICYA; SAAS 3;
SATA 46, 76

**Pinkwater, Manus**
    See Pinkwater, Daniel Manus
    See also SATA 8

**Pinsky, Robert**  1940-. . . . . . . **CLC 9, 19, 38**
    See also CA 29-32R; CAAS 4; DLBY 82

**Pinta, Harold**
    See Pinter, Harold

**Pinter, Harold**
    1930- . . . . . **CLC 1, 3, 6, 9, 11, 15, 27, 58,**
                **73; DA; WLC**
    See also CA 5-8R; CANR 33; CDBLB 1960
    to Present; DLB 13; MTCW

**Pirandello, Luigi**
    1867-1936 . . . . . . **TCLC 4, 29; DA; WLC**
    See also CA 104

**Pirsig, Robert M(aynard)**
    1928- . . . . . . . . . . . . . . . . . . . **CLC 4, 6, 73**
    See also CA 53-56; CANR 42; MTCW;
    SATA 39

**Pisarev, Dmitry Ivanovich**
    1840-1868 . . . . . . . . . . . . . . . . **NCLC 25**

**Pix, Mary (Griffith)**  1666-1709 . . . . . . **LC 8**
    See also DLB 80

**Pixerecourt, Guilbert de**
    1773-1844 . . . . . . . . . . . . . . . . **NCLC 39**

**Plaidy, Jean**
    See Hibbert, Eleanor Alice Burford

**Planche, James Robinson**
    1796-1880 . . . . . . . . . . . . . . . . **NCLC 42**

**Plant, Robert**  1948- . . . . . . . . . . . . . **CLC 12**

**Plante, David (Robert)**
    1940- . . . . . . . . . . . . . . **CLC 7, 23, 38**
    See also CA 37-40R; CANR 12, 36;
    DLBY 83; MTCW

**Plath, Sylvia**
    1932-1963 . . . . . **CLC 1, 2, 3, 5, 9, 11, 14,**
                **17, 50, 51, 62; DA; PC 1; WLC**
    See also CA 19-20; CANR 34; CAP 2;
    CDALB 1941-1968; DLB 5, 6; MTCW

**Plato**  428(?)B.C.-348(?)B.C.. . . . **CMLC 8; DA**

**Platonov, Andrei** . . . . . . . . . . . . . . . . **TCLC 14**
    See also Klimentov, Andrei Platonovich

**Platt, Kin**  1911- . . . . . . . . . . . . . . . . . **CLC 26**
    See also AAYA 11; CA 17-20R; CANR 11;
    JRDA; SAAS 17; SATA 21

**Plick et Plock**
    See Simenon, Georges (Jacques Christian)

**Plimpton, George (Ames)**  1927-. . . . . **CLC 36**
    See also AITN 1; CA 21-24R; CANR 32;
    MTCW; SATA 10

**Plomer, William Charles Franklin**
    1903-1973 . . . . . . . . . . . . . . . . **CLC 4, 8**
    See also CA 21-22; CANR 34; CAP 2;
    DLB 20; MTCW; SATA 24

**Plowman, Piers**
    See Kavanagh, Patrick (Joseph)

**Plum, J.**
    See Wodehouse, P(elham) G(renville)

**Plumly, Stanley (Ross)**  1939- . . . . . . **CLC 33**
    See also CA 108; 110; DLB 5

**Plumpe, Friedrich Wilhelm**
    1888-1931 . . . . . . . . . . . . . . . . **TCLC 53**
    See also CA 112

**Poe, Edgar Allan**
    1809-1849 . . . . . **NCLC 1, 16; DA; PC 1;**
                **SSC 1; WLC**
    See also CDALB 1640-1865; DLB 3, 59, 73,
    74; SATA 23

**Poet of Titchfield Street, The**
    See Pound, Ezra (Weston Loomis)

**Pohl, Frederik**  1919- . . . . . . . . . . . . . **CLC 18**
    See also CA 61-64; CAAS 1; CANR 11, 37;
    DLB 8; MTCW; SATA 24

**Poirier, Louis**  1910-
    See Gracq, Julien
    See also CA 122; 126

**Poitier, Sidney**  1927-. . . . . . . . . . . . . **CLC 26**
    See also BW; CA 117

**Polanski, Roman**  1933- . . . . . . . . . . . **CLC 16**
    See also CA 77-80

**Poliakoff, Stephen**  1952- . . . . . . . . . . **CLC 38**
    See also CA 106; DLB 13

**Police, The**. . . . . . . . . . . . . . . . . . . . **CLC 26**
    See also Copeland, Stewart (Armstrong);
    Summers, Andrew James; Sumner,
    Gordon Matthew

**Pollitt, Katha**  1949- . . . . . . . . . . . . . **CLC 28**
    See also CA 120; 122; MTCW

**Pollock, (Mary) Sharon**  1936-. . . . . . **CLC 50**
    See also CA 141; DLB 60

**Pomerance, Bernard**  1940-. . . . . . . . **CLC 13**
    See also CA 101

**Ponge, Francis (Jean Gaston Alfred)**
    1899-1988 . . . . . . . . . . . . . . . . **CLC 6, 18**
    See also CA 85-88; 126; CANR 40

**Pontoppidan, Henrik**  1857-1943 . . . **TCLC 29**

**Poole, Josephine** . . . . . . . . . . . . . . . **CLC 17**
    See also Helyar, Jane Penelope Josephine
    See also SAAS 2; SATA 5

**Popa, Vasko**  1922- . . . . . . . . . . . . . . **CLC 19**
    See also CA 112

**Pope, Alexander**
    1688-1744 . . . . . . . . . . **LC 3; DA; WLC**
    See also CDBLB 1660-1789; DLB 95, 101

**Porter, Connie (Rose)**  1959(?)- . . . . . **CLC 70**
    See also CA 142

**Porter, Gene(va Grace) Stratton**
    1863(?)-1924 . . . . . . . . . . . . . . **TCLC 21**
    See also CA 112

**Porter, Katherine Anne**
    1890-1980 . . . . . . **CLC 1, 3, 7, 10, 13, 15,**
                **27; DA; SSC 4**
    See also AITN 2; CA 1-4R; 101; CANR 1;
    DLB 4, 9, 102; DLBY 80; MTCW;
    SATA 23, 39

**Porter, Peter (Neville Frederick)**
    1929-. . . . . . . . . . . . . . . . . **CLC 5, 13, 33**
    See also CA 85-88; DLB 40

**Porter, William Sydney**  1862-1910
    See Henry, O.
    See also CA 104; 131; CDALB 1865-1917;
    DA; DLB 12, 78, 79; MTCW; YABC 2

**Portillo (y Pacheco), Jose Lopez**
    See Lopez Portillo (y Pacheco), Jose

**Post, Melville Davisson**
    1869-1930 . . . . . . . . . . . . . . . . **TCLC 39**
    See also CA 110

**Potok, Chaim**  1929-. . . . . . . **CLC 2, 7, 14, 26**
    See also AITN 1, 2; CA 17-20R; CANR 19,
    35; DLB 28; MTCW; SATA 33

**Potter, Beatrice**
    See Webb, (Martha) Beatrice (Potter)
    See also MAICYA

**Potter, Dennis (Christopher George)**
    1935- . . . . . . . . . . . . . . . . . . . . **CLC 58**
    See also CA 107; CANR 33; MTCW

**Pound, Ezra (Weston Loomis)**
    1885-1972 . . . . . . **CLC 1, 2, 3, 4, 5, 7, 10,**
                **13, 18, 34, 48, 50; DA; PC 4; WLC**
    See also CA 5-8R; 37-40R; CANR 40;
    CDALB 1917-1929; DLB 4, 45, 63;
    MTCW

**Povod, Reinaldo**  1959-. . . . . . . . . . . **CLC 44**
    See also CA 136

**Powell, Anthony (Dymoke)**
    1905- . . . . . . . . . . **CLC 1, 3, 7, 9, 10, 31**
    See also CA 1-4R; CANR 1, 32;
    CDBLB 1945-1960; DLB 15; MTCW

**Powell, Dawn**  1897-1965 . . . . . . . . . **CLC 66**
    See also CA 5-8R

**Powell, Padgett**  1952-. . . . . . . . . . . . **CLC 34**
    See also CA 126

**Powers, J(ames) F(arl)**
    1917-. . . . . . . . **CLC 1, 4, 8, 57; SSC 4**
    See also CA 1-4R; CANR 2; DLB 130;
    MTCW

**Powers, John J(ames)**  1945-
    See Powers, John R.
    See also CA 69-72

**Powers, John R.** . . . . . . . . . . . . . . . . **CLC 66**
    See also Powers, John J(ames)

**Pownall, David**  1938-. . . . . . . . . . . . **CLC 10**
    See also CA 89-92; CAAS 18; DLB 14

**Powys, John Cowper**
    1872-1963 . . . . . . . . . . . **CLC 7, 9, 15, 46**
    See also CA 85-88; DLB 15; MTCW

**Powys, T(heodore) F(rancis)**
    1875-1953 . . . . . . . . . . . . . . . . . **TCLC 9**
    See also CA 106; DLB 36

**Prager, Emily**  1952-. . . . . . . . . . . . . **CLC 56**

**Pratt, E(dwin) J(ohn)**
    1883(?)-1964 . . . . . . . . . . . . . . . **CLC 19**
    See also CA 141; 93-96; DLB 92

**Premchand**. . . . . . . . . . . . . . . . . . . . **TCLC 21**
    See also Srivastava, Dhanpat Rai

**Preussler, Otfried**  1923-. . . . . . . . . . **CLC 17**
    See also CA 77-80; SATA 24

**Prevert, Jacques (Henri Marie)**
    1900-1977 . . . . . . . . . . . . . . . . . **CLC 15**
    See also CA 77-80; 69-72; CANR 29;
    MTCW; SATA 30

**Prevost, Abbe (Antoine Francois)**
    1697-1763 . . . . . . . . . . . . . . . . . . **LC 1**

**Price, (Edward) Reynolds**
    1933- . . . . . . . **CLC 3, 6, 13, 43, 50, 63**
    See also CA 1-4R; CANR 1, 37; DLB 2

**Price, Richard**  1949- . . . . . . . . . . **CLC 6, 12**
    See also CA 49-52; CANR 3; DLBY 81

**Prichard, Katharine Susannah**
    1883-1969 . . . . . . . . . . . . . . . . . **CLC 46**
    See also CA 11-12; CANR 33; CAP 1;
    MTCW; SATA 66

**Priestley, J(ohn) B(oynton)**
1894-1984 ............ **CLC 2, 5, 9, 34**
See also CA 9-12R; 113; CANR 33;
  CDBLB 1914-1945; DLB 10, 34, 77, 100,
  139; DLBY 84; MTCW

**Prince** 1958(?)- ................. **CLC 35**

**Prince, F(rank) T(empleton)** 1912- .. **CLC 22**
See also CA 101; CANR 43; DLB 20

**Prince Kropotkin**
See Kropotkin, Peter (Aleksieevich)

**Prior, Matthew** 1664-1721 ........... **LC 4**
See also DLB 95

**Pritchard, William H(arrison)**
1932- ....................... **CLC 34**
See also CA 65-68; CANR 23; DLB 111

**Pritchett, V(ictor) S(awdon)**
1900- ....... **CLC 5, 13, 15, 41; SSC 14**
See also CA 61-64; CANR 31; DLB 15,
  139; MTCW

**Private 19022**
See Manning, Frederic

**Probst, Mark** 1925- .............. **CLC 59**
See also CA 130

**Prokosch, Frederic** 1908-1989 .... **CLC 4, 48**
See also CA 73-76; 128; DLB 48

**Prophet, The**
See Dreiser, Theodore (Herman Albert)

**Prose, Francine** 1947- ............. **CLC 45**
See also CA 109; 112

**Proudhon**
See Cunha, Euclides (Rodrigues Pimenta) da

**Proulx, E. Annie** 1935- ........... **CLC 81**

**Proust, (Valentin-Louis-George-Eugene-)**
  **Marcel**
1871-1922 ... **TCLC 7, 13, 33; DA; WLC**
See also CA 104; 120; DLB 65; MTCW

**Prowler, Harley**
See Masters, Edgar Lee

**Prus, Boleslaw** .................. **TCLC 48**
See also Glowacki, Aleksander

**Pryor, Richard (Franklin Lenox Thomas)**
1940- ....................... **CLC 26**
See also CA 122

**Przybyszewski, Stanislaw**
1868-1927 .................. **TCLC 36**
See also DLB 66

**Pteleon**
See Grieve, C(hristopher) M(urray)

**Puckett, Lute**
See Masters, Edgar Lee

**Puig, Manuel**
1932-1990 ... **CLC 3, 5, 10, 28, 65; HLC**
See also CA 45-48; CANR 2, 32; DLB 113;
  HW; MTCW

**Purdy, Al(fred Wellington)**
1918- ............... **CLC 3, 6, 14, 50**
See also CA 81-84; CAAS 17; CANR 42;
  DLB 88

**Purdy, James (Amos)**
1923- ........... **CLC 2, 4, 10, 28, 52**
See also CA 33-36R; CAAS 1; CANR 19;
  DLB 2; MTCW

**Pure, Simon**
See Swinnerton, Frank Arthur

**Pushkin, Alexander (Sergeyevich)**
1799-1837 ...... **NCLC 3, 27; DA; WLC**
See also SATA 61

**P'u Sung-ling** 1640-1715 ............ **LC 3**

**Putnam, Arthur Lee**
See Alger, Horatio, Jr.

**Puzo, Mario** 1920- ......... **CLC 1, 2, 6, 36**
See also CA 65-68; CANR 4, 42; DLB 6;
  MTCW

**Pym, Barbara (Mary Crampton)**
1913-1980 ........... **CLC 13, 19, 37**
See also CA 13-14; 97-100; CANR 13, 34;
  CAP 1; DLB 14; DLBY 87; MTCW

**Pynchon, Thomas (Ruggles, Jr.)**
1937- ..... **CLC 2, 3, 6, 9, 11, 18, 33, 62,**
                **72; DA; SSC 14; WLC**
See also BEST 90:2; CA 17-20R; CANR 22;
  DLB 2; MTCW

**Q**
See Quiller-Couch, Arthur Thomas

**Qian Zhongshu**
See Ch'ien Chung-shu

**Qroll**
See Dagerman, Stig (Halvard)

**Quarrington, Paul (Lewis)** 1953- .... **CLC 65**
See also CA 129

**Quasimodo, Salvatore** 1901-1968 ... **CLC 10**
See also CA 13-16; 25-28R; CAP 1;
  DLB 114; MTCW

**Queen, Ellery** ................... **CLC 3, 11**
See also Dannay, Frederic; Davidson,
  Avram; Lee, Manfred B(ennington);
  Sturgeon, Theodore (Hamilton); Vance,
  John Holbrook

**Queen, Ellery, Jr.**
See Dannay, Frederic; Lee, Manfred
  B(ennington)

**Queneau, Raymond**
1903-1976 ........... **CLC 2, 5, 10, 42**
See also CA 77-80; 69-72; CANR 32;
  DLB 72; MTCW

**Quevedo, Francisco de** 1580-1645 .... **LC 23**

**Quiller-Couch, Arthur Thomas**
1863-1944 .................. **TCLC 53**
See also CA 118; DLB 135

**Quin, Ann (Marie)** 1936-1973 ....... **CLC 6**
See also CA 9-12R; 45-48; DLB 14

**Quinn, Martin**
See Smith, Martin Cruz

**Quinn, Simon**
See Smith, Martin Cruz

**Quiroga, Horacio (Sylvestre)**
1878-1937 ............ **TCLC 20; HLC**
See also CA 117; 131; HW; MTCW

**Quoirez, Francoise** 1935- .......... **CLC 9**
See also Sagan, Francoise
See also CA 49-52; CANR 6, 39; MTCW

**Raabe, Wilhelm** 1831-1910 ....... **TCLC 45**
See also DLB 129

**Rabe, David (William)** 1940- ... **CLC 4, 8, 33**
See also CA 85-88; CABS 3; DLB 7

**Rabelais, Francois**
1483-1553 ........... **LC 5; DA; WLC**

**Rabinovitch, Sholem** 1859-1916
See Aleichem, Sholom
See also CA 104

**Radcliffe, Ann (Ward)** 1764-1823 .. **NCLC 6**
See also DLB 39

**Radiguet, Raymond** 1903-1923 .... **TCLC 29**
See also DLB 65

**Radnoti, Miklos** 1909-1944 ....... **TCLC 16**
See also CA 118

**Rado, James** 1939- ............... **CLC 17**
See also CA 105

**Radvanyi, Netty** 1900-1983
See Seghers, Anna
See also CA 85-88; 110

**Raeburn, John (Hay)** 1941- ........ **CLC 34**
See also CA 57-60

**Ragni, Gerome** 1942-1991 ......... **CLC 17**
See also CA 105; 134

**Rahv, Philip** 1908-1973 ........... **CLC 24**
See also Greenberg, Ivan
See also DLB 137

**Raine, Craig** 1944- ............... **CLC 32**
See also CA 108; CANR 29; DLB 40

**Raine, Kathleen (Jessie)** 1908- ... **CLC 7, 45**
See also CA 85-88; DLB 20; MTCW

**Rainis, Janis** 1865-1929 ......... **TCLC 29**

**Rakosi, Carl** ..................... **CLC 47**
See also Rawley, Callman
See also CAAS 5

**Raleigh, Richard**
See Lovecraft, H(oward) P(hillips)

**Rallentando, H. P.**
See Sayers, Dorothy L(eigh)

**Ramal, Walter**
See de la Mare, Walter (John)

**Ramon, Juan**
See Jimenez (Mantecon), Juan Ramon

**Ramos, Graciliano** 1892-1953 ..... **TCLC 32**

**Rampersad, Arnold** 1941- ......... **CLC 44**
See also CA 127; 133; DLB 111

**Rampling, Anne**
See Rice, Anne

**Ramuz, Charles-Ferdinand**
1878-1947 .................. **TCLC 33**

**Rand, Ayn**
1905-1982 ...... **CLC 3, 30, 44, 79; DA;**
                              **WLC**
See also AAYA 10; CA 13-16R; 105;
  CANR 27; MTCW

**Randall, Dudley (Felker)**
1914- ................... **CLC 1; BLC**
See also BW; CA 25-28R; CANR 23;
  DLB 41

**Randall, Robert**
See Silverberg, Robert

**Ranger, Ken**
See Creasey, John

**Ransom, John Crowe**
1888-1974 ......... **CLC 2, 4, 5, 11, 24**
See also CA 5-8R; 49-52; CANR 6, 34;
  DLB 45, 63; MTCW

**Rao, Raja** 1909- .............. **CLC 25, 56**
See also CA 73-76; MTCW

**Rosenfeld, Samuel** 1896-1963
See Tzara, Tristan
See also CA 89-92

**Rosenthal, M(acha) L(ouis)** 1917-... **CLC 28**
See also CA 1-4R; CAAS 6; CANR 4;
DLB 5; SATA 59

**Ross, Barnaby**
See Dannay, Frederic

**Ross, Bernard L.**
See Follett, Ken(neth Martin)

**Ross, J. H.**
See Lawrence, T(homas) E(dward)

**Ross, Martin**
See Martin, Violet Florence
See also DLB 135

**Ross, (James) Sinclair** 1908-....... **CLC 13**
See also CA 73-76; DLB 88

**Rossetti, Christina (Georgina)**
1830-1894 ... **NCLC 2; DA; PC 7; WLC**
See also DLB 35; MAICYA; SATA 20

**Rossetti, Dante Gabriel**
1828-1882 ........ **NCLC 4; DA; WLC**
See also CDBLB 1832-1890; DLB 35

**Rossner, Judith (Perelman)**
1935- .................. **CLC 6, 9, 29**
See also AITN 2; BEST 90:3; CA 17-20R;
CANR 18; DLB 6; MTCW

**Rostand, Edmond (Eugene Alexis)**
1868-1918 .......... **TCLC 6, 37; DA**
See also CA 104; 126; MTCW

**Roth, Henry** 1906-.......... **CLC 2, 6, 11**
See also CA 11-12; CANR 38; CAP 1;
DLB 28; MTCW

**Roth, Joseph** 1894-1939......... **TCLC 33**
See also DLB 85

**Roth, Philip (Milton)**
1933- ..... **CLC 1, 2, 3, 4, 6, 9, 15, 22,**
**31, 47, 66; DA; WLC**
See also BEST 90:3; CA 1-4R; CANR 1, 22,
36; CDALB 1968-1988; DLB 2, 28;
DLBY 82; MTCW

**Rothenberg, Jerome** 1931-....... **CLC 6, 57**
See also CA 45-48; CANR 1; DLB 5

**Roumain, Jacques (Jean Baptiste)**
1907-1944 ............ **TCLC 19; BLC**
See also BW; CA 117; 125

**Rourke, Constance (Mayfield)**
1885-1941 ................. **TCLC 12**
See also CA 107; YABC 1

**Rousseau, Jean-Baptiste** 1671-1741 ... **LC 9**

**Rousseau, Jean-Jacques**
1712-1778 .......... **LC 14; DA; WLC**

**Roussel, Raymond** 1877-1933 ..... **TCLC 20**
See also CA 117

**Rovit, Earl (Herbert)** 1927-........ **CLC 7**
See also CA 5-8R; CANR 12

**Rowe, Nicholas** 1674-1718.......... **LC 8**
See also DLB 84

**Rowley, Ames Dorrance**
See Lovecraft, H(oward) P(hillips)

**Rowson, Susanna Haswell**
1762(?)-1824 ................ **NCLC 5**
See also DLB 37

**Roy, Gabrielle** 1909-1983....... **CLC 10, 14**
See also CA 53-56; 110; CANR 5; DLB 68;
MTCW

**Rozewicz, Tadeusz** 1921-........ **CLC 9, 23**
See also CA 108; CANR 36; MTCW

**Ruark, Gibbons** 1941- ............. **CLC 3**
See also CA 33-36R; CANR 14, 31;
DLB 120

**Rubens, Bernice (Ruth)** 1923-... **CLC 19, 31**
See also 25-28R; CANR 33; DLB 14;
MTCW

**Rudkin, (James) David** 1936- ...... **CLC 14**
See also CA 89-92; DLB 13

**Rudnik, Raphael** 1933-............. **CLC 7**
See also CA 29-32R

**Ruffian, M.**
See Hasek, Jaroslav (Matej Frantisek)

**Ruiz, Jose Martinez** ............... **CLC 11**
See also Martinez Ruiz, Jose

**Rukeyser, Muriel**
1913-1980 .......... **CLC 6, 10, 15, 27**
See also CA 5-8R; 93-96; CANR 26;
DLB 48; MTCW; SATA 22

**Rule, Jane (Vance)** 1931-......... **CLC 27**
See also CA 25-28R; CAAS 18; CANR 12;
DLB 60

**Rulfo, Juan** 1918-1986.... **CLC 8, 80; HLC**
See also CA 85-88; 118; CANR 26;
DLB 113; HW; MTCW

**Runeberg, Johan** 1804-1877...... **NCLC 41**

**Runyon, (Alfred) Damon**
1884(?)-1946 ................ **TCLC 10**
See also CA 107; DLB 11, 86

**Rush, Norman** 1933-............. **CLC 44**
See also CA 121; 126

**Rushdie, (Ahmed) Salman**
1947- ................ **CLC 23, 31, 55**
See also BEST 89:3; CA 108; 111;
CANR 33; MTCW

**Rushforth, Peter (Scott)** 1945- ..... **CLC 19**
See also CA 101

**Ruskin, John** 1819-1900......... **TCLC 20**
See also CA 114; 129; CDBLB 1832-1890;
DLB 55; SATA 24

**Russ, Joanna** 1937-.............. **CLC 15**
See also CA 25-28R; CANR 11, 31; DLB 8;
MTCW

**Russell, George William** 1867-1935
See A. E.
See also CA 104; CDBLB 1890-1914

**Russell, (Henry) Ken(neth Alfred)**
1927- ...................... **CLC 16**
See also CA 105

**Russell, Willy** 1947-.............. **CLC 60**

**Rutherford, Mark** ................ **TCLC 25**
See also White, William Hale
See also DLB 18

**Ruyslinck, Ward**
See Belser, Reimond Karel Maria de

**Ryan, Cornelius (John)** 1920-1974 ... **CLC 7**
See also CA 69-72; 53-56; CANR 38

**Ryan, Michael** 1946- ............. **CLC 65**
See also CA 49-52; DLBY 82

**Rybakov, Anatoli (Naumovich)**
1911-................... **CLC 23, 53**
See also CA 126; 135

**Ryder, Jonathan**
See Ludlum, Robert

**Ryga, George** 1932-1987 .......... **CLC 14**
See also CA 101; 124; CANR 43; DLB 60

**S. S.**
See Sassoon, Siegfried (Lorraine)

**Saba, Umberto** 1883-1957 ........ **TCLC 33**
See also CA 144; DLB 114

**Sabatini, Rafael** 1875-1950 ....... **TCLC 47**

**Sabato, Ernesto (R.)**
1911- .............. **CLC 10, 23; HLC**
See also CA 97-100; CANR 32; HW;
MTCW

**Sacastru, Martin**
See Bioy Casares, Adolfo

**Sacher-Masoch, Leopold von**
1836(?)-1895 .............. **NCLC 31**

**Sachs, Marilyn (Stickle)** 1927- ..... **CLC 35**
See also AAYA 2; CA 17-20R; CANR 13;
CLR 2; JRDA; MAICYA; SAAS 2;
SATA 3, 68

**Sachs, Nelly** 1891-1970 ........... **CLC 14**
See also CA 17-18; 25-28R; CAP 2

**Sackler, Howard (Oliver)**
1929-1982 ................... **CLC 14**
See also CA 61-64; 108; CANR 30; DLB 7

**Sacks, Oliver (Wolf)** 1933- ........ **CLC 67**
See also CA 53-56; CANR 28; MTCW

**Sade, Donatien Alphonse Francois Comte**
1740-1814 ................. **NCLC 3**

**Sadoff, Ira** 1945-................. **CLC 9**
See also CA 53-56; CANR 5, 21; DLB 120

**Saetone**
See Camus, Albert

**Safire, William** 1929-............. **CLC 10**
See also CA 17-20R; CANR 31

**Sagan, Carl (Edward)** 1934-........ **CLC 30**
See also AAYA 2; CA 25-28R; CANR 11,
36; MTCW; SATA 58

**Sagan, Francoise** ........ **CLC 3, 6, 9, 17, 36**
See also Quoirez, Francoise
See also DLB 83

**Sahgal, Nayantara (Pandit)** 1927-... **CLC 41**
See also CA 9-12R; CANR 11

**Saint, H(arry) F.** 1941- .......... **CLC 50**
See also CA 127

**St. Aubin de Teran, Lisa** 1953-
See Teran, Lisa St. Aubin de
See also CA 118; 126

**Sainte-Beuve, Charles Augustin**
1804-1869 ................. **NCLC 5**

**Saint-Exupery, Antoine (Jean Baptiste Marie**
**Roger) de** 1900-1944 ... **TCLC 2; WLC**
See also CA 108; 132; CLR 10; DLB 72;
MAICYA; MTCW; SATA 20

**St. John, David**
See Hunt, E(verette) Howard, Jr.

**Saint-John Perse**
See Leger, (Marie-Rene Auguste) Alexis
Saint-Leger

**Schneider, Leonard Alfred** 1925-1966
See Bruce, Lenny
See also CA 89-92

**Schnitzler, Arthur**
1862-1931 . . . . . . . . . . **TCLC 4; SSC 15**
See also CA 104; DLB 81, 118

**Schor, Sandra (M.)** 1932(?)-1990 . . . **CLC 65**
See also CA 132

**Schorer, Mark** 1908-1977 . . . . . . . . . **CLC 9**
See also CA 5-8R; 73-76; CANR 7;
DLB 103

**Schrader, Paul (Joseph)** 1946- . . . . . . **CLC 26**
See also CA 37-40R; CANR 41; DLB 44

**Schreiner, Olive (Emilie Albertina)**
1855-1920 . . . . . . . . . . . . . . . . . . **TCLC 9**
See also CA 105; DLB 18

**Schulberg, Budd (Wilson)**
1914- . . . . . . . . . . . . . . . . . . . . **CLC 7, 48**
See also CA 25-28R; CANR 19; DLB 6, 26,
28; DLBY 81

**Schulz, Bruno**
1892-1942 . . . . . . . . **TCLC 5, 51; SSC 13**
See also CA 115; 123

**Schulz, Charles M(onroe)** 1922- . . . . **CLC 12**
See also CA 9-12R; CANR 6; SATA 10

**Schumacher, E(rnst) F(riedrich)**
1911-1977 . . . . . . . . . . . . . . . . . . **CLC 80**
See also CA 81-84; 73-76; CANR 34

**Schuyler, James Marcus**
1923-1991 . . . . . . . . . . . . . . . . **CLC 5, 23**
See also CA 101; 134; DLB 5

**Schwartz, Delmore (David)**
1913-1966 . . . . . . **CLC 2, 4, 10, 45; PC 8**
See also CA 17-18; 25-28R; CANR 35;
CAP 2; DLB 28, 48; MTCW

**Schwartz, Ernst**
See Ozu, Yasujiro

**Schwartz, John Burnham** 1965- . . . . **CLC 59**
See also CA 132

**Schwartz, Lynne Sharon** 1939- . . . . . **CLC 31**
See also CA 103; CANR 44

**Schwartz, Muriel A.**
See Eliot, T(homas) S(tearns)

**Schwarz-Bart, Andre** 1928- . . . . . . . **CLC 2, 4**
See also CA 89-92

**Schwarz-Bart, Simone** 1938- . . . . . . . . **CLC 7**
See also CA 97-100

**Schwob, (Mayer Andre) Marcel**
1867-1905 . . . . . . . . . . . . . . . . . **TCLC 20**
See also CA 117; DLB 123

**Sciascia, Leonardo**
1921-1989 . . . . . . . . . . . . . . **CLC 8, 9, 41**
See also CA 85-88; 130; CANR 35; MTCW

**Scoppettone, Sandra** 1936- . . . . . . . . **CLC 26**
See also AAYA 11; CA 5-8R; CANR 41;
SATA 9

**Scorsese, Martin** 1942- . . . . . . . . . . . **CLC 20**
See also CA 110; 114

**Scotland, Jay**
See Jakes, John (William)

**Scott, Duncan Campbell**
1862-1947 . . . . . . . . . . . . . . . . . . **TCLC 6**
See also CA 104; DLB 92

**Scott, Evelyn** 1893-1963 . . . . . . . . . . **CLC 43**
See also CA 104; 112; DLB 9, 48

**Scott, F(rancis) R(eginald)**
1899-1985 . . . . . . . . . . . . . . . . . . **CLC 22**
See also CA 101; 114; DLB 88

**Scott, Frank**
See Scott, F(rancis) R(eginald)

**Scott, Joanna** 1960- . . . . . . . . . . . . . **CLC 50**
See also CA 126

**Scott, Paul (Mark)** 1920-1978 . . . . **CLC 9, 60**
See also CA 81-84; 77-80; CANR 33;
DLB 14; MTCW

**Scott, Walter**
1771-1832 . . . . . . . . **NCLC 15; DA; WLC**
See also CDBLB 1789-1832; DLB 93, 107,
116; YABC 2

**Scribe, (Augustin) Eugene**
1791-1861 . . . . . . . . . . . . . . . . . **NCLC 16**

**Scrum, R.**
See Crumb, R(obert)

**Scudery, Madeleine de** 1607-1701 . . . . . **LC 2**

**Scum**
See Crumb, R(obert)

**Scumbag, Little Bobby**
See Crumb, R(obert)

**Seabrook, John**
See Hubbard, L(afayette) Ron(ald)

**Sealy, I. Allan** 1951- . . . . . . . . . . . . **CLC 55**

**Search, Alexander**
See Pessoa, Fernando (Antonio Nogueira)

**Sebastian, Lee**
See Silverberg, Robert

**Sebastian Owl**
See Thompson, Hunter S(tockton)

**Sebestyen, Ouida** 1924- . . . . . . . . . . . **CLC 30**
See also AAYA 8; CA 107; CANR 40;
CLR 17; JRDA; MAICYA; SAAS 10;
SATA 39

**Secundus, H. Scriblerus**
See Fielding, Henry

**Sedges, John**
See Buck, Pearl S(ydenstricker)

**Sedgwick, Catharine Maria**
1789-1867 . . . . . . . . . . . . . . . . . **NCLC 19**
See also DLB 1, 74

**Seelye, John** 1931- . . . . . . . . . . . . . . . **CLC 7**

**Seferiades, Giorgos Stylianou** 1900-1971
See Seferis, George
See also CA 5-8R; 33-36R; CANR 5, 36;
MTCW

**Seferis, George** . . . . . . . . . . . . . . . **CLC 5, 11**
See also Seferiades, Giorgos Stylianou

**Segal, Erich (Wolf)** 1937- . . . . . . . **CLC 3, 10**
See also BEST 89:1; CA 25-28R; CANR 20,
36; DLBY 86; MTCW

**Seger, Bob** 1945- . . . . . . . . . . . . . . . **CLC 35**

**Seghers, Anna** . . . . . . . . . . . . . . . . . . **CLC 7**
See also Radvanyi, Netty
See also DLB 69

**Seidel, Frederick (Lewis)** 1936- . . . . . **CLC 18**
See also CA 13-16R; CANR 8; DLBY 84

**Seifert, Jaroslav** 1901-1986 . . . . . **CLC 34, 44**
See also CA 127; MTCW

**Sei Shonagon** c. 966-1017(?) . . . . . . **CMLC 6**

**Selby, Hubert, Jr.** 1928- . . . . . **CLC 1, 2, 4, 8**
See also CA 13-16R; CANR 33; DLB 2

**Selzer, Richard** 1928- . . . . . . . . . . . . **CLC 74**
See also CA 65-68; CANR 14

**Sembene, Ousmane**
See Ousmane, Sembene

**Senancour, Etienne Pivert de**
1770-1846 . . . . . . . . . . . . . . . . . **NCLC 16**
See also DLB 119

**Sender, Ramon (Jose)**
1902-1982 . . . . . . . . . . . . . . **CLC 8; HLC**
See also CA 5-8R; 105; CANR 8; HW;
MTCW

**Seneca, Lucius Annaeus**
4B.C.-65 . . . . . . . . . . . . . . . . . . **CMLC 6**

**Senghor, Leopold Sedar**
1906- . . . . . . . . . . . . . . . . . **CLC 54; BLC**
See also BW; CA 116; 125; MTCW

**Serling, (Edward) Rod(man)**
1924-1975 . . . . . . . . . . . . . . . . . . **CLC 30**
See also AITN 1; CA 65-68; 57-60; DLB 26

**Serna, Ramon Gomez de la**
See Gomez de la Serna, Ramon

**Serpieres**
See Guillevic, (Eugene)

**Service, Robert**
See Service, Robert W(illiam)
See also DLB 92

**Service, Robert W(illiam)**
1874(?)-1958 . . . . . . **TCLC 15; DA; WLC**
See also Service, Robert
See also CA 115; 140; SATA 20

**Seth, Vikram** 1952- . . . . . . . . . . . . . . **CLC 43**
See also CA 121; 127; DLB 120

**Seton, Cynthia Propper**
1926-1982 . . . . . . . . . . . . . . . . . . **CLC 27**
See also CA 5-8R; 108; CANR 7

**Seton, Ernest (Evan) Thompson**
1860-1946 . . . . . . . . . . . . . . . . . **TCLC 31**
See also CA 109; DLB 92; JRDA; SATA 18

**Seton-Thompson, Ernest**
See Seton, Ernest (Evan) Thompson

**Settle, Mary Lee** 1918- . . . . . . . . **CLC 19, 61**
See also CA 89-92; CAAS 1; CANR 44;
DLB 6

**Seuphor, Michel**
See Arp, Jean

**Sevigne, Marie (de Rabutin-Chantal) Marquise
de** 1626-1696 . . . . . . . . . . . . . . **LC 11**

**Sexton, Anne (Harvey)**
1928-1974 . . . . **CLC 2, 4, 6, 8, 10, 15, 53;
DA; PC 2; WLC**
See also CA 1-4R; 53-56; CABS 2;
CANR 3, 36; CDALB 1941-1968; DLB 5;
MTCW; SATA 10

**Shaara, Michael (Joseph Jr.)**
1929-1988 . . . . . . . . . . . . . . . . . . **CLC 15**
See also AITN 1; CA 102; DLBY 83

**Shackleton, C. C.**
See Aldiss, Brian W(ilson)

**Shacochis, Bob** . . . . . . . . . . . . . . . . . **CLC 39**
See also Shacochis, Robert G.

Shacochis, Robert G.  1951-
See Shacochis, Bob
See also CA 119; 124

Shaffer, Anthony (Joshua)  1926-.... **CLC 19**
See also CA 110; 116; DLB 13

Shaffer, Peter (Levin)
1926- .......... **CLC 5, 14, 18, 37, 60**
See also CA 25-28R; CANR 25;
CDBLB 1960 to Present; DLB 13;
MTCW

Shakey, Bernard
See Young, Neil

Shalamov, Varlam (Tikhonovich)
1907(?)-1982 ................ **CLC 18**
See also CA 129; 105

Shamlu, Ahmad  1925- ............ **CLC 10**

Shammas, Anton  1951-........... **CLC 55**

Shange, Ntozake
1948- .... **CLC 8, 25, 38, 74; BLC; DC 3**
See also AAYA 9; BW; CA 85-88; CABS 3;
CANR 27; DLB 38; MTCW

Shanley, John Patrick  1950-....... **CLC 75**
See also CA 128; 133

Shapcott, Thomas William  1935- ... **CLC 38**
See also CA 69-72

Shapiro, Jane..................... **CLC 76**

Shapiro, Karl (Jay)  1913-.. **CLC 4, 8, 15, 53**
See also CA 1-4R; CAAS 6; CANR 1, 36;
DLB 48; MTCW

Sharp, William  1855-1905 ........ **TCLC 39**

Sharpe, Thomas Ridley  1928-
See Sharpe, Tom
See also CA 114; 122

Sharpe, Tom.................... **CLC 36**
See also Sharpe, Thomas Ridley
See also DLB 14

Shaw, Bernard.................. **TCLC 45**
See also Shaw, George Bernard

Shaw, G. Bernard
See Shaw, George Bernard

Shaw, George Bernard
1856-1950 .... **TCLC 3, 9, 21; DA; WLC**
See also Shaw, Bernard
See also CA 104; 128; CDBLB 1914-1945;
DLB 10, 57; MTCW

Shaw, Henry Wheeler
1818-1885 ................ **NCLC 15**
See also DLB 11

Shaw, Irwin  1913-1984...... **CLC 7, 23, 34**
See also AITN 1; CA 13-16R; 112;
CANR 21; CDALB 1941-1968; DLB 6,
102; DLBY 84; MTCW

Shaw, Robert  1927-1978 ........... **CLC 5**
See also AITN 1; CA 1-4R; 81-84;
CANR 4; DLB 13, 14

Shaw, T. E.
See Lawrence, T(homas) E(dward)

Shawn, Wallace  1943- ............ **CLC 41**
See also CA 112

Sheed, Wilfrid (John Joseph)
1930- ................ **CLC 2, 4, 10, 53**
See also CA 65-68; CANR 30; DLB 6;
MTCW

Sheldon, Alice Hastings Bradley
1915(?)-1987
See Tiptree, James, Jr.
See also CA 108; 122; CANR 34; MTCW

Sheldon, John
See Bloch, Robert (Albert)

Shelley, Mary Wollstonecraft (Godwin)
1797-1851 ........ **NCLC 14; DA; WLC**
See also CDBLB 1789-1832; DLB 110, 116;
SATA 29

Shelley, Percy Bysshe
1792-1822 ........ **NCLC 18; DA; WLC**
See also CDBLB 1789-1832; DLB 96, 110

Shepard, Jim  1956-............... **CLC 36**
See also CA 137

Shepard, Lucius  1947-........... **CLC 34**
See also CA 128; 141

Shepard, Sam
1943- ........ **CLC 4, 6, 17, 34, 41, 44**
See also AAYA 1; CA 69-72; CABS 3;
CANR 22; DLB 7; MTCW

Shepherd, Michael
See Ludlum, Robert

Sherburne, Zoa (Morin)  1912-...... **CLC 30**
See also CA 1-4R; CANR 3, 37; MAICYA;
SAAS 18; SATA 3

Sheridan, Frances  1724-1766........ **LC 7**
See also DLB 39, 84

Sheridan, Richard Brinsley
1751-1816 ... **NCLC 5; DA; DC 1; WLC**
See also CDBLB 1660-1789; DLB 89

Sherman, Jonathan Marc.......... **CLC 55**

Sherman, Martin  1941(?)-......... **CLC 19**
See also CA 116; 123

Sherwin, Judith Johnson  1936-... **CLC 7, 15**
See also CA 25-28R; CANR 34

Sherwood, Frances  1940-.......... **CLC 81**

Sherwood, Robert E(mmet)
1896-1955 ................. **TCLC 3**
See also CA 104; DLB 7, 26

Shiel, M(atthew) P(hipps)
1865-1947 ................. **TCLC 8**
See also CA 106

Shiga, Naoya  1883-1971........... **CLC 33**
See also CA 101; 33-36R

Shimazaki Haruki  1872-1943
See Shimazaki Toson
See also CA 105; 134

Shimazaki Toson.................. **TCLC 5**
See also Shimazaki Haruki

Sholokhov, Mikhail (Aleksandrovich)
1905-1984 ................. **CLC 7, 15**
See also CA 101; 112; MTCW; SATA 36

Shone, Patric
See Hanley, James

Shreve, Susan Richards  1939-...... **CLC 23**
See also CA 49-52; CAAS 5; CANR 5, 38;
MAICYA; SATA 41, 46

Shue, Larry  1946-1985............ **CLC 52**
See also CA 117

Shu-Jen, Chou  1881-1936
See Hsun, Lu
See also CA 104

Shulman, Alix Kates  1932-...... **CLC 2, 10**
See also CA 29-32R; CANR 43; SATA 7

Shuster, Joe  1914-............... **CLC 21**

Shute, Nevil..................... **CLC 30**
See also Norway, Nevil Shute

Shuttle, Penelope (Diane)  1947-..... **CLC 7**
See also CA 93-96; CANR 39; DLB 14, 40

Sidney, Mary  1561-1621 .......... **LC 19**

Sidney, Sir Philip  1554-1586.... **LC 19; DA**
See also CDBLB Before 1660

Siegel, Jerome  1914-............. **CLC 21**
See also CA 116

Siegel, Jerry
See Siegel, Jerome

Sienkiewicz, Henryk (Adam Alexander Pius)
1846-1916 .................. **TCLC 3**
See also CA 104; 134

Sierra, Gregorio Martinez
See Martinez Sierra, Gregorio

Sierra, Maria (de la O'LeJarraga) Martinez
See Martinez Sierra, Maria (de la
O'LeJarraga)

Sigal, Clancy  1926-................ **CLC 7**
See also CA 1-4R

Sigourney, Lydia Howard (Huntley)
1791-1865 ................ **NCLC 21**
See also DLB 1, 42, 73

Siguenza y Gongora, Carlos de
1645-1700 .................... **LC 8**

Sigurjonsson, Johann  1880-1919... **TCLC 27**

Sikelianos, Angelos  1884-1951 .... **TCLC 39**

Silkin, Jon  1930- ............. **CLC 2, 6, 43**
See also CA 5-8R; CAAS 5; DLB 27

Silko, Leslie Marmon
1948-................ **CLC 23, 74; DA**
See also CA 115; 122

Sillanpaa, Frans Eemil  1888-1964... **CLC 19**
See also CA 129; 93-96; MTCW

Sillitoe, Alan
1928-.......... **CLC 1, 3, 6, 10, 19, 57**
See also AITN 1; CA 9-12R; CAAS 2;
CANR 8, 26; CDBLB 1960 to Present;
DLB 14, 139; MTCW; SATA 61

Silone, Ignazio  1900-1978 .......... **CLC 4**
See also CA 25-28; 81-84; CANR 34;
CAP 2; MTCW

Silver, Joan Micklin  1935- ........ **CLC 20**
See also CA 114; 121

Silver, Nicholas
See Faust, Frederick (Schiller)

Silverberg, Robert  1935-........... **CLC 7**
See also CA 1-4R; CAAS 3; CANR 1, 20,
36; DLB 8; MAICYA; MTCW; SATA 13

Silverstein, Alvin  1933-........... **CLC 17**
See also CA 49-52; CANR 2; CLR 25;
JRDA; MAICYA; SATA 8, 69

Silverstein, Virginia B(arbara Opshelor)
1937-...................... **CLC 17**
See also CA 49-52; CANR 2; CLR 25;
JRDA; MAICYA; SATA 8, 69

Sim, Georges
See Simenon, Georges (Jacques Christian)

**Simak, Clifford D(onald)**
1904-1988 ................ **CLC 1, 55**
See also CA 1-4R; 125; CANR 1, 35;
DLB 8; MTCW; SATA 56

**Simenon, Georges (Jacques Christian)**
1903-1989 ...... **CLC 1, 2, 3, 8, 18, 47**
See also CA 85-88; 129; CANR 35;
DLB 72; DLBY 89; MTCW

**Simic, Charles** 1938-... **CLC 6, 9, 22, 49, 68**
See also CA 29-32R; CAAS 4; CANR 12,
33; DLB 105

**Simmons, Charles (Paul)** 1924-..... **CLC 57**
See also CA 89-92

**Simmons, Dan** 1948-............. **CLC 44**
See also CA 138

**Simmons, James (Stewart Alexander)**
1933-...................... **CLC 43**
See also CA 105; DLB 40

**Simms, William Gilmore**
1806-1870 ................. **NCLC 3**
See also DLB 3, 30, 59, 73

**Simon, Carly** 1945-.............. **CLC 26**
See also CA 105

**Simon, Claude** 1913-....... **CLC 4, 9, 15, 39**
See also CA 89-92; CANR 33; DLB 83;
MTCW

**Simon, (Marvin) Neil**
1927-.......... **CLC 6, 11, 31, 39, 70**
See also AITN 1; CA 21-24R; CANR 26;
DLB 7; MTCW

**Simon, Paul** 1942(?)-............. **CLC 17**
See also CA 116

**Simonon, Paul** 1956(?)-.......... **CLC 30**
See also Clash, The

**Simpson, Harriette**
See Arnow, Harriette (Louisa) Simpson

**Simpson, Louis (Aston Marantz)**
1923-................ **CLC 4, 7, 9, 32**
See also CA 1-4R; CAAS 4; CANR 1;
DLB 5; MTCW

**Simpson, Mona (Elizabeth)** 1957-... **CLC 44**
See also CA 122; 135

**Simpson, N(orman) F(rederick)**
1919-...................... **CLC 29**
See also CA 13-16R; DLB 13

**Sinclair, Andrew (Annandale)**
1935-...................... **CLC 2, 14**
See also CA 9-12R; CAAS 5; CANR 14, 38;
DLB 14; MTCW

**Sinclair, Emil**
See Hesse, Hermann

**Sinclair, Iain** 1943-.............. **CLC 76**
See also CA 132

**Sinclair, Iain MacGregor**
See Sinclair, Iain

**Sinclair, Mary Amelia St. Clair** 1865(?)-1946
See Sinclair, May
See also CA 104

**Sinclair, May**................. **TCLC 3, 11**
See also Sinclair, Mary Amelia St. Clair
See also DLB 36, 135

**Sinclair, Upton (Beall)**
1878-1968 ...... **CLC 1, 11, 15, 63; DA;**
**WLC**
See also CA 5-8R; 25-28R; CANR 7;
CDALB 1929-1941; DLB 9; MTCW;
SATA 9

**Singer, Isaac**
See Singer, Isaac Bashevis

**Singer, Isaac Bashevis**
1904-1991 .... **CLC 1, 3, 6, 9, 11, 15, 23,**
**38, 69; DA; SSC 3; WLC**
See also AITN 1, 2; CA 1-4R; 134;
CANR 1, 39; CDALB 1941-1968; CLR 1;
DLB 6, 28, 52; DLBY 91; JRDA;
MAICYA; MTCW; SATA 3, 27;
SATA-Obit 68

**Singer, Israel Joshua** 1893-1944 ... **TCLC 33**

**Singh, Khushwant** 1915-.......... **CLC 11**
See also CA 9-12R; CAAS 9; CANR 6

**Sinjohn, John**
See Galsworthy, John

**Sinyavsky, Andrei (Donatevich)**
1925-...................... **CLC 8**
See also CA 85-88

**Sirin, V.**
See Nabokov, Vladimir (Vladimirovich)

**Sissman, L(ouis) E(dward)**
1928-1976 ................. **CLC 9, 18**
See also CA 21-24R; 65-68; CANR 13;
DLB 5

**Sisson, C(harles) H(ubert)** 1914-..... **CLC 8**
See also CA 1-4R; CAAS 3; CANR 3;
DLB 27

**Sitwell, Dame Edith**
1887-1964 ........ **CLC 2, 9, 67; PC 3**
See also CA 9-12R; CANR 35;
CDBLB 1945-1960; DLB 20; MTCW

**Sjoewall, Maj** 1935-............... **CLC 7**
See also CA 65-68

**Sjowall, Maj**
See Sjoewall, Maj

**Skelton, Robin** 1925-.............. **CLC 13**
See also AITN 2; CA 5-8R; CAAS 5;
CANR 28; DLB 27, 53

**Skolimowski, Jerzy** 1938-......... **CLC 20**
See also CA 128

**Skram, Amalie (Bertha)**
1847-1905 ................. **TCLC 25**

**Skvorecky, Josef (Vaclav)**
1924-................. **CLC 15, 39, 69**
See also CA 61-64; CAAS 1; CANR 10, 34;
MTCW

**Slade, Bernard**................. **CLC 11, 46**
See also Newbound, Bernard Slade
See also CAAS 9; DLB 53

**Slaughter, Carolyn** 1946-.......... **CLC 56**
See also CA 85-88

**Slaughter, Frank G(ill)** 1908-...... **CLC 29**
See also AITN 2; CA 5-8R; CANR 5

**Slavitt, David R(ytman)** 1935-.... **CLC 5, 14**
See also CA 21-24R; CAAS 3; CANR 41;
DLB 5, 6

**Slesinger, Tess** 1905-1945 ........ **TCLC 10**
See also CA 107; DLB 102

**Slessor, Kenneth** 1901-1971........ **CLC 14**
See also CA 102; 89-92

**Slowacki, Juliusz** 1809-1849 ..... **NCLC 15**

**Smart, Christopher** 1722-1771........ **LC 3**
See also DLB 109

**Smart, Elizabeth** 1913-1986........ **CLC 54**
See also CA 81-84; 118; DLB 88

**Smiley, Jane (Graves)** 1949-.... **CLC 53, 76**
See also CA 104; CANR 30

**Smith, A(rthur) J(ames) M(arshall)**
1902-1980 ................... **CLC 15**
See also CA 1-4R; 102; CANR 4; DLB 88

**Smith, Betty (Wehner)** 1896-1972... **CLC 19**
See also CA 5-8R; 33-36R; DLBY 82;
SATA 6

**Smith, Charlotte (Turner)**
1749-1806 ................. **NCLC 23**
See also DLB 39, 109

**Smith, Clark Ashton** 1893-1961 .... **CLC 43**
See also CA 143

**Smith, Dave**................. **CLC 22, 42**
See also Smith, David (Jeddie)
See also CAAS 7; DLB 5

**Smith, David (Jeddie)** 1942-
See Smith, Dave
See also CA 49-52; CANR 1

**Smith, Florence Margaret**
1902-1971 ................... **CLC 8**
See also Smith, Stevie
See also CA 17-18; 29-32R; CANR 35;
CAP 2; MTCW

**Smith, Iain Crichton** 1928-....... **CLC 64**
See also CA 21-24R; DLB 40, 139

**Smith, John** 1580(?)-1631 .......... **LC 9**

**Smith, Johnston**
See Crane, Stephen (Townley)

**Smith, Lee** 1944-.............. **CLC 25, 73**
See also CA 114; 119; DLBY 83

**Smith, Martin**
See Smith, Martin Cruz

**Smith, Martin Cruz** 1942-......... **CLC 25**
See also BEST 89:4; CA 85-88; CANR 6,
23, 43

**Smith, Mary-Ann Tirone** 1944-..... **CLC 39**
See also CA 118; 136

**Smith, Patti** 1946- .............. **CLC 12**
See also CA 93-96

**Smith, Pauline (Urmson)**
1882-1959 ................. **TCLC 25**

**Smith, Rosamond**
See Oates, Joyce Carol

**Smith, Sheila Kaye**
See Kaye-Smith, Sheila

**Smith, Stevie** ............. **CLC 3, 8, 25, 44**
See also Smith, Florence Margaret
See also DLB 20

**Smith, Wilbur A(ddison)** 1933-..... **CLC 33**
See also CA 13-16R; CANR 7; MTCW

**Smith, William Jay** 1918- .......... **CLC 6**
See also CA 5-8R; CANR 44; DLB 5;
MAICYA; SATA 2, 68

**Smith, Woodrow Wilson**
See Kuttner, Henry

**Smolenskin, Peretz** 1842-1885.... **NCLC 30**

**Smollett, Tobias (George)** 1721-1771 .. **LC 2**
See also CDBLB 1660-1789; DLB 39, 104

**Snodgrass, W(illiam) D(e Witt)**
1926- ............ **CLC 2, 6, 10, 18, 68**
See also CA 1-4R; CANR 6, 36; DLB 5;
MTCW

**Snow, C(harles) P(ercy)**
1905-1980 ....... **CLC 1, 4, 6, 9, 13, 19**
See also CA 5-8R; 101; CANR 28;
CDBLB 1945-1960; DLB 15, 77; MTCW

**Snow, Frances Compton**
See Adams, Henry (Brooks)

**Snyder, Gary (Sherman)**
1930- ............ **CLC 1, 2, 5, 9, 32**
See also CA 17-20R; CANR 30; DLB 5, 16

**Snyder, Zilpha Keatley** 1927- ...... **CLC 17**
See also CA 9-12R; CANR 38; CLR 31;
JRDA; MAICYA; SAAS 2; SATA 1, 28,
75

**Soares, Bernardo**
See Pessoa, Fernando (Antonio Nogueira)

**Sobh, A.**
See Shamlu, Ahmad

**Sobol, Joshua**.................... **CLC 60**

**Soderberg, Hjalmar** 1869-1941 .... **TCLC 39**

**Sodergran, Edith (Irene)**
See Soedergran, Edith (Irene)

**Soedergran, Edith (Irene)**
1892-1923 .................. **TCLC 31**

**Softly, Edgar**
See Lovecraft, H(oward) P(hillips)

**Softly, Edward**
See Lovecraft, H(oward) P(hillips)

**Sokolov, Raymond** 1941- ........... **CLC 7**
See also CA 85-88

**Solo, Jay**
See Ellison, Harlan

**Sologub, Fyodor** .................. **TCLC 9**
See also Teternikov, Fyodor Kuzmich

**Solomons, Ikey Esquir**
See Thackeray, William Makepeace

**Solomos, Dionysios** 1798-1857 ... **NCLC 15**

**Solwoska, Mara**
See French, Marilyn

**Solzhenitsyn, Aleksandr I(sayevich)**
1918- ...... **CLC 1, 2, 4, 7, 9, 10, 18, 26,**
**34, 78; DA; WLC**
See also AITN 1; CA 69-72; CANR 40;
MTCW

**Somers, Jane**
See Lessing, Doris (May)

**Somerville, Edith** 1858-1949 ...... **TCLC 51**
See also DLB 135

**Somerville & Ross**
See Martin, Violet Florence; Somerville,
Edith

**Sommer, Scott** 1951- ............ **CLC 25**
See also CA 106

**Sondheim, Stephen (Joshua)**
1930- ................. **CLC 30, 39**
See also AAYA 11; CA 103

**Sontag, Susan** 1933-... **CLC 1, 2, 10, 13, 31**
See also CA 17-20R; CANR 25; DLB 2, 67;
MTCW

**Sophocles**
496(?)B.C.-406(?)B.C..... **CMLC 2; DA;**
**DC 1**

**Sorel, Julia**
See Drexler, Rosalyn

**Sorrentino, Gilbert**
1929- ............ **CLC 3, 7, 14, 22, 40**
See also CA 77-80; CANR 14, 33; DLB 5;
DLBY 80

**Soto, Gary** 1952-........ **CLC 32, 80; HLC**
See also AAYA 10; CA 119; 125; DLB 82;
HW; JRDA

**Soupault, Philippe** 1897-1990 ...... **CLC 68**
See also CA 116; 131

**Souster, (Holmes) Raymond**
1921- .................... **CLC 5, 14**
See also CA 13-16R; CAAS 14; CANR 13,
29; DLB 88; SATA 63

**Southern, Terry** 1926- ............. **CLC 7**
See also CA 1-4R; CANR 1; DLB 2

**Southey, Robert** 1774-1843 ....... **NCLC 8**
See also DLB 93, 107, 142; SATA 54

**Southworth, Emma Dorothy Eliza Nevitte**
1819-1899 ................. **NCLC 26**

**Souza, Ernest**
See Scott, Evelyn

**Soyinka, Wole**
1934- ....... **CLC 3, 5, 14, 36, 44; BLC;**
**DA; DC 2; WLC**
See also BW; CA 13-16R; CANR 27, 39;
DLB 125; MTCW

**Spackman, W(illiam) M(ode)**
1905-1990 .................. **CLC 46**
See also CA 81-84; 132

**Spacks, Barry** 1931-............. **CLC 14**
See also CA 29-32R; CANR 33; DLB 105

**Spanidou, Irini** 1946- ............. **CLC 44**

**Spark, Muriel (Sarah)**
1918- ........ **CLC 2, 3, 5, 8, 13, 18, 40;**
**SSC 10**
See also CA 5-8R; CANR 12, 36;
CDBLB 1945-1960; DLB 15, 139; MTCW

**Spaulding, Douglas**
See Bradbury, Ray (Douglas)

**Spaulding, Leonard**
See Bradbury, Ray (Douglas)

**Spence, J. A. D.**
See Eliot, T(homas) S(tearns)

**Spencer, Elizabeth** 1921- ......... **CLC 22**
See also CA 13-16R; CANR 32; DLB 6;
MTCW; SATA 14

**Spencer, Leonard G.**
See Silverberg, Robert

**Spencer, Scott** 1945-............. **CLC 30**
See also CA 113; DLBY 86

**Spender, Stephen (Harold)**
1909- ............. **CLC 1, 2, 5, 10, 41**
See also CA 9-12R; CANR 31;
CDBLB 1945-1960; DLB 20; MTCW

**Spengler, Oswald (Arnold Gottfried)**
1880-1936 .................. **TCLC 25**
See also CA 118

**Spenser, Edmund**
1552(?)-1599 .... **LC 5; DA; PC 8; WLC**
See also CDBLB Before 1660

**Spicer, Jack** 1925-1965 ...... **CLC 8, 18, 72**
See also CA 85-88; DLB 5, 16

**Spiegelman, Art** 1948- ........... **CLC 76**
See also AAYA 10; CA 125; CANR 41

**Spielberg, Peter** 1929- ............. **CLC 6**
See also CA 5-8R; CANR 4; DLBY 81

**Spielberg, Steven** 1947- ........... **CLC 20**
See also AAYA 8; CA 77-80; CANR 32;
SATA 32

**Spillane, Frank Morrison** 1918-
See Spillane, Mickey
See also CA 25-28R; CANR 28; MTCW;
SATA 66

**Spillane, Mickey** ................ **CLC 3, 13**
See also Spillane, Frank Morrison

**Spinoza, Benedictus de** 1632-1677 .... **LC 9**

**Spinrad, Norman (Richard)** 1940-... **CLC 46**
See also CA 37-40R; CAAS 19; CANR 20;
DLB 8

**Spitteler, Carl (Friedrich Georg)**
1845-1924 ................. **TCLC 12**
See also CA 109; DLB 129

**Spivack, Kathleen (Romola Drucker)**
1938- ..................... **CLC 6**
See also CA 49-52

**Spoto, Donald** 1941-............. **CLC 39**
See also CA 65-68; CANR 11

**Springsteen, Bruce (F.)** 1949- ...... **CLC 17**
See also CA 111

**Spurling, Hilary** 1940-............ **CLC 34**
See also CA 104; CANR 25

**Squires, (James) Radcliffe**
1917-1993 ................. **CLC 51**
See also CA 1-4R; 140; CANR 6, 21

**Srivastava, Dhanpat Rai** 1880(?)-1936
See Premchand
See also CA 118

**Stacy, Donald**
See Pohl, Frederik

**Stael, Germaine de**
See Stael-Holstein, Anne Louise Germaine
Necker Baronn
See also DLB 119

**Stael-Holstein, Anne Louise Germaine Necker**
**Baronn** 1766-1817 .......... **NCLC 3**
See also Stael, Germaine de

**Stafford, Jean** 1915-1979... **CLC 4, 7, 19, 68**
See also CA 1-4R; 85-88; CANR 3; DLB 2;
MTCW; SATA 22

**Stafford, William (Edgar)**
1914-1993 .............. **CLC 4, 7, 29**
See also CA 5-8R; 142; CAAS 3; CANR 5,
22; DLB 5

**Staines, Trevor**
See Brunner, John (Kilian Houston)

**Stairs, Gordon**
See Austin, Mary (Hunter)

**Stannard, Martin** 1947-........... **CLC 44**
See also CA 142

**Stanton, Maura** 1946- ............. **CLC 9**
See also CA 89-92; CANR 15; DLB 120

**Tate, (John Orley) Allen**
  1899-1979 .... **CLC 2, 4, 6, 9, 11, 14, 24**
  See also CA 5-8R; 85-88; CANR 32;
  DLB 4, 45, 63; MTCW

**Tate, Ellalice**
  See Hibbert, Eleanor Alice Burford

**Tate, James (Vincent)** 1943- ... **CLC 2, 6, 25**
  See also CA 21-24R; CANR 29; DLB 5

**Tavel, Ronald** 1940- .............. **CLC 6**
  See also CA 21-24R; CANR 33

**Taylor, Cecil Philip** 1929-1981 ..... **CLC 27**
  See also CA 25-28R; 105

**Taylor, Edward** 1642(?)-1729.... **LC 11; DA**
  See also DLB 24

**Taylor, Eleanor Ross** 1920- ........ **CLC 5**
  See also CA 81-84

**Taylor, Elizabeth** 1912-1975 ... **CLC 2, 4, 29**
  See also CA 13-16R; CANR 9; DLB 139;
  MTCW; SATA 13

**Taylor, Henry (Splawn)** 1942- ...... **CLC 44**
  See also CA 33-36R; CAAS 7; CANR 31;
  DLB 5

**Taylor, Kamala (Purnaiya)** 1924-
  See Markandaya, Kamala
  See also CA 77-80

**Taylor, Mildred D.** ................ **CLC 21**
  See also AAYA 10; BW; CA 85-88;
  CANR 25; CLR 9; DLB 52; JRDA;
  MAICYA; SAAS 5; SATA 15, 70

**Taylor, Peter (Hillsman)**
  1917- ...... **CLC 1, 4, 18, 37, 44, 50, 71;
  SSC 10**
  See also CA 13-16R; CANR 9; DLBY 81;
  MTCW

**Taylor, Robert Lewis** 1912- ........ **CLC 14**
  See also CA 1-4R; CANR 3; SATA 10

**Tchekhov, Anton**
  See Chekhov, Anton (Pavlovich)

**Teasdale, Sara** 1884-1933. ......... **TCLC 4**
  See also CA 104; DLB 45; SATA 32

**Tegner, Esaias** 1782-1846. ........ **NCLC 2**

**Teilhard de Chardin, (Marie Joseph) Pierre**
  1881-1955 ................... **TCLC 9**
  See also CA 105

**Temple, Ann**
  See Mortimer, Penelope (Ruth)

**Tennant, Emma (Christina)**
  1937- .................... **CLC 13, 52**
  See also CA 65-68; CAAS 9; CANR 10, 38;
  DLB 14

**Tenneshaw, S. M.**
  See Silverberg, Robert

**Tennyson, Alfred**
  1809-1892 .. **NCLC 30; DA; PC 6; WLC**
  See also CDBLB 1832-1890; DLB 32

**Teran, Lisa St. Aubin de** .......... **CLC 36**
  See also St. Aubin de Teran, Lisa

**Teresa de Jesus, St.** 1515-1582 ...... **LC 18**

**Terkel, Louis** 1912-
  See Terkel, Studs
  See also CA 57-60; CANR 18; MTCW

**Terkel, Studs** .................... **CLC 38**
  See also Terkel, Louis
  See also AITN 1

**Terry, C. V.**
  See Slaughter, Frank G(ill)

**Terry, Megan** 1932- ............. **CLC 19**
  See also CA 77-80; CABS 3; CANR 43;
  DLB 7

**Tertz, Abram**
  See Sinyavsky, Andrei (Donatevich)

**Tesich, Steve** 1943(?)- ......... **CLC 40, 69**
  See also CA 105; DLBY 83

**Teternikov, Fyodor Kuzmich** 1863-1927
  See Sologub, Fyodor
  See also CA 104

**Tevis, Walter** 1928-1984 ......... **CLC 42**
  See also CA 113

**Tey, Josephine** ................. **TCLC 14**
  See also Mackintosh, Elizabeth
  See also DLB 77

**Thackeray, William Makepeace**
  1811-1863 .... **NCLC 5, 14, 22, 43; DA;
  WLC**
  See also CDBLB 1832-1890; DLB 21, 55;
  SATA 23

**Thakura, Ravindranatha**
  See Tagore, Rabindranath

**Tharoor, Shashi** 1956- ............ **CLC 70**
  See also CA 141

**Thelwell, Michael Miles** 1939- ..... **CLC 22**
  See also CA 101

**Theobald, Lewis, Jr.**
  See Lovecraft, H(oward) P(hillips)

**Theodorescu, Ion N.** 1880-1967
  See Arghezi, Tudor
  See also CA 116

**Theriault, Yves** 1915-1983 ........ **CLC 79**
  See also CA 102; DLB 88

**Theroux, Alexander (Louis)**
  1939- .................... **CLC 2, 25**
  See also CA 85-88; CANR 20

**Theroux, Paul (Edward)**
  1941- ........ **CLC 5, 8, 11, 15, 28, 46**
  See also BEST 89:4; CA 33-36R; CANR 20;
  DLB 2; MTCW; SATA 44

**Thesen, Sharon** 1946- ............ **CLC 56**

**Thevenin, Denis**
  See Duhamel, Georges

**Thibault, Jacques Anatole Francois**
  1844-1924
  See France, Anatole
  See also CA 106; 127; MTCW

**Thiele, Colin (Milton)** 1920- ....... **CLC 17**
  See also CA 29-32R; CANR 12, 28;
  CLR 27; MAICYA; SAAS 2; SATA 14,
  72

**Thomas, Audrey (Callahan)**
  1935- .................. **CLC 7, 13, 37**
  See also AITN 2; CA 21-24R; CAAS 19;
  CANR 36; DLB 60; MTCW

**Thomas, D(onald) M(ichael)**
  1935- ................. **CLC 13, 22, 31**
  See also CA 61-64; CAAS 11; CANR 17;
  CDBLB 1960 to Present; DLB 40;
  MTCW

**Thomas, Dylan (Marlais)**
  1914-1953 ... **TCLC 1, 8, 45; DA; PC 2;
  SSC 3; WLC**
  See also CA 104; 120; CDBLB 1945-1960;
  DLB 13, 20, 139; MTCW; SATA 60

**Thomas, (Philip) Edward**
  1878-1917 ................. **TCLC 10**
  See also CA 106; DLB 19

**Thomas, Joyce Carol** 1938- ........ **CLC 35**
  See also AAYA 12; BW; CA 113; 116;
  CLR 19; DLB 33; JRDA; MAICYA;
  MTCW; SAAS 7; SATA 40

**Thomas, Lewis** 1913-1993 ........ **CLC 35**
  See also CA 85-88; 143; CANR 38; MTCW

**Thomas, Paul**
  See Mann, (Paul) Thomas

**Thomas, Piri** 1928- ............... **CLC 17**
  See also CA 73-76; HW

**Thomas, R(onald) S(tuart)**
  1913- .................. **CLC 6, 13, 48**
  See also CA 89-92; CAAS 4; CANR 30;
  CDBLB 1960 to Present; DLB 27;
  MTCW

**Thomas, Ross (Elmore)** 1926- ...... **CLC 39**
  See also CA 33-36R; CANR 22

**Thompson, Francis Clegg**
  See Mencken, H(enry) L(ouis)

**Thompson, Francis Joseph**
  1859-1907 ................. **TCLC 4**
  See also CA 104; CDBLB 1890-1914;
  DLB 19

**Thompson, Hunter S(tockton)**
  1939- .................. **CLC 9, 17, 40**
  See also BEST 89:1; CA 17-20R; CANR 23;
  MTCW

**Thompson, James Myers**
  See Thompson, Jim (Myers)

**Thompson, Jim (Myers)**
  1906-1977(?) ................. **CLC 69**
  See also CA 140

**Thompson, Judith** ................. **CLC 39**

**Thomson, James** 1700-1748........ **LC 16**

**Thomson, James** 1834-1882 ...... **NCLC 18**

**Thoreau, Henry David**
  1817-1862 ..... **NCLC 7, 21; DA; WLC**
  See also CDALB 1640-1865; DLB 1

**Thornton, Hall**
  See Silverberg, Robert

**Thurber, James (Grover)**
  1894-1961 ... **CLC 5, 11, 25; DA; SSC 1**
  See also CA 73-76; CANR 17, 39;
  CDALB 1929-1941; DLB 4, 11, 22, 102;
  MAICYA; MTCW; SATA 13

**Thurman, Wallace (Henry)**
  1902-1934 .............. **TCLC 6; BLC**
  See also BW; CA 104; 124; DLB 51

**Ticheburn, Cheviot**
  See Ainsworth, William Harrison

**Tieck, (Johann) Ludwig**
  1773-1853 ................. **NCLC 5**
  See also DLB 90

**Tiger, Derry**
  See Ellison, Harlan

**Tilghman, Christopher** 1948(?)- ..... **CLC 65**

**Tuohy, John Francis**  1925-
See Tuohy, Frank
See also CA 5-8R; CANR 3

**Turco, Lewis (Putnam)**  1934- ... **CLC 11, 63**
See also CA 13-16R; CANR 24; DLBY 84

**Turgenev, Ivan**
1818-1883 ...... **NCLC 21; DA; SSC 7;**
**WLC**

**Turner, Frederick**  1943-.......... **CLC 48**
See also CA 73-76; CAAS 10; CANR 12,
30; DLB 40

**Tusan, Stan**  1936-................ **CLC 22**
See also CA 105

**Tutu, Desmond M(pilo)**
1931-.................. **CLC 80; BLC**
See also BW; CA 125

**Tutuola, Amos**  1920- ... **CLC 5, 14, 29; BLC**
See also BW; CA 9-12R; CANR 27;
DLB 125; MTCW

**Twain, Mark**
... **TCLC 6, 12, 19, 36, 48; SSC 6; WLC**
See also Clemens, Samuel Langhorne
See also DLB 11, 12, 23, 64, 74

**Tyler, Anne**
1941- ........ **CLC 7, 11, 18, 28, 44, 59**
See also BEST 89:1; CA 9-12R; CANR 11,
33; DLB 6; DLBY 82; MTCW; SATA 7

**Tyler, Royall**  1757-1826.......... **NCLC 3**
See also DLB 37

**Tynan, Katharine**  1861-1931 ....... **TCLC 3**
See also CA 104

**Tytell, John**  1939- .............. **CLC 50**
See also CA 29-32R

**Tyutchev, Fyodor**  1803-1873 ..... **NCLC 34**

**Tzara, Tristan** .................... **CLC 47**
See also Rosenfeld, Samuel

**Uhry, Alfred**  1936-.............. **CLC 55**
See also CA 127; 133

**Ulf, Haerved**
See Strindberg, (Johan) August

**Ulf, Harved**
See Strindberg, (Johan) August

**Ulibarri, Sabine R(eyes)**  1919- ..... **CLC 83**
See also CA 131; DLB 82; HW

**Unamuno (y Jugo), Miguel de**
1864-1936 .... **TCLC 2, 9; HLC; SSC 11**
See also CA 104; 131; DLB 108; HW;
MTCW

**Undercliffe, Errol**
See Campbell, (John) Ramsey

**Underwood, Miles**
See Glassco, John

**Undset, Sigrid**
1882-1949 ........ **TCLC 3; DA; WLC**
See also CA 104; 129; MTCW

**Ungaretti, Giuseppe**
1888-1970 ............. **CLC 7, 11, 15**
See also CA 19-20; 25-28R; CAP 2;
DLB 114

**Unger, Douglas**  1952-............. **CLC 34**
See also CA 130

**Unsworth, Barry (Forster)**  1930-.... **CLC 76**
See also CA 25-28R; CANR 30

**Updike, John (Hoyer)**
1932- ...... **CLC 1, 2, 3, 5, 7, 9, 13, 15,**
**23, 34, 43, 70; DA; SSC 13; WLC**
See also CA 1-4R; CABS 1; CANR 4, 33;
CDALB 1968-1988; DLB 2, 5; DLBD 3;
DLBY 80, 82; MTCW

**Upshaw, Margaret Mitchell**
See Mitchell, Margaret (Munnerlyn)

**Upton, Mark**
See Sanders, Lawrence

**Urdang, Constance (Henriette)**
1922-....................... **CLC 47**
See also CA 21-24R; CANR 9, 24

**Uriel, Henry**
See Faust, Frederick (Schiller)

**Uris, Leon (Marcus)**  1924-...... **CLC 7, 32**
See also AITN 1, 2; BEST 89:2; CA 1-4R;
CANR 1, 40; MTCW; SATA 49

**Urmuz**
See Codrescu, Andrei

**Ustinov, Peter (Alexander)**  1921-.... **CLC 1**
See also AITN 1; CA 13-16R; CANR 25;
DLB 13

**V**
See Chekhov, Anton (Pavlovich)

**Vaculik, Ludvik**  1926-............. **CLC 7**
See also CA 53-56

**Valenzuela, Luisa**  1938-... **CLC 31; SSC 14**
See also CA 101; CANR 32; DLB 113; HW

**Valera y Alcala-Galiano, Juan**
1824-1905 ................. **TCLC 10**
See also CA 106

**Valery, (Ambroise) Paul (Toussaint Jules)**
1871-1945 .......... **TCLC 4, 15; PC 9**
See also CA 104; 122; MTCW

**Valle-Inclan, Ramon (Maria) del**
1866-1936 ............. **TCLC 5; HLC**
See also CA 106; DLB 134

**Vallejo, Antonio Buero**
See Buero Vallejo, Antonio

**Vallejo, Cesar (Abraham)**
1892-1938 ............. **TCLC 3; HLC**
See also CA 105; HW

**Valle Y Pena, Ramon del**
See Valle-Inclan, Ramon (Maria) del

**Van Ash, Cay**  1918-.............. **CLC 34**

**Vanbrugh, Sir John**  1664-1726 ...... **LC 21**
See also DLB 80

**Van Campen, Karl**
See Campbell, John W(ood, Jr.)

**Vance, Gerald**
See Silverberg, Robert

**Vance, Jack** .................... **CLC 35**
See also Vance, John Holbrook
See also DLB 8

**Vance, John Holbrook**  1916-
See Queen, Ellery; Vance, Jack
See also CA 29-32R; CANR 17; MTCW

**Van Den Bogarde, Derek Jules Gaspard Ulric**
**Niven**  1921-
See Bogarde, Dirk
See also CA 77-80

**Vandenburgh, Jane** ................ **CLC 59**

**Vanderhaeghe, Guy**  1951- ......... **CLC 41**
See also CA 113

**van der Post, Laurens (Jan)**  1906- ... **CLC 5**
See also CA 5-8R; CANR 35

**van de Wetering, Janwillem**  1931- .. **CLC 47**
See also CA 49-52; CANR 4

**Van Dine, S. S.** ................. **TCLC 23**
See also Wright, Willard Huntington

**Van Doren, Carl (Clinton)**
1885-1950 ................. **TCLC 18**
See also CA 111

**Van Doren, Mark**  1894-1972..... **CLC 6, 10**
See also CA 1-4R; 37-40R; CANR 3;
DLB 45; MTCW

**Van Druten, John (William)**
1901-1957 .................. **TCLC 2**
See also CA 104; DLB 10

**Van Duyn, Mona (Jane)**
1921-.................. **CLC 3, 7, 63**
See also CA 9-12R; CANR 7, 38; DLB 5

**Van Dyne, Edith**
See Baum, L(yman) Frank

**van Itallie, Jean-Claude**  1936-....... **CLC 3**
See also CA 45-48; CAAS 2; CANR 1;
DLB 7

**van Ostaijen, Paul**  1896-1928 ..... **TCLC 33**

**Van Peebles, Melvin**  1932- ...... **CLC 2, 20**
See also BW; CA 85-88; CANR 27

**Vansittart, Peter**  1920-............ **CLC 42**
See also CA 1-4R; CANR 3

**Van Vechten, Carl**  1880-1964 ...... **CLC 33**
See also CA 89-92; DLB 4, 9, 51

**Van Vogt, A(lfred) E(lton)**  1912-..... **CLC 1**
See also CA 21-24R; CANR 28; DLB 8;
SATA 14

**Varda, Agnes**  1928- .............. **CLC 16**
See also CA 116; 122

**Vargas Llosa, (Jorge) Mario (Pedro)**
1936- ....... **CLC 3, 6, 9, 10, 15, 31, 42;**
**DA; HLC**
See also CA 73-76; CANR 18, 32, 42; HW;
MTCW

**Vasiliu, Gheorghe**  1881-1957
See Bacovia, George
See also CA 123

**Vassa, Gustavus**
See Equiano, Olaudah

**Vassilikos, Vassilis**  1933-......... **CLC 4, 8**
See also CA 81-84

**Vaughn, Stephanie**................. **CLC 62**

**Vazov, Ivan (Minchov)**
1850-1921 ................. **TCLC 25**
See also CA 121

**Veblen, Thorstein (Bunde)**
1857-1929 ................. **TCLC 31**
See also CA 115

**Vega, Lope de**  1562-1635.......... **LC 23**

**Venison, Alfred**
See Pound, Ezra (Weston Loomis)

**Verdi, Marie de**
See Mencken, H(enry) L(ouis)

**Verdu, Matilde**
See Cela, Camilo Jose

Wellman, Manly Wade 1903-1986 .. **CLC 49**
See also CA 1-4R; 118; CANR 6, 16, 44;
SATA 6, 47

Wells, Carolyn 1869(?)-1942 ...... **TCLC 35**
See also CA 113; DLB 11

Wells, H(erbert) G(eorge)
1866-1946 ....... **TCLC 6, 12, 19; DA;**
**SSC 6; WLC**
See also CA 110; 121; CDBLB 1914-1945;
DLB 34, 70; MTCW; SATA 20

Wells, Rosemary 1943-........... **CLC 12**
See also CA 85-88; CLR 16; MAICYA;
SAAS 1; SATA 18, 69

Welty, Eudora
1909- ...... **CLC 1, 2, 5, 14, 22, 33; DA;**
**SSC 1; WLC**
See also CA 9-12R; CABS 1; CANR 32;
CDALB 1941-1968; DLB 2, 102;
DLBY 87; MTCW

Wen I-to 1899-1946 ............. **TCLC 28**

Wentworth, Robert
See Hamilton, Edmond

Werfel, Franz (V.) 1890-1945 ...... **TCLC 8**
See also CA 104; DLB 81, 124

Wergeland, Henrik Arnold
1808-1845 ................. **NCLC 5**

Wersba, Barbara 1932-........... **CLC 30**
See also AAYA 2; CA 29-32R; CANR 16,
38; CLR 3; DLB 52; JRDA; MAICYA;
SAAS 2; SATA 1, 58

Wertmueller, Lina 1928- .......... **CLC 16**
See also CA 97-100; CANR 39

Wescott, Glenway 1901-1987....... **CLC 13**
See also CA 13-16R; 121; CANR 23;
DLB 4, 9, 102

Wesker, Arnold 1932- ........ **CLC 3, 5, 42**
See also CA 1-4R; CAAS 7; CANR 1, 33;
CDBLB 1960 to Present; DLB 13;
MTCW

Wesley, Richard (Errol) 1945-....... **CLC 7**
See also BW; CA 57-60; CANR 27; DLB 38

Wessel, Johan Herman 1742-1785 .... **LC 7**

West, Anthony (Panther)
1914-1987 ................. **CLC 50**
See also CA 45-48; 124; CANR 3, 19;
DLB 15

West, C. P.
See Wodehouse, P(elham) G(renville)

West, (Mary) Jessamyn
1902-1984 ............... **CLC 7, 17**
See also CA 9-12R; 112; CANR 27; DLB 6;
DLBY 84; MTCW; SATA 37

West, Morris L(anglo) 1916-..... **CLC 6, 33**
See also CA 5-8R; CANR 24; MTCW

West, Nathanael
1903-1940 ........... **TCLC 1, 14, 44**
See also CA 104; 125; CDALB 1929-1941;
DLB 4, 9, 28; MTCW

West, Owen
See Koontz, Dean R(ay)

West, Paul 1930- ............ **CLC 7, 14**
See also CA 13-16R; CAAS 7; CANR 22;
DLB 14

West, Rebecca 1892-1983 .. **CLC 7, 9, 31, 50**
See also CA 5-8R; 109; CANR 19; DLB 36;
DLBY 83; MTCW

Westall, Robert (Atkinson)
1929-1993 ................. **CLC 17**
See also AAYA 12; CA 69-72; 141;
CANR 18; CLR 13; JRDA; MAICYA;
SAAS 2; SATA 23, 69; SATA-Obit 75

Westlake, Donald E(dwin)
1933- .................... **CLC 7, 33**
See also CA 17-20R; CAAS 13; CANR 16,
44

Westmacott, Mary
See Christie, Agatha (Mary Clarissa)

Weston, Allen
See Norton, Andre

Wetcheek, J. L.
See Feuchtwanger, Lion

Wetering, Janwillem van de
See van de Wetering, Janwillem

Wetherell, Elizabeth
See Warner, Susan (Bogert)

Whalen, Philip 1923- ........... **CLC 6, 29**
See also CA 9-12R; CANR 5, 39; DLB 16

Wharton, Edith (Newbold Jones)
1862-1937 ...... **TCLC 3, 9, 27, 53; DA;**
**SSC 6; WLC**
See also CA 104; 132; CDALB 1865-1917;
DLB 4, 9, 12, 78; MTCW

Wharton, James
See Mencken, H(enry) L(ouis)

Wharton, William (a pseudonym)
......................... **CLC 18, 37**
See also CA 93-96; DLBY 80

Wheatley (Peters), Phillis
1754(?)-1784 .... **LC 3; BLC; DA; PC 3;**
**WLC**
See also CDALB 1640-1865; DLB 31, 50

Wheelock, John Hall 1886-1978.... **CLC 14**
See also CA 13-16R; 77-80; CANR 14;
DLB 45

White, E(lwyn) B(rooks)
1899-1985 ............. **CLC 10, 34, 39**
See also AITN 2; CA 13-16R; 116;
CANR 16, 37; CLR 1, 21; DLB 11, 22;
MAICYA; MTCW; SATA 2, 29, 44

White, Edmund (Valentine III)
1940- ..................... **CLC 27**
See also AAYA 7; CA 45-48; CANR 3, 19,
36; MTCW

White, Patrick (Victor Martindale)
1912-1990 .. **CLC 3, 4, 5, 7, 9, 18, 65, 69**
See also CA 81-84; 132; CANR 43; MTCW

White, Phyllis Dorothy James 1920-
See James, P. D.
See also CA 21-24R; CANR 17, 43; MTCW

White, T(erence) H(anbury)
1906-1964 ................... **CLC 30**
See also CA 73-76; CANR 37; JRDA;
MAICYA; SATA 12

White, Terence de Vere 1912-...... **CLC 49**
See also CA 49-52; CANR 3

White, Walter F(rancis)
1893-1955 ................. **TCLC 15**
See also White, Walter
See also CA 115; 124; DLB 51

White, William Hale 1831-1913
See Rutherford, Mark
See also CA 121

Whitehead, E(dward) A(nthony)
1933- ...................... **CLC 5**
See also CA 65-68

Whitemore, Hugh (John) 1936-..... **CLC 37**
See also CA 132

Whitman, Sarah Helen (Power)
1803-1878 ................. **NCLC 19**
See also DLB 1

Whitman, Walt(er)
1819-1892 ..... **NCLC 4, 31; DA; PC 3;**
**WLC**
See also CDALB 1640-1865; DLB 3, 64;
SATA 20

Whitney, Phyllis A(yame) 1903-.... **CLC 42**
See also AITN 2; BEST 90:3; CA 1-4R;
CANR 3, 25, 38; JRDA; MAICYA;
SATA 1, 30

Whittemore, (Edward) Reed (Jr.)
1919- ...................... **CLC 4**
See also CA 9-12R; CAAS 8; CANR 4;
DLB 5

Whittier, John Greenleaf
1807-1892 .................. **NCLC 8**
See also CDALB 1640-1865; DLB 1

Whittlebot, Hernia
See Coward, Noel (Peirce)

Wicker, Thomas Grey 1926-
See Wicker, Tom
See also CA 65-68; CANR 21

Wicker, Tom ...................... **CLC 7**
See also Wicker, Thomas Grey

Wideman, John Edgar
1941- ......... **CLC 5, 34, 36, 67; BLC**
See also BW; CA 85-88; CANR 14, 42;
DLB 33

Wiebe, Rudy (Henry) 1934-... **CLC 6, 11, 14**
See also CA 37-40R; CANR 42; DLB 60

Wieland, Christoph Martin
1733-1813 ................. **NCLC 17**
See also DLB 97

Wieners, John 1934-.............. **CLC 7**
See also CA 13-16R; DLB 16

Wiesel, Elie(zer)
1928- ........... **CLC 3, 5, 11, 37; DA**
See also AAYA 7; AITN 1; CA 5-8R;
CAAS 4; CANR 8, 40; DLB 83;
DLBY 87; MTCW; SATA 56

Wiggins, Marianne 1947-.......... **CLC 57**
See also BEST 89:3; CA 130

Wight, James Alfred 1916-
See Herriot, James
See also CA 77-80; SATA 44, 55

Wilbur, Richard (Purdy)
1921- ......... **CLC 3, 6, 9, 14, 53; DA**
See also CA 1-4R; CABS 2; CANR 2, 29;
DLB 5; MTCW; SATA 9

Wild, Peter 1940-................ **CLC 14**
See also CA 37-40R; DLB 5

Wilde, Oscar (Fingal O'Flahertie Wills)
1854(?)-1900 .... **TCLC 1, 8, 23, 41; DA;**
**SSC 11; WLC**
See also CA 104; 119; CDBLB 1890-1914;
DLB 10, 19, 34, 57, 141; SATA 24

Wilder, Billy .................... CLC 20
See also Wilder, Samuel
See also DLB 26

Wilder, Samuel  1906-
See Wilder, Billy
See also CA 89-92

Wilder, Thornton (Niven)
1897-1975 ...... CLC 1, 5, 6, 10, 15, 35,
82; DA; DC 1; WLC
See also AITN 2; CA 13-16R; 61-64;
CANR 40; DLB 4, 7, 9; MTCW

Wilding, Michael  1942- ........... CLC 73
See also CA 104; CANR 24

Wiley, Richard  1944- ............. CLC 44
See also CA 121; 129

Wilhelm, Kate .................... CLC 7
See also Wilhelm, Katie Gertrude
See also CAAS 5; DLB 8

Wilhelm, Katie Gertrude  1928-
See Wilhelm, Kate
See also CA 37-40R; CANR 17, 36; MTCW

Wilkins, Mary
See Freeman, Mary Eleanor Wilkins

Willard, Nancy  1936- ........... CLC 7, 37
See also CA 89-92; CANR 10, 39; CLR 5;
DLB 5, 52; MAICYA; MTCW;
SATA 30, 37, 71

Williams, C(harles) K(enneth)
1936- .................... CLC 33, 56
See also CA 37-40R; DLB 5

Williams, Charles
See Collier, James L(incoln)

Williams, Charles (Walter Stansby)
1886-1945 ............... TCLC 1, 11
See also CA 104; DLB 100

Williams, (George) Emlyn
1905-1987 .................. CLC 15
See also CA 104; 123; CANR 36; DLB 10,
77; MTCW

Williams, Hugo  1942- ............ CLC 42
See also CA 17-20R; DLB 40

Williams, J. Walker
See Wodehouse, P(elham) G(renville)

Williams, John A(lfred)
1925- ................ CLC 5, 13; BLC
See also BW; CA 53-56; CAAS 3; CANR 6,
26; DLB 2, 33

Williams, Jonathan (Chamberlain)
1929- ...................... CLC 13
See also CA 9-12R; CAAS 12; CANR 8;
DLB 5

Williams, Joy  1944- .............. CLC 31
See also CA 41-44R; CANR 22

Williams, Norman  1952- ......... CLC 39
See also CA 118

Williams, Tennessee
1911-1983 ..... CLC 1, 2, 5, 7, 8, 11, 15,
19, 30, 39, 45, 71; DA; DC 4; WLC
See also AITN 1, 2; CA 5-8R; 108;
CABS 3; CANR 31; CDALB 1941-1968;
DLB 7; DLBD 4; DLBY 83; MTCW

Williams, Thomas (Alonzo)
1926-1990 .................... CLC 14
See also CA 1-4R; 132; CANR 2

Williams, William C.
See Williams, William Carlos

Williams, William Carlos
1883-1963 .... CLC 1, 2, 5, 9, 13, 22, 42,
67; DA; PC 7
See also CA 89-92; CANR 34;
CDALB 1917-1929; DLB 4, 16, 54, 86;
MTCW

Williamson, David (Keith)  1942- .... CLC 56
See also CA 103; CANR 41

Williamson, Jack ................. CLC 29
See also Williamson, John Stewart
See also CAAS 8; DLB 8

Williamson, John Stewart  1908-
See Williamson, Jack
See also CA 17-20R; CANR 23

Willie, Frederick
See Lovecraft, H(oward) P(hillips)

Willingham, Calder (Baynard, Jr.)
1922- ..................... CLC 5, 51
See also CA 5-8R; CANR 3; DLB 2, 44;
MTCW

Willis, Charles
See Clarke, Arthur C(harles)

Willy
See Colette, (Sidonie-Gabrielle)

Willy, Colette
See Colette, (Sidonie-Gabrielle)

Wilson, A(ndrew) N(orman)  1950- .. CLC 33
See also CA 112; 122; DLB 14

Wilson, Angus (Frank Johnstone)
1913-1991 ........ CLC 2, 3, 5, 25, 34
See also CA 5-8R; 134; CANR 21; DLB 15,
139; MTCW

Wilson, August
1945- .. CLC 39, 50, 63; BLC; DA; DC 2
See also BW; CA 115; 122; CANR 42;
MTCW

Wilson, Brian  1942- .............. CLC 12

Wilson, Colin  1931- ............ CLC 3, 14
See also CA 1-4R; CAAS 5; CANR 1, 22,
33; DLB 14; MTCW

Wilson, Dirk
See Pohl, Frederik

Wilson, Edmund
1895-1972 .......... CLC 1, 2, 3, 8, 24
See also CA 1-4R; 37-40R; CANR 1;
DLB 63; MTCW

Wilson, Ethel Davis (Bryant)
1888(?)-1980 ................. CLC 13
See also CA 102; DLB 68; MTCW

Wilson, John  1785-1854 ......... NCLC 5

Wilson, John (Anthony) Burgess  1917-1993
See Burgess, Anthony
See also CA 1-4R; 143; CANR 2; MTCW

Wilson, Lanford  1937- ....... CLC 7, 14, 36
See also CA 17-20R; CABS 3; DLB 7

Wilson, Robert M.  1944- ........ CLC 7, 9
See also CA 49-52; CANR 2, 41; MTCW

Wilson, Robert McLiam  1964- ..... CLC 59
See also CA 132

Wilson, Sloan  1920- ............. CLC 32
See also CA 1-4R; CANR 1, 44

Wilson, Snoo  1948- .............. CLC 33
See also CA 69-72

Wilson, William S(mith)  1932- ..... CLC 49
See also CA 81-84

Winchilsea, Anne (Kingsmill) Finch Counte
1661-1720 .................... LC 3

Windham, Basil
See Wodehouse, P(elham) G(renville)

Wingrove, David (John)  1954- ...... CLC 68
See also CA 133

Winters, Janet Lewis .............. CLC 41
See also Lewis, Janet
See also DLBY 87

Winters, (Arthur) Yvor
1900-1968 ............... CLC 4, 8, 32
See also CA 11-12; 25-28R; CAP 1;
DLB 48; MTCW

Winterson, Jeanette  1959- ........ CLC 64
See also CA 136

Wiseman, Frederick  1930- ........ CLC 20

Wister, Owen  1860-1938 ........ TCLC 21
See also CA 108; DLB 9, 78; SATA 62

Witkacy
See Witkiewicz, Stanislaw Ignacy

Witkiewicz, Stanislaw Ignacy
1885-1939 .................. TCLC 8
See also CA 105

Wittig, Monique  1935(?)- .......... CLC 22
See also CA 116; 135; DLB 83

Wittlin, Jozef  1896-1976 .......... CLC 25
See also CA 49-52; 65-68; CANR 3

Wodehouse, P(elham) G(renville)
1881-1975 ... CLC 1, 2, 5, 10, 22; SSC 2
See also AITN 2; CA 45-48; 57-60;
CANR 3, 33; CDBLB 1914-1945;
DLB 34; MTCW; SATA 22

Woiwode, L.
See Woiwode, Larry (Alfred)

Woiwode, Larry (Alfred)  1941- ... CLC 6, 10
See also CA 73-76; CANR 16; DLB 6

Wojciechowska, Maia (Teresa)
1927- ....................... CLC 26
See also AAYA 8; CA 9-12R; CANR 4, 41;
CLR 1; JRDA; MAICYA; SAAS 1;
SATA 1, 28

Wolf, Christa  1929- ........ CLC 14, 29, 58
See also CA 85-88; DLB 75; MTCW

Wolfe, Gene (Rodman)  1931- ....... CLC 25
See also CA 57-60; CAAS 9; CANR 6, 32;
DLB 8

Wolfe, George C.  1954- ........... CLC 49

Wolfe, Thomas (Clayton)
1900-1938 ... TCLC 4, 13, 29; DA; WLC
See also CA 104; 132; CDALB 1929-1941;
DLB 9, 102; DLBD 2; DLBY 85; MTCW

Wolfe, Thomas Kennerly, Jr.  1931-
See Wolfe, Tom
See also CA 13-16R; CANR 9, 33; MTCW

Wolfe, Tom ......... CLC 1, 2, 9, 15, 35, 51
See also Wolfe, Thomas Kennerly, Jr.
See also AAYA 8; AITN 2; BEST 89:1

Wolff, Geoffrey (Ansell)  1937- ..... CLC 41
See also CA 29-32R; CANR 29, 43

**Wolff, Sonia**
See Levitin, Sonia (Wolff)

**Wolff, Tobias (Jonathan Ansell)**
1945- . . . . . . . . . . . . . . . . . . . CLC 39, 64
See also BEST 90:2; CA 114; 117; DLB 130

**Wolfram von Eschenbach**
c. 1170-c. 1220 . . . . . . . . . . . . . CMLC 5
See also DLB 138

**Wolitzer, Hilma** 1930- . . . . . . . . . . . CLC 17
See also CA 65-68; CANR 18, 40; SATA 31

**Wollstonecraft, Mary** 1759-1797. . . . . . LC 5
See also CDBLB 1789-1832; DLB 39, 104

**Wonder, Stevie** . . . . . . . . . . . . . . . . CLC 12
See also Morris, Steveland Judkins

**Wong, Jade Snow** 1922- . . . . . . . . . . CLC 17
See also CA 109

**Woodcott, Keith**
See Brunner, John (Kilian Houston)

**Woodruff, Robert W.**
See Mencken, H(enry) L(ouis)

**Woolf, (Adeline) Virginia**
1882-1941 . . . . . . TCLC 1, 5, 20, 43; DA;
SSC 7; WLC
See also CA 104; 130; CDBLB 1914-1945;
DLB 36, 100; DLBD 10; MTCW

**Woollcott, Alexander (Humphreys)**
1887-1943 . . . . . . . . . . . . . . . . . TCLC 5
See also CA 105; DLB 29

**Woolrich, Cornell** 1903-1968. . . . . . . CLC 77
See also Hopley-Woolrich, Cornell George

**Wordsworth, Dorothy**
1771-1855 . . . . . . . . . . . . . . . . NCLC 25
See also DLB 107

**Wordsworth, William**
1770-1850 . . . . NCLC 12, 38; DA; PC 4;
WLC
See also CDBLB 1789-1832; DLB 93, 107

**Wouk, Herman** 1915- . . . . . . . . . CLC 1, 9, 38
See also CA 5-8R; CANR 6, 33; DLBY 82;
MTCW

**Wright, Charles (Penzel, Jr.)**
1935- . . . . . . . . . . . . . . . . . CLC 6, 13, 28
See also CA 29-32R; CAAS 7; CANR 23,
36; DLBY 82; MTCW

**Wright, Charles Stevenson**
1932- . . . . . . . . . . . . . . . . CLC 49; BLC 3
See also BW; CA 9-12R; CANR 26;
DLB 33

**Wright, Jack R.**
See Harris, Mark

**Wright, James (Arlington)**
1927-1980 . . . . . . . . . . . . CLC 3, 5, 10, 28
See also AITN 2; CA 49-52; 97-100;
CANR 4, 34; DLB 5; MTCW

**Wright, Judith (Arandell)**
1915- . . . . . . . . . . . . . . . . . . CLC 11, 53
See also CA 13-16R; CANR 31; MTCW;
SATA 14

**Wright, L(aurali) R.** 1939- . . . . . . . . CLC 44
See also CA 138

**Wright, Richard (Nathaniel)**
1908-1960 . . . . CLC 1, 3, 4, 9, 14, 21, 48,
74; BLC; DA; SSC 2; WLC
See also AAYA 5; BW; CA 108;
CDALB 1929-1941; DLB 76, 102;
DLBD 2; MTCW

**Wright, Richard B(ruce)** 1937- . . . . . . CLC 6
See also CA 85-88; DLB 53

**Wright, Rick** 1945- . . . . . . . . . . . . . CLC 35
See also Pink Floyd

**Wright, Rowland**
See Wells, Carolyn

**Wright, Stephen** 1946- . . . . . . . . . . . CLC 33

**Wright, Willard Huntington** 1888-1939
See Van Dine, S. S.
See also CA 115

**Wright, William** 1930- . . . . . . . . . . . CLC 44
See also CA 53-56; CANR 7, 23

**Wu Ch'eng-en** 1500(?)-1582(?) . . . . . . . LC 7

**Wu Ching-tzu** 1701-1754 . . . . . . . . . . . LC 2

**Wurlitzer, Rudolph** 1938(?)- . . . CLC 2, 4, 15
See also CA 85-88

**Wycherley, William** 1641-1715 . . . . LC 8, 21
See also CDBLB 1660-1789; DLB 80

**Wylie, Elinor (Morton Hoyt)**
1885-1928 . . . . . . . . . . . . . . . . . TCLC 8
See also CA 105; DLB 9, 45

**Wylie, Philip (Gordon)** 1902-1971. . . CLC 43
See also CA 21-22; 33-36R; CAP 2; DLB 9

**Wyndham, John**
See Harris, John (Wyndham Parkes Lucas)
Beynon

**Wyss, Johann David Von**
1743-1818 . . . . . . . . . . . . . . . . NCLC 10
See also JRDA; MAICYA; SATA 27, 29

**Yakumo Koizumi**
See Hearn, (Patricio) Lafcadio (Tessima
Carlos)

**Yanez, Jose Donoso**
See Donoso (Yanez), Jose

**Yanovsky, Basile S.**
See Yanovsky, V(assily) S(emenovich)

**Yanovsky, V(assily) S(emenovich)**
1906-1989 . . . . . . . . . . . . . . . CLC 2, 18
See also CA 97-100; 129

**Yates, Richard** 1926-1992 . . . . . CLC 7, 8, 23
See also CA 5-8R; 139; CANR 10, 43;
DLB 2; DLBY 81, 92

**Yeats, W. B.**
See Yeats, William Butler

**Yeats, William Butler**
1865-1939 . . . . . TCLC 1, 11, 18, 31; DA;
WLC
See also CA 104; 127; CDBLB 1890-1914;
DLB 10, 19, 98; MTCW

**Yehoshua, A(braham) B.**
1936- . . . . . . . . . . . . . . . . . . CLC 13, 31
See also CA 33-36R; CANR 43

**Yep, Laurence Michael** 1948- . . . . . . CLC 35
See also AAYA 5; CA 49-52; CANR 1;
CLR 3, 17; DLB 52; JRDA; MAICYA;
SATA 7, 69

**Yerby, Frank G(arvin)**
1916-1991 . . . . . . . . . CLC 1, 7, 22; BLC
See also BW; CA 9-12R; 136; CANR 16;
DLB 76; MTCW

**Yesenin, Sergei Alexandrovich**
See Esenin, Sergei (Alexandrovich)

**Yevtushenko, Yevgeny (Alexandrovich)**
1933- . . . . . . . . . . . CLC 1, 3, 13, 26, 51
See also CA 81-84; CANR 33; MTCW

**Yezierska, Anzia** 1885(?)-1970 . . . . . CLC 46
See also CA 126; 89-92; DLB 28; MTCW

**Yglesias, Helen** 1915- . . . . . . . . . . . CLC 7, 22
See also CA 37-40R; CANR 15; MTCW

**Yokomitsu Riichi** 1898-1947 . . . . . . TCLC 47

**Yonge, Charlotte (Mary)**
1823-1901 . . . . . . . . . . . . . . . . TCLC 48
See also CA 109; DLB 18; SATA 17

**York, Jeremy**
See Creasey, John

**York, Simon**
See Heinlein, Robert A(nson)

**Yorke, Henry Vincent** 1905-1974 . . . CLC 13
See also Green, Henry
See also CA 85-88; 49-52

**Young, Al(bert James)**
1939- . . . . . . . . . . . . . . . . . CLC 19; BLC
See also BW; CA 29-32R; CANR 26;
DLB 33

**Young, Andrew (John)** 1885-1971. . . . CLC 5
See also CA 5-8R; CANR 7, 29

**Young, Collier**
See Bloch, Robert (Albert)

**Young, Edward** 1683-1765. . . . . . . . . . LC 3
See also DLB 95

**Young, Marguerite** 1909- . . . . . . . . . CLC 82
See also CA 13-16; CAP 1

**Young, Neil** 1945- . . . . . . . . . . . . . . CLC 17
See also CA 110

**Yourcenar, Marguerite**
1903-1987 . . . . . . . . . . . . CLC 19, 38, 50
See also CA 69-72; CANR 23; DLB 72;
DLBY 88; MTCW

**Yurick, Sol** 1925- . . . . . . . . . . . . . . . CLC 6
See also CA 13-16R; CANR 25

**Zabolotskii, Nikolai Alekseevich**
1903-1958 . . . . . . . . . . . . . . . . TCLC 52
See also CA 116

**Zamiatin, Yevgenii**
See Zamyatin, Evgeny Ivanovich

**Zamyatin, Evgeny Ivanovich**
1884-1937 . . . . . . . . . . . . . . TCLC 8, 37
See also CA 105

**Zangwill, Israel** 1864-1926. . . . . . . TCLC 16
See also CA 109; DLB 10, 135

**Zappa, Francis Vincent, Jr.** 1940-1993
See Zappa, Frank
See also CA 108; 143

**Zappa, Frank** . . . . . . . . . . . . . . . . . . CLC 17
See also Zappa, Francis Vincent, Jr.

**Zaturenska, Marya** 1902-1982. . . . CLC 6, 11
See also CA 13-16R; 105; CANR 22

**Zelazny, Roger (Joseph)** 1937- . . . . . CLC 21
See also AAYA 7; CA 21-24R; CANR 26;
DLB 8; MTCW; SATA 39, 57

**Zhdanov, Andrei A(lexandrovich)**
    1896-1948 . . . . . . . . . . . . . . . . . **TCLC 18**
  See also CA 117

**Zhukovsky, Vasily**   1783-1852 . . . . **NCLC 35**

**Ziegenhagen, Eric** . . . . . . . . . . . . . . . . **CLC 55**

**Zimmer, Jill Schary**
  See Robinson, Jill

**Zimmerman, Robert**
  See Dylan, Bob

**Zindel, Paul**   1936- . . . . . . . . . **CLC 6, 26; DA**
  See also AAYA 2; CA 73-76; CANR 31;
    CLR 3; DLB 7, 52; JRDA; MAICYA;
    MTCW; SATA 16, 58

**Zinov'Ev, A. A.**
  See Zinoviev, Alexander (Aleksandrovich)

**Zinoviev, Alexander (Aleksandrovich)**
    1922- . . . . . . . . . . . . . . . . . . . . . . **CLC 19**
  See also CA 116; 133; CAAS 10

**Zoilus**
  See Lovecraft, H(oward) P(hillips)

**Zola, Emile (Edouard Charles Antoine)**
    1840-1902 . . . . . . **TCLC 1, 6, 21, 41; DA;**
                                                    **WLC**
  See also CA 104; 138; DLB 123

**Zoline, Pamela**   1941- . . . . . . . . . . . . . **CLC 62**

**Zorrilla y Moral, Jose**   1817-1893 . . **NCLC 6**

**Zoshchenko, Mikhail (Mikhailovich)**
    1895-1958 . . . . . . . . . . **TCLC 15; SSC 15**
  See also CA 115

**Zuckmayer, Carl**   1896-1977 . . . . . . . **CLC 18**
  See also CA 69-72; DLB 56, 124

**Zuk, Georges**
  See Skelton, Robin

**Zukofsky, Louis**
    1904-1978 . . . . . . . **CLC 1, 2, 4, 7, 11, 18**
  See also CA 9-12R; 77-80; CANR 39;
    DLB 5; MTCW

**Zweig, Paul**   1935-1984 . . . . . . . . **CLC 34, 42**
  See also CA 85-88; 113

**Zweig, Stefan**   1881-1942 . . . . . . . . **TCLC 17**
  See also CA 112; DLB 81, 118